A TEXTBOOK OF
PHYSIOLOGICAL
PSYCHOLOGY

A TEXTBOOK OF
PHYSIOLOGICAL
PSYCHOLOGY

Sebastian Peter Grossman

DEPARTMENT OF PSYCHOLOGY
THE UNIVERSITY OF CHICAGO

John Wiley & Sons, Inc.   NEW YORK   LONDON   SYDNEY

PREFACE

This book is intended as a textbook for graduate and undergraduate students in biopsychology, neurophysiology, and neuroanatomy. Extensive citation of primary sources should also make it a useful reference for research workers in these and allied fields.

Physiological psychology is not a separate science in the traditional sense. It has become a distinct field of study because its subject matter is at the frontier of so many biological sciences that the traditionally trained expert in any one of them can no longer work effectively in physiological psychology. Relevant research is conducted by psychologists, physiologists, anatomists, pharmacologists, and chemists, to name only some of the more important contributors of data and theory. The flood of research papers in each of these professions is such that no one individual can keep informed in all of them. Yet an understanding of behavior is possible only if we can study the physical and chemical events which occur when we perceive a change in our environment, recall relevant information, and respond in accordance with our needs and desires.

The problem is reduced to manageable proportions if we emphasize the word *relevant* in the definition of our task. No man can master all these fields, but it is possible to obtain expertise in the aspects of each discipline that are directly relevant to our problems. This expertise permits us to conduct research which uses anatomical, physiological, and chemical techniques and concepts to study psychological processes.

Even this relatively modest approach has become increasingly difficult because of rapid developments in some areas of physiological psychology. Further specialization may become necessary, and some areas have already moved in this direction. The clearest example is the rapidly expanding field of psychopharmacology. Largely as the result of the recent discovery of various mood-altering drugs and the current interest in pharmacological explanations of physiological and psychological processes (such as synaptic transmission, information coding, and memory), this field has become large and complex and can no longer be treated adequately within the framework of physiological psychology. No effort is made in this book to do so. The investigation of perceptual processes and related sensory mechanisms similarly has become so complex that it requires separate treatment by qualified specialists and should be the subject of a separate course. This book accordingly discusses only the perceptual and sensory processes necessary for an understanding of the general problems which are introduced by the many complex transformations that must occur before changes in physical energy can be translated into patterns of neural activity. Part Two attempts to illustrate these problems by discussing the transformation of radiant energy into neural impulses which give rise to visual perceptions and by presenting a more general survey of reticular influences on sensation and perception.

The subject matter of this book is thus defined as the physiological and chemical processes (and their anatomical substrates) that intervene between the arrival of sensory signals in the central nervous system and the elaboration of appropriate responses to them. These mediating processes can be variously classified; it has been convenient to establish a somewhat arbitrary dichotomy which gives rise to Parts Three and Four of this book. Chapters 6 through 11 (Part Three) contain discussions of motivational mechanisms that determine whether a change in the organism's internal or external environment requires an overt reaction. Chapters 12 through 16 (Part Four) contain discussions of the problems raised by the plasticity of the organism's response repertoire (that is, the anatomical, physiological, and biochemical mechanisms responsible for learning, recall, and forgetting).

The four parts of this book are aimed at different levels of sophistication. The first provides a brief introduction or review of the aspects of neurophysiology and neuroanatomy that are essential for an understanding of subsequent sections. The treatment of neuroanatomy is more extensive than that traditionally found in textbooks in physiological psychology, providing the reader with a ready reference for discussion of the research literature. The second part presents somewhat more detailed and extensively documented discussions of a sensory system (vision), the classical motor systems, and reticular mechanisms.

Parts Three and Four contain the main body of information on the subject of physiological psychology. The areas covered in these chapters are too complex to permit complete coverage of all experimental data and theoretical issues. An effort has been made, however, to present extensive and representative samples of historically important as well as currently active areas of research and to discuss the evidence for both sides of all issues. Sufficient literature citations are provided to give the reader easy access to primary and secondary sources for further study. Interpretative conclusions have largely been omitted (except in the chapters which deal expressly with theoretical issues) because they often obscure rather than illuminate the important variables. It is hoped that the experimental literature is presented in sufficient detail to permit the interested reader to form his own generalizations and conclusions.

This book would not have been completed without the encouragement and assistance of my wife Lore. In a sense, it is her book as much as it is mine, for I would never have had the patience and endurance to accomplish the many administrative and clerical tasks which she so diligently and proficiently performed.

I am also indebted to my students who, over the years, have contributed in so many ways to this book. Most chapters have benefited from seminar and class discussions, and many of my students, particularly Mr. Thomas Green, have given of their time to assist in readying the manuscript for the printer.

I would also like to thank the many individuals who have permitted reproduction of their data and illustrations. Part One, in particular, has benefited greatly from the generosity of Professors Elizabeth Crosby, E. L. House, E. W. Lauer, T. Humphrey, B. Pansky, T. L. Peele, T. C. Ruch, and R. C. Truex, who made many of their excellent photographs and drawings available to me.

Last, but not least, I want to express my appreciation for the cooperation of the publishers who have granted permission to reproduce illustrations from many books and journals. A detailed list of illustration credits is given on pages 883 to 886.

SEBASTIAN PETER GROSSMAN

Chicago, Illinois
January 1967

CONTENTS

Chapter 2   ANATOMY OF THE NERVOUS SYSTEM, 43

PART TWO   179

Chapter 4   THE MOTOR SYSTEM AND MECHANISMS OF BASIC SENSORY-MOTOR INTEGRATION, 241

Chapter 5   THE RETICULAR FORMATION AND NONSPECIFIC THALAMIC PROJECTION SYSTEM, 288

PART THREE   311

Chapter 9   EMOTIONAL BEHAVIOR, 498

Chapter 10   REWARDING AND AVERSIVE EFFECTS OF CENTRAL STIMULATION, 564

Chapter 14   **CONSOLIDATION, 797**

PART ONE

CHAPTER ONE

General and Neuronal Cytology

THE CELL

All living organisms are constructed of essentially similar building blocks called *cells*. Cells vary in size, shape, and function but generally have the same basic structure: this structure consists of (1) an outer *membrane* which is a selectively permeable border and maintains an equilibrium of certain chemical and electrical properties, (2) the *cytoplasm* which makes up the main body of the cell and supports the major metabolic processes, and (3) the *cell nucleus* which regulates the activities of the cell on the basis of genetic information (see Figure 1.1).

The Membrane

The *membrane* acts as a selective filter which permits certain substances (such as nutrients) to enter the cell and denies access to other chemicals which might be harmful or disruptive to normal functional processes. It contains the essential chemical constitutents of the cell but permits the outward passage of waste products or other substances the cell may secrete. Since many chemicals (the *electrolytes*) are composed of molecules which dissociate into positively charged and negatively charged ions, the cell membrane may contain more positively charged ions on one side than on the other. When this happens, the membrane is said to be *polarized*.

One of the functions of the cell membrane is to maintain an equal number of ions on either side of itself. When a mechanical, chemical, or electrical disturbance outside the cell removes some of the ions from the outer wall of the cell membrane, a compensatory movement of ions takes place and restores the equilibrium. If the membrane is polarized, this movement of ions to the outside of the cell disturbs the previous relationship between positive and negative electrical charges. When this occurs, the cell is said to be *irritated*. Complex mechanisms, which we will discuss in detail later, subsequently set into motion a chain reaction which reverses the movement of ions and reestablishes the electrical potential. This repair process may require a chain reaction of ion exchange along the membrane which results in the *conduction* of the irritation to all parts of the cell membrane. *Irritability* and *conductivity* are important properties of all cells.

The Cytoplasm

The *cytoplasm* makes up the main body of the cell. The chemical composition and anatomical

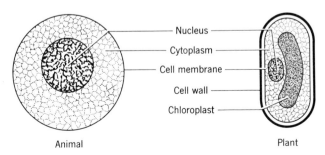

Fig. 1.1 Structural plan of animal and plant cells. Animal cells lack the cell wall and the chloroplast, which contains the green pigment *chlorophyll*. (From Carlson and Johnson, 1949.)

Nucleus

Cytoplasm

Cell membrane

Cell wall

Chloroplast

Animal

Plant

microstructure of cytoplasmic material vary greatly among different cells, largely as the result of *differentiation* (the process by which cells develop and use a particular capability to the virtual exclusion of others). However, many structural and functional properties are common to the cytoplasm of all cells.

Cells perform their various functions by means of complex chemical reactions which require energy. This energy is supplied by nutrients which are metabolized in the cytoplasmic portion of the cell. Some chemical reactions alter the size or shape of some molecules in a way that changes the shape of the cell itself. When these processes are reversible, a cell can alternate between two physical states and display *contractility*. This, of course, is the basis of movement.

The various metabolic processes taking place inside the cell cytoplasm may produce novel combinations of basic chemical substances. Often, these new compounds are needed by the cell itself and do not enter the general circulation. However, sometimes the new substance is secreted through the membrane into the immediate environment of the cell or into the circulatory system for general distribution. Specialized secretory cells make up the important glandular system of higher organisms.

The Nucleus

The *nucleus* of a cell may be compared to the central office of a factory. It contains *deoxyribonucleic acid* (DNA) which carries genetic information and determines the functional properties of each cell. The genetic information is passed on by means of *genes* which make up the *chromosomal* portion of the nucleus. Another nucleic acid (*ribonucleic acid* or RNA) transfers the information from the nucleus to the cytoplasm.

The simplest living organisms are made up of a single cell; the cell absorbs nutrients directly from its environment and transforms them into energy which is used to maintain essential vital processes. The membrane properties of irritability and conductivity permit the cell to react to changes in its environment. These reactions consist of modifications of the metabolic processes in the cytoplasm and may produce contraction (and movement) or secretion.

Evolutionary developments have resulted in the survival of increasingly complex organisms which are composed of more than one cell. These cooperative cellular arrangements are of mutual benefit only to the extent that they permit functional specialization. In a process called *differentiation*, cells of multicellular organisms specialize in a particular function, often to the virtual exclusion of others. Such specialization results in *receptors* (cells which are particularly sensitive to environmental changes), *conductors* (cells which specialize in the rapid propagation of a local membrane irritation), and *effectors* (cells which respond to most stimuli by initiating chemical reactions that change the overall dimensions of the cell). There are, of course, other specialized cells which perform such essential functions as secretion, intermediary metabolism, and structural support, but these will not be of major concern in the following discussion.

THE CONSTITUENTS OF PROTOPLASM

The basic constituent of cells is called *protoplasm*. Ordinary water (H_2O) makes up 60 to 99% of all protoplasmic material. This abundance of water assures that important chemicals can go into solution and become uniformly distributed throughout the cell. Since chemical reactions occur more readily between substances in solution than between solids, the high water content of protoplasm also assures a rapid and complete interaction between protoplasmic constituents.

Furthermore, the presence of water permits the splitting of certain molecules (called *electrolytes*) into smaller components called *ions*. Ions possess electrical charges, and solutions containing ions conduct electricity. There are three basic classes of electrolytes: (1) *acids* which, in solution, yield positively charged hydrogen ions (H^+); (2) *bases* or *alkalies* which always yield a negatively charged hydroxyl ion (OH^-); and (3) *salts* which yield neither H^+ nor OH^-. (Some compounds dissociate into both H^+ and OH^-.) Many of the important properties of cells, such as irritability and conductivity, depend on an unequal distribution of electrical charges inside and outside the cell membrane.

Protoplasm contains, in addition to water, a variety of *inorganic salts*. The nature and distribution of these salts is very similar in living cells and in cells found in seawater, presumably because all protoplasmic material has evolved from the sea. The most common salts in protoplasm are (in decreasing order of relative concentration) chloride, sodium, potassium, calcium, and manganese. Salts make up only about 0.9% of the total body weight but exert important influences on cellular functions.

Three major groups of organic compounds, carbohydrates, fats, and proteins, are found in living cells. The *carbohydrates* are composed of carbon, hydrogen, and oxygen and are commonly divided into three subclasses. The simplest sugars or *monosaccharides* ($C_6H_{12}O_6$), such as glucose, are plentiful in nature and provide many of the nutrients used in living organisms. The double sugars or *disaccharides* are composed of two molecules of simple sugar, the union usually producing a loss of a single water molecule:

$$2C_6H_{12}O_6 \rightarrow C_{12}H_{22}O_{11} + H_2O$$

A large number of simple sugar molecules combine to form the compound sugars or *polysaccharides* which make up the *starches*. Animal starches are called *glycogens* and serve as a storage form of carbohydrates, particularly in liver and muscle cells. Glycogen is readily converted into a glucose compound which is a necessary part of all combustion processes in the cell. Carbohydrates mainly serve this "fuel" function; they may also be incorporated into the structure of protoplasmic material, serving as building material for the cells.

Glucose normally makes up about 0.1% of the weight of mammalian cells. The irritability of cells in the brain is sharply increased whenever a significant fall in sugar occurs. This hyperirritability may lead to motor seizures and death. The concentration of blood glucose is normally maintained within narrow limits by a number of cooperating mechanisms, including the liver, the pancreas, and the adrenal gland. The failure of any one of the contributing mechanisms causes death. For example, a common malfunction of the pancreas results in a chronically lowered blood sugar concentration and induces unconsciousness and death. (The common disease *diabetes* is reflected by the opposite condition, a dangerously high glucose level.)

Fats are also composed of carbon, hydrogen, and oxygen, but their molecular structure differs importantly from that of carbohydrates (fats contain much less oxygen in proportion to carbon and hydrogen). Before fat can be absorbed by living organisms, it must be broken down by the enzymatic action of digestive juices into its component parts, *glycerol* and *fatty acids.* Fats, like carbohydrates, serve as fuel and provide energy for the many chemical reactions which form the basis of all cellular responses.

Fats contain twice as much energy per unit weight as carbohydrates and are therefore useful as energy stores. However, the conversion of fat to energy is a relatively slow process, and the organism typically exhausts all its stores of the more readily available and convertible carbohydrates (glycogen) before drawing on its fat stores.

Fats are incorporated into both intracellular and membrane components of cells and make up a significantly greater fraction of protoplasmic structure than do carbohydrates. Fat is a poor conductor of heat, and its subdermal (i.e., below the skin) deposits very effectively conserve body temperature.

Proteins are the last of the three major organic constituents of protoplasmic materials. Proteins consist of very complex and large molecules which are made up of carbon, hydrogen, oxygen, and nitrogen as well as traces of sulfur and phosphorus. Protein molecules can be split into simpler molecules called *amino acids;* these have been called the building blocks of cells. Amino acids are complex molecules themselves. They are differentiated from other substances because they contain an amino (NH_2) group as well as a COOH complex which is responsible for the acidity of the compound. More than twenty amino acids are presently known, and a great variety of proteins can be created from the many possible combinations and permutations of these basic building blocks.

Every species appears to have some characteristic proteins which differ less from those of closely related species than from those of organisms further removed in evolutionary development. Protein molecules are the basic structural components of all animal tissues. They can also provide energy because a rearrangement of atoms can transform protein into combustible glucose. When an organism is starved to the point where nearly all normally occurring stores of glucose and glycogen have been exhausted, the cells begin to burn themselves in a final effort to maintain essential life processes.

Closely related to the proteins are complex substances called *enzymes;* these are important catalysts (i.e., substances which promote chemical reactions without providing energy for the reaction). The precise structure of most enzymes is not known. Enzymes, organic catalysts which are manufactured by all living cells, are indispensable for the chemical reactions which sustain basic life processes. The breakdown of protein into amino acids or the transformations of complex starches into simple sugars are good examples. These reactions occur almost continuously in the digestive tract because of the enzymatic action of gastric juices and are essential for the transformation of foodstuffs into materials useful to the organism. Intracellular chemical reactions depend to a large measure on oxidation processes which usually respond much too slowly at normal body temperatures to be useful in the rapid reactions of most cells. Enzymes speed up this essential process and thus facilitate all cellular reactions. Moreover, most of the chemical constituents of cells are essentially inert and inactive until activated by specific enzymatic processes. Some enzymes are secreted into the bloodstream and other body cavities; there they act extracellularly to transform complex chemical substances into components which can pass through the cell membrane and be used in intracellular reactions. Enzymes have such a highly selective action that it is now believed that a specific enzyme may exist for every chemical reaction which can occur in protoplasm.

Two substances are functionally if not structurally related to enzymes. *Hormones* are complex compounds which are manufactured and secreted by specialized gland cells. *Vitamins* cannot be produced by the organism and must constantly be supplied from external sources. Hormones as well as vitamins are indispensable to normal cellular activity; however, like enzymes, they do not supply energy to chemical reactions and do not form any important part of the structure of protoplasm.

The proteins which constitute protoplasm occur in *colloidal suspensions*. This state multiplies the reactive surface area of the protein molecules and increases the rate of intracellular chemical reactions. Certain rearrangements of the relationship between the solid particles and the watery portion of colloidal suspensions result in changes in the consistency of substances from semisolid or *gel* states to almost watery or *sol* states. Plasma membranes are composed of gelled protoplasm which maintains the structure of the cell. The cytoplasmic portion of the cell (exclusive of certain inclusions) is made up of protoplasm in the sol or liquid state. Sol-to-gel and gel-to-sol conversions are involved in cellular activities which temporarily change the shape or configuration of the cell. Ameboid movements as well as the clotting of blood exposed to air are good examples of such transformations. The clotting reaction of blood is particularly interesting. Special protein molecules (fibrinogen) are suspended in a sol state in normal blood. At the site of injury, a sol-to-gel

transformation occurs, produces a blood clot, and closes the wound.

ENERGY RELATIONSHIPS

The term metabolic processes refers to all the chemical reactions which occur in cells or within the cavities of the organism. *Anabolic* processes result in the manufacture of compounds which are essential to the survival of cells, and *catabolic* processes destroy or decompose cellular constituents. In most normal cells protoplasm is continuously catabolized (destroyed) and replaced by concurrent anabolic processes.

The energy for these reactions is derived from oxidation (i.e., combustion). One basic mechanism is *aerobic oxidation,* a combustion process which requires free oxygen. Respiratory movements provide the oxygen which is needed for these essential reactions. A second type of combustive process, *anaerobic oxidation,* derives oxygen (and energy) from a reaction with other compounds. In living cells this *fermentation* process yields vital energies which permit survival, at least for some period of time, in the absence of free oxygen. Mammalian cells can extract only a very limited quantity of energy from anaerobic reactions and are therefore extremely dependent on a constant supply of free oxygen. Other types of cells (such as yeast) can maintain themselves indefinitely in the complete absence of oxygen; some cells (certain bacteria, for instance) even perish in the presence of free oxygen.

EXCHANGE OF MATERIALS ACROSS PROTOPLASMIC MEMBRANES

The constant chemical activity of cells requires a continuous supply of basic materials as well as the speedy removal of poisonous waste products of metabolic activity. Several transport mechanisms achieve this movement of molecules across the cell membrane.

Diffusion

Diffusion is caused by the continuous motion which is typical of ions and molecules in solution. This motion produces frequent collisions of the individual particles and results in the migration of molecules from regions of high concentration (and frequent collisions) to areas of relatively low concentration, until all portions of the solution are equiconcentrated. Materials used in intracellular reactions are nearly always present in greater concentrations outside the cell membrane and tend to diffuse into the cell. Waste products, on the other hand, are always more concentrated in the intracellular spaces and tend to diffuse out.

In complex, multicellular organisms, diffusion also plays a role in getting essential materials to the cell and removing waste products from its environment; this is an obvious requirement if the diffusion mechanism is going to do its job in the long run. For example, oxygen diffusion from the lung cavities transfers this important molecule to the bloodstream. The oxygen then moves by diffusion across the capillary walls of the blood vessels to the interstitial spaces. Finally, it crosses the cell membrane into the intracellular compartment where it is used up in aerobic oxidation processes. The waste product of this combustion, *carbon dioxide,* follows the same route in reverse and is finally expelled in the processes of exhalation. Diffusion can only occur across a *permeable membrane.* All membranes in the organism are freely permeable to oxygen and carbon dioxide but present impregnable or partial barriers to other molecules.

Filtration

Filtration refers to the movement of molecules or ions across a membrane as the result of mechanical pressure differences. In vertebrates and some invertebrates, the fluid of the blood is above atmospheric pressure whereas the interstitial fluids are at atmospheric pressure. A gradient of mechanical pressure consequently develops and forces water and certain ions and molecules through the capillary walls of the blood vessels into the interstitial spaces. This filtration process is very efficient and probably accounts for most of the movement of metabolites from the blood into the interstitial spaces.

Osmotic Exchange of Water

Truly permeable membranes (i.e., membranes which do not provide a barrier to any molecule or ion) exist, but they are very rare in biological organisms. The opposite situation is similar; truly impermeable membranes which do not permit the exchange of any particles are rare. Most biological membranes obstruct the passage of some materials and permit the transfer of others, i. e., they are *semipermeable* or *selectively permeable.* Not all cellular membranes are permeable to the same materials, and important differences in *relative* permeability exist (i.e., some substances move more easily through some membranes than through others). Many of the organism's most important processes depend on such selective permeability. For instance, ions readily pass through the walls of capillaries but may find a relative or even absolute barrier at the cell wall. Ionic concentration differences across the cell membrane result and are responsible for important properties such as excitability and conductivity.

Various factors determine the permeability of a membrane to a particular substance. One limiting factor, obviously, is *size;* the molecules may simply exceed the diameter of the available openings in the cell wall. Size probably explains why complete protein molecules cannot enter most organic cells whereas protein constituents, the amino acids, can do so with ease. *Solubility* is another important determinant of permeability. Substances that are easily soluble in fat generally pass through cellular membranes without difficulty because they can attack the fatty portions of the cell wall and, in effect, enlarge the available opening. Permeability is also determined by the *electrical potential* which usually arises across a cell membrane as a direct result of the membrane's selective permeability to some ions. The intracellular compartment of nerve cells, for instance, is negative with respect to the interstitial spaces which surround the cell. This potential difference favors the movement of positively charged particles into the cell and the outflow of negatively charged ions from it.

Osmosis refers to the movement of water which occurs as a direct result of unequal concentrations of some substance. The two concentrations are separated by a semipermeable membrane which is impermeable to that substance. For example, if sugar is added to one of two compartments which contain an equal amount of water and are separated by a membrane that is impermeable to sugar, water will move from the area of zero concentration to the area of high concentration. This movement of water continues until the mechanical (i.e., gravitational) pressure produced by the unequal volumes equals the osmotic pressure (see Figure 1.2).

The reasons for this movement of water molecules are complex. One important factor seems to be the relative size of the molecules on each side of the membrane. The water molecules on both sides of the membrane move about and have an equal tendency to cross the partition into the adjacent compartment. However, many of the

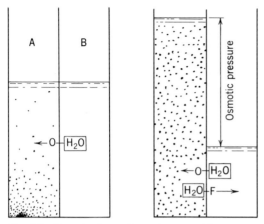

Fig. 1.2 Osmosis. A membrane impermeable to sugar prevents the dissolving sugar molecules from diffusing into chamber B. Water migrates from B to A, and equilibrium is established (right) when the osmotic flow of water (O) is equalized by the filtration of water (F) in the opposite direction. (From Carlson and Johnson, 1949.)

water molecules in the sugar-containing compartment are bound to sugar and are thus prevented from crossing the membrane. Consequently, there are more freely diffusing water molecules available on the side which contains no sugar, and a relative movement of water in the direction of the sugar solution results.

Osmotic pressure gradients exist whenever two solutions of unequal concentration are separated by a membrane which is impermeable to the solute. In the multicellular organism, such osmotic pressure gradients are common and account for the regulation of the organism's fluid balance.

Osmotic pressure gradients are also responsible for some difficulties which are encountered in the clinic and the laboratory. Cells which are removed from an organism for the purpose of study must be maintained in an environment which avoids the development of osmotic gradients across the cell membrane. If a typical mammalian cell were maintained in pure water, the cell would soon balloon and burst because of a rapid influx of water. If enough sodium chloride is added to the environment of the cell to make a 0.9% NaCl solution, only little movement of fluid occurs. This, it turns out, is the normal extracellular concentration of these ions; cells can be maintained in such a *physiological solution* although other essential ions such as potassium are not present. Substances to be injected into an organism must be dissolved in such physiological saline in order to avoid tissue damage.

TYPES OF CELLS

Receptors

Cells which have selectively developed the property of irritability serve to transduce physical energy into chemical reactions. In the most general case a receptor relays information about any change in its environment to the organism. Since it is clearly impractical for the organism to respond to any and all changes in physical energy in the same fashion, receptors are further specialized to be preferentially sensitive to specific forms of physical energy (such as mechanical, chemical, etc.).

In man and in most of the animal species which are of interest to the psychophysiologist, four general classes of receptors can be found; these are preferentially sensitive to thermal, chemical, mechanical, and visual energies, respectively. This specialization is relative rather than absolute. All receptors remain sensitive to all forms of energy (though much more energy is needed in some instances than in others). Some receptors (such as the rod and cone cells of the eye) serve almost exclusively as transducers of energy. Others (such as the mechanical and thermal receptors of the skin) combine the properties of receptors and conductors.

Effectors

Two basic classes of effectors can be distinguished. *Muscle* cells have specialized in the property of contractility; they respond to stimulation by initiating chemical processes which change the configuration of the cell. In vertebrates three varieties of muscle cells exist. The simplest *smooth* muscle has developed a special substance, the *fibrillae,* which change in shape and produce the overall deformation of the cell. Smooth muscles are found primarily in the viscera. *Striated* muscles have developed two types of fibrillae, one dark and the other light in appearance. These are arranged in an orderly sequence, giving the muscle a striated appearance. Striated muscles make up all the somatic musculature of the vertebrate organism. The third type of muscle contains the same light and dark fibrillae organized in what appears to be a random network. This muscle is found exclusively in the heart and has therefore been called *cardiac* muscle.

The second class of effector is the *gland* cell. This cell responds to irritating stimulation of the cell membrane by producing novel chemical substances which are eventually secreted through the cell membrane. Basically, there are two types of gland cells. *Duct* glands discharge their secretions into body cavities such as the stomach or intestine; and *ductless* glands empty directly into the bloodstream. The secretions of duct glands typically have a much more localized effect than those of ductless glands.

Conductors

Cells which specialize in conduction of irritability are called *neurons* or *nerve* cells (see Figure 1.3). They typically develop long narrow processes which serve to transmit excitation, often over great distances. The main body of a neuron is called the *soma* or *perikaryon.* The processes of the cell are called *axons* and *dendrites.* Dendrites are typically short processes which conduct irritation *toward* the body of the cell (i.e., in an *afferent* direction in relation to the cell body). Generally, a cell has many diffusely branched dendrites but has only a single, relatively long axon. The axon conducts irritation *away* from the cell

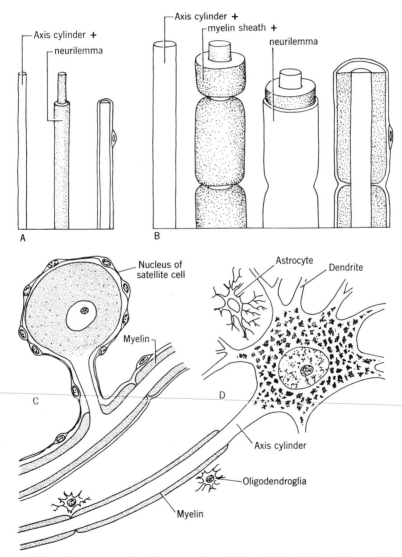

Fig. 1.3 Schematic representation of a nonmyelinated fiber, A, the right-hand figure of the group showing the fiber cut longitudinally. B shows components of a myelinated fiber. The various layers of the nerve fiber are exaggerated in certain respects. C is a dorsal root ganglion cell with its unipolar process dividing into peripheral and central branches. D is a multipolar cell of the spinal cord, with associated neuroglial cells. (From Gardner, 1963.)

(i.e., in an *efferent* direction in relation to the cell body). At its peripheral end an axon typically branches into *terminal arborizations*. Axons relate to the body or dendrites of other nerve cells or directly to muscle membranes via *end feet*, often called *terminal buttons*. The junction between the end feet and the dendrites or soma of the next cell is called a *synapse*. Approximately 100 Å separate the cell membranes at synaptic junctions. Axons are surrounded by a fatty sheath (the *myelin sheath*); in the peripheral nervous system the sheath is surrounded by *neurilemmal* cells and in the central nervous system by *glial* cells. The myelin is lipid in nature and therefore turns black when osmic acid is applied (the "Marchi" stain) and blue or black after treatment with hematoxylin (the "Weigert" stain) (see Figure 1.4). Axons vary greatly with respect to the degree of myelinization. Large-diameter fibers typically are heavily myelinated and appear white on gross inspection. Smaller fibers are poorly myelinated or essentially unmyelinated and appear gray. Axons are commonly called nerve fibers, a term which generally includes the myelin sheath. The term *node of Ranvier* is applied to interruptions in the myelin sheath which typically occur at regular intervals. In the peripheral nervous system each segment of

axon between successive nodes of Ranvier is composed of a single *Schwann* cell which forms the neurilemmal sheath. Axons typically enter and leave the central nervous system in bundles called *nerves*.

The soma of nerve cells varies in diameter from 5 to about 100 micra. Their dendrites are typically short (in the order of a few hundred micra), but some cells in the somatosensory system have dendritic processes several feet long. The axons of neurons range from a few micra to several feet in length. The cell membrane is made up of alternating layers of proteins and lipids approximately 100 to 150 Å in diameter; these are periodically interrupted by water-filled pores about 3 Å in diameter. The cell nucleus is normally located in the center of nerve cells and contains a prominent nucleolus.

The cytoplasm is a viscous substance which contains a variety of inclusions. The most important of these are the following.

1. The *Nissl bodies* consist of nucleoproteins (largely ribonucleic acid) and are typically scattered uniformly through the cytoplasmic portion of the cell. They are generally present in dendritic processes but are absent from the axon and even the portion of the soma from which the axon originates (the *axon hillock*). Nissl bodies stain blue with such basic cell dyes as cresyl violet, toluidine blue, or methylene blue. Their distribution in the cell soma is often used as an index of cellular injury. (Injury to a nerve cell produces *chromatolysis*, a reaction which is characterized by rearrangement of the Nissl bodies near the periphery of the cell body and eventual disappearance of all Nissl substance.) (See Figure 1.5.)

2. The *Golgi apparatus* is a network of protoplasmic material which stains easily with neutral red. It is typically concentrated around the nucleus of the cell, although it has also been found in the dendritic processes. It responds to injury to the cell by *retispersion* reactions which include a displacement and eventual dissolution of the Golgi apparatus. This reaction typically takes place before any changes can be observed in the Nissl substance.

3. The *mitochondria* are phospholipid-protein inclusions which often appear in granules or filaments. They are fairly evenly distributed throughout the body of neurons, generally occupying a position between the Nissl substance and the Golgi apparatus. A sharp increase in the number of mitochondria has been reported as a consequence of damage to cell processes (see Figure 1.6).

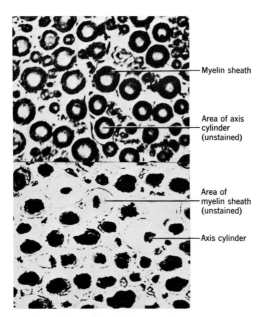

Myelin sheath

Area of axis cylinder (unstained)

Area of myelin sheath (unstained)

Axis cylinder

Fig. 1.4 Photomicrographs of cross sections of dorsal roots (rabbit). The fibers in the upper half of the figure are stained by the Weigert method to show myelin sheaths, those in the lower half by a silver method to demonstrate axis cylinders. (From Gardner, 1963.)

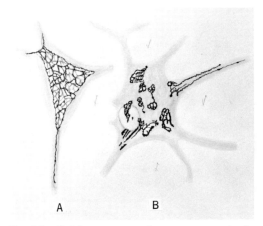

Fig. 1.5 Golgi apparatus and motor neurons in the rabbit. A, normal appearance in cell of the sublingual nucleus; B, appearance in similar cell, 4 days after cutting the sublingual nerve. (From Peele, 1961.)

4. *Neurofibrils* extend from the dendrites through the soma of the neuron into the axon. The filaments are often contorted and range from 75 to 200 Å in diameter.

Neurons are typically surrounded by *glial* cells which vary greatly in size and shape. *Neuroglial* cells (*astrocytes* and *oligodendrocytes*) serve primarily supportive and protective functions. *Microglial* cells are phagocytes which take up, transform, and remove the products of normal and abnormal disintegration of neurons.

Astrocytes typically have vascular feet which connect the cell to neighboring blood vessels. It is generally assumed that these vascular connections serve primarily the purpose of secretion or excretion from the glial cell. However, the converse, i.e., uptake of nutrients from the bloodstream, may also take place. Astrocytes typically have many additional processes which contain granular materials. The precise termination of these processes is not known. Astrocytes may proliferate in response to injury or disintegrate (see Figure 1.7).

Oligodendrocytes are poorly staining glial cells of fairly constant size and configuration. They typically have only a few processes. According to their primary location in the brain, they are classified as *satellite* cells (found around the soma of nerve cells) or *perivascular* and *interfascicular* cells (found along blood vessels and nerve fibers). Oligodendrocytes are responsible for the formation and maintenance of myelin in the central nervous system.

Connective Cells

Some cells specialize in the manufacture of long fibrous strands which make up the bulk of connective tissue. These tightly interwoven fibers give the connective tissue a tough elastic consistency. Connective cells are found in all parts of the organism and generally provide a framework for other cells. A special type of connective cell is capable of manufacturing calcium-phosphorus compounds which harden into rigid structural members; this cell makes up the bones and cartilage tissues of the organism.

Epithelial Cells

These are typically thin and flat or tall and columnar supportive or connective cells which line the exposed surfaces of the organism.

Fat Cells

Special "storage" cells, which exist in most complex organisms, have developed the ability to store large amounts of fat. The bulk of these cells is composed of inert fat. The cell cytoplasm and nucleus are compressed into a thin wall which surrounds the fat.

Organization of cells. Groups of cells of common functional properties constitute a *tissue*. In higher organisms several different tissues may cooperate in a particular function and thus form an *organ*, such as the heart. Organs may be further organized into *organ systems* such as the digestive system or the circulatory system.

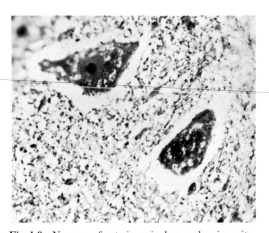

Fig. 1.6 Neurons of anterior spinal gray, showing mitochondria stained and Golgi apparatus in a negative image for the kitten. Photomicrograph, ×645. (From Peele, 1961.)

Blood vessel   Astrocyte

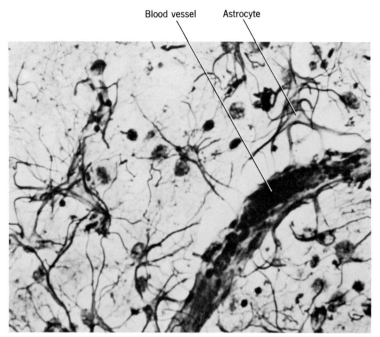

Fig. 1.7 Photomicrograph of a section of human cerebral cortex stained for astrocytes. The cortex had been involved by an infection which had caused astrocytes to increase in number. The leader to the indicated astrocyte ends on the nucleus. Note how the extensions of this cell attach to the adjacent blood vessel. (From Gardner, 1963.)

THE NEURON AND ITS BASIC MECHANISM OF ACTION

Ionic Transport across a Cell Membrane

Each cell of the organism is surrounded by *interstitial fluids* (i.e., those *extracellular fluids* which are in direct contact with cell membranes). This fluid is similar in most respects to the aqueous solution inside the cell body which is called *intracellular fluid.* Nutrient materials and waste products cross the cell membrane easily. A number of mechanisms reduce the permeability of this membrane to substances which are either essential or harmful to the metabolism of the cell.

One of the most important differences between extracellular and intracellular fluids is a marked imbalance in the concentrations of certain ions. This imbalance is directly responsible for some of the electrochemical events which underly the important membrane properties of irritability and conductivity. The concentrations of sodium (Na^+) and chloride (Cl^-) are much higher in the interstitial fluids than inside the cell. The concentrations of potassium (K^+) and organic anions (A^-), on the other hand, are much higher in the cytoplasm than in the interstitial fluids. The inequality of these concentrations is related to the fact that the cell membrane represents a selective barrier to ion movement; thus, the ions diffuse through the cell wall at only a fraction of their normal rate. This inequality combines with active transport mechanisms which maintain a low intracellular concentration of sodium and a relatively high concentration of potassium.

The ion imbalance between the interior and exterior of a cell creates an electrical potential across the cell membrane which may reach 50 to 90 millivolts. This *steady* or *resting potential* influences the transport of ions across the membrane. Since the inside of the cell is negative in relation to the interstitial fluid, cations ($+$) tend to move into the cell and anions ($-$) move out of it. Potassium tends to flow out of the cell because of its high initial concentration but also tends to diffuse *into* the cell because of the distribution of electrical charges on both sides of the membrane. These two tendencies almost cancel each other, so that only a slight tendency remains for K^+ to move out of the cell. Chloride is subject to similar opposing forces. There normally is little or no net diffusion of Cl^- through the cell membrane; the tendency of chloride to diffuse into the cell because of excessive extracellular concentrations is exactly balanced by electrical opposition to the movement of negatively charged ions into the cell.

The situation is quite different for Na^+ and A^-. Here the concentrations and the electrical differences act in concert. The cell membrane is nearly impermeable to A^-, and there is little or no movement of anions. The membrane is less permeable to Na^+ than to K^+, but a steady movement of sodium into the cell takes place. The intracellular concentration of Na^+ nevertheless remains nearly constant in living cells, probably because some active transport mechanism requiring metabolic energy produces a compensatory movement of sodium ions out of the cell. This active transport is usually accompanied by the uptake of potassium and has been called the *sodium-potassium pump*. The transmembrane potential (i.e., the resting potential) arises because the cell membrane is much more permeable to potassium than to sodium and because the active sodium transport maintains the intracellular sodium concentrations at a low, steady value.

A cell at rest is said to be in a state of *polarization*. Any external or internal (metabolic) influence which changes the polarization of the cell membrane also modifies its excitability. For instance, a state of hyperpolarization can be induced by a movement of potassium into the cell, resulting in a marked decrease in its excitability threshold. A loss of K^+ ions, on the other hand, produces depolarization and lowers the threshold. Transient changes in the ionic permeability of the cell membrane produce momentary fluctuations in the transmembrane potential. These electrochemical changes are propagated along the cell membrane and may be transmitted to adjacent neurons across the synapse. It is these transient electrochemical events that carry all information in the nervous system. They are also responsible for the special properties which permit the transduction of physical energies into information which is useful to the nervous system.

The propagated disturbance is called an *impulse*. Its electrical correlate constitutes an *action potential*. The energy for the transmission of nerve impulses is derived from the metabolic activity of the nerve cell itself, not from the physical stimulus which originated the ionic disturbance. As the action potential moves along a cell membrane, successive sections of the neuron become negative in relation to the surrounding portions of the cell. This area of negativity may

encompass several centimeters in larger fibers. If one attaches two electrodes as in Figure 1.8, a sudden negative potential can be recorded; this potential is followed by its mirror image as the traveling disturbance reaches the second electrode. The distance between the two portions of the wave is determined by the distance between the electrodes. The passage of the action potential is described in its entirety by half of this diphasic wave.

It is customary to damage the area under the second electrode in order to study the electrical potential. The resulting monophasic nerve impulse has been studied in great detail. One type of action potential is common to all nerve cells. Its size and speed of conduction may vary between neurons. Typically, the potential differences accompanying the propagation of an action potential is in the order of 100 millivolts and persists for only a few milliseconds.

The ionic changes that underlie the development of the action potential are complex. Basically, a brief and highly specific increase in the membrane permeability to Na^+ permits sodium to flow into the cell until the membrane potential approaches the Na^+ equilibrium potential. When the membrane permeability to sodium increases above its permeability to potassium, Na^+ ions are driven into the cell because the extracellular con-

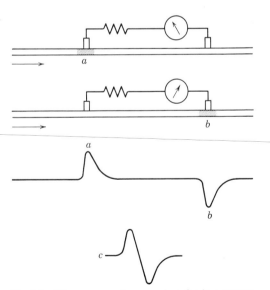

Fig. 1.8 The passage of a nerve impulse in a nonconducting medium. The record obtained when the two electrodes are close together, as shown at *c*, gives the appearance of a diphasic wave. (From Brazier, 1961.)

centrations of sodium are normally higher than those inside the cell. The membrane potential (negative inside the cell) acts to further this movement of positive ions. The momentary 500-fold increase in permeability to sodium is the result of the rapid reduction in membrane voltage which occurs as a direct consequence of suprathreshold stimulation. Once the increased permeability of the membrane has induced an influx of sodium into the cell, a chain reaction is started which produces further depolarization.

The cell returns to a polarized state because the increased permeability to Na^+ is transient and because the membrane permeability to potassium increases as the membrane potential approaches zero. The resting membrane is preferentially permeable to potassium, whereas the active membrane is preferentially permeable to sodium. The electrochemical changes which are responsible for the action potential can therefore be described simply as a sudden change from a potassium to a sodium membrane.

The propagation of an action potential depends on the following ionic changes. When a spike potential is initiated, the membrane potential in the active region is near the sodium equilibrium potential. The potential of neighboring inactive sections of the membrane is near the potassium equilibrium potential. Consequently, charges flow along the outside of the membrane from the inactive to the active region. Here they enter the cell and return through the intracellular fluid to the inactive section, where they again flow out of the cell. The local circuit which is thus set up lowers the membrane voltage in the inactive region. When this potential difference reaches threshold, the inactive region becomes active, permeability to sodium increases, and the membrane potential decreases to the equilibrium potential of sodium. In this fashion the action potential moves away from the stimulating electrode at a constant speed in all directions.

In myelinated fibers this process is modified by the insulator properties of the fatty myelin sheath. The electrical membrane of the cell is in effective contact with the extracellular fluid only at the regularly spaced nodes of Ranvier; the distance between successive nodes is described by a ratio of about 100:1 for fiber diameter to distance between successive nodes. Since an interchange of ions can take place only at these periodic interruptions of fiber insulation, the action potential hops along the fiber from node to node; this condition is described as *saltatory conduction*. Since only

small portions of the cell membrane must be depolarized for saltatory conduction to occur, the velocity of conduction is about twenty times greater in myelinated than in unmyelinated fibers.

It has been suggested that the neurohumor acetylcholine may play an important role in the generation and propagation of action potentials in nerve fibers. This hypothesis suggests that acetylcholine, which depolarization liberates from a bound and inactive form, increases cell membrane permeability to sodium by combining with a "receptor" protein. Repolarization of the membrane occurs when the liberated acetylcholine is destroyed by cholinesterase, which is typically present in high concentrations. This interpretation is parsimonious, since it explains the propagation of nerve impulses along an axon in terms of the same mechanisms which have been proposed for the transmission of impulses from one neuron to another. However, recent experimental evidence suggests that some nerves do not synthesize acetylcholine in appreciable quantities (but do conduct nerve impulses adequately).

Electrical Properties of the Cell Membrane of Neurons

The propagation of action potentials is subject to the *all-or-none law*. This law states that once a neuron has been stimulated to the point where a traveling disturbance is created, the size of this response and the speed of its conduction are independent of the intensity of the stimulation. Neurons vary with respect to the size and conduction velocity of their action potentials, but the response of a given cell remains constant. This law does not apply to the initiation and propagation of excitation at each end of the often very long nerve cells; these may be determined by different electrochemical processes. Furthermore, the size and conduction velocity of the action potential of a given cell depends on the state of the cell at the time of stimulation. The size of the potential may be severely affected by fatigue (such as may be created by the recent passage of another action potential) or by a disturbance of cellular metabolism as produced by various drugs.

Figure 1.9 illustrates the events following electrical stimulation of a nerve fiber. Most of the electrical current flows from the anode to the cathode along the low-resistance pathway provided by the extracellular fluid and has little effect on the fiber itself. Some of the current flows from the anode through the cell membrane into the cell and then flows through the axoplasm

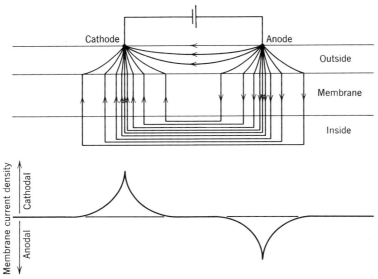

Fig. 1.9 Current distribution in the nerve fiber during passage of constant current from an external source. Only a segment of fiber is shown. Lines with directional marks indicate approximate paths of flow of the current. Closely spaced lines indicate high current density. The current spreads from electrodes in all available directions and passes through the membrane over a wide area. Note that the current spreads laterally into extrapolar regions. The lateral spread of penetrating current lines is illustrated (below) by a plot of density of current lines (membrane current) against distance along nerve. The current falls off exponentially with distance from the electrode. As electrodes are brought closer together, cathodal and anodal effects interfere in the interpolar region. The transmembrane potential at a point is altered proportionately to the current density at that point. (From Woodbury and Patton, 1961.)

to the cathode. Since the membrane provides *resistance* to this current flow, a potential drop opposite in sign to that of the resting membrane potential occurs at the cathode (where the current flows *out* of the cell). This results in *hypopolarization* or depolarization of the cell membrane. Current flows *inward* at the anode, producing an increase in the transmembrane potential or a state of *hyperpolarization*. If the membrane at the cathode is reduced to the threshold value for the cell, an action potential originates while the excitability is decreased at the anode.

This interpretation of neuron response to stimulation considers the nerve fiber merely as a pure resistance. However, the high-resistance cell membrane separates highly conductive media in the external and internal fluid compartments. This arrangement constitutes a capacitance which affects the time course and spatial properties of the transmembrane potential. Voltage is proportional to the charge on the capacitor, and some of the charges on the membrane must be neutralized if the voltage is to be reduced. This process takes time, and the membrane capacitance hinders the

development of changes in the transmembrane potential.

The changes in membrane potential which are produced by the application of a stimulating current are greatest at the electrode and diminish exponentially as a function of distance from the point of application (see bottom of Figure 1.9).

The strength of an abruptly applied and terminated (square pulse) current required to exceed a cell's threshold and initiate an action potential is a function of the duration of current flow. The membrane capacitance is charged gradually so that the change in transmembrane potential is maximal only after an appreciable period of time. This delay implies that a cell threshold is a function of stimulus duration, a relationship which is shown in the strength-duration curve shown in Figure 1.10.

Subthreshold stimulation of a nerve fiber does not evoke an action potential. Instead, it produces temporary changes in the cell threshold which may determine the cell's reaction to subsequent stimulation. When a brief "conditioning" stimulus is applied a few milliseconds before the presentation

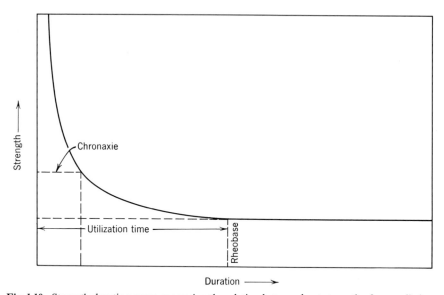

Fig. 1.10 Strength-duration curve expressing the relation between least strength of an applied current and least time during which it must flow in order to reach the threshold. There is a minimal current density below which excitation does not occur, but strength-duration curves do not express subliminal events. Since utilization time is difficult to measure accurately, Lucas, Lapicque, and others have taken as a measure of excitability the time during which current twice rheobase must flow in order to excite. This time interval is called *chronaxy* (chronaxie) or *excitation time*. (From Woodbury and Patton, 1961.)

of a "test" stimulus, the intensity of the test shock required to elicit an action potential will be lower than normal. This facilitation persists for a short time after the conditioning stimulus is presented, because the voltage changes induced by it disappear only gradually. The lowered threshold is not spatially confined to the site of stimulation; rather, it extends on either side, decreasing exponentially to the resting threshold level. When a prolonged conditioning stimulus is presented, a temporary increase in excitability occurs at the stimulating electrode (the cathode). This increase summates with test stimuli which are applied shortly after the onset of the conditioning stimulus. The facilitatory effect decreases even though the conditioning stimulus is maintained, a phenomenon referred to as *accommodation*. After the conditioning stimulus is withdrawn, the membrane excitability at the cathode falls below the resting level and recovers slowly. This state is known as *postcathodal depression*. At the anode, opposite changes in excitability develop, as shown in Figure 1.11.

Suprathreshold stimulation of a nerve depolarizes the cell membrane at the cathode (*catelectrotonus*); at the same time that the membrane under the anode becomes hyperpolarized (*anelectrotonus*).

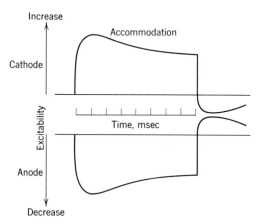

Fig. 1.11 Excitability changes in a nerve during the passage of a current for a short period of time. Note that the nerve under the negative electrode (cathode) increases in excitability very quickly, but that this excitability slowly decreases (accommodation) as the current continues to flow and drops very abruptly when the current is turned off. In fact, the nerve momentarily becomes less sensitive to stimuli than it was before the current was applied. Converse changes occur in that part of the nerve under the positive electrode (anode). (From Gardner, 1963.)

When the stimulating current is terminated, the membrane returns to its normal resting level.

When a constant current is maintained, a nerve fiber eventually ceases to respond, because the excitation of the nerve fiber depends on the rate of change in the transmembrane potential. The existence of a *minimal gradient* of excitation is suggested by the fact that a stimulus which increases only gradually in intensity fails to elicit a response from the nerve in spite of clearly suprathreshold intensities. The reduced efficiency of persisting or gradually increasing stimuli is also known as accommodation. There is little or no accommodation in nerve fibers carrying "pain" information, and generally less accommodation in sensory than in motor nerves. It has been suggested that the effects of subthreshold or prolonged stimuli are related to the fact that the nerve cell does not behave as an inert conductor but generates forces which tend to oppose externally applied currents.

Recovery from suprathreshold stimuli occurs along a time course which is closely related to the phenomena just described. Once the threshold of a cell is exceeded by stimulation, a complex series of electrochemical changes occur; we have called this the action potential (see Figure 1.12). Following a brief buildup of subthreshold changes in the transmembrane potential (the local process), a very brief (typically less than 0.5 millisecond) *spike potential* arises; this represents the information-carrying portion of the action potential. During the propagation of this spike potential, the nerve fiber is in a state of *absolute refractoriness* (i.e., it cannot be excited by any stimulus, regardless of its intensity). This state puts an upper limit on the maximum number of impulses which can be conducted by a neuron. The limit has been calculated and demonstrated experimentally to be about 2000 impulses per second.

The absolute refractory period coincides roughly with the rising portion of the spike poten-

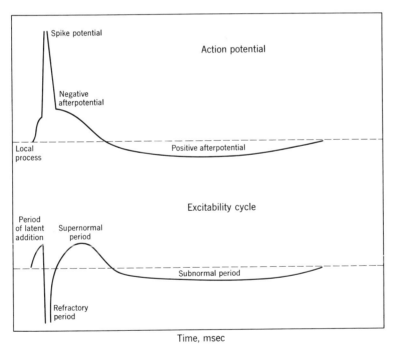

Time, msec

Fig. 1.12 The action potential and the excitability cycle of nerve fibers. The duration of the first two phases has been exaggerated in proportion to the second two phases in order to display all phases clearly. In the action potential "local process" refers to the period when purely local changes, including the electronic potentials, occur at the site of stimulation. These changes are accompanied by a period of latent addition in the excitability of the fiber. The spike potential is the "nervous impulse" and corresponds to the refractory period. The negative and positive after potentials correspond, respectively, to the supernormal and subnormal periods of excitability. (From Morgan and Stellar, 1950.)

tial and the early stages of the falling phase. It is followed by a more prolonged period of *relative refractoriness,* which corresponds to the transition period between the spike potential and the negative after potential which subsequently develops. During this 3- to 5-millisecond period of relative refractoriness, only very intense stimuli elicit a propagated action potential, and the size of the spike potential is smaller than normal (see Figure 1.13). The smaller spike potentials are propagated at a slower conduction rate than usual.

The spike potential is followed by a *negative afterpotential* which is of much lower amplitude than the spike potential and typically lasts 5 to 15 milliseconds. During this period the nerve fiber is in a state of heightened excitability and responds to subthreshold stimulation.

This *period of supernormality* is followed by a relatively long (50 to 80 milliseconds) *positive afterpotential,* which is correlated with a period of *subnormality.* During this time the nerve fiber is less excitable than normal, and conduction velocities are lower. The positive afterpotential is assumed to represent a continuation of the same electrochemical events which are responsible for the period of relative refractoriness.

The repetition rate of stimuli greatly influences the excitability of nerve fibers. Rapidly repeated stimuli shorten the negative and increase the positive afterpotentials, prolong the refractory period, and delay the recovery phase. Rapidly repeated stimuli may produce inhibitory rather than excitatory effects. This inhibition was first described by Wedensky, who observed that a fatigued muscle responded only to the first of a series of rapidly repeated stimuli but continued to respond adequately to stimuli presented at a lower repetition rate. The conditions for *Wedensky's inhibition* are met whenever the repetition rate is adjusted so that successive stimuli fall within the relative refractory period of the immediately preceding stimulus. This adjustment produces subnormal spike potentials which may be unable to excite a fatigued muscle, or to be propagated along partially blocked nerve fibers or synapses.

Before we turn to a discussion of conduction mechanisms at cell junctions, it may be useful to represent the electrical properties of nerve fibers in terms of a simple electrical circuit. A cell membrane has a relatively high electrical resistance because ions are able to permeate it only at a slow rate. It has capacitance because it separates two low-resistance media, the extracellular and intracellular fluids. If we think of a nerve fiber as being composed of short segments, we can draw equivalent electrical circuits which would show the same response to an applied current as the nerve cell (see Figure 1.14).

Transmission of Information between Neurons

Neurons communicate with one another at axodendritic or axosomatic junctions where the terminal arborizations of one cell come into close contact with the dendrites or somata of other neurons. At these *synaptic* junctions, only a few hundred Angstrom units separate adjacent cells, and transmission of the action potential becomes possible. The electrical disturbance does not simply jump the gap between adjacent cells as was initially assumed. Instead, the arrival of an action potential at the end feet of an axon stimulates secretory activity of small vesicles which contain neurohumoral substances in inactive or bound form. When liberated, these chemicals become active and diffuse across the synaptic gap. They subsequently interact with specific receptor sites located on the postsynaptic membrane and produce a change in the transmembrane potential of the adjacent cell.

There appear to be many different neural transmitters, and it is generally assumed today that the action of the various neurohumors may differ significantly. Some (the excitors) are thought to depolarize the postsynaptic membrane by reducing the potential difference between the inside and the outside of the postsynaptic cell membrane. This electrotonic potential is not, itself, propagated; it decays exponentially with distance from the site of transmitter action much like the electro-

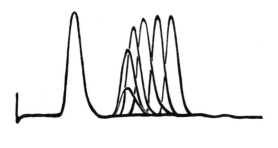

Fig. 1.13 The relatively refractory period of motor fibers in a frog's nerve. Successive pictures have been superimposed so that the first responses are coincident. Paired maximal stimuli were given, the second following the first at intervals of 1.4, 1.6, 2.0, 2.6, 3.6, and 4.4 msec. Time marker, 1 msec. (From von Brücke et al., 1941.)

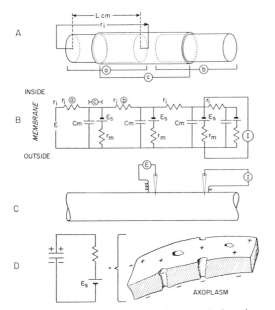

Fig. 1.14 Derivation of the approximate equivalent electrical circuit of a long, thin, cylindrical axon. In an electrical circuit diagram a straight line (————) represents an ideal conductor (zero resistance), a zigzag line (—∧∧—) represents an ideal resistance (no capacitance between its terminals), and —|⊢— represents an ideal capacitor (infinite resistance between its terminals). In A, the axoplasm and membrane are each marked off into halfway overlapping segments L cm long (accurate representation of the nerve requires that L be no more than about 0.05 cm). Any segment of axoplasm has a resistance (r_i) which is in series with the adjoining segments. Thus the upper line in B consists of a series of resistors, each of which is the electrical equivalent of the correspondingly labeled segment of axoplasm in A. Extracellular fluid is large and is assumed to have no resistance; this is represented by the lower horizontal line in B. The equivalent circuit of a segment of membrane (c) must be connected between intracellular and extracellular fluid equivalents at the juction of two r_i's. For example, segment c is connected between the axoplasmic segments a and b.

C, experimental arrangement for measuring cable properties. Compare with B, where a current source is shown applied across the membrane at one point; the "transmembrane potential" of the equivalent circuit can be measured at any other point.

D, derivation of the equivalent circuit of a membrane segment. The equivalent consists of a capacitor (c_m) representing the insulating, ion-impermeable regions of membrane in parallel with a resistor (r_m) representing the ion-permeable regions of membrane. (For convenience, the ion-permeable region is indicated by pores penetrating the membrane.) A battery of potential ε_s is connected in series with r_m to signify the existence of a steady transmembrane potential. (From Woodbury and Patton, 1961.)

tonic response to electrical stimulation of a nerve fiber. The *excitatory postsynaptic potential* (EPSP) may (1) involve a sufficiently large area of the postsynaptic membrane to generate a propagated action potential, (2) produce a subthreshold depolarization which decays without further affecting the electrical properties of the postsynaptic membrane, or (3) produce a subthreshold depolarization of the postsynaptic membrane which summates either with adjacent areas of depolarization (due to the action of a transmitter which is released from another button) or with previous or subsequent changes in the postsynaptic membrane potential to elicit a propagated action potential.

Other transmitter substances (the inhibitors) are thought to increase the potential difference across the postsynaptic cell membrane. This induces a state of hyperpolarization and reduces the neuron's level of excitability. These *inhibitory postsynaptic potentials* (IPSP) are thought to be the basic mechanism of inhibitory processes in the nervous system (see Figure 1.15).

All postsynaptic potentials are local, graded responses which are not propagated, decay with time, and summate temporally as well as spatially. The size of the postsynaptic potential is related to the intensity of the presynaptic electrical activ-

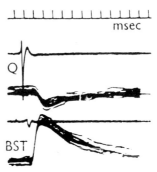

Fig. 1.15 Intracellular recordings of hyperpolarization during inhibition and depolarization during excitation. In the record marked Q the superimposed sweeps show the response of a biceps-semitendinosus motor neuron to stimulation of the group Ia afferents of the monosynaptic pathway to its anatagonist muscle (the quadriceps). The downward deflection indicates hyperpolarization (and inhibition). In the record marked BST the response of the same cell to stimulation of its own monosynaptic arc is a depolarization indicative of heightened excitability. Above each of the multiple sweeps is the afferent volley recorded from the stimulated L6 dorsal root, negatively downward. Only the last represents a propagated potential change. (From Coombs et al., 1955b.)

ity. The intensity of the presynaptic electrical activity is presumed to be related to the quantity of transmitter substance which is released; this quantity, in turn, determines the size of the area of the postsynaptic membrane which becomes hyper- or hypopolarized (see Figure 1.16).

Some cells exhibit depolarizing as well as hyperpolarizing postsynaptic potentials. Others are endowed with apparently more specific response mechanisms and show either only excitatory or only inhibitory postsynaptic potential changes. All muscle fibers and some neurons develop only depolarizing postsynaptic potentials. Gland cells, on the other hand, always show a hyperpolarization reaction to any form of stimulation. Most neurons in the vertebrate nervous system show both excitatory and inhibitory reactions. (The commonly used terms "excitatory" and "inhibitory" postsynaptic potentials are not, strictly speaking, synonymous with "depolarizing" and "hyperpolarizing," although common usage tends in that direction. Some muscle fibers generate depolarization potentials but no propagated electrical "excitation.")

These two electrically opposing states may coexist temporally in different parts of the cell membrane; in fact, they interact to determine the response of the cell. The transmission of information is thus *not* completed by the generation of a depolarizing or excitatory postsynaptic potential. The chain of transmission is broken if the intensity or area of the excitatory potential is insufficient to exceed the postsynaptic threshold or to overcome the inhibition which may be simultaneously generated by other hyperpolarizing inputs to the same cell. The hyperpolarizing (inhibitory) postsynaptic potential is itself the end result of synaptic transmission initiated by a spike potential. This spike potential represents excitatory activity in the presynaptic cell and requires a depolarizing (excitatory potential) influence to become a propagated electrical disturbance.

It seems unlikely, at present, that the sign of the postsynaptic potential is determined by the transmitter substance itself. *Acetylcholine,* for instance, is known to produce depolarization (i.e., "excitation") at neuromuscular junctions, but it hyperpolarizes the pacemaker cells of the heart muscle. However, the chemical composition of a transmitter substance may affect synaptic transmission

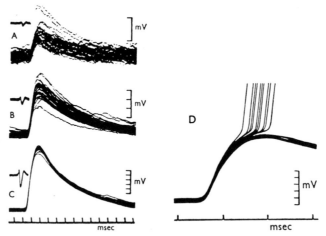

Fig. 1.16 Postsynaptic potentials recorded by a microelectrode from inside a motor neuron in the spinal cord of a cat. The responses shown were evoked monosynaptically by stimulation of the dorsal root and were recorded from an anterior horn cell. In A, B, and C the afferent volleys were of three different strengths, as indicated by their size in the insets (all recorded at the same amplification). The motor neuron responses were correspondingly graded as shown by the scales of amplification to the right of each record. All records depict the superposition of about 40 traces (positively up). In A, B, and C the degree of depolarization was insufficient to trigger a spike potential. In D from another neuron, spikes have been generated following ten of the stimuli and rise out of the picture. (From Coombs et al., 1955a.)

in other ways. For instance, transmitters that consist of large, complex molecules are not likely to be stored in great quantities in the presynaptic membrane. Action potentials arriving at such a synapse would produce only a few postsynaptic potentials and would soon exhaust the transmitter stores. The complexity of the molecular structure of the transmitter substance also affects the rapidity of transmission across the synapse, since the speed of diffusion is a function of molecular dimension and structure. Labile transmitter substances (such as acetylcholine) produce only brief and transient effects on the postsynaptic membrane. Other substances which are less rapidly destroyed produce larger and more prolonged electrical disturbances. The duration and stability of a postsynaptic potential may also be influenced by the nature of the chemical bond between the transmitter substance and its receptor site on the postsynaptic membrane.

The transmission of information across a synaptic junction interposes a delay which may be as long as several milliseconds. (Typically, the synaptic delay is about 0.3 to 0.4 millisecond.) This delay is presumably related to (1) the secretory activity of the presynaptic vesicles, (2) the diffusion of the transmitter substance across the approximately 100 Å gap which separates the pre- and postsynaptic membrane, (3) the chemical reactions required to bind the transmitter to its receptor site and develop the postsynaptic potential, and (4) the electrogenic reactions necessary to transform the postsynaptic potential into a propagated spike potential.

The identification of specific transmitter substances has been exceedingly difficult, partly because the quantities released at a synaptic junction are very small. Historically, the first suggestion that synaptic transmission might be based on the release of specific neurohumoral substances was made by Dubois-Reymond. Subsequent work by Otto Loewi demonstrated that stimulation of the vagus nerve resulted in the liberation of a substance (he called it vagus substance) which produced an inhibitory effect on cardiac muscle. Loewi also observed that stimulation of sympathetic fibers resulted in the secretion of an "accelerator" substance which produced opposite effects on cardiac muscle. Later investigations have shown that the vagus substance is *acetylcholine* and that this neurohumoral substance acts as a transmitter at all neuromuscular junctions in the somatomotor and the parasympathetic nervous system. Loewi's "accelerator" substance turned

out to be an epinephrine-like neurohumor which has recently been shown to resemble *norepinephrine*. Norepinephrine is now known to act as a transmitter substance at neuromuscular junctions in the sympathetic nervous system. However, not all neuromuscular junctions in the sympathetic nervous system are *adrenergic* (i.e., selectively sensitive to epinephrine or norepinephrine). The neuroglandular junctions at the sweat glands, although they form part of the sympathetic portion of the automatic nervous system, are specifically activated by acetylcholine. Certain sympathetic vasodilator fibers (neurons which initiate an increase in the diameter of blood vessels) also appear to release acetylcholine.

Acetylcholine has also been found to be the transmitter substance at neural junctions in the ganglia of the sympathetic nervous system. The substance is present in relatively high concentrations throughout the central nervous system, and there is much circumstantial evidence to suggest that at least some synapses in the central nervous system (CNS) may be cholinergically mediated. Epinephrine and norepinephrine are nonrandomly distributed in the central nervous system and are known to affect central nervous activity. Some recent evidence links the activity of specific portions of the central nervous system to the action of adrenergic substances. However, it is difficult to demonstrate conclusively that any substance acts as a neurohumoral transmitter in the central nervous system, because even a small portion of the brain contains literally millions of synaptic junctions which may not be homogeneous with respect to their transmissive properties. The central nervous system contains many chemical substances which could potentially serve as transmitters of neural impulses. One of the important frontiers in modern biological science is the determination of specific transmitters in the central nervous system. Generally, a transmitter must meet the following criteria: (1) it must mimic the action of neural action potentials; (2) its effectiveness must change as a function of the same chemical or neural manipulations which are known to modify neural excitation; (3) it must occur naturally, preferably in a nonrandom distribution; and (4) a naturally occurring antagonist must inactivate the suspected neurohumor with the rapidity required for the transmission of as many as 2000 discrete neural potentials per second.

Strictly speaking, no presently known chemical fulfills all these requirements. However, a number of substances meet a sufficient number of criteria to be suspect. Others produce such marked effects on central nervous functions that an explanation in terms of a direct or indirect (i.e., metabolic) action on the transmission properties of certain parts of the brain appears reasonable. Perhaps the most promising of these suspected transmitters is *serotonin* (5-hydroxytryptamine) and metabolically related substances which have been found to be selectively active in many parts of the brain. *Gamma-aminobutyric acid* (GABA) may be an inhibitory transmitter in the sense that it inactivates postsynaptic membranes.

Rather than present largely speculative evidence for the central transmission properties of these suspected substances, it may be more instructive to discuss in some detail the properties of the two neurohumors which are known to have transmitter functions in the peripheral nervous system.

Acetylcholine is present in many neural tissues in a bound, inactive form which is not hydrolyzed (i.e., destroyed) by its antagonist, *cholinesterase*. Nerve tissue is known to synthesize acetylcholine by a process involving the acetylation of choline. Acetylcholine may have two rather distinct actions at neuroeffector and synaptic junctions. At neuroeffector junctions in the parasympathetic nervous system, the heart, and endocrine gland cells, acetylcholine produces effects very similar to those of muscarine (a poison derived from certain species of mushrooms). The term *muscarinic* has been employed to describe these effects. At synaptic junctions in sympathetic ganglia and at skeletal neuroeffector junctions, acetylcholine acts more like the alkaloid nicotine, which first stimu-

lates (depolarizes) and then paralyzes or inhibits (hyperpolarizes) the activity of cells in autonomic ganglia and skeletal muscles. These effects are called *nicotinic*.

Atropine and related alkaloids selectively block the muscarinic action of acetylcholine, whereas *nicotine* and *curare* selectively prevent the nicotinic action of the neurohumor. The precise mechanism of action of these *blocking agents* is not known. Atropine prevents all muscarinic responses to exogenous (i.e., injected) acetylcholine, regardless of whether the normal effects are excitatory (as in the intestine) or inhibitory (as in the heart). However, this blocking agent is only moderately effective in preventing the response to neural stimulation in the same systems. In other instances, atropine is equally effective in blocking the effects of exogenous and endogenous acetylcholine. It is possible that these differences are related to different releaser mechanisms. Atropine may block acetylcholine which is extracellularly released by cholinergic nerves but does not prevent the effects of intracellularly liberated acetylcholine (see Table 1.1).

Structures innervated by cholinergic nerves are stimulated by three *parasympathomimetic* agents: (1) *choline esters* such as acetylcholine, methacholine, carbachol, and bethanechol; (2) *cholinesterase inhibitors* such as physostigmine, neostigmine, and diisopropylfluorophosphate; and (3) *naturally occurring alkaloids* such as pilocarpine, arecoline, and muscarine.

The cholinesters typically possess three distinct pharmacological actions, muscarinic, nicotinic, and curariform. Slight changes in the side chains of these esters produce substances which almost

TABLE 1.1
Structural formulas of choline and related choline esters

Choline	$(CH_3)_3{\equiv}N{\cdot}CH_2{\cdot}CH_2OH$ $\quad\quad\quad\mid$ $\quad\quad\quad OH$
Acetylcholine	$(CH_3)_3{\equiv}N{\cdot}CH_2{\cdot}CH_2{\cdot}O{\cdot}COCH_3$ $\quad\quad\quad\mid$ $\quad\quad\quad OH$
Methacholine (Acetyl-β-methylcholine)	$(CH_3)_3{\equiv}N{\cdot}CH_2{\cdot}CH(CH_3){\cdot}O{\cdot}COCH_3$ $\quad\quad\quad\mid$ $\quad\quad\quad OH$
Carbachol (Carbaminoylcholine)	$(CH_3)_3{\equiv}N{\cdot}CH_2{\cdot}CH_2{\cdot}O{\cdot}CONH_2$ $\quad\quad\quad\mid$ $\quad\quad\quad OH$
Bethanechol (Carbaminoyl-β-methylcholine)	$(CH_3)_3{\equiv}N{\cdot}CH_2{\cdot}CH(CH_3){\cdot}O{\cdot}CONH_2$ $\quad\quad\quad\mid$ $\quad\quad\quad OH$

exclusively exert only one of these actions. For instance, *succinylcholine* is an excellent curariform agent but has only weak muscarinic and ganglionic effects; the esters of *β-methylcholine* exhibit only muscarinic responses; and the aromatic *benzoylcholine* exhibits properties similar to those of nicotine. *Carbachol* has strong nicotinic actions and is markedly resistant to destruction by cholinesterase, a property which makes this substance a very useful experimental drug.

When a nerve is stimulated, acetylcholine is released in an active form and is rapidly destroyed by cholinesterase. It is found in varying concentrations in nearly all parts of the nervous system. The concentrations of acetylcholine and cholinesterase are typically higher in gray matter than in white matter, presumably because of the presence of cells and synaptic junctions. In the embryonic nervous system, the appearance of high concentrations of cholinesterase accompanies functional development. This enzyme is present in very large quantities and acts sufficiently rapidly to destroy an amount of acetylcholine equal to what is required to stimulate a postsynaptic potential within the refractory period of a nerve. For instance, in a single frog muscle endplate, enough cholinesterase has been found to destroy 1.6×10^9 molecules of acetylcholine in 1 millisecond. Cholinesterase is inhibited by a large number of drugs which thereby protect acetylcholine from hydrolysis and intensify and prolong its excitatory action upon neural tissue. The most powerful drugs in this category are physostigmine, neostigmine, and diisopropylfluorophosphate (DFP).

Epinephrine (adrenaline) is the major active principle of the adrenal medulla. It is composed of two basic constituents, 1, 2-*dihydroxybenzene* (*catechol*) and *ethanolamine*. Epinephrine acts directly on certain smooth muscles which are innervated by the sympathetic portion of the autonomic nervous system. Denervation of structures which normally receive adrenergic innervation greatly increases their sensitivity to circulating epinephrine.

Demethylated epinephrine (*norepinephrine, noradrenaline*) is released by postganglionic fibers of the sympathetic nervous system and appears to act as the transmitter substance at this neuromuscular junction. (Actually, norepinephrine constitutes only about 80% of the compound which is liberated upon stimulation of the postganglionic fibers. The other 20% are made up largely of epinephrine.) Norepinephrine also occurs naturally in the adrenal medulla.

Possible metabolic precursors of norepinephrine are *dihydroxyphenyleserine* and *hydroxytyramine (dopamine)*. Although specific antagonists have not been described for any of the catecholamines, it has been suggested that enzymes such as *monoamine oxidase* may play an important role in the inactivation of epinephrine and norepinephrine. Several *adrenergic blocking agents* have been described which selectively inhibit the response of effector cells to stimulation of postganglionic adrenergic fibers. These blocking agents act directly on the postsynaptic membrane. *Dibenamine* (N,N-dibenzyl-β-chloroethylamine) and *dibenzyline* (phenoxybenzamine) are typical examples of a group of β-haloalkylamines which produce a highly specific and effective blockage of adrenergic receptors. They generally are more effective against circulating epinephrine than adrenergic nerve stimulation. This may be true because the blocking agents prevent the circulating epinephrine from penetrating the effector cells, whereas sympathetic nerve impulses may cause the release of the transmitter *within* the effector cell. However, several experimental observations suggest that this explanation may not be sufficient. Dibenamine and dibenzyline block the excitatory response of smooth muscle and exocrine glands to adrenergic stimuli, but they do not prevent the inhibitory responses of some smooth muscles and the response of mammalian cardiac muscle.

Other drugs have adrenergic blocking properties (e.g., ergot alkaloids, tolazoline, phentolamine, benzodioxans, etc.), but the action of these substances is much less specific. They typically induce a variety of physiological and pharmacological changes which are unrelated to their adrenergic blocking property.

The possible role of norepinephrine and related catecholamines as central nervous system transmitters is poorly understood. Norepinephrine and serotonin are nonrandomly distributed in the brain, particularly in subcortical portions. Infusions of these catecholamines into arteries supplying specific portions of the brain produce only minor effects on nervous function, because these amines do not readily cross the blood-brain barrier. Efforts to increase or decrease the brain concentration of catecholamines more indirectly have generally produced marked behavioral and electrophysiological changes. However, the selectivity of the pharmacological procedures in these studies is suspect. Direct applications of adrenergic substances or blocking agents to selected portions of the central nervous system have recently been shown to elicit specific behavioral and electrophysiological changes. It is not certain, however, that the observed modifications in neural function are caused by a transmitter action of the injected substances.

The Compound Action Potential of Nerve Trunks

Although nerve fibers are basically alike, they vary in such important parameters as conduction speed, threshold of excitation, and maximal rate of impulse conduction. These variations imply that the electrical activity of a nerve or nerve trunk is different from that recorded from a single fiber; some of the more obvious differences will be briefly discussed here.

acts as a volume conductor under these circumstances and the recorded potentials are very distorted.

The volume effect on the compound action potential of peripheral nerves can be minimized by suspending the nerve in an insulating medium such as mineral oil. If both electrodes of the recording apparatus are placed on the outside of a nerve trunk, no potential difference is recorded in the resting state, because the exterior of a nerve trunk is at the same electrical potential throughout its length. As an action potential approaches, the first electrode becomes negative with respect to the second. As the potential travels further along the nerve fiber, this relationship is reversed, creating a diphasic potential as shown in Fig-

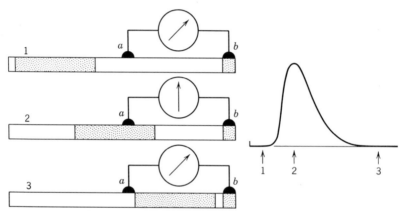

Fig. 1.17   Monophasic recording of the nerve action potential. *Left,* small stippled area under *b* indicates the nerve has been injured at this point. Consequently a steady injury potential is recorded in 1, *b* being negative to *a*. As the action potential (long stippled area) progresses to *a* in 2, *a* and *b* become equipotential. In 3, the action potential progresses beyond *a* and *b* is once more negative to *a*. *Right,* recorded monophasic action potential; numbered arrows indicate instantaneous potentials recorded at three stages of conduction shown at left. (From Patton, 1961.)

If recording electrodes are placed on the outside of a nerve trunk, a complex *compound action potential* is recorded. This represents the sum of neural activity within the nerve trunk, modified to some extent by the medium which surrounds the nerve. The modification occurs because nerve fibers are surrounded by a conducting medium, i.e., the nerve acts as a *volume conductor*. The extent of the influence of the surrounding medium is a function of its volume in relation to that of the nerve fibers which generate the electrical activity. The effect of volume is especially noticeable when the electrical activity of the entire brain or spinal cord is recorded or when the electrical activity of the heart is recorded through electrodes which are placed on the surface of the body. The entire body

ure 1.8. If the distance between the recording electrodes is shorter than the wavelength of the action potential (i.e., the length of the nerve trunk which is occupied by the total action potential), the amplitude as well as the time course of the electrical changes are distorted. They are distorted because the electrical disturbance reaches the second electrode before repolarization is completed under the first electrode. The effects of this are particularly annoying because the conduction velocity of individual nerves inside a nerve trunk varies. The disturbances which are transmitted by rapidly conducting fibers may reach the second electrode at the same time that the action potential of more slowly conducting fibers reaches the first. The electrical events at the two electrodes cancel each other, since the procedure only permits the recording of potential differences between the two electrodes.

These problems can be circumvented if conduction in the nerve trunk is blocked by crushing, burning, cutting, or anesthetizing the fibers under the second electrode (see Figure 1.17). Since the second electrode is now in contact with a portion of the nerve membrane in which the steady potential has been reduced to zero, an *injury* or *demarcation potential* can be recorded between the two electrodes. This injury potential reaches only about one-fourth to one-third the amplitude of the resting potential, since current can flow between the two electrodes through the axoplasm of each fiber and through the external medium which surrounds the nerve trunk. The extent of this shunting is related to the relative level of resistance inside and outside the nerve. Shunting can be minimized (thus maximizing the demarcation potential) by increasing the resistance of the external medium. When the recording devices are connected in this fashion, the arrival of action potentials results in a negative deflection in the steady demarcation potential; this is called a *monophasic compound action potential.* (It is conventional to indicate negativity by an *upward* deflection.)

The compound action potential which is monophasically recorded from peripheral nerves usually has an irregular contour which shows several distinct elevations (see Figures 1.18 and

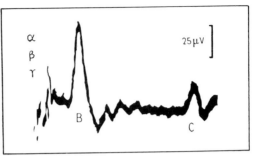

Fig. 1.19 The *B* and *C* elevations of the compound action potential of a mixed nerve trunk. From the same nerve at the same conduction distance as in Fig. 1.18. The *A* complex has preceded these elevations and is not shown here. Note the great increase in amplification used in order to show these small elevations. (From Brazier, 1961, after Erlanger and Gasser, 1937.)

1.19). After a maximal stimulus is applied to a compound nerve (i.e., a stimulus of sufficient intensity to elicit a response from all nerve fibers in the trunk), three major negative deflections occur in the action potential called *A, B,* and *C* waves, respectively.

The first and by far the largest *A* wave consists of a number of distinct portions. The first *alpha* component is so large that the other portions cannot be seen at an amplification which permits visualization of the entire alpha deflection. It is a very rapid and sudden negative deflection which is complete within less than a millisecond. The second component, *beta,* is much smaller and not quite so brief. The third or *gamma* component consists of a very low-amplitude deflection which is much more prolonged. It is customary to distinguish a fourth *delta* component of the *A* wave, although this portion is often not observable; at best, it consists only of a change in the slope of the falling portion of the gamma component.

The *A* wave is followed by a low-amplitude *B* wave. This wave is not generally subdivided into distinct components, although its often irregular shape suggests additional classification at times. The *B* wave is followed, after a considerable delay, by a very small *C* wave which is of even lower amplitude.

The individual components of this compound action potential are related to the conduction velocity and size of the individual fibers which make up the nerve trunk. The large *A* wave reflects the activity of very large, rapidly conducting fibers which typically make up the bulk of most peripheral nerves. There is a distinct distribution of

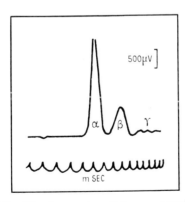

Fig. 1.18 The A complex of the compound action potential of a mixed nerve trunk recorded 13.1 cm from the point of stimulation. The full amplitude of the alpha elevation, which is the response of the largest fiber of the A group, is outside the limits of the record. The beta and gamma elevations are the responses of the less rapidly conducting fibers of the A group. Peroneal nerve of the bullfrog. (From Brazier, 1961, after Erlanger and Gasser, 1937.)

fiber diameters within this class of fibers (called *A* fibers) which is reflected in the alpha, beta, gamma, and delta components of the *A* wave. The largest and most rapidly conducting fibers of the *A* class give rise to the alpha component. Slightly smaller and slower *A* fibers produce the beta deflection, and still smaller and slower conducting fibers of this group conduct the gamma and delta components of the *A* wave. The *B* and *C* waves are produced by activity in still smaller and more slowly conducting fibers.

Fiber diameter ranges from less than 1 micron to about 20 micra, and conduction velocity is linearly related to fiber diameter—at least in myelinated fibers. The separation between individual components of the compound action potential widens as recording electrodes are placed farther and farther from the site of stimulation. The contour of the compound nerve potential is a function of the distribution of fiber sizes in the nerve from which recordings are obtained. Since there are wide variations among peripheral nerves with respect to the relative distribution of fiber sizes, a great variation in the shape of action potentials exists. All nerves contain rapidly conducting *A* fibers, and a large *A* wave is always present. The individual components of the *A* wave are not always distinguishable because the distribution of fibers within the nerve may not be distinctly multimodal. The *B* and *C* waves are often not seen with submaximal stimuli because the threshold of excitation is also closely

related to fiber size (the larger the fiber, the lower its threshold). Some peripheral nerve trunks do not contain the very small and unmyelinated fibers which give rise to the *C* wave or may not contain a sufficient concentration of small fibers of similar diameter to produce a clear and distinct deflection. The properties of mammalian nerves are summarized in Table 1.2.

Typically, peripheral nerves are mixed (i.e., contain both sensory afferents and motor efferents). Somatic nerves tend to show a bimodal distribution of afferent fibers with peaks in the 1- to 5-micron and 6- to 12-micron ranges, respectively. Muscle nerves usually have a third group of larger fibers with a diameter in the 12- to 21-micron range. Motor nerves also contain a large number of very small unmyelinated *C* fibers which are postganglionic axons of the autonomic nervous system.

Efferent (i.e., motor) fibers tend to be distributed bimodally with peaks in the 2- to 8-micron and 12- to 20-micron ranges. These correspond to two distinct sections in the compound action potential which can be recorded from deafferented efferent nerves.

Fibers of differing overall diameter vary not only in conduction velocity and threshold but also with respect to the duration and size of the afterpotential which follows the propagation of a spike potential. The distribution of afterpotentials in a nerve trunk results in compound afterpotentials which may change the excitability of the nerve

TABLE 1.2

Properties of mammalian nerve fibers

	A	B	s.C	d.r.C
Fiber diameter, microns	1–22	≤3	0.3–1.3	0.4–1.2
Conduction speed, meters/sec.	5–120	3–15	0.7–2.3	0.6–2.0
Spike duration, msec	0.4–0.5	1.2	2.0	2.0
Absolutely refractory period, msec	0.4–1.0	1.2	2.0	2.0
Negative afterpotential amplitude, % of spike	3–5	none	3–5	none
duration, msec	12–20	–	50–80	–
Positive afterpotential amplitude, % of spike	0.2	1.5–4.0	1.5	*
duration, msec	40–60	100–300	300–1000	*
Order of susceptibility to asphyxia	2	1	3	3
Velocity-diameter ratio	6	?	?	1.73 average

* A post-spike positivity 10 to 30% of spike amplitude and decaying to half size in 50 msec is recorded from d.r.C fibers. This afterpositivity differs from the positive afterpotential of other fibers. The A fibers are myelinated, somatic, afferent and efferent fibers. The B fibers are myelinated, efferent, preganglionic axons found in autonomic nerves. The C fibers are unmyelinated, the s.C group being the efferent postganglionic sympathetic axons, and the d.r.C group the small unmyelinated afferent axons found in peripheral nerves and dorsal roots. (From Patton, 1961.)

for as long as 1000 milliseconds. The negative afterpotential typically ranges from 12 to 80 milliseconds, and the positive afterpotential may persist for up to a full second. The excitability changes which accompany these persisting afterpotentials are similar to those that have been described in detail for the single nerve fiber.

Action potentials recorded from nerve tracts in the central nervous system: It is impossible to change the conduction properties of the environment of a nerve inside the central nervous system. Thus, volume conduction becomes a knotty problem. Since the nerve trunk is embedded in conductive tissue, its action potentials can be recorded from a relatively wide area around the nerve. Localizing the activity which occurs in response to a particular stimulus presents a problem. One solution is suggested by the changes observed in the action potential when one of the recording electrodes damages or enters the nerve trunk. If the action potential which is recorded from inside the central nervous system is of a distinctly biphasic (actually, triphasic) nature, the origin of the potential is in doubt. When this potential changes to a monophasic potential, the assumption can be made that the movement of the recording electrode has damaged active fibers.

Another peculiarity of volume conduction should be pointed out. Recording electrodes placed inside a volume conductor will record a potential only as long as the conducting structures are unequally or oppositely polarized. No potential is recorded when the tissue is completely polarized or depolarized because every solid angle is matched by an equal and electrically opposite solid angle. It follows from the property of volume conduction that slow changes in membrane polarization which have long decay constants in

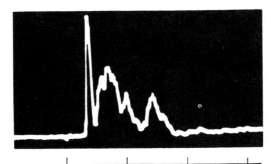

Fig. 1.21 Discharges in a ventral spinal root following stimulation of the dorsal root of the same segment. The initial spike response is from the two-neuron arc; the irregular discharges following it are from the multineuron pathways. Time marker, 5 msec. (From Lloyd, 1943.)

relation to conduction time cannot be recorded. The positive and negative afterpotentials of the spike potential typically fall into this category and cannot be visualized by recordings from a volume conductor.

Potentials recorded from the surface of the spinal cord in response to a single shock stimulus to an afferent nerve appear very rapidly (all the delay being accounted for by the conduction time of the afferent fibers) and are typically triphasic in contour (see Figure 1.20). This potential can be recorded from a relatively large section of the cord. It is typically followed first by a slow negative potential and then by a long-lasting positive potential. These slow potentials have been collectively called *intermediary cord potentials.* The slow negative potential may represent the activity of cells within the spinal cord or may reflect depolarization processes in the terminal arborizations of the afferent fibers.

Potentials recorded from the ventral root (i.e., the initial segment of motor nerves as they leave the spinal cord) following stimulation of the dorsal root (i.e., the terminal portion of an afferent or sensory nerve before it enters the spinal cord) take the form of a sharp spike; the spike is followed by a number of irregular potentials (see Figure 1.21). The spike appears after an interval which corresponds well to the delay interposed by a single synapse. It seems to reflect the response of motor nerves to afferents arriving via the *monosynaptic reflex arc.* The smaller potentials represent the motor neurons' responses to stimulation which is multisynaptically conducted through the cord. There are a number of these potentials, because the same stimulus is conducted

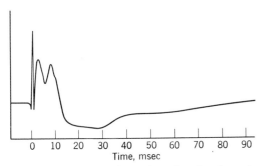

Fig. 1.20 Recording from electrodes placed on the dorsal surface of the spinal cord. Response to a single afferent volley applied to the dorsal root. (From Gasser, 1937. *Harvey Lectures,* Charles C Thomas.)

to the motor neurons via a number of different paths which involve different numbers of synapses.

Stimulation of afferent nerve fibers or sense organs produces similar compound action potentials at the ventral root. An analysis of the effects of a single stimulus to the afferent (sensory) nerve from a particular muscle shows that potentials are generated in a number of areas of the cord. A functional analysis of the physiological consequences of such an afferent barrage indicates that afferents from a particular muscle (1) mediate excitatory responses in motor neurons which connect directly to that muscle, (2) facilitate the responses of motor neurons related to its synergists, and (3) inhibit the activity of motor neurons which connect to antagonistic muscles at the same joint.

Potentials recorded from the dorsal root have been reported to consist of a sharp spike potential which is followed by slow negative potentials. The slow potentials are capable of both temporal and spatial summation and appear to be decrementally conducted from the sensory cell body in the dorsal root.

These slow potentials can be recorded without interference from the spike potential if the stimulating electrodes are placed on the cut end of a dorsal root fiber and if the recording is obtained from adjacent dorsal roots. This method permits a more detailed analysis of the contour of the potential and indicates that the slow negative potential is typically preceded by four other potentials (see Figure 1.22). The first three potentials may represent electrotonic spread from the cord that originates from the spike potential in the dorsal column of the cord. The fourth appears to be related to postsynaptic activity.

The *dorsal root electrotonus* is a slow negative potential and is always recorded from the dorsal

root following the propagation of a spike potential. Presumably reflecting the activity of interneurons in the cord, it invades all neurons of the same electrical sign. Similar electrotonic potentials can be recorded from the ventral root.

We can often record spike potentials which are conducted antidromically (i.e., toward the periphery in a sensory nerve) riding on the contour of these slow potentials. The interval between the arrival of the sensory potential conducted dromically and the potential conducted antidromically varies between 2.5 and 15 milliseconds. It has been suggested that these *dorsal root reflexes* may serve to inhibit excessive input in the sensory fiber.

The Spontaneous Electrical Activity of the Brain

The neurons of the central nervous system appear to be continuously active, even in the absence of distinct stimulation to sensory end organs. Electrodes placed outside or inside the brain do not record distinct action potentials unless a particular sensory modality is being discretely stimulated. However, low-amplitude fluctuating potentials are always present, which were first described by Caton about 100 years ago.

This "spontaneous" activity of the cells of the nervous system has been studied extensively during the past 50 years, but we still do not know precisely how or where the rhythmic oscillations originate. Initially it was thought that the slow potential changes represented a summation of action potentials. According to this hypothesis, the relatively large and slow waves characterizing the brain at rest are composed of action potentials generated in synchrony. The relatively fast and low-amplitude potentials characteristic of the brain during arousal may be composed of action potentials occurring asynchronously (and hence tending to cancel each other).

Much work has been directed toward the discovery of the "pacemaker" likely to be responsible for the rhythmic summation of neural activity during rest. Various theories have been proposed to account for this phenomenon. Chemical and neural pacemakers have been postulated. The chemical pacemakers are thought to determine cellular metabolism in the brain and influence the spontaneous discharges of neurons by regulating the metabolic activity underlying the generation of action potentials. The neural pacemakers might act in a more complex fashion. It has been suggested that synchrony may be caused by a waxing and waning of excitation in complexly

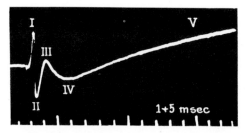

Fig. 1.22 Sequence of potential changes recorded from a dorsal root adjacent to the root stimulated (bullfrog). (From Lloyd and McIntyre, 1949.)

interrelated networks of neurons; the sum of all synaptic delays in the network being the pacing element.

It has recently been proposed that the oscillation potentials might represent fluctuations in neural excitability rather than actual spike discharges. This approach promises to be fruitful in the future. Currently, recordings of the electrical activity of specific parts of the brain as an index of changes in neural activity are being made, but the genesis of the recorded potentials is not known.

Despite extensive research during the past 30 years, it has been impossible to determine close correlations between behavioral or functional changes and specific alterations in the gross activity of the brain or the locally recorded activity of specific brain structures. The only clear example of such a correlation is a relationship between the overall state of rest and relaxation and a preponderance of high-voltage slow (8 to 12 cycles per second) waves in many parts of the brain. This *alpha rhythm* is "blocked" as soon as the organism orients toward a stimulus. The large high-amplitude waves are replaced by fast (30 to 60 cycles per second) low-amplitude wave patterns which appear much more irregular than the relatively synchronous alpha waves (see Figure 1.23). It has recently been shown that this *alpha-blocking, desynchronization,* or *arousal* reaction can be induced by electrical stimulation of the midbrain reticular formation and that damage to this complex network of interneurons abolishes this response (see Figure 1.24).

Electroencephalogram (EEG) is the generic term for a graphic recording of the oscillatory potentials from the brain. The EEG is typically obtained by connecting the recording electrodes to an ink writer via several stages of differential amplification; these stages magnify the potential differences between two adjacent electrodes in the brain (bipolar recording technique) or between a single electrode in the brain and an "indifferent" electrode located outside the central nervous system. The term *electrocorticogram* is reserved for electroencephalograms obtained from the surface of the cortex (the lateral and dorsal aspect of the brain in man and higher mammals).

In man, the electroencephalogram can be recorded from electrodes which are superficially

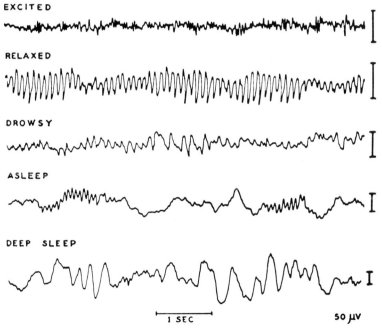

Fig. 1.23 Electroencephalographic records during excitment, relaxation, and varying degrees of sleep. In the fourth strip runs of 14/sec rhythm, superimposed on slow waves, are termed "sleep spindles." Note that excitement is characterized by a rapid frequency and small amplitude, and that varying degrees of sleep are marked by increasing irregularity and by the appearance of slow waves. (From Jasper, 1941. *Epilepsy and cerebral localization,* Charles C Thomas.)

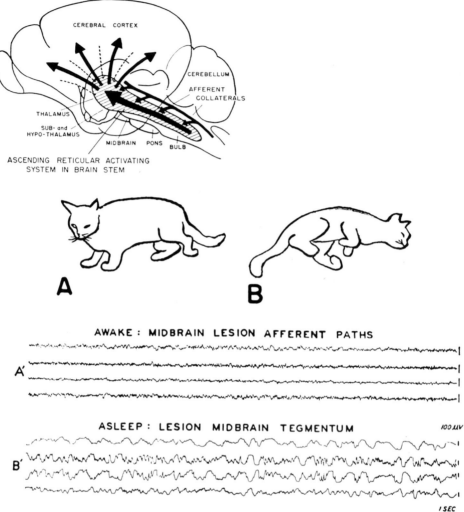

Fig. 1.24 *Top,* sagittal section of the cat brain showing neural basis of arousal response. *Bottom,* typical behavior and EEG records of cats with midbrain lesion sparing tegmentum (A and A′) and with lesion of tegmentum (B and B′). Cat B appeared continuously asleep or comatose during postoperative survival. (From Towe and Ruch, 1961.)

attached to the skull (see Figure 1.25). This clinical tool permits the discovery of gross electrical disturbances in the brain. The recordings are typically obtained in monopolar fashion, permitting the localization of abnormal discharge foci. (The distance between the active recording electrode and the discharge focus determines the amplitude of the recorded potential.) A phase-reversal analysis of bipolar recordings is also occasionally used. The electrical activity of ventral aspects of the brain can be recorded from special electrodes which are inserted into the nasopharyngeal cavity or the external auditory canal.

At any point in time, the electroencephalogram contains different frequencies, and it is often difficult to determine the dominant frequency by visual analysis of the EEG record. Computer analyses of the frequency and/or amplitude spectrum of the EEG show that most, if not all, frequencies are represented at any point in time and that so-called dominant frequencies merely occur more often than others. The normal frequency range is from about 1 cycle per second to around 60 to 80 cycles per second, and the resting EEG typically shows a spectrum such as that in Figure 1.26. Common frequencies in this spectrum have been named

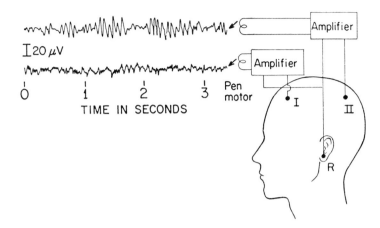

Fig. 1.25 Arrangement for recording EEG. The potential difference between frontal lead (I) and reference lead (R) shows low amplitude, fast activity of waking, relaxed human. Simultaneously, occipital lead (II) shows higher amplitude, slower activity. (From Towe and Ruch, 1961.)

(such as delta, theta, alpha, beta, and gamma). These names do not imply established functional differences (see Figure 1.26).

Alpha waves (8 to 12 cycles per second) are typical of the relaxed or drowsy organism. Slightly faster activity (about 12 to 15 cycles per second), which typically occurs in trains, is characteristic of sleep in man. These *spindle* waves alternate during sleep with very slow (1 to 2 cycles per second) *delta* waves. Slightly faster (4 to 7 cycles per second) *theta* waves are commonly recorded from certain subcortical parts of the brain and have been interpreted as a possible sign of inhibitory activity. Fast and typically low-amplitude activity (above 20 cycles per second) is generally referred to as *beta* activity. Some investigators refer to very fast (above 50 cycles per second) waves as *gamma* activity.

Repetitive electrical stimulation of certain parts of the brain (the intralaminar nuclei of the thalamus) produces diphasic potentials in the electro-encephalogram of the cortex. The amplitude of this potential may wax and wane at a frequency which approximates that of the alpha wave (8 to 10 cycles per second). These *recruiting responses* are believed to be similar to spontaneous "burst" activity which is seen in the cortical EEG in the absence of specific sensory stimulation. Evoked responses are potentiated during such bursts of 8 to 10 cycles per second activity in the EEG. It has been suggested that the excitability of the cortex may be reflected in the waxing and waning of this activity and that the thalamic nuclei from which recruiting responses can be elicited may exercise some measure of control over excitability. These relationships will be discussed in greater detail in the section on reticular mechanisms.

INITIATION OF IMPULSES AT THE RECEPTOR

Receptor functions may be exercised by specialized terminal arborizations of dendritic por-

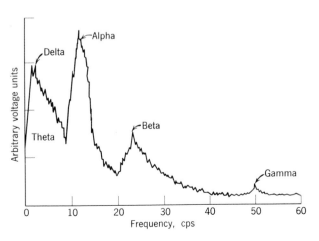

Fig. 1.26 The frequency spectrum of brain waves. Alpha waves, 10 cps; beta waves, 20 to 25 cps; gamma waves, 40 to 60 cps; and delta waves, 1 to 2 cps. Waves of 4 to 7 cps, between the delta and alpha waves, are called theta waves. (From Morgan and Stellar, 1950.)

tions of nerve cells or by specialized cells which act as selective transducers of particular forms of physical energy into neural impulses. A single receptor may command a "private line" into the central nervous system or may feed information into a neural pathway which is also used by other receptors.

Most higher organisms have receptors specialized to transduce mechanical, thermal, electromagnetic, and chemical energies. Most receptors are preferentially sensitive to only one form of energy, although all will respond to excessive (i.e., damaging) stimulation in all modalities. In addition, there seem to be receptors which are very insensitive to all types of physical energies and respond only to potentially damaging intensities of stimulation in any modality. The pain receptors fall into the latter category.

The specificity of receptors for skin senses has been challenged recently. Receptors presumed to be selectively sensitive to thermal or mechanical stimulation have been described. However, it seems that these specialized receptors are not *essential* for the sensations of warmth, cold, pressure, or tactile stimulation. We do not mean to imply that receptor specificity does not exist in the skin senses. Recent single-unit studies (recordings of the activity of single nerve fibers) have shown that receptors sensitive to mechanical deformation are usually very insensitive to thermal stimuli and that temperature receptors are not normally sensitive to mechanical stimulation. Moreover, it has been observed that pain and temperature receptors apparently communicate only with nerve fibers of very small diameter, whereas receptors sensitive to mechanical stimulation are part of large-diameter fibers.

A *sensory unit* is defined as those receptors that are part of or connect to a single afferent (i.e., sensory) neuron. Particularly in the skin senses, many receptors may contribute information to a single sensory neuron, and the *receptive field* is large. The receptive fields of skin senses, for instance, may reach 40 square centimeters in the cat. Spatial discrimination within such a field is possible because neighboring receptive fields overlap. Information about the location of stimuli within a particular area can therefore be derived from the pattern of activity generated in adjacent receptive fields.

All sensory units represent independent channels of information processing which transmit information about specific changes in the physical and chemical environments to the central nervous

system. The information is coded in terms of activity patterns in each single unit and related central pathways. Important, information-carrying factors are (1) the interval between impulses and the duration of the activity in the sensory neuron, and (2) the sensitivity of the receptor, the size and location of the receptive field, and the nature of the physical energy to be transduced.

The Receptor Potential

The action of physical energies on nerve endings or specialized receptor cells does not directly induce the electrochemical events responsible for the initiation and propagation of action potentials. Instead, a graded *generator potential* develops and initiates the action potential. The term generator potential refers to all graded potential changes in sense organs directly related to the initiation of action potentials in the associated afferent nerves. The term *receptor potential* applies only to generator potentials that occur in a single receptor.

A good example of a generator potential which is not a receptor potential is the alternating potential recorded from the basilar membrane of the cochlea during the application of a sound wave. This potential change, which occurs across multicellular compartments, is called *microphonic potential*. It appears to be responsible for the initiation of action potentials in the eighth (auditory) nerve. It serves the same function as the receptor potential in a single nerve, although the anatomical distribution of the electrical events is much greater.

Receptor potentials have been recorded from olfactory, photo, and mechanical receptors. The magnitude of receptor potentials is a function of stimulus intensity (see Figure 1.27). A certain

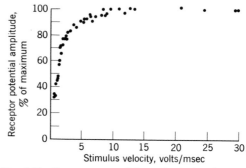

Fig. 1.27 Receptor potential amplitude in relation to the velocity of the mechanical stimulus with displacement constant in a Pacinian corpuscle. The stimulus velocity is given in arbitrary units. (From Gray and Sato, 1953.)

threshold magnitude of the receptor potential is required before action potentials can be initiated. Once this threshold is crossed, increases in the magnitude of the receptor potential are reflected by the frequency of action potentials in the associated afferent nerve. In frog muscle spindle, for instance, there is a linear relationship between the amplitude of the receptor potential and the frequency of nerve discharge. Our information is still quite limited in this important area. The amplitude of the receptor potential seems to increase up to an asymptotic limit. The rate of rise of the receptor potential may, in addition, be related to the intensity of the stimulus. In certain mechanoreceptors (such as muscle spindles and Pacinian corpuscles), the velocity of the mechanical displacement (or more generally, the rate at which the physical environment of the receptor changes) influences the amplitude of the receptor potential as well as its rate of rise to maximal values.

The duration of a receptor potential is a direct function of the stimulus duration. A phenomenon similar to summation occurs when the stimulus intensity is increased. True summation of receptor potentials occurs when two brief stimuli are presented in close succession (see Figure 1.28). In this way, a number of subthreshold stimuli can produce additive effects which result in a propagated action potential, a phenomenon which may be responsible for the maximal sensitivity of receptors.

If the repetition rate of successive stimuli is slow, such that the receptor potential generated by the first stimulus has had time to decay completely before the next stimulus arrives, the opposite reaction (i.e., depression) occurs at least in some receptors. Stimuli arriving within a few milliseconds after the decay of a receptor potential produce generator potentials that are smaller than normal. Antidromically conducted impulses from the associated neuron may also produce inhibitory effects.

Afferent Nerve Activity

Recent microelectrode studies have shown that action potentials do not originate from the same site as receptor potentials. In typical receptor cells the propagated impulse appears to be generated in the cell body, whereas the receptor potential develops in the cell's dendritic processes. Specialized receptor cells may show slightly different arrangements, but the basic principle (i.e., the spatial separation of the receptor and action potential) is maintained. The Pacinian corpuscle, for instance,

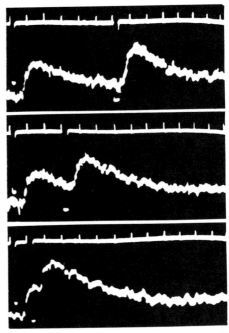

Fig. 1.28 Summation of receptor potentials with different intervals between stimuli. *Upper trace*, stimulus signal and time in milliseconds. *Lower trace*, receptor potentials. (From Gray and Sato, 1953.)

consists of a very fine, unmyelinated nerve ending which is encapsulated by several layers of tissue. About halfway through the receptor, the nerve ending acquires a myelin sheath. The first node of Ranvier typically lies within the cell body. The receptor potential seems to be generated only at the unmyelinated portion of the nerve ending, whereas the action potential arises in the myelinated portion, usually near the first node of Ranvier.

The clear distinction between the receptor and action potentials is maintained when the action of pharmacological agents is considered. Procaine (a local anesthetic), for instance, blocks action potentials in concentrations that do not affect the receptor potential. Cocaine similarly blocks nerve activity without affecting receptor potentials.

The application of acetylcholine to receptor cells has been shown to increase or initiate the discharge of related afferent neurons. The application of this neurohumor directly to these neurons produces no comparable effects. This fact constitutes presumptive evidence for a direct facilitatory action of acetylcholine on receptor functions, most probably the receptor potential itself. It is

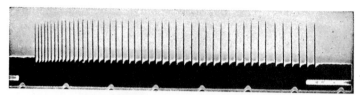

Fig. 1.29   Record showing adaptation of sense organ (photoreceptor). The stimulus was maintained at constant strength throughout, but the interval between discharges steadily diminished. The signal indicates duration of stimulus application. Time marker, 0.2 sec. (From Bronk, 1934.)

currently assumed that acetylcholine depolarizes the membrane of the unmyelinated terminal portions of the sensory nerve fiber or receptor cell and thus facilitates the development of the receptor potential. This interpretation is, however, contradicted by the observation that low doses of curare, nicotine, or hexamethonium block this action of acetylcholine but generally have no effect on the reaction of the receptor to normal stimuli. Acetylcholine may therefore not be an intermediary in the normal process of excitation of receptors, although the drug modifies the excitability of receptors under special conditions. Stimulation of sympathetic nerves or application of epinephrine to skin receptors similarly facilitates receptor potentials.

Receptors can be classified according to their response to maintained stimulation. *Phasic receptors* respond to a prolonged stimulus by initiating a burst of rapid nerve discharges. The rate of firing decreases rapidly with time and may reach zero. This *adaptation* process occurs much more slowly in *tonic* receptors, which show only a gradual decline in the frequency of action potential discharge. Tonic receptors typically reach

steady values directly related to the intensity of the maintained stimulus (see Figure 1.29).

Tonic receptors signal information to the central nervous system about physical or chemical stimuli always present but varying in intensity (or concentration). The clearest examples, although by no means the only ones, are the kinesthetic receptors in the tendons and joints which relay information about the relative positions of limbs. Individual receptors respond only to a specific and restricted range of stimulus intensities. Within this range there is an almost perfect relationship between stimulus intensity and impulse frequency (see Figure 1.30).

The *Weber-Fechner law* states that the smallest detectable increment in the intensity of a stimulus is constant. This venerable psychophysical law appears to be valid for individual receptor cells when one considers the minimal increment in stimulus intensity required to produce an increase in firing frequency.

Tonic receptors tend to "overreact" to changes in the environment. It appears that this excessive reaction carries much of the information to which organisms respond. A sudden increase in the in-

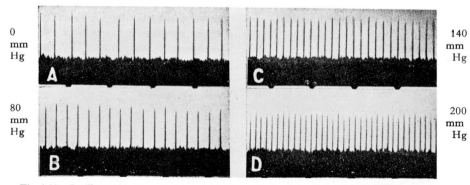

Fig. 1.30   Oscillographic records showing relation of frequency of discharge to intensity of stimulation. The single end organ in the carotid sinus was stimulated by four different pressures within the sinus. Time marker, 0.2 sec. (From Bronk and Stella, 1935.)

tensity of a steady stimulus, for instance, produces an increase in receptor discharge that greatly exceeds the firing level normally associated with that stimulus intensity. The firing rate declines to normal levels as the receptor adapts to the new stimulus intensity. Conversely, when there is a sudden drop in stimulus intensity, the firing rate decreases to a value much below that appropriate to the stimulus and then the rate gradually recovers.

Phasic sensory receptors operate on somewhat different principles. They do not discharge at a constant and controlled rate which is related to the intensity of some pervasive stimulus. Instead, they respond distinctly to the onset and/or termination of stimuli which are not constantly present in the organism's environment. Phasic receptors adapt very rapidly to maintained stimuli.

The most common type of phasic receptor responds to the presentation of a discrete stimulus by initiating a rapid burst of action potentials; these gradually diminish when the stimulus is maintained. The receptors of different modalities have typical response latencies and threshold values for the velocity of stimulus change.

Some receptors respond only to the onset and/or cessation of a stimulus by initiating a single potential or burst of potentials. Such ON, OFF, or ON-OFF receptors are particularly common in the visual system. The stimulus change in these instances must not always be absolute; ON receptors may fire in response to a sudden increase in stimulus intensity and OFF receptors in response to a sudden decrease (see Figure 1.31).

The basic mechanisms of receptor function are only superficially understood. It is assumed that all receptors generate receptor potentials at portions of the cell membrane which are unable to conduct an action potential. The energy required to initiate and maintain this generator potential does not derive from the physical energy provided by the stimulus but arises from the electrochemical gradients of the principal ions in the cell. It has been suggested that changes in the membrane potential, which signal changes in stimulus intensity, may be related to an alteration in the capacity of the receptor membrane. However, changes in ionic permeability similar to those occurring at the site of direct nerve stimulation may produce the observed electrical changes. The change in membrane permeability may be the direct result of the action of physical energies supplied by the stimulus; this may be true for mechanical deformation. The change may also depend on the action of chemical intermediaries, which seems to be more likely with photic receptors.

Evoked Potentials in the Central Nervous System

The stimulation of a peripheral sensory receptor initiates a generator potential which, when superthreshold, sets up an action potential. This potential is then propagated toward the central nervous system by an associated sensory nerve fiber. The body of this sensory nerve fiber is located in the dorsal root (for cutaneous and kinesthetic impulses), and its axon extends some distance into the spinal cord. The action potential is then routed through complex pathways (which will be discussed in the next section) to *specific sensory projection areas* located in the cortical mantle. If recording electrodes are placed in or on such a primary projection area or in or near the sensory pathway which conducts impulses to

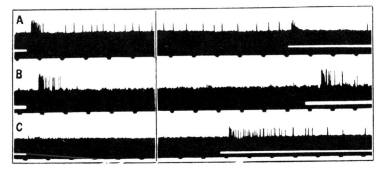

Fig. 1.31 Three types of impulse discharge from single fibers of the optic nerve of the frog. A, maintained response; B, ON-OFF response; C, OFF response. The occlusion of the white horizontal bar in each record indicates the period of illumination. Time marker, 1 + 0.5 sec. (From Hartline, 1938.)

this area, a clear and distinct electrical response to peripheral sensory stimulation can be recorded.

These *evoked potentials* can best be visualized in organisms which are under sufficient barbiturate anesthesia to depress the background EEG activity. (They are not seen with such anesthetics as ether or chloroform which block transmission of afferent potentials.) The evoked potential typically consists of an initial, short-latency (8 to 10 milliseconds) spike potential followed by a larger and more gradual deflection (see Figure 1.32). The first of these potentials, the *primary evoked potential,* can usually be recorded only from a fairly restricted portion of the brain. This area is assumed to be the exact locus of the sensory representation of the physical stimulus to the related sensory receptor. The evoked potential reaches the cortical projection areas on the side contralateral to the stimulated receptor via the classical sensory pathways. A slow *secondary evoked potential* can be recorded from most areas of the cortex and seems to reach it via different pathways which bypass the sensory relays of the thalamus.

Evoked potentials recorded from unanesthetized subjects are often difficult to detect because they are superimposed on the spontaneous (EEG) activity of the brain. Recent technological developments have provided "averaging" devices which summate the evoked response to several hundred stimuli. The spontaneous electrical activity of the brain is random with respect to the time of stimulation, and repeated averaging of the EEG tends to cancel the spontaneous activity. However, the evoked potentials always occur within some specific time interval after the application of stimulation; hence the potentials tend to summate and become more prominent with each repetition.

Recent investigations have used microelectrodes (with a tip diameter of 0.5 to 5 micra) to record the electrical response of single nerve cells in the brain. The response of single neurons to discrete sensory stimulation may take the form of an increase or decrease in the spontaneous discharge frequency of that neuron or in the elicitation of one or more spike potentials. These are similar, if not identical, to the spike potentials which are recorded from nerve cells in the peripheral nervous system (see Figure 1.33).

It has not been possible to establish a definite relationship between the evoked potential which is recorded through macroelectrodes (with a tip diameter of 50 to 1000 micra) and the spike response of single units.

BASIC PROPERTIES OF EFFECTOR CELLS

The Basic Effector Unit

The *basic effector unit* is not a single motor cell or even a group of muscle fibers. Instead, the *motor unit* is defined on the basis of common in-

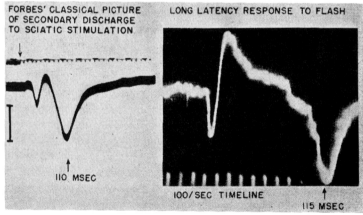

Fig. 1.32 *Left,* response from the contralateral sensory-motor cortex to stimulation (at the arrow) of the sciatic nerve in a cat under pentobarbital anesthesia. The record shows the primary response followed later by the larger secondary response. Vertical calibration mark, 200 μV. The black dots at the top of the illustration represent 0.04-sec intervals. Negativity is recorded upward. (From Forbes and Morison, 1939.) *Right,* primary and long-latency response to a flash recorded from the visual cortex of a cat under pentobarbital anesthesia. (From Brazier, 1958.)

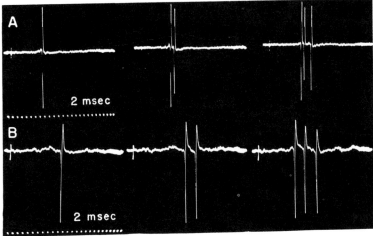

Fig. 1.33 Unit spikes of two units (A, B) recorded from the monkey postcentral gyrus, showing variation in initial spike latency and number of spikes per discharge when sampled at three different times. Note the general consistency of the spike shape for each unit. Negativity is recorded downward. (From Towe and Amassian, 1958.)

nervation. It consists of a single motor neuron, its axon, and the group of muscle fibers which are innervated by the terminal arborizations from the axon. Muscle responses, therefore, are graded not in terms of muscle fiber units but in terms of the total number of muscle fibers innervated by a single axon.

The average size of a motor unit varies greatly. In the intrinsic muscles of the eye, which must be capable of very exact and fine adjustments, the ratio of muscle fibers to motor axons is very small, and it is not uncommon to find that one neuron serves only three or four motor fibers. On the other hand, large muscles which typically react as a whole, such as the biceps, often have innervation ratios of 200:1 or more.

The weakest possible response of a muscle is the contraction of a single motor unit. As stimulation increases, more motor units are activated (a process called recruitment), and the individual motor units discharge more frequently. If the stimulation is further increased, the frequency of neural discharges reaches tetanic limits and the individual twitch responses summate to form a tetanus. Although a single motor unit follows the *all-or-nothing* law of responding, the muscle as a whole does not.

Recent electronmicroscopic analyses of muscle tissue have shown a striking parallel between the structural organization of the units and subunits of a muscle fiber. The elongated proteins inside a filament as well as the filaments within a muscle fibril and the fibrils within a muscle fiber are all longitudinally oriented, as shown in Figure 1.34. The building blocks of the contractile cells are two proteins, *actin* and *myosin,* consisting of long molecular chains. During contraction the filaments of actin and myosin slide past each other and produce a shortening of the muscle cell.

The contraction process is initiated by a depolarization of the muscle cell membrane that occurs as the result of synaptic transmission of an action potential. The latency between membrane depolarization and the mechanical contraction response is of the order of 1 millisecond.

Contraction of a muscle fiber results in either a shortening of the cell or the development of tension, or both. Contracting muscles may shorten and thus produce gross movement. Since weight is carried through space in any movement of a limb, this type of contraction has been called *isotonic* (equal tension). Contractions that cause tension (i.e., a force which opposes other influences such as gravity but does not itself move a limb) are called *isometric* (equal length). This type of contraction is usually employed to prevent movement. A third type of muscular activity, *lengthening,* occurs when the forces opposing an isometric contraction are sufficiently large to stretch or lengthen the muscle while it is actively contracting. This type of muscular activity is typically found whenever muscles operate as antagonistic pairs (see Table 1.3).

The energy consumed in the process of muscu-

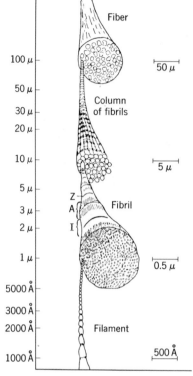

100 μ

50 μ

30 μ

20 μ

10 μ

5 μ

3 μ

2 μ

1 μ

5000 Å

3000 Å

2000 Å

1000 Å

Fiber

50 μ

Column of fibrils

5 μ

Z
A   Fibril
I

0.5 μ

Filament

500 Å

Fig. 1.34 Logarithmic extension diagram of the skeletal muscle fiber structure. (From Woodbury and Ruch, 1961.)

lar contractions derives from a number of chemical reactions. The basic process involves the gradual breakdown of glycogen into lactic acid, an energy-liberating process which requires no free oxygen (anaerobic). However, the reaction that restores the muscle to its resting state (the reconversion of lactic acid to glycogen) is an aerobic reaction which takes the following form:

Lactic acid $+ O_2 \rightarrow CO_2 + H_2O +$ Energy

This apparently complex and roundabout method of energy transfer is related to the fact that almost no molecular oxygen can be stored in or about

muscle cells. When a muscular contraction occurs, there are consequently little or no oxygen stores available for the liberation of energy by aerobic means. However, the contraction itself stimulates the circulatory system, and the blood flow to the active muscle is stepped up. This process brings greater quantities of oxygen to the muscle, and enough oxygen can be removed from the blood to permit the aerobic reconstitution of glycogen.

Energy transformations always involve an energy loss because heat is produced, and the muscle is no exception. Only about 20 to 30% of the energy liberated in the conversion of glycogen to lactic acid is converted into mechanical work. The remaining 70 to 80% is liberated as heat and is used to maintain normal body temperature.

The brief response of a skeletal muscle to a single maximal volley of action potentials in related motor neurons is called a *twitch*. The basic form of all twitch contraction curves is similar for all striated muscles, but the duration and amplitude of the response vary among different types of muscles and species of animals. The distribution of muscle response latencies appears to be roughly bimodal. Some very fast muscles react within 5 to 10 milliseconds after the arrival of the action potential. Superficial extensors typically fall into the fast-reacting muscle category, having response latencies of about 20 to 35 milliseconds. Deep muscles, on the other hand, particularly those that move a large joint, react slowly; reaction times of over 100 milliseconds are typical. Generally, fast muscles appear pale or almost white. The slower muscles appear red because of a greater concentration of myoglobin. Fast muscles tend to be used for rapid phasic movements of distinct muscle groups, whereas slow muscles typically regulate phasic adjustments such as posture.

Summation or Facilitation

Summation or *facilitation* occurs when two maximal stimuli are presented in rapid succession to

TABLE 1.3

Classes of muscle contraction

Type of Contraction	Function	External Force Opposing Muscle	External Work by Muscle	Rate of Energy Supply
Shortening (isotonic)	Acceleration	Less	Positive	Increases
Isometric (constant length)	Fixation	Equal	None	
Lengthening	Deceleration	Greater	Negative	Decreases

From Woodbury and Ruch, 1961.

a muscle or to related neurons. An increase in the intensity of stimulation of a muscle or muscle-related neuron produces a correlated increase in the intensity of contraction up to the point where all fibers of the muscle are activated. Further increases in the intensity of a "maximal" stimulus do not produce a further increase in the muscle response (see Figure 1.35). However, if two maximal stimuli are presented in sufficiently close succession so that the second is presented during the contraction response to the first, a greater response occurs than to a single maximal stimulus. The intensity of this facilitatory effect is a function of the interstimulus interval (the higher the repetition rate, the greater the response) when the interstimulus interval is longer than the refractory period of the muscle membrane. Tetanic facilitation is based on a summation of mechanical events rather than electrical events and should not be compared to neural facilitation during the supernormal period.

If several stimuli are delivered at a very rapid rate, progressive summation occurs; each stimulus then adds a diminishing increment of facilitation until the contraction of the muscle is maintained. This tension is called *tetanus*. Partial or incomplete tetanus occurs when the repetition rate of successive stimuli is too low to maintain the contraction response.

Neuromuscular Transmission

The propagation of an action potential across a neuromuscular junction occurs by means of a neurohumoral transmitter substance. At all skeletal muscle junctions the neurohumor is called *acetylcholine.* The sequence of events can be summarized as follows. (1) The arrival of an action potential at the terminal arborization of an axon stimulates the secretion or liberation of stored acetylcholine. The transmitter then diffuses across the small gap between the nerve and the endplate of the muscle. (2) Upon its arrival at the endplate, acetylcholine interacts with a specific receptor complex. This interaction increases the permeability of the endplate membrane to all ions and decreases the membrane potential toward zero. (3) If this change in the membrane potential is sufficient to produce a suprathreshold depolarization of the endplate, an electrical impulse is propagated from the endplate in all directions. (4) The acetylcholine is rapidly destroyed by an enzyme (*acetylcholinesterase*) which is stored in high concentrations in the muscle endplate.

It has been possible to study the acetylcholine-induced changes in the endplate membrane in

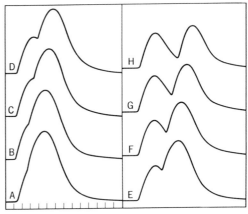

Fig. 1.35 Summation of muscular contraction by double stimulation. Isometric records of the median head of the gastrocnemius responding to two stimuli in succession. Intervals in milliseconds between stimuli in different records are A, 24; B, 32; C, 40; D, 48; E, 57; F, 69; G, 77; H, 88. Time is recorded below record A in 20-msec intervals. (From Woodbury and Ruch, 1961.)

some detail since the blocking agent *curare* can be administered in doses which interfere with neuromuscular transmission sufficiently to reduce the endplate potential (e.p.p.) below the threshold for a propagated action potential. It is then possible to study the properties of the endplate potential in isolation. In a curarized preparation the endplate potential recorded in response to stimulation of a motor nerve consists of a nonpropagated monophasic response (see Figure 1.36). The size (but not the configuration) of this response is a function of the concentration of the blocking agent.

At the normal (i.e., noncurarized) neuromuscular junction, endplate potentials are typically sufficient to produce a propagated action potential which is conducted along the muscle membrane in a manner analogous to that described for unmyelinated nerve fibers. In mammalian muscle the typical conduction velocity is about 5 meters per second.

Special Properties of Cardiac and Smooth Muscles

Cardiac muscle essentially consists of striated muscle fibers which are not arranged in orderly, parallel fashion as in skeletal muscle; rather, the fibers branch and appear to fuse with each other, producing what appears to be a continuous net or syncytium. This peculiar anatomical arrangement is thought to be responsible for the simultaneity of action which characterizes the heart

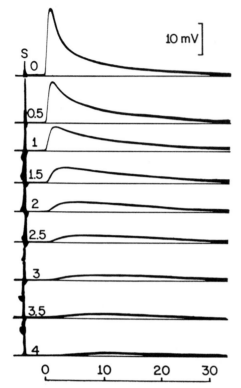

Fig. 1.36 Transmembrane potential changes produced in a curarized muscle fiber by stimulation of the motor nerve to the muscle. *Abscissa,* time in milliseconds, *Ordinate,* change in transmembrane potential in millivolts. S, stimulus artefact, signaling time of stimulus to motor nerve. The number by each curve is the distance of the intracellular recording microelectrode from the muscle endplate. As the distance is increased, the recorded potential becomes smaller and slower. (From Fatt and Katz, 1951.)

muscle. The operation of the cardiac pump depends, in fact, on a synchronous contraction of large portions of the heart. This spontaneous and synchronous activity occurs in the absence of direct innervation. The normal stimulus for the contraction of cardiac muscle is a depolarization of the muscle fiber membrane. The depolarization is brought about by propagated action potentials here as in other muscle fibers. However, this action potential is conducted without apparent decrement from one cardiac muscle fiber to another. A stimulus applied to any portion of a ventricle elicits electrical changes which rapidly spread to all other portions of that segment of the heart in a process called *local circuit activation.*

The typical action potential recorded from cardiac muscle is several hundred milliseconds in duration and roughly equals the duration of the resulting contraction. There is a direct relationship between heart rate and the duration of action potentials recorded from the heart muscle; the action potential duration is roughly one-half the interval between successive heart beats.

Stimulation of any portion of the heart can initiate a propagated action potential. However, a specialized "pacemaker" region in the sinoatrial node appears to determine the rate of cardiac contractions because its intrinsic rate is faster than that of other portions of the heart. The membrane potential of cells in this pacemaker region has no stable value but gradually falls toward zero during the diastolic phase of cardiac activity. When this *pacemaker potential* reaches a threshold, an action potential is generated and is propagated to all other portions of the heart. The pacemaker cell membrane then repolarizes until the membrane potential approaches the equilibrium potential for potassium.

There are essentially two varieties of smooth muscles. *Visceral smooth muscles* make up the walls of the gastrointestinal tract and the urogenital tract. They do not show the cross-striations typical of skeletal or cardiac muscle and contract only very slowly. *Multi-unit smooth muscle* is found in some very small muscles such as the nictitating membrane of the cat, the intrinsic eye muscles, or the precapillary sphincters. A single stimulation of the innervation of a multi-unit smooth muscle often sets up a prolonged response resembling incomplete tetanus. This reaction is presumably caused by the release of a transmitter substance (norepinephrine) at the endplate which is not rapidly destroyed and persists for several hundred milliseconds. Slow responses are typical of this type of muscle (see Figure 1.37).

The action potentials of visceral muscle differ widely from tissue to tissue. Some resemble cardiac potentials, and syncytial conduction has been reported; however, the syncytial connections appear to be much less efficient than in the heart. The size of action potentials from most visceral tissues (such as the intestine and uterus) is only a few millivolts.

The Gland Cells

The *gland cells* are also effectors, although their action and structure differ from those of muscle cells. Secretory cells are typically cuboidal or columnar in shape and possess clearly defined cytoplasmic inclusions. During the process of secretion, these *secretory granules* contract and

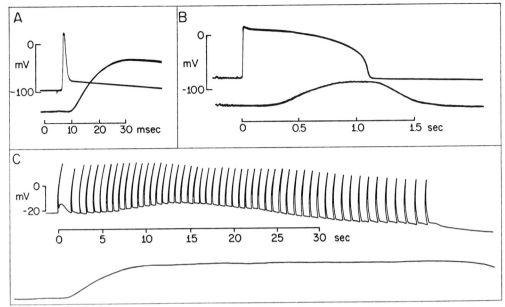

Fig. 1.37 Simultaneously recorded transmembrane potentials and contraction in three types of muscle. A, isolated frog skeletal muscle fiber. B, whole frog ventricle; action potential recorded from one cell. C, strip of pregnant rat uterus (smooth muscle); action potential recorded from one cell. *Ordinates,* lower trace, arbitrary units of contractile tension. (From Ruch et al., 1961.)

may even disappear, changing the overall appearance of the cell. Secretion from glandular cells may make use of osmotic, filtration, or diffusion gradients; however, secretion can continue even when strong physical forces oppose the action. Secretion usually results in the liberation of new, specific substances which are manufactured by the gland cell and are not available from any other source. The secretory process may be initiated by the arrival of neural impulses or by the presence of particular chemical substances (often compounds secreted by other gland cells) at the glandular membrane.

BIBLIOGRAPHY

Brazier, Mary A. B. Studies of evoked responses by flash in man and cat. In *The reticular formation of the brain.* H. H. Jasper, L. D. Proctor, R. S. Knighton, W. C. Noshay, & R. T. Costello, Eds. Boston: Little, Brown, 1958.

Brazier, Mary A. B. *The electrical activity of the nervous system* (2nd ed.). New York: Macmillan, 1961.

Bronk, D. W. The mechanism of sensory end organs. *Res. Publ., Ass. Res. Nerv. ment. Dis.,* 1934, **15**, 60–82.

Bronk, D. W., & Stella, G. The response to steady pressures of single end organs in the isolated carotid sinus. *Amer. J. Physiol.,* 1935, **110**, 708–714.

Buchthal, F., & Kaiser, E. The rhedogy of the cross striated muscle fiber with particular reference to isotonic conditions. *Dan. Biol. Medd.,* 1951, **21**(7), 1–318.

Carlson, J., & Johnson, V. *The machinery of the body.* Chicago: Univ. of Chicago Press, 1949.

Coombs, J. S., Eccles, J. C., & Fatt, P. Excitatory synaptic action in motoneurons. *J. Physiol. (London),* 1955a, **130**, 374–395.

Coombs, J. S., Eccles, J. C., & Fatt, P. The inhibitory suppression of reflex discharges from motoneurons. *J. Physiol. (London),* 1955b, **130**, 396–413.

Cooper, S., & Eccles, J. C. The isometric responses of mammalian muscles. *J. Physiol. (London),* 1930, **69**, 377–385.

Erlanger, J., & Gasser, H. S. *Electrical signs of nervous activity.* Philadelphia: Univ. of Pennsylvania Press, 1937.

Fatt, P., & Katz, B. An analysis of the end-plate potential recorded with an intracellular electrode. *J. Physiol. (London),* 1951, **115**, 320–370.

Forbes, A., & Morison, B. R. Cortical response to sensory stimulation under deep barbiturate narcosis. *J. Neurophysiol.,* 1939, **2**, 112–128.

Gardner, E. *Fundamentals of neurology* (4th ed.). Philadelphia: Saunders, 1963.

Gasser, H. S. The control of excitation in the nervous system. *Harvey Lect.,* 1937, **32**, 169–193.

Gray, J. A. B. Initiation of impulses at receptors. In *Handbook of physiology. Vol. I.* J. Field, H. W. Magoun, & V. E. Hall, Eds. Baltimore: Williams and Wilkins, 1959.

Gray, J. A. B., & Sato, M. Properties of the receptor potential in Pacinian corpuscles. *J. Physiol. (London)*, 1953, **122**, 610–636.

Hartline, H. K. The response of single optic nerve fibers of the vertebrate eye to illumination of the retina. *Amer. J. Physiol.*, 1938, **121**, 400–415.

Hodgkin, A. L., & Horowitz, P. The differential action of hypertonic solutions on the twitch and action potential of a muscle fibre. *J. Physiol. (London)*, 1957, **136**, 17–18.

Jasper, H. H. In Penfield, W.,& Erickson, T. C., *Epilepsy and cerebral localization*. Springfield, Ill.: Thomas, 1941.

Lindsley, D. B., Schreiner, L. H., Knowles, W. B., & Magoun, H. W. Behavioral and EEG changes following chronic brainstem lesions in the cat. *EEG clin. Neurophysiol.*, 1950, **2**, 483–498.

Lloyd, D. P. C. Reflex action in relation to pattern and peripheral source of afferent stimulation. *J. Neurophysiol.*, 1943, **6**, 111–119.

Lloyd, D. P. C., & McIntyre, A. K. On the origins of dorsal root potentials. *J. gen. Physiol.*, 1949, **32**, 409–443.

Marcora, J. W. D. In Maximow, A. A., & Bloom, W., *Textbook of histology* (7th ed.). Philadelphia: Saunders, 1952, p. 185.

Morgan, C. T., & Stellar, E. *Physiological psychology*. New York: McGraw-Hill, 1950.

Patton, H. D. Special properties of nerve trunks and tracts. In Ruch, T. C., Patton, H. D., Woodbury, J. W., & Towe, A. L. *Neurophysiology*. Philadelphia: Saunders, 1961.

Peele, T. L. *The neuroanatomical basis for clinical neurology* (2nd ed.). New York: Blakiston Division, McGraw-Hill, 1961.

Ruch, T. C. Somatic sensation. In Ruch, T. C., Patton, H. D., Woodbury, J. W., & Towe, A. L. *Neurophysiology*. Philadelphia: Saunders, 1961.

Towe, A. L., & Amassian, V. E. Patterns of activity in single cortical units following stimulation of the digits in monkeys. *J. Neurophysiol.*, 1958, **21**, 292–311.

Towe, A. L., & Ruch, T. C. Association areas and the cerebral cortex in general. In Ruch, T. C., Patton, H. D., Woodbury, J. W., & Towe, A. L. *Neurophysiology*. Philadelphia: Saunders, 1961.

Von Brücke, E. T., Early, M., & Forbes, A. Recovery of responsiveness in motor and sensory fibers during the relative refractory period. *J. Neurophysiol.*, 1941, **4**, 80–91.

Woodbury, J. W., & Patton, H. D. Action potential; cable and excitable properties of the cell membrane. In Ruch, T. C., Patton, H. D., Woodbury, J. W., & Towe, A. L. *Neurophysiology*. Philadelphia: Saunders, 1961.

Woodbury, J. W., & Ruch, T. C. Muscle. In Ruch, T. C., Patton, H. D., Woodbury, J. W., & Towe, A. L. *Neurophysiology*. Philadelphia: Saunders, 1961.

CHAPTER TWO

Anatomy of the Nervous System

In the course of embryological development, the nerve cells of the organism collect in a tubular structure which persists, in modified form, in the adult. The portion of the tube that ends up in the head develops into the *brain* and the remainder forms the *spinal cord*. Together they constitute the *central nervous system* (CNS).

Information reaches cells in the central nervous system via *afferent* or *sensory* nerves which project to every portion of the body. The transmission of information from the central nervous system to the peripheral effectors (muscles and glands) occurs via *efferent* or *motor* nerves. *Spinal* nerves (those sensory and motor nerves that enter and originate from the spinal cord) leave the spinal cord at regular intervals. *Cranial* nerves (those sensory and motor nerves that enter and originate from the brain) are irregularly spaced. The cranial and spinal nerves and their peripheral ramifications form the *peripheral nervous system* (PNS).

Before we proceed with a more detailed discussion of the nervous system, a few terms should be explained. It is common to discuss the location of parts of the body in relation to three imaginary planes (see Figure 2.1). The *sagittal* plane divides the body into right and left parts. The *median* plane is the sagittal plane that dissects the body into *equal* right and left halves. The *coronal* (or *frontal*) plane divides the body into front and back parts (i.e., the coronal plane runs at right angles to the sagittal plane). The *horizontal* plane divides the body into upper and lower parts.

In man, the front of the body (in the upright position) is considered to be *anterior*, the back *posterior*. *Superior* refers to higher structures and *inferior* to lower ones. These terms are usually used only when a reference point is provided.

Cranial (toward the head) refers to higher structures in a more absolute sense and *caudal* (toward the tail) to lower structures.

In animals, the same terms are used in a slightly different way because the basic orientation of the body is changed. Structures toward the front of the organism are called *ventral*, those located near the back are called *dorsal*. *Cranial* and *anterior* become synonymous, as do *caudal* and *posterior*.

THE CENTRAL NERVOUS SYSTEM

THE SPINAL CORD

The central nervous system basically serves two primary functions. It interconnects sensory receptors and motor effectors which are often located in very different portions of the organism. It also permits an integration of the various sensory inputs and resulting motor efferents to assure that the organism is going in only one direction at the same time. In higher organisms this integrative function has become quite complex and includes such refinements as storage mechanisms for sensory information and related mechanisms which permit a comparison of the stored information with present input.

The overall design of the nervous system reflects these basic functions. *Sensory* pathways bring information into the central nervous system and distribute it to its various parts; *motor* pathways bring detailed information from various portions of the brain and spinal cord to the muscles and glands; and, in between, a complex feltwork of *associative*, *internuncial*, or *intercalary* neurons (these terms are essentially used interchangeably) perform the many integrative processes.

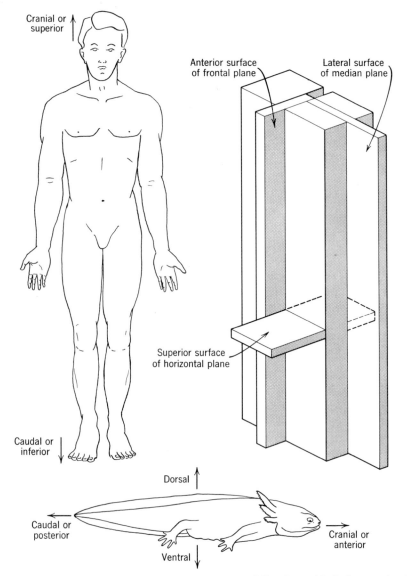

Cranial or superior

Anterior surface of frontal plane

Lateral surface of median plane

Superior surface of horizontal plane

Caudal or inferior

Dorsal

Caudal or posterior

Cranial or anterior

Ventral

Fig. 2.1 The anatomical position and synonymous terms of direction; a block diagram showing the primary planes and surfaces; and an amphibian, illustrating comparative anatomical nomenclature. (From Gardner, 1963.)

Gross Anatomy

This organization is most easily seen in the spinal cord (see Figures 2.2 and 2.3). If we transect the spinal cord, two portions can be clearly distinguished. A white outer portion contains the ascending and descending pathways which connect the peripheral nerves with the brain. A butterfly-shaped gray inner section contains the interneurons of the cord which permit some measure of local integration of the sensory and motor func-

tions. In the simplest case, a sensory neuron may enter the spinal cord, send an axon through the gray matter, and connect directly with a motor neuron which is located near the ventral surface of the spinal gray. This is a *monosynaptic* reflex connection. Other examples of simple, *segmental* reflex connections are provided by sensory neurons which enter the spinal gray and then synapse on a short-axon interneuron which communicates directly with a motor neuron located within the same segment of the cord.

Sensory neurons project axons into the spinal cord; the axons either ascend directly in the large sensory pathways in the posterior (dorsal) portion of spinal white matter or enter the spinal gray to synapse with interneurons which then project to the ascending sensory pathways. However, collaterals from the primary sensory axon frequently ascend or descend only a short distance in the cord; they then connect either directly to motor neurons or to interneurons which, in turn, synapse with spinal motor neurons. These collaterals often form *suprasegmental* reflex connections which permit an integration of reflex activity at the spinal level.

In man, the spinal cord does not extend through the entire length of the bony structure (the *vertebral column*) which surrounds the delicate neural tissue. The vertebral column continues to grow after the development of the nervous system has been completed. Spinal cord segments consequently lie somewhat higher than the corresponding vertebrae (see Figure 2.4). The caudal termination of the spinal cord (the *conus terminalis*) typically lies near the first or second lumbar vertebrae. The remainder of the vertebral column is taken up by the collection of long nerve roots (the *cauda equina*) which project from the caudal portion of the cord downward to the appropriate vertebral segments.

The spinal cord is divided into equal halves by the *anterior* and *posterior median longitudinal fissures* (see Figure 2.5). The *anterolateral* and *posterolateral* fissures further divide each half into approximately equal thirds. The two halves of the spinal cord appear roughly symmetrical. They are joined by a narrow commissure of gray and white matter. The gray commissure of the cord contains the *central canal*, which may contain cerebrospinal fluid.

The spinal cord (as well as the brain) is covered by three membranes (the *meninges*) which separate the delicate neural tissues from the bony en-

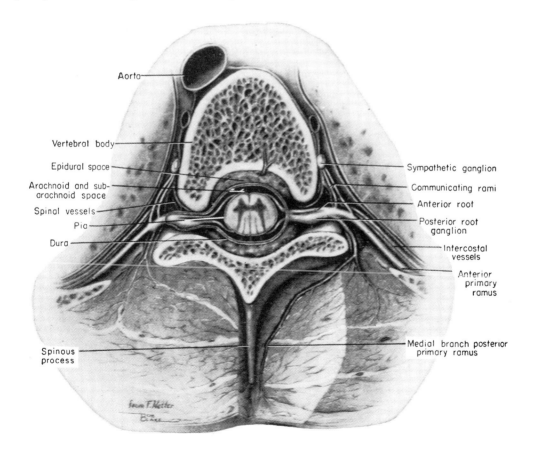

Fig. 2.2 Transverse section through the thoracic spine and spinal cord. (From Peele, 1961, redrawn after F. Netter, *Vol. I. Nervous System.* Courtesy Ciba, Inc.)

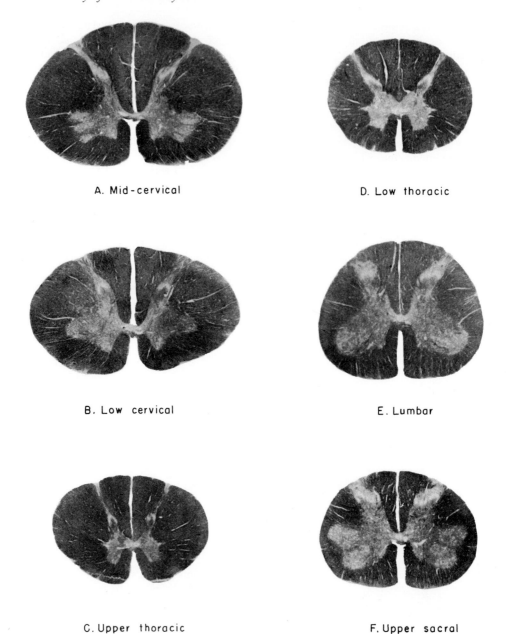

A. Mid-cervical

D. Low thoracic

B. Low cervical

E. Lumbar

C. Upper thoracic

F. Upper sacral

Fig. 2.3   Representative sections from various levels of the human spinal cord, × 5.4. (From Peele, 1961.)

casement of the central nervous system. The outermost membrane, the *dura mater,* is fibrous and tough; the innermost *pia mater,* is soft and pliable. Between is a thick, flexible *arachnoid* membrane. The pia and arachnoid are often collectively called the *leptomeninx.* The cranial portions of these meninges will be discussed in detail later (see Figure 2.6).

In the spinal cord the dura is separated from the periosteum of the vertebrae by *epidural space* which is usually filled with fat and venous plexuses. The spinal dura forms a sac; this sac is firmly attached to the *foramen magnum* and connects loosely to the ligaments which project from the vertebrae all along the vertebral column. At the level of the second sacral vertebra, the dura is

The Spinal Cord 47

pierced by the *filum terminale* which contains the tapering end portion of the spinal cord and cauda equina. The spinal dura is innervated by spinal nerves and receives its blood supply from regional spinal arteries.

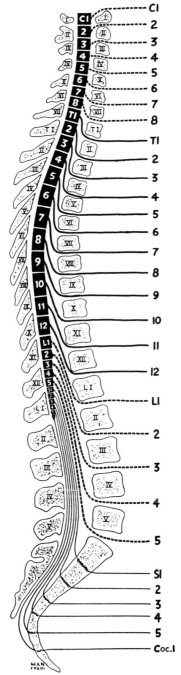

Fig. 2.4 The relations of the spinal cord segments and spinal nerves to the bodies and spinous processes of the vertebrae. (From Haymaker and Woodhall, 1953.)

The spinal pia is attached to the arachnoid membrane by the *septum posticum* which runs along the posterior longitudinal fissure. The pia extends laterally into discrete processes known as *dentate ligaments* which attach to the dura. The spinal pia is innervated by meningeal branches of spinal nerves and receives its blood supply from regional spinal arteries.

At each vertebral segment of the cord, spinal nerves enter and leave in a discrete pattern. The sensory nerves form distinct bundles (one on either side) called the *posterior* or *dorsal spinal roots* which enter the posterior portion of the cord. The axons which arise from motor cells in the anterior and lateral portions of the cord leave the vertebral column via two *anterior* or *ventral roots* (one on either side).

Blood Supply

The spinal cord has a rich arterial blood supply. Small arteries arise from each vertebral artery. These unite to form the *anterior spinal artery* which runs in the anterior longitudinal sulcus. It is joined at many anterior roots by *radicular arteries;* these arise from the *lateral spinal arteries* which supply the vertebrae, the periosteum, and the dura mater.

The anterior spinal artery gives rise to *sulcal arteries* which enter the spinal cord proper and branch to form the *intramedullary vessels*. These supply primarily the gray matter and internal aspects of the surrounding white matter of the cord. Other branches from the anterior spinal artery, the *coronal arteries,* surround the outside of the cord and supply most of its white matter (see Figure 2.7). An additional source of arterial supply are the posterior spinal arteries which derive from cranial arteries (the vertebral or posterior inferior cerebellar artery) and run along the dorsal surface of the cord, medial to the point of entrance of the sensory root fibers.

The pattern of venous drainage is similar. The *anterior venous trunk* runs parallel to the anterior spinal artery. They collect venous drainage from *radicular* and *sulcal veins* which generally follow the same course as the arteries of the same name. In the posterior portion of the cord, a single midline venous trunk as well as a pair of posterolateral trunks is usually present (see Figure 2.8).

Microscopic Anatomy

The butterfly or H-shaped gray (cellular) portion of the spinal cord is divided into *posterior* (or *dorsal*) *horns,* anterior (or *ventral*) *horns,* and the *intermediate columns* which connect the

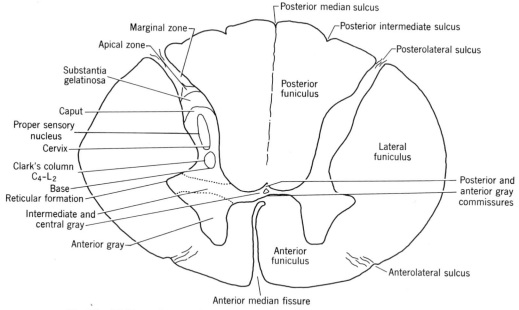

Fig. 2.5   Divisions of gray and white matter within the spinal cord. (From Peele, 1961.)

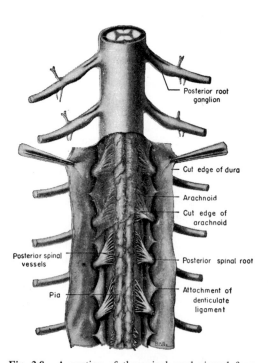

Fig. 2.6   A portion of the spinal cord viewed from behind, with dura incised and some arachnoid cut away to show relations of meninges to the cord and roots. The spinal subarachnoid space can be visualized through the filmy arachnoid. (From Peele, 1961.)

anterior and posterior portions of the cord. The narrow bridge of cells which connects the symmetrical right and left portions of the cord is called the *gray commissure*. It is surrounded by white fibers which also connect the two lateral portions of the cord. These connections are called the *anterior* and *posterior white commissures.*

In the anterior horn of the spinal cord, large cells predominate; these send axons to the musculature of the trunk. Particularly in the cervical and lumbar portions of the cord, the anterior horns are heavily populated by motor neurons which innervate the limb musculature. These motor neurons tend to be typographically organized so that distal muscles are supplied by dorsolaterally located nerve cells. These lower motor neurons represent the *final common path* of Sherrington and are classed as *general somatic motor* fibers. Axons from descending motor nerves, interneurons, or collaterals from peripheral sensory neurons terminate on these ventral horn cells. Associative neurons are also distributed through the anterior horn. Some form distinct groupings, or *nuclei* which tend to have common functions. An example of such a grouping is the *anterior commissural nucleus* of the most medial part of the anterior gray. This nucleus contains cells which project across the central commissure to ventral horn cells on the other side of the cord.

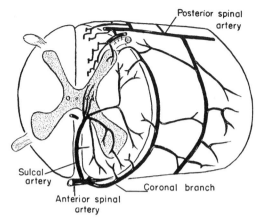

Fig. 2.7 Intrinsic arterial supply of the human spinal cord. (From Peele, 1961.)

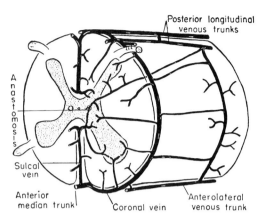

Fig. 2.8 Intrinsic venous drainage of the human spinal cord. (From Peele, 1961.)

The lateral portion of the spinal gray is made up of smaller motor cells which innervate smooth muscle, cardiac muscle, and glands. These *preganglionic motor neurons* of the spinal sympathetic and parasympathetic divisions of the autonomic nervous system form distinct nuclei called *intermediolateral cell columns.* Their axons are classed as *general visceral motor* fibers.

The cells of primary sensory neurons of the peripheral nervous system are located in the dorsal roots. These *pseudounipolar* cells have very long (up to several feet in length) "dendritic" processes which conduct sensory information toward the soma of the sensory neuron. Equally long axons project into the dorsal or posterior portion of the spinal cord. (The peripheral nerves will be discussed in a subsequent section.)

The posterior gray is divided into (1) the *marginal zone* or *Lissauer's fasciculus* (see Figure 2.5),

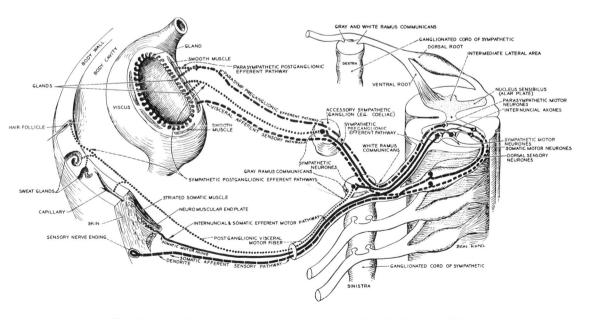

Fig. 2.9 Somatic and visceral spinal reflex pathways. (From Rubinstein, 1953.)

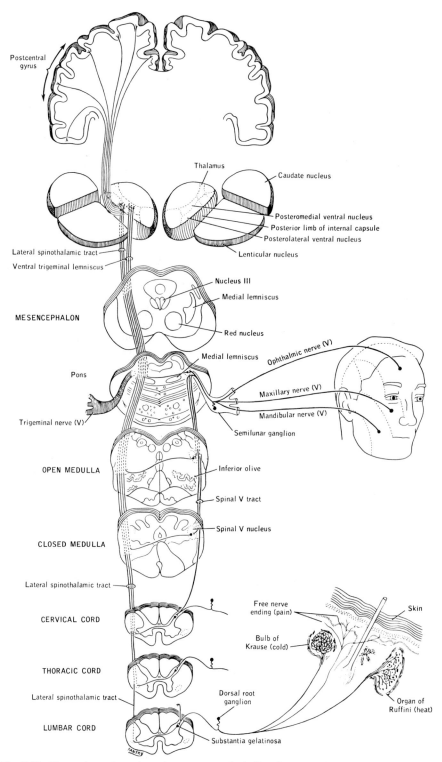

Fig. 2.10 The pathway for pain and temperature, including the types of receptors. (From House and Pansky, 1960.)

which forms the posterolateral portion of the posterior gray and contains segmental and intersegmental association neurons as well as axons from the lateral division of posterior root fibers; (2) the *substantia gelatinosa,* which surrounds the head (or "caput") of the dorsal horns—it contains primarily small cells and poorly myelinated axons; (3) the *substantia spongiosa* or *body* of the posterior gray which is subdivided into a posterior portion called *caput,* an intermediary portion called *cervix,* and an anterior part called *basal* portion. The body of the dorsal horns contains many large cells which tend to group into two distinct columns. The caput and cervix contain the *proper sensory* (or *central*) *nucleus,* which receives many collaterals from the sensory neurons in the dorsal roots and projects centrally via the spinothalamic and spinotectal tracts. The second column, the *dorsal nucleus,* is located in the medial portion of the basal section. Low lumbar and sacral portions of the dorsal nucleus are called the *nucleus of Stilling.* More cranial parts are known as *Clark's nucleus.* Cells located in the Stilling nucleus contribute fibers to the ventral spinocerebellar tract; those in Clark's nucleus project via the dorsal spinocerebellar tract.

The white matter which surrounds the spinal gray is made up largely of myelinated axons (hence the white appearance) which tend to group in large bundles or *funiculi.* The longitudinal fissures of the cord separate the *posterior, lateral,* and *anterior* funiculi. Within these large bundles smaller subdivisions can be detected. These *fiber tracts* or *fasciculi* contain mostly long ascending or descending axons.

The sensory components of the spinal cord originate in the dorsal roots. These roots contain two classes of fibers: *somatic afferents* from striated muscles, the skin, and subcutaneous tissues; and *visceral afferents* from smooth muscles, the heart, and the glands.

Two distinct fiber bundles connect the dorsal root with the spinal cord. The *lateral bundle* contains small- and medium-sized fibers which enter Lissauer's fasciculus and transmit information about temperature and pain stimuli to the body and viscera. These fibers typically divide into short ascending and descending branches which synapse on neurons of the *proper sensory nucleus.* These *secondary sensory neurons* project thin, myelinated axons across the anterior commissure into the *lateral spinothalamic tract* (see Figure 2.10). Collaterals from the lateral bundle may also ascend in Lissauer's fasciculus and may

synapse with cells in this tract which project further upward. In this way an *uncrossed* pathway which projects pain and temperature impulses toward the cranium is produced. The neurons in Lissauer's fasciculus also project axons or collaterals to association cells in the substantia gelatinosa. These send *intra*segmental as well as *inter*segmental projections to motor neurons and thus complete spinal reflex connections.

The pain and temperature fibers of the lateral spinothalamic tract assume either an anterior position in the lateral funiculus or a posterior position in the anterior funiculus (see Figure 2.16). Fibers from caudal portions of the cord tend to be pushed posteriorly and laterally by incoming fibers from higher segments of the cord. This movement produces a distinct topographic representation, as shown in Figure 2.11. Axons from the spinothalamic tracts terminate in the thalamus or in the reticular formation of the brainstem. As the tract reaches the brainstem, its fibers are scattered through a fairly large area dorsal to the inferior olive. The fibers ascend through the ventrolateral tegmentum of the pons and midbrain and terminate in the posterolateral ventral nucleus of the thalamus. As the lateral spinothalamic tract ascends, it gives off collaterals to the posterior gray of the spinal cord and the reticular formation of the medulla, pons, and mesencephalon. Projections to the hypothalamus, substantia

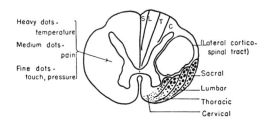

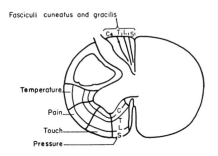

Fig. 2.11 Various concepts of the spinothalamic tracts. (From Peele, 1961. *Top,* after Walker, 1940; *bottom,* after Foerster, 1936.)

nigra, and midline nuclei of the thalamus have also been reported. In the midbrain a reorientation of the fibers of the lateral spinothalamic tract occurs. Axons which carry impulses from the lower limbs run most dorsally, those from the arms and body slightly more ventrally, and fibers from the head (the *quintothalamic* tract) most ventrally. From the posterolateral ventral nucleus of the thalamus, pain and temperature impulses are transmitted via the internal capsule to neurons located in the *postcentral gyrus* of the *parietal lobe* of the cortex. Dull and poorly localized pain and intense temperature stimuli can be appreciated even when the projections to the cortex are cut. However, all localization or fine discriminations depend on the cortical mechanisms.

The lateral spinothalamic tract is sometimes sectioned in patients suffering from intractable pain. Unilateral transection of this tract results in a more or less complete loss of pain and temperature sensitivity on the contralateral side of the body, which generally begins about one dermatome below the section (see Figure 2.12). Bilateral destruction of the pain pathways is required for the alleviation of pain sensations from the viscera.

The second major division of the projection from the dorsal root to the spinal cord, the *medial bundle,* contains primarily large myelinated fibers from neuromuscular and neurotendinous spindles, Pacinian corpuscles, and encapsulated and naked tactile receptors. These fibers enter the

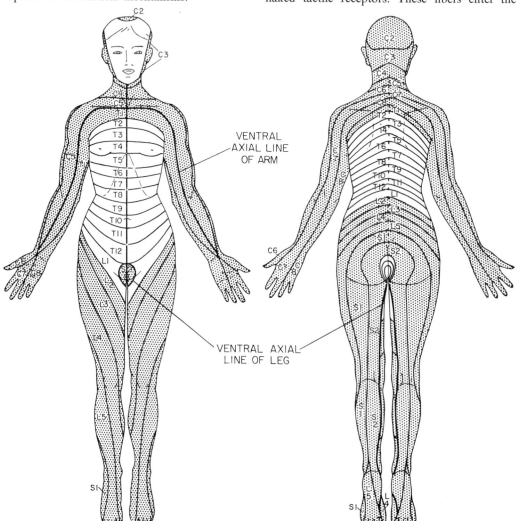

Fig. 2.12 The pattern of cutaneous innervation of the dermatomes. (From J. J. Keegan and F. D. Garrett, *Anat. Rec.,* 1948, **102,** 411.)

spinal cord near the dorsal portion of the posterior horn and typically divide into long ascending and descending branches; these give off collaterals to several spinal cord segments above and below the segment of entry. Some of these collaterals form monosynaptic reflex connections (such as the myotatic reflex) which are complete within the segment of entry. Some cross to the other side of the cord via the posterior commissure and terminate at cells of Clark's nucleus.

The ascending branches of the medial bundle fibers enter the posterior funiculus where they form large nerve tracts which project to the brainstem. Two distinct bundles in the upper half of the cord can be described. The *fasciculus gracilis* takes up the medial portion of the posterior funiculus. It carries impulses which arise from the lower segments of the body (those innervated by nerves entering the sacral, lumbar, and lower six thoracic segments of the cord). The *fasciculus cuneatus* takes up the lateral portion of the posterior funiculus. It carries impulses which arise from the upper segments of the body (those innervated by nerves entering the upper six thoracic and all cervical segments of the cord). The components of both fasciculi are arranged in a topographic order. Fibers arising from the lower portion of the body run medially, those from the upper portion run laterally. The *secondary sensory neuron* for this uncrossed pathway for touch and pressure stimuli is located in the *nuclei gracilis* and *cuneatus* in the caudal portion of the medulla. The axons from these secondary cells form the *internal arcuate fiber tract;* this tract crosses the midline underneath the fourth ventricle and ascends to the *posterolateral ventral nucleus* of the thalamus in a large fiber bundle called the *medial lemniscus.* This distinct fiber bundle runs along the ventral tegmentum of the brainstem and gives off collaterals to the reticular formation, the midline nuclei of the thalamus, the substantia nigra, and the globus pallidus and hypothalamus. From the posterolateral ventral nucleus of the thalamus, projections are made through the internal capsule to the postcentral gyrus of the parietal lobe (see Figures 2.13 and 2.14).

Destruction of fibers in this important sensory tract impairs the sensations of touch and light pressure as well as important kinesthetic sensations which convey information about the position and movement of the body. *Hypotonia* (a reduction in the resistance of skeletal muscles to passive stretch) then occurs; it combines with a loss of feedback from the muscles to produce a condition called *sensory ataxia* which is characterized by uncoordinated and awkward movements.

Fibers of the medial bundle which carry information about deep pressure and touch may take a number of different pathways to the brain. The ascending and descending branches of these fibers typically synapse at neurons located in the cervical and basal portion of the spinal gray. These secondary sensory neurons then project axons through the anterior commissure to the other side of the cord; there they form the *ventral spinothalamic tract* which ascends in the anterior portion of the anterior fasciculus (see Figure 2.14). Some of the axons from the secondary neurons in this pathway do not cross but join the ventral spinothalamic tract on the *same* side of the cord. The ventral spinothalamic tract, therefore, is a mixed tract which carries information from both sides of the body. The axons from this tract join the medial lemniscus in the rostral brainstem and terminate in the posterolateral ventral nucleus of the thalamus. Their cortical projection is similar to that of the lateral spinothalamic tract.

Some axons from the secondary sensory nuclei in the basal and cervical portion of the spinal gray form a relatively short tract; this *spinotectal tract* ascends in the lateral funiculus and terminates in the nuclei of the *superior* and *inferior colliculi* in the *tectum* of the midbrain.

Collaterals from primary sensory axons which enter with the medial bundle may also terminate in Clark's column, either on the same or contralateral side of the cord. From here, axons are projected to the lateral column where they ascend just ventral to Lissauer's tract. Although some fibers may cross and join the tract on the opposite side of the cord, this *dorsal spinocerebellar tract* is largely an uncrossed connection between the sensory endings in muscles and tendons and the motor centers of the cerebellum (see Figure 2.15). A *ventral spinocerebellar tract* of similar origin is primarily a crossed tract which carries sensory feedback from the musculature on the contralateral side of the body to the cerebellum. The dorsal spinocerebellar tract enters the cerebellum via the *inferior cerebral peduncle* (or *restiform body*). The ventral tract enters via the *brachium conjunctivum.*

In addition, there are several sensory pathways which connect secondary cells in the posterior spinal gray with the lower portions of the brainstem. The *spino-olivary tract* is primarily a crossed pathway which ascends in the ventral

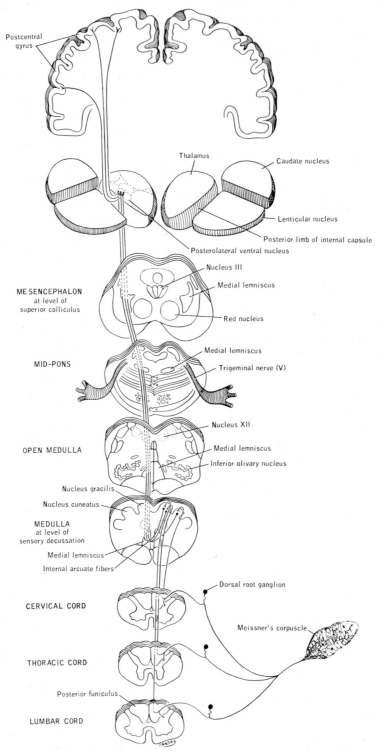

Fig. 2.13 Pathway for tactile discrimination. (From House and Pansky, 1960.)

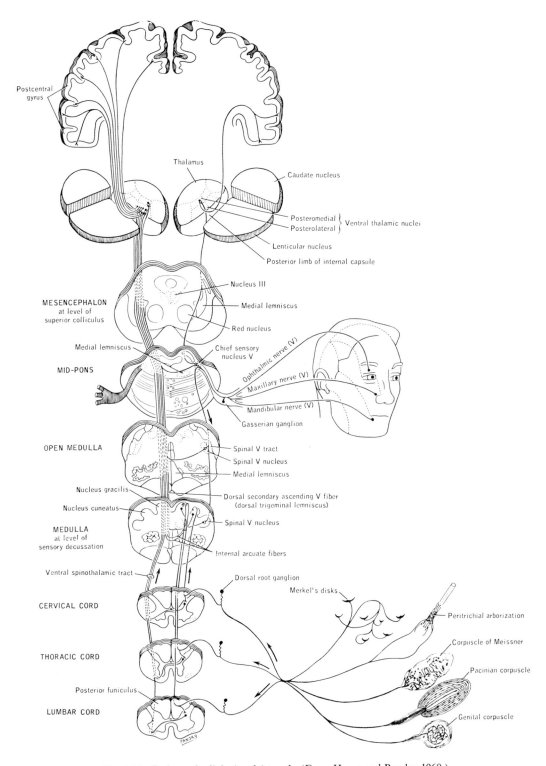

Fig. 2.14 Pathway for light (crude) touch. (From House and Pansky, 1960.)

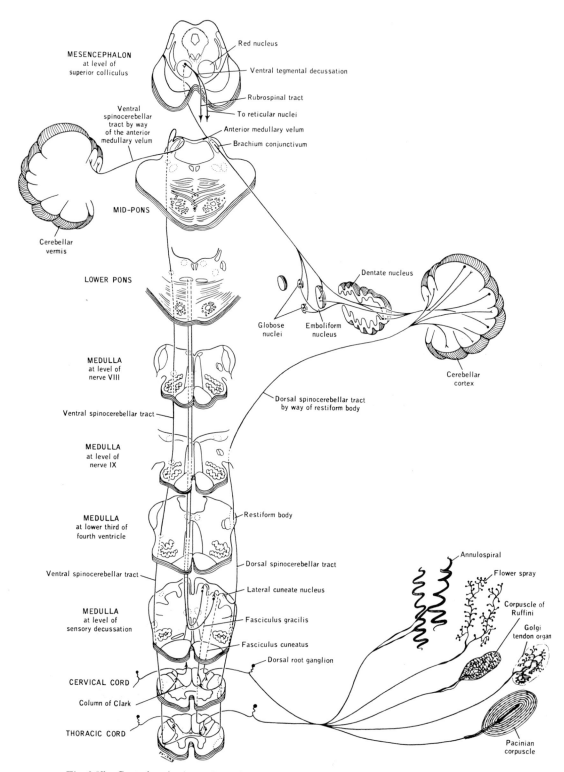

Fig. 2.15 Central projections of muscle and tendon receptors. (From House and Pansky, 1960.)

funiculus and the most ventral portion of the lateral funiculus and terminates in the *inferior olivary nucleus* of the medulla. The *spinoreticular tract* contains largely uncrossed fibers which ascend in the lateral funiculus and terminate in the lateral reticular nucleus of the medulla. The information which is relayed in these pathways eventually reaches the cerebellum via olivocerebellar and reticulocerebellar connections.

The motor components of the spinal cord consist of two major groups, the *pyramidal* and *extrapyramidal* pathways (see Figure 2.16). Large pyramidal cells in the precentral portion of the frontal lobe and the postcentral gyrus of the parietal lobe project long axons through the *internal capsule* into the *cerebral peduncle,* and then on to the *basilar portion* of the *pons* and along the ventral border of the *medulla* where they form clearly visible bulges or *pyramids.* Most of these axons then *decussate* (i.e., cross to the other side of the

medulla) before descending into the posterior portion of the lateral funiculus as the *lateral corticospinal tract.* The uncrossed fibers from the pyramidal tract enter the medial portion of the anterior funiculus as the *ventral corticospinal tract* (see Figure 2.17). The long fibers from these tracts may terminate directly on the large multipolar motor neurons which are found in the anterior portion of the dorsal horn or on interneurons which, in turn, project directly or indirectly to the motor neurons. The fibers of these pyramidal motor tracts are myelinated, and many of them originate from specific layers of cells in the cortex (the Betz cells in the fifth cortical layer). The exact origin of some of the smaller fibers in this tract is not known; however, all appear to have a facilitatory effect on spinal motor neurons which control *specific* movements.

The extrapyramidal motor tracts of the spinal cord arise from various subcortical nuclei which receive afferents from the cortical motor areas.

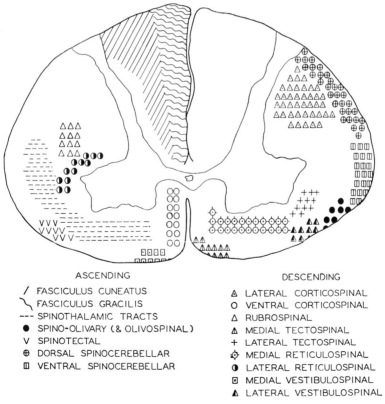

ASCENDING

/ FASCICULUS CUNEATUS
⌝ FASCICULUS GRACILIS
--- SPINOTHALAMIC TRACTS
● SPINO-OLIVARY (& OLIVOSPINAL)
V SPINOTECTAL
⊕ DORSAL SPINOCEREBELLAR
▥ VENTRAL SPINOCEREBELLAR

DESCENDING

△ LATERAL CORTICOSPINAL
O VENTRAL CORTICOSPINAL
▵ RUBROSPINAL
▲ MEDIAL TECTOSPINAL
+ LATERAL TECTOSPINAL
⬦ MEDIAL RETICULOSPINAL
◑ LATERAL RETICULOSPINAL
▤ MEDIAL VESTIBULOSPINAL
▲ LATERAL VESTIBULOSPINAL

Fig. 2.16 Spinal cord pathways. For purposes of clarity, no pathway is duplicated on the two sides. Those in the anterior funiculus in particular are shown more discretely than they actually occur. Associative tracts are not shown. (From Peele, 1961.)

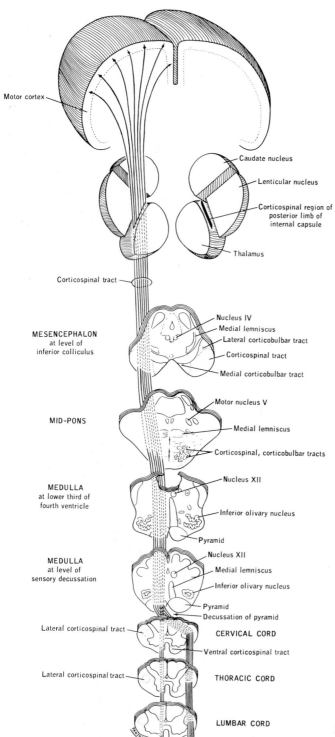

Motor cortex

Caudate nucleus

Lenticular nucleus

Corticospinal region of
posterior limb of
internal capsule

Thalamus

Corticospinal tract

MESENCEPHALON
at level of
inferior colliculus

Nucleus IV
Medial lemniscus
Lateral corticobulbar tract
Corticospinal tract
Medial corticobulbar tract

MID-PONS

Motor nucleus V

Medial lemniscus

Corticospinal, corticobulbar tracts

MEDULLA
at lower third of
fourth ventricle

Nucleus XII

Inferior olivary nucleus

Pyramid

MEDULLA
at level of
sensory decussation

Nucleus XII
Medial lemniscus
Inferior olivary nucleus

Pyramid
Decussation of pyramid

Lateral corticospinal tract

CERVICAL CORD

Ventral corticospinal tract

Lateral corticospinal tract

THORACIC CORD

LUMBAR CORD

Fig. 2.17 The corticospinal pathway.
(From House and Pansky, 1960.)

58

A more detailed description of the central portions of this complex system of interrelated pathways will be presented later. Only the spinal pathways which form the lowest portion of this system will be discussed here.

Efferent fibers from the red nucleus of the midbrain form the *rubrotegmentospinal tract* which descends in the medial portion of the lateral funiculus of the cord after decussating in the midbrain. It ends primarily in the upper segments of the cord and synapses with interneurons located in the intermediate gray (see Figure 2.18).

Cells located in the reticular nuclei of the pons and medulla (particularly near the motor nucleus of the vagus) project axons along the *medial reticulospinal tract.* This tract enters the anterior funiculus of the cord and terminates directly on motor cells of the ventral horn or on closely associated interneurons. Both crossed and uncrossed components have been described. Other reticular nuclei of the medulla (particularly those in the vicinity of the motor nucleus of the trigeminal nerve) give rise to the *lateral reticulospinal tract* which enters the lateral funiculus and descends as far as lumbar segments of the cord. This primarily crossed pathway seems to be particularly important in the coordination of movement. In contrast to the medial reticulospinal pathways (which appear to carry primarily facilitatory impulses), the lateral reticulospinal tracts carry primarily inhibitory impulses (see Figure 2.19).

Neurons in or near the colliculi of the midbrain project axons into the *medial* and *lateral tectospinal tracts;* these carry to the ventral horn motor cells information that permits postural adjustments to auditory and visual stimuli. Both tracts contain crossed as well as uncrossed elements. The medial tectospinal tract enters the anterior funiculus of the spinal cord; the lateral reaches the lateral funiculus.

Neurons in the lateral vestibular nuclei of Deiters give rise to axons which descend in the anterior funiculus of the cord as the *lateral vestibulospinal tract.* This uncrossed pathway terminates primarily on the motor neurons of the ventral horn. Fibers from all other vestibular nuclei enter the spinal cord in the anterior funiculus and usually run parallel to a tract called the medial longitudinal fasciculus (see Figure 2.20). The fibers of this *medial vestibulospinal tract* terminate primarily in the cervical portion of the cord. Both the lateral and medial vestibulospinal tracts appear to carry information which is essential for postural adjustments to proprioceptive stimuli. Fibers

from the fastigial nuclei of the cerebellum decussate in the inferior cerebellar commissure and enter the ventral funiculus. This *uncinate fasciculus* terminates in cervical portions of the cord.

In addition to these large ascending and descending fiber systems, a number of tracts in the spinal cord essentially begin and terminate within the cord itself. Most of these *associative tracts* have both ascending and descending components arising from association nuclei all along the cord and terminating either on association neurons or on ventral horn motor cells. Most of these associative tracts run along the outer surface of the spinal gray and, in effect, form an outer shell around the gray matter. These are the *fasciculi proprii* or *propriospinal system.* Other tracts, such as the *medial longitudinal fasciculus,* form distinct pathways in the spinal white matter. Less obviously part of the association system, although commonly classed with it, are tracts formed by descending branches of primary sensory fibers, largely from the medial bundle. These fibers may terminate directly on anterior horn cells and thus form basic reflex connections or synapse with interneurons several segments below their segment of entry. The *fasciculus fascicularis* and the *septomarginal fasciculus* are prominent examples of this type of pathway in the cord.

THE BRAINSTEM

The Medulla and Pons

The cranial aspects of the spinal cord communicate with the *bulbar* portion of the brainstem via the *foramen magnum,* a large opening in the bony calvarium which surrounds the brain. This most caudal portion of the brainstem is called the *medulla oblongata.* It extends from the lower border of the foramen magnum rostralward to the *striae medullares,* white stripes which cross the floor of the fourth ventricle and serve as convenient landmarks in this portion of the brain.

The central canal of the spinal cord continues into the medulla and gradually widens to a rhomboid-shaped canal called the *fourth ventricle.* The widest part of the fourth ventricle is at the rostral border of the medulla.

The floor of the fourth ventricle contains a number of landmarks (see Figure 2.21). In the caudal portion of the ventricle, the *hypoglossal trigone* appears; it forms a noticeable elevation on either side of the midline fissure and marks the position of the *hypoglossal* (XII cranial) nerve. Immediately lateral to the hypoglossal trigone is another

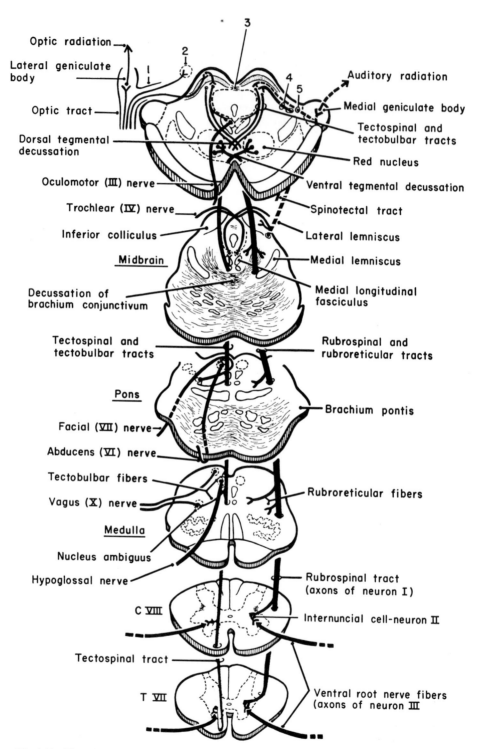

Fig. 2.18 The rubrospinal, rubroreticular, tectospinal, and tectobulbar tracts. These are extrapyramidal and reflex pathways. Other midbrain structures include 1, the brachium of the superior colliculus; 2, pretectal area; 3, commissure of superior colliculus; 4, spinotectal tract; 5, collicular fibers from lateral lemniscus. (From Truex, 1959.)

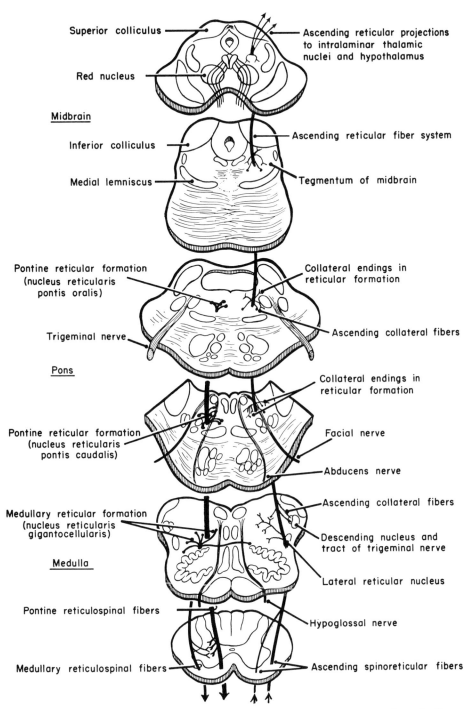

Fig. 2.19 Ascending and descending reticular fiber systems. Ascending spinoreticular and collateral reticular projections are shown on the right. This system gives off collateral fibers at various brainstem levels and is augmented by rostrally projecting reticular fibers. Pontine reticulospinal fibers (medial reticulospinal tract) are uncrossed and originate largely from the nucleus reticularis pontis caudalis. Medullary reticulospinal fibers (lateral reticulospinal tract) are predominantly uncrossed and arise from the nucleus reticularis gigantocellularis. Fibers from these sources are not sharply segregated in the spinal cord. (From Truex and Carpenter, 1964.)

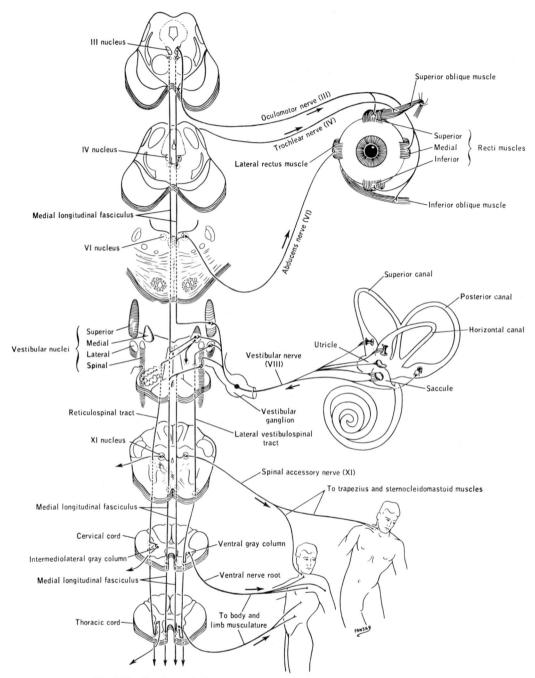

III nucleus

Superior oblique muscle

Oculomotor nerve (III)

Trochlear nerve (IV)

IV nucleus

Lateral rectus muscle

Superior
Medial   } Recti muscles
Inferior

Inferior oblique muscle

Medial longitudinal fasciculus

Abducens nerve (VI)

VI nucleus

Superior canal

Posterior canal

Horizontal canal

Superior
Medial
Lateral
Spinal

} Vestibular nuclei

Utricle

Vestibular nerve
(VIII)

Saccule

Reticulospinal tract

Vestibular
ganglion

Lateral vestibulospinal
tract

XI nucleus

Spinal accessory nerve (XI)

To trapezius and sternocleidomastoid muscles

Medial longitudinal fasciculus

Cervical cord

Ventral gray column

Intermediolateral gray column

Ventral nerve root

Medial longitudinal fasciculus

Thoracic cord

To body and
limb musculature

Fig. 2.20   Simple vestibular reflex pathways. (From House and Pansky, 1960.)

elevation, the *ala cinerea,* which overlies the dorsal motor nucleus of the *vagus* (X cranial) nerve. The lower portion of the fourth ventricle has been called the *calamus scriptorius.* In front of the hypoglossal trigone is the *medial eminence* which extends into the pontine portion of the brainstem.

In the lower part of the medial eminence is located the nucleus of the *abducens* (VI cranial) nerve. The lateral portion of the floor of the fourth ventricle is largely taken up by the *acoustic area* which indicates the location of the major *vestibular nuclei* and the *dorsal cochlear nucleus.*

The surface of the brainstem contains several important landmarks (see Figure 2.22). On the dorsal surface of the medulla, fissures and ridges represent a direct extension of the dorsal median fissure and posterior funiculi of the spinal cord. These ridges mark the course of the fasciculi gracilis and cuneatus and their termination in the *nuclei gracilis* and *cuneatus*. Lateral to the cuneate fasciculus, a third ridge on the surface of the medulla, the *tuberculum trigeminum*, marks the location of the nucleus and spinal tract of the

trigeminal (V cranial) nerve. The roots of the *spinal accessory* (XI cranial), *vagus* (X cranial), and *glossopharyngeal* (IX cranial) nerves leave the medulla ventrolaterally to the tuberculum trigeminum.

A conspicuous elevation on the ventrolateral surface of the medulla is called the *inferior olivary eminence*. It overlies an important relay nucleus, the *inferior olivary nucleus*. The ventral surface of the medulla is taken up by the *pyramids*, pronounced ridges which mark the location of the

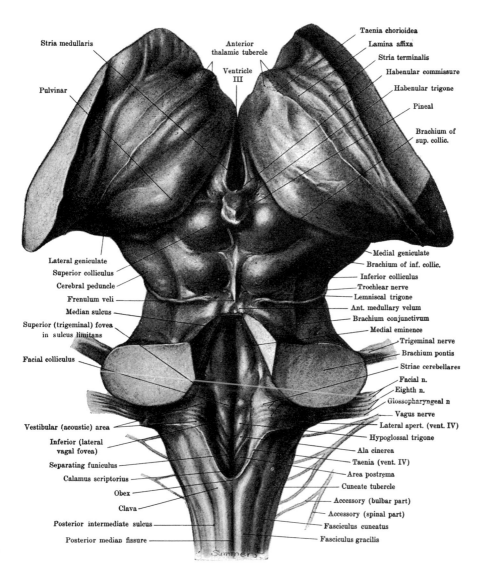

Fig. 2.21 Dorsal surface of the brainstem. The cerebellum has been removed to show the structures on the floor of the fourth ventricle (rhomboid fossa). (From Mettler, 1948.)

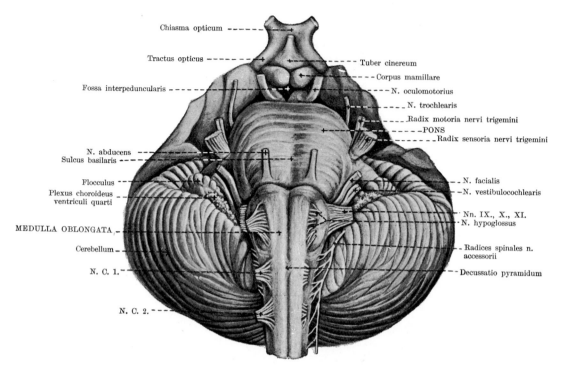

Chiasma opticum

Tractus opticus

Fossa interpeduncularis

Tuber cinereum

Corpus mamillare

N. oculomotorius

N. trochlearis

Radix motoria nervi trigemini

PONS

Radix sensoria nervi trigemini

N. abducens

Sulcus basilaris

Flocculus

Plexus choroideus ventriculi quarti

MEDULLA OBLONGATA

Cerebellum

N. C. 1.

N. C. 2.

N. facialis

N. vestibulocochlearis

Nn. IX., X., XI.

N. hypoglossus

Radices spinales n. accessorii

Decussatio pyramidum

Fig. 2.22   Ventral surface of the brainstem and upper spinal cord. (From Kiss and Szentágothai, 1964.)

corticospinal fiber system. The root of the *hypoglossal* (XII cranial) nerve arises between the inferior olivary eminence and the pyramids.

The pontine portion of the brainstem is identified by large, transversely running pontocerebellar fiber tracts which project to the cerebellum as the *middle cerebellar peduncle* or *brachium pontis.* The upper half of the medulla projects to the cerebellum via the *inferior cerebellar peduncle* or *restiform body.* A third fiber bundle, the *brachium conjunctivum* or *superior cerebellar peduncle,* connects the cerebellum with anterior parts of the brainstem.

The roots of the *abducens* (VI cranial) nerve leave the ventral medulla as it merges with the pontine portion of the brainstem. The roots of the *facial* (VII cranial) and *acoustic* (VIII cranial) nerves leave the brainstem at the same rostrocaudal level but considerably lateral to the origin of the abducens (see Figures 2.23 and 2.24).

The major fiber tracts of the spinal cord maintain their peripheral position in the bulbar portion of the brainstem. The fiber tracts of the posterior funiculi (fasciculi gracilis and cuneatus) retain their dorsal position; the tracts which originate in the lateral funiculi remain in the lateral field of the medulla (with the exception of the lateral corticospinal tract which runs in the ventral part of the medulla). Fiber tracts which course through the medial portion of the anterior funiculi run in the midline of the medulla and pons. Tracts which run in the more lateral portion of the anterior funiculi assume an intermediate position in the brainstem.

Secondary fibers from the nuclei gracilis and cuneatus descend into the bulbar portion of the brainstem and then cross the midline just rostral to the decussation of the pyramidal motor system; they then ascend in the medial portion of the brainstem to the thalamus in the *medial lemniscus.* The topographical organization of impulses which characterize the cuneate and gracilis tracts is maintained. In the medulla proprioceptive and tactile impulses from the contralateral foot run ventrally; those from the neck run dorsally. The axis of the medial lemniscus changes position in the pontine portion of the brainstem. (The widest part of this oval bundle assumes a horizontal orientation.)

The *spinal tract* and *nucleus* of the *trigeminal*

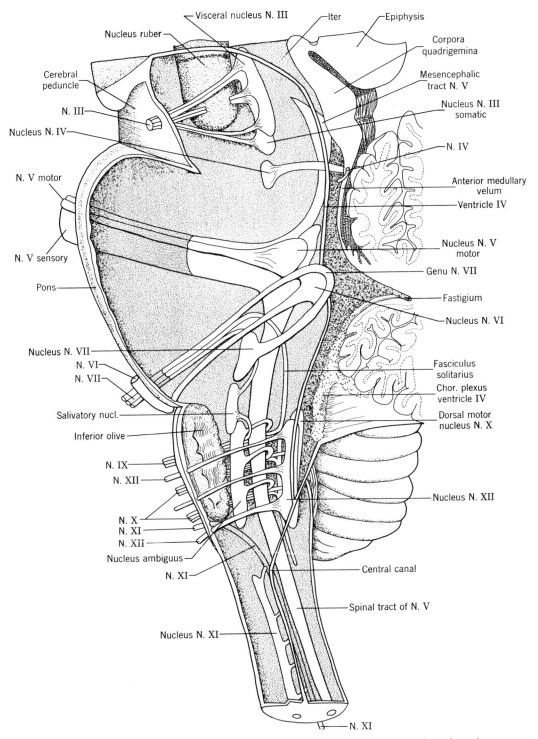

Fig. 2.23 Nuclei and intramedullary course of some of the cranial nerves, somewhat schematic, viewed from the median sagittal surface. The right brainstem is represented as a hollow from which all other brain substance has been removed. (From Truex, 1959.)

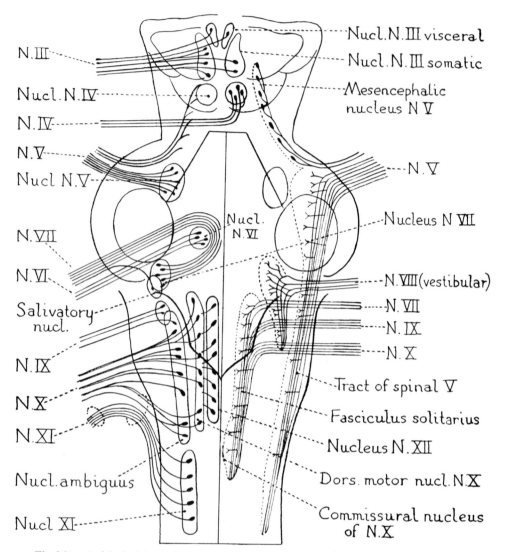

Fig. 2.24   Nuclei of origin, nuclei of termination, and intramedullary course of the cranial nerves, projected on the dorsal surface of the brainstem. (From Truex, 1959.)

nerve lie along the lateral aspect of the medulla. The tract extends into the caudal half of the pons where it joins the *sensory* nucleus of the trigeminal nerve. Throughout the length of the medulla and caudal pons, secondary fibers which form small fascicles emerge. These ascend in an oblique direction and eventually cross the midline of the brainstem before joining the medial lemniscus on the other side of the brain. These fibers make up the *ventral ascending tract of the fifth cranial nerve.*

The *lateral spinothalamic tract,* which carries pain and temperature information from contralateral parts of the body, runs along the lateral

surface of the medulla. It maintains essentially the same topographic organization throughout its course. Impulses from the lower extremities are carried in the lateral portion of the tract. Those from higher parts of the body run in the more medial sections. The lateral spinothalamic tract eventually joins the medial lemniscus in its course to the thalamus. *Spinotectal* fibers accompany the lateral spinothalamic fibers in the bulbar and pontine sections of the brainstem. These spinotectal projections terminate in the superior colliculi of the midbrain.

The *dorsal spinocerebellar tract* ascends in the dorsolateral portion of the medulla and enters the restiform body. The *ventral spinocerebellar tract* runs along the lateral aspects of the medulla and pons; it maintains a close association with fibers from the lateral spinothalamic tract until it enters the brachium conjunctivum at midpontine levels. *Spino-olivary tracts* terminate in the olivary nuclei which are located in the ventrolateral portion of the caudal medulla.

The corticospinal motor system is the major descending pathway in the pons and medulla. In the ventral part of the medulla it forms the *pyramidal* elevations. At the very caudal end of the medulla, most fibers (about 85%) of this pathway cross the midline and descend on the contralateral side of the spinal cord. These *motor decussations* form one of the major landmarks of the caudal medulla (see Figure 2.25).

The descending tracts of the lateral funiculus of the spinal cord (the *rubrotegmentospinal, lateral tectotegmentospinal,* and *lateral reticulospinal* tracts) course through the lower portion of the

pons in the lateral tegmental area. From here they project along the lateral surface of the medulla and into the lateral funiculi. The *vestibulospinal tracts* originate in the vestibular nuclei in the floor of the fourth ventricle and run dorsal to the olivary nuclei toward the cord.

Several transverse levels are usually distinguished in the bulbar and pontine section of the brainstem: (1) the level of the motor decussations (see Figure 2.5); (2) the level of the vagus, bulbar accessory, and hypoglossal nerves (see Figures 2.6 and 2.7); (3) the level of the acoustic and glossopharyngeal nerves (see Figure 2.8); (4) the level of the facial and abducens nerves (see Figure 2.9); (5) the trigeminal level (see Figure 2.10); and (6) the pretrigeminal level (see Figure 2.11).

The level of the pyramidal decussations (see Figure 2.25). The dorsal portion of this transitional section of the brainstem is taken up by the fasciculi gracilis and cuneatus and their nuclei.

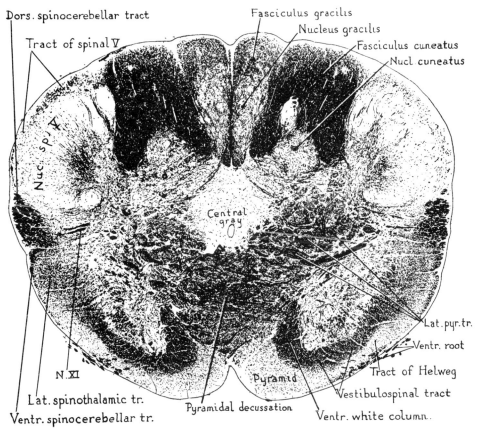

Fig. 2.25 Transverse section of the medulla through the decussation of the pyramidal tracts. Weigert's myelin stain. (From Truex and Carpenter, 1964.)

The substantia gelatinosa and Lissauer's tract, which carry pain and temperature impulses from the body, merge at upper cervical levels of the cord with the nucleus and spinal tract of the trigeminal (V cranial) nerve; this nerve carries pain and temperature impulses from the face. The dorsal and ventral spinocerebellar, spino-olivary, and spinocerebellar tracts of the lateral funiculi continue to run on the lateral surface of the caudal medulla. The lateral corticospinal pathways move from the lateral funiculus of the cord to the ventromedial aspect of the caudal medulla. Also represented in the lateral medulla are the rubrotegmental, lateral reticulospinal, lateral spinothalamic, and spinotectal tracts. The lateral proprius region of the spinal cord is continuous with the reticular formation of the lower brainstem.

The descending fibers of the corticospinal tracts separate in the lower medulla into lateral and ventral corticospinal components. Most of the fibers cross the midline in the ventral medulla and enter the lateral corticospinal tract which descends in the lateral funiculi of the cord. Some fibers do not cross but enter directly into the ventral funiculi. The decussation of the pyramidal motor system is the most conspicuous landmark of the transitional region between the spinal cord and the caudal medulla.

The central portion of the transitional area is taken up by several cell masses. The rostral half of the spinal nucleus of the *accessory* (XI cranial) nerve extends into the caudal medulla, where it becomes continuous with the nucleus *retroambigualis*. The substantia gelatinosa of the cord becomes essentially continuous with the nucleus of the spinal tract of the trigeminal (V cranial) nerve.

The level of the vagal, accessory, and hypoglossal nerves and nuclei (see Figure 2.26 and 2.27). Immediately anterior to the level of the motor decussations, three major cranial nerve nuclei begin and extend almost to the anterior border of the medulla. Overlying these important nuclei are the fasciculi and nuclei cuneatus and gracilis and, in the more anterior portions, the fourth ventricle.

Near the midline and beneath the cranial nerve nuclei the *nucleus of the raphé* and associated fibers appear. Some portions of this complex system of cells and fibers constitute part of the ascending reticular formation; others project specifically into the cerebellum. The major ascending fiber tracts (medial longitudinal fasciculus, medial reticulospinal and medial tectospinal tracts, and

medial lemniscus) run adjacent to the midline above the pyramidal motor fibers.

A dark-staining cell mass, the *arcuate nucleus,* is located dorsal to the pyramids. It receives afferents from the corticospinal tracts and projects to the cerebellum.

Much of the ventrolateral portion of the medulla at this transverse level is taken up by the irregularly shaped *inferior olivary nucleus.* This nucleus is the origin of the olivospinal and olivocerebellar tracts and the terminus of spino-olivary and cerebello-olivary connections.

The reticular gray takes up the area between the inferior olivary complex and the periventricular part of the medulla. The lateral aspects of the brainstem at this level contain the *lateral reticular nucleus* which is subdivided into an area containing primarily large cells (*pars magnocellularis*) and an area containing primarily small cells (*pars parvocellularis*). The lateral reticular nucleus projects to the cerebellum and receives afferents from the fastigial nucleus of the cerebellum.

The level of the acoustic and glossopharyngeal nerves (see Figure 2.28). The fourth ventricle reaches its widest point at this level. The composition of the ventral two-thirds of the medulla has not essentially changed. In the dorsal portion of the brainstem, several important nuclei take up the floor of the fourth ventricle and the dorsal and dorsolateral surface of the medulla.

In the midline region of the floor of the fourth ventricle, the *dorsal paramedian nucleus* projects to the cerebellum. The *nucleus prepositus* which develops immediately lateral to the dorsal paramedian nucleus separates the dorsal portion of the hypoglossal nerve nucleus from the caudal portion of the abducens nerve nucleus. Still more laterally, the *inferior salivatory nucleus* lies at the level of the entering roots of the glossopharyngeal nerve and forms part of the glossopharyngeal complex. Axons from this nucleus distribute through the glossopharyngeal nerve to the otic ganglion of the ear which projects postganglionic fibers to the parotid gland. The general sensory components of the glossopharyngeal nucleus enter the adjacent *fasciculus solitarius* and terminate in the *nucleus parasolitarius* which is located slightly more caudally. Taste fibers which enter the brainstem with the glossopharyngeal nerve (primarily from the posterior third of the tongue) also enter the fasciculus solitarius; however, they terminate near their level of entrance in the dorsally situated *gustatory nucleus* (also called the *dorsal visceral gray nu-*

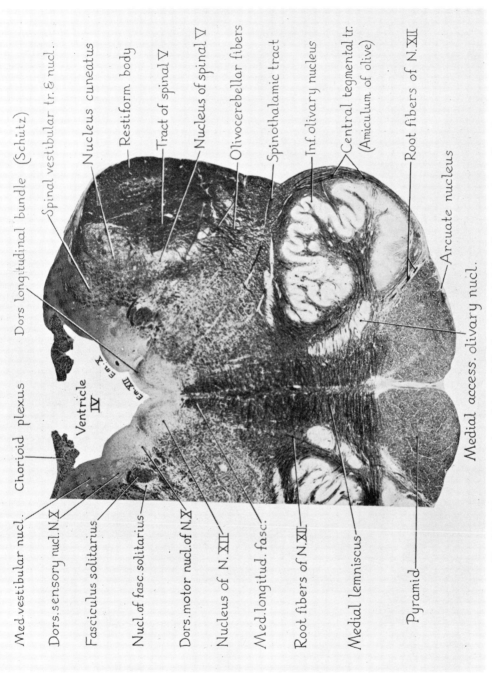

Med.vestibular nucl.

Chorioid plexus

Dors longitudinal bundle (Schütz)

Spinal vestibular tr.& nucl.

Nucleus cuneatus

Restiform body

Tract of spinal V

Nucleus of spinal V

Olivocerebellar fibers

Spinothalamic tract

Inf.olivary nucleus

Central tegmental tr.
(Amiculum of olive)

Root fibers of N.XII

Arcuate nucleus

Medial access. olivary nucl.

Dors.sensory nucl. N.X

Fasciculus solitarius

Nucl.of fasc.solitarius

Dors.motor nucl.of N.X

Nucleus of N. XII

Med.longitud. fasc.

Root fibers of N.XII

Medial lemniscus

Pyramid

Ventricle IV

Em.XII

Em.X

Fig. 2.26 Transverse section of the medulla through the inferior olive. Weigert's myelin stain. Em.X, eminentia vagi; Em.XII, eminentia hypoglossi. (From Truex and Carpenter, 1964.)

69

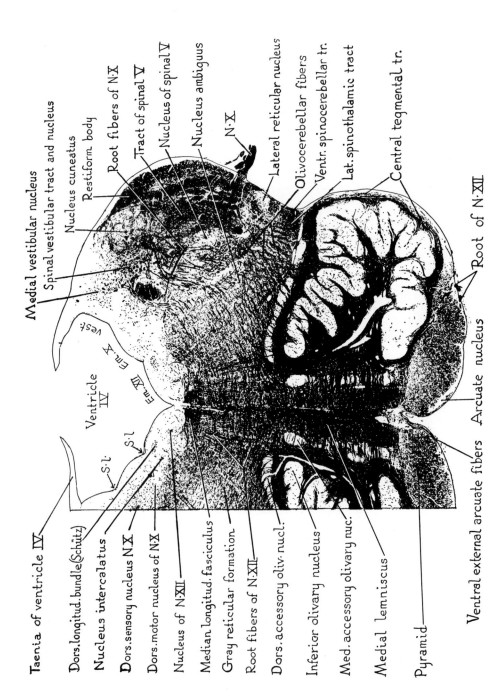

Taenia of ventricle IV

Dors. longitud. bundle (Schütz)

Nucleus intercalatus

Dors. sensory nucleus N·X

Dors. motor nucleus of N·X

Nucleus of N·XII

Median longitud. fasciculus

Gray reticular formation

Root fibers of N·XII

Dors. accessory oliv. nucl.

Inferior olivary nucleus

Med. accessory olivary nuc.

Medial lemniscus

Pyramid

Ventricle IV

Medial vestibular nucleus

Spinal vestibular tract and nucleus

Nucleus cuneatus

Restiform body

Root fibers of N·X

Tract of spinal V

Nucleus of spinal V

Nucleus ambiguus

N·X

Lateral reticular nucleus

Olivocerebellar fibers

Ventr. spinocerebellar tr.

Lat. spinothalamic tract

Central tegmental tr.

Root of N·XII

Arcuate nucleus

Ventral external arcuate fibers

Fig. 2.27 Transverse section of the medulla through the middle of the olive. Weigert's myelin stain. Em.X, eminentia vagi (ala cinerea); Em.XII, eminentia hypoglossi; S.l., sulcus limitans; vest., area vestibularis. (From Truex, 1959.)

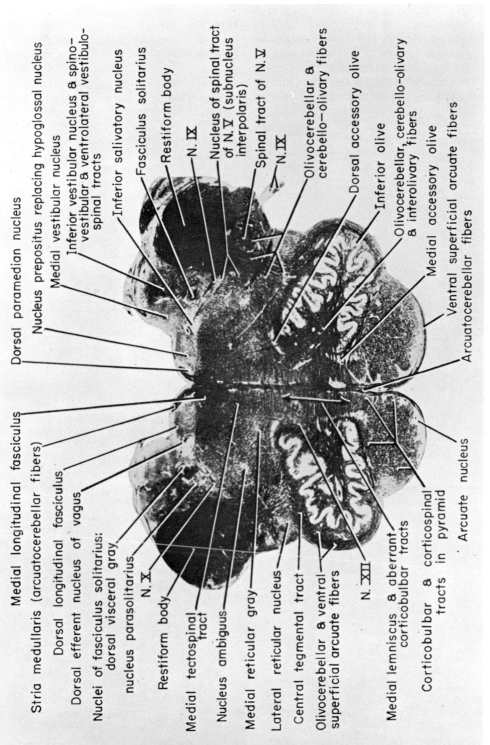

Fig. 2.28 Transverse section of the medulla at the most rostral levels of the vagus nerve (left side) and the most caudal levels of the glossopharyngeal nerve (right side). Weil preparation. (From Crosby et al., 1962.)

Medial longitudinal fasciculus

Stria medullaris (arcuatocerebellar fibers)

Dorsal longitudinal fasciculus

Dorsal efferent nucleus of vagus

Nuclei of fasciculus solitarius:
dorsal visceral gray

nucleus parasolitarius

N. X

Restiform body

Medial tectospinal tract

Nucleus ambiguus

Medial reticular gray

Lateral reticular nucleus

Central tegmental tract

Olivocerebellar & ventral superficial arcuate fibers

N. XII

Medial lemniscus & aberrant corticobulbar tracts

Corticobulbar & corticospinal tracts in pyramid

Arcuate nucleus

Dorsal paramedian nucleus

Nucleus prepositus replacing hypoglossal nucleus

Medial vestibular nucleus

Inferior vestibular nucleus & spino-vestibular & ventrolateral vestibulo-spinal tracts

Inferior salivatory nucleus

Fasciculus solitarius

Restiform body

N. IX

Nucleus of spinal tract of N. V (subnucleus interpolaris)

Spinal tract of N. V

N. IX

Olivocerebellar & cerebello-olivary fibers

Dorsal accessory olive

Inferior olive

Olivocerebellar, cerebello-olivary & interolivary fibers

Medial accessory olive

Ventral superficial arcuate fibers

Arcuatocerebellar fibers

71

cleus). This nucleus projects axons to the medial lemniscus and to the posterior ventral nucleus of the dorsal thalamus.

Fibers of the *acoustic* (VIII cranial) nerve enter the brainstem at the level of the glossopharyngeal nerve. The incoming fibers bifurcate and distribute along the dorsal and lateral border of the inferior cerebellar peduncle before terminating in the dorsolateral gray of the medulla. The area of termination has been subdivided into the *dorsal* and *ventral cochlear nuclei*.

The dorsal cochlear nucleus forms a prominent elevation in the lateral portion of the fourth ven-

tricle. Secondary fibers from the ventral cochlear nucleus traverse the midline of the brainstem in a distinctive pattern (the *trapezoid body*) to reach the lateral lemniscus of the contralateral side. Here they ascend to the midbrain where many of them terminate in the inferior colliculi. Most of the fibers from the dorsal cochlear nucleus follow a similar path. They decussate in the midline and eventually join the lateral lemniscus of the opposite side. Some of the secondary neurons in the dorsal cochlear nucleus project directly into the lateral lemniscus of the same (ipsilateral) side of the stem (see Figure 2.29).

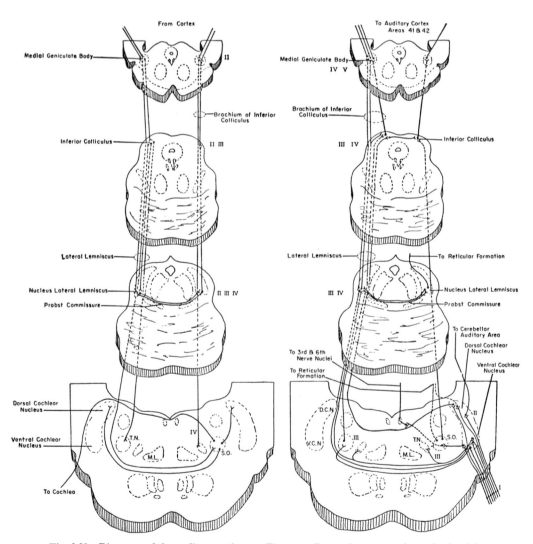

Fig. 2.29 Diagrams of the auditory pathways. The ascending pathways are shown in the right diagram, the descending tracts in the left. M.L., medial lemnicus; S.O., superior olive; T.N., trapezoid nuclei. (From Peele, 1961.)

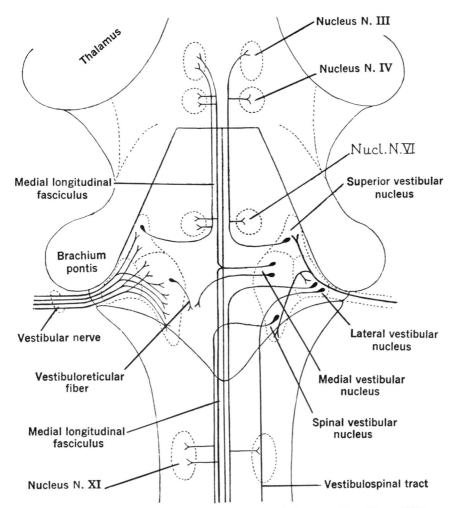

Nucleus N. III

Thalamus

Nucleus N. IV

Nucl. N. VI

Superior vestibular
nucleus

Medial longitudinal
fasciculus

Brachium
pontis

Vestibular nerve

Lateral vestibular
nucleus

Vestibuloreticular
fiber

Medial vestibular
nucleus

Medial longitudinal
fasciculus

Spinal vestibular
nucleus

Nucleus N. XI

Vestibulospinal tract

Fig. 2.30 Some of the principal connections of the vestibular nerve. (From Truex, 1959.)

The lateral lemnisci project collaterals to a number of small nuclei which collectively are called the *nuclei of the lateral lemniscus.* Axons from these nuclei project back into the lateral lemnisci or to the inferior colliculus or medial geniculate nucleus of the contralateral side. These projections are partly responsible for the bilateral representation of each ear at higher levels of the central nervous system. (A further exchange of information takes place at the level of the colliculi through the inferior collicular commissure.)

Many of the fibers from the superior olivary nucleus enter the vestibular root of the *auditory* (VIII cranial) nerve on the contralateral side of the brainstem. This olivocochlear bundle serves important controlling functions with respect to auditory input.

Fibers from the vestibular division of the eighth cranial nerve terminate in a cluster of *vestibular nuclei* which are distributed in the floor of the fourth ventricle, medial to the cochlear nuclei and the restiform body. The principal vestibular nuclei are the *medial nucleus of Schwalbe,* the *superior nucleus of Bechterew,* the *lateral Deiters nucleus,* and the *inferior spinal nucleus.* The medial, lateral, and inferior nuclei are present at the bulbar-pontine border and take up much of the widest portion of the floor of the fourth ventricle. The superior nucleus is located more anteriorly at the level of the facial and abducens nuclei (see Figure 2.30).

The medial and superior vestibular nuclei project to the homolateral flocculonodular lobe and fastigial nuclei of the cerebellum. The latter, in turn, project to the lateral and superior vestibular nuclei. Fibers from all vestibular nuclei enter the

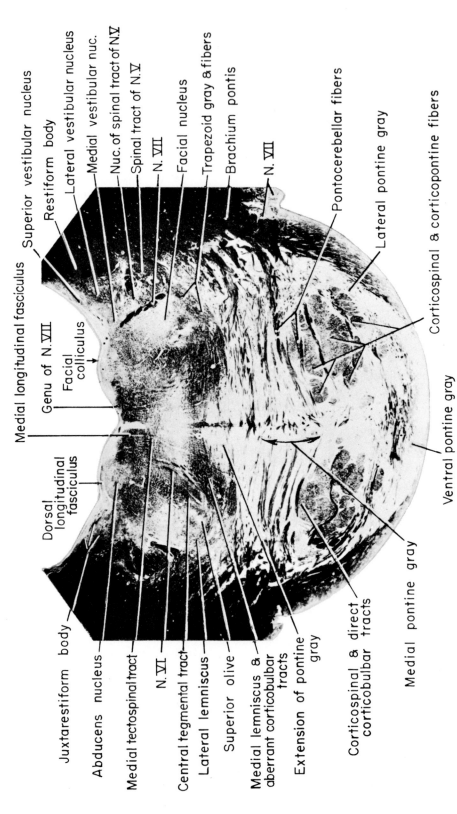

Superior vestibular nucleus

Restiform body

Lateral vestibular nucleus

Medial vestibular nuc.

Nuc. of spinal tract of N.V

Spinal tract of N.V

N. VII

Facial nucleus

Trapezoid gray & fibers

Brachium pontis

Medial longitudinal fasciculus

Genu of N. VII

Facial colliculus

N. VII

Pontocerebellar fibers

Lateral pontine gray

Corticospinal & corticopontine fibers

Ventral pontine gray

Juxtarestiform body

Abducens nucleus

Medial tectospinal tract

N. VI

Central tegmental tract

Lateral lemniscus

Superior olive

Medial lemniscus & aberrant corticobulbar tracts

Extension of pontine gray

Dorsal longitudinal fasciculus

Corticospinal & direct corticobulbar tracts

Medial pontine gray

Fig. 2.31 Transverse section through the caudal third of the pons at the level of the facial and abducens nerves and nuclei. Weil preparation. Magnified about 5 times. Subnucleus rostralis of the nucleus of the spinal tract of nerve V is present at this level. (From Crosby et al., 1962.)

medial longitudinal fasciculi on both sides of the brainstem. Some of the ascending fibers in this tract enter the abducens nucleus of the pontine area which supplies motor fibers to the lateral rectus muscle of the eye. Other fibers enter the *parabducens* nucleus which projects to the oculomotor areas. These connections are responsible for the reflex turning of the eyes in the direction opposite to that of the turning head. The medial vestibular nuclei also project fibers to the reticular gray of the brainstem and to the dorsal motor nucleus of the vagus, a connection which is responsible for motion sickness. The reticular connections permit vestibulospinal influences on postural adjustments. In addition, there are several distinct vestibulospinal pathways. Some of the fibers which join the medial longitudinal fasciculi descend into the spinal cord as the *medial vestibulospinal* tract. From the lateral vestibular nucleus another large fiber bundle, the *ventrolateral vestibulospinal* tract, originates; it terminates in direct relation to motor neurons in the ventral horn of the cord.

At the level of the glossopharyngeal and acoustic nerves, the large traversing fiber bundles marking the basal portion of the pontine section of the brainstem begin to appear. These bundles consist of pontocerebellar fibers which arise largely from cells in the pontine gray (cell masses in the base of the pons). These cells receive afferents from cortical, subcortical, and even spinal projections.

The level of the facial and abducens nerves (see Figure 2.31). One of the clearest landmarks of this portion of the pons is the medial lemniscus which runs parallel to the floor of the fourth ventricle. Dorsolateral to this prominent fiber bundle is the *superior olivary nucleus* which receives fibers from the cochlear nuclei and contributes axons to the lateral lemnisci.

The tegmental gray matter medial to the superior olivary nucleus is divided into a number of nuclei (the *nucleus motorius dissipatus, inferior central tegmental nucleus, nucleus papilliformis*). The afferent or efferent connections and functional importance of these cell masses is not known.

Lateral and dorsolateral to the superior olivary nucleus, the prominent *facial nucleus* of the facial (VII cranial) nerve appears. The seventh nerve emerges from the brainstem at this level. The motor nucleus of the facial nerve is located in the lower third of the pons, immediately adjacent to the spinal tract and nucleus of the trigeminal (V cranial) nerve (see Figure 2.32).

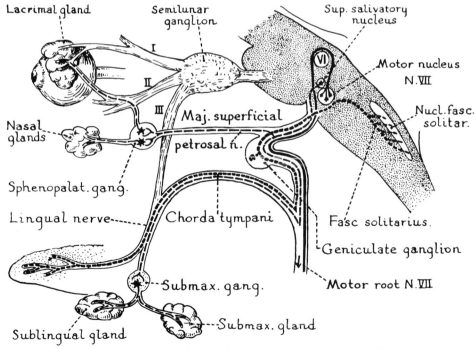

Fig. 2.32 Components of the facial nerve (intermediofacial). I, ophthalmic; II, maxillary; and III, mandibular ramus of trigeminal nerve. (From Truex and Carpenter, 1964.)

Slightly lateral to the motor nucleus of the facial nerve is the *superior salivatory nucleus*. It projects efferents along the facial nerve to the sphenopalatine ganglion which controls the secretions of the lachrymal glands, and to the submandibular ganglion which controls the secretions of the sublingual salivary glands. Some of the components of the facial nerve originate in the *dorsal visceral gray* of the pons. These carry taste impulses from the anterior two-thirds of the tongue.

Dorsal to the superior salivatory nucleus and the lateral portion of the tegmental gray is the *abducens nucleus* which projects afferents to the rectus muscle of the eye. Lateral and dorsolateral to the abducens nucleus, the lateral and superior vestibular nuclei persist. The dorsal half of this level of the brainstem is enveloped by the brachium pontis and restiform body.

The ventral third of the caudal pons is taken up by corticospinal and corticobulbar motor fibers, and by the ventral and medial pontine gray. The ascending and descending bundles of the lateral spinal cord and medulla continue their course in the ventrolateral pons, between the spinal tract of the trigeminal dorsally and the pontocerebellar fibers ventrally.

The level of the trigeminal nerves (see Figure 2.33). The medial third of the pontine brainstem is essentially similar to the lower portion just described. The main changes are in the dorsal tegmental section where the facial and abducens nuclei have been replaced by the *motor and sensory nuclei of the trigeminal* (V cranial) nerve. The fibers which emerge from these nuclei course through the tegmentum and basal portion of the brainstem to emerge in line with the root of the facial nerve.

The motor nucleus of the trigeminal nerve supplies the muscles of mastication. The efferent components of this important cranial nerve supply most of the head with cutaneous innervation. The sensory nucleus of the fifth cranial nerve (as well as the nucleus of the spinal tract) projects to the thalamus (see Figure 2.34).

The pretrigeminal level (see Figure 2.35). In the rostral third of the pons, the fourth ventricle narrows to form the *aqueduct of Sylvius*. The ventral two-thirds of the pons are taken up by *medial, lateral,* and *ventral* portions of the *pontine gray,* corticospinal and corticobulbar fibers, and some pontocerebellar fibers. The brachium pontis assumes a position on the dorsolateral surface of the lower two-thirds of the brainstem. The pretrigeminal portion of the pons does not contain nuclei of cranial nerves. However, fibers from the trochlear nucleus of the lower brainstem cross through the anterior medullary velum (which forms the roof of the fourth ventricle) before they emerge from the dorsal surface of the brainstem.

Several important changes take place in the dorsal third of the pons at this level. The cranial nerve nuclei and the superior olivary nuclei which characterize the more caudal sections of the pons have disappeared. The medial part of the central tegmental gray is now taken up by a large nuclear mass called the *superior central tegmental nucleus.* Laterally and slightly beneath it is an elongated cell mass called the *lateroventral tegmental nucleus;* directly above the superior central tegmental nucleus lies the *dorsal tegmental nucleus.* A heavily pigmented section of the tegmental gray lateral to the dorsal tegmental nucleus is called the *nucleus of the locus caeruleus.* These nuclei of the tegmental gray are bordered laterally by the brachium conjunctivum. On the dorsolateral surface of the pons are found the *dorsal* and *ventral* nuclei of the lateral lemniscus.

The Midbrain (see Figure 2.36)

The rostral aspect of the pons is continuous with the mesencephalon. The caudal border of the inferior colliculi (prominent elevations on the dorsal surface of the midbrain) serves as a convenient landmark for the posterior border of the midbrain. The cranial or rostral border of the mesencephalon is described by a convexoconcave line from the posterior commissure dorsally to the mammillary bodies ventrally.

The dorsolateral fissure serves as a convenient boundary between the *tectal* portion of the midbrain which takes up approximately the dorsal third of the brainstem and the *tegmental* portion which makes up the medial aspect. The ventrolateral fissure similarly separates the ventral third or *basis pedunculi* from the tegmentum.

Four prominent elevations can be seen on the dorsal surface of the midbrain. These are called *anterior* and *posterior corpora quadrigemina* or *superior* (anterior) and *inferior* (posterior) *colliculi.*

Two very large fiber bundles, the *cerebral peduncles,* make up the basis pedunculi, which carries corticospinal and corticobulbar fibers of the pyramidal motor system.

The tectum. The most prominent aspects of the tectal area of the midbrain are the colliculi. The *inferior colliculi* are composed of a nucleus

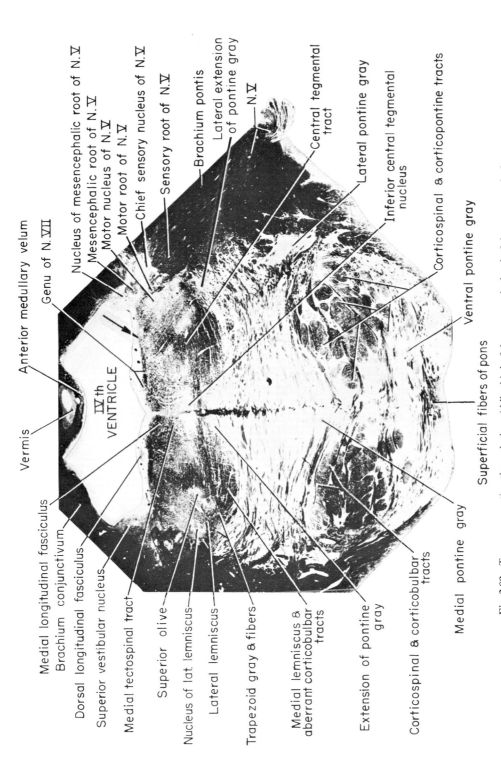

Vermis

Anterior medullary velum

Genu of N. VII

Nucleus of mesencephalic root of N. V

Mesencephalic root of N. V

Motor nucleus of N. V

Motor root of N. V

Chief sensory nucleus of N. V

Sensory root of N. V

Brachium pontis

Lateral extension of pontine gray

N. V

Central tegmental tract

Lateral pontine gray

Inferior central tegmental nucleus

Corticospinal & corticopontine tracts

Ventral pontine gray

Superficial fibers of pons

Medial longitudinal fasciculus

Brachium conjunctivum

Dorsal longitudinal fasciculus

Superior vestibular nucleus

Medial tectospinal tract

Superior olive

Nucleus of lat. lemniscus

Lateral lemniscus

Trapezoid gray & fibers

Medial lemniscus & aberrant corticobulbar tracts

Extension of pontine gray

Corticospinal & corticobulbar tracts

Medial pontine gray

IV th VENTRICLE

Fig. 2.33 Transverse section through the middle third of the pons at the level of the motor and of the chief sensory nuclei of the trigeminal nerve and its emerging root fibers. The arrow points to the crossing trigeminal fibers. Weil preparation. (From Crosby et al., 1962.)

77

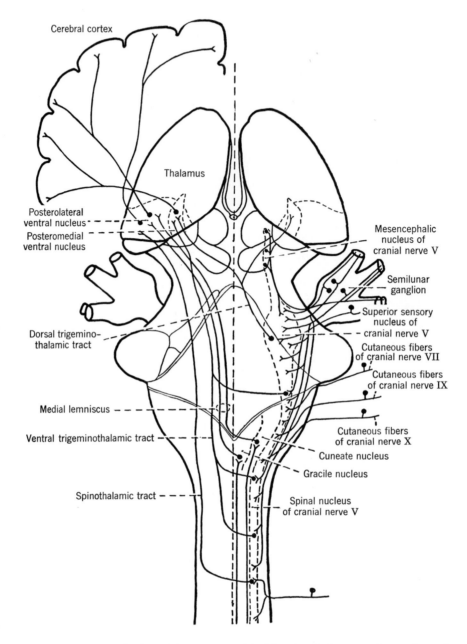

Fig. 2.34 Thalamic projections of the sensory nuclei of the trigeminal nerve and general somatic afferent pathways. (From Larsell, 1951.)

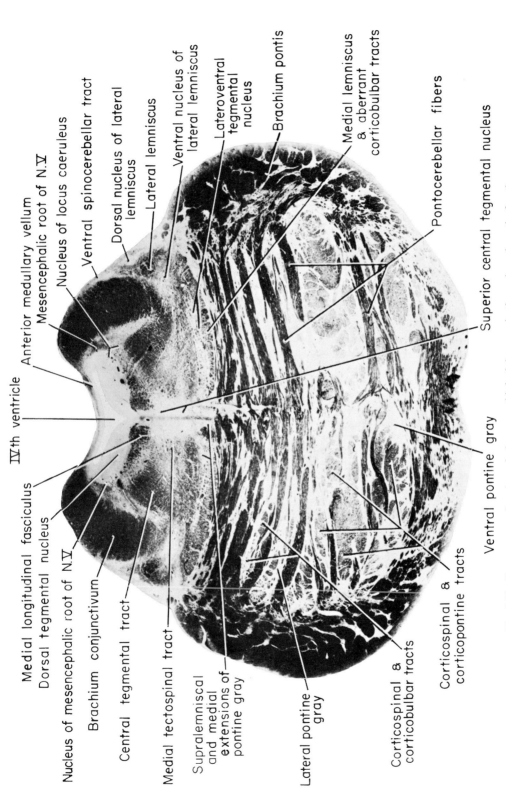

Medial longitudinal fasciculus

IVth ventricle

Dorsal tegmental nucleus

Nucleus of mesencephalic root of N.V

Brachium conjunctivum

Central tegmental tract

Medial tectospinal tract

Supralemniscal and medial extensions of pontine gray

Lateral pontine gray

Corticospinal & corticobulbar tracts

Corticospinal & corticopontine tracts

Ventral pontine gray

Anterior medullary vellum
Mesencephalic root of N.V
Nucleus of locus caeruleus
Ventral spinocerebellar tract
Dorsal nucleus of lateral lemniscus
Lateral lemniscus
Ventral nucleus of lateral lemniscus
Lateroventral tegmental nucleus
Brachium pontis
Medial lemniscus & aberrant corticobulbar tracts
Pontocerebellar fibers
Superior central tegmental nucleus

Fig. 2.35 Transverse section through the upper third of the pons in the region where the fourth ventricle is narrowing down toward the cerebral aqueduct. Weil stain. (From Crosby et al., 1962.)

79

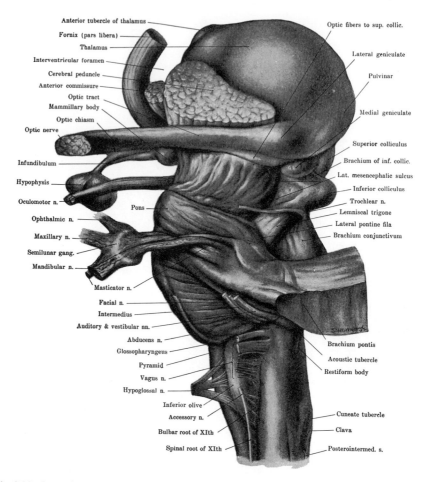

Fig. 2.36 Lateral aspect of the brainstem and cranial nerves. The cerebellum and structures surrounding the thalamus have been removed. (From Mettler, 1948.)

surrounded by a distinct layer of fibers and cells called the *collicular capsule.* The inferior colliculus on each side of the brain is connected to the inferior colliculus on the other side by fibers which run in the *intercollicular gray* or the *inferior collicular commissure* (see Figures 2.37 and 2.38).

The inferior colliculi represent a major relay station for the lateral lemniscus; this tract terminates in such a way that discrete patterns of sensory inputs, corresponding to the frequency of auditory signals, are formed. The major efferent connections of the inferior colliculi occur via the *peduncle of the inferior colliculi* which courses through the midbrain beneath the superior colliculi and terminates in the medial geniculate nuclei of the thalamus.

The *superior colliculi* are made up of distinct

layers of cells and fibers (see Figure 2.39). The striations have been studied in some detail (see Figure 2.40). The ventral-most portion of the superior colliculi, the *stratum zonale,* is composed largely of fibers from the corticotectal tract which arises in the audio-visual association areas of the cortex. The next layer, the *stratum griseum superficiale,* consists of short-axon interneurons which communicate between the stratum zonale and the underlying *stratum opticum.* Terminal fibers from the optic tract make up this third layer of the superior colliculi. A distinct pattern of projection is maintained; fibers from the inferior retinal quadrant reach the medial and rostral parts of the optic stratum, and fibers from the superior retinal quadrant project to the lateral and ventral portions of the collicular stratum. The *intermediate*

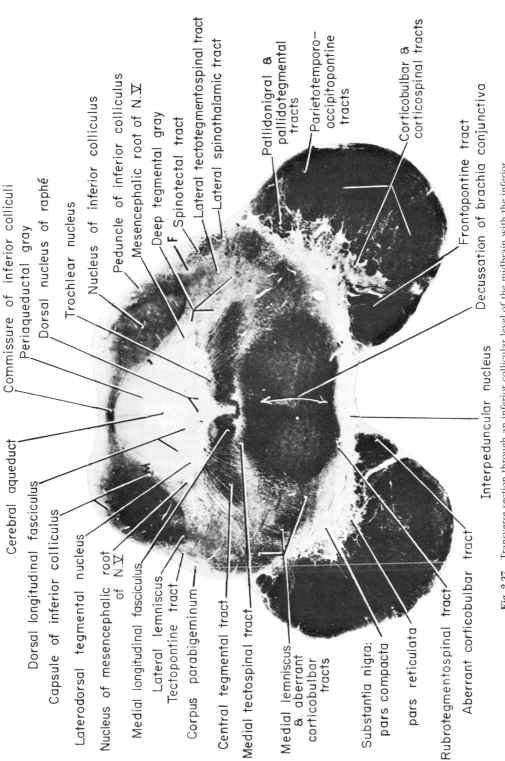

Cerebral aqueduct

Commissure of inferior colliculi

Periaqueductal gray

Dorsal longitudinal fasciculus

Dorsal nucleus of raphé

Capsule of inferior colliculus

Trochlear nucleus

Laterodorsal tegmental nucleus

Nucleus of inferior colliculus

Nucleus of mesencephalic root of N.Ⅴ

Peduncle of inferior colliculus

Medial longitudinal fasciculus

Mesencephalic root of N.Ⅴ

Lateral lemniscus

Deep tegmental gray

Tectopontine tract

F Spinotectal tract

Corpus parabigeminum

Lateral tectotegmentospinal tract

Central tegmental tract

Lateral spinothalamic tract

Medial tectospinal tract

Pallidonigral & pallidotegmental tracts

Medial lemniscus & aberrant corticobulbar tracts

Parietotemporo– occipitopontine tracts

Substantia nigra: pars compacta

Corticobulbar & corticospinal tracts

pars reticulata

Frontopontine tract

Rubrotegmentospinal tract

Decussation of brachia conjunctiva

Aberrant corticobulbar tract

Interpeduncular nucleus

Fig. 2.37 Transverse section through an inferior collicular level of the midbrain with the inferior colliculus dorsally, the trochlear nucleus indenting the medial longitudinal fasciculus, and the massive decussation of the brachia conjunctiva in the tegmentum and the cerebral peduncles ventrally. L and M, lateral and medial medullary laminae, respectively, of the capsule of the inferior colliculus; F, frontal nucleus of lateral lemniscus. Weil preparation. (From Crosby et al., 1962.)

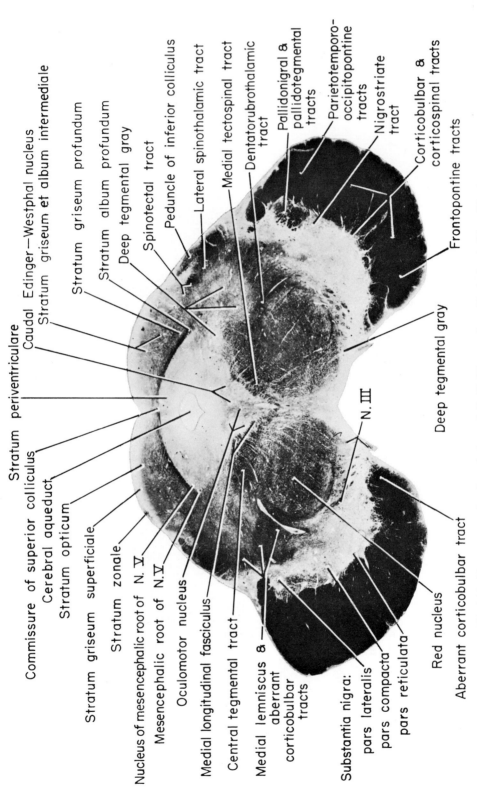

Fig. 2.38 Transverse section through the caudal half of the superior collicular level of the midbrain with the superior colliculus dorsally, the oculomotor nucleus dorsomedial to the medial longitudinal fasciculus, the red nucleus more lateroventrally in the tegmentum, and the basis pedunculi ventrally. Weil preparation. (From Crosby et al., 1962.)

Stratum periventriculare

Commissure of superior colliculus
Cerebral aqueduct
Stratum opticum

Caudal Edinger—Westphal nucleus
Stratum griseum et album intermediale

Stratum griseum profundum

Stratum album profundum

Deep tegmental gray

Spinotectal tract

Peduncle of inferior colliculus

Lateral spinothalamic tract

Medial tectospinal tract

Dentatorubrothalamic tract

Pallidonigral & pallidotegmental tracts

Parietotemporo-occipitopontine tracts

Nigrostriate tract

Corticobulbar & corticospinal tracts

Frontopontine tracts

Stratum griseum superficiale
Stratum zonale
Nucleus of mesencephalic root of N. Ⅴ
Mesencephalic root of N.Ⅴ
Oculomotor nucleus
Medial longitudinal fasciculus
Central tegmental tract
Medial lemniscus & aberrant corticobulbar tracts
Substantia nigra:
pars lateralis
pars compacta
pars reticulata

N. Ⅲ

Deep tegmental gray

Red nucleus

Aberrant corticobulbar tract

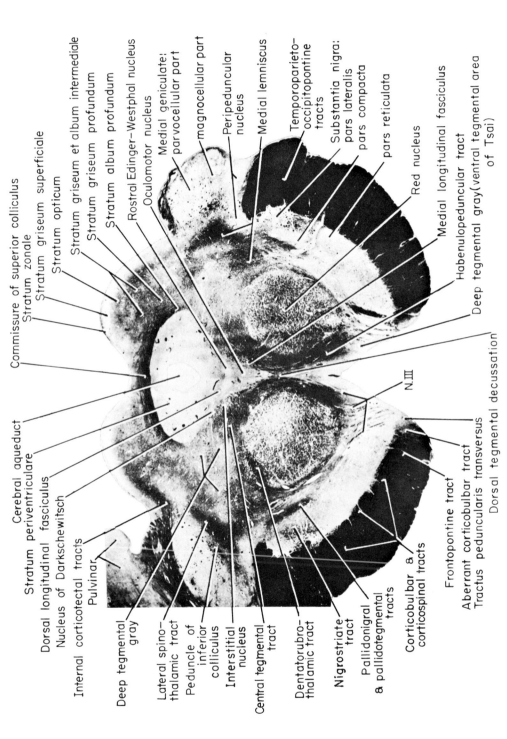

Fig. 2.39 Transverse section through the rostral half of the superior collicular level of the midbrain. Weil preparation. (From Crosby et al., 1962.)

Cerebral aqueduct
Stratum periventriculare
Dorsal longitudinal fasciculus
Nucleus of Darkschewitsch
Internal corticotectal tracts
Pulvinar

Deep tegmental gray

Lateral spino-thalamic tract
Peduncle of inferior colliculus
Interstitial nucleus
Central tegmental tract
Dentatorubro-thalamic tract
Nigrostriate tract
Pallidonigral & pallidotegmental tracts
Corticobulbar & corticospinal tracts
Aberrant corticobulbar tract
Frontopontine tract
Tractus peduncularis transversus

Commissure of superior colliculus
Stratum zonale
Stratum griseum superficiale
Stratum opticum
Stratum griseum et album intermediale
Stratum griseum profundum
Stratum album profundum
Rostral Edinger–Westphal nucleus
Oculomotor nucleus
Medial geniculate; parvocellular part
magnocellular part
Peripeduncular nucleus
Medial lemniscus
Temporoparieto-occipitopontine tracts
Substantia nigra; pars lateralis
pars compacta
pars reticulata
Red nucleus
Medial longitudinal fasciculus
Habenulopeduncular tract
Deep tegmental gray (ventral tegmental area of Tsai)

N. III

Dorsal tegmental decussation

83

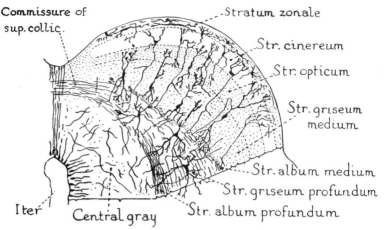

Fig. 2.40   Cells of the superior colliculus reconstructed from Golgi preparations. (From Truex and Carpenter, 1964.)

gray and white layers (or *strata griseum et album intermediale*) consist of several distinct bands of cells and fibers. These layers receive afferents from the corticotectal tract which arises from the visual cortex (areas 18 and 19) of the cerebral hemisphere. These connections serve as part of the neural circuit that controls eye movements. Other sensory afferents are contributed to this layer of the superior colliculi by spinotectal and thalamotectal tracts; this fact suggests an extensive integrative function. The *deep gray layer* (or *stratum griseum profundum*) interconnects the intermediate gray and white layers with the *stratum album* (or *deep white layer*) which represents the origin of the major efferents from the superior colliculi. These efferents include (1) the *medial tectospinal* tract, which projects to bulbar motor centers before entering the spinal cord—it enters the anterior funiculus and terminates primarily at interneurons connecting to ventral horn motor cells in the upper half of the cord; (2) the *tectorubral* tract, which projects to the red nucleus and other motor centers of the brainstem; (3) the *tectotegmental* tract, which projects a short distance into the tegmental gray underlying the superior colliculi; and (4) the *tectopontine* tract, which projects visual impulses to the pontine gray for relay to the cerebellum. Additional connections to the oculomotor nuclei, the habenular complex of the thalamus, and the supraoptic region of the hypothalamus have been described. The last layer of the superior colliculi, the *periventricular layer* (or *stratum periventriculare*), receives auditory afferents from the inferior colliculi as well as olfactory and cutaneous afferents from the tectal component of the

dorsal longitudinal fasciculus.

The ventral surface of the midbrain, anterior to the superior colliculi, is taken up by the *pretectal nuclei*. These nuclei receive afferents from the visual pathways for the completion of the light reflex (a reduction in pupillary diameter with increased illumination) as well as projections from the occipital and preoccipital areas of the cerebral cortex. The major efferent connections of the pretectal nuclei are to the Edinger-Westphal nucleus located slightly dorsally to the main oculomotor nuclei. The Edinger-Westphal nucleus projects to the ciliary ganglion of the eye.

The tegmentum. The midbrain tegmentum contains the *trochlear complex* ventral to the inferior colliculi. This complex projects fibers of the trochlear (IV cranial) nerve across the midline and dorsalward to their point of emergence from the dorsal surface of the brainstem, just behind the inferior colliculi. The trochlear complex consists of a number of functionally and anatomically related nuclei. The *trochlear nucleus* and *accessory trochlear nucleus* project efferent fibers to the superior oblique muscles of the eye—those muscles responsible for eye movement. Proprioceptive receptors in these muscles return afferent inputs to the trochlear complex of the midbrain.

Anteromedial to the trochlear nucleus and just beneath the superior colliculi is the *oculomotor* (III cranial) nerve nucleus. The caudal portions of the oculomotor nuclei of each side fuse to form a centrally located *nucleus of Perlia*. This nuclear complex projects efferents to the intrinsic eye muscles. The oculomotor nuclei also receive proprioceptive afferents from the orbital eye muscles. Surrounding the oculomotor nucleus on its rostral and medial side is the *Edinger-Westphal* nucleus which projects fibers toward the eye with the oculomotor nerve. At present it is thought that the Edinger-Westphal nucleus may receive inputs from the pretectal nuclei and send efferents to the ciliary ganglion which synapse with postganglionic fiber connections to the sphincter muscles of the pupil. This pathway is believed to be involved in the pupillary accommodation reflex to strong visual stimuli.

Dorsal and dorsolateral to the trochlear and oculomotor nuclei a large cell mass, the *periaqueductal gray*, appears. The dorsal part of this gray matter is continuous with the central layer of the superior colliculi. The lateral section consists of a largely undifferentiated mass of cells which adjoins the mesencephalic root and nucleus of the trigeminal nerve. The lateral section is continuous with the innermost layer of the inferior colliculus. The ventral portion of the periaqueductal gray arises caudally from pontine periaqueductal gray matter and continues rostrally as the diencephalic periventricular gray. The periaqueductal gray contains some poorly myelinated fibers (the *dorsal longitudinal fasciculus of Schütz*) which interconnect hypothalamic and midbrain reticular nuclei.

The ventral portion of the periaqueductal gray differentiates into a number of distinct nuclei. The *nucleus of Darkschewitsch* extends anteriorly from the dorsal boundary of the Edinger-Westphal complex to the caudal part of the diencephalon. The *interstitial nucleus of Cajal* runs parallel to it in a slightly more ventrolateral position. Both nuclei receive afferents from the vestibular nuclei, the basal ganglia, and the occipital cortex of the cerebrum. The nucleus of Darkschewitsch projects efferents to the medial longitudinal fasciculus of Schütz. The interstitial nucleus projects largely to the interstitiospinal fasciculi.

The *deep tegmental gray of the midbrain* ventral to the periaqueductal gray shows several distinct cell accumulations. The most prominent of these is the *red nucleus*. The large-celled portion of the nucleus, the *pars magnocellularis*, is a dark-red-staining cellular mass which is almost completely encapsulated by large fiber systems. The small-celled portion or *pars parvocellularis* overlaps with the anterior section of the large-celled portion. It forms the dorsal section of the red nucleus which extends into the ventral thalamus.

The red nucleus receives (1) cerebellorubral afferents from the dentate, globose, and emboliform nuclei of the cerebellum; (2) corticorubral fibers from the homolateral frontal association areas of the cortex of the cerebrum; and (3) collaterals from the superior colliculi, the lenticular fasciculus, and the ansa lenticularis.

The major descending efferent pathway from the red nucleus is the crossed rubrospinal tract; this tract projects collaterals to the motor nuclei of the trigeminal and facial nerve nuclei and to the nucleus ambiguus in its course through the lower brainstem. The caudal aspects of the red nucleus also project to the thalamus and to the dentate nucleus of the cerebellum. The pars parvocellularis of the red nucleus discharges primarily upward along the rubrothalamic tract to the nucleus ventralis lateralis of the thalamus which projects to the motor and premotor areas of the cerebral cortex. The red nucleus is part of the extrapyramidal motor system which maintains muscle tonus and stabilizes limb movements.

The remainder of the deep tegmental gray of the midbrain is divided on the basis of largely anatomical considerations into an almost infinite number of small nuclear masses. Most of the cells of this area are part of the multisynaptic projection system of the reticular formation of the brainstem, which we shall discuss in detail later. Many of the nuclear clusters in this midbrain gray receive afferents from the cerebellum, the hypothalamus, the basal ganglia, and motor areas of the cerebral cortex in addition to collaterals from the ascending sensory tracts. The cerebral cortex projects to the tegmental gray either along widely dispersed independent fibers or along axons which run with the ansa lenticularis or lenticular fasciculus. These axons arise primarily from cells in the premotor areas and occipital and preoccipital regions. The basal ganglia project to the midbrain gray primarily by way of the lenticular fasciculus which arises in the globus pallidus; it discharges to the nucleus of Darkschewitsch, the interstitial nucleus, the red nucleus, and to the undifferentiated portions of the deep gray.

The transitional area between the hypothalamus (mammillary body) and the cerebral peduncle contains the *ventral tegmental gray* which has differentiated into several distinct nuclear masses. The rostral portion of the ventral tegmentum, ventral to the red nucleus, is called the *area of Tsai*. In addition to its cellular component, this area contains a profusion of fibers of passage which make it essentially impossible to study the functional significance of this area with techniques now available. Some optic fibers have been traced into the area of Tsai, and an efferent discharge to the oculomotor nuclei has been described.

In most animals (except man) the caudal portion of the ventral tegmental gray forms a large and distinct *interpeduncular nucleus* which receives afferents from the habenulopeduncular tract and projects to the dorsal tegmentum.

The tegmentum of the midbrain contains a large number of fibers of passage. The lateral lemniscus enters the caudal portion of the tegmentum, but then turns dorsalward to terminate in the inferior colliculus. The medial lemniscus surrounds the periaqueductal gray throughout its course in the midbrain; it now contains distinct segments corresponding to the lateral spinothalamic tract, the ventral spinothalamic tract, the fibers ascending in the funiculi gracilis and cuneatus, and some taste fibers. In its course through the midbrain, the medial lemniscus moves toward the dorsal surface of the brainstem. In the anterior portion of the midbrain, this tract lies immediately below the superior colliculi and dorsolateral to the red nucleus.

In the medial portion of the periaqueductal gray runs an important coordinating fiber system, the *medial longitudinal fasciculus* (see Figure 2.39). It contains (1) vestibular fibers from the vestibular nuclei which project largely to the nucleus of Darkschewitsch and the interstitial nucleus, (2) short fibers which interconnect the various motor nuclei of the brainstem, and (3) an extrapyramidal component which carries impulses from the lenticular fasciculus to the nucleus of the longitudinal fasciculus. These fibers connect to motor nuclei of the brainstem as well as to anterior horn cells of the spinal cord.

The *dorsal longitudinal fasciculus* runs slightly more dorsally in the periventricular gray. It projects collaterals to the superior colliculi and most reticular nuclei of the brainstem and receives afferents from most of these nuclei.

The basis pedunculi. The ventral portion of the midbrain contains a small amount of nuclear gray matter and the very extensive corticospinal and corticobulbar fiber system (see Figure 2.41).

The major nucleus of this area, the *substantia nigra,* extends from the upper pontine portion of the stem into the diencephalon. Its neurons have a large amount of *melanin* pigment which gives the area its characteristic black appearance. The *pars lateralis* makes up the lateral aspect of the rostral portion of the substantia nigra. It receives afferents from the globus pallidus and putamen and

discharges to the tectal area. The *pars compacta* and *pars reticulata* receive afferents from the cortex (premotor, parietal, and island of Reil), the striatum, pallidum, and tectum. They project largely along the *comb bundle* through the internal capsule into the lenticular nucleus.

The cerebral peduncles contain distinct corticospinal and corticobulbar components. The corticospinal fibers arise in the pre- and postcentral gyri of the cortex and occupy the middle two-thirds of each peduncle. The fibers continue without synaptic interruption through the lower brainstem to the motor decussations where approximately 80% of them cross the midline and enter the lateral funiculi of the cord (see Figure 2.42).

The corticobulbar fibers arise from cortical motor areas and take up the lateral third of the cerebral peduncle. They distribute widely through the lower brainstem. Their distribution is bilateral with respect to the oculomotor, trigeminal, and facial nuclei, and the nucleus ambiguus. The abducens and hypoglossal nuclei receive largely crossed fibers from the contralateral cortex. Distinct fiber bundles that run on the side of the pyramidal fiber tracts at the base of the midbrain contain fibers which project from the frontal, temporal, occipital, and parietal lobes of the cerebral cortex to the pontine area of the brainstem. These fibers are the first portion of the corticopontocerebellar system.

The Diencephalon (see Figure 2.43)

The brainstem extends anteriorly and dorsally from the midbrain into the diencephalon. Laterally, the diencephalon is bounded by the posterior limb of the internal capsule and the tail of the caudate nucleus. It extends anteriorly to an imaginary line which intersects the interventricular foramen dorsally to the upper border of the chiasmatic ridge ventrally.

The aqueduct of Sylvius widens as it enters the diencephalon and forms the third ventricle. The third ventricle continues into the telencephalon and communicates laterally through the interventricular foramen with the lateral ventricles of the cerebral hemispheres.

The diencephalon is commonly divided into the following major portions. (1) The *hypothalamus* constitutes the ventral-most portion of the diencephalon and contains the floor and walls of the third ventricle. (2) The *epithalamus* consists primarily of the habenular complex, the pineal organ, and the posterior commissure. (3) The *ventral*

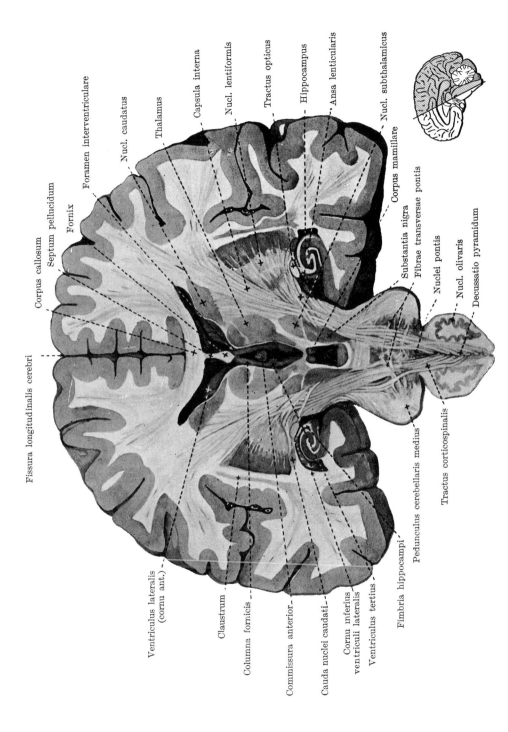

Fissura longitudinalis cerebri

Corpus callosum
Septum pellucidum
Fornix
Foramen interventriculare
Nucl. caudatus
Thalamus
Capsula interna
Nucl. lentiformis
Tractus opticus
Hippocampus
Ansa lenticularis
Nucl. subthalamicus
Corpus mamillare
Substantia nigra
Fibrae transversae pontis
Nuclei pontis
Nucl. olivaris
Decussatio pyramidum

Ventriculus lateralis
(cornu ant.)
Claustrum
Columna fornicis
Commissura anterior
Cauda nuclei caudati
Cornu inferius
ventriculi lateralis
Ventriculus tertius
Fimbria hippocampi
Pedunculus cerebellaris medius
Tractus corticospinalis

Fig. 2.41 Oblique frontal section of the brain, posterior view. (From Kiss and Szentágothai, 1964.)

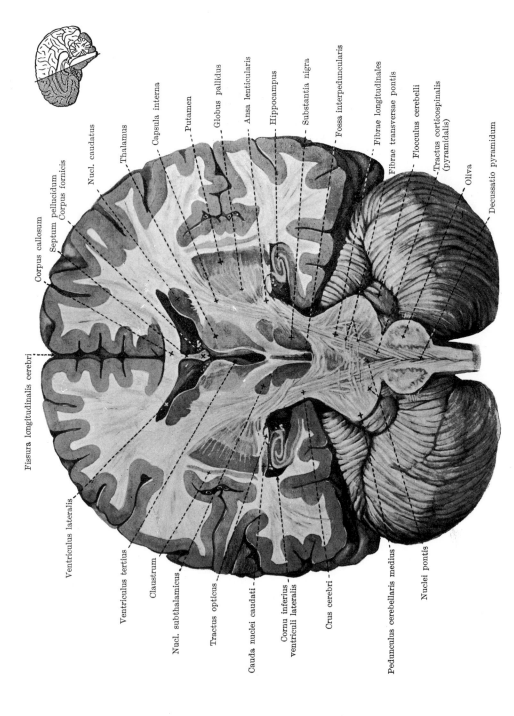

Fissura longitudinalis cerebri

Corpus callosum
Septum pellucidum
Corpus fornicis
Nucl. caudatus
Thalamus
Capsula interna
Putamen
Globus pallidus
Ansa lenticularis
Hippocampus
Substantia nigra
Fossa interpeduncularis
Fibrae longitudinales
Fibrae transversae pontis
Flocculus cerebelli
Tractus corticospinalis
(pyramidalis)
Oliva
Decussatio pyramidum

Ventriculus lateralis
Ventriculus tertius
Claustrum
Nucl. subthalamicus
Tractus opticus
Cauda nuclei caudati
Cornu inferius
ventriculi lateralis
Crus cerebri
Pedunculus cerebellaris medius
Nuclei pontis

Fig. 2.42 Oblique frontal section of the brain, anterior view. (From Kiss and Szentágothai, 1964.)

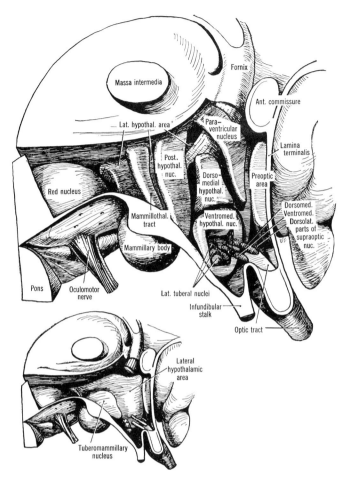

Fig. 2.43   The diencephalon, seen from the midline. (From Mettler, 1948, after an original drawing by Haymaker, to be published by Charles C Thomas.)

thalamus or *subthalamus* represents a continuation of the midbrain tegmentum and contains portions of the red nucleus and substantia nigra. (4) The *dorsal thalamus or thalamus proper* is a highly complex mass of nuclei from fiber systems which coordinate most projections from the brainstem to the important cerebral cortex.

The hypothalamus. The hypothalamus extends from the rostral border of the midbrain to the tip of the chiasmatic ridge, where it terminates posterior to the preoptic area. It extends from the ventral surface of the brain dorsally to the subthalamic nuclei. Laterally, it is bounded by the internal capsule and the ascending limbs of the optic tracts.

The hypothalamus can be divided into three zones along its anterior-posterior axis. The *periventricular* zone surrounds the third ventricle.

Immediately lateral to it is the *medial zone*. The lateral-most third of the hypothalamus is called the *lateral zone*.

The periventricular zone. The periventricular zone consists essentially of an extension of the periventricular gray of the midbrain. It contains small fibers as well as cells which are widely dispersed except in the ventral part of the tuberal region; here the cells form a distinct, deep-staining *arcuate* or *periventricular nucleus* which provides a convenient landmark for this portion of the brainstem.

The medial hypothalamic zone. The caudal portion of the ventral hypothalamus shows two round elevations in the medial zone called *mammillary bodies*. They contain the *medial* and *lateral mammillary nuclei*. The lateral mammillary nucleus receives afferents from the hippocampus and dentate gyrus via the fornix. The medial mammillary nuclei project the *mammillothalamic* tract to the anterior nucleus of the thalamus proper.

The *posterior hypothalamic* area extends forward from the mammillary bodies to the *ventromedial* and *dorsomedial nuclei.*

The *dorsal hypothalamic area* separates the dorsomedial nuclei from the subthalamus. It extends from the posterior hypothalamic area to the level of the paraventricular nuclei.

The anterior portion of the medial zone of the hypothalamus is formed by the *anterior hypothalamic area,* an irregularly shaped cell mass which extends rostrally into the medial preoptic area.

A very dark-staining *supraoptic nucleus* overlies the lateral aspects of the optic tracts. It is functionally related to an equally dark-staining *paraventricular* nucleus which adjoins the third ventricle at chiasmatic levels.

The lateral hypothalamic zone.

This zone is a largely undifferentiated mass of cells and fibers which extends along the lateral border of the hypothalamus from the lateral preoptic area to the level of the midbrain. In the caudal portion of the lateral zone, lateral to the mammillary bodies and posterior hypothalamic area, the deep-staining *tuberomammillary* and *mammillo-infundibular* nuclei appear.

Several elongated cell concentrations can be traced through the entire length of the lateral hypothalamic zone. Lateral, posterior, and anterior groups of these *lateral tuberal nuclei* have been distinguished by some writers. It is customary, however, to refer to all but the caudalmost portion of the lateral hypothalamus as the *lateral hypothalamic area.*

The fiber connections of the hypothalamus.

The hypothalamus receives afferents from the cerebral cortex, the thalamus, the globus pallidus, and amygdaloid nuclei, as well as from the spinal cord, brainstem cranial nerve nuclei, and the visual system.

The most prominent afferent fiber bundle to the hypothalamus is the *fornix;* the fornix arises from the pyramidal cells of the hippocampus and dentate gyrus and ends in the posterior hypothalamus, primarily in the mammillary nuclei. Collaterals from the fornix have also been traced into the rostral hypothalamus and preoptic area, as well as into the habenular complex of the epithalamus (see Figure 2.44).

A large ascending and descending fiber tract, the *medial forebrain bundle,* interconnects the ventromedial rhinencephalic areas with the preoptic area and lateral hypothalamus. Many of the medial forebrain bundle fibers continue through the hypothalamus to the midbrain tegmentum. These fibers project collaterals into the lateral hypothalamic areas.

The amygdaloid nuclei project a major fiber bundle, the *stria terminalis,* to the preoptic and anterior hypothalamic areas. Some projections to the ventromedial nuclei of the hypothalamus have also been reported.

The hypothalamus also receives anatomically less distinct efferents from several sources: (1) The *dorsal gray of the brainstem* projects to the mammillary bodies via the medial lemniscus, the mammillary peduncle, and the dorsal longitudinal fasciculus. (2) The *frontal cortex of the cerebrum* projects to the mammillary body and various other hypothalamic nuclei via the septal area which discharges into the medial forebrain bundle. These cortical projections arise chiefly from the precentral gyrus (area 6) of the frontal lobe. Other fiber connections from the cortex to various hypothalamic areas have been traced through the dorsomedial or anterior nuclei of the thalamus. (3) *Projections from visceral and somatosensory nuclei* in the brainstem and cord have been traced through the medial lemniscus, the mammillary peduncle, and a multisynaptic pathway which originates in the nucleus parasolitarius.

The hypothalamus may also receive afferents from all sensory systems, either directly along pathways from subthalamic sensory relay nuclei or indirectly from the multisynaptic relay system in the reticular formation of the brainstem which courses through the hypothalamus. The evidence for these connections is largely physiological rather than anatomical.

The efferent connections of the hypothalamus are made largely via large fiber tracts (see Figure 2.45). The *mammillothalamic tract* arises from the medial mammillary nucleus; it projects to the anterior nucleus of the thalamus, which appears to serve largely as a relay nucleus. It projects to the cingulate gyrus of the medial cerebral cortex and forms an important hypothalamocortical pathway. This connection is not entirely a one-way street but contains corticohypothalamic components.

The medial mammillary nuclei also project caudally into the brainstem along a large fiber

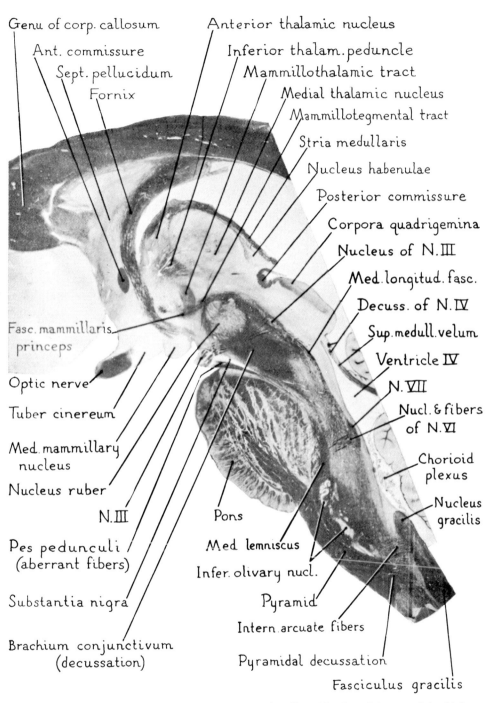

Genu of corp. callosum
Ant. commissure
Sept. pellucidum
Fornix

Anterior thalamic nucleus
Inferior thalam. peduncle
Mammillothalamic tract
Medial thalamic nucleus
Mammillotegmental tract
Stria medullaris
Nucleus habenulae
Posterior commissure
Corpora quadrigemina
Nucleus of N. III
Med. longitud. fasc.
Decuss. of N. IV
Sup. medull. velum
Ventricle IV
N. VII
Nucl. & fibers of N. VI
Chorioid plexus
Nucleus gracilis

Fasc. mammillaris princeps
Optic nerve
Tuber cinereum
Med. mammillary nucleus
Nucleus ruber
N. III
Pes pedunculi (aberrant fibers)
Substantia nigra
Brachium conjunctivum (decussation)

Pons
Med. lemniscus
Infer. olivary nucl.
Pyramid
Intern. arcuate fibers
Pyramidal decussation
Fasciculus gracilis

Fig. 2.44 Sagittal section of the brainstem through the pillar of fornix and the root of the third nerve. Weigert's myelin stain. (From Truex and Carpenter, 1964.)

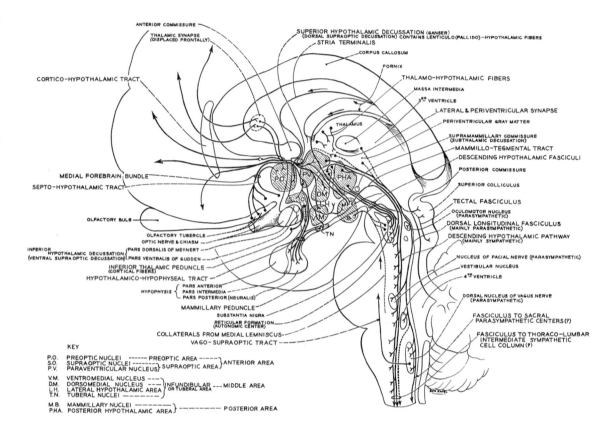

Fig. 2.45 Midline sagittal section of the diencephalon, showing the principal nuclear groupings and discharge paths of the hypothalamus. (From Rubinstein, 1953.)

bundle called the *mammillotegmental tract*. This tract is joined by fibers from many other hypothalamic nuclei. It terminates diffusely in the medial and lateral reticular nuclei of the brainstem.

A large *periventricular fiber system* arises from the posterior hypothalamic area, the tuberal nuclei, and the supraoptic nuclei. Some of the fibers from this pathway terminate in the midline and dorsomedial of the thalamus which are in reciprocal connection with hypothalamic as well as cortical areas. The majority of the periventricular fibers project toward the brainstem. These may end in the tectal or tegmental (reticular) nuclei of the midbrain, pons, and medulla, or they may continue into the anterior and lateral funiculi of the spinal cord. These descending pathways carry largely autonomic efferents (such as pupillodilator, vasomotor, and sudomotor) to sympathetic as

well as parasympathetic nuclei and ganglia.

The many small, unmyelinated fibers of the hypothalamo-hypophyseal tract arise in the supraoptic and paraventricular nuclei of the hypothalamus. From here they project into the infundibulum and terminate in the neurohypophysis (i.e., the neural lobe of the hypophyseal or pituitary gland). These fibers control the secretory activity of the neural lobe of the pituitary and may act as a transport system for hormones manufactured in the hypothalamic nuclei. These functions will be discussed in detail later.

The hypothalamus has been called the head-ganglion of the autonomic nervous system because it appears to be the highest center of integration for many visceral functions. In addition, it seems to regulate or participate in the regulation of many processes which are related to such psychological variables as hunger, thirst, sexual arousal, and emotion. These functional aspects will also be discussed in detail later.

The epithalamus (see Figure 2.46). The *pineal gland* or *epiphysis cerebri* develops from the posterior roof of the diencephalon and projects outward from the dorsal surface of the brainstem, just rostral to the superior colliculi. It receives fibers from the habenular and posterior commissures, but these fibers may have little functional significance. The major innervation of the pineal gland derives from postganglionic neurons in the cervical ganglia which project centrally via the nervi conarii. The functions of this gland have not yet been established; they appear to be related to the regulatory system which controls many biological functions in relation to changes in the relative amount of daylight.

The *habenular complex* consists of medial and lateral habenular nuclei which are situated anterodorsally to the dorsomedial nuclei of the thalamus. The habenula receives afferents from the hippocampus via the *medial corticohabenular tract;* from

the amygdala and hippocampal gyrus via the *lateral corticohabenular tract;* from the hypothalamus and preoptic area via the *preopticohabenular tract;* and from the superior colliculi via the *tectohabenular* fibers. It projects efferents to the dorsomedial nucleus of the thalamus, the dorsal tegmental nucleus (which projects through the longitudinal fasciculus to parasympathetic nuclei), and the interpeduncular nucleus (via the habenulopeduncular tract of Meynert).

The posterior commissure lies on the boundary between the midbrain and the diencephalon, just dorsal to the junction of the aqueduct of Sylvius with the third ventricle. This commissure is essentially a large, crossing-fiber bundle which contains axons from cells in many parts of the brain. Some axons originate in the globus pallidus and terminate in the midbrain tegmentum, particularly the red nucleus. Others run from the visual (occipital) cortex of the cerebrum to the superior colliculi, or interconnect the colliculi on the two sides of the brainstem. The posterior commissure also interconnects the colliculi with the pretectal

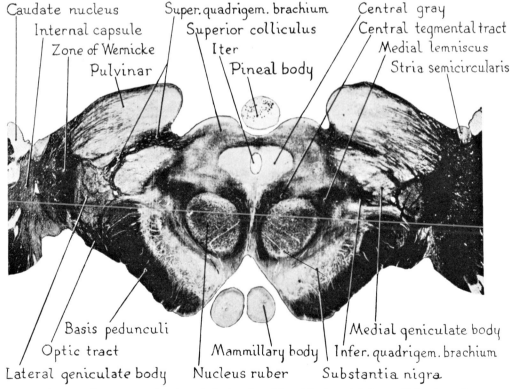

Caudate nucleus
Internal capsule
Zone of Wernicke
Pulvinar
Super. quadrigem. brachium
Superior colliculus
Iter
Pineal body
Central gray
Central tegmental tract
Medial lemniscus
Stria semicircularis

Basis pedunculi
Optic tract
Lateral geniculate body
Mammillary body
Nucleus ruber
Medial geniculate body
Infer. quadrigem. brachium
Substantia nigra

Fig. 2.46 Transverse section through the junction of the midbrain and thalamus. Weigert's myelin stain. (From Truex and Carpenter, 1964.)

nuclei; it sets up a major diffuse projection system between the globus pallidus and the midbrain, particularly the nucleus of Darkschewitsch, the interstitial nucleus of Cajal, and the nucleus of the posterior commissure.

Cells surrounding the aqueduct just behind the posterior commissure form a plate-like structure called the *subcommissural organ.* It is made up largely of secretory cells which discharge into the cerebrospinal fluid of the third ventricle.

The subthalamus (see Figure 2.44). The subthalamus or ventral thalamus lies sandwiched between the hypothalamus ventrally and the dorsal thalamus or thalamus proper dorsally. It is composed primarily of the zona incerta, the fields of Forel, the entopeduncular nucleus, the subthalamic nucleus, and the rostral extensions of the substantia nigra and red nucleus.

The *zona incerta,* nucleus of the fields of Forel, and subthalamic nucleus border the dorsolateral hypothalamus and ventral aspects of the thalamus. The zona incerta contains cells and fibers. The major afferents into it arise from the globus pallidus (via the lenticular fasciculus) and the lenticular nucleus (via the fasciculus subthalamicus); these project fibers through the zona incerta and extend collaterals into it. The zona incerta projects into the tegmentum of the midbrain and forms a link in an important striato-incerto-tegmento-olivary fiber system.

The *nucleus of the field of Forel* lies on the medial border of the zona incerta. It receives afferents from the striatum via the lenticular fas-ciculus and the ansa lenticularis and projects via the same fiber bundles to the tegmentum of the midbrain.

The *entopeduncular nucleus* is a loose collection of cells which follow the course of the ansa lenticularis through the diencephalon. This nucleus appears to receive and project fibers through the ansa lenticularis and, possibly, the inferior thalamic peduncle.

The *subthalamic nucleus* is stretched out along the medial border of the internal capsule. It is connected to the lenticular nucleus by the subthalamic fasciculus and may project to the putamen and caudate via more diffuse fiber connections. All these connections appear to be efferent as well as afferent. Although no discrete anatomical pathways have been established, the subthalamic nucleus also appears to have connections to the zona incerta, the field of Forel, the red nucleus, and some portions of the substantia nigra.

The substantia nigra and red nucleus have been discussed in some detail in the description of the anatomy of the midbrain. They continue forward into the subthalamic area and interconnect extensively with the internal capsule and basal ganglia in their rostral extension.

The dorsal thalamus (see Figure 2.47). The dorsal thalamus or, more conventionally, the *thalamus,* takes up the center of the brain, dorsal to the hypothalamus and subthalamus and medial to the internal capsule. Each side of the thalamus is divided into *internal* and *external* segments by nar-

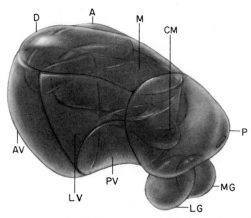

Fig. 2.47   A reconstruction of the left half of a human thalamus. Only the larger thalamic nuclei are shown. A, anterior nucleus; AV, anterior ventral; CM, centrum medianum; D, dorsal nuclei of lateral mass; LG, lateral geniculate; LV, lateral ventral; M, medial nucleus; MG, medial geniculate; P, pulvinar; PV, posterior ventral. (From Peele, 1961.)

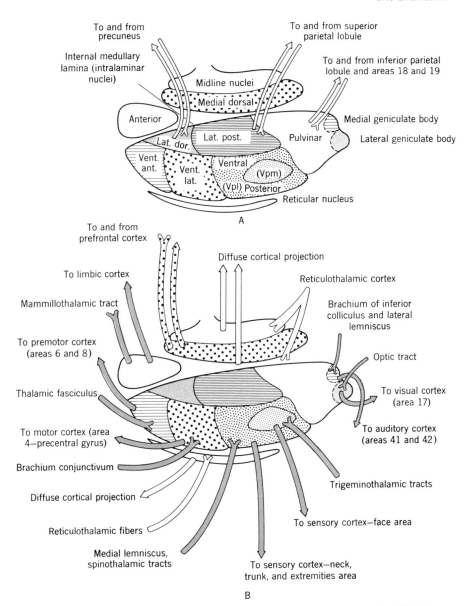

Fig. 2.48 Major thalamic nuclei, dorsolateral view. A, identification of nuclei of the left thalamus; B, principal afferent and efferent fiber connections of the thalamic nuclei. The ventral posteromedial (Vpm) and larger ventral posterolateral (Vpl) nuclear subdivisions of the ventral posterior nucleus are indicated. Medial and lateral geniculate bodies (metathalamus) and reticular nuclei are included. (From Truex and Carpenter, 1964.)

row bands of fibers called *medullary laminae.* A similar sheet of fibers, the external medullary lamina, separates the external segments of the thalamus from the reticular nucleus, which in turn surrounds the main mass of the thalamus and keeps it separate from the internal capsule. The following discrete nuclear masses within the thalamus are commonly distinguished (see Figures 2.48 and 2.49).

The anterior nuclei. Three major nuclei, the *anteromedial, anterodorsal,* and *anteroventral* nuclei, take up the anterior portion of the thalamus. The anteroventral nucleus is most prominent in

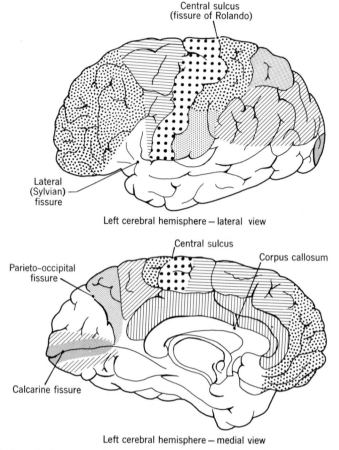

Fig. 2.49 Left cerebral cortex, to demonstrate projection areas of the thalamocortical nerve fibers. (From Truex and Carpenter, 1964.)

the human brain. All three receive afferents from the mammillary bodies via the mammillothalamic tract and project to the cerebral cortex. The anteromedial nucleus projects to the inferior surface of the frontal pole and to anterior portions of the cingulate gyrus. The anteroventral sends fibers to areas 23 and 24 of the cingulate gyrus. The antero-dorsal nucleus projects to area 29 (the retrosplenial portion) of the cingulate gyrus (see Figure 2.50).

The midline nuclei. The phylogenetically oldest nuclei of the thalamus are found in its midline. They are typically well developed in macrosmatic animals and tend to deteriorate in higher mammals. Several distinct nuclei have been described. The area immediately surrounding the third ventricle has been divided into the *anterior* and *posterior paraventricular nuclei*. The anterior nucleus

extends from the stria medullaris to the habenular complex, the posterior from the habenula to the pretectal periventricular gray (see Figure 2.51).

The *parataenial nucleus* is made up of cells which are scattered around the fibers of the stria medullaris. Directly caudal to the anterodorsal nucleus (and dorsal to the cells of the parataenial nucleus) is the *intero-anterodorsal nucleus*. Almost directly in the center of the thalamus are the *rhomboid* and *central medial nuclei*. These nuclei make up the *massa intermedia* which connects the two sides of the thalamus in many species.

The most ventrally located of the midline nuclei is the *nucleus reuniens*. It projects backward from the caudal border of the anterior tubercle to the middle of the massa intermedia. The caudal portion of the periventricular gray of the thalamus has not been divided into distinct nuclei.

The afferent connections of the midline nuclei

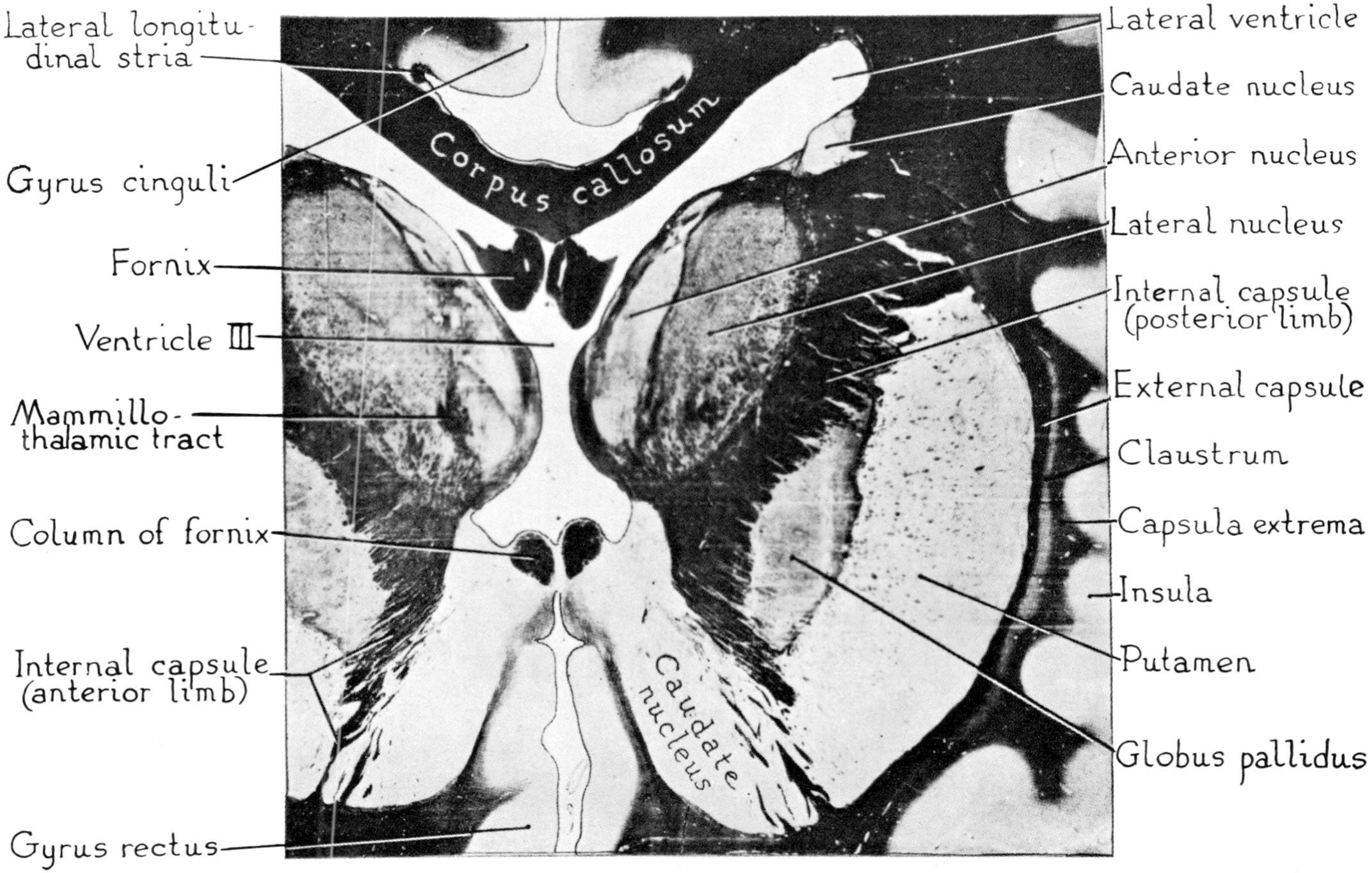
Lateral longitudinal stria
Gyrus cinguli
Fornix
Ventricle III
Mammillo-thalamic tract
Column of fornix
Internal capsule (anterior limb)
Gyrus rectus
Corpus callosum
Caudate nucleus
Lateral ventricle
Caudate nucleus
Anterior nucleus
Lateral nucleus
Internal capsule (posterior limb)
External capsule
Claustrum
Capsula extrema
Insula
Putamen
Globus pallidus

Fig. 2.50 Transverse section through the basal ganglia and the rostral portion of the thalamus. Weigert's myelin stain. (From Truex and Carpenter, 1964.)

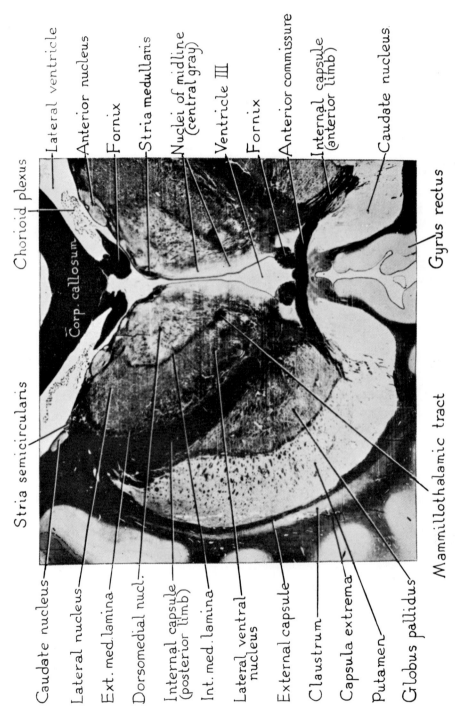

Chorioid plexus

Stria semicircularis

Caudate nucleus

Lateral ventricle

Anterior nucleus

Fornix

Stria medullaris

Nuclei of midline (central gray)

Ventricle III

Fornix

Anterior commissure

Internal capsule (anterior limb)

Caudate nucleus

Gyrus rectus

Corp. callosum

Caudate nucleus

Lateral nucleus

Ext. med. lamina

Dorsomedial nucl.

Internal capsule (posterior limb)

Int. med. lamina

Lateral ventral nucleus

External capsule

Claustrum

Capsula extrema

Putamen

Globus pallidus

Mammillothalamic tract

Fig. 2.51 Transverse section through the diencephalon and basal ganglia at the level of the anterior commissure. Weigert's myelin stain. (From Truex and Carpenter, 1964.)

include fibers from the spinothalamic tracts, the quintothalamic (trigeminothalamic) tracts, and the medial lemniscus. Anatomically less distinct are afferents from the tectal and pretectal area and other thalamic nuclei.

The midline nuclei project diffusely to many, if not all, areas of the cortex, as shown by extensive degeneration following decortication. However, no distinct anatomical pathways for this functionally important projection have been demonstrated, and the possibility exists that the pathway may be indirect, i.e., via one or more subcortical relays. The midline nuclei also project to the hypothalamus, basal ganglia, and amygdaloid complex.

The medial nuclei. The midline nuclei are surrounded by a group of well-developed nuclear masses called the midline group. The *dorsomedial* nucleus extends from the anteroventral nuclei dorsally to the nuclei centrum medianum and parafasciculus caudally. Laterally, it projects to the internal medullary lamina. The dorsomedial nucleus has reciprocal connections with the hypothalamus, the pretectal region, the prefrontal cortex, and other thalamic nuclei (see Figure 2.52).

The nucleus *centrum medianum* separates the dorsomedial and lateral nuclei of the thalamus from the red nuclei. The nucleus is almost entirely enclosed in fibers from the internal medullary lamina; it neither receives nor projects distinct fiber bundles. Some evidence has been presented suggesting the existence of afferent inputs from the trigeminal and vagus, the medial geniculate, the dentate nucleus of the cerebellum, and the cerebral motor cortex. The nucleus centrum medianum projects, apparently, via diffuse fiber connections to the caudate and putamen.

Several smaller nuclei are commonly distinguished in the medial thalamus. The *nucleus submedius* extends caudally from the posterior border of the anteromedial nucleus of the anterior group. Lateral to the central medial nucleus and anterior to the centrum medianum, a small *paracentral* nucleus forms within the internal medullary lamina. The lateral portion of the laminae is taken up by the *central lateral* nucleus which surrounds the dorsal half of the dorsomedial nuclei. The *parafascicular* nucleus completes the medial area, taking up a position ventral to the caudal part of the dorsomedial nucleus. The afferent and efferent projections of these smaller medial nuclei are largely unknown.

The lateral nuclei. The lateral nuclei extend from the caudal border of the thalamus to its dorsal limits.

The *pulvinar* nucleus constitutes the caudal thalamus, beginning just ahead of the superior colliculi. It contains several distinct cell masses and projects to a number of cortical and subcortical regions. It receives afferents from the amygdaloid complex and the preoccipital and occipital areas (via collaterals from the corticotectal fiber bundle). Cells in the caudal portion of the pulvinar project to the occipitotemporal and parietotemporal cortex; those of the rostral pulvinar project to the parietal cortex.

The dorsal portion of the pulvinar is separated from the pretectal area by the small nucleus *suprageniculatus*. Its connections are not well established.

The *posterolateral* nucleus extends forward and laterally from the rostral border of the pulvinar. It is separated from the dorsomedial nucleus by the internal medullary lamina and its nuclei. The posterolateral nucleus is reciprocally connected to the surrounding thalamic nuclei and projects diffusely to the parietal cortex. It receives some corticothalamic afferents, primarily from the parietal and frontal cortices.

The *dorsolateral* nucleus extends dorsomedially to the lateral posterior nucleus, near the dorsal surface of the thalamus. It is reciprocally interconnected by surrounding thalamic nuclei and projects to the inferior parietal cortex.

The ventral nuclei. The ventral surface of the thalamus is divided into several large nuclear masses. The *posteroventral* nucleus is the largest nucleus of this group. It lies ventrolateral to the dorsomedial nucleus and ventromedial to the lateral nuclei. The posteroventral nucleus approaches the third ventricle medially and may communicate with its counterpart across the midline via the *interventral commissure*. The lateral portion of the posteroventral nucleus, the nucleus *ventralis posterolateralis*, receives terminal fibers from the gracilis and cuneate components of the medial lemniscus. These fibers carry information about tactile and proprioceptive stimuli from all parts of the body.

The ventral and lateral spinothalamic fiber system, which carries information about pain and pressure from all portions of the body, also terminates in the region of the posteroventral nucleus. Primitive temperature and "itch" sensations may be related to projections of the spinothalamic system to the nucleus ventralis posterolateralis. The quintothalamic fibers which carry tactile, temperature, and pain impulses from the face project contralaterally to the medial portion

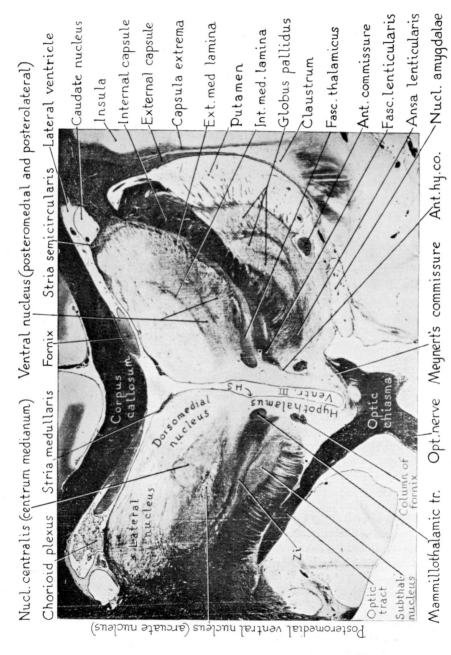

Nucl. centralis (centrum medianum)   Ventral nucleus (posteromedial and posterolateral)

Chorioid plexus   Stria medullaris   Fornix   Stria semicircularis   Lateral ventricle

Caudate nucleus

Insula

Internal capsule

External capsule

Capsula extrema

Ext. med. lamina

Putamen

Int. med. lamina

Globus pallidus

Claustrum

Fasc. thalamicus

Ant. commissure

Fasc. lenticularis

Ansa lenticularis

Nucl. amygdalae

Corpus callosum

Dorsomedial nucleus

Lateral nucleus

Hypothalamus   Ventr. III   CHS   HS

Optic chiasma

Column of fornix

Zi

Optic tract

Subthal. nucleus

Mammillothalamic tr.   Opt. nerve   Meynert's commissure   Ant. hy. co.

Posteromedial ventral nucleus (arcuate nucleus)

Fig. 2.52 Transverse section through the diencephalon and basal ganglia at the level of the optic chiasma. The right side is cut at a higher level than the left. Weigert's myelin stain. Ant. hy. co., anterior hypothalamic commissure; Hs, hypothalamic sulcus; Zi, zona incerta. The gray stripe separating the external medullary lamina from the internal capsule constitutes the reticular nucleus which ventrally becomes continuous with the zona incerta. (From Truex and Carpenter, 1964.)

of the posteroventral nucleus, the nucleus *ventralis posteromedialis.* This portion of the nucleus also receives gustatory impulses from secondary ascending taste fibers and general visceral impulses from the gastrointestinal tract and the urinary bladder.

The posteroventral nucleus projects to the paracentral and postcentral area of the cerebral cortex (somatic sensory area 1) through the posterior limb of the internal capsule; it also receives some afferents from this portion of the parietal lobe. Extensive projections to the basal ganglia have also been reported.

The lateral portion of the posteroventral nucleus is continuous with the *lateroventral (ventralis lateralis)* nucleus which receives crossed afferents from the rubrothalamic and dentatothalamic tracts and from the thalamic fasciculus. The latter carries fibers from the globus pallidus. Afferents from the motor cortex (area 6) have also been described. Efferent projections of the lateroventral nucleus reach the motor areas of the cortex (areas 4 and 6). Some evidence of somatotopic organization of these projections has been reported.

The rostral-most aspect of the ventral thalamus is taken up by the *anteroventral (ventralis anterior)* nucleus. It receives afferents from the globus pallidus and the frontal cortex. Anatomically, it has been difficult to trace the efferent connections of this nucleus. On the basis of electrophysiological information, the anteroventral nucleus is assumed to project diffusely to nearly all parts of the cerebral cortex.

The metathalamus. The metathalamus makes up the transitional area between the mesencephalon and the caudal portion of the thalamus. The *dorsal pretectal area* extends from immediately anterior to the superior colliculi to the caudal border of the pulvinar nucleus of the thalamus. It contains undifferentiated gray matter (sometimes referred to as the large-cell nucleus of the optic tract) and receives fibers from the optic tract.

Rostral and lateral to the superior colliculi, ventral to the pretectal area and pulvinar nucleus, the *medial geniculate body* appears. It receives fibers from the inferior colliculi and lateral lemnisci. It discharges through the auditory radiations to the homolateral auditory areas of the temporal operculum. The frequency of auditory signals is tonotopically projected to the medial geniculate nucleus in some species. The nucleus projects to the primary auditory area (AI) of the cortex as well as the secondary auditory area (AII) and the surrounding auditory "association" cortex (EP).

Lateral to the rostral portion of the medial geniculate nucleus, the *lateral geniculate body* appears on the surface of the brain. The dorsal portion of the lateral geniculate has six distinct layers of cells. These layers alternate with equally distinct layers of fibers and give the nucleus a striped appearance. The principal afferent input to the lateral geniculate body is the optic tract. It terminates in such a way that crossed fibers reach layers 1, 4, and 6 and uncrossed fibers distribute to layers 2, 3, and 5. The ventral portion of the lateral geniculate receives fibers largely from the superior colliculi and projects mainly to the midbrain tegmentum. The dorsal nucleus of the lateral geniculate body projects through the *geniculocalcarine tract* (the visual radiations) to the visual cortex. Topographic localization is maintained in such a way that the medial portion of the lateral geniculate (the superior retinal quadrant) is projected to the superior lip of the calcarine fissure whereas impulses from the lateral portion (inferior retinal quadrant) project to the inferior lip. The macular projections terminate most posteriorly on the visual cortex; those from more peripheral portions of the retina terminate in more anterior sections.

The reticular nucleus. The dorsal thalamus is essentially enveloped by a thin band of cells which form a boundary between the external medullary lamina and the internal capsule. This area is continuous with the zona incerta, and the reticular nucleus is often classified as a subthalamic nucleus. The reticular nucleus projects in an orderly fashion to apparently all portions of the cortex. The anterior aspects of the nucleus project to the frontal cortex, the more posterior portions to the parietal, temporal, and visual cortices. There is also evidence for an extensive interconnection with other thalamic nuclei and with the globus pallidus. Electrophysiological evidence indicates that a close functional relationship exists between the reticular nucleus and the intralaminar and midline nuclei of the thalamus.

The Telencephalic Nuclei (Figures 2.53 to 2.59)

The dorsal portion of the brainstem consists of a group of nuclei collectively called *basal ganglia.* This includes the *globus pallidus,* the *putamen,* the *caudate* nucleus, the *claustrum,* the *substantia innominata,* and the *amygdaloid complex.* The putamen and globus pallidus are often collectively

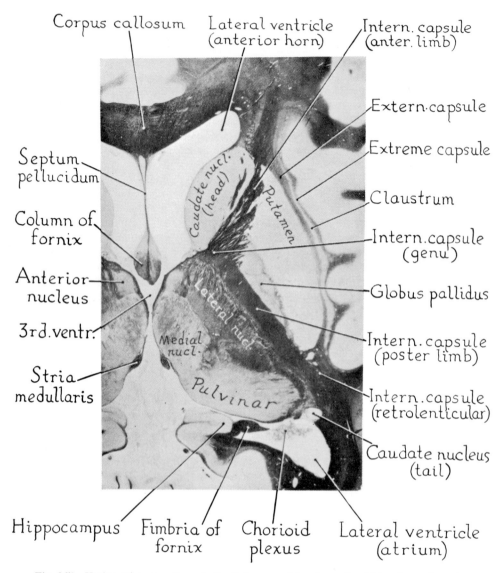

Corpus callosum   Lateral ventricle   Intern. capsule
                   (anterior horn)   (anter. limb)

Septum pellucidum

Column of fornix

Anterior nucleus

3rd. ventr.

Stria medullaris

Caudate nucl. (head)

Putamen

Lateral nucl.

Medial nucl.

Pulvinar

Extern. capsule

Extreme capsule

Claustrum

Intern. capsule (genu)

Globus pallidus

Intern. capsule (poster limb)

Intern. capsule (retrolenticular)

Caudate nucleus (tail)

Hippocampus   Fimbria of fornix   Chorioid plexus   Lateral ventricle (atrium)

Fig. 2.53 Horizontal section through the thalamus and basal ganglia. Weigert's myelin stain. (From Truex and Carpenter, 1964.)

called *lenticular* or *lentiform* nucleus; the term *corpus striatum* (or *striatum*) is collectively applied to the lenticular and caudate nuclei. The caudate and putamen are sometimes called *neostriatum,* the globus pallidus *paleostriatum* (or *pallidum*), and the amygdala *archistriatum* (see Figure 2.54).

The *head of the caudate* nucleus (the *nucleus accumbens septi*) is located in the anterior portion of the lateral ventricle. It projects a thin "tail" medially along the dorsolateral aspect of the thalamus and downward into the inferior horn of the lateral ventricle, where it terminates in the

corticomedial part of the amygdala. In its course along the medial and superior wall of the lateral ventricle, the tail of the caudate nucleus is accompanied by the stria terminalis, which arises in the amygdaloid complex and projects to the diencephalon.

The ventral aspects of the head of the caudate nucleus are adjacent to the putamen. The two nuclei are incompletely separated by fibers from the anterior limb of the internal capsule. Medially, the putamen is bordered by the globus pallidus, separated from it only by a thin band of fibers called the *outer* or *external medullary lamina*. The globus pallidus is usually divided into an inner and an outer segment by the *internal medullary lamina* or stria. A similar fiber tract, the *external capsule*, separates the putamen from the laterally located claustrum. The *extreme capsule* forms a boundary between the claustrum and the overlying cortex of the cerebrum. The ventral aspects of the claustrum and putamen extend into the amygdaloid complex.

The striatum is separated from the thalamus by the *internal capsule*, which forms the major pathway between the cortex and the brainstem. The *anterior limb* of the internal capsule separates the head of the caudate from the lenticular nucleus; the *genu*, or middle portion of the internal capsule, separates the lenticular and caudate nuclei from the thalamus; and the *posterior limb* separates the lenticular nucleus from the posterior thalamus. The internal capsule is crossed by

fibers which interconnect the thalamus and caudate nucleus with the lenticular nucleus.

The striatum. The lenticular nuclei receive corticostriate fibers from areas 4, 6, and 8 of the frontal lobe; from areas 2, 5, and 7 of the parietal lobe; from areas 23 and 24 of the cingulate gyrus; and from the temporal pole and island of Reil. Some of these fibers enter the lenticular complex via the internal capsule; others pass into the external capsule and course ventralward before terminating in the putamen or globus pallidus. The motor areas of the frontal cortex (areas 2, 4, 6, and 8) are also connected to the lenticular nuclei via collaterals from the corticospinal tracts. The caudate nucleus receives projections largely from the "suppressor" areas of the frontal cortex (areas 2s, 4s, 8s, and 19s).

Thalamostriate fibers may (1) pass through the caudate and course ventralward with the posterior

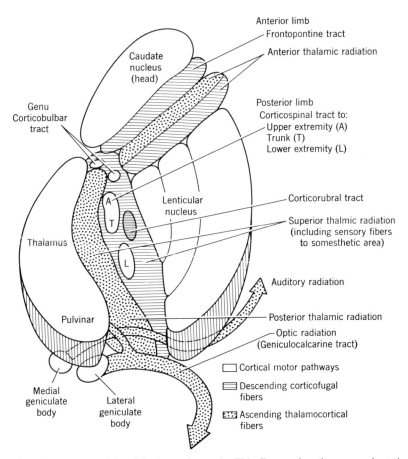

Fig. 2.54 Components of the right internal capsule. This diagram has the same orientation as Figure 2.53. (From Truex and Carpenter, 1964.)

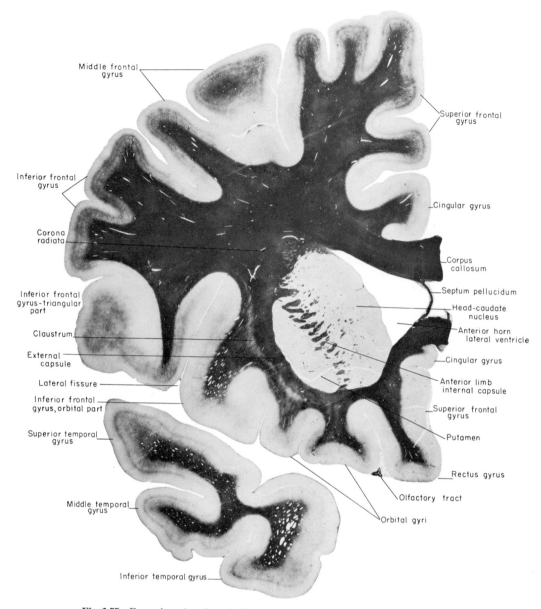

Fig. 2.55 Frontal section through the cerebral hemisphere. (From Jelgersma, 1931.)

limb of the internal capsule before entering the medial side of the putamen, or (2) reach the internal capsule directly and enter the putamen and outer segments of the globus pallidus. The lateral, ventral, and dorsomedial nuclei of the thalamus are particularly heavy contributors to the thalamostriate connection system. There is some evidence for a reciprocal innervation between the lenticular nuclei and the thalamus, but the anatomic documentation for these connec-

tions is not well established. A pallidothalamic projection along the thalamic fasciculus which interconnects the globus pallidus and the antero-ventral nucleus of the thalamus has been found. The fibers of this fasciculus pass medially in the zona incerta and fields of Forel before ascending to the ventral nuclei of the anterior thalamus.

The major afferents to the striatum from lower portions of the brainstem arise from the substantia nigra of the midbrain. These nigrostriate fibers interdigitate with the fibers of the internal capsule and form the *comb bundle*. Most of the nigrostriate fibers terminate in the putamen.

The principal direction of conduction within the striatum is from the caudate to the putamen and globus pallidus and from the putamen to the globus pallidus. The fiber projections between the putamen and globus pallidus make up most of the medullary laminae which separate the two nuclear masses. The globus pallidus and caudate nucleus also discharge to the substantia innominata positioned ventral to the lateral aspects of the lenticular nucleus.

Several major fiber bundles bear the efferent

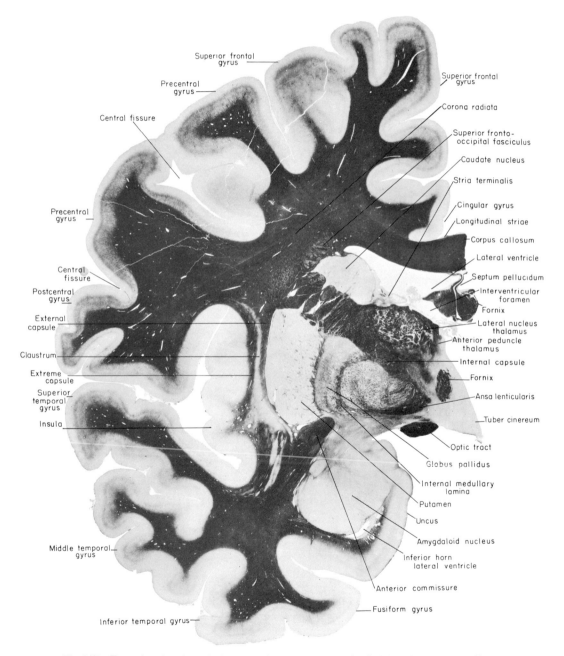

Fig. 2.56   Frontal section through the cerebral hemisphere at the level of the tuber cinereum. (From Jelgersma, 1931.)

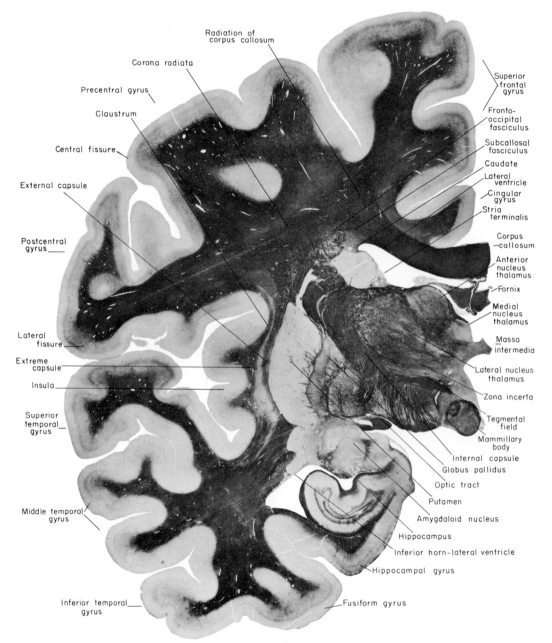

Radiation of
corpus callosum

Corona radiata

Precentral gyrus

Claustrum

Central fissure

External capsule

Postcentral
gyrus

Lateral
fissure

Extreme
capsule

Insula

Superior
temporal
gyrus

Middle temporal
gyrus

Inferior temporal
gyrus

Superior
frontal
gyrus

Fronto-
occipital
fasciculus

Subcallosal
fasciculus

Caudate

Lateral
ventricle

Cingular
gyrus

Stria
terminalis

Corpus
callosum

Anterior
nucleus
thalamus

Fornix

Medial
nucleus
thalamus

Massa
intermedia

Lateral nucleus
thalamus

Zona incerta

Tegmental
field

Mammillary
body

Internal capsule

Globus pallidus

Optic tract

Putamen

Amygdaloid nucleus

Hippocampus

Inferior horn-lateral ventricle

Hippocampal gyrus

Fusiform gyrus

Fig. 2.57 Frontal section through the cerebral hemisphere at the level of the mammillary bodies. (From Jelgersma, 1931.)

outflow from the striatum. The *pallidohypo-thalamic fasciculus* projects fibers from the globus pallidus to the ventromedial hypothalamus. The fibers synapse on cells projecting to the midbrain tegmentum. The *lenticular fasciculus* (also called the H_2 bundle of Forel) projects from the globus pallidus to the zona incerta of the subthalamic region. These fiber bundles synapse on cells which project to the midbrain tegmentum and the olivary nuclei of the medulla, or continue into the field of Forel where they synapse with cells projecting to the nucleus of Darkschewitsch, the interstitial nucleus of Cajal, the red nucleus, and the surrounding tegmental gray. These connections establish a major efferent pathway to the motor nuclei of the brainstem and to the anterior horn cells of the spinal cord. The *subthalamic fasciculus* interconnects the globus pallidus and putamen with the subthalamic nucleus of the other side of the brain. This pathway carries reciprocal connections and provides the basis for

pallidonigral interactions. The *ansa lenticularis* originates in the putamen and globus pallidus and terminates largely in the nucleus of the field of Forel. Secondary fibers from this nucleus then continue the ansa lenticularis into midbrain, where they terminate in the red nucleus, the deep gray surrounding that nucleus, and the lateral

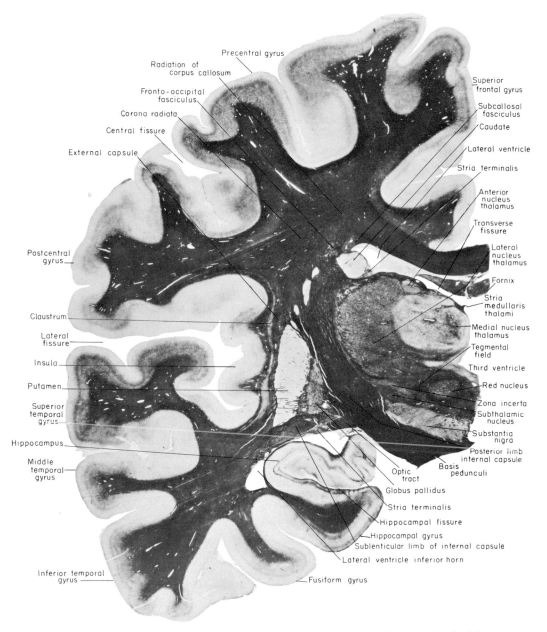

Fig. 2.58 Frontal section through the cerebral hemisphere at the plane of the rostral end of the red nucleus. (From Jelgersma, 1931.)

tegmental gray. From here, tegmentobulbar and tegmentospinal tracts which provide important pathways for lenticular efferents arise.

Functionally, the striatum has been shown to be part of several important neural circuits. The cerebral cortex and thalamus project afferents to the globus pallidus. From here, the afferents are relayed via the lenticular fasciculus, the ansa lenticularis, and subthalamic fasciculus to nuclei in the midbrain which project to bulbar motor nuclei and motor neurons of the spinal cord. The lower centers, in turn, project to midbrain nuclei which are connected to the subthalamic nucleus and striatum via nigrostriatal, tegmentostriatal, and tegmentosubthalamostriatal fiber bundles. These afferents from lower portions of the brainstem synapse largely in the putamen, which projects fibers along the thalamic fasciculus to the anteroventral nucleus of the thalamus. From here, the circuit to the cortex, particularly to the motor and premotor areas near the central fissure, is completed.

Another circuit involves projections from the "suppressor" areas of the cortex to the caudate nucleus. The projections are then relayed to the lenticular nuclei for discharge along the thalamic fasciculus to the ventral nuclei of the thalamus. From here, the information is carried to the motor and premotor areas of the frontal cortex.

The striatum provides an important link between many other parts of the brain. Damage to the striatum is clinically associated with muscular tremor, hypertonicity, and loss of automatic associated movements.

The claustrum. The claustrum is a thin sheet of cells that are separated from the cortex of the island of Reil only by the extreme capsule. Its posterior aspects are continuous with the amygdaloid complex. The claustrum receives fibers from both of the fiber bundles (the external and extreme capsule) which surround it. It also receives afferents from the fronto-occipital fiber bundle and the superior longitudinal fiber bundle of the cortex. The claustrum projects to the inferior frontal gyrus of the frontal lobe as well as to portions of the island of Reil and operculum. Its subcortical connections include fibers in the ansa peduncularis and ansa lenticularis. The functional significance of this area is not established.

The amygdala (see Figure 2.56). The amygdaloid complex lies at the tip of the inferior horn of the lateral ventricle. It is surrounded by the periamygdaloid cortex of the hippocampal gyrus and is bordered by the hippocampus proper at the posterior border. The amygdala is continuous with the tail of the caudate nucleus and with the ventral part of the claustrum and putamen. The amygdaloid complex contains two major nuclear masses, the *corticomedial* and the *basolateral* groups.

The corticomedial complex includes (1) the *anterior amygdaloid* area which represents the transitional zone between the anterior perforated space and the substantia innominata on the one hand and the amygdaloid complex on the other. This area contains the *diagonal band of Broca* which connects the parolfactory area of Broca with the lenticular nucleus and amygdaloid complex; (2) the *nuclei of the lateral olfactory tract* which continue from the anterior amygdaloid area posteriorly and are made up of deep-staining cells; (3) the *medial amygdaloid nucleus* which surrounds the dorsal aspects of the nucleus of the lateral olfactory tract; (4) the *cortical amygdaloid nucleus* which is located posterior to the lateral olfactory tract and ventral to the medial nucleus; and (5) the *central nucleus* which forms a distinct cellular mass between the corticomedial and the basolateral groups of nuclei.

The basolateral complex contains the *lateral amygdaloid nucleus* which forms the lateral-most portion of the amygdala. This nucleus is continuous with portions of the claustrum and with the cortical matter surrounding it. Medial and dorsomedial to it is the *basal amygdaloid nucleus* which is continuous with the overlying cortical matter. The basal and cortical nuclei are separated by the *accessory basal nucleus* which is also continuous with the overlying cortex.

The *lateral olfactory tract* projects to the anterior amygdaloid area, the nucleus of the lateral olfactory tract, and the medial amygdaloid nucleus. These nuclei, in turn, send into the stria terminalis fibers which enter the preoptic and anterior hypothalamic areas as the precommissural component of the stria. Some of these fibers decussate in the anterior commissure and project to the preoptic and anterior hypothalamic areas of the contralateral side of the brain. Other fibers from the stria terminalis join the stria medullaris and terminate in the habenular complex. Finally, a component of the stria terminalis joins the fornix for distribution in the posterior hypothalamic region. The central amygdaloid nucleus projects fibers into the *longitudinal association bundle*

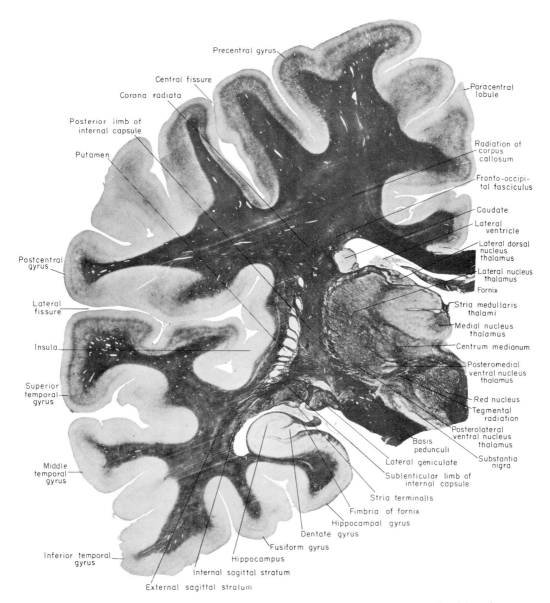

Fig. 2.59 Frontal section through the cerebral hemisphere at the plane of the middle of the red nucleus. (From Jelgersma, 1931.)

which terminates in the anterior hypothalamic area (see Figure 2.60).

The basolateral nuclei project to the amydaloid complex of the contralateral hemisphere via the anterior commissure. They have extensive interconnections with the corticomedial nuclei; however, the major efferent outflow appears to take a diffuse route which makes use of the intimate relationship of this portion of the amygdala with the surrounding cortical tissue. The hippocampal and dentate gyri in particular receive extensive afferents from the basolateral nuclei. This interchange sets up an important pathway between the amygdaloid complex and the posterior hypothalamus and midbrain tegmentum via the *fornix* which arises in part from the hippocampal gyrus. Multisynaptic connections both to the orbital surface of the cortical hemispheres and to the cingulate gyrus of the midline have also been demonstrated.

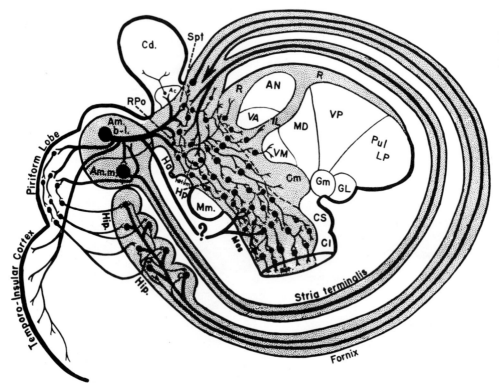

Fig. 2.60 Neuronal organization of the amygdaloid projection system as revealed by electrophysiological studies. Ac, nucleus accumbens; Am. b-1., basolateral subdivision of amygdala; Am.m., corticomedial subdivision of the amygdala; AN, anterior thalamic nuclei; Cd., caudate nucleus; Cl, inferior colliculus; Cm, centrum medianum; CS, superior colliculus; GL, lateral geniculate body; Gm, medial geniculate body; Ha, anterior hypothalamus; Hip., hippocampus; Hp, posterior hypothalamus; IL, intralaminar nuclei of thalamus; LP, nucleus lateralis posterior thalami; MD, nucleus medialis dorsalis thalami; Mes, mesencephalon; Mn., mammillary body; NHvm, nucleus ventromedialis hypothalami; Pul, pulvinar; R, nucleus reticularis thalami; Ret, reticular formation; RPo, regio preoptica; Spt, septum; and Va, nucleus ventralis anterior thalami. The dotted area represents the subcortical integrative areas regulating "global" mechanisms and the limbic structures projecting into it. (From Gloor, 1960.)

Blood Supply of the Brainstem (see Figure 2.61)

The brainstem is supplied by a number of large *regional arteries*. The bulbar portion of the stem derives its blood largely from the *vertebral* arteries, the pontine section from the *basilar* artery, and the midbrain from the *anterior* and *posterior chorioidal arteries* and the *posterior cerebral arteries*.

Vessels that branch from the regional arteries and penetrate the ventral surface of the brainstem are called *paramedian* arteries. In the posterior portion of the medulla, paramedian arteries arise from the *anterior spinal* arteries. The paramedian arteries of the anterior medulla, the pons, and

the midbrain arise primarily from the *basilar* artery.

Vessels that branch from the regional arteries and run transversely around the brainstem before penetrating its lateral surface are called *short circumferential* arteries. *Long circumferential* arteries run completely around the brainstem before entering the dorsal surface. The short circumferential arteries of the caudal medulla arise from the basilar or vertebral arteries. A long circumferential artery of vertebral origin supplies the rostral medulla and restiform body. The pontine area is supplied by a number of short circumferential arteries arising from the basilar artery and by a long circumferential artery from the *superior cerebellar* artery.

The midbrain region has no short circumferential arteries. Instead, a number of long circumferential arteries (the *quadrigeminal, anterior* and *posterior chorioidal, accessory chorioidal,* and *posterior cerebral*) project short, penetrating vessels into the lateral area en route to the dorsal section of the brainstem.

The venous drainage of the medulla, pons, and midbrain is essentially similar to the arterial supply. The *anterior* and *posterior median medullary* veins are connected to subpial plexuses. Caudally, these veins are continuous with the anterior and posterior spinal venous trunks. Rostrally, the anterior median medullary vein is continuous with the *median pontine* vein which drains the medial and ventrolateral regions.

Paramedian radicles drain the ventrolateral and lateral midbrain into the *interpeduncular venous plexus* which is continuous with the *basal* vein. The dorsal midbrain drains into the *internal cerebral* vein or the *great vein of Galen.*

The hypothalamus receives most of its blood directly from small arteries which arise from the *circle of Willis* and from the *ophthalmic* artery. Venous drainage from the hypothalamus occurs largely via the basal vein which drains into the great vein of Galen.

The thalamus receives five major arteries. The *thalamoperforating* artery arises from the posterior cerebral artery and enters the brain just posterior to the mammillary bodies. The *thalamogeniculate* artery also arises from the posterior cerebral and approaches the thalamus from its ventral surface. The *thalamotuberal* artery arises from the *posterior communicating* artery of the circle of Willis and enters the diencephalon anterior to the mammillary bodies. The *chorioidal* vessels arise from the anterior and posterior chorioidal arteries and enter the diencephalon from the third ventricle. The *lenticulo-optic* arteries arise from the middle cerebral artery.

Radicles of the *small vein of Galen* drain the superior and central portion of the thalamus. The ventral thalamus drains either into radicles of the basal veins or into small veins which empty into

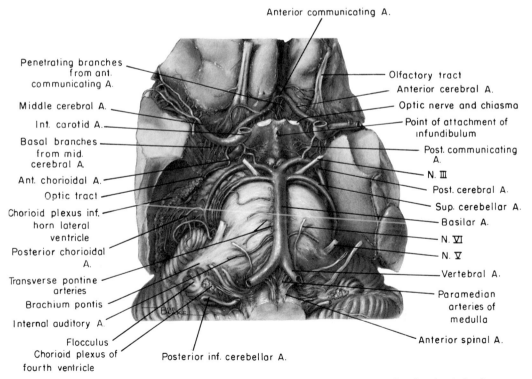

Anterior communicating A.

Penetrating branches from ant. communicating A.

Middle cerebral A.

Int. carotid A.

Basal branches from mid. cerebral A.

Ant. chorioidal A.

Optic tract

Chorioid plexus inf. horn lateral ventricle

Posterior chorioidal A.

Transverse pontine arteries

Brachium pontis

Internal auditory A.

Flocculus

Chorioid plexus of fourth ventricle

Posterior inf. cerebellar A.

Olfactory tract

Anterior cerebral A.

Optic nerve and chiasma

Point of attachment of infundibulum

Post. communicating A.

N. III

Post. cerebral A.

Sup. cerebellar A.

Basilar A.

N. VI

N. V

Vertebral A.

Paramedian arteries of medulla

Anterior spinal A.

Fig. 2.61 The principal arteries at the base of the brain and especially those forming the circle of Willis. The temporal lobes have been partially dissected away, and on the left the inferior horn of the lateral ventricle has been opened. (From Peele, 1961.)

the veins and *cavernous sinuses* at the base of the brain.

The middle cerebral artery projects a number of arteries toward the head of the caudate, globus pallidus, putamen, and internal capsule. The posterior portion of the lenticular nucleus is supplied by the anterior choriodal artery, and the thalamogeniculate branch from the posterior cerebral artery.

The basal ganglia drain into the great vein of Galen, the *terminal* vein, and the middle cerebral vein.

THE CEREBRAL HEMISPHERES

Gross Anatomy

The telencephalon consists of a small, medially located portion composed largely of the preoptic

area and the anterior commissure, and two large lateral portions, the cerebral hemispheres, which in man and in the higher mammals have become so extensive that they obscure much of the brainstem.

The surface of the cerebral hemispheres is convoluted, forming a number of ridges (*gyri*) and grooves (*sulci* or *fissures*) (see Figure 2.62). The anterior end of the hemispheres has been called the *frontal pole*, and the posterior end the *occipital pole*.

Along the lateral surface of the hemispheres, a deep fissure, the *lateral* or *Sylvian fissure,* marks the border between the *frontal* and *parietal lobes* (above the lateral fissure) and the *temporal lobe* (below the fissure). The anterior portion of the temporal lobe is called the *temporal pole*.

The walls of the lateral fissure are formed by folds of cortical tissue. A large area of surface

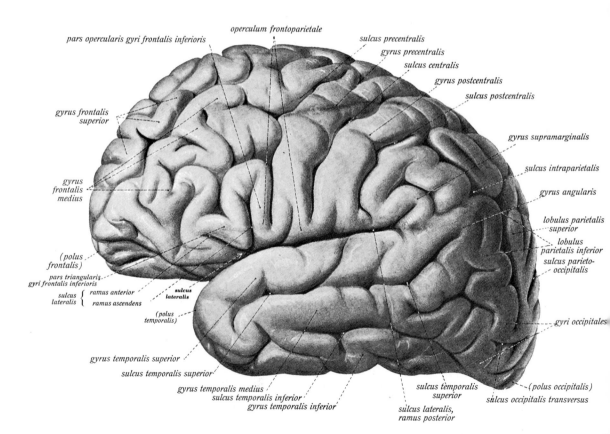

Fig. 2.62   Lateral surface of the human brain. (From Sobotta, 1963.)

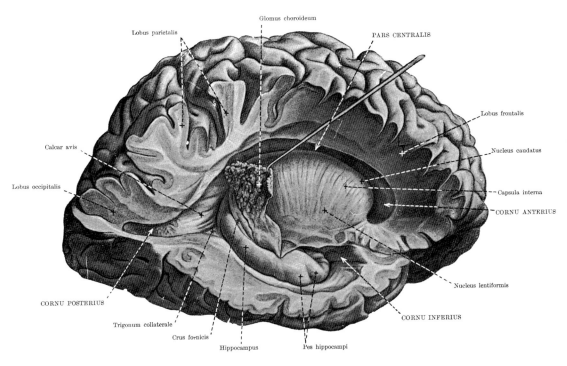

Glomus choroideum

Lobus parietalis

PARS CENTRALIS

Lobus frontalis

Nucleus caudatus

Calcar avis

Capsula interna

Lobus occipitalis

CORNU ANTERIUS

Nucleus lentiformis

CORNU POSTERIUS

CORNU INFERIUS

Trigonum collaterale

Crus fornicis

Hippocampus

Pes hippocampi

Fig. 2.63   The lateral ventricle of the cerebral hemisphere. (From Kiss and Szentágothai, 1964.)

cortex, the *island of Reil,* is buried in the folds of the fissure. The outer border of the island of Reil is marked by the *circular* or *limiting* fissure (see Figure 2.81).

The *central* fissure runs at about a 70° angle to the lateral fissure; it extends from the medial surface of the hemisphere, over its lateral aspect, and almost into the lateral fissure.

The region anterior to the central fissure and above the temporal lobe makes up the *frontal lobe.* Just in front of and parallel to the central fissure, the *precentral* gyrus develops; it is bordered anteriorly by the *precentral* fissure. Two major sulci, the *superior* and *inferior frontal* fissures, project anteriorly from the precentral fissure and form the *superior, middle,* and *inferior frontal gyri.* These major convolutions are, in turn, furrowed by smaller sulci which further subdivide them.

The region posterior to the central fissure and dorsal to the lateral fissure makes up the *parietal lobe,* which extends posteriorly to the *parieto-occipital fissure.* The parietal lobe is subdivided

by the *postcentral fissure* into the postcentral gyrus and a large *parietal lobule.* This lobule is, in turn, divided into superior and inferior portions by the *intraparietal fissure* projecting posteriorly, roughly at right angles to the postcentral fissure. In man the inferior parietal lobule is further subdivided into the *supramarginal* gyrus and the *angular* gyrus.

The parieto-occipital fissure forms the anterior border of the *occipital lobe* which makes up the posterior aspect of the cerebral hemispheres. This fissure does not project to the ventral surface of the hemispheres; it is therefore customary to complete the anterior border of the occipital lobe by an imaginary line which extends the parieto-occipital fissure to a small indentation on the ventrolateral surface of the temporal lobe called the *occipital notch.* The most prominent fissure of the occipital lobe, the *calcarine fissure,* originates on the medial surface of the hemispheres; it then continues onto the lateral surface and divides the occipital lobe into superior and inferior aspects.

The *temporal lobe* makes up the remaining portion of the lateral and lateroventral surface of the hemispheres. This lobe is bounded dorsally by the lateral fissure and posteriorly by the imaginary line between the parieto-occipital fissure and the occipital notch. Two major fissures, the *superior* and *middle temporal fissures,* parallel the lateral fissure and subdivide the lateral portion of the temporal lobe into *superior, middle,* and *inferior gyri.*

The ventral aspect of the medial surface of the hemisphere is formed by a large commissural fiber bundle, the *corpus callosum,* which interconnects the two hemispheres along the medial third of their anterior-posterior extent. The thick, posterior portion of the corpus callosum is known as the *splenium,* the main body is the *corpus,* and the sharp bend in its anterior portion is the *genu* (see Figure 2.64).

Dorsal to the corpus callosum is the *cingulate gyrus.* It is separated from the cortex of the dorsomedial surface by the *cingulate sulcus.* The caudal portion of the medial surface is taken up by the occipital lobe; this lobe is divided medially by the calcarine fissure into a superior portion, the *cuneus,* and an inferior portion, the *lingula.*

The cingulate gyrus curves around the splenium of the corpus callosum and becomes continuous through the *isthmus* with the *hippocampal gyrus* of the ventral surface of the temporal lobe. These three gyri, the hippocampal, isthmus, and cingulate, constitute the *fornicate* or *limbic* lobe. The term limbic lobe is, however, often applied to a more extensive portion of the cerebrum, including the *anterior* and *posterior parolfactory gyri,* the *olfactory bulb* and *stalk,* and the *prepyriform* cortex. It becomes then essentially synonymous with the term rhinencephalon.

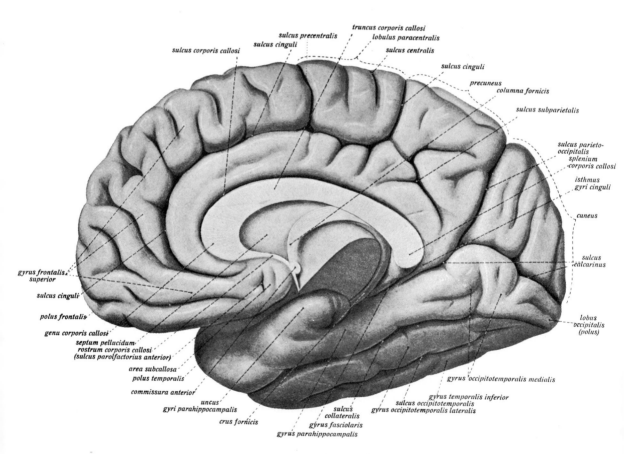

Fig. 2.64   Medial surface of the human brain. (From Sobotta, 1963.)

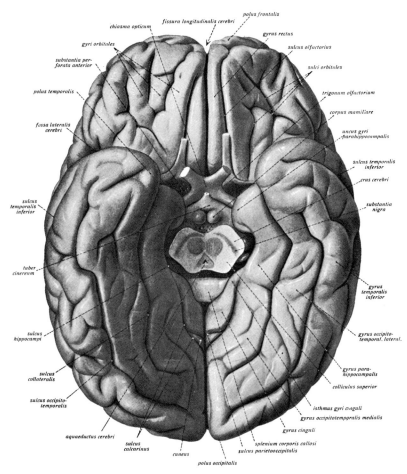

Fig. 2.65   Ventral surface of the human brain. (From Sobotta, 1963.)

The *ventral surface* of the cerebral hemispheres is constituted of temporal and frontal cortex and olfactory apparatus (see Figure 2.65).

The *olfactory bulb* and *stalk* parallel the *olfactory sulcus* which marks the medial border of the ventral portion of the frontal lobe. The stalk divides into *medial* and *lateral olfactory striae* which enclose the *olfactory trigone* and *anterior perforated area* on the ventral surface of the brain.

The frontal lobe forms a distinct *gyrus rectus* medial to the olfactory stalk and a number of *orbital gyri* lateral to it.

The temporal lobe forms the *fusiform gyrus* on the ventral surface of the hemisphere; the gyrus extends from the *inferior temporal fissure* laterally to the *collateral fissure* medially. The latter separates temporal neocortex from the rhinencephalic cortex of the hippocampal gyrus. The *hippocampal gyrus* and its anteromedial extension, the *uncus*, are sometimes considered part of the temporal lobe.

The cerebral hemispheres contain large *lateral ventricles* which communicate with the third ventricle at the *interventricular foramen* (see Figures 2.66 and 2.67). The *anterior horns* of the lateral ventricle extend rostrally into the frontal lobes. The *main body of the ventricle* is located directly beneath the corpus callosum. The *posterior horn* of the lateral ventricle extends posteriorly into the occipital lobe, and the *inferior horn* curves dorsalward and forward into the medial aspect of the temporal lobe. The caudate nucleus accompanies almost the entire length of the lateral ventricle. Capillary plexuses (the *chorioid plexus*) of modified ependymal cells project into the medial and posterior portion of the lateral ventricle. These plexuses are composed of secretory cells which form cerebrospinal fluid from venous blood.

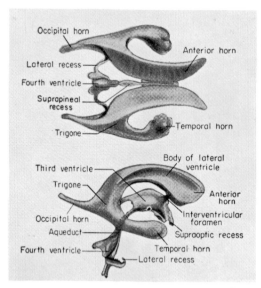

Fig. 2.66   Casts of the ventricular system. (From Peele, 1961.)

A cross-sectional view shows that the cerebral hemispheres contain a thin, gray outer layer of cells, the *cortex* (or rind) of the hemispheres, and a thicker, white inner layer of fibers. These fibers make up the many pathways which interconnect all portions of the hemispheres.

The Fiber System of the Cerebral Hemispheres

There are three major classes of cerebral fiber connections, *projection* fibers, *commissural* fibers, and *association* fibers.

The *projection fibers* originate in the cerebral hemispheres and project to subcortical portions of the brain. Some of these projections follow a diffuse course to lower centers, but most join major efferent fiber systems from the hemispheres. Some of the corticostriate and corticotegmental projections are good examples of a diffuse discharge system from the cortex. The internal and external capsule and fornix are the major specific fiber bundles which originate in the cerebral hemispheres.

The *internal capsule* projects to lower aspects of the brain along the medial border of the lenticular nucleus. It is bordered medially by the caudate nucleus and the dorsal thalamus. It carries corticotectal, corticotegmental, corticorubral, corticobulbar, and corticospinal fibers. Projection fibers that enter the internal capsule must interdigitate with the transverse fibers of the corpus callosum before forming the solid sheet of fibers which make up the capsule. They do so in distinct bundles which appear to radiate out to the cortex. This distinctive formation is called the *corona radiata*.

The *external capsule* is a sheet of fibers which

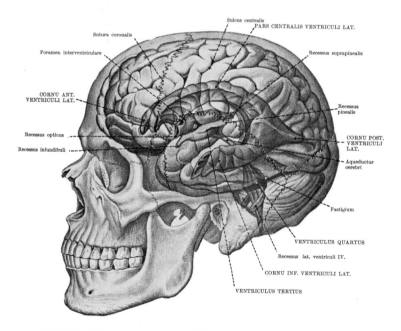

Fig. 2.67   The ventricular system. (From Kiss and Szentágothai, 1964.)

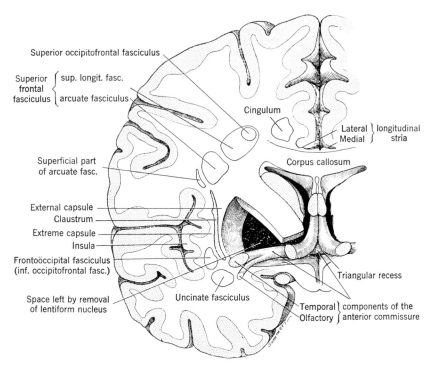

Fig. 2.68 The major long association fiber systems of the cerebral hemisphere. (From Mettler, 1948.)

collect from the corona radiata and project along the lateral border of the putamen. Some of these fibers terminate in the striatum; other fibers join pallidofugal efferents and form the lenticular fasciculus which projects to the midbrain tegmentum.

The *commissural fibers* interconnect the two hemispheres. The major commissural system is the *corpus callosum* which forms the roof of the anterior horn and the body of the lateral ventricle. The corpus callosum interconnects essentially all aspects of the cerebral hemispheres. A smaller fiber bundle, the *anterior commissure,* traverses the midline just anterior and dorsal to the preoptic area. It interrelates the olfactory bulb and nucleus, anterior perforated space, prepyriform cortex, hippocampus, amygdala, and temporal neocortex with the corresponding structures in the contralateral hemisphere (see Figure 2.68). The *hippocampal commissure* crosses the hemispheres just beneath the splenium of the corpus callosum. It originates from the hippocampus and the hippocampal gyrus and discharges either to the corresponding structures in the contralateral hemisphere or via the fornix system to contralateral portions

of the hypothalamus and the midbrain.

All parts of a cerebral hemisphere are extensively interconnected via long or short *association fibers.* The short association fibers may begin and terminate in the cortex without entering the white matter of the hemispheres; or they may pass through the white matter for some distance before re-entering the cellular layers of the cortex in the same hemisphere. The short association fibers are often poorly myelinated and exist in such profusion that no pattern of interconnections has yet been determined.

The long association fibers, on the other hand, form relatively discrete bundles or tracts which interconnect specific areas of the hemispheres. The *cingulum* overlies the corpus callosum near the medial surface of the hemispheres. It extends from the parolfactory area of Broca anteriorly to the hippocampal gyrus medially and posteriorly. Some of its components run the entire length of the cingulum, and others enter and terminate during its course. The *uncinate fasciculus* connects the hippocampal gyri, temporal neocortex, and amygdaloid area with the frontal cortex. The *inferior* and *superior occipitofrontal fasciculi* carry fibers which interconnect the occipital and temporal cortex with the frontal lobe and island of Reil. The *inferior longitudinal fasciculus* interconnects the occipital lobe with the cortex of the temporal and parietal lobes and the hippocampal gyrus. The *superior longitudinal fasciculus* interconnects the dorsomedial aspects of the frontal, parietal, and occipital lobes. Other association bundles include (1) the *orbitofrontal bundles* which interconnect ventral and dorsal portions of the frontal lobe; and (2) the *extreme capsule*, which runs along the ventral surface of the island of Reil, and appears to carry fibers which interconnect various portions of the deep layer of cortical matter (see Figures 2.69 and 2.70).

The Cortex of the Cerebral Hemispheres

About two-thirds of the outer cellular layers of the hemispheres which make up the cortex of the hemispheres are buried within sulci and fissures. In man, the average thickness of the cortex is approximately 2.5 millimeters, and the weight of the cellular layers makes up about one-third of the total weight of the hemispheres. The cortices of both hemispheres contain somewhere around 10 to 15 billion cells.

On the basis of cytoarchitectonic and phylogenetic considerations, three types of cortical tissues are commonly distinguished. The phylogenetically oldest and structurally simplest (three-layer) cortex is called *paleopallium* or *allocortex*. The youngest and most complex (six-layer) cortex is called *neopallium, neocortex,* or *isocortex.* A transitional type, which may contain four to five layers of cells, is called *archipallium* or *juxtallocortex.*

The Neocortex

The neocortex makes up essentially all the dorsal and lateral aspects of the cerebral hemispheres and extends into the ventral surface. It always contains six distinct layers of cells which give it a laminated appearance.

On the basis of cellular constituents (see Figure 2.71), the following six cortical layers can be distinguished. (1) An outer, sparsely populated layer is composed primarily of plexuses formed by the apical dendrites and collaterals from cells in lower layers. (2) A second layer contains primarily small pyramidal and some granular cells which entend dendrites into the first layer and project axons to most lower layers. (3) A

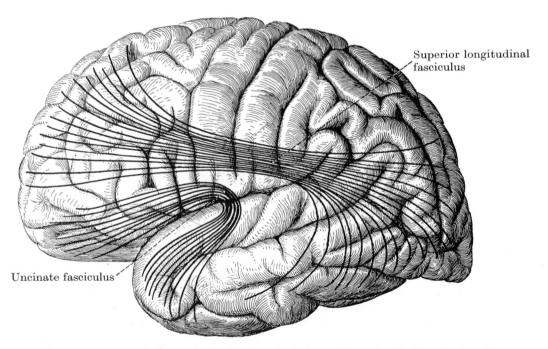

Superior longitudinal fasciculus

Uncinate fasciculus

Fig. 2.69 The superior longitudinal and uncinate fasciculi, superimposed on the lateral surface of the cerebral hemisphere. (From Sobotta, 1963.)

Cingulum   Arcuate fibers (cerebral)

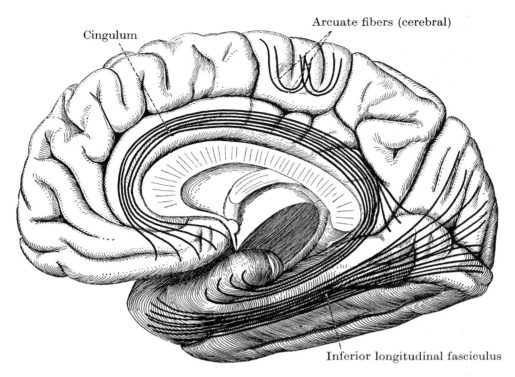

Inferior longitudinal fasciculus

Fig. 2.70   The cingulum, the arcuate fibers, and the inferior longitudinal fasciculus, superimposed on the medial surface of the cerebral hemispheres. (From Sobotta, 1963.)

very thick third layer is composed of large pyramidal cells which receive terminal connections from specific afferent fiber systems and project axons to most other cortical layers as well as the white matter of the hemispheres for distribution to other areas of the cortex. (4) The outer segment of the fourth layer contains primarily star pyramids which project dendritic processes vertically to the outermost layer of the cortex and horizontally within the fourth layer itself. The inner segment of the fourth layer contains primarily small star cells whose dendrites typically terminate within the fourth layer. (5) The fifth cortical layer contains pyramidal cells of various sizes which project long axons into the white matter. These may terminate within the cerebral hemispheres or project caudally as part of the corticofugal fiber systems. (6) The innermost layer of the neocortex contains primarily spindle cells which project dendrites into the fourth and fifth layers. Axons from these cells form the long and short association fibers of the white matter.

Specific afferents from subcortical sources form a plexus (*the outer stripe of Baillarger*) in the fourth cortical layer and some project to the third layer. Cells of layers 5 and 6 project apical dendrites into the higher layers for direct as well as indirect contact with these afferents. Cells of layers 1 and 2 do not synapse with specific afferents. The nonspecific thalamic projection fibers terminate primarily on neurons of the sixth cortical layer.

On the basis of variations in the development and cell density of these cortical layers in different portions of the hemispheres, several types of neocortical tissue have been described. Various maps of the neocortical mantle have been constructed on the basis of these cytoarchitectonic considerations. The most commonly used system (and the one which will be used in this discussion) is that proposed by Brodmann over 50 years ago. It contains 53 numbered subdivisions (see Figure 2.72). More recently, attempts have been made to use a functionally oriented mapping system based on thalamocortical projections (see Figure 2.73).

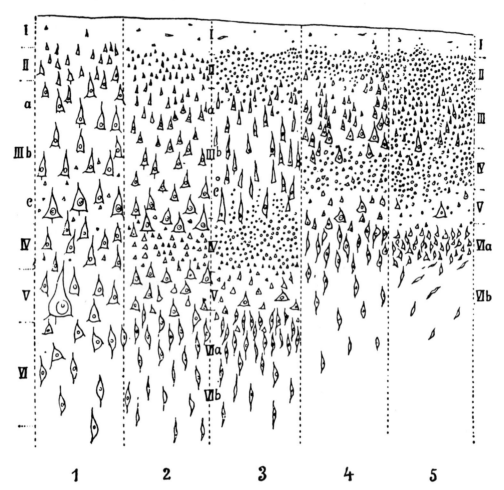

Fig. 2.71 The five fundamental structural types of cerebral cortex: 1, agranular; 2, frontal; 3, parietal; 4, polar; 5, granular. (From Peele, 1961, after Economo, 1929.)

The frontal lobe. The frontal lobe includes the primary and secondary motor areas of the cortex, and a large expanse of cortical matter which has been called the "association" area for want of more detailed knowledge of its functions (see Figure 2.74).

The *primary motor area* (Brodmann area 4) occupies most of the precentral gyrus. Anteriorly, it is bounded by a "suppressor" area (area 4s). Layer 5 of the motor area contains many giant pyramidal cells of Betz which give rise to many of the long, myelinated fibers of the corticobulbar and corticospinal tracts. Other fibers of the pyramidal motor system arise from smaller pyramidal cells located in the primary motor area as well as areas 6 and 8 of the frontal lobe and the sensory-motor areas of the postcentral gyrus

(areas 3, 2, and 1 of Brodmann). Direct stimulation of area 4 has shown a specific topographic pattern of innervation (see Figure 2.75).

Other pathways arise from the primary motor area of the frontal lobe. Most project to motor centers of the brainstem and spinal cord and form part of the extrapyramidal motor system (see Figure 2.76). The axons of these tracts arise primarily in the fifth and sixth layers of the precentral gyrus and pass to the caudate, putamen, globus pallidus, thalamus, red nucleus, substantia nigra, and subthalamus.

The precentral gyrus receives afferents from areas 3, 2, 1, 5, 21, and 22 of the temporal lobe and areas 6, 8, 9, and 10 of the frontal lobe.

Area 4 projects association fibers to areas 1, 5, and 7 of the parietal lobe, to the secondary motor

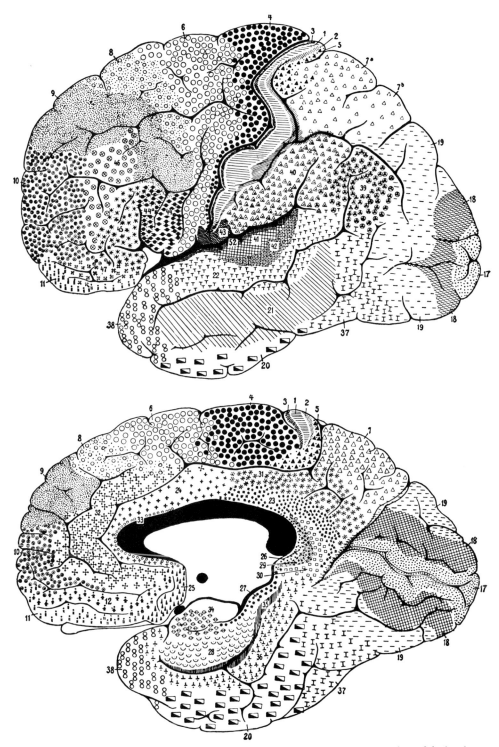

Fig. 2.72 Cytoarchitectural maps of the human cerebral cortex. *Top*, convex surface of the hemisphere; *bottom*, medial surface. (From Peele, 1954, after Brodmann, 1914.)

121

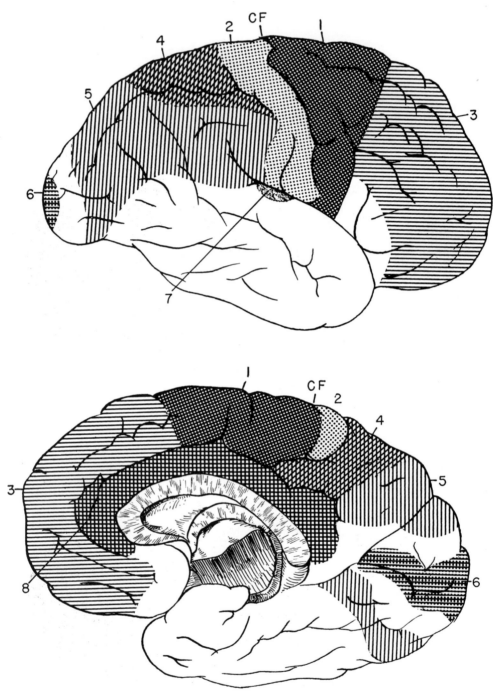

Fig. 2.73 Divisions of the human cerebral cortex according to thalamocortical projections. CF, central fissure. *Top*, lateral surface; *bottom*, medial hemispheric surface. 1, central region, with projections from anterior and lateral ventral nuclei; 2, central region, with projections from posterior ventral nuclei; 3, frontal region, fibers from the dorsomedial nucleus; 4, parieto-temporo-occipital region, with fibers from the lateral dorsal and lateral posterior nuclei; 5, parieto-temporo-occipital region, with fibers from the pulvinar; 6, an occipital region receiving fibers from the lateral geniculate; 7, a supratemporal region, with fibers from the medial geniculate; 8, a limbic region, with fibers from the anterior nuclei. (From Peele, 1961.)

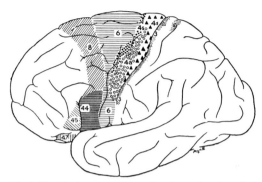

Fig. 2.74 The human precentral and associated cortical areas on the lateral hemispheric surface. (From Peele, 1961.)

area at the foot of the central fissure, and to areas 4 and 6 of the frontal lobe.

Stimulation of the anterior portion of the precentral gyrus (area 4s) produces a general relaxation of muscular tension and terminates spontaneous activity. This "suppressor" effect is independent of direct connections between areas 4 and 4s; it seems to be mediated by subcortical projections which connect area 4s with the caudate, globus pallidus, nucleus ventralis anterior of the thalamus, and primary motor cortex.

A secondary sensory-motor area which appears to lack specific somatotopic organization of its projections has been demonstrated at the base of the precentral and postcentral gyri.

The frontal cortex immediately anterior to areas 4 and 4s is also related to the motor system. The posterior portion of area 6 contributes to the pyramidal and extrapyramidal fiber system. Stimulation of this area typically gives rise to gross limb movements. The more anterior portions of area 6 and the adjacent area 8 project largely to the basal ganglia and bulbar motor nuclei. Stimulation of these areas often results in movements of the head or eyes.

Corticobulbar efferents also arise from area 44 located ventrally to area 8. The premotor areas 6 and 8 are reciprocally connected to the primary motor area of the precentral gyrus as well as to portions of the cingulate gyrus and the parietal lobe. These areas project afferents to the putamen, globus pallidus, red nucleus, and midbrain via corticostriate and corticorubral pathways and fibers which join the ansa lenticularis.

The frontal cortex anterior to areas 6, 8, and 44 is commonly treated together as the *prefrontal* cortex. This portion includes Brodmann areas 9,

10, 11, and 12 and constitutes the "association" areas.

The prefrontal cortex receives and projects many of the major long association bundles which interconnect the various segments of each hemisphere. There is thus ample opportunity for the prefrontal cortex to interact with essentially all other portions of the cortex, and this is one of the reasons for the designation of this area as "association" cortex.

Areas 9 and 10 and the orbitofrontal surface of the prefrontal cortex also receive very prominent thalamocortical projections from the dorsomedial nuclei. Physiological evidence exists for a multisynaptic connection between the intralaminar and midline nuclei of the thalamus and the prefrontal cortex.

Efferent connections to the motor areas, the lenticular nucleus, and various thalamic nuclei have been described. Projections from areas 9 and 10 to the dorsomedial thalamus play an important role in a corticohypothalamic pathway which descends into the hypothalamus via periventricular fibers.

The functional role of the prefrontal areas is far from clear. Electrical stimulation of some areas of the frontal lobe produces changes in various autonomic functions (such as gastric motility and blood pressure). Destruction of some aspects of the prefrontal cortex has been reported to reduce "emotionality" or general affective

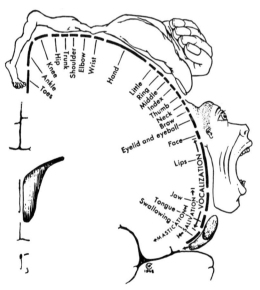

Fig. 2.75 The localization pattern on the human motor cortex. (From Penfield and Rasmussen, 1950.)

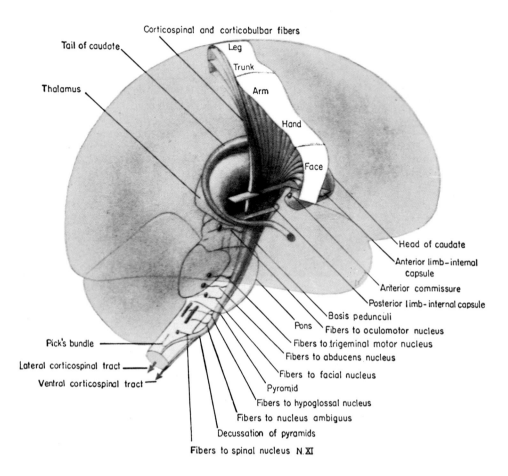

Corticospinal and corticobulbar fibers
Tail of caudate
Leg
Trunk
Arm
Thalamus
Hand
Face
Head of caudate
Anterior limb–internal capsule
Anterior commissure
Posterior limb–internal capsule
Basis pedunculi
Pons
Fibers to oculomotor nucleus
Fibers to trigeminal motor nucleus
Fibers to abducens nucleus
Pick's bundle
Fibers to facial nucleus
Lateral corticospinal tract
Pyramid
Ventral corticospinal tract
Fibers to hypoglossal nucleus
Fibers to nucleus ambiguus
Decussation of pyramids
Fibers to spinal nucleus N. XI

Fig. 2.76 The course of corticospinal and corticobulbar fibers. The lenticular nucleus has been removed. The "leg" area continues on the medial hemispheric surface. The finer divisions of these major areas are not shown for purposes of simplification. The "wavy" contour of the corticobulbar fibers passing to cranial nerve motor nuclei denotes decussation. (From Peele, 1961.)

reactions to sensory input. (This fact spurred the clinical use of frontal lobotomy in cases of severe mental illness.) Such manipulation also tends to reduce man's intellectual abilities, and the use of this technique in hospitals was gradually eliminated as a result of this realization. The affective response to pain stimuli also seems to be greatly reduced, and frontal lesions have been made in patients suffering from intractable pain.

The parietal lobe. The parietal lobe contains the primary somatic sensory projection areas (Brodmann areas 1, 2, and 3) and the somatosensory association cortex of areas 5 and 7. In man and higher primates it also includes areas 39 and 40 of the angular and supramarginal gyri which are related to speech. Area 19 is functionally re-

lated to the occipital cortex and projects into the posteroventral corner of the parietal lobe (as well as the posterodorsal corner of the temporal lobe).

The somesthetic cortex of areas 3, 2, and 1 receives specific sensory projections from the posterolateral ventral nuclei of the thalamus; these nuclei relay somatosensory impulses from the spinothalamic, medial lemniscal, and trigeminolemniscal fiber systems. The somatotopic organization of impulses in these fiber systems is reflected in a distinct topographic organization of the somatosensory projections on the postcentral gyrus (areas 3, 2, and 1) (see Figure 2.77).

This sensory representation of the contralateral body surface largely coincides with the pattern of motor projections on the precentral gyrus. Moreover, there is some overlap between the

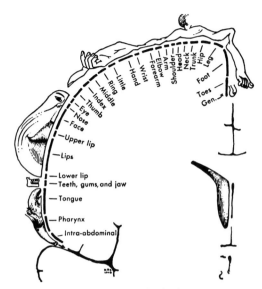

Fig. 2.77 A sensory homunculus laid upon a cross section of the hemisphere and drawn somewhat in proportion to the extent of sensory cortex devoted to its component parts. The length of the black lines within the cortex surface more accurately indicates the comparative extent of each representation. (From Peele, 1961, after Penfield and Rasmussen, 1950.)

sensory and the motor systems, as shown in Figure 2.78.

The most posterior portion of the somatosensory projections has been called area 2s. Stimulation of this region reduces the activity in areas 3, 2, and 1. Area 2s is therefore often classed as a "suppressor" area. Like most other suppressor areas, it is connected with the caudate nucleus.

A second sensory area, which is coexistent with the secondary motor area and lacks topographic organization, has been demonstrated near the base of the central fissure.

The somatosensory projection areas are closely related to the adjacent "association" areas of the parietal lobe (areas 5 and 7), the occipital and frontal lobe, and the cingulate gyrus and hippocampus. They project to the red nuclei of the brainstem, the posteroventral nucleus of the thalamus, and the motor nuclei and ventral horn cells of the brainstem and spinal cord. They also contribute to the extrapyramidal motor system and project diffusely to the basal ganglia and motor nuclei of the midbrain.

Areas 5 and 7 of the superior parietal lobe, the somatosensory association areas, are reciprocally connected to the lateral dorsal and lateral posterior

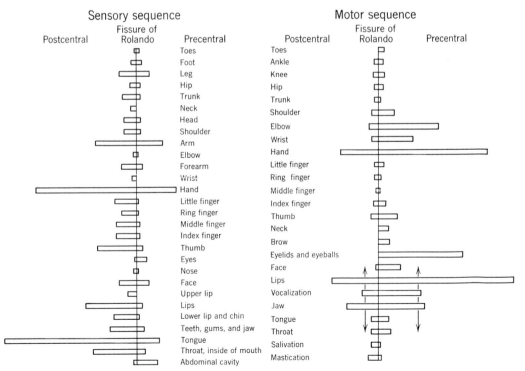

Fig. 2.78 Motor and sensory sequences in the human pre- and postcentral gyrus. (From Penfield and Boldrey, 1937.)

nuclei of the thalamus. Some pyramidal and extrapyramidal components of the motor system originate in this portion of the parietal cortex. The somatosensory association areas are profusely interconnected with the primary somatosensory projection areas, the visual cortex, and parts of the cingulate gyrus.

Area 19 is located at the junction of the temporal, parietal, and occipital lobes. It is closely related, anatomically, to the adjacent visual association areas (area 18); it represents a motor center which appears to be specifically concerned with the control of vertical or oblique eye movements. This control is exercised via direct corticotectal pathways. The posterior components of area 19 may also serve more general visual association functions.

Areas 39 and 40 can be distinguished only in primates and man and have been described as parietal association areas. Lesions in the angular gyrus (area 39) produce marked speech disturbances in man. Damage to the supramarginal gyrus (area 40) causes a related impairment in man's ability to understand spoken words.

The occipital lobe. The occipital lobe contains the primary visual projection area (area 17) and the visual association area (area 18) as well as the posterior portion of area 19 just described (see Figure 2.79).

The geniculocalcarine projections terminate in a specific pattern in the *striate* cortex of the occipital lobe. (The name striate cortex derives from the fact that Baillarger's stripe is particularly well developed in this part of the brain because the visual radiations course through it.) Macular projections terminate most caudally in the calcarine fissure, followed by paramacular and peripheral projections progressively more anterior.

Area 17, the striate cortex, projects to the visual association areas (area 18) and may contribute some fibers to area 19. It does not receive many fibers from the major intrahemispheric association bundles.

The *parastriate* cortex, which surrounds area 17 and extends anteriorly to area 19 and the border of the occipital lobe, has been called the visual association area. It does not have a marked stripe

Parieto-occipital fissure

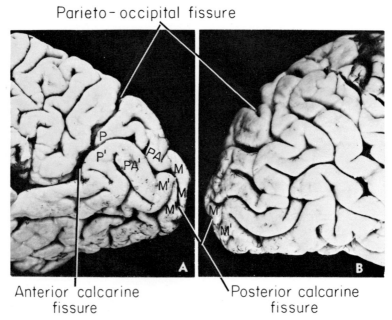

Anterior calcarine fissure

Posterior calcarine fissure

Fig. 2.79   Occipital region of the human right cerebral hemisphere from A, the medial surface; B, the lateral surface. The letters indicate the projection of the retina on the superior and inferior lips of the calcarine fissure. On the superior lip, M, PA, and P represent the projection of the macular, paramacular, and peripheral portions, respectively, of the contralateral superior nasal and the homolateral superior temporal retinal quadrants. On the inferior lip of the calcarine fissure, M', PA', and P' represent the projection of the macular, paramacular, and peripheral portions, respectively, of the contralateral inferior nasal and the homolateral inferior temporal retinal quadrants. (From Crosby et al., 1962.)

of Baillarger and does not receive direct fibers from the visual system. The major afferent input to area 18 arises from the primary visual projection area of the striate cortex. The parastriate cortex is reciprocally connected through the long association bundles of the hemispheres to the somatosensory, auditory, and frontal association areas as well as the primary somatosensory and motor areas which surround the central fissure. It projects corticotectal and corticomesencephalic fibers to the superior colliculi and pretectal nuclei for the control of eye movements.

The temporal lobe. The temporal lobe of the hemispheres is a relatively late embryologic and phylogentic development. It is divided into distinct areas by the superior, middle, and inferior temporal and the fusiform gyri. On the basis of cytoarchitectonic considerations, the temporal lobe has been further subdivided into a large number of areas which do not correspond to discrete *functional* units. We do not, in fact, know very much about the functional role of many of the temporal lobe areas. Most of it is therefore classified as an "association" area.

One of the exceptions to this rule is the relatively large *primary auditory projection* area which takes up areas 41 and 42 of the superior temporal gyrus and opercular surface. These areas are related to two obliquely transverse gyri known as the *anterior* and *posterior convolutions of Heschl*. The major portion of these areas is hidden in the lateral fissure and can be seen only when the walls of the operculum are opened. Area 52 on the insular side of area 41, and area 22 which surrounds area 42 on the lateral surface of the temporal lobe, serve as *auditory association areas* (see Figure 2.80).

Auditory stimuli are tonotopically projected to at least two distinct portions of the temporal lobe in many animals. In the cat, for instance, the basal coils of the cochlea are represented in the rostral portion of auditory area I and the apical portion is projected to more caudal sections of the primary auditory area. This pattern is exactly reversed in auditory area II which is located slightly ventral to the first one (see Figure 2.80). Additional representations of auditory stimuli in the cat have been located in the *posterior ectosylvian gyrus* (EP) which is located immediately posterior to the primary auditory projection areas.

The medial geniculate body projects fibers to the auditory cortex of the temporal lobe (auditory areas I and II as well as the ectosylvian gyrus) via the auditory radiations which pass through the

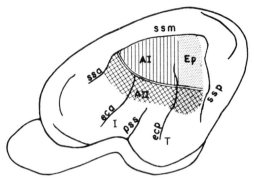

Fig. 2.80 The primary (AI, auditory I) and secondary (AII, auditory II) auditory areas and the posterior ectosylvian area (Ep) of the cat: *eca* and *ecp* are the anterior and posterior ectosylvian sulci, respectively; *pss* is the pseudosylvian sulcus; *ssa, ssm,* and *ssp* are the anterior, middle, and posterior branches of the suprasylvian sulcus; I and T are the insular and temporal cortices. (From Rose and Woolsey, 1958. Copyright 1958 by the Regents of the University of Wisconsin. Reproduced with permission.)

sublenticular portion of the internal capsule. Fibers from the auditory areas pass over corticogeniculate and corticotectal tracts to the medial geniculate and inferior colliculus. The primary auditory projection areas also contribute association fibers to the surrounding areas of the parietal and temporal cortex, to the island of Reil, and to portions of the frontal lobe (particularly the frontal eye fields and area 4 of the precentral gyrus).

The auditory association areas are closely interconnected with primary auditory projection areas 41 and 42 and adjacent portions of the parietal, occipital, and temporal cortex. In man, these areas serve interpretative functions with respect to auditory stimuli. Damage to area 22 produces an inability to understand or interpret sounds without apparent primary sensory impairment. Stimulation of area 22 yields movements of the extremities and the head, presumably via connections between the temporal cortex and the basal ganglia and more direct corticotectal fibers. Area 52 is anatomically closely related to the primary auditory areas, but its functional role in audition has not yet been clarified, largely because of its secluded location inside the lateral fissure.

The general "association" areas of the temporal lobe are closely interrelated via short association fibers and project extensively into the inferior fronto-occipital and inferior longitudinal fasciculi. Through these and other pathways, the temporal lobe is profusely interconnected with the occipital, parietal, and frontal association areas, as well as the primary sensory projection areas. The opercular aspects of the temporal lobe are closely related to the cortex of the island of Reil and the inferior frontal regions.

The temporal lobe projects efferents into the pyramidal and extrapyramidal motor system, in part through corticostriate connections and corticotegmental fascicles. It also projects to the pulvinar and ventral nuclei of the thalamus. Corticotectal and corticopontine projections have been described in some species.

Electrical stimulation of many temporal lobe foci produces movements of the body or head. A discrete somatotopic organization of this motor representation has been described for some species. Several autonomic functions (respiratory arrest, changes in blood pressure, etc.) are also affected by electrical stimulation of some portions of the temporal lobe.

Lesions or tumor growth in the temporal lobe of man most frequently cause "associative" disturbances such as visual or auditory aphasias and agnosias. The rostral portion of the temporal lobe, including the temporal pole, may be related to emotional and motivational mechanisms. Large lesions in this part of the brain produce placidity, hypersexuality, and lowered emotional reactivity.

The island of Reil. The island of Reil is separated from the surrounding *opercular* cortex of the frontal, parietal, and temporal operculum by the *limiting* or *central fissure*. It is totally buried in the fold of the lateral fissure and can be visualized only when the temporal lobe is retracted. The island is divided into a small *posteroinferior* and a large *anterosuperior region* by the *central fissure*. These can be further subdivided into a number of regions on the basis of smaller sulci and gyri (see Figure 2.81).

Because of the island's secluded location, we know relatively little about the relationship of this portion of the cortex to the rest of the brain. It appears to be interconnected with the surrounding opercula of the frontal, parietal, and temporal lobes and may project some fibers through the claustrum to the putamen.

Some parts of the island appear to be definitely related to specific motor projections which, in some species, may represent a secondary motor

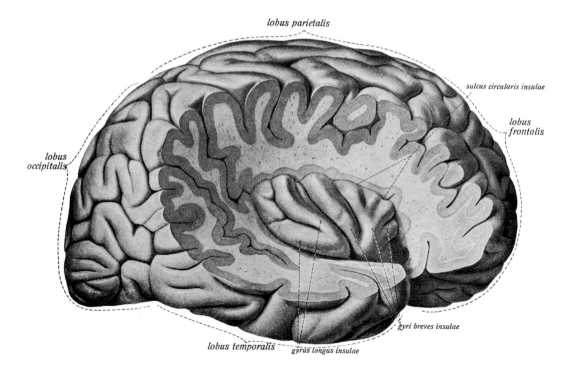

Fig. 2.81 Lateral surface of the human brain. Part of the cortex has been removed to show the location of the island of Reil. (From Sobotta, 1963.)

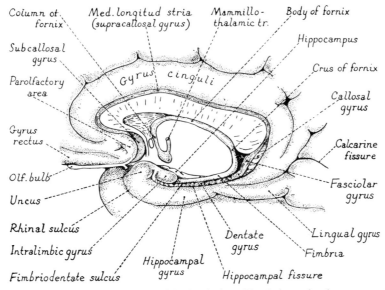

Fig. 2.82 Portion of the medial surface of the hemisphere. The thalamus has been removed and the hippocampal gyrus pulled downward to expose the structures related to the hippocampal fissure. (From Truex, 1959.)

area. This projection begins ventral to the primary motor area of the precentral gyrus and continues ventrally into the insular cortex. Visceral sensory representations (particularly from the gastric tract) have been described in man, and a number of viscermotor responses (respiratory arrest, changes in blood pessure, salivation, and piloerection) have been observed following electrical stimulation of the insular cortex in a variety of species.

The cortical representation of gustatory stimuli may be located in or very near the island of Reil. Some investigators have reported a specific projection of taste fibers to the island itself; others have localized the gustatory projections in the opercular cortex which surrounds the superior aspects of the island of Reil (i.e., the ventral-most portion of the postcentral gyrus of the parietal lobe).

The cingulate region. The cingulate region includes the neocortical aspects of the medial surface of the hemispheres (see Figure 2.82). Its principal constituents are the *cingulate gyrus* which is subdivided into areas 23, 24, 31, and 33; and the *isthmus* which includes areas 26, 29, and 30.

The anteromedial nucleus of the thalamus projects to the precallosal portion of the cingulate gyrus, the anterodorsal nucleus projects to the retrosplenial area, and the anteroventral nucleus

projects to the supracallosal region. Most of these projections carry impulses of hypothalamic origin.

One of the major association bundles of the hemispheres, the cingulum, is largely confined to the cingulate region and relates it to neighboring portions of the frontal, parietal, and occipital cortex.

Specific interconnections between area 24 and frontal areas 6, 8, 9, and 10 of the frontal lobe and between areas 11, 12, and 13 of the orbitofrontal cortex and the rostral cingulate gyrus have been described.

Efferents to subcortical areas have been traced from the cingulate region to (1) the midbrain tegmentum (via the internal and external capsule and lenticular fasciculus); (2) most areas of the hypothalamus (via diffuse projection pathways); (3) the anterior and dorsomedial nuclei of the thalamus (via diffuse pathways); (4) the caudate nucleus (via the subcallosal bundle); and (5) the globus pallidus (via the internal capsule).

Electrical stimulation of the cingulate region has produced specific patterns of movement of the head, neck, and body, suggesting a somatotopic organization of motor functions. These somato-motor movements can occur even after the primary motor cortex of the precentral gyrus has been destroyed. Stimulation of the cingulate region also affects such autonomic functions as blood pressure, respiration, cardiovascular responses, pilomotor and sudomotor reactions, and salivation. Lesions in the cingulate area typically produce low emotional reactivity, apathy, indifference to all sensory inputs, and akinesia.

The Rhinencephalon

Areas of the cerebrum that are constituted of allo- or juxtallocortex develop phylogenetically with the olfactory system. Although many of these areas are not directly related to olfactory function, all are commonly included in the rhinencephalon or "smell brain." On the basis of functional considerations, it has become customary to include the amygdaloid nuclei, cingulate gyrus, and even hypothalamus, in the rhinencephalon. This inclusion is inappropriate in the present context. A purely anatomical definition of the rhinencephalon includes the olfactory nerve, bulb, and stalk, the anterior olfactory nucleus, the anterior perforated area, the parolfactory area of Broca (septal area), the diagonal band of Broca and its nucleus, the hippocampus, the prepyriform cortex, and portions of the hippocampal gyrus which meet the criteria for juxtallocortex (see Figure 2.83).

The primary fibers of the olfactory system project very thin, poorly myelinated, and exceedingly slow-conducting axons through the *cribriform plate* to the anteroventral surface of the brain where the axons enter the *olfactory bulb* in a sector-like pattern. The bulb is attached to the cerebral hemispheres by a long and thin *olfactory stalk* which bifurcates into two *olfactory trigones* as it approaches the surface of the brain. The olfactory bulb and stalk are made up of primitive cortex which shows no lamination.

Toward the caudal end of the bulb, scattered cells of the *anterior olfactory nucleus* appear; these cells form an often discontinuous ring around the center portion of the olfactory bulb. In the embryo and the adult of some species, this center portion contains an olfactory ventricle which is connected to the lateral ventricle of the cerebral hemispheres. The anterior olfactory nucleus receives afferents only from olfactory fibers which course through the bulb; this nucleus projects only along the olfactory tract and serves presumably to "amplify" olfactory signals on the way to the central nervous system. The anterior olfactory nucleus continues into the olfactory trigones and becomes continuous with the prepyriform gray which surrounds the lateral olfactory tract.

The olfactory stalk divides into a *lateral* and a *medial olfactory tract* as the olfactory fibers enter the cerebral hemispheres. Immediately behind the olfactory trigone is the *anterior perforated substance* which receives terminal fibers from the medial and lateral olfactory tracts and discharges to the epithalamus and hypothalamus.

Immediately dorsal to the anterior perforated

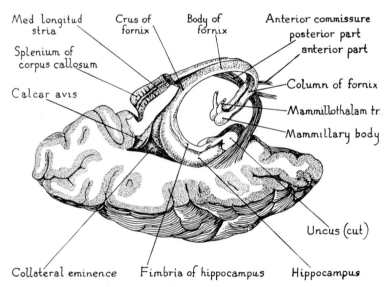

Fig. 2.83 Dissection of the right hemisphere showing inferior and posterior horns of the lateral ventricle, hippocampus, fornix, and anterior commissure. (From Truex and Carpenter, 1964.)

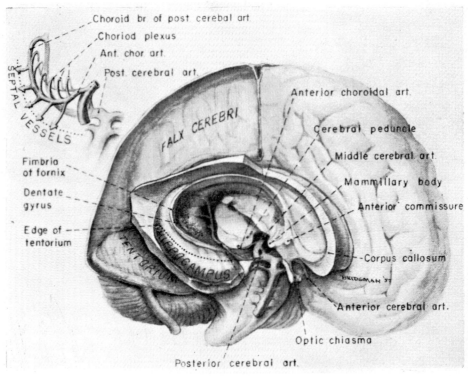

Fig. 2.84 A dissected human hippocampus. The hemisphere has been partially removed, the midbrain is cut across, and the third ventricle is exposed. The dotted line represents the edge of the tentorium which, as shown in the diagrammatic insert, crosses at right angles to the vessels supplying the hippocampus. (From Green, 1960.)

substance, on the medial surface of the hemispheres and extending upward to the subcallosal gyrus, is the *parolfactory area of Broca*, or *septal area*. It is divided into a *lateral septal area* which projects into the lateral ventricles and is continuous dorsally with the *septum pellucidum*, and a *medial* septal area which is dorsally continuous with the septum pellucidum and the *septohippocampal nucleus*. The septum pellucidum is a thin sheet of cells and fibers which connects the fornix and the corpus callosum. Both septal areas and the septum pellucidum receive fibers from the medial olfactory tract and are reciprocally related to the hypothalamus and hippocampus.

The *hippocampal formation* is a large and complex archipallial structure which takes up a considerable portion of the central section of each hemisphere (see Figures 2.84 and 2.85). It is continuous with the anterior olfactory nucleus through its anterior extension, the *lamina terminalis*. In the human brain the hippocampal formation extends from the septal region over the corpus callosum and ventrally into the rostral end of the temporal lobe. The *dorsal hippocampus*, which runs along the corpus callosum, is quite narrow. The *posteroventral hippocampus* broadens and forms the floor of the inferior horn of the lateral ventricle.

The hippocampal formation is separated from the adjacent allocortex by the *hippocampal* fissure. In the temporal region this fissure separates the hippocampal formation from the hippocampal gyrus; in the dorsal section it is continuous with the supracallosal sulcus which separates the dorsal portions of the hippocampus (the *supracallosal gyrus*) from the cingulate gyrus.

The hippocampus proper (*Ammon's horn*, or *cornu ammonis*) consists of three-layer cortex. It extends along the floor of the fourth ventricle and is covered by the ependymal lining of the ventricle and a sheet of myelinated fibers called the *alveus*. These fibers are continuous with the distinct fiber bundle called the *fimbria* which develops along

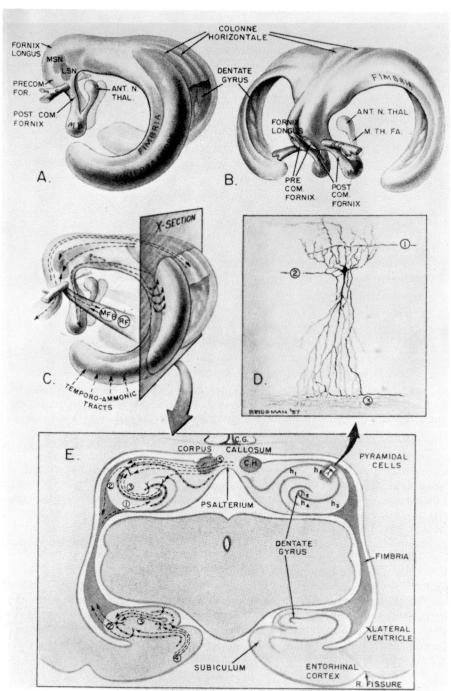

Fig. 2.85 Hippocampus of the cat. A, dissection from the left side. B, same from the front. C, same as A but showing some of the conduction paths; MFB, median forebrain bundle; RF, reticular formation. D, termination of afferents about a hippocampal pyramid: (1) from the alveus, (2) from dentate granule cells, and (3) from the temporoammonic tract. E, schematic cross section at the level shown in C, showing (1) afferents from the fimbria to the dentate gyrus, (2) axons of pyramidal cells, (3) dentatopyramidal fibers, (4) temporoammonic fibers, and (5) fibers from colonne horizontale and psalterium; h_1 to h_5 show the approximate locations of pyramidal neuron fields. The rudimentary supracallosal hippocampus is omitted for simplicity. (From Green, 1960.)

the medial border of the hippocampus. Most of the fibers in the fimbria do not join the body of the fornix; rather, they form the *postcommissural fornix* which projects around the anterior commissure into the hypothalamus and mammillary bodies or joins the *precommissural fornix* which enters the septum.

The fornices of the two hemispheres, as they join in the dorsal portions of the brain, are separated by two parallel bands of fibers called the *horizontal columns.* These bundles contain fibers which project to the hippocampus from the septum. The hippocampi of the two hemispheres are profusely interconnected through the *hippocampal commissure.*

The *dentate gyrus* or *fascia dentata* is a narrow band of cortex which is almost entirely surrounded by the hippocampus and is continuous with the hippocampus in the hippocampal fissure. Posteriorly, the three-layer cortex of the dentate gyrus is continuous with the supracallosal gyrus. Anteriorly, it continues along the inferior surface of the uncus and projects across the medial surface of the uncus as the *bands of Giacomini.*

The hippocampus is continuous ventromedially with the *presubiculum* which separates it from the *subicular area.* The dentate gyrus and subiculum are composed of rudimentary cortex with only a few cell layers. The subiculum is continuous with the presubicular area (area 27); this area is made up of five-layer cortex and extends to the hippocampal gyrus on the ventromedial surface of the brain (see Figure 2.86).

The *pyriform lobe* begins in the lumen of the island of Reil and extends into the folds of the lateral fissure as the *lateral olfactory gyrus;* this gyrus then extends laterally to the border of the anterior perforated substance. The lateral olfactory gyrus projects along the inner surface of the temporal lobe and becomes continuous posteriorly with the *hippocampal gyrus.* The rostral portion of the hippocampal gyrus is called the *uncus.* The hippocampal gyrus is separated from neocortical tissue by the rhinal fissure. The lateral olfactory gyrus, which extends to the rostral portion of the amygdaloid complex, is also called *prepyriform area.* As the lateral olfactory gyrus spreads over the amygdaloid nuclei, the area becomes known as the *periamygdaloid region.* The major portion of the anterior hippocampal gyrus is called the *entorhinal area.* This area marks the terminal portion of the pyriform lobe.

The fiber connections of the rhinencephalon

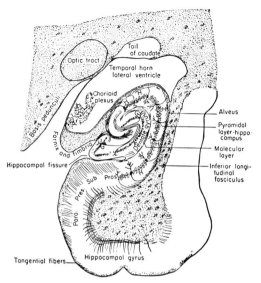

Fig. 2.86 Orientation of the hippocampus and dentate gyrus. G, granule cell of dentate gyrus; H, hippocampus; Para, parasubiculum; Pres, presubiculum; Pros, prosubiculum; Sub, subiculum. (From Peele, 1961.)

are highly complex and, as yet, incompletely understood (see Figure 2.87). The olfactory tract divides into medial and lateral striae as it enters the cerebral hemispheres. The medial olfactory stria projects to the septum pellucidum, the subcallosal gyrus, the septal area, the olfactory trigone, and the anterior hippocampus. The lateral olfactory stria projects to the prepyriform area, the anterior perforated space, and various nuclei of the corticomedial amygdala.

All areas of the brain which receive afferents from the medial olfactory stria project through the stria medullaris into the habenular complex. These areas also interconnect with the preoptic and hypothalamic areas through the *medial forebrain bundle* which originates, at least in part, in the septal area and terminates in the ventromedial area of the hypothalamus.

The terminal structures of the lateral olfactory stria (the amygdala and prepyriform area) also project to the hypothalamus via the *stria terminalis* and more diffuse amygdalohypothalamic fiber systems. They project to the habenular complex via *amygdalohabenular fascicles.* The corticomedial nuclei of the amygdala also discharge to the basolateral region which is profusely interconnected with the hippocampal gyrus, and through it, with the lateral surface of the temporal lobe and the hippocampus proper. The hippo-

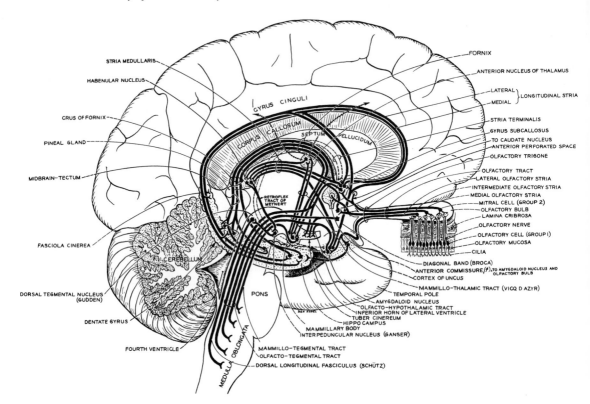

Fig. 2.87 The olfactory system, projected on the medial surface of the human brain. (From Rubinstein, 1953.)

campal gyrus is also reciprocally connected with the cingulate gyrus and entorhinal area. All along its course through the cerebral hemispheres, the hippocampus and related structures receive and project short association fibers into the surrounding neocortical mantle. Although the anatomical proof for these connections is not very strong, ample physiological evidence suggests that sensory impulses from all sensory modalities reach the hippocampus.

The principal efferent pathway from the hippocampus is the *fornix*. It arises from the hippocampus, the dentate and hippocampal gyri, and associated portions of the prosubiculum. Some fibers of the fornix enter the septal area, the nucleus of the diagonal band of Broca, the preoptic area, the habenula, and the rostral hypothalamic and subthalamic nuclei. The majority of the fibers, however, terminate in the homolateral medial mammillary nucleus. Precommissural components of the fornix cross the midline and terminate in septal, preoptic, and anterior hypothalamic nuclei. The fornix contains commissural

fibers which interrelate the fornices of the two hemispheres; these fibers cross the midline in the *commissure of the fornix* or *psalterium*.

The rhinencephalon of man and most higher mammals is only in part related to olfaction. Instead, most of its components, notably the septal nuclei, hippocampal formation, and functionally related areas, seem to be concerned with the regulation of complex associative and regulatory processes which are reflected in such pyschological functions as motivation, emotion, and perhaps memory. The effects of electrical stimulation and ablation of portions of the rhinencephalon are too complex to be summarized here. They will be treated in some detail in subsequent sections of the discussion.

THE CEREBELLUM

The cerebellum consists of a number of deep nuclei which are surrounded mainly by medullated fibers and extensively convoluted, multilayer cortex. The superior surface of the cerebellum is separated from the occipital lobe of the cerebrum by a double layer of dura called *tentorium cerebelli.* The ventral surface covers the pontine and upper bulbar portions of the brainstem. The cerebellum extends laterally beyond the limits of the brainstem into the cerebellar fossae of the calvarium.

On gross inspection, the cerebellum can be subdivided into a worm-like central portion called *vermis,* two *lateral lobes* or *hemispheres,* and two ventral projections from the posterior cerebellum called *flocculi* (see Figure 2.88). The vermis and flocculi are phylogenetically old and are collectively called *paleocerebellum.* The large lateral hemispheres consist of more recently developed tissue and are called *neocerebellum.*

The secondary subdivisions of the cerebellum have been made largely on the basis of prominent fissures and gyri rather than by functional units (see Figure 2.89). Three major sections are recognized.

1. The relatively small portion of the cerebellum which extends anteriorly from the *primary* or *preclival* fissure is divided by the *precentral* and *postcentral* fissures into three distinct sections. The medially situated vermis forms the *lingula, central,* and *culmen.* The cerebellar hemispheres are essentially absent at the anterior lingual area. They develop posterior to the precentral fissure and form an *anterior lobe.* This lobe is divided by the postcentral fissure into an anterior portion called *ala centralis* and a posterior section called *anterior crescentic* or *semilunar lobule.*

2. The *posterior lobe* makes up the main portion of the cerebellum. It is furrowed by a number of large fissures (the *postclival, great horizontal, postpyramidal,* and *prepyramidal* fissures) which divide it into five prominent gyri. The vermis forms (proceeding posteriorly from the primary fissure) (1) the *declivus,* (2) the *folium vermis,* (3) the *tuber,* (4) the *pyramis,* and (5) the *uvula.* The corresponding portions of the lateral hemispheres are (1) the *posterior semilunar lobule* (or *lobulus simplex* when the declivus is included), (2) the *posterior superior lobule* or *crus I,* (3) the *posterior*

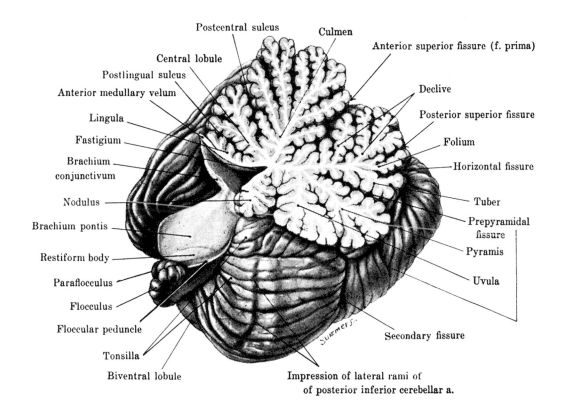

Fig. 2.88 Sagittal section through the cerebellum. (From Mettler, 1948.)

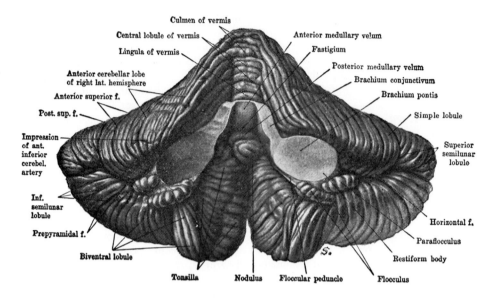

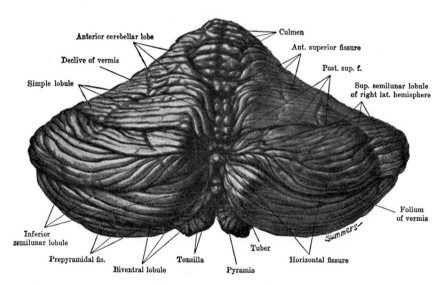

Fig. 2.89 The superior (top) and inferior (bottom) surfaces of the cerebellum. The anterior and posterior crescentic lobules are sometimes called the anterior and posterior semilunar lobules, and the posterior superior and the posterior inferior lobules are often termed the anterior and the posterior quadrangular lobules, respectively. (From Mettler, 1948.)

inferior lobule or *crus II,* (4) the *biventral lobule* or *dorsal paraflocculus,* and (5) the *tonsil* or *ventral paraflocculus.* The posterior portion of the posterior inferior lobule or crus II is sometimes called the *gracile* or *paramedian* lobule. The posterior tonsil or ventral paraflocculus forms a distinct ridge which is called the *accessory paraflocculus*

(see Figure 2.90).

3. The cerebellum posterior to the postnodular fissure consists of two parts. The most caudal portion of the vermis is called the *nodule.* From it project two distinct lobules called the *flocculus.* Together the nodule and flocculus constitute the *flocculonodular lobe.*

The cortical mantle of the cerebellum forms distinct parallel folds or *folia* which contain an inner core of medullated fibers surrounded by several discrete layers of cells. The inner *granular layer* contains *granule* cells which receive the terminal arborizations from *mossy fibers*. These fibers originate exclusively external to the cerebellum and represent the major afferent input to it. The granule cells project axons into the outer molecular layer of the cerebellar cortex. Here, the axons bifurcate and form fiber bundles which run parallel to the cortical surface. The granular layer also contains *Golgi* cells; these cells project short, profusely branching axons to the granule cells and extend their dendrites into the molecular layer of the cortex (see Figure 2.91).

The external *molecular layer* of the cerebellar cortex contains relatively few cells. Those present in this layer are largely *stellate* cells which project ascending as well as descending dendritic processes in a transverse direction to the folium. Stellate cells in the inferior parts of the molecular layer have profusely branching axons which form complicated nests or baskets around the *Purkinje* cells, located between the molecular and granular layers. The *basket* cells of the molecular layer receive afferents from *climbing* fibers which may carry information from intra- as well as extra-cerebellar sources.

The Purkinje cells are the major source of efferent projections from the cerebellar cortex to its deep nuclei. Their axons always emerge from the inferior end of the cell and project numerous collaterals to adjacent areas of the cortex. These recurrent collaterals form plexuses which terminate on Purkinje and Golgi cells. The dendritic processes of Purkinje cells always project into the molecular layer of the cortex, where they form distinct leaf-shaped plexuses.

Four nuclei are buried deep in the white matter of each side of the cerebellum. Starting medially, they are called the *fastigial, globose, emboliform,* and *dentate* nuclei. The dentate nucleus is highly convoluted and resembles the inferior olivary nucleus of the medulla. Its lateral aspects receive axons from Purkinje cells located in the neocerebellum, the paraflocculus, and the anterior semilunar lobule. The emboliform and globose nuclei are often collectively called the *nucleus interpositus*. They receive axons from Purkinje cells in the central lobule and culmen, the superior and inferior semilunar lobules, and the biventral

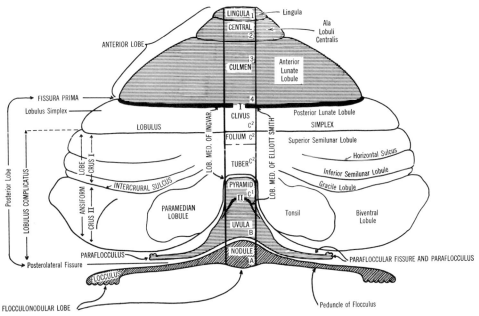

Fig. 2.90 Schematic representation of the cerebellum. The cross-hatched area is archicerebellum, the horizontally hatched areas are paleocerebellum, and the white area is neocerebellum. The terminology of comparative anatomy is given in capital letters. Older nomenclature, still in clinical use, is given in capital and lower-case lettering. (From Rubinstein, 1953.)

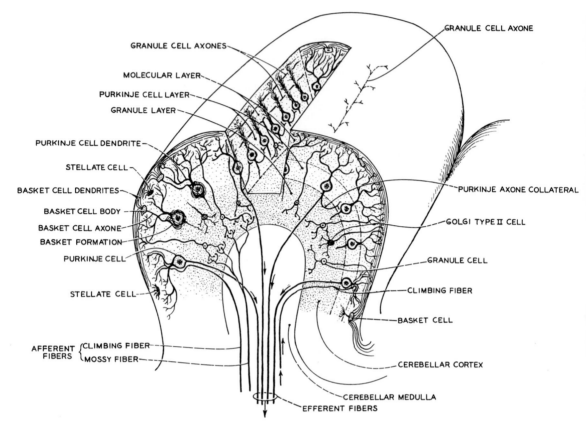

GRANULE CELL AXONES

MOLECULAR LAYER

PURKINJE CELL LAYER

GRANULE LAYER

PURKINJE CELL DENDRITE

STELLATE CELL

BASKET CELL DENDRITES

BASKET CELL BODY

BASKET CELL AXONE

BASKET FORMATION

PURKINJE CELL

STELLATE CELL

AFFERENT FIBERS { CLIMBING FIBER / MOSSY FIBER

GRANULE CELL AXONE

PURKINJE AXONE COLLATERAL

GOLGI TYPE II CELL

GRANULE CELL

CLIMBING FIBER

BASKET CELL

CEREBELLAR CORTEX

CEREBELLAR MEDULLA

EFFERENT FIBERS

Fig. 2.91   Diagram of a folium of the cerebellum. (From Rubinstein, 1953.)

lobule. The fastigial nuclei (also called *tectal* or *roof* nuclei) receive projections from the vermian part of the cerebellar cortex.

Aside from some projections from the flocculus, uvula, nodulus, and anterior lobule to the vestibular nuclei of the brainstem (via the *angular bundle* and brachium conjunctivum), the efferent projections from the cerebellum arise exclusively from these four nuclei. The dentate and interpositus nuclei project via the brachium conjunctivum to the contralateral red nucleus and lateroventral nuclei of the thalamus. This *dentatorubrothalamic pathway* then continues to the precentral gyrus of the cerebrum, and the circuit is completed via corticopontocerebellar projections. The fastigial nuclei project (1) an uncrossed *fastigiobulbar* pathway through the juxtarestiform body to the ipsilateral vestibular nuclei, dorsal reticular formation of the medulla, and cranial nerve motor nuclei; and (2) a crossed projection to the com-

plementary structures on the other side of the brainstem via the *uncinate fasciculus* (see Figure 2.92).

All afferent projections to the cerebellum must cross through the three cerebellar peduncles. The restiform body contains afferents from *vestibulo-cerebellar, olivocerebellar, dorsal spinocerebellar,* and *external arcuate* pathways. The brachium pontis carries largely *pontocerebellar* projections, and the brachium conjunctivum contains *ventral spinocerebellar, trigeminocerebellar,* and *tecto-cerebellar* tracts (see Figure 2.93).

The vestibulocerebellar projections originate in the vestibular nerve and nuclei of the brainstem and terminate in the homolateral flocculus, the homolateral half of the nodulus, uvula, and lingula, and directly in the fastigial nuclei. The dorsal spinocerebellar projections arise from Clark's column and course through the restiform body. The ventral spinocerebellar fibers arise

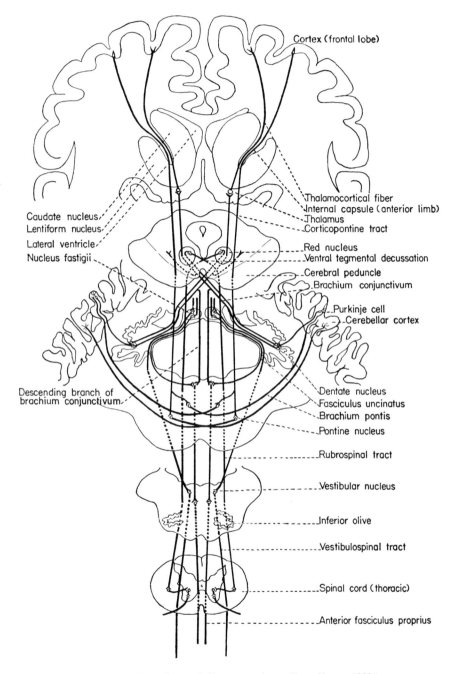

Cortex (frontal lobe)

Thalamocortical fiber
Internal capsule (anterior limb)
Thalamus
Corticopontine tract

Caudate nucleus
Lentiform nucleus

Lateral ventricle
Nucleus fastigii

Red nucleus
Ventral tegmental decussation
Cerebral peduncle
Brachium conjunctivum

Purkinje cell
Cerebellar cortex

Descending branch of
brachium conjunctivum

Dentate nucleus
Fasciculus uncinatus
Brachium pontis
Pontine nucleus

Rubrospinal tract

Vestibular nucleus

Inferior olive

Vestibulospinal tract

Spinal cord (thoracic)

Anterior fasciculus proprius

Fig. 2.92   The major cerebellar connections. (From Kuntz, 1950.)

139

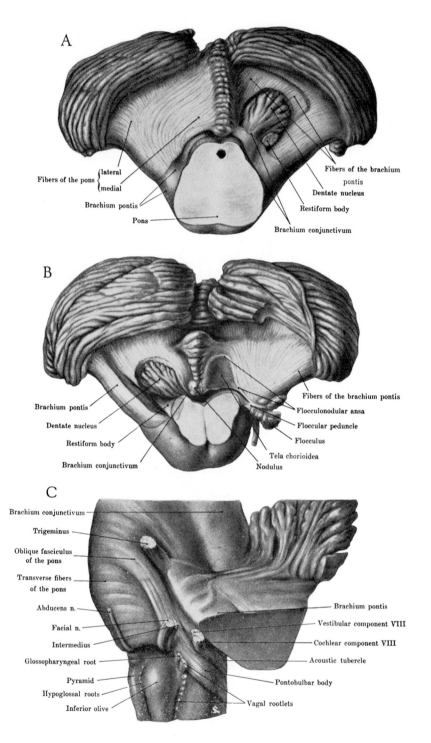

Fig. 2.93 A, superior surface of the cerebellum after exposure of the brachium pontis on the right and the brachium conjunctivum on the left. B, ventral view of the cerebellum after exposure of the restiform body and brachium pontis. C, lateral view of the cerebellum and brainstem after exposure of the pontobulbar body. (From Mettler, 1948.)

from the posterior gray of the spinal cord, cross the midline, and enter the cerebellum via the brachium conjunctivum. All spinocerebellar fibers terminate in the medial portion of the anterior lobe (central lobule and culmen) and the paramedian and simplex lobule of the posterior lobe. Reticulocerebellar fibers from the medulla enter the cerebellum via the restiform body and terminate in the same areas as the spinocerebellar projections. Olivocerebellar fibers arise from the inferior olive of the medulla and project via the restiform body to all portions of the cerebellum except the flocculus. A major portion of the cerebellar afferents consists of corticopontocerebellar fibers which arise primarily from the precentral

gyrus of the cortex (although all cerebral lobes have some projections to the cerebellum). All corticocerebellar fibers relay in ipsilateral pontine nuclei which project primarily via the brachium pontis into the lateral neocerebellum. Lesser projections to the vermian part of the posterior lobe and portions of the anterior lobe have been described (see Figure 2.94).

The white matter of the cerebellum contains a profusely interconnected system of long and short *association* fibers; these fibers permit projections between adjacent folia as well as between the vermian and hemispheric portions of the cerebellum. Extensive *corticonuclear* projections connect the cortical layers which receive almost all

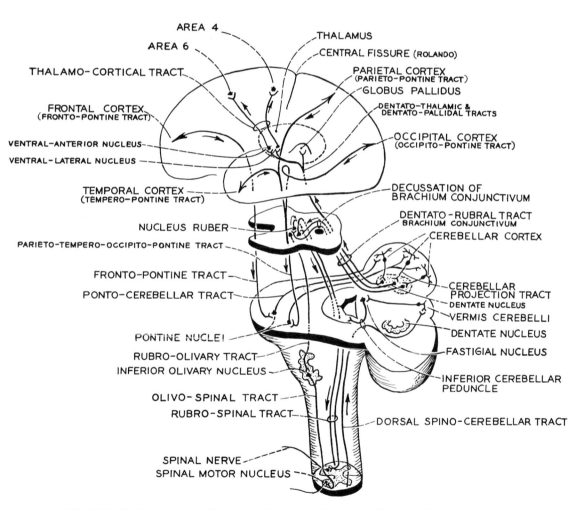

Fig. 2.94 Cerebropontocerebellar connections and efferent cerebellar projections to the thalamus, globus pallidus, red nucleus, inferior olivary nucleus, and spinal cord. (From Rubinstein, 1953.)

afferents to the cerebellum with the cerebellar nuclei which originate most efferent projections from the cerebellum. This corticonuclear projection tends to be organized so that the medially located vermian portion of the cortex projects to the medial (fastigial) nuclei; the paravermian portions of the hemispheres project to the nucleus interpositus, and the lateral aspects of the cerebellar cortex project to the dentate nuclei. These projections are typically uncrossed.

The cerebellum serves largely as a coordinating center for motor responses that are primarily reflexive or "automatic" in nature. Destruction of all or part of the cerebellum does not result in the total loss of a particular motor function. Instead, the general impairment of movement that occurs affects particularly the execution of complex movements. However, this impairment is also reflected in abnormal muscle tonus (hypotonia) and in a tendency to stumble and fall (ataxia).

Selective damage to the flocculonodular lobe results in a disturbance of equilibrium which is typically compensated after some time, presumably by bulbar vestibular mechanisms. Lesions in the neocerebellum cause atonia, tremor, and disorders of voluntary movement. Destruction of the paleocerebellar cortex produces an increase in extensor tone, lack of coordination, and "cerebellar fits." Lesions in the cerebellar nuclei result in deficits similar to those seen after damage to the cortical area that projects to the nucleus in question (see Figure 2.95).

The cerebellum receives extensive projections from all sensory systems, and it has been suggested that some portions of the cerebellum may serve as primitive sensory projection centers. Stimulation of tactile receptors results in a somatotopically organized pattern of projections on the cerebellar cortex ipsilateral to the locus of stimulation. A comparable and overlapping

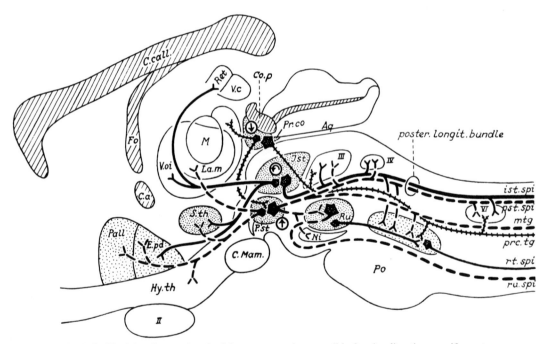

Fig. 2.95 Nuclei and tracts involved in posture and responsible for the direction-specific motor effects of mesodiencephalic stimulation. Rotation movements are regulated by the interstitial nucleus (*Ist*) and its fiber systems (———). Raising movements are regulated by the praestitial nucleus (*P.st*) and its fiber systems (— — —). This tonically active nucleus sends short fibers to the nucleus ruber magnocellularis (*Ru*) from which arises the rubrospinal tract (*ru.spi*). Lowering movements are regulated by the praecommissural nucleus (*Pr.co*) and its fiber systems (+++). The efferent fibers constitute the praecommissurotegmental tract. All descending fiber tracts of the direction-specific systems send collaterals to the nuclei of the ocular muscles (nerves III, IV, and VI) and the reticular formation. (From Jung and Hassler, 1960.)

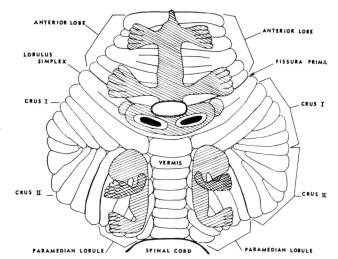

Fig. 2.96 The areas of projection of tactile impulses on the cerebellum of the cat. The anterior area on which the body plan is projected includes the lobulus simplex with the anterior lobe and is an ipsilateral projection. The posterior projection is bilateral, primarily in the paramedian lobules. It extends into crus I and crus II laterally and into pyramis medially. (From Snider, 1952.)

projection of proprioceptive impulses has been reported. Visual as well as auditory projections have been demonstrated in the lobulus simplex, the folium vermis, the tuber, the pyramis, and the paravermian portion of the posterior hemisphere (see Figures 2.96 and 2.97). Direct tectocerebellar and tectopontocerebellar pathways for this projection exist.

Electrical stimulation of the cerebellum produces specific motor effects which result in movements of the ipsilateral extremities and face. A somatotopic projection of motor functions in the anterior lobe has been demonstrated for the cat, dog, and monkey. The posterior aspects of the body are represented in the anterior portion of the anterior lobe; the more superior segments of the body are represented in more posterior parts of the anterior lobe (see Figure 2.98). A second somatotopic projection of motor functions in the posterior lobe has been described.

Stimulation of the cerebellar cortex may facilitate or inhibit movements which are elicited by stimulation of the cerebral cortex or by peripheral stimulation to reflex connections.

Stimulation of the cerebellum also produces specific autonomic responses. Excitation of the anterior lobe inhibits vasoconstrictor and respiratory mechanisms, and stimulation of the median lobule of the posterior lobe produces parasympathomimetic effects on pupillary responses.

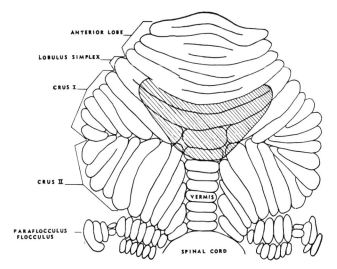

Fig. 2.97 The area of projection of auditory and visual impulses on the cerebellum of the cat as determined by click and photic stimulation. The two areas are co-extensive, and the combined audiovisual area lies mainly in the lobulus simplex, folium vermis, and tuber vermis but extends into crus I and crus II. (From Snider, 1952.)

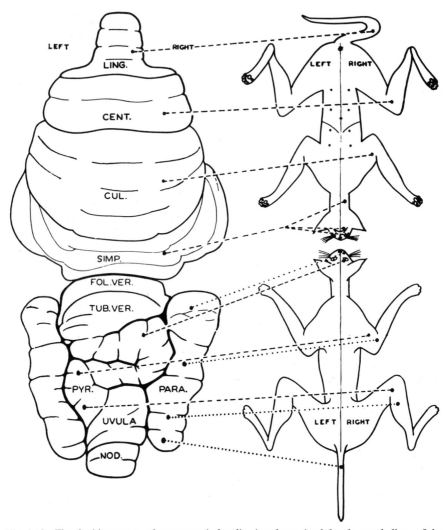

Fig. 2.98 The double pattern of somatotopic localization determined for the cerebellum of the cat by observation of overt movements elicited ipsilaterally (top) and bilaterally (bottom) by stimulation of the decerebrate animal. The lobules of the cerebellar vermis are labeled from the top to the bottom of the figure as follows: lingula, central, culmen, (lobulus) simplex, folium vermis, tuber vermis, pyramis, uvula, and nodule; the paraflocculus is labeled on the right side. (From Hampson et al., 1952.)

The blood supply of the cerebellum derives largely from the *anterior* and *posterior inferior cerebellar* arteries and the *superior cerebellar* artery. The anterior inferior cerebellar artery supplies the flocculus, the lateral hemispheric region of the inferior semilunar and biventral lobules, and the vermian portions of the folium, tuber, and pyramis. The posterior inferior cerebellar artery supplies the posterior and inferior cerebellum, including the posterior hemisphere, the uvula, the flocculonodular lobe, and the caudal portion of the cerebellar nuclei. The superior cerebellar artery supplies the anterior portion of the cerebellar nuclei as well as the brachium conjunctivum and some anterior lobe cortex. The superior aspects of the cerebellum drain into the *superior cerebellar* veins which empty into the straight, the transverse, or the superior petrosal sinuses. The ventral parts of the cerebellum drain into the inferior cerebellar artery which in turn empties into the *inferior petrosal sinus* and the *occipital sinus.*

THE PERIPHERAL NERVOUS SYSTEM

The brain and spinal cord communicate with the organism's environment via nerves which arise or terminate in the central nervous system and project to peripheral sensory receptors and effectors. Sensory receptors are distributed throughout the body. They translate changes in physical energy in the external or internal environment into neural impulses which can be used by the many integrative mechanisms of the central nervous system. The end product of this integration must, in turn, be transduced into mechanical energy by the peripheral effectors (muscles and glands) to provide an overt response to the environment. The peripheral nerves which connect the receptors and muscles to the central nervous system and to related cellular masses outside the brain and spinal cord make up the peripheral nervous system. It is customary to distinguish somatosensory, somatomotor, and autonomic components. The latter group contains both sensory and motor branches. A distinction is made between the spinal and cranial portions of the peripheral nervous system. Twelve pairs of cranial nerves originate largely from the lower portions of the brainstem, and 31 pairs of segmentally arranged spinal nerves project from the spinal cord.

THE SPINAL NERVES

The spinal nerves arise from intervertebral foramina and are composed of efferent and afferent fibers. Each spinal nerve arises from the cord by a *dorsal (afferent) root* and a *ventral (efferent) root*. The dorsal root contains the pseudobipolar cells of the afferent fibers. These cells project axons into the spinal cord and receive long "dendritic" processes from the peripheral sense organs. The cell body of the efferent cells is located in the ventral horn of the spinal cord. The ventral root contains only axons of these motor cells. The ventral and dorsal roots unite a short distance from the cord to form a common nerve trunk. This mixed spinal nerve divides again shortly after the confluence of the dorsal and ventral roots to form several distinct branches or *rami* as shown in Figure 2.99. (1) The *dorsal ramus* supplies the muscles and sensory endings of the back, (2) the *ventral ramus* supplies the ventral and lateral aspects of the trunk, (3) the *meningeal ramus* re-

turns to the intervertebral foramen and supplies the meninges and vertebral column, and (4) the *ramus communicans* arises from the thoracic and first two lumbar nerves and connects the spinal column to the sympathetic ganglia, which form a *paravertebral chain* along the thoracic and upper lumbar sections of the cord. The ramus communicans is composed of two distinct sections. The *white ramus communicans* contains myelinated sympathetic motor fibers and sensory fibers from the viscera; the *gray ramus communicans* contains poorly myelinated sympathetic fibers which arise from cells in the paravertebral ganglia and travel to the blood vessels and glands of the trunk and extremities. *Parasympathetic motor* nerves arise from the second, third, and fourth sacral spinal nerves in place of the ramus communicans. These fibers bypass the paravertebral ganglia and terminate in plexuses near the viscera to be innervated.

The dorsal and ventral rami divide to form deep and superficial nerves, which in turn branch repeatedly and eventually terminate on single receptors or effectors. The deep peripheral nerves contain somatomotor fibers to the striped musculature of the trunk, autonomic motor fibers to the blood vessels, and sensory (proprioceptive) fibers from receptors in the muscles, tendons, and joints. The superficial peripheral nerves contain primarily sensory fibers from receptors in the skin and autonomic motor fibers to blood vessels, hair cells, and glands.

Some of the spinal nerves take part in the formation of plexuses which give rise to mixed spinal nerves. These plexuses contain fibers from several anterior and posterior spinal roots and upset the segmental organization of the peripheral nerve

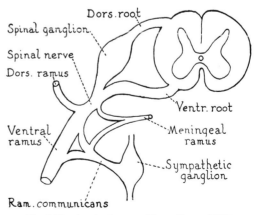

Fig. 2.99 A spinal nerve. (From Truex, 1959.)

supply. A *cervical plexus* is formed from parts of
the upper four cervical nerves, a *brachial plexus*
from the lower four cervical and upper thoracic
nerves, a *lumbar plexus* from the first three lumbar
nerves, and a *lumbosacral plexus* from the lower
lumbar and all sacral nerves. Each *myotome*
(muscle segment) is originally connected to a
specific pair of spinal roots. However, the myo-
tomes split, regroup, and migrate in the course of
embryological development and necessitate the
intermixing of spinal nerves.

Although the segmental projection of sensory
impulses is affected to some extent by the intermixing of spinal nerves, a clear pattern of innervation is retained. This is possible because a single
dermatome (the area of the skin that is supplied
by a single dorsal root) may be innervated by fibers
which travel with several peripheral nerves (see
Figures 2.100 and 2.101).

The neurilemmal sheath of peripheral nerve
fibers is surrounded by a sticky substance called
endoneurium. Several endoneurial tubes collect in

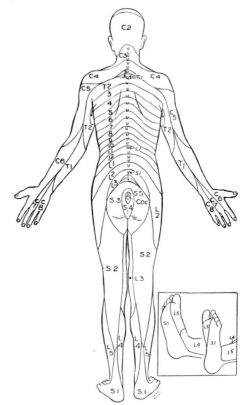

Fig. 2.101 Back view of the human dermatomes.
Arrows in the region of the spinal column point to the
spinous processes of the first thoracic, first lumbar, and
first sacral vertebrae. C, cervical; T, thoracic; L, lumbar;
S, sacral. (From Truex, 1959.)

fascicles; these fascicles are surrounded by tough,
collagenous connective tissue called *perineurium*
and are connected by elastic connective tissue
called *epineurium* (see Figure 2.102). Every layer
of connective tissue contains blood vessels arising
from regional arteries. The many ascending and
descending branches of regional arteries anasto-
mose to form a continuous arterial channel within
each nerve. The venous drainage generally follows
a similar pattern.

Peripheral Termination of Afferent Spinal Nerves

The afferent components of spinal nerves (i.e.,
the long "dendritic" process of cells in the dorsal
root ganglion) terminate near the external or
internal surface of the organism and form receptor
mechanisms which specialize in the transduction
of particular types of physical energy into neural
signals. Structurally, two types of receptors have

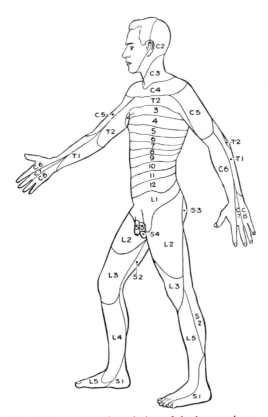

Fig. 2.100 A ventrolateral view of the human dermatomes. C, cervical; T, thoracic; L, lumbar; S, sacral.
(From Truex, 1959.)

been described, *free nerve endings* and *encapsulated nerve endings*. *General somesthetic receptors* (touch, pressure, pain, temperature, kinesthetic, and visceral sensors) and *special sense organs* (the eye, ear, nose, and taste receptors) may be distinguished. A topographic classification into *exteroceptors, proprioceptors,* and *interoceptors* is used widely, although these distinctions have little functional significance (see Figure 2.103).

Exteroceptors include cutaneous, visual, auditory, and olfactory receptors and are selectively sensitive to changes in the external environment of the organism. *Interoceptors* (or *visceroceptors*) include chemoreceptors and pressure, temperature, and pain receptors located in the interior

endings are found in the skin, the serous membranes of the heart, alimentary canal, and blood vessels, as well as in smooth and striped muscle. They are preferentially sensitive to light touch, deep pressure, or pain.

Encapsulated nerve endings are found in a variety of shapes and sizes, and specific functional properties have been attributed to many of them. The question of selective sensitivity is not as clear as one might expect, and we shall merely discuss some representative encapsulated endings here. All consist essentially of a free nerve ending that invades a capsule or cylinder of epithelial or muscle tissue. These receptor structures are believed to aid in the transduction of physical energy into

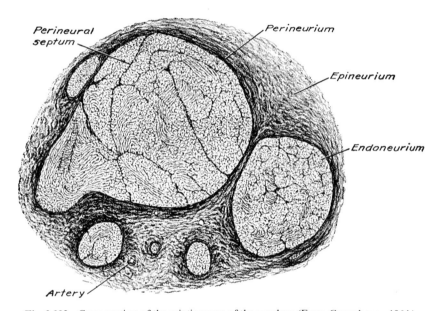

Fig. 2.102 Cross section of the sciatic nerve of the monkey. (From Copenhaver, 1964.)

surfaces of the body (such as the mouth, throat, stomach, intestines, and the walls of the blood vessels) and respond to changes in the internal environment. *Proprioceptors,* a special class of interoceptor, are selectively sensitive to changes in the overall position of the body or of one of its extremities. The tension and pressure receptors of the muscles, tendons, and joints, as well as the receptors of the labyrinth, fall into this category.

Free nerve endings are formed in many parts of the body when poorly myelinated fibers approach a cutaneous surface. The myelin sheath is lost as the terminal arborizations of the fiber develop extensive plexuses. Terminal fibrils from these plexuses serve as sensory receptors. Free nerve

biochemical changes which can produce specific irritation of the free nerve ending and initiate a nerve impulse (see Figure 2.104).

Perhaps the most representative example of an encapsulated receptor is the *Pacinian corpuscle*. It is found primarily in the periosteum, ligaments, and joint capsule as well as in subcutaneous tissue, the walls of many viscera, and internal organs. These pressure receptors consist of a free nerve ending which is surrounded by a thick, laminated capsule. This complex structure sometimes contains more than 30 layers of concentrically arranged collagenous fibers, separated by layers of flattened lamellar cells.

Meissner's tactile corpuscle is an example of a

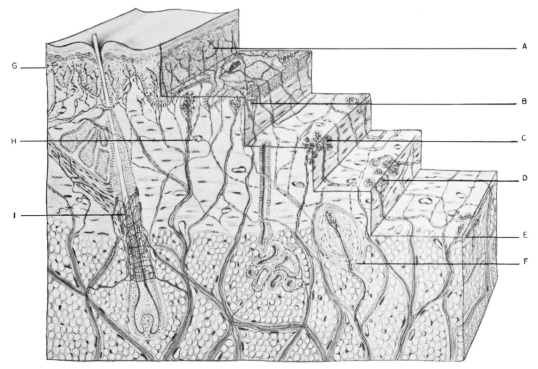

Fig. 2.103 The cutaneous innervation. A, beaded nerve nets subserving pain (probably fast pain); B, Meissner's corpuscle, subserving touch; C and D, groups of Krause's end bulbs, subserving cold (these lie at variable depths beneath the skin surface); E, group of Ruffini endings, subserving warmth; F, Pacinian corpuscle, subserving pressure; G, Merkel's disks, subserving touch; H, beaded nerve fibers derived from nerve nets, subserving pain and associated with blood vessels (probably slow pain); I, nerve terminals about the sheath of a hair, subserving touch. (From Peele, 1961.)

Border between inner and
outer bulbs

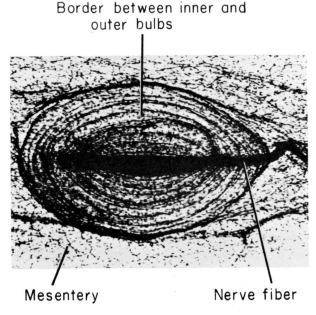

Mesentery   Nerve fiber

Fig. 2.104 Longitudinal view of a Pacinian corpuscle from the mesentery of the cat. Methylene blue injection, photomicrograph, $\times$ 150. (From Crosby et al., 1962.)

smaller encapsulated ending. Its free nerve ending is surrounded by several delicate parallel layers of connective tissue which enclose a semifluid core. The free nerve ending forms a complex pattern of terminal arborizations which are oriented exclusively parallel to the surface of the skin. This intricate structural arrangement accounts for the superb sensitivity of Meissner's corpuscles to minute changes in tactile stimulation. The corpuscle is found in such sensitive areas as the glans penis, the tips of the fingers, and the lips.

The *neuromuscular* and *neurotendinous endings* are unique because they contain a large amount of muscular or tendinous tissue inside the sensory receptor structure. The neuromuscular ending is surrounded by a double-walled sheath of connective tissue which is continuous with the connective tissue of the muscle. Several intrafusal muscle fibers are present within such a capsule, but extensive branching and anastomosis generally occur between the individual fibers. The central portion of the intrafusal muscle fibers, the *nuclear bag*, does not contract. Each end or *polar* portion (also called the *myotube*) appears to have its own motor innervation (small "gamma" efferents) and can act as an independent contractile unit (see Figure 2.105).

The sensory fiber loses its myelin sheath as it enters the muscle spindle and forms flattened, ribbon-like terminals. These terminals spiral around the intrafusal muscle fiber or parallel it for some distance, giving off many claw-like projections which entwine the muscle fiber. In addition to these *annulospiral endings*, a second type of neuromuscular terminal results from the still more profuse branching of the sensory nerve fiber around the intrafusal muscle. These *flower-spray* (or arborescent) *endings* are found largely in the noncontractile myotube region of the intrafusal muscle fiber. With these two receptors, the muscle spindle senses the degree of stretch in the surrounding muscles as well as the degree of contraction of its own intrafusal fibers. The muscle spindle serves as the afferent link of stretch (*myotatic*) reflexes which are important in postural adjustment.

Peripheral Terminations of Efferent Spinal Nerves

The motor fibers of spinal nerves are axons from anterior horn cells and from smaller cells in the medial portion of the spinal gray. The former give rise to large (10- to 15-micron diameter) *alpha* fibers which project to skeletal muscle fibers. The latter project smaller (4- to 5-micron), poorly mye-

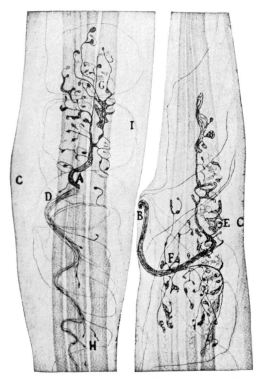

Fig. 2.105 Neuromuscular spindle. A, coarse nerve fiber with arborescent (flower-spray) terminations at G; B, coarse fiber with spiral and annular terminations at E and F; H, motor fibers; I, fine unmyelinated fibers; C, connective tissue capsule. (From Truex and Carpenter, 1964.)

linated motor fibers to the intrafusal muscle fibers of the muscle spindle. These *gamma efferents* represent the efferent link of reflex connections that are responsible for muscle tone and posture.

The large, myelinated alpha fibers from the anterior horn cells branch, often profusely, before terminating on several muscle fibers. A single anterior horn cell and all the muscle fibers it innervates constitute a *motor unit.* A single anterior horn cell may innervate one or as many as 100 muscle fibers.

Motor fibers terminate in grape-like arborizations on distinct elevations (called *endplates*) which develop on the surface of skeletal (striped) muscle fibers. The nerve and its coverings are not continuous with the muscle fiber but form a synaptic relationship at the *myoneural junction* (see Figure 2.106). Impulses are transmitted across the several hundred angstrom units which separate the neuron from the muscle by means of a chemical transmitter which is liberated from the neuron. The unmyelinated motor fibers of the autonomic

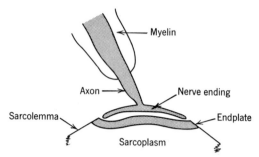

Fig. 2.106 Neuromyal junction. (From Wenger et al., 1956, after Couteau, 1947.)

nervous system often form extensive intramuscular plexuses. Terminal arborizations arise from these plexuses and terminate in fine loops on the muscle fiber.

Degeneration and Regeneration of Peripheral Nerves

When a peripheral nerve is sectioned some distance from the cell body, the soma of the cell undergoes a series of *chromatolytic* changes. The cell eventually regenerates an axonal process which tends to grow in the direction of the organ previously innervated. The severed axon stump distal to the cut degenerates (this is called *Wallerian* degeneration), leaving behind neurilemma tubules and scar tissue to guide the regenerating axon terminal to the appropriate organ. These regenerative processes occur in unmyelinated or poorly myelinated axons as well as in myelinated fibers, but they have not been demonstrated in the central nervous system.

THE CRANIAL NERVES

Most of the cranial nerves originate from nuclei in the brainstem. Some contain specialized fiber systems which represent *special somatic* or *visceral afferents* (such as visual, auditory, vestibular, or olfactory inputs to the brain). Others contain *specialized visceral efferents* from the brain, or *general somatic* and *visceral efferents* and *afferents* to all portions of the head, neck, and shoulders. The nuclei of the cranial nerves tend to be organized so that somatic afferent fiber systems terminate in an interrupted column of cells in the lateral portion of the brainstem; visceral afferents terminate in a band of nuclei located slightly more medially; visceral efferents terminate in still more medially located nuclei and the somatic

efferents generally arise from cells near the midline (see Figure 2.23). Many of the cranial nerves are mixed and therefore arise from, and project to, several of these nuclear masses. Two of the cranial nerves (olfactory and optic) are not, strictly speaking, peripheral nerves, but represent subcortical and even cortical tissue which has migrated to the periphery. However, they are generally included in the discussion of cranial nerves on functional grounds (see Table 2.1).

The Olfactory System (the I Cranial Nerve)

The primary olfactory receptors are small cells which are located in the *olfactory membrane.* A coarse projection from this receptor, the *olfactory rod,* extends to the surface of the *olfactory epithelium.* This rod is equipped with approximately ten *olfactory hairs* which project into the olfactory mucosa. The mucosa of the olfactory caverns provides a fluid medium in which the gaseous odors affecting the chemoreceptors of the olfactory system can be dissolved.

The olfactory receptor also has very fine unmyelinated processes which join the *olfactory nerve* on its way to the central nervous system. Fascicles of this nerve penetrate the *cribriform plate* and enter the olfactory bulb. Here, they synapse with the dendritic arborizations (*glomeruli*) of *mitral* cells. Axons from these secondary neurons constitute the olfactory bulb and olfactory tracts which course posteriorly along the ventromedial aspect of the cerebrum. The caudal portion of the olfactory bulb contains cells of the anterior olfactory nucleus. These cells receive collaterals from the mitral cells and project back to them, forming a feedback loop which may act as an amplification mechanism for olfactory impulses.

The posterior section of the olfactory bulb is continuous with the olfactory tracts. These tracts join the main mass of the cerebral hemispheres at the *anterior perforated substance.* The olfactory tract divides at this junction into *lateral* and *medial olfactory striae,* which surround the *olfactory trigone.* The medial olfactory stria projects to the septum pellucidum, the septal area, the subcallosal gyrus, and the olfactory trigone, as well as to the contralateral anterior olfactory nucleus (via the anterior commissure). The lateral olfactory stria projects to the prepyriform cortex and to the corticomedial nuclei of the amygdala. The connections of these primary olfactory projection areas were discussed in the section on the rhinencephalon.

The Visual System (the II Cranial Nerve)

The second cranial nerve is not, strictly speaking, a peripheral nerve. The visual receptors and associated pathways develop from the central nervous system and migrate to the periphery. They resemble cortical tissue rather than peripheral receptor mechanisms. The optic nerve is classed as a cranial nerve purely on the basis of functional considerations.

The primary visual receptors, the *rods* and *cones*, are located in the *retina* of the eye. The retina has three major layers of cells. The innermost layer, which is farthest from the light, contains the photosensitive elements. It is separated from the inner lining of the eye (the *sclera*) by a densely pigmented *chorioidal* layer.

The two types of visual receptors are nonran-domly distributed in the retina. Cones, which are responsible for the perception of color and fine detail, are densely packed in the central portion of the eye, the *fovea centralis*. Rods, which are responsible for night vision, are not found in this part of the eye. They begin to occur in the peri-foveal regions and increase in number and relative density toward the periphery of the retina. Conversely, the number of cones decreases proportionately.

A human eye contains approximately 6.5 million cones. Many of these establish a "private line" to the visual projection centers of the central nervous system. The rods typically share communication lines to the central nervous system and are much more numerous; the best estimates range from 110 to 130 million per eye (see Figures 2.107, 2.108, 2.109).

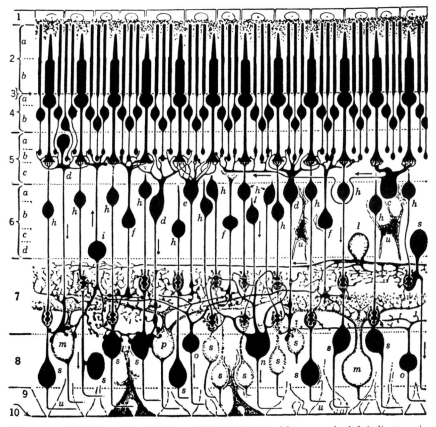

Fig. 2.107 Structure of the primate retina. The numbers and letters at the left indicate various layers and zones. The other letters indicate elements as follows: *c*, horizontal cell; *d*, mop bipolar; *e*, brush bipolar; *f*, flat bipolar; *h*, midget bipolar; *i*, centrifugal bipolar (amacrine cell); *l*, internal association cell (amacrine cell); *m*, *o*, and *p*, diffuse ganglion cells; *n*, short ganglion cell; *s*, midget ganglion cell; *u*, "radial fibers" of Müller. (From Polyak, 1957.)

Outline of the cranial nerves

TABLE 2.1

Nerves	Components		Function	Central Connection	Cell Bodies	Peripheral Distribution
I. Olfactory	Afferent	Special visceral	Smell	Olfactory bulb and tract	Olfactory epithelial cells	Olfactory nerves
II. Optic	Afferent	Special somatic	Vision	Optic nerve and tract	Ganglion cells of retina	Rods and cones of retina
III. Oculomotor	Efferent	Somatic	Ocular movement	Nucleus III	Nucleus III	Branches to Levator palpebrae, Rectus superior, medius, inferior, Obliquus inferior
	Efferent	General visceral	Contraction of pupil and accommodation	Nucleus of Edinger-Westphal	Nucleus of Edinger-Westphal	Ciliary ganglion; Ciliaris and Sphincter pupillae
	Afferent	Proprioceptive	Muscular sensibility	Nucleus mesencephalicus V	Nucleus mesencephalicus V	Sensory endings in ocular muscles
IV. Trochlear	Efferent	Somatic	Ocular movement	Nucleus IV	Nucleus IV	Branches to Obliquus superior
	Afferent	Proprioceptive	Muscular sensibility	Nucleus mesencephalicus V	Nucleus mesencephalicus V	Sensory endings in Obliquus superior
V. Trigeminal	Afferent	General somatic	General sensibility	Trigeminal sensory nucleus	Trigeminal ganglion (Gasserian)	Sensory branches of ophthalmic maxillary and mandibular nerves to skin and mucous membranes of face and head
	Efferent	Special visceral	Mastication	Motor V nucleus	Motor V nucleus	Branches to Temporalis, Masseter, Pterygoidei, Mylohyoideus, Digastricus, Tensores tympani and palatini
	Afferent	Proprioceptive	Muscular sensibility	Nucleus mesencephalicus V	Nucleus mesencephalicus V	Sensory endings in muscles of mastication
VI. Abducent	Efferent	Somatic	Ocular movement	Nucleus VI	Nucleus VI	Branches to Rectus lateralis
	Afferent	Proprioceptive	Muscular sensibility	Nucleus mesencephalicus V	Nucleus mesencephalicus V	Sensory endings in Rectus lateralis
VII. Facial	Efferent	Special visceral	Facial expression	Motor VII nucleus	Motor VII nucleus	Branches to facial muscles, Stapedius, Stylohyoideus, Digastricus
	Efferent	General visceral	Glandular secretion	Nucleus salivatorius	Nucleus salivatorius	Greater superficial petrosal nerve, sphenopalatine ganglion, with branches of maxillary V to glands of nasal mucosa. Chorda tympani, lingual nerve, submaxillary ganglion, submaxillary and sublingual glands
	Afferent	Special visceral	Taste	Nucleus tractus solitarius	Geniculate ganglion	Chorda tympani, lingual nerve, taste buds, anterior tongue

Nerve	Component	Function	Nucleus	Nucleus/Ganglion	Distribution
	Afferent General visceral	Visceral sensibility	Nucleus tractus solitarius	Geniculate ganglion	Great superficial petrosal, chorda tympani and branches
	Afferent General somatic	Cutaneous sensibility	Nucleus spinal tract of V	Geniculate ganglion	With auricular branch of vagus to external ear and mastoid region
VIII. Acoustic	Afferent Special somatic	Hearing	Cochlear nuclei	Spiral ganglion	Organ of Corti in cochlea
	Afferent Proprioceptive	Sense of equilibrium	Vestibular nuclei	Vestibular ganglion	Semicircular canals, saccule, and utricle
IX. Glossopharyngeal	Afferent Special visceral	Taste	Nucleus tractus solitarius	Inferior ganglion IX	Lingual branches, taste buds, posterior tongue
	Afferent General visceral	Visceral sensibility	Nucleus tractus solitarius	Inferior ganglion IX	Tympanic nerve to middle ear, branches to pharynx and tongue, carotid sinus nerve
	Efferent General visceral	Glandular secretion	Nucleus salivatorius	Nucleus salivatorius	Tympanic, lesser superficial petrosal nerves, otic ganglion, with auriculo-temporal V to parotid gland
	Efferent Special visceral	Swallowing	Nucleus ambiguus	Nucleus ambiguus	Branch to Stylopharyngeus
X. Vagus	Efferent General visceral	Involuntary muscle and gland control	Dorsal motor nucleus X	Dorsal motor nucleus X	Cardiac nerves and plexus; ganglia on heart. Pulmonary plexus; ganglia, respiratory tract. Esophageal, gastric, celiac plexuses; myenteric and submucous plexuses, muscle and glands of digestive tract down to transverse colon
	Efferent Special visceral	Swallowing and phonation	Nucleus ambiguus	Nucleus ambiguus	Pharyngeal branches, superior and inferior laryngeal nerves
	Afferent General visceral	Visceral sensibility	Nucleus tractus solitarius	Ganglion nodosum	Fibers in all cervical, thoracic, and abdominal branches; carotid and aortic bodies
	Afferent Special visceral	Taste	Nucleus tractus solitarius	Ganglion nodosum	Branches to region of epiglottis and taste buds
	Afferent General somatic	Cutaneous sensibility	Nucleus spinal tract V	Jugular ganglion	Auricular branch to external ear and meatus
XI. Accessory	Efferent Special visceral	Swallowing and phonation	Nucleus ambiguus	Nucleus ambiguus	Bulbar portion, communication with vagus, in vagus branches to muscles of pharynx and larynx
	Efferent Special somatic	Movements of shoulder and head	Lateral column of upper cervical spinal cord	Lateral column of upper cervical spinal cord	Spinal portion, branches to Sternocleidomastoideus and Trapezius
XII. Hypoglossal	Efferent General somatic	Movements of tongue	Nucleus XII	Nucleus XII	Branches to extrinsic and intrinsic muscles of tongue

From Gray, 1959.

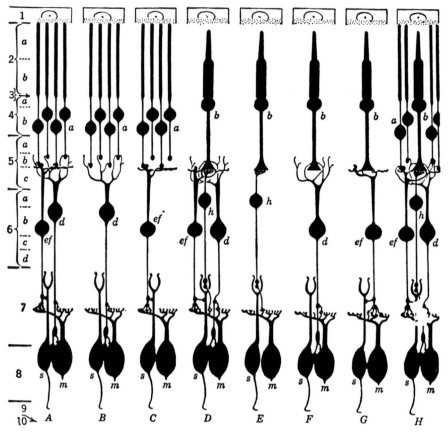

Fig. 2.108 Grouping of the primate retinal cells into functional systems. (For the identification of elements, see Fig. 2.107.) A, rod system; B, rod system with a single intermediate link (mop bipolar); C, rod system with only the brush or flat bipolar as the next link; D, cone system; E, pure cone system with midget bipolar as intermediate link; F, cone with mop bipolar as intermediate link; G, cone system with either the brush or flat bipolar cell as intermediate link; H, common rod-and-cone system. (From Polyak, 1957.)

The rods contain rhodopsin (visual purple) which bleaches to xanthopsin (visual yellow or retinene) and leucopsin (visual white or vitamin A) on exposure to light. The process is largely reversible in the dark. The cones contain several light-sensitive substances which undergo complex changes when they are exposed to specific wavelengths.

Groups of rods project to a single bipolar cell. Peripherally located cones may share a bipolar cell or project to bipolar cells which also receive terminal arborizations from rods. The cones in the foveal area establish typically a 1:1 relationship with the second-order elements in the visual pathways. These monosynaptic bipolar cells are called *midget bipolars*.

Some bipolar cells are in dendritic relationship with the third relay in the visual pathway, the *ganglion cells*. These centrifugal bipolar cells project axons laterally across the retina and terminate on rods and cones.

The *ganglion cells* may either continue a private line to the central nervous system or connect polysynaptically with a number of bipolar cells (typically those that have already collected information from several receptor cells). Fibers from these ganglion cells make up the *optic* (II cranial) *nerve*. The human optic nerve contains roughly one million fibers which are topographically organized according to their point of origin (see Figure 2.111).

At the optic chiasma a partial decussation of the optic nerve fibers takes place. Fibers from the temporal half of the retina remain in the ipsi-lateral *optic tract*, whereas those from the nasal half decussate and enter the contralateral optic tract. The postchiasmatic optic tract thus contains a bilateral representation of visual inputs.

Approximately 80% of the optic fibers terminate in the *lateral geniculate body* of the thalamus. The remaining 20% project to the superior colliculi and pretectal area and serve as the afferent link of the pupillary light reflex and motor adjustments concerned with eye movements.

The optic tract fibers terminate in the lateral geniculate body in the characteristic pattern which reflects their origin on the retina. Projections from the nasal quadrants of the contralateral retina terminate in layers 1, 4, and 6; uncrossed fibers from the temporal quadrants of the ipsilateral eye terminate in layers 2, 3, and 5. Projections from the macular portion of the retina take up the medial aspects of the caudal medial geniculate; those from more peripheral portions of the retina are projected to anterior and lateral segments of the nucleus (see Figure 2.110).

All the cells of the lateral geniculate nucleus project via the *geniculocalcarine tract* to the ipsilateral primary visual reception area of the occipital cortex. This tract passes through the posterior limb of the internal capsule and into the *outer stripe of Baillarger* (also called the *stripe of Gennari*) in the striate cortex. The topographic organization of the visual projections is maintained in the geniculocalcarine tract as well as in its terminations on the occipital cortex (see Figure 2.111). The visual system thus establishes a point-to-point relationship between specific peripheral receptors and central projection sites. Damage to the visual projections at any stage produces predictable and highly specific losses in visual ability.

The Innervation of the Eye Muscles (Cranial Nerves III, IV, and VI)

The *oculomotor* (III cranial) nerve arises from cells that form a V-shaped nucleus in the central

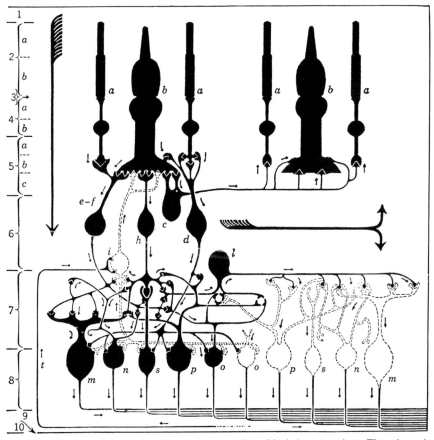

Fig. 2.109 The essential elements of the primate retina with their connections. The schema indicates the direction of propagation of impulses from the receptors to other elements in the retina, to the brain, and back to the retina. For key see Fig. 2.107. (From Polyak, 1957.)

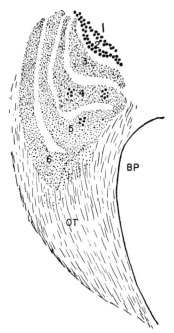

Fig. 2.110 Horizontal section through the human lateral geniculate (dorsal nucleus). The large-celled laminae are the most superficial. BP, basis pedunculi; OT, optic tract fibers approaching the geniculate. (From Peele, 1961.)

gray of the midbrain; this nucleus lies dorsomedial to the red nucleus (see Figure 2.112). Several components of the oculomotor nucleus have been distinguished. The most prominent of these are the *lateral nucleus*, the *nucleus of Perlia,* and the *paramedian* and *caudal central nuclei.* The *anterior central* nucleus and the *Edinger-Westphal* nucleus are anatomically as well as functionally associated with the anterior portion of the oculomotor complex; the *trochlear* (IV cranial) nucleus is often embedded in its posterior projections. The nucleus of the *abducens* (VI cranial) nerve lies slightly more posterior in the floor of the fourth ventricle.

Fibers of the oculomotor nerve course through the ventral portion of the midbrain and emerge from the *interpeduncular fossa.* The nerve supplies somatic efferents to the ipsilateral *levator* and *superior rectus,* the contralateral *inferior rectus,* both the ipsilateral and the contralateral *internal rectus,* and the *inferior oblique* muscles. Preganglionic parasympathetic fibers from the Edinger-Westphal nucleus accompany the oculomotor nerve to the *ciliary* ganglion for synapses with cells projecting to the sphincter muscles of the iris (see Figure 2.113).

The *trochlear* (IV cranial) nerve contains somatic efferent fibers from cells distributed in the ventral portion of the central gray of the midbrain. The fibers course dorsocaudally and decussate before emerging from the dorsal surface of the brainstem caudal to the inferior colliculi. The trochlear nerve innervates the contralateral *superior oblique* muscles of the eye.

The *abducens* (VI cranial) nerve arises from nuclei located below the floor of the fourth ventricle in the caudal third of the pons. The root fibers turn ventrally and caudally from their origin, course through the pons, and emerge from its caudal border in line with the hypoglossal roots. These fibers supply the *external rectus* muscle of the eye. Smaller fibers arise from the closely adjacent *parabducens nucleus* and project to the abducens and oculomotor nuclei.

All three of these oculomotor nerves also contain relatively small somatic afferent components which arise primarily from muscle spindles in the ocular muscles. These spindle afferents carry proprioceptive information that is important in the voluntary control of eye movement and position.

Eye movements may be voluntary or may occur reflexly in response to visual, vestibular, or auditory stimulation. The oculomotor nuclei do not receive afferents directly from the cortical and subcortical projections of these senses; rather they receive secondary inputs from the centers for conjugate eye movements in the midbrain tegmentum and tectum. Afferents from the superior colliculi appear to be particularly essential for vertical movements, projections from the parabducens nuclei for horizontal movements, and fibers from the nucleus of Perlia for convergence.

The Trigeminal (V Cranial) Nerve

The large trigeminal nerve supplies general somatic afferents and some general somatic efferents to the skin and mucous membranes of the head. It has three distinct divisions, called the *ophthalmic, maxillary,* and *mandibular* nerves. All three emerge from the *Gasserian* or *semilunar ganglion* which lies in a depression of the temporal bone (see Figure 2.114).

The smallest of the three divisions of the trigeminal nerve, the *ophthalmic* nerve, divides into three branches, the *frontal, lacrimal,* and *nasociliary* soon after it emerges from the Gasserian ganglion. The frontal branch contains general somatic afferents from the cutaneous surface of the superior portion of the head. The lacrimal

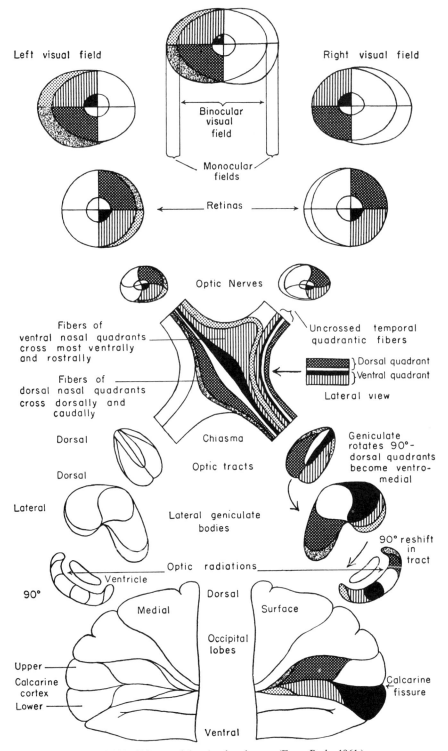

Fig. 2.111 Schema of the visual pathways. (From Peele, 1961.)

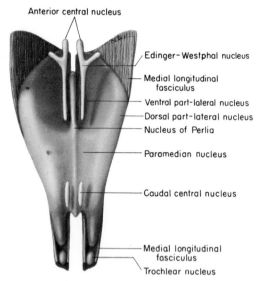

Anterior central nucleus

Edinger-Westphal nucleus

Medial longitudinal fasciculus

Ventral part-lateral nucleus

Dorsal part-lateral nucleus

Nucleus of Perlia

Paramedian nucleus

Caudal central nucleus

Medial longitudinal fasciculus

Trochlear nucleus

Fig. 2.112 Oculomotor and trochlear nuclei of the human. (From Peele, 1961.)

branch carries sympathetic fibers to the lacrimal gland, and the nasociliary branch projects to the ciliary ganglion. In addition to these major divisions, the ophthalmic nerve receives sympathetic fibers from the carotid plexus and sends afferents to the oculomotor, trochlear, and abducens nerves.

The *maxillary* division supports the spheno-palatine ganglion, the skin of the face below and lateral to the eyes and nose, the mucous mem-

branes of the maxillary and sphenoid sinuses, the nasal septal conchae, and the upper teeth and gums.

The *mandibular* division supplies afferents to the dura, the mucous membranes in the anterior two-thirds of the tongue, the lower teeth and gums, the skin of the lower face and anterior ear, and the paraotid, submaxillary, and sublingual glands. Its motor components supply special visceral efferents to a number of muscles in the facial region of the head. The motor fibers are related to the *motor nucleus* of the trigeminal nerve which is located in the medial third of the pons ventrolateral to the floor of the fourth ventricle. The motor fibers emerge from the brainstem as a distinct nerve root which lies inferior to the Gasserian ganglion. The motor nucleus receives afferents from corticobulbar, tectobulbar, and rubroreticulobulbar tracts, as well as from the medial longitudinal fasciculus.

The *sensory nuclei* of the trigeminal nerve form an irregulary shaped, long cellular mass which extends from approximately the fourth cervical level of the spinal cord to the upper pontine segments of the brainstem. General somatic afferents from the skin and mucous membranes of the head carry pain, temperature, and touch impulses. These fibers arise from pseudo-unipolar cells in the Gasserian ganglion. These cells extend their central projections into the brainstem, where they bifurcate into short ascending and long descending limbs. Fibers carrying pain and temperature

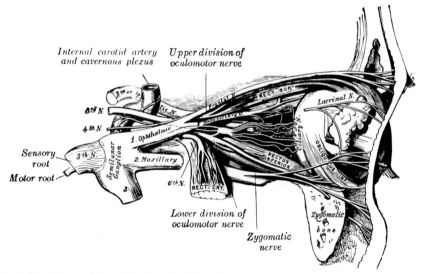

Internal carotid artery and cavernous plexus

Upper division of oculomotor nerve

Lacrimal N.

3ª or

tic N.

RECT. SUP.

Frontal N.

8ª N.

4ᵗʰ N.

1. Ophthalmic

Ciliary N.

OBLIQUUS SUP.

Sensory root

5ᵗʰ N.

2. Maxillary

RECTUS INFERIOR

OBLIQUUS INF.

Semilunar ganglion

Motor root

3

6ᵗʰ N.

RECT. LAT.

Lower division of oculomotor nerve

Zygomatic bone

Zygomatic nerve

Fig. 2.113 Nerves of the orbit, side view. The ciliary ganglion is shown but not labeled. (From Gray, 1959.)

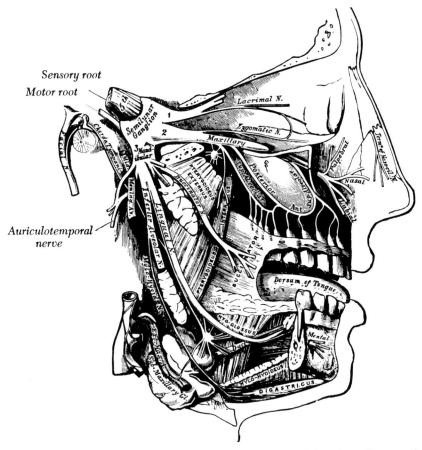

Fig. 2.114 Distribution of the maxillary and mandibular nerves and the submaxillary ganglion. (From Gray, 1959.)

impulses descend in the brainstem and upper cord as the *spinal tract* of the trigeminal; they terminate all along its course in an immediately adjacent gray matter called the *spinal nucleus* of the trigeminal. The organization of fibers as well as their termination in the spinal tract and nucleus of the trigeminal nerve follow specific topographic patterns which are related to their origin in the periphery. Trigeminal fibers that carry impulses from tactile and pressure receptors ascend in the brainstem and terminate around the *main sensory nucleus* of the trigeminal in the medial segments of the pons, slightly ventral and lateral to the floor of the fourth ventricle. Fibers carrying proprioceptive afferents from the muscles of mastication and from teeth and gums do not arise from cells in the semilunar ganglion; rather, they originate inside the central nervous system in the *mesencephalic nucleus* which extends rostrally to the level of the posterior commissure. Other

proprioceptive components of the trigeminal arise from the Gasserian ganglion.

The spinal and main sensory nuclei of the trigeminal project to the motor nuclei of the medulla and spinal cord to complete a number of crossed reflex arcs. Some fibers also pass upward to the trigeminal, oculomotor, facial, and hypoglossal nuclei. Long ascending fibers project to the thalamus along the trigeminothalamic or quinothalamic tracts and terminate in the posteroventral nuclei of the thalamus. Crossed as well as uncrossed quintothalamic projections have been described; these projections may course through the upper brainstem in discrete trigeminal lemnisci (see Figure 2.34).

The Facial (VII Cranial) Nerve

The facial nerve contains afferent projections from taste receptors of some sections of the mouth, cutaneous impulses from portions of the ear, visceral impulses from palatal and nasal membranes, and proprioceptive impulses from facial muscles. Its efferent components innervate striated muscles of the face, scalp, and ear as well as several parasympathetic ganglia that supply the submaxillary, sublingual, and lacrimal glands.

The facial *motor nucleus* lies in the lateral aspects of the pontine tegmentum just ventrolateral to the spinal nucleus and tract of the trigeminal. Fibers from the motor nucleus course through the floor of the fourth ventricle and form the genu of the facial nerve. From here they project to the lateral surface of the brainstem and emerge from it near the caudal border of the pons. The fibers accompany the auditory (VIII cranial) nerve to the internal auditory meatus. Here the visceral efferent components join the glossopalatine nerve. The somatic efferents continue through the meatus and project to the parotid gland where they divide into temporal, zygomatic, buccal, mandibular, and cervical branches. The visceral efferents arise from the *superior salivatory nucleus* which lies dorsomedial to the main facial nucleus. Preganglionic parasympathetic fibers from this nucleus pass through the chorda tympani nerve and finally join the lingual nerve for distribution to the submaxillary ganglion (see Figure 2.115).

The *sensory fibers* of the facial nerve arise from the *geniculate ganglion* which lies near the distal end of the auditory meatus and form the *glossopalatine nerve* (or *nervus intermedius*). Some of these fibers innervate taste buds on the anterior two-thirds of the tongue. They are distributed via the chorda tympani and lingual nerves. Other fibers innervate the cutaneous surface of the ear and are distributed via the auricular branch of the facial nerve. A third projection system to the palatal and nasal mucous membranes passes through the petrosal and sphenopalatine ganglia.

The facial nuclei receive afferents from cortical, striate, hypothalamic, tectal, pontine, and bulbar sources. They are extensively interconnected with the brainstem nuclei of most other cranial nerves; these nuclei complete such reflexes as the adjustment of tension on the stapedius muscle of the ear in response to intense auditory stimulation, the coordination of eyelid and eye movements, and the blink reflex to strong visual stimulation.

The Auditory and Vestibular Systems

The cochlear division of the VIII cranial nerve. The primary auditory neurons are located in the *spiral ganglion*. Dendritic processes from these cells terminate on hair cells in the cochlea.

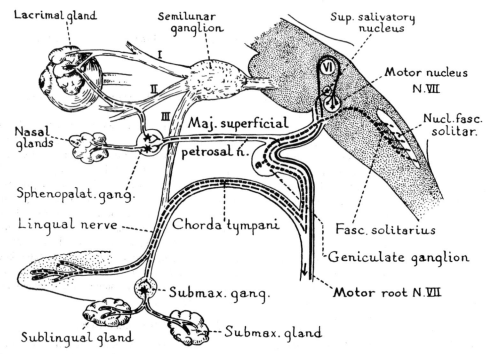

Fig. 2.115 Components of the facial nerve (intermediofacial): I, opthalmic; II, maxillary; and III, mandibular ramus of trigeminal nerve. (From Truex and Carpenter, 1964.)

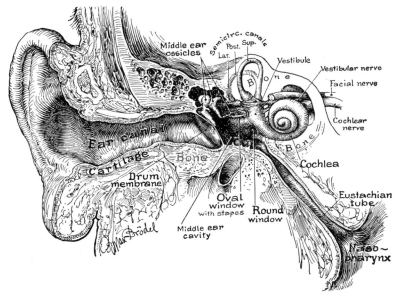

Fig. 2.116   Gross anatomy of the external, middle, and internal ear. (From Peele, 1961.)

Deformation of these hair cells by vibration represents the primary auditory stimulus (see Figure 2.116).

Sound waves reach the auditory receptors via the external ear which is designed to conduct and amplify sound. The arrival of sound waves at the *tympanic membrane* or eardrum activates the *malleus* (hammer), a small bone that is attached to the inner surface of this membrane. The malleus articulates with another bone, the *incus* (or anvil), which in turn connects to the third ossicle in this chain, the *stapes* (or stirrup). The base of the stapes is attached to the *round window* which separates the middle ear from the cochlea. The tension on this mechanical transducer system is varied by two muscles: the *tensor tympani* attaches to the malleus and receives innervation from the trigeminal nerve, and the *stapedius* attaches to the neck of the stapes and is innervated by the facial nerve.

The inner ear consists of a bony cochlear canal which is incompletely divided by the *lamina spiralis* into a medial *scala tympani* and a lateral *scala vestibuli*. The scalae are filled with endolymphatic fluid and communicate at the apex of the cochlea (called the *helicotrema*) where the lamina spiralis is absent (see Figures 2.117 and 2.118).

The bony lamina spiralis contains a *cochlear*

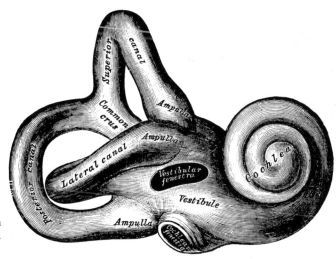

Fig. 2.117   Right osseous labyrinth with spongy bone removed, lateral view. (From Gray, 1959.)

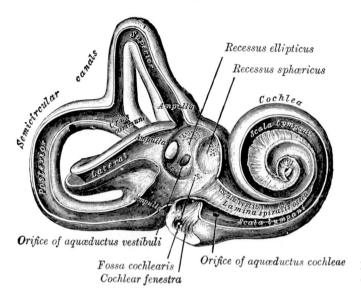

Recessus ellipticus

Recessus sphæricus

Orifice of aquæductus vestibuli

Fossa cochlearis
Cochlear fenestra

Orifice of aquæductus cochleae

Fig. 2.118   Interior of the right osseous labyrinth. (From Gray, 1959.)

duct which is separated from the scala tympani only by a thin *basilar membrane.* The roof of the cochlear duct is formed by *Reissner's vestibular membrane* which separates the duct from the scala vestibuli. At the wide portion of the snail-like cochlea, the scala tympani is separated from the middle ear only by a thin membrane called the round window. The scala vestibuli is continuous with the *vestibule.*

The hair cells, which transduce sound waves into neural activity, are located in a complex receptor organ called the *organ of Corti.* It consists of a variety of supporting cells and the auditory receptors. The organ of Corti forms a ridge on the upper surface of the basilar membrane. A tunnel of tall supporting cells runs down the center of this ridge. A single row of "inner" hair cells forms along the medial surface of this tunnel, and three rows of "outer" hair cells are arranged along its lateral surface. A thin *tectorial membrane* rests on top of the hair cells (see Figures 2.119 and 2.120).

Dendritic projections from the bipolar cells of the spiral ganglion come in contact with these hair cells. Two types of connections are recognized: (1) *radial fibers* with terminals about several internal hair cells and (2) *spiral fibers* with terminals about external as well as internal hair cells.

Axons from cells in the spiral ganglion form the cochlear division of the auditory nerve. This nerve enters the medulla rostrolaterally to the restiform body and terminates in the *ventral* and *dorsal cochlear nuclei.* Secondary fibers from these nuclei

ascend in the brainstem in three distinct bundles, the *dorsal, intermediate,* and *ventral auditory striae.* These secondary auditory fibers decussate either in the *median raphé* or the *trapezoid body* and terminate in (1) the *nucleus of the trapezoid body,* (2) the *contralateral superior olivary nucleus,* (3) the *reticular formation of the rostral medulla and pons,* (4) the *nuclei of the lateral lemniscus,* or (5) the *inferior colliculus.* Tertiary auditory projections from the superior olive and the trapezoid nucleus terminate in the inferior colliculus or pass directly to the *medial geniculate body* of the thalamus (see Figure 2.121).

The inferior colliculus relays auditory impulses to the ipsilateral medial geniculate via the *brachium of the inferior colliculus.* It also projects crossed fibers to the contralateral inferior colliculus and contralateral medial geniculate. Bilateral representation of auditory signals is further assured by an extensive exchange of fibers between the nuclei of the lateral lemnisci via the *commissure of Probst.*

Some of the auditory relay nuclei have extensive afferent as well as efferent connections with other cranial nerve nuclei for the completion of numerous auditory reflex circuits.

The *medial geniculate nuclei* receive tertiary and quarternary fibers which carry information from ipsilateral receptors as well as contralateral receptors. The majority of the cells in the medial geniculate project through the posterior limb of the internal capsule to the primary auditory projection cortex in the *superior transverse gyri* of the

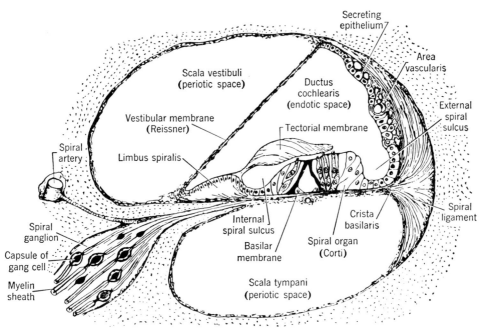

Fig. 2.119 Cross section of a cochlear canal. The ductus cochlearis (or scala media) contains the organ of Corti with its hair cells, the ultimate end organs of hearing. (From Rasmussen, 1943.)

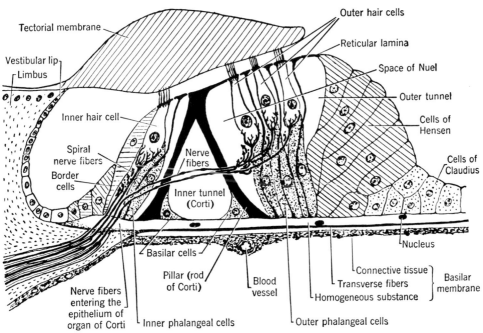

Fig. 2.120 Cross section of the organ of Corti. The outer hair cells are supported by their respective phalangeal cells, which rest in turn on the movable basilar membrane. The phalangeal cells supporting the inner hair cells rest on bone. Motion of the basilar membrane distorts the hair cells. (From Rasmussen, 1943.)

163

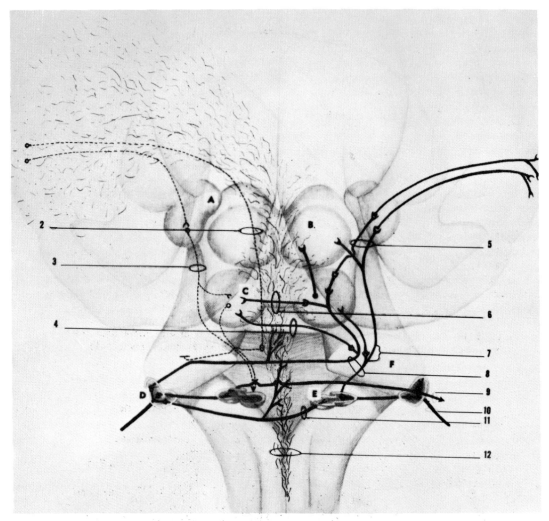

Fig. 2.121   Main features of the known connections of the auditory pathways in the cat. A, medial geniculate body; B, superior colliculus; C, inferior colliculus; D, cochlear nucleus; E, superior olive; F, cut section of brachium pontis; 2, corticopontocerebellar pathway; 3, recurrent fibers throughout the auditory projection pathway; 4, commissure of Probst; 5, brachium of inferior colliculus; 6, commissure of inferior colliculus; 7, nucleus lateral lemniscus; 8, lateral lemniscus; 9, olive cochlear bundle; 10, cochlear nerve; 11, trapezoid body; 12, reticular system (diffuse projection to cerebral cortex). (From Ades, 1959.)

temporal lobe. Some degree of tonotopic organization of the auditory projection system is maintained throughout its complex pathways.

The primary cortical projections of auditory signals are located in areas 41 and 42 of the temporal and opercular cortex. Areas 52 and 22, which surround the primary projection areas, are considered to be auditory association areas in man. Recent physiological investigations have suggested a more extensive cortical projection of the auditory system.

The vestibular division of the VIII cranial nerve. The primary neurons of the vestibular branch of the VIII cranial nerve are located in the *ganglion of Scarpa* deep in the internal auditory meatus. Dendritic processes of these bipolar neurons terminate about hair cells in the *maculae sacculi* and *cristae*, complex receptor organs in the inner ear.

The inner ear or labyrinth consists of a number of interconnected cavities in the temporal bone. Three major divisions, the *vestibule, semicircular canals,* and *cochlea,* are recognized. The membranous labyrinth formed in these caverns generally follows the contours of the petrous bones and is separated from them by the perilymphatic space (see Figure 2.122).

The three semicircular canals are arranged at right angles to one another and represent the three planes of space. Each of the canals has a marked dilatation at one end, the *ampullae.* These ampullae have patches of sensory epithelium, *cristae,* which contain vestibular receptors. The exposed hairs of these cells are embedded in a gelatinous membrane, the *cupula.* This membrane deflects the hairs of the vestibular receptors and initiates nervous impulses whenever the endolymphatic fluids of the semicircular canals come into motion. Rotatory and angular accelerations are the principal sources of stimulation for the ampullar receptors (see Figures 2.123 and 2.124).

The *utricle* and *saccule* of the vestibule contain similar patches of sensory epithelim, the *maculae.* The longitudinal axes of these maculae are approximately perpendicular to one another. The hair cells of these sensory organs are covered by a gelatinous membrane which contains calcareous crystals called *otoliths.* Linear movement or changes in head position provide the primary stimuli to the vestibular receptors of the maculae.

Axons from neurons in the vestibular ganglion of Scarpa form the vestibular branch of the auditory nerve. This branch projects toward the brainstem in close association with the cochlear division and enters the medulla anteromedial to the auditory fibers as a distinct bundle. Most fibers of the vestibular nerve terminate in the vestibular nuclei of the brainstem. Some fibers project directly to the nodulus, uvula, lingula, and fastigial nuclei of the cerebellum (see Figure 2.125).

There are four vestibular nuclei. The *medial* or *Schwalbe's nucleus* lies near the floor of the fourth ventricle just medial to the *lateral* or *Deiters' nucleus.* The lateral nucleus is contiguous rostrally with the *superior* or *Bechterew's nucleus* and caudally with the *spinal* or *descending nucleus.*

Two descending pathways originate in the vestibular system. The uncrossed *lateral vestibulospinal tract* originates primarily from Deiters' nucleus. The crossed *medial vestibulospinal tract* carries fibers from the lateral, medial, and spinal vestibular nuclei.

There are several important ascending pro-

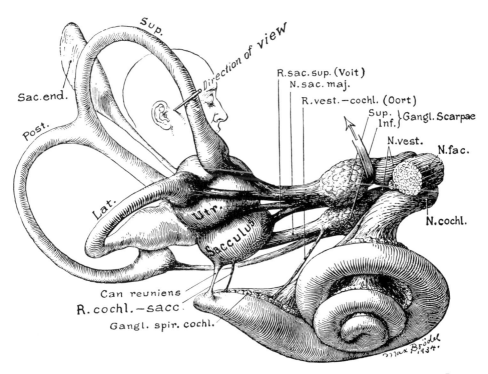

Fig. 2.122 Nerve supply of the vestibular apparatus and cochlea. (From M. Hardy, *Anat. Rec.,* 1934, **59,** 412.)

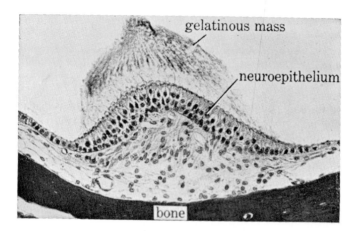
gelatinous mass

neuroepithelium

bone

Fig. 2.123 Ampullary crista of the posterior semicircular canal, guinea pig labyrinth. The gelatinous mass containing processes of hair cells has shrunk in fixation of the tissues. Photomicrograph, ×90. (From Nonidez and Windle, 1949.)

jections. *Vestibulocerebellar* fibers interconnect the superior, medial, and spinal vestibular nuclei with the flocculus, nodulus, and fastigial nuclei. *Vestibuloreticular* projections from the superior and medial nuclei distribute widely throughout the bulbar and pontine reticular formation. *Vestibulomesencephalic* fibers ascend to the oculomotor nuclei for the completion of reflex circuits. Vestibular impulses are directly or indirectly distributed to some thalamic nuclei, the superior temporal lobe, and premotor areas of the frontal lobe.

The Glossopharyngeal (IX Cranial) Nerve

Fibers from a number of nuclei in the lower medulla collect to form the glossopharyngeal nerve which emerges from the medulla in association with the vagus and spinal accessory nerves. Its *sensory components* arise from cells which are located within the jugular foramen in the *inferior* and *superior petrosal ganglia* (see Figure 2.126).

Special visceral afferents from these ganglia represent the most important innervation of the taste buds *(circumvallate papillae)* on the posterior third of the tongue. These taste fibers synapse centrally on cells in the nucleus of the tractus solitarius which projects secondary fibers to the posteromedial ventral nucleus of the thalamus. Some of the secondary taste fibers may project to cells at the semilunar nucleus which directly or indirectly connect to the parietal lobe of the cerebrum.

General somatic afferents from the superior petrosal ganglion carry impulses from cutaneous receptors in part of the ear and concha.

General visceral afferents arising from the inferior petrosal ganglion carry pain and tactile impulses from the posterior third of the tongue,

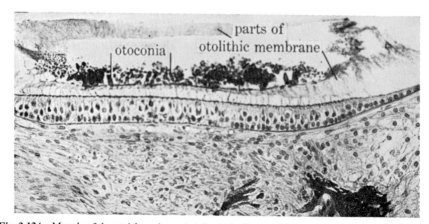
otoconia

parts of
otolithic membrane

Fig. 2.124 Macula of the utricle, guinea pig labyrinth. The otolithic membrane has been deformed in preservation of the tissues; otoconia are present. Photomicrograph, ×90. (From Nonidez and Windle, 1949.)

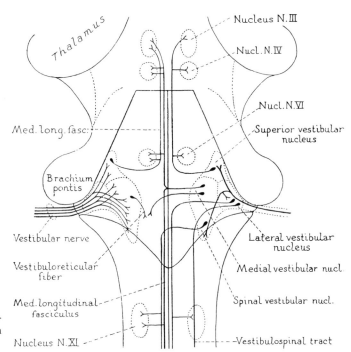

Nucleus N.III

Nucl. N.IV

Nucl. N.VI

Superior vestibular nucleus

Thalamus

Med. long. fasc.

Brachium pontis

Vestibular nerve

Vestibuloreticular fiber

Med. longitudinal fasciculus

Lateral vestibular nucleus

Medial vestibular nucl.

Spinal vestibular nucl.

Nucleus N.XI

Vestibulospinal tract

Fig. 2.125 Some of the principal connections of the vestibular nerve. (From Truex, 1959.)

the mucous membrane of the uvula, the soft palate, and the Eustachian tubes. There are also some sensory fibers from pressor receptors in the carotid that complete the afferent link of important carotid sinus reflexes by synapsing on cells near the nucleus of the tractus solitarius.

The motor fibers of the glossopharyngeal nerve arise in part from the rostral portion of the *nucleus ambiguus* which is located in the ventrolateral portion of the bulbar tegmentum just ventromedial to the spinal nucleus of the trigeminal. These fibers innervate the pharynx. Parasympathetic preganglionic fibers from the inferior salivatory nucleus join the glossopharyngeal nerve; they are then distributed to the otic ganglion which projects postganglionic fibers to the parotid gland. These fibers are involved in the secretion of saliva.

The nucleus ambiguus receives extensive afferents from sensory nuclei of various cranial nerves for the completion of reflex responses such as gagging, coughing, or swallowing. Corticobulbar projections provide voluntary control over the motor functions that are mediated by the glossopharyngeal nerve.

The Vagus (X Cranial) Nerve

The tenth cranial nerve is a large mixed nerve and innervates a great number of widely separated stuctures. It emerges from the medulla dorsal to the inferior olive and projects through the jugular foramen which contains the superior *jugular ganglion* and the inferior *nodose ganglion*. The cell bodies of all afferent components of the vagus are collected in these ganglia (see Figure 2.127).

A small *meningeal* nerve arises directly from the jugular ganglion and supplies portions of the dura. The *auricular* nerve also projects directly from the jugular ganglion to the aural portion of the face. Most of the vagal fibers project caudally and form a *pharyngeal plexus* which also contains fibers from the glossopharyngeal nerve and the sympathetic trunk. The vagus gives rise to the following major branches: the *superior* and *inferior laryngeal*, the *cardiac, bronchial, pulmonary, esophageal, abdominal,* and *pericardiac* nerves.

Preganglionic parasympathetic fibers to smooth muscles of the intestines and cardiac muscles of the heart arise from the *dorsal motor nucleus* of the vagus, located in the caudal portion of the floor of the fourth ventricle. General somatic efferents arise from the nucleus ambiguus of the ventrolateral tegmentum.

Dendritic processes from cells in the nodose ganglion carry taste impulses from the epiglottis. The central projections from these cells reach the nucleus solitarius for distribution to the accessory semilunar ganglion or the posteromedial ventral nucleus of the thalamus. The auricular branch of the vagus carries sensory fibers from

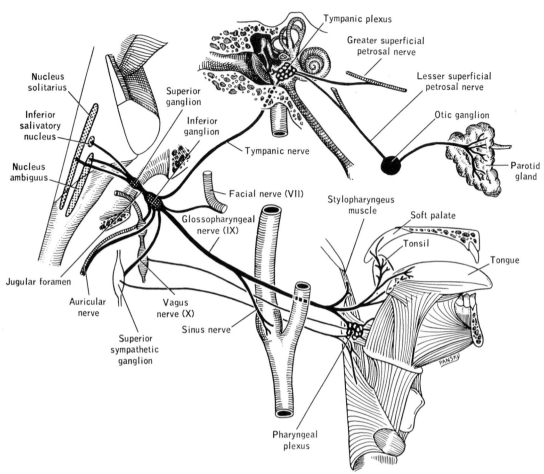

Fig. 2.126 Course, distribution, and relations of the glossopharyngeal nerve (IX). (From House and Pansky, 1960.)

some portions of the ear. The central projections of these cells terminate in the spinal nucleus of the trigeminal. General visceral afferents from portions of the pharynx, larynx, and the membranes of the thoracic and abdominal viscera are carried by dendritic processes of cells from the nodose ganglion. These cells project to the postvagal portion of the nucleus solitarius, which is sometimes called the *dorsal sensory nucleus* of the vagus.

The motor nuclei of the vagus receive afferents from neighboring sensory nuclei of the brainstem for the completion of various reflex patterns. Voluntary control of pharyngeal and laryngeal muscles is provided by projections from the precentral gyrus of the cerebrum.

The Spinal Accessory (XI Cranial) Nerve

The eleventh cranial nerve is a pure motor nerve. It has two *bulbar components:* (1) pregan-

glionic parasympathetic fibers which arise from the dorsal motor nucleus of the vagus and rejoin the distribution system of the vagus, and (2) special visceral efferents which arise from the nucleus ambiguus and project to the musculature of the pharynx. The *spinal portion* of the spinal accessory nerve arises from ventral horn cells in the upper five cervical segments and emerges from the surface of the upper cord via several distinct rootlets. The spinal fibers innervate the sternocleidomastoid and trapezius muscles of the neck (see Figure 2.128).

The Hypoglossal (XII Cranial) Nerve

The hypoglossal nerve is primarily a motor nerve which innervates the musculature of the tongue. Its fibers arise from the hypoglossal nucleus situated under the *hypoglossal trigone* in the floor of the fourth ventricle. (The nucleus of the hypoglossal nerve is located at upper cervical levels of the cord in most lower animals.) The principal function of the hypoglossal nerve is to carry general somatic efferents to the tongue. However, general visceral efferents from the *nucleus of Roller* and general somatic afferents from proprioceptors in the tongue may also use this pathway.

The hypoglossal nucleus receives afferents from the nucleus of the tractus solitarius and the spinal nucleus of the trigeminal for the completion of several reflex arcs that involve movements of the tongue. It also receives direct and indirect corticobulbar projections which provide a pathway for voluntary control of tongue movements.

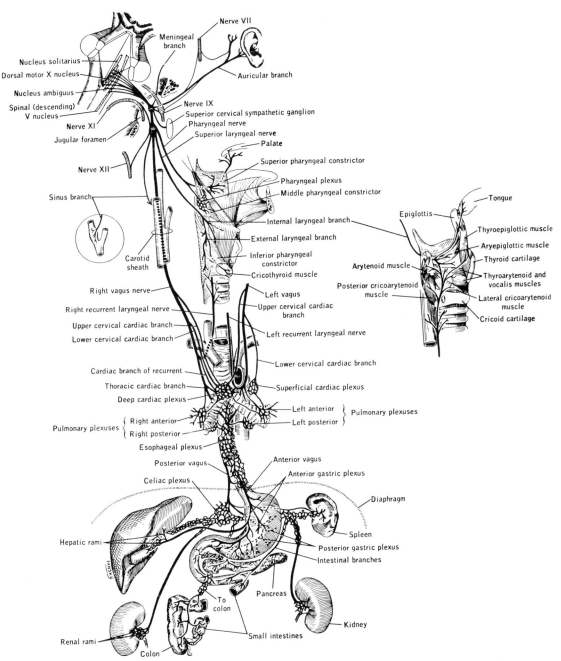

Fig. 2.127 Course, relations, and complete distribution of the vagus nerve (X). (From House and Pansky, 1960.)

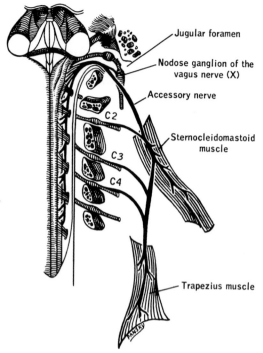

Fig. 2.128 Course, distribution, and relations of the spinal accessory nerve (XI). (From House and Pansky, 1960.)

THE AUTONOMIC NERVOUS SYSTEM

The aspects of the peripheral and central nervous system that are concerned with the regulation of visceral functions comprise the *autonomic, visceral,* or *vegetative* nervous system: the *somatic* nervous system, on the other hand, is concerned with sensory inputs from exteroceptors and with control of skeletal (striped) muscles.

The central representation of the autonomic nervous system (ANS) is closely intermingled with the somatic aspects of the brain and spinal cord. Some central autonomic pathways and nuclei have been demonstrated. However, most of the cells and fibers that integrate autonomic functions at central levels are diffusely distributed in the nuclei and tracts of the somatosensory and somatomotor systems.

Peripherally, the autonomic nervous system is anatomically, physiologically, and, to some extent, pharmacologically distinct from the somatic nervous system. This separateness is particularly true for the motor components that form distinct ganglia outside the central nervous system.

Visceral afferents arise from cells that are intermingled with somatosensory cells in the dorsal root ganglia and may reach the viscera via somatic nerves as well as autonomic nerves.

These anatomic distinctions led Langley to propose a definition of the autonomic nervous system that included only its peripheral visceromotor components. Although many anatomists still follow Langley's restricted usage of the term, functional considerations suggest that the broader definition contained in the opening paragraph of this chapter may be more useful.

GROSS SUBDIVISIONS

The peripheral autonomic nervous system consists of a *sympathetic* or *thoracicolumbar* division and a *parasympathetic* or *craniosacral* division. The primary motor neurons of both branches are located inside the central nervous system and project to secondary efferent cells collected in prominent, peripheral *ganglia*. In contrast to the somatomotor system which projects efferents directly to the peripheral musculature, *preganglionic* and *postganglionic components* of the autonomic nervous system can be distinguished (see Figure 2.129).

Three types of autonomic ganglia have been described. *Vertebral ganglia* are extensively interconnected by ascending and descending fibers and form a *ganglionic trunk* or *chain* along the ventrolateral surface of the spinal cord. *Collateral ganglia* are formed in mesenteric plexuses which surround the major visceral arteries. *Terminal ganglia* are widely distributed throughout the viscera, usually within a short distance of the structures that receive the postganglionic efferents.

The preganglionic fibers of the sympathetic nervous system arise from cells in the intermediolateral and intermediomedial gray of the spinal cord. They project through the ventral roots of all thoracic and upper two lumbar nerves and leave the spinal nerve soon after its formation. They project to the vertebral ganglia of the sympathetic chain via the *white ramus communicans.*

The parasympathetic division contains two anatomically distinct sections. The *cranial outflow* comprises visceral motor fibers from the oculomotor, facial, glossopharyngeal, and vagus cranial nerve nuclei of the brainstem. Its projections reach either *cranial autonomic ganglia* (such as the ciliary, otic, sphenopalatine, and submandibular ganglia) or *terminal ganglia* in the heart, lungs, and stomach. The *sacral outflow* contains visceral efferents from nuclei in the lower cord and pro-

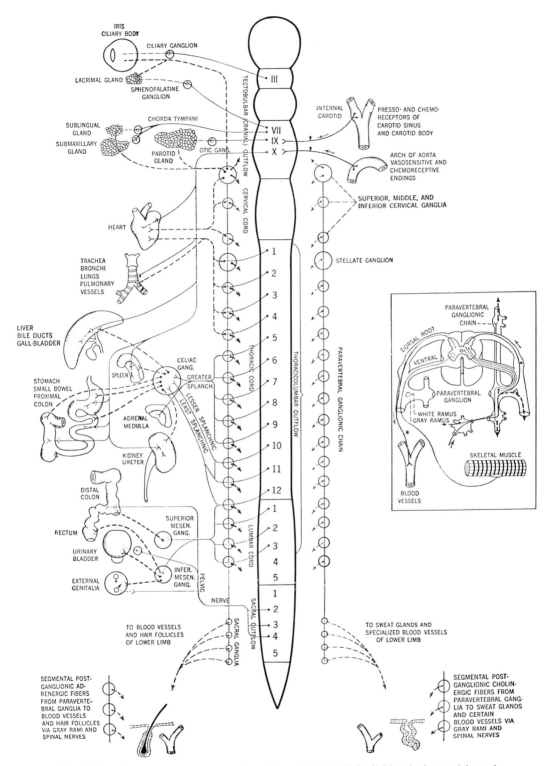

Fig. 2.129 The autonomic nervous system. The parasympathetic division is the cranial-sacral outflow, the sympathetic division the thoracicolumbar outflow. Preganglionic fibers (———), postganglionic fibers (— — —). (From Goodman and Gilman, 1965.)

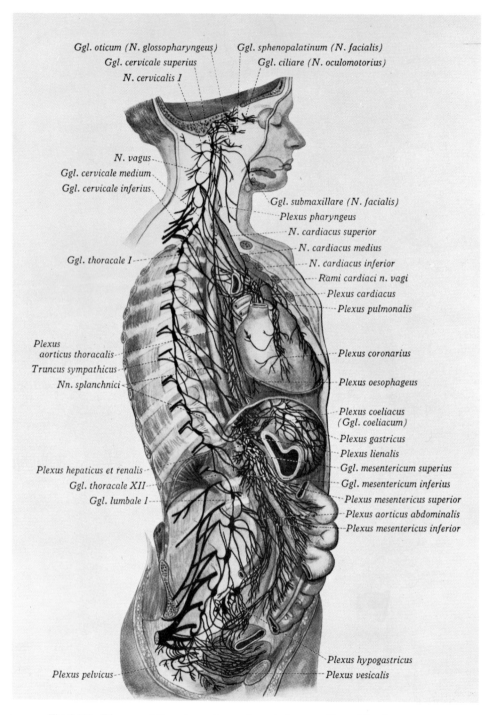

Ggl. oticum (N. glossopharyngeus)   Ggl. sphenopalatinum (N. facialis)
    Ggl. cervicale superius   Ggl. ciliare (N. oculomotorius)
        N. cervicalis I

                N. vagus
        Ggl. cervicale medium
        Ggl. cervicale inferius

                                    Ggl. submaxillare (N. facialis)
                                    Plexus pharyngeus
                                    N. cardiacus superior
                                    N. cardiacus medius
                                    N. cardiacus inferior
        Ggl. thoracale I   Rami cardiaci n. vagi
                                    Plexus cardiacus
                                    Plexus pulmonalis

                                    Plexus coronarius
Plexus
    aorticus thoracalis   Plexus oesophageus
Truncus sympathicus
    Nn. splanchnici   Plexus coeliacus
                                    (Ggl. coeliacum)
                                    Plexus gastricus
                                    Plexus lienalis
Plexus hepaticus et renalis   Ggl. mesentericum superius
    Ggl. thoracale XII   Ggl. mesentericum inferius
        Ggl. lumbale I   Plexus mesentericus superior
                                    Plexus aorticus abdominalis
                                    Plexus mesentericus inferior

                                    Plexus hypogastricus
    Plexus pelvicus   Plexus vesicalis

Fig. 2.130 Diagram of the autonomic ganglia and plexuses. (From Woerdeman, 1950.)

jects directly to terminal ganglia in the pelvic viscera.

Most visceral structures receive both sympathetic and parasympathetic innervation. The two divisions of the autonomic nervous system often, though by no means always, act antagonistically, and a delicate balance of opposing sympathetic and parasympathetic influences exists in many visceral functions.

THE SYMPATHETIC DIVISION

The preganglionic, myelinated axons of visceromotor cells from the thoracic and upper lumbar sections of the spinal cord project through the white ramus communicans to the vertebral chain ganglia; these ganglia parallel the ventrolateral aspects of the spinal cord from the base of the skull to the coccyx. The preganglionic fibers may (1) synapse on secondary (postganglionic) motor cells either within the ganglion of entry or in higher or lower segments of the chain, or (2) project through the sympathetic chain and form the *splanchnic nerves* which terminate in prevertebral ganglia (see Figure 2.130).

The *greater* and *lesser splanchnic nerves* arise from lower thoracic segments of the cord and project to prevertebral ganglia in the *celiac plexus*. The *least splanchnic nerve* arises from the lowest thoracic segment and projects to ganglia in the *renal plexus*. The *celiac plexus* extends from the diaphragm to the renal arteries and gives rise to a number of smaller nerve plexuses (the phrenic, suprarenal, spermatic or ovarian, gastric, hepatic, splenic, and superior mesenteric). It contains the *celiac, aorticorenal,* and *superior mesenteric ganglia* from which unmyelinated postganglionic fibers project to the smooth muscles of the viscera.

The upper segments of the *vertebral chain*, adjacent to the cervical sections of the spinal cord, contain the *superior, middle,* and *inferior cervical ganglia*. The preganglionic afferents to these ganglia arise primarily from upper thoracic sections of the cord and ascend in the sympathetic chain. The lower portions of the vertebral chain generally follow the segmental organization of the spinal cord and form twelve thoracic, three to four lumbar, and four to five sacral ganglia. The caudal segments of the lateral chains fuse to form a single coccygeal ganglion. The lower ganglia receive afferents from lower thoracic and upper lumbar sections of the cord; these afferents descend in the vertebral chain for several segments before synapsing on postganglionic cells (see Figure 2.131).

The cells of the vertebral chain project un-

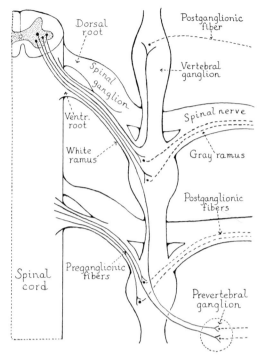

Fig. 2.131 Portion of the sympathetic trunk showing course of preganglionic and postganglionic fibers. (From Truex, 1959.)

myelinated (gray) fibers to all spinal nerves via the *gray rami communicans*. These fibers innervate blood vessels and glands of the walls of the viscera. Fibers from the cervical ganglia may (1) enter cranial nerves IX, X, XI, and XII, (2) enter the upper spinal nerves, or (3) project to plexuses surrounding the carotid arteries. The cervical sympathetic outflow innervates the heart, the blood vessels, sweat glands and hairs of the head and face, the pharynx, the dilator muscles of the iris and the submandibular, sublingual, and parotid glands.

The synaptic transmission of impulses from sympathetic preganglionic fibers to the soma or dendrites of postganglionic cells is based on the liberation of the neurohumor *acetylcholine;* the system is thus *cholinergic.* However, the transmission of impulses at the sympathetic neuroeffector junction between postganglionic fibers and smooth or cardiac muscle and glands occurs via the release of *norepinephrine* (or *noradrenaline*); that is, the system is *adrenergic.*

THE PARASYMPATHETIC DIVISION

The cells of the craniosacral or parasympathetic division project axons directly to *terminal ganglia*

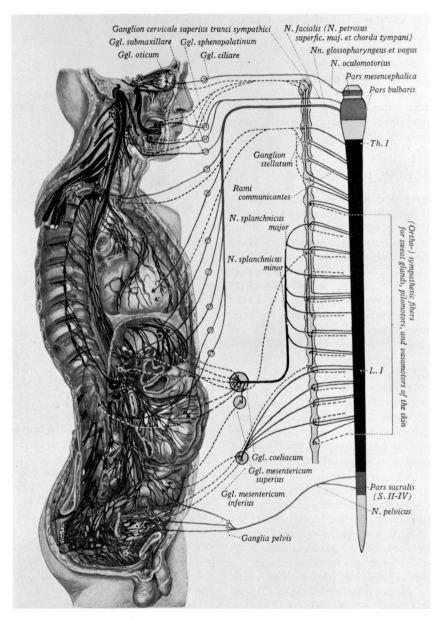

Fig. 2.132 Diagram of the peripheral terminations of the autonomic nervous system. (From Woerdeman, 1950.)

located near the structure to be innervated. There are four major terminal ganglia in the cranial portion of the system. (1) The *ciliary ganglion,* located near the optic nerve, receives preganglionic afferents from the oculomotor nerve. It innervates the smooth muscles of the iris and ciliary body. (2) The *sphenopalatine ganglion,* located in the spheno-palatine fossa, receives afferents from the superficial petrosal nerve (a branch of the facial or VII

cranial nerve). It projects to the lacrimal glands and the blood vessels and glands of the mucous membranes of the palate and nose. (3) The *sub-mandibular ganglion,* located in the immediate vicinity of the submaxillary gland, receives afferents from the chorda tympani (a branch of the facial nerve). It projects to the submaxillary and sublingual glands and to portions of the mouth. (4) The *otic ganglion,* adjacent to the mandibular nerve, receives afferents from the lesser superficial petrosal nerve (a branch of the glossopharyngeal or IX cranial nerve) and innervates the parotid gland.

The major source of parasympathetic fibers in the cranial division is the vagus (X cranial) nerve. Preganglionic afferents are distributed via the vagus to the pharynx and larynx, the pulmonary, cardiac, and esophageal plexuses and the stomach, and the plexuses of the lower intestine—the *plexuses of Auerbach and Meissner*. Postganglionic fibers from these relay stations reach terminal ganglia in the heart and bronchial musculature, the walls of the stomach and lower gastrointestinal tract, the liver, pancreas, and kidney.

The *sacral outflow* of the parasympathetic division consists mainly of preganglionic fibers which leave the second, third, and fourth spinal segments of the spinal cord and form the *pelvic nerve*. They end in terminal ganglia in the *pelvic plexus* and the *myenteric* and *submucosal* plexuses of the colon and rectum. From here, postganglionic fibers project to the accessory generative organs, the bladder, the colon, and the rectum (see Figure 2.132).

The transmission of impulses at the parasympathetic neuroeffector junction as well as at ganglionic synapses occurs via the release of acetylcholine.

SENSORY ASPECTS OF THE AUTONOMIC NERVOUS SYSTEM

All viscera contain sensory receptors that project via autonomic and somatic spinal and cranial nerves to cells in the cerebrospinal ganglia. The sensory components of the sympathetic nerves originate in the dorsal root ganglia of the thoracic and upper lumbar segments of the cord; they pass through the white ramus communicans and the vertebral chain to pressure and pain receptors in the thoracic and abdominal viscera.

The vagus contains afferents from cells in the *nodose ganglion* that carry sensory information from the heart, lungs, and abdominal viscera. The sacral division of the parasympathetic nervous system projects visceral afferents from cells in the sacral dorsal roots to sensory receptors in the bladder, rectum, and genital organs.

GROSS CHANGES IN AUTONOMIC FUNCTIONS

The following are examples of increased parasympathetic functions: (1) pupillary constriction (myosis) and accommodation of optic muscles; (2) increased secretion of the submaxillary, sublingual, and lacrimal glands; (3) inhibition of cardiac functions and coronary vasoconstriction; (4) constriction of bronchial musculature; (5) increased peristalsis of the digestive tract and increased secretion of hydrochloric acid in the stomach; (6) inhibition of anal and vesical (urinary) sphincter muscles; (7) vasodilation of cutaneous vessels.

Excitation of sympathetic functions results in (1) dilatation of the pupils (mydriasis); (2) increase in salivary and lacrimal gland secretions; (3) acceleration of cardiac activity and coronary vasodilatation; (4) dilation of the bronchi; (5) inhibition of peristalsis and vasoconstriction of intestinal blood vessels; (6) contraction of anal and internal (renal) sphincters; (7) vasoconstriction, excitation of pilomotor muscles, and secretion of sweat glands.

Dysfunctions of the autonomic nervous system are related to many clinical disorders. *Angina pectoris,* a cardiac condition which ranks among the most frequent causes of death in the United States, appears to be intimately related to excessive vasoconstriction of the coronary arteries and to a resultant ischemia of the heart muscles. *Peptic ulcers,* another common affliction of modern man, is related to an oversecretion of hydrochloric acid and abnormal gastric motility.

Drugs that stimulate, mimic, or enhance the activity of the two divisions of the autonomic nervous system are called *sympathomimetic* or *parasympathomimetic* drugs. Substances that block the transmission of impulses in the autonomic nervous system are called *sympatholytic* (or *adrenolytic*) and *parasympatholytic* (or *cholinolytic*) drugs.

CENTRAL LEVELS OF INTEGRATION

The hypothalamic portion of the diencephalon is considered to be the "headganglion" of the autonomic nervous system. Stimulation in the anterior hypothalamus and preoptic area tends to excite the parasympathetic division (contraction of the bladder, a fall in blood pressure, pupillary constriction, cardiac slowing or arrest, increased secretion of gastric juices, and increased motility of the stomach and intestine). Stimulation of the posterior hypothalamus generally produces sympathetic reactions (pupillary dilatation, increased blood pressure, inhibition of gastric secretion and motility, etc.). This distinction is relative rather than absolute; isolated sympathetic responses can be elicited from the anterior nuclei of the hypothalamus, and some parasympathetic functions are represented in the posterior diencephalon.

Autonomic responses have also been elicited by stimulation of a number of cortical regions, and evoked potentials have been recorded from many cortical sites following the stimulation of interoceptors. These cortical autonomic projections are particularly numerous in the orbital portions of the frontal lobe and in the cortex of the rhinencephalon. The extensive and diffuse cortical representation of visceral functions in the rhinencephalon has given rise to the term *visceral brain* to describe the old and transitional cortex.

Individual autonomic responses may also be integrated at lower levels of the brainstem and the cerebellum. Stimulation of the deep cerebellar nuclei produces such autonomic responses as pupillary dilatation and changes in the muscular tension of intestinal structures. Vasomotor responses appear to be at least partly regulated by "centers" in the lower medulla. Respiratory movements are controlled by a bulbar respiratory center located dorsal to the inferior olivary nucleus and by a subsidiary pneumotaxic center which takes up part of the ventrolateral tegmentum of the pons.

The major autonomic fiber projections in the central nervous system course through the brainstem in the dorsal longitudinal fasciculus of Schütz and in several diffuse fiber bundles which enter the anterior and lateral funiculi of the spinal cord.

SOME FUNCTIONAL CONSIDERATIONS

The autonomic nervous system permits the organism to adjust to changes in the internal environment. Since these alterations of the *milieu interne* are often the direct result of changes in the external environment, the autonomic nervous system cannot function in isolation. Although *viscerovisceral* reflexes are by far the most common type of autonomic integration, a number of important *viscerosomatic* reflex connections produce changes in somatic motor functions in response to stimuli arising in the viscera. *Somatovisceral* reactions (responses of the smooth muscles of the viscera to peripheral stimuli) are also common; and even *viscerosensory* interactions (i.e., modifications of somatosensory functions as the result of visceral stimulation) have been reported. The most common of these reactions is the phenomenon of referred pain. The sensation of pain, usually in an extremity, is caused by stimulation of visceral receptors not represented in the area to which the sensation is attributed.

BIBLIOGRAPHY

Ades, H. W. Central auditory mechanisms. In *Handbook of physiology*. Vol. I. J. Field, H. W. Magoun, & V. E. Hall, Eds. Baltimore: Williams and Wilkins, 1959.

Bender, M. B., & Kanzer, M. G. Dynamics of homonymous hemianopias and preservation of central vision. *Brain,* 1939, **62,** 404–421.

Bonin, G. von. Architecture of the precentral motor cortex and some adjacent areas. In *The precentral motor cortex* (2nd ed.). Paul C. Bucy, Ed. Urbana: Univ. of Illinois Press, 1949, 8–82.

Brodmann, K. From Physiologie des Gehirns. In *Die allgemeine Chirurgie der Gehirnkrankheiten,* Neue Deutsche Chirurgie, Vol. 11. Stuttgart: Enke, 1914.

Copenhaver, W. M. *Bailey's textbook of histology* (15th ed.). Baltimore: Williams and Wilkins, 1964.

Couteau, R. Contribution à l'étude de la synapse myoneurode. *Rev. canad. Biol.,* 1947, **6,** 563–711.

Crosby, Elizabeth C., Humphrey, T., & Lauer, E. W. *Correlative anatomy of the nervous system.* New York: Macmillan, 1962.

Economo, C. von. *The cytoarchitectonics of the human cerebral cortex.* S. Parker (Humphrey Milford), Trans. New York: Oxford Univ. Press, 1929.

Foerster, O. In *Handbuch der Neurology.* O. Bumke & O. Foerster, Eds. Berlin: Springer, 1936.

Gardner, E. *Fundamentals of neurology* (4th ed.). Philadelphia: Saunders, 1963.

Gloor, P. Amygdala. In *Handbook of physiology. Vol. II.* J. Field, H. W. Magoun, & V. E. Hall, Eds. Baltimore: Williams and Wilkins, 1960.

Goodman, L. S., & Gilman, A. *The pharmacological basis of therapeutics* (3rd ed.). New York: Macmillan, 1965.

Gray, H. Peripheral nervous system. In *Anatomy of the human body* (27th ed.). C. M. Goss, Ed. Philadelphia: Lea and Febiger, 1959.

Green, J. D. The hippocampus. In *Handbook of physiology. Vol. II.* J. Field, H. W. Magoun, & V. E. Hall, Eds. Baltimore: Williams and Wilkins, 1960.

Hampson, J. L., Harrison, C. R., & Woolsey, C. N. Cerebro-cerebellar projections and somatotopic localization of motor function in the cerebellum. *Res. Publ., Ass. Res. nerv. ment. Dis.,* 1952, **30,** 299–316.

Hardy, M. Observations on the innervation of the macula sacculi in man. *Anat. Rec.,* 1934, **59,** 403–418.

Haymaker, W., & Woodhall, B. *Peripheral nerve injuries* (2nd ed.). Philadelphia: Saunders, 1953.

Herren, R. Y., & Alexander, L. Sulcal and intrinsic blood

vessels of human spinal cord. *Arch. Neurol. Psychiat. (Chicago)*, 1939, **41**, 678–687.

House, E. L., & Pansky, B. *Neuroanatomy.* New York: McGraw-Hill, 1960.

Hyndman, O. R., & Van Epps, C. Anterior chordotomy. Further observations on physiological results and optimum manner of performance. *Arch. Neurol. Psychiat. (Chicago)*, 1943, **50**, 129–148.

Jelgersma, G. *Atlas anatomicum cerebri humani.* Amsterdam: Scheltema and Holkema, 1931.

Jung, R., & Hassler, R. The extrapyramidal motor system. In *Handbook of physiology. Vol. II.* J. F. Field, H. W. Magoun, & V. E. Hall, Eds. Baltimore: Williams and Wilkins, 1960.

Kappers, C. U. A., Huber, G. C., & Crosby, Elizabeth C. *The comparative anatomy of the nervous system of vertebrates.* New York: Macmillan, 1936.

Keegan, J. J., & Garrett, F. D. The segmental distribution of the cutaneous nerves in the limbs of man. *Anat. Rec.*, 1948, **102**, 409–437.

Kiss, F., & Szentágothai, J. *Atlas of human anatomy. Vol. III* (17th ed.). London: Pergamon Press, 1964.

Kuntz, A. *A textbook of neuro-anatomy* (5th ed.). Philadelphia: Lea and Febiger, 1950.

Larsell, O. *Anatomy of the nervous system* (2nd ed.). New York: Appleton-Century-Crofts, 1951.

Mettler, F. A. *Neuroanatomy* (2nd ed.). St Louis, Mo.: Mosby, 1948.

Netter, F. H. *The Ciba collection of medical illustrations. Vol. I. Nervous system.* Summit, N. J.: Ciba Pharmaceutical Products Co., 1953, p. 58.

Nonidez, J. F., & Windle, W. F. *Textbook of histology.* New York: McGraw-Hill, 1949.

Peele, T. L. *The neuroanatomical basis for clinical neurology* (2nd ed.). New York: Blakiston Division, McGraw-Hill, 1961.

Penfield, W., & Boldrey, E. Somatic motor and sensory representation in the cerebral cortex of man as studied by electrical stimulation, *Brain*, 1937, **60**, 389–443.

Penfield, W., & Rasmussen, T. *The cerebral cortex of man. A clinical study of localization of function.* New York: Macmillan, 1950.

Polyak, S. L. *The retina.* Chicago: Univ. of Chicago Press, 1941.

Polyak, S. L. *The vertebrate visual system.* H. Klüver, Ed. Chicago: Univ. of Chicago Press, 1957.

Rasmussen, A. T. *Outlines of neuroanatomy.* Dubuque, Iowa: Brown, 1943.

Rose, J. E., & Woolsey, C. N. *Cortical connections and functional organization of the thalamic auditory system of the cat.* Madison: Univ. of Wisconsin Press, 1958.

Rubinstein, H. S. *The study of the brain.* New York: Grune and Stratton, 1953.

Snider, R. S. Interrelations of cerebellum and brain stem. *Res. Publ., Ass. Res. nerv. ment. Dis.*, 1952, **30**, 267–281.

Sobotta, J. In *Atlas of human anatomy. Vol. III* (8th English ed.). F. H. J. Figge, Ed., New York: Hafner, 1963.

Truex, R. C. *Strong and Elwyn's human neuroanatomy* (4th ed.). Baltimore: Williams and Wilkins, 1959.

Truex, R. C., & Carpenter, M. B. *Strong and Elwyn's human neuroanatomy* (5th ed.). Baltimore: Williams and Wilkins, 1964.

Walker, A. E. The spinothalamic tract in man. *Arch. Neurol. Psychiat. (Chicago)*, 1940, **43**, 284–298.

Weddell, G. The anatomy of cutaneous sensibility. *Brit. Med. Bull.*, 1945, **3**, 733.

Wenger, M. A., Jones, F. N., & Jones, M. H. In *Physiological psychology.* New York: Henry Holt, 1956.

Woerdeman, M. W. *Atlas of human anatomy. Vol. II.* Philadelphia: Blakiston, 1950.

PART TWO

CHAPTER THREE

Vision

THE PHYSICAL PROPERTIES OF
THE VISUAL STIMULUS

The necessary and sufficient condition for the excitation of biological photoreceptors is the presence of a threshold quantity of *radiant energy*. The properties of this particular form of energy must be examined before we can investigate its transformation into proportional biological signals by the visual receptors of the eye.

Radiant energy travels through space at a constant speed of about 186,000 miles per second (mps). It is periodic with respect to time and space, and this periodicity can be measured in terms of energy *frequency* or its inverse, *wavelength*. The velocity of radiant energy is defined by the product of its wavelength and its frequency. Velocity is reduced by $1/n$ (where n equals the *refractive index* of the medium) whenever energy travels through a medium other than a vacuum. Since the refractive index does not affect the frequency of radiant energy, the wavelength must also be divided by n.

Biological photoreceptors are poor detectors of radiant energy. Light that is visible to man and most vertebrates has a wavelength of about 400 to 700 millimicra ($m\mu$) and a frequency range from 7×10^{14} to 4×10^{14} cycles per second (cps). This range represents only a tiny sliver of the spectrum of radiant energy (see Figure 3.1). Wavelengths just below the visible portion of the spectrum are called *ultraviolet* (UV), those just above it *infrared*. Most natural sources of radiant energy emit wavelengths that are not restricted to the visible portion of the spectrum.

Radiant energy can be considered to be propagated in the form of transverse electromagnetic waves moving in a plane that is at right angles to the direction of travel. It is useful to consider all waves of radiant energy to be caused by the motion of charged particles. The movement of nuclear particles, for instance, produces very short gamma waves; the movement of electrons in the inner and outer shells of the atom is responsible for the propagation of X-rays and visible light, respectively; infrared waves result from the movement of whole atoms or molecules. The very long radio waves are caused by the movement of electrons through metals.

This *electromagnetic wave theory* involves serious contradictions when we consider the production or destruction of radiant energy. However, the problem can be solved by assuming that the exchange between matter and radiant energy is a discontinuous process. This *corpuscular theory of radiation* suggests that radiant energy consists of discrete *quanta*, the size of which is directly related to the frequency of the radiation.

Radiation that passes through a particular surface area carries a certain amount of energy per second called *radiant flux* (P). It is measured in watts or ergs per second and is analogous to the "power" concept in electricity. Radiant flux per unit area is called *irradiation*.

Any surface that emits radiant energy is a *source*. An object that produces radiant energy is a *primary source;* when it merely reflects the energy from a primary source it is a *secondary source*. A *point source* is so small in relation to its distance from the observer (subtending less than 10 min of arc) that it has no discernible dimensions. The emission of radiant energy from a point source is measured in terms of its *radiant intensity*. The radiation of larger, *extended sources* can be assessed in two ways. The total radiant flux in all directions is measured in terms of *radiant emittance*. The energy from a primary extended source that is received at a specific point in space is measured in terms of *radiance*. The unit of measure-

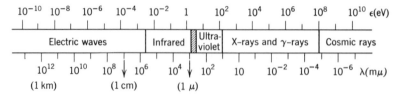

Fig. 3.1 Range of radiations, scaled in wavelengths (millimicra) and in quanta (electron volts). Visible light is represented by the cross-hatched region. (From Le Grand, 1957.)

ment for both radiance and radiant emittance is watts per square centimeter.

Since the spectral composition of radiant energy affects its properties, a visual stimulus must be specified in terms of its components, i.e., in terms of *spectral radiance,* or *spectral radiant emittance.*

THE BIOLOGICAL PHOTORECEPTOR

The physical properties of radiant energy are only imperfectly recognized by biological photoreceptors. As long as only a single wavelength is presented, the visual stimulus is adequately described in terms of radiant energy. However, the optic receptors respond differentially to various portions of the visible spectrum, and a compound stimulus consisting of several wavelengths produces effects that are not simply related to the radiant energies of its components. It is therefore necessary to consider some of the properties of the visual receptor before we can adequately specify the properties of the visual stimulus.

Biological photoreceptors are commonly found in specialized structures, the eyes. The optic properties of these receptor organs significantly alter the physical stimulus and must therefore briefly be considered at this point.

The human eye is almost spherical except for a marked anterior protruberance called the *cornea.* The entire structure is enveloped in a protective covering, the *sclera,* which is continuous with the cornea at the *limbus.* The sclera is lined by a heavily pigmented, nutrient membrane, the *chorioid,* which is continuous in the anterior sections of the eye with the *ciliary body.* This accumulation of fine muscles adjusts the diameter of the lens and thus permits focusing. The ciliary body projects a pigmented membrane, the *iris,* across part of the anterior section of the eye. The iris is pierced by an adjustable opening, the *pupil,* which controls the influx of radiant energy. The inside of the eye is covered by the *retina,* a light-sensitive layer of cells which contains two types of photo-

receptors, the *rods* and *cones.* A soft, biconvex *lens* is attached to the ciliary body by a thin membranous sheath called *zonule.* The lens consists of several distinct tissue layers which are arranged in an onion-like fashion. The space between the cornea and the lens is filled with the clear, *aqueous body.* The space between the lens and the retina is filled with a viscous jelly called *vitreous body* (see Figure 3.2).

THE ACTION OF RADIANT ENERGY ON THE PHOTORECEPTOR

In order to calculate the basic properties of the retinal image of a physical stimulus, a "standard eye" with the following dimensions has been used: refractive index of vitreous body, 1.336; object focal length, 16.68 mm; image focal length, 22.29 mm. Using these values, we can calculate the area of a retinal image $y' = 16.68u$ (where u is the *visual angle*). This is unfortunately only a rough approximation, since the eye is not truly spherical. (The visual angle can be defined for this purpose as the angle between a straight line joining the eye to the extremities of a diameter of the source.)

Distortions Resulting from the Physical Structure of the Eye

The photosensitive properties of the retina vary as a function of *eccentricity* (i.e., the angle between the point of fixation and the source). Maximum

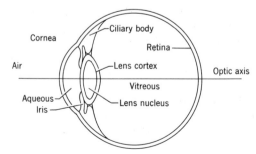

Fig. 3.2 Gullstrand's schematic eye. (From Fry, 1959.)

sensitivity obtains when the retinal image falls on the *fovea,* the central portion of the retina which contains only cone receptors and has its center coincide with the image of the point of fixation.

A straight line interconnecting the center of the eye with the point of fixation forms the *visual axis.* This must be clearly distinguished from the *optical axis* which projects at a 5° angle from the visual axis (see Figure 3.3).

The limits of the *visual field* (the area within which a point source can be perceived without movement of the eye or head) can be calculated by assuming theoretical values for the radius of the curvature of the cornea (8 mm) and the distance between the cornea and the iris (3.6 mm). The theoretical limit is presented by radiant energy which passes from source A to point M on the cornea (see Figure 3.3). The ray of energy passes through the center of the pupil and is refracted along the line MB. We can calculate the visual field as follows: cos $MOP = OP/MB = 0.55$; angle $MOP = 56°38'$. Sine of angle of refraction PMO is identical, hence sin $AMN = 0.55 \times 1.336 = 0.735$; and angle of incidence $AMN = 47°17'$. The angle between the incident light and the optical axis is therefore 104°. Correcting for the deviation from the visual axis, the visual field is approximately 109° by this calculation, a good fit to empirical measurements of the temporal half of the visual field. (The nasal half rarely exceeds 60°, and the upper and lower halves of the visual field usually have values between 70 and 80°.)

The response of biological photoreceptors is not only a function of the radiant flux (P) of a stimulus but also a function of the temporal parameters (t) of stimulation. A visual stimulus must have a duration of several milliseconds to initiate a response from biological photoreceptors. Once this threshold is reached, the response of the visual system is determined by the radiant flux; however, the present state and recent history of the photoreceptor must be considered carefully. All photic receptors show *adaptation* to the ambient level of illumination and change their sensitivity as a result of light or dark adaptation. Furthermore, the various sections of the retina are to some extent interrelated, so that the effect of a visual stimulus to a restricted portion of the visual field is influenced by the distribution of visual flux in adjacent portions of the retina. This *simultaneous contrast* phenomenon may cause facilitatory or *summation* effects when the total radiant flux is

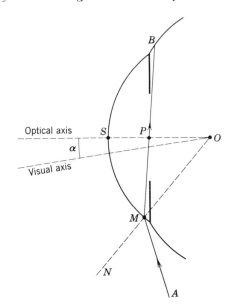

Fig. 3.3 Theoretical limit of the visual field. (From Le Grand, 1957.)

integrated, regardless of distribution. Facilitation occurs most frequently when approximately equal sources project to adjacent portions of the retina. The effects of the weaker of two unequal retinal images are inhibited when sources of very different radiance are used.

Photometric Considerations

We have considered the physical properties of the visual stimulus and the distortions produced by the physical properties of the eye. For this initial section of our discussion, absolute radiometric concepts were useful and adequate. However, when we consider the response of the biological organism, it immediately becomes obvious that this system responds very differently from our idealized eye; another system of measurement, *photometric quantities,* must therefore be introduced.

It may be best to approach this problem by means of a series of examples. If two sources S_1 and S_2 emit monochromatic radiations of equal wavelengths ($\lambda_1 = \lambda_2$) and uniform radiance ($L_{e_1} = L_{e_2}$), a biological organism can perceive the equality of the radiances without difficulty. However, when the wavelength of the radiations is not similar ($\lambda_1 \neq \lambda_2$), differences in color will be perceived and will tend to obscure the equality of the radiances. On the other hand, slight differences in the wavelength can be compensated by differences in the radiance of the two sources. It is thus possible to write an equation

$$V_{\lambda_1}L_{e_1} = V_{\lambda_2}L_{e_2}$$

where $V_{\lambda_1}/V_{\lambda_2}$ is an empirically derived ratio. By arbitrarily fixing the value of V for a certain wavelength as unity, we can define the *relative luminous efficiency* of all monochromatic radiations.

The relationship between V_λ and L across the visible spectrum describes its *relative luminous efficiency function*. Estimates of this relationship have been obtained by various methods. The least complicated, but cumbersome, technique relies on simultaneous comparisons of all possible pairs of visible wavelengths. A simplification of this procedure, the step-by-step method, takes direct comparisons of neighboring wavelengths at selected portions of the spectrum. A third possibility, the flicker method, applies the technique of successive comparisons. White light (a source emitting roughly equivalent radiances of all wavelengths of the visible spectrum) is rapidly alternated with a source emitting monochromatic light of some specific wavelength. The radiance (L_e) of the monochromatic light is then adjusted to minimize flicker, and the entire process is repeated with another wavelength. Relative luminous efficiency can then again be calculated from the formula

$$V_{\lambda_1}L_{e_1} = V_{\lambda_2}L_{e_2}$$

A number of luminous efficiency curves have been published (Coblentz and Emerson, 1918; Hyde et al., 1918; Gibson and Tyndall, 1923). The international Committee for Weights and Measurement (C.I.E.) has adopted an *average luminous efficiency curve* which was first proposed by Gibson and Tyndall in 1924 (see Figure 3.4).

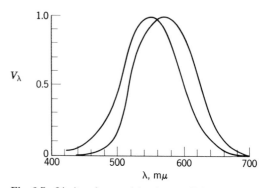

Fig. 3.5 Limits of normal luminous efficiency curves. (From Le Grand, 1957, after Coblentz and Emerson, 1918.)

The C.I.E. curve is roughly bell-shaped with a maximum around 555 mμ. A fairly good estimation of this important function can be derived from an empirical formula suggested by Moon and Spencer (1943):

$$V_\lambda = A Y^{-p} \exp(-q/\lambda)$$

Or

$$\log V_\lambda = \log A - p \log \lambda - 0.43429q/\lambda$$

where $A = 32.4107$, $p = 182.1905$, and $q = 100.937$.

The accuracy of the mathematical fit can be increased by adding coefficients (Walsh, 1953), but the computations become too complicated for practical use.

Individual luminous efficiency curves may differ significantly from the C.I.E. average. An example of such variance is shown in Figure 3.5. An estimate of the displacement of an individual from the population average can be obtained by determining his Y/B (yellow-blue) ratio (Ives, 1915). It is possible to mix solutions of potassium bichromate (yellow) and copper sulfate (blue) so that the average observer judges them to be of equal luminosity when they are, in fact, illuminated by identical sources. The Y/B ratio of the average observer is thus arbitrarily placed at unity. An individual who is more sensitive than the average person to long wavelengths would judge the yellow solution to be more luminous than the blue and show a Y/B ratio greater than unity. An observer who is particularly sensitive to the shortwave end of the visible spectrum would have a Y/B ratio smaller than unity.

The data that were averaged for the C.I.E. curve were obtained under rather rigid experimental conditions and under very low levels of retinal illumination. A closer look at individual data

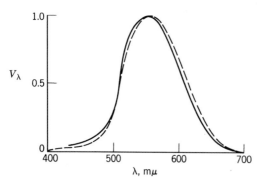

Fig. 3.4 Relative luminous efficiency curves by the step-by-step method (——) and the flicker method (– – –). (From Le Grand, 1957.)

shows that the shape of the relative luminosity curve is a function of a great number of variables which were held constant in these experiments. The size and luminance of the photometric field, the eccentricity of the retinal image, and the nature of the surrounding field are only some of the more important examples of such variables.

Perhaps the most important factor is the level of illumination (or degree of dark adaptation). The scotopic luminous efficiency function of dark-adapted observers differs rather sharply from the photopic efficiency functions, particularly at the upper end of the visual spectrum (see Figure 3.6). This discrepancy accounts for the well-known Purkinje shift in apparent brightness, i.e., blue and red surfaces which were equated for brightness in daylight appear unequal at night, the blue being much brighter. The average maximum scotopic efficiency lies near 507 mμ, or approximately 48 mμ below that of the photopic efficiency function (the photopic curve shown in Figure 3.6 has been shifted to the low end of the spectrum by 48 mμ to make the maxima coincide and to permit a direct comparison of the form of the two functions).

The Purkinje effect distorts all photometric measures to such an extent that they are practi-

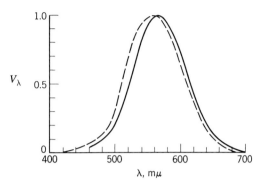

Fig. 3.7 The photopic luminous efficiency curve according to Jainski (——) and the C.I.E. curve (– – –). (From Le Grand, 1957.)

cally useless unless standard daylight conditions can be maintained. Such distortion implies that the law of proportionality, which has been assumed to relate the luminances of different sources, is not generally applicable. If two sources of equal apparent brightness are dimmed to such an extent that dark adaptation occurs, the two sources may have appreciably different apparent luminances, depending on their spectral composition. In view of these problems, it is necessary to specify the source intensity whenever numerical values for photometric quantities are quoted.

Scotopic functions are obtained whenever the retinal illumination is below 10^{-3} candelas/meter^2, the subject is dark-adapted, and the image of the source is projected on extrafoveal portions of the retina. (The definition of a *candela* is that a full radiator at the temperature of the solidification of platinum possesses a luminance of exactly 60 candelas/cm^2. A *full radiator* [or *black-body radiator*] is defined as a hollow cavity that is completely enclosed except for a small opening through which radiation is emitted. At low temperatures the opening looks black because the light that enters the cavity is largely absorbed after multiple reflections and diffusions occur. The full radiator is an important theoretical source of radiant energy because its properties are fully defined by its temperature.) Foveal vision is photopic, even at low levels of illumination, and the standard C.I.E. curve can be used. Strictly speaking, the C.I.E. average was obtained under impure conditions which were actually intermediate between photopic and scotopic and does not coincide precisely with the photopic luminous efficiency curve (see Gibson, 1940; Jainski, 1938; Lüthy, 1942; Jaggi, 1939). A direct comparison of the two curves is presented in Figure 3.7.

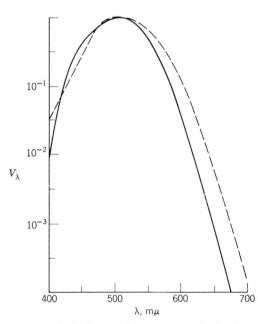

Fig. 3.6 The C.I.E. curve for scotopic relative luminous efficiency V_λ' plotted logarithmically against wavelength (solid line). The broken line shows the photopic curve V_λ shifted 48 mμ toward the violet. (From Le Grand, 1957.)

Although the literature is not entirely unanimous on this point, it seems that the maximum efficiency of the photopic curve is displaced toward the upper end of the visible spectrum (approximately 565 mμ). Values below the C.I.E. standard are typically obtained above 600 mμ, suggesting an inverse Purkinje effect at the very long wavelengths. A systematic shift toward higher values is found at the shortwave end of the visible spectrum.

These observations have given rise to the *duplicity theory of vision;* this theory states that the eye cannot be treated as a uniform photoreceptor but must be considered a combination of two types of receptors, (1) a daylight receptor which functions at high levels of illumination and has a spectral sensitivity described by the photic luminous efficiency curve and (2) a night receptor which functions at very low levels of illumination and has a spectral sensitivity defined by the scotopic luminous efficiency curve. A nonrandom distribution of these two types of receptors must be assumed.

A *mean* or *standard observer* can be defined by means of the C.I.E. average luminous efficiency curve; the transition from radiometric to photometric terms is accomplished via this imaginary visual system. We have seen that the perception of a source depends not only on its radiance L_e, but also on the product VL_e. The photometric equivalent of radiance, called *luminance* (L), is therefore defined as

$$L = K_m V_\lambda L_e$$

where K_m is a constant determined by the units of measurement for L and L_e. *Luminous efficiency* (K_λ) is determined as

$$K_\lambda = K_m V_\lambda$$

and K_m therefore describes the *maximum luminous efficiency*. The reciprocal of the maximum luminous efficiency, $1/K_m$, represents the *mechanical equivalent of light*.

The luminance of a source has several interesting properties. We have already seen the *law of transitivity* in operation. If two pairs of luminances L_1L_2 and L_2L_3 appear identical, a pair formed by the extreme members L_1L_3 also appears identical. The *law of proportionality* states that two areas that appear to be equally bright remain so when the sources are multiplied by the same number. The *additivity law* proposes that the luminance of a compound stimulus is an integral function of the luminances of its components.

All photometric quantities can be described by a single unit because they can be derived from this concept of luminance. *Luminous intensity* (I), the counterpart of radiant intensity, is directly related to luminance; *luminous flux* (F) is related to the product of the luminous intensity and the solid angle, and *illuminance* is a direct function of luminous flux (E) or luminous emittance (M) per unit area.

Luminous intensity is measured in candelas (cd), an arbitrary measure which replaces a number of obsolete standards, such as the international candle and Hefner's candle. The unit of luminous flux is the *lumen* (candela $\times$ steradian); illumination or illuminance is measured in *phot* (lumen $\times$ cm^2) or *lux* (lumen $\times$ meter^2). The lux is equal to a *meter-candle*. A nonmetric *footcandle* (10.764 lux) is sometimes used.

Many units of luminance have been employed. Common units are the *stilb* (cd/cm^2), the *nit* (cd/meter^2), or equivalent nonmetric measures cd/ft^2 or cd/in.^{2}. Another system has made use of the perfect source described by Lambert's law (i.e., a source which has a constant radiance, independent of the direction of view). The illumination of one phot on a perfect diffusing surface produces a luminance of one *equivalent phot* or *lambert*. In this system are also the *equivalent lux* or *apostilb*, which describe the luminance of a perfect diffusing surface with an illumination of one lux. The nonmetric system uses the *equivalent footcandle* (efc) or *footlambert* which represents the luminance of a perfect diffuser with an illumination of 1 lumen/ft^2.

The appearance of an extended source is determined by its luminance. Retinal illumination is always proportional to the luminance, regardless of size or distance of the source. The relationship between the luminance and resultant retinal illumination is in part a function of the transmittive properties (i.e., the refractory index) of the optical media that separate the source from the retina. Since the refractory index of air is almost unity (1.0003), we can generally disregard this factor and concentrate on the influence of the membranes and fluids of the eye. First, a small quantity (about 2%) of the incident light is reflected by the outer surface of the cornea. Some attempts have been made to calculate the absorption of radiant energy in the media of the eye by assuming that the eye has absorption characteristics similar to those of water. This assumption permits some interesting speculations about the nature of the biological photoreceptors. For instance, infrared radiations above 1400 mµ are completely absorbed by the media of the eye (i.e., transformed into heat). However, almost half of the infrared waves below 1000 mµ reach the retina, suggesting that the photoreceptors themselves are insensitive to wavelengths above 700 mµ (the upper limit of the visible portion of the spectrum). Measurements of the actual absorption properties of vertebrate eyes (Goldmann et al., 1950; Lenoble and Le Grand, 1953) have indicated that the actual values are quite close to those predicted in this theoretical schema.

The theoretical model does not, unfortunately, work at the other end of the visible spectrum, since water is almost totally transparent for ultraviolet wavelengths. Actual measurements (Hosoya, 1929) have suggested, however, that the lower limits of the visible spectrum may be determined by the absorption properties of the optical media. The cornea and vitreous body absorb ultraviolet wavelengths below about 300 mµ, a value which agrees well with the absorption band of the lens in children. As a person becomes older, the ultraviolet absorption band of his lens moves gradually higher, until it may exceed 400 mµ in the aged. The existence of wide individual differences with respect to the upper limits of ultraviolet absorption explains some of the variance found in the relative luminous efficiency curves for different observers.

The transparency of the eye has been investigated empirically (Ludvigh and MacCarthy, 1938; Solomon, 1950; Wald, 1949; Weale, 1954), and the general conclusion from these studies is surprising. The transparency of the media of the eye, particularly in older persons, appears to be very low. There is loss from absorption, particularly at the lower wavelengths, and a great deal of diffusion scatters the projection of flux on the parts of the retina that are not involved in the direct projection of the image of the source.

Another factor that affects the illumination of the retina is the size of the pupil. Light falling on the retina elicits optic reflexes which adjust the diameter of the pupil to the intensity of the incident light. This reflex protects the retina from sudden extreme changes in illumination, but it is of only limited value because the pupil has a rather restricted range of possible apertures (about 2 to 8 mm in man for a ratio of approximately 25:1). Normal eyes show *isocoria*, i.e., equal pupil diameters in both eyes even though they may receive different amounts of light. The temporal course of the pupillary response (as well as its limited range) suggests that this protective reflex serves primarily to help the photoreceptors adjust to changes in ambient illumination. The pupil constricts sharply within 200 to 400 msec after a sharp increase in illumination. The pupil continues to contract for a few seconds, and the small aperture is maintained for a few minutes. Gradually, however, the retina adapts to the new level of illumination and the pupillary muscles relax, permitting a return to almost normal levels. Decreases in illumination produce an opposite sequence of events which also returns the eye to nearly its normal level. Since the effect of illumination appears to be relatively independent of wavelength, a crude estimation of relative luminous efficiency functions can be obtained by measuring pupillary dilation in response to radiant energy from different portions of the spectrum. This measure lacks precision, largely because short wavelengths seem to produce disproportionately large effects on the pupillary reflex. Other factors that affect pupillary diameter and may interfere with its usefulness as an index of relative luminous efficiency include (1) eccentricity (pupillary diameter increases as a function of the angular distance between the point of fixation and the center of the source), (2) accommodation and convergence (contraction), (3) emotionality (dilatation), (4) irritation (contraction), and (5) fatigue (dilatation).

It is possible to consider retinal illumination without referring to pupillary diameter, simply by projecting into the eye a light beam that is so small as to take up only part of the pupillary aperture. Such a *Maxwellian view* can be achieved by focusing the image of a point source by means of a lens onto the plane of the observer's pupil. Stiles and Crawford (1933a, b) discovered a peculiar phenomenon with respect to Maxwellian images. If two point sources of equal intensity are focused on the plane of the pupil, and if the image of one of them is in the center of the pupil but the other is near its border, the image in the center will appear much brighter although the retinal illumination provided by the two sources is equal (see Figure 3.8). It appears from these observations that a peripheral point of entry into the eye is less effective than a central entry through the pupil. Several empirical equations have been suggested to quantify this effect; perhaps the simplest has been proposed by Moon and Spencer (1943). The relative directional efficiency (η) of a point of entry is determined by its distance (r) from the point of maximum efficiency (which is not always

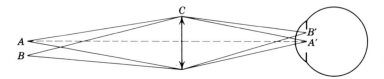

Fig. 3.8   The Stiles-Crawford effect. (From Le Grand, 1957.)

in the exact center of the pupil). The complete formula reads

$$\eta = 1 - 0.085r^2 + 0.022r^4$$

The Stiles-Crawford effect is minimal at low intensities (it may even be reversed for some observers), and is greater at the extremes of the visible spectrum. It severely affects an otherwise convenient measure of retinal illumination, the *troland* (or photon). The troland represents the product of the luminance (L) of an extended source (expressed in cd/meter²) and the area (S) of the pupil (expressed in mm²) and assumes equal directional efficiency. Because of the Stiles-Crawford effect, the area (S) of the pupil is not a useful factor. Instead, an effective pupil area S_e which takes into account the unequal transmittive efficiency of the pupil must be calculated. Assuming that the Stiles-Crawford effect is additive, the effective pupil area can be determined from the following formula:

$$S_e = \frac{1}{4}d^2\left[1 - 0.085\left(\frac{d^2}{8}\right) + 0.002\left(\frac{d^4}{48}\right)\right]$$

The product S_eL provides an estimate of the *effective retinal illumination level* which is expressed in terms of *effective trolands*.

Variations of the area of projection of a narrow beam of monochromatic radiant energy also produce a change in the subjective response to color. This modification is too large to be attributable to the concurrent change in the level of illumination, but seems to be directly related to the obliquity of the projection on the retina.

The Trivariance of Vision

The vertebrate eye is an unusual photoreceptor. Its response is not univariant, as for almost all other photoreceptors, but trivariant (i.e., requires the determination of three variables). The eye's response to monochromatic radiation can be determined completely by two quantities, its wavelength (λ) and its radiant flux (P) or related measures such as radiance. The response of the eye to polychromatic radiation requires an additional specification of the energy distribution (E_λ) within the visible spectrum.

The addition of two monochromatic luminances, $L_1 + L_2$ (i.e., the additive superposition of flux on the same part of the retina), always produces a light; the appearance of this light can be exactly reproduced by adding a pure monochromatic luminance L to white light. This basic law of the trivariance of vision can be expressed as

$$L_1S_1 + L_2S_2 \equiv L_wW + L_\lambda\lambda$$

where λ is the dominant wavelength of the mixture.

Luminances are always additive, but colors can neutralize each other (i.e., the addition of two monochromatic lights L_1 and L_2 can result in white light, a sensation of colorlessness). Colors with this property are said to be *complementary*. Complementaries neutralize each other only if the ratio of luminances is suitably chosen. If the ratio is inappropriate, the mixture has the color of the dominant wavelength but appears to be diluted with white. The addition of wavelengths near the extremes of the spectrum does not produce white light but a new radiation called *purple*. There is a complete range of pure purples from violet to red, and these can be visualized to complete a circular spectrum of colors. The purples are complementary to monochromatic radiations between 492 and 567 mμ (green) which do not have a complementary monochromatic radiation within the normal visible spectrum; it has become customary to specify a purple radiation in terms of the wavelength of its spectral complementary.

Several important experimental facts about color mixtures have been stated as *Grassmann's law:* the terms of a colorimetric equation are *additive*, they can be *multiplied* by the same number, they are *associative* (the sum of several luminances can be replaced by any other sum which is equivalent to it), and they are *transitive* (two mixtures, each of which appears identical with a third, are themselves equivalent). It follows directly from these laws that (1) the sum of any number of pure luminances is equivalent to white light plus a single pure luminance, and that (2) the appearance of any light can be exactly reproduced by the addition of a pure luminance to white light.

It is customary to replace the three variables

λ, L_w, and L_λ by the total luminance of the mixture ($L = L_w + L_\lambda$) and the *colorimetric purity ratio* ($p_c = L_\lambda/L$). This factor is unity for monochromatic lights and zero for white light. Thus there is a distinction between *luminous variables* (in this case the luminance of the mixture) and *chromatic variables* (the wavelength λ and the colorimetric purity ratio p_c). With this conceptual framework, it is useful to think of vision as being divided into a *luminous univariance* and a *chromatic bivariance.*

It is necessary to introduce here the concept of *tristimulus value* (*C*): this is defined as the ratio of the radiant flux (*P*) of a reference stimulus to a radiant flux (*e*) arbitrarily chosen as the unit of radiant flux for that reference stimulus. If we select three monochromatic radiations, λ_1, λ_2, and λ_3, as reference stimuli, we can determine corresponding tristimulus values by computing the values for $C_1 = P_1/e_1$, etc. This simple transformation permits the use of different units of magnitude for the components of a color mixture.

If $\lambda_1 < \lambda_2 < \lambda_3$, and if λ_1 and λ_3 are too far apart to be complementary, $C_1 + C_2$ results in a mixture of white light plus a single monochromatic radiation (or purple). It is then possible to select C_1 and C_2 for which the mixture is complementary to λ_2, and the sum of C_1, C_2, and C_3 is white light:

$$C_1 + C_2 + C_3 = C_w W$$

If λ_1 and λ_3 are too closely adjacent in the spectrum to be complementary, values can be chosen for the two wavelengths so that

$$C_1 + C_3 = C_w W + C_2$$

This can be written as

$$C_1 - C_2 + C_3 = C_w W$$

and is a mathematical expression for the impor-

tant empirical observation that the tristimulus values of C_2 can have negative values. It can be shown mathematically that any monochromatic light is equivalent to the *algebraic* sum of suitable amounts of three reference lights, and that one of the tristimulus values must be negative. If the sources are not monochromatic, all three trichromatic stimulus values may be positive.

In practice, all colors can be defined solely by their chromatic variables, and only relative values are needed to describe the three tristimulus values. Every light can be identified by two of the *chromaticity coordinates* or *trichromatic coefficients* (*c*); these are defined (with their sums equal to unity) as

$$c_1 = \frac{C_1}{C_1 + C_2 + C_3}$$

and

$$c_2 = \frac{C_2}{C_1 + C_2 + C_3}$$

$$c_3 = \frac{C_3}{C_1 + C_2 + C_3}.$$

The chromaticity coordinates can be represented in an equilateral *Maxwellian color triangle* with a height of unity (see Figure 3.9). In this diagram any light of coordinates c_i is represented by a point *M*, whose distance from the sides is equal to the coordinates, i.e., $MN_i = c_i$. The sum of the lengths MN_i is equal to the height of the triangle. The reference stimuli are represented by the corners of the triangle. To circumvent the inconvenience of oblique coordinates, a rectangular *chromaticity diagram* can be constructed in which the chromaticity coordinates c_1 and c_2 are abscissa and ordinate of the system respectively; the term c_3 is not represented but can be calculated, since the three coordinates sum to unity. In this system the reference stimuli are shown by points on the

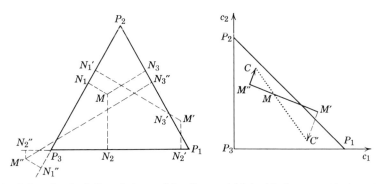

Fig. 3.9 Color triangle (left) and chromaticity diagram (right) with the geometrical construction illustrating the center-of-gravity rule. (From Le Grand, 1957.)

axes at unit distance from the origin and by the origin itself.

Several empirical determinations of chromaticity coordinates have been undertaken. The classical investigation was reported by Maxwell (1890) who selected monochromatic radiations at 630 mμ (red), 528 mμ (green), and 457 mμ (blue) as reference stimuli. Subsequent investigators have continued to use red, green, and blue reference stimuli, and the systems have been known as *RGB* systems. An *average chromaticity function* was adopted by the C.I.E. on the basis of corrected average data from two major investigations by Wright (1929) and Guild (1931). This function uses the *RGB* system with reference stimuli at 700, 546.1, and 435.8 mμ (see Figure 3.10). Its spectrum locus is identical to the straight line *RG*, so that the physical addition of red and green can essentially reproduce all intermediate radiations. The luminous values of the reference standards can be calculated on the basis of the average luminous efficiency curve, and the actual values turn out to be $l_r = 1$; $l_g = 4.59$; $l_b = 0.06$. The luminous unit of any stimulus can be calculated from the formula $l_s = l_r r + l_g g + l_b b$. Stimuli with a luminous value of zero lie on the line

$$l_r r + l_g g + l_b b = 0$$

which has been called the *alchyne.* Points on this line define stimuli that have no luminous flux regardless of tristimulus value.

The *RGB* systems are not very convenient for practical colorimetric calculations because one of the chromaticity coordinates is always negative. Furthermore, the apparent psychological "primacy" of the reference stimuli induces the experimenter to attribute special qualities to these arbitrary points. It has therefore become customary to select imaginary reference stimuli in an *XYZ* system (see Figure 3.11) which is based on the following considerations. The points representing two of the reference stimuli, *X* and *Z*, are on the alchyne, and the tristimulus values *X* and *Z* therefore have no luminous flux. The tristimulus value for *Y* is equal to the luminous flux, i.e., l_x and l_z are equal to zero; l_y is equal to one. The sides *X Y* and *YZ* of the triangle formed by the reference stimuli are tangents to the spectrum locus. The system is based on an equi-energy spectrum (i.e., the source *W* is at the center of the diagram).

The tristimulus values of the *XYZ* system are related to the tristimulus values of the *RGB* system

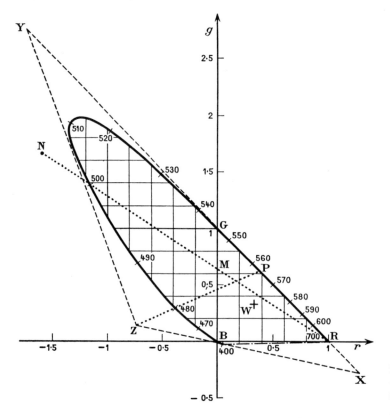

Fig. 3.10 The *RGB* chromaticity diagram as defined by the C.I.E. (From Le Grand, 1957.)

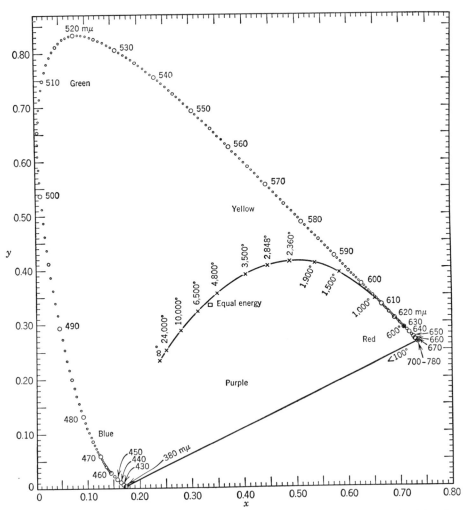

Fig. 3.11   The x, y chromaticity diagram of the I.C.I. system. The abscissa is the ratio of the tristimulus value X to the sum of all three $(X + Y + Z)$. The ordinate is the ratio of Y to this sum. The parts of the spectrum locus are identified by wavelength in millimicra. The region bounded by this locus and the straight line (purple border) joining its extremes represent all chromaticities producible by actual stimuli. The central curved line represents the chromaticities of the complete radiator and is called the Planckian locus. Points on this locus are identified by the temperature of the radiator expressed on the Kelvin scale. (From Judd, 1951.)

as follows:

$$X = 2.7689R + 1.7517G + 1.1302B$$
$$Y = R + 4.5907G + 0.0601B$$

and

$$Z = 0.0565G + 5.5943B$$

The chromaticity coordinates can be calculated from these values using the relationship

$$\frac{x}{X} = \frac{y}{Y} = \frac{z}{Z} = X + Y + Z.$$

(see Table 3.1).

Primary light sources can be specified colorimetrically by their three tristimulus values using the formulas

$$X = \Sigma a\bar{x}E_\lambda \Delta\lambda$$
$$Y = \Sigma a\bar{y}E_\lambda \Delta\lambda$$
$$Z = \Sigma a\bar{z}E_\lambda \Delta\lambda$$

where Σ denotes a summation over all equal intervals $\Delta\lambda$ in the visible spectrum (such as the summation of 97 intervals of a 5-mμ width between 377.5 and 772.5 mμ). E_λ is the value of the spectral

TABLE 3.1

Chromaticity coordinates (x, y, z) of the spectrum colors

Wavelength, mμ	Chromaticity Coordinates			Wavelength, mμ	Chromaticity Coordinates		
	x	y	z		x	y	z
380	0.1741	0.0050	0.8209	550	0.3016	0.6923	0.0061
385	0.1740	0.0050	0.8210	555	0.3373	0.6589	0.0038
390	0.1738	0.0049	0.8213	560	0.3731	0.6245	0.0024
395	0.1736	0.0049	0.8215	565	0.4087	0.5896	0.0017
				570	0.4441	0.5547	0.0012
400	0.1733	0.0048	0.8219				
405	0.1730	0.0048	0.8222	575	0.4788	0.5202	0.0010
410	0.1726	0.0048	0.8226	580	0.5125	0.4866	0.0009
415	0.1721	0.0048	0.8231	585	0.5448	0.4544	0.0008
420	0.1714	0.0051	0.8235	590	0.5752	0.4242	0.0006
				595	0.6029	0.3965	0.0006
425	0.1703	0.0058	0.8239				
430	0.1689	0.0069	0.8242	600	0.6270	0.3725	0.0005
435	0.1669	0.0086	0.8245	605	0.6482	0.3514	0.0004
440	0.1644	0.0109	0.8247	610	0.6658	0.3340	0.0002
445	0.1611	0.0138	0.8251	615	0.6801	0.3197	0.0002
				620	0.6915	0.3083	0.0002
450	0.1566	0.0177	0.8257				
455	0.1510	0.0227	0.8263	625	0.7006	0.2993	0.0001
460	0.1440	0.0297	0.8263	630	0.7079	0.2920	0.0001
465	0.1355	0.0399	0.8246	635	0.7140	0.2859	0.0001
470	0.1241	0.0578	0.8181	640	0.7190	0.2809	0.0001
				645	0.7230	0.2770	0.0000
475	0.1096	0.0868	0.8036				
480	0.0913	0.1327	0.7760	650	0.7260	0.2740	0.0000
485	0.0687	0.2007	0.7306	655	0.7283	0.2717	0.0000
490	0.0454	0.2950	0.6596	660	0.7300	0.2700	0.0000
495	0.0235	0.4127	0.5638	665	0.7311	0.2689	0.0000
				670	0.7320	0.2680	0.0000
500	0.0082	0.5384	0.4534				
505	0.0039	0.6548	0.3413	675	0.7327	0.2673	0.0000
510	0.0139	0.7502	0.2359	680	0.7334	0.2666	0.0000
515	0.0389	0.8120	0.1491	685	0.7340	0.2660	0.0000
520	0.0743	0.8338	0.0919	690	0.7344	0.2656	0.0000
				695	0.7346	0.2654	0.0000
525	0.1142	0.8262	0.0596				
530	0.1547	0.8059	0.0394	700	0.7347	0.2653	0.0000
535	0.1929	0.7816	0.0255	705	0.7347	0.2653	0.0000
540	0.2296	0.7543	0.0161	710	0.7347	0.2653	0.0000
545	0.2658	0.7243	0.0099	715	0.7347	0.2653	0.0000

From Judd, 1951.

emittance of the source; by arbitrarily selecting the value for $a \, \Delta\lambda$ at unity, relative expressions for X, Y, and Z can be found according to the simplified formulas $X = \Sigma \bar{x} E_\lambda$; $Y = \Sigma \bar{y} E_\lambda$; $Z = \Sigma \bar{z} E_\lambda$. Given the spectral distribution E_λ of a source, its chromaticity coordinates can be easily calculated with this formula.

An alternate system for specifying the color of a source is to determine its dominant wavelength (λ) and its colorimetric purity (p_c), provided that white light is conventionally specified. Using the diagram presented in Figure 3.12, let O stand for the source of achromatic light and M the light to be specified. The dominant wavelength λ is the monochromatic radiation which corresponds to L, the point on the spectrum locus which lies in a straight line connecting points O and L through the point M. The *colorimetric purity* (p_c) cannot be read directly from the graph. It is estimated by the *excitation purity* (p_e) which can be derived as follows:

$$P_e = \frac{OM}{OL} = \frac{x - x_0}{x_\lambda - x_0} = \frac{y - y_0}{y_\lambda - y_0}$$

(The coordinates x and y are those of the point L'' on the line of the pure purples.) Lines of equal excitation purity can be then drawn with O at the center, as shown in Figure 3.13.

DISPARITIES BETWEEN THE PHYSICAL AND PSYCHOLOGICAL PROPERTIES OF VISUAL STIMULI

Some interesting differences between psychological and physical determinations of stimulus parameters must now be discussed. On the basis of physical measurements, all monochromatic radiations are "simple," and there is no valid reason for selecting any one wavelength or number of wavelengths as primary. However, some colors (such as red) subjectively appear to be simple (i.e., of a unitary character), whereas others (such as orange) seem to be mixtures of more primary hues. Most observers agree on purplish-red, yellow, and blue as simple or primary colors.

Similarly, all monochromatic radiations have a purity equal to unity, but the psychological correlate of purity (saturation) varies as a function of wavelength (see Figure 3.13). For instance, violet is described as maximally saturated, red assumes an intermediate position, and yellow is considered to have little saturation or color. The psychological sensation of saturation also varies as a function of luminance, being low at both low and very high

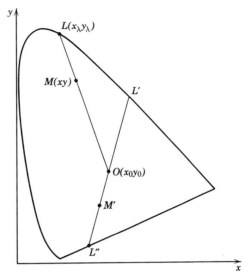

Fig. 3.12 The definition of dominant wavelength. (From Le Grand, 1957.)

levels of luminance (Hunt, 1952, 1953). The optimal level of luminance is not constant over the visible spectrum. The extremes require relatively little luminance to reach maximal saturation, but the medial portions of the spectrum require very high intensities (Purdy, 1931b).

Finally, hue, the psychological correlate of wavelength, varies to some degree as a function of luminance. Increases in luminance shift subjective color perception toward the blue and yellow portions of the spectrum. Violet and blue-green lights take on a bluer appearance, and red and yellow-green appear yellower. This *Bezold-Brücke effect* suggests that there may be two distinct maxima in the spectrum corresponding to yellow and blue which somehow "dominate" the rest of the wavelengths. The green portion presumably separates these two spheres of influence. Purdy (1931a) has presented data suggesting that the magnitude of the Bezold-Brücke effect can be large. For intance, the color of 525 mμ at 1000 trolands was matched at 545 mμ when the intensity was lowered to 100 trolands, a shift of more than 5% of the entire visible spectrum.

Perhaps the most interesting interaction of physical properties and psychological reactions occurs when the purity of a spectral radiation is changed. It has long been known (Aubert, 1865; Müller, 1931) that the addition of white light to a monochromatic radiation results in a considerable change in apparent color (hue). Several more recent investigations (Newhall et al., 1943; Mac-

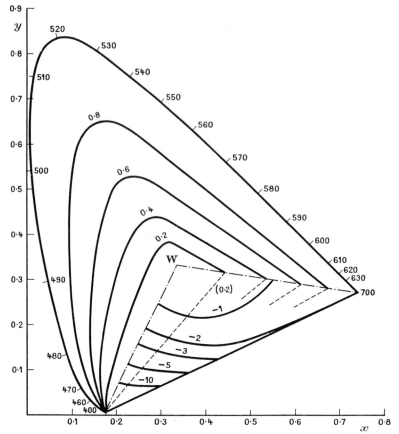

Fig. 3.13   Curves of equal colorimetric purity, with *W* as achromatic light. (From Le Grand, 1957.)

Adam, 1956) have verified and systematically studied this effect.

Psychological correlates of the luminance variable are quite difficult to define. For a primary source, there is really no corresponding psychological variable: the subjective sensation of *luminosity* is practically invariant over a wide range of luminance values because the visual receptor adapts rapidly. Secondary sources give rise to a distinct psychological attribute called *brightness*. This is a measure of the reflection of a surface in relation to the reflection of its background. (If such comparisons are precluded, it is impossible to determine whether a dark surface is well illuminated or a light surface poorly so.)

The psychological scale of brightness does not correspond simply and directly to the physical reflection of a surface. Fechner (1860) suggested over 100 years ago that the relationship between brightness and reflection might be described by the expression

$$A = a \log (1 + b\rho)$$

where *a* and *b* are constant and ρ is a measure of reflectance. Plateau (1873) thought that a monomial expression $A = a\rho^b$ might present a better theoretical figure. More recent experimental observations (Newhall et al., 1943) indicate that the hyperbolic formula may provide the better approximation (see Figure 3.14).

THE ABSOLUTE THRESHOLD

In the preceding discussion we have repeatedly pointed out that the biological photoreceptor is an imperfect transducer of radiant energy. Even within the visible spectrum there is a wide range of photic stimuli which do not contain sufficient energy to excite the vertebrate eye. The minimal quantity of radiant energy that elicits a response from a biological photoreceptor constitutes its *absolute threshold*.

The simplest and safest definition of the absolute threshold is not in terms of an absolute value; rather, the definition covers a range of stimulus values such that luminances greater than the upper limit are always perceived and values below the lower limit are never seen. The size of this range presumably tells us something about the precision of our measurements.

Direct measures of the absolute threshold have been obtained in a number of experimental situations. The simplest, but most artifact-prone, method consists of presenting the observer with a mechanical control device which directly varies the intensity of the test field. The subject repeatedly adjusts the control device to the lowest setting that permits the unambiguous perception of the test field. He thereby establishes a range of values the mean of which presumably represents an estimate of the absolute threshold. Early psychophysicists, Fechner and Wundt, predicted a more elaborate technique, the *method of limits*. This method requires the investigator to present alternate sequences of stimuli of increasing and decreasing intensity; in this way a *range of just perceptible luminances* (the lowest intensities of the ascending series which can just be perceived) and

a *range of just not perceptible luminances* (the highest intensities of the descending series which can definitely not be perceived) are established. The *arithmetic* average of the mean of the upper and lower ranges is then considered to be the absolute threshold.

A somewhat different conceptualization of the absolute threshold employs probability mathematics. Within the range of values between superthreshold intensities which are always perceived and subthreshold intensities which never produce a sensation, some intensity levels (those closer to the upper limit of the range of uncertainty) are more likely to elicit a response than others. Assuming that the range of uncertainty is established solely by random error, a normal Gaussian distribution of the errors can be assumed; the precision of measurement would be inversely proportional to the standard error of this distribution. The normal, S-shaped probability integral can then be applied, and the absolute threshold is defined as the mean (and median) of this distribution.

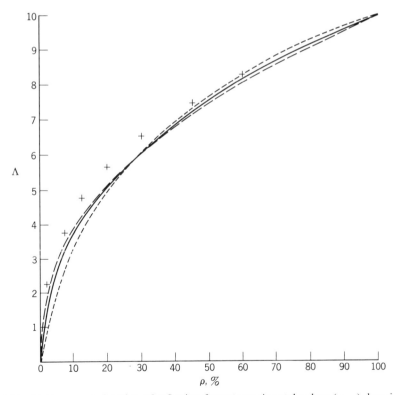

Fig. 3.14 Lightness as a function of reflection factor: experimental values (———), logarithmic formula (-----), hyperbolic formula (– – – –), experimental results with a black background (+). (From Le Grand, 1957.)

A practical application of this technique involves the *method of constant stimuli*; this method consists of repeated presentations of a few selected luminances which are known to be distributed fairly evenly in the range of uncertainty. The proportion of "yes" responses to each stimulus value is recorded, and the data are fitted to a normal cumulative probability curve. The mean (threshold) value is then obtained by interpolation. Various statistical refinements, such as the *method of least squares*, can be used to improve the fit of the empirical observations to the probability function.

In spite of its shortcomings, the vertebrate photoreceptor is a sensitive detector of radiant energy. We can calculate that the minimal energy flux of a stimulus of 10° apparent diameter required to elicit a response from a human observer is somewhere in the neighborhood of 9×10^{-16} watt. If we assume an energy loss of about 50% because of the absorption and diffusion properties of the ocular media, and an equal energy distribution over the retinal area which corresponds to a stimulus of that size (i.e., approximately 6.65 mm^2), the energy density on the retina is only about 7×10^{-15} watt/cm^2, about 40,000 times more sensitive than good photographic emulsions.

The Effect of Dark Adaptation

The absolute threshold varies as a function of dark adaptation. A subject who enters a dimly lit room after spending some time outdoors on a bright, sunny day will initially see nothing (i.e., his absolute threshold is almost infinity). As his eye adapts to the lowered level of illumination, the threshold moves progressively lower until he can distinguish every feature of the environment.

Dark adaptation is a biphasic phenomenon (see Figure 3.15). The first, relatively brief phase

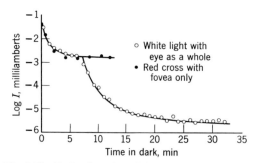

Fig. 3.15 Dark adaptation of the eye as a whole, showing separable functions for cones and rods. (From Hecht, 1934.)

represents photopic adaptation which typically reaches asymptotic values within 5 to 8 min. It is followed by a longer and more marked phase of scotopic adaptation which is not complete until about 60 min after the initial exposure to darkness. The overall change in threshold may exceed a 10,000-fold increase in sensitivity.

If the test conditions are maintained absolutely constant, there is surprisingly little intraobserver variability from one day to the next. In fact, some experimenters (Sheard, 1944), for instance, have suggested that the intrasubject variance for trained observers may approach the probable error of measurement and thus may reflect statistical rather than biological variations. The intersubject variability, on the other hand, is considerable, even for subjects judged to have "normal" vision. Several studies have reported standard deviations in excess of 0.2 log unit, indicating a total range of well over 1.2 log units (0.6 unit on either side of the mean). Much of this intersubject variance is related to the age of the observer.

The nature of the adaptation function can be significantly altered by preadaptation to a bright surface of uniform luminance. The adaptation function is thereby displaced laterally by an extension of the photopic adaptation phase, particularly when the duration of the preadaptation phase (t_0) exceeds 3 min, and the intensity of the preadaptation field (L_0) is high. Preadaptation also reduces the slope of the photopic and scotopic curves, particularly when L_0 is large.

When stimuli above 650 mμ (red) are used, only the photopic phase of dark adaptation occurs, regardless of the position of the retinal image. With stimuli below about 460 mμ (blue), only the scotopic function obtains. Monochromatic radiations from the middle of the spectrum (yellow-green) result in a biphasic adaptation function similar to that seen with white light.

The effects of dark adaptation do not disappear immediately when the illumination is raised. Particularly at moderate levels of ambient illumination, the effects of dark adaptation are reversed only very gradually. The absolute threshold remains significantly lowered for nearly an hour under most low-luminance conditions.

Other Factors Affecting the Absolute Threshold

The position of the retinal image. If we investigate the response to point sources, a pattern of retinal sensitivity that is predictable from its anatomical composition emerges. The central foveal region, which contains only cone receptors, has by far the lowest thresholds of the light-adapted eye; however, the region shows only the photopic phase of dark adaptation and loses its advantage when the completely dark-adapted eye is tested. Following complete adaptation, a central scotoma can be demonstrated, and the central foveal region is totally blind to many stimuli that are easily visible to peripheral receptors. This produces an interesting, totally automatic shift of the point of fixation from the fovea to an area with an eccentricity (distance from the center of the fovea) of about 2°.

Peripheral sensitivity is not, of course, uniform. In the dark-adapted eye, the absolute threshold seems to be the lowest about 10 to 20° from the center of the fovea and then gradually increases as the periphery of the retina is approached. The edge of the visual field has an absolute threshold under dark-adaptation conditions roughly equivalent to that of the fovea.

The size of the retinal image. This variation in sensitivity suggests that the size and location of the stimulus interact significantly. The area (S) of the retinal image is determined by the solid angle (w) subtended by the source at the eye ($S = 278w$). Variations of the solid angle shift the dark-adaptation curve parallel to the ordinate axis (Wald, 1938). This shift implies that the absolute threshold (L) is so related to the time (t) of onset of darkness and the solid angle of the object that

$$\log L = \log C - k \log w$$

where C is a function of t, and k varies with the eccentricity of the retinal image. An alternate expression for this relationship is

$$Lw^k = C$$

In the anatomically homogenous fovea, the luminous flux sums completely, regardless of area, provided that the apparent diameter (visual angle) of the stimulus does not exceed a few minutes of arc. The exponent k then becomes unity, and the absolute threshold is described by *Ricco's law*, $Lw = C$. This simple relationship holds for peripheral as well as foveal vision when the size of the stimulus does not exceed a few minutes of arc (partly because the anatomic composition of a small peripheral area can be considered to be uniform). If the visual angle varies between 7′ and 1°, k takes on a value of 0.3 to 0.5, and the foveal threshold is approximated by *Piéron's law*:

$$L^3 \sqrt{w} = C$$

Empirically, the value of k has been shown to

vary between 0.5 and unity as a function of object size and the eccentricity of the retinal image (Weinstein and Arnulf, 1946; Wald, 1938).

The absolute threshold of one eye is totally independent of the state of adaptation of the other (Crawford, 1940), but the binocular threshold of dark-adapted eyes appears to be slightly lower than that of either eye alone. Some of the earlier workers had reported that binocular thresholds were only half of the monocular value, but a survey of the more recent lierature (see Le Grand, 1957) suggests a more modest degree of summation.

Length of stimulus exposure. When the exposure time of the stimulus (t) is very brief (below about 100 msec), the threshold becomes a direct function of the product of time (t) and luminous flux (L): this is *Bloch's law*. For larger values of t the summation is only partial, and the product Lt increases with exposure time [$Lt = L_\infty (t + t_0)$] where t_0 is a constant. This relationship has been called the *Blondel-Rey law*. The linear function is not the best approximation of the empirical relationship because the response of the retina is not uniform but varies systematically as a function of eccentricity. Galifret and Piéron (1947) have suggested that a parabolic function with an exponent descriptive of this change in retinal responsivity may provide a better fit of the data.

The spectral composition of the stimulus. The absolute threshold is significantly affected by the wavelength of the stimulus, as we might expect on the basis of the luminous efficiency function. Threshold measurements reported by Wald (1945) suggest that aside from a small deviation at the shortwave end of the spectrum, the reciprocal of the foveal threshold measured in energy units (E), agrees almost perfectly with the photopic luminous efficiency curve (see Figure 3.16).

A comparison between the monochromatic and achromatic thresholds of the foveal and peripheral retinae shows that certain monochromatic stimuli are seen as colorless. The ratio of threshold for color to that for light (the *photochromatic interval*) is a function of wavelength. For peripheral vision the interval reaches a value of 100 at the lower end of the visible spectrum and gradually diminishes at higher wavelengths until it is essentially unity above 650 mμ. In the fovea the difference between chromatic and achromatic thresholds is typically much smaller and less clearly a function of wavelengths. Here, the psychological variable of saturation (i.e., purity)

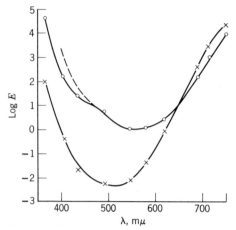

Fig. 3.16 The foveal threshold (circles) and the extra-foveal threshold (crosses) as functions of wavelength. The broken line is the photopic luminous efficiency curve. (From Le Grand, 1957.)

appears to be the more important determinant of the size of the photochromatic interval, with unsaturated yellow giving the largest values (Galifret and Piéron, 1947).

DIFFERENTIAL THRESHOLDS

Brightness (Luminance) Discrimination

The *differential luminance threshold* may be defined as the minimal increment in luminance (ΔL) that must be added to a particular stimulus to produce a just noticeable difference between L and $L/\Delta L$. Most commonly, this differential threshold is measured by some variant of the method of simultaneous contrast. Typically, the luminance of one portion of the visual field is fixed, and the subject is required to match it by adjusting the luminance of a variable portion. As discussed earlier, various psychophysical techniques are available for such measurements; the relative desirability of individual measures is largely a function of the law of diminishing returns, i.e., the ratio of increased precision to increased effort.

The differential threshold remains approximately constant over wide ranges of absolute luminances. The absolute size of the minimal increment ΔL required to detect a difference between two adjacent stimuli represents a roughly constant fraction (about 0.01) of the absolute luminance of the stimuli. This is *Weber's law*.

The differential threshold may be as low as 0.005 if the two parts of the field are not separated

by a distinct boundary. The introduction of a dark line may quadruple the differential threshold (Le Grand, 1933).

The absolute value of the differential threshold is significantly affected by the size of the test object and the duration of the stimulus exposure (see Figure 3.17). The influence of these variables is greatest at low levels of luminance and peripheral vision. The wavelengths of the test stimuli do not affect the size of the differential threshold unless very low luminances are used (Hecht et al., 1938).

Fechner (1860) used Weber's law as the basis for his famous proposition that the sensation (S) is proportional to the logarithm of the stimulus ($S = K \log_e L +$ constant). Weber's fraction is relatively inconstant. Moon and Spencer (1944) reviewed the available data and concluded that

$$\Delta L = c(a + \sqrt{L})^2$$

where c is a variable descriptive of subjective variance and a is a constant that equals 0.456 if L is expressed in candelas per square meter under conditions of high luminance. Under conditions of low luminance, ΔL may be larger than L and can be described adequately by the following empirical relationship:

$$\Delta L = L_s\left[1 + \left(\frac{L}{b}\right)^{0.63}\right]$$

(where L_s is the absolute threshold of the test stimulus and L is the luminance of the background).

Dark adaptation tends to reduce the differential threshold (Durup and Rousselot, 1939) as long as large test patches of low absolute luminance are used. However, this reduction does not imply a close correlation between the absolute and differential thresholds under other test conditions.

Color (Wavelength) Discrimination

A comparison of monochromatic radiations of constant luminance can be achieved if the stimuli are specified on the basis of either their chromaticity coordinates or their dominant wavelengths and purities. If we investigate spectral colors with a purity equal to unity, an interesting distribution of differential thresholds over the visible spectrum emerges. The upper end of the spectrum (above about 680 mμ) has a differential threshold of infinity and is therefore called the *region of constant hue*. The shortwave end of the spectrum is characterized by very large differential thresholds, whereas the middle, particularly those areas that

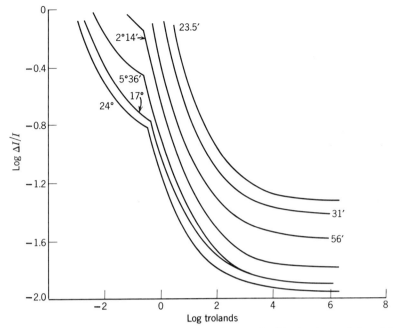

Fig. 3.17 Human intensity discrimination as dependent on the illumination and size of the test object. Each curve is for a separate size of test object. The visual angles subtended are indicated on the curves. (From Steinhardt, 1936. Reproduced by permission of the Rockefeller University Press.)

correspond to distinctly different "primary" colors, has very low threshold values. Normal observers show two pronounced and almost equal minimal threshold regions in the neighborhood of 490 mμ (the transition from blue to green) and 590 mμ (the transition from yellow to orange); some observers also show a third minimum near 440 mμ.

In the region of maximal spectral efficiency, differential thresholds may be of the order of 0.2 mμ, provided the test objects are fairly large and the retinal illumination is high. A sample distribution of differential thresholds is shown in Figure 3.18 (data from Wright, 1946).

The differential color threshold is remarkably insensitive to purity changes at the short (blue) end of the spectrum. Above 490 mμ the threshold rises sharply and systematically with purity deviations from unity. The contour of the threshold distribution (in contrast to its absolute level) does not appear to be affected at all by the addition of white light (Tyndall, 1933).

The threshold for purity changes (i.e., the minimal quantity of monochromatic luminance which must be added to a white light of a given luminance to produce a sensation of color) has itself been investigated (Priest and Brickwedde, 1938). As we might expect, the differential purity thresh-

old is largest in the yellow region (about 570 mμ) where the observer can detect a change in luminance before seeing the added color. In the region of constant hue, the differential purity threshold reaches asymptotic values for which $\Delta p = 0.005$. The threshold values fall sharply at the shortwave end of the distribution, and Δp may fall below 0.001 at 400 mμ. If a just noticeable quantity of white light is added to a monochromatic radiation, the threshold value for Δp varies little as a function of wavelength; the average value for a 2° field then is about 0.02 (Wright and Pitt, 1935).

The differential threshold for color should be calculable from the chromaticity diagram, the

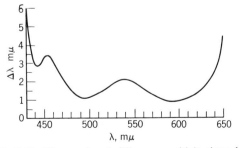

Fig. 3.18 The wavelength difference sensitivity throughout the spectrum. (From Wright and Pitt, 1934.)

relevant measure being the length of the straight line interconnecting the two radiations which are to be compared. The *XYZ* system does not serve well in this context because the distances between points that represent just distinguishable hues are not nearly constant in different portions of the diagram. Many attempts have been made to correct this basic fault of the otherwise useful system by a variety of linear transformations (Judd, 1935; Sinden, 1938; Breckenridge and Schaub, 1939). The results have not been encouraging. Perhaps the simplest and most useful of these transformations has been suggested by MacAdam (1942) using rectangular coordinates *U* and *V* and maintaining zero luminances for two of the reference stimuli. MacAdam's transformation is

$$U = \tfrac{2}{3}X, \quad V = Y, \quad W = -0.5X + 1.5Y + 0.5Z$$

TEMPORAL FACTORS IN VISION

Brief Stimuli

If a trained observer is asked to adjust the apparent brightness of a constant stimulus (L_a) to that of a very brief flash of light (L), a number of interesting phenomena can be recorded. At very low levels of luminance, the value of L_a is always below that of L and approaches L asymptotically as the duration (t) of the comparison stimulus exceeds several seconds. At high levels of luminosity, on the other hand, L_a is adjusted to values several times higher than that of the comparison stimulus if the duration of L is below a second or two. The asymptotic value of L_a is equal to L for values of t in excess of 3 to 4 sec. The initial overshoot was discovered by Broca and Sulzer in 1904 and is still called the *Broca-Sulzer phenomenon*. It has been suggested that the overshoot may represent the true, initial reaction of photoreceptors and that this reaction is inhibited by the continuing action of radiant energy. Circumstantial support for such an interpretation can be adduced from the observation that the successive presentation of very brief visual stimuli to the same area of the retina partially inhibits the apparent luminosity of the compound when the interstimulus interval is somewhere between 0.04 and 0.07 sec (Baumgardt and Segal, 1946).

The apparent duration of visual stimuli shorter than 150 to 200 msec is constant. When such stimuli are repeated at rapid regular intervals, a steady stimulus is perceived, provided the frequency of repetition exceeds the critical fusion frequency (c.f.f.). The luminance (L_m) of this steady stimulus is given by *Talbot's law:*

$$L_m = \frac{1}{t} \int_0^t L \, dt$$

The c.f.f. increases as a function of the mean luminance, a relationship which is described by *Porter's law,*

$$N = a \log L_m + b$$

except for a sharp change in the slope of the relationship that occurs in the low-luminance end of the function. Since the values of N are very different for day and night vision, Piéron has suggested a different formula, $N = a (L_m)^n$; the exponent n is different for day (0.25) and night (0.14) vision. The range of values for N is from 3 to 4 per second at very low levels of illumination to about 100 per second or more at very high levels.

At high levels of luminance, the c.f.f. is essentially independent of the wavelength of the source. This is not true at low luminances where the Purkinje effect becomes a factor. Dark adaptation lowers the c.f.f. if retinal illumination is high. At very low levels (below about 10 trolands), N increases after a brief initial decline for peripheral (but not foveal) vision.

At moderate intensities and low repetition rates, the subjective correlate of flicker frequency is almost identical to N. However, this correlation breaks down near the c.f.f. At very low illumination levels, repetition rates near the 3 to 4 per second fusion threshold produce subjective sensations comparable to those elicited by a repetition rate of 20 per second. At higher levels of luminance, flicker frequencies just below a high luminance threshold of 50 per second give rise to essentially the same subjective sensations.

One of the most surprising phenomena in this area is the relative stability of the c.f.f. with relatively drastic changes in the light-dark ratio (LDR) or pulse length to frequency ratio of the flicker (Bartley, 1959).

The c.f.f. is significantly affected, on the other hand, by changes in the illumination of retinal areas adjacent to the retinal image of the intermittent stimulus. The c.f.f. is slightly lowered with very low intensity illumination of adjacent areas of the retina. It is sharply *increased* when the illumination of the adjacent or surrounding field is increased beyond some minimal level, the value of this threshold being a function of the intensity of the intermittent stimulus.

The sensation of flicker is a peculiarly variable phenomenon. If a large source is presented at flicker frequencies just below the threshold value for the luminance of the field, the flicker appears to move from the periphery of the field at low levels of retinal illumination to the center at very high levels. At frequencies much below the c.f.f., the entire stimulus object appears to flicker at all levels of luminance. The perception of the light and dark phases of the flickering stimulus becomes greatly exaggerated at very low repetition rates (i.e., the light phase has an apparent luminance which greatly exceeds its actual value and the dark phase appears unnaturally black). Painful sensations and even disorientations in time and space may be reported under these conditions.

A different form of flicker sensation can be produced by alternating achromatic and monochromatic lights. The sensation of flicker in these conditions may be due to differences in luminance or to wavelength change itself. At very high levels of luminance, the fusion frequency for color is essentially constant across the visible spectrum, suggesting that luminance is the determining factor. At moderate intensities, the c.f.f. is lowest near 570 mμ (about 10 per second) and increases sharply toward each end of the spectrum (Troland, 1916). The purity of the colors has only a very limited influence on the c.f.f. (Galifret and Piéron, 1949).

Constant Stimuli

Constant visual stimuli of a duration (t) greater than several seconds give rise to a complex sensation which appears to be constituted of a number of distinct phases (see Figure 3.19).

A brief, initial *latent phase* (A-B) intervenes between the onset of the stimulus and the initial phase of the sensation. This interval is related to (1) the time required for a summation of the radiant energies of the stimulus to the level of the absolute threshold of the photoreceptor, (2) the time required for the photochemical reactions to transduce this radiant energy into proportional physiological signals, and (3) the delay imposed by the transmission of impulses from the photoreceptor to the primary projection and association areas of the central nervous system. The latter process involves several synaptic delays as well as the actual time required for the transmission of impulses along the optic nerve. The absolute intensity of the stimulus affects the duration of the latent phase to some extent.

The *initial or initiatory phase* (B-C-D) of the visual sensation is characterized by a perceptible increase in the subjective intensity of the sensation

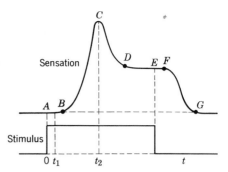

Fig. 3.19 Diagram illustrating the course of the sensation resulting from a constant stimulus. (From Le Grand, 1957.)

to some maximum value followed by a fall to asymptotic levels. This overshoot phenomenon is analogous to the Broca-Sulzer effect previously described for brief stimulus durations.

The *stable phase* (D-E) is shown in Figure 3.19 as a period of constant sensation. This is appropriate for relatively short stimuli; it must be modified for longer durations because adaptation processes reduce the intensity of sensation as a function of time.

When the stimulus is removed, the sensation remains essentially unchanged for some time (E-F) because the same factors that were responsible for the latent phase are still operating. The sensation then declines gradually (F-G), a phenomenon called *persistence*. Piéron (1939) has suggested that the duration of the period E-F is inversely proportional to $\sqrt{L}$ and the total duration of the *extinction phase* (E-G) increases as a function of L.

A number of *afterimages* (not indicated in Figure 3.19) may occur if the luminance of the stimulus is fairly high. If the test stimulus consists of white light, a stream of successive color sensations covering the entire spectrum may occur. With stimuli of a specific spectral wavelength, the afterimages tend to alternate between the corresponding hue and its complementary color.

SPATIAL FACTORS IN VISION

Throughout the preceding discussion we have repeatedly mentioned interactions between adjacent portions of the retina. A closer look at some of these relationships may now be useful. *Spatial summation* has been demonstrated with respect to absolute thresholds for peripheral vision. The threshold of a test stimulus that consists of two adjacent segments increases as a function of the distance between their retinal representations, up to a maximum separation of about 150 mμ when individual components become distinctly visible. The interaction of foveal representations stops at a separation of only 10 min (Beitel, 1934). These summation effects are only seen when the two stimuli have low and roughly equivalent luminance levels. If one stimulus appears brighter than the other, an inhibitory reaction occurs, and the perception of the weaker stimulus is reduced or totally absent.

A special example of these spatial interaction effects is the influence of the luminance (L_0) of the background of two stimuli of luminances L and ΔL which are to be compared for apparent brightness. The differential threshold is lowest when the luminance of the background is identical to that of the standard ($L_0 = L$), and highest when L_0 is much above L. The differential threshold is also significantly affected by the presentation of a very bright light a small distance from the test field. This *glare* phenomenon has been studied extensively by Holladay (1926) and Stiles (1929). The inhibitory effect can be quantified empirically, and the differential threshold then becomes equal to that appropriate to a stimulus of a luminance L plus β, where $\beta = 10\ E\theta^{-2}$ and θ is the angular distance in degrees of the glare stimulus from the test field. The apparent diameter of the source and the spectral composition of its radiation are essentially constant.

SOME PERCEPTUAL PHENOMENA

In the preceding sections of this chapter we have attempted to (1) specify the properties of a visual stimulus and its effect on biological photoreceptors, and (2) describe the corresponding subjective sensations of human observers. The human nervous system does not, however, restrict itself to a simple reaction to isolated visual stimuli; rather, it responds often very peculiarly to spatial and temporal relationships between complex visual stimuli. These complex sensations are not simply and directly related to the physical properties of the component stimuli, and we do not understand the integrative action of the nervous system well enough to discuss the physical or physiological basis for them at this time. These "higher-order" sensations are therefore typically treated as "perceptions"; this concept presumably implies the operation of complex integrative processes which somehow transform simple sensations into quasi-sensory experiences that are not adequately described by reference to their physical properties.

As our understanding of neural mechanisms progresses, these apparently complex phenomena reduce to relatively simple interaction processes, and one may hope that we may someday be able to discuss sensory mechanisms without taking refuge behind "perceptual" concepts. We are not yet anywhere near this point, however, and our discussion could not be complete without at least a cursory treatment of these phenomena.

The simplest visual stimulus is homogeneous with respect to color (wavelength), saturation (purity), and brightness (radiance). If such a *Ganzfeld* is sufficiently large to encompass the total visual field, the observer perceives the visual stimulus as devoid of surface, limits, or other dimensions (Koffka, 1935). If a gradient of illumination is introduced into a *Ganzfeld,* so that the brightness difference between immediately adjacent areas is not above the differential threshold (although the difference of the extremes clearly exceeds this liminal value), the entire visual field assumes an apparent brightness that corresponds roughly to the *average* illumination of the visual field. If a boundary is introduced to separate the field into two equal sections, the brightness of each half appears internally uniform; however, a brightness difference exists between halves and a clear step function separates them. These effects illustrate the tendency toward *assimilation* (homogeneity) and the role of *contours* (contrast); both are quite common in visual perception.

If distinct gradients of color, saturation, or brightness are introduced into the visual field, the tendency toward homogeneity cannot maintain the illusion of a uniform field; distinct segments then take on dimensions of size, shape, color, or brightness which are noticeably different from the rest of the field. Aspects of the visual field that are spatially adjacent or very similar with respect to some of their basic properties tend to form compound stimuli. They appear to be separated from the rest of the visual field by distinct contours or boundaries. These "figures," as the Gestalt psychologists have called compound stimuli in contradistinction to the homogeneous "ground" of the visual field, are the basic units of visual perception.

The perception of space is fundamental to the interpretation of compound stimuli as figures. Traditionally, a number of visual and kinesthetic stimuli have been considered essential to the perception of spatial relationships. The most common of these stimuli are the following. (1) *Linear Perspective.* Parallel lines appear to approach each other in the distance. (2) *Relative Size.* The largest figures in the visual field appear closest. (Both of these influences are related to the fact that a constant distance between two stimuli subtends a smaller angle at the eye when viewed from a distance.) (3) *Aerial Perspective.* Because uniformity is commonly associated with objects viewed at some distance, the relative amount of contrast can be used as a cue for distance. (4) *Interposition.* Objects that appear to cover other figures are seen as closer (the essential cue here appears to be the continuity of the contours of objects). (5) *Accommodation* and *Convergence.* The proprioceptive feedback from the oculomotor muscles changes as a function of distance. (6) *Stereoscopic Information.* The retinal images of an object are not identical in the two eyes. The extent of the difference is a function of distance, since it depends on variations in the convergence angle of the eyes.

Gibson (1950) has suggested that the sensation of *depth* may be defined by considering *gradients of texture,* a concept which encompasses most, if not all, of the individual variables which are traditionally considered. Rows or columns of objects which diminish in size and increase in density from the bottom of the visual field toward the top create a perception of a receding slanting plane. A gradual change in such a gradient produces the perception of a corner; a distinct break constitutes an edge (see Figure 3.20).

The sensation of motion presents an interesting perceptual problem. Under the best conditions, a stimulus must be displaced in space at a minimal rate of about 2 min of arc per second before continuous movements rather than discrete images are perceived. The exact value of this *absolute movement threshold* is influenced by the intensity and size of the stimulus as well as by the relative brightness of the background. Ekman and Dahlbaeck (1956) have reported that the apparent velocity of a moving stimulus increases approximately as the square of its objective velocity. A remarkably low differential velocity threshold of 30 sec of arc has been reported by Graham et al. (1948).

Several interesting, if poorly understood, motion phenomena have been reported. For instance, the *apparent velocity* of moving objects is higher when the image of the object is projected on foveal portions of the retina rather than peripheral portions. However, apparent velocity is reduced if eye movements follow the direction of the movement. (This is the Aubert-Fleischl paradox.) More surprising, perhaps, is Hazelhoff's effect, which describes the sensation resulting from the sudden presentation of a stationary dot in the middle of a square which is moving rapidly across the visual field. The dot temporarily appears to be outside and ahead of the square when it is first presented.

This effect raises the problem of *apparent motion,* one of the traditional concerns of workers in perception. The subjective sensation of apparent

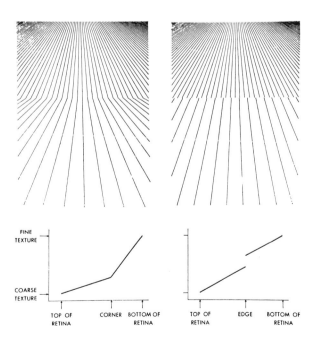

Fig. 3.20 Depth from gradients. *Left,* a change of gradient corresponding to a corner; *right,* a jump between two gradients corresponding to an edge. (From Gibson, 1950.)

movement does not correspond in any obvious way to the physical properties of the stimulus. A brief discussion of the basic observations may be of interest.

The simplest case of apparent motion is what has been called an *afterimage of motion*. For instance, if a horizontally striped surface is moved rapidly in either vertical direction, an apparent motion of the striped pattern in the direction opposite to the actual movement becomes noticeable. This apparent motion persists for some time after the actual movement of the stimulus surface is stopped. A similar phenomenon can be observed when a disk with a spiral pattern is rotated at moderate speeds. The spiral appears alternately to contract and expand, and the pulsating motion is temporarily transposed to other fixed objects when the observer changes his point of fixation.

Another type of apparent motion occurs when the actual movement of "ground" is attributed to the "figure" portion of the visual field. The classical demonstration of such *induced motion* is the movement of luminous objects in a dark room. For instance, the motion of a luminous rectangle imparts apparent motion to a stationary luminous point inside it. Actual movement of both components of the stimulus in opposite directions gives rise to the illusion that the dot moves at the combined speeds within a stationary rectangle. Johanssen (1950) has suggested that the apparent motion of two luminous dots actually moving along straight intersecting lines may reflect the end result of a vector analysis of the geometrical situation.

The clearest example of apparent motion in the complete absence of physical movement (*autokinetic motion*) occurs when a single-point source is suspended in a dark room. In the total absence of a reference framework, this point appears to move about erratically; the extent of the apparent motion is so great that explanations in terms of eye movements are not adequate to account for the phenomenon.

Apparent motion can also be created by the serial presentation of static visual patterns. The classical example of such *stroboscopic motion* is the motion picture. The basic principles of this form of apparent movement have been investigated in situations where single pairs of stimuli are presented in succession. Wertheimer's classic study of this phenomenon showed that successive presentations of two stimuli result in two distinct sensations (but no movement) as long as the interstimulus interval exceeds 200 msec. At very short intervals (below about 30 msec), both stimuli are perceived simultaneously. Only at some intermediate range of values is motion from the location of the first of the stimuli to the location of the second perceived. The optimal interval for the elicitation of apparent movement is a joint function of the distance between the two stimuli and the intensity. Any increase in distance must be compensated by a proportional increase in intensity, and vice versa. The direction of the apparent motion is a function of the relative intensity and spatial pattern of the stimuli.

Apparent motion can affect the perception of spatial relationships. If three lights are presented at equal distances along a horizontal plane in a darkroom and each light is alternately illuminated only briefly, the apparent distance between the lights is a function of the relative repetition rate. If the interstimulus interval between *a* and *b* is longer than that between *b* and *c* (but all intervals are within the range of apparent movement), the distance between *a* and *b* will appear longer than the physically identical distance between *b* and *c*.

It has been shown that the perception of apparent movement is not peculiar to man. Monkeys react to moving pictures much as they would to other animals outside their reach (Klüver, 1933), and several varieties of fish have been shown to respond to a pattern of apparent movement (Gaffron, 1934).

Perhaps the most unusual aspect of man's perception of visual stimuli is the constancy of the apparent size and shape of objects in spite of vast differences in their distance and orientation to the eye and consequent differences in the size and shape of retinal images. This constancy can best be appreciated when we consider the fact that a circle, viewed obliquely, continues to be perceived as a circle although the retinal image has the form of an ellipse. An ellipse that projects precisely the same retinal image is easily distinguished from the circle. However, this constancy effect is not perfect. The subjective perception usually falls somewhere between the actual retinal projection and the "constant" image. This tendency has been called a *conceptual compromise* by Brunswik (1934, 1956); he proposed the following empirical formula to determine the relative effect of the constancy tendency,

$$BR = \frac{R - S}{C - S}$$

where R is the subject's overt response, S is the response tendency according to the "law of retinal image," and C is the response predicted by the "law of constancy." Thouless (1931a, b) quantified the "partial regression to the real object" in the same terms, using a logarithmic expression:

$$TR = \frac{\log R - \log S}{\log C - \log S}$$

Helson (1943) attempted to explain color constancies in terms of adaptation levels and contrast phenomena. He suggested that the "weighted geometric mean of the reflectance of all parts of the visual scene" establishes an adaptation level which affects the perception of other colors by imparting the hue of its complementary color to all reflectances above the adaptation level. All colors near the adaptation level appear to have very low saturation, according to Helson's hypothesis, and may actually appear achromatic.

Similar interpretations of brightness constancy have been proposed by Wallach (1939) and others. The usefulness of such hypotheses is limited by the frequently observed directionality of the contrast effect. For instance, a bright background reduces the apparent brightness of a stimulus that is less bright than the surround, but a dim surround generally has little if any effect on the apparent brightness of a stimulus that is brighter than the background.

Brightness, as well as color, constancies have been demonstrated in monkeys (Köhler, 1917; Locke, 1935), birds (Katz and Révész, 1921), and fish (Burkamp, 1923). Size and form constancies have been reported in monkeys (Zeigler and Leibowitz, 1958), cats (Gunter, 1951), and birds (Götz, 1926).

The many well-known *geometric illusions* (see Figure 3.21) may be examples of constancy effects. Tausch (1954) has recently revived interest in this possibility by suggesting that an illusion may be produced by the "release" of specific behavioral response patterns by inappropriate stimuli because of a misapplied tendency to maintain size or shape constancy. An example of this phenomenon is shown in Figure 3.22. The perceptual image of a table has to be considerably modified, with respect to size as well as angular composition, if the concept of a rectangular object is to be maintained when the table is viewed from a frontal perspective. A drawing of a table must contain similar

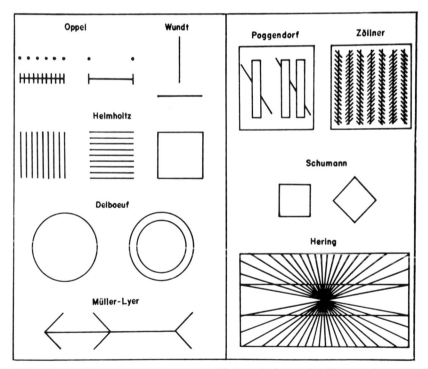

Fig. 3.21 Some of the classical optic-geometric illusions. *Left,* so-called illusions of extent; *right,* illusions of angles. Both extent and angle are affected simultaneously in several of these patterns, e.g., in the Müller-Lyer illusion (lower left) and in Schumann's upright and rotated squares (middle right). (From Teuber, 1960.)

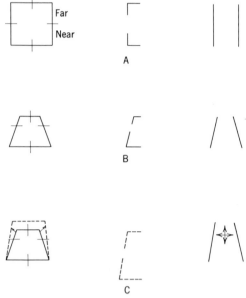

Fig. 3.22   Illusions as misapplied constancies. A, the appearance of a square surface (e.g., a table top) seen from in front and slightly from above is distorted by the laws of geometrical optics, as shown in B. The perceptual process is thought to operate on this pattern by counter-distortion, resulting in the changes schematized in C. Such a process would involve apparent lengths, sizes, and angles. (From Teuber, 1960.)

modifications if a perspective drawing is to result. Tausch suggests that the sensation of converging lines or apparently distorted angles may evoke a perceptual constancy reaction which attempts to reconstruct a rectangular or otherwise "normal" image. "Prototypical" constancies similar to our example are assumed to exist for every geometric illusion.

A sequential rather than simultaneous interaction between stimuli has been described by Köhler (1940) and others as *figural aftereffects.* This interesting distortion of the physical stimulus may be related to constancy and contrast phenomena; it has been suggested as a possible "explanation" of at least some types of geometric illusions (Köhler and Fishback, 1950). The aftereffects are induced by the prolonged inspection of a geometric pattern (such as a series of curved lines) which exaggerates one of the dimensions of a subsequently projected test stimulus. An apparently compensatory perceptual reaction (of unknown origin and dimensions) takes place, and the test stimulus is distorted in the direction opposite to that of the original pattern (see Figure 3.23).

THE TRANSDUCTION OF PHYSICAL ENERGY INTO PHYSIOLOGICAL SIGNALS

The Chemistry of Photoreceptor Processes

Radiant energy, in order to affect neural processes, must be absorbed by specialized substances called pigments. Since such pigments undergo catabolic changes in the presence of light, some chemical mechanisms must be available for the rapid and continual regeneration of photosensitive pigments. A priori, we might expect to find more than one type of photosensitive substance because the eye appears to be differentially sensitive to radiant energies of different wavelengths. Several pigments have been isolated to date, *iodopsin* and *cyanopsin* in the color-sensitive cones and *rhodopsin* and *porphyropsin* in the rod receptors. Each pigment is a protein that owes its photosensitive properties to *carotenoid chromophores.*

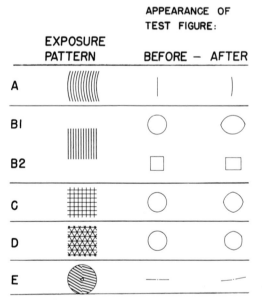

Fig. 3.23   Aftereffects induced by active scanning of various patterned fields. A, scanning the set of curved lines for 1 min induces apparent curvature in an objectively straight line; the curved line shown at the right is now called straight. Analogous transformations are shown under B-E. Scanning the set of vertical lines for 1 min induces horizontal elongation and distortion of circles (B1) and converts squares into rectangles (B2). C and D, checkered fields convert circles into polygons. E, scanning for 1 min within the circle converts a horizontal line as shown. In a sense, the bias induced by the special exposure fields sets up new equivalence classes; polygons are now circles, etc. (From Teuber, 1960.)

Four chemical constituents interact in the rods or cones to transduce radiant energy into proportional physiological signals: (1) a basic substance called *opsin*, (2) *alcohol dehydrogenase*, the enzyme that catalyzes the conversion, (3) *cozymase*, the coenzyme of the system, and (4) vitamin A_1 or A_2. We also have the four carotenoid chromophores which are stereoisomeric with those of the visual pigments.

The rod pigments, rhodopsin and porphyropsin, have been the most extensively investigated. Their reaction is so similar to that of the cone pigments that we can use the model about to be developed in the subsequent treatment of cyanopsin and iodopsin.

In the presence of light, rhodopsin is converted to an orange intermediate called *lumirhodopsin*. As the reaction continues, *metarhodopsin* is formed; it dissociates in the presence of water into *retinene* and *opsin* (see Figure 3.24).

Retinene is reduced to vitamin A by the concerted action of alcohol dehydrogenase, the enzyme and cozymase (NAD or niacin adenine dinucleotide, formerly DPN or diphosphopyridine nucleotide), and the coenzyme. This reaction involves the transfer of hydrogen from the coenzyme to the aldehyde group of retinene, thereby reducing it to the alcohol group of the vitamin (see Figure 3.25).

We have essentially described the known chemical reaction of rhodopsin to light. A vital last step is still missing; we cannot explain how the end products, retinene and/or opsin, produce the bioelectric excitation of the neural mechanisms which must occur if action potentials are to be propagated in central portions of the visual system. We can be fairly certain that retinene, at least in the form that we know it, cannot initiate the rapid and explosive neural responses, partly because it is released only very slowly at physiological temperatures and pH values, and partly because it appears to be a relatively inert substance. Opsin, on the other hand, undergoes a number of important transformations in response to light; these changes might be responsible for the final step in the photoreceptor conversion. It

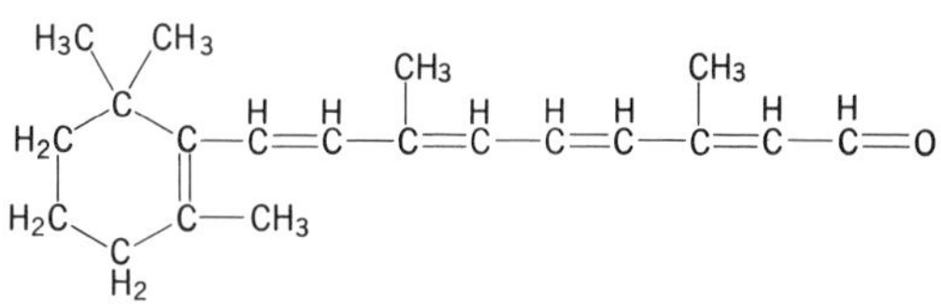

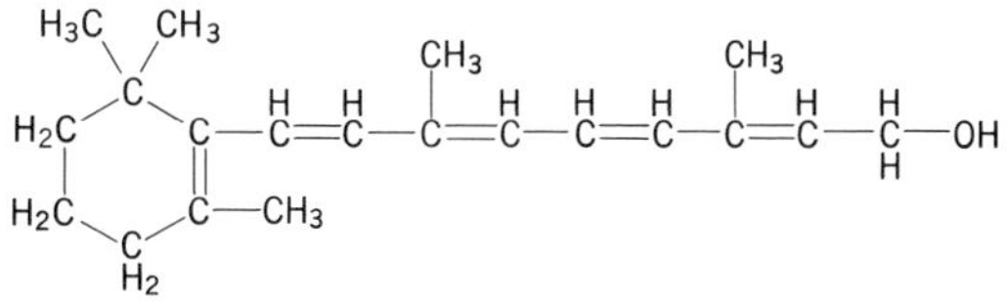

Fig. 3.25 Vitamin A.

has been suggested (Wald and Brown, 1951–1952; Radding and Wald, 1955–1956; Wald, 1959) that the ion concentration of the photoreceptor may be directly modified by the liberation of ion-binding groups (sulfhydryl and an acid-binding group) from opsin.

An important question remains to be asked about the regeneration of the photosensitive pigments which must take place if the photoreceptors are to respond to changes in illumination. The problem appears to be solved quite easily and practically by a continuous and rapid resynthesis of rhodopsin (or other visual pigments) from retinene and opsin or from vitamin A and opsin. The former is a spontaneous reaction which requires neither an enzyme nor an external source of energy. In the dark, opsin and retinene interact to form rhodopsin. The energy liberated in this reaction is used to oxidize vitamin A to retinene. Retinene cannot accumulate because the process is self-limiting (see Figure 3.26).

The eyes of freshwater fishes and some amphibia do not contain rhodopsin but a related pigment called *porphyropsin*. This substance undergoes essentially the same bleaching and regeneration cycles as rhodopsin, but slightly different forms of retinene and vitamin A are involved in the conversion process (compare Figures 3.27 and 3.28). The two rod pigments have almost identical opsins and differ only with respect to their carotenoids.

Fig. 3.24 Retinene.

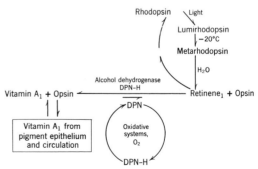

Fig. 3.26 Diagram of the rhodopsin system. (From Hubbard and Wald, 1951.)

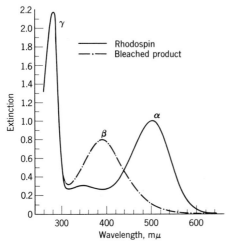

Fig. 3.27 Absorption spectra of bullfrog rhodopsin and of the product of its bleaching in aqueous digitonin solution, pH 5.55. Rhodopsin possesses three absorption maxima: the α-band, mainly responsible for the spectral sensitivity of rod vision; the β-band, which, like the α-band, belongs to the prosthetic group; and the γ-band, produced by the protein opsin. On bleaching, the α- and β-bands are replaced by the retinene band at about 385 mμ; the opsin band remains unchanged. (From Wald, 1949.)

The cone pigment *iodopsin*, on the other hand, has carotenoids that are identical to those of rhodopsin, but has different opsins. The conversion cycle of rhodopsin describes the chemical reactions that occur in the cone receptor on exposure to light (and subsequent regeneration in the dark) if we replace the opsin (scotopsin) of the rod system with the opsin (photopsin) of the cone system (see Figure 3.26).

A fourth visual pigment, *cyanopsin*, has a maximal absorption near 620 mμ; it has been synthesized by Wald and his colleagues, who combined cone opsin with retinene$_2$ (the carotenoid that combines with rod opsin to form porphyropsin). A comparison of the absorption spectrum of this pigment with the spectral sensitivity of freshwater fish (see Figure 3.29) indicates that cyanopsin may be the photopic counterpart of porphyropsin in freshwater fishes and amphibia.

The selective and specific action of the visual pigments is nowhere better illustrated than in a direct comparison of their absorption spectra with the spectral sensitivities of rods and cones. (Some corrections of the spectral sensitivity data usually must be made to allow for colored ocular structures.) Some examples are shown in Figures 3.30 and 3.31. The spectral sensitivity measurements used in these comparisons are obtained by recording the minimal quantity of radiant energy at each wavelength which evokes an electrophysiological response from a selected portion of the retina.

It has generally been assumed that the sensitivity changes that occur during light or dark adaptation are directly related to the bleaching and resynthesis of visual pigments. Rushton and his co-workers (Rushton, 1957; Rushton et al., 1955; Campbell and Rushton, 1955) devised an ingenious technique for estimating this relationship. They measured the bleaching and resynthesis of rhodopsin in the intact eye by comparing the peripheral retinal reflection of blue-green light (which is largely absorbed by rhodopsin) with the retinal reflection of orange (which is only poorly absorbed by the pigment of the rods). These studies show that the rhodopsin content of the

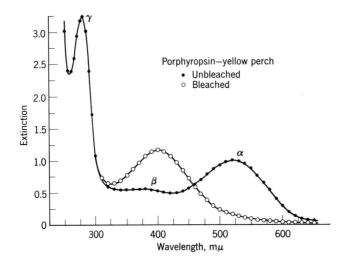

Fig. 3.28 Absorption spectra of porphyropsin and of the product of its bleaching (pH 7.0) from the freshwater yellow perch, *Perca flavescens*. Porphyropsin, like rhodopsin, possesses three absorption bands: the α-band at about 522 mμ, the β-band at about 377 mμ, and the γ-band (opsin) at about 280 mμ. On bleaching, the α- and β-bands are replaced by the absorption band of retinene$_2$, at about 400 mμ. (From Wald et al., 1959.)

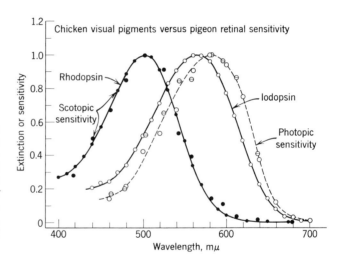

Fig. 3.29 The absorption spectrum of cyanopsin compared with Granit's electrophysiological measurements of the spectral sensitivity of cone vision in a freshwater fish, the tench, and in the European tortoise, *Testudo graeca*. (From Wald et al., 1953, AAAS.)

Fig. 3.30 Absorption spectra of chicken rhodopsin and iodopsin, compared with the spectral sensitivities of dark- and light-adapted pigeons. The latter were measured electrophysiologically and are plotted in terms of the reciprocals of the numbers of incident quanta needed to evoke a constant electrical response. (From Wald et al., 1954–1955. Reproduced by permission of the Rockefeller University Press.)

Fig. 3.31 Absorption spectra of porphyropsin and cyanopsin (lines, small circles) compared with the spectral sensitivities of rod and cone vision in a freshwater fish, the tench (broken line, large circles). The spectral sensitivities were measured electrophysiologically in opened eyes from which the cornea and lens had been removed. (From Wald, 1959.)

209

rod-containing peripheral retina falls exponentially during exposure to light, reaching an asymptote that is characteristic of the intensity of the stimulus (see Figure 3.32). In the dark the rhodopsin content rises to roughly normal values within about 30 min.

A comparison of Rushton's results with the temporal course of dark and light adaptation suggests that the relationship between sensitivity and visual pigment concentration is not simple. A clear covariance becomes apparent only when the concentration of rhodopsin is compared to the logarithm of visual sensitivity (expressed as the reciprocal of energy). Wald (Wald, 1954; Wald et al., 1954–1955) suggested that such a relationship would be expected if the photoreceptor were a compartmentalized structure, each compartment being capable of essentially independent responses to light. According to this hypothesis, the absorption of a single quantum of radiant energy by such a compartment suffices to discharge most of its visual pigment. This renders the compartment temporarily incapable of further excitation although the remaining pigments continue to absorb light. The rod receptor is entirely inexcitable only when all compartments have been discharged (i.e., when each compartment has absorbed at least one quantum of light). Mathematical extensions of this concept imply that the logarithm of sensitivity should be proportional to the concentration of visual pigments in the eye.

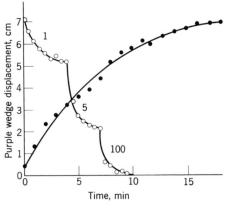

Fig. 3.32 Bleaching and resynthesis of rhodopsin in the human retina 15° temporal to the fovea. *Open circles,* on exposing the eye successively to lights of increasing brightness, the rhodopsin content falls each time to a new steady-state level at which the rate of bleaching is balanced by the regeneration rate. *Filled circles,* in the dark, rhodopsin regenerates. (From Campbell and Rushton, 1955.)

The relationship between sensitivity and pigment concentration appears to be general. Rushton (1957) has demonstrated that the synthesis of cone pigments in the dark occurs much more rapidly than the synthesis of rod pigments and that the course of synthesis follows the photopic phase of dark adaptation. These observations are corroborated by Wald's (1954–1955) data on the rate of synthesis of rhodopsin and iodopsin *in vitro.* Wald showed that the synthesis of iodopsin is essentially complete within 5 min whereas that of rhodopsin continues for about 1 hr.

THE ELECTRICAL ACTIVITY OF THE VISUAL SYSTEM

The Electroretinogram (ERG) and Related Phenomena

A *resting potential* (or *corneoretinal potential*) of about 6 mV exists between the cornea and the back of the eye. The potential is cornea positive in vertebrates and appears to be independent of illumination. It was first described by du Bois-Reymond over 100 years ago and has been largely neglected in recent years except as a convenient measure of eye movements. Its exact origin is still unknown.

Holmgren reported in 1866 that this resting potential showed sudden, systematic changes at the onset of illumination. Dewar and M'Kendrick discovered in 1873 that these "action potentials" derived from the retina itself; the first *electroretinogram* (ERG), i.e., a complete record of the polyphasic response of the eye to light as a function of time, was published by Gotch in 1903.

The electroretinogram is obtained in animals by recording the potential changes existing between electrodes on the cornea and those on some portion of the posterior surface of the eye, preferably near the optic tract. An approximation of the ERG can be obtained from human observers by placing one electrode on the forehead and the other (a chlorinated silver wire inserted into a saline solution that is in contact with the cornea) on the cornea (Karpe, 1948).

The ERG is a complex, multiphasic mass response which originates from the retina and shows several distinct phases and components. When the eye is first exposed to a light stimulus, a small negative potential (the *a*-wave) occurs; it is followed by a large, positive potential, the *b*-wave. In mixed retinae each of these waves contains distinct photopic and scotopic components which are differentially affected by dark adaptation (Johnson, 1958).

This ON effect (the *a*- and *b*-wave complex) is followed by a gradually rising positive potential, the *c*-wave, which approaches some asymptotic maximum and declines only very slowly after the stimulation is terminated. A few hundred milliseconds after the cessation of stimulation, a small positive deflection in the slope of the *c*-wave often occurs. This *d*-wave or OFF effect is not seen in the human ERG.

The *b*- and *c*-waves have been shown to consist of several overlapping components that have different rise times and amplitudes. The origin of the slower components has been assigned to rod receptors, that of the faster ones to cones (Granit and Wrede, 1937).

The interval between the stimulus onset and the appearance of the first, negative (*a*-wave) component of the ERG averages only about 40 msec; latencies as brief as 10 msec are common. The reciprocal of the duration of the latent period is roughly a linear function of the logarithm of the luminance of the stimulus. In pure cone or mixed eyes, the latency of the ERG is also affected by the wavelength of the stimulus and by the adaptation level of the eye. Distinct latency functions for scotopic and photopic vision which largely parallel the photopic and scotopic luminous efficiency curves can be obtained (Granit and Wrede, 1937).

Granit (1933, 1955, 1959) suggested that the ERG may represent a composite of three distinct electrical responses, as shown schematically in Figure 3.33. The interaction between a slow positive component (I) and a rapid second, positive component (II) is thought to give rise to the two major deflections of the ERG, the initial response to light onset (the *b*-wave) and the gradual *c*-wave which follows it. The small initial negative deflection (the *a*-wave) is thought to be produced by the third, negative component of the ERG. The small *d*-wave that rides the declining *c*-wave after the termination of stimulation may be caused by the differential rate of decay of the three components (primarily the rapid decay of the third, negative component).

Component I is negligible at low levels of retinal illumination and disappears almost completely when the eye is thoroughly light adapted. It may reflect some aspect of the photopic response to light since it is completely absent from cone retinae.

Component II correlates well, in amplitude as well as temporal characteristics, with the overall response of the optic nerve. Its contours are much more variable than those of the other components; a double, initial undulation and several smaller subsequent fluctuations are not uncommon.

The third, negative component may have inhibitory rather than excitatory functions. It precedes the positive components and produces the small, negative *a*-wave which may serve to terminate all retinal responses to preceding stimuli and thus "ready" the photoreceptors for a simple response to the new stimulus (Le Grand, 1957). The third component is very small or absent when the luminance of the stimulus is low.

The composition of the retina is reflected in the ERG. Pure cone retinae give rise to an ERG that does not show the secondary slow potential (the *c*-wave) and may even fall to negative levels between the initial ON response (the *b*-wave) and the OFF response (*d*-wave). The pure cone ERG typically has a large *a*-wave, indicating a disproportionate influence of the third component.

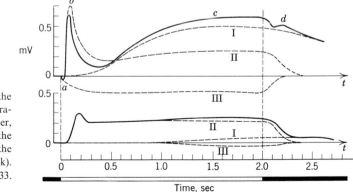

Fig. 3.33 Electroretinogram of the cat: size of stimulus, 3.4×10^{-4} steradian; luminance, 50 cd/meter² upper, 0.5 cd/meter² lower. The line below the time scale indicates the presence of the stimulus (white) or its absence (black). According to data from Granit, 1933. (From Le Grand, 1957.)

The pure rod ERG resembles more closely our model, except that the OFF response (*d*-wave) is absent; however, a corresponding signal can be recorded from the optic nerve.

Pure rod and most mixed retinae respond to flickering light with repeated, positive *b*-waves. Pure cone ERG's show repeated modulations of the negative *a*-wave and of the small positive *d*-wave as well as undulations of the *b*-wave. The fluctuations of the ERG are synchronous with the flicker frequency up to some maximal level; however, there is no simple correlation between the critical fusion frequency and the disappearance of these oscillations (Bernhard, 1940), contrary to some early reports by Sachs (1929) and others. Subjective sensations of flicker have been reported while the ERG response appeared perfectly smooth, presumably because the human ERG reflects primarily the activity of the rods, which have a lower c.f.f. than cone receptors. The oscillatory undulations in the ERG may be the result of alternating excitation from component II and inhibition from the activity of component III (Le Grand, 1957).

The ERG reflects interesting spatial interaction phenomena. Simultaneous stimuli to closely adjacent points of the retina produce a summation of the ERG potential. When the two stimuli are presented in close succession, separate ERG responses can be recorded, but the *b*-wave of the response to the second stimulus may be reduced or totally absent (Granit et al., 1935).

The ERG response is roughly proportional to the logarithm of the stimulus intensity, which suggests that the generator potentials that sum to produce the ERG may also be logarithmically

related to luminous intensity. This prediction has been generally confirmed by microelectrode studies of the visual generator potential (Granit, 1955).

The second, positive component of the ERG varies systematically as a function of log luminance. Figure 3.34 presents the characteristic sigmoid function which relates the amplitude to the two major derivatives of this component, the *b*- and *c*-waves, to the log stimulus intensity.

Some interesting correlations between ERG recordings and the state of adaptation have been reported. In mammals light adaptation eliminates the first, positive component of the ERG and greatly reduces the second; the *b*-wave eventually disappears and the ERG response is minimal, consisting essentially of a negative *a*-wave which gradually returns to the resting potential. Dark adaptation results in the gradual reappearance of the ERG's positive components, particularly the *b*-wave, which becomes its most prominent deflection. The Purkinje shift is reflected in this *b*-wave portion of the ERG (Kohlrausch, 1931a, b).

The ERG contains components that are differentially sensitive to radiations of specific wavelengths. The amplitude of the *b*-wave of the frog's ERG, for instance, has been shown to vary as a function of wavelength and the state of dark adaptation. The dark-adapted eye showed a maximum response at about 510 mμ (a shift of 50 mμ from the light-adapted maximum of about 560 mμ). The amplitude of the *c*-wave in the frog was found to duplicate roughly the contour of the scotopic luminous efficiency function (Granit and Wrede, 1937; Granit and Munsterhjelm, 1937). In man, the *b*-wave corresponds most closely to the relative scotopic luminous efficiency function (Riggs et al., 1949). At the blue end of the spectrum, the ERG measure typically overestimates spectral sensitivity, presumably because the blue light is diffused more extensively so that the electrical activity of a greater portion of the retinal surface can sum to produce the ERG response (Riggs, 1958).

The spectral sensitivity of the ERG has been investigated by Japanese workers (Toida and Goto, 1954) who reported that the small *d*-wave component of the OFF response may have specific spectral maxima in the region of red, green, and blue. An even more complex relationship has been reported by Adrian (1945). Radiations in the red portion of the spectrum were found to produce large, negative (*a*-wave) deflections, followed by relatively small *b*-waves. Stimuli from the blue, shortwave portion of the spectrum, on the other

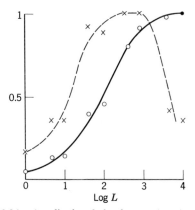

Fig. 3.34 Amplitude of the *b*-wave (——) and the *c*-wave (– – –) of the dark-adapted eye, as a function of luminance, according to Granit. (From Le Grand, 1957.)

hand, elicited little or no *a*-wave responses but large *b*-wave responses.

The origin of the various components of the ERG is still in doubt. It has been suggested (Granit, 1947, 1955) that the first, positive component may reflect the decomposition of visual pigments. The second component may be related to the activity of the bipolar cells; it cannot, as had previously been assumed, reflect the activity of the receptor cells because the potential is very sensitive to potassium chloride which does not affect the response of rudimentary retinae containing only receptor cells (Therman, 1940). The third, negative component may reflect the centrifugal action of higher central mechanisms which is transmitted to the receptor elements via the horizontal cells. On the basis of extensive toxicity studies, Noell (1953), on the other hand, concluded that the first component reflected the transport of ions through the pigment epithelium, the second component represented synaptic activity between the receptor and the bipolar cells, and the third consisted of two distinct potentials that originated from the outer processes of the receptor cells themselves.

Patterns of Neural Discharge from Retinal Elements

Electrophysiological recordings from the whole optic nerve (Adrian and Matthews, 1927a, b) demonstrate a burst of action potentials in response to visual stimuli. If a constant stimulus is presented for an extended period of time, the frequency of the optic nerve discharge attains a maximum and then gradually declines to some asymptotic value. Termination of the stimulus causes a sudden increase in the rate of discharge followed by a gradual return to the resting level (defined by spontaneous discharges).

Hartline and his associates (Hartline, 1938a, 1940; Hartline and Graham, 1932; Hartline and McDonald, 1947) isolated single optic nerve fibers and demonstrated that the compound response of the optic nerve was constituted of three types of components, represented by distinct anatomical units (see Figure 3.35). About 20% of the fibers in the optic nerve of the frog (the type A fibers) respond to the onset of light with a rapid burst of action potentials and continue to respond to maintained stimuli at a lower, steady frequency. (The latencies of these ON responses are bimodally distributed, and two classes of ON fibers are sometimes distinguished.) About 50% of the fibers (the B or ON-OFF fibers) respond only to the onset and termination of visual stimuli. The remaining 30% (the C or OFF fibers) respond only to the cessation of stimulation with a high-frequency burst of impulses which slows only gradually and outlasts the stimulus by several seconds. The OFF response is inhibited by a second presentation of the stimulus, the latency of the inhibition being shorter than that of the positive response of the type A and B fibers. The correlation between this inhibitory effect and the negative (*a*-wave) deflection of the ERG is rather good, but causal relationships have not been established. The firing rate of all these fibers appears to be a function of stimulus intensity (see Figure 3.36).

Our understanding of the visual system has been greatly advanced by the development of microdissection (Hartline, 1935, 1938, 1940a, b, c) and microelectrode recording techniques which have permitted a detailed analysis of single-cell activity in the retina (Granit, 1947, 1950; Rushton, 1949, 1953; Kuffler, 1952, 1953).

This approach has suggested that the eye may contain successive layers of functionally superimposed receptive fields. Generally, several receptors converge on a single bipolar cell and several bipolar cells on a single ganglion cell. The

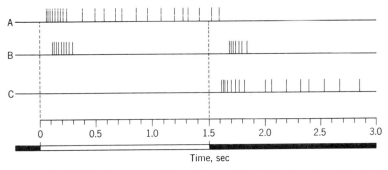

Fig. 3.35 The three kinds of responses of the optic nerve fibers in the frog. According to Hartline, 1940b. (From Le Grand, 1957.)

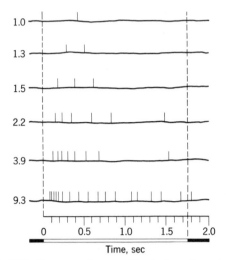

Fig. 3.36 Response of a nerve fiber in the guinea pig at different values of luminance. The absolute threshold is taken as unity. (From Granit, 1955.)

activity of a single optic nerve fiber thus reflects the activity of a relatively large number of primary visual receptors. An apparent exception to this rule is the connection between the foveal cone receptors, individual midget bipolars, and single ganglion cells; this connection results in what appears to be a "private line" to the central nervous system. Even here, some overlap of receptive fields exists, suggesting an interaction between "private line" connections at some level of integration.

A particularly interesting example of the extensive interaction between individual retinal elements has been demonstrated in studies of the ON, OFF, and ON-OFF responses to light. Hartline's initial work (Hartline, 1938) suggested that a single response category might be characteristic of a particular type of optic nerve fiber and that the ratio of response categories might correlate with some basic visual capability of the eye under study. More recent investigations of this subject (Granit, 1955, 1959), suggest that such a classification may be, at least in part, misleading and artifactual; it has been found that the same units can give ON, OFF, or ON-OFF responses, depending on the intensity and wavelength of the stimulus and the portion of the receptive field affected (Granit, 1944, 1950; Granit and Tansley, 1948; Gernandt, 1948). It was observed that the relative intensity and duration of ON or OFF responses of an ON-OFF unit varied as a function of stimulus intensity (Granit, 1944; Donner and Willmer, 1950) and

that the ON and OFF responses could be selectively inhibited or emphasized by polarizing the retina with a small direct current. Anodal currents facilitate the response of OFF units and tended to inhibit the discharge of ON units. Cathodal currents produced opposite effects. Mixed, ON-OFF units respond variably to anodal as well as cathodal currents (Granit, 1948).

Granit (1951) investigated the effects of stimuli presented in such rapid succession that the ON and OFF responses collide. He found that the two response types interact competitively rather than additively: only one of the responses is propagated, essentially unchanged, while the other is completely suppressed. These and related observations led Granit (1955, 1959) to hypothesize that the retina may contain two basically antagonistic response systems which compete for the same central connections under some conditions. The ON system normally responds to threshold stimulation by initiating a series of propagated action potentials as well as a steady potential that inhibits the OFF system for the duration of the stimulation. The response of the OFF system represents a release from this inhibition, its duration presumably being a function of the duration and amplitude of the visual stimulus.

This interaction theory assumes very extensive interconnections between retinal elements as well as convergence toward the central nervous system. It has long been known that the receptive field of a single optic nerve fiber is typically of the order of 1mm or more, and some observations reported by Thomson (1953) and Kuffler (1952, 1953) support Granit's notion of extensively interacting antagonistic systems in the retina. Hartline's (1938) earlier microdissection studies had shown that the absolute threshold varied extensively within the receptive field of a single fiber (see Figure 3.37).

Kuffler (1952, 1953) demonstrated in a series of elegant investigations on the intact cat eye that antagonistic responses could be obtained from the same visual field and that the distribution of ON, ON-OFF, and OFF responses within a single receptive field could be modified by changing the intensity of the illumination (see Figure 3.38).

Some receptive fields were characterized by (1) a central zone from which only ON responses could be elicited; (2) a transitional area giving ON-OFF responses, and (3) a fringe area from which only OFF responses could be recorded. Other receptive fields showed an opposite pattern of organization, the outer fringe being part of the ON

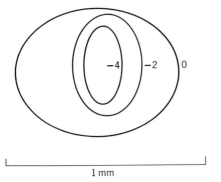

1 mm

Fig. 3.37 Chart of the receptive field of a single optic nerve fiber of the frog. Each line encloses a retinal region within which the exploring spotlight (relative size shown above left, the log of the intensity given on the line) produced a response from the fiber. On each line the indicated intensity was the threshold; the set of curves constitutes a contour map of the distribution of the retinal sensitivity to light with reference to this particular fiber. (From Hartline, 1940c.)

system. Kuffler's results also showed the type of competitive interaction suggested by Granit. When stimuli were simultaneously projected onto the same receptive field so that one stimulated only the ON zone and the other only the OFF zone, the response of the related fiber depended entirely on the relative intensity of the stimuli. When both stimuli were of roughly equivalent intensity, a weak and relatively brief ON response, followed by an equally reduced OFF response, was recorded. When the stimulus to the ON area was more intense, the OFF responses were inhibited and the ON responses prolonged. Conversely, when the stimulus to the OFF zone was stronger, little or no reaction to the stimulus onset occurred, but its offset was marked by a pronounced discharge.

Barlow (1953a, b) reported related observations from the frog retina. He found that the entire receptive field gave ON-OFF responses similar to those seen in the transitional zone of Kuffler; the ON region may have been so small in this species that pure ON responses could not be obtained. Illumination of an area surrounding this receptive field inhibited all responses to concurrent stimulation of the field. However, no clear response to the inhibitory stimulus itself could be seen, and a direct analogy to Kuffler's OFF system may not be appropriate. One of Kuffler's (1952) observations may be of interest in this context. He noted that the overall size of a receptive field decreased when background illumination increased (i.e., stimulation of retinal areas surrounding the visual field

tended to inhibit the response to stimulation of the visual field itself).

Wagner et al. (1963) have recently shown that the nature of the response from a given receptive field may also depend on the wavelength of the stimulus. These workers found that some of the receptive fields of the goldfish retina gave clear ON responses to low-intensity stimulation of some parts of the visible spectrum, but not to others. OFF responses could be obtained from the same receptive fields only with relatively high levels of illumination when the same wavelength was used. Other fields showed a clearly opposite organization or gave ON and OFF responses to stimuli of the same wavelength and intensity.

The inhibitory or competitive interaction of retinal elements has been studied in some detail by Ratliff and his associates in the compound eye of the *Limulus* (horseshoe crab) (Ratliff, 1961; Ratliff and Hartline, 1959; Ratliff et al., 1958). An ommatidium of a *Limulus* eye contains ten to twelve visual receptor cells and one bipolar neuron (the eccentric cell). The central process of the eccentric cell joins the optic tract and appears to carry all the information from its ommatidium of origin.

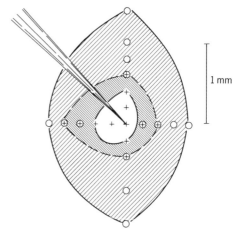

1 mm

Fig. 3.38 Distribution of discharge patterns within the receptive field of a ganglion cell (located at tip of electrode) of the cat retina. The exploring spot was 0.2 mm in diameter, about 100 times the threshold at the center of the field. Background illumination was approximately 25 mc. In the central region (crosses) ON discharges were found, whereas in the diagonally hatched part only OFF discharges occurred (circles). In the intermediary zone (horizontally hatched) discharges were ON-OFF. Note that a change in the conditions of illumination (background, etc.) altered the discharge pattern distribution. (From Kuffler, 1953.)

Ratliff found that the number and frequency of discharges in the axon of such an eccentric cell could be decreased by illumination of ommatidia adjacent to the ommatidium of origin. The magnitude of this inhibitory effect varied as a function of the intensity, area, and pattern of the inhibitory stimulation (Hartline et al., 1956). The effect was not directional, since the simultaneous illumination of two adjacent ommatidia produced mutual inhibition. (The response of each of the two units is smaller than it would be if the stimulus did not extend to both.) Hartline and Ratliff (1957) have described this interaction by means of two simultaneous linear equations,

$$r_1 = e_1 - K_{1,2}(r_2 - r^\circ_{1,2})$$
$$r_2 = e_2 - K_{2,1}(r_1 - r^\circ_{2,1})$$

where r refers to the response of each ommatidium in terms of discharge frequency, e equals the excitation supplied by the stimulus, and K is the "inhibitory coefficient." The term r° refers to the threshold of excitation which must be exceeded before inhibitory influences can arise.

Hartline and Ratliff (1958) extended these observations by showing that the inhibitory influences of two ommatidia (which were sufficiently far apart to exert no mutual inhibition on each other, but were close enough to a third ommatidium to inhibit its activity) combined in a simple additive fashion. Hartline and Ratliff (1958) used this information to quantify the activity of n interacting ommatidia by a set of linear equations, each with $n - 1$ inhibitory terms which are combined as follows,

$$r_p = e_p - \sum_{j=1}^{n} K_{p,j}(r_j - r^\circ_{p,j})$$

where $p = 1, 2, \ldots, n$, $j \neq p$, and $r_j \nless r^\circ_{p,j}$. The threshold value for the inhibitory effect increases as a roughly linear function of the distance between the interacting ommatidia (Ratliff and Hartline, 1959). This increase is reflected in the equation above by an increase in the threshold $(r^\circ_{p,j})$ and a decrease in the inhibitory coefficient $(K_{p,j})$.

MacNichol (MacNichol, 1956; MacNichol and Hartline, 1948) found that the inhibitory effect on neighboring elements greatly exaggerated the difference in relative firing frequency of adjacent units during changes in illumination. A sudden increase in illumination produced a sharp rise in the firing rate of the directly stimulated ommatidium. After some time the rate of discharge settled down to a new steady rate which was lower than that of the initial response. The excessive initial reactions produced an extreme inhibition during the transient phase of the response, and the firing rate of neighboring ommatidia showed a momentary sharp decrease so that the difference between the stimulated and unstimulated elements was greatly exaggerated.

It is not entirely clear to what extent we can generalize these observations of interaction phenomena in the compound eye of the horseshoe crab to the more complexly organized eye of man and other mammals. It is tempting to agree with Ratliff's (1961) suggestion that complex responses in the optic nerve of the Limulus have properties that appear to be analogous if not identical to those observed in vertebrate eyes and that the model which has been discussed in these pages may serve as a useful guide to our investigations of the more complex systems.

In our concern over the effects of specific visual stimuli, we must not forget that the visual system, like other sensory systems, maintains a steady level of spontaneous activity which is largely independent, though not always unaffected, by retinal illumination. Granit (1941a) studied this phenomenon by means of retinal microelectrodes and observed some peculiar relationships. He found that all ganglion cells in the retina showed some spontaneous activity and that visual stimuli increased or decreased the firing rate of most cells. The overall level of discharge from the light-adapted retina was depressed by visual stimuli and increased sharply by dark adaptation. Some units did not respond to visual stimulation but continued to show almost constant rates of spontaneous discharge at all levels of illumination. (Similar light-resistant elements have been described by Kuffler, 1953.)

Several investigators (Claes, 1939; Ingvar, 1954) have shown that the normal electrophysiological (EEG) activity of the visual cortex depends on the integrity of the retina but not on the presence of visual stimulation. Granit (1955) has suggested that the spontaneous activity of retinal elements may serve to maintain this normal cortical pattern in the dark and that the apparently light-insensitive elements may provide specialized "tonic" sensory inputs which specifically serve this function. He proposed that these tonic excitatory influences on cortical functions may be mediated via the brainstem reticular formation.

Centrifugal influences on retinal function have been demonstrated by Granit (1953). Ramón y Cajal (1933) and others have indicated that motor projections from the mesencephalic reticular formation may reach the retina of most vertebrates. The functional significance of these connections was demonstrated in experiments showing that reticular stimulation affected receptor sensitivity. Granit observed that electrical stimulation (50 to 200 cps) of the mesencephalic reticular formation doubled the response of retinal units to a constant visual stimulus. The reticular stimulation had to be maintained for some time before this facilitatory effect became noticeable, and some measure of facilitation remained for several seconds after the cessation of the electrical stimulus to the brainstem. Reticular stimulation was also found to produce a marked rise in the spontaneous activity of the retinal elements. Granit also observed that prolonged and intense stimulation of the reticular formation so greatly increased the duration of the retinal response to light that the ON and OFF components of the response merely modulated a continuous discharge and were often barely discernible.

Very interesting results were obtained by Granit and his associates when the threshold responses of single retinal elements (most probably ganglion cells and optic nerve fibers) to stimuli of different wavelengths (colors) were recorded by microelectrode techniques (Granit, 1941a, b, c, d, 1942a, b, c, 1943a, b, c, 1945a, b, c, 1949).

Two basically different spectral sensitivity functions called *dominator* and *modulator* functions were observed. Some units responded to all wavelengths within the visible spectrum, although marked variations in threshold occurred. In the vertebrate eye, two slightly different types of such broad-band dominator functions were observed, a *scotopic dominator* curve with a maximum near 500 mμ and a *photopic dominator* curve with a maximum near 560 mμ (Granit, 1943; Donner and Granit, 1949). The shape of the scotopic dominator function was found to coincide almost perfectly with the absorption spectrum of rhodopsin, the pigment found in vertebrate eyes (Rushton, 1952). The photopic dominator functions of vertebrate eyes have been shown to correspond to the absorption spectrum of iodopsin (see the discussion of photochemical processes beginning on p. 206).

Other retinal units responded only to a comparatively narrow band of wavelengths. These *modulator* functions typically have maxima near wavelengths that correspond to blue, green, yellow, and red colors, although not all eyes have four types of modulator units (see Figure 3.39). There is some question about the "yellow" modulator, since it is difficult to distinguish between spectral sensitivity curves with maxima at 580 mμ (yellow) and 600 mμ (red) with the microelectrode techniques. Granit (1942, 1945, 1955) has tended to support a tricolor theory of color vision for mixed eyes such as man's, based on distinct modulator functions for blue, green, and red. Other species (such as the snake) appear to have only red and green modulator units, and some animals (such as rats) which have pure rod retinae do not show any distinct modulator response.

The clear distinction between spectral responses of retinal units breaks down, to some extent, because different modulators converge on a single ganglion cell. Granit's (1941) recordings have

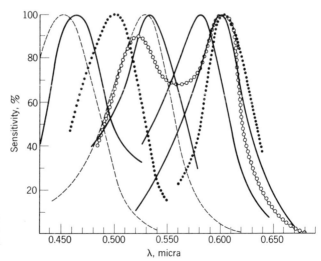

Fig. 3.39 Modulator curves: rat (· · ·), guinea pig (– – –), frog (——), snake (∘-∘-∘). Equal quantum intensity spectrum. (From Granit, 1943a.)

been obtained largely from ganglion cells, and he reported the frequent occurrence of cells that appear to collect information from more than one modulator. The modulator curves obtained from such cells may have two or more maxima and represent composites of individual modulator functions.

Granit (1947, 1955) has suggested that the scotopic and photopic dominator curves (and, by implication, the related visual pigments) are responsible only for the translation of brightness (luminance) differences into photoreceptor signals. The modulator functions, which presumably reflect the absorption spectra or other photochemical reactions of more specific and so far unknown visual pigments, are thought to describe the organism's response to color (i.e., wavelength and saturation of the visual stimulus).

Much interest has recently been generated by the demonstration of slow, graded potentials which appear to originate in the bipolar layers of the retina and may be analogous to the "generator potentials" described for other sensory systems (Svaetichin, 1953; MacNichol and Svaetichin, 1958; Tomita, 1963).

Three basic types of slow potentials have been recorded. *Luminosity* (*L*) *potentials* have been recorded primarily from the retinae of fishes; their amplitude appears to vary as a function of wavelengths in much the same way as the broad-band dominator curve of single-cell discharge. The luminosity potential is considered to be related to

a luminosity or brightness receptor system, because (1) it can be recorded from retinae that do not possess known color receptors and (2) the function that describes the spectral amplitude distribution of these potentials is not distorted by selective adaptation to light of a specific wavelength.

The amplitude of the *yellow-blue* (*Y-B*) and *red-green* (*R-G*) *potentials* is more complexly distributed over the visible spectrum in a bimodal fashion. The maximum amplitude of the negative portion of the *Y-B* potential lies near 475 mμ (blue). The amplitude distribution then goes through an area of essentially zero response near 540 mμ and reaches a positive maximum near 580 mμ, the yellow band of the spectrum. The red-green amplitude function is similarly biphasic, the negative maximum being near 515 mμ and the positive near 600 or 620 mμ (see Figures 3.40, 3.41, 3.42).

The *R-G* and *Y-B* potentials are subject to selective adaptation (i.e., the response to specific wavelengths can be inhibited by prolonged exposure to that wavelength) particularly in the regions of maximal sensitivity. This selective adaptation suggests the action of four distinct color receptors, but further information is needed before we can interpret the effects of those large, positive and negative potentials on the initiation and propagation of action potentials.

A very interesting group of studies has recently attempted to demonstrate a correlation between

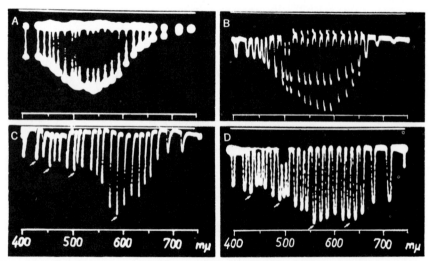

Fig. 3.40 Spectral response curves of the L type: A obtained from the Lutianidae sp. caught at a depth of 30 to 70 meters; B, C, and D obtained from shallow-water fish. (From Svaetichin and MacNichol, 1958.)

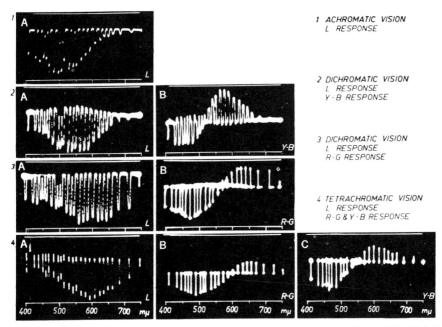

Fig. 3.41 Different types of spectral response curve recordings. (From Svaetichin and MacNichol, 1958.)

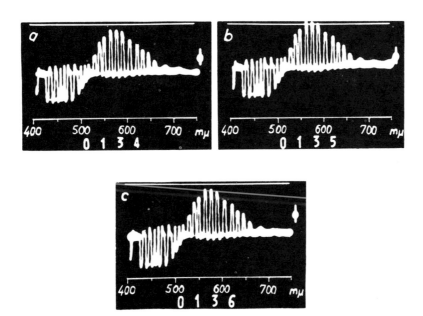

Fig. 3.42 *Y-B* type of spectral response curves obtained in sequence from the same cell. The flattening of the peaks of the spectral response curve in the blue region of the spectrum is due to a saturation effect not present when less intense illumination is used. (From Svaetichin and MacNichol, 1958.)

anatomically and functionally distinct components of the frog eye (Lettvin et al., 1959; Maturana, 1959; Maturana et al., 1960; Lettvin et al., 1961). These workers recorded the optic tract fiber response to visual stimuli and found five different classes of optic fibers that responded sufficiently distinctly to specific aspects of the visual field to warrant the assumption that fundamentally distinct visual processes might be represented.

1. THE BOUNDARY DETECTORS. Small, unmyelinated fibers, which related to receptive fields of only 2 to 4° in diameter, were found to respond maximally to brightness contrast, provided the boundaries between the different portions of the visual field were sharp. Changes in contrast did not in themselves affect the response of these detectors, but any movement of the boundary elicited maximal responses.

2. THE CONVEX BOUNDARY DETECTORS. Similar small, unmyelinated fibers related to only slightly larger retinal fields; they were found to respond preferentially to boundaries with measurable curvature and maximally to boundaries in motion or just at rest following motion. The largest responses were obtained from such fibers when the darker area was smaller and convex in relation to the lighter portion of the visual field. Centripetal movement of such an object set up long-lasting discharges.

3. THE CHANGING CONTRAST DETECTORS. A relatively small number of larger myelinated fibers with conduction velocities between 1 and 5 meters/sec and fairly large receptive fields were found to respond only to changes in contrast. The response was maximal when the boundary between adjacent areas of different brightness was sharp and moving rapidly.

4. THE DIMMING DETECTORS. Myelinated fibers with very large receptive fields and high conduction velocities (about 10 meters/sec) were found to respond to any reduction in illumination (corresponding to one of Granit's OFF receptors).

5. UNCLASSIFIED DETECTORS. A few very large myelinated fibers respond to changes in illumination with a frequency which is roughly inversely proportional to the intensity of the stimulus. These fibers are found to respond slowly to changes in the overall level of illumination. They are "unclassified" because they occur only rarely.

Lettvin et al. (1961) suggested that these functional categories may be correlated with five anatomically distinct types of ganglion cells in the retina of the frog (see Figure 3.43).

1. THE ONE-LEVEL RESTRICTED FIELD CELL. This smallest of the ganglion cells projects planar bushes of dendritic terminals into the inner level of the inner plexiform layer of the retina. It is thought to mediate the response of boundary detectors.

2. THE ONE-LEVEL BROAD FIELD CELL. This largest of the ganglion cells projects dendritic processes to the outer level of the inner plexiform layer. The dendritic arborizations ramify extensively and

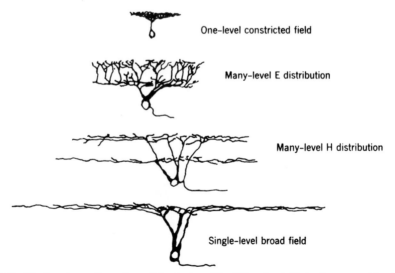

One-level constricted field

Many-level E distribution

Many-level H distribution

Single-level broad field

Fig. 3.43 The four types of ganglion cell (exclusive of the diffuse dendritic tree) compared for shape and relative size on the same scale. (From Lettvin et al., 1961.)

cover a large portion of the retina. The cell is believed to mediate the response of the dimming receptors.

3. THE MANY-LEVEL H DISTRIBUTION CELL. This medium-sized ganglion cell projects dendrites to both the inner and the outer levels of the inner plexiform layer. It is believed to be concerned with the response of changing contrast receptors.

4. THE MANY-LEVEL E DISTRIBUTION CELL. This small ganglion cell projects profusely branching dendrites to the inner level of the inner plexiform layer. It is thought to respond preferentially to convex boundary detectors.

5. THE DIFFUSE TREE CELL. This rare ganglion cell projects dendrites in all directions throughout the plexiform layer. The dendritic terminations do not show the planar organization character-istic of the other four classes. This cell is believed to mediate the response of the unclassified detec-tors (largely because both are only very infre-quently encountered).

THE TRANSFER AND PROCESSING OF VISUAL INFORMATION IN THE CENTRAL NERVOUS SYSTEM

The visual system consists of (1) the retina which contains the primary photoreceptors as well as the first (bipolar) and second (ganglion cell) relays of the system; (2) the optic nerve which partially decussates at the optic chiasma in such a fashion that each postchiasmatic optic tract carries information from the nasal half of the contralateral retina and the temporal half of the ipsilateral retina; (3) relay nuclei in the brainstem, including the lateral geniculate body, superior colliculi, and pretectal area; (4) the optic radiations from the geniculate body to the visual cortex; and (5) the primary visual projection areas of the occipital cortex.

The Optic Tract

In the cat four types of optic tract fibers can be distinguished on the basis of fiber size, termination in the central nervous system, and conduction velocity. The largest and fastest-conducting group of fibers terminates in the lateral geniculate body on cells that project to the primary visual projec-tion areas of the occipital cortex. The next smaller and slower group of fibers terminates in other layers of the lateral geniculate body on cells that project to the lateral nuclei of the thalamus. A third smaller and slower group of optic tract fi-bers projects to the pretectal area, and the smallest

and slowest fibers terminate in the superior col-liculi.

Direct stimulation of the optic tract produces a single distinct spike discharge in the dorsal nucleus of the lateral geniculate body. This spike potential may be synaptically conducted to the visual cor-tex; or it may die, presumably because inhibitory influences increase the threshold of the geniculate synapse so that more than one optic tract impulse must act concurrently to produce a propagated response. Very strong stimulation of the optic tract elicits a second spike potential which arrives at the geniculate level after much longer delays and may be followed by still another, slow potential change (Bishop and O'Leary, 1940, 1942).

The postsynaptic geniculate response to the first of these spikes is directly conducted to the visual cortex. The second, more slowly conducted spike potential excites geniculate cells in layer B which project to the lateral thalamic nuclei. From here, the potential or some proportional signal is transmitted to the visual cortex where the elec-trical disturbance arrives after a considerable delay.

The Geniculate Body

Several investigators have suggested that the optic tract impulses may be significantly modified at the synapse in the lateral geniculate body (Evarts and Hughes, 1957a, b; Schoolman and Evarts, 1959; Bishop et al., 1959). It may there-fore be worthwhile to discuss in detail a few recent studies in this field.

Many of the neurons in the dorsal nucleus of the geniculate are spontaneously active when the animal is maintained in complete darkness (De Valois et al., 1962; Hubel, 1960). Arden and Soederberg (1961) have recently reported that the spontaneous discharge of geniculate neurons is not rhythmic, as is true of the retinal elements. Rather, the discharge tends to occur in rapid, brief bursts which typically contain no more than a few spike potentials. The within-burst frequency of these discharges has been calculated to be about 300 cps, but this information may be meaningless considering the small number of spikes per burst. Arden and Liu (1960) have shown that the within-burst interspike intervals tend to be distributed so that the shortest intervals (1 to 10 msec) occur most frequently. Such an irregular distribution of resting activity would not be expected if the genic-ulate cells passively relayed the retinal input. Further indication of interaction processes has been reported by Granit and Phillips (1956) who found that the within-burst amplitude of the geniculate spikes may wax and wane.

The source of this "spontaneous" activity has been investigated in some detail (see Arden and Soederberg, 1961). In the *encéphale isolé* preparation, many of the cells of the lateral geniculate body continue to show spontaneous activity, even when the input from the retina is completely blocked. In the *cerveau isolé* preparation, on the other hand, all spontaneous activity ceased when the retinal inputs were blocked. This finding suggests that the spontaneous activity of the geniculate cells may reflect external influences from the cortex and brainstem. The latter appears to be the more important source of the two since "decortication" of an encéphale isolé preparation had only little effect on spontaneous activity.

The resting activity of geniculate neurons was also found to vary as a function of general "arousal," with some cells showing an increased rate of firing during EEG and behavioral activation, others a decrement. Some of the cells showed additional rhythmic variations in the level of base activity.

Electrical stimulation of some portions of the brainstem reticular formation has been shown to increase the rate of spontaneous discharge of some geniculate neurons (Ogawa, 1963). Sudden auditory or olfactory stimuli increased the geniculate response to light as well as the resting level of spontaneous discharge. Maintained or frequently repeated presentations of visual stimuli tended to reduce the response of geniculate neurons (Mancia et al., 1959; Arden and Soederberg, 1961).

The response of single geniculate cells to visual stimuli has been investigated by Arden and Liu (1960). They found that not all neurons in the lateral geniculate nucleus responded to visual inputs to the retina with a distinct spike potential. Some were found to be totally unaffected; others responded only briefly with bursts of activity which were similar to those seen in the resting record. Rapidly repeated visual stimuli (flicker) often elicited synchronized single-spike or short-burst discharges; these were so similar to the resting activity that only the precise temporal relationship between the stimuli and the geniculate responses distinguished active from inactive units. Increases in stimulus intensity often did not affect the amplitude or frequency of the single-cell responses but did improve the synchrony between the stimuli and the spike potentials.

Bishop et al. (1958) have emphasized that a single spike potential in an optic tract fiber may not be sufficient to induce postsynaptic excitation of a comparable potential in the geniculate. Instead, a graded slow postsynaptic potential which may represent subthreshold facilitatory effects is induced. Only if several optic tract fibers converge on a single geniculate neuron and discharge simultaneously or nearly so, can these facilitatory effects sum to evoke propagated postsynaptic potentials; this clearly represents another step in the progressive convergence which characterizes the visual system.

Hubel and Wiesel (1961; Hubel, 1963) have shown that the retinal receptive fields of a single geniculate cell are composed of discrete concentric ON, ON-OFF, and OFF zones much like the receptive fields of retinal ganglion cells; they also demonstrated that the individual cells appear to interact competitively as they do when the recordings are obtained directly from the retina. However, recent observations reported by Bartley and Nelson (1963) suggest some interesting differences between the response of geniculate and retinal units. The retinal response to stimulation of ON or OFF zones consists essentially of a brief burst of spike potentials. The number and frequency of within-burst potentials varies, at least partly, as a function of stimulus intensity and duration as well as the absolute size of the stimulus (which determines the size of the inhibitory influence from neighboring areas of the retina). Beyond these continuous variations there is no physical characteristic which might categorize the retinal response into a few distinct classes. This is not the case at the geniculate level. Relatively intense visual stimuli elicit three successive groups of ON responses which arrive at the geniculate body after characteristically different latencies (about 30, 140, and 380 msec, respectively). Two distinct OFF responses (with latencies of about 30 and 170 msec) have also been reported. The functional significance of these groupings is not immediately obvious.

De Valois (1960) has reported that some of the geniculate neurons respond to changes in wavelengths in a way that suggests their function as pure brightness transducers. That is, a plot of the sensitivity threshold as a function of wavelengths tends to duplicate or at least approximate (1) the scotopic luminous efficiency curve, (2) the broad-band dominator function of some retinal units, and (3) the decomposition curve of the visual pigment rhodopsin. Other units responded with distinct ON effects to stimuli of the red portion of the spectrum and gave OFF responses to green stimuli. Still others gave ON responses to stimuli from the shortwave (blue) end of the visible spectrum and OFF responses to yellow. These red-green and yellow-blue units typically did not respond to white light, presumably because approximately equal ON and OFF influences canceled each other. These observations are particularly important in view of the *R-G* and *B-Y* generator potentials which Svaetichin (1953) and others have recorded from portions of the retina. It may be that these slow potentials are not merely general excitatory or inhibitory influences on retinal events, as some authors have suggested. Instead, they may carry essential information which in some way becomes coded in the spike activity of the optic tract and at least partially uncoded by geniculate cells with specific spectral sensitivities.

A recent analysis of related findings in the rabbit (Hill, 1962) suggests that our understanding of the mechanisms responsible for this coding may be hindered by species differences. Hill recorded the spectral sensitivity of geniculate neurons in the rabbit and recorded a large variety of response categories. Some ON units responded maximally to a specific wavelength and provided spectral sensitivity curves that were not unlike the narrow-band modulator functions of Granit. Other units had two or more maxima, suggesting the convergence of a number of different primary receptors of rather different spectral sensitivity. Although the definition of maxima in these units is not as restricted as one might wish, Hill believed he was able to detect five distinct peaks in the neighborhood of 435, 460, 500, 580, and 635 mμ. Only two types of maximal OFF responses (with peaks near 450 and 500 mμ) were found, but this discrepancy between the number of ON and OFF units may represent little more than sampling error. Some units responded with a clear ON response to stimuli of one band of wavelengths and gave equally distinct OFF responses at other portions of the visible spectrum.

The Superior Colliculi

We mentioned in our discussion of the anatomy of the visual system that the projections to the superior colliculi are topographically organized and that this subcortical relay station may be primarily concerned with the completion of various reflex responses.

What remains to be discussed briefly is recent microelectrode work (Maturana et al., 1959; Lettvin et al., 1961) which suggests an interesting *functional* organization of the retinocollicular projections. These workers found that the retina is fully and registrally represented in the four layers of the superior colliculus. They also observed that the five types of visual detectors which they isolated in the frog retina may be differentially distributed so that the boundary detectors are located in the outer layer of the colliculus and the dimming detectors in the deepest layer.

Two novel detector classes appear to be represented in the tectal area which surrounds the colliculi. Neurons called *newness cells* cover the entire visual field with extensively overlapping visual fields of about 30° diameter. These neurons respond only briefly to any sharp change in illumination or movement; the frequency of the discharge is related to the suddenness, speed, and direction of the change. Repeated movements in the same direction produced adaptation.

A second type of tectal neuron appeared to have a "receptive field" covering most, if not all, of the visual field except for a small "null" region. Stimuli that are projected entirely within this null region do not elicit a response; however, when the same stimulus appears anywhere else in the visual field, a burst of impulses occurs which continues as long as the object moves. If it stops for about 2 min, the discharge of this *sameness* neuron dies away and erupts again as soon as the object moves again.

Cortical Mechanisms

The cortical representation of vision has been extensively studied. An imposing body of detailed and sometimes isolated facts and several not entirely compatible theoretical schemes exist for their interpretation. It is salutary, therefore, merely to discuss the major findings in this field and present a brief summary of the individual interpretations rather than attempt an integration of the sometimes incompatible systems.

Before we embark on this discussion, it may be worthwhile to point out that not all visual abilities are dependent on cortical projections. The most thorough description of the behavior of animals with total lesions of the striate cortex has been provided by Klüver (1942). The animals (monkeys) retained many of the simple light reflexes, such as pupillary constriction in response to a sudden increase in illumination, and could get around remarkably well in a familiar environment. Klüver concluded, on the basis of extensive tests, that the monkeys could no longer discriminate differences in brightness (i.e., luminance per unit area) but could respond quite adequately to absolute differences in total luminance. The absolute threshold for responses to visual stimuli did not appear to be appreciably increased, and the animals performed some remarkable discriminations as long as the total luminance of the discriminanda could be used as a differential cue. Monkeys without visual cortices cannot discriminate intermittency (flicker) if the total luminance of the steady and intermittent sources is set to be equal; they do not respond to differences in wavelength but they may discriminate color on the basis of luminance differences. Similarly, they cannot discriminate objects on the basis of shape or contour if the total luminance of the discriminanda is equivalent.

The macroelectrode studies of Bishop and Bartley. Bishop and Bartley investigated the gross electrophysiology of the visual cortex and related portions of the brain for well over 30 years (Bishop, 1933; Bartley and Bishop, 1933; Bishop and Clare, 1952a, b; Bishop and O'Leary, 1938; Bartley, 1959). These studies provide the background for all the more recent microelectrode investigations, some of which we shall discuss.

Bishop and Clare (1952a) reported that the simplest cortical response pattern was obtained by applying single-shock stimulation to the proximal stump of the dissected optic tract. The primary response appeared to be conducted directly to the fourth layer of the visual cortex and to spread from there to all other layers. This resulted in a compound, three-spike response which may reflect the successive activation of three distinct cell populations. Subsequent detailed studies of this compound potential (Bishop and Clare, 1953a, b) showed that a number of smaller spike potentials intervened between each of the large potentials.

On the basis of these and related experimental observations, Clare and Bishop (1955) suggested that the fibers of the optic radiations terminate directly on short-axon cells of the fourth cortical layer. These cells project to pyramidal cells of the same region. Axons from the pyramidal cells join the short and long association pathways of the cortical white matter or return (largely via recurrent collaterals) to short-axon cells in all layers of the visual cortex. These short-axon cells project in turn to a second set of pyramidal cells which start another cycle of interconnections and excitation much like the first. Clare and Bishop suggested that the three large spike potentials of the cortical response to optic tract stimulation might

represent the successive activation of three different populations of pyramidal cells; the intervening, low-amplitude spike responses may reflect the activity of three distinct and successively excited populations of short-axon cells. They also suggested that the slow, direct-current potential shifts observed in the visual cortex following intense and/or prolonged stimulation may reflect activity in the apical dendrites of the pyramidal cells.

The arrival of spike potentials in the visual cortex also results in a number of slow-wave responses which have been attributed to different layers of the cortical mantle. The first of these responses is a slow, surface-positive wave; this wave is thought to reflect the state of polarization of the apical dendrites of neurons which are generating and propagating the spike potentials (see Figure 3.44).

This initial slow wave is followed by two distinct waves of surface negativity. The first and smaller of these deflections may reflect the conduction of activity from the cell bodies to the surface of the cortex via apical dendrites. The second, larger potential seems to result from neuronal discharges localized in the fourth layer of the cortical mantle (see Bishop and Clare, 1952a, b, 1953a, b for further details).

Electrical responses similar to those observed after optic tract stimulation have been elicited by direct electrical stimulation of specific layers of the occipital cortex (Bishop and Clare, 1953). Surface stimulation of the cortical mantle elicited only a slow, negative potential. A biphasic response was obtained from the upper layers of the striate cortex, the initial phase being surface-positive. Stimulation of the lower layers produced two or three distinct spike potentials, and stimulation near the terminations of the optic radiations reproduced the complete sequence of spike and slow potentials normally seen after optic tract stimulation.

Observations of cortical responses outside the primary visual projection area (Clare and Bishop, 1954) showed evoked potentials that were similar in form and complexity to those seen in the occipital cortex itself but only about one-eighth of the amplitude of the primary responses. The responses of part of the ventromedial suprasylvian gyrus in the cat (an audiovisual association area) occurred about 1 msec after the response of the occipital cortex and seemed to be related to the second major spike discharge in the primary response.

Bartley's earlier studies (1936) of the evoked responses to retinal stimulation demonstrated that specific portions of the retina selectively fired

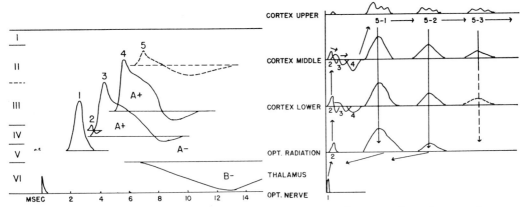

Fig. 3.44 *Left,* tentative inferences concerning the origin of cortical responses drawn from experimental data. Roman numerals at left indicate conventional cortical layers and furnish a scale of depth. Numerals 1 to 5 refer to cortical spikes; A+, underlying surface-positive waves; B−, late surface-negative wave which appears to arise from lower layers of cortex; A−, the early surface-negative wave, only occasionally well developed in the normal cortex but large under strychnine where it becomes the most prominent potential element of the record. (From Bishop and Clare, 1952.)

Right, Responses of the optic pathway of the rabbit. At least four elements of the response, following the activation of the optic nerve, can be distinguished in some records, although any two adjacent elements, each presumably complex, may be confluent in a single response. The last of these four may be repeated several times at intervals of about 0.2 sec following a single shock. A discharge of the corticofugal fibers during at least the first of these repetitive cortical discharges appears to facilitate the thalamic neurons to a second discharge from the optic nerve. This is indicated by the long vertical arrows pointing downward. Abscissas, time; ordinates, voltage. (From Bishop and O'Leary, 1936.)

specific portions of the visual projection cortex and that both spatial and temporal summation or inhibition existed. Simultaneous stimulation of two neighboring retinal points typically produced distinct cortical responses in each of the two areas that corresponded to the site of stimulation. If recording electrodes were placed at points intermediate between the cortical representations of the two retinal areas, a single response could sometimes be observed; this response tended to show summation when the two retinal areas were concurrently excited. If the presentation of two visual stimuli was separated in time as well as in space, a facilitatory summation effect occurred, even in the areas of direct cortical representation of each stimulus, until the interstimulus interval exceeded some maximal value (around 150 to 175 msec). The response to the second stimulus was often totally suppressed once this interval was exceeded.

Bartley also found that the size of the visual stimulus was systematically and positively related to the latency ("implicit time" in Bartley's terminology) between the retinal stimulation and the peak of the initial spike of the cortical response (see Figure 3.45).

He also reported some interesting observations concerning the temporal interactions between evoked responses in the cortex. Using brief light flashes separated by relatively long periods of darkness, he recorded distinct responses to the onset and termination of the stimulation. Unlike their interaction in lower portions of the visual system, the gross ON and OFF responses of the visual cortex could coexist. Bartley pointed out that the response latencies for ON responses appeared to be significantly shorter than those for OFF responses. Progressive shortening of the dark interval that separated successive light flashes eventually resulted in the all-but-simultaneous arrival of ON responses to the next stimulus and OFF responses to the preceding stimulus. Bartley suggested that this coincidence might be responsible for the critical fusion frequency (c.f.f.) of flashing stimuli.

Bartley's findings have interesting implications for our understanding of the processing of positive and negative states. He observed that OFF re-

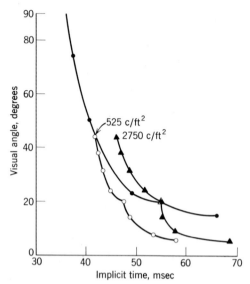

Fig. 3.45 The relation between implicit time of the rabbit's cortex and the visual angle of the target. Note the break in curves at or near 20°. This break suggests that the increase in target size beyond this point does not involve further spatial summation at the retina, and that further reduction in implicit time is a continuation of the effect from increasing the intensity of incidental stray illumination of the retina. (From Bartley, 1935.)

sponses could be conducted in the visual pathways almost concurrently with ON reactions to stimulation of the same receptive fields in the retina. However, successive ON responses could not be processed unless they occurred a minimum of about 80 msec apart. This finding suggests that the ON and OFF responses from a given retinal field may be able to use separate pathways to the cortex in spite of their apparently competitive interaction at lower levels of the system (Bartley, 1936b).

Bishop (1933) found that the amplitude of the individual cortical evoked responses to repetitive visual stimuli was essentially random unless the presentation of the stimuli was "tuned" to the spontaneous activity of the cortex or vice versa. Using a maximal shock to the optic tract to initiate reorganization of the spontaneous rhythm of the visual cortex (the basic rhythm is not affected but is shifted in time), Bishop found that the spacing of subsequent stimuli, so that their arrival at the cortex coincided or conflicted with the natural rhythm, could significantly affect the magnitude of the evoked response (see Figure 3.46).

A marked tuning of the cortical activity was demonstrated when the stimuli were repeated at

exactly twice the spontaneous EEG frequency of the occipital cortex. The initial lack of response gradually changed to submaximal "following" of the stimulus frequency, as shown in Figure 3.47.

Facilitatory effects have been recorded at cortical as well as geniculate levels. The inhibitory phase following a cortical evoked potential is characterized by a slow, surface-negative wave. Under some circumstances this period of negativity may be preceded by a number of brief undulations which seem to correlate with a facilitatory state of the visual pathways (Bishop and O'Leary, 1938, 1940).

Halstead and his associates have suggested that the spontaneous EEG rhythm of the visual cortex may be capable of following the frequency of intermittent visual stimuli up to the c.f.f. (Halstead et al., 1942a, b). This "photic driving" response has recently been used in a number of experiments on the pathways used by conditioned responses to visual stimuli. Further discussion is given in our section on the electrophysiological correlates of the learning process.

The microelectrode studies of Hubel and Wiesel. Hubel and Wiesel have recently reported a series of microelectrode studies which have significantly enhanced our understanding of the visual system (Hubel, 1959, 1960, 1963; Hubel and Wiesel, 1959, 1961, 1962).

The initial studies of this series showed that many cortical cells did not respond to visual stimuli that covered large sections of the visual field; however, the cells discharged vigorously when only restricted foci on the retina were illuminated. Furthermore, stimuli that were moved across the visual field often elicited a response from single cortical cells which did not respond to any stationary stimuli. The cells of

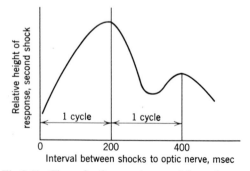

Fig. 3.46 The cycle of responsiveness of the optic cortex of the rabbit as determined by paired stimulation. (From S. H. Bartley, *J. cell. comp. Physiol,* 1936, **8**, 48.)

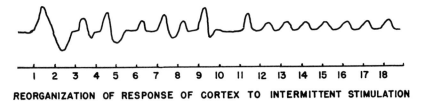

REORGANIZATION OF RESPONSE OF CORTEX TO INTERMITTENT STIMULATION

Fig. 3.47 The response of the optic cortex of the rabbit to rapidly repeated stimulation of the optic nerve. At first the pulses are delivered more frequently than the cortex is able to respond. Later, the several channels capable of being activated become distributed in time in such a way that no single channel needs to respond to successive pulses for there to be a cortical response. (From S. H. Bartley, *J. cell. comp. Physiol,* 1936, **8,** 49.)

the visual cortex were found to exhibit a surprising amount of "spontaneous" activity in the absence of retinal illumination. Marked changes in discharge frequency occurred without corresponding changes in retinal illumination.

In subsequent studies Hubel and Wiesel showed that most neurons of the occipital cortex respond selectively to stimulation of a small retinal field. The maintained activity of cortical cells could be partially inhibited by the projection of small visual stimuli to specific portions of this receptive field, and the termination of such an inhibitory stimulus produced a sudden burst of cortical discharge. The projection of the same stimulus to other portions of the same retinal field gave ON responses. A thorough study of 45 such cortical units showed that most of the receptive fields of neurons in the occipital cortex had distinct excitatory and inhibitory regions, although the relative size of these antagonistic regions varied greatly. Simultaneous stimulation of excitatory and inhibitory regions caused mutual inhibition, i.e., the ON response to the onset of stimulation as well as the OFF response to its termination were shorter than normal. Simultaneous stimulation of the entire receptive field (or the entire retina) did not typically affect the spontaneous activity of the cortical neurons. Summation effects were always observed when the stimulation was confined to either the excitatory or inhibitory regions; the response was maximal when the contours of the stimulus were adjusted to cover most or all of the excitatory or inhibitory region of a particular receptive field (see Figures 3.48, 3.49).

Almost all the receptive fields were organized so that an oblong central excitatory or inhibitory zone was flanked by thin bands of points which responded in the opposite fashion. The relative size of the central and opposing lateral areas varied considerably, and some receptive fields appeared to have only one flanking region or had flanking regions of very unequal influence. Receptive fields were observed with horizontal, oblique, or vertical axes (the axis of a receptive field being defined as a straight line that runs through the center of the field in a direction determined by its maximal extent). The outer boundary (i.e., size) of the receptive fields of cortical neurons depended greatly on the intensity of the stimulus and background illumination and tended to be much more poorly defined than the size of receptive fields of retinal or geniculate cells.

The peculiar geometric pattern of the receptive fields of cortical units suggested the use of long slits of light which could be rotated around the center of the receptive field so that minimal and maximal coverage of the same receptive field could be obtained by the same stimulus. Hubel and Wiesel found that the changing proportion of excitatory and inhibitory influences that could be obtained by such a procedure was reflected in the response of the cortical cells (see the example reproduced in Figure 3.50).

A number of interesting phenomena were observed when slits of light were moved across the visual field. Movement was found to be a more effective stimulus than any stationary source. However, the orientation (axis) of the oblong stimulus and the direction of its movement were also important determinants of the cortical response. For instance, any horizontal movement of a vertically oriented slit across the receptive field shown in Figure 3.47 produced a marked response. Vertical movement of a horizontally oriented slit of the same dimensions across the same visual field did not produce a clear cortical reaction (see Figure 3.51). The differential effect was found to be related to the relative orientation of the slit to the receptive field. If the slit covered the excitatory and inhibitory areas simultaneously, little or no response could be detected; however, a marked reaction was always recorded when the

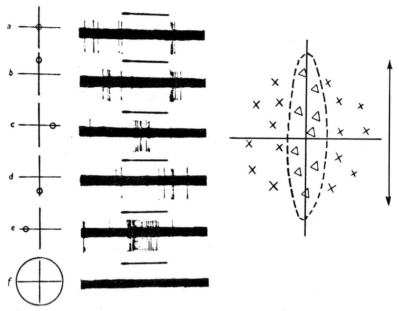

Fig. 3.48 Responses of a cell in the cat's striate cortex to a 1° spot of light. The receptive field is located in the eye contralateral to the hemisphere from which the unit was recorded, close to and below the area centralis, just nasal to the horizontal meridian. No response was evoked from the ipsilateral eye. The complete map of the receptive field is shown at right: ×, areas giving excitation; △, areas giving inhibitory effects; scale, 4°. Axes of this diagram are reproduced to the left of each record; *a*, 1° (0.25 mm) spot shone in the center of the field; *b-e*, 1° spot shone on four points equidistant from center; *f*, 5° spot covering the entire field. Background illumination, 0.17 log mc; stimulus intensity, 1.65 log mc; duration of each stimulus, 1 sec; positive deflexions upward. (From Hubel and Wiesel, 1959.)

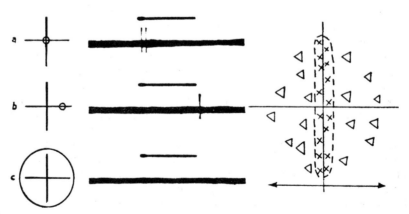

Fig. 3.49 Responses of a unit to stimulation with circular spots of light. The receptive field is located in the area centralis of the contralateral eye (this unit could also be activated by the ipsilateral eye). *a*, 1° spot in the center region; *b*, same spot displaced 3° to the right; *c*, 8° spot covering the entire receptive field. (From Hubel and Wiesel, 1959.)

228

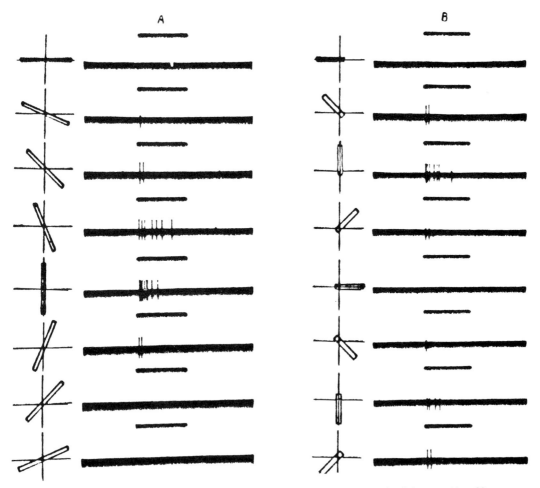

Fig. 3.50 Same unit as in Figure 3.49. A, responses to shining a rectangular light spot, $1° \times 8°$; center of slit superimposed on center of receptive field; successive stimuli rotated clockwise, as shown left. B, responses to $1° \times 5°$ slit oriented in various directions, with one end always covering the center of the receptive field. Note that this central region evoked responses when stimulated alone. Stimulus duration, 1 sec. (From Hubel and Wiesel, 1959.)

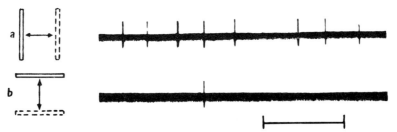

Fig. 3.51 Same unit as in Figures 3.49 and 3.50. Receptive field shown in Figure 3.49. Responses to a slit ($1° \times 8°$) moved transversely back and forth across the receptive field: *a*, slit moved horizontally; *b*, slit moved vertically. (From Hubel and Wiesel, 1959.)

slit was moved across the antagonistic areas successively. Distinct excitatory responses always occurred when a slit was moved across a receptor field characterized by a particularly well-developed flanking excitatory region, separated by a band of inhibitory influences. Some units were found to give different responses to movement in some planes or directions; some responded preferentially to motion in only one direction but not at all to movement in the reverse direction. This directional sensitivity was commonly associated with unequal flanking regions. For instance, an obliquely oriented unit with an inhibitory center flanked by one very large excitatory region on one side and a very small and weak excitatory region on the other responded differentially to a slit stimulus which was oriented so that its axis paralleled that of the receptive field. Downward motion of the stimulus elicited intense responses from the cortical unit, but upward motion did not affect the resting discharge.

Most of the units responded only to stimulation of one receptive field in either the ipsilateral or the contralateral eye. A few responded to receptive fields in roughly homologous regions of both retinae. Although these receptive fields were always similar in composition and orientation, the cortical cells often responded better to stimulation of one of the two fields. Simultaneous excitation of both receptive fields yielded summation effects, provided the stimuli were confined to either the excitatory or the inhibitory zones of both receptive fields. Competitive interaction (inhibition) could be produced by simultaneous stimulation of antagonistic zones in the two receptive fields. The cortical unit did not respond at all, for instance, if the inhibitory regions of the receptive field of the right eye were stimulated concurrently with the excitatory region of the left eye.

The microelectrode studies of Jung and Baumgartner. A group of German workers (Baumgarten and Jung, 1952; Baumgartner, 1955; Baumgartner and Jung, 1955; Baumgartner and Hakas, 1959, 1960; Jung, 1958a, b, 1961; Jung et al., 1952; Jung and Baumgartner, 1955) have analyzed the response of single units in the visual cortex to diffuse visual light and simple pattern stimuli. This work is particularly interesting because an effort is made to interpret the observations in terms of perceptual problems.

Jung and his colleagues have attempted to build a remarkably simple theoretical framework for the visual system; their plan reduces its apparent complexity to an interaction between only two basically antagonistic systems which respond selectively to "brightness information" and "darkness information" respectively. Before we discuss these systems, a brief presentation of their empirical data will be made.

Using glass-capillary microelectrodes, Jung and Baumgartner recorded the responses of single cells in the occipital cortex to diffuse light, intermittent flashes of light, or a grid of alternating light and dark stripes (the pattern stimulus). Figure 3.52 shows the five basic response categories that were encountered. Since a particular cortical cell always responded in a characteristic fashion, a corresponding classification of neurons that parallels the response types shown in Figure 3.52 was suggested.

By far the largest category, the A neurons, did not respond to diffuse light. Some of these cells did react to flicker, movement, or contrast between adjacent areas of different brightness. Jung suggested that all the cells of this category may respond to highly specialized visual inputs rather than to gross differences of illumination as studied in these experiments. Since most of the A-type neurons were fired or facilitated by thalamic, reticular, or vestibular stimulation, the authors further proposed that these cells might perform additional stabilizing functions by providing a constant overall level of cortical excitation regardless of gross changes in retinal illumination.

Brightness information per se appeared to be received by the B-type neurons. These neurons responded promptly and vigorously to the onset of any threshold value visual stimulus and maintained an increased level of firing throughout the presence of such a stimulus. They constitute about one-fourth of the neural population of the striate cortex. The B-type neurons appear to be functionally related to the ON elements of the ganglion and geniculate levels.

A few neurons, the very rare C-type cells, responded to the onset as well as to the termination of all visual stimuli by a brief but definite period of inhibition of the spontaneous activity. These responses were found only very rarely, and it is not entirely clear that a distinct population of cells must be responsible for them, since C responses to stimulation of one eye have been recorded from units which respond to stimulation of the other eye with perfectly healthy B-type reactions (Grüsser and Grüsser-Cornehls, 1960).

A similar inhibition of spontaneous activity occurred in the response of D-type neurons to

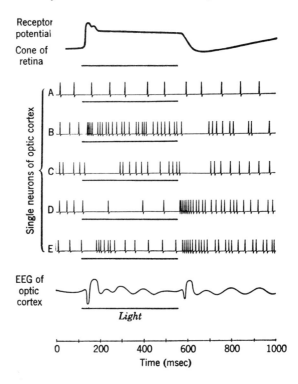

Fig. 3.52 Five types of neuronal responses of the visual cortex to light and dark stimulation and their relation to receptor excitation and to the EEG. The topmost graph shows the receptor potential recorded with microelectrode, intracellularly from the cone layer of the retina. The bottom graph shows cortical potentials with the ON and OFF effect from a gross electrode recording on the cortical surface (macrorhythms). Graphs A-E, schematic representation of discharges of different neuronal types: A neuron, no reaction to light or dark; B neuron, activated by light, inhibited by dark with delayed afteractivation (similar to on element of retina); C neuron, inhibitory break for both light and dark; D neuron, inhibited by light and activated by dark (reciprocal of B neuron, similar to OFF element of retina); E neuron, pre-excitatory inhibition precedes delayed activation by light, early activation by dark (similar to ON-OFF elements of retina). (From Jung et al., 1957.)

the onset of any brief or maintained stimulus; however, the main response of these D-type neurons, a marked burst of activity, occurred after the cessation of the stimulation (Jung et al., 1957).

Frequently indistinct from the D-type neurons is a class of cells that show very similar inhibitory reactions to the light onset as well as marked OFF responses after its cessation; however, they also give a burst of rapid activity shortly after the stimulus onset (i.e., immediately after the initial period of inhibition).

Perhaps the most interesting property of these response categories is that they appear to be specific to photic stimulation of the retina. Electrical stimulation of the optic nerve (Grüsser and Grützner, 1958; Grützner et al., 1958) or the nonspecific nuclei of the thalamus (Creutzfeld and Akimoto, 1957–1958) produced very different responses from single cells in the visual cortex and did not interfere with the cortical response to photic stimulation (Jung, 1961).

Recent investigations of the cortical reaction to alternating stripes of light and darkness (a grid pattern which is moved in discrete steps across the visual field) by Baumgartner and Hakas (1959, 1960) demonstrated that the response of each of the five neuronal classes was reversed in the dark. This reciprocity of the response of single units

to alternating light-dark cycles is demonstrated for two of the response classes (the B and D responses) in Figure 3.53. Jung (1961) pointed out that the excessive response of both types of units to the transition from light to dark and vice versa correlates nicely with the perceptual experience of simultaneous contrast (portions of a white field which are immediately adjacent to a sharply bounded black field appear whiter than parts which are farther removed from the boundary).

Baumgartner and Hakas (1960) have used the differential response to light and dark segments of a grid stimulus as an estimate of the size of the central core of the receptive field (i.e., the portion that gives uniform excitatory or inhibitory responses) of retinal, geniculate, and cortical cells. The central core of the receptive field (and presumably the entire receptive field) of cortical cells appeared to be smaller by at least 50% than that of retinal cells. This finding is surprising in view of the well-documented convergence toward the central nervous system.

A very interesting convergence of heterogeneous inputs from geniculate, reticular, and vestibular as well as optic afferents on single cells in the cortex has been observed in Jung's laboratory (Jung, 1961). Specific retinal and nonspecific thalamic inputs were found to converge on most

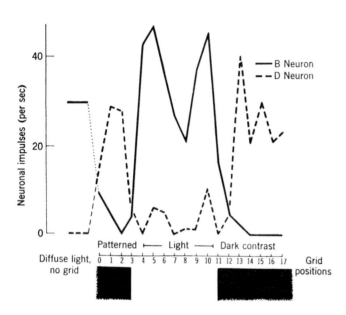

Fig. 3.53 Responses to contrast pattern and diffuse light in a cortical B and D neuron from the same experiment (from unpublished experiments of Baumgartner). The responses to light-on are plotted for spike frequencies per second on the ordinate (spikes counted in the first 500 msec following light-on) in relation to the projections of the receptive field to contrast pattern and diffuse light on the abscissa.

The bright stripe has a visual angle of 5°41′ and is exposed in grid positions 3 to 11 by steps moving across the receptive fields of the neurons from left to right. Reciprocal activation and inhibition of the two antagonistic neurons and contrast enhancement of the discharge at the border of bright and dark stripes are clearly shown in the peaks and troughs of the upper graphs. This neuronal behavior may be explained satisfactorily by two factors: (1) reciprocal inhibition of antagonistic neurons in the same receptive field, and (2) lateral inhibition of synergic neurons in the surrounding field. (From Jung, 1961.)

neurons in area 17. Thalamic stimulation did not affect the cortical response to visual stimuli (Creutzfeld and Akimoto, 1957–1958) but raised the c.f.f. (the maximum stimulus repetition rate to which the cortical cells responded in a 1:1 fashion) of striate cells (Creutzfeld and Grüsser, 1959). Stimulation of the reticular formation tended to lower the c.f.f. of most cortical cells.

Some peculiar sensory interactions have been reported by Grüsser and his associates (Grüsser et al., 1959; Grüsser and Grüsser-Cornehls, 1959, 1960). Their findings suggest extensive projections from the vestibular nuclei of the brainstem. Most cells in the visual cortex gave distinct ON or OFF responses to labyrinthine stimulation and showed significantly modified reactions to light during labyrinthine excitation. The c.f.f. of most cortical cells was increased by stimulation of the labyrinth.

A study of the effects of binocular stimulation suggests that most cells in the visual cortex respond only to afferents from either the ipsilateral *or* the contralateral retina. Some competitive interaction occurred in about 30% of the cells studied. True binocular convergence (equivalence of stimuli to either eye) was found in only about 10% of the cells tested. Jung (1961) suggested that this preponderance of monocular representations at

the level of the primary visual projections correlates nicely with the psychophysical observation that each eye develops independent images which may only "secondarily" be fused by associative processes into stereoscopic images.

Jung (1959a, b) has attempted to integrate the findings from these single-cell studies with some of the basic phenomena of visual perception, an important step in the direction to which we must turn if this complex area is ever to be understood.

The subjective sensation of brightness is logarithmically related to the intensity of illumination per unit area according to the (not entirely adequate) Weber-Fechner law of perception. Jung suggested that the sensation of brightness may find a direct correlate in the activity of the B-type neurons, since their discharge rate also increases roughly as a logarithmic function of stimulus intensity. Differences in brightness (i.e., contrast) may be signaled by the activity of the D-type neurons whose firing rate appears to be inversely related to retinal illumination.

Adaptation, as studied by the "stopped image" technique (the stimulus is projected to precisely the same spot on the retina by means of mirrors which are attached to the eye and cancel the effects of saccadic eye movements), has a direct correlate in the discharge frequency of some cortical neurons (Grüsser, 1960).

Simple afterimages can be considered to be spontaneous alternations of patterns of light and dark phases of retinal illuminations. Jung and his associates have observed apparently spontaneous alternations of excitatory and inhibitory responses of cortical neurons during and following the presentation of light-dark patterns of retinal illumination. The time course of these spontaneous alternations seemed roughly comparable to that of afterimages.

The limited interaction between binocular inputs also appears to have psychophysical correlates. Under most circumstances the interaction is competitive rather than additive. Binocular summation is a correspondingly rare phenomenon, whereas binocular rivalry occurs frequently when different stimuli are presented to corresponding points of the two retinae.

We have already discussed the correlation between simultaneous contrast and the excessive response of some cortical neurons to sharply defined transitional areas between light and dark segments of the visual field (see Figure 3.53). Similar mechanisms may contribute to a number of psychophysical relationships between intermittent stimulation and the corresponding subjective sensation. The c.f.f. of single cortical neurons (the maximal rate of repetitive stimulation to which single cells can respond in a 1:1 fashion) has been shown to equal roughly the subjective c.f.f. (the maximal rate of repetitive stimulation which permits the perception of distinct stimuli). Both rates covary as a function of a number of variables. For instance, the neuronal as well as the subjective c.f.f. varies as a function of luminance (brightness) of the light phase (Porter's law). Maximal subjective brightness and the highest discharge rate of B-type neurons in the visual cortex occur at a flicker frequency (about 10/sec) which is lower than the c.f.f. (the Brücke-Bartley effect) (Bartley, 1959; Grüsser and Creutzfeld, 1957).

The subjective c.f.f. is also known to vary as a function of attention because of reticular influences, and the c.f.f. of single striate cells can be changed by electrical stimulation of the nonspecific thalamic nuclei and midbrain reticular formation (Jung et al., 1957; Creutzfeld and Grüsser, 1959). The repetition rate of flicker presented to one eye does not affect the perception of flicker in the other eye except at values very close to the monocular c.f.f. The response rate of single cortical neurons shows a similar lack of interaction under these conditions (Jung, 1961).

Jung suggested that the scotopic functions of the visual system can be understood in terms of only two antagonistic systems: (1) a *brightness system* which is composed of B-type neurons and a *darkness system* which consists of D-type neurons. The discharge frequency of the B neurons is positively related to the luminance of the stimulus and the perception of brightness; that of the D neurons correlates inversely with brightness. The E units of the visual cortex are thought to correspond to retinal ON-OFF units which are particularly common in peripheral portions of the retina and are believed to function specifically as motion detectors. The response pattern of the E neurons is in most respects so similar to that of the D-type cells that Jung suggested darkness system which includes E and D units. This theory essentially reduces scotopic aspects of the visual system to an ON (B-type neurons) and OFF (D- and E-type neurons) mechanism. (The C units are so rarely found as to be negligible, and the A neurons, by definition, do not participate in simple visual sensations.) The coordination of the ON and OFF parts of this system is thought to be based on two principal processes, *reciprocal inhibition* of antagonistic neurons of the same region and *lateral inhibition* of synergistic neurons of neighboring areas.

BIBLIOGRAPHY

Adrian, E. D. The electric response of the human eye. *J. Physiol. (London)*, 1945, **104**, 84–104.

Adrian, E. D., & Matthews, R. The action of light on the eye. I: The discharge of impulses in the optic nerve and its relation to the electric change in the retina. *J. Physiol. (London)*, 1927a, **63**, 378–414.

Adrian, E. D., & Matthews, R. The action of light on the eye. II: The processes involved in retinal excitation. *J. Physiol. (London)*, 1927b, **64**, 279–301.

Arden, G. B., & Liu, Y. M. Some types of response of single cells in the rabbit lateral geniculate body to stimulation of the retina by light and to electrical stimulation of the optic nerve. *Acta physiol. scand.*, 1960a, **48**, 36–48.

Arden, G. B., & Liu, Y. M. Some responses of the lateral geniculate body of the rabbit to flickering light stimuli. *Acta physiol. scand.*, 1960b, **48**, 49–62.

Arden, G. B., & Soederberg, U. The transfer of optic information through the lateral geniculate body of the rabbit. In *Sensory communication.* W. A. Rosenblith, Ed. Cambridge, Mass.: M.I.T. Press, 1961.

Aubert, H. *Physiologie der Netzhaut.* Breslau: Thieme, 1865.

Barlow, H. B. Action potentials from the frog's retina. *J. Physiol. (London)*, 1953a, **119**, 58–68.

Barlow, H. B. Summation and inhibition in the frog's retina, *J. Physiol. (London)*, 1953b, **119**, 69–88.

Bartley, S. H. The time of occurrence of the cortical response as determined by the area of the stimulus object. *Amer. J. Physiol.*, 1935, **110**, 666–674.

Bartley, S. H. A comparison of the electrogram of the optic cortex with that of the retina. *Amer. J. Physiol.*, 1936a, **117**, 338–348.

Bartley, S. H. Temporal and spatial summation of extrinsic impulses with intrinsic activity of cortex. *J. cell. comp. Physiol.*, 1936b, **8**, 41–62.

Bartley, S. H. Central mechanisms of vision. In *Handbook of physiology. Vol. I.* J. Field, H. W. Magoun, & V. E. Hall, Eds. Baltimore: Williams and Wilkins, 1959.

Bartley, S. H., & Bishop, G. H. The cortical response to stimulation of the optic nerve in the rabbit. *Amer. J. Physiol.*, 1933, **103**, 159–172.

Bartley, S. H., & Nelson, T. M. Some relation between sensory end results and neural activity in the optic pathway. *J. Psychol.*, 1963, **55**, 121–143.

Baumgardt, E., & Segal, J. La fonction inhibitrice dans le processus visuel. *C. R. Soc. Biol. (Paris)*, 1946, **140**, 231.

Baumgarten, R. von, & Jung, R. Microelectrode studies on the visual cortex. *Rev. neurol.*, 1952, **87**, 151–155.

Baumgartner, G. Reaktionen einzelner Neurone im optischen Cortex der Katze nach Lichtblitzen. *Pflüg. Arch. ges. Physiol.*, 1955, **261**, 457–469.

Baumgartner, G., & Hakas, P. Reaktionen einzelner Opticusneurone und corticaler Nervenzellen der Katze im Hell-Dunkel-Grenzfeld (Simultankontrast). *Pflüg. Arch. ges. Physiol.*, 1959, **270**, 29.

Baumgartner, G., & Hakas, P. Vergleich der receptiven Felder einzelner on-Neurone des N. opticus, des Corpus geniculatum laterale und des optischen Cortex der Katze. *Zbl. ges. Neurol. Psychiat.*, 1960, **155**, 243–244.

Baumgartner, G., & Jung, R. Hemmungphaenomene an einzelnen corticalen Neuronen und ihre Bedeutung fuer die Bremsung convulsiever Entladungen. *Arch. Sci. biol.*, 1955, **39**, 474–486.

Beitel, R. J., Jr. Spatial summation of subliminal stimuli in the retina of the human eye. *J. gen. Psychol.*, 1934, **10**, 311–327.

Bernhard, C. G. Contributions to neurophysiology of optic pathway. *Acta physiol. scand.*, 1940, **1**, 1–94.

Bernhard, C. G., & Skoglund, C. R. Selective suppression with ethyl alcohol of inhibition in optic nerve and of negative component P^{III} of electroretinogram. *Acta physiol. scand.*, 1941, **2**, 10–21.

Bishop, G. H. Cyclic changes in excitability of optic pathway of rabbit. *Amer. J. Physiol.*, 1933, **103**, 213–224.

Bishop, G. H., & Clare, M. H. Relations between specifically evoked and "spontaneous" activity of optic cortex. *EEG clin. Neurophysiol.*, 1952a, **4**, 321–330.

Bishop, G. H., & Clare, M. H. Sites of origin of electric potentials in striate cortex. *J. Neurophysiol.*, 1952b, **15**, 201–220.

Bishop, G. H., & Clare, M. H. Responses of cortex to direct electrical stimuli applied at different depths. *J. Neurophysiol.*, 1953a, **16**, 1–19.

Bishop, G. H., & Clare, M. H. Sequence of events in optic cortex response to volleys of impulses in radiation. *J. Neurophysiol.*, 1953b, **16**, 490–498.

Bishop, G. H., & O'Leary, J. Components of the electrical response of the optic cortex of the rabbit. *Amer. J. Physiol.*, 1936, **117**, 292–308.

Bishop, G. H., & O'Leary, J. Potential records from optic cortex of cat. *J. Neurophysiol.*, 1938, **1**, 391–404.

Bishop, G. H., & O'Leary, J. Electrical activity of the lateral geniculate of cats following optic nerve stimuli. *J. Neurophysiol.*, 1940, **3**, 308–322.

Bishop, G. H., & O'Leary, J. Factors determining form of potential record in vicinity of synapses of dorsal nucleus of lateral geniculate body. *J. cell. comp. Physiol.*, 1942, **19**, 315–331.

Bishop, P. O., Burke, W., & Davis, R. Synapse discharge by single fibre in mammalian visual system. *Nature (London)*, 1958, **182**, 728–730.

Bishop, P. O., Burke, W., & Davis, R. Activation of single lateral geniculate cells by stimulation of either optic nerve. *Science*, 1959, **130**, 506–507.

Breckenridge, F. C., & Schaub, W. R. Rectangular uniform-chromaticity-scale coordinates *J. opt. Soc. Amer.*, 1939, **29**, 370.

Broca, A. La sensation luminense en fonction du temps. *J. Physiol. Path. gén.*, 1902, **4**, 632–640.

Broca, A., & Sulzer, D. La sensation luminense en fonction du temps pour les lumières colorées; experiences avec les milieux absorbants. *J. Physiol. Path. gén.*, 1904, **6**, 55–68.

Brunswik, E. *Wahrnehmung und Gegenstandswelt.* Leipzig: Deuticke, 1934.

Brunswik, E. *Perception and the representative design of psychological experiments.* Berkeley: Univ. of California Press, 1956.

Burkamp, W. Versuche über das Farbenwiederkennen der Fische. *Z. Sinnesorgan.*, 1923, **55**, 133–170.

Campbell, F. W., & Rushton, W. A. H. Measurement of scotopic pigment in living human eye. *J. Physiol. (London)*, 1955, **130**, 131–147.

Claes, E. Contribution à l'étude physiologique de la fonction visuelle. I: Analyse oscillographique de l'activité spontanée et sensorielle de l'aire visuelle corticale chez le chat non anesthésié. *Arch. int. Physiol.*, 1939, **48**, 181–237.

Clare, M. H., & Bishop, G. H. Response from association area secondarily activated from optic cortex. *J. Neurophysiol.*, 1954, **17**, 271–277.

Clare, M. H., & Bishop, G. H. Dendritic circuits: properties of cortical paths involving dendrites. *Amer. J. Psychiat.*, 1955a, **111**, 818–825.

Clare, M. H., & Bishop, G. H. Properties of dendrites; apical dendrites of cat cortex. *EEG clin. Neurophysiol.*, 1955b, **7**, 85–98.

Coblentz, W. W., & Emerson, W. B. Relative sensibility of the average eye to light of different colors. *Bull. Bur. Stand.*, 1918, **14**, 167

Crawford, B. H. Ocular interaction in its relation to measurements of brightness threshold. *Proc. roy. Soc. (London)*, *B*, 1940, **128**, 552–559.

Creutzfeld, O., & Akimoto, H. Konvergenz und gegenseitige Beeinflussung von Impulsen aus der Retina und den unspezifischen Thalamuskernen an einzelnen Neuronen des optisohen Cortex. *Arch. Psychiat. Nervenkr.*, 1957–1958, **196**, 520–548.

Creutzfeld, O., & Grüsser, O. J. Beeinflussung der Flimmerreaktion einzelner corticaler Neurone durch elektrische Reize unspezifischer Thalamuskerne. *Proceedings of the first international congress of neurological sciences, Brussels, 1957. Vol. III. EEG Clinical Neurophysiology and Epilepsy*, London: Pergamon Press, 1959.

De Valois, R. L. Color vision mechanisms in the monkey. *J. gen. Physiol.*, 1960, **43**, 115–128.

De Valois, R. L., Jacobs, G. H., & Jones, A. E. Effects of increments and decrements of light on neural discharge rate. *Science*, 1962, **136**, 986–987.

Dewar, J., & M'Kendrick, J. G. On the physiological action of light. *J. Anat. Physiol.*, 1873a, **7**, 275–282.

Dewar, J., & M'Kendrick, J. G. On the physiological action of light. *Trans. roy. Soc. Edinburgh*, 1873b, **27**, 141–166.

Donner, K. O., & Granit, R. Scotopic dominator and state of visual purple in the retina. *Acta physiol. scand.*, 1949, **17**, 161–169.

Donner, K. O., & Willmer, E. N. An analysis of the response from single visual-purple-dependent elements in the retina of the cat. *J. Physiol. (London)*, 1950, **111**, 160–173.

Durup, G., & Rousselot, L. Seuils absolus et seuils differentiels en vision nocturne. *Année psychol.*, 1939, **40**, 171.

Ekman, G., & Dahlbaeck, B. *Psychology lab reports*. Stockholm: Stockholm Univ. Press, 1956, 31.

Evarts, E. V., & Hughes, J. R. Relation of posttetanic potentiation to subnormality of lateral geniculate potentials. *Amer. J. Physiol.*, 1957, **188**, 238–244.

Fechner, G. T. *Elemente der Psychophysik*. Leipzig: Breitkopf and Haertel, 1860.

Fry, G. A. The image-forming mechanism of the eye. In *Handbook of physiology. Vol. I*. J. Field, H. W. Magoun, & V. E. Hall, Eds. Baltimore: Williams and Wilkins, 1959.

Gaffron, M. Untersuchungen über das Bewegungssehen bei Libbellenlarven, Fliegen und Fischen. *Z. vergl. Physiol.*, 1934, **20**, 299–337.

Galifret, Y., & Piéron, H. La relation quantité-durée dans l'excitation lumineuse par radiations monochromatiques. *Année psychol.*, 1947, **43**, 231–248.

Galifret, Y., & Piéron, H. Vitesse de réaction et intensité de sensation donées experimentales sur le problème d'une courbe signoide des vitesses. *Année psychol.*, 1949, **47**, 1–16.

Gernandt, B. E. The form variations of the spike recorded by a microelectrode applied on to the mammalian retina. *Acta physiol. scand.*, 1948a, **15**, 88–92.

Gernandt, B. E. Polarity of dark adapted retinal on/off-elements as a function of wave-length. *Acta physiol. scand.*, 1948b, **15**, 286–289.

Gibson, J. J. *The perception of the visual world*. Boston: Houghton Mifflin, 1950.

Gibson, K. S. Spectral characteristics of test solutions used in heterochromatic photometry. *J. opt. Soc. Amer.*, 1924, **9**, 113.

Gibson, K. S. Spectral luminosity factors. *J. opt. Soc. Amer.*, 1940, **30**, 51.

Gibson, K. S., & Tyndall, E. P. T. Visibility of radiant energy. *Bull. Bur. Stand.*, 1923, **19**, 131.

Götz, W. Experimentelle Untersuchungen zum Problem der Sehgrössenkonstanz beim Haushuhn. *Z. Psychol.*, 1926, **99**, 247–260.

Goldmann, H., Koenig, H., & Maeder, F. Die Durchlaessigkeit der Augenlinse fuer Infrarot. *Ophthalmologica*, 1950, **120**, 198–205.

Gotch, F. The time relations of the photo-electric changes in the eyeball of the frog. *J. Physiol. (London)*, 1903, **29**, 388–410.

Graham, C. H. An investigation of binocular summation. I: The fovea. *J. gen. Psychol.*, 1930, **3**, 494–510.

Graham, C. H., Baker, K. E. Hecht, M., & Lloyd, V. V. Factors influencing thresholds for monocular movement parallax. *J. exp. Psychol.*, 1948, **38**, 205–223.

Granit, R. The components of the retinal action potential and their relation to the discharge in the optic nerve. *J. Physiol. (London)*, 1933, **77**, 207–240.

Granit, R. Rotation of activity and spontaneous rhythms in the retina. *Acta physiol. scand.*, 1941a, **1**, 370–379.

Granit, R. The "red'' receptor of Testudo. *Acta physiol. scand.*, 1941b, **1**, 386–388.

Granit, R. Isolation of colour-sensitive elements in a mammalian retina. *Acta physiol. scand.*, 1941c, **2**, 93–109.

Granit, R. A relation between rod and cone substances based on scotopic and photopic spectra of Cyrinus, Tinca, Anguilla and Testudo. *Acta physiol. scand.*, 1941d, **2**, 334–346.

Granit, R. Colour receptors of the frog's retina. *Acta physiol. scand.*, 1942a, **3**, 137–151.

Granit, R. Spectral properties of the visual receptor elements of the guinea pig. *Acta physiol. scand.*, 1942b, **3**, 318–328.

Granit, R. The photopic spectrum of the pigeon. *Acta physiol. scand.*, 1942c, **4**, 118–124.

Granit, R. A physiological theory of colour perception. *Nature (London)*, 1943a, **151**, 11–14.

Granit, R. "Red" and "green" receptors in the retina of Tropidonotus. *Acta physiol. scand.*, 1943b, **5**, 108–115.

Granit, R. The spectral properties of the visual receptors of the cat. *Acta physiol. scand.*, 1943c, **5**, 219–229.

Granit, R. Stimulus intensity in relation to excitation and pre- and post-excitatory inhibition in isolated elements of mammalian retinae. *J. Physiol. (London)*, 1944, **103**, 103–118.

Granit, R. Some properties of post-excitatory inhibition studies in the optic nerve with micro-electrods. *Vet. akad. arkiv. Zool.*, 1945a, **11**, A 36.

Granit, R. The electrophysiological analysis of the fundamental problem of colour reception. Thomas Young Oration No. 14. *Proc. phys. Soc. (London)*, 1945b, **57**, 447–463.

Granit, R. The colour receptors of the mammalian retina. *J. Neurophysiol.*, 1945c, **8**, 195–210.

Granit, R. *Sensory mechanisms of the retina.* London: Oxford Univ. Press, 1947.

Granit, R. Neural organization of the retinal elements, as revealed by polarization. *J. Neurophysiol.*, 1948, **11**, 239–251.

Granit, R. The effect of two wave-lengths of light upon the same retinal element. *Acta physiol. scand.*, 1949, **18**, 281–294.

Granit, R. Reflex self-regulation of the muscle concentration and autogenic inhibition. *J. Neurophysiol.*, 1950a, **13**, 351–372.

Granit, R. The organization of the vertebrate retinal elements. *Ergebn. Physiol.*, 1950b, **46**, 31–70.

Granit, R. The antagonism between the on- and off-systems in the cats retina. *Année psychol.*, 1951, **50**, 129–134.

Granit, R. Effecter på retina vid stimulering i hjaernan. *Proc. Swed. ophthalmol. Soc. Nov.*, 1953.

Granit, R. *Receptors and sensory perception.* New Haven, Conn.: Yale Univ. Press, 1955.

Granit, R. Neural activity in the retina. In *Handbook of physiology. Vol. I.* J. Field, H. W. Magoun, & V. E. Hall, Eds. Baltimore: Williams and Wilkins, 1959.

Granit, R., & Munsterhjelm, A. The electrical response of dark-adapted frog's eyes to monochromatic stimuli. *J. Physiol. (London)*, 1937, **88**, 436–458.

Granit, R., & Phillips, C. G. Excitatory and inhibitory processes acting upon individual Purkinje cells of the cerebellum in cats. *J. Physiol. (London)*, 1956, **133**, 520–547.

Granit, R., & Tansley, K. Rods, cones and the localization of preexcitatory inhibition in the mammalian retina. *J. Physiol. (London)*, 1948, **107**, 54–66.

Granit, R., & Wrede, C. M. The electrical responses of light-adapted frog's eyes to monochromatic stimuli. *J. Physiol. (London)*, 1937, **89**, 239–256.

Granit, R., Rubinstein, B., & Therman, P. O. A new type of interaction experiment with retinal action potential. *J. Physiol. (London)*, 1935, **85**, 34.

Grüsser, O. J. Rezeptorabhaengige Potentiale der Katzenretina and ihre Reaktionen auf Flimmerlicht. *Pflüg. Arch. ges. Physiol.*, 1960, **271**, 511–525.

Grüsser, O. J., & Cornehls, U. Reaktionen einzelner Neurone im optischen Cortex der Katze nach elektrischer Labyrinthpolarisation. *Pflüg. Arch. ges. Physiol.*, 1959, **270**, 31.

Grüsser, O. J., & Creutzfeld, O. Eine neurophysiologische Grundlage des Bruecke-Bartley-Effektes: Maxima der Impulsfrequenz retinaler und corticaler Neurone bei Flimmerlicht mittlerer Frequenzen. *Pflüg. Arch. ges. Physiol.*, 1957, **263**, 668–681.

Grüsser, O. J., & Grüsser-Cornehls, U. Mikroelektrodenuntersuchungen zur Konvergenz vestibulaerer und retinaler Afferenzen an einzelnen Neuronen des optischen Cortex der Katze. *Pflüg. Arch. ges. Physiol.*, 1960, **270**, 227–238.

Grüsser, O. J., & Grützner, A. Reaktionen einzelner Neurone des optischen Cortex der Katze nach elektrischen Reizserien des Nervus opticus. *Arch. Psychiat. Nervenkr.*, 1958, **197**, 405–432.

Grützner, A., Grüsser, O. J., & Baumgartner, G. Reaktionen einzelner Neurone im optischen Cortex der Katze nach elektrischer Reizung des Nervus opticus. *Arch. Psychiat. Nervenkr.*, 1958, **197**, 377–404.

Grüsser, O. J., Grüsser-Cornehls, U., & Saur, G. Reaktionen einzelner Neurone im optischen Cortex der Katze nach elektrischer Polarisation des Labyrinths. *Pflüg. Arch. ges. Physiol.*, 1959, **269**, 593–612.

Guild, J. The colorimetric properties of the spectrum. *Phil. Trans. roy. Soc. London, A*, 1931, **230**, 149.

Gunter, R. Visual size constancy in the cat. *Brit. J. Psychol.*, 1951, **42**, 288–293.

Halstead, W. C., Knox, G. W., & Walker, A. E. Modification of cortical activity by means of intermittent photic stimulation. *J. Neurophysiol.*, 1942a, **5**, 349–355.

Halstead, W. C., Knox, G. W., Woolf, J. I., & Walker, A. E. Effects of intensity and wavelength on driving cortical activity in monkeys. *J. Neurophysiol.*, 1942b, **5**, 483–486.

Hartline, H. K. Impulses in single optic nerve fibers of the vertebrate retina. *Amer. J. Physiol.*, 1935, **113**, 59.

Hartline, H. K. The response of single optic nerve fibers of the vertebrate eye to illumination of the retina. *Amer. J. Physiol.*, 1938a, **121**, 400–415.

Hartline, H. K. The discharge of impulses in the optic nerve of Pecten in response to illumination of the eye. *J. cell. comp. Physiol.*, 1938b, **11**, 465–478.

Hartline, H. K. The receptive field of the optic nerve fibers. *Amer. J. Physiol.*, 1940a, **130**, 690–699.

Hartline, H. K. The effects of spatial summation in the retina on the excitation of the fibers of the optic nerve. *Amer. J. Physiol.*, 1940b, **130**, 700–711.

Hartline, H. K. The nerve messages in the fibers of the visual pathway. *J. opt. Soc. Amer.,* 1940c, **30,** 239–247.

Hartline, H. K., & Graham, C. H. Nerve impulses from single receptors in the eye. *J. cell. comp. Physiol.,* 1932, **1,** 277–295.

Hartline, H. K., & McDonald, P. R. Light and dark adaptation of single photoreceptor elements in the eye of Limulus. *J. cell. comp. Physiol.,* 1947, **30,** 225–253.

Hartline, H. K., & Ratliff, F. Inhibitory interaction of receptor units in the eye of the Limulus. *J. gen. Physiol.,* 1957, **40,** 357–376.

Hartline, H. K., & Ratliff, F. Spatial summation of inhibitory influences in the eye of Limulus, and the mutual interaction of receptor units. *J. gen. Physiol.,* 1958, **41,** 1049–1066.

Hartline, H. K., Wagner, H. G., & Ratliff, F. Inhibition in the eye of Limulus. *J. gen. Physiol.,* 1956, **39,** 651–673.

Hecht, S. Chapter 14. In *Handbook of general experimental psychology.* C. A. Murchison, Ed. Worchester, Mass.: Clark Univ. Press, 1934.

Hecht, S., Peskin, J. C., & Patt, M. Intensity discrimination in human eye; relation between $\Delta I/I$ and intensity for different parts of spectrum. *J. gen. Physiol.,* 1938, **22,** 7–19.

Helson, H. Some factors and implications of color constancy. *J. opt. Soc. Amer.,* 1943, **33,** 555–567.

Hill, R. M. Unit responses of the rabbit lateral geniculate nucleus to monochromatic light on the retina. *Science,* 1962, **135,** 98–99.

Holladay, L. L. The fundamentals of glare and visibility. *J. opt. Soc. Amer.,* 1926, **12,** 271–320.

Holladay, L. L. Action of a light-source in the field of view in lowering visibility. *J. opt. Soc. Amer.,* 1927, **14,** 1–15.

Holmgren, F. Method att objectivera effected av ljusintryck på retina. *Upsala laekareforenings forh.,* 1865–1866, **1,** 177–191.

Hosoya, H. Über die Altersverschiedenheit der Ultraviolettabsorption der menschlichen Augenmedien. *Tohoku J. exp. Med.,* 1929, **13,** 510.

Hubbard, R. The molecular weight of rhodopsin and the nature of the rhodopsin-digitonin complex. *J. gen. Physiol.,* 1953–1954, **37,** 381–399.

Hubbard, R., & Wald, G. The mechanism of rhodopsin synthesis. *Proc. nat. Acad. Sci. (Washington),* 1951, **37,** 69–79.

Hubel, D. H. Cortical unit responses to visual stimuli in nonanesthetized cats. *Amer. J. Ophthalmol.,* 1958, **46,** 110–121.

Hubel, D. H. Single unit activity in striate cortex of unrestrained cats. *J. Physiol. (London),* 1959, **147,** 226–238.

Hubel, D. H. Single unit activity in lateral geniculate body and optic tract of unrestrained cats. *J. Physiol. (London),* 1960, **150,** 91–104.

Hubel, D. H. Integrative processes in ventral visual pathway of the cat. *J. opt. Soc. Amer.,* 1963, **53,** 58–66.

Hubel, D. H., & Wiesel, T. N. Receptive fields of single neurons in the cat's striate cortex. *J. Physiol. (London),* 1959, **148,** 574.

Hubel, D. H., & Wiesel, T. N. Integrative action in the cat's lateral geniculate body. *J. Physiol. (London),* 1961, **155,** 385–398.

Hubel, D. H., & Wiesel, T. N. Receptive fields, binocular interaction and functional architecture in the cat's visual cortex. *J. Physiol (London),* 1962, **160,** 106–154.

Hunt, R. W. G. Light and dark adaptation and the perception of color. *J. opt. Soc. Amer.,* 1952, **42,** 190–199.

Hunt, R. W. G. The perception of color in 1° fields for different states of adaptation. *J. opt. Soc. Amer.,* 1953, **43,** 479–484.

Hyde, E. P., Forsythe, W. E., & Cady, F. E. The visibility of radiation. *Astrophys. J.,* 1918, **48,** 65.

Ingvar, D. H. Effects of reticular stimulation upon neuronally isolated cortex. Observations at his institute, 1954. Cited by R. Granit. *Receptors and sensory perception.* New Haven, Conn.: Yale Univ. Press, 1955.

Ives, H. E. Physical photometry. *Am. Illum. Eng. Soc. Trans.,* 1915a, **10,** 101–125.

Ives, H. E. The transformation of color-mixture equations from one system to another. *J. Frank. Inst.,* 1915b, **180,** 673–701.

Jainski, K. Dissertation. Berlin: Tech. Hochschule, 1938.

Jaggi, M. Beitrag zur Kenntnis der spektralen Hellempfindlichkeit des menschlichen Auges auf Grund flimmerphotometrischer Messungen. *Helv. Phys. Acta,* 1939, **12,** 77–108.

Johanssen, G. *Configurations in event perception.* Uppsala: Almqvist, 1950.

Johnson, E. P. The character of the B-wave in the human electroretinogram. *A.M.A. Arch. Ophthalmol.,* 1958, **143,** 565–591.

Judd, D. B. A Maxwell triangle yielding uniform chromaticity scales. *J. opt. Soc. Amer.,* 1935, **25,** 24–35.

Judd, D. B. Basic correlates of the visual stimulus. In *Handbook of experimental psychology.* S. S. Stevens, Ed. New York: Wiley, 1951.

Jung, R. Coordination of specific and nonspecific afferent impulses at single neurons of the visual cortex. In *The reticular formation of the brain.* H. H. Jasper, L. D. Proctor, R. S. Knighton, W. C. Noshay, & R. T. Costello, Eds. Boston: Little, Brown, 1958a.

Jung, R. Excitation, inhibition and coordination of cortical neurons. *Exp. Cell Res.,* 1958b, Suppl. 5, 262–271.

Jung, R. Microphysiology of cortical neurons and its significance for psychophysiology. In Festschrift Prof. C. Estable. *An. Facult. Med. Montevideo,* 1959a, **44,** 323–332.

Jung, R. Mikrophysiologie des optischen Cortex: Koordination der Neuronenentladungen nach optischen, vestibulaeren und unspezifischen Afferenzen und ihre Bedeutung fuer die Sinnesphysiologie. *Fifteenth general assembly of the Japanese medical congress, Tokyo,* 1959b, **5**, 693–698.

Jung, R. Neuronal integration in the visual cortex and its significance for visual information. In *Sensory communication.* W. A. Rosenblith, Ed. Cambridge, Mass.: M.I.T. Press, 1961.

Jung, R., & Baumgartner, G. Hemmungsmechanismen und bremsende Stabilisierung an einzelnen Neuronen des optischen Cortex: Ein Beitrag sur Koordination corticaler Errengungsvorgaenge. *Pflüg. Arch. ges. Physiol.,* 1955, **261**, 434–456.

Jung, R., Baumgarten, R. von, & Baumgartner, G. Mikroableitungen von einzelnen Nervenzellen im optischen Cortex: Die lichtaktivierten B-Neurone. *Arch. Psychiat. Nervenkr.,* 1952, **189**, 521–539.

Jung, R., Creutzfeld, O., & Grüsser, O. J. Die Mikrophysiologie kortikaler Neurone und ihre Bedeutung fuer die Sinnes- und Hirnfunktionen. *Dtsch. med. Wschr.,* 1957, **82**, 1050–1059.

Karpe, G. The basis of clinical electroretinography. *Acta Ophthalmol.,* 1945, Suppl. 24, 1–118.

Karpe, G. Apparatus and method for clinical recording of electroretinogram. *Doc. Ophthalmol.,* 1948a, **2**, 268–276.

Karpe, G. Early diagnosis of siderosis retinae by use of electroretinography. *Doc. Ophthalmol.,* 1948b, **2**, 277–296.

Katz, D., & Révész, G. Experimentelle Studien zur vergleichenden Psychologie. *Z. angew. Psychol.,* 1921, **18**, 307–320.

Klüver, H. *Behavior mechanisms in monkeys.* Chicago: Univ. of Chicago Press, 1933, reprinted 1957.

Klüver, H. Functional significance of the geniculostriate system. *Biol. Symposia,* 1942, **7**, 253–299.

Köhler, W. Die Farbe der Sehdinge beim Schimpansen und beim Haushuhn. *Z. Psychol.,* 1917, **77**, 248–255.

Köhler, W. *Die physischen Gestalten in Ruhe und im stationären Zustand.* New York: Liveright, 1940.

Köhler, W., & Fishback, J. The destruction of the Müller-Lyer illusion in repeated trials. I: An examination of two theories. *J. exp. Psychol.* 1950, **40**, 267–398.

Koffka, K. *Handbuch der normalen und pathologischen Physiologie. Vol. XII.* A. Bethe, G. V. Bergmann, G. Embden, & A. Ellinger, Eds. Berlin: Springer, 1931.

Koffka, K. *Principles of gestalt psychology.* New York: Harcourt, Brace, 1935.

Kohlrausch, A. Elektrische Erscheinungen am Auge. *Handbuch norm. path. Physiol.,* 12, 1931a, **2**, 1394–1496.

Kohlrausch, A. Tagessehen, Daemmersehen, Adaption. *Handbuch norm. path. Physiol.,* 12, 1931b, **2**, 1499–1594.

Kuffler, S. W. Neurons in the retina: organization, inhibition and excitation problems. *Cold. Spr. Harb. Symp. quant. Biol.,* 1952, **17**, 281–292.

Kuffler, S. W. Discharge patterns and functional organization of mammalian retina. *J. Neurophysiol.,* 1953, **16**, 37–68.

Le Grand, Y. Sur la précision en photométrie visuelle. *Rev. d'Opt.,* 1933, **12**, 145.

Le Grand, Y. *Light, colour and vision.* New York: Wiley, 1957.

Lenoble, J., & Le Grand, Y. L'absorption du cristallin dans l'infrarouge. *Rev. d'Opt.,* 1953, **32**, 641–648.

Lettvin, J. Y., Maturana, H. R., McCulloch, W. S., & Pitts, W. H. What the frag's eye tells the frog's brain. *Proc. Inst. Radio Engr.,* 1959, **47**, 1940–1951.

Lettvin, J. Y., Maturana, H. R., Pitts, W. H., & McCulloch, W. S. Two remarks on the visual system of the frog. In *Sensory communication.* W. A. Rosenblith, Ed. Cambridge, Mass.: M.I.T. Press, 1961.

Locke, N. M. Color constancy in the rhesus monkey and in man. *Arch. Psychol.,* 1935, **28**, 193.

Ludvigh, E., & MacCarthy, E. F. Absorption of visible light by the refractive media of the human eye. *Arch. Ophthalmol.* 1938, **20**, 37.

Lüthy, H. Über die Abhängigkeit der Flimmer-Hellempfindlichkeit des menschlichen Auges von den Messbedingungen. *Helv. Phys. Acta,* 1942, **15**, 343.

MacAdam, D. L. Visual sensitivities to color differences in daylight. *J. opt. Soc. Amer.,* 1942, **32**, 247.

MacAdam, D. L. Chromatic adaptation. *J. opt. Soc. Amer.,* 1956, **46**, 500–513.

MacNichol, E. F., Jr. Visual receptors as biological transducers. In *Molecular structure and functional activity of nerve cells. Amer. Inst. biol. Sci. Publ.,* 1956, **1**, 34–53.

MacNichol, E. F., Jr., & Hartline, H. K. Responses to small changes of light intensity by the light-adapted photoreceptors. *Fed. Proc.,* 1948, **7**, 76.

MacNichol, E. F., Jr., & Svaetichin, G. Electric responses from the isolated retinas of fishes. *Amer. J. Ophthalmol.,* 1958, **46**, 26–40.

Mancia, M., Meulders, M., & Santibañez, H. G. Changes of photically evoked potentials in the visual pathway of the cerveau isole cat. *Arch. ital. Biol.,* 1959, **97**, 376–398.

Maturana, H. R. Number of fibres in the optic nerve and the number of ganglion cells in the retina of Anurans. *Nature (London),* 1959, **183**, 1406.

Maturana, H. R. Lettvin, J. Y., McCulloch, W. S., & Pitts, W. H. Evidence that cut optic nerve fibers in a frog regenerate to their proper places in the tectum. *Science,* 1959, **130**, 1709–1710.

Maturana, H. R., Lettvin, J. Y., Pitts, W. H., & McCulloch, W. S. Physiology and anatomy of vision in the frog. *J. gen. Physiol.,* 1960, Suppl. 43, 129–175.

Maxwell, J. C. *Scientific papers. Vol. I.* Cambridge: Cambridge Univ. Press, 1890.

Moon, P., & Spencer, D. E. Analytical representation of standard response curves. *J. opt. Soc. Amer.,* 1943, **33**, 89.

Moon, P., & Spencer, D. E. Visual data applied to lighting design. *J. opt. Soc. Amer.*, 1944, **34**, 605.

Müller, G. E. Kleine Beiträge zur Psychophysiologie der Farbenempfindung. *Z. Sinnesphysiol.*, 1931, **62**, 53–110, 167–202.

Newhall, S. M., Nickerson, D., & Judd, D. B. Final report of the O.S.A. Subcommittee on the spacing of the Munsell Colors. *J. opt. Soc. Amer.*, 1943, **33**, 385.

Noell, W. K. *Studies on the electrophysiology and the metabolism of the retina.* Randolph Field, Texas: USAF School of Aviation Medicine, 1953, 122.

Ogawa, T. Midbrain reticular influences upon single neurons in lateral geniculate nucleus. *Science*, 1963, **139**, 343–344.

Piéron, H. Physiologie de la vision. *Traité d'ophthalmologie. Vol. II.* Paris: Masson, 1939.

Plateau, J. A. Sur la mésure des sensations physiques et sur la loi qui lie l'intensité de ces sensations à l'intensité de la cause excitante. *Pogg. Ann.*, 1873, **150**, 465–476.

Priest, I. G., & Brickwedde, F. G. The minimum perceptible colorimetric purity as a function of dominant wave-length. *J. opt. Soc. Amer.*, 1938, **28**, 133.

Purdy, D. McL. On the saturation and chromatic threshold of the spectral colours. *Brit. J. Psych.*, 1931a, **21**, 283.

Purdy, D. McL. Spectral hue as a function of intensity. *Amer. J. Psychol.*, 1931b, **43**, 541.

Radding, C. M., & Wald, G. Acid-base properties of rhodopsin and opsin. *J. gen. Physiol.*, 1955–1956, **39**, 909–933.

Ramón y Cajal, S. La rétine des vertébrés. *Trav. Lab. Rech. biol. Univ. Madrid.*, 1933, **28**, App. 1–142.

Ratliff, F. Inhibitory interaction and the detection and enhancement of contours. In *Sensory communication.* W. A. Rosenblith, Ed. Cambridge, Mass.: M.I.T. Press, 1961.

Ratliff, F., & Hartline, H. K. The response of the Limulus optic nerve fibers to patterns of illumination on the receptor mosaic. *J. gen. Physiol.*, 1959, **42**, 1241–1255.

Ratliff, F., Miller, W. H., & Hartline, H. K. Neural interaction in the eye and the integration of receptor activity. *Ann. N.Y. Acad. Sci.*, 1958, **74**, 210–222.

Riggs, L. A. The human electroretinogram. *A.M.A. Arch. Ophthalmol.*, 1958, **60**, 739–754.

Riggs, L. A., Berry, R. N., & Wayner, M. A. A comparison of electrical and psychophysical determinations of the spectral sensitivity of the human eye. *J. opt. Soc. Amer.*, 1949, **39**, 427–436.

Rushton, W. A. The structure responsible for action potential spikes in the cat's retina. *Nature (London)*, 1949, **164**, 743–744.

Rushton, W. A. Apparatus for analyzing the light reflected from the eye of the cat. *J. Physiol. (London)*, 1952, **117**, 47.

Rushton, W. A. Electric records from the vertebrate optic nerve. *Brit. med. Bull.*, 1953, **9**, 68–74.

Rushton, W. A. Physical measurement of cone pigment in the living human eye. *Nature (London)*, 1957, **179**, 571–573.

Rushton, W. A., Campbell, F. W., Hagins, W. A., & Brindley, G. S. The bleaching and regeneration of rhodopsin in the living eye of the albino rabbit and of man. *Optica Acta*, 1955, **1**, 183–190.

Sachs, E. Die Aktionsströme des menschlichen Auges, ihre Beziehung zu Reiz und Empfindung. *Klin. Wschr.*, 1929, **8**, 136–137.

Schoolman, A., & Evarts, E. V. Responses to lateral geniculate radiation stimulation in cats with implanted electrodes. *J. Neurophysiol.*, 1959, **22**, 112–129.

Sheard, C. Dark adaptation. *J. opt. Soc. Amer.*, 1944, **34**, 464.

Sinden, R. H. A further search for the ideal color system. II: A reconsideration of the Helmholtz line element. *J. opt. Soc. Amer.*, 1938, **28**, 339–347.

Solomon, F. L'absorption sélective de la lumière par le cristallin. *Rev. d'Opt.*, 1950, **29**, 632–647.

Steinhardt, J. Intensity discrimination in the human eye. *J. gen. Physiol.*, 1936, **20**, 185–209.

Stiles, W. S. Effect of glare on brightness difference threshold. *Proc. roy. Soc. (London)*, B, 1929a, **104**, 322–351.

Stiles, W. S. Scattering theory of effect of glare on brightness difference threshold. *Proc. roy. Soc. (London)*, B, 1929b, **105**, 131–146.

Stiles, W. S., & Crawford, B. H. Luminous efficiency of rays entering eye pupil at different points. *Proc. roy. Soc. (London)*, B, 1933a, **112**, 428–450.

Stiles, W. S., & Crawford, B. H. The liminal brightness increment as a function of wave-length for different conditions of the foveal and parafoveal retina. *Proc. roy. Soc. (London)*, B, 1933b, **113**, 496.

Svaetichin, G. The cone action potential. *Acta physiol. scand.*, 1953, **29**, Suppl. 106, 565–600.

Svaetichin, G., & MacNichol, E. F., Jr. Retinal mechanisms for chromatic and achromatic vision. *Ann. N.Y. Acad. Sci.*, 1958, **74**, 385–399.

Tausch, R. Optische Täuschungen als artifizielle Effekte der Gestaltungsprozesse von Grössen- und Formenkonstanz in der natürlichen Raumwahrnehmung. *Psychol. Forsch.*, 1954, **24**, 299–348.

Teuber, H. L. Perception. In *Handbook of physiology. Vol. III.* J. Field, H. W. Magoun, & V. E. Hall, Eds. Baltimore: Williams and Wilkins, 1960.

Therman, P. O. Neurophysiology of the retina. *Acta Soc. Scient. Fenn., Nova Ser. B*, 1938, **2**(1), 74.

Therman, P. O. Action potentials of squid eye. *Amer. J. Physiol.*, 1940, **130**, 239–248.

Thomson, L. C. The localization of function in the rabbit retina. *J. Physiol. (London)*, 1953, **119**, 191–209.

Thouless, R. H. Phenomenal regression to the real object. *Brit. J. Psychol.*, 1931a, **21**, 339–359.

Thouless, R. H. Phenomenal regression to the "real" object. *Brit. J. Psychol.*, 1931b, **22**, 1–30.

Toida, N., & Goto, M. Some mechanisms of color reception found by analyzing the electroretinogram of the frog. *Jap. J. Physiol.,* 1954, **4,** 260.

Tomita, T. Electrical activity in the vertebrate retina. *J. opt. Soc. Amer.,* 1963, **53,** 49–57.

Troland, L. T. Notes on flicker photometry: flicker photometer frequency as a function of the color of the standard, and of the measured, light. *J. Frank. Inst.,* 1916, **181,** 853–855.

Tyndall, E. P. T. Chromaticity sensibility of wave-length difference as a function of purity. *J. opt. Soc. Amer.,* 1933, **23,** 15.

Wagner, H. G., MacNichol, E. F., Jr., & Wolbarsht, M. L. Functional basis for "on"-center and "off"-center receptive fields in the retina. *J. opt. Soc. Amer.,* 1963, **53,** 66–70.

Wald, G. The porphyropsin visual system. *J. gen Physiol.,* 1938–1939, **22,** 775–793.

Wald, G. Human vision and the spectrum. *Science,* 1945, **101,** 653.

Wald, G. Photochemistry of vision. *Doc. Ophthalmol.,* 1949, **3,** 94–137.

Wald, G. On mechanism of visual threshold and visual adaptation. *Science,* 1954, **119,** 887–892.

Wald, G. The photoreceptor process in vision. In *Handbook of physiology. Vol. I.* J. Field, H. W. Magoun, & V. E. Hall, Eds. Baltimore: Williams and Wilkins, 1959.

Wald, G., & Brown, P. K. The role of sulfhydryl groups in the bleaching and synthesis of rhodopsin. *J. gen. Physiol.,* 1952, **35,** 797–821.

Wald, G.; Brown, P. K., & Smith, P. H. Cyanopsin, a new pigment of cone vision. *Science,* 1953, **118,** 505–508.

Wald, G., Brown, P. K., & Smith, P. H. Iodopsin. *J. gen. Physiol.,* 1954–1955, **38,** 623–681.

Wald, G., Brown, P. K., & Brown, P. S. Unpublished observations. As cited by Wald. The photoreceptor process in vision. In *Handbook of physiology. Vol. I.* J. Field, H. W. Magoun, & V. E. Hall, Eds. Baltimore: Williams and Wilkins, 1959.

Wallach, H. On constancy of visual speed. *Psychol. Rev.,* 1939, **46,** 541–552.

Walsh, J. W. T. *Photometry* (2nd ed.). London: Constable, 1953.

Weale, R. A. Light absorption by the lens of the human eye. *Optica Acta,* 1954, **1,** 107–110.

Weinstein, C., & Arnulf, A. Contribution à l'étude des seuils de perception de l'oeil *Comm. Lab. Inst. Opt.,* 1946, **2,** 1.

Wright, W. D. *A re-determination of the trichromatic mixture data.* Medical Research Council, Report of the Committee on the Physiology of Vision, VII. Special Report Series, No. 139, London, 1929.

Wright, W. D. *Researches on normal and defective colour vision.* London: Kimpton, 1946.

Wright, W. D., & Pitt, F. H. G. Hue discrimination in normal colour vision. *Proc. phys. Soc. (London),* 1934, **46,** 463.

Wright, W. D., & Pitt, F. H. G. The colour-vision characteristics of two trichromats. *Proc. phys. Soc. (London),* 1935, **47,** 205–217.

Zeigler, H. P., & Leibowitz, H. A methodological study of "shape constancy" in the rhesus monkey. *J. comp. physiol. Psychol.,* 1958, **51,** 155–160.

CHAPTER FOUR

The Motor System and Mechanisms of Basic Sensory-Motor Integration

BASIC REFLEX MECHANISMS

Basic Effector Mechanisms

The basic effector mechanism of the organism is a muscle. Skeletal muscles are composed of extrafusal and intrafusal muscle fibers. These join to form a unit which is attached to the bones of the body by tendons. Muscles maintain the position or initiate the movement of limbs by adjusting the relative contraction (flexion or shortening) or relaxation (extension or elongation) of individual muscle groups. Visceral and cardiac muscles exert their influence largely by varying the pressure on the fluid and semifluid contents of the viscera. A second effector system, the glands, exerts its influence by discharging hormonal substances into the bloodstream or body cavities.

The activity of all effector units is controlled by the sensory input to the organism, either directly via reflex regulatory mechanisms or indirectly via voluntary influences of cortical origin. Most of the influences that control the activity of the motor systems are exercised via neural mechanisms. The activity of visceral muscles and glands is to some extent under hormonal regulation.

The skeletal (somatic) muscles of the body receive afferents directly from motor cells located in the ventral horn of the spinal cord and in the brainstem. Sherrington (1898a, b) called these neurons the *final common path* of the motor system because many complex influences may interact in the central nervous system to determine the activity of one of these motor cells. Visceral muscles receive afferents from motor cells located in ganglia outside the central nervous system. These ganglia are innervated by motor cells in the ventrolateral spinal gray and by many of the cranial nerve nuclei of the brainstem. The addi-

tional synapse in the visceral motor system is one of the reasons why it responds typically in a less specific fashion than somatic muscle.

The Monosynaptic Reflex Arc

The motor neurons of the spinal cord that project axons to the peripheral muscles or ganglia are controlled by a variety of influences. The simplest sensory-motor relationship is a *monosynaptic reflex arc* which consists of only two neurons: a dorsal horn cell receives sensory information via its long, pseudodendritic processes and projects into the spinal cord an axon that terminates directly on the second neuron of the arc, the ventral horn motor cell. (The sensory input to this feedback system comes from the annulospiral endings of the muscle spindles.) Such simple, monosynaptic reflex arcs are not common in higher animals. They are found primarily as part of the feedback system which maintains muscular tonus and basic postural adjustments. They have nevertheless been studied in great detail because their simplicity permits experimental control over most aspects of the feedback loop.

The interaction between sensory and motor systems generally involves a number of intervening links which receive sensory information from other parts of the body as well as voluntary influences from higher levels of integration (see Figure 4.1).

The Multisynaptic Reflex Arc

The disynaptic tendon reflexes. The simplest of these *multisynaptic* connections between sensory receptors and muscle fibers is the *disynaptic reflex arc*. This three-neuron system links the Golgi tendon organs via a single *interneuron* with the motor neurons that innervate the related muscle fibers. This reflex mechanism is antagonistically

241

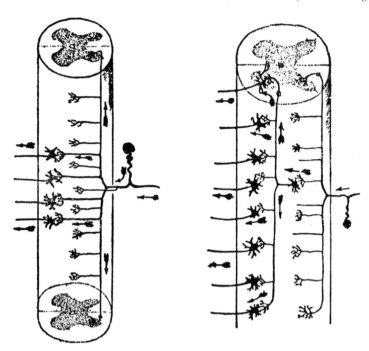

Fig. 4.1 Circumscribed reflex mechanism of Ramón y Cajal (left), showing direct connection between afferent collaterals and motor neurons, and diffuse reflex mechanism of Ramón y Cajal (right), in which an interneuron is intercalated between afferent fibers and neurons. (From Patton, 1965a.)

related to the monosynaptic stretch reflex. Stretching a muscle initially produces afferents in the annulospiral endings which are part of the monosynaptic *myotatic* reflex arc. This neural input elicits a reflex contraction which tends to return the limb to its original position, thus maintaining postural adjustments. If the stretch is continued in spite of this initial counterreaction, the Golgi tendon organs are stimulated. Inhibitory influences are then conducted across the disynaptic reflex arc and eventually override the excitatory influences of the monosynaptic reflex to permit movement of the limb.

The relationship between the sensory endings in the muscles (the intrafusal receptors and Golgi tendon organs) and the activity of the related muscle has been extensively investigated and serves as a useful model of basic sensory-motor interactions (Eldred, 1955).

The role of the spindle and tendon receptors. The muscle spindle consists of between four and six intrafusal fibers which form a single organ. Each intrafusal fiber (see Figure 4.2) consists of a central *nuclear bag* region which is noncontractile, and two individually contractile *polar regions* which are separated from the nuclear bag by *transitional* or *myotube regions*. The *primary* or *annulospiral endings* are usually located on the nuclear bag. The *secondary* or *flower-spray endings*

tend to be found in the transitional myotube region. In some species only one spindle receptor may be present. The fibers that innervate the annulospiral endings are among the largest (20 mμ) and fastest conducting (up to 100 meters/sec) in the body. The secondary, flower-spray endings receive smaller (and slower) fibers.

The polar regions of the intrafusal fibers receive small (gamma) motor fibers which conduct at about 20 to 40 meters/sec. The extrafusal muscle fibers and some intrafusal fibers receive large (alpha) motor fibers which conduct at much higher rates (about 60 to 80 meters/sec). (See Figure 4.3.)

The muscle spindles also receive a number of very fine (0.5 mμ) unmyelinated fibers which project afferents from free nerve endings (pain receptors) or efferents of the visceromotor system to the blood vessels of the intrafusal fibers.

Not all the sensory feedback from muscles derives from the intrafusal spindle receptors. The Golgi tendon organs which are located at the junction of tendons and muscles or at the origin of the muscle spindles themselves (Barker, 1948) cooperate closely with the spindle receptors to regulate muscle tonus. They are generally innervated by large, rapidly conducting fibers.

Both Golgi tendon organs and spindle receptors are stimulated by mechanical distortion produced by an increase or decrease in the normal tension of the associated muscles. Muscle spindles are arranged "in parallel" to the extrafusal fibers. Contraction of the extrafusal muscle therefore inhibits the activity of the receptor. Tendon organs are connected "in series" with the extrafusal muscle and are stimulated by increasing contraction (see Figure 4.4).

The pioneering single-fiber recordings of Matthews (1929, 1931a, b, 1933) have elucidated these relationships in detail. The spindle (annulospiral) receptors were found to have an exceedingly low threshold. Even a few grams of stretch elicited sustained firing. Any contraction of the extrafusal muscle interrupted this rhythmic activity but increased the discharge of the tendon organs. The tendon receptors also responded to stretch but had relatively high thresholds (100 to 200 grams). They did not normally discharge

under conditions of tonic stretch when the spindle receptors were active. The latter always responded to contraction of the extrafusal fibers by an inhibition of discharge; however, stimulation of the high-threshold gamma efferents to the polar regions produced a contraction of the intrafusal fiber itself and a marked increase in spindle receptor discharge. The contraction response of the intrafusal fiber did not measurably affect the stretch of the extrafusal muscle and was therefore not generally reflected in the activity of the tendon organs.

The annulospiral endings of the muscle spindle are believed to form the receptor system responsible for the phasic and tonic monosynaptic stretch or myotatic reflexes; these play an important role in the control of posture and movement. (The clinically important knee jerk or ankle jerk

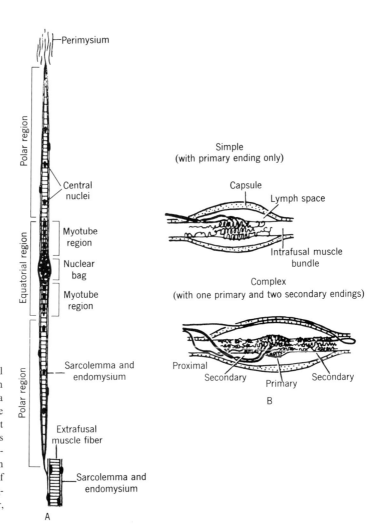

Fig. 4.2 A, a single intrafusal muscle fiber; each polar region has been shortened to about a third of its typical length. B, the equatorial regions of two rabbit muscle spindles illustrating types of sensory innervation. The intrafusal muscle bundle is shown in outline only, and the area of nuclear bags is indicated by exaggerated swelling. (From Barker, 1948.)

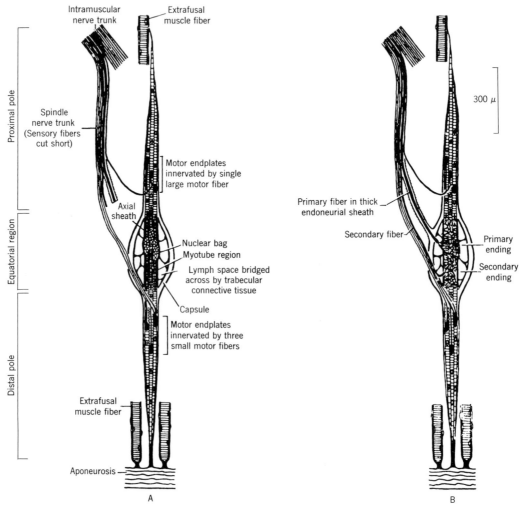

Fig. 4.3 An idealized rabbit muscle spindle. Polar regions have been shortened to about half their typical lengths. In A, the motor innervation is shown, but the sensory innervation has been omitted to demonstrate the morphology of the equatorial region. Motor endplates are represented as black disks. B, the same spindle with the addition of a sensory innervation comprising one primary and one secondary ending. (From Barker, 1948.)

are special examples of this type of reflex.) The Golgi tendon organs appear to be the afferent link in a number of disynaptic reflex arcs which protect the muscles from overload by mediating *autogenic inhibitory influences* on the same motor neurons. Examples of such protective reflexes are the *clasp-knife lengthening reflex* which causes the sudden relaxation of a contracted muscle exposed to intense and prolonged stretch, and *Phillipson's compensatory reflex* contraction of the extensor muscles of the contralateral limb.

The flexion and crossed extensor reflexes. The *flexion reflex* is a good example of a more com-plex, multisynaptic reflex connection. It is best studied in unanesthetized spinal preparations to avoid confounding influences of higher integra-tive mechanisms and drug-related distortions. (Chronic spinal preparations are obtained by complete transection of the cord at low thoracic levels. A more complete "high-spinal" or "decapi-tate" preparation, which requires artificial respi-ration, is obtained by cord transection at the highest cervical vertebra.)

The basic flexion reflex consists of a contraction of the flexor muscles ipsilateral to the source of painful stimulation. A reciprocal connection of the afferents with ipsilateral motor neurons provides concurrent inhibitory influences to the antagonistic extensor muscles. This interaction results in simultaneous relaxation of the extensors and permits movement of the stimulated limb away from the source of noxious stimulation.

The simple flexion reflex is often associated with a contraction of the extensor muscles and a relaxation of the flexor muscles of the corresponding contralateral extremity. This *crossed extensor* reflex is related to sensory inputs from collateral branches of the afferent neurons or interneurons which form the basic flexion reflex. Such an antagonistic pattern of innervation on the two sides of the cord is known as *double reciprocal innervation*.

The gamma efferent feedback loop. It has been shown that sensory information from receptors in muscles and tendons may directly or indirectly initiate activity in the corresponding muscles. This sensory-motor interaction is not based on a simple unidirectional exchange of information, however. The sensitivity of the afferent link of the

reflex systems is determined by the activity of the gamma efferents to the muscle spindles. Activation of these "fusimotor" fibers elicits contraction responses from the polar regions of the intrafusal muscle spindles. This process increases the tension of the nuclear bag and myotube region and produces a mechanical distortion of the spindle receptor. As a result of this stimulation, the background activity of the spindle receptors increases and their sensitivity is raised. The contractions of the intrafusal fibers are not sufficient to affect the tension of the extrafusal muscle fibers directly. The resulting positive bias on the spindle receptors may drastically change the activity in the afferent feedback to the alpha motor neurons of the ventral horn and thus determine the contraction of the muscle.

Some of Kuffler's single-cell studies illustrate these relationships well (Kuffler et al., 1951; Hunt and Kuffler, 1951a, b, 1954). The data given in Figure 4.5 show that electrical stimulation of single fusimotor fibers increased the spindle receptor response to varying degrees of stretch,

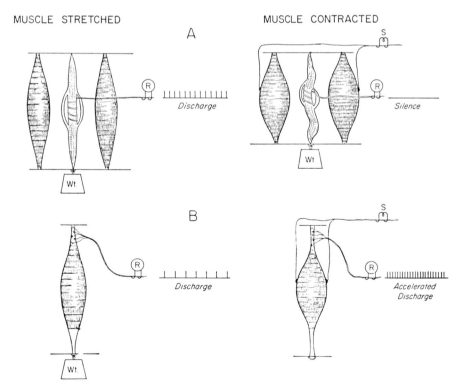

Fig. 4.4 Relation of muscle spindles and tendon organs to muscle fibers. A, the spindle is arranged "in parallel" with muscle fibers so that muscle contraction slackens tension on the spindle. B, the tendon organ is arranged "in series" with muscle fibers so that both passive and active contractions of muscle cause the receptor to discharge. (From Patton, 1965b.)

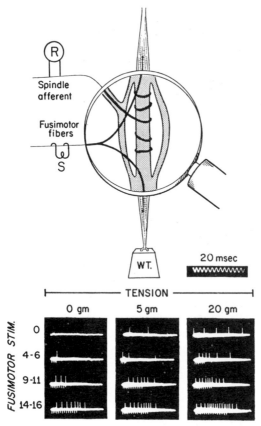

Fig. 4.5 Effects of tension and fusimotor stimulation on the discharge rate of the spindle ending. Upward deflections in traces are action potentials of a single isolated spindle afferent fiber. Small deflections below the base line in some records are shock artefacts produced by stimulating fusimotor fibers. Note that the discharge rate depends on both passive tension and fusimotor activity. (From Patton, 1965b.)

muscle tension which reflects the activity in the gamma efferent circuit. Hunt (Hunt, 1951; Hunt and Paintal, 1958) has demonstrated that the fusimotor system maintains a tonic discharge which varies as a function of afferents to the fusimotor neurons in the spinal cord. Many centers in the brainstem, cerebellum, and cerebral cortex influence these fusimotor neurons. The resting activity of the system appears to be determined primarily by direct afferents from the related muscle because the spontaneous activity is abolished by dorsal root transection.

Kuffler's work also demonstrates that the fusimotor activity is affected significantly by cutaneous stimuli such as touch, pressure, or pain. Such stimulation increases the gamma efferent discharge to flexor muscles and inhibits the input to ipsilateral extensors. The fusimotor activity in the contralateral musculature follows an opposite pattern, so that the alpha and gamma systems respond similarly for the simple flexion reflexes. Patton (1965a, b) has suggested that this arrangement may compensate for the decreased spindle discharge which normally signals the reduced tension of the reflexly contracted muscles. The gamma efferent system thus maintains the proportionality between spindle activity and external stretch under varying conditions of muscular contractions. Hunt and Paintal (1958) reported that the tendon receptors do not directly affect the activity of the gamma efferent system.

The fusimotor system and the resultant feedback loop are a very important part of the reflex mechanisms that maintain posture and permit locomotion. The full measure of this contribution will become evident when we discuss the many central influences that act on this peripheral biasing mechanism.

The reflex arcs discussed so far are completed within the spinal cord. They are normally under both inhibitory and excitatory control of many central mechanisms (Granit and Kaada, 1952), but they can basically function in the absence of these influences. Some of the simplest reflex arcs (the flexion and myotatic reflexes) are completed within one segment of the spinal cord and are often called *segmental reflexes*. Others (such as the crossed extensor reflex) involve many segments of the cord and may be combined into complex reactions to compound stimuli. These *intersegmental reflexes* may involve the simultaneous or successive activation of several simple cooperative or competitive reflex connections and result in complex response patterns such as locomotion.

the extent of the facilitation being a function of stimulus frequency. Each muscle receives a number of fusimotor fibers. Branches from each fusimotor (gamma efferent) fiber reach a number of spindles and provide a complex feedback mechanism for the graded biasing of the spindle receptor sensitivity; such a mechanism may override even the suppression of spindle activity which normally occurs during contraction of the extrafusal muscles (see Figure 4.6).

Figure 4.7 shows the pathways involved in the simple monosynaptic stretch reflex. In this feedback system the activity of the afferent link is complexly determined by (1) the extrafusal muscle tension which results from activity in the primary alpha efferents, and (2) the intrafusal

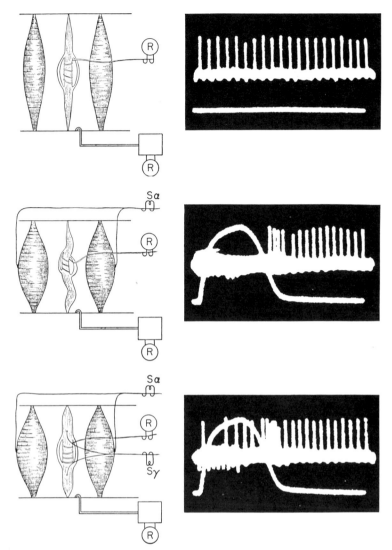

Fig. 4.6 Effect of fusimotor stimulation on the silent period in spindle discharge during muscle contraction. *Thick line in traces,* record from spindle afferent fiber; *thin line,* tension of muscle. *Upper trace,* sustained tension (15 grams) elicits rhythmic firing of receptor. *Middle trace,* discharge ceases during muscle twitch because spindles are relieved from stretch. *Lower trace,* fusimotor stimulation (indicated by shock artefacts extending beneath base line) takes up "slack" in spindle and permits sustained discharge even during muscle contraction. (From Patton, 1965b.)

Spinal shock. If the higher influences are suddenly removed by spinal cord transection, a period of almost complete areflexia results. In man and primates this *spinal shock* is severe and often prolonged. Lower species show a much briefer period of hyporeflexia, suggesting less influence from higher control mechanisms.

During the first two or three weeks after high spinal transection, all reflex activity is absent in man. The first of the basic reflexes to return is the protective flexion response to noxious stimulation. This reaction is often exaggerated and may be accompanied by a "mass reflex" response of normally unrelated visceral mechanisms (bladder and rectal contractions, sweating, etc.). The extensor reflexes rarely attain this state of hyperreflexia. The limbs tend to remain flaccid and regain but little tonus.

The depression of reflex activity following spinal cord transection is not caused by surgical

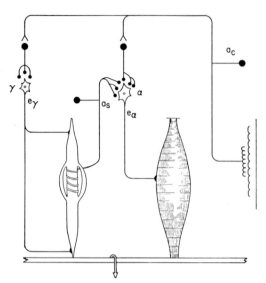

Fig. 4.7 The "peripheral loop" of the stretch reflex mechanism: a_c, cutaneous afferent path; a_s, spindle afferent path; e_α and e_γ, alpha and gamma (fusimotor) efferent pathways, respectively. (From Patton, 1965b.)

insult; rather, it is a direct consequence of the sudden removal of central influences which, in the intact animal, continually bombard the lower motor neurons. This finely balanced mixture of facilitatory and inhibitory influences normally maintains a degree of subliminal excitation which permits maximal responses to local afferents that would not otherwise be capable of eliciting a response.

Suprasegmental reflexes. The various segmental and intersegmental reflexes are organized into complex postural and locomotor reactions by reflex centers in the brainstem, cerebellum, and cerebral cortex. The resulting *suprasegmental reflexes* are often determined by complex sensory feedback mechanisms from muscle spindles, tendon organs, joint receptors, specialized end organs in the vestibular system, and even cutaneous and distance receptors. In reaction to constantly changing inputs from a multitude of sensory receptors, these suprasegmental reflexes are constantly adjusted to maintain posture under widely changing environmental conditions.

The simplest postural reflexes are the *positive* and *negative supporting reactions* which maintain the basic position of the body. These reflexes consist of the simultaneous contraction (or relaxation) of the flexor and extensor muscles of a limb and provide rigidity for support or flaccidity

for movement of the limb. Postural adjustments are supported by *tonic attitudinal reflexes* which maintain certain basic relationships between the limbs, head, and trunk. More complex vestibular and kinesthetic reflexes are involved in the *righting reactions*, a reflexive adjustment that returns the body to its normal position. Perhaps the greatest complexity of reflexive control is demanded by the *placing* and *hopping reactions*. The former consists of the reflexive placing of feet on solid ground, the latter of a series of hops which result in the proper placement of a limb under the body so that maximal support is obtained.

Very complex central integrative mechanisms are involved in the control of some of these reflex adjustments. We will return to a discussion of the integration of posture and locomotion after we present a detailed treatment of the central organization of the motor system.

THE PYRAMIDAL MOTOR SYSTEM

The pyramidal motor system was defined anatomically long before its precise origin and function were known. The classical definition includes all cortical cells which project axons through the pyramids of the ventral medulla descending into the spinal cord. On the basis of functional considerations, it has become customary to include the "aberrant pyramidal fibers" which project from the cortex to the cranial nerve motor nuclei of the brainstem. These fibers arise from the same cortical regions as the corticospinal projections and accompany them in their course through the internal capsule and peduncles of the midbrain, but they depart from them at pontine levels and do not traverse the pyramids. Some corticoreticular projections do course through the bulbar pyramids and are therefore technically —though incorrectly—included in the pyramidal motor pathway (Swank, 1934a, b).

The Effects of Pyramidal Tract Transection (Pyramidotomy)

The most direct, though not necessarily the most complete, story about the functional properties of the pyramidal motor system is obtained by transecting it unilaterally or bilaterally in the bulbar segment of the brainstem. This has been done in rats (Barron, 1934), dogs (Starlinger, 1895), cats (Tower, 1936), and monkeys (Tower, 1942). Unilateral transections always result in contralateral paresis, the severity of the deficit being markedly greater in primates and man than in lower species. The most prominent feature of the deficit is the nearly complete loss of the precise movements which are essential for any type of skilled or learned pattern of motor coordination. Some voluntary movements are commonly retained, but the motions tend to be clumsy, poorly coordinated with postural adjustments, and often ineffectual because of poor aim and lack of specificity. In addition to the basic paretic symptom, the skeletal muscles typically show some hypotonia, atrophy, and marked inhibition of simple reflex activity. Pure pyramidal tract lesions do not, as is often falsely stated in clinical texts, produce spasticity (Patton and Amassian, 1960).

We must be cautious in the interpretation of the effects of experimental pyramidotomy (transection of the corticospinal fibers at bulbar levels) because the pyramidal tract fibers give off many collaterals to various nuclei and pathways of the mesencephalic and pontine brainstem (Ramón y Cajal, 1899, p. 967). Since the cortical cells from which the pyramidal tract fibers originate typically do not degenerate following pyramidotomy, significant influences of pyramidal origin may remain after the tract has been completely transected at the bulbar level.

Electrical Stimulation of the Pyramidal Tract

It is therefore useful to supplement our knowledge with information from experiments that have applied electrical stimulation to the pyramidal motor fibers. The results of cortical stimulation studies will be discussed in a later section because it appears impossible to affect either the pyramidal or the extrapyramidal systems selectively with this technique (Patton and Amassian, 1954).

Brookhart (1952) has studied the effects of bulbar pyramidal tract stimulation in anesthetized monkeys. He observed that single stimuli did not normally suffice to elicit a response from skeletal muscles. Prolonged stimulation, which presumably permitted temporal summation of impulses, was usually required to elicit a stable contraction response. Each group of muscles had a definite threshold in terms of train and pulse duration of the stimulus.

Landau (1952, 1953) has reported that complex patterns of movement ("walking," "scratching") were elicited by pyramidal tract stimulation in decerebrate cats; he also observed a number of autonomic responses such as changes in heart rate, piloerection, and pupillary dilatation.

The Electrical Response of the Pyramidal Tract to Cortical Stimulation

Electrical stimulation of the motor cortex or of the immediately inferior white matter produces a complex electrical response that can be recorded from various loci in the lower pyramidal tract (see Figure 4.8). The initial deflection is a positive wave (called D wave) which arrives at the bulbar decussation or upper segments of the cord after such brief latencies (0.7 to 1.0 msec) that the possibility of an intervening synapse can be excluded. The D wave is typically followed 2.0 to 2.5 msec later by a variable number of positive deflections (the I waves) which have properties suggesting at least one synaptic delay. The indirect I waves appear to be of cortical origin since they are not seen after stimulation of the white matter (see Patton and Amassian, 1954).

A detailed analysis of the response of various components of the pyramidal tract to cortical stimulation has led Patton and Amassian (1960) to conclude that the I waves may be caused by the re-excitation of the same cortical neurons (the Betz cells of the motor cortex) that give rise to the primary D waves. Since the amplitude of the I waves may significantly exceed that of the D waves, more than a simple, repetitive discharge of the same neurons must be involved. It seems that cortical stimulation simultaneously excites primary motor neurons which give rise to the D waves and longitudinally oriented interneurons which re-excite the same motor neurons plus adjacent ones which escaped direct stimulation.

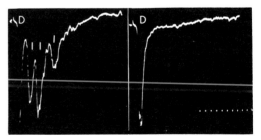

Fig. 4.8 Pyramidal tract responses to stimulation of the motor cortex and white matter in the monkey (Dial anesthesia). The recording electrode is in the lateral column at cord segment C_1. Downward deflection indicates positivity at the exploring electrode. *Left,* stimulus to the contralateral motor cortex; D and I waves are labeled. *Right,* stimulus to white matter after ablation of the motor cortex; only the D wave persists. Time, 1 msec. (From Patton and Amassian, 1960.)

The relatively long delay of the *I* waves (which suggests at least two or three synaptic delays) may be caused by a third link in this chain, the excitation spreading from longitudinal cells to Golgi-type II interneurons before returning to the Betz cells. The *I* waves thus may represent an activity that is composed partly of repetitive discharges from the same cells which gave rise to the *D* waves and partly of the delayed discharge of neighboring cortical cells outside the direct field of the electrical stimulus.

The Cortical Origin of the Pyramidal Tract

Degeneration studies. Complete removal of one cortical hemisphere (Mettler, 1944) results in the total degeneration of the fibers which make up the bulbar pyramid. The precise origin of the corticospinal tract in the cortex has remained a point of contention. Pyramidotomy produces cortical degeneration that is largely confined to the internal lamina of area 4 of the precentral gyrus; however, only the giant Betz cells appear to be affected by these degenerative influences. Recent cell counts have indicated that no more than 2 or 3% of the pyramidal tract fibers can originate from these cells. (There are only about 34,000 giant Betz cells in the cortex; there are more than one million corticospinal tract fibers.) Selective ablation studies (Lassek, 1942; Walberg and Brodal, 1953) have suggested that (1) only about 30 to 40% of the pyramidal tract fibers arise from the traditional motor areas of the precentral gyrus; (2) many corticospinal fibers arise from the sensory projection areas of the parietal lobe; and (3) even the temporal and occipital cortex appear to contribute significant numbers of pyramidal fibers. It is clear that traditional views about the origin and functions of this motor system must be revised.

Electrophysiological techniques. A number of more specific maps of the cortical representations of the pyramidal system have been obtained by a variety of electrophysiological stimulation and recording techniques. One approach has been the mapping of cortical points from which clear *D*-wave responses in the bulbar pyramids can be elicited. Using this technique, Patton and Roscoe (see Patton and Amassian, 1960) found two discrete pyramidal motor projections on the cortex of the cat; one projection included all the anterior and parts of the posterior sigmoid gyri, the other included parts of the ectosylvian gyrus. Surrounding these "primary" regions were extensive "fringe areas" from which only *I* responses could be obtained. This observation suggests that overt

muscular responses may be elicited by cortical stimulation of areas which project to, but are not themselves a principal part of, the pyramidal motor system—an important note to remember in subsequent sections of the discussion. Some electrophysiological experiments have succeeded in recording a very extensive spread of excitation following stimulation of the motor cortex which just exceeded the threshold for overt movements. It is thus difficult to evaluate the significance of stimulation studies that have mapped the cortical representation of the motor system on the basis of overt movements elicited by cortical stimulation (Lilly, 1956; Lilly et al., 1956). These maps may be much more extensive than the distribution of primary corticospinal projection neurons of either the pyramidal or the extrapyramidal motor system.

Woolsey and Chang (1948) first recorded the antidromically conducted responses to electrical stimulation of the bulbar pyramids from the cortex of cats and monkeys. The propagation of impulses from the site of stimulation to the cell body produces a distinct electrical response at the cell soma which is not normally conducted to other cells. A number of maps have been constructed with this technique (see Figure 4.9) which are typically somewhat larger than those based on *D*-wave origins. Patton and Towe (see Patton and Amassian, 1960) discovered one possible explanation for this discrepancy. Some of the cortical cells from which only *I*-wave responses could be elicited were fired antidromically by stimulation of the bulbar pyramids. This reaction may reflect little more than volume conduction or possibly spread of the pyramidal tract stimulus to the overlying sensory pathways. More research is needed to clarify this issue.

The pyramidal tract response to peripheral stimuli. The relationship between sensory input and pyramidal motor system discharge has been investigated in experiments concerned with the response of pyramidal tract fibers to electrical stimulation of peripheral sensory nerves. When care is taken to place the recording electrode into the pyramidal tract to avoid pickup from the overlying lemniscal system, a simple positive or positive-negative wave appears within 10 to 20 msec (the shorter latencies are recorded for contralateral stimulation) after peripheral stimulation. The wave persists for about 15 msec, suggesting the repetitive and asynchronous activation of cortical motor neurons (Adrian and Moruzzi, 1939). Such responses can be obtained from ipsi-

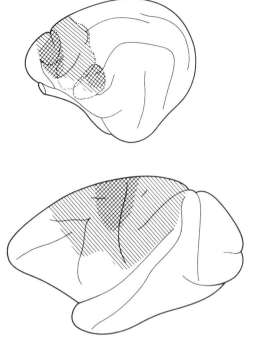

Fig. 4.9 Cortical regions from which antidromic potentials are recorded following stimulation of the bulbar pyramid in the cat (top) and monkey (bottom). Crosshatched areas, large responses; hatched areas, small responses. (From Woolsey and Chang, 1948.)

lateral as well as contralateral stimulation, although the former tends to have longer latencies and may be more fragile (in the sense that it is more easily affected by asphyxia, barbiturates, etc.).

The pyramidal tract responds to peripheral sensory stimulation during the positive phase of the cortical reaction to that stimulation. The initial, negative phase of the cortical response precedes the pyramidal tract reaction by about 4.5 msec. Since the corticobulbar conduction time in the pyramidal fibers amounts to only about 0.5 msec, a delay of about 4 msec occurs at the level of the Betz cells (i.e., the cells of origin for the pyramidal tract).

Microelectrode recordings of the response of cortical motor cells to peripheral stimulation suggests that the delay may be the result of several interacting mechanisms. Some time may be required for temporal summation or related processes to occur. The pyramidal motor cells typically respond to a single peripheral volley with a burst of spike responses. The discharge latency of different cortical cells varies consider-

ably. Patton and Towe (see Patton and Amassian, 1960) have estimated that 44.6% of the cortical pyramidal neurons initiate spike responses before the gross electrical response of the cortex reaches peak positivity. In the region of mean positivity itself, 51.4% of the units began to fire (see Figure 4.10). The reasons for the delay of the pyramidal tract response become apparent when one considers the latency distributions of the responses of single cortical units.

The spinal termination of pyramidal fibers. The anatomical course of the pyramidal tract through the internal capsule, pons, and lower brainstem has been described in some detail in Chapter 2. Degeneration studies (Barnard and Woolsey, 1956) have shown that some degree of topographical organization exists in the upper portions of the pyramidal pathways; however, the pattern of the projections gets lost in the medulla. Prominent *D*-wave responses to cortical stimulation are generally recorded only from the contralateral lateral column of the spinal cord, although uncrossed pyramidal fibers have been identified anatomically. These fibers may terminate in high cervical segments and thus escape detection by recording techniques.

Most pyramidal tract fibers terminate in upper portions of the cord; few if any connect directly to ventral horn motor cells. Recent degeneration studies by Chambers and Liu (cited by Patton and Amassian, 1960) demonstrated that most of the pyramidal fibers synapse on interneurons located at the base of the dorsal horn or in the intermediate gray of the cord. Electrophysiological studies have shown that short latency (4 to 5 msec) responses to electrical stimulation of the bulbar pyramids can be recorded only from the outer basilar regions of the cord. Cells located at the base of the dorsal horn and in the intermediate gray responded after significantly longer latencies (10 and 20 msec respectively) and typically required more prolonged stimulation (Lloyd, 1944).

Pyramidal tract stimulation at the bulbar level facilitates three-neuron reflex discharges with a latency of about 9 msec and monosynaptic reflex activity with a latency of about 12 msec. The delay between bulbar stimulation and the arrival of the first pyramidal volley is about 4 to 5 msec. This suggests that another 4 to 5 msec must be taken up—perhaps by temporal summation—at the interneuron level before the pyramidal activity can have an effect on spinal reflexes. An additional 3 msec are lost in synaptic delays and perhaps in further summation before the ventral

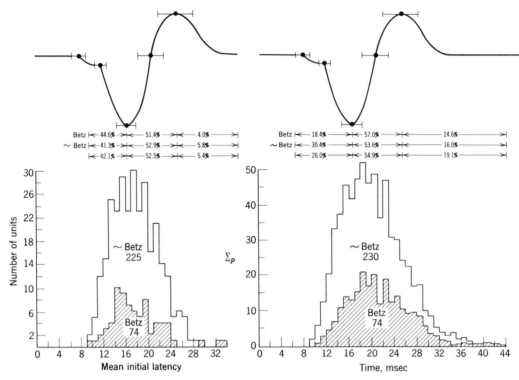

Fig. 4.10 Firing times of orthodromically excited cortical cells of chloralose-anesthetized cats, related to surface cortical potential. *Left, upper trace,* reconstructed average surface cortical response (somatosensory area I) to stimulating contralateral footpad; horizontal brackets, standard deviations of measured points in time. *Below,* distribution of initial latencies of 132 cortical cells responding to forepaw stimulation; numbers bracketed by arrows indicate proportions of Betz, non-Betz, and total populations firing the first spike within the indicated time periods. *Right, upper trace* surface potential as in the left part. *Below,* summation of firing probabilities at indicated times (abscissa) for 140 cortical cells. (From Patton and Amassian, 1960.)

horn motor cell itself can be affected (see Figure 4.11).

The pyramidal tract is not entirely efferent. Some direct sensory afferents from the upper segments of the spinal cord, projections from the cuneate and gracile nuclei of the medulla, and intermediate sensory relays via the pyramidal tract all reach the cortex. In man, these afferents make up only about 4% of the pyramidal tract fibers (Nathan and Smith, 1955), and no functional significance has been assigned to them. It might be worth remembering, however, that 4% of one million amounts to 40,000 afferent fibers, an ascending pathway of potential importance.

THE EXTRAPYRAMIDAL MOTOR SYSTEM

All central mechanisms that affect motor activity and do not discharge via the pyramidal tracts are part of the extrapyramidal motor system. This negative conceptualization is related to the historical origin of the term. The notion of an extrapyramidal motor system was created by the neurological and physiological investigators of the nineteenth century to explain the persistence of muscular activity after total transection of the pyramidal tracts. This explanation has unfortunately resulted in the erroneous conclusion that the extrapyramidal motor system must be secondary or supplementary in nature. Nothing could be more false, as a brief look at phylogenetic data will demonstrate. The pyramidal motor system is relatively new phylogenetically. It is totally absent in lower vertebrates and only poorly developed in some relatively "high" representatives of this most advanced subphylum. Even in man, this system is not indispensible. Recent experiments have shown that voluntary movements can be executed even when the pyramidal tracts are completely transected. The peculiar contribution of pyramidal influences appears to be the precise control of small groups of muscles, largely in the distal extremities (fingers, toes, etc.). It provides little more than expendable facilitatory influences on basic postural and locomotor functions.

The extrapyramidal motor system consists of several interacting components which are to some extent anatomically and functionally distinct (see Figure 4.12): the system contains (1) cortical neurons from most if not all sections of the cerebral hemispheres; (2) the striatum and pallidum of the telencephalic basal ganglia; (3) certain diencephalic nuclei (the subthalamic nucleus and the nuclei ventralis anterior, ventralis lateralis, and medialis of the thalamus); (4) mesencephalic structures (the red nucleus and substantia nigra); (5) certain reticular and cranial nerve nuclei of the lower brainstem; and (6) the cerebellum.

Cortical Mechanisms

The complexity of the cortical influence on extrapyramidal motor functions is best appreciated when we recall the multitude of afferent and efferent pathways that interconnect the subcortical components of this diffuse system with literally all parts of the cerebral hemispheres. Very extensive cortical projections originate from the primary and secondary motor areas of the frontal lobe (areas 4 and 6). However, ablation and stimulation experiments have suggested a much more extensive distribution of cortical extrapyramidal motor projections. For instance, complete bilateral destruction of areas 4 and 6 leaves the postural and locomotor reactions of monkeys essentially intact (Fulton and Dow, 1938). Electrical stimulation of many regions of the frontal, parietal, and temporal lobes has elicited motor responses of varying precision, even after the pyramidal tract or the primary motor areas have been destroyed (Vogt and Vogt, 1907, 1919; Tower, 1936; Penfield and Jasper, 1954).

The origin of the cortical contributions is so widespread and diffuse that it has been impossible, with presently available techniques, to isolate functionally distinct centers or pathways in the cerebral cortex. Subcortical integration of extrapyramidal influences as well as the largely "automatic" nature of the motor adjustments suggest that the cortical influences may serve largely to

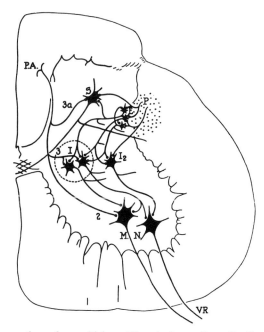

Fig. 4.11 Spinal connections of pyramidal tract fibers in the cat. E, small cells of the external basilar region; I, intermediate gray nucleus of Ramón y Cajal; I₂, other neurons of the intermediate region; M.N., motor neurons; P, pyramidal tract; P.A., primary afferent collaterals; S, solitary cells of the dorsal horn; VR, ventral root; 2, 3, and 3a, terminal collaterals of the primary afferent system. (From Lloyd, 1941.)

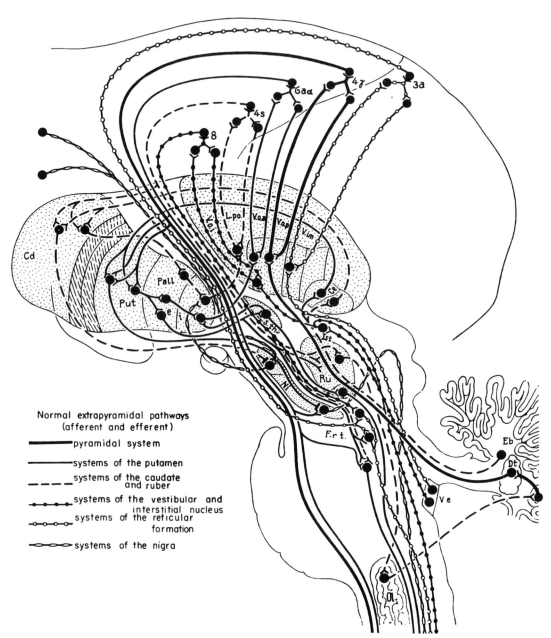

Fig. 4.12 Fiber connections of the extrapyramidal motor system with the afferent and efferent pathways. (From Jung and Hassler, 1960.)

provide detailed sensory information and, perhaps, end products of some "associative" processes, to regulatory mechanisms of striatal, pallidal, and cerebellar origin.

The Basal Ganglia

The telencephalic nuclei of the striatum and pallidum appear to be major integrative centers for the extrapyramidal motor system. The striatum exerts strong inhibitory influences on cortical mechanisms concerned with the regulation of voluntary motor activity. This inhibitory influence is essential for man's ability to concentrate on the performance of specific motor reactions to restricted aspects of the total sensory input. The pallidum appears to be less immediately related to the central control of motor responses; rather, it discharges directly to peripheral motor neurons.

Pallidal lesions. Partial unilateral destruction of the pallidum produces no marked motor deficits in cats or dogs; however, if the putamen is invaded by the lesion, postural reflexes are significantly impaired and the contralateral extremities show marked hypertonicity (Jung and Hassler, 1960). Small bilateral lesions in the pallidum of monkeys fail to elicit changes in motor activity (Kennard, 1944a, b). Larger bilateral damage produces catalepsy and inactivity (F. A. Mettler, 1945, 1954).

The pallidum in man has been totally or partially removed to control *Parkinson's disease* (characterized by a sharp increase in muscle tone, tremor at rest, and an impairment of voluntary activity because of a complete loss of autonomic movements). Partial destruction of the pallidum suppresses rigidity and reduces tremor, but the effects do not seem to be selective. The excessive motor activity that characterizes other hyperkinetic diseases is also reduced by partial pallidal damage; moreover, complete unilateral removal of the pallidum produces transitory drowsiness, a marked impairment of contact with the environment, and an arrest of spontaneous activity. Bilateral lesions tend to emphasize these symptoms and induce permanent deficits in spontaneous activity, "self-awareness," and "critical capacity."

Pallidal stimulation. Electrical stimulation of the putamen produces tonic-clonic movements, even when the motor cortex has been removed (von Bechterew, 1909–1911). Cortical motor responses are inhibited by stimulation of the anterior pallidum (Hodes et al., 1951) but are facilitated by high-frequency stimulation of the posterior pallidum (Peacock and Hodes, 1951).

Stimulation of the pallidum in man produces temporary arousal, even when the patient is in deep anesthesia. Unanesthetized patients (local anesthetics only) become disoriented and stop responding to their environment during pallidal stimulation. These behavioral changes are often associated with respiratory arrest and high-voltage EEG activity in both cortical hemispheres.

Lesions in the striatum. Bilateral destruction of the striatum in animals produces a syndrome of "obstinate progression" (Magendie, 1841; Schiff, 1858). Small bilateral lesions in the caudate do not affect the motor activity of cats or monkeys; larger ablations induce circling movements and obstinate progression (Mettler and Mettler,

1942). Extrapyramidal motor symptoms, such as tremor or spasticity, have not been reported after experimental striatal damage. Kennard (1944a, b) has shown that these disturbances appear only after combined lesions in the striatum and motor cortices (areas 6 or 8).

In man extensive damage of the striatum causes *Huntington's chorea*, a disease that is characterized by rapid, involuntary movements, general hypotonia, an impairment of voluntary movements because of poor coordination (*asynergism*), and lack of postural support.

Lesions in the putamen result in a variety of symptoms which may be *choreiform* or *athetotic* (the athetoid syndrome is characterized by slow, repetitious, involuntary movements and the assumption of abnormal postures, particularly of the extremities).

Smaller striatal lesions do not typically produce clinical disorders unless additional damage to other portions of the extrapyramidal motor system occurs. Large lesions have been reported to elicit both static tremor and tremor at rest.

Stimulation in the striatum. Electrical stimulation of the caudate nucleus produces a number of reactions; their precise nature varies as a function of stimulus frequency and intensity. Some of the earlier studies (Hassler, 1956a, b, c) reported turning of the head and body in a contralateral direction to the site of low-frequency stimulation. Forman and Ward (1957) demonstrated that specific parts of the body appeared to be somatotopically represented in the caudate so that selective contralateral movements could be elicited from specific sites.

A number of distinct inhibitory reactions have been evoked by caudate stimulation. Some of the earlier studies (Mettler et al., 1939; Hodes et al., 1952) observed a general inhibition of cortical motor effects during caudate stimulation. Hess (1948) reported "motor sleep" (characterized by a marked lack of spontaneous activity and a raising of the overall threshold of motor response to any sensory stimulation) following prolonged caudatal stimulation. Other workers induced sleep in man and monkeys (Heath and Hodes, 1952) or elicited a complete temporary arrest of all movements (Hunter and Jasper, 1949).

Later experiments by Buchwald and his associates (Buchwald et al., 1961a; Heuser et al., 1961; Buchwald et al., 1961b; Buchwald et al., 1961c) have shown that low-frequency stimulation of the caudate nucleus evokes rhythmic spindle activity in the motor cortex as well as sleep or behavioral arrest. High-frequency stimulation desynchronized the cortical EEG and produced behavioral arousal. High-frequency stimulation (300 pulses per second) superimposed on low-frequency stimulation (0.2 to 0.5 pulse per second) reversed the inhibitory effects of the latter (see Figures 4.13 and 4.14).

Buchwald et al. (1961a, b, c) interpreted these findings to suggest two separate and opposing caudate systems: one, activated by low-frequency stimulation, inhibits cortical processes; the other, stimulated by high-frequency inputs, exerts facilitatory effects. These two systems are thought to act in opposition to the reticular arousal system. In view of the large and consistent literature which suggests primary inhibitory functions, Buchwald et al. proposed that the caudate nucleus may

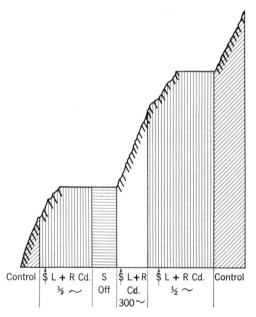

Fig. 4.13   Effect of high- and low-frequency stimulation of the caudate nucleus on the rate of bar pressing for a food reward (ratio of reinforcement, 1 unit of food/12 presses). The slope of the curve is proportional to the rate of response. Control: responses for food reward before caudate stimulation. $ L+R Cd. ($\frac{1}{2}$~): bilateral stimulation of caudate nuclei at a rate of 1 p/2 sec first slows and then stops pressing. Stimulation parameters (suprathreshold for spindle production): 0.1-msec pulse duration, 50 volts. Off: caudate stimulation is stopped; the cat still does not respond. $ L+R Cd. (300~): bilateral high-frequency stimulation of caudate nuclei (300 p/sec, 0.01-msec pulse duration, 70 volts) causes immediate return to the control rate of bar pressing. (From Buchwald et al., 1961c.)

normally function as part of a negative feedback loop; this loop receives inputs from the nonspecific thalamic projection system and discharges to the cortex via the nucleus ventralis anterior of the thalamus.

Stevens et al. (1961) reported related observations. High-frequency stimulation as well as direct applications of cholinergic drugs to the caudate nucleus elicited hyperactivity and contralateral circling. Low-frequency stimulation and the long-term effects of cholinergic stimulation induced behavioral and electrophysiological sleep and inhibited the performance of conditioned avoidance responses.

Electrical activity of the basal ganglia. The electrical activity of the caudate and putamen appears to be peculiarly related to that of the cortex, hippocampus, and thalamus. The normal low-voltage "spontaneous" activity of the striatum is replaced by high-voltage discharges as soon as the cortical connections are severed. Electrical stimulation of the caudate may induce very slow activity which correlates with periods of relative "inactivity" in the cortical EEG and similar periods of slow activity in the hippocampus and nonspecific thalamic system (Umbach, 1955). The electrical activity of some of the nonspecific thalamic nuclei and hippocampus can be synchronized by low-frequency stimulation of the caudate nucleus (Shimamoto and Verzeano, 1954).

Segundo and Machne (1956) have presented an interesting analysis of microelectrode recordings from single cells in the caudate and putamen (see Figure 4.15). Roughly 60% of the neurons recorded from the putamen responded to somatic stimulation of skin and muscle receptors with either a decrease or an increase of the resting activity. Neurons in the pallidum gave only excitatory responses. The authors suggested on the basis of their observations that the striatum and pallidum may contribute motor impulses to a neural circuit that is concerned with the integration of complex sensory and motor patterns.

Diencephalic Nuclei

The subthalamic nucleus. The pallidum receives extensive inputs from the subthalamic nucleus. Many of the pallidal syndromes can be duplicated by subthalamic damage or stimulation. Choreiform hyperkinesia has been produced in experimental animals by even partial destruction of this nucleus (Carpenter and Carpenter, 1951; Whittier and Mettler, 1949); however, neither the severity nor the duration of the disturbances appeared to

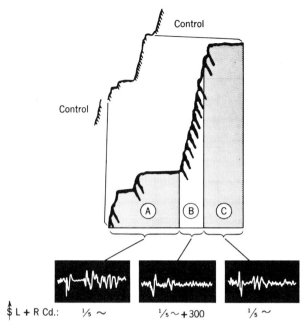

Fig. 4.14 Effect of simultaneous low- and high-frequency stimulation of the caudate nuclei on a bar-pressing response. Oscilloscope tracing on the left shows evoked potential and "caudate spindle" elicited by low-frequency (1 p/5 sec) stimulation. The response rate during this stimulation (A) falls to zero. The middle trace shows abolition of spindling by simultaneous low- and high-frequency (300 p/sec) stimulation of the caudate nuclei. The response rate returns to the control values (B). The trace on the right shows the recurrence of the caudate spindle when the high-frequency stimulation is discontinued. Bar pressing is again inhibited (C). (From Buchwald et al., 1961c.)

be related to the extent of the subthalamic damage. Unilateral destruction of the subthalamic nucleus in man causes *hemiballismus*; this disease is characterized by violent involuntary movements which begin in proximal muscle groups and gradually spread to the extremities (Jakob, 1923). Electrical stimulation of this region in cats has been shown to elicit rhythmic locomotor responses or complete circling movements to the side opposite the side of stimulation (Waller, 1940).

Jung and Hassler (1960) concluded on the basis of these and related clinical observations that the subthalamic nuclei may exercise overall control of rhythmic movements of the limbs.

Thalamic nuclei. The striatum receives extensive inputs from the nucleus centrum medianum of the thalamus which appears to integrate sensory information from all modalities as well as from cerebellar and reticular afferents. This pathway influences overall cortical excitability and regulates the motor components of sleep. The experimental support for this interpretation consists largely of the following observations. Low-frequency stimulation of some parts of the centrum medianum induces electrophysiological as well as behavioral sleep (Hess et al., 1953), respiratory inhibition, and a depression of reflex activity (Hess, 1954a, b). High-frequency stimulation produces a cortical recruiting response and behavioral as well as electrophysiological arousal (Hanbery and Jasper, 1953). Partial destruction does not produce overt motor deficits in spite of the apparently crucial position of this thalamic nucleus in the extrapyramidal system (Hassler, 1955a, b).

Most of the efferent projections from the pallidum terminate in the ventrolateral (VL) and anteroventral (VA) nuclei of the thalamus. Electrical stimulation of discrete points within these nuclei elicits distinct movements, usually of the contralateral extremities. Extensive damage typically results in lack of postural control, contralateral ataxia, and mimetic paralysis of facial muscles. Smaller therapeutic lesions are often performed to reduce the resting tremor and *myoclonic movements* (rapid arhythmic contrac-

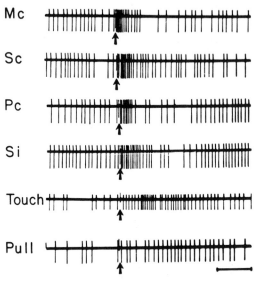

Fig. 4.15 Neuronal activity in the putamen following various afferent stimuli. The effects of single shock stimuli (7 volts, 0.1 msec) at the arrow to contralateral median (Mc), contralateral sciatic (Sc), contralateral peroneal (Pc), and ipsilateral sciatic (Si) nerves. *Below,* responses elicited by lightly touching the fur at the base of the tail (touch) or by stretching the contralateral gastrocnemius muscle (pull); application of such stimuli occurred approximately at the arrow. Downward deflection represents a positive signal, and time calibration indicates 500 msec. (From Segundo and Machne, 1956.)

tions of single muscles or small muscle groups) which characterize some hyperkinetic motor disorders. Selective damage to the *nucleus ventro-oralis anterior* and *nucleus lateropolaris* has been reported to abolish completely the rigor of Parkinson's disease and the hyperkinetic symptoms of athetosis and *torsion dystonia* (spasmodic rotations of the trunk and excessive muscular contractions which prevent voluntary movement). See Jung and Hassler, 1960, for details.

Grossman et al. (1965) have shown that cholinergic stimulation of the reticular nucleus or midline nuclei of the thalamus extensively inhibited all recently learned behavior and prevented the establishment of novel conditioned responses in the rat. Similar observations have been reported in the cat by Buchwald and Ling (1965).

Mesencephalic Structures

The substantia nigra. One of the most important way stations of the extrapyramidal motor system is the substantia nigra of the midbrain. It appears to provide essential "starter" impulses

which facilitate phasic muscular contractions. Clinical and experimental observations indicate that this function may be exercised, at least in part, via the gamma efferent system which biases postural reflex adjustments. It has been shown that gamma efferent excitation (presumably mediated via the nigroreticulospinal pathway) precedes the alpha neuron discharge in many types of movements. This influence is thought to be essential for (1) postural adjustments that are necessary for the completion of phasic motor responses and (2) a "priming" of the musculature involved in the phasic responses so that rapid and exact movements of specific muscle groups can be organized by the subsequent alpha neuron discharge. (A marked lowering of the spindle receptor thresholds might be one way to produce such a selective increase in sensitivity.) These generalizations are based largely on the following experimental and clinical observations.

Lesions confined to the substantia nigra are responsible for most of the complex motor syndrome commonly seen in Parkinson's disease. The excessive muscle tone that produces the characteristic rigidity of Parkinsonism is related to an enhancement of the myotatic (tonic) component of the stretch reflex. This hypertonicity and the commonly observed inability to initiate voluntary movements are thought to be caused by a loss of central control over some aspects of the gamma efferent system. (The gamma efferents adjust the sensitivity of the annulospiral receptors. A loss of such regulation results in a loss of control over the length of a muscle and its adaptation to changes in tonic stretch.)

Two additional symptoms that are often seen in Parkinson's disease, *paralysis agitans* and *akinesia* (loss of automatic movements and general motor stiffness), are caused by lesions in the substantia nigra. Only tremor, which sometimes accompanies Parkinson's disease, does not appear to be directly related to lesions in the substantia nigra; rather, tremor represents the result of additional striatal damage or loss of striatal connections (Hassler, 1938, 1939).

Experimental lesions in the substantia nigra have produced evidence of postural tremor, probably because of damage to ascending fiber systems (Peterson et al., 1949; Bishop et al., 1948). Electrical stimulation elicits few, if any, distinct motor movements: swallowing and chewing have been reported by some of the earlier workers (von Bechterew, 1909–1911). However, stimulation tends to increase the extensor tonus of anterior limbs (Mettler, 1943) and reduce the amplitude of cortically evoked motor responses (Mettler et al., 1939).

The nucleus ruber. An analysis of the functional significance of influences from the red nucleus of the midbrain is complicated by its heterogeneous composition and by its location in a portion of the brainstem that is crossed by many important ascending and descending fiber tracts. Early experiments suggested that the results obtained from rodents and carnivores differ significantly from those seen in primates and man. This distinction can presumably be attributed to basic anatomical differences. The nucleus ruber of the rodent and carnivore is primarily composed of large cells that discharge into the crossed rubrospinal tract. The red nucleus of primates and man, on the other hand, consists primarily of small cells that discharge into the central tegmental tract and synapse in the reticular formation of the lower brainstem.

Unilateral destruction of the red nucleus in the cat produces transitory ataxia and a contralateral decrease in muscle tone and proprioceptive reflex activity (Ingram and Ranson, 1932). Bilateral lesions produce extensor rigidity and increased resistance to passive movement as well as hyperkinetic disorders of an athetotic-choreiform nature (Lafora, 1955). It is, unfortunately, not entirely clear to what extent these effects may be attributable to the interruption of fiber tracts or to the involvement of neighboring motor nuclei of the brainstem. Similar problems must be considered in the monkey, in which coarse tremor (Keller and Hare, 1934), transitory ataxia, asynergia, and tremor (Mettler and Carpenter, cited by Jung and Hassler, 1960) have been observed after rubral lesions.

Two distinct syndromes have been reported in man. The upper rubral syndrome includes coarse static and action tremor, hemiataxia, and hemiparesis (Chiray et al., 1923). The lower syndrome consists of contralateral hemiasynergia, unilateral athetotic movements, and rhythmic myoclonic contractions of the muscles of extremities.

The only clear motor effect of electrical stimulation of the red nucleus is an upward motion of the head and anterior segments of the trunk (Hassler, 1956a, b, c). More complex movements have been reported by some investigators, but these seem to be related to incidental excitation of adjacent aspects of the reticular formation (Ingram et al., 1932).

Jung and Hassler (1960) have recently suggested that the small-celled component of the red nucleus may exercise an important regulatory influence on motor functions of the cerebral cortex. The large-celled elements may perform a corresponding function for cerebellar motor processes.

Brainstem Reticular and Vestibular Mechanisms

The reticular formation of the medulla and lower pons exerts important regulatory controls over the spinal motor mechanisms, presumably via a direct effect on the gamma efferent system. Magoun and Rhines (1946; Rhines and Magoun, 1946) first demonstrated that the bulbar portion of the brainstem, superior to the inferior olivary nucleus, contained a number of facilitatory and inhibitory regions (see Figure 4.16) from which spinal reflex activity could be significantly affected. Electrical stimulation of the inhibitory region reduced (1) all basic spinal reflexes, (2) motor responses caused by cortical stimulation, and (3) decerebrate rigidity. The bulbar inhibitory center appears to be functionally related to the "inhibitory area" (4s) of the precentral motor cortex (McCulloch et al., 1946).

A larger and more diffuse facilitatory area is found in the reticular formation of the ventral diencephalon, midbrain tegmentum, and pontine gray. Stimulation of these facilitatory regions reinforces the excitatory inputs to the spinal

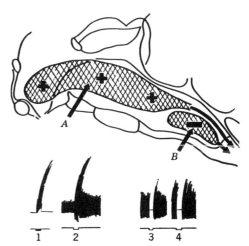

Fig. 4.16 A midsagittal plane of the cat's brainstem, showing by cross-hatching the facilitatory (+) and inhibitory (−) areas of Magoun and Rhines. *Below*, typical records showing facilitation (A) and inhibition (B) of the patellar reflex (1 and 3) and of cortical motor response (2 and 4). The lowest line is a stimulus signal. (From Niemer and Magoun, 1947.)

motor neurons and facilitates reflex responses, even in decorticate preparations. Rhines and Magoun (1947) have suggested that the facilitatory region of the brainstem reticular formation may reinforce the discharge of the pyramidal motor system.

Although the reticular mechanisms are commonly labeled positive and negative, their influence is not uniform. Stimulation of the midline inhibitory center inhibits extensor tonus but elicits flexor contraction. Stimulation of the facilitatory area inhibits flexion but induces or facilitates extensor reflexes, such as those that dominate in decerebrate rigidity (Sprague and Chambers, 1954).

The vestibular nuclei of the lower brainstem also exert a major facilitatory influence on the spinal motor neurons, largely on tonic (postural) reflex responses. The vestibular influence on postural adjustments is essential for the maintenance of equilibrium and orientation in space.

The influence of these brainstem mechanisms is seen most clearly in the decerebrate animal; such an animal shows excessive extensor rigidity, presumably because of an unchecked influence of the reticular and vestibular facilitatory mechanisms. This rigidity is enhanced by additional destruction of the cerebellum (see the following discussion).

The Cerebellum

The cerebellum is a major integrative center for postural adjustments, locomotion, and a number of other reflex adjustments. Although it has been studied extensively, many of the earlier investigations failed to provide adequate controls to rule out a spread of stimulation or damage to the immediately adjacent brainstem.

The anterior lobe of the cerebellum primarily regulates activity in the lower portions of the extrapyramidal system. It exerts its effects via direct descending pathways that project to interneurons in the spinal cord. Some projections to the red nucleus, the reticular formation of the brainstem tegmentum, and the vestibulospinal system also exist. Both facilitatory and inhibitory effects have been reported. The posterior lobe, on the other hand, acts primarily on ascending systems and modifies the activity of cerebral motor functions.

As a whole, the cerebellum functions as a regulator of the tonus of striated skeletal muscles rather than as an initiator of distinct muscle responses. It exerts its influence, at least in part, by controlling the gamma efferent discharge and regulating the time-space pattern of alpha motor activity. These generalizations are based on the following evidence.

Ablation of the cerebellum. Total destruction of the cerebellum produces a complex motor syndrome that shows distinct recovery phases. Initially, animals in which the cerebellum has been destroyed are excessively active but are unable to stand because of extensor rigidity. They show clonic movements of the hindlimbs and rigid extensions of the forelimbs. The general hyperactivity of spinal motor mechanisms is also reflected in excessive tendon and other postural reflexes.

Gradually, the animals start to compensate for the excessive facilitatory influences on spinal motor neurons which are caused by the release of tonic inhibition of cerebellar origin. Such compensation often leads to atonia and asthenia; the initial righting responses end in total collapse because the limbs cannot bear the weight of the animal. Eventually, the animal regains locomotion of a lumbering and unsure nature, but a basic lack of control over phasic contraction responses remains. This cerebellar ataxia includes massive coarse tremor in the upper half of the body and poor timing and execution of locomotor movements. Most reflexes are poorly executed as well as hyperexcitable; however, some individual responses such as scratching reflexes appear to be largely protected (Dusser de Barenne, 1937; Rademaker, 1931; Lewandowsky, 1907; Thomas, 1897).

Unilateral destruction of the cerebellar cortex produces essentially comparable ipsilateral deficits. Such effects are more obvious because the response of the affected side can be immediately compared with the intact side.

The anterior lobe. Electrical stimulation of the vermian portion of the anterior lobe markedly modifies alpha motor neuron discharge. The direction of the effect appears to be area-dependent, although some reports suggest that stimulation of a particular point may facilitate some motor patterns but inhibit others. The most famous of the inhibitory effects is the collapse of decerebrate rigidity which follows electrical stimulation of the anterior cerebellum (Sherrington, 1897; Bremer, 1922a, b). The effect is all the more dramatic because it is largely restricted to the ipsilateral side of the body.

Stimulation of the anterior cerebellum also inhibits the extensor tonus and crossed extensor re-flexes in normal animals (Sprague and Chambers, 1954). Compensatory contractions of the flexor muscles are not normally seen (Moruzzi, 1950a, b). A number of other motor functions may also be inhibited. Vasomotor responses (Moruzzi, 1938a, b), galvanic skin reflexes (Wang and Brown, 1956), and skeletal muscle responses induced by cerebral stimulation (Snider et al., 1949) have been inhibited by electrical stimulation of the anterior cerebellum. Some of these effects may be related to the marked inhibition of muscle spindle activity which has been reported in a number of studies (Granit, 1955; Granit et al., 1952).

Facilitatory influences have been obtained from the same areas. Moruzzi (1950a, b) demonstrated that a lowering of the frequency of stimulation often sufficed to convert the extensor inhibition normally seen after cerebellar stimulation into a pronounced extensor facilitation. He suggested that the anterior lobe of the cerebellum may have frequency-specific afferent or efferent connections which provide for excitatory as well as inhibitory influences to the same structures. Other investigators (Sprague and Chambers, 1954; Pompeiano, 1955, 1956) have found that the contralateral inhibition of extensor tonus (seen after stimulation of the anterior cerebellum in decerebrate animals) can be converted into a marked facilitation of extensor tonus by a slight decrease in the intensity of the stimulating current. A peculiar rebound facilitation of the ipsilateral extensor tonus has been reported to follow the initial inhibition in decerebrate animals (Bremer, 1922a, b). Mechanisms for this effect are not yet understood.

We have discussed the stimulation effects as if the anterior lobe were essentially equipotential. Strictly speaking, this is not true; however, the spread of excitation is normally so extensive that little somatotopic organization can be detected. With very minimal currents, some investigators (Snider et al., 1949; Hampson et al., 1952) have succeeded in demonstrating a functional organization of the anterior vermis, the tail of the animal being represented in the lingula, the hindlimbs in the centralis, and the forelimb in the culmen.

Ablation of the anterior lobe of the cerebellum in quadrupeds results in a pronounced extensor rigidity of the extremities and in some ataxia and tremor of the trunk and head muscles (Chambers and Sprague, 1955a, b; Lindsley et al., 1949; Snider and Woolsey, 1941). The existing rigidity of decerebrates is intensified by additional damage to the anterior cerebellum (Dow, 1938a, b). The

symptoms are less pronounced in the primate (Fulton and Conner, 1939). Complete removal of the anterior lobe produces disturbances of postural adjustments, voluntary movements, and simple reflex activity, as well as some tremor; however, the marked extensor rigidity characteristic of the quadruped does not typically appear (see also Carrera and Mettler, 1947).

The posterior lobe. The effects of stimulation of the posterior vermis on postural reflex adjustments are similar to those seen after stimulation of the anterior aspects of the vermis (Hampson et al., 1952; Sprague and Chambers, 1954). Stimulation of the posterior cerebellar cortex, on the other hand, produces primarily ascending effects which modify the activity of the cerebral motor cortices. Electrical stimulation of the posterior cerebellar cortex has been reported to increase the rate and amplitude of cerebrocortical EEG discharges (Walker, 1938). Similar changes in the EEG of the cortical motor areas have been produced by chemical stimulation (strychnine, picrotoxin, Metrazol) of the ansiform lobule (Canestari et al., 1955; Crepax and Fadiga, 1956). Electrical (Mollica et al., 1953) or chemical (Crepax and Fadiga, 1956) stimulation of the vermis, on the other hand, produces electrophysiological "arousal" and changes the direct-current level of the electrocortical response (Dondey and Snider, 1955).

These electrophysiological changes are accompanied by functional modifications in the cerebral cortex. The threshold of motor cells in the cerebral cortex to electrical stimulation is significantly lowered during stimulation of the ansiform lobule or posterior vermis (Dusser de Barenne, 1937). Overt movements that are elicited by electrical stimulation of the cerebral motor cortex can be facilitated or inhibited by concurrent stimulation of the lateral vermis, culmen, and posterior hemisphere (Snider et al., 1947; Snider and Magoun, 1949; Snider et al., 1949).

Stimulation of various cerebellar points (ansiform lobule, paramedian, and posterior vermis) in unanesthetized animals produces complex patterns of movement which often start with the assumption of abnormal postures. These "seizure-like" response patterns appear to be independent of external influences, since they persist after decortication and peripheral deafferentation (Clark, 1939a, b; Clark and Ward, 1949, 1952).

Destruction of the posterior vermis essentially reproduces the exaggerated postural tonus and disturbances of voluntary movement that characterize the anterior vermian lesion effect. Fulton and Dow (1937) have described in some detail the ataxic and postural disturbances observed in primates following posterior lobe damage. Tremor, dysmetria, and poorly organized complex reflex responses are typically seen in lower vertebrates in addition to ataxia and hypotonia (Bremer, 1935). Partial destruction, restricted to Crura I and II, has been reported to have no effect as long as the underlying nuclei were spared (Chambers and Sprague, 1955a, b).

The cerebellar nuclei. The fastigial nuclei are the major recipients of afferents from the anterior lobe. Complete destruction of these nuclei in the cat produces spasticity. Unilateral destruction results in contralateral spasticity and atonia of the ipsilateral limbs. Removal of the anterior lobe in the decerebrate cat produces increased ipsilateral rigidity and contralateral release. Additional destruction of the fastigial nuclei reverses the pattern; the rigidity appears contralaterally and disappears ipsilaterally (Sprague and Chambers, 1953).

The interpositus and dentate nuclei receive afferents from the posterior sections of the cerebellar cortex. Unilateral destruction of the intermediate nuclei (globose and emboliform) in the cat and rabbit produce tremor, ataxia, and loss of ipsilateral placing reactions (Snider, 1940; Chambers and Sprague, 1955a, b). Lesions of the dentate nuclei produced hypoactivity and some impairment of placing and hopping reactions.

Some functional considerations. The primary role of the cerebellum in the control of motor functions is the tonic regulation of posture. The cerebellum may exert its effects either directly on the spinal motor neurons or indirectly via a modification of the activity of other portions of the extrapyramidal motor system. Posture depends on the tonic discharge of spinal cord motor neurons. The cerebellum affects this tonic discharge in a number of ways. The hypertonicity commonly observed after cerebral damage may be caused by a release of cerebellar inhibition of vestibulospinal pathways (DeVito et al., 1956), or by reticulospinal mechanisms that regulate the gamma efferent discharge (Granit, 1955). The cerebelloreticulospinal pathway is probably also involved in the hypotonic disturbances frequently seen as part of the cerebellar syndrome. Bremer (1936a, b) and others have suggested that some of the inhibitory effects of cerebellar damage may be

the result of a removal of facilitatory influences on the cerebral cortex.

POSTURE, LOCOMOTION, AND COMPLEX VOLUNTARY MOVEMENTS

Postural Adjustments

Posture refers to the complex muscular adjustments that resist the displacement of the body or any of its parts by gravity. Man's upright posture requires the continual integration of afferent information from literally tens of thousands of receptors which monitor the body's position in relation to the environment. The principal sources of information are (1) the muscle spindle receptors and tendon organs which signal the relative state of tension of individual muscles: (2) the Ruffini endings and tendon organs which are sensitive to flexor and extensor movements or rotation of joints; and (3) the specialized vestibular receptors of the inner ear which respond to the position of the head in relation to the basic planes of space. Additional important information may arise from slowly adapting mechanoreceptors in the skin and in the walls of the viscera; distance receptors also provide information about the position of the body in relation to its environment.

Basic resistive or compensatory adjustments for minute deviations of individual limbs or the entire body from a voluntarily selected posture occur automatically and continually throughout every minute of life. Resistive mechanisms such as the simple stretch reflex oppose the movement of a limb and initiate its return to the basic position. The compensatory mechanisms initiate active movements to restore the status quo after a disturbance can no longer be corrected by the resistive mechanisms.

The details of the neural and muscular cooperation that makes these complex adjustments possible are only poorly understood. To start at the effector end of the feedback loop, one can ask how the continual tension of distinct muscles can be maintained by nervous and muscular systems which appear to be incapable of continual intense activity. Motor neurons are capable of sustained firing for up to 30 or 40 min (Lindsley, 1935); however, this ability cannot account for long-term postural adjustments unless the minute adjustments in muscle tension which continually occur result in sufficiently detailed feedback changes to alternately inhibit and stimulate individual neurons and muscle fibers of the system.

There is some experimental evidence for distinct tonic and phasic motor systems, including separate peripheral motor neurons and distinct muscle fibers. Tonic contractions of muscles in some amphibia, for instance, are mediated by a distinct class of ventral root fibers which innervate a special, small type of muscle (Kuffler and Gerard, 1947; Kuffler and Williams, 1953). Larger motor neurons innervate large muscle fibers that appear to be capable only of short, phasic contractions. In mammals a similar, though less absolute, distinction can be made between "red" muscles which are concerned primarily with sustained, postural contractions and "white" muscles which respond more rapidly and discretely as part of phasic muscular responses (Needham, 1926). Furthermore, there is considerable evidence suggesting that some single muscle units are preferentially activated in the course of voluntary movements, whereas others react more promptly to signals for postural adjustments (Denny-Brown, 1949). Histological evidence suggests that the motor neurons which innervate "tonic" muscles are smaller than those related to the "phasic" muscle fibers (Denny-Brown, 1929). Electrophysiological recordings of motor neuron activity have suggested that some units (presumably those innervating "tonic" muscles) fire at uniform, relatively low rates, whereas others respond more erratically, alternating rapid bursts with longer periods of silence (Kawakami, 1954a, b, c). Eccles and his associates (1957) have suggested that motor neurons can be divided into two overlapping distributions on the basis of their response to stimulation. Intracellular recordings showed that the tonic units had longer after-hyperpolarization and slower conduction rates than phasic units and were generally more easily stimulated through monosynaptic reflex arcs.

The importance of tonic reflex contractions in the maintenance of posture has been questioned in the past decades. Clemmesen (1951) has even suggested that the concept of muscle tone be discarded in favor of an analysis of the passive elastic tensions and forces in muscles and tendons which are essentially independent of neural facilitation. This notion is supported by the demonstration that the muscles of the distal joints appear to be largely inactive during normal standing in man (Hoeffer, 1941; Weddel et al., 1944) and that denervation of the lower foot does not seem to impair the pigeon's ability to balance on that foot alone (Chauveau, 1891).

Clemmesen's extreme view is not shared by most muscle physiologists, but it is clear that man's ability to stand derives in part from the elasticity of the ligaments and muscles and the mechanical properties of supporting joints. Thus, Joubert and Gueguen (1955) have found the elastic tension of the calf muscle to be essentially identical to the gravitational forces that tend to pull the body foward. Eldred (1960) has suggested that tonic influences may be less important in the postural adjustments of man than frequent, intermittent, corrective contractions of a phasic nature. Quadrupeds must depend more heavily on tonic mechanisms because their limbs are normally maintained in a partially flexed position.

The principal postural reflexes were discussed in the opening section of this chapter. All basic reactions appear to be integrated by spinal mechanisms and can be elicited from spinal animals after some recuperation from spinal shock. However, many facilitatory and inhibitory influences are normally exerted by central mechanisms that significantly modify these simple responses and integrate them into more complex response patterns. The contribution of particular portions of the central nervous system has been studied by recording the motor deficits resulting from progressively higher brainstem transections.

The *spinal* cat shows weak stretch reflexes, some crossed extensor reflexes, and some compensatory ipsilateral extensor reactions.

Bulbospinal animals with low brainstem transections just above the level of the medulla cannot right themselves, walk, or stand spontaneously. The deficit is related to an extreme facilitation of extensor reflexes and positive supporting reactions. The animals do have well-developed tonic neck and labyrinthine reflexes which adjust the position of the limbs in accordance with the position of the head. The tonic neck reflex is responsible for (1) an increase in the extensor tonus of forelimbs and hindlimbs ipsilateral to the direction of movement of the jaw; (2) an extension of the forelimbs and a relaxation of the hindlimbs in response to dorsal flexion of the head; and (3) a relaxation of the forelimbs and an extension of the hindlimbs following ventral flexion of the head. The labyrinthine reflexes are responsible for the maximal extension of all limbs when the animal is placed on its back and for the minimal extension of the limbs when the animal is prone with the snout tilted 45° to the horizontal plane.

High decerebrate cats and dogs with brainstem transections in the midbrain (just above the red nucleus) do not show decerebrate rigidity; they display rudimentary righting reflexes after an initial period of recovery. Primates also retain some basic righting reflexes but are typically unable to stand because they are very dependent on cortical integration of motor functions.

Several distinct reflexes contribute to the righting reaction. Feedback from asymmetrical stimulation of cutaneous and pressure receptors of the body surfaces results in the *body-on-head* righting reflex which causes corrective movements of the head when the body is in a horizontal position. The *body-righting reflex* represents a similar reaction to selective cutaneous stimulation of the upper surfaces of the body. The reflex results in the assumption of a horizontal position by the hindquarters, regardless of the position of the upper body segments. The primary righting reflexes are of *labyrinthine* origin. Because of sensory feedback from the otoliths, the head always assumes a horizontal position, irrespective of the position of the rest of the body.

In addition to this static labyrinthine reflex, several other reflexes are elicited by linear or angular acceleration. Linear acceleration elicits the *vestibular placing reactions* (extension of forelegs and spreading of the toes in response to rapid downward motion of the whole body). Angular acceleration (movement around the vertical axis of the body) elicits a number of reflex adjustments of the muscular tonus of the neck, limbs, and trunk. The most pronounced acceleratory reflex reaction is *nystagmus*, a rapid movement of the eyes in order to maintain fixed reference points in the rapidly spinning environment. The eyes move rapidly in the direction of the rotation and fixate on some stationary point in the environment. Fixation is maintained as long as the rotation permits, but the eye eventually must move to a new fixation. This alternation of slow eye movements and rapid readjustments is called nystagmus.

Once the head has been turned in response to labyrinthine and *head-on-body* reflex adjustments, proprioceptors in the neck muscles are stimulated and complete a *neck-righting reflex* which acts to bring the body itself into a horizontal position. Even in the absence of cues from the labyrinth, neck proprioceptors, and cutaneous feedback, the normal animal will display *optic righting reflexes* in response to visual cues. These reflexes are cortically mediated and do not, of course, function in the high decerebrate.

High-decerebrate primates show a characteristic pattern of abnormal postural reflexes. In the

lateral position the fore and hindlimbs of the upper half of the body are flexed, and the hands and feet show a strong, involuntary "grasp reflex." The forelimbs and hindlimbs of the lower body half are extended (see Figure 4.17).

Two basic postural reflex adjustments are notably absent from the decorticate animal: the *placing reactions* which assure that the limbs are in an optimal position for standing, and the *hopping reactions* which restore a normal upright posture when the equilibrium of the organism has been disrupted.

Locomotion

Locomotion is essentially a problem of high-order postural adjustments. All basic reflex mechanisms that contribute to the organism's ability to stand or to adjust its position in relation to the environment, are involved. The simple stretch reflex, for instance, is essential for restraining antagonists in alternating contractions and for limiting the excursions of limbs in motion. The positive supporting reaction, which is the primary standing reflex, is also basic to the static phase of movement. More complex postural reflexes maintain or restore the equilibrium of the body during and after movement.

Some reflex adjustments are peculiar to locomotion. We have already mentioned the *negative supporting reactions;* these permit the organism to lift a leg off the ground and swing it forward, largely because the movement is unopposed by gravitational forces. These reactions alternate with the *extensor thrust reflex* which represents a positive supporting reaction in response to changes in the tension around the toe pads. This reflex involves primarily the musculature of the hip

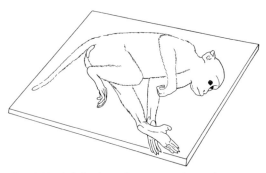

Fig. 4.17 Thalamic reflex posture in a decorticate monkey. Note that the lowermost extremities are extended and the uppermost are flexed. (From Bieber and Fulton, 1938.)

(Moruzzi, 1950a, b). The basic postural reflexes are aided by kinetic *progression reflexes* based on sensory feedback from the vestibular system.

Although the total pattern of muscular adjustments required to complete coordinated movements is complex, the basic reflexes that contribute the motion itself are simple. Reflex flexion of one hindleg initiates a reflex extension of the opposite hindleg and a flexor extension of the diagonal forelimb (Sherrington, 1898a). The apparently complex sequence of reflexes that constitute locomotion may occur purely reflexly. Movement of the head in relation to the trunk reflexly elicits a progression of proprioceptive reflexes which successively induce the contraction of neck, forelimb, and hindlimb muscles; these may result in motion because secondary crossed and uncrossed compensatory reflex adjustments occur.

Complex Voluntary Movements

Survey of neural and muscular mechanisms. Complex skilled movements are the end product of the selective activation and/or inhibition of a large number of specific muscles. The pattern of excitation must be coordinated so that the combined action of all units results in an organized spatiotemporal sequence of motor responses. These complex motions are poorly described in terms of specific action of each of the muscle groups which may contribute to them. A particular complex movement is specified primarily by its consequences and may never be precisely duplicated in terms of the specific pattern of activation or inhibition of individual muscle groups.

Tower (1940, 1949) has shown that the execution of skilled patterns of movement, although dependent on postural support, depends primarily on cortical influences that are transmitted to the primary motor neurons via the pyramidal motor system. A detailed analysis of the cortical representation of the motor system (Bucy, 1949; Phillips, 1956) indicates that two types of pyramidal motor mechanisms may exist. In some areas (notably the precentral gyrus), points that represent individual muscles or even muscle units can be found. Other regions seem to harbor much more diffuse and overlapping representations of muscle groups or even of complex movements.

Bernhard and Bohm (1954) have described a functional division of the corticospinal tract which may maintain this distinction. On the basis of electrophysiological (Lloyd, 1941) and histological (Szentágothai, 1948) evidence, it has been assumed that all corticospinal fibers terminate on internuncial neurons in the spinal cord. However, Bernhard and Bohm (1954) discovered a direct monosynaptic pathway between the motor cortex and the spinal motor neurons. Paillard (1960) subsequently suggested that a group of large, myelinated fibers that arise from the giant Betz cells of the precentral gyrus and make up about 3 to 4% of the pyramidal tract may be responsible for this direct pathway to the spinal motor neuron. Bernhard and Bohm suggested that these fast-conducting monosynaptic connections may play a special role in the control of skilled movements, perhaps as an anatomical substrate for the phasic, "episodic" organization of motor impulses which Tower (1949) proposed to be one of the two complementary components of the corticospinal control of movement. The other phasic aspect of this system would presumably be exercised by the polysynaptic connections of the pyramidal motor system. This distinction has been made explicit by Paillard (1955) with respect to the "motor scotoma" reported by Pribram and his associates (1955). (Motor scotoma refers to the loss of specific skilled movements of the extremities following precentral damage which is not accompanied by a general loss of voluntary movement in the affected limb.) It is possible, in view of some recent observations (Jung and Hassler, 1960), that the sparing of voluntary movement may, in part, be related to extrapyramidal mechanisms; however, a contribution of aspects of the pyramidal system that are perhaps both functionally and anatomically distinct appears to be a more likely explanation.

Tower's extensive investigations have shown that coordinated, voluntary movements can be elicited by cortical stimulation only from proximal muscle groups after transection of the pyramidal tract (Tower, 1940). Hess (1949) suggested that the extrapyramidal influences provide merely a framework that permits the execution of skilled movements.

The clinical study of specific motor disorders and their relationship to damage in restricted portions of the brain (see reviews by Penfield and Rasmussen, 1950; Penfield and Jasper, 1954) has indicated that the motor cortex is activated by impulses from essentially all cortical and many subcortical regions. Some investigators (see Paillard, 1960, p. 1694) have spoken of the motor cortex as "a funnel of convergence for the stream of patterned impulses which produce voluntary movements." Circumcision of cortical areas or transection of the transcortical pathways has little or no effect on function (Penfield, 1940; Sperry,

1947; Lashley, 1952). It appears therefore that the relationship between different areas of the cortex must be relayed by subcortical mechanisms.

Penfield (Penfield, 1954; Penfield and Jasper, 1954) has suggested that the subcortical integrative coordination of this corticocortical flow of information may be achieved by a "centrencephalic" system of centers and pathways (see Figure 4.18). Although Penfield did not specify the anatomical structures involved in this integrative mechanism, we may assume, on the basis of its functional assignment, that the mesencephalic reticular formation and nonspecific thalamic projection system most closely fit the suggested pattern of action.

The details of this subcortical, integrative process and its anatomical representation remain to be specified, but the general concept of such a coordinating system is all but inescapable in view of the experimental and clinical literature of the past decades. The hypothesized system presumably originates the impulses that selectively and specifically facilitate or inhibit restricted cortical functions. It thus represents, in some sense, the "highest" controlling mechanism in the brain. A subcortical seat of the "highest" processes may be disquieting to some investigators, but the arrangement appears eminently sensible in view of the integrative function of reticular processes (see the following discussion).

The great importance of sensory information in the control and coordination of skilled voluntary movements is intuitively obvious and has been demonstrated in many clinical and experimental situations. It is clear that visually guided movements cannot be exercised when the visual feedback is eliminated; however, even less conspicuous sensory inputs appear to be essential. For instance, deafferentation of a limb produces motor deficits that are difficult to distinguish from those produced by major insult to the motor system itself. Sensory feedback is not only essential for the control of skilled movements, but the selective sensitivity of particular muscle groups and the postural adjustments that are important prerequisites for the initiation and successful completion of any movement are also directly determined by sensory feedback from the muscles themselves.

An analysis of the role of servomechanisms in movement. The coordination and adjustment of muscle tonus and phasic contractions of individual muscle groups in response to a kaleidoscope of ever-changing sensory input are best analyzed in terms of interlocking servomechanisms. The individual components of such a system are interconnected so that any discrepancy between the current state of a muscle and the intended outcome of the movement results in automatic, corrective action. Such a multiple-feedback system continues to operate, essentially automatically and without supervision from higher centers, until the intended action is completed. Once the integrative mechanisms of the brain have arrived at a master plan for the movement and initiate its inception, individual motor adjustments may essentially take care of themselves.

Many attempts have been made to apply this analogy to various homeostatic and neural processes (Hoagland, 1949; McCulloch, 1949), and several specific models which attempt to describe the interaction between sensory input and motor control in this fashion have been published (Brown and Campbell, 1948; Ruch, 1951a, b; Paillard, 1960). Some of the basic properties of such feedback systems and a schematic diagram of some of the suggested closed-loop feedback circuits in the central nervous system are shown in Figures 4.19 and 4.20.

Some of these servomechanisms are directly related to receptors in the muscle to be controlled and have therefore been called "output-informed"

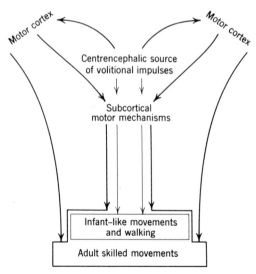

Fig. 4.18 Hypothetical diagram of the stream of nerve impulses producing adult skilled movements (in heavy lines). The impulses come from the centrencephalic area to each Rolandic motor cortex and from there descend to subcortical motor mechanisms and peripheral bulbospinal motor neurons. In fine lines are shown the course of nerve impulses producing voluntary action without involvement of the motor cortex. (From Paillard, 1960.)

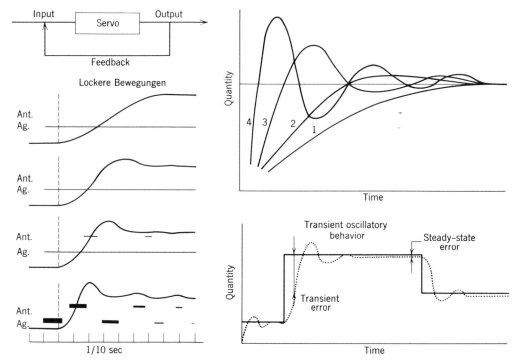

Fig. 4.19 *Upper left,* the principle of organization of a servomechanism unit. *Lower left,* distribution of the muscular activity in two antagonistic groups of muscles, the agonists (Ag.) and antagonists (Ant.), at four stages of increasing speed of movement. The electromyographic activity of each group is schematized by a line, the thickness of which varies with intensity. The mechanographic record shows the increasing tendency to oscillation when the speed of execution is increasing. The final position is achieved only by a transient oscillatory movement. (From Wachholder, 1928.)

Upper right, transient stability of a physical system with varying degrees of damping. Curves 2, 3, and 4 are progressively underdamped and show increasing degrees of oscillatory behavior. Curve 1 is overdamped and shows great stability at the expense of a long response time. A servomechanism shows a similar mode of functioning. Compare these curves with those shown at left. (From Brown and Campbell, 1948.)

Lower right, response of a human subject in a tracking experiment. The diagram illustrates the several kinds of errors observed between the response ($\cdots$) and the command (——) during a sudden change in the latter. Steady-state and transient errors, as well as transient oscillatory behavior, are also characteristic of the performance of a servomechanism. (From Ruch, 1951a.)

feedback circuits. Others interconnect integrative mechanisms in the central nervous system and receive only secondary (i.e., processed) information. These systems have been called "input-informed" circuits.

Many of the postural adjustments that constantly occur depend on output-informed feedback systems which respond automatically to sensory feedback from muscles, tendons, joints, and cutaneous receptors. The control of precise movements represents a special example of this relationship. The central reticulospinal and vestibulospinal control over the gamma efferents which bias the sensitivity of the spindle receptors is an excellent example of the influence of higher-order

feedback mechanisms on the lower systems. The gamma afferents return information to the cerebellum and other central integrative centers; they establish several higher-order feedback connections which interact to permit the precise control of individual muscles. The corticocerebellocortical system has been described as still a higher level of feedback integration of the input-informed variety. Ruch (1951a) has suggested that this loop may serve to amplify and extend in time the motor influences that arise from the cortex. In this scheme the cerebellum performs functions similar to those of the comparator of the electromechanical models. It "compares" the commands issued from the cerebral cortex with feedback from mus-

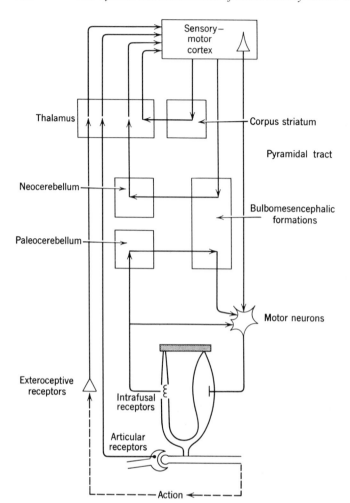

Fig. 4.20 Examples of output- and input-informed circuits which play a part in the control of motor command. (From Paillard, 1960.)

cle spindles and may arrive at compromise instructions which result in the cortical output as well as corrective action in the peripheral muscles.

Paillard (1960) has recently argued that this type of analysis, when applied to all levels of the nervous system, suggests a circular pattern of integration, as shown in Figure 4.21. This scheme of the nervous system conceptualizes the dynamic output of each state of neural integration (as well as that of the entire organism) as the end product of a continuous flow of neural impulses from sensory receptors to the effector organ via a number of closed feedback loops.

The acquisition of skilled movements. This type of analysis has some interesting implications for the initial development of skilled motor movements. The organism's repertoire of complex movements is very small at birth, not only because

the control over the many individual muscles is still missing, but also because many of the specific motor acts which characterize the adult are acquired rather than innate. All the individual muscular contractions which make up a skilled movement are undoubtedly functional at birth or soon thereafter. However, the spatiotemporal pattern of muscular activity which is peculiar to a skilled voluntary motion has to be learned, and this requires a series of progressive adjustments in the feedback systems just discussed. A sequence of successive approximations can usually be discerned in the course of motor learning; this process starts with unnecessarily massive and effortful motions, usually involving much if not all of the body, progresses through a number of stages of increasing refinement (these characterize the commonly observed plateaux of skilled motor performance), and eventually reaches a level of integration which is characterized by minimal effort and highly specialized responses from specific muscle groups. The most difficult aspect of this process is the disruption or inactivation of existing patterns of sensory-motor integration; these previously satisfied the requirements of the organism but now interfere with the establishment of the novel feedback systems. This interference is, of course, smallest in the infant, who is capable of acquiring remarkably complex patterns of motor coordination with relative ease. In the mature individual many well-established sensory-motor patterns exist, and it is quite difficult to "teach an old dog new tricks" (as anyone will testify who ever attempted to learn to ride a bicycle after the age of 25).

During the initial stage of acquiring a complex, skilled movement, man and most animals rely very heavily on feedback from the optic system. Corrections are made primarily as a result of visually perceived deviations of the limb or extremity from the target. During this stage all skilled movements are effortful, require great "concentration," and demand the attention of most if not all integrative systems. This concentration is shown by the often complete lack of response to stimuli of other modalities: the individual is oblivious to his environment. As learning progresses, more and more of the control is relegated to feedback circuits; these circuits rely on proprioceptive information from the muscles that are used in the act itself or support related postural responses. Each segment of the movement or muscle contraction thus becomes a signal for the next, initiating a sequence of events which can proceed essentially automatically (i.e., on the basis of local feedback systems rather than "higher" control) once the movement is initiated. Eventually information from the eye is used only to initiate the sequence, and the response itself is guided by local

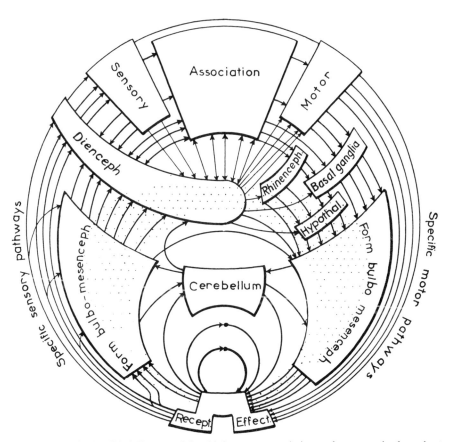

Fig. 4.21 Highly simplified diagram of the chief sensory, associative, and motor paths throughout the nervous system, illustrating the circular organization of the sensory-motor relations at any level. Only the output-informed circuits are represented. Some direct sensory connections to various higher structures have been intentionally omitted. (From Paillard, 1960.)

circuits. This partial automation undoubtedly accounts for the resistance of some overlearned response patterns (such as feeding, drinking, etc.) to central nervous system damage.

The acquisition of skilled movements can thus be discussed in terms of three basic processes: (1) the initial establishment of novel spatiotemporal combinations of reflexive, innate, or previously learned movements; (2) the inhibition or disruption of other innate or learned sensory-motor feedback systems which interfere with the performance of the novel response pattern; and (3) the transfer of feedback control to kinetic sensory mechanisms and progressively lower levels of integration.

THE ENDOCRINE SYSTEM

Complex organisms respond to changes in the environment not only by initiating or inhibiting muscular activity, but also by secreting a variety of chemical substances called hormones; these are essential, rate-limiting factors in many metabolic processes. Hormonal reactions have been neglected by psychophysiologists partly because the activity of the specific secretory organs is difficult to measure. This neglect is unfortunate because hormonal influences control many metabolic functions that determine the organism's response to specific environmental events. The influence is clearest, perhaps, for the sex hormones, which determine the sexual responsiveness of the organism and represent an important aspect of sexual motivation. However, many other subtler and less well-understood hormonal influences affect motivational mechanism and determine directly or indirectly the organism's response to its environment. Pituitary hormones, for instance, regulate diuretic water loss, carbohydrate metabolism, and related conversion mechanisms, thus significantly affecting the organism's need for food and water. Other endocrine glands secrete neurohumors which may act directly on the reticular formation and thus influence the overall state of arousal or reactivity to the environment. Many other hormonal mechanisms potentially affect the organism's response to specific environmental changes, and closer attention to such non-neural factors will contribute significantly to our understanding of psychophysiological relationships.

Introduction

Hormones are chemical substances secreted by endocrine glands. These glands form a reciprocating system which regulates the rates of many metabolic processes as well as the development and function of many tissues. Endocrine glands typically secrete hormones that not only affect certain metabolic processes, but also stimulate or inhibit other glands. These may, in turn, secrete hormones that affect the activity of the gland which started the cycle. The activity of the endocrine system is also closely linked functionally and developmentally to the nervous system. Certain endocrine glands can act independently of neural influences, but they are normally activated by neural mechanisms and may be considered nonspecific extensions of the nervous system.

Hormones may be defined more precisely as specific chemical substances which are manufactured and secreted by specific organs. They are discharged into the general circulation for transport to distant sites of action. Hormones regulate the *rates* of specific processes without contributing energy or matter to the tissues on which they act. Although we do not yet know the details of this process, hormones undoubtedly exert their effects by inhibiting or exciting enzyme systems. This means that hormones cannot initiate new processes but merely modulate existing functions—a distinction which tends to be forgotten frequently.

The production and secretion of specific hormones are affected not only by other hormones and neural influences, but also by general nutritional and metabolic conditions in the organism. Any change in the secretory activity of an endocrine gland affects the activity of other glands of the system. This interaction complicates the interpretation of experimental or clinical observations of the effects of artificial or pathologic increases or decreases of a specific hormone.

Before we turn to a consideration of particular hormone systems and their role in behavior, one last point should be emphasized. Although there may be exceptions to this rule, the endocrine system tends to act in a homeostatic fashion. The response of specific endocrine glands to neural or hormonal stimuli tends to return the organism to a resting state (i.e., a state that was interrupted by the introduction of the stimulus which activated the gland).

The Hypophysis

The hypophysis (or pituitary gland) has been called the master gland of the organism because it secretes a variety of hormones which significantly influence the activity of all other glands of the endocrine system. Embryologically, this gland is formed by two distinct types of tissue. The anterior, glandular portion derives from epithelial tissue called Rathke's pouch. The posterior, neural portion originates from neurectoderm from the floor of the third ventricle. In most species the gland rests in a depression of the sphenoid bone, the sella turcica, located beneath the ventral surface of the diencephalon.

The hypophysis is conveniently divided into a posterior lobe (*neurohypophysis*) and an anterior lobe (*adenohypophysis*). The neurohypophysis is in turn subdivided into three parts: the *median eminence of the tuber cinereum,* the *infundibular stem,* and the *neural lobe* proper. The adenohypophysis is subdivided into the *pars distalis* (the anterior lobe proper), the *pars tuberalis,* and the *pars intermedia.* The main secreting portion of the adenohypophysis is the pars distalis. The glandular (anterior) lobe and the neural (posterior) lobe of the hypophysis are, in effect, two independent organs. No functional relationship between the two aspects of the gland have yet been established, and we shall treat them separately in our discussion (see Heller, 1957; Harris, 1955).

The adenohypophysis. This important portion of the pituitary gland has intrigued scientists for many centuries. The secretory action of the anterior lobe, particularly the pars distalis, is under neural control, and its activity is modulated by environmental events. We still do not know precisely how this neural control is exercised, since the adenohypophysis has few, if any, neural innervations. It has been suggested that the adenohypophysis may (1) be under the control of the peripheral autonomic nervous system via sympathetic fibers from the facial nerves; (2) have a direct innervation from the base of the brain via the stalk of the gland; or (3) be activated by chemical means through either the systemic blood supply of the gland or the hypophyseal portal blood supply.

Although many experimenters have reported neural components in the anterior lobe, other investigations by Rasmussen (1938) and Green (1954) fail to corroborate these findings. Harris (1960) suggests in an excellent review of this material that the earlier positive results may be attributed to the use of silver techniques which not only stain neurons but may also impregnate connective tissue. These and functional considerations suggest that the activity of the anterior lobe is not under direct neural control but may be activated primarily, if not solely, by chemical

means. Since the systemic blood supply of the adenohypophysis is extremely variable across species (whereas the functions of this gland remain remarkably stable), recent workers have tended to agree that the portal blood supply which is nearly identical over species must be the connecting link between the gland and the nervous system. The blood in these portal vessels has been shown to flow from the median eminence of the tuber cinereum to the pars distalis of the pituitary gland. It has been suggested that the well-known influence of hypothalamic neurons on the activity of this gland may be exercised by the liberation of some neurohumoral substance into the capillaries of the hypothalamic blood supply; the substance is then transported to the pars distalis via the portal blood supply. No direct evidence for this suggestion is available as yet, but it appears to be the best working hypothesis at the moment (Ingram, 1956) (see Figure 4.22).

Hormones of the adenohypophysis. The anterior lobe of the pituitary gland manufactures and secretes six major hormonal substances. Four of these, the two gonadotrophins, adrenotrophin, and thyrotrophin, control the activity of other endocrine glands. The remaining two hormones, the lactogenic hormone and the growth hormone, act primarily on metabolic processes, although they too effect other glands. The trophic hormones are essential to the morphological development and normal functioning of their respective target glands. The secretion of these hormones tends to vary with the physiological state of the organism (see Sawyer, 1961, for extensive review). The gonadotrophins act directly on the gonads and thus influence sexual behavior (see Young, 1961; Villee, 1961; Velardo, 1958). The *follicle-stimulating hormone* (FSH) induces the development of ovarian follicles in the female and stimulates the growth of the seminiferous tubules and the maintenance of spermatogenesis in the male. The second gonadotrophin has been called *luteinizing hormone* (LH) or *interstitial-cell-stimulating hormone* (ICSH). In the female, this hormone acts synergistically with the follicle-stimulating hormone to regulate the final stages of follicular development, ovulation, and *estrogen* secretion. It also induces luteinization and the secretion of the gonadal hormone *progesterone.* In the male, LH (or ICSH) stimulates the development of the interstitial tissues of the testes and the secretion of *androgen,* the male gonadal hormone.

Thyrotrophin and *adrenocorticotrophin* (ACTH) are essential for the normal growth and secretory

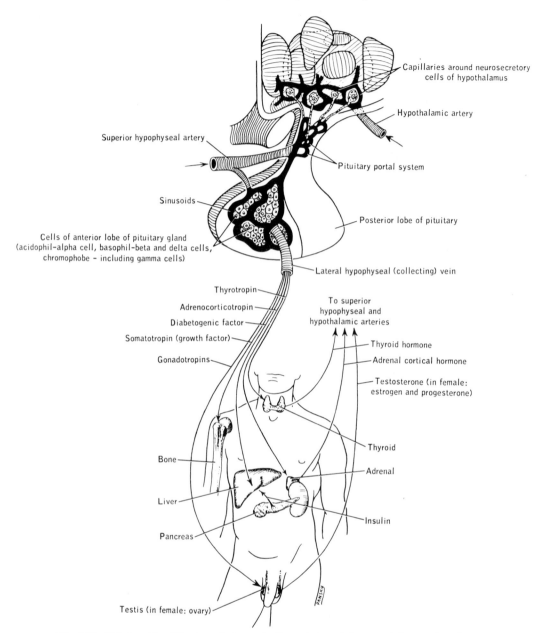

Fig. 4.22   Relationship of the hypothalamus to the anterior pituitary and thus to the other endocrines, the liver, and the bone marrow. (From House and Pansky, 1960.)

function of the thyroid and adrenal glands, respectively. Since we will discuss these organs in some detail later in this chapter, the trophic action of the pituitary hormones need not be described here.

The *lactogenic hormone* (*prolactin*) is responsible for the initiation and maintenance of lactation by mammary glands that have been primed for

action by the previous secretion of ovarian hormones (Linzell, 1959). The lactogenic hormone also affects the ovaries by aiding in the maintenance of the corpora lutea; it has also been called *luteotrophin*.

The *growth hormone* (*somatotrophin*) accelerates the growth of bones and tissues in both young and adult organisms. Chronic treatment with this hormone produces gigantism. Following hypophysectomy, the organism fails to develop properly, and a condition of hypophyseal dwarfism appears (Smith et al., 1955).

In addition to these specific effects, a variety of general metabolic processes depend on some aspect of anterior pituitary secretion. Among the more important symptoms of anterior pituitary damage are a disturbance of the carbohydrate metabolism (commonly in the form of hypoglycemia) and an increased utilization of carbohydrates and fats. Some of the metabolic reactions may be caused by indirect effects on the adrenal cortex. It has been suggested that the various metabolic effects of pituitary hormones may have in common a direction of action which is opposite to that of insulin.

The neurohypophysis. The posterior lobe of the pituitary gland, in contrast to the anterior portion, is richly innervated, primarily by the *supraopticohypophyseal tract* which originates from the paraventricular and supraoptic nuclei of the hypothalamus. If this tract is transected, the pars nervosa of the hypophysis shows pronounced atrophic changes and becomes largely nonfunctional. Conversely, if the posterior lobe is removed, degenerative changes are seen in the supraoptic and paraventricular nuclei (see Figure 4.23).

The secretory activity of the neurohypophysis appears to be completely under neural control, but there is some question about how this control is exercised. The most likely explanation of the intimate hypothalamo-neurohypophyseal relationship is provided by the *neurosecretory theory*. This hypothesis proposes that the hormones of the posterior pituitary are manufactured by cells in the supraoptic and paraventricular nuclei of the hypothalamus. The hormones are transported down the axons of the hypothalamic neurons and are *stored* in the neurohypophysis. They are liberated into the blood system upon the arrival of *neural* impulses that travel along the same axons which are responsible for the transport of the hormonal substances from the hypothalamus to the pituitary. According to this view, the fibers of the supraopticohypophyseal tract serve the dual function of neural secretomotor innervation and neurosecretory transport system (see Harris, 1960, for further details of this mechanism).

Hormones of the neurohypophysis. Three types of hormonal factors of neurohypophyseal origin

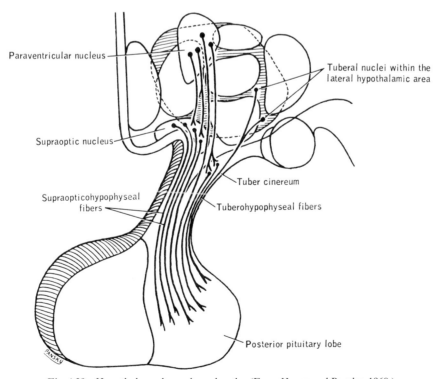

Fig. 4.23 Hypothalamo-hypophyseal paths. (From House and Pansky, 1960.)

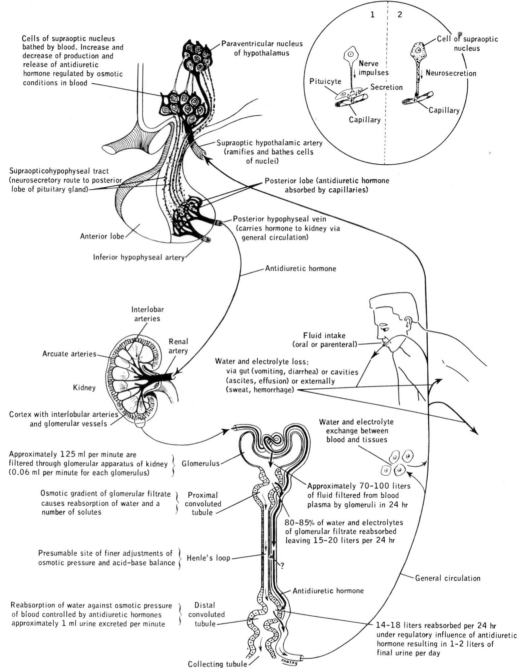

Cells of supraoptic nucleus bathed by blood. Increase and decrease of production and release of antidiuretic hormone regulated by osmotic conditions in blood

Paraventricular nucleus of hypothalamus

1 | 2

Nerve impulses

Cell of supraoptic nucleus

Pituicyte

Secretion

Neurosecretion

Capillary

Capillary

Supraoptic hypothalamic artery (ramifies and bathes cells of nuclei)

Supraopticohypophyseal tract (neurosecretory route to posterior lobe of pituitary gland)

Posterior lobe (antidiuretic hormone absorbed by capillaries)

Anterior lobe

Posterior hypophyseal vein (carries hormone to kidney via general circulation)

Inferior hypophyseal artery

Antidiuretic hormone

Interlobar arteries

Renal artery

Fluid intake (oral or parenteral)

Arcuate arteries

Water and electrolyte loss: via gut (vomiting, diarrhea) or cavities (ascites, effusion) or externally (sweat, hemorrhage)

Kidney

Cortex with interlobular arteries and glomerular vessels

Water and electrolyte exchange between blood and tissues

Approximately 125 ml per minute are filtered through glomerular apparatus of kidney (0.06 ml per minute for each glomerulus)

Glomerulus

Approximately 70–100 liters of fluid filtered from blood plasma by glomeruli in 24 hr

Osmotic gradient of glomerular filtrate causes reabsorption of water and a number of solutes

Proximal convoluted tubule

80–85% of water and electrolytes of glomerular filtrate reabsorbed leaving 15–20 liters per 24 hr

Presumable site of finer adjustments of osmotic pressure and acid-base balance

Henle's loop

?

General circulation

Antidiuretic hormone

Reabsorption of water against osmotic pressure of blood controlled by antidiuretic hormones approximately 1 ml urine excreted per minute

Distal convoluted tubule

14–18 liters reabsorbed per 24 hr under regulatory influence of antidiuretic hormone resulting in 1–2 liters of final urine per day

Collecting tubule

PANSKY

Fig. 4.24 Control of water excretion and water balance. Theories of the origin of the antidiuretic hormone. 1, pituicytes release the antidiuretic hormone under nervous influence. 2, hormone produced as a neurosecretion by cells in the supraoptic nucleus and conducted by nerve fibers to the posterior lobe for storage or absorption. (From House and Pansky, 1960.)

have been isolated. *Antidiuretic hormone* (ADH) acts on the renal tubules to regulate the concentration of urine and thus contributes to the regulation of the organism's fluid balance. Removal of the posterior lobe results in the constant secretion of very dilute urine, a condition called polyuria. The secretion of ADH is under the control of hypothalamic neurons which appear to be selectively sensitive to the osmolarity of the hypothalamic blood supply. As the osmotic pressure rises, more ADH is secreted, and the dilution of the urine is decreased so that as much water is retained in the body as is commensurate with the excretory needs of the organism. When the fluid balance of the body becomes positive and the osmotic pressure of the blood drops, less ADH is secreted and urinary dilution increases (Thorn, 1958) (see Figure 4.24).

The second neurohypophyseal hormone, *oxytocin*, acts primarily on the lactating breast and the uterus. The release of oxytocin is elicited by stimulation of the female reproductive organs and the nipples of the breast. This hormone is responsible for the expulsion of milk from the mammary glands and plays an important role in parturition and sperm transport in the uterus (Berde, 1961). The third and least understood component of neurohypophyseal origin is *vasopressin*, a hormone which directly or indirectly affects peripheral vasomotor activity. Injections of posterior pituitary extract produce arteriolar and capillary constriction and thus elevate blood pressure (see Figure 4.25).

The Adrenals

The adrenal glands, like the pituitary, are functionally and morphologically two distinct organs. The larger glandular portion (the adrenal cortex) arises from urogenital mesoderm and surrounds the neural portion (the adrenal medulla) in the adult mammal. The medullary tissue develops from sympathetic ganglia and remains intimately connected with the sympathetic nervous system via the splanchnic nerve (Moon, 1961).

The *adrenal cortex* is composed of three distinct layers of cells which contain large amounts of fats and ascorbic acid (see Figure 4.26). These cells show a remarkable power of regeneration; even small remnants of this gland may regenerate until it is, at least functionally, replaced. Secretions from the adrenal cortex are essential to a variety of metabolic processes. Complete removal of the gland leads to death within 5 to 15 days unless substitution therapy is instituted. The principal symptoms observed following adrenocortical removal are lack of appetite, nausea, diarrhea, asthenia, hypoglycemia, hemoconcentration, and renal failure. In man, a similar syndrome of adrenal insufficiency called Addison's disease occurs frequently. An excessive excretion of sodium and chloride ions by the kidney is responsible for a movement of water into the cells and a consequent diminuition of extracellular fluids. Adrenalectomized animals are unable to draw on stored body proteins and cannot maintain a normal carbohydrate metabolism. This inability is responsible

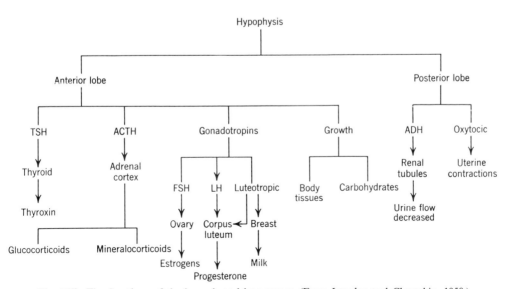

Fig. 4.25 The functions of the hypophyseal horomones. (From Langley and Cheraskin, 1958.)

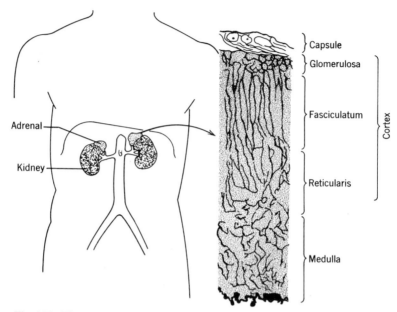

Fig. 4.26 The anatomy of the adrenal glands. (From Langley and Cheraskin, 1958.)

for a precipitous drop in blood sugar during fasting (see Figure 4.27).

These divergent effects are not caused by the secretion of a few distinct hormones. A variety of different hormonal substances have been isolated from the adrenal cortex, and more may be discovered as chemical techniques improve. So far, 28 different steroids that appear to have specific hormonal functions have been isolated. (See Figure 4.28 for a structural analysis of some important steroids.) Even when all of these have been extracted from adrenal cortex extract, an *amorphous* fraction which contains one or more

additional active substances of unknown chemical structure remains. Among the active steroids that have been isolated are several *androgenic* substances (*adrenosterone, estrone, progesterone*) which affect sexual behavior (Wolstenholme and O'Connor, 1960). The secretory functions of the adrenal cortex are under the exclusive control of the adrenotrophic hormone (ACTH) which is liberated by the adenohypophysis (see Figure 4.29).

The *adrenal medulla* is made up of modified sympathetic ganglion cells which secrete *epinephrine* (adrenalin) and *norepinephrine* (noradrenaline)

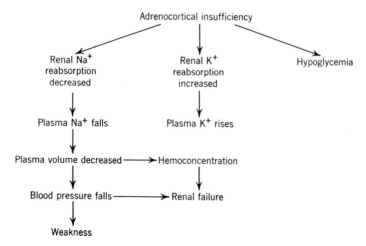

Fig. 4.27 The influence of adrenal insufficiency on electrolyte balance. (From Langley and Cheraskin, 1958.)

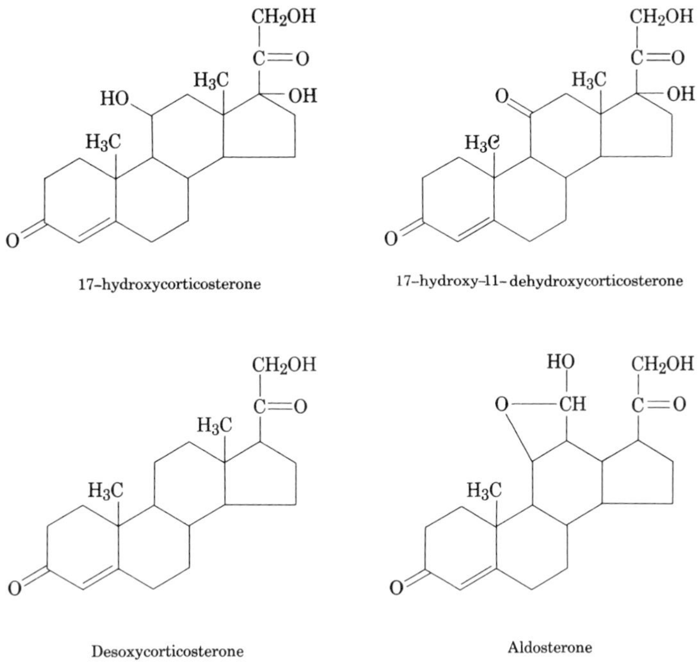

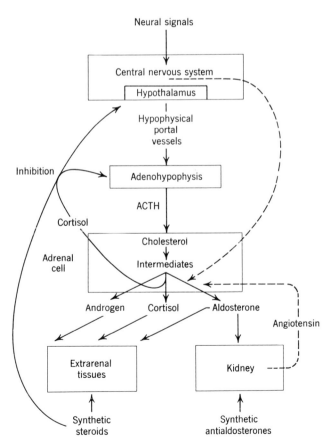

Fig. 4.28 The structural formulas of adrenal steroids. (From Langley and Cheraskin, 1958.)

17-hydroxycorticosterone

17-hydroxy-11-dehydroxycorticosterone

Desoxycorticosterone

Aldosterone

Fig. 4.29 Neuroendocrine control of the adrenal cortical function. (From J. Tepperman, *Metabolic and endocrine physiology.* Copyright 1962 by Year Book Medical Publications, Inc. Used by permission of Year Book Medical Publishers.)

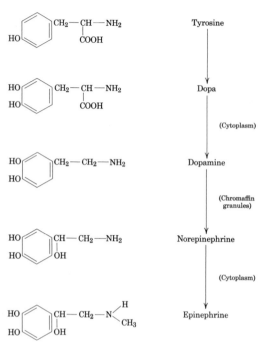

Fig. 4.30 Synthesis of catecholamine hormones. (From J. Tepperman, *Metabolic and endocrine physiology.* Copyright 1962 by Year Book Medical Publications, Inc. Used by permission of Year Book Medical Publishers.)

(see Figure 4.30). The secretory organs are connected with preganglionic fibers of the sympathetic nervous system, and their activity seems to be controlled completely via these neural pathways. The level of epinephrine secretion varies as a function of the general level of stimulation of the nervous system. Very little or none is secreted under basal conditions (sleep), but even relatively mild stimulation (such as that produced by walking) produces a marked secretory activity. Very strong stimuli, particularly if prolonged, painful, or "emotional," flood the entire organism with catecholamines (Vane et al., 1960).

Norepinephrine acts as the transmitter agent for postganglionic sympathetic impulses. Circulating epinephrine therefore produces effects that are identical to general sympathetic neural discharge. An intact nerve supply is not essential to this action of epinephrine, suggesting that it exerts its effects directly on the effector cells. Epinephrine generally has a vasoconstrictor action, although moderate doses may produce dilatation of the vessels in skeletal and cardiac muscles. It has a powerful stimulating effect on the myocardium, increasing both the frequency and force of contractions. As a direct result of its vasomotor and cardiomuscular effects, epinephrine tends to raise blood pressure, pulse rate, and cardiac output. The hormone produces variable effects on smooth muscles (usually in the direction of contraction) and increases the rate of glycogenolysis in liver and muscle, producing hyperglycemia. It also stimulates the secretion of adrenotrophin, thyrotrophin, and gonadotrophin by the adenohypophysis, thereby indirectly extending its effects to other metabolic processes.

The Pancreas

The pancreas secretes a single hormonal substance called *insulin*, but this agent is so essential to many metabolic processes that the pancreas has been studied extensively. Only about 2% of the pancreatic cells (found in the islets of Langerhans) are secretory organs (see Figure 4.31). A lack of pancreatic secretion produces polyuria, glycosuria, ketonuria, marked wasting of the body, and death in a comatose state. These are also the symptoms of diabetes mellitus, a rather common disorder caused by pancreatic hypofunction. This condition was almost invariably fatal until the pancreatic hormone was synthesized.

Insulin is a protein that is rapidly inactivated by digestive enzymes. Therefore, it is usually ad-

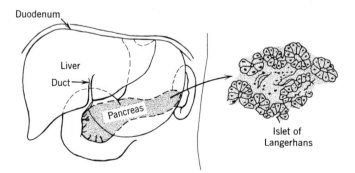

Fig. 4.31 Anatomy of the pancreas. (From Langley and Cheraskin, 1958.)

ministered in combination with *protamine* or *globin*, with which it forms relatively insoluble complexes. Of the many insulin targets, perhaps most important are carbohydrate and fat metabolism. Insulin-deficient organisms show severe hyperglycemia and glycosuria. Administered carbohydrates are not as readily utilized as in the normal animal, and carbohydrate combustion is severely reduced or absent. The formation of lipids from carbohydrates is impaired, and fat catabolism appears increased. More generally, there is a decrease in the organism's ability to utilize carbohydrates for oxidative purposes, fat formation, and glycogen storage. Fats and proteins are used in greater quantities to supply the needed energy, severely depleting the fat and protein stores (Williams, 1960) (see Figure 4.32).

The normal rate of insulin secretion varies as a function of carbohydrate intake and has been shown to be regulated by the concentration of glucose in the blood.

The Thyroid Gland

In most species the thyroid gland consists of two lobes located on either side of the trachea (see Figure 4.33). Thyroid tissue derives from the pharyngeal floor and consists of small follicles filled with a gelatinous substance called thyroid colloid. The thyroid is innervated extensively by postganglionic fibers from the cervical ganglia of the sympathetic chain and by fibers traveling with the vagus (X) nerve. This innervation is not essential to thyroid function, but it indirectly affects secretory activity by controlling the circulation of blood through the gland (Hamolsky and Freedberg, 1960).

The thyroid gland contains an extraordinarily high concentration of *iodine* which is normally stored in organic combination with thyroglobulin, the protein of the colloid. Two iodine-containing substances can be isolated from thyroid tissue. Most of the iodine occurs in the form of *diio-*

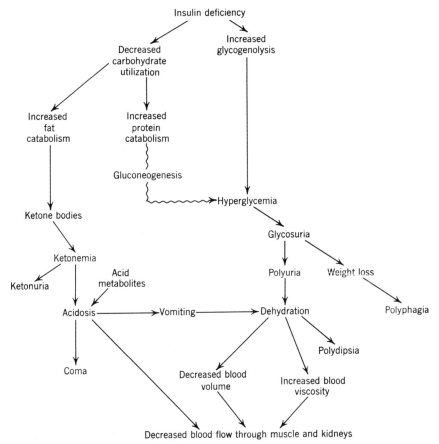

Fig. 4.32 Sequence of events resulting from insulin deficiency. (From Langley and Cheraskin, 1958.)

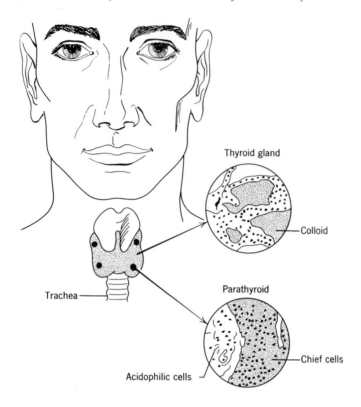

Fig. 4.33 The anatomy of the thyroid and parathyroid glands. (From Langley and Cheraskin, 1958.)

dotyrosine which has little, if any, hormonal action. Roughly 25% of the available iodine is found in the form of *thyroxin*, the major hormone of the thyroid gland (Rawson, 1960) (see Figure 4.34).

The presence of thyroid tissue is not essential to survival, but severe metabolic disturbances result from thyroxin deficiency. In young organisms, a partial inhibition of growth and development is observed; in man, this leads to a condition known as *cretinism,* characterized by dwarfism and severe mental deficiency. In the adult organism, thyroxin deficiency produces a marked slowing of the basal metabolic rate, a reduction of

pulse rate, cardiac output, and circulation, as well as a general hyporeactivity to external stimulation. Clinically even more prevalent is a hyperthyroid condition that is characterized by an elevated metabolic rate, diuresis, depletion of liver glycogens, and a marked hypersensitivity of the autonomic nervous system which is reflected in nervousness and emotional hyperreactivity.

The activity of the thyroid gland is almost entirely determined by the secretion of thyrotrophic hormone by the anterior pituitary gland. Both the formation and secretion of thyroxin are affected by this hormone.

The Parathyroid Glands

A variable number (commonly two pairs) of small glands are usually found in the immediate vicinity of the thyroid glands. Parathyroid tissue resembles that of the thyroid but is devoid of colloid. The "parathyroid hormone" has not yet been chemically identified, but an extract can be prepared from parathyroid tissue which counteracts apparently all the symptoms of hypoparathyroid function. Although this extract may contain several discrete substances, it is commonly assumed that there is only one active parathyroid hormone because the principal action

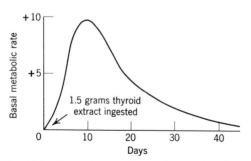

Fig. 4.34 The delayed effects of thyroxin. (From Langley and Cheraskin, 1958.)

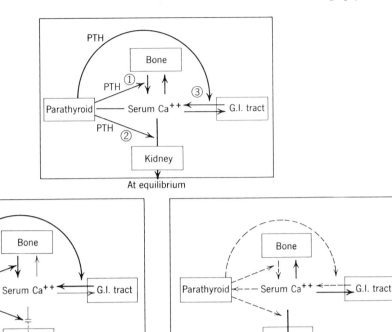

Fig. 4.35 Serum calcium ion homeostasis and the parathyroid glands. (From J. Tepperman, *Metabolic and endocrine physiology.* Copyright 1962 by Year Book Medical Publications, Inc. Used by permission of Year Book Medical Publishers.)

of the parathyroid extract concerns only the very closely related metabolisms of calcium and phosphorus (see Figure 4.35). The product of the concentrations of these ions is always constant, and a strict reciprocal relationship exists between them in pure solutions. Such a precise correspond- ence does not obtain in body fluids because of the presence of other salts, but a change in the concentration of one of these ions is generally followed by an inverse change in the other (Greep and Talmage, 1960).

When the parathyroid hormone is absent, the

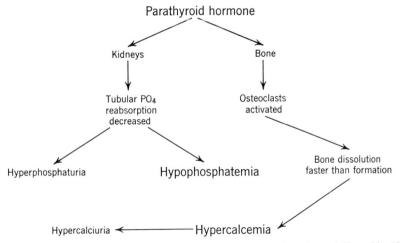

Fig. 4.36 The mechanism of parathyroid hormone action. (From Langley and Cheraskin, 1958.)

serum calcium concentration falls with a consequent rise in serum phosphate levels (see Figure
4.36). The urinary excretion of both salts is diminished. The low calcium level produces an extreme hyperirritability of the nervous system and
leads to tetany, convulsion, and death. An acute
overdosage of the hormone, on the other hand,
produces a shock-like state and death from circulatory collapse caused, at least in part, by the
ensuing phosphaturia.

The secretory activity of the parathyroid glands
is governed by the calcium concentration of the
blood, but no intermediary mechanism has yet
been discovered. Neither direct neural control nor
pituitary trophins have been established to date
(Rasmussen, 1961).

BIBLIOGRAPHY

Adrian, E. D., & Moruzzi, G. Impulses in the pyramidal tract. *J. Physiol. (London)*, 1939, **97**, 153–
199.

Barker, D. The innervation of the muscle spindles.
Quart. J. micr. Sci., 1948, **89**, 143–186.

Barnard, J. W., & Woolsey, C. N. A study of localization
in the corticospinal tracts of monkey and cat. *J.
comp. Neurol.*, 1956, **105**, 25–50.

Barron, D. H. The results of unilateral pyramidal section in the rat. *J. comp. Neurol.*, 1934, **60**, 45–56.

Berde, B. *Recent progress in oxytocin research.* Springfield, Ill.: Thomas, 1961.

Bernhard, C. G., & Bohm, E. Cortical representation
of the cortico-motoneuronal system in monkeys.
Experientia, 1954, **10**, 312–315.

Bieber, I., & Fulton, J. F. Relation of the cerebral cortex
to the grasp reflex and to postural and righting
reflexes. *Arch. Neurol. Psychiat. (Chicago)*, 1938, **39**,
433–454.

Bishop, G. M., Clare, M. H., & Price, J. Patterns of
tremor in normal and pathological conditions.
J. appl. Physiol., 1948, **1**, 123–147.

Bremer, F. Contribution à l'étude de la physiologie du
cerevelet la fonction inhibitrice du paléo-cere-
bellum. *Arch. int. Physiol.*, 1922a, **19**, 189–226.

Bremer, F. La strychnine et les phénomènes d'inhibition.
C. R. Soc. Biol. (Paris), 1922b, **87**, 1055–1057.

Bremer, F. *Traité de physiologie normale et pathologique.*
R. LeCervelet, G. H. Roger, & L. Binet, Eds. Paris:
Masson, 1935.

Bremer, F. Nouvelles recherches sur le mécanisme du
sommeil. *C. R. Soc. Biol. (Paris)*, 1936a, **122**,
460–463.

Bremer, F. Activité electrique du cortex cérébral dans
les états de sommeil et de veille chez le chat. *C. R.
Soc. Biol. (Paris)*, 1936b, **122**, 464–467.

Brookhart, J. M. Study of cortico-spinal activation of
motor neurons. *Res. Publ., Ass. Res. nerv. ment.
Dis.*, 1952, **30**, 157–173.

Brown, G. S., & Campbell, D. S. *Principles of servomechanisms.* New York: Wiley, 1948.

Buchwald, N. A., & Ling, S. G. Behavioral response to
intracerebral administrations of carbachol. *Fed.
Proc.*, 1965, **24**, 523.

Buchwald, N. A., Wyers, E. J., Okuma, T., & Heuser, G.
The "caudate-spindle." I: Electrophysiological
properties. *EEG clin. Neurophysiol.*, 1961a, **13**,
509–513.

Buchwald, N. A., Heuser, G., Wyers, E. J., & Lauprecht,
C. W. The "caudate-spindle." III: Inhibition by
high frequency stimulation of subcortical structures. *EEG clin. Neurophysiol.*, 1961b, **13**, 525–530.

Buchwald, N. A., Wyers, E. J., Lauprecht, C. W., &
Heuser, G. The "caudate-spindle." IV: A behavioral index of caudate-induced inhibition. *EEG
clin. Neurophysiol.*, 1961c, **13**, 531–537.

Bucy, P. C. *The precentral motor cortex* (2nd ed.).
Urbana: Univ. of Illinois Press, 1949.

Canestrari, R., Crepax, P., & Machne, X. Modifications
de l'activité électrique du gyrus sygmoidien du
chien et du chat par application de strychnine sur
le cortex néocérébelleux. *Arch. Psicol. Neurol.
Psichiat.*, 1955, **16**, 19–31.

Carpenter, M. B., & Carpenter, C. S. Analysis of somatotopic relations of the corpus Luysi in man and
monkey. *J. comp. Neurol.*, 1951, **95**, 349–370.

Carrea, R. M. E., & Mettler, F. A. Physiological consequences following extensive removals of the cerebellar cortex and deep cerebellar nuclei and effect
of secondary cerebral ablations in the primate.
J. comp. Neurol., 1947, **87**, 169–288.

Chambers, W. W., & Sprague, J. M. Functional localization in cerebellum. *A.M.A. Arch. Neurol. Psychiat.*, 1955a, **74**, 653–680.

Chambers, W. W., & Sprague, J. M. Functional localization in the cerebellum. *J. comp. Neurol.*, 1955b,
103, 105–129.

Chauveau, B. On the sensorimotor nerve-circuit of
muscles. *Brain*, 1891, **14**, 145–178.

Chiray, E., Foix, C., & Nicolesco, J. Hémitremblement
du type de la sclérose en plaques, par lésion rubro-
thalamo sous-thalamique. Syndrome de la région
supéro-externe du noyan rouge, avec attiente
silencieuse ou non du thalamus. *Rev. neurol.*, 1923,
39, 305–310.

Clark, S. L. Motor seizures accompanying small cerebellar lesions in cats. *J. comp. Neurol.*, 1939a, **71**,
41–57.

Clark, S. L. Responses following electrical stimulation
of the cerebellar cortex in the normal cat. *J. Neurophysiol.*, 1939b, **2**, 19–35.

Clark, S. L., & Ward, J. W. The electroencephalogram in
cerebellar seizures. *EEG clin. Neurophysiol.*, 1949,
1, 299–304.

Clark, S. L., & Ward, J. W. Observations on the mechanism of experimental cerebellar seizures. *J. Neurophysiol.*, 1952, **15**, 221–234.

Clemmesen, S. Some studies on muscle tone. *Proc. roy. Soc. Med.*, 1951, **44**, 637–646.

Crepax, P., & Fadiga, E. La stimolazione chimica della corteccia cerebrale di gatto. *Arch. Sci. biol.*, 1956, **40**, 66–80.

Denny-Brown, D. E. The histological features of striped muscle in relation to its functional activity. *Proc. roy. Soc. (London)*, B, 1929, **104**, 371–411.

Denny-Brown, D. E. Interpretation of the electromyogram. *A.M.A. Arch. Neurol. Psychiat.*, 1949, **61**, 99–128.

DeVito, R. V., Brusa, A., & Arduini, A. Cerebellar and vestibular influences on Deitersian units. *J. Neurophysiol.*, 1956, **19**, 241–253.

Dondey, M., & Snider, R. S. Slow potential shifts following cerebellar stimulation. *EEG clin. Neurophysiol.*, 1955, **7**, 265–272.

Dow, R. S. Effect of lesions in the vestibular part of the cerebellum in primates. *A.M.A. Arch. Neurol. Psychiat.*, 1938a, **40**, 500–520.

Dow, R. S. The electrical activity of the cerebellum and its functional significance. *J. Physiol. (London)*, 1938b, **94**, 67–86.

Dusser de Barenne, J. *Handbuch der Neurologie.* O. Bumke & O. Foerster, Eds. Berlin: Springer, 1937.

Eccles, J. C., Eccles, M., & Lundberg, A. The convergence of monosynaptic excitatory afferents onto many different species of alpha motoneurones. *J. Physiol. (London)*, 1957, **137**, 22–50.

Eldred, E. Some brain structures which influence muscle spindles. *Fed. Proc.*, 1955, **14**, 43.

Eldred, E. Posture and locomotion. In *Handbook of physiology. Vol. II.* J. Field, H. W. Magoun, & V. E. Hall, Eds. Baltimore: Williams and Wilkins, 1960.

Forman, D., & Ward, J. W. Responses to electrical stimulation of caudate nucleus in cats in chronic experiments. *J. Neurophysiol.*, 1957, **20**, 230–244.

Fulton, J. F., & Connor, G. Physiological basis of three major cerebellar syndromes. *Trans. Amer. neurol. Ass.*, 1939, **65**, 53–57.

Fulton, J. F., & Dow, R. S. Cerebellum: summary of functional localization. *Yale J. Biol. Med.*, 1937, **10**, 89–119.

Fulton, J. F., & Dow, R. S. Postural neck reflexes in the labyrinthectomized monkey and their effect on the grasp reflex. *J. Neurophysiol.*, 1938, **1**, 455–462.

Granit, R. *Receptors and sensory perception.* New Haven, Conn.: Yale Univ. Press, 1955.

Granit, R., & Kaada, B. Influence of stimulation of central nervous structures on muscle spindles in cat. *Acta physiol. scand.*, 1952, **27**, 130–160.

Granit, R., Job, C., & Kaada, B. Activation of muscle spindles in pinna reflex. *Acta physiol. scand.*, 1952, **27**, 161–168.

Green, J. D. The comparative anatomy of the hypophysis with special reference to its blood supply and innervation. *Amer. J. Anat.*, 1951, **88**, 225–290.

Green, J. D. Electrical activity in the hypothalamus and hippocampus of conscious rabbits. *Anat. Rec.*, 1954, **118**, 304.

Greep, R. O., & Talmage, R. V. *The parathyroids.* Springfield, Ill.: Thomas, 1960.

Grossman, S. P., Peters, R. H., Freedman, P. E., & Willer, H. I., Behavioral effects of cholinergic stimulation of the thalamic reticular formation. *J. comp. physiol. Psychol.*, 1965, **59**, 57–65.

Hamolsky, M. W., & Freedberg, A. S. The thyroid gland. *New Engl. J. Med.*, 1960, **262**, 23–28, 70–78, 129–137.

Hampson, J. L., Harrison, C. R., & Woolsey, C. N. Cerebrocerebellar projections and somatotopic localization of motor function in cerebellum. *Res. Publ., Ass. Res. nerv. ment. Dis.*, 1952, **30**, 299–316.

Hanbery, J., & Jasper, H. H. Independence of diffuse thalamocortical projection system shown by specific nuclear destructions. *J. Neurophysiol.*, 1953, **16**, 252–271.

Harris, G. W. *Neural control of the pituitary gland.* London: Edward Arnold, 1955.

Harris, G. W. Central control of pituitary secretion. In *Handbook of physiology. Vol. II.* J. Field, H. W. Magoun, & V. E. Hall, Eds. Baltimore: Williams and Wilkins, 1960.

Hassler, R. Zur Pathologie der Paralysis agitans und des postenzephalitischen Parkinsonismus. *J. Psychol. Neurol.*, 1938, **48**, 387–476.

Hassler, R. Zur pathologischen Anatomie des senilen und des parkistonistischen Tremor. *J. Psychol. Neurol.*, 1939, **49**, 193–230.

Hassler, R. *Symposium de tálamo.* Sixth Latin-American Congress of Neurocirculation. 1955a, III, 754.

Hassler, R. The pathological basis of tremor and parkinsonism. *Excerpta med.* Sect. 8. *Neurol. Psychiat.*, 1955b, **8**, 769.

Hassler, R. Die extrapyramidalen Rindensysteme und die zentrale Regelung der Motorik. *Dtsch. Z. Nervenheilk.* 1956a, **175**, 233–258.

Hassler, R. Die zentralen Apparate der Wendebewegungen I: Ipsiversive Wendungen durch Reizung einer direkten vestibulo-thalamischen Bahn im Hirnstamm der Katze. *Arch. Psychiat.*, 1956b, **194**, 456–481.

Hassler, R. *Abstract of communication of the 20th international physiological congress*, 1956c, **405**, 1004.

Heath, R. G., & Hodes, R. S. Induction of sleep by stimulation of caudate nucleus in macaque rhesus and man. *Trans. Amer. Neurol. Ass.*, 1952, **77**, 204–210.

Heller, H. *The neurohypophysis.* New York: Academic Press, 1957.

Hess, R., Jr., Koella, W. P., & Akert, K. Cortical and subcortical recordings in natural and artificially induced sleep in cats. *EEG clin. Neurophysiol.*, 1953, **5**, 75–90.

Hess, W. R. Zwischenhirn und Motorik. *Helv. physiol. pharmacol. Acta*, 1948, Suppl. 5 (entire issue).

Hess, W. R. *Das Zwischenhirn: Syndrome, Lokalizationen, Funktionen.* Basel: Schwabe, 1949.

Hess, W. R. *Das Zwischenhirn* (2nd ed.). Basel: Schwabe, 1954a.

Hess, W. R. *Diencephalon, autonomic and extrapyramidal functions.* New York: Grune and Stratton, 1954b.

Heuser, G., Buchwald, N. A., & Wyers, E. J. The "caudate-spindle." II: Facilitatory and inhibitory caudate-cortical pathways. *EEG clin. Neurophysiol.,* 1961, **13**, 519–524.

Hoagland, H. Rhythmic behavior of the nervous system. *Science,* 1949, **109**, 157–164.

Hodes, R. S., Peacock, S. M., & Heath, R. G. Influence of the forebrain on somato-motor activity. *J. comp. Neurol.,* 1951, **94**, 381–408.

Hodes, R. S., Heath, R. G., & Hendley, C. D. Cortical and subcortical electrical activity in sleep. *Trans. Amer. Neurol. Ass.,* 1952, **77**, 201–203.

Hoeffer, P. F. A. Innervation and "tonus" of striated muscle in man. *A.M.A. Arch. Neurol. Psychiat.,* 1941, **46**, 947–972.

House, E. L., & Pansky, B. *Neuroanatomy.* New York: McGraw-Hill, 1960.

Hunt, C. C. The reflex activity of mammalian small nerve fibers. *J. Physiol. (London),* 1951, **115**, 456.

Hunt, C. C., & Kuffler, S. W. Further study of efferent small-nerve fibres to mammalian muscle spindles. Multiple spindle innervation and activity during contraction. *J. Physiol. (London),* 1951a, **113**, 283–297.

Hunt, C. C., & Kuffler, S. W. Stretch receptor discharges during muscle contraction. *J. Physiol. (London),* 1951b, **113**, 298–315.

Hunt, C. C., & Kuffler, S. W. Motor innervation of skeletal muscle: multiple innervation of individual muscle fibres and motor unit function. *J. Physiol. (London),* 1954, **126**, 293–303.

Hunt, C. C., & Paintal, A. S. Spinal reflex regulation of fusimotor neurones. *J. Physiol. (London),* 1958, **143**, 195–212.

Hunter, J., & Jasper, H. H. Effects of thalamic stimulation in unanesthetized cats: arrest reactions and petit mal-like seizures, activation patterns, and generalized convulsions. *EEG clin. Neurophysiol.,* 1949, **1**, 305–324.

Ingram, W. R. The hypothalamus. *Clin. Symposia,* 1956, **8** (4), CIBA Pharmaceutical Products.

Ingram, W. R., & Ranson, S. W. Effects of lesions in the red nuclei in cats. *A.M.A. Arch. Neurol. Psychiat.,* 1932, **28**, 482–512.

Ingram, W. R., Ranson, S. W., Hannet, F. I, Zeiss, F. R., & Terwilliger, E. H. Results of stimulation of the tegmentum with the Horsley-Clarke stereotaxic apparatus. *A.M.A. Arch. Neurol. Psychiat.,* 1932, **28**, 513–541.

Jakob, A. *Die Extrapyramidalen Erkrankungen.* Berlin: Springer, 1923.

Joubert, G., & Gueguen, J. Y. Examen mécanique et électromyographique du triceps sural d'un sujet debout. Importance respective des tensions élastiques et contractiles déployées. *C. R. Soc. Biol. (Paris),* 1955, **149**, 499–502.

Jung, R., & Hassler, R. The extrapyramidal motor system. In *Handbook of physiology. Vol. II.* J. Field, H. W. Magoun, & V. E. Hall, Eds. Baltimore: Williams and Wilkins, 1960.

Kawakami, M. Electro-myographic study on the functional differentiation of the hand and foot muscles. *Jap. J. Physiol.,* 1954a, **4**, 1–6.

Kawakami, M. Electro-myographic investigation on the human external sphincter muscle of anus. *Jap. J. Physiol.,* 1954b, **4**, 196–204.

Kawakami, M. Electro-myographic study of the human abdominal muscles affected by sexual hormones. *Jap. J. Physiol.,* 1954c, **4**, 274–289.

Keller, A. D., & Hare, W. K. The rubrospinal tracts in the monkey. *A.M.A. Arch. Neurol. Psychiat.,* 1934, **32**, 1253–1272.

Kennard, Margaret A. Experimental analysis of the functions of the basal ganglia in monkeys and chimpanzees. *J. Neurophysiol.,* 1944a, **7**, 127–148.

Kennard, Margaret A. *The precentral motor cortex.* P. Bucy, Ed. Urbana: Univ. of Illinois Press, 1944b.

Kuffler, S. W., & Gerard, R. W. The small-nerve motor system to skeletal muscle. *J. Neurophysiol.,* 1947, **10**, 383–394.

Kuffler, S. W., & Williams, E. M. V. Properties of the "slow" skeletal muscle fibres of the frog. *J. Physiol. (London),* 1953, **121**, 318–340.

Kuffler, S. W., Hunt, C. C., & Quilliam, J. P. Function of medullated small-nerve fibers in mammalian ventral roots: efferent muscle spindle innervation. *J. Neurophysiol.,* 1951, **14**, 29–54.

Lafora, G. R. Myoclonus: physiological and pathological considerations. *Excerpta med.* Sect. 8. *Neurol. Psychiat.,* 1955, **8**, 769–770.

Landau, W. M. Patterns of movement elicited by medullary pyramidal stimulation in the cat. *EEG clin. Neurophysiol.,* 1952, **4**, 527–546.

Landau, W. M. Autonomic responses mediated via the corticospinal tract. *J. Neurophysiol.,* 1953, **16**, 299–311.

Langley, L. L., & Cheraskin, E. *The physiology of man.* New York: McGraw-Hill, 1958.

Lashley, K. S. Functional interpretation of anatomic patterns. *Res. Publ., Ass. Res. nerv. ment. Dis.,* 1952, **30**, 529–547.

Lassek, A. M. The pyramidal tract. *J. nerv. ment. Dis.,* 1942, **95**, 721–729.

Lewandowsky, M. *Die Funktion des zentralen Nervensystems.* Jena: Fischer, 1907.

Lilly, J. C. Distribution of "motor" functions in the cerebral cortex in the conscious intact monkey. *Science,* 1956, **124**, 937.

Lilly, J. C., Hughes, J. R., & Galkin, T. W. Gradients of motor function in the whole cerebral cortex of the unanesthetized monkey. *Fed. Proc.,* 1956, **15**, 119.

Lindsley, D. B. Electrical activity of human motor units during voluntary contraction. *Amer. J. Physiol.*, 1935, **114**, 90–99.

Lindsley, D. B., Schreiner, L. H., & Magoun, H. W. An electromyographic study of spasticity. *J. Neurophysiol.*, 1949, **12**, 197–205.

Linzell, J. L. Physiology of the mammary glands. *Physiol. Rev.*, 1959, **39**, 534–576.

Lloyd, D. P. C. The spinal mechanism of the pyramidal system in cats. *J. Neurophysiol.*, 1941, **4**, 525–546.

Lloyd, D. P. C. Functional organization of the spinal cord. *Physiol. Rev.*, 1944, **24**, 1–17.

McCulloch, W. S. Mechanisms for spread of epileptic activation of brain. *EEG clin. Neurophysiol.*, 1949, **42**, 71–84.

McCulloch, W. S., Graf, G., & Magoun, H. W. Cortico-bulbo-reticular pathway from area 4-s. *J. Neurophysiol.*, 1946, **9**, 127–132.

Magendie, F. *Leçons sur les fonctions et les maladies du systeme Nerveux.* Paris: Steinheil, 1841.

Magoun, H. W., & Rhines, Ruth. An inhibitory mechanism in the bulbar reticular formation. *J. Neurophysiol.*, 1946, **9**, 165–171.

Matthews, B. H. C. Specific nerve impulses. *J. Physiol.* (*London*), 1929, **67**, 169–190.

Matthews, B. H. C. The response of a single end organ. *J. Physiol.* (*London*), 1931a, **71**, 64–110.

Matthews, B. H. C. The response of a muscle spindle during active contraction of a muscle. *J. Physiol.* (*London*), 1931b, **72**, 153–174.

Matthews, B. H. C. Nerve endings in mammalian muscle. *J. Physiol.* (*London*), 1933, **78**, 1–33.

Mettler, F. A. Extensive unilateral cerebral removals in primate; physiological effects and resultant degeneration. *J. comp. Neurol.*, 1943, **79**, 185–245.

Mettler, F. A. On the origin of the fibers in the pyramid of the primate brain. *Proc. Soc. exp. Biol. Med.*, 1944, **57**, 111–113.

Mettler, F. A. Effects of bilateral simultaneous subcortical lesions in primate. *J. Neuropathol. exp. Neurol.*, 1945, **4**, 99–122.

Mettler, F. A. Fiber connections of the corpus striatum of the monkey and baboon. *J. comp. Neurol.*, 1954, **82**, 169–204.

Mettler, F. A., & Mettler, C. C. The effects of striatal injury. *Brain*, 1942, **65**, 242–255.

Mettler, F. A., Ades, H. W., Lipman, E., & Culler, E. A. The extrapyramidal system. *A.M.A. Arch. Neurol. Psychiat.*, 1939, **41**, 984–995.

Mollica, A., Moruzzi, G., & Naquet, R. Décharges réticulaires induites par la polarisation du cervelet: leurs rapports avec le tonus postural et la réaction de'éveil. *EEG clin. Neurophysiol.*, 1953, **5**, 571–584.

Moon, H. D. *The adrenal cortex.* New York: Paul Hoeber, 1961.

Moruzzi, G. Azione del paleocerebellum sui reflessi vasomotori. *Arch. Fisiol.*, 1938a, **38**, 36–74.

Moruzzi, G. Sur les rapports entre le Paléocervelet et les réflexes vasomoteurs. *Année Physiol.*, 1938b, **14**, 605–612.

Moruzzi, G. Effects at different frequencies of cerebellar stimulation upon postural tonus and myotatic reflexes. *EEG clin. Neurophysiol.*, 1950a, **2**, 463–469.

Moruzzi, G. *Problems in cerebellar physiology.* Springfield, Ill.: Thomas, 1950b.

Nathan, P. W., & Smith, M. C. Spino-cortical fibers in man. *J. Neurol. Neurosurg. Psychiat.*, 1955, **18**, 181–190.

Needham, D. M. Red and white muscle. *Physiol. Rev.*, 1926, **6**, 1–28.

Niemer, W. T., & Magoun, H. W. Reticulo-spinal tracts influencing motor activity. *J. comp. Neurol.*, 1947, **87**, 367–379.

Paillard, J. *Réflexes et régulations d'origine proprioceptive chez l'homme.* Paris: Arnette, 1955.

Paillard, J. The patterning of skilled movements. In *Handbook of physiology. Vol. III.* J. Field, H. W. Magoun, & V. E. Hall, Eds. Baltimore: Williams and Wilkins, 1960.

Patton, H. D. Spinal reflexes and synaptic transmission. In Ruch, T. C., Patton, H. D., Woodbury, J. W., & Towe, A. L. *Neurophysiology* (2nd ed.). Philadelphia: Saunders, 1965a.

Patton, H. D. Reflex regulation of movement and posture. In Ruch, T. C., Patton, H. D., Woodbury, J. W., Towe, A. L. *Neurophysiology* (2nd ed.). Philadelphia: Saunders, 1965b.

Patton, H. D., & Amassian, V. E. Single- and multiple-unit analysis of cortical stage of pyramidal tract activation. *J. Neurophysiol.*, 1954, **17**, 345–363.

Patton, H. D., & Amassian, V. E. The pyramidal tract: its excitation and functions. In *Handbook of physiology. Vol. II.* J. Field, H. W. Magoun, & V. E. Hall, Eds. Baltimore: Williams and Wilkins, 1960.

Peacock, S. M., & Hodes, R. S. Influence of the forebrain on somato-motor activity. *J. comp. Neurol.*, 1951, **94**, 409–428.

Penfield, W. L'écorce cérébrale chez l'homme. *Année psychol.*, 1940, **39**, 1–32.

Penfield, W. Mechanisms of voluntary movement. *Brain*, 1954, **77**, 1–17.

Penfield, W., & Jasper, H. H. *Epilepsy and the functional anatomy of the human brain.* Boston: Little, Brown, 1954.

Penfield, W., & Rasmussen, T. *The cerebral cortex of man.* New York: Macmillan, 1950.

Peterson, E., Magoun, H. W., McCulloch, W. S., & Lindsley, D. B. Production of postural tremor. *J. Neurophysiol.*, 1949, **12**, 371–384.

Phillips, C. G. Cortical motor threshold and the thresholds and distribution of excited Betz cells in the cat. *Quart. J. exp. Physiol.*, 1956, **41**, 70–84.

Pompeiano, O. Sulle rispaste crociate degli arti a stimolazione della corteccia vermania del lobus anterior nel gatto decerebrato. *Boll. Soc. ital. Biol. sper.*, 1955, **31**, 808–816.

Pompeiano, O. Sul meccanismo delle risposte posturali

crociate alla stimolazione di an emiverme del *lobus anterior* nel Gatto decerebrato. *Arch. Sci. biol.*, 1956, **40**, 513.

Pribram, K. H., Kruger, L., Robinson, F., & Berman, A. J. Effects of precentral lesions on behavior of monkeys. *Yale J. Biol. Med.*, 1955, **28**, 428–443.

Rademaker, C. G. *Das Stehen.* Berlin: Springer, 1931.

Ramón y Cajal, S. *Histologie du système nerveux de l'homme et des vertébrés. Vol. I.* Paris: Maloine, 1899.

Ramón y Cajal, S. *Histologie du système nerveux,* Paris: Maloine, 1909.

Rasmussen, A. T. Innervation of the hypophysis. *Endocrinology,* 1938, **23**, 263.

Rasmussen, H. Parathyroid hormone. *Amer. J. Med.,* 1961, **30**, 112–128.

Rawson, R. W. Modern concepts of thyroid physiology (symposium). *Ann. N.Y. Acad. Sci.,* 1960, **86**, 311–676.

Rhines, Ruth, & Magoun, H. W. Brainstem facilitation of cortical motor responses. *J. Neurophysiol.,* 1946, **9**, 219–229.

Rhines, Ruth, & Magoun, H. W. *Spasticity and the extrapyramidal system.* Springfield, Ill.: Thomas, 1947.

Ruch, T. C. Motor systems. In *Handbook of experimental psychology.* S. S. Stevens, Ed. New York: Wiley, 1951a.

Ruch, T. C. Sensory mechanisms. In *Handbook of experimental psychology.* S. S. Stevens, Ed. New York: Wiley, 1951b.

Ruch, T. C., Patton, H. D., Woodbury, J. W., & Towe, A. L. *Neurophysiology.* Philadelphia: Saunders, 1965.

Sawyer, W. H. Neurohypophysial hormones. *Pharmacol. Rev.,* 1961, **13**, 225–277.

Schiff, J. M. I. Muskel- und Nervenphysiologie. In *Lehrbuch der Physiologie des Menschen. Vols. I and II.* Lahr: Schauenburg, 1858, 1859.

Segundo, J. P., & Machne, X. Unitary responses to afferent volleys in lenticular nucleus and claustrum. *J. Neurophysiol.,* 1956, **19**, 325–339.

Sherrington, C. S. Double (antidrome) conduction in the central nervous system. *Proc. roy. Soc. (London), B,* 1897, **61**, 234–246.

Sherrington, C. S. Decerebrate rigidity, and reflex coordination of movements. *J. Physiol. (London),* 1898a, **22**, 319–332.

Sherrington, C. S. Experiments in examination of the peripheral distribution of the fibers of the posterior roots of some spinal nerves. *Phil. Trans. roy. Soc. London, B,* 1898b, **90**, 49–186.

Shimamoto, T., & Verzeano, M. Relations between caudate and diffusely projecting thalamic nuclei. *J. Neurophysiol.,* 1954, **17**, 278–288.

Smith, R. W., Jr., Graebler, O., & Long, C. N. H. *The hypophysial growth hormone, nature and actions.* New York: McGraw-Hill, 1955.

Snider, R. S. Functional studies following lesions of nucleus interpositus in rabbit. *Bull. Johns Hopk. Hosp.,* 1940, **67**, 139–153.

Snider, R. S., & Magoun, H. W. Facilitation produced by cerebellar stimulation. *J. Neurophysiol.,* 1949, **12**, 335–345.

Snider, R. S., & Woolsey, C. N. Extensor rigidity in cats produced by simultaneous ablation of the anterior lobe of the cerebellum and the pericruciate areas of the cerebral hemispheres. *Amer. J. Physiol.,* 1941, **133**, 454.

Snider, R. S., McCulloch, W. S., & Magoun, H. W. A cerebello-bulbo-reticular pathway for suppression. *J. Neurophysiol.,* 1949, **12**, 325–334.

Snider, R. S., Magoun, H. W., & McCulloch, W. S. A suppressor cerebello-bulbo-reticular pathway from anterior lobe and paramedian lobules. *Fed. Proc.,* 1947, **6**, 207.

Sperry, R. W. Cerebral regulation of motor coordination in monkeys following multiple transection of sensorimotor cortex. *J. Neurophysiol.,* 1947, **10**, 275–294.

Sprague, J. M., & Chambers, W. W. Regulation of posture in intact and decerebrate cat. I: Cerebellum, reticular formation, vestibular nuclei. *J. Neurophysiol.,* 1953, **16**, 451–463.

Sprague, J. M., & Chambers, W. W. Control of posture by reticular formation and cerebellum in the intact, anesthetized and unanesthetized and in the decerebrated cat. *Amer. J. Physiol.,* 1954, **176**, 52–64.

Starlinger, J. Die Durchschneidung beider Pyramiden beim Hunde. *Neurol. Zbl.,* 1895, **14**, 390–394.

Stevens, J. R., Kim, C., & MacLean, P. Stimulation of caudate nucleus. *Arch. Neurol. (Chicago),* 1961, **4**, 47–54.

Swank, R. L. The relationship between the circumolivary pyramidal fascicles and the pontobulbar body in man. *J. comp. Neurol.,* 1934a, **60**, 309–318.

Swank, R. L. Aberrant pyramidal fascicles in the cat. *J. comp. Neurol.,* 1934b, **60**, 355–359.

Szentágothai, J. Anatomical considerations of monosynaptic reflex arcs. *J. Neurophysiol.,* 1948, **11**, 445–454.

Tepperman, J. *Metabolic and endocrine physiology.* Chicago: Year Book Medical Publications, 1962.

Thomas, A. *Le cervelet: étude anatomique, clinique et physiologique.* Paris: Steinheil, 1897.

Thorn, N. A. Mammalian anti-diuretic hormone. *Physiol. Rev.,* 1958, **38**, 169–195.

Tower, S. S. Extrapyramidal action from the cat's cerebral cortex: motor and inhibitory. *Brain,* 1936, **59**, 408–444.

Tower, S. S. Pyramidal lesion in the monkey. *Brain,* 1940, **63**, 36–90.

Tower, S. S. The production of spasticity in monkeys by lesions in the pons. *Anat. Rec.,* 1942, Suppl. 82, 450–451.

Tower, S. S. In *The precentral motor cortex* (2nd ed.). P. C. Bucy, Ed. Urbana: Univ. of Illinois Press, 1949.

Umbach, W. The role of the nucleus caudatus in subcortical relationships. *EEG clin. Neurophysiol.,* 1955, **7**, 665.

Vane, J. R., Wolstenholme, G. E. W., & O'Connor, M. *Adrenergic mechanisms.* Ciba Foundation Symposium. Boston: Little, Brown, 1960.

Velardo, J. T. *Endocrinology of reproduction.* New York: Oxford Univ. Press, 1958.

Villee, C. A. *Control of ovulation.* New York: Pergamon Press, 1961.

Vogt, C., & Vogt, O. Zur kenntnis der elektrisch erregbaren Hirnrinden-Gebiete bei den Säugetieren. *J. Physiol. Neurol.,* 1907, **8**, 277–456.

Vogt, C., & Vogt, O. Allgemeinere Ergebnisse unserer Hirnforschung. *J. Physiol. Neurol.,* 1919, **25**, 279–461.

Von Bechterew, W. *Die Funktionen der Nervenzentralen. Vols. I–III.* Jena: Fischer, 1909–1911.

Wachholder, K. *Willkürliche Haltung und Bewegung insbesondere im Lichte elektrophysiologische Untersuchunger.* Müchen: Bergmann, 1928.

Walberg, F., & Brodal, A. Pyramidal tract fibres from temporal and occipital lobes: experimental study in cat. *Brain,* 1953, **76**, 491–508.

Walker, A. E. An oscillographic study of cerebello-cerebral relationships. *J. Neurophysiol.,* 1938, **1**, 16–23.

Waller, W. H. Progression movements elicited by subthalamic stimulation. *J. Neurophysiol.,* 1940, **3**, 300–307.

Wang, S. C., & Brown, V. W. Suprasegmental inhibition of an autonomic reflex. *J. Neurophysiol.,* 1956, **19**, 564–572.

Weddell, G., Feinstein, B., & Pattle, R. E. The electrical activity of voluntary muscle in man under normal and pathological conditions. *Brain,* 1944, **67**, 178–257.

Whittier, J. R., & Mettler, F. A. Studies on subthalamus of rhesus monkey; anatomy and fiber connections of subthalamic nucleus of Luys. *J. comp. Neurol.,* 1949, **90**, 281–319.

Williams, R. H. *Diabetes.* New York: Paul Hoeber, 1960.

Wolstenholme, G. E. W., & O'Connor, M. *Metabolic effects of adrenal hormones.* Ciba Foundation Study Group 6. Boston: Little, Brown, 1960.

Woolsey, C. N., & Chang, H.-T. Activation of the cerebral cortex by antidromic volleys in the pyramidal tract. *Res. Publ., Ass. Res. nerv. ment. Dis.* 1948, **27**, 146–161.

Young, W. C. *Sex and internal secretions.* Baltimore: Williams and Wilkins, 1961.

CHAPTER FIVE

The Reticular Formation and Nonspecific Thalamic Projection System

THE RETICULAR FORMATION OF THE BRAINSTEM

Gross Functional and Structural Considerations

The primitive nervous system is the simplest model for the study of sensory-motor interactions. Aside from specific receptor and effector processes, the phylogenetically primitive nervous system consists almost exclusively of an undifferentiated mass of typically short-axon cells. In the course of phylogenetic development, distinct cell masses (nuclei) and fiber bundles arise, and only remnants of the *formatio reticularis* (so called because its microscopic appearance resembles that of a reticulum or fishnet) persist in the upper half of the spinal cord and the central core of the brainstem. It is difficult to distinguish clearly between reticular and nonreticular mechanisms at many levels of the brainstem. Anatomically, the reticular formation is not a truly undifferentiated mass of cells and short, connecting fibers; rather, it tends to show distinct cellular groupings which have led to the classification of 98 nuclear masses (Olszewski, 1954). Some of the long-recognized nuclei of the diencephalon and midbrain (such as the red nucleus and substantia nigra) may functionally and developmentally be part of the reticular formation rather than of specific sensory or motor systems.

Histological studies have pointed out that the majority of the cells in the brainstem reticular formation may not be of the short-axon type which has been assumed to provide local, polysynaptic interactions in this complex system. Very long reticular connections have also been described (Scheibel and Scheibel, 1958). The apparent lack of physical grouping of these projection fibers into anatomically distinct bundles should not be interpreted a priori to imply functional diversity (see Figure 5.1).

Much of the nonspecificity of the reticular formation is undoubtedly a reflection of our ignorance. We may expect to progress on the road which has led in a relatively short period of 20 years to the demonstration of a number of specific and anatomically distinct functional mechanisms. It seems probable that the reticular formation may some day be defined on purely functional rather than anatomical grounds. The reticular functions are indeed complex and apparently diffuse; however, every addition to our knowledge has tended to bring out specificity where we had suspected nothing but a complete lack of differentiation.

Some very specific regulatory functions have long been known to be exercised by specific groups of cells in the brainstem reticular formation. These functions appear to be related primarily to the reflexive control of visceral or "semiautomatic" skeletal responses, such as gastrointestinal secretions, vasomotor tonus, and respiration. In the last two decades, it has become apparent that the reticular formation (or more specifically, some parts of it) also exert pronounced effects on sensory input, cortical activity, and tonic as well as phasic motor reactions of the skeletal musculature. Moreover, higher-order integrative processes, which are thought to give rise to such complex manifestations of neural activity as motivation, emotion, and learning, have been related, imperfectly as it were, to the activity of the reticular formation.

It is a reflection of our ignorance that we must speak of "the influence of reticular mechanisms" on such factors as "the reception, conduction, and integration of all sensory signals" or on "motor functions concerned in phasic or tonic muscular control" (French, 1960). It may be true that the reticular formation, by reason of its peculiar anatomical structure, may be uniquely suited to perform certain integrative processes that are potentially useful in all sensory or motor functions. However, it is not "the reticular formation" as a whole that is performing these functions; the influence is not so nonspecific that it concurrently affects all sensory input or motor integration. Individual aspects of this apparently undifferentiated mass of cells acquire greater and greater functional and anatomical specificity as we collect more information about them. It now appears almost certain that specific parts of the reticular formation monitor and control the input of particular sensory modalities (see the discussion of the role of reticular mechanisms in habituation and arousal) and affect the tonic or phasic activity of specific muscle groups in accordance with the requirements of the moment.

The vestiges of the embryologically and phylogenetically prominent spinal reticular formation are commonly considered to be a separate spinal system of internuncial neurons. This lower reticular formation is particularly well developed in the upper half of the cord and projects direct as well as multisynaptic pathways to all levels of the brainstem.

Following Ramón y Cajal's (1909) usage, the reticular formation proper may be considered to extend from the lower border of the medulla to the diencephalon. Its anterodorsal extent is a matter of some debate. The subjects of this altercation are some of the hypothalamic and subthalamic nuclei, the nonspecific projection nuclei of the thalamus (which will be discussed later), and some aspects of the septal area. Throughout its course in the brainstem, the reticular formation is centrally located; it is surrounded on all sides by the pathways and nuclei of the specific sensory projections and the pyramidal and extrapyramidal motor systems (some aspects of the latter are sometimes considered to be part of the brainstem reticular formation). A description of the many cell masses and fiber bundles in the reticular formation which have been demonstrated in recent years will not be attempted, largely because we do not yet understand the functional significance of most of the anatomical distinctions. We will, instead, follow current usage and discuss the reticular formation in terms of apparent functional units which are largely defined in terms of general "excitatory" or "inhibitory" influences and grossly defined classes of events such as "receptor sensitivity," "cortical activity," or "motor adjust-

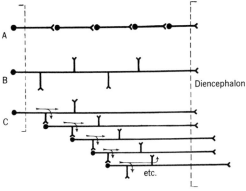

Fig. 5.1 Several possible conduction circuits through the reticular core of the brainstem. A shows the type of chaining of short-axoned cells which has been hypothesized by Moruzzi and Magoun and by a number of other workers to explain conduction characteristics marked by slow transmission, long latency, and recruiting. B shows a single long-axoned cell, reaching from bulb (dotted line at left) to diencephalon and illustrating the type of conductor which has been found in very large numbers in the reticular formation. C illustrates that the many collaterals of long conductors, as in B, may provide for more circuitous paths through the reticular core, producing increasing lateral dispersion and increasingly long conduction times and longer latencies. (From Scheibel and Scheibel, 1958.)

ments." Though clearly inadequate, these functional descriptions are the best the field has presently to offer, and we shall attempt to derive as much benefit as possible from their use.

The reticular formation of the brainstem receives a profusion of collaterals from all ascending sensory pathways. Additional spinoreticular pathways synapse on cells scattered throughout the longitudinal extent of the brainstem reticular formation (Nauta, 1958; Morin, 1953; Brodal, 1949; Putnam, 1938). Collaterals from cranial nerve nuclei are also prevalent.

The microscopic anatomy of the brainstem reticular formation shows an organization peculiar to this part of the brain. The cells of the central core of the brainstem are characterized by extensive and profusely branching dendritic fields which permit the channeling of impulses from a number of spatially divergent sources to a single neuron. Physiologically, such channeling results in a convergence of afferents from many different sources on a single reticular neuron and permits the integrative activity ascribed to the system as a whole. It is not uncommon, for instance, to find single cells in the midbrain reticular formation which fire or inhibit firing in response to peripheral stimulation of sensory receptors from a variety of modalities as well as from cerebellar or cortico-thalamic inputs. The central core of the reticular formation is characterized by cells which have diffusely branching dendritic fields and short axons. The reticular cells of the lateral areas of the brainstem project bifurcating axons into the medial portion, one leg typically taking an ascending course, the other a descending one. Scheibel and Scheibel (1958) have studied these anatomical relationships in some detail and have concluded that (1) the afferents to the reticular formation tend to arrive in a plane that is roughly perpendicular to the long axis of the brainstem; (2) the degree of overlap of the collateral afferent plexuses complemented by an equally overlapping arrangement of the dendritic fields is so great that specificity of input cannot be maintained; and (3) the long ascending and descending branches of the reticular cell axons project a profusion of collaterals which arise from all levels of the axon

and radiate perpendicularly to the course of the axon, as shown in Figure 5.2.

Corticofugal influences on the reticular formation have been shown to originate in the motor cortex (Rossi and Brodal, 1956), the sensory-motor cortex (Ramón y Cajal, 1909; McCulloch et al., 1946), the temporal lobe (Mettler, 1935), the orbitofrontal cortex (Wall et al., 1951), and the various rhinencephalic areas (Adey et al., 1956). Some of these corticoreticular fibers course through the internal capsule and upper brainstem in the company of the pyramidal tract and enter the reticular formation primarily in the lateral pontine tegmentum and dorsal medulla (Rossi and Brodal, 1956). However, most of the cortico-reticular connections are so diffuse and poorly localized that an anatomical description of their pathways does not yet exist.

The intralaminar and midline nuclei of the thalamus are so intimately related functionally and anatomically to the reticular formation of the lower brainstem that many authors consider them

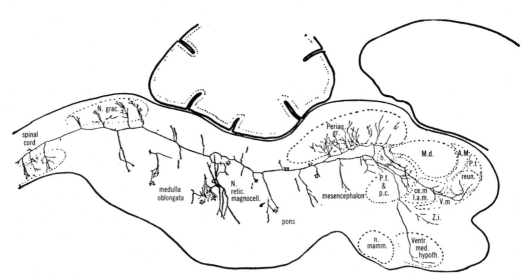

Fig. 5.2 Sagittal section of a 2-day-old rat, showing a single large reticular cell of the magnocellular nucleus. It emits an axon which bifurcates into a caudal and a rostral segment. The caudal segment gives off many collaterals to the adjacent reticular formation, to the nucleus gracilis, and to the ventral nuclei of the spinal cord. The rostrally running segment gives off collaterals to the reticular formation and to the periaqueductal gray substance, and then appears to supply the parafascicular and paracentral nuclei, the center median and interanteromedian nuclei, and reuniens nucleus, and the ventromedial hypothalamus, as well as the zona incerta.

N. grac., nucleus gracilis; N. retic. magnocell., magnocellular reticular nucleus; Periaq. gr., periaqueductal gray; A. M., anterior medialis nucleus; reun., nucleus reuniens; P.f. & p.c., parafascicularis and paracentralis nuclei; Ce.m., nucleus centralis medialis; I.a.m., nucleus anteromedialis inferior; V.m., ventralis medialis; M.d., nucleus medialis dorsalis; Z.i., zona incerta; h., habenula; n. mamm., mammillary body; Ventr. med. hypoth., ventromedial hypothalamic area; Pt., parataenial nucleus. (From Scheibel and Scheibel, 1958.)

to be part of a general reticular system. The thalamic nuclei project diffusely to most areas of the cortex and receive extensive corticofugal afferents via a number of connections. The pathways taken by the thalamocortical influences are not yet clear. Complete decortication produces degenerative changes only in the reticular nuclei of the thalamus (Rose and Woolsey, 1949). The more prominent intralaminar and midline nuclei show little or no cellular necrosis. Cells of the midine and intralaminar nuclei do degenerate following extensive damage to the rhinencephalon, striatum, and amygdaloid complex (Rose and Woolsey, 1949) suggesting possibly specific thalamopaleocortical and thalamostriatal connections (see Droogleever-Fortuyn and Stefens, 1951). Jasper (1954) has suggested, largely on the basis of these degeneration studies, that the neocortical projections of the midline and intralaminar nuclei may be mediated by the reticular nuclei that essentially surround the thalamus.

The reticular formation of the lower brainstem projects to the cortex either directly via diffuse extrathalamic projections which course through the ventrolateral diencephalon (Nauta, 1958; Scheibel and Scheibel, 1958) or indirectly via a number of reticulothalamic connections. A number of diffuse projections to the midline nuclei were isolated by Lewandowsky (1904) over 60 years ago, and distinct lateral reticulothalamic, tegmentothalamic, and tectothalamic pathways to the midline and intralaminar nuclei have more recently been described (Whitlock and Schreiner, 1954).

The reticular formation receives important extrapyramidal motor inputs from the basal ganglia, indirectly via the thalamic nuclei (Ranson and Ranson, 1942) and directly from the fastigial nuclei of the cerebellum (Sprague et al., 1957; McMasters, 1957). Cells in the bulbar portion of the reticular formation project extensively to the cerebellum, and a reticulostriatal connection is established via the midline and intralaminar nuclei of the thalamus.

Reticular Influences on Sensory Mechanisms

Recent experimental observations suggest that a significant disparity exists between the physical energy which constantly impinges on the various receptors of our sensorium and the world we perceive. Only in the anesthetized state do the classical sensory pathways conduct impulses that are consistently and reliably related to the environment. In the awake animal, this input is distorted by a variety of influences which arise from a number of central mechanisms and are channeled into and integrated by the reticular formation of the brainstem.

An analysis of this integrative process led Livingston (1959) to suggest that the impulses conducted through the primary sensory pathways may not, by themselves, provide a sufficient basis for perception. Instead, each sensory input may need to be organized and integrated with information from other concurrently active sensory systems as well as from association areas and storage mechanisms of the central nervous system. The end product of this complex interaction rather than the primary sensory input gives rise to the subjective perception of the environment.

The central nervous system apparently uses the diffuse interconnections between sensory systems and higher centers of association which the brainstem reticular formation provides to achieve this integration of sensory inputs. On the basis of information which may arise from any or all parts of the central nervous system, the reticular formation maintains a complex and constantly fluctuating state of excitation that biases the sensitivity of specific sensory modalities. The net effect of this biasing influence on the sensory receptor or conduction pathways may be facilitatory or inhibitory. However, available evidence suggests that the reticular formation maintains a tonic inhibitory influence on all sensory mechanisms. Facilitatory effects may be achieved by a decrease in this tonic inhibitory influence rather than by active facilitation.

The inhibitory influence of the reticular formation is typically smallest whenever the sensory signal is novel, sudden, or intense, or when that signal assumes special significance as a cue for other stimuli. It is largest when the sensory input duplicates information classed as "unimportant" and already stored in the memory mechanisms of the brain. (The process of initial arousal and progressive habituation is discussed in some detail in Chapter 12.)

When viewed in this way, the sensory system is not physiologically or anatomically distinct from other integrative or motor systems in the central nervous system. Areas of the brain implicated in complex motivational or associative processes receive extensive sensory inputs and, in turn, modify the sensory signals at all levels of the input system. The motor system similarly requires constant and detailed sensory feedback for the regulation of postural and phasic movements; it, in turn, modifies the sensory input largely via the gamma efferents and related connections to the receptor organs.

The sensory receiving areas of the cortex do not provide the first, or even the most important, step in sensory integration, as has been assumed in the past. Instead, sensory information appears to be modified initially at the receptor level and subsequently at synaptic relays along the primary or extralemniscal pathways. Much of the sensory information is lost or greatly distorted by central influences which reflect the organism's previous experience, current state of attention, other concurrent sensory inputs, or the general state of reactivity.

It is no longer possible to think of sensation or perception as the end products of a relatively simple transducer activity at the receptor level followed by undistorted transmission of the sensory signal to a "primary" cortical projection field, a field which then somehow decodes the signal and, perhaps with the aid of signals from "association" areas, initiates neural activity which is the direct correlate of perception.

Instead, we must consider a number of related systems which transmit sensory information or impulses that affect their transmission in other systems: (1) the classical (lemniscal) sensory pathways to the primary cortical projection areas; (2) the extralemniscal pathways which provide an alternate, often polysynaptic, route to the higher centers and find a more general cortical distribution; (3) the integrative pathways of the reticular formation which conduct sensory impulses along nonspecific pathways and provide connections between all parts of the brain and the relay stations of the lemniscal and extralemniscal pathways; and (4) the pyramidal and extrapyramidal motor systems which interconnect the cortex, basal ganglia, brainstem nuclei, reticular formation, cerebellum, and spinal motor neurons and exercise a significant control over receptor sensitivity. Interaction between these systems could occur at all levels of the reticular formation.

The experimental evidence for this interpretation will be summarized briefly in the following section. (More complete discussions can be found in reviews by Jasper et al., 1958; Granit, 1959; Lindsley, 1960; Livingston, 1959.)

The control of receptor functions. The "spontaneous" firing rate of ganglion cells in the retina and the responsiveness of such cells to visual stimuli can be facilitated or inhibited by electrical stimulation of the midbrain tegmentum (Granit,

1955). The effect appears to be initiated by efferent fiber projections to the retina which originate in or course through the midbrain reticular formation (Ramón y Cajal, 1909–1911).

The sensitivity of the auditory receptors appears to be similarly controlled. Stimulation of the bul-

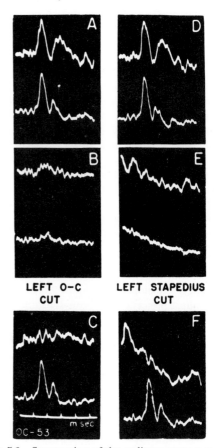

Fig. 5.3 Suppression of the auditory nerve response by olivocochlear and stapedius mechanisms. A, control auditory nerve responses to a click applied to each ear, right recording above left. B, suppression of both left and right responses with shocks at 100/sec delivered to the decussation of the olivocochlear bundle in the floor of the fourth ventricle. This high frequency of stimulation tetanizes the stapedius muscle, thus eliminating interference from that source (see E). C, following transection of the left olivocochlear bundle, the suppression shown in B occurs only on the right. D, another control response showing that the lesion made between B and C has not interfered with the auditory nerve response from either ear. E, single shocks to the same medullary location 13 msec before the test clicks suppress the eighth nerve responses from either ear (stapedius effect). F, following cutting of the tendon of the left stapedius muscle, the suppression shown in E is seen only on the right. (From Galambos, 1956.)

bar portion of the brainstem near the superior olivary nucleus inhibits the auditory nerve's response to auditory stimuli (Galambos, 1956) (see Figure 5.3). The effect is mediated by efferents which originate near the superior olive and project through the olivocochlear bundle to the contralateral cochlea. Here the efferents terminate in the vicinity of the synapse between the primary receptor cells and the auditory tract fibers (Rasmussen, 1953).

Stimulation of the anterior commissure, amygdaloid area, prepyriform cortex, or olfactory tubercle inhibits the activity of the olfactory bulb. Lesions in the anterior commissure augment the activity of the olfactory system, suggesting the operation of a tonic effect in the intact animal (Kerr and Hagbarth, 1955). The effects appear to be mediated by efferents that arise from the primary olfactory projections in the rhinencephalon and terminate on granule cells near the synaptic junction between olfactory receptors and the cells that give rise to olfactory bulb fibers (Ramón y Cajal, 1909–1911).

The efferent control over muscle receptors has already been discussed in some detail. The intrafusal muscles receive special gamma efferents which adjust the tension of the intrafusal fiber without significantly affecting the stretch of the extrafusal muscle. This process modifies the "resting" activity of the spindle receptors and biases their sensitivity (Hunt and Kuffler, 1951; Granit and Kaada, 1952; Kuffler and Hunt, 1952) (see Figure 5.4).

The touch receptors of the skin appear to be controlled by visceral efferents from the sympathetic branch of the autonomic nervous system. Stimulation of these fibers facilitates touch receptor sensitivity. Since the neuroeffector transmission in the sympathetic system occurs via the release of adrenergic substances, the touch receptors are also subject to a generalized facilitation which is a function of the level of circulating epinephrine and norepinephrine (Loewenstein, 1956).

Control of transmission in central relay stations. Stimulation of the brainstem reticular formation (and, to a lesser extent, of the parietal cortex, anterior cingulate gyrus, and anterior cerebellar vermis) inhibits the conduction of sensory impulses in the ventral and lateral funiculi of the cord. The activity of the primary somatosensory pathways in the dorsal column is not affected, presumably because no synapse intervenes between the dorsal root fiber (which is directly stimulated in these studies) and the site of recording (Hagbarth and Kerr, 1954). Transmission in the

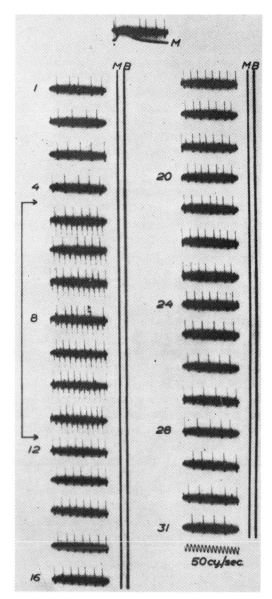

Fig. 5.4 Effect of brainstem reticular (midbrain tegmentum) stimulation on a gastrocnemius muscle spindle afferent discharge. *Above*, contraction of 134 grams at low myograph sensitivity to demonstrate the silent period of the large muscle spindle afferent unit. Initial tension throughout, 52 grams. Light Dial anesthesia. 1 to 4, control before reticular stimulation; 5 to 11, during stimulation; 12 to 31, after stimulation. Consecutive sweeps at 2-sec intervals. Myograph (M) alongside film. Distance M-B (base line) corresponds to 10 grams. Note that stimulation of the brainstem reticular formation, without altering the muscle tension, accelerates the spindle's rate of firing and that this effect persists more than half a minute. (From Granit and Kaada, 1952.)

first central relay in the primary somatosensory pathway (the nuclei cuneatus and gracilis in the bulbar brainstem) is significantly inhibited by reticular stimulation. Damage to the midpontine reticular formation increases the amplitude of the activity in the lemniscal pathways, suggesting normal tonic inhibitory effects (Scherrer and Hernández-Peón, 1955; Hernández-Peón et al., 1956) (see Figure 5.5).

The effects of the brainstem reticular formation on transmission in the thalamic somatosensory nuclei are complex. Typically, one effect is inhibitory; it does not completely suppress conduction but reduces the amplitude and duration of the potentials that are conducted to the cortex. Lesions in the central brainstem and barbiturate anesthesia (which selectively affects the polysynaptic reticular formation) increase the amplitude and duration of the thalamic projections (King et al., 1957). The transmission of visual (Hernández-Peón et al., 1956) and auditory (Jouvet and Desmedt, 1956) signals through the specific relay nuclei of the midbrain and thalamus is also partly inhibited by stimulation of the midbrain reticular formation.

The central control over sensory reception, conduction, and perception is exercised by an efferent system; this system originates in the cortex of the cerebrum (and perhaps the cerebellum) and essentially parallels the entire course of the primary sensory pathways, picking up additional influences from integrative centers along the way. The cortex thus determines to some extent its own sensory input by modifying the signals that arise in the primary and extralemniscal pathways. Examples of such corticifugal influences are shown in Figure 5.6.

Reticular Influences on Tonic and Phasic Motor Functions

The reticular formation of the brainstem transmits many of the influences that modulate the basic pattern of spinal reflex connections in accordance with postural requirements or specific motor "commands" from cortical or related extrapyramidal centers. Excitation of the reticular formation may produce sufficient spinal facilitation to elicit movements (Snider and Stowell, 1944); it may even effect complete postural adjustments such as contralateral extension of the limbs combined with ipsilateral contraction (Sprague and Chambers, 1954). More typically, reticular influences act primarily to facilitate or inhibit spinal motor mechanisms and thus *modify* rather than elicit postural and phasic movements.

The reticular influences are transmitted over

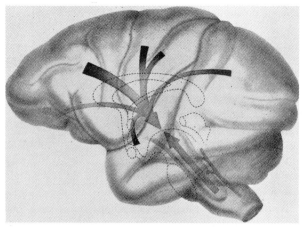

Fig. 5.5 Corticofugal pathways and collaterals of classical afferent pathways converging on the reticular formation of the lower brainstem. Stimulation of widespread cortical areas gives rise to electric potentials in the reticular formation, hence functional connection by assumed corticoreticular paths. Afferent impulses from all sources and impulses originating in the cortex are capable of exciting the ascending reticular activating system (ARAS), which in turn maintains the cortex and behavior in a state of arousal and alertness and perhaps selectively controls attention. (From French et al., 1955.)

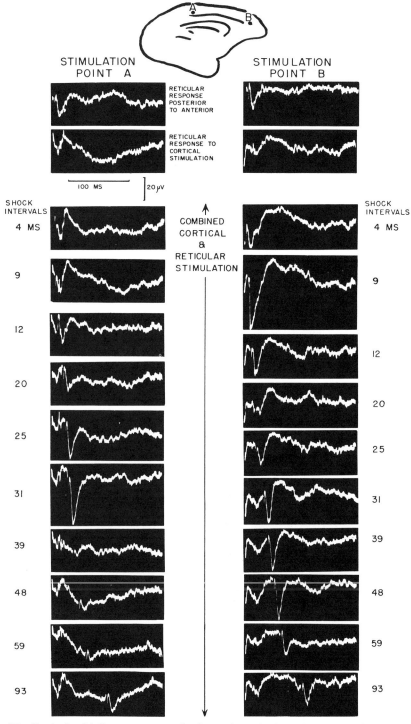

Fig. 5.6 Corticofugal influences on a conduction pathway in the brainstem reticular formation. Responses recorded from bipolar electrodes in the anterior brainstem show the effects of single cortical shocks on volleys ascending from a test stimulation site in the posterior brainstem. Left column, effects of cortical shocks applied to point A on the medial surface of the monkey hemisphere. Right column, effects on the same pathway of shocks applied to a more anterior cortical site, point B. Note that ascending brainstem volley is facilitated when cortical shock is delivered to point A 31 msec before posterior brainstem test shock, whereas facilitation from point B occurs at 9 and again at 48 msec, at which moments the brainstem pathway is being inhibited from point A. This reaction illustrates the principle that a number of cortical sites can exert a controlling influence on ascending systems intrinsic to the brainstem, thereby being able, presumably, to interfere with mechanisms involved in sensation. (From Adey et al., 1957.)

rapidly conducting bilateral spinal pathways (Magoun, 1950a, b) which terminate primarily on spinal interneurons rather than on ventral horn motor cells (Lloyd, 1941a, b). The reticular influences on spinal motor activity are to some extent self-perpetuating, since the effects of reticular stimulation outlast the stimulus by several seconds (Kleyntjens et al., 1955).

At least some motor effects are produced by reticulospinal influences on gamma efferents; these efferents control the muscle receptor sensitivity and thus bias the afferent signals to many of the local reflex arcs as well as to higher centers of motor integration such as the cerebellum (Granit and Kaada, 1952; Granit, 1955) (see Figure 5.7).

Early studies of the descending influences of the brainstem reticular formation by Magoun and Rhines (1946, 1947) emphasized the existence of distinct facilitatory and inhibitory influences which were thought to derive from anatomically distinct sections of the brainstem. More recent studies have suggested that the anatomical distinction between facilitatory and inhibitory areas is not as absolute as the results of the initial investigations indicated. Inhibitory effects have been obtained from some areas of the upper brainstem which were originally thought to be facilitatory only (Austin, 1952); reciprocal effects have been observed from a number of points in both lower and upper segments of the central core of the brainstem (Sprague, 1953; Sprague and Chambers, 1954).

Inhibitory influences. Magoun and Rhines (1946, 1947) first described the total inhibition of reflexly or cortically elicited movement during electrical stimulation of lower, bulbar portions of the reticular formation. Subsequent studies showed that inhibitory influences could be elicited from all portions of the brainstem reticular formation and from related nuclei in the thalamus and septal area (Hodes et al., 1951; Austin, 1952). The observed inhibition of movement is typically

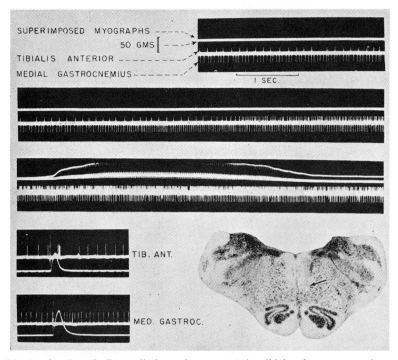

Fig. 5.7 Acceleration of afferent discharge from an anterior tibial and a gastrocnemius muscle spindle upon stimulation of the contralateral ventromedial reticular formation. Repetitive stimulation began at the second line of continuous tracing and progressively increased to 5 volts. Electrolytic decerebration with chloralose, 20 mg/kg. The left leg was denervated except for the medial gastrocnemius and anterior tibial nerves; the right sciatic nerve and lower sacral roots were severed. Note the acceleration of both spindles, the threshold of the gastrocnemius being lower. The tibial muscle eventually contracted. (From Eldred and Fujimori, 1958.)

most prominent ipsilateral to the site of stimulation (Niemer and Magoun, 1947); it may be reciprocal (Sprague, 1953) or nonreciprocal (Magoun and Rhines, 1946), depending on the locus and parameters of stimulation. Reticular inhibition may be mediated by a special class of spinal interneurons, the Renshaw cells (Eccles et al., 1954). All spinal reflex patterns are susceptible to reticular inhibition, but investigations reported later show that the simple, monosynaptic stretch reflex (which is beginning to look rather complex) may be particularly sensitive to such inhibitory influences (Gernandt and Thulin, 1955).

Facilitatory influences. Spinal reflex patterns or cortically evoked movements can be facilitated by stimulation of many points, particularly in rostral portions of the reticular formation (midbrain and pontine tegmentum, periaqueductal gray, subthalamic and hypothalamic nuclei, midline and intralaminar nuclei of the thalamus, and parts of the septum (see Peacock and Hodes, 1951; Magoun and Rhines, 1946, 1947). The effects are transmitted over rapidly conducting spinal pathways; these paths are sufficiently distinct from the reticulospinal tracts that carry inhibitory influences to permit differential sectioning in some studies (Niemer and Magoun, 1947). The effects may be reciprocal or nonreciprocal, depending on the site of stimulation (Sprague and Chambers,

1954). Multisynaptic reflex patterns appear to be particularly susceptible to reticular facilitation (Gernandt and Thulin, 1955), but facilitation of monosynaptic myotatic reflexes has also been observed (Austin, 1952).

Reticular Influences on Cortical Functions

Interest in reticular mechanisms has largely been stimulated by the Moruzzi and Magoun (1949) discovery of the reticular control of cortical activity and correlated behavioral fluctuations in arousal from sleep to wakefulness (for details, see reviews by French, 1960; Lindsley, 1960) (see Figure 5.8).

In the 1930's the important observations of Hess and his associates (see Hess's 1949 and 1954 reviews of this material) suggested that sleep and wakefulness appeared to be controlled by centers in the diencephalon. The work of Moruzzi and Magoun (1949) and subsequent investigators demonstrated that the state of cortical activity, as reflected in the gross EEG pattern, and behavioral arousal were functions of reticulocortical inputs which depend on the transmission of sensory information to the brainstem reticular formation.

The reticular formation or, more specifically, the portion of it devoted to the ascending reticular activating system (ARAS), is capable of some autochthonous activity (Moruzzi, 1954). How-

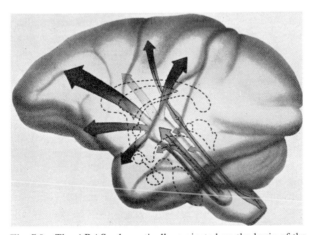

Fig. 5.8 The ARAS schematically projected on the brain of the monkey. The reticular formation, consisting of the multineuronal, multisynaptic central core of the region from medulla to hypothalamus, receives collaterals from specific or classical sensory pathways and projects diffusely upon the cortex. Impulses via specific sensory pathways are brief, discrete, direct, and of short latency in contrast to those via the unspecific ARAS which are persistent, diffuse, and of long latency. (From Lindsley, 1960.)

ever, the proper functioning of the arousal system requires sensory input, not to the cortex but directly to the reticular formation itself. Behavioral coma and electrophysiologically defined sleep are the result of complete deafferentation, presumably not because of a direct effect on cortical mechanisms (which are inactive in the face of intact inputs from the primary sensory pathways when the reticulocortical projections are destroyed) but because the reticular formation cannot function without sensory inputs. Several studies have shown that stimuli to cutaneous and muscle receptors are much more effective in maintaining reticular activity than inputs from specialized distance receptors such as the eye or nose (French et al., 1952; Arduini and Moruzzi, 1953).

Since the blocking effect of anesthetics is exerted primarily on synaptic mechanisms (see Brazier, 1954), it is possible to show that depression of the polysynaptic reticulocortical input results in both cortical and overt behavioral inhibition although the primary sensory pathways to the cortex remain functional (French et al., 1953). During anesthesia or following extensive damage to the brainstem reticular formation, the organism is comatose, and the cortical electrical activity is characterized by high-voltage slow discharges (Lindsley et al., 1950). Conversely, rapid electrical stimulation of the reticular formation or nonspecific thalamic projection nuclei of sleeping animals arouses them and desynchronizes the cortex (Segundo et al., 1955). Slow stimulation rates which approximate the frequency of the cortical EEG during sleep (8 to 12 cps) induce sleep or drowsiness, as originally shown by Hess (1929) and replicated by Akimoto and his associates (Akimoto et al., 1956b).

The many brainstem transection studies of the past 20 years (see Lindsley, 1960, for a review of this material) have shown that the reticular formation cannot maintain wakefulness or organized muscular activity without cortical assistance. If we add the observation French, 1952; Bremer and Terzuolo, 1952, 1954) that arousal can be obtained by direct cortical stimulation, the importance of corticoreticular influences becomes apparent. It may be more useful to think of the "ascending" reticular arousal system as a higher-order feedback circuit which includes descending and ascending connections; this concept is elaborated in some detail in Chapter 4 on basic sensory-motor interactions.

A discussion of the arousal functions of the reticular formation would be incomplete with-

out considering neurohumoral factors. Cortical arousal can be elicited by injections of cholinergic (Bradley, 1958) and adrenergic (Bonvallet et al., 1954) substances into the blood supply of the brainstem or directly into the reticular formation itself (Grossman, unpublished observations). Behavioral observations (Grossman, 1966; Grossman and Grossman, 1966) suggest that different portions of the reticular formation may respond to adrenergic and cholinergic substances (see also the excellent discussion of this matter by Rothballer, 1956, and Table 5.1).

At least some adrenergic effects may be related to changes in the general circulating level of catecholamines. Bonvallet and his associates (Bonvallet et al., 1954) have suggested that the arousal response to environmental events may have an initial, neural component, followed by a more prolonged "tonic" phase produced by the action of adrenergic substances that are released by the adrenal medulla during any novel, sudden, or otherwise stressful stimulation.

Some studies have suggested that the reticular influences on cortical and spinal mechanisms may themselves be mediated, at least in part, by humoral transport systems. For instance, Ingvar (1955, 1958) observed cortical desynchronization responses to reticular stimulation in sections of cortex that were neurologically completely isolated from the rest of the brain. Dell (1958) reported that the myotatic stretch reflex of the decerebrate animal may be facilitated by peripheral epinephrine administrations.

The importance of adrenergic mechanisms has been emphasized by the behavioral effects of various tranquilizers (reserpine, chlorpromazine) and psychotropic drugs (such as LSD-25) which are structurally related (all have indole or indolelike moieties) to adrenergic substances.

An analysis of the effects of adrenergic and cholinergic substances and related blocking agents reveals some peculiar dissociations between electrophysiological and behavioral arousal; these make the value of the gross cortical EEG as an index of cortical activity questionable. For instance, peripheral injections of atropine in moderate doses do not impair an animal's overt, behavioral responsiveness to the environment; however, the high-voltage slow-wave activity which characterizes electrophysiologically defined sleep is induced (Bradley and Elkes, 1953a, b). Conversely, reserpine is a very potent behavioral depressant which induces drowsiness and reduces the organism's behavioral responsiveness without

TABLE 5.1

Behavioral and electrophysiological changes believed to be caused by a direct drug action on the reticular formation

| Drug | Conscious Animal | | Encéphale Isolé | Cerveau Isolé |
	Behavior	Electrical Activity	Electrical Activity	Electrical Activity
Physostigmine	Normal	Fast, low-amplitude activity	Fast, low-amplitude activity	Fast, low-amplitude activity
Atropine	Normal or excited	High-amplitude slow waves and spindles	High-amplitude slow waves and spindles	High-amplitude slow waves and spindles
Amphetamine	Excited	Fast, low-amplitude activity	Fast, low-amplitude activity	No effect
LSD-25	Excited	Fast, low-amplitude activity	No effect	No effect
Chlorpromazine	Drowsy and indifferent	Slow and 5–8 cps. activity	Increased slow activity and spindles	No effect

From Bradley, 1958.

significantly changing the cortical EEG. Chlorpromazine similarly does not induce electrophysiological sleep or modify the cortical arousal threshold to stimulation of the thalamic nuclei; however, behavioral reactivity is significantly reduced, and the threshold for behavioral arousal responses to thalamic stimulation is increased tenfold (Killam et al., 1957). The behavioral responses to these drugs are particularly puzzling because the responsiveness of the reticular formation or of the reticulocortical projections appears to be largely unaffected (Killam and Killam, 1958). It has been suggested that chlorpromazine may in fact increase the inhibitory activity of the brainstem reticular formation and thus modify the arousal value of sensory inputs.

Central Influences on Reticular Functions

Cortical influences. In the course of the recent emphasis on the "arousal" functions of the reticular formation, reticulocortical influences have been perhaps unduly stressed. Cortical activity is markedly affected by damage to or stimulation of the brainstem reticular formation, but the interaction between these structures in the intact animal is a two-way process. (Essentially all areas of the cortex project directly or indirectly to the central core of the brainstem, as was first shown by Ramón y Cajal, 1909–1911.)

The inhibitory corticoreticular projection has historically received the most experimental attention, partly because it transmits the inhibitory effects of the many cortical "suppressor" areas which have been described in considerable detail in the past few decades (McCulloch et al., 1946). More recent investigations have shown that facilitatory as well as inhibitory effects can be obtained from essentially all areas of the cortex and even from the same site of stimulation, depending on the parameters of stimulation and the state of the organism. Single cells in the reticular formation sometimes increase their firing rate in response to cortical stimulation and decrease it in response to the same stimulation at other times, presumably because of other inputs to either the cortical or reticular cells (Baumgarten and Mollica, 1954). Gross changes in the response of the reticular formation to cortical stimulation as a function of stimulus parameters have been reported by several workers (Eliasson, 1952; Segundo et al., 1955).

Cerebellar influences. Facilitatory as well as inhibitory influences also arise from the cerebellum, partly in response to sensory feedback from the muscle receptors which complete a suprasegmental gamma neuron feedback system. Facilitatory and excitatory effects can be elicited from stimulation of the same cerebellar site, the nature of the effect being a function of the frequency of stimulation and the state of the organism (Snider et al., 1949). Moruzzi (1950) suggested that the direction of the cerebellar influence may, under normal circumstances, be controlled by the discharge frequency of the cerebellar neurons.

The cerebellar influence on the reticular formation appears to be represented in a somatotopically organized pattern. Electrical stimulation at threshold intensities often facilitates or inhibits the activity of single muscles or muscle fibers (Nulsen et al., 1948). This finding is surprising in view of the assumed lack of specificity of reticulospinal projections; it may lead to a re-examination of this question, particularly since microelectrode studies (Scheibel et al., 1955) have indicated point-to-point relationships between some cerebellar and reticular cells. Chambers and Sprague (1955) have suggested that the vermis of the cerebellum may be relatively nonspecifically related to the central reticular formation and mediate impulses related to gross postural adjustments. The paraventral cerebellar cortex, on the other hand, may project more selectively to cells in the lateral portion of the reticular formation and influence the specific action of individual muscles as part of a phasic activation.

Basal ganglia. Some aspects of the brainstem reticular formation are often considered part of the extrapyramidal motor system. Such an interpretation is tempting because (1) no direct pathways can be demonstrated between the basal ganglia or cerebellum and the spinal motor neuron; (2) at least some of the important relay nuclei of the extrapyramidal motor system (such as the red nucleus and substantia nigra of the midbrain) are developmentally part of the reticular formation; (3) many of the basal ganglia project to or receive afferents from thalamic nuclei which are part of the nonspecific projection system; and (4) stimulation of the striatum does not typically elicit movements but facilitates or inhibits motions that are reflexly or cortically evoked in much the same fashion as stimulation of the brainstem reticular formation.

Stimulation or destruction of various aspects of the striatopallidal system has been shown to produce facilitatory as well as inhibitory influences (Bucy, 1949; Magoun, 1954; see also the discussion of the extrapyramidal motor system in Chapter 4). These may reflect cortical influences on the basal ganglia or activity in complex feedback circuits between the basal ganglia, the red nucleus and substantia nigra, the cerebellum, thalamus, and cortex (Bucy, 1949).

THE NONSPECIFIC THALAMIC PROJECTION SYSTEM

Anatomical Considerations

The nonspecific thalamic projection system represents the rostral continuation of the brainstem reticular formation which projects to the cortex preferentially, though not exclusivelly, through the thalamic nuclei. The nonspecific thalamic projection system is composed of a profusely interconnected polysynaptic neuronal network in the internal medullary lamina, the midline nuclei, and the reticular nucleus of the thalamus (see Figure 5.9). Fibers from the centrum medianum project medioventrally to and through the nucleus ventralis medialis (VM); they pass into the nucleus ventralis anterior (VA) and the dorsal aspects of the reticular nucleus (RT). Fibers from the dorsolateral regions of the nonspecific system project preferentially to the posterior cortex; those from the ventromedial thalamus project to the frontal and allocortical parts of the cerebrum. A fairly precise topographic organization of the nonspecific thalamic projections to the cortex has been reported (Hanbery and Jasper, 1953).

The anatomical pathways for this nonspecific projection system are still subject to debate. It has been suggested that most influences that arise from midline and intralaminar nuclei may be relayed to the cortex via the reticular nucleus; this is the only part of the system with direct cortical projections (Rose, 1952, Hanbery et al., 1954; Hanbery and Jasper, 1953). Other workers have traced a pathway from the midline and intralaminar nuclei to or through the caudate nucleus. It has been suggested that the caudatocortical projections may be a major component of the nonspecific projection system. Recruiting responses typical of the nonspecific thalamic projection system (see later) can be obtained by stimulation of the caudate nucleus; however, Jasper (1960) has pointed out that the recruiting responses recorded following thalamic stimulation may arrive at the cortex after much shorter latencies than those commonly seen following caudate stimulation, suggesting the existence of a more direct route to the cortex. (See Nauta and Whitlock, 1954; Nashold et al., 1955; Akimoto et al, 1956a for physiological and anatomical information on this topic.)

Several other discharge pathways exist. The

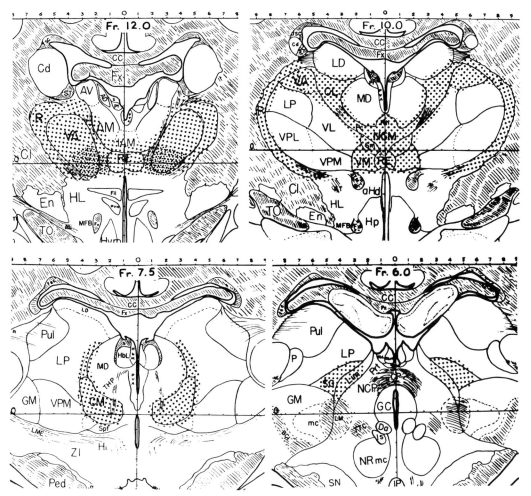

Fig. 5.9 The thalamic reticular system. Stippled areas indicate recruiting responses to local repetitive stimulation in the cat. Cross sections of stereotaxic frontal planes (Fr.) 12, 10, 7.5, and 6 are shown. The double stippling in the ventral portion of the nucleus ventralis anterior indicates the region where rostrally conducting pathways are dense. (From Jasper, 1960.)

centrum medianum has anatomically and physiologically documented efferent connections to the putamen. Impulses from the nonspecific thalamic projection system may reach the cortex via striatothalamic or direct striatocortical connections (McLardy, 1948, 1951). The intralaminar and midline nuclei are also extensively interconnected with the specific projection and association nuclei of the thalamus. They not only establish an extensive system of thalamic integration but also gain access to several direct thalamocortical projection systems. Since recruiting responses are least prominent, if not totally absent, in the specific sensory projection areas of the cortex, the nonspecific system does not appear to use the specific

sensory pathways. Anatomical and electrophysiological evidence supports the proposition that pathways from the thalamus to the association areas of the frontal, parietal, and temporal lobes of the cerebrum may carry impulses originating in the nonspecific thalamic projection nuclei (Starzl and Magoun, 1951; Starzl and Whitlock, 1952). Even the relatively small recruiting responses which can be recorded from the specific sensory projection areas do not seem to result from activity in the primary sensory pathways since the related specific relay nuclei of the thalamus can be completely ablated without suppressing these responses (Hanbery and Jasper, 1953). Some investigators have shown that the recruiting responses of the sensory projection areas may be even larger than normal following destruction of the associated specific relay nuclei of the thalamus. This indicates some degree of competitive interaction between the specific and nonspecific systems (Jasper et al., 1955) (see Figure 5.10).

The Recruiting Response

Electrical stimulation of the nonspecific thalamic projection nuclei produces characteristic cortical responses which are used to define the anatomical limits of the nonspecific projection system and its direct connections (see Figures 5.10–5.14). A single shock to the intralaminar nuclei produces a spindle burst (see Figure 5.11A and B) which typically appears first in the frontal cortex and only late in posterior association areas (see Figure

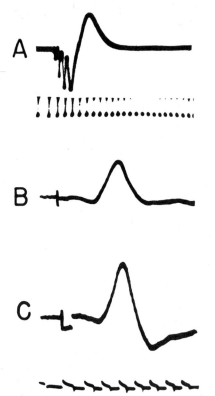

Fig. 5.10   Oscilloscope tracings of A, specific visual evoked potential in response to a single shock to the lateral geniculate body (time marker, 2 msec); B, recruiting potential from recording electrodes in the visual cortex response to stimulating the nucleus ventralis anterior, and C, recruiting response from the same electrode site in the visual cortex after destruction of the lateral geniculate body. Time marker, 10 msec. (From Hanbery and Jasper, 1953.)

5.12). Repetitive stimulation at or near the resting rhythm of the cortex (6 to 12 cps) elicits distinct recruiting responses (see Figure 5.11C) which may have a gradually waxing and waning amplitude; such responses totally obliterate the normal EEG activity. Complex response patterns or complete arrest of all cortical activity may be obtained by high-frequency, high-intensity stimulation of some aspects of the nonspecific thalamic systems.

Microelectrode studies of the recruiting response (Li et al., 1956a, b) have shown that it represents a wave of depolarization which originates in the superficial layers of the cortex. The individual cortical cells that respond to stimulation of the specific sensory systems and relay nuclei of the thalamus are not typically fired by afferents from the nonspecific nuclei, although their threshold to subsequent stimulation of the sensory systems may be significantly lowered. Other cells are fired by the ascending portion of the recruiting wave, but the initial recruiting waves always precede unit firing. This sequence of events suggests that the recruiting response may be analogous to synaptic or dendritic potentials and may initiate rather than reflect unit activity. Some spontaneously active cortical cells respond to the recruiting waves by adjusting their discharge rate upward or downward so that pools of neighboring neurons fire synchronously. This mechanism permits important thalamic influences on the timing of cortical activity. Such cortical driving is effective only when the frequency of thalamic stimulation (and of the recruiting responses of the cortex) approximates the spontaneous rhythmic activity of the cortex.

It has been suggested that the recruiting response may reflect successive increments of depolarization in dendritic networks and that such dendritic responses are mediated by distinct axodendritic synaptic connections which differ functionally from the axosomatic synapses of the specific sensory systems (see Chang, 1952; Bishop, 1956).

Repetitive stimulation of specific sensory nuclei of the thalamus at or near the resting rhythm of the cortex produces "augmenting" responses in the sensory projection areas; these are distinguishable from the recruiting responses only by the short-latency evoked potentials which initiate each response (Morison and Dempsey, 1943). This observation may indicate that components of the nonspecific projection systems are represented in the specific sensory projections, as suggested by the anatomical observation that axodendritic

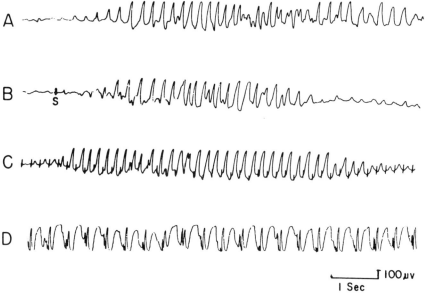

Fig. 5.11 Effect of stimulation in the nucleus centralis medialis of the cat on electrical activity of the anterior suprasylvian gyrus. The animal was under light pentobarbital anesthesia. A, spontaneous spindle burst; B, a single 1-msec shock (s) "tripping" a spindle burst; C, repetitive stimulation at 5/sec showing waxing and waning of recruiting response; D, spike and wave response to stimulation at 2.5/sec. (From Jasper, 1960.)

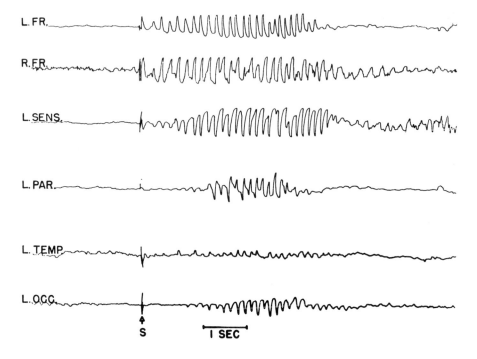

Fig. 5.12 Tripping of spindle bursts in six different cortical areas in response to a single shock in the nucleus centralis medialis of the cat under pentobarbital anesthesia. (From Jasper, 1960.)

synapses can be found in sensory projection areas (Nauta and Whitlock, 1954). Or it may merely show that the dendritic potential is not peculiar to the nonspecific thalamic system (see Figure 5.13).

Functional Relationships

The nonspecific thalamic projection nuclei are intimately related to the lemniscal and extra-lemniscal sensory systems via direct collaterals from all primary pathways, reciprocal intrathalamic connections, and afferents from the brainstem reticular formation. Activation of the nonspecific system may modify the response of the cortical sensory projection areas to afferents in the specific sensory pathways by inhibiting or facilitating the elaboration of signals in various cortical layers or by modifying the aftereffect of the sensory volley. The surface-negative component of the primary evoked potential is most markedly affected by signals in the nonspecific projections (see Figure 5.14) (Jasper and Ajmone-Marsan, 1950).

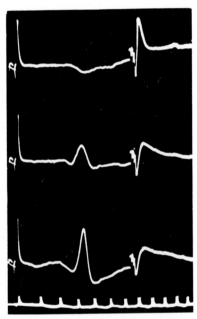

Fig. 5.13 Oscilloscope records of recruiting and specific evoked potentials from the visual cortex obtained simultaneously by repetitive stimulation with paired shocks. The initial shock was applied to the nucleus ventralis anterior followed by a test shock to the lateral geniculate body 62 msec later. Note the reciprocal relationship between the variations in the recruiting wave and the amplitude of the surface-negative component of the specific evoked potential. Time marker, 10 msec. (From Jasper and Ajmone-Marsan, 1950.)

The nonspecific thalamic projections are related to the motor system by direct thalamostriatal projections, pathways to the motor areas of the cortex, and reciprocal connections with the brainstem reticular formation. Cortically induced movement can be facilitated by stimulation of the intralaminar nuclei (Jasper, 1949), although the threshold of the pyramidal cells of the motor cortex does not appear to be affected by recruiting responses (Brookhardt and Zanchetti, 1956).

By far the most important interconnections of the nonspecific thalamic system relate to its function as the dorsal extension of the midbrain reticular formation. Electrophysiological and behavioral activation can be obtained from stimulation of the nonspecific projection nuclei of the thalamus, and large lesions in the anterior portions of the system produce behavioral coma and electrophysiological sleep patterns very much like stimulation or ablation of lower portions of the reticular formation. The effects of thalamic stimulation and ablation are rarely as severe or prolonged as those seen in the midbrain, presumably because alternate, extrathalamic reticulocortical pathways can maintain some measure of influence on the cortex (Lindsley et al., 1949; Lindsley et al., 1950).

Stimulation of the midbrain reticular formation does not typically elicit cortical recruiting responses; it may even block the recruiting response to concurrent thalamic stimulation (Moruzzi and Magoun, 1949). On the other hand, stimulation of the nonspecific projection nuclei of the thalamus rarely produces the maintained behavioral and electrophysiological arousal typical of the response to midbrain stimulation.

Sharpless and Jasper (1956) have demonstrated that two basically different types of cortical activation may exist: a brief "phasic" activation response thought to be related to the activity of the nonspecific thalamic system and a prolonged "tonic" activation which presumably results from extrathalamically mediated activity in the midbrain reticular formation (see also the discussion of arousal mechanisms in Chapter 12 on electrophysiological correlates of the learning process).

Behavioral studies suggest that excitation of the thalamic system tends to produce sleep or behavioral inhibition, whereas midbrain stimulation generally results in activation and arousal (Hunter and Jasper, 1949; Grossman et al., 1965). Jasper (1960) has suggested that the thalamic and midbrain portions of the reticular formation may also differ with respect to their specificity of action. The "nonspecific" thalamic projections are spe-

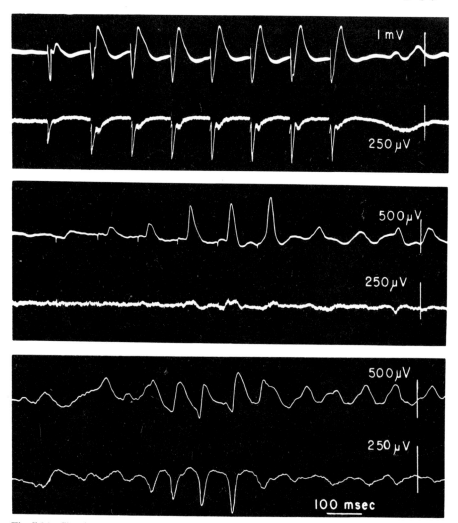

Fig. 5.14 Simultaneous recordings from the anterior sigmoid gyrus (upper trace) and medullary pyramid (lower trace). *Top,* augmenting responses initiated in an unanesthetized cat by stimulation of the nucleus ventralis lateralis; note the "relayed" pyramidal volleys. *Middle,* similar recordings from another preparation, recruiting response initiated by stimulation of the nucleus reuniens; note the stability of the pyramidal recording. *Bottom,* recordings taken during a spontaneous spindle burst in an unanesthetized cat with mesencephalic thermocoagulation; note the relayed spindle waves in the pyramidal recording. (From Brookhart and Zanchetti, 1956.)

cific and modify the activity of restricted portions of the cortex. The midbrain reticular formation, on the other hand, seems to control a more general activating influence which affects all cortical areas regardless of the modality of the arousing stimulus. It is possible that this general influence may provide an essential background of activation against which the specific activation of localized cortical areas can be used to "direct attention" to particular events in the environment. Much more information is needed, particularly about the organization of the midbrain reticular formation, before we can answer this critical question.

BIBLIOGRAPHY

Adey, W. R., Merrillees, C. R., & Sunderland, S. The entorhinal area; behavioral, evoked potential, and histological studies of its interrelationships with brainstem regions. *Brain,* 1956, **79,** 414.

Adey, W. R., Segundo, J. P., & Livingston, R. B. Corticifugal influences on intrinsic brainstem conduction in cat and monkey. *J. Neurophysiol.*, 1957, **20**, 1.

Akimoto, H., Negishi, K., & Yamada, K. Studies on thalamo-cortical connection in cat by means of retrograde degeneration method. *Folia psychiat. neurol. jap.*, 1956a, **10**, 39–82.

Akimoto, H., Yamaguchi, N., Okabe, K., Nakagawa, T., Nakamura, I., Abe, K., Torii, H., & Masahashi, K. On the sleep induced through electrical stimulation of dog thalamus. *Folia psychiat. neurol. jap.*, 1956b, **10**, 117.

Arduini, A., & Moruzzi, G. Sensory and thalamic synchronization in the olfactory bulb. *EEG clin. Neurophysiol.*, 1953, **5**, 235–250.

Austin, G. M. Suprabulbar mechanisms of facilitation and inhibition of cord reflexes. *Res. Publ., Ass. Res. nerv. ment. Dis.*, 1952, **30**, 196–222.

Baumgarten, R. von, & Mollica, A. Der Einfluss sensibler Reizung auf die Entladungsfrequenz Kleinhirnabhängiger Reticulariszellen. *Arch. ges. Physiol.*, 1954, **259**, 79–96.

Bishop, G. H. Natural history of the nerve impulse. *Physiol. Rev.*, 1956, **36**, 376.

Bonvallet, M., Dell, P., & Hiebel, G. Tonus sympathique et activité électrique corticale. *EEG clin. Neurophysiol.*, 1954, **6**, 119.

Bradley, P. B. The central action of certain drugs in relation to the reticular formation of the brain. In *The reticular formation of the brain.* H. H. Jasper, L. D. Proctor, R. S. Knighton, W. C. Noshay, & R. T. Costello, Eds. Boston: Little, Brown, 1958.

Bradley, P. B., & Elkes, J. The effect of amphetamine and *d*-lysergic acid diethylamide (LSD$_{25}$) on the electrical activity of the brain of the conscious cat. *J. Physiol. (London)*, 1953a, **120**, 13.

Bradley, P. B., & Elkes, J. The effect of atropine, hyoseyamine, physostigmine, and neostigmine on the electrical activity of the brain of the conscious cat. *J. Physiol. (London)*, 1953b, **120**, 14.

Brazier, Mary A. B. *Brain mechanisms and consciousness.* E. D. Adrian, F. Bremer, H. H. Jasper, & J. F. Delafresnaye, Eds. Springfield, Ill.: Thomas, 1954.

Bremer, F., & Terzuolo, C. Rôle de l'écorce cérébrale dans le processus du réveil. *Arch. int. Physiol.*, 1952, **60**, 228–231.

Bremer, F., & Terzuolo, C. Contribution à l'étude des mécanismes physiolobiques du maintien de l'activité vibile du cerveau interaction de la formation réticulée et de l'ecorée cérèbrale dans le processus du réveil. *Arch. int. Physiol.*, 1954, **62**, 157.

Brodal, A. Spinal afferents to the lateral reticular nucleus of the medulla oblongata in the cat. *J. comp. Neurol.*, 1949, **91**, 259–296.

Brookhart, J. M., & Zanchetti, A. The relation between electro-cortical waves and responsiveness of the cortico-spinal system. *EEG clin. Neurophysiol.*, 1956, **8**, 427–444.

Bucy, P. C., Ed. *The precentral motor cortex.* Urbana: Univ. of Illinois Press, 1949.

Chambers, W. W., & Sprague, J. W. Functional localization in the cerebellum. I: Organization in longitudinal cortico-nuclear zones and their contribution to the control of posture, both extrapyramidal and pyramidal. *J. comp. Neurol.*, 1955, **103**, 105–129.

Chang, H. T. Cortical neurons with particular reference to the apical dendrites. *Cold Spr. Harb. Symp. quant. Biol.*, 1952, **17**, 189–202.

Dell, P. *The reticular formation of the brain.* H. H. Jasper, L. D. Proctor, R. S. Knighton, W. C. Noshay, & R. T. Costello, Eds. Boston: Little, Brown, 1958.

Droogleever-Fortuyn, J. As cited by Jasper, H. H. In *Handbook of physiology. Vol. II.* J. Field, H. W. Magoun, & V. E. Hall, Eds. Baltimore: Williams and Wilkins, 1960, p. 1308, Fig. 1.

Droogleever-Fortuyn, J., & Stefens, R. On the anatomical relations of the intralaminar and midline cells of the thalamus. *EEG clin. Neurophysiol.*, 1951, **3**, 393–398.

Eccles, J. C., Fatt, P., & Koketsu, K. Cholinergic and inhibitory synapses in a pathway from motor-axon collaterals to motor neurons. *J. Physiol. (London)*, 1954, **126**, 524–562.

Eldred, E., & Fujimori, B. Relations of the reticular formation to muscle spindle activation. In *The reticular formation of the brain.* H. H. Jasper, L. D. Proctor, R. S. Knighton, W. C. Noshay, & R. T. Costello, Eds. Boston: Little, Brown, 1958.

Eliasson, S. Cerebral influence on gastric motility in cat. *Acta physiol scand.*, 1952, **26**, 1.

French, J. D. Brain lesions associated with prolonged unconsciousness. *A.M.A. Arch. Neurol. Psychiat.*, 1952, **68**, 727–740.

French, J. D. The reticular formation. In *Handbook of physiology. Vol. II.* J. Field, H. W. Magoun, & V. E. Hall, Eds. Baltimore: Williams and Wilkins, 1960.

French, J. D., Amerongen, F. K. von, & Magoun, H. W. An activating system in brainstem of monkey. *A.M.A. Arch. Neurol. Psychiat.*, 1952, **68**, 577–590.

French, J. D., Hernández-Peón, R., & Livingston, R. B. Projections from cortex to cephalic brainstem (reticular formation) in monkey. *J. Neurophysiol.*, 1955, **18**, 74.

French, J. D., Verzeano, M., & Magoun, H. W. An extralemniscal sensory system in the brain. *A.M.A. Arch. Neurol. Psychiat.*, 1953, **69**, 505.

Galambos, R. Suppression of auditory nerve activity by stimulation of efferent fibers to cochlea. *J. Neurophysiol.*, 1956, **19**, 424.

Gernandt, B. E., & Thulin, C. A. Reciprocal effects upon spinal motoneurons from stimulation of bulbar reticular formation. *J. Neurophysiol.*, 1955, **18**, 113–129.

Granit, R. *Receptors and sensory perception.* New Haven, Conn.: Yale Univ. Press, 1955.

Granit, R. Neural activity in the retina. In *Handbook of physiology. Vol. I.* J. Field, H. W. Magoun, & V. E. Hall, Eds. Baltimore: Williams and Wilkins, 1959.

Granit, R., & Kaada, B. R. Influence of stimulation of central nervous structures on muscle spindles in cat. *Acta physiol. scand.*, 1952, **27**, 130–150.

Grossman, S. P. Acquisition and performance of avoidance responses during chemical stimulation of the midbrain reticular formation. *J. comp. physiol. Psychol.*, 1966, in press.

Grossman, S. P., & Grossman, Lore. Effects of chemical stimulation of the midbrain reticular formation on appetitive behavior. *J. comp. physiol. Psychol.*, 1966, in press.

Grossman, S. P., Peters, R. H., Freedman, P. E., & Willer, H. I. Behavioral effects of cholinergic stimulation of the thalamic reticular formation. *J. comp. physiol. Psychol.*, 1965, **50**, 57–65.

Hagbarth, K. E., & Kerr, D. I. B. Central influences on spinal afferent conduction. *J. Neurophysiol.*, 1954, **17**, 295.

Hanbery, J., & Jasper, H. H. Independence of the diffuse thalamo-cortical projection system shown by specific nuclear destruction. *J. Neurophysiol.*, 1953, **16**, 252.

Hanbery, J., Ajmone-Marsan, C., & Dilworth, M. Pathways of non-specific thalamocortical projection system. *EEG clin. Neurophysiol.*, 1954, **6**, 103.

Hernández-Peón, R., Scherrer, H., & Velasco, M. Central influences on afferent conduction in the somatic and visual pathways. *Acta neurol. lat.-amer.*, 1956, **2**, 8.

Hess, W. R. Lokalisatorische Ergebnisse der Hirnreizversuche mit Schlafeffect. *Arch. Psychiat.*, 1929, **88**, 813.

Hess, W. R. *Das Zwischenhirn: Syndrome, Lokalisationen, Funktionen.* Basel: Schwabe, 1949.

Hess, W. R. *Diencephalon: autonomic and extrapyramidal functions.* New York: Grune and Stratton, 1954.

Hodes, R. S., Peacock, S. M., & Heath, R. G. Influence of the fore-brain on somato-motor activity. *J. comp. Neurol.*, 1951, **94**, 381–408.

Hunt, C. C., & Kuffler, S. W. Further study of efferent small-nerve fibers to mammalian muscle spindles. Multiple spindle innervation and activity during contraction. *J. Physiol. (London)*, 1951, **113**, 283.

Hunter, J., & Jasper, H. H. Effect of thalamic stimulation in unanesthetized animals. *EEG clin. Neurophysiol.*, 1949, **1**, 305.

Ingvar, D. H. Reproduction of the 3 per second spike and wave EEG pattern by subcortical electrical stimulation in cats. *Acta physiol. scand.*, 1955, **33**, 137–150.

Ingvar, D. H. *The reticular formation of the brain.* H. H. Jasper, L. D. Proctor, R. S. Knighton, W. C. Noshay, & R. T. Costello, Eds. Boston: Little, Brown, 1958.

Jasper, H. H. Diffuse projection systems: the integrative action of the thalamic reticular system. *EEG clin. Neurophysiol.*, 1949, **1**, 405.

Jasper, H. H. *Brain mechanisms and consciousness.* E. D.

Adrian, F. Bremer, H. H. Jasper, & J. F. Delafresnaye, Eds. Springfield, Ill.: Thomas, 1954.

Jasper, H. H. Unspecific thalamocortical relations. In *Handbook of physiology. Vol. II.* J. Field, H. W. Magoun, & V. E. Hall, Eds. Baltimore: Williams and Wilkins, 1960.

Jasper, H. H., & Ajmone-Marsan, C. Thalamocortical integrating mechanisms. *Res. Publ., Ass. Res. nerv. ment. Dis.*, 1950, **30**, 493.

Jasper, H. H., Naquet, R., & King, E. E. Thalamocortical recruiting responses in sensory receiving areas in the cat. *EEG clin. Neurophysiol.*, 1955, **7**, 99.

Jasper, H. H., Proctor, L. D., Knighton, R. S., Noshay, W. C., & Costello, R. T., Eds. *The reticular formation of the brain.* Boston: Little, Brown, 1958.

Jouvet, M., & Desmedt, J. E. Contrôle central des messages acoustiques afferents. *C. R. Acad. Sci. (Paris)*, 1956, **243**, 1916–1917.

Kerr, D. I. B., & Hagbarth, K. E. An investigation of olfactory centrifugal fiber system. *J. Neurophysiol.*, 1955, **18**, 362.

Killam, E. E., & Killam, K. *The reticular formation of the brain.* H. H. Jasper, L. D. Proctor, R. S. Knighton, W. C. Noshay, & R. T. Costello, Eds. Boston: Little, Brown, 1958.

Killam, E. E., Killam, K., & Shaw, T. The effects of psychotherapeutic compounds on central afferent and limbic pathways. *Ann. N.Y. Acad. Sci.*, 1957, **66**, 784.

King, E. E., Naquet, R., & Magoun, H. W. Alterations in somatic afferent transmission through thalamus by central mechanisms and barbiturates. *J. Pharmacol. exp. Therap.*, 1957, **119**, 48–63.

Kleyntjens, F., Koizumi, K., & McBrooks, C. Stimulation of suprabulbar reticular formation. *Arch. Neurol. Psychiat. (Chicago)*, 1955, **73**, 425–438.

Kuffler, S. W., & Hunt, C. C. Mammalian small-nerve fibers: system for efferent nervous regulation of muscle spindle discharge. *Res. Publ., Ass. Res. nerv. ment. Dis.*, 1952, **30**, 24–47.

Lewandowsky, M. *Untersuchungen über die Leitungsbahnen des Truncus cerebri und ihrem Zusammenhang mit denen der Medulla spinalis und des Cortex cerebri.* Jena: Fischer, 1904.

Li, C. L., Cullen, C., & Jasper, H. H. Laminar microelectrode studies of specific somatosensory cortical potentials. *J. Neurophysiol.*, 1956a, **19**, 111–130.

Li, C. L., Cullen, C., & Jasper, H. H. Laminar microelectrode analysis of cortical unspecific recruiting responses and spontaneous rhythms. *J. Neurophysiol.*, 1956b, **19**, 131.

Lindsley, D. B. Attention, consciousness, sleep and wakefulness. In *Handbook of physiology. Vol. III.* J. Field, H. W. Magoun, & V. E. Hall, Eds. Baltimore: Williams and Wilkins, 1960.

Lindsley, D. B., Bowden, J. W., & Magoun, H. W. Effect upon EEG of acute injury to the brainstem activating system. *EEG clin. Neurophysiol.*, 1949, **1**, 475.

Lindsley, D. B., Schreiner, L. H., Knowles, W. B., &

Magoun, H. W. Behavioral and EEG changes following chronic brainstem lesions in the cat. *EEG clin. Neurophysiol.*, 1950, **2**, 483.

Livingston, R. B. Central control of receptors and sensory transmission systems. In *Handbook of physiology. Vol. I.* J. Field, H. W. Magoun, & V. E. Hall, Eds. Baltimore: Williams and Wilkins, 1959.

Lloyd, D. P. C. Activity in neurons of the bulbospinal correlation system. *J. Neurophysiol.*, 1941a, **4**, 115–134.

Lloyd, D. P. C. The spinal mechanism of the pyramidal system in cats. *J. Neurophysiol.*, 1941b, **4**, 525–546.

Loewenstein, W. R. Modulation of cutaneous mechanoreceptors by sympathetic stimulation. *J. Physiol. (London)*, 1956, **132**, 40.

McCulloch, W. S., Graf, G., & Magoun, H. W. Cortico-bulbo-reticular pathway from area 4-s. *J. Neurophysiol.*, 1946, **9**, 127.

McLardy, T. Projection of the centromedian nucleus of the human thalamus. *Brain*, 1948, **71**, 290–303.

McLardy, T. Diffuse thalamic projection to cortex: an anatomical critique. *EEG clin. Neurophysiol.*, 1951, **3**, 183–188.

McMasters, R. E. Efferent projections of the deep nuclei of the cerebellum of the cat. *Anat. Rec.*, 1957, **127**, 331–332.

Magoun, H. W. Caudal and cephalic influences of brainstem reticular formation. *Physiol. Rev.*, 1950, **30**, 459–474.

Magoun, H. W. *Parkinsonism and its treatment.* L. J. Doshay, Ed. Philadelphia: Lippincott, 1954.

Magoun, H. W., & Rhines, Ruth. An inhibitory mechanism in the bulbar reticular formation. *J. Neurophysiol.*, 1946, **9**, 165–171.

Magoun, H. W., & Rhines, Ruth. *Spasticity: the stretch reflex and extrapyramidal systems.* Springfield, Ill.: Thomas, 1947.

Mettler, F. A. Corticifugal connections of cortex of *Macaca mulatta. J. comp. Neurol.*, 1935a, **61**, 221.

Mettler, F. A. Corticifugal connections of cortex of *Macaca mulatta;* frontal region. *J. comp. Neurol.*, 1935b, **61**, 509.

Mettler, F. A. Corticifugal connections of cortex of *Macaca mulatta;* parietal region. *J. comp. Neurol.*, 1935c, **62**, 263.

Mettler, F. A. Corticifugal fiber connections of cortex of *Macaca mulatta;* temporal region. *J. comp. Neurol.*, 1935d, **63**, 25.

Morin, F. Afferent projections to the midbrain tegmentum and their spinal course. *Amer. J. Physiol.*, 1953, **172**, 483–496.

Morison, R. S., & Dempsey, E. W. Mechanism of thalamocortical augmentation and repetition. *Amer. J. Physiol.*, 1943, **138**, 297–308.

Moruzzi, G. *Problems in cerebellar physiology.* Springfield, Ill.: Thomas, 1950.

Moruzzi, G. *Brain mechanisms and consciousness.* E. D. Adrian, F. Bremer, H. H. Jasper, & J. F. Delafresnaye, Eds. Springfield, Ill.: Thomas, 1954.

Moruzzi, G., & Magoun, H. W. Brainstem reticular formation and activation of the EEG. *EEG clin. Neurophysiol.*, 1949, **1**, 455.

Nashold, B. S., Hanbery, J., & Olszewski, J. Observations on the diffuse thalamic projections. *EEG clin. Neurophysiol.*, 1955, **7**, 609–620.

Nauta, W. J. H. *The reticular formation of the brain.* H. H. Jasper, L. D. Proctor, R. S. Knighton, W. C. Noshay, & R. T. Costello, Eds. Boston: Little, Brown, 1958.

Nauta, W. J. H., & Whitlock, D. G. *Brain mechanisms and consciousness.* E. D. Adrian, F. Bremer, H. H. Jasper, & J. F. Delafresnaye, Eds. Oxford: Blackwell, 1954.

Niemer, W. T., & Magoun, H. W. Reticulo-spinal tracts influencing motor activity. *J. comp. Neurol.*, 1947, **87**, 367–379.

Nulsen, F. E., Black, S. P. W., & Drake, C. G. Inhibition and facilitation of motor activity by the anterior cerebellum. *Fed. Proc.*, 1948, **7**, 86.

Olszewski, J. *Brain mechanisms and consciousness.* E. D. Adrian, F. Bremer, H. H. Jasper, & J. F. Delafresnaye, Eds. Springfield, Ill.: Thomas, 1954.

Peacock, S. M., & Hodes, R. S. Influence of the forebrain on somato-motor activity. *J. comp. Neurol.*, 1951, **94**, 409–426.

Pribram, K. H. The intrinsic systems of the forebrain. In *Handbook of physiology. Vol. II.* J. Field, H. W. Magoun, & V. E. Hall, Eds. Baltimore: Williams and Wilkins, 1960.

Putnam, T. J. Relief from unilateral paralysis agitans by section of the pyramidal tract. *A.M.A. Arch. Neurol. Psychiat.*, 1938, **40**, 1049–1050.

Ramón y Cajal, S. *Histologie du système nerveux de l'homme et des vertébrés* (reprinted from original, 1909–1911). Madrid: Consejo Superior de Investigaciones Cientificas, 1952–1955.

Ranson, S. W., & Ranson, S. W., Jr. Efferent fibers of corpus striatum. *Res. Publ., Ass. Res. nerv. ment. Dis.*, 1942, **21**, 69–76.

Rasmussen, G. L. Further observations of the efferent cochlear bundle. *J. comp. Neurol.*, 1953, **99**, 61.

Rose, J. E. Cortical connections of reticular complex of thalamus. *Res. Publ., Ass. Res. nerv. ment. Dis.*, 1952, **30**, 454–479.

Rose, J. E., & Woolsey, C. N. Organization of the mammalian thalamus and its relationship to the cerebral cortex. *EEG clin. Neurophysiol.*, 1949, **1**, 391–404.

Rossi, G. F., & Brodal, A. Corticofugal fibres to the brainstem reticular formation: an experimental study in the cat. *J. Anat.*, 1956, **90**, 42.

Rothballer, A. B. Studies on the adrenaline-sensitive component of the reticular activating system. *EEG clin. Neurophysiol.*, 1956, **8**, 603.

Scheibel, M. E., & Scheibel, A. B. Structural substrates for integrative patterns in the brainstem reticular core. In *The reticular formation of the brain.* H. H. Jasper, L. D. Proctor, R. S. Knighton, W. C. Noshay, & R. T. Costello, Eds. Boston: Little, Brown, 1958.

Scheibel, M. E., Scheibel, A. B., Mollica, A., & Moruzzi, G. Convergence and interaction of afferent impulses on single units of reticular formation. *J. Neurophysiol.*, 1955, **18**, 309.

Scherrer, H., & Hernández-Peón, R. Inhibitory influence of reticular formation upon synaptic transmission in bracilus nucleus. *Fed. Proc.*, 1955, **14**, 132.

Segundo, J. P., Arana, R., & French, J. D. Behavioral arousal by stimulation of the brain in the monkey. *J. Neurosurg.*, 1955, **12**, 601.

Sharpless, S., & Jasper, H. H. Habituation of the arousal reaction. *Brain*, 1956, **79**, 655.

Snider, R. S., & Stowell, A. Receiving areas of the tactile, auditory, and visual systems in the cerebellum. *J. Neurophysiol.*, 1944, **7**, 331–357.

Snider, R. S., McCulloch, W. S., & Magoun, H. W. A cerebello-bulbo-reticular pathway for suppression. *J. Neurophysiol.*, 1949, **12**, 325–334.

Sprague, J. M. Stimulation of reticular formation in intact, unanesthetized and in decerebrated cats. *Fed. Proc.*, 1953, **12**, 137.

Sprague, J. M., & Chambers, W. W. Control of posture by reticular formation and cerebellum in the intact, anesthetized and unanesthetized and in the decerebrated cat. *Amer. J. Physiol.*, 1954, **176**, 52–64.

Sprague, J. M., Cohen, D., & Chambers, W. W. Efferent cerebellar pathways to brainstem. *Anat. Rec.*, 1957, **127**, 372 (abstract).

Starzl, T. E., & Magoun, H. W. Organization of the diffuse thalamic projection system. *J. Neurophysiol.*, 1951, **14**, 133–146.

Starzl, T. E., & Whitlock, D. G. Diffuse thalamic projection system in monkey. *J. Neurophysiol.*, 1952, **15**, 449–468.

Wall, P. D., Glees, P., & Fulton, J. F. Corticofugal connexions of posterior orbital surface in rhesus monkey. *Brain*, 1951, **74**, 66.

Whitlock, D. G., & Schreiner, L. H. Some connections of the midline region and centre median nucleus of the thalamus of the cat. *Anat. Rec.*, 1954, **118**, 368.

PART THREE

CHAPTER SIX

Hunger and the Regulation
of the Organism's Energy Balance

Hunger has traditionally served as the proto-type of primary motivation in the psychological laboratory. Its physiological parallel, the question of energy balance, has been studied extensively in the physiological laboratory; it represents one of the most important mechanisms which permit the organism to maintain a constant internal environment in the face of constantly changing external conditions.

Although we know a great deal about the psychological aspects of hunger and the physiological and biochemical mechanisms that contribute to the organism's energy balance, it is, in fact, difficult to define precisely what is meant by either concept. We do not yet understand the contribution of the many peripheral and central physiologic mechanisms well enough to define the antecedents of feeding behavior in this fashion. Psychologic theory and observation have generally disregarded the important relationship between hunger and the organism's energy balance and provide little more than pragmatically useful, but theoretically inconclusive, "operational" definitions. Some surveys of the literature (Carlson, 1916; M. I. Grossman, 1955) suggest that hunger may be defined as "a complex of sensations," but what about lower organisms which lack a sufficiently developed nervous system to experience complex sensations? Are insects not hungry merely because the regulation of their feeding behavior appears to be relatively simple (Dethier and Bodenstein, 1957)?

The ingestion of nutrient substances is a necessary condition for the survival of all living organisms. Our interest in the complex organization of man and higher mammals should not obscure the fact that the regulation of food intake (and hunger) must be a universal property of all organisms.

THE ORGANISM'S ENERGY BALANCE

Before delving into the complex problem of how the organism maintains a constant relationship between energy output and energy input, it is necessary to take a brief look at just what is being regulated.

Implicit in the early physiological theories of hunger (Haller, 1776; Darwin, 1801; Carlson, 1916; Cannon, 1934) is the assumption that peripheral, gastric mechanisms regulate food intake on the basis of information from the gastrointestinal tract itself, and are essentially independent of chemical or nervous changes elsewhere in the body. Carlson (1916) presents this position in his conclusion that "the gastric hunger mechanism is primarily automatic or independent of blood changes as well as central nervous influences." It must have been clear even to these pioneering physiologists that variations in food intake affect more than the digestive tract; however, they made little or no provision for feedback mechanisms which must correlate gastric activity with the needs of the organism.

More recent investigations of this problem have arrived at the notion of an overall energy balance which the organism attempts to maintain at equilibrium; however, the specific mechanisms which contribute to the regulation, i.e., precisely what is regulated, are still the subject of debate.

Cowgill (1928) reported a linear relationship between body length and log calorie expenditure per hour (64 cal/hr/meter^2 of body surface). He maintained that this relationship held under widely varying conditions of energy output. On an *ad libitum* feeding schedule, the animals maintained a constant body weight indefinitely and adjusted their intake when the energy content of the diet was altered. Gasnier and Mayer (1939a,

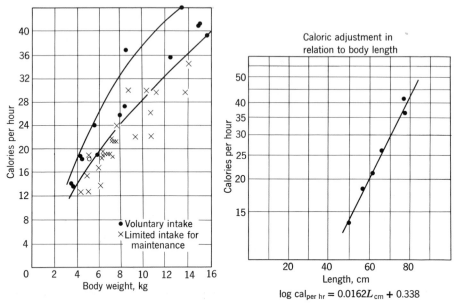

Fig. 6.1 Caloric adjustments of dogs (indicated by circles). Cases of limited intake designed to secure maintenance are represented by crosses. The area between the lines may be regarded as representing the zone of caloric adjustment. (From Cowgill, 1928.)

b, c, d, e) demonstrated that the body constituents other than water and nitrogen remained almost constant over a period of 80 days under controlled temperature and humidity conditions. A nearly perfect linear proportionality was found to exist between energy input as measured by the energy equivalent of the food, feces, and urine, and energy output as determined by environmental temperature. Caloric intake increased following the exposure to cold but decreased sharply when the temperature was raised above normal levels. Gasnier and Mayer concluded from their extensive observations that the organism's energy balance appeared to be subject to two cooperating regulatory influences. A short-term, day-to-day regulation would permit relatively large deviations from the ideal proportionality between energy input and energy output, and a long-term regulation would somehow compensate for these errors.

This conclusion is supported by observations from experiments that have manipulated the organism's energy output more drastically. Mayer et al. (1954) found that exercise disrupted the feeding pattern of rats, but the animals rapidly adjusted their food intake to counterbalance the stepped-up output almost precisely. Rats running in a treadmill from 1 to 5 hr per day showed a linear increment in food intake with increasing

output and maintained a constant body weight. The regulatory mechanism appeared to operate only within a normal range. Very brief (20 to 60 min) or very prolonged (over 5 hr) periods of exercise were not adequately compensated and resulted in a decrease in body weight.

The proportionality between energy input and output is apparently maintained even in animals with central nervous system lesions which produce hyperphagia (overeating). Lundbaek and Stevenson (1947), for instance, found that both normal and hyperphagic animals adjusted their daily food consumption to maintain constant caloric intake when switched from a high-carbohydrate to a high-fat diet. A shift in the opposite direction interfered with the caloric regulation, but the disturbance appeared to be temporary. Kennedy (1950) similarly reported that young rats adjusted their food intake when their diet was diluted with up to 75% of non-nutrient roughage and maintained a constant caloric intake. In these studies hyperphagic animals with a markedly different input-output ratio also maintained a constant relationship and make the adjustments even more rapidly than normal animals. This regulation broke down when the hyperphagic animals reached a maximum body weight and stopped overeating.

In subsequent studies Kennedy (1952) found

that hyperphagic animals also can maintain a constant input-output ratio when the energy output is manipulated by changes in the environmental temperature. The regression line of food intake on rate of weight gain was found to be identical at 23 and 34° Celsius. The relationship between environmental temperature and food intake has suggested to some investigators (Brobeck, 1947–1948) that food intake and hunger may be regulated as part of the organism's temperature regulation. This hypothesis and related empirical observations will be discussed in detail later in this chapter.

Many factors may contribute to a disturbance of an organism's energy balance. Genetically obese mice, for instance, become fat on a normal diet because of a marked decrease in energy output. Some lesions in the central nervous system (i.e., in the frontal cortex) drastically increase the organism's energy input; however, this change may not be reflected in body weight because a concurrent rise in locomotor activity compensates for the abnormal input. Lesions in other parts of the brain (i.e., the hypothalamus) may produce a sharp increase or decrease in food intake which is not balanced by a compensatory change in the energy output mechanisms and thus leads to adiposity or death.

These observations suggest that hunger may be the end result of a variety of complex and continually interacting regulatory mechanisms. A closer look at the experimental literature in this field supports such an interpretation.

HISTORICAL DEVELOPMENTS

Peripheral Theories

Hunger and appetite have been favorite topics of literary essays throughout the history of man. (See informative and entertaining reviews of this material by Sternberg, 1908, 1910, 1911.) The first scientific treatises on the subject of hunger and appetite date back to some of the natural scientists of the eighteenth and nineteenth centuries.

Haller (1776) proposed that hunger seemed to be a sensation of exclusively peripheral origin which arises as a direct consequence of the stimulation of sensory nerves from the stomach. A similar interpretation was supported by Erasmus Darwin (1801), although he disagreed with Haller about the mechanisms which produce the stimulation. Where Haller proposed that the "hunger-nerves" in the mucosa of the gastrointestinal tract

may be stimulated by a "grinding or rubbing (tritus) of the delicate and vilous folds the gastric mucosa against each other, through a motion or contraction inherent in the stomach," Darwin thought that the sensation of hunger might indeed be caused by an opposite condition—the atonicity and absence of contractions in the empty stomach.

Johannes Müller, in his famous *Handbuch der Physiologie des Menschen* (1844), supported a purely peripheral interpretation of hunger and suggested that hunger sensations may reflect merely the absence of some positive sensation which is normally generated in the gastrointestinal tract during the digestion of foods.

Another group of investigators (von Voit, 1881; Stiller, 1915) accepted the gastric origin of the hunger sensations without committing themselves to a specific mechanism of stimulation. Soemmering (1794) and Bostock (1836) proposed that the stimulation of gastric nerves might be caused by the release of gastric juices.

The theory of hunger as a purely negative phenomenon has failed to attract much attention or support from later workers, but stomach contractions became widely accepted as the physiological basis and correlate of hunger (Vierordt, 1871; Knapp, 1906; Hertz, 1911), even before Cannon and Washburn (1912) demonstrated a correlation between such "hunger contractions" and the report of hunger sensations in man.

Central Theories

Diametrically opposed to these peripheral interpretations of the origin of hunger are such central hypotheses as Magendie's (1826) postulation of a hypothetical, neural center in the brain, believed to give rise to periodic hunger sensations irrespective of any sensations from the stomach. Such autonomous central mechanisms were accepted by many influential physiologists of the nineteenth century (Tiedemann, 1836; Schiff, 1867; Ewald, 1893; Wundt, 1902); their preoccupation with central influences has prompted many of the experiments that have provided the empirical basis for more recent and less radical central theories of hunger. Bardier (1911), for instance, proposed that a "hunger center" somewhere in the brain responded to changes in blood composition which occur during privation and to nervous afferents from all organs of the body. The afferent impulses were believed to be initiated by a depletion of nutrients from the blood.

The core of this theory—that some changes take

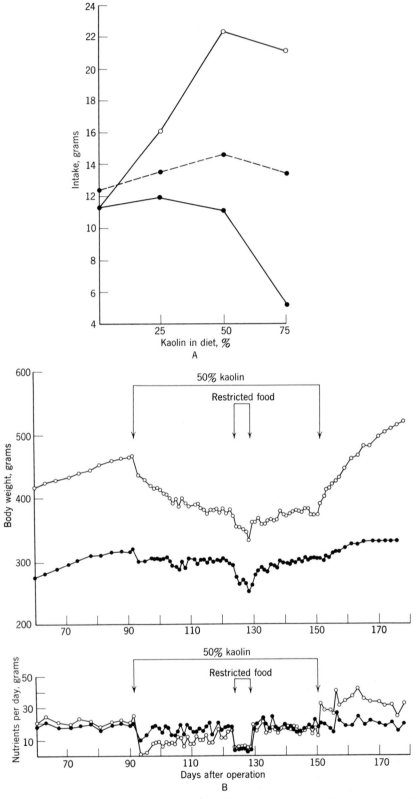

Fig. 6.2 A, effect of dilution of diet with kaolin on daily intake of normal male rats: total solids eaten (o—o), nutrient intake (●—●), water intake (●---●). B, reaction of one animal with ventromedial nucleus damage (open circles) and one control animal (filled circles) to a 50% kaolin mixture. (From Kennedy, 1950.)

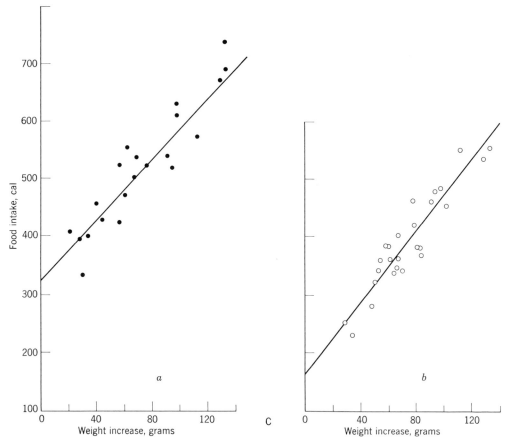

Fig. 6.2 (continued)   C, Linear regression of food intake on the weight gain of hyperphagic rats during 14-day periods of maximal weight gain *a*, at 75°F; *b*, at 94°F. (From Kennedy, 1952.)

place in the blood of deprived organisms which directly or indirectly stimulate a hunger center in the brain—has been accepted by many physiologists of the nineteenth century (Longet, 1868; Roux, 1897; Foster, 1891; Schlessinger, 1893) and continues to play an important role in theoretical thinking today.

Early clinical investigations of obesity (Mohr, 1840; Fröhlich, 1902; Erdheim, 1904) supported the notion of a hunger center located at the base of the brain and have led to extensive studies of the role of the hypothalamus in the control of food intake.

Historically, then, there are two diametrically opposed traditions, one supporting an exclusively peripheral theory, the other a primarily, if not exclusively, central one. The empirical evidence and theoretical thought of the past 50 years and the concurrent attempt to integrate these divergent views will now be discussed.

PERIPHERAL MECHANISMS

Before discussing the experimental observations which have suggested the operation of various peripheral neural and chemical factors, we will present a brief review of the digestive system, since most of the peripheral influences arise directly from the intestinal tract.

The Structure and Function of the Digestive System

Gross anatomy. The digestive system is designed to permit the ingestion of foodstuffs, their reduction to simpler substances, the absorption of nutrients, electrolytes, and water, and the removal of waste products.

Food is ingested into the mouth. Here it is broken down into smaller particles for transport through the pharynx and esophagus to the stom-

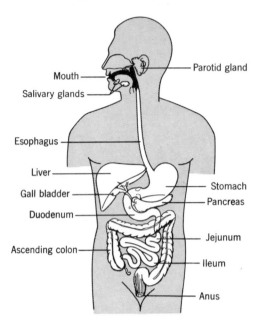

Fig. 6.3   The alimentary tract. (From Guyton, 1961.)

ach. This is an important step in the digestive process, for the nutrients of most fruits and vegetables cannot be digested unless the tough, indigestible cellulose membrane which surrounds them is broken in the process of mastication. The utilization of other foodstuffs is also facilitated, for digestive enzymes can act only on the surface of food particles; thus, the smaller the particles, the greater the total surface area of the original intake and the faster the digestion.

The stomach serves largely to store foodstuffs and mix them with gastric secretions until a semifluid mixture called chyme results. Chyme is then transported to the small intestine at a rate that is adjusted to be maximally suitable to the digestion and absorption of the nutrients in it.

The mixing of the foodstuffs in the stomach is accomplished by small and relatively weak *tonus waves* of muscular activity; these occur about once every 20 sec in man and gradually spread over much of the stomach, traveling in the direction of the pylorus. The movement of food through the stomach results from large *peristaltic waves* which arise in the antrum and spread into the duodenum. A third type of contraction, commonly called *hunger contraction,* occurs primarily in the empty stomach.

The rate at which foods move into the duodenum is determined largely by the intensity of the peristaltic waves, but is also influenced by the

fluidity of the chyme (a function of the type of food, degree of mastication, intensity of tonus waves, and length of storage in the stomach) and the receptivity of the small intestine (determined by the amount of chyme previously moved to the duodenum, the acidity of the chyme, and the type of foods represented). The peristaltic activity may be slowed down either by a direct *enterogastric reflex* (which involves only neurons to and from the stomach) or by the secretion of a hormone, *enterogastrone.* These inhibiting influences are elicited when the chyme is acid, fat, or other than isotonic, or when the small intestine is already full.

In the small intestine the chyme is further mixed with secretions from the intestinal glands and is propelled forward toward the colon by peristaltic waves which are initiated by the *gastroenteric* reflex response to distension of the walls of the stomach. This reflex response consists of an increase in the intensity and frequency of the muscular contractions and secretions from the walls of the small intestine and is mediated by neurons of the *myenteric plexus.*

The waste products of the digestive process eventually pass through the *ileocaecal valve* from the *ileum* into the *caecum* of the *colon.* Here the fecal matter continues to be mixed so that every bit of it is eventually exposed to the surface of the large intestine. This exposure permits the absorption of water and electrolytes, the primary function of the proximal half of the colon.

The fecal matter is gradually propelled toward the descending colon and anus by mass movements of the musculature of the colon initiated by *duodenocolic* reflex responses to the entrance of foods into the duodenum.

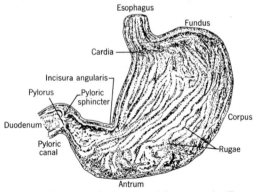

Fig. 6.4   Functional anatomy of the stomach. (From Guyton, 1961.)

Basic secretory functions. The gastrointestinal tract contains glands that secrete *mucus* to lubricate and protect the system and, particularly in its upper portions, glands that secrete essential *digestive enzymes* which permit a breakdown of foodstuffs for assimilation. The digestive secretions occur in response to the presence of specific foodstuffs in particular portions of the alimentary canal. Even the constituents of the individual secretions may vary as a function of the foodstuffs that are to be attacked. Moreover, the quantity of the enzymes secreted in response to the ingestion of foods is usually precisely enough, not more or less, to provide adequate digestion, a remarkable mechanism indeed.

The first source of digestive secretions are the *salivary glands* (the parotid, submaxillary, sublingual, and buccal glands). Saliva contains a *serous* secretion which carries the enzyme for the digestion of starches (*ptyalin*) and a *mucous* secretion which lubricates the buccal cavity and esophageal and pharyngeal passages. The activity of the salivary glands is regulated largely by the inferior and superior salivary nuclei of the bulbar-pontine region of the brainstem. Salivation may be elicited by central influences (as when one thinks of biting into a fresh lemon), buccal stimulation (the normal response to foods in the mouth), and gastrointestinal stimuli (the salivation elicited by nausea).

The *pyloric* and *cardiac glands* of the stomach secrete only a very thin mucus which serves mainly to protect the stomach walls from digestive influences of the gastric enzymes and to thin the chyme for further transport. The *digestive glands* of the stomach contain a variety of cells that serve a variety of functions. The *neck* cells secrete mucus, the *chief* cells secrete digestive enzymes, and the *parietal* cells secrete hydrochloric acid. The principal digestive enzyme, *pepsin*, is stored in the chief cells in an inactive form called *pepsinogen*. It is activated by hydrochloric acid from the parietal cells and requires a pH of 5 or lower to retain its proteolytic (protein-digesting) activity.

When food enters the stomach, an intermediate hormone called *gastrin* is released from the antral portion of the stomach. This hormone is absorbed into the blood and subsequently stimulates the gastric glands, possibly by initiating the release of histamine from some unknown donor. Since the gastric secretions continue for some time after food has left the stomach, it is assumed that the lower intestine may also secrete some hormones that affect the activity of the gastric glands. No specific substances have as yet been isolated.

By far the most important influence on the secretory activity of the gastric glands originates centrally and is transmitted to the stomach via the vagus nerve. Stomach secretions may also be inhibited by (1) an enterogastric reflex which originates from pressure receptors in the small intestine and exerts its effect on the glands of the stomach via the vagus nerve, (2) the release of the hormone enterogastrone in response to the presence of fat and, to a lesser extent, sugar in the small intestine, and (3) local inhibitory reflex responses to a fall in gastric pH.

The presence of foods in the upper portions of the small intestine causes the release and activation of a polypeptide hormone called *secretin* which stimulates the pancreas to secrete a mixture of *sodium bicarbonate* and *sodium chloride;* this mixture acts to neutralize the very acidic chyme and thus stops the peptic activity of the gastric enzyme which would otherwise digest the walls of the small intestine. Another hormone, *pancreozymin*, is released from the small intestine upon the arrival of chyme, particularly if it contains intermediate products of protein digestion *protoses* and *peptones*. Pancreozymin acts on the pancreas to elicit the secretion of digestive enzymes.

The pancreatic juices contain enzymes for the digestion of proteins (*trypsin, chymotrypsin,* and *carboxypolypeptidase*), carbohydrates (*pancreatic amylase*), and fats (*pancreatic lipase*). These enzymes are stored in an inactive form and are activated by specific foodstuffs upon release into the upper intestine. Pancreatic secretions occur in response to hormonal (see above) or neural stimulation. The latter relies on vagal efferents from the central nervous system and local reflex connections.

The presence of fats in the upper intestine causes the release of a hormone called *cholecystokinin* from the intestinal mucosa; cholecystokinin elicits rhythmic contractions of the gallbladder. These contractions, in conjunction with the peristaltic activity of the gastrointestinal tract, initiate the release of *bile*. This substance is continuously secreted by the liver and is stored in the gallbladder until needed. It contains no digestive enzymes but is essential for the digestion of fats. It emulsifies fat globules and renders the end product of fat digestion soluble for absorption through the gastrointestinal mucosa.

Immediately inside the duodenum, *Bruner's glands* secrete mucus in response to various intestinal hormones, vagal efferents from the central nervous system, or local reflex stimulation. These secretions protect the duodenal walls from digestion. *Paneth cells* in the mucosa of the small intestine secrete *peptidases* which split polypeptides into amino acids; *intestinal lipases* which split neutral fats into glycerol and fatty acids; *intestinal amylases* which split carbohydrates into disaccharides; and *sucrases, maltases,* and *isomaltases* which split the disaccharides into absorbable monosaccharides. Larger glands, the *crypts of Lieberkühn,* secrete a substance called *succus entericus* which provides the final steps of digestion before the foodstuffs can be absorbed. It breaks proteins into amino acids, carbohydrates into monosaccharides, and neutral fats into fatty acids and glycerol. The rate of secretion of this important enzyme is determined by the relative distension of the small intestine.

The glands of the large intestine secrete primarily mucus needed to protect the walls of the colon.

The innervation of the gastrointestinal tract. The *intramural nerve plexus* accompanies the entire length of the gastrointestinal tract from the esophagus to the anus. It consists essentially of two layers of neurons, the outer, *myenteric plexus* (also called *Auerbach's plexus*) and the inner, *Meissner's plexus.* Stimulation of the intramural plexus increases the tonus of the gut and the amplitude, rate, and velocity of the rhythmic contractions of its walls. The intramural plexus is responsible for the many local reflex responses which coordinate peristaltic movements and initiate the secretion of gastric enzymes and mucus.

The gastrointestinal tract also receives extensive sympathetic and parasympathetic fibers from the central nervous system. Cranial parasympathetic fibers reach the esophagus, stomach, pancreas, gallbladder, small intestine, and upper portions of the large intestine via the vagus nerve. Sacral parasympathetics reach the distal half of the large intestine via the *nervi erigentes.* The postganglionic neurons of the parasympathetic system lie largely in Auerbach's plexus. Sympathetic efferents to the digestive system project through the sympathetic chain and synapse on ganglion cells in the *celiac* and *mesenteric ganglia.*

Sympathetic stimulation generally inhibits the activity of the digestive system (it excites the anal and ileocaecal sphincter muscles, but this also serves inhibitory purposes). Parasympathetic stimulation produces more specific facilitatory effects on local reflex activity and causes a general increase in tonus and activity.

Digestion and absorption. Natural foods (carbohydrates, proteins, and fats) cannot be absorbed in their natural form and are totally useless until broken down into smaller particles in the process of digestion.

Digestion. Most carbohydrates are *polysaccharides,* combinations of *monosaccharides* that are bound together when a hydrogen ion is removed from one monosaccharide and a hydroxyl group from another. Digestion, or the breakdown of the polysaccharides, consists essentially of a return of the missing hydrogen and hydroxyl ions in a process of *hydrolysis.*

There are three major sources of carbohydrates, *sucrose* (cane sugar), *lactose* (found in milk), and *starches* (grains and most other vegetables).

Up to 40% of the polysaccharides are hydrolyzed in the mouth to simpler disaccharides, by the enzyme ptyalin. The gastric enzymes have only a small hydrolyzing effect. In the small intestine the enzyme pancreatic amylase hydrolyzes all polysaccharides to disaccharides. The four enzymes of the small intestine (lactase, sucrase, maltase, and isomaltase) then reduce the corresponding disaccharides (*lactose, sucrose, maltose,* and

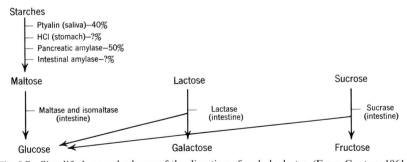

Fig. 6.5 Simplified general scheme of the digestion of carbohydrates. (From Guyton, 1961.)

isomaltose) to simple sugars. The end product of the digestive process of most natural carbohydrates is about 80% *glucose,* 10% *fructose,* and 10% *galactose* which can be absorbed.

Most dietary fats are *triglycerides* which contain *glycerol* and *fatty acids.* Almost all the neutral fats pass intact through the mouth and stomach and are digested in the small intestine, largely by the enzymatic action of enteric and pancreatic lipase. This process is aided by the bile salts which reduce the surface tension of the fat globules and thus encourage their destruction. The digestion of fats may stop at the monoglyceride stage or continue until all fat is broken down into glycerol and fatty acids.

Proteins are made up of long chains of amino acids which are connected by *peptide linkages.* Proteins (found largely in meats and vegetables) are hydrolyzed to intermediate products (*polypeptides, proteoses,* and *peptones*) by the enzyme pepsin. This process is typically complete by the time the food leaves the stomach. In the small intestine the proteins are attacked by pancreatic enzymes (trypsin, chymotrypsin, and carboxypolypeptidases) which reduce them to smaller polypeptide molecules or even to amino acids. The final hydrolysis of polypeptides into amino acids is initiated by enzymes of the small intestine called *amino polypeptidases* and *dipeptidases.*

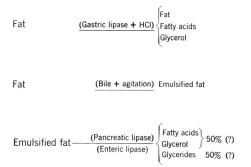

Fig. 6.6 Simplified scheme of fat digestion. (From Guyton, 1961.)

Absorption. The absorption of the breakdown products of the digestive process through the gastrointestinal mucosa may occur simply as the result of *diffusion* (i.e., the transmembrane transport of substances as a result of molecular movements along a diffusion gradient) or may require *active transport* (the movement of substances against a concentration gradient or an electrical gradient).

Water and many of the electrolytes diffuse readily through the mucosa of the upper intestine. This diffusion may be facilitated by electrical gradients (the diffusion of negative ions from the gut appears to be accomplished in this fashion).

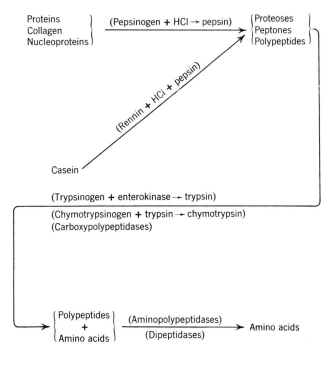

Fig. 6.7 Simplified scheme of protein digestion. (From Guyton, 1961.)

Most of the nutrients require active transport mechanisms which are believed to operate on a common principle. The substance to be transported combines with a *carrier,* and the combination diffuses through the walls of the mucosal cells. On the other side of the mucosa, the substance is enzymatically released and the carrier returns to pick up another "cargo." Both the combination and the release require energy.

Most carbohydrates are absorbed in the form of simple sugars which require active transport. Specific transport mechanisms exist for each type of monosaccharide, and each consequently has characteristic rates of absorption. However, there also seems to be a degree of competitive interaction between the individual transport mechanisms that suggests the operation of a common transport mechanism.

Proteins in the form of amino acids are generally absorbed in much the same manner. Some dipeptides and even whole protein molecules may be absorbed, but this requires special, as yet unknown, transport facilities.

Fats, on the other hand, may diffuse through the intestinal membranes in the form of fatty acids, glycerol, and monoglycerides. (No active transport mechanism has been isolated to date which seems to be specific to the fats.) Once in the interstitial spaces, the fatty acids recombine with glycerol or mono- and diglycerides to form new triglycerides. These small globules of fat pass through the lymphatic channels into the venous system. The absorption of many fatty acids requires the presence of bile salts.

The monovalent electrolytes (sodium, potassium, chloride, nitrate, and bicarbonate) are easily absorbed through the walls of the upper intestine. For some of these substances (notably sodium), an active transport mechanism exists; this mechanism in turn establishes electrochemical gradients which facilitate the movement of other ions through the mucosa. The polyvalent ions (such as calcium, magnesium, and sulfate) are poorly absorbed and are generally not used by the body in any significant quantities.

Water may simply diffuse across the walls of the gastric tract because of osmotic pressure gradients or be actively transported by a specific transport system.

Sodium and chloride are also absorbed from the upper portion of the upper half of the *large* intestine. This creates osmotic gradients which permit the absorption of most of the water in the fecal matter.

Peripheral Factors in the Regulation of Food Intake

Local theories of motivation, such as Cannon's (1934) theory of hunger, propose that neurophysiological changes may indeed occur centrally as well as peripherally as a result of deprivation. However, these are thought *not* to operate directly on the motivational states of the organism, but to affect peripheral mechanisms which in turn produce direct drive stimulation (Cannon, 1929, 1932, 1934).

Such an interpretation is supported by a large body of clinical and experimental evidence; the coincidence of peripheral stimulation such as stomach contractions or dryness of the oral and pharyngeal cavities with the sensation of hunger or thirst respectively has been reported (Cannon and Washburn, 1912; Carlson, 1913; Cannon, 1929, 1932, 1934; Gregersen and Cizek, 1956; Wolf, 1958). Introspection suggests that peripheral stimulation is an important factor in sexual arousal as well as the sensation of thirst and hunger.

Cannon's theory of hunger is analogous to the James-Lange theory of emotion which suggests that emotional states arise as a *consequence* of overt responses to the environment. The local theory of hunger would say that we are hungry because we feel stomach contractions; a more centrally oriented theorist would claim that we have stomach contractions because we are hungry.

The experimental literature of the past 50 years favors the centralist position in this issue, as well as in the analogous case of the James-Lange theory. We do not mean to suggest that stomach contractions, local chemical changes, or other peripheral factors may not play an important role in the regulation of food intake. Even if the "master control" for hunger is localized in some part of the central nervous system, as the experimental evidence suggests, stimuli of peripheral origin may be necessary to activate this central mechanism following a period of privation and inhibit it after satiation. Our understanding of these signals is an integral and necessary part of the larger problem of hunger.

In this connection, another point needs to be emphasized. Great importance is placed by most central theorists on the fact that the organism appears to be quite capable of regulating food intake when the contribution of individual peripheral mechanisms has been eliminated. Such evidence represents an important contribution to our knowledge in demonstrating the nonessentiality of such mechanisms; however, it does not show that the mechanisms do not cooperate with other factors in the intact organism.

The role of stomach contractions. Until very recently, most experimental investigations of the regulation of food intake or the physiological basis of hunger were directed toward peripheral mechanisms. The stomach and its periodic motility were of particular interest to the earlier investigators because of the concurrent theoretical emphasis on local sensory factors. A direct and causal relationship between the motility of the stomach and food intake had to be established if hunger was to be explained by sensory afferents from the gastrointestinal tract.

Denervation studies. Well before the turn of the century this problem was studied extensively in the physiological laboratories of Europe (Sédillot, 1829; Schiff, 1867; Longet, 1868; Ewald, 1893). Many of these early studies were concerned with the effects of partial or complete removal of the innervation of the stomach (vagi and splanchnic nerves) in man as well as experimental animals. The results generally agreed that denervation had little or no effect on hunger sensations in man or on the regulation of food intake in a variety of species. It seemed clear by the turn of the century that stomach contractions cannot play an *essential* role in the regulation of food intake and hunger unless the regulatory function of the stomach is exercised by non-neural (i.e., chemical) mechanisms.

The denervation experiments have been replicated more recently (Bash, 1939; Morgan and Morgan, 1940; Harris et al., 1947) and essentially the same results have been obtained. Denervation of the stomach in human patients (M. I. Grossman et al., 1947) similarly does not affect regulation of food intake or the sensation of appetite. Vagotomy (which eliminates gastric contractions) as well as splanchnectomy (which eliminates afferent impulses from the stomach) do not diminish hunger sensations. All studies agree that complete denervation of the stomach disturbs the regulation of food intake only very temporarily, presumably because of a general postsurgical debility rather than the elimination of essential stimuli specifically related to hunger.

Regulation of intake without stomach. Clinical case histories of individuals without stomachs (the esophagus is connected directly to the in-testine) seem to rule out a hormonal or chemical regulation, at least as far as the stomach itself is concerned. Such patients show a normal desire for food and are perfectly capable of regulating food intake within normal limits. The frequency of meals is necessarily larger since only relatively small quantities can be stored in the upper intestine, but the total daily intake remains normal (Wangenstein and Carlson, 1931; MacDonald et al., 1947).

Rats whose stomachs have been surgically removed (1) learn a maze that leads to food reward as well and as rapidly as normal controls, (2) obtain normal scores in an obstruction box experiment when the reinforcement for crossing an electrified grid is food, and (3) show as much activity in connection with the accustomed time of feeding as do control animals (Tsang, 1938).

Correlation of hunger sensations with stomach motility. The nonessentiality of sensory impulses from the stomach is well established at this point, but this does not prove that stomach contractions do not contribute to the regulation of feeding behavior in the intact organism.

Many experiments have demonstrated that periods of gastric motility correlate well with reports of hunger sensations in man. The first of these experiments was reported by Cannon and Washburn in 1912 and forms the basis of Cannon's influential theory of motivation. In these experiments, stomach motility was monitored for extended periods of time before, during, and after the usual time of eating by means of X-ray observations as well as pneumographic recordings from a balloon swallowed into the stomach. The contractions of the empty stomach were found to coincide rather precisely with hunger sensations. Each separate contraction appeared to be synchronous with a single "hunger pang."

Carlson (1912–1913a, b, c) has demonstrated that these contractions stimulate sensory nerves, not in the gastric mucosa as had been assumed in the past but in the submucosa or muscularis. The afferent impulses are then carried by the sympathetic nervous system to the medulla where they affect respiratory and cardiac centers (Carlson, 1914a, b, 1916). From here they are relayed to the midbrain and thalamus (Quigley, 1955).

The nature of these contractions has been studied extensively by a variety of techniques, and there is little doubt of their reality, periodicity, and correlation with hunger sensations (Meschan and Quigley, 1938).

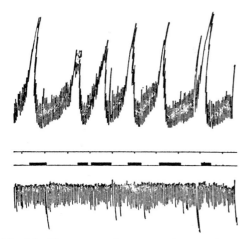

Fig. 6.8 The top record represents intragastric pressure (the small oscillations due to respiration, the large to contractions of the stomach); the second record is time in minutes (10 min); the third record is the report of hunger pangs; the lowest record is respiration registered by means of a pneumograph about the abdomen. The scale is half the original size. (From Cannon and Washburn, 1912.)

The emphasis on central mechanisms during the past 20 years has diminished interest in gastric feedback; it is obvious, however, that the integrative mechanisms of the central nervous system cannot operate without neural or chemical information from peripheral sources. We shall briefly consider some of the parameters of local gastric activity in the hope that some of the information will be helpful in understanding one neglected aspect of this feedback system.

The periodic motility of the alimentary canal is a constant feature in a variety of animals. Motility is not peculiar to mammals but has been demonstrated in the empty crop of the pigeon (Rogers, 1916). The precise localization of the contractions that seem to correlate with the sensation of hunger in man has been the subject of much dispute. Carlson (1912–1913a, b, c, 1916) suggested that hunger pangs are primarily related to muscular spasms in the fundic portion of the stomach. Subsequent experimental investigations have implicated the antral musculature (Templeton and Quigley, 1930) and the corpus and fundus of the stomach (Quigley et al., 1929). It has always been taken for granted that hunger must be related to the activity of the stomach itself, but much of the experimental literature does not support this interpretation. Ivy et al. (1925) reported many years ago that there appears to be a close temporal

coincidence of duodenal and stomach activity, and that the onset of duodenal contractions nearly always precedes the activation of the stomach. Many subsequent investigations have replicated these findings and have shown that hunger sensations correlate with duodenal activity, even in the complete absence of stomach contractions (Quigley and Solomon, 1930; Meschan and Quigley, 1938; Brody et al., 1940; Quigley and Read, 1942). These results confirm earlier reports which implicated the circular constriction of the lower portion of the digestive tract as the essential component in "hunger contractions" (Martin and Rogers, 1927).

Quigley and his students have shown that gastric contractions are not inhibited by the placement of non-nutritive or even nutritive substances into the stomach. However, stomach and duodenal activity does disappear, even in the completely denervated stomach, when nutritive foods are allowed to enter the upper intestine (Quigley and Phelps, 1934; Quigley and Meschan, 1941; Quigley et al., 1941; Quigley and Read, 1942; Quigley et al., 1942). Gastric activity is inhibited when fat is introduced into the duodenum (Gershon-Cohen and Shay, 1937), the jejunum (Waugh, 1936), or even the lower ileum or colon (Quigley and Hallaran, 1932). Nervous connections to the stomach are not necessary for this effect (M. I. Grossman, 1950). Even gastric hypermotility (induced by insulin injections) disappears when nutritive substances (dextrose or sugar) are allowed to enter the duodenum (Quigley et al., 1929).

Stomach motility is presumably inhibited by the secretion of enterogastrone (M. I. Grossman, 1950); this hormone is released from the mucosa of the upper small intestine when fat or sugar is present. Enterogastrone also inhibits the secretory activity of the stomach (Kosaka and Lim, 1930). Janowitz and M. I. Grossman (1951) have reported that the experimental administration of enterogastrone inhibits gastric contractions but does *not* affect food intake.

That duodenal rather than stomach contractions may be the crucial element in the much maligned hunger contractions is important. Most of the arguments against a possible regulatory function of this mechanism are based on experimental evidence from gastrostomized subjects or on denervation studies which have not adequately controlled for duodenal factors. That possible afferents from the duodenum or jejunum contribute significantly to the regulation of food intake has not yet been ruled out, and the possibility of

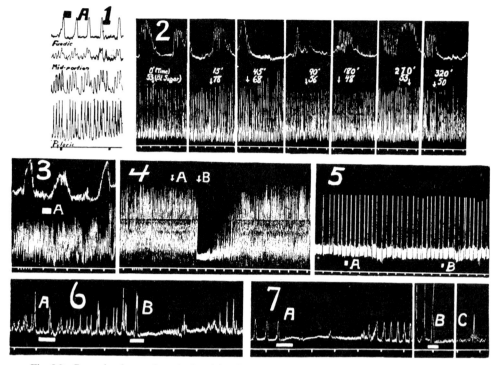

Fig. 6.9 Records of gastrointestinal activity. 1, normal dog, 40 hr since fed (H. S. F.), 4 balloons in stomach; A, intravenous injection 10 grams glucose 30 cc). 2, normal dog, 40 H. S. F., record from colon and stomach. At 0′ injected intravenously 0.25 gram/kg glucose (50%).

3, normal dog, 34 H. S. F., record from ileum and stomach. At A injected intravenously 15 grams glucose (50%). "True" blood sugar 10 min before injection; 79 mg/100 cc, 60 min after injection 160. 4, normal dog, 18 H. S. F., record from stomach; A, intravenous injection of 10 grams glucose (50%); B, intravenous injection of 0.5 cc oxytocin. 5, vagotomized dog, 40 H. S. F. record from stomach; A, intravenous injection of 50 grams glucose (50%); B, intravenous injection of 30 cc 0.9% NaCl.

6, normal dog (with cannula to duodenum), 20 H. S. F., record from stomach; A, 50 cc 0.9% NaCl into duodenum; B, 50 cc cane sugar (isotonic) into duodenum. 7, normal dog (with cannula to duodenum), 40 H. S. F., record from stomach; A, 50 cc glucose (5%) into duodenum; B, 35 min later, 50 cc lactose (isotonic) into duodenum; C, 28 min later. Time marker, 5 min. (From Quigley and Hallaran, 1932.)

a chemical mediation of this control has not even been explored.

Carlson (1916) surveyed the literature on the effects of removal or denervation of the stomach and concluded that "the gastric hunger mechanism is primarily automatic or independent of blood changes as well as of central nervous control, but, in the normal individual, chemical changes of the blood as well as nervous influences from the brain and spinal cord, augment or decrease this primary automatism in a way to correlate it with the needs of the organism."

Subsequent investigations have shown that the motility of the gastrointestinal tract is not an automatism, even though neural influences are non-

essential. This is shown most convincingly in studies using a denervated Haidenhain pouch (a small stomach which is made of gastrointestinal tissue and is implanted somewhere in the body cavity). Some of the earlier studies showed that such an isolated pouch exhibited rhythmic contractions which were synchronous with those of the stomach and showed identical variations as a function of food deprivation or feeding (Robins and Boyd, 1923; Bercowitz, 1923; Farrell and Ivy, 1926). The pouch contractions were inhibited when food was placed into the small intestine, but the injection of nutritive substances into the pouch did not inhibit stomach contractions (Robins and Boyd, 1923; Quigley et al., 1934).

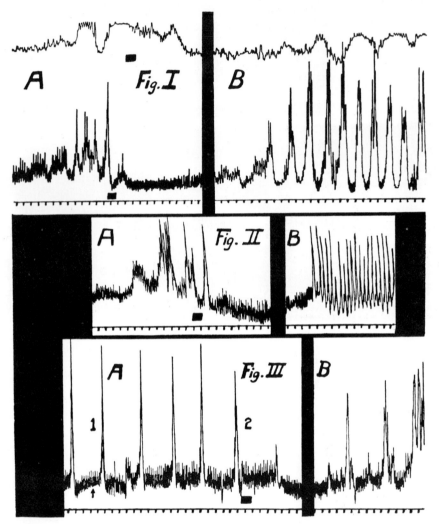

Fig. 6.10 Records of gastrointestinal activity. 1, simultaneous records from main stomach (lower) and autotransplanted pouch (upper) showing typical initiation of spontaneous motility almost simultaneously in both regions. The horizontal band indicates injection of one egg yolk into the main stomach. Inhibition of the main stomach followed in 1 min, inhibition of the pouch in 6 min. The first portion of B, 35 min after start of egg yolk administration, shows recovery beginning in pouch and stomach (complete recovery of tone did not occur in this experiment). Time marker, 1 min.

2, record from vagotomized, splanchnectomized, and celiac ganglionectomized stomach; A, spontaneous initiation of motility. The horizontal band indicates injection of one egg yolk into the stomach. Gastric inhibition occurred in 3 min. The first portion of record B, 45 min after beginning of egg yolk administration, shows return of gastric motility.

3, record from pouch of entire stomach. A1, completion of perfusion of the pouch with one and one-half egg yolk—no effect; A2, introduction of one egg yolk into the duodenum, gastric inhibition in 4 min. First portion of record B, 49 min after beginning of egg yolk injection, shows return of gastric motility. (From Quigley et al., 1934.)

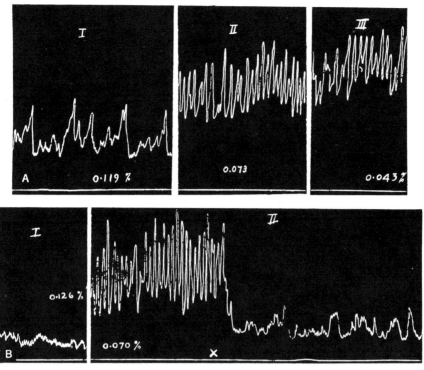

Fig. 6.11 Records of gastrointestinal activity. A, water manometer tracings of gastric "hunger contractions." I, before injection of insulin, blood sugar 0.119. II, 60 min after injection of 40 units insulin, blood sugar 0.073. III, 120 min after the insulin injection, blood sugar 0.043. Showing the augmentation of gastric hunger contractions and tonus parallel with insulin hypoglycemia in normal dogs.

B, water manometer tracing of the gastric "hunger contractions." I, before insulin injections, blood sugar 0.126. II, 90 min after injection of 40 units of insulin, blood sugar 0.070. *x*, intravenous injection of 10 grams glucose. Showing initiation of gastric tetany parallel with insulin hypoglycemia and inhibition of this tetany by glucose. (From Bulatão and Carlson, 1924b.)

The effects of glucose and insulin on stomach motility. These observations suggest that the activity of the gastrointestinal tract, and perhaps hunger itself, may be under hormonal rather than neural control, and a voluminous and controversial body of experimental observations has accumulated on this issue.

Luckhardt and Carlson (1915) reported the now classic observation that the transfusion of blood from starving dogs could serve as a temporary stimulus for hunger contractions in sated animals. The authors suggested that these results might be caused by a decrease in blood sugar or glycogen reserves; this hypothesis can be fairly easily tested, since the blood sugar level can be lowered experimentally by insulin administrations and raised by direct injections of glucose.

These techniques have been used by many investigators, and the early results looked promising.

Intravenous injections of glucose decreased the gastric motility in hungry animals, and the administration of insulin increased the motility of the stomach. Control injections of hypertonic saline had no effect (Bulatão and Carlson, 1924a, b). Insulin-induced hypoglycemia also increased the motility of the duodenum, and such duodenal contractions were associated with subjective sensations of hunger in man (Quigley et al., 1929; Quigley and Templeton, 1939). The insulin-induced increase in gastric motility was reduced or abolished by intravenous glucose injections (Bulatão and Carlson, 1924a, b; Regan, 1933).

The situation, unfortunately, is not so clear as these early experimental findings suggest. Insulin or glucose injections do not affect the motility of the isolated Haidenhain pouch (Stucky et al., 1928; Templeton and Quigley, 1930), and the normal activity of the gastrointestinal tract does

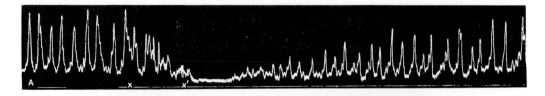

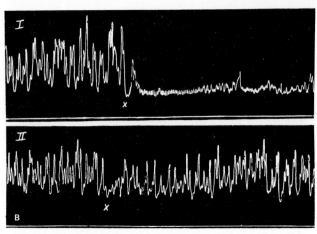

Fig. 6.12   Records of gastrointestinal activity. A, water manometer tracing of gastric "hunger contractions." x–x', intravenous injection of 10 grams glucose (50% solution), showing inhibition of the gastric tonus and hunger contractions by hyperglycemia. Total time of record, 60 min.

B, water manometer tracings of gastric "hunger contractions." Ix, intravenous injection of 10 grams glucose. IIx, intravenous injection of 10 grams lactose. Showing absence of inhibition from lactose hyperglycemia. (From Bulatão and Carlson, 1924b.)

not correlate very highly with variations in blood sugar (Mulinos, 1933). Moreover, the insulin-induced hypermotility of the stomach can be inhibited by drugs (atropine) which do not affect the blood sugar level (Wilder and Schultz, 1931), and some types of experimentally (phlorizin) induced hypoglycemias are associated with a *decrease* in gastric motility rather than the expected increase (Quigley and Lindquist, 1930). Finally, there is some evidence that the glucose-induced inhibition of gastric motility may be an artifact of the injection procedure. Intravenous injections of inactive substances such as saline have been reported to produce a temporary inhibition of gastric activity which was comparable to that elicited by injections of glucose intravenously or directly into the stomach (Quigley and Hallaran, 1932).

To summarize the possible contribution of gastric motility briefly: hunger contractions may not originate in the stomach itself, but reflect duodenal activity. The initiation and inhibition of periodic contractions of the gastrointestinal tract appear to be independent of neural mechanisms,

but reflect hormonal influences. A relationship between specific hormonal factors and gastric motility has not yet been established. Blood sugar concentrations covary with stomach motility, but the correlation is far from perfect, and some important exceptions have been demonstrated.

Stomach distension as a factor in satiety. The digestion and assimilation of all nutrient substances require considerable time, and any mechanism designed to regulate the food intake per meal rather than the frequency of feeding must be independent of slow chemical changes which depend on the assimilation of the ingested foodstuffs. The stomach itself is the most obvious source of neural satiety signals; it is equipped with sensitive stretch receptors which meter gastric distension and send impulses to the central nervous system via afferent fibers which travel with the vagus nerve (Paintal, 1954).

The possible contribution of the gastric distension signals to satiety has been investigated in two different experimental situations. The first systematic study of this problem (Adolph, 1947) investigated the effects of variations in the "nutritive density" of the diet on food intake. It was found that rats increased their daily food intake and maintained a constant caloric intake when the proportion of non-nutritive material (water or kaolin) in their diet was small. A compromise between excessive distension of the digestive tract and insufficient nutrient intake was effected when the concentration of the admixture was high. Strominger et al. (1953) have also reported that food intake (exclusive of roughage) was not at all affected by the addition of non-nutritive cellulose to the diet. Other studies have observed a less complete and only gradual adjustment of the tendency to ingest a constant daily volume regardless of caloric content (Janowitz and M. I. Grossman, 1949a).

A different approach to this problem has suggested that the signals that arise from a distended stomach may be important cues for the cessation of feeding only when the physical limits of the system are approached. Janowitz and M. I. Grossman (1949b) put fistulae into the stomach of normal and esophagostomized dogs and injected food directly into the stomach at various intervals before the normal daily feeding. Intragastric injections of up to 20% of the normal daily intake 20 min before the normal feeding time did not affect subsequent oral intake. Injections of larger quantities reduced subsequent intake even when the injected material was non-nutritive. Preloading with any quantity of food 4 hr before the normal feeding had no effect. The sham feeding of esophagostomized animals (the esophagus is severed from the stomach, and its lower portion is externalized so that food does not reach the stomach) was not inhibited by stomach loading. Subsequent experiments (Janowitz and M. I. Grossman, 1951) showed that the prefeeding of small but calorically significant quantities of foods 20 min before the regular feeding time had no effect on subsequent oral intake. Larger quantities showed a depressant effect.

Long-range studies of the effects of intragastric prefeedings have suggested that most organisms adjust only very gradually and incompletely to excessive caloric intake if the nutrients are injected long enough before feeding time to assure that the stomach is no longer distended when the animal feeds orally.

Share et al. (1952), for instance, reported that up to 33% of the normal caloric intake could be injected daily without affecting total oral intake when the injections were given 4 hr after the time of feeding. The average daily intake was not significantly affected even when this procedure was continued for several weeks. A small decrease in oral consumption appeared when the intragastric injections exceeded 33%, but the total caloric intake (oral plus fistula) greatly exceeded normal levels. Janowitz and Hollander (1953) similarly found that daily intragastric injections of up to 175% of the normal caloric intake had little or no immediate effect on oral intake. Compensatory adjustments began to be made only after several weeks, and the intake remained depressed for four or five weeks after the intragastric feeding was terminated. These findings suggest that sensory feedback from the mouth and upper portions of the gastrointestinal tract may provide important signals for the regulation of intake per meal; such signals are only gradually overridden by neural or humoral signals from some calorimeter which attempts to balance the body's energy equation in the long run.

The intragastric feeding technique has been used recently by Epstein and Teitelbaum (1962 a, b) to show that animals are capable of regulating their caloric intake even when no food passes through their mouths. Rats were trained to leverpress for small intragastric injections of a liquid diet. After some period of adjustment, the animals were quite able to regulate their daily intake and body weight over periods of time up to 44 days. Most remarkable, immediate adjustments were made when the nutritive density of the diet was reduced by 50% by the addition of water or increased by the withdrawal of water. Similarly precise compensatory adjustments were made when the size of the individual injection was halved or doubled. The constant caloric intake was maintained when the ratio of lever presses to reinforcements was changed. (See also Teitelbaum and Epstein, 1963.)

A related question, the rewarding or drive-reducing properties of foods intragastrically administered, has been investigated by Neal Miller and his students (Kohn, 1951; Miller and Kessen, 1952; Berkun et al., 1952). The experiments of these men have shown that (1) food injected directly into the stomach *is* rewarding to a hungry animal though significantly less so than food ingested by mouth; (2) non-nutritive substances do not have rewarding properties; and (3) mere mechanical stimulation or distension of the stomach is negatively reinforcing, i.e., the animals learn a response to avoid such stimulation. The authors

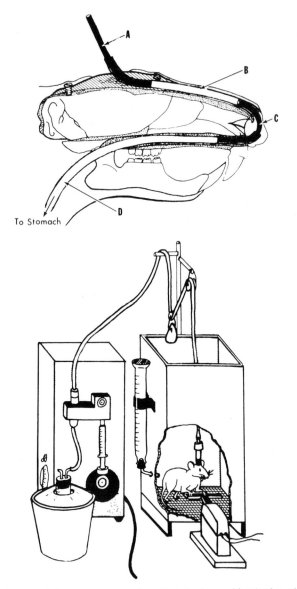

Fig. 6.13 *Top,* Course of the nasopharyngeal gastic tube in a midsagittal section of the rat's head. A, 22-gauge stainless steel; B, 24-gauge polyvinyl tubing; C, 22-gauge stainless steel; D, PE50 polyethylene tubing. *Bottom,* the apparatus for intragastric self-injection by the rat. (From Epstein and Teitelbaum, 1962b.)

concluded that the local contribution of the oral-pharyngeal mechanism (such as taste, smell, and swallowing) appears to be real, though relatively small and nonessential to drive reduction, and that simple distension of the stomach is not sufficient to produce even temporary changes in the hunger drive. Sharma et al. (1961) have recently reported that the inflation of intragastric balloons with water or air produced a significant increase

in the electrical activity of the ventromedial nuclei of the hypothalamus (i.e., the satiety center); however, the significance of this result remains to be evaluated.

It may be concluded that signals from the stomach lead to the cessation of feeding only when the limits of the system are approached. These signals may, under normal circumstances, contribute to the regulation of food intake and

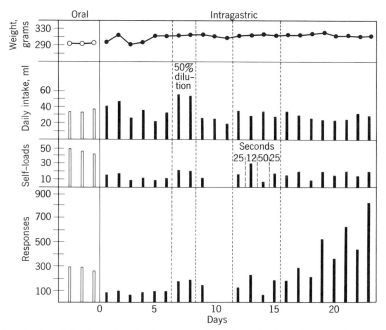

Fig. 6.14 Body weight, daily food intake, the number of self-loads, and the number of daily responses during 3 days of oral food intake and 25 days of intragastric intake in the normal rat. (From Epstein and Teitelbaum, 1962b.)

energy exchange by limiting the size of each meal, but they cannot regulate daily intake; this is shown by the fact that intragastrically administered nutrients do not affect oral intake if the stomach is permitted to empty before feeding time. The overriding influence of a "calorimeter" is suggested by the subject's eventual adjustment to the excessive caloric intake. The recent intragastric self-injection experiments suggest that animals can regulate intake when the feedback from taste, smell, and other sensory receptors from the mouth and throat is eliminated, but this does not imply a regulation based on direct signals from the stomach.

The role of blood sugar in the regulation of hunger and satiety. The preceding discussion of gastric factors suggests that the purely local peripheral mechanisms of motility and distension do not provide *essential* signals for the regulation of food intake. The initiation of feeding behavior may primarily depend on central mechanisms which can operate without immediate sensory feedback from the gastrointestinal tract. However, any central control mechanism must be capable of adjusting food intake in accordance with the changing requirements of the organism, and some means of communication must exist. Moreover,

hunger is reduced so rapidly in most species that a restoration of the organism's energy balance cannot account for the cessation of food intake. The satiety signals must almost certainly originate in the gastrointestinal tract; they must be transmitted to the central regulatory mechanisms by means of some system which cannot rely on neural pathways, since denervation of the stomach does not seem to interfere at all with the regulation of intake.

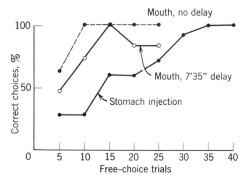

Fig. 6.15 Percentage of correct choices in a maze when the milk reinforcement was either delivered directly into the stomach or given orally. (From Miller and Kessen, 1952.)

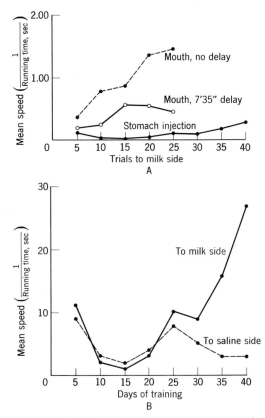

Fig. 6.16 A, speed of running to a compartment in which milk reinforcements were either delivered directly into the stomach or given orally. B, a comparison of the running speeds to compartments in which milk or isotonic saline was injected directly into the stomach. (From Miller and Kessen, 1952.)

Ever since Luckhardt and Carlson (1915) demonstrated that blood from starving dogs could serve as a stimulus for hunger contractions, interest has centered around the possibility that some breakdown product of metabolic activity in the blood might act as the essential signal which informs the central regulatory mechanisms of the state of the organism's energy balance.

Since the frequency of food intake (and the periodicity of hunger) is relatively high in most species, the hormonal mechanisms must show rapid and large fluctuations as a function of energy intake and loss and must have an immediate effect on the central nervous system. Fat and protein metabolisms are too slow to meet these criteria (Mayer, 1952, 1953a, b). Carbohydrate metabolism, on the other hand, is relatively rapid and operates with only minimal body reserves. Even a few hours suffice to deplete the liver glyco-

gen stores and produce a marked drop in blood sugar, in spite of continuing efforts of the organism to synthesize glycogen from body proteins.

Moreover, glucose is utilized preferentially by all tissues and almost exclusively by the central nervous system. Low glucose levels starve the brain and result in rapid death, suggesting that the regulation of its metabolism may, indeed, be of primary importance. The body's carbohydrate stores are the first to be seriously depleted when the energy output increases. The availability of carbohydrates determines the rate of glycogen synthesis from body proteins (Engel, 1949) as well as the rate of fat oxidation (Geyer et al., 1953) and thus influences all metabolic processes.

Mayer's glucostatic theory of hunger. These considerations, as well as early clinical and experimental evidence, led Jean Mayer to postulate a *glucostatic* regulation of hunger and food intake. As originally proposed, this hypothesis assumed that the central nervous system contains "glucoreceptors" which are preferentially sensitive to the concentration of sugar in the blood and initiate feeding whenever the absolute level falls below some minimal value. This hypothesis cannot account for a number of clinical observations, such as the overeating of diabetic patients who have an elevated blood sugar level, the abnormally high blood sugar levels which characterize many forms of pathological obesity, and the phenomenon of "hunger diabetes" (a starved man continues to eat in spite of rapidly rising blood sugar levels).

Mayer (1953b, 1955) has suggested that the absolute level of sugar in the blood may not accurately reflect the *utilization* of sugar in the brain, because glucose must cross the cell membranes of the glucoreceptors before it can be used. This transmembrane transport depends on a number of chemical reactions (phosphorylation through hexokinase reactions) which may be retarded under some circumstances; thus, central glucose utilization may be low in spite of an elevated absolute level of sugar in the blood. Mayer suggested that the difference in sugar concentration between the arterial blood supply to the brain and the venous drainage from the brain may be the best measure of central glucose utilization.

Thus modified, the *glucostatic theory* states that glucoreceptors in the central nervous system (most probably in the hypothalamus) may be preferentially sensitive to the rate of sugar utilization. Low utilization rates (which under normal circumstances reflect a low availability of glucose) initiate neural activity which elicits hunger sensations and food intake. High utilization rates (which under normal circumstances reflect a high absolute level of blood sugar) inhibit this neural activity and stop feeding behavior.

The glucostatic theory has enjoyed considerable interest and support. It is a very appealing theoretical system because it links the central regula-

tory mechanisms directly to the metabolic processes that determine the organism's homeostatic balance. It provides an almost satisfactory explanation of why the neural feedback from the gastrointestinal tract should be nonessential. The explanation is not totally satisfying because the onset of satiety, as measured by the cessation of feeding, often precedes the absorption of a quan-

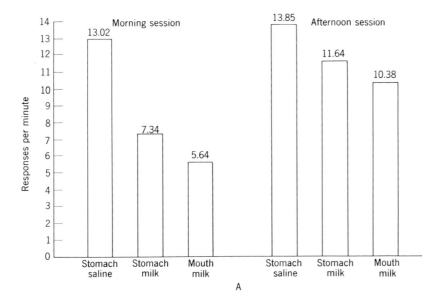

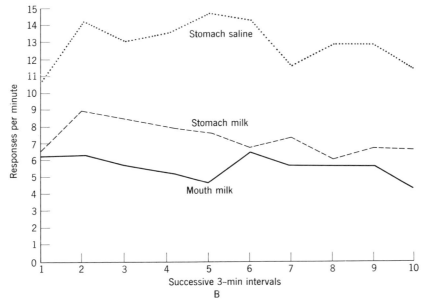

Fig. 6.17 A, the immediate and delayed effect on hunger of three methods of prefeeding. B, the immediate effect on hunger of three methods of prefeeding. (From Kohn, 1951.)

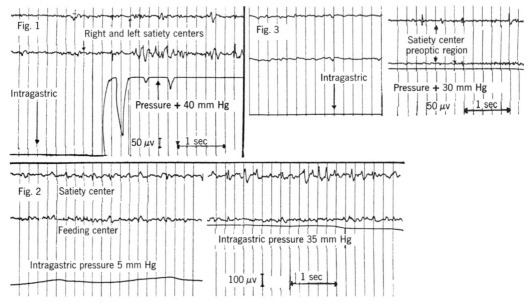

Fig. 6.18 1, Bipolar recording of activity of left and right satiety centers of a cat with the intragastric pressure recorded through a water-filled-balloon catheter system. On raising intragastric pressure to +40 mm Hg, high-voltage irregular waves appear in the satiety regions.

2, Bipolar recording of activity of right satiety and feeding centers in a monkey. On raising the intragastric pressure, high-voltage irregular waves appear in the satiety region, but no such change occurs in the feeding region.

3, Bipolar recording of activity of left satiety center and preoptic region of a cat. On raising the intragastric pressure, spikes appear in the satiety region and not in the preoptic region. (From Sharma et al., 1961.)

tity of glucose sufficient to significantly affect the availability of sugar in the brain; this, however, is a relatively minor defect. Other and more serious questions arise when we inspect the experimental support for the theory.

The effects of insulin-induced hypoglycemia on food intake and hunger. The theory is quite handsomely supported by clinical and experimental observations about the effects of insulin on food intake and hunger. Short (1929) lowered the blood sugar of patients suffering from malnutrition by periodic injections of insulin and reported that the resulting hypoglycemia was reliably associated with an impressive improvement of appetite and weight gain. A number of clinical and experimental investigations failed to replicate these results in the early 1930's, and the suggestion was advanced that Short's results were due to a placebo effect (Freyberg, 1935; McIntyre and Burke, 1937). Later studies of this problem (Barnes and Keeton, 1940) indicated that the negative effects were caused by the rapid absorption of insulin; they demonstrated convincingly

that marked changes in food intake can be produced when the insulin is administered in a slowly absorbing compound (*protamine zinc insulin* is commonly used for this purpose since the basic protein protamine is relatively insoluble in body fluids). An elegant demonstration of this effect has been published by MacKay and associates (MacKay et al., 1940). Repeated injections of protamine insulin produced a doubling of the normal daily intake, whereas standard insulin had no effect. To prove that the insulin effect on food intake was, in fact, related to its depressant action on blood sugar, these workers removed the adrenal medulla (thus preventing the secretion of epinephrine which normally raises the concentration of sugar in the blood). The resulting hypoglycemia increased food intake and produced a substantial weight gain. The effect of insulin on food intake is independent of neural connection to and from the stomach, suggesting that the insulin-induced hypoglycemia may act directly on the central glucoreceptors (M. I. Grossman et al., 1947; M. I. Grossman and Stein, 1948).

The theoretical implications of these observations are unfortunately not so clear. The organism's response to insulin is quite complex. Initially, the absolute hypoglycemia which develops is accompanied by an increase in peripheral arteriovenous glucose differences. As the absolute blood sugar concentration begins to recover, the arteriovenous differences fall to near resting levels. Hunger sensations arise only when this has occurred; however, they persist through another rise in A-V differences and through a continued rise in absolute blood sugar (Somogyi, 1951b; M. I. Grossman, 1955). Moreover, the rate of glucose utilization of the brain as a whole appears not to be affected by insulin (Himwich et al., 1941), necessitating the assumption (Mayer, 1955) that the postulated glucoreceptors of the hypothalamus react to insulin like peripheral tissue rather than like the rest of the brain. This assumption raises a problem in Mayer's theory, with respect to the well-demonstrated appetite depressant effects of epinephrine. Epinephrine injections produce *hyperglycemia* and a decreased peripheral arteriovenous glucose difference, but epinephrine has no effect on the central utilization of glucose; it may even increase the local consumption of glucose in the hypothalamus (Somogyi, 1951a; Keller and Roberts, 1953).

The effects of glucose injections on food intake and hunger. If a lowering of the blood sugar level normally produces a decreased central sugar utilization and thus stimulates the central mechanisms which regulate food intake and hunger, it should be possible to induce satiety and cessation of feeding in deprived animals by intravenous injections of glucose in quantities which are not themselves calorically significant. A number of investigations have attempted to test this prediction, and the results have, unfortunately, not been entirely harmonious.

M. I. Grossman and his associates (Hanson and Grossman, 1948; Janowitz and Grossman, 1948, 1949a) have reported that intravenous or intraperitoneal injections of even calorically significant quantities of glucose fail to produce a depression in food intake greater than that seen after control injections of saline. In man, glucose injections, regardless of the site of administration, produced only a small depression of hunger sensations which was said to be "very much smaller than that produced by eating a small breakfast." The depression of hunger was not reliably greater than that produced by control injections of saline, and M. I. Grossman suggested that the small effects might be due to a placebo reaction.

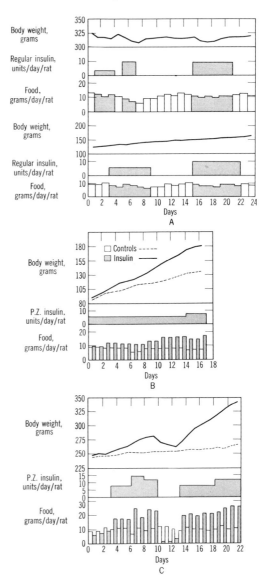

Fig. 6.19 A, experiments illustrating the failure of regular insulin to influence the food intake or body weight of the rat. The first experiment is from data obtained on a single rat; the second represents the averages from a group of three rats.

B, C, typical examples of the marked effect of protamine zinc insulin on the food intake and body weight of the rat. In both experiments the figures are averages for groups of four rats. (From E. M. MacKay, J. W. Calloway, and R. H. Barnes, *J. Nutr.,* 1940, **20**, Figures 1 and 2.)

On the other hand, there are clinical reports which suggest that calorically adequate diets are associated with large arteriovenous glucose differences which decrease only very shortly before mealtime; submaintenance diets are characterized

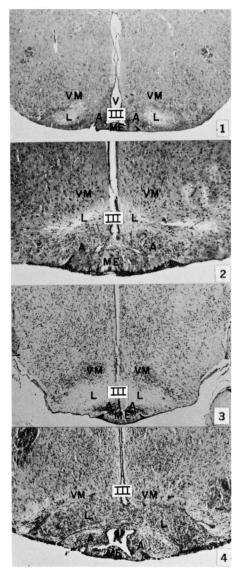

Fig. 6.20 Sections through the infundibular region of the hypothalamus of mice treated with goldthioglucose. ME, median eminence; VM, nucleus ventralis medialis; A, nucleus arcuatus; III, third ventricle; L, lesion.

Bilateral hypothalamic lesions unassociated with weight gain in $C_{57}BL$ strain mice. Dose, 0.35 mg/gram body weight; duration of experiment, 2 days; stain, romanes silver. ×23.

2, Bilateral hypothalamic lesions unassociated with weight gain in CBA strain mice. Dose, 0.18 mg/gram body weight; duration of experiment, 19 days; stain, hematoxylin and eosin. ×23.

3, Hypothalamic lesion associated with marked weight gain in CBA strain mice. Dose, 0.35 mg/gram body weight; duration of experiment, 2 days; stain, toluidin blue. ×45.

4, Hypothalamic lesion associated with moderate weight gain in $C_{57}BL$ strain mice. Dose, 1.2 mg/gram

by small arteriovenous differences which fall rapidly after the ingestion of meals (Mayer, 1952). Attempts have been made to quantify this relationship, and van Itallie (1953; van Itallie et al., 1953) reported a satisfactory correlation between diminishing arteriovenous glucose differences and the subjective sensation of hunger. The findings appear to be significant, although these clinical observations lack some of the procedural refinements which are very desirable in such experiments. Stunkard and Wolf (1954) have also reported that the injection of a highly concentrated glucose solution promptly abolished gastric contractions as well as hunger sensations. The inhibition was associated with large arteriovenous glucose differences, and hunger as well as stomach motility returned when these differences began to decline. Mayer and Bates (1952) have also reported that injections of glucose and epinephrine which resulted in marked hyperglycemia significantly reduced food intake. They concluded that the observed depression could not be dependent on the nutritional value of the sugar injections since other nutritive substances (sucrose and fats) did not produce comparable effects. This is unfortunately not so clear as one might wish, since the sucroses must be metabolized before they can be utilized by the organism, whereas the glucose is immediately available. Archdeacon et al. (1949) had earlier reported a similar depression of intake following glucose injections.

Some important support for Mayer's hypothesis, particularly the hypothesized glucoreceptors, their localization in the hypothalamus, and direct involvement in the control of feeding behavior, has been obtained in recent investigations of the histological and behavioral effects of goldthioglucose. Gold is very toxic to all living tissue, and the combination of gold and glucose produces central nervous system damage which, at least in the mouse, is concentrated in the hypothalamic area. Injections of goldthioglucose also produce marked hyperphagia (overeating) and obesity (Marshall et al., 1955; Larsson and Ström, 1957; Larsson, 1957; Liebelt and Perry, 1957). Mayer has suggested that the effects on food intake are precisely those predicted by his theory and are caused by selective damage to the glucoreceptors.

Anand et al. (1961b) have recently supported Mayer's hypothesis further with the demonstration that the electrical activity of the hypothalamic satiety center (see the following discussion of cen-

body weight; duration of experiment, 19 days; stain, hematoxylin and eosin. ×45. (From Liebelt and Perry, 1957.)

tral mechanisms) appeared significantly decreased by experimental hyperglycemia, whereas the electrical activity of the excitatory feeding center appeared diminished. Hypoglycemia produced opposite, though less reliable, effects.

Less favorable to Mayer's hypothesis are some findings by Epstein (1960a). He observed absolutely no change in food intake following the injection of glucose directly into the portions of the hypothalamus that seem to be directly concerned with the initiation or cessation of feeding behavior. Injections of procaine or hypertonic saline, on the other hand, affected food intake significantly.

Long-term regulation and the possible influence of lipostatic mechanisms. Mayer (1955) has suggested that the short-term, day-to-day regulation of food intake and hunger may depend on glucostatic controls, but that the long-range adjustment of energy intake to energy output may be mediated by a corrective mechanism which spontaneously mobilizes a quantity of fat directly proportional to the total fat content of the body. The coefficient of proportionality presumably depends on such factors as nature of diet, exercise, and temperature, as well as the constitution of the organism, i.e., its genetic makeup, basic metabolism, etc. Such an automatic mechanism would account for weight constancy, for any increase in fat content would be followed by increased availability of utilizable fat. This lipostatic mechanism is a logical adjunct to the glucostatic hypothesis in view of the close interrelation between the carbohydrate and fat metabolisms. There is, however, little or no direct evidence for such a regulation; we cannot judge its usefulness until further evidence becomes available.

Conclusions. Any peripheral factors found to be involved in the control of food intake must act in the capacity of information carriers; they must activate or inhibit centers in the central nervous system, rather than act as autonomous regulatory mechanisms, as was implied by the original local theories. The nature and *modus operandi* of such peripheral factors are not yet clear, and we may gain a more complete understanding of the problem by investigating the central aspects of hunger regulation. The study of the principally affected nervous mechanisms may, in turn, provide us with information relevant to the peripheral transmitters that affect these structures. Before we discuss central regulation, let us briefly review the status of the peripheral factors.

The situation is best summarized by the statement that mechanisms such as gastric motility

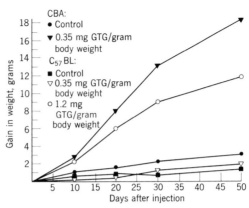

Fig. 6.21   Response in terms of weight gain to varying doses of goldthioglucose in CBA and $C_{57}BL$ inbred mice. Each group represents 15 to 25 mice. (From Liebelt and Perry, 1957.)

and distension, blood sugar levels, and other metabolic changes correlate with food intake and, in man, with the sensation of hunger, at least under normal conditions. None of these mechanisms, however, has been unambiguously shown to be *essential* to a satisfactory regulation of the organism's energy balance.

The evidence that demonstrates the nonessentiality of the purely mechanical gastric factors of contraction and distension is quite conclusive; however, some questions remain about the importance of these mechanisms in other portions of the gastrointestinal tract. The standard (extirpation) techniques cannot answer this question, and we may be forced to approach the problem somewhat more indirectly, possibly by studying the affected structures in the brain.

The situation is complex when we consider metabolic factors. It seems likely, if not certain, that at least the inhibitory influences of satiation originate in the gastrointestinal tract and are transmitted to the central nervous system via some non-nervous, chemical system. However, we do not at present know of a chemical transmission system which could operate with sufficient speed and precision to fulfill the requirements of the satiety mechanism. The central mechanism responsible for the initiation of feeding and hunger must respond promptly to the metabolic needs of the entire organism. Hunger is not initiated by nervous impulses from the stomach, and it is improbable that an assessment of the metabolic requirements of the entire organism should depend on nervous influences from any specific portion of the body. Instead, the initiation and the cessation of feeding behavior may depend on humoral mechanisms; we have discussed one possible information carrier. The evidence for an exclusively glucostatic regulation of hunger is at present far from complete, and other possibilities should be explored. It is possible that the demonstrated correlation between blood sugar concentration and food intake may not be descriptive of a causal relationship, or that this mechanism, though real, may be merely one of several hormonal systems which transmit information to central neural mechanisms.

Although it is essential that this problem continue to be investigated directly, a more indirect approach may be profitable as well. Following the demonstration of regulatory centers in the central nervous system, we can attempt to discover possible specific chemical affinities which might suggest how the activity of these central mechanisms is regulated. In the following section we shall see what progress has been made in the precise localization of neural systems which appear to contribute directly or indirectly to the regulation of feeding behavior and hunger.

CENTRAL MECHANISMS

Historically, the first area of the central nervous system to be implicated in the regulation of food intake and hunger motivation was the hypothalamus. Although many other regions of the brain have subsequently been related to the regulation of feeding behavior, the hypothalamic mechanisms continue to attract a predominant share of both theoretical and experimental attention. Electrical stimulation or extirpation of relatively small and well-defined regions of the ventral aspect of the diencephalon produce drastic and sometimes irreversible changes in food intake and food motivation. The hypothalamus is directly and intimately connected to all regions of the central nervous system that influence feeding behavior; it is often concluded that the hypothalamus may contain the master control which integrates the information from various peripheral as well as central sources.

The feeding and satiety centers of the ventral hypothalamus have been the subject of extensive experimental study over the past 50 years, and relatively much is known about their operation. Extrahypothalamic mechanisms have only recently attracted serious attention, and most of the available data on their function are by-products of studies not specifically designed to investigate the problem of hunger motivation. Much more information is needed before we can talk intelligently about possible interrelationships between extra- and intrahypothalamic factors. It is clear that the hypothalamic mechanisms must receive and integrate information from peripheral as well as central sources, and exercise their effect on behavior through some more general integrative mechanisms; such mechanisms would translate the motivational forces that may be generated by the hypothalamic activity into gross behavioral responses.

We have already considered some of the peripheral mechanisms which may serve as information carriers and shall point out additional factors in our discussion of the hypothalamic systems. The available information on higher central mechanisms is still only rudimentary, and little is known about integrative processes. We shall therefore confine our treatment of the extrahypothalamic mechanisms to a brief description of some experiments which suggest that feeding behavior may be more complexly regulated than has been assumed in the past.

Many of the clinical and experimental reports that have implicated the hypothalamus as a possible integrative center for hunger motivation and feeding behavior come from investigations designed to study pathological obesity. Considerable attention will be devoted to this topic, for much evidence for the hypothalamic regulation of satiety has been accumulated in the course of these studies, and hypotheses about specific physiological mechanisms have been tested. Psychologists and neurophysiologists have only recently designed experiments to answer questions about the motivational aspects of this problem. Because the distinction between studies undertaken to investigate pathological obesity and those aimed more specifically at the mechanisms regulating feeding behavior and hunger is often very difficult to make, it will be convenient to consider them both together.

The Anatomy of the Hypothalamus

To establish a convenient frame of reference for the material to be presented in the following sections, we shall briefly review the anatomical topography of the diencephalon.

The hypothalamus has been subdivided into a number of discrete nuclei on the basis of the anatomical localization of cell concentrations and fiber bundles as well as infiltrating fiber tracts. This classification should imply little more than a convenient means of descriptive communication, for many of the nuclei contain several histologically different types of neurons. Physiological functions corresponding to these subdivisions have been identified for only a few of the pairs of nuclei, and most functional localization is at best regional at the present time.

Proceeding in an anterior-posterior direction, the first cell concentration generally grouped with the hypothalamus, though more properly a part of the telencephalon, is the *preoptic area*. This region has been implicated in the regulation of temperature and other autonomic functions and is closely related to the olfactory regions laterally. Further caudally, the anterior and lateral regions appear. The former region contains the *paraventricular* nuclei near the third ventricle, ventromedial to the fornix, and the *supraoptic* nuclei. Both pairs of nuclei send fibers down the infundibular stalk into the posterior lobe of the pituitary and have been shown to participate in the regulation of hypophyseal functions. Also situated in this general region are the nucleus *suprachiasmaticus* and the nucleus *supraopticus diffusus*. This portion of the hypothalamus is closely connected to the ansa peduncularis as well as to the inferior thalamic peduncle, both of which are believed to establish important connections with the septum pellucidum, insula, and thalamus. In the lateral portion of the hypothalamus, the *lateral hypothalamic area* continues caudally, now separated from the medial structures by the fornix which passes caudally through the tuber cinerum. Medially, the *dorsomedial* and *ventromedial* nuclei appear; these are particularly well defined in lower animals and serve as landmarks for this region. Considerable attention will be devoted to this area because it appears to contain neural elements which help regulate feeding behavior and satiation. The *ventromedial* nucleus has important direct connections to the globus pallidus, the orbital portion of the frontal lobe, and the amygdaloid complex. The medial portion of this region of the hypothalamus also has rich connections with the thalamus, partly via the *periventricular* nuclei which, at their lower end, expand into the *periventricular-arcuate* nuclei. In the posterior portion of the hypothalamus we find the mammillary region, characterized by the formation of the *subthalamic* nucleus and the compression of the hypothalamus by the ventromedial drift of the internal capsules; the region also contains an expansion of the subthalamic area. The *posterior* nucleus arises between the third ventricle and the subthalamic area, giving rise to important descending afferent pathways.

The hypothalamus is the most richly vascular

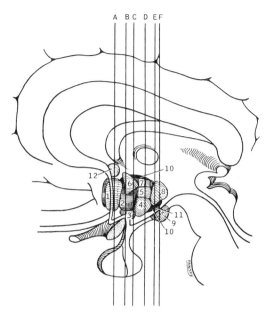

Fig. 6.22 General topography of the hypothalamus, indicating the planes for the vertical sections shown in Figures 6.24 and 6.25. 1, preoptic nuclei; 2, anterior hypothalamic area; 3, supraoptic nucleus; 4, ventromedial nucleus; 5, dorsomedial nucleus; 6, paraventricular nucleus; 7, dorsal hypothalamic area; 8, posterior hypothalamic area; 9, mammillary body; 10, lateral hypothalamic area; 11, intercalated nucleus; 12, anterior commissure. (From House and Pansky, 1960.)

region of the central nervous system; it is also in direct contact with the cerebrospinal fluid, since its medial aspects border the third ventricle. This suggests that chemical or osmotic variations of the blood may exert a direct effect on hypothalamic tissue. Recent studies of the distribution of isotopically labeled chemicals have also shown that the blood-brain barrier which prevents the entry of many drugs into the central nervous system is at least partially "porous" in the region of the diencephalon.

Historical Background

Hyperphagia (overeating) and obesity following injury or tumor growth in the general region of the hypothalamus have been reported in the clinical literature for well over 100 years. The precise anatomical localization of responsible structures has only recently been achieved, after nearly half a century of heated dispute; the physiological mechanisms mediating the control of these regions are, even today, subject to much speculation.

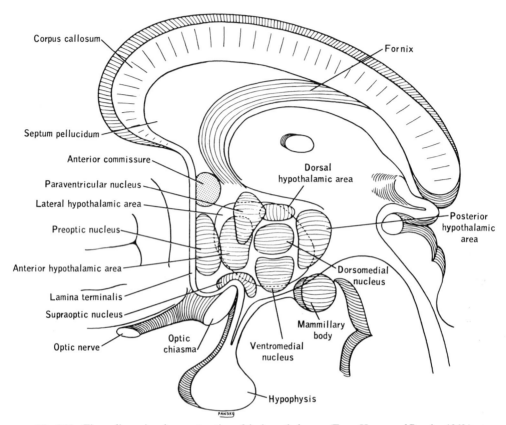

Fig. 6.23   Three-dimensional reconstruction of the hypothalamus. (From House and Pansky, 1960.)

Mohr (1840) gave the first detailed account of the symptomatology of what is now known to be hypothalamic obesity. No inquiry into the etiology of the phenomenon appears to have been undertaken until Babinski (1900) and Fröhlich (1902) published their observations. On the basis of extensive clinical data, these workers suggested that pathological obesity or "Fröhlich's syndrome" was caused by an endocrine imbalance due to hypopituitarism (an impairment of the secretory activity of the hypophysis). Only two years later, this view was challenged by Erdheim (1904) on the basis of the observation that tumors near the base of the brain could cause obesity without extensive damage to the pituitary, and that no particular type of tumor seemed to be associated with the disease. Erdheim proposed that the locus of the affected mechanism was to be found in the region of the base of the brain rather than the pituitary itself.

The first experimental evidence in support of this theory was obtained by Aschner (1912), who showed that surgical removal of the pituitary

failed to produce obesity and overeating unless the lesions extended into the overlying hypothalamus. Other investigators continued to attribute experimentally produced obesity and hyperphagia to the pituitary. They denied hypothalamic damage in their investigations and supported Fröhlich's interpretation of the phenomenon as an endocrine imbalance of hypophyseal origin (Crowe et al., 1910; Bell, 1917; Dott, 1923; Keller and Noble, 1935, 1936).

Subsequent investigations (Camus and Roussy, 1913, 1920, 1922) showed that even complete removal of the anterior lobe of the pituitary failed to produce obesity in the dog unless the lesions extended into the hypothalamus. P. E. Smith (1927, 1930) compared the effects of hypothalamic lesions with those produced by hypophysectomy (surgical removal of the gland, often accompanied by incidental damage to the ventral hypothalamus). The pituitary was approached by a parapharyngeal route (i.e., via the roof of the mouth) to minimize incidental damage to the hypothalamus. These experiments showed that lesions restricted to the hypothalamus produced obesity as well as genital dystrophy (a symptom often seen in clinical cases of hypothalamic obesity). Removal of the pituitary did not induce obesity, but was followed by a cessation of normal growth (hypophyseal dwarfism) and atrophy of the thyroids and gonads.

All these early studies failed to produce other than inferential evidence in support of a causal relationship between hypothalamic damage and the phenomenon under study; none of the experimenters succeeded in restricting the obesity-producing lesions to the hypothalamus itself. However, they focused the attention of subsequent and better-equipped researchers on this region of the diencephalon by eliminating anatomical structures previously believed to be involved in the etiology of adiposity (obesity).

The first pure case of hypothalamic obesity which showed no direct damage to the pituitary is mentioned by Bailey and Bremer (1921); they reported a series of investigations concerned

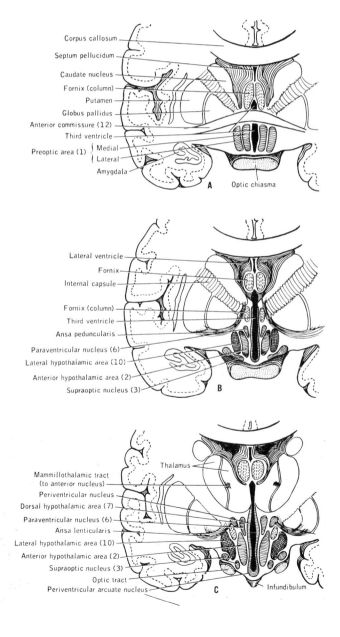

Fig. 6.24 Planes A, B, and C of Figure 6.22. (From House and Pansky, 1960.)

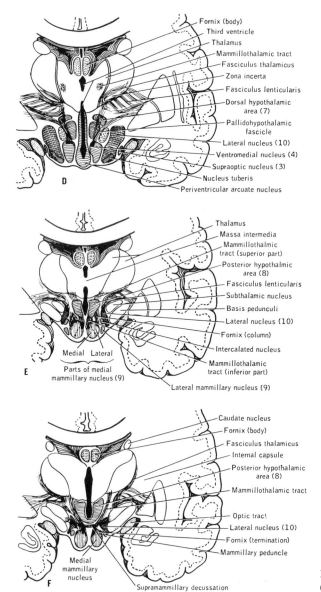

Fornix (body)
Third ventricle
Thalamus
Mammillothalamic tract
Fasciculus thalamicus
Zona incerta
Fasciculus lenticularis
Dorsal hypothalamic area (7)
Pallidohypothalamic fascicle
Lateral nucleus (10)
Ventromedial nucleus (4)
Supraoptic nucleus (3)
Nucleus tuberis
Periventricular arcuate nucleus

D

Thalamus
Massa intermedia
Mammillothalmic tract (superior part)
Posterior hypothalmic area (8)
Fasciculus lenticularis
Subthalamic nucleus
Basis pedunculi
Lateral nucleus (10)
Fornix (column)
Intercalated nucleus
Mammillothalamic tract (inferior part)
Lateral mammillary nucleus (9)

Medial Lateral
Parts of medial mammillary nucleus (9)

E

Caudate nucleus
Fornix (body)
Fasciculus thalamicus
Internal capsule
Posterior hypothalamic area (8)
Mammillothalamic tract
Optic tract
Lateral nucleus (10)
Fornix (termination)
Mammillary peduncle

Medial mammillary nucleus

F
Supramammillary decussation

Fig. 6.25   Planes D, E, and F of Figure 6.22. (From House and Pansky, 1960.)

primarily with the etiology of diabetes insipidus (persistent passage of urine low in specific gravity and free of sugar and albumin) in the dog. They reported that lesions restricted to the hypothalamus produced transient or permanent polyuria (excessive excretion of dilute urine), frequently accompanied by adiposity, hyperphagia, genital dystrophy, and polydipsia (excessive water intake). Before discussing the extensive literature that has appeared since these developments, we would like to mention Hetherington's (1943) investigation which provided the unequivocal proof

required to bring this long-standing controversy to an end. Hetherington demonstrated convincingly that hypothalamic lesions produce adiposity whether or not the anterior lobe of the pituitary has been damaged, and that no amount of pituitary damage will cause obesity as long as the hypothalamus remains unaffected by the lesions. More specifically, it was shown that hypophysectomized rats, which were observed for a sufficient time to allow maximal atrophy of the thyroids, adrenals, and gonads (75 to 80 days), did not show any sign of hyperphagia or developing obesity. Additional lesions in the ventromedial nuclei of the hypothalamus clearly produced obesity which was superimposed on the previously developed pituitary dwarfism. These experiments were made possible by the development and modification of the Horsely-Clark stereotaxic instrument for use on the rat (Clark, 1939), allowing the accurate placement of restricted electrolytic lesions.

Following the definitive demonstration of the causal relationship between localized hypothalamic damage and Fröhlich's syndrome by Hetherington and Ranson (1940, 1942a, b) and Hetherington (1941, 1943), a large number of reports have appeared in the medical, physiological, and psychological literature of the past two decades; these attempt (1) to provide a more specific localization of the structures concerned with the regulation of energy input and output, (2) to investigate the physiological systems that excite or inhibit these central control mechanisms, and (3) to investigate the psychological (i.e., motivational) properties of the phenomenon. An answer to the latter question depends, to some extent at least, on the satisfactory solution to the first problem; therefore, anatomical localization of the affected hypothalamic areas will be discussed first, in spite of the fact that only relatively recently has much progress been made in this field.

Specific Hypothalamic Mechanisms for the Control of Food Intake, Adiposity, and Hunger

The satiety mechanism. *Localization.* Few of the early studies of experimental obesity provided sufficiently specific histological evidence to allow a mapping of the cell concentrations responsible for the observed behavioral changes. Interpretation of the descriptions available from this period is complicated by the presence of both additional extrahypothalamic and intrahypothalamic damage which may have interfered with important nervous connections to hypothalamic regions reported "undamaged and unaffected." Many of the early investigators relied on Warner's (1929) report that crude surgical lesions in the hypothalamus produce pathological changes only in the directly affected nuclei, and that even immediately adjacent areas show no histological abnormalities. It is quite clear today that these findings were due to insufficient staining techniques. Further confusion was created by experimental reports which claimed hypothalamic obesity and changes in food intake following damage to various portions of the diencephalon. Bailey and Bremer (1921)

reported obesity following large lesions in the posterior hypothalamus between the pituitary stalk and anterior border of the mammillary bodies. Other investigators (Crooke and Gilmore, 1938; Biggart and Alexander, 1939) attributed experimentally produced obesity to damage to the anterior hypothalamus. Heinbecker et al. (1944) suggested that lesions interrupting axons from cells in the caudal portion of the periventricular nuclei interfere with fat metabolism and hence produce obesity. The free-hand surgical ablations made in these studies undoubtedly damaged many additional fiber tracts and nuclei; none of these results has been replicated by later investigators who have used more precise stereotaxic techniques.

Following the development of the Horsely-Clark stereotaxic instrument, the region in or near the ventromedial nuclei of the hypothalamus was implicated in experimental studies using more accurate placements of restricted electrolytic lesions. Hetherington and Ranson (1940) reported obesity following lesions restricted to the "area of the ventromedial and arcuate nuclei," and Hetherington (1941) obtained results from lesions in the medial half of the lateral hypothalamus as well as in the dorsomedial nuclei. Further studies by Hetherington and Ranson (1942a, b) showed that obesity could be produced by damage to a relatively large area of the tuberal and posterior portion of the hypothalamus; however, the most effective lesions were located in, or ventrolateral to, the ventromedial nuclei.

A series of subsequent studies (Brobeck et al., 1943a, b; Brooks, 1946a, b, c; Brooks et al., 1946a, b) confirmed Hetherington's findings and suggested that the ventromedial nuclei must be involved, directly or indirectly, if obesity is to result. Kennedy (1950) and Bruce and Kennedy (1951) replicated earlier findings (Hetherington and Ranson, 1942a; Brobeck et al., 1943a) which had shown that these nuclei need not be destroyed completely in order to produce experimental obesity. Marked hypothalamic obesity (and hyperphagia) occurred as the result of lesions ventrolateral to the ventromedial nuclei. Mayer and Barnett (1955) have found that such lesions need not be bilateral as had been assumed in the past. They report that unilateral lesions do produce the classical hypothalamic hyperphagic syndrome, although the magnitude of this effect is only roughly one-half that usually observed after bilateral lesions.

It has been suggested that although the neurons

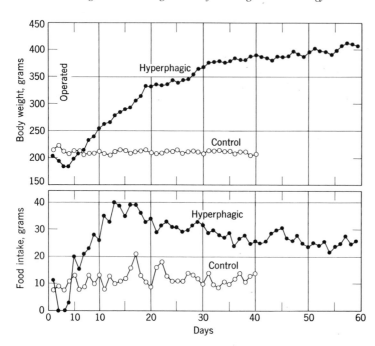

Fig. 6.26 Postoperative body weight and daily food intake of a hyperphagic animal compared to those of a normal unoperated control animal. (From Teitelbaum, 1961.)

involved in the regulation of food intake are located *in* the ventromedial nuclei, their axons extend from the inferior and lateral borders of these nuclei into the region above and lateral to the mammillary bodies, and project from there to the mesencephalic tegmentum (Hetherington, 1944; Brobeck et al., 1943a; Wheatley, 1944; Brobeck, 1946). Such a contention is supported by a number of studies showing that obesity as well as hyperphagia can be produced by bilateral lesions posterior to the ventromedial nuclei. Bailey and Bremer (1921) reported obesity in dogs following ablation of the posterior hypothalamus, and Heinbecker et al. (1944) obtained similar results with lesions in the periventricular nuclei. In monkeys, hyperphagia has been produced by lesions in the posteroventral portions of the thalamus as well as the rostral aspects of the mesencephalic tegmentum (Ruch et al., 1941, 1942). Larsson (1954) has reported that electrical stimulation of the brainstem near the dorsal motor nucleus of the vagus produces polyphagia (overeating and indiscriminate eating of normally unacceptable substances) in goats.

Recent evidence from studies employing electrical stimulation of the ventromedial nuclei (Anand and Dua, 1955a, b) shows that the analogous result, a decrease of food intake (though not complete aphagia), may be caused by excitation of neurons in this region. That the activity of the ventromedial nuclei may be related to a "stopping of feeding" is further suggested by direct recordings of the electrical activity of this region. Brobeck et al. (1956) found that intravenous injections of Benzedrine or Dexedrine (appetite depressants which are structurally related to epinephrine) produced EEG changes similar to those seen during barbiturate anesthesia in all parts of the hypothalamus except the medial nuclei. The ventromedial nuclei showed a prolonged increase in both frequency and amplitude. These results suggest that the appetite-depressing action of these drugs may be directly related to an excitatory action on the inhibitory mechanism of the medial hypothalamus.

Some consternation has recently been created by reports suggesting that the hyperphagia and obesity commonly seen after ventromedial damage might be an artifact of the lesioning technique and reflect lateral stimulation rather than the removal of an inhibitory mechanism. Reynolds (1963) made presumably comparable lesions in the hypothalamus with the conventional direct-current technique and with a radio-frequency technique which is thought to prevent the plating effect of the direct currents. He found that the conventional techniques produced hyperphagia and obesity, but he saw little or no effect after lesions made with the radio-frequency current. He concluded that the hyperphagia might be caused by metal particles which are knocked off the metal electrode during the passage of a direct anodal current and possibly invade and stimulate the lateral hypothalamic feeding center. A priori, this is not a very likely hypothesis, since the hyperphagia and obesity described in many early studies relied on surgical means of ablation rather than electrical. An alternative hypothesis—that the lesion might produce scar tissue which irritates and stimulates the adjacent feeding center— also seems unlikely in view of the many studies (see Morgane, 1960) which have shown that lesions immediately anterior or posterior to the lateral

hypothalamic feeding center do not affect food or water intake. A study by Hoebel (1965) demonstrated that hyperphagia and obesity can be obtained by radio-frequency lesions in the ventromedial hypothalamus, suggesting that both of the proposed explanations may not account for Reynold's findings. Just why he obtained the largely negative results is not yet clear, but different results might have been observed if more palatable foods had been used. It has been reported in a number of studies (see Teitelbaum, 1961; Teitelbaum and Epstein, 1962, 1963) that the development of hyperphagia depends in no

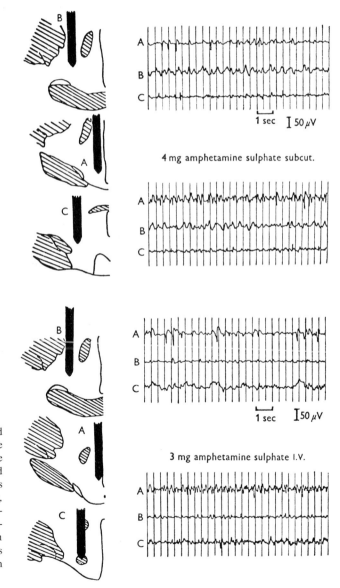

Fig. 6.27 *Top,* electrical activity recorded from A, the medial hypothalamus; B, the rostrolateral hypothalamus; and C, the caudolateral hypothalamus. Upper record before, lower record after subcutaneous injection of 4 mg amphetamine. *Bottom,* electrical activity of A, the medial hypothalamus; B, the rostrolateral hypothalamus; and C, the caudal hypothalamus in the plane of the fornix after intravenous injection of 3 mg amphetamine. (From Brobeck et al., 1956.)

small measure on the nature of the diet, a point perhaps not considered sufficiently in Reynold's experiments.

Anatomical changes due to lesions or stimulation of the ventromedial hypothalamus. The peripheral effects of hyperphagia-producing lesions in the hypothalamus have been studied extensively in the hope of finding information relevant to the peripheral mediating mechanisms that respond to the central changes. The most striking modification of the anatomical structure of the organism with lesions in the ventromedial region of the hypothalamus is the enormous quantity of surplus fat deposited. It has been reported (P. E. Smith, 1927; Hetherington and Weil, 1940) that surplus fat deposits make up as much as 74% of the total body weight in hypothalamic-obese animals, clearly satisfying Fenton's (1956) definition of obesity. The greatly augmented food intake also causes excessive distension and hypertrophy of the gastrointestinal walls, as well as structural and functional abnormalities of the kidney. Dilation and necrosis of the tubules, hyalinization of the renal tubules, and albumin as well as erythrocytes and cast deposits in the urine have been reported (Brobeck et al., 1943a).

Most clinical and experimental studies have reported hypoplasia of the gonads and genitalia following ventromedial hypothalamic lesions (Fröhlich, 1902; Bailey and Bremer, 1921; Hetherington and Ranson, 1942b).

Obesity and genital hypoplasia do not, however, seem to be invariably related. Brooks et al. (1942) and Hetherington and Ranson (1942b) found that localized lesions can produce one of these conditions without necessarily causing the appearance of the other. D'Angelo (1959) reported that bilateral lesions in the arcuate nuclei and the median eminence of the hypothalamus produced atrophy of the reproductive tract and reduced thyroid function in adult female rats without disturbing the regulation of food intake.

The organ most drastically affected by hypothalamic damage is the liver, which is yellow and dilated to almost double its normal size following obesity-producing lesions. In the fed state, the liver of the hypothalamic-obese animal may contain twice the normal percentage of ether-extractable lipids, which indicates that the total quantity of hepatic fat may be approximately four times the normal amount (Tepperman et al., 1943a, b, c).

A number of investigators have noticed a yellowing of the albino rat's fur, which tends to become sparse and show scaly cutaneous tissue hypersensitive to local infections (Hetherington and Ranson, 1940; Graef et al., 1944). Animals with hypothalamic lesions also appear to be subject to a great variety of nonspecific ailments which eventually bring about death, long before the normal life-span has been completed (Hetherington and Ranson, 1940; Brooks, 1946b; Ingram, 1960).

A review of the literature (see Sheehan, 1940) suggests that lesions in various portions of the hypothalamus may produce gastrointestinal erosions. In the monkey, Hoff and Sheehan (1935) observed acute mucosal perforations following lesions in the tuber cinereum, and A. D. Keller (1936) reported similar erosions and hemorrhage in dogs following lesions at the level of the optic chiasma. French et al. (1952) have shown that lesions in the anterior hypothalamus produce submucosal hemorrhages, whereas lesions in the posterior diencephalon induce gastric ulcers. Maire and Patton (1956) have observed hemorrhaging erosions in the upper GI tract in rats after preoptic lesions. Feldman (Feldman et al., 1961) has recently concluded that gastrointestinal lesions are produced much more frequently by hypothalamic damage than by destruction of any other part of the central nervous system. Presumably, these gastrointestinal effects of hypothalamic damage are due to an increased secretion of hydrochloric acid.

These findings are of particular interest, for clinical studies of ulcer patients have shown that a greatly increased frequency of food intake tends to alleviate the pain associated with gastrointestinal erosion. Also of interest in this connection is the finding that the desire to eat in human subjects appears to be correlated with the secretion of hydrochloric acid (HCl). Cancer patients show normal appetites as long as HCl is secreted, but lose the desire to eat as soon as this secretion stops (Gilmour, 1958). It is possible that the abnormal food intake observed after ventromedial nucleus lesions may, at least in part, be caused by the local gastric irritation rather than by a direct effect on the central regulation of hunger.

Such a conclusion is supported by data from electrical stimulation studies. Beattie (1932) reported 30 years ago that electrical stimulation of the infundibular region of the hypothalamus caused the appearance of small hyperemic patches in the gastric mucosa. Wang et al. (1940) observed a blanching of the small intestine during stimulation of the anterior hypothalamus. Stimulation of discrete areas of the lateral aspect of the anterior

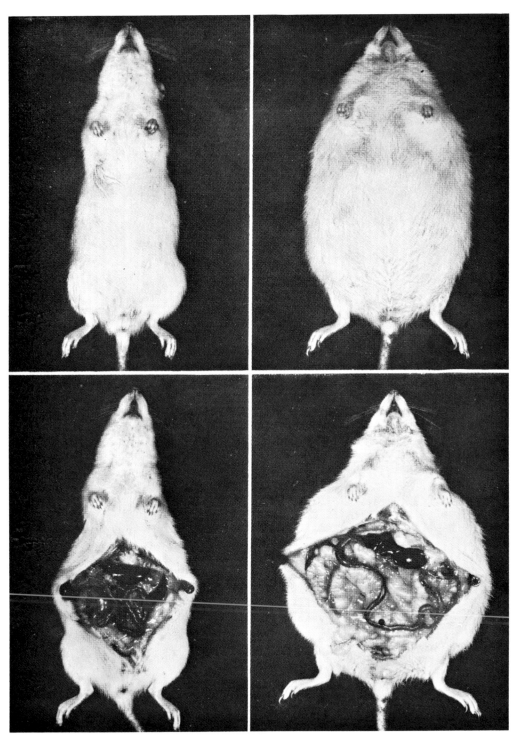

Fig. 6.28 Comparison of one hypothalamic obese rat and one control rat at autopsy, nineteen weeks after operation. (From Kennedy, 1950.)

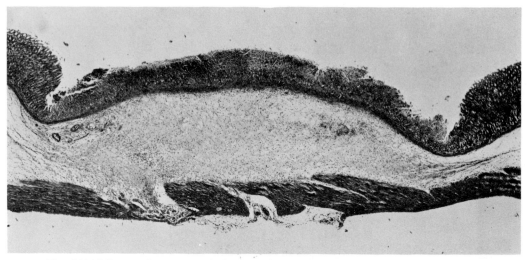

Fig. 6.29   Microscopic appearance of typical hemorrhagic erosion of the gastric mucosa following preoptic hypothalamic lesions. (From Maire and Patton, 1956.)

hypothalamus (including the medial forebrain bundle) produces a marked increase in gastric acidity (Porter et al., 1953) in addition to acute gastrointestinal erosions and hemorrhage (Feldman et al., 1961).

Wang et al. (1940) demonstrated that the effects of hypothalamic stimulation on the gastrointestinal tract are mediated by two mechanisms. The immediate changes in the gastrointestinal tract are produced by vagal stimulation. They are characterized by a sudden onset and relatively brief latencies and are totally abolished by bilateral vagotomy (transection of the vagus nerve). A more delayed excitatory response to hypothalamic stimulation (occurring after 40 to 60 sec) is not affected by transection of the vagi. This effect shows a gradual onset and typically persists for several minutes after the cessation of hypothalamic stimulation. Wang et al. suggested that this delayed response may be due to pituitary gland secretions which are known to have definite effects on the gastrointestinal tract (Geiling, 1926; van Dyke, 1936). Although Wang's evidence is not quite conclusive, this interpretation has considerable face validity, for it is well known that secretion of the posterior lobe of the pituitary may be initiated by electrical stimulation of the anterior hypothalamus (Clark and Wang, 1939) including the hypophyseal stalk itself (Haterius and Ferguson, 1938).

French et al. (1953) observed that electrical stimulation of the anterior hypothalamus produced an early rise in gastric secretion which is at a peak within 1 hr after stimulation. Such a response appears to be due to vagal stimulation, since bilateral vagotomy completely abolished this effect. Stimulation of the posterior hypothalamus produced a delayed (3 to 4 hr) rise in gastric secretion which was not affected by transection of the vagi and appeared to be related to secretions from the anterior pituitary and adrenal cortex.

Several studies have shown that hypothalamic stimulation may have pronounced effects on gastric motility. Immediate cessation of peristalsis and loss of muscular tone in the stomach and small intestine have been reported (Kabat et al., 1935). Hypermotility has also been reported (Wang et al., 1940). Beattie (1932; Beattie and Sheehan, 1934) found that electrical stimulation of the anterior hypothalamus had an excitatory effect on gastric activity, whereas stimulation of the posterior portion of the diencephalon inhibited gastric motility. The excitatory component of this regulation appears to be independent of vagal influences, since not only hypermotility but also hypersecretion can be elicited by hypothalamic stimulation in vagotomized animals (Wang et al., 1940; Heslop, 1938a, b).

Physiological mechanisms.   The experimental evidence considered so far does little more than establish the clinically important, but theoretically inconclusive, fact that certain regions of the hypothalamus appear to be involved in the regulation of food intake, and that Fröhlich's syndrome (extreme obesity) reflects restricted hypothalamic

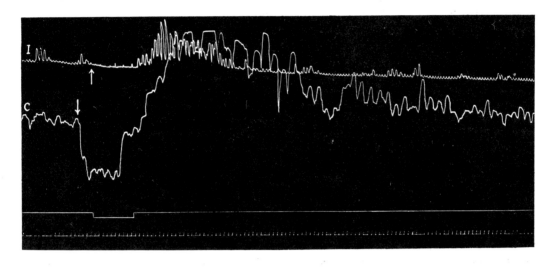

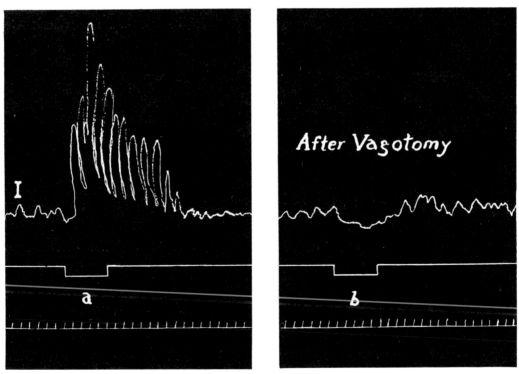

Fig. 6.30 *Top,* kymograph tracings showing the delayed excitatory responses of the small intestine (I) and colon (C) with loss of colonic tone during electrical stimulation of the hypothalamus, beginning at the arrow. Small excursions of the tracing (I) are respiratory. Time marker, 6 sec. *Bottom,* kymograph tracings showing the immediate excitatory response of the small intestine (I) in the tracing (a) which was abolished after vagatomy (b). Time marker, 6 sec. (From Wang et al., 1940.)

damage. How are the observed changes in food intake and body weight related to the activity of these hypothalamic centers, and what physiological mechanisms may be affected by these central mechanisms?

Bilateral destruction of the ventromedial nuclei of the hypothalamus produces two prominent symptoms, overeating and obesity. Although the relationship between these two effects appears obvious at first glance, the question of causality is not so clearly answered when one takes a closer look at the experimental evidence. The early clinical and experimental investigations of the effects of hypothalamic lesions reported obesity, but they failed to observe hyperphagia. Most recent studies suggest that overeating plays an important role in the development of hypothalamic obesity; it is not clear that this is the only factor. Both symptoms may be produced by a basic change in the organism's energy balance which reflects the activity of many different physiological mechanisms.

FAT METABOLISM. Bates et al. (1955a, b) have shown storage of excessive quantities of surplus fat to be responsible for up to 90% of the increase in body weight following ventromedial lesions in the hypothalamus. The simplest explanation of this effect is a primary disorder of the fat metabolism from either decreased lipid oxidation or increased fat synthesis. Various implications of this hypothesis have been tested in the past 50 years. The results of these experiments generally agree that the simplest explanation does not seem to be the correct one. Abnormal fat metabolism plays an essential but apparently secondary role in the etiology of hypothalamic obesity (Brobeck, 1946); however, interesting metabolic changes which are not characteristic of other forms of obesity occur.

Obese rats and monkeys on limited feeding schedules metabolize tissue fats at normal rates of conversion (Brooks et al., 1942; Brobeck et al., 1943a), and their respiratory quotient (a convenient measure of metabolic rate) is well within the normal range (Tepperman et al., 1943a). When fed on an *ad libitum* schedule, these animals show a fat turnover that amounts only to approximately 5% of the control level. Such a drastic decrease is not found in other types of obesity, suggesting that this effect is not merely secondary to the raised food intake (Bates et al., 1955a, b).

The greatly increased synthesis of fat in the hypothalamic animal appears to be a direct result of the abnormal eating habits. Carbohydrates are transformed into fat at a greatly accelerated rate

in the experimentally obese rat, but this change in the conversion rate does not appear until some time after the lesions have been made (Tepperman et al., 1943a). Overeating, however, starts immediately after the anesthesia wears off and is greatest during the first 48 hr after the operation. Normal animals show similarly accelerated conversion reactions when trained to eat their daily ration within a brief (1 to 3 hr) period which corresponds roughly to the feeding habits of the hypothalamic animals. Dickerson et al. (1953) have reported that the carbohydrate metabolism of normal animals trained to eat their daily ration in a brief feeding session showed abnormalities similar to those seen in the lesioned rat. These data suggest that the abnormal synthesis of fat may be directly related to the changed feeding habits of the animal with ventromedial lesions.

The abnormal carbohydrate metabolism in hypothalamic hyperphagia produces important secondary effects. Insulin cannot be liberated rapidly enough to dispose of the accelerated carbohydrate intake. This lack causes hyperglycemia (which, according to Mayer's original hypothesis, should lead to an immediate cessation of eating), glycosuria, and diabetes mellitus (disturbance of carbohydrate metabolism due to deficient pancreatic secretion of insulin) (Ranson et al., 1938; Brobeck et al., 1943b; Tepperman et al., 1943b; Ruch and Patton, 1946).

INCREASED ENERGY INPUT (HYPERPHAGIA). Nearly all the early clinical and experimental investigations of the "ventromedial lesion syndrome" failed to report any change in food intake. The resulting obesity was commonly attributed to metabolic disorders or to a decline in general activity.

Subsequent studies of this phenomenon (Tepperman et al., 1941; Brooks et al., 1942; Brobeck et al., 1943a; Wheatley, 1944; Brooks, 1946c) have shown that obesity-producing lesions always result in overeating. There is, however, no general agreement in the recent literature regarding the relative importance of this effect or the physiological mechanisms which may be responsible for it.

That overeating is a direct consequence of hypothalamic damage is suggested by the onset of voracious eating as soon as the animal returns to consciousness after the operation (Brobeck et al., 1943a). The food intake of the hypothalamic hyperphagic animal is typically greatest during the first 48 hr after the operation and declines gradually as the body becomes more and more obese. Excessive feeding and rapid weight gain (the *dynamic phase* of hypothalamic hyperphagia, as Brobeck has called it) persist for several months. As the animal attains its maximum weight (two to three times normal), the food intake levels off to near normal quantities (the *static phase* of hyperphagia), and no further increase in body weight occurs. The gradual decrease of food consumption at this stage does not indicate a partial functional recovery of the hypothalamic mechanisms but reflects the physical limitations of the organism. Once a maximum "ceiling" has been reached, the organism is unable to tolerate further increases in body size, and an unknown shut-off mechanism begins to limit food intake. If the animals are deprived after stabilizing their maximum weight during the static phase of obesity and are starved until they reach their preoperative weight level, a new dynamic phase (characterized by excessive eating and rapid weight gain) occurs as soon as free access to food is restored (Brobeck et al., 1943a; Brooks and Lambert, 1946; Brooks, 1945; Brooks and Lockwood, 1945).

Numerous investigations have reported significant correlations between food intake and weight gain in animals with ventromedial nucleus lesions. However, there still remains an unsettled controversy about whether this hyperphagia can account for all the adiposity (Hetherington, 1941; Hetherington and Ranson, 1942a; Brobeck et al., 1943a; Brooks and Marine, 1946; Brooks and Lambert, 1946; Brooks et al., 1946a, b).

Several experiments have attempted to investigate this problem in pair-feeding situations which maintain the total food intake and/or total feeding time constant for normal and operated animals (Tepperman et al., 1943a; Brooks et al., 1946a, b; Brooks and Lambert, 1946). The results of these studies are unfortunately not as clear-cut as one might desire. Most hyperphagic animals fail to gain weight at higher than normal rates when maintained on a diet determined by the food intake of normal controls. However, some animals with ventromedial nucleus lesions appear to be able to outgain their normal controls even on the same amount of food. The weight gain in these cases is not nearly so pronounced as that under *ad libitum* feeding conditions. The abnormal feeding habits of the hypothalamic hyperphagic animal disappear in the static phase of the obesity; however, spaced feeding schedules that approximate the pattern of normal food intake do not prevent the development of adiposity. These findings sug-

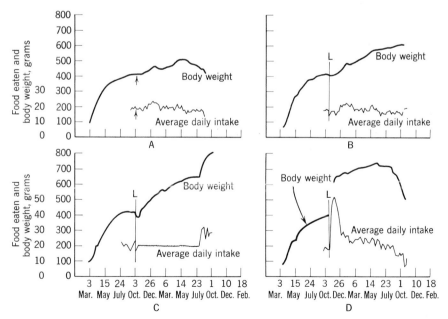

Fig. 6.31 A, weight change and food intake of a normal rat. Arrows indicate the time at which lesions were made in littermates. B, littermate with a ventromedial lesion pair-fed with the normal. C, littermate with lesion limited to its preoperative average food intake. D, littermate with lesion fed *ad libitum*. L, hypothalamic lesions made; *ad lib, ad libitum* feeding begun. (From Brooks and Lambert, 1946.)

gest that hypothalamic lesions affect the organism's energy balance not only by a direct increase in food intake, but also via some disturbance of the output mechanism. Before we turn to brief consideration of this possibility, another aspect of hypothalamic hyperphagia should be mentioned.

Teitelbaum and Epstein (Teitelbaum, 1961) have suggested that lesions in the ventromedial nuclei may produce a defect in the regulation of body weight rather than a disturbance of the food intake mechanism per se. This hypothesis proposes that the ventromedial hypothalamus may contain receptors for an as yet unknown circulating hormonal metabolite which may signal the state of the animals' fat deposits. This notion finds some support in Hervey's work with parabiotic rats. (The circulatory systems of such animals are joined to permit an exchange of blood.) This work is in need of replication, since some of the findings are unclear, but the results are interesting. If one

of a pair of parabiotic rats is made hyperphagic by bilateral ventromedial lesions, the other member of the pair becomes aphagic and loses weight (Hervey, 1959). This may indicate that the ventromedial nuclei of the normal partner respond to some change in the blood that is circulated between the two animals.

DISTURBANCES OF GENERAL ACTIVITY. Hetherington (1941) reported in one of his earlier studies of localized hypothalamic lesions that an enormous decrease of activity rather than an increase in food intake seemed to be responsible for the observed obesity. A subsequent investigation supported this hypothesis. Hetherington and Ranson (1942a) measured the activity of animals in an activity wheel and found that total running decreased significantly after ventromedial nucleus lesions. Mayer et al. (1955) have more recently replicated these findings in the mouse. Bilateral lesions in the

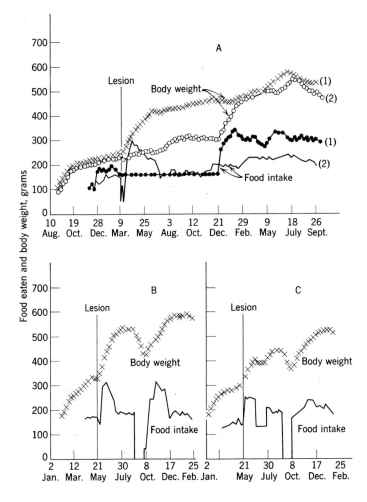

Fig. 6.32   A, weight gain and food intake of two animals with ventromedial lesions. Number 1 was permitted free access to food and water and showed marked dynamic and static phases of the hypothalamic syndrome. Number 2 was limited to its preoperative intake (which it received in eight equal parts, delivered at 3-hr intervals). B, C, weight changes during and after food limitation and starvation in obese animals. (From Brooks and Lambert, 1946.)

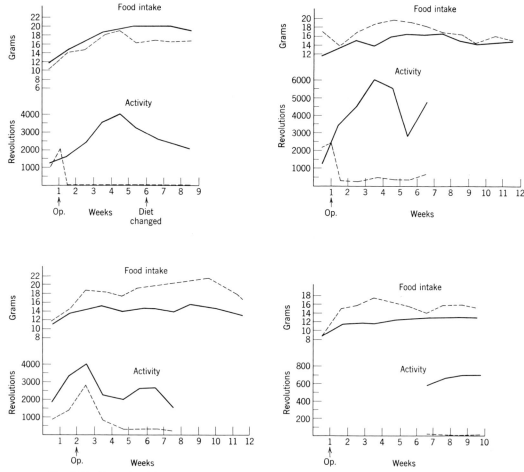

Fig. 6.33   Records of food intake and spontaneous activity (running) of obese rats with hypothalamic lesions (– – –) and of their normal littermate controls (——). (From Hetherington and Ranson, 1942a.)

ventromedial nuclei (infringing on the paraventricular and arcuate nuclei) produced pronounced obesity and hyperphagia as well as an almost total suppression of spontaneous activity to approximately 2 to 3% of normal.

Brooks's (1946a, b) findings suggest that these results must be evaluated with caution. Twelve to 24 hr after surgery, hyperactivity was manifested and was followed in a few days by a sharply decreased activity. However, the change in the activity pattern was found to be independent of the eventual appearance of hyperphagia and obesity. Furthermore, the activity of obese animals was depressed for only a relatively brief period of time (returning to normal levels well before the end of the dynamic phase of obesity) when the activity measures were taken in a tambour cage.

This return to normal activity levels may not be observed in the activity wheel because the obese animal may be unable to run.

Decreased activity may nevertheless cause the relatively greater weight gain of hypothalamic animals in a pair-feeding situation, since all relevant studies were conducted well within the period of lowered activity. The inactive animal may store as fat the surplus energy expended in locomotion by the more active controls (Brobeck, 1945).

It should be pointed out that inactivity does not invariably lead to obesity; this would be the case if inactivity were a significant factor. Hetherington and Ranson (1942a) and Brooks (1946b, c) found that disturbances of the activity rhythm occurred in animals which failed to become either hyperphagic or obese.

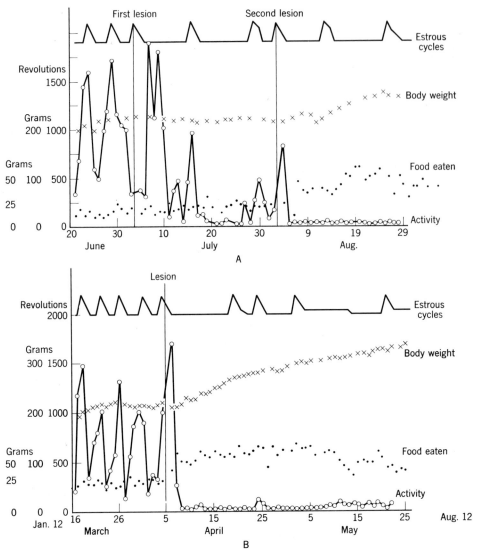

Fig. 6.34 A, body weight, food intake, activity changes, and modifications of the estrous cycle induced by hypothalamic lesions. The first lesion produced a reduction in activity and a modification of estrous rhythm but no hyperphagia or obesity. The second lesion produced a further reduction in activity and a mild degree of obesity. B, abolition of running activity and the development of obesity after operation. (From Brooks, 1946c.)

HEAT PRODUCTION. Another potential explanation of at least some of the weight gain of hypothalamic animals may involve reduced heat production. The organism's heat exchange is severely disturbed for several days following hypothalamic damage. The animal may divert energy normally dissipated as heat into excess fat storage, thus contributing to obesity (Brobeck, 1946, 1957a, b, c). The amount of energy liberated appears to be too small in comparison with total energy intake to account for all the ensuing obesity; however, it

may explain the relatively small effect seen in the pair-feeding situation. The proposed mechanism cannot easily account for the obesity of animals maintained on an *ad libitum* feeding schedule, since a number of studies (Bruhn and Keller, 1941; Brobeck et al., 1943a; Brooks and Marine, 1946; Mayer and Greenberg, 1953) have demonstrated that the initial decrease in total heat production is followed by an enormous increase as the animal begins to gain weight. (The heat production of animals at or near maximum weight has been shown to be nearly twice normal, a value which corresponds well to their increased total body weight.)

The possibility that the rate of heat production may be a factor in the regulation of the organism's energy balance, and thus directly or indirectly influence the feeding behavior of the organism, is an intriguing one. Structures in the preoptic area and anterior hypothalamus have been shown to participate in the regulation of heat dissipation, and neurons stimulated by falling blood temperatures have been found throughout the hypothalamus (Teague and Ranson, 1936; Ranson et al., 1937; Magoun et al., 1938; Clark et al., 1939; Andersson and Persson, 1957). We shall return to this matter after a brief discussion of the lateral hypothalamic feeding mechanism.

SENSORY FACTORS. When non-nutritive substances are added to their food, normal animals tend to compensate for this dilution by a proportional increase in total intake. Teitelbaum (1955) found that animals with bilateral lesions in the ventromedial nuclei of the hypothalamus cannot affect a comparable regulation. When as little as 25% cellulose is added to their diet, food consumption *decreases* drastically, particularly in the static phase of hypothalamic obesity, where even small amounts of roughage suffice to suppress eating for as long as a week. These results seem to be due to sensory (taste) factors, since similar results were obtained when a bitter substance was added to the diet. Normal animals continue to eat a normal daily ration when small amounts of quinine are

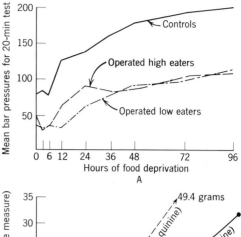

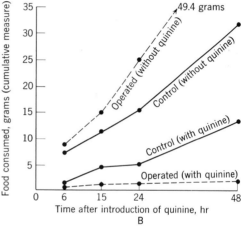

Fig. 6.36   A, effect of hypothalamic lesions on the rate of bar pressing after various intervals of food deprivation. The rate of bar pressing (reinforced at 5-min intervals) increases with hours of food deprivation; the performance of both operated subgroups is poorer than that of the control rats.

B, effect of a bitter taste on the food intake of rats with hypothalamic lesions. With a bland-mixture, synthetic high-fat diet, the cumulative curves show a higher food intake for the operated animals than for the controls; with a bitter mixture (1024 mg quinine/100 grams) the food intakes of both groups are reduced, and the direction of the difference between them is reversed. (From Miller et al., 1950, AAAS.)

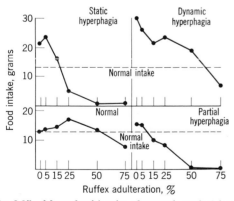

Fig. 6.35   Mean food intake of normal, static (obese) hyperphagic, partial hyperphagic, and dynamic (non-obese) hyperphagic animals as a function of percentage of cellulose (Ruffex) adulteration. The dashed lines represent the normal intake of rats fed the standard diet. (From Teitelbaum, 1955.)

mixed in with their food. Hypothalamic animals, on the other hand, eat practically nothing. Conversely, these animals overeat by a great amount when their food is sweetened with dextrose, whereas normal rats tend to maintain a relatively constant caloric intake.

These results suggest that the sensory aspects of food are more critical to the hyperphagic animal than to the normal animal. Their overall motivation for food may actually be lower than normal. This conclusion was first drawn by Miller et al.

(1950) who found that hyperphagic animals were less willing to work for food than the normal control animals, although they would eat much more on a palatable *ad libitum* diet. Teitelbaum (1957) has confirmed this result and has found that hyperphagic animals do not increase their general activity as much as normal animals when they are deprived of food. To the extent that such random activity is a prerequisite for getting food, this result again suggests a lowered motivational level.

The pattern of food intake of normal and hyperphagic animals was compared by Teitelbaum and Campbell (1958). They found that hyperphagic animals on a liquid diet do not eat more quickly or more frequently than their normal controls. They do, however, consume more food per meal, suggesting that the impairment may be primarily related to the ability to stop eating, rather than to a generally increased motivation to ingest food. On a solid diet, hyperphagic animals not only eat larger meals but also return to the food cup more frequently. The authors suggested that the greater bulk of the solid diet made it physically impossible for the hyperphagic animals to obtain a sufficient number of calories per meal to sustain their total caloric intake at a constant level. Williams and Teitelbaum (1959) further investigated this problem and found that both normal and hyperphagic animals can maintain a constant caloric intake when the diet is diluted by 50% water (the constant caloric intake of the hyperphagic animals is, of course, much higher than that of normal rats). This caloric regulation is apparently not seen in experiments using cellulose admixtures because of the increased sensitivity of these animals to sensory factors.

Possible contribution of affective mechanisms. The ventromedial nuclei play an apparently important role in the central regulation of a number of motivational functions other than hunger or satiety. Particularly the control of emotional behavior or affective reactions to stimuli of all modalities seems to be intimately related to this area

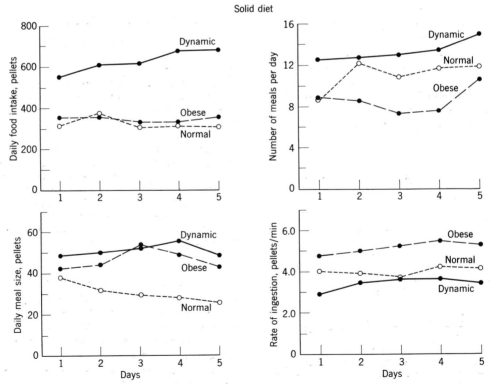

Fig. 6.37 Patterns of ingestion by normal, dynamic hyperphagic, and obese hyperphagic animals on a solid diet. The daily meal size, the number of meals per day, and the rate of ingestion during each meal represent the patterns of ingestion that produced the total amount ingested daily. (From Teitelbaum and Campbell, 1958.)

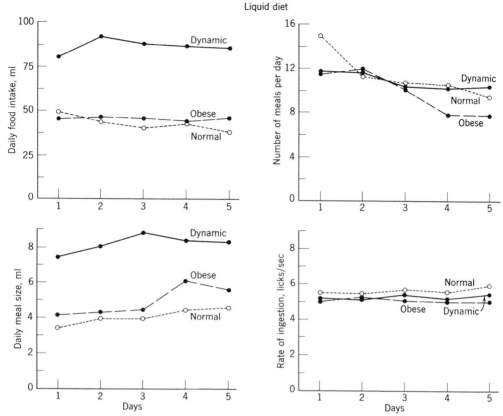

Fig. 6.38 Patterns of ingestion by normal, dynamic, and obese hyperphagic animals on a liquid diet. The daily meal size, number of meals per day, and rate of ingestion during each meal represent the patterns of ingestion that produced the total amount ingested daily. (From Teitelbaum and Campbell, 1958.)

of the hypothalamus (Wheatley, 1944; Hess, 1949). It is possible that very diverse functions may be regulated by neural circuits which overlap extensively at some point in the brain; however, the influence of the ventromedial nuclei on feeding behavior is sufficiently peculiar to suggest an alternative hypothesis. Could the effects on feeding behavior be secondary to a more general change in the organism's affective response to all stimuli?

Such an interpretation is not as unlikely as it may seem at first glance. Lesions in the ventromedial hypothalamus cause overeating and obesity only when palatable foods are available. Little effect is seen when the food is slightly stale, and hypophagia, or even aphagia, can be observed when the diet is made bitter or otherwise unpalatable by the admixture of quinine or roughage (Miller et al., 1950; Teitelbaum, 1955, 1957). It is possible that this finickiness may indicate a basic disturbance of food motivation which is reflected

in an increased response to taste as a motivating aspect of the situation (Teitelbaum and Epstein, 1963). However, this interpretation does explain why animals with ventromedial lesions are less willing than normals to work for food in a simple lever-pressing situation (Miller et al., 1950; Teitelbaum, 1957).

Miller (1964) has proposed that the peculiar reaction to ventromedial lesions suggests that the food motivation of the animals may in fact be lower than normal and that the overeating may be related to an interference with a satiety mechanism which normally inhibits the basic feeding center. This interpretation is generally accepted today and has been incorporated into psychophysiological theories of motivation (Stellar, 1954, 1960) which suggest that distinct inhibitory centers restrain the primary, excitatory mechanisms. In combination with the suggested exaggeration of taste influences, this interpretation accounts for the data fairly well, although some important questions remain to be resolved.

It is possible that the hypothalamic lesions produce separate and potentially independent effects on a variety of overlapping neural circuits concerned with food motivation, satiety, taste or taste motivation, emotional responsiveness, sexual behavior, etc. However, a simpler and more parsimonious interpretation may be possible. Ventromedial damage is known to increase sharply an animal's emotional responsiveness to all stimuli (Wheatley, 1944). We cannot yet adequately assess positive affective responses in animals, and the literature, therefore, has stressed the negative aspects of this change ("rage"); however, it seems likely that the change in the organism's threshold for affective responses may be a general one. The "finickiness" of the ventromedial animal might then reflect a change in its affective response to taste rather than a change in the intensity or quality of the sensation itself.

A simple interpretation of the apparently contradictory effects of ventromedial lesions on appetitive behavior becomes possible if a general rather than a specific change in affect is assumed. The animals should in fact eat more when the food is palatable, but should be more sensitive

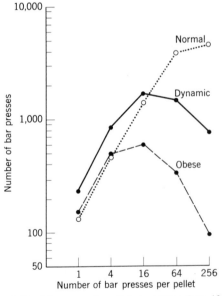

Fig. 6.39 Mean number of bar presses (per 12-hr period) of normal, obese hyperphagic, and dynamic (nonobese) hyperphagic animals as a function of the number of bar presses required to obtain each pellet. (From Teitelbaum, 1957.)

than normal to unpleasant tastes. They should work less for food than normals because of the exaggerated response to handling, the test situation, the deprivation regimen, and the requirement of having to work for their daily bread. Even the peculiar observation that ventromedial animals respond more sharply than normals to nonreinforcement can be predicted on the basis of this hypothesis. The performance of animals with ventromedial lesions drops sharply as the reward conditions of an aperiodic reward schedule are gradually worsened (Teitelbaum, 1957).

Some experimental support for this hypothesis has now become available (S. P. Grossman, 1966). In replication of earlier studies, it was observed that small, bilateral lesions in the dorsal portion of the ventromedial nuclei increased food intake but decreased performance of food-rewarded instrumental (lever-pressing and maze) responses. Water consumption was not impaired (presumably because the taste of water is neutral), but the performance of water-reinforced responses decreased precipitously as the probability of reinforcement was decreased. A simple avoidance response in a shuttle box, on the other hand, was reliably facilitated by the lesions, as one would predict if a general lowering of the threshold for all affective responses to the environment had occurred.

These results were replicated in a subsequent experiment which showed that the application of a cholinergic blocking agent (atropine) to the ventromedial nuclei did not reliably affect food intake, but significantly impaired the performance of appetitive (food- or water-rewarded) instrumental responses. The shuttle box avoidance behavior was again facilitated.

Krasne (1962) has reported related findings which support our hypothesis. Electrical stimulation of the ventromedial nuclei not only interfered with feeding behavior, as was previously reported (Teitelbaum and Epstein, 1962), but also stopped drinking in thirsty rats. The animals could be taught an instrumental response to terminate such stimulation, suggesting that the effects of stimulation had aversive properties. Krasne also found (see Miller, 1964) that lesions in the ventromedial hypothalamus resulted in an exaggerated response to quinine dilutions of the animals' water supply.

Contradictory results have been reported by Hamilton and Brobeck (1964b), who found that ventromedial lesions increased the food intake of monkeys but did not seem to affect the animals'

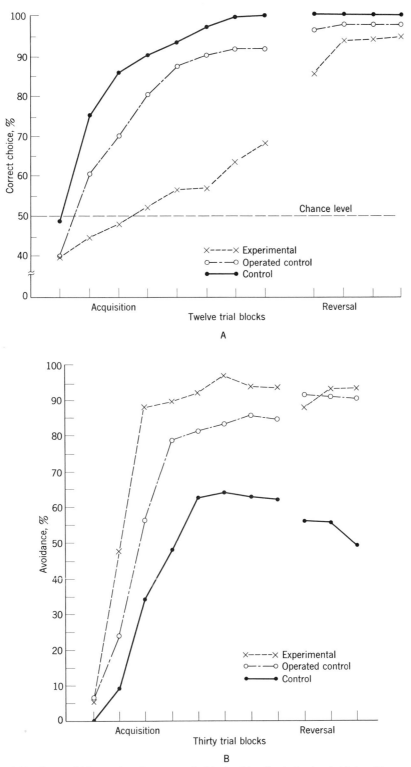

Fig. 6.40 A, acquisition and performance of a black-white discrimination habit in a T-maze apparatus. The experimental animals received atropine during the acquisition phase, the operated control animals only during the reversal period. B, acquisition and performance of an escape-avoidance habit in a shuttle box apparatus. The experimental animals received atropine during the acquisition phase, the operated controls only during the reversal phase. (From S. P. Grossman, 1966.)

response to quinine adulteration of the food or nonreinforcement. These conclusions are based on very few animals, but they may indicate important procedural (a fixed-ratio schedule of reinforcement was used) or species differences. The latter appears to be more likely, since Poirier and his associates have described some peculiar reactions to ventromedial lesions (obesity without hyperphagia) in monkeys (Poirier et al., 1962a, b). Further information is needed before we can evaluate these findings.

The lateral hypothalamic feeding center. *Localization.* At about the same time that Hetherington's investigations firmly established the precise localization of the ventromedial satiety center, a report by Brügger (1943) suggested that the hypothalamus might also contain a complementary feeding center. Brügger found that electrical stimulation of the perifornical region lateral to the ventromedial nuclei elicited voracious eating of both edible and inedible substances in cats. Prolonged stimulation of this region evoked compulsive eating which persisted for as long as 20 min after the termination of stimulation. This drive was restricted to edible substances in only two of the 34 animals tested. In many instances both eating and drinking were elicited by the stimulation.

This early report was all but forgotten until Anand and Brobeck (1951a, b) reported that small bilateral lesions, restricted to the lateral hypothalamic region, lateral to the ventromedial

nuclei, produced complete and permanent aphagia. Even animals that had previously been made hyperphagic by bilateral ventromedial lesions became completely aphagic when lateral lesions were added. Histological examinations of the affected portion of the lateral hypothalamus showed that it contained cells from the lateral hypothalamic nucleus as well as a large number of fibers from the medial forebrain bundle, the stria terminalis, and the fornix. Anand and Brobeck suggested that this region contains an excitatory feeding mechanism which apparently takes precedence over the more medially located satiety center.

Teitelbaum and Stellar (1954) investigated this region further and reported two important findings: lateral lesions always produced *both* aphagia and adipsia, and these effects did not appear to be permanent. After the operation, the animals completely refused freely available food and water and eventually died of starvation and dehydration. However, if the animals were kept alive by artificial feeding and watering with a stomach tube, a gradual recovery process was completed within 6 to 75 days.

The histological composition of the lateral hypothalamic area has recently led several investigators to ask whether the observed changes in feeding and drinking behavior are in fact due to the stimulation or ablation of localized cell concentrations rather than of fibers of passage. This region of the diencephalon is characterized by a relatively sparse cell population and a proliferation of fibers belonging mainly to the prominent medial forebrain bundle and pallidofugal fibers. Morgane (1960, 1961a) has shown that the medial forebrain bundle is not essential in the regulation of basic feeding and drinking behavior. Large lesions in this fiber tract anterior and/or posterior to the feeding center did not have a pronounced and permanent effect on either food or water intake.

Morgane also found, however, that the effects of lesions lateral to the ventromedial nuclei differed significantly, depending on whether the damage was in the mid-lateral or far-lateral hypothalamus. Mid-lateral lesions produced a temporary aphagia and adipsia which was easily reversed following a relatively brief period of intragastric feeding and watering. Far-lateral lesions, on the other hand, produced more drastic effects which persisted for as long as 45 days of intragastric feeding without showing any signs of improvement. Histological examination showed

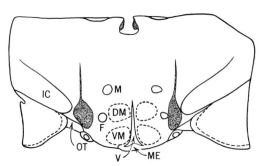

Fig. 6.41 Section through rat hypothalamus in the tuberal region, rostral to the pituitary stalk and caudal to the optic tract. The heavily shaded areas represent bilateral lesions in the lateral hypothalamus which result in aphagia, weight loss, and eventual death from starvation. DM, dorsomedial nucleus of the hypothalamus; F, fornix; IC, internal capsule; M, mamillothalamic tract; ME, median eminence; OT, optic tract; V, third ventricle; VM, ventromedial nucleus of the hypothalamus. (From Anand and Brobeck, 1951b.)

that the far-lateral lesions produced degeneration in the pallidofugal fiber systems.

Subsequent experiments (Morgane, 1961b) demonstrated that the adipsia and aphagia characteristic of lateral hypothalamic lesions could be reproduced by damage to the origin of these fiber bundles in the internal segments of the globi pallidi. Morgane (1961c) has attempted to differentiate the mid-lateral syndrome from the far-lateral in terms of motivational and metabolic systems. Electrical stimulation of the far-lateral region, in the dispersion field of the pallidofugal fiber systems, induced eating in satiated animals. Sated animals crossed electrically charged grids to bar-press for food on various reinforcement schedules. Stimulation of the more medial region (containing the medial forebrain bundle) also elicited feeding, but never grid crossing. Lesions or stimulation of the medial forebrain bundle (MFB) anterior or posterior to the feeding center did not interfere with the eating behavior elicited by electrical stimulation of either the mid-lateral or far-lateral region. However, grid crossing and lever pressing could no longer be elicited from the far-lateral region after MFB lesions.

Morgane suggested that a metabolic feeding center may be located in the far-lateral region and may be directly related to pallidofugal fibers, whereas the hunger-motivating system is composed of the more medial components of the medial forebrain bundle. The apparently motivational effects of far-lateral stimulation are explained by a possible potentiation of the medial hunger center. According to this view, the essential facilitating mechanism responsible for starting the hunger drive crosses the hypothalamus at the ventromedial level. On the other hand, the reduction of the hunger drive is related to collaterals from the medial forebrain bundle which cross medially and posteriorly to join the periventricular fiber system.

Collins (1954) has obtained evidence suggesting that the caudal continuation of this fiber system may take a tegmental route. Small lesions in the midbrain tegmentum produced complete aphagia and adipsia and a resultant loss in body weight. The animals ate when spoon-fed, but food- and water-seeking behavior appeared to be entirely eliminated. Electrical stimulation of tegmental regions increased food intake of a preferred diet, but no indiscriminate feeding was observed. Collins suggested that these effects may be produced by the interruption or stimulation of fibers collected from the medial preoptic and anterior hypothalamic areas; these fibers travel along the ventromedial angle of the medial forebrain bundle and are joined by a tract originating in the ventromedial nuclei.

Recovery from lesions. The demonstration of a gradual return to apparently normal regulation of food and water intake after a period of intragastric feeding and watering has raised some interesting questions about the possible contribution of extrahypothalamic mechanisms. Although very careful and extensive studies of this problem have been made (Teitelbaum, 1961; Teitelbaum and Epstein, 1962), it is not yet clear whether this "recovery of function" results from an incomplete destruction of the hypothalamic mechanisms or from an increase in the activity of extrahypothalamic systems.

The recovery is at least in part mediated by the tissue that surrounds the lateral lesion, as was shown by the observation (Teitelbaum and Epstein, 1962) that additional lesions adjacent to the original ones caused a return to aphagia and adipsia in completely recovered rats. The initial recovery may thus reflect a gradual return to normal activity in areas surrounding the lesion and subjected to physical trauma, edema, or gliosis during and after the passage of direct current.

Teitelbaum has maintained that recovery from lateral hypothalamic lesions can always be obtained, provided that proper care is taken to feed and water the animal for a sufficient period of time. The effect of a second lesion, on the other hand, suggests that recovery may occur only because not all the hypothalamic feeding center is generally removed. One of the problems in this area has been the proliferation of conflicting results and the possibility of species differences. Teitelbaum and Stellar (1954) observed complete recovery in rats as early as 6 days after the operation, and even shorter recovery periods have been reported (Miller, 1965). Anand et al. (1955), on the other hand, reported that cats with bilateral lesions in the lateral hypothalamus remain aphagic in spite of continued intragastric feeding. The animals completely refused all food, even when it was placed directly in their mouths, and died of starvation when the artificial feeding was discontinued after four weeks. Morgane (1961a, b, c) has reported that rats with far-lateral or pallidal lesions do not show the typical recovery. The period of force-feeding in all these experiments was unfortunately not sufficiently long to rule out completely an eventual recovery. Teitelbaum has repeatedly suggested that the lateral hypothalamic animal may be particularly sensitive and that recovery may require very careful handling. This, too, may be a factor in the negative findings.

The problems of lateral hypothalamic aphagia and adipsia as well as the parameters of recovery have been extensively and carefully studied in Teitelbaum's laboratory (Teitelbaum, 1961, 1962; Teitelbaum and Epstein, 1962, 1963), and four distinct recovery phases were identified. During the first stage the animals refuse all foods and do not drink at all. They eventually die unless artificial feeding and watering is instituted. If food or milk is placed directly into the mouth of these animals, they will spit it out and attempt to wipe it off their face and paws. The duration of this stage is variable (no direct correlation with either the location or the extent of the lesion has been reported), but is nearly always sufficient to cause death unless corrective measures (intragastric feeding) are employed. In the second stage wet and especially palatable foods such as milk and milk chocolate are accepted, although not in sufficient quantities to maintain life. Dry foods and water are still entirely refused.

During the third and perhaps most interesting phase, the animals are able to regulate their caloric intake when wet and palatable foods are available. They still refuse dry food and water and die of starvation and dehydration if only a standard laboratory diet is provided. These animals work (i.e., press a bar) to obtain liquid food

which is injected directly into their stomach (Epstein, 1960b), suggesting that the taste component is no longer essential for the elicitation of feeding behavior. At this stage adipsia appears to be the primary cause of the remaining disturbance of the food-intake regulation. If the liquid diet is replaced by dry laboratory food, the animals continue to eat for several days but completely refuse water. They become completely dehydrated unless liquids are supplied by intragastric injections, and their food intake drops to zero within 2 or 3 days. This effect is in marked contrast to the first two stages, where adequate hydration does not prevent the appearance of complete aphagia. During this third phase of the lateral starvation syndrome, animals can be made "hyperphagic by additional lesions in the ventromedial nuclei" (Williams and Teitelbaum, 1959; Teitelbaum and Epstein, 1962). When ventromedial and lateral lesions are made simultaneously, the animal starves to death unless force-feeding is instituted. Once the animal has recovered from the aphagia, however, pronounced hyperphagia appears unless adequate hydration is provided.

Finally, most rats with lateral hypothalamic lesions accept water and maintain a normal regulation of caloric intake and body weight even on a dry-food diet. Superficially, these animals appear normal in this fourth stage of the recovery process. However, permanent deficits in the animals' ability to regulate their water exchange remain (Teitelbaum, 1961). Some of the animals do not

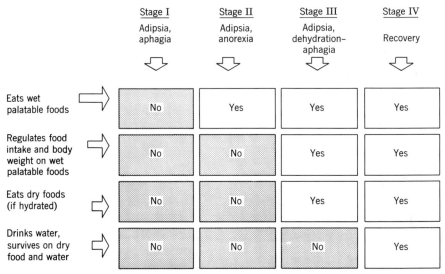

	Stage I Adipsia, aphagia	Stage II Adipsia, anorexia	Stage III Adipsia, dehydration– aphagia	Stage IV Recovery
Eats wet palatable foods	No	Yes	Yes	Yes
Regulates food intake and body weight on wet palatable foods	No	No	Yes	Yes
Eats dry foods (if hydrated)	No	No	Yes	Yes
Drinks water, survives on dry food and water	No	No	No	Yes

Fig. 6.42 Stages of recovery seen in the lateral hypothalamic syndrome. The critical behavioral events are listed on the left. (From Teitelbaum and Epstein, 1962.)

increase their water consumption in response to artificial dehydration. Many of them fail to adjust their rate of drinking to a schedule that allows access to water for only several hours per day. The hypersensitivity to bitter tastes also remains. Control rats maintain a normal daily water intake even when their water supply is heavily diluted with quinine. Rats who have apparently recovered from lateral hypothalamic lesions completely refuse water (and eventually die) when the concentration of quinine is several hundred times lower than that needed to deter normal animals. When similar quinine solutions are injected directly into the rats' stomachs, the adipsic animals continue to accept dry food and survive. A similar deficit remains with respect to food intake. Here, too, very small admixtures of quinine suffice to induce a complete refusal of dry food and result in the eventual death of the animal.

Some interesting findings about the source of the influence that mediates the recovery have been obtained by Teitelbaum and Cytawa (1965). Bilateral lateral hypothalamic lesions were made, and the animals were permitted to recover from the resulting aphagia and adipsia. After a 24-hr period of food deprivation, potassium chloride (KCl) was applied to the cortex in an effort to induce a "spreading depression" of cortical functions (see the discussion of the effects of reversible cortical lesions on learning and memory in Chapter 13). This treatment inhibited all food and water intake in control and lateral hypothalamic animals. However, the control animals recovered from the effects of the cortical depression within a few hours; they usually began to eat liquid food after only 2 or 3 hr and accepted normal laboratory pellets and water 6 to 8 hr after the KCl application. After 24 hr, these animals had ingested a normal daily ration of both food and water and no longer showed any noticeable impairment. The body weight recovered more slowly, but reached normal levels within 4 to 6 days. Rats with lateral hypothalamic lesions, on the other hand, appeared to relapse into the initial stages of hypothalamic aphagia and adipsia. One animal refused food and water for 4 days and died. Another was maintained by tube feeding for 8 days before regaining the ability to regulate its intake of a liquid diet. It did not accept pellets until the sixteenth day after the KCl administration and did not drink water until the twenty-first day. Recovery was complete only after 27 days. Teitelbaum and Cytawa suggested that cortical influences may be essential for the functioning of the remnants of the lateral hypothalamic feeding center.

The independence of the effects on food and water intake. Teitelbaum's experiments suggest that the changes in feeding elicited by electrical stimulation or ablation of the lateral hypothalamic area may be independent of the concomitant effects on water intake. That these two mechanisms do in fact operate independently has been demonstrated in a series of studies concerned with the neuropharmacological properties of this region (S. P. Grossman, 1960, 1962a, b, 1964a, b, c, d). In these experiments double cannulae were sterotaxically implanted into the lateral hypothalami of rats. Crystalline chemicals were then repeatedly applied directly to the lateral hypothalamus of unrestrained animals. It was found that injections of adrenergic transmitter substances (epinephrine or norepinephrine) elicit voracious and prolonged eating in fully satiated animals. Injections of cholinergic transmitter substances (acetylcholine or carbachol) into the identical site in the same animals produce vigorous and prolonged drinking. Although the overt effects of chemical stimulation persisted only for 30 to 50 min, the animals consumed as much as 50 to 75% of their normal daily intake during the 1-hr test period following these injections. The total intake was nearly dou-

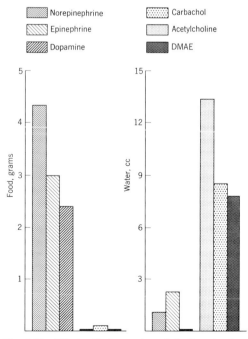

Fig. 6.43 Effects of adrenergic and cholinergic stimulation of the hypothalamus on food and water intake of sated animals during a 1-hr poststimulation period. (From S. P. Grossman, 1964d.)

bled on the day of stimulation, and a considerable weight gain was observed following adrenergic stimulation. The chemical stimulation appeared to have selective motivational effects. Following adrenergic stimulation, the animals greatly increased the rate of bar pressing for food but did not work at all for water. After the injection of carbachol, on the other hand, performance on the water bar increased significantly, but the animals did not work for food. Subsequent experiments demonstrated that the effects of central chemical stimulation could be blocked selectively by the systemic administration of the appropriate (i.e., sympathetic or parasympathetic) blocking agents. Normal hunger was also sharply reduced by the systemic or central administration of sympathetic blocking agents, and normal thirst was inhibited by the injection of parasympathetic blocking agents. The combined evidence from these experiments can best be summarized by the postulation of two anatomically overlapping systems of neural elements at the level of the hypothalamus; these systems participate in the regulation of food and water intake and appear to be selectively sensitive to adrenergic and cholinergic stimulation, respectively. The differential excitation and inhibition

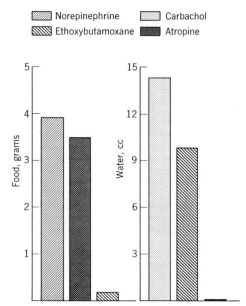

Fig. 6.45   Effects of adrenergic and cholinergic stimulation of the hypothalamus 1 hr after the systemic injection of adrenergic (ethoxybutamoxane) and cholinergic (atropine) blocking agents. (From S. P. Grossman, 1964d.)

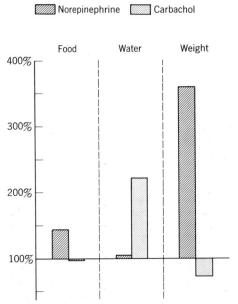

Fig. 6.44   Effects of adrenergic and cholinergic stimulation of the hypothalamus on food and water intake and body weight during a 24-hr poststimulation period. The results are expressed as a percentage of a base line which represents the average of pre- and poststimulation control tests. (S. P. Grossman, 1964d.)

of a single neural mechanism appear unlikely (in spite of the fact that all placements showed both effects) because the relative magnitude of the eating and drinking effects varied considerably between subjects. The demonstrated effectiveness of adrenergic and cholinergic blocking agents to selectively reduce normal hunger and thirst, respectively, suggests that neurochemical "coding" may be a functional property of these hypothalamic systems in the intact animal.

Miller and his associates (see Miller, 1965, for a review of this material) have continued this line of investigation. To ascertain whether the effects of the blocking agents may be caused by possible peripheral effects, atropine sulfate (which readily crosses the blood-brain barrier) and atropine methyl nitrate (which does not get into the brain as rapidly) were injected peripherally. Drinking was inhibited much more rapidly and completely by the atropine sulfate.

Next, the effects of centrally and peripherally administered norepinephrine and carbachol were compared. Direct injections of norepinephrine into the hypothalamus elicited feeding, the best response occurring to about 22 μg of the drug. When the same dose was injected intraperitoneally (into the body cavity), no feeding responses were elic-

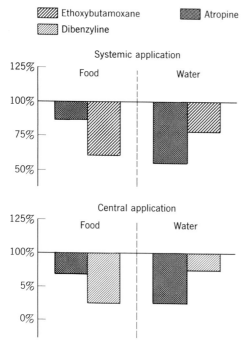

Fig. 6.46 Effects of systemically or centrally administered adrenergic (ethoxybutamoxane or dibenzyline) and cholinergic (atropine) blocking agents on food and water intake of deprived animals. The results are expressed as a percentage of a base line which represents the average of pre- and poststimulation control tests. (From S. P. Grossman, 1964d.)

ited. The feeding of hungry animals, in fact, was found to be severely depressed, in agreement with the common observation that related drugs such as amphetamine are useful appetite depressants (Epstein, 1959). Peripheral injections of epinephrine also raised the threshold for the elicitation of feeding responses by electrical stimulation of the lateral hypothalamus, a most interesting observation.

In an extension of this work, it was found that electrical stimulation, which elicits feeding responses, also increases blood sugar during tests in which food is not present. Direct injections of norepinephrine into the lateral hypothalamus also produce a rise in blood sugar (as well as a small fall in body temperature), suggesting that the injection may have activated a general mechanism for the correction of nutritional deficits. The specificity of these effects is questioned, however, by the observation that carbachol produced an even larger effect on both blood sugar and body temperature.

Some of these observations were made in ex-

periments using liquid rather than crystalline injections to avoid possible artifacts which might result from nonphysiological concentrations of the transmitter substance. Miller et al. (1964) have replicated S. P. Grossman's (1960, 1962a, b) results using aqueous solutions in an attempt to establish precise dose-response relationships. They found that doses of carbachol as small as 0.047 μg reliably elicited drinking responses; the most effective dose was somewhere near the normal concentration of cholinergic substances in brain tissue. The smallest dose of norepinephrine that reliably elicited feeding responses was 0.8 μg, considerably higher than that of carbachol, but still within a reasonable physiological range. Norepinephrine and carbachol applications to the motor cortex, in doses larger than those found to be most effective at the level of the hypothalamus, did not evoke noticeable responses. Very much larger doses, comparable to those that elicited convulsive behavior when applied to the hypothalamus, produced movement and convulsion when applied to the motor cortex.

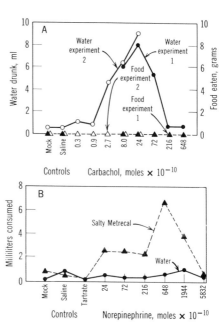

Fig. 6.47 A, dose-response curve for drinking elicited by injections of carbachol into the lateral hypothalamus of rats which had eaten and drunk to satiation. No eating is elicited. B, dose-response curve for consumption of a liquid food (salty Metrecal) elicited by injection of norepinephrine into the lateral hypothalamus of rats which had eaten and drunk to satiation. Negligible amounts of water are consumed. (From Miller, 1965, © AAAS.)

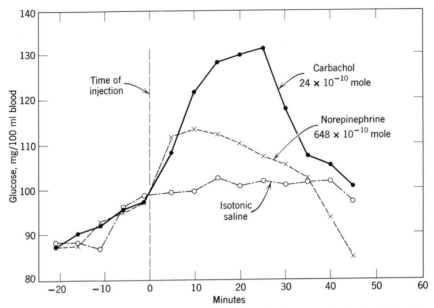

Fig. 6.48   Effects on blood glucose of injecting norepinephrine and carbachol into the lateral hypothalamus of rats. As compared with an injection of isotonic saline, an injection of the dose of norepinephrine that is optimum for eliciting eating produces an increase in blood glucose. However, an injection of the dose of carbachol that is optimum for eliciting drinking produces an even greater increase. No food or water is given during the tests. (From Miller, 1965, © AAAS.)

Stein and Seifter (1962) have demonstrated that the response to carbachol appears to be mediated by muscarinic synapses in the hypothalamus. Wolf and Miller (1964) have shown that lesions in the lateral hypothalamus abolished or severely depressed the response of other parts of the limbic system to chemical stimulation, whereas lesions in other parts of the brain appeared to have only transient effects on the response of the hypothalamus to chemical stimulation.

"Stimulus-bound" and delayed effects of electrical stimulation. Many early investigations of the effects of electrical stimulation of the lateral hypothalamic region reported some gnawing, biting, and eating in response to such stimulation, but only a delayed effect on food intake (Brügger, 1943; Hess, 1954). Delgado and Anand (1953) failed to observe any immediate effects of chronic electrical stimulation, but they report a large (up to 70%) increase in food intake on the day following stimulation. The intake of solid foods returned to normal within 2 days unless stimulation was resumed, but milk consumption (drinking?) remained elevated by as much as 300% for 4 to 5 days. The authors concluded that the results suggested the operation of some unknown humoral

factor (blood sugar levels were unaffected by the stimulation). These experiments were replicated and extended by Anand and Dua (1955a, b). No immediate effect of chronic hypothalamic stimulation (1 hr daily, 2 msec/5 min) was observed, but food intake increased significantly for 2 to 3 days after the stimulation. In these experiments a rise in blood sugar level was recorded following electrical stimulation, and the authors suggested that food intake may have been affected indirectly via this change in blood glucose. Similar stimulation of the ventromedial nuclei produced some decrease in the average daily food intake, but no corresponding change in blood glucose was reported.

More recent experiments have found that electrical stimulation of *specific points* within the lateral hypothalamus reliably elicit immediate feeding responses in satiated animals. Coons and Miller (cited by Miller, 1957, 1960) have observed stimulus-bound feeding which starts immediately after the onset of stimulation and terminates promptly when the current is interrupted. During such stimulation rats perform a previously learned bar-pressing response for food, even when their efforts are only infrequently rewarded. Lever pressing and feeding stop almost immediately

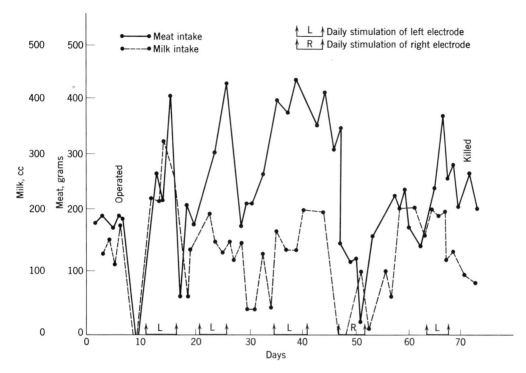

Fig. 6.49 Meat and milk intake chart of a cat. The left electrode was in the lateral region of the middle hypothalamus and the right in the lateral region of the posterior hypothalamus. (From Anand and Dua, 1955b.)

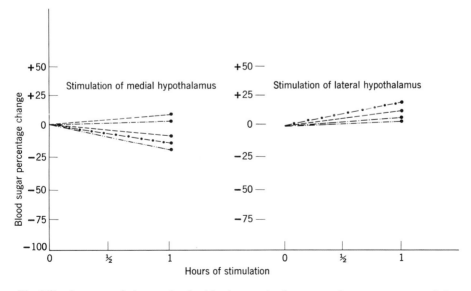

Fig. 6.50 Averages of changes in the blood sugar levels, expressed as a percentage of the prestimulatory levels, obtained by stimulation of the hypothalamic regions. (From Anand and Dua, 1955a.)

after the cessation of electrical stimulation. Although many points in the lateral hypothalamus apparently show either feeding or drinking in response to electrical stimulation, others elicit only feeding. A thirsty (but food-sated) animal will turn away from the drinking tube and begin eating when such a region is stimulated.

O. A. Smith, Jr. (1961) reported that electrical stimulation of some points in the lateral hypothalamus produces feeding which persists for as long as 10 min after cessation of the stimulation. He noted an additional delayed effect which resulted in a significantly raised food intake during the 24-hr period following electrical stimulation. Smith also observed that stimulation of some points in the lateral area elicited indiscriminate eating or chewing of edible as well as inedible substances. This effect appeared to be entirely stimulus-bound. Larsson (1955) found that electrical stimulation of an area just caudal to the optic chiasma and extending back through the entire hypothalamus elicits feeding in goats. He further reported that direct injections of hypertonic saline solutions into this area also produced feeding responses. These findings have been replicated by Epstein (1960a). In a beautifully counterbalanced experiment, Epstein demonstrated that direct injections of hypertonic saline into the lateral hypothalamus induced feeding; however, food intake was stopped or reduced by similar injections into the ventromedial nuclei. Conversely, procaine (a local anesthetic) reduced food intake in the lateral hypothalamus but increased feeding in the ventromedial nucleus.

Wyrwicka et al. (1960) found that electrical stimulation of the lateral hypothalamus in goats (1) elicited stimulus-bound feeding, (2) evoked previously learned instrumental responses for food reward, and (3) motivated the learning of new responses if such behavior was reinforced by food rewards. Several other studies (Morgane, 1961a; S. P. Grossman, 1962a) have shown that satiated animals will work to obtain food during electrical or chemical stimulation of the lateral hypothalamus.

Motivational versus motor aspects of hypothalamic aphagia. Since Anand and Brobeck's initial demonstration of aphagia and adipsia following lateral hypothalamic lesions, it has generally been assumed that the failure to eat and drink reflects a direct interference with hunger and thirst. This interpretation is supported by the many studies demonstrating that feeding or drinking responses can be obtained by electrical (Miller, 1957, 1960) or chemical (S. P. Grossman, 1960, 1962a, b) stimulation of this area. However, Baillie and Morrison (1963) observed that rats with lateral lesions pressed a lever to obtain intragastric injections of food, although they did not eat the food by mouth. This suggests that some or all of the deficit may be related to a motor impairment; i.e., the animal may be hungry but somehow unable to eat. This interpretation is supported by Morgane's (1961) observation that lesions in the

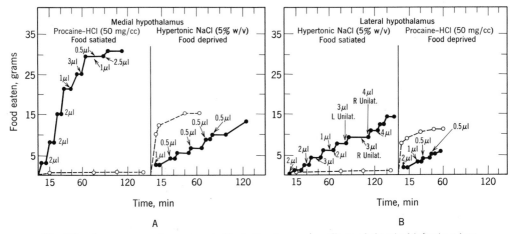

Fig. 6.51 A, summary of experiments illustrating two major effects of chemical injections into the medial hypothalamus, i.e., elicitation of eating by procaine-HCl and suppression of eating by hypertonic saline. B, summary of experiments illustrating two major effects of chemical injections into the lateral hypothalamus, i.e., initiation of eating by hypertonic saline and suppression of eating by procain-HCL. Experimental animal (●—●), normal control (○----○). (From Epstein, 1960a.)

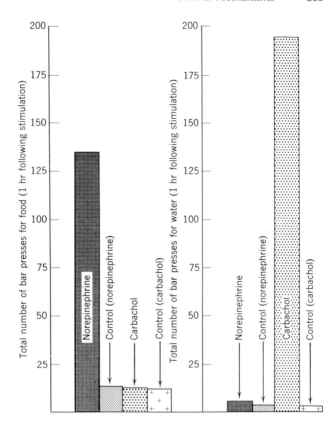

Fig. 6.52 Effects of adrenergic and cholinergic stimulation of the hypothalamus of satiated rats on rate of bar pressing for food and water rewards on a 30-sec variable-interval schedule. Control levels were determined during a 1-hr period preceding each stimulation. (From S. P. Grossman, 1962a.)

globus pallidus or its efferent fiber systems produce aphagia as severe as that seen after hypothalamic lesion. (The globus pallidus is considered to be an integral part of the extrapyramidal motor system.) Morgane suggests, in fact, that the efficacy of the hypothalamic lesions may be due to the interruption of pallidofugal fibers rather than to a destruction of a hypothalamic feeding center itself.

These observations have led Rodgers et al. (1965) to a most interesting series of experiments designed to study the possible involvement of motor functions. In these studies the recovery of feeding and drinking was observed in lateral hypothalamic rats given a choice between feeding themselves by mouth with highly palatable foods or pressing a lever to obtain an injection of 0.2 cc of a liquid diet. The results showed that all rats resumed oral feeding before intragastric regulation could be seen. Some animals never showed aphagia with respect to the palatable foods but refused to bar-press for intragastric food injections. Others were completely aphagic and adipsic for varying lengths of time, but they always accepted the palatable foods before beginning to

bar-press for intragastric injections. Rodgers et al. suggested that the effects reported by Baillie and Morrison might have occurred because only an unpalatable diet was offered by mouth and that the very transient effects observed in this study might reflect finickiness rather than true hypothalamic aphagia. The observations of Rodgers and associates suggest that the deficits seen after lateral hypothalamic damage are caused by motivational effects rather than motor effects.

Hunger and the regulation of body temperature. Strang and McClugage (1931) suggested, over 30 years ago, that satiety may be related to the heat stress which is imposed on the organism during the assimilation of nutrients. Some early support for such an interpretation became available when Booth and Strang (1936) reported a few years later that satiety, as measured by the cessation of feeding, was accompanied by cutaneous vasodilatation and a consequent rise in skin temperature.

Brobeck (1947–1948, 1951, 1957a, b, c) has extended this notion and proposed what might be called a *thermoregulatory* theory of hunger; this

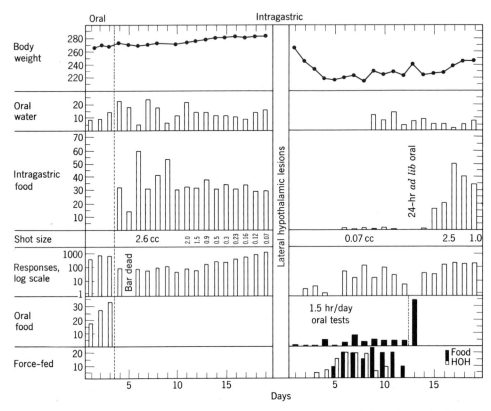

Fig. 6.53 A typical recovery from the effects of lateral hypothalamic lesions. The animal ate palatable food on the first postoperative day and drank water on the ninth. Intragastric feeding did not return until the sixth postoperative day, and the animal did not regulate its intragastric intake until the stomach load was increased from 0.07 to 2.5 ml (fifteenth postoperative day). (From Rodgers et al., 1965.)

theory holds that the organism's energy equation may be balanced by a temperature-regulating mechanism, and that food intake is regulated as a part of the normal control of body temperature. In Brobeck's words, "animals eat to keep warm and stop eating to prevent hyperthermia."

This hypothesis does not preclude the operation of other mechanisms that have been proposed to account for the initiation or cessation of feeding. For instance, Mayer's glucostatic control might well operate within the framework of a more general energy-regulating system. The correlation of low blood sugar with hunger would be expected, in fact, because low arterial glucose levels rapidly induce signs of heat deficiency such as piloerection and shivering. Hypoglycemia reduces the resting heat production and activates the heat conservation mechanisms. Hyperglycemia, which is not unambiguously related to food intake, does not affect the temperature mechanisms.

Brobeck (1957a, b, c) has suggested that the

thermoregulatory mechanism cannot account for all phases of the food-intake regulation and proposed the following sequence of relationships between the various mechanisms which have been implicated in the control of feeding behavior.

When food is taken, sensory receptors from the mouth, pharynx, esophagus, and stomach signal to the nervous system that eating is in progress. The amount of food eaten may be limited, first, by this sensory input. Within a few minutes after eating, the rate of heat production begins to rise. Extra heat is produced centrally and stimulates receptors in the hypothalamic preoptic region. This "central-heating" effect causes peripheral vasodilatation and inhibits feeding. Only when this central-heat production ceases can hunger arise once more.

Brobeck's interesting hypothesis has stimulated much research designed to show correlations between food intake and (1) environmental temperature, (2) the specific dynamic action (SDA)

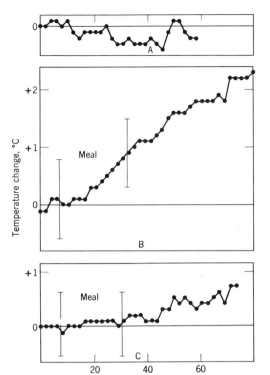

Fig. 6.54 Composite curves of the temperature reactions of the skin during the control period with the meal omitted (A) and of persons of normal weight (B) and obese persons (C) before, during, and after a meal of meat to the level of satiety. (From Booth and Strang, 1936.)

of the diet, and (3) body or brain temperature. A brief survey of this material will now be presented.

The effects of environmental temperature. Brobeck (1947–1948) measured food intake under various environmental temperatures and reported that rats ate practically nothing when the temperature rose above 94°F. He suggested that food intake might be inhibited because the organism cannot accept the additional heat stress caused by the ingestion and assimilation of nutrients. Kennedy (1952) has questioned this interpretation, since changes in environmental temperature also elevate the organism's standard metabolism. He replicated Brobeck's observation that animals exposed to heat temporarily reduce food intake, but he also observed that a similar inhibition occurs when the animals are first exposed to cold, and that the level of intake returns to normal as soon as the animals become acclimated to the new conditions. Other investigators have reported that rats acclimated to very low environmental tem-

peratures continue to show an elevated metabolic rate which is associated with an increased utilization of carbohydrates (Bates and Sellers, 1953; Weiss, 1960).

Although more information may be necessary before we can be certain, it seems that the relationship between food intake and environmental temperature may reflect the activity of an "emergency" mechanism which comes into play only when a drastic change in the environment occurs. Small day-to-day fluctuations as well as (within limits) the absolute level of the environmental temperature do not seem to be important determinants of food intake. These conclusions support the hypothesis that suggests a relationship between the temperature regulation of the organism and food intake, but they do not indicate that this mechanism may be an essential part of the day-to-day regulation of hunger.

The specific dynamic action of foods. After food is ingested, the metabolic rate increases as a result of the many chemical reactions associated with digestion, absorption, and storage of foods in the body. The change in metabolic rate is called the *specific dynamic action* (SDA) of foods. The magnitude of this effect varies significantly for the various major constituents of the diet (the SDA of fat is lowest of all nutrients; that of protein is highest because it must undergo oxidative deamination before oxidation).

Strominger and Brobeck (1953) have suggested that the satiety value of specific diets should be correlated with their SDA if the thermostatic theory of satiety is, in fact, correct. Diets high in protein should be accepted in smaller quantities than a diet high in fat. An experimental test of this hypothesis showed that neither "bulk" nor calories were maintained constant when the composition of the diet was changed, but food intake seemed to be adjusted roughly in proportion to the SDA of the diets (see Strominger et al., 1953).

Lyon et al. (1953) have also reported a good correlation between dietary composition (which reflects SDA) and the rate of weight gain in genetically obese mice; similar relationships have been observed in normal mice (Mickelsen et al., 1955). Other workers have demonstrated that the exclusive feeding of a high-protein diet prevents obesity on an *ad libitum* feeding schedule (Fenton, 1953), and that the appearance of obesity following ventromedial lesions depends on a high fat content in the diet (Lundbaek and Stevenson, 1947). These findings have been confirmed in the mouse by Mayer et al. (1955), who found that the rate of weight gain in hypothalamic hyperphagic animals is greatest on a high-fat diet (1.8 grams per day) and lowest on a high-protein diet (1.1 grams per day).

The relationship between body and brain temperature and food intake.

A number of the earlier workers in this field (Burton and Murlin, 1935; Booth and Strang, 1936; Sheard et al., 1941) reported a fairly good correlation between small temperature fluctuations, measured peripherally or centrally, and food intake. A recent study of the diurnal temperature patterns in sheep (Mendel and Raghaven, 1964) indicates that the suggested relationship may be much more complex than initially suggested. Body temperature, measured in the external jugular vein and internal carotid artery, rose slightly during the feeding period itself, but remained remarkably constant between periods of feeding. The temperature of the body cavity fell during the feeding period, and the rectal, skin, and subcutaneous temperature measures showed no significant covariance with feeding. Diurnal patterns of body temperature were observed, and these patterns shifted when the animals were deprived of food. However, the close correlation between food intake and temperature change predicted by Brobeck's hypothesis was not evident.

Some interesting evidence in favor of Brobeck's hypothesis has been reported by Andersson and Larsson (1961). Using rather large thermode implants in the goat brain, these workers found that local cooling of the preoptic area and rostral hypothalamus inhibited drinking in thirsty animals and induced feeding in spite of persisting dehydration. Warming of the same area had the opposite effects. Hungry goats stopped eating after about 30 sec of central heating and began to drink large quantities of water. A rise or fall of about 10°C at the surface of the implant, required to produce this behavior, resulted in a temperature change of about 1 to 1.5°C at a distance of 6 mm from the thermode.

An interpretation of these effects is complicated by the grossly unphysiological nature of the temperature change. Experiments by S. P. Grossman and Rechtschaffen (1966) have shown that the temperature of the preoptic area (and of other portions of the brain) of cats varies no more than about 1.0°C over a period of many days and does *not* covary (except temporarily as the result of local heating or cooling effects transmitted directly from the roof of the mouth) with food or liquid intake, food deprivation, or satiety. These measures of central temperature change were accurate

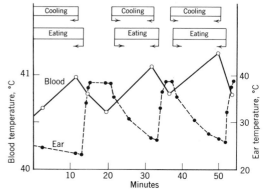

Fig. 6.55 Part of an experiment in which the preoptic area and rostral hypothalamus of a goat were repeatedly cooled. The goat had free access to hay during the experiment, which started at normal feeding time. The increasing blood temperature during the periods of central cooling was due to shivering and peripheral vasoconstriction. During the intervals between periods of central cooling, heat-loss mechanisms were mobilized, which worked to put the body temperature back to a normal level. The animal was eating hay with a seemingly good appetite during the periods of central cooling, but he stopped eating simultaneously to the onset of peripheral vasodilatation (rise of ear temperature) following discontinuation of central cooling. Toward the end of the experiment central cooling induced eating in spite of a blood temperature well above 41°C. (From Andersson and Larsson, 1961.)

to about 0.1°C and should have reflected any central-heating effect that might be associated with food intake. These observations do not rule out the possibility that the small peripheral changes in temperature following a meal may elicit neural signals to the central mechanisms which control feeding behavior; however, a direct central-heating effect, as suggested by Brobeck's theory and the results of Andersson and Larsson's study, does not seem to operate.

The clear effects reported by Andersson and Larsson remain an enigma. It is possible that the excessive heating or cooling of the preoptic area may have had a general, stimulating effect on neighboring neural tissue, but this does not, by itself, account for the apparent specificity of the effects. Andersson and Larsson reported that damage to the preoptic heat-loss center by proton irradiation produced adipsia but had little or no effect on food intake. This suggests that the apparent specificity may reflect a local effect of heating and cooling on mechanisms related to water intake and a perhaps more general effect on the posteriorly located feeding center.

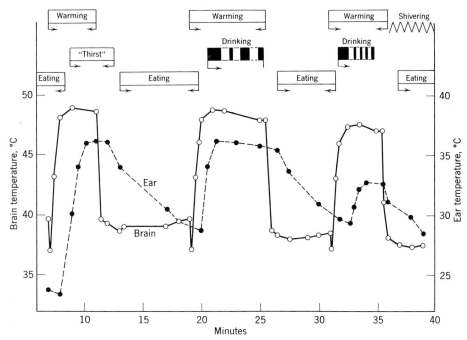

Fig. 6.56 Results of warming the preoptic area and rostral hypothalamus in the previously hungry goat. Brain temperature was recorded close to the surface of the thermode. The goat was fed hay at the beginning of the experiment and had free access to water except during the first period of central warming. During the periods of warming, eating stopped simultaneously to the onset of peripheral vasodilatation (rise of ear temperature) and started again when ear surface temperature had begun to fall after discontinuation of central warming. The perfusion of the thermode with warm water induced a strong urge to drink. During the first period of central warming, when the water container was temporarily removed, this urge was evidenced by the animal's licking the drops of water coming from the outlet tubing of the thermode ("thirst") and later on by repeated drinking of large amounts of water during the periods of central warming. (From Andersson and Larsson, 1961.)

Miller's recent observation on the effects of chemical stimulation of lateral hypothalamic feeding and drinking centers provide some interesting information in this connection. Miller (1965) reported that injections of norepinephrine which elicited feeding behavior also produced a small fall in body temperature, an effect which supports Brobeck's hypothesis. However, an even larger fall in temperature was produced by injections of carbachol which elicited drinking and *suppressed* feeding responses.

Electrophysiological observations on the central glucostat. Recent electrophysiological observations by Anand and his associates have provided some interesting correlations between the activity of the central feeding and satiety centers and various peripheral events that may be related to food intake.

Sharma et al. (1961) showed that gastric disten-

sion, caused by inflating a water-filled balloon in the stomach, produced high-voltage, irregular waves and spike discharges in the satiety center of the ventromedial hypothalamus, but had no effect on the electrophysiological (EEG) activity of the lateral feeding center. Normally occurring gastric hunger contractions did not affect the electrical activity of any area in the hypothalamus. This observation supports M. I. Grossman's (1955) suggestion that stomach distension may be a regulatory factor only at the extremes of distension.

Sharma and associates also observed in these studies that intravenous injections of glucagon (a substance of pancreatic or digestive tract origin which mobilizes hepatic glycogen and thereby raises the concentration of blood glucose) increased the electrical activity of the ventromedial area and reduced stomach motility after an initial delay sufficient to produce a marked rise in blood

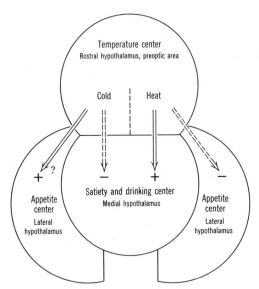

Fig. 6.57 A tentative explanation of the alimentary effects of cooling and warming the preoptic area and rostral hypothalamus. The suggested explanation of the effect of warming on food intake is in accordance with Brobeck's (1948, 1960) thermostatic theory. (From Andersson and Larsson, 1961.)

sugar and arteriovenous glucose differences. The inhibition of gastric contractions by glucagon was abolished by ventromedial lesions, suggesting that this effect may be mediated by the satiety center.

Additional experiments (Anand et al., 1961a, b, 1962) showed that hyperglycemia, regardless of origin, always produced an increase in the electrical (EEG) activity of the ventromedial satiety center and a slight diminution of the activity of the lateral feeding centers. Hypoglycemia produced opposite effects. Following a meal, the electrical activity of the ventromedial area was shown to increase gradually, the rate of change correlating roughly with the development of arteriovenous glucose differences.

Anand et al. (1964) showed that the activity of individual neurons in the hypothalamic feeding and satiety centers varied as a function of arteriovenous glucose differences. The activity of single cells from the ventromedial area increased during a period of increased glucose utilization and decreased during hypoglycemia. Single cells from the lateral hypothalamus responded in an opposite fashion. The greatest change in unit activity did not correlate with the maximal change in blood sugar level, but with variations in the arteriovenous utilization rate. These effects were

shown to be independent of the osmotic effects of the hypertonic glucose injections, for hypertonic saline did not produce comparable effects.

These electrophysiological observations are very important and need to be followed up in some detail. They are, unfortunately, subject to most of, if not all, the criticisms that can be raised against any EEG or unit-activity study. The EEG changes are typically not unique to changes in satiety, glucose utilization, or gastric motility, and a more exact treatment of the data (perhaps in terms of a probability analysis) is badly needed. The unit-activity data are more convincing, but one wonders just how representative the activity of a few carefully selected units may be of the state of excitation or inhibition in a major integrative center. Much more work using this potentially rewarding approach is needed before we can evaluate the results of electrophysiological observations.

A number of other studies have suggested that the hypothalamus may harbor the central "glucostat" which regulates food intake either autonomously or in cooperation with other regulatory mechanisms. We have already mentioned some of the studies showing that goldthioglucose (a gold-glucose compound which is rapidly absorbed from the small intestine and has toxic effects on body tissues when present in large quantities) is selectively deposited in the ventromedial hypothalamus of mice (Marshall and Mayer, 1954; Mayer and Marshall, 1956) and produces local lesions and hyperphagia. This effect may be caused by a special affinity of glucose for glucoreceptors in this area of the brain, although the compound also accumulates in other parts of the body which do not have known glucoreceptor functions.

Recent tissue respiration studies have further shown that in the intact, sated animal the medial hypothalamic region takes up significantly more radioactively labeled glucose and oxygen than the lateral feeding center (Anand et al., 1961c). The lateral feeding center, on the other hand, takes up more labeled potassium than the medial area when the animals are deprived (Forssberg and Larsson, 1954); this finding has also been interpreted to support the glucostatic function of this part of the brain (Mayer, 1955).

Herberg (1960, 1962) has recently shown that intraventricular injections of glucose significantly reduced the food intake of hungry animals, whereas similar injections of fructose, glucagon, or insulin were without effect.

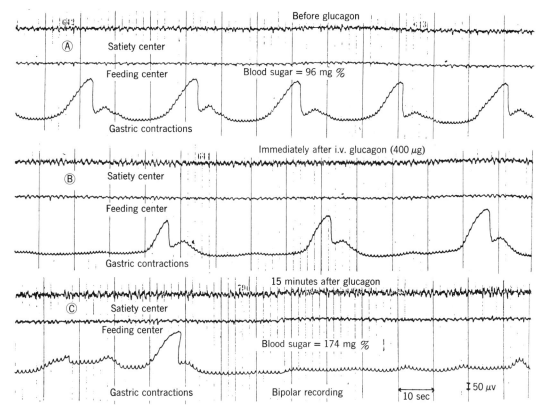

Fig. 6.58 Bipolar recording of the activity of the satiety and feeding centers and gastric motility of a monkey. A, slow-moving record. After giving 400 μg glucagon intravenously, the blood sugar rises. Simultaneously, the activity of the satiety center increases and gastric contractions are inhibited. C, no change in the activity of the feeding center occurs. Such a change appears only after about 15 min, when blood sugar rises, and not immediately after injection as in B. (From Sharma et al., 1961.)

Summary of the hypothalamic contribution to hunger. The following conclusions are offered in summary.

Feeding behavior (and presumably its psychological correlate, hunger) is controlled, at least in part, by two interacting regulatory mechanisms at the level of the hypothalamus. The excitatory component of this system is located in the lateral hypothalamus at the same rostrocaudal plane as the inhibitory mechanism, in or near the ventromedial nuclei of the hypothalamus. Some evidence suggests that the excitatory mechanism may, in fact, contain a distinct metabolic component, involving pallidofugal fiber systems, and a motivational component which is mediated via the medial forebrain bundle.

Electrical and chemical stimulation of the excitatory system in satiated animals elicits feeding which appears to have all of the specific motivational properties of normal hunger. During or after such stimulation, animals will work to obtain food even when their efforts are only aperiodically reinforced. Extirpation of this region produces aphagia and adipsia, although there is some question about the permanence of this phenomenon. If animals with such lesions are maintained by intragastric feeding and watering, they will eventually recover. It is not clear whether this is merely due to a recovery of function within this hypothalamic mechanism (i.e., lesions do not eliminate all the tissue concerned with the regulation of feeding behavior), or to a true shift of function to other, possibly extrahypothalamic, mechanisms. Extirpation or stimulation of this region also affects the regulation of water intake or thirst but does not appear to be the primary cause of the observed effects on food intake.

Bilateral lesions of the inhibitory or satiety

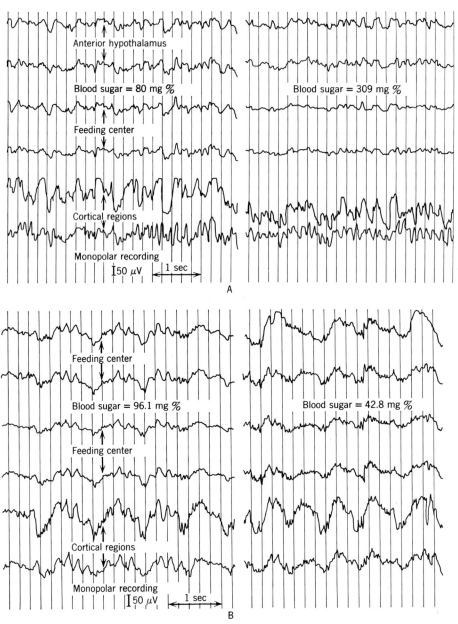

Fig. 6.59 A, monopolar recordings from a cat with a reference electrode on the left ear. Hyperglycemia has reduced the voltage of the electrical activity of the feeding centers from 70–75 to 20–25 μV. No significant change is observed in the electrical activity of the anterior hypothalamus and cortical regions. B, monopolar recordings from a cat with a reference electrode on the left ear. Hypoglycemia has produced a slight increase in the frequency of the electrical activity of the feeding centers from 11–12 waves/sec to 13–14 waves/sec. (From Anand et al., 1961a.)

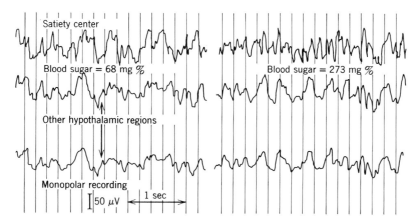

Fig. 6.60 Monopolar recordings from a cat with a reference electrode on the ear before and after intravenous glucose injection. Hyperglycemia has increased the frequency of the electrical activity of the satiety center from 6–7 waves/sec to 9–10 waves/sec without changing the amplitude. No significant change in the electrical activity of other hypothalamic regions is seen. (From Anand et al., 1961a.)

mechanisms located in or near the ventromedial nuclei produce hyperphagia and obesity. The adiposity is primarily produced by overeating, although a decrease in activity as well as several metabolic disturbances may contribute to the hypothalamic obesity. Electrical stimulation of these nuclei induces hypophagia (but never complete aphagia). In the case of the satiety mechanism there is doubt about the motivational character of the observed effects. Lesions of the ventromedial nuclei do produce overeating when palatable food is freely available. However, the animals will not work as hard to obtain food as do normal animals, and they appear hypersensitive to the sensory aspects of their diets. They actually consume less food than normal controls when cellulose or quinine is added to their meals. It has been suggested that such lesions may interfere with the mechanism of stopping eating rather than with the hunger mechanism itself, but recent observations suggest more general affective processes may also be involved.

Little evidence is as yet available about the physiological mechanisms which in turn excite or inhibit these hypothalamic centers or the means by which they exert their influence. The two most prominent hypotheses offered in explanation of the first question are Mayer's glucostatic theory and Brobeck's thermoregulatory hypothesis. Mayer's theory proposes that the stimulus for hunger is a drop in the rate of central glucose utilization. The thermoregulatory theory suggests that the regulation of food intake, which may be an integral part of the organism's energy exchange,

is related to the heat-loss and heat-conservation mechanisms of the hypothalamus. Either or both of these mechanisms may be important for the regulation of feeding behavior; however, much additional evidence is required to explain negative experimental evidence before we can accept either of them.

Other Central Influences

Experimental investigations of the allocortical and juxtallocortical portions of the cerebrum have almost invariably shown that extirpation or electrical stimulation of limbic system structures produces changes in feeding behavior or "eating automatisms."

The temporal lobe and amygdala. One of the first investigations of temporal lobe functions (Brown and Schaefer, 1888) reported that large bilateral lesions of the temporal lobe produce hyperphagia in monkeys. More recently, Fuller et al. (1957) found that lesions in the "pyriform-amygdala-hippocampal complex" double the average daily food intake of cats during the first two weeks after the operation. This abnormal intake was reflected in a pronounced weight gain, but both food intake and body weight returned to normal after one month. Temporal lobectomies in man (see the discussion in Chapter 9 on emotion), often produce "compulsive mouthing" as well as overeating and changes in food preference.

Fulton (1951) reports that more restricted lesions, destroying only the amygdaloid complex, cause almost constant nibbling and greatly prolonged feeding. Morgane and Kosman (1959a, b) observed hyperphagia with lesions of the pyriform lobe and amygdaloid complex and have related these effects to the close anatomical relationship between the amygdala and hypothalamic systems. Anand and Brobeck (1952) failed to modify food intake by similar amygdaloid lesions, but they observed that spontaneous activity and body temperature were decreased markedly—though temporarily—following such lesions. This finding may have interesting implications for Brobeck's thermoregulatory control of food intake, although the authors did not discuss this point further.

Green et al. (1957) attempted to localize more precisely the amygdaloid component that must be affected to produce changes in feeding behavior. They found that lesions restricted to the junction of the basal and lateral nuclei reliably evoked overeating, whereas lesions in other portions of the amygdala failed to do so. Wood (1958), on the other hand, found that small lesions in the central and medial nuclei were effective in producing hyperphagia. Green et al. (1957) have reported that lesions of the anterior part of the amygdala may, in fact, produce aphagia, and similar results have been obtained by Koikegami et al. (1955, 1958). Anand and Brobeck (1952) found that such aphagia was only temporary in cats. Anand et al. (1958) found that lesions restricted to the amygdala and periamygdaloid region produced temporary aphagia or hypophagia in cats and monkeys. Temporal lobe lesions which did not involve the amygdaloid complex were followed by hyperphagia. Very extensive damage to the temporal lobe cortex (including the amygdala) produced an initial period of hypophagia, followed by pronounced and long-lasting hyperphagia. The changes in feeding behavior were more pronounced in monkeys than in cats, suggesting the possibility of encephalization, even with respect to the limbic system.

The relationship between specific areas of the amygdaloid complex and food intake has recently been investigated in detail. S. P. Grossman and Lore Grossman (1963) found that very small bilateral lesions in the posterioventral amygdala of rats produced a marked rise in both food and water intake, but the effects were not permanent. Subsequent experiments demonstrated that apparently permanent hyperphagia and hyperdipsia could be obtained by slightly larger lesions in the posterior amygdala, whereas lesions in the anterior amygdaloid complex increased food intake but reduced water consumption.

Electrical stimulation of the anterior region inhibited food intake in deprived animals but increased water consumption. Stimulation of the posterior area inhibited both food and water intake.

Subsequent studies of the effects of chemical stimulation of the amygdaloid complex (S. P. Grossman, 1964a) suggest that the amygdala may exert indirect influences on feeding and drinking behavior and that such behavior may require activity in other, possibly hypothalamic, centers. Adrenergic stimulation of the ventral amygdala of deprived animals reliably increased food-motivated bar-pressing responses but decreased water-motivated responses. This pattern was reversed after the central application of an adrenergic blocking agent. Cholinergic stimulation of the same area increased water intake but reduced food consumption. The cholinergic blocking agent atropine reliably reversed these effects, whereas other control substances did not affect food or water intake. None of the neurohumoral substances affected food or water intake in sated animals, suggesting that the activity of the amygdala may modulate the activity of other, possibly hypothalamic, mechanisms (see S. P. Grossman, 1964b).

These investigations provided some support for the hypothesis that both excitatory and inhibi-

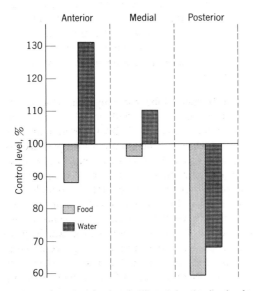

Fig. 6.61 Food and water intake of deprived animals during 1 hr of "chronic" electrical stimulation of the ventral amygdala. Data are expressed as a percentage of the average intake on control tests without electrical stimulation. (From S. P. Grossman and Lore Grossman, 1963.)

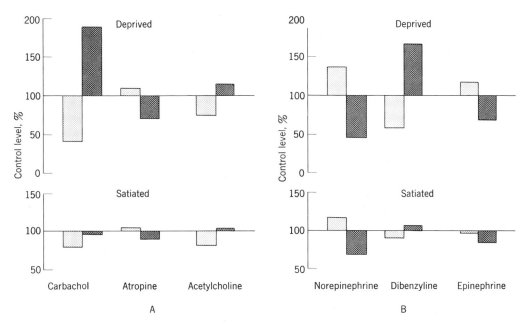

Fig. 6.62 A, average bar-pressing performance for food (gray) and water (black) after cholinergic stimulation or blockade of the ventral amygdala. The data are expressed as a percentage of the average pre- and poststimulation control level. B, after adrenergic stimulation or blockade. (From S. P. Grossman, 1964a.)

tory mechanisms may be represented in the amygdaloid area. Some recent observations by Robinson (1964) suggest, however, that the neural circuit that mediates feeding behavior may be much more diffusely represented than has been assumed. Robinson used "roving" monopolar electrodes to explore large portions (almost 6000 discrete points) of the brain of monkeys; he found that food and water intake and such functionally related activities as ejection of foodstuffs from the mouth and vomiting could be elicited from many portions of the brain, notably from the limbic system and related diencephalic nuclei. A stochastic analysis of the data suggested that the concept of neural centers either in the hypothalamus or in other parts of the brain does not appear to be useful. Feeding and drinking responses could be obtained from a wide region of the brain, and even within the traditional feeding center of the lateral hypothalamus many other unrelated activities were at times elicited. Although the probability of obtaining a feeding response to electrical stimulation was greatest in the lateral hypothalamus, fully 85% of the feeding responses were elicited by stimulation outside this region. Unless we assume that the hypothalamic responses are qualitatively superior, the notion of a feeding center no longer seems appropriate.

The hippocampal formation. Fuller et al. (1957) have reported that lesions involving the hippocampal-amygdaloid area produced a 100% increase in food consumption during the first two postoperative weeks, but the effect gradually disappeared. This lack of permanence is reminiscent of the temporary hyperphagia following minute posterior amygdaloid lesions in the Grossman and Grossman (1963) study; these findings may reflect amygdaloid influences rather than hippocampal influences, although the study is often cited in support of a hippocampal involvement in food intake. Ehrlich (1963) has reported that lesions more clearly restricted to the hippocampus proper produced a significant increase in food and water intake; however, the records were unfortunately maintained for a 3-day test period only, and the long-term effects cannot be assessed. Recent observations (S. P. Grossman, unpublished studies) have shown that very small lesions in the entorhinal area, which surrounds the ventral hippocampus and may be functionally related to it, often produce peculiar effects which suggest significant metabolic disturbances (increased intake without weight gain; weight gain without apparent increase in food intake). More detailed studies are needed to clarify the contribution of this portion of the brain.

A number of experiments have recently suggested that animals with hippocampal lesions generally perform a food-rewarded instrumental response better than normals or animals with neocortical damage; however, it is not entirely clear that these effects are related to a primary change in food motivation. Ehrlich (1963) found that rats with dorsal hippocampal lesions ran faster in a straight alley for food reward than normals and also pressed a bar at significantly higher rates under partial reinforcement conditions. Peretz (1963) similarly found that bar pressing for food rewards was facilitated, and the experimental extinction of the response was retarded, by hippocampal lesions. The delayed extinction had previously been noted by Teitelbaum (1960) and Correll (1957). Grossman and Mountford (1964), on the other hand, found that chemical interference with hippocampal functions significantly hindered the performance of a simple food-rewarded discrimination response. Correll (1957) earlier reported slower running speeds in hippocampal animals than in normal animals in a simple straight-alley study.

An interpretation of these results is difficult because hippocampal lesions also result in marked changes of "affect" (lesions usually increase the animals' reactivity, and the handling of such an animal in a food-rewarded situation may be more stressful than normal) or general activity (the animals appear unable to withhold punished responses and display a general rise in locomotor activity which might account for the more rapid running and higher performance seen in some of the studies).

The frontal granular cortex. Because of its intimate connections with subcortical and limbic structures which contribute to the regulation of various emotional and motivational responses, the frontal cortex is typically treated as a functional part of this circuit rather than as a part of the neocortical sensory-motor systems. That this is an appropriate assignment is shown when we consider the effects of frontal cortex lesions or stimulation on food intake or on food-rewarded instrumental responses.

Extensive frontal damage in the monkey has been reported to produce extreme hyperphagia which results in a consumption of as much as 300% of the normal daily intake (Fulton et al., 1932; Watts and Fulton, 1934). More restricted damage to the frontal poles of cats and dogs (Richter and Hawkes, 1939), the prefrontal lateral cortex (Brutkowski, 1959a, b, c), or the premotor

areas (Bykov, 1957) has been reported to induce ravenous eating, polyphagia (ingestion of indigestible substances), and excited behavior in food-rewarded learning situations. Ruch and Shenkin (1943) found only a relatively mild and temporary effect on food intake following damage restricted to area 13; they reported that the net effect of the lesion on body energy levels was in fact negative, since a very large increase in locomotor activity compensated for the increased energy intake. Anand et al. (1958) have reported that lesions in the frontal lobe that included or were restricted to the posterior orbital gyrus of cats always produced a *decrease* in food intake, whereas lesions that spared this region produced varying degrees of hyperphagia. Pribram and Bagshaw (1953) have reported significantly increased oral activity and polyphagia following lesions in the frontotemporal cortex.

Electrical stimulation studies have generally supported the hypothesis that some aspects of the granular prefrontal cortex may be concerned with the regulation of food intake. MacLean and Delgado (1953), for instance, reported that both chemical and electrical stimulation of frontotemporal cortex produced sniffing, licking, and biting, as well as voracious eating. Similar results have been reported by Schaltenbrandt and Cobb (1931), Rioch and Brenner (1938), and Kaada (1951).

Kirschbaum (1951) emphasized, in a review of the clinical literature on the behavioral effects of frontal lobe tumors or lesions, that an excessive drive for food and bulimia occur almost invariably following frontal lobe damage. Hofstatter et al. (1945) have suggested that the overeating and rapid weight gain may be particularly characteristic of lesions involving the lower medial and orbital frontal cortex. Bulimia has also been reported in a recent review of the symptoms of frontal lobe damage (Hécaen, 1964).

The thalamus. Cobb (1944) reported that the destruction of connections between the frontal lobes and the thalamus produced overeating in man. Andersson and Larsson (1956) were unable to replicate these findings in the dog, but a number of investigators have reported drastic changes in food intake following restricted thalamic damage. Ruch et al. (1941, 1942), for instance, reported that lesions in the arcuate nucleus of the thalamus interfere with the sensation of taste and result in marked hyperphagia and obesity. The effect on food intake did not seem to be directly related to the loss of taste: lesions slightly more rostral failed to produce the hyperphagia but still caused a complete loss of gustatory sensations. Maire (1956) reported that electrical stimulation of the anterior thalamus elicited feeding behavior or induced seizure activity which was followed by ravenous eating. O. A. Smith, Jr. et al. (1961) found that stimulation of the anteroventral nuclei of the thalamus of rats elicited similar seizure activity and subsequent ravenous eating; however, they failed to observe any facilitation of food-rewarded lever-pressing behavior.

Conclusions. Although it is clear that the regulation of primary motivational processes is not an exclusively hypothalamic function, the nature of the many, and often diffusely organized, extrahypothalamic influences is not yet understood. Robinson's (1964) interesting observations suggest that we may have to think of a complexly and diffusely organized system of overlapping circuits which, perhaps because of purely geographic arti-

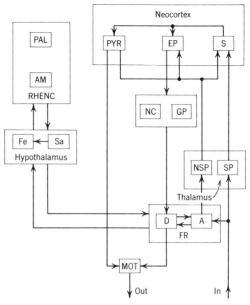

Fig. 6.64 The main anatomical divisions of the central nervous system implicated in the elaboration of feeding responses. A, ascending reticular system; AM, subcortical components of the limbic system; D, descending reticular system; EP, extrapyramidal system; Fe, lateral area; FR, reticular formation; GP, globus pallidus; MOT, lower motor mechanisms; NC, nucleus caudatus; NSP, nonspecific ascending system; PAL, cortical components of the limbic system; PYR, pyramidal system; RHENC, rhinencephalon; S, cortical sensory areas; Sa, ventromedial area; SP, specific ascending pathways. (From de Ruiter, 1963.)

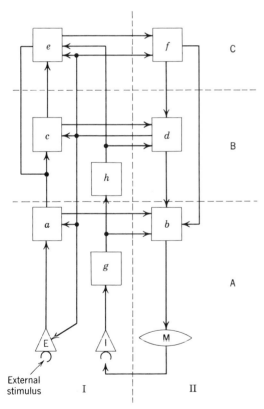

Fig. 6.63 The general principle of connections in the feeding network. A, lower "reflex" level; B, level of the reticular formation and associated structures; C, cortical level; I, systems gathering and evaluating information; II, executive systems; E, exteroceptor; I, internal receptor; M, effector. (From de Ruiter, 1963.)

facts, appear most concentrated in the hypothalamus. What is needed at present is a careful study of the functional role of the extrahypothalamic mechanisms in situations that permit a clear decision about the potential involvement of hypothalamic influences.

In a discussion of this problem, de Ruiter (1963) has developed the scheme that we are presenting in the last illustrations of this chapter. The diagrams are essentially self-explanatory and may, as de Ruiter suggests, orient us toward areas where information is most needed. They do not at present represent more than a pictorial summary of the often-conflicting experimental literature, and we must be careful to accept the suggested pathways and centers with a grain of salt.

SUMMARY

All data of modern psychology represent some measurable aspect of a gross behavioral reaction

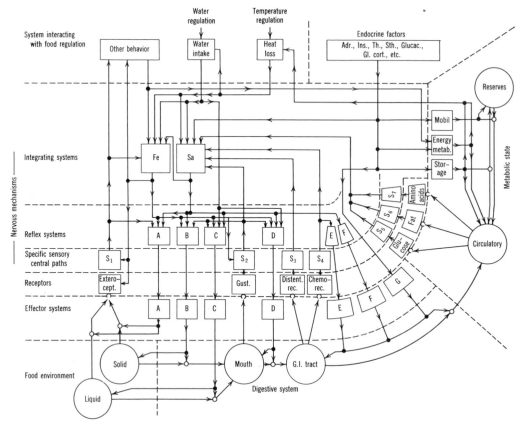

Fig. 6.65 Synthetic diagram of present data on the network of nutritional homeostasis. A, B, C, D, patterns of movement involved in the acquisition and ingestion of food (e.g., approach, mastication, sucking, and deglutition, respectively); E, F, peristalsis and digestion; G, intestinal absorption; Fe, hunger mechanism; Sa, satiety mechanism; S_1–S_7, afferent pathways of various external and internal receptors. The circles indicate the sites occupied by the various nutrients, outside and inside the body. (From de Ruiter, 1963.)

to stimulation of exteroceptive nervous processes. The organism's response depends not only, and in special instances not even primarily, on the particular parameters of external stimulation, but also on organismic variables which may be classified as motivational factors.

The past 50 years of experimental investigation have greatly advanced our understanding of the effects of environmental conditions, and techniques have become available for the recording and quantification of the response measures. Motivational factors, on the other hand, have generally remained hypothetical constructs of insufficient specificity and substance to allow more than indirect and partial control and manipulation. The conceptual motivational structure employed by most psychological theorists is still based on Cannon's classical statement of the local

theory of thirst and hunger (Cannon, 1934), in spite of excellent evidence to the contrary.

Motivation has in the past decades become one of the basic concepts in modern theories of learning, personality, and social behavior. It is therefore important to seek a better empirical and theoretical understanding of the physiological mechanisms that mediate these behaviors. The present state of our knowledge does not allow a concise treatment of the subject. A considerable body of experimental fact has become available for each of the primary drives, but this information has not been successfully integrated into a general theory of motivation based on the operation of physiological mechanisms.

When we talk about the physiology of hunger, we are concerned with the neural and hormonal mechanisms that regulate the organism's energy intake. How does the organism "know" when to ingest food and when to stop? Just how constant is the balance of caloric intake and energy expenditure?

Historically, it was believed that food intake was primarily, if not exclusively, regulated by sensations of a purely peripheral origin. We are hungry because our stomach is empty and satiated because it is full. This eminently sensible theory is not, unfortunately, correct. Stomach contractions may correlate with hunger sensations in man, and severe gastric distension with the feeling of satiety; however, neither of these factors appears to be essential either to the sensation of hunger or to an adequate regulation of energy intake.

More modern theories of hunger have been based on the assumption that a central nervous system mechanism regulates food intake. Beginning with clinical reports of severe disturbances of the energy-exchange mechanism following tumor growth at the base of the brain, much experimental interest has centered on hypothalamic mechanisms. The available evidence today suggests that an excitatory control mechanism may be located in the lateral hypothalamus at the same rostrocaudal coordinates as a medial inhibitory or satiety mechanism.

Lesions in the satiety mechanism of the ventromedial nuclei produce overeating and obesity. The organism doubles or triples its normal body weight and returns to a more normal food intake only when the physical limitations of the body prevent further adiposity. Electrical stimulation of this area induces a reduction of food intake in hungry animals and, if prolonged, may lead to hypophagia.

It is not clear, however, that this mechanism is specifically involved in the regulation of hunger. Hyperphagic animals do not show a raised level of motivation as measured by their willingness to work for food or accept bitter or diluted foods. It has been suggested that the function of the satiety mechanism may be primarily to induce "stopping of eating." Some recent observations indicate that the inhibitory function of the ventromedial satiety mechanism may be general rather than specific, but further information is needed.

It is clear that the ingestion of food must either excite an inhibitory mechanism or reduce the activity in a feeding center more directly. What we do not yet know is how this hypothetical mechanism is apprised of the fact that sufficient food has been consumed. The "messenger" is probably not of neural origin, since stomach denervation does not seem to interfere with food regulation. Of the many possible humoral factors, only blood sugar has received much theoretical and experimental interest. Some evidence suggests that the carbohydrate metabolism may covary directly with hunger, but we do not yet have sufficient evidence to accept a glucostatic theory of hunger or satiety without reservation.

Lesions in the more lateral excitatory mechanism produce complete aphagia and adipsia. Animals with bilateral lesions in this area die of starvation and dehydration while sitting on a mountain of food and next to a bottle of fresh water. The failure to eat does not depend on dehydration. Most animals recover from the effects of lateral lesions if they are maintained by intragastric feeding and watering for several weeks or months. Electrical stimulation of this area induces feeding and drinking in satiated animals. Chemical stimulation induces feeding or drinking, depending on the nature of the stimulating substance; these responses suggest that the mechanisms regulating food and water intake are physiologically and functionally distinct in spite of the apparent anatomical overlap.

It has been suggested that this lateral mechanism may have two distinct components, a metabolic control which operates via pallidofugal fibers and a motivational mechanism which depends on the medial forebrain bundle.

We do not know at this time how these mechanisms are apprised of the fact that the organism's energy stores are depleted. This process presumably requires information from both peripheral and central structures and may depend on either neural or hormonal factors. Mayer's glucostatic hypothesis suggests that these hypothalamic mechanisms may be preferentially sensitive to the level of sugar in the blood or to the utilization of glucose in the brain. Brobeck's thermoregulatory hypothesis suggests that the regulation of food intake may be an integral part of the organism's general energy exchange; the latter is most directly related to the heat-loss and heat-conservation mechanisms which have been demonstrated in the anterior and posterior hypothalamus. Both theories can point to an impressive array of experimental support, but many negative data argue against an uncritical acceptance of either notion.

Changes in food intake have been observed following lesions or electrical stimulation of various allocortical and juxtallocortical structures.

The effects may be as clear-cut as those observed after hypothalamic damage or stimulation but typically are not so specific. The activity of the hypothalamic centers must be integrated at higher (i.e., cortical) levels in order to produce well-directed behavioral responses, but how this integration takes place is at present only poorly understood.

Much research remains to be done before we can complete the cycle from the depletion of the organism's energy stores to the execution of food-seeking and feeding responses. Future research in this field will have to concentrate on the physiological mechanisms that excite or inhibit the hypothalamic centers and on the integrative processes that translate the resultant hypothalamic activity into overt behavior.

BIBLIOGRAPHY

Adams, T. Hypothalamic temperature in the cat during feeding and sleep. *Science,* 1963, **139**, 609–610.

Adolph, E. F. Urges to eat and drink in rats. *Amer. J. Physiol.,* 1947, **151**, 110–125.

Anand, B. K. Nervous regulation of food intake. *Physiol. Rev.,* 1961, **41**, 677–708.

Anand, B. K., & Brobeck, J. R. Hypothalamic control of food intake in rats and cats. *Yale J. Biol. Med.,* 1951a, **24**, 123.

Anand, B. K., & Brobeck, J. R. Localization of a feeding center in the hypothalamus of the rat. *Proc. Soc. exp. Biol. Med.,* 1951b, **77**, 323–324.

Anand, B. K., & Brobeck, J. R. Food intake and spontaneous activity of rats with lesions in the amygdaloid nuclei. *J. Neurophysiol.,* 1952, **15**, 421–431.

Anand, B. K., & Dua, S. Blood sugar changes induced by electrical stimulation of the hypothalamus of the cat. *Ind. J. med. Res.,* 1955a, **43**, 123–127.

Anand, B. K., & Dua, S. Feeding responses induced by electrical stimulation of the hypothalamus in cat. *Ind. J. med. Res.,* 1955b, **43**, 113–122.

Anand, B. K., Dua, S., & Schoenberg, K. Hypothalamic control of food intake in cats and monkeys. *J. Physiol. (London),* 1955, **127**, 143–152.

Anand, B. K., Dua, S., & Chhina, G. S. Higher nervous control over food intake. *Ind. J. med. Res.,* 1958, **46**, 277–287.

Anand, B. K., Dua, S., & Singh, B. Electrical activity of the hypothalamic "feeding centres" under the effect of changes in blood chemistry. *EEG clin. Neurophysiol.,* 1961a, **13**, 54–59.

Anand, B. K., Subberwal, U., Manchanda, S. K., & Singh, B. Glucoreceptor mechanism in the hypothalamic feeding centres. *Ind. J. med. Res.,* 1961b, **49**, 717–724.

Anand, B. K., Talwar, G. P., Dua, S., & Mhatre, R. M. Glucose and oxygen consumption of hypothalamic feeding centers. *Ind. J. med. Res.,* 1961c, **49**, 725–732.

Anand, B. K., Chhina, G. S., & Singh, B. Effect of glucose on the activity of hypothalamic "feeding centers." *Science,* 1962, **138**, 597–598.

Anand, B. K., Chhina, G. S., Sharma, K. N., Dua, S., & Singh, B. Activity of single neurons in the hypothalamic feeding centers: effect of glucose. *Amer. J. Physiol.,* 1964, **207**, 1146–1154.

Andersson, B., & Larsson, S. Water and food intake and the inhibitory effect of amphetamine on drinking and eating before and after pre-frontal lobotomy in dogs. *Acta physiol. scand.,* 1956, **38**, 22–30.

Andersson, B., & Larsson, B. Influence of local temperature changes in the preoptic area and rostral hypothalamus on the regulation of food and water intake. *Acta physiol. scand.,* 1961, **52**, 75–89.

Andersson, B., & Persson, N. Pronounced hypothermia elicited by prolonged stimulation of the "heat-loss center" in unanesthetized goats. *Acta physiol. scand.,* 1957, **41**, 277–282.

Archdeacon, J. W., Presnell, M. W., & Walton, C. J. Effects of atropine on food ingestion and water drinking in dogs. *Amer. J. Physiol.,* 1949, **157**, 149.

Aschner, B. Über die Funktion der Hypophyse. *Pflüg. Arch. ges. Physiol.,* 1912, **146**, 1–146.

Babinski, M. J. Tumeur du corps pituilaire, sans acromégalie, et avec arrêl de développement des organs génitaux. *Rev. neurol..* 1900, **8**, 531.

Bailey, P., & Bremer, F. Experimental diabetes insipidus. *Arch. intern. Med.,* 1921, **28**, 773–803.

Baillie, P., & Morrison, S. D. The nature of the suppression of food intake by lateral hypothalamic lesions in rats. *J. Physiol. (London),* 1963, **165**, 227–245.

Baker, D. G., & Sellers, E. A. Carbohydrate metabolism in the rat exposed to a low environmental temperature. *Fed. Proc.,* 1953, **12**, 8.

Bardier, E. *Les fonctions digestives.* Paris: O. Doin, 1911.

Barnes, B. O., & Keeton, R. W. Experimental obesity. *Amer. J. Physiol.,* 1940, **129**, 305.

Bash, K. W. An investigation into a possible organic basis for the hunger drive. *J. comp. Psychol.,* 1939, **28**, 109–134.

Bates, M. W., Nauss, S. F., Hagman, N. C., & Mayer, J. Fat metabolism in three forms of experimental obesity: body composition. *Amer. J. Physiol.,* 1955a, **180**, 301–309.

Bates, M. W., Mayer, J., & Nauss, S. F. Fat metabolism in three forms of experimental obesity: fatty acid turnover. *Amer. J. Physiol.,* 1955b, **180**, 309–311.

Beattie, J. Relation of tuber cinereum to gastric and cardiac functions, preliminary note. *Canad. med. Ass. J.,* 1932, **26**, 278.

Beattie, J., & Sheehan, D. The effect of hypothalamic stimulation on gastric motility. *J. Physiol. (London),* 1934, **81**, 218–227.

Bell, W. B. Experimental operation on the pituitary. *Quart. J. exp. Physiol.,* 1917, **11**, 77

Bercowitz, Z. Studies on the motility of denervated Heidenhain pouch. *Amer. J. Physiol.,* 1923, **72**, 109.

Berkun, M. M., Kessen, M. L., & Miller, N. E. Hunger-reducing effects of food by stomach fistula versus food by mouth, measured by a consumatory response. *J. comp. physiol. Psychol.,* 1952, **45**, 550–554.

Biggart, J. H., & Alexander, G. L. Experimental diabetes insipidus. *J. Path. Bact.,* 1939, **48**, 405.

Booth, G., & Strang, J. M. Changes in temperature of the skin following the ingestion of food. *Arch. intern. Med.,* 1936, **57**, 533–543.

Bostock, J. *An elementary system of physiology.* London: Baldwin, 1836.

Brobeck, J. R. Effects of variations in activity, food intake, and environmental temperature on weight gain in albino rat. *Amer. J. Physiol.,* 1945, **143**, 1–5.

Brobeck, J. R. Mechanisms of the development of obesity in animals with hypothalamic lesions. *Physiol. Rev.,* 1946, **26**, 541–559.

Brobeck, J. R. Food intake as a mechanism of temperature regulation. *Yale J. Biol. Med.,* 1947–1948, **20**, 545–552.

Brobeck, J. R. Hypothalamic control of food intake in rats and cats. *Yale J. Biol. Med.,* 1951, **24**, 123–139.

Brobeck, J. R. Neural regulation of food intake. *Ann. N.Y. Acad. Sci.,* 1955, **63**, 44–55.

Brobeck, J. R. Mechanisms concerned with appetite. *Pediatrics,* 1957a, **20**, 549–552.

Brobeck, J. R. Neural control of hunger, appetite, and satiety. *Yale J. Biol. Med.,* 1957b, **29**, 565–574.

Brobeck, J. R. Neural factors of obesity. *Bull. N.Y. Acad. Med.,* 1957c, **33**, 762–770.

Brobeck, J. R. Regulation of feeding and drinking. In *Handbook of physiology. Vol. II.* J. Field, H. W. Magoun, & V. E. Hall, Eds. Baltimore: Williams and Wilkins, 1960, 1197–1206.

Brobeck, J. R., Tepperman, J., & Long, C. N. H. Experimental hypothalamic hyperphagia in the albino rat. *Yale J. Biol. Med.,* 1943a, **15**, 831–853.

Brobeck, J. R., Tepperman, J., & Long, C. N. H. The effect of experimental obesity upon carbohydrate metabolism. *Yale J. Biol. Med.,* 1943b, **15**, 893–903.

Brobeck, J. R., Larsson, S., & Reyes, E. A study of the electrical activity of the hypothalamic feeding mechanism. *J. Physiol. (London),* 1956, **132**, 358–364.

Brody, D. A., Werle, J. M., Meschan, I., & Quigley, J. P. Intralumen pressures of the digestive tract, especially the pyloric region. *Amer. J. Physiol.,* 1940, **130**, 791.

Brooks, C. McC. A study of the respiratory quotient in obesity. *Fed. Proc.,* 1945, **4**, 9.

Brooks, C. McC. Activity and the development of obesity. *Fed. Proc.,* 1946a, **5**, 12.

Brooks, C. McC. A study of the respiratory quotient in experimental hypothalamic obesity. *Amer. J. Physiol.,* 1946b, **147**, 727–734.

Brooks, C. McC. The relative importance of changes in activity in the development of experimentally produced obesity in the rat. *Amer. J. Physiol.,* 1946c, **147**, 708–716.

Brooks, C. McC., & Lambert, E. F. A study of the effect of limitation of food intake and the method of feeding on the rate of weight-gain during hypothalamic obesity in the albino rat. *Amer. J. Physiol.,* 1946, **147**, 695–707.

Brooks, C. McC., & Lockwood, R. L. A study of the effect of hypothalamic lesions on the eating habits of rats. *Fed. Proc.,* 1945, **4**, 9.

Brooks, C. McC., & Marine, D. N. A study of oxygen consumption in obesity. *Fed. Proc.,* 1946, **5**, 12.

Brooks, C. McC., Lambert, E. F., & Bard, P. Experimental production of obesity in the monkey (*Macaca mulatta*). *Fed. Proc.,* 1942, **1**, 11.

Brooks, C. McC., Lockwood, R. L., & Wiggins, M. L. A study of the effect of hypothalamic lesions on the eating habits of the albino rat. *Amer. J. Physiol.,* 1946a, **147**, 735–742.

Brooks, C. McC., Marine, D. N., & Lambert, E. F. A study of the food-feces ratios and of the oxygen consumption of albino rats during various phases of experimentally produced obesity. *Amer. J. Physiol.,* 1946b, **147**, 717–726.

Brown, S., & Schaefer, E. A. An investigation into the functions of the occipital and temporal lobes of the monkey's brain. *Phil. Trans. roy. Soc. London,* 1888, **179**, 303–327.

Bruce, H. M., & Kennedy, G. C. The central nervous control of food and water intake. *Proc. roy. Soc. (London),* B, 1951, **138**, 528–544.

Bruch, H. The Fröhlich Syndrome. *Amer. J. Dis. Child.,* 1939, **58**, 1282–1289.

Brügger, M. Fresstrieb als hypothalmisches Symptom. *Helv. physiol. pharmacol. Acta,* 1943, **1**, 183–198.

Bruhn, J. M., & Keller, A. D. The effect of experimentally produced obesity on energy and water metabolism. *Amer. J. Physiol.,* 1941, **133**, 229.

Brutkowski, S. Effects of prefrontal ablations on salivation during the alimentary unconditioned reflex and after its cessation. *Acta Biol. exp. (Warsaw),* 1959a, **19**, 281–289.

Brutkowski, S. Comparison of classical and instrumental alimentary conditioned reflexes following bilateral prefrontal lobectomies in dogs. *Acta Biol. exp. (Warsaw),* 1959b, **19**, 291–299.

Brutkowski, S. The solutions of a difficult inhibitory task (alternation) by normal and prefrontal dogs. *Acta Biol. exp. (Warsaw),* 1959c, **19**, 301–312.

Bulatão, E., & Carlson, A. J. The relation of blood sugar to the gastric hunger contractions. *Amer. J. Physiol.,* 1924a, **68**, 148.

Bulatão, E., & Carlson, A. J. Contribution to the physiology of the stomach. Influence of experimental changes in blood sugar level on gastric hunger contractions. *Amer. J. Physiol.,* 1924b, **69**, 107.

Burton, A. C., & Murlin, J. R. Temperature distribution, blood flow and heat storage in the body in basal conditions and after injection of food. *J. Nutr.,* 1935, **9**, 281–300.

Bykov, K. M. *The cerebral cortex and the internal organs.*

W. H. Gantt, Trans. New York: Chemical Publishing Co., 1957.

Camus, J., & Roussy, G. Hypophysectomie et polyurie expérimentales. *C. R. Soc. Biol. (Paris)*, 1913, **75**, 483–486.

Camus, J., & Roussy, G. Syndrome adipso-génital et polyurie expérimentale. *Rev. neurol.*, 1920, **36**, 1201.

Camus, J., & Roussy, G. Les syndromes hypophysaires. *Rev. neurol.*, 1922, **38**, 622–639.

Cannon, W. B. *Bodily changes in pain, hunger, fear, and rage* (2nd ed.). New York: Appleton, 1929.

Cannon, W. B. *The wisdom of the body.* New York: Norton, 1932, 101.

Cannon, W. B. Hunger and thirst. In *Handbook of general experimental psychology.* C. Murchison, Ed. Worcester, Mass.: Clark Univ. Press, 1934, 247–263.

Cannon, W. B., & Washburn, A. L. An explanation of hunger. *Amer. J. Physiol.*, 1912, **29**, 444–454.

Carlson, A. J. The character of the movements of the empty stomach in man. *Amer. J. Physiol.*, 1912–1913a, **31**, 309.

Carlson, A. J. The relation between the contractions of the empty stomach and the sensation of hunger. *Amer. J. Physiol.*, 1912–1913b, **31**, 175–192.

Carlson, A. J. The influence of the gastric hunger contractions on the cardiac and vasomotor centers, and on the reflex excitability of the spinal cord. *Amer. J. Physiol.*, 1912–1913c, **31**, 318.

Carlson, A. J. The influence of stimulation of the gastric mucosa on gastric hunger contractions. *Amer. J. Physiol.*, 1913, **32**, 245.

Carlson, A. J. The hunger contractions of the empty stomach during prolonged starvation. *Amer. J. Physiol.*, 1914a, **33**, 95.

Carlson, A. J. The nervous control of the gastric hunger mechanism. *Amer. J. Physiol.*, 1914b, **34**, 155.

Carlson, A. J. *The control of hunger in health and diseases.* Chicago: Univ. of Chicago Press, 1916.

Carr, W. J. The effect of adrenalectomy upon the NaCl taste threshold in rat. *J. comp. physiol. Psychol.*, 1952, **45**, 377–380.

Ciba. *The Ciba collection of medical illustrations. Vol. VIII. The hypothalamus.* Summit, N. J.: Ciba Pharmaceutical Products Co., 1956.

Clark, G. The use of the Horseley-Clarke instrument on the rat. *Science*, 1939, **90**, 92.

Clark, G., & Wang, S. C. The liberation of a pressor hormone following stimulation of the hypothalamus. *Amer. J. Physiol.*, 1939, **127**, 597.

Clark, G., Magoun, H. W., & Ranson, S. W. Hypothalamic regulation of body temperature. *J. Neurophysiol.*, 1939, **2**, 61–80.

Cobb, S. Technique of interviewing a patient with psychosomatic disorder. *Med. Clin. N. Amer.*, 1944, **282**, 1210–1216.

Collins, E. Localization of an experimental hypothalamic and midbrain syndrome simulating sleep. *J. comp. Neurol.*, 1954, **100**, 661–697.

Cooke, R. E. The behavioral response of infants to heat stress. *Yale J. Biol. Med.*, 1952, **24**, 334.

Correll, R. E. The effect of bilateral hippocampal stimulation on the acquisition and extinction of an instrumental respose. *J. comp. physiol. Psychol.*, 1957, **50**, 624–629.

Cottle, W., & Carlson, L. D. Adaptive changes in rats exposed to cold: caloric exchange. *Amer. J. Physiol.*, 1954, **178**, 305–308.

Cowgill, G. R. The energy factor in relation to food intake: experiments on the dog. *Amer. J. Physiol.*, 1928, **85**, 45–64.

Crooke, A. C., & Gilmore, J. R. A description of the effect of hypophysectomy on the growing rat, with the resulting histological changes in the adrenal and thyroid glands and the testicles. *J. Path. Bact.*, 1938, **47**, 522.

Crowe, S. J., Cushing, H., & Homans, J. Experimental hypophysectomy. *Bull. Johns Hopk. Hosp.* 1910, **21**, 127.

D'Angelo, S. A. Thyroid hormone administration and ovarian and adrenal activity in rats bearing hypothalamic lesions. *Endocrinology*, 1959, **64**, 685–701.

Darwin, E. *Zoonomia (London)*, 1801, **3**, 322.

Delgado, J. M. R. Responses evoked in waking cat by electrical stimulation of motor-cortex. *Amer. J. Physiol.*, 1952, **171**, 436–446.

Delgado, J. M. R., & Anand, B. K. Increased food intake induced by electrical stimulation of the lateral hypothalamus. *Amer. J. Physiol.*, 1953, **172**, 162–168.

De Ruiter, L. The physiology of vertebrate feeding behavior: towards a synthesis of the ethological and physiological approaches to problems of behavior. *Z. Tierpsychol.*, 1963, **20**, 498–516.

Dethier, V. G., & Bodenstein, D. Hunger in the blowfly. *Z. Tierpsychol.*, 1957, **15**, 129.

Dickerson, V. C., Tepperman, J., & Long, C. N. H. The role of the liver in the synthesis of fatty acids from carbohydrates. *Yale J. Biol. Med.*, 1953, **15**, 875.

Dott, N. M. An investigation into the functions of the pituitary and thyroid glands. I: Technique of their experimental surgery and summary of results. *Quart. J. exp. Physiol.*, 1923, **13**, 241–282

Ehrlich, A. Effects of tegmental lesions on motivated behavior in rats. *J. comp. physiol. Psychol.*, 1963, **56**, 390–396.

Engel, F. L. Stimulation of nitrogen metabolism by adrenal-cortical extract during insulin hypoglycemia. *J. clin. Endocrinol.*, 1949, **9**, 657–658.

Epstein, A. N. Suppression of eating and drinking by amphetamine and other drugs in normal and hyperphagic rats. *J. comp. physiol. Psychol.*, 1959, **52**, 37–45.

Epstein, A. N. Reciprocal changes in feeding behavior produced by intra-hypothalamic chemical injections. *Amer. J. Physiol.*, 1960a, **199**, 969–974.

Epstein, A. N. Water intake without the act of drinking. *Science*, 1960b, **131**, 497–498.

Epstein, A. N., & Teitelbaum, P. A water-tight swivel joint permitting chronic injection into moving animals. *J. appl. Physiol.*, 1962a, **17**, 171–172.

Epstein, A. N., & Teitelbaum, P. Regulation of food intake in the absence of taste, smell, and other oropharyngeal sensations. *J. comp. physiol. Psychol.,* 1962b, **55**, 753–759.

Erdheim, J. Über Hypophysenganggeschwulste und Hirncholesteatome *S.-B. Akad. Wiss. Wien.,* 1904, **113**, Abt. III, 537–726.

Ewald, J. R. *Klinik der Verdauungskrankheiten.* Cologne: Bergmann, 1893.

Farrell, J. I., & Ivy, A. C. Studies on the motility of the transplanted gastric pouch. *Amer. J. Physiol.,* 1926, **76**, 227.

Feldman, S. E., Larsson, S., & Lepkovsky, S. Aphagia in chickens. *Amer. J. Physiol.,* 1957, **191**, 259.

Feldman, S. E., Behar, A. J., & Birnbaum, D. Gastric lesions following hypothalamic stimulation. *Arch. Neurol. (Chicago),* 1961, **4**, 308–317.

Fenton, P. F. Studies in obesity. I: Nutritional obesity in mice. *J. Nutr.,* 1953, **49**, 319–331.

Fenton, P. F. Growth and fat deposits in the mouse. A definition of obesity. *Amer. J. Physiol.,* 1956, **184**, 52.

Forssberg, A., & Larsson, S. Studies of isotope distribution and chemical composition in the hypothalamic region of hungry and fed rats. *Acta physiol. scand.,* 1954, **32**, Suppl. 115, Pt. II, 41–63.

Foster, M. *Textbook of physiology.* London: Macmillan, 1891.

French, J. D., Porter, R. W., Amerongen, F. K. von, & Raney, R. B. Gastrointestinal hemorrhage and ulceration associated with intracranial lesions; clinical and experimental study. *Surgery,* 1952, **32**, 395–407.

French, J. D., Longmire, R. L., Porter, R. W., & Movius, H. J. Extravagal influences on gastric HCl secretion induced by stress stimuli. *Surgery,* 1953, **34**, 621–632.

Freyberg, R. H. A study of the value of insulin in undernutrition. *Amer. J. med. Sci.,* 1935, **190**, 28.

Fröhlich, A. Dr. Alfred Froehlich stellt einen Fall von Tumor der Hypophyse ohne Akromegalie vor. *Wien. klin. Rdsch.,* 1902, **15**, 883.

Fröhlich, A. Case-material in Bruch, H. The Fröhlich syndrome. *Amer. J. Dis. Child.,* 1939, **58**, 1282–1289.

Fuller, J. L., Rosvold, H. E., & Pribram, K. H. The effects on affective and cognitive behavior in the dog of lesions of the pyriform amygdala-hippocampal complex. *J. comp. physiol. Psychol.,* 1957, **50**, 89–96.

Fulton, J. F. *Frontal lobotomy and affective behavior.* New York: Norton, 1951, 78–82.

Fulton, J. F., & Bailey, P. Tumors on the region of the third ventricle: their diagnosis and relation to pathological sleep. *J. nerv. ment. Dis.,* 1929, **69**, 1–26.

Fulton, J. F., Jacobsen, C. F., & Kennard, Margaret A. A note concerning the relation of the frontal lobes to posture and forced grasping in monkeys. *Brain.* 1932, **55**, 524–536.

Gasnier, A., & Mayer, A. Récherches sur la régulation de la nutrition. I: Analités et côtés des mécanismes régulateurs. *Ann Physiol. Physicochim. biol.,* 1939a, **15**, 145–156.

Gasnier, A., & Mayer, A. Récherches sur la régulation de la nutrition. II: Les méchanismes régulateurs de la nutrition chez le lapin domestique. *Ann. Physiol. Physicochim. biol.,* 1939b, **15**, 157–185.

Gasnier, A., & Mayer, A. Récherches sur la régulation de la nutrition. III: Méchanismes régulateurs de la nutrition et intensité du métabolisme. *Ann. Physiol. Physicochim. biol.,* 1939c, **15**, 186–194.

Gasnier, A., & Mayer, A. Récherches sur la régulation de la nutrition. IV. Différences entre deux races de lapins domestiques. *Ann. Physiol. Physicochim. biol.,* 1939d, **15**, 195–209.

Gasnier, A., & Mayer, A. Récherches sur la régulation de la nutrition. V: Caractères individuals. *Ann Physiol. Physicochim. biol.,* 1939e, **15**, 210–214.

Geiling, E. The pituitary body. *Physiol. Rev.,* 1926, **6**, 62–123.

Gershon-Cohen, J., & Shay, H. Experimental studies on gastric physiology in man; study of pyloric control. Role of milk and cream in the normal and in subjects with quiescent duadenal ulcer. *Amer. J. Roentgenol.,* 1937, **38**, 427–446.

Geyer, R. P., Bowie, E. J., & Bates, J. C. Effects on fasting and pyruvate on palmitic acid metabolism. *J. biol. Chem.,* 1953, **200**, 271–274.

Gianturco, C. Some mechanical factors of gastric physiology, study II. *Amer. J. Roentgenol.,* 1934, **31**, 745.

Gilmour, J. Clinical aspects of carcinoma of stomach in diagnosis. *Brit. med. J.,* 1958, **5073**, 745–748.

Graef, I., Negrin, J., & Page, I. H. The development of hepatic cirrhosis in dogs after hypophysectomy. *Amer. J. Path.,* 1944, **20**, 823.

Green, J. D., Clemente, C. D., & de Groot, J. Rhinencephalic lesions and behavior in cats. *J. comp. Neurol.,* 1957, **108**, 505–546.

Gregersen, M. I., & Cizek, L. Total water balance, thirst, fluid deficits and excess. In *Medical physiology,* Philip Bard, Ed. St. Louis, Mo.: Mosby, 1956, 763–779.

Grossman, M. I. Gastrointestinal hormones. *Physiol. Rev.,* 1950, **30**, 33–90.

Grossman, M. I. Integration of current views on the regulation of hunger and appetite. *Ann. N.Y. Acad. Sci.,* 1955, **63**, 76–91.

Grossman, M. I., & Stein, I. F. The effect of vagotomy on the hunger-producing action of insulin in man. *J. appl. Physiol.,* 1948, **1**, 263.

Grossman, M. I., Cummins, G. M., & Ivy, A. C. The effect of insulin on food intake after vagotomy and sympathectomy. *Amer. J. Physiol.,* 1947, **149**, 100.

Grossman, S. P. Eating or drinking elicited by direct adrenergic or cholinergic stimulation of hypothalamus. *Science,* 1960, **132**, 301–302.

Grossman, S. P. Direct adrenergic and cholinergic stimulation of hypothalamic mechanisms. *Amer. J. Physiol.,* 1962a, **202**, 872–882.

Grossman, S. P. Effects of adrenergic and cholinergic

blocking agents on hypothalamic mechanisms. *Amer. J. Physiol.,* 1962b, **202,** 1230–1236.

Grossman, S. P. Behavioral effects of chemical stimulation of the ventral amygdala. *J. comp. physiol. Psychol.,* 1964a, **57,** 29–36

Grossman, S. P. Effects of chemical stimulation of the septal area on motivation. *J. comp. physiol. Psychol.,* 1964b, **58,** 194–200.

Grossman, S. P. Some neurochemical properties of the central regulation of thirst. In *Thirst, first international symposium on thirst in the regulation of body water.* M. J. Wayner, Ed. New York: Pergamon Press, 1964c.

Grossman, S. P. Behavioral effects of direct chemical stimulation of central nervous system structures. *Int. J. Neuropharmacol.,* 1964d, **3,** 45–58.

Grossman, S. P. The VMH: a center for affective reactions, satiety, or both? *Int. J. Physiol. Behav.,* 1966, **1,** 1–10.

Grossman, S. P., & Grossman, Lore. Food and water intake following lesions or electrical stimulation of the amygdala. *Amer. J. Physiol.,* 1963, **205,** 761–765.

Grossman, S. P., & Mountford, Helen. Effects of chemical stimulation of the dorsal hippocampus on learning and performance. *Amer. J. Physiol.,* 1964, **207,** 1387–1393.

Grossman, S. P., & Rechtschaffen, A. Long-term variations in brain temperature in relation to food-intake and a thermoregulatory theory of energy regulation. *Amer. J. Physiol.,* submitted.

Guyton, A. C. *Textbook of medical physiology* (2nd ed., illustrated). Philadelphia: Saunders, 1961.

Haller, A. Fames et sitis. *Elementa Physiol.,* 1776, **6,** 185.

Hamilton, C. L. Interactions of food intake and temperature regulation in the rat. *J. comp. physiol. Psychol.,* 1963, **56,** 476–488.

Hamilton, C. L., & Brobeck, J. R. Food intake and temperature regulation in rats with rostral hypothalamic lesions. *Amer. J. Physiol.,* 1964a, **207,** 291–297.

Hamilton, C. L., & Brobeck, J. R. Hypothalamic hyperphagia in the monkey. *J. comp. physiol. Psychol.,* 1964b, **57,** 271–278.

Hanson, M. E., & Grossman, M. I. The failure of intravenous glucose to inhibit food intake in dogs. *Fed. Proc.,* 1948, **7,** 50.

Harris, S. C., Ivy, A. C., & Searle, L. M. Mechanisms of amphetamine-induced loss of weight; consideration of theory of hunger and appetite. *J. Amer. med. Ass.,* 1947, **134,** 1468–1475.

Haterius, H. O., & Ferguson, J. Evidence for the hormonal nature of the oxytocic principle of the hypophysis. *Amer. J. Physiol.,* 1938, **124,** 314.

Hécaen, H. Mental symptoms associated with tumors of the frontal lobe. In *The frontal granular cortex and behavior.* J. M. Warren & K. Akert, Eds. New York: McGraw-Hill, 1964.

Heinbecker, P., White, H. L., & Rolf, D. Experimental obesity in the dog. *Amer. J. Physiol.,* 1944, **141,** 549.

Herberg, L. J. Hunger reduction produced by injecting glucose into the lateral ventricle of the rat. *Nature (London),* 1960, **187,** 245–246.

Herberg, L. J. Physiological drives investigated by means of injections into the cerebral ventricles of the rat. *Quart. J. exp. Psychol.,* 1962, **14,** 8–14.

Hertz, A. F. *The sensibility of the alimentary canal.* London: Oxford Medical Publications, 1911.

Hervey, G. R. The effects of lesions in the hypothalamus in parabiotic rats. *J. Physiol. (London),* 1959, **145,** 336–352.

Heslop, T. S. The nervous control of gastric secretion, an experimental study. *Brit. J. Surg.,* 1938a, **25,** 884.

Heslop, T. S. The hypothalamus and gastric motility. *Quart. J. exp. Physiol.,* 1938b, **28,** 335–340.

Hess, W. R. *Das Zwischenhirn: Syndrome, Lokalisationen, Functionen.* Basel: Schwabe, 1949.

Hess, W. R. *Diencephalon: autonomic and extrapyramidal functions.* New York: Grune and Stratton, 1954.

Hetherington, A. W. The relation of various hypothalamic lesions to other phenomena in the rat. *Amer. J. Physiol.,* 1941, **133,** 326–327.

Hetherington, A. W. The production of hypothalamic obesity in rats already displaying chronic hypopituitarism. *Amer. J. Physiol.,* 1943, **140,** 89–91.

Hetherington, A. W. Non-production of hypothalamic obesity in the rat by lesions rostral or dorsal to the ventro-medial hypothalamic nuclei. *J. comp. Neurol.,* 1944, **80,** 33.

Hetherington, A. W., & Ranson, S. W. Hypothalamic lesions and adiposity in the rat. *Anat. Rec.,* 1940, **78,** 149.

Hetherington, A. W., & Ranson, S. W. The spontaneous activity and food intake of rats with hypothalamic lesions. *Amer. J. Physiol.,* 1942a, **136,** 609–617.

Hetherington, A. W., & Ranson, S. W. Effect of early hypophysectomy on hypothalamic obesity. *Endocrinology,* 1942b, **31,** 30–34.

Hetherington, A. W., & Weil, A. The lipoid, calcium, phosphorous and iron content of rats with hypothalamic and hypophyseal damage. *Endocrinology,* 1940, **26,** 723–727.

Himwich, H. E. *Brain metabolism and cerebral disorders.* Baltimore: Williams and Wilkins, 1941.

Himwich, H. E., Bowman, K. M., Daly, C., Fazwkas, J. F., Wortis, J., & Goldfarb, W. Cerebral blood flow and brain metabolism during insulin hypoglycemia. *Amer. J. Physiol.,* 1941, **132,** 640.

Hinde, R. A. Appetitive behavior, consummatory act, and the hierarchial organization of behavior with special reference to the great tit. *Behavior,* 1953, **5,** 189.

Hoebel, B. G. Hypothalamic lesions by electrocauterization: disinhibition of feeding and self-stimulation. *Science,* 1965, **149,** 452–453.

Hoebel, B. G., & Teitelbaum, P. Hypothalamic control of feeding and self-stimulation. *Science,* 1962, **135,** 375–377.

Hoff, E. C., & Sheehan, D. Experimental gastric secretion following hypothalamic lesions in monkeys. *Amer. J. Path.*, 1935, **11**, 789–802.

Hofstatter, L., Smolik, E. A., & Busch, A. K. Prefrontal lobotomy in treatment of chronic psychosis. *Arch. Neurol. Psychiat. (Chicago)*, 1945, **53**, 125–130.

Holmes, J. E., & Miller, N. E. Effects of bacterial endotoxin on water intake, food intake, and body temperature in the albino rat. *J. exp. Med.*, 1963, **118**, 649–658.

House, E. L., & Pansky, B. *Neuroanatomy.* New York: McGraw-Hill, 1960.

Ingram, W. R. Central autonomic mechanisms. In *Handbook of physiology, Vol. II.* J. Field, H. W. Magoun, & V. E. Hall, Eds. Baltimore: Williams and Wilkins, 1960.

Ivy, A. C., Vloedman, D. A., & Keane, J. The small intestine in hunger. *Amer. J. Physiol.*, 1925, **72**, 99.

Janowitz, H., & Grossman, M. I. The effect of parenteral administration of glucose and protein hydrolysate on food intake of the rat. *Amer. J. Physiol.*, 1948, **155**, 28.

Janowitz, H. D., & Grossman, M. I. Effect of intravenously administered glucose on food intake in the dog. *Amer. J. Physiol.*, 1949a, **156**, 87.

Janowitz, H. D., & Grossman, M. I. Effect of variations in nutritive density on intake of food in dogs and cats. *Amer. J. Physiol.*, 1949b, **158**, 184–193.

Janowitz, H. D., & Grossman, M. I. Some factors affecting the food intake of normal dogs and dogs with esophagostomy and gastric fistulae. *Amer. J. Physiol.*, 1949c, **159**, 143–148.

Janowitz, H. D., & Grossman, M. I. Hunger and appetite: some definitions and concepts. *J. Mt. Sinai Hosp.*, 1949d, **16**, 231–240.

Janowitz, H. D., & Grossman, M. I. Effect of pre-feeding alcohol and bitters on food intake of dogs. *Amer. J. Physiol.*, 1951, **164**, 182.

Janowitz, H. D., & Hollander, F. Effect of prolonged intragastric feeding on oral ingestion. *Fed. Proc.*, 1953, **12**, 72.

Janowitz, H. D., & Ivy, A. C. Rate of blood-sugar levels in spontaneous and insulin-induced hunger in man. *J. appl. Physiol.*, 1949, **1**, 643.

Kaada, B. R. Somato-motor, autonomic and electrocorticographic responses to electrical stimulation of "rhinencephalic" and other structures in primates, cats and dogs. *Acta physiol. scand.*, 1951, **24**, Suppl. 83, 285.

Kabat, H., Anson, B. J., Magoun, H. W., & Ranson, S. W. Stimulation of the hypothalamus with special reference to its effect on gastro-intestinal motility. *Amer. J. Physiol.*, 1935, **112**, 214.

Keller, A. D. Ulceration in the digestive tract of the dog following intracranial procedures. *Arch. Path.*, 1936, **21**, 127–164.

Keller, A. D., & Noble, W. M. Adiposity with normal sex functions following extirpation of the posterior lobe of the hypophysis in the dog. *Amer. J. Physiol.*, 1935, **113**, 79.

Keller, A. D., & Noble, W. M. Further observations on enhanced appetite with resultant adiposity following removal of the posterior lobe of the hypophysis. *Amer. J. Physiol.*, 1936, **116**, 90.

Keller, M. R., & Roberts, S. Epinephrine stimulation of pituitary metabolism. *Fed. Proc.*, 1953, **12**, 76.

Kennedy, G. C. The hypothalamic control of food intake in rats. *Proc. roy. Soc. (London), B*, 1950, **137**, 535–548.

Kennedy, G. C. The role of depot fat in the hypothalamic control of food intake in the rat. *Proc. roy. Soc. (London), B*, 1952, **140**, 578–592.

Kirschbaum, W. R. Excessive hunger as a symptom of cerebral origin. *J. nerv. ment. Dis.*, 1951, **113**, 95.

Knapp, M. I. The nature and cause of hunger, appetite and anorexia. *Amer. Med.*, 1906, **10**, 333.

Kohn, M. Satiation of hunger from food injected directly into the stomach versus food ingested by mouth. *J. comp. physiol. Psychol.*, 1951, **44**, 412–422.

Koikegami, H., Fuse, S., Yokoyama, T., Watanabe, T., & Watanabe, H. Contributions of the comparative anatomy of the amygdaloid nuclei of mammals with some experiments of their distruction or stimulation. *Folia psychiat. neurol. jap.*, 1955, **8**, 336–368.

Koikegami, H., Fuse, S., Hiroki, S., Kazami, T., & Kageyama, Y. On the inhibitory effect upon the growth of infant animals or on the obesity in adult cat induced by bilateral destruction of the amygdaloid nuclear region. *Folia phychiat. neurol. jap.*, 1958, **12**, 207–223.

Kosaka, T., & Lim, R. Mechanism of inhibition of gastric secretion by fat; role of bile and cystokinin. *Chin. J. Physiol.*, 1930, **4**, 213–220.

Krasne, F. B. General disruption resulting from electrical stimulus of ventromedial hypothalamus. *Science*, 1962, **138**, 822–823.

Larsson, S. On hypothalamic organization of the nervous mechanism regulating food intake. *Acta physiol. scand.*, 1954, **32**, Suppl. 115, 63.

Larsson, S. On the hypothalamic organization of the nervous mechanisms regulating food intake. *Acta physiol. scand.*, 1955, **32**, 1–40.

Larsson, S. Food preferences in obesity caused by goldthioglucose. *Acta physiol. scand.*, 1957, **40**, 368–376.

Larsson, S., & Ström, L. Some characteristics of goldthioglucose obesity in the mouse. *Acta physiol. scand.*, 1957, **38**, 298–308.

Liebelt, R. A., & Perry, J. H. Hypothalamic lesions associated with goldthioglucose-induced obesity. *Proc. Soc. exp. Biol. Med.*, 1957, **95**, 774.

Longet, F. A. *Traité de physiologie.* Paris: Masson, 1868.

Luckhardt, A. B., & Carlson, A. J. Contributions to the physiology of the stomach. XVII: On the chemical control of the gastric hunger mechanism. *Amer. J. Physiol.*, 1915, **36**, 37.

Lundbaek, K., & Stevenson, J. A. F. Reduced carbohydrate intake after fat feeding in normal rats and rats with hypothalamic hyperphagia. *Amer. J. Physiol.*, 1947, **151**, 530–537.

Lyon, J. B., Dowling, Marian T., & Fenton, P. F. Studies on obesity. II: Food intake and oxygen consumption. *J. Nutr.,* 1953, **51**, 65–70.

McCleary, R. A. Taste and post-ingestion factors in specific hunger behavior. *J. comp. physiol. Psychol.,* 1953, **46**, 411–421.

MacDonald, R. M., Ingelfinger, F. J., & Belding, H. W. Late effects of total gastrostomy in man. *New Engl. J. Med.,* 1947, **237**, 887.

McIntyre, A. R., & Burke, J. C. The tolerance of the albino rat for insulin. *Amer. J. Physiol.,* 1937, **119**, 364.

MacKay, E. M., Calloway, J. W., & Barnes, R. H. Hyperalimentation in normal animals produced by protamine-insulin. *J. Nutr.,* 1940, **20**, 59.

MacLean, P. D., & Delgado, J. M. R. Electrical and chemical stimulation of fronto-temporal portion of limbic system in waking animal. *EEG clin. Neurophysiol.,* 1953, **5**, 91–100.

Magendie, F. *Lehrbuch der Physiologie.* Tübingen: Ostrander, 1826.

Magoun, H. W., Harrison, F., Brobeck, J. R., & Ranson, S. W. Activation of heat-loss mechanisms by local heating of the brain. *J. Neurophysiol.,* 1938, **1**, 101.

Maire, F. W. Eating and drinking responses elicited by diencephalic stimulation in unanesthetized rats. *Fed. Proc.,* 1956, **15**, 124.

Maire, F. W., & Patton, H. D. Neural structures involved in the genesis of "preoptic pulmonary edima," gastric erosions and behavior changes. *Amer. J. Physiol.,* 1956, **184**, 345–350.

Marshall, N. B., & Mayer, J. Energy balance in goldthioglucose obesity. *Amer. J. Physiol.,* 1954, **178**, 271–274.

Marshall, N. B., Barnett, R. J., & Mayer, J. Hypothalamic lesions in goldthioglucose injected mice. *Proc. Soc. exp. Biol. Med.,* 1955, **90**, 240.

Martin, C. L., & Rogers, F. T. Hunger pain. *Amer. J. Roentgenol.,* 1927, **17**, 222.

Mayer, J. The glucostatic theory of regulation of food intake and the problem of obesity. *Bull. New Engl. med. Cent.,* 1952, **14**, 43.

Mayer, J. Genetic, traumatic and environmental factors in the etiology of obesity. *Physiol. Rev.,* 1953a, **33**, 472–508.

Mayer, J. Glucostatic mechanisms of regulation of food intake. *New Engl. J. Med.,* 1953b, **249**, 13–16.

Mayer, J. Regulation of energy intake and the body weight. The glucostatic theory and the lipostatic hypothesis. *Ann. N.Y. Acad. Sci.,* 1955, **63**, 15–43.

Mayer, J., & Barnett, R. J. Obesity following unilateral hypothalamic lesions in rats. *Science,* 1955, **121**, 599.

Mayer, J., & Bates, M. W. Blood glucose and food intake in normal and hypophysectomized alloxan-treated rats. *Amer. J. Physiol.,* 1952, **168**, 812–819.

Mayer, J., & Greenberg, R. Hyperthemia in hypothalamic hyperphagia. *Amer. J. Physiol.,* 1953, **173**, 523–525.

Mayer, J., & Marshall, N. B. Specificity of goldthioglucose for ventromedial hypothalamic lesions and hyperphagia. *Nature (London),* 1956, **178**, 1399–1400.

Mayer, J., Marshall, N. B., Vitale, J. J., Christensen, J. H., Mashayekhi, M. B., & Stare, F. J. Exercise, food intake and body weight in normal rats and genetically obese adult mice. *Amer. J. Physiol.,* 1954, **177**, 544–547.

Mayer, J., French, R. G., Zighera, C. F., & Barnett, R. J. Hypothalamic obesity in the mouse. *Amer. J. Physiol.,* 1955, **182**, 75–82.

Mendel, V. E., & Raghaven, G. V. A study of diurnal temperature patterns in sheep. *J. Physiol. (London),* 1964, **174**, 206–216.

Meschan, I., & Quigley, J. P. Spontaneous motility of the pyloric sphincter and adjacent regions of the gut in the unanesthetized dog. *Amer. J. Physiol.,* 1938, **121**, 350.

Mickelsen, O. S., Takahashi, S., & Craig, C. Experimental obesity. I: Production of obesity in rats by feeding high-fat diets. *J. Nutr.,* 1955, **57**, 541.

Miller, N. E. Experiments on motivation. *Science,* 1957, **126**, 1271–1278.

Miller, N. E. Motivational effects of brain stimulation and drugs. *Fed. Proc.,* 1960, **19**, 846–853.

Miller, N. E. Some psychophysiological studies of motivation and of the behavioral effects of illness. *Bull. Brit. psychol. Soc.,* 1964, **17**, 55.

Miller, N. E. Chemical coding of behavior in the brain. *Science,* 1965, **148**, 328–338.

Miller, N. E., & Kessen, M. L. Reward effects of food via stomach fistula compared with those of food via mouth. *J. comp. physiol. Psychol.,* 1952, **45**, 555–564.

Miller, N. E., Bailey, C. J., & Stevenson, J. A. F. "Decreased hunger" but increased food intake resulting from hypothalamic lesions. *Science,* 1950, **112**, 256–259.

Miller, N. E., Gottesman, Kay S., & Emery, Nona. Dose response to carbachol and norepinephrine in rat hypothalamus. *Amer. J. Physiol.,* 1964, **206**, 1384–1388.

Mohr, B. Hypertrophie der Hypophyse cerebri und dadurch bedingter Druck auf die Hoehengrundflaeche insbesondere auf die Sehnerven, dass Chiasma derselben, und dem laengseitigen Hoehenschenkel. *Wschr. ges. Heilkunde,* 1840, **6**, 565–574.

Montemurro, D. G., & Stevenson, J. A. F. The localization of hypothalamic structures in the rat influencing water consumption. *Yale J. Biol. Med.,* 1955-1956, **28**, 396–403.

Montemurro, D. G., & Stevenson, J. A. F. Adipsia produced by hypothalamic lesions in the rat. *Canad. J. Biochem.,* 1957, **35**, 31–37.

Morgan, C. T., & Morgan, J. D. Studies in hunger. II: The relation of gastric denervation and dietary sugar to the effect of insulin upon food intake in the rat. *J. gen. Psychol.,* 1940, **57**, 153–163.

Morgane, P. J. Medial forebrain bundle and hypothalamic "feeding" centers. *Fed. Proc.,* 1960, **19,** 292 (abstract).

Morgane, P. J. Electrophysiological studies of feeding and satiety centers in the rat. *Amer. J. Physiol.,* 1961a, **201,** 838–844.

Morgane, P. J. Evidence of a "hunger motivational" system in the lateral hypothalamus of the rat. *Nature (London),* 1961b, **191,** 672–674.

Morgane, P. J. Medial forebrain bundle and "feeding centers" of the hypothalamus. *J. comp. Neurol.,* 1961c, **117,** 1–26.

Morgane, P. J., & Kosman, A. J. A rhinencephalic feeding center in the cat. *Amer. J. Physiol.,* 1959a, **197,** 158–162.

Morgane, P. J., & Kosman, A. J. A rhinencephalic feeding in the cat. *Fed. Proc.,* 1959b, **18,** 108.

Morrison, S. D., & Mayer, J. Adipsia and aphagia in rats after lateral subthalamic lesions. *Amer. J. Physiol.,* 1957, **191,** 248.

Mulinos, M. G. The gastric hunger mechanism. IV: The influence of experimental alterations in blood sugar concentration on the gastric hunger contractions. *Amer. J. Physiol.,* 1933, **104,** 371.

Müller, J. *Handbuch der Physiologie des Menschen.* Coblenz: Hölscher, 1844, 398.

Novin, D., & Miller, N. E. Failure to condition thirst induced by feeding dry food to hungry rats. *J. comp. physiol. Psychol.,* 1962, **55,** 373–374.

Paintal, A. S. A study of gastric stretch receptors. Their role in the peripheral mechanism of satiation of hunger and thirst. *J. Physiol. (London),* 1954, **126,** 255–270.

Peretz, E. The effect of hippocampal ablation on the strength of food-obtained responses. *Amer. Psychologist,* 1963, **18,** 464.

Pfaffman, C., & Bare, J. K. Gustatory nerve discharges in normal and adrenalectomized rats. *J. comp. physiol. Psychol.,* 1950, **43,** 320–324.

Poirier, L. J., Mouren-Mathieu, Anne-Marie, & Richer, Claude-Lise. Neuroanatomical study of obese and non-obese hypothalamic monkeys in relation to food intake, locomotor activity, and temperature regulation. *Canad. J. Biochem.,* 1962a, **40,** 1185–1193.

Poirier, L. J., Mouren-Mathieu, Anne-Marie, & Richer, Claude-Lise. Obesity in the absence of absolute hyperphagic in monkeys with hypothalamic lesions. *Rev. canad. Biol.,* 1962b, **21,** 127–134.

Porter, E., Movius, H. J., & French, J. D. Hypothalamic influences on HCl secretion of the stomach. *Surgery,* 1953, **33,** 875–880.

Pribram, K. H., & Bagshaw, M. Further analysis of the temporal lobe syndrome utilizing fronto-temporal ablations. *J. comp. Neurol.,* 1953, **99,** 347.

Quigley, J. P. The role of the digestive tract in regulating the ingestion of food. *Ann. N.Y. Acad. Sci.,* 1955, **63,** 6–14.

Quigley, J. P., & Hallaran, W. R. The independence of spontaneous gastro-intestinal motility and blood-sugar levels. *Amer. J. Physiol.,* 1932, **100,** 100–102.

Quigley, J. P., & Lindquist, J. L. Action of phlorizine on hunger contractions in the normal and vagotomized dog. *Amer. J. Physiol.,* 1930, **92,** 690.

Quigley, J. P., & Meschan, I. Inhibition of the pyloric sphincter region by the digestion-products of fat. *Amer. J. Physiol.,* 1941, **134,** 803.

Quigley, J. P., & Phelps, K. R. The mechanism of gastric motor inhibition from ingested carbohydrates. *Amer. J. Physiol.,* 1934, **109,** 133.

Quigley, J. P., & Read, M. R. The spontaneous motility of the pyloric sphincter and its relation to gastric evacuation "the pyloric diagraph." *Amer. J. Physiol.,* 1942, **137,** 234.

Quigley, J. P., & Solomon, V. Action of insulin on the motility of the gastro-intestinal tract. *Amer. J. Physiol.,* 1930, **91,** 488.

Quigley, J. P., & Templeton, R. D. Action of insulin on the motility of the gastro-intestinal tract. *Amer. J. Physiol.,* 1939, **91,** 482.

Quigley, J. P., Johnson, V., & Solomon, E. I. Action of insulin on the motility of the gastro-intestinal tract. I: Action on the stomach of normal fasting man. *Amer. J. Physiol.,* 1929, **90,** 89.

Quigley, J. P., Zettleman, H. J., & Ivy, A. C. Analysis of the factors involved in the gastric motor inhibition by fats. *Amer. J. Physiol.,* 1934, **108,** 643.

Quigley, J. P., Werle, J. M., Ligon, E. W., & Read, M. R. The influence of fats on the motor activity of the pyloric sphincter region and on the process of gastric evacuation studied by the balloon-water manometer and by the optical manometer-fluoroscopic techniques. *Amer. J. Physiol.,* 1941, **134,** 132.

Quigley, J. P., Read, M. R., Radzow, K. H., Meschan, I., & Werle, J. M. The effect of hydrochloric acid on the pyloric sphincter, the adjacent portions of the digestive tract and on the process of gastric evacuation. *Amer. J. Physiol.,* 1942, **137,** 153.

Ranson, S. W., Fisher, C., & Ingram, W. R. Hypothalamic regulation of temperature in the monkey. *Arch. Neurol. Psychiat. (Chicago),* 1937, **38,** 445–465.

Ranson, S. W., Fisher, C., & Ingram, W. R. Adiposity and diabetes mellitus in a monkey with hypothalamic lesions. *Endocrinology,* 1938, **23,** 175–181.

Regan, I. F. The action of insulin on the motility of the empty stomach. *Amer. J. Physiol.,* 1933, **104,** 90.

Reynolds, R. W. Ventromedial hypothalamic lesions without hyperphagia. *Amer. J. Physiol.,* 1963, **204,** 60–62.

Richter, C. P. Total self-regulatory functions in animals and human beings. *Harvey Lect.,* 1942–1943, **38,** 63–103.

Richter, C. P., & Hawkes, C. D. Increased spontaneous activity and food intake produced in rats by removal of the frontal poles of the brain. *J. Neurol. Psychiat.,* 1939, **2,** 231.

Rioch, D. Mck., & Brenner, C. Experiments on the

striatum and rhinencephalon. *J. comp. Neurol.,* 1938, **68,** 491–507.

Robins, R. B., & Boyd, T. E. The fundamental rhythm of the Heidenhain pouch movements and their reflex modifications. *Amer. J. Physiol.,* 1923, **67,** 166.

Robinson, B. W. Forebrain alimentary responses: some organizational principles. In *Thirst, first international symposium on thirst in the regulation of body water.* M. J. Wayner, Ed. New York: Pergamon Press, 1964.

Rodgers, W. L., Epstein, A. N., & Teitelbaum, P. Lateral hypothalamic aphagia: motor failure or motivational deficit? *Amer. J. Physiol.,* 1965, **208,** 334–342.

Rogers, F. T. Contributions to the physiology of the stomach. XXXIV: The hunger mechanism of the pigeon and its relation to the central nervous system. *Amer. J. Physiol.,* 1916, **41,** 555.

Roux, J. La faim. Étude physiopsychologique. *Bull. Soc. Anthrop. (Lyon),* 1897 (monograph).

Ruch, T. C., & Patton, H. D. Obesity in animals with hypothalamic lesions. *Physiol. Rev.,* 1946, **26,** 541–559.

Ruch, T. C., & Shenkin, H. A. The relation of area 13 on orbital surface of frontal lobes to hyperactivity and hyperphagia in monkeys. *J. Neurophysiol.,* 1943, **6,** 349–360.

Ruch, T. C., Blum, M., & Brobeck, J. R. Taste disturbances from thalamic lesions in monkeys. *Amer. J. Physiol.,* 1941, **133,** 433.

Ruch, T. C., Patton, H. D., & Brobeck, J. R. Hyperphagia and adiposity in relation to disturbances of taste. *Fed. Proc.,* 1942, **1,** 76.

Schaltenbrandt, G., & Cobb, S. Clinical and anatomical studies of two cats without neocortex. *Brain,* 1931, **53,** 449–488.

Schiff, M. *Physiologie de la digestion.* Florence: 1867; Berlin: Hirschwald, 1868.

Schlessinger, H. Beitrag zur Kenntniss des Hungergefühls. *Wien. klin. Wschr.,* 1893, **6,** 566.

Scott, W. W., Scott, C. C., & Luckhardt, A. B. Observations on the blood sugar level before, during and after hunger periods in humans. *Amer. J. Physiol.,* 1938, **123,** 243.

Sédillot, C. E. *Du nerf vague et ses fonctions.* Paris: Terziolo, 1829.

Share, I., Martyniuk, E., & Grossman, M. I. Effect of prolonged intragastric feeding on oral food intake in dogs. *Amer. J. Physiol.,* 1952, **169,** 229.

Sharma, K. N., Anand, B. K., Dua, S., & Singh, B. Role of stomach in regulation of activities of hypothalamic feeding centers. *Amer. J. Physiol.,* 1961, **201,** 593–598.

Sheard, C., Williams, M. M. D., & Morton, B. T. Skin temperature of the extremities under various environmental and physiological conditions. In *Temperature,* American Institute of Physics. New York: Reinhold, 1941.

Sheehan, D. The hypothalamic and gastrointestinal regulation. *Res. Publ., Ass. Res. nerv. ment. Dis.,* 1940, **20,** 589–616.

Sherrington, C. S. The parts of the brain below cerebral cortex, viz. medulla oblongata, pons, cerebellum, corpora quatrigemina, and region of thalamus. In *Textbook of physiology,* E. A. Sharpey-Schäfer, Ed. Edinburgh: Pentland, 1900.

Short, J. J. Increasing weight with insulin. *J. Lab. clin. Med.,* 1929, **14,** 330.

Smith, O. A., Jr. Food intake and HT stimulation. In *Electrical stimulation of the brain,* D. E. Sheer, Ed. Austin: Univ. of Texas Press, 1961.

Smith, O. A., Jr., McFarland, W. L., & Teitelbaum, H. Motivational concomitants of eating elicited by stimulation of the anterior thalamus. *J. comp. physiol. Psychol.,* 1961, **54,** 484–488.

Smith, P. E. The disabilities caused by hypophysectomy and their repair. The tuberal (hypothalamic) syndrome in the rat. *J. Amer. med. Ass.,* 1927, **88,** 158–161.

Smith, P. E. Hypophysectomy and a replacement therapy in the rat. *Amer. J. Anat.,* 1930, **45,** 205.

Soemmering, S. T. *De corporis humani fabrica,* 1794, **6,** 237.

Somogyi, M. Studies of arteriovenous differences in blood sugar. V: Effect of epinephrine on the rate of glucose assimilation. *J. biol. Chem.,* 1951a, **186,** 513–516.

Somogyi, M. Effect of insulin hypoglycemia on alimentary hyperglycemia. *J. biol. Chem.,* 1951b, **193,** 859–871.

Stein, L., & Seifter, J. Muscarinic synapses in the hypothalamus. *Amer. J. Physiol.,* 1962, **202,** 751–756.

Stellar, E. The physiology of motivation. *Psychol. Rev.,* 1954, **61,** 522.

Stellar, E. Drive and motivation. In *Handbook of physiology. Vol. III.* J. Field, H. W. Magoun, & V. E. Hall, Eds. Baltimore: Williams and Wilkins, 1960.

Stellar, E., Hyman, R., & Somet, S. Gastric factors controlling water intake and salt-solution drinking. *J. comp. physiol. Psychol.,* 1954, **47,** 220–226.

Sternberg, W. Die Appetitlosigkeit. *Zbl. Physiol.,* 1908, **22** (monograph).

Sternberg, W. Die Physiologische Grundlage des Hungergefühls. *Z. Sinnesphysiol.,* 1910, **45,** 71.

Sternberg, W. Der Appetit in der exacten Medizin. *Z. Sinnesphysiol.,* 1911, **45,** 433.

Stiller, B. Die Pathologie des Appetits. *Arch. Verdau.-Kr.,* 1915, **21,** 23.

Strang, J. M., & McClugage, H. B. The specific dynamic action of food in abnormal states of nutrition. *Amer. J. med. Sci.,* 1931, **182,** 49–81.

Strominger, J. L., & Brobeck, J. R. A mechanism of regulation of food intake. *Yale J. Biol. Med.,* 1953, **25,** 383.

Strominger, J. L., Brobeck, J. R., & Cort, R. L. Regulation of food intake in normal rats and in rats with hypothalamic hyperphagia. *Yale J. Biol. Med.,* 1953, **36,** 55–74.

Stucky, C. S., Rose, W. B., & Cowgill, G. R. Studies in the physiology of vitamins. VI: The effect of insulin on gastric motility in vitamin B deficiency. *Amer. J. Physiol.,* 1928, **87**, 85.

Stunkard, A. J., & Wolf, H. G. Correlation of arterio-venous glucose differences, gastric hunger contractions and the experience of hunger in man. *Fed. Proc.,* 1954, **13**, 147.

Teague, R. S., & Ranson, S. W. The role of the anterior hypothalamus in temperature regulation. *Amer. J. Physiol.,* 1936, **117**, 562–570.

Teitelbaum, H. The effect of hippocampal lesions on extinction of an operant response. Paper read at the annual meeting of the Canadian Psychological Association, 1960.

Teitelbaum, P. Sensory control of hypothalamic hyperphagia. *J. comp. physiol. Psychol.,* 1955, **48**, 158–163.

Teitelbaum, P. Random and food-directed activity in hyperphagic and normal rats. *J. comp. physiol. Psychol.,* 1957, **50**, 486–490.

Teitelbaum, P. Disturbances in feeding and drinking behavior after hypothalamic lesions. In *Nebraska symposium on motivation,* M. R. Jones, Ed. Lincoln: Univ. of Nebraska Press, 1961, 39–69.

Teitelbaum, P. Motivational correlates of hypothalamic activity. *Proceedings of the 22nd international physiological congress, Leyden, Holland. Vol. I, Pt. II,* 1962. Also in *Excerpta medica,* International Congress Series No. 47, 697–704.

Teitelbaum, P., & Campbell, B. A. Ingestion patterns in hyperphagic and normal rats. *J. comp. physiol. Psychol.,* 1958, **51**, 135–141.

Teitelbaum, P., and Cytawa, J. Spreading depression and recovery from lateral hypothalamic damage. *Science,* 1965, **147**, 61–63.

Teitelbaum, P., & Epstein, A. N. The lateral hypothalamic syndrome: recovery of feeding and drinking after lateral hypothalamic lesions. *Psychol. Rev.,* 1962, **69**, 74–90.

Teitelbaum, P., & Epstein, A. N. The role of taste and smell in the regulation of food and water intake. In *Proceedings of the first international symposium on olfaction and taste.* London: Pergamon Press, 1963.

Teitelbaum, P., & Stellar, E. Recovery from the failure to eat, produced by hypothalamic lesions. *Science,* 1954, **120**, 894–895.

Templeton, R. D., & Johnson, V. Further observations on the nature of hunger contractions in man. *Amer. J. Physiol.,* 1929, **88**, 173.

Templeton, R. D., & Quigley, J. P. Action of insulin on motility of gastro-intestinal tract; action on Heidenhain pouch. *Amer. J. Physiol.,* 1930, **91**, 467–474.

Tepperman, J., Brobeck, J. R., & Long, C. N. H. A study of experimental hypothalamic obesity in the rat. *Amer. J. Physiol.,* 1941, **133**, 468–469 (abstract).

Tepperman, J., Brobeck, J. R., & Long, C. N. H. The effects of hypothalamic hyperphagia and of alterations in feeding habits on the metabolism of the albino rat. *Yale J. Biol. Med.,* 1943a, **15**, 855–879.

Tepperman, J., Engel, F. L., & Long, C. N. H. Review

of adrenal cortical hypertrophy. *Endocrinology,* 1943b, **32**, 373–402.

Tepperman, J., Engel, F. L., & Long, C. N. H. Effect of high protein diets on size and activity of adrenal cortex in albino rat. *Endocrinology,* 1943c, **32**, 403–409.

Tiedemann, F. *Physiologie des Menschen.* Darmstadt: Leste, 1836.

Tsang, Y. C. Hunger motivation in gastrectomized rats. *J. comp. Psychol.,* 1938, **26**, 1–17.

Van Dyke, H. B. *The physiology and pharmacology of the pituitary body. Vol. I.* Chicago: Univ. of Chicago Press, 1936.

Van Itallie, T. B. Peripheral assimilation of fructose in man. *Proc. Soc. exp. Biol. Med.,* 1953, **84**, 713–715.

Van Itallie, T. B., Beaudoin, R. & Mayer, J. Arterio-venous glucose differences, metabolic hypoglycemia and food intake in man. *J. clin. Nutr.,* 1953, **1**, 208–216.

Vierordt, K. *Grundriss der Physiologie.* Tübingen: Hölzchen, 1871.

Von Voit, C. Hunger und Durstgefühl. In *Hermann's Handbuch der Physiologie,* 1881, **5**, 560.

Wang, S. C., Clark, G., Dey, F. L., & Ranson, S. W. Further study on the gastro-intestinal motility following stimulation of the hypothalamus. *Amer. J. Physiol.,* 1940, **130**, 81–88.

Wangenstein, O. H., & Carlson, A. J. Hunger sensations in a patient after total gastrectomy. *Proc. Soc. exp. Biol. Med.,* 1931, **28**, 545–547.

Warner, F. J. Experimental lesions in the hypothalamus of the guinea pig. *J. nerv. ment. Dis.,* 1929, **69**, 661–665.

Watts, J. W., & Fulton, J. F. Intussusception—the relation of the cerebral cortex to intestinal motility in the monkey. *New Engl. J. Med.,* 1934, **210**, 883–896.

Waugh, J. M. Effect of fat introduced into jejunum by fistula on motility and emptying time of stomach. *Arch. Surg.,* 1936, **33**, 451–466.

Weber, E. H. In *Wagner's Handwörterbuch der Physiologie.* Braunschweig: Vieweg, 1846.

Weiss, A. K. An analysis of the metabolic responses of rats exposed to cold. *Amer. J. Physiol.,* 1960, **196**, 913–918.

Wheatley, M. D. The hypothalamus and affective behavior in cats. *Arch. Neurol. Psychiat. (Chicago),* 1944, **52**, 296–316.

Wilder, R. L., & Schultz, F. W. The action of atropine and adrenaline on gastric tonus and hypermotility induced by insulin hypoglycemia. *Amer. J. Physiol.,* 1931, **96**, 54.

Williams, D. R., & Teitelbaum, P. Some observations on the starvation resulting from lateral hypothalamic lesions. *J. comp. physiol. Psychol.,* 1959, **4**, 458–465.

Wolf, A. V. *Thirst, physiology of the urge to drink and problems of water level.* Springfield, Ill.: Thomas, 1958.

Wolf, G., & Miller, N. E. Lateral hypothalamic lesions: effects on drinking elicited by carbachol in preoptic area and posterior hypothalamus. *Science,* 1964, **143**, 585–587.

Wood, D. C. Behavioral changes following discrete lesions of temporal lobe structures. *Neurology,* 1958, **8**, 215–220.

Wundt, W. *Physiologische Psychologie.* Leipzig: Engelmann, 1902.

Wyrwicka, W., Dobrzecka, C., & Tarnecki, R. The effect of electrical stimulation of the hypothalamic feeding center in satiated goats on alimentary conditioned reflexes, type II. *Acta Biol. exp. (Warsaw),* 1960, **20**, 121–136.

CHAPTER SEVEN

Physiological Mechanisms of Thirst

In the course of phylogenetic development some organisms develop the ability to establish within the body conditions that differ significantly from those of the environment. Claude Bernard, the great French physiologist, suggested more than 200 years ago that it was this development that enabled animals to leave the sea and venture onto land. Gradually, the organism attains the ability to regulate its *milieu interne* or internal environment so precisely that it becomes entirely independent of the protective sea.

The primary need of any living organism is a continuous and adequate supply of oxygen. Oxygen is abundantly available on land at all but the highest elevations and rarely presents a problem once an organism has developed a physical apparatus for its intake. Almost equally important, however, is the maintenance of a constant fluid level in the body. Living tissue depends very directly on water for all metabolic processes. In fact, the principal constituent of all cells is water. The supply of water presents no difficulty to the organism living in the sea. As the organism ventures forth onto land, however, the precise regulation of water intake becomes an acute problem. Water is continuously excreted and secreted by the body in the process of waste removal and temperature regulation.

As long as water is freely available, the intact organism manages to maintain its water balance within surprisingly narrow limits. Adolph (1943b) demonstrated that in man this range amounts to ±0.22% of body weight. When water loss exceeds 0.5% of total body weight, man becomes thirsty and seeks water. If *water balance* is defined as gain minus loss from any source, this behavior can be described as an attempt to maintain a water balance of zero. A *positive water balance* is created when the organism retains an abnormal amount of water. This may be caused either by the excessive ingestion or infusion of liquids, or by a disturbance of the secretory or excretory functions. Such a disturbance may be produced by damage to the sweat glands or by an interruption of urinary flow. When an organism is overloaded with water, various regulatory mechanisms immediately begin to operate to return the balance to zero. When the organism is deprived of water for even relatively short periods of time, a *negative water balance* develops. The immediate reaction to this negative balance is a sharp reduction of urinary excretion and of perspiration. This response tends to restore the body's water balance temporarily. However, waste products must continually be eliminated, and temperature regulation depends very directly on perspiration. The organism therefore continues to lose water (i.e., increases the negative water balance) and must eventually replenish its supply if it is to survive. When the negative balance reaches a critical level, the organism will normally seek and consume an amount of water that is directly proportional to the deficit. The body then returns to a zero balance. When an animal drinks, we assume that it is "thirsty." If this were the whole story, we could define our intervening variable in terms of the relative water balance of the organism. Unfortunately, a negative water balance is not *always* accompanied by a subjective sensation of thirst and may not lead to the ingestion of water. Conversely, one can be intensely "thirsty" without having a negative water balance. The consumption of spicy foods often elicits thirst (and drinking) when the organism's water balance is, in fact, positive. If, on the other hand, we define thirst in terms of the subjective sensations that normally

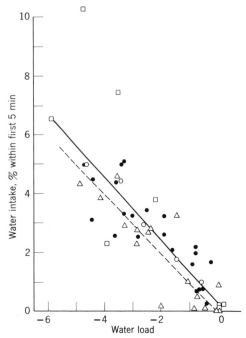

Fig. 7.1 Water intakes of dogs offered water at the end of dehydration periods of various lengths of time. Large circles mark the mean for each percent of water deficit. (From Adolph, 1943b. Copyright 1943 by The Ronald Press Co.)

precede drinking, we shall find ourselves hard-pressed to demonstrate the essential nature of any particular sensory mechanism.

Classically, thirst has been defined as a complex of sensations that arise from the mouth and throat. Early theories of thirst were concerned exclusively with the origin and analysis of such subjective sensations and their reactions to various changes in the organism's water balance. Drinking was assumed to be a direct consequence of such drive stimulation, and total water intake was believed to be proportional to the intensity of these sensations. We shall discuss these local or peripheral-origin theories in greater detail when we consider the possible contribution of peripheral neural or humoral mechanisms. It is sufficient to note here that such factors do not appear to be essential for the regulation of drinking and cannot be postulated as the physiological basis of thirst.

Thirst cannot be defined in terms of water deficit, absolute dehydration, or negative water load, for these states do not necessarily lead to water ingestion. Conversely, water consumption is not a reliable index of water deficit (Adolph et al., 1947). If subjective sensations cannot be trusted,

what precisely do we mean when we say an organism is "thirsty"? These persistent problems of definition are only too common in almost all areas of physiological psychology. They reflect the present state of our ignorance about the complex interrelationships among the many physiological variables that affect as basic a regulatory mechanism as fluid exchange. It can only be hoped that our definitions will improve as additional data become available. This can occur, however, only if we can proceed with relevant research projects, and we must first arrive at some working definition of our principal variable.

Since much of the experimental work depends on animals, a definition in terms of subjective experience is not very useful. Measures of absolute water deficit are so difficult to obtain that a working hypothesis in terms of the organism's fluid balance would be very impractical. What remains is the cautious acceptance of an operational definition of thirst in terms of time of deprivation. This is not a very satisfactory or precise measure, for water intake—and presumably thirst—depends on a great number and variety of additional factors. The large individual differences in water intake of a group of animals with a common deprivation history conveniently hide this problem. However, as long as we remain aware of the shortcomings of such a definition, we can proceed with our research and attempt to unravel some of the complexities of the mechanisms that determine the organism's water intake and thirst.

On a more theoretical level, we might propose another working hypothesis. This would define thirst as the end result of the operation of a variety of physiological mechanisms which contribute to the regulation of the organism's fluid balance. Some of these factors are well established; others are just beginning to be investigated; still others may be obscure now. This approach lacks specificity and elegance but allows us to investigate the matter unfettered by theoretical biases and predilections. As we proceed with our discussion of the research literature, the advantages of this eclectic position will become obvious.

We have studiously avoided the problem of conscious experience by phrasing our definition in terms of physiological mechanisms. To pursue a parallelistic philosophy, we might assume that the conscious sensations of thirst are correlated with variations in some or all of the neural and/or hormonal mechanisms that participate in the regulation of water intake. This problem is cur-

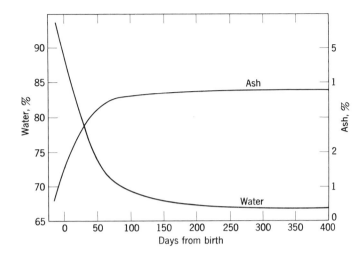

Fig. 7.2 Water and ash content of the rat as a function of age. Chemical maturity is attained as curves level off. (From Wolf, 1958. *Thirst: physiology of the urge to drink and problems of water lack.* Charles C Thomas.)

rently not open to scientific investigation, and an answer to this question is not demanded for the purpose of our research efforts. We can proceed to theorize about the physiological aspects of thirst without being enmeshed in philosophical discussions.

THE EXCHANGE OF BODY FLUIDS

Because the regulation of thirst is intimately related to the regulation of body fluids in general, we might briefly consider some of the basic aspects of this regulatory system. The water content of adult mammals is approximately 70 to 75% of total body weight exclusive of fat deposits (McClure and Aldrich, 1923; Shohl, 1939). Young

animals contain considerably more water per kilogram of body weight than old ones, partly because mature tissue has greater rigidity and tensile strength, and partly because there is a relative increase in the amount of body fat with age.

Water is as necessary for growth as is food Kudo (1921a, b). If the water intake of young animals is restricted, growth will be arrested, even if a normal or a superfluous amount of food is consumed. The organism continuously loses water through the lungs and skin, and considerable amounts of fluid are lost in the form of urine. In order to maintain a zero fluid balance, water must be supplied at regular intervals.

It will be helpful for subsequent discussions to consider the transport of water in the body. Three

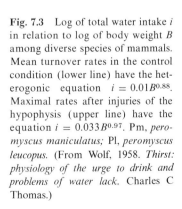

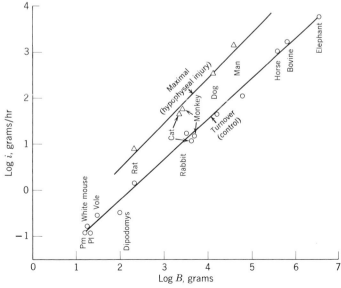

Fig. 7.3 Log of total water intake i in relation to log of body weight B among diverse species of mammals. Mean turnover rates in the control condition (lower line) have the heterogonic equation $i = 0.01B^{0.88}$. Maximal rates after injuries of the hypophysis (upper line) have the equation $i = 0.033B^{0.97}$. Pm, *peromyscus maniculatus;* Pl, *peromyscus leucopus.* (From Wolf, 1958. *Thirst: physiology of the urge to drink and problems of water lack.* Charles C Thomas.)

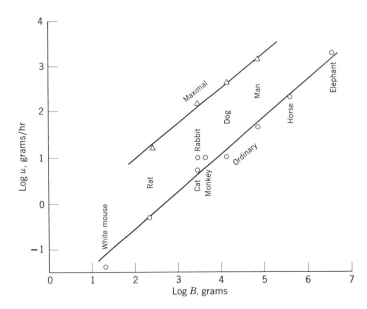

Fig. 7.4 Log of urinary water output u in relation to log of body weight B among diverse species of mammals. "Ordinary" rates (lower line) are those of water balance, "maximal" rates (upper line) those during continued forced administration of water by stomach. Heterogonic equations are $u = 0.0064B^{0.82}$ for ordinary rates and $u = 0.26B^{0.78}$ for maximal rates. (From Wolf, 1958. *Thirst: physiology of the urge to drink and problems of water lack.* Charles C Thomas.)

principal mechanisms perform this function, diffusion, filtration, and osmosis. *Diffusion* across a membrane occurs when two solutions of different concentrations are separated by a membrane that is permeable to the solute. This process is due solely to the action of kinetic molecular energy. *Filtration* refers to the passage of water and solutes through a membrane by some mechanical force such as blood pressure, hydrostatic pressure, or gravity. *Osmosis* is a process by which water molecules pass through a semipermeable membrane when the solutions on either side of the membrane have unequal concentrations of some solute. If, for example, two sodium chloride solutions of unequal concentration are separated by a semipermeable membrane, water will flow through the membrane from the less concentrated solution into the more concentrated solution. This process tends to bring about an equalization of the two concentrations. Wolf (1958) has stated that a solution does not have any osmotic pressure in itself. He writes: "*What is called the osmotic pressure denotes the hydrostatic pressure excess which would be produced in a solution if a semipermeable membrane (one permitting passage of solvent but not solute particles), rather than a permeable membrane, separated that solution in a manometric chamber of constant volume from its solvent, the latter at constant pressure.*"

Osmotic pressure is measured by freezing point depression, vapor pressure lowering, or boiling point elevation. We shall be less concerned with osmotic pressure per se than with *effective osmotic*

pressure, which refers to the part of the total osmotic pressure of a solution that governs the tendency of the solvent to pass across a boundary or membrane. The effective osmotic pressure is the product of the total osmotic pressure of a solution and the ratio of the number of dissolved particles which do not permeate the membrane to the total number of particles in the solution. An equivalent term for effective osmotic pressure is *tonicity*.

A practical example may clarify these relationships. If we consider a cell suspended in a solution of sodium chloride of such a concentration that there is no net fluid transmission across the membrane, we have an *isotonic* solution; there is no change in cellular volume because the intracellular and extracellular fluids have the same osmotic pressure. If we add sodium choride to the extracellular fluid (i.e., the medium in which our cell lives), we have created a *hypertonic* solution; water begins to move out of the cell, and cell volume decreases. Conversely, if we withdraw sodium chloride from the extracellular fluid to a point at which the concentration of sodium chloride is actually higher inside the cell than it is outside, we have a *hypotonic* extracellular environment; fluid then flows into the cell, thereby increasing its volume. If, on the other hand, we add urea to the extracellular fluid, no change in effective osmotic pressure or tonicity is produced because the cell membrane is permeable to urea. However, we *have* changed total osmotic pressure as measured by standard freezing point or vapor pressure measurements. (Actually, there are brief transient changes in effective osmotic pressure even in this instance which arise while the equilibrium is being re-established between the two solutions. Because the solute [urea] passes through the cell membrane fairly rapidly, we can disregard this temporary shift in effective osmotic pressure.)

Directly related to these considerations is the distinction between absolute and relative hydration or dehydration. When the total body fluids fall below the normal level (i.e., when a condition of negative water balance exists), the organism is said to be in a state of *absolute dehydration*. *Relative dehydration*, on the other hand, refers to a deficit of water in relation to the concentration of certain extracellular electrolytes, especially sodium. If we withdraw one liter of water from an organism, a state of absolute dehydration exists. If the withdrawn fluid contains normal concentrations of electrolytes, no relative dehydration is created because the relative concentration of these agents remains constant. If we add sodium chloride to the extracellular fluids without adding a proportional amount of water, we have created a relative dehydration without any disturbance of the absolute level of hydration.

Relative dehydration (i.e., an increase in the concentration of electrolytes in the extracellular fluid) produces hypertonicity with respect to the intracellular fluids and a consequent change in effective osmotic pressure. This pressure gradient results in the movement of water from the cells into the interstitial spaces with a consequent reduction in cell volume. Relative hydration produces the opposite effect. Adding water to the extracellular fluid dilutes the electrolyte concentration (hypotonicity) and causes a shift in the effective osmotic pressure so that water moves into the cells and increases cellular volume. We shall see later how these factors may affect the regulation of fluid intake and thirst.

HISTORICAL CONSIDERATIONS

Scientific interest in the regulation of water intake and thirst dates back several hundred years to the physiological research centers which began to flourish at European universities during the eighteenth century. As early as 1821, Rullier was able to summarize a considerable research literature relevant to the "urge to drink" and point to a bewildering variety of theoretical interpretations of these data. Magendie, one of the great pioneers of French physiology, suggested in 1822 that thirst should be considered an "instinctive

sentiment" which "does not admit of any explanation"; however, the majority of physiological scientists of this era disagreed with his pessimistic views, and experimental as well as theoretical interest continued unabated. Soon three fairly distinct groups of theoretical notions emerged. These have survived relatively unchanged.

Most of the physiological workers in the field of dipsology assumed that the regulation of water intake and thirst was directly and causally related to the local sensations that normally accompany thirst in man. Although these local-origin theories remained quite influential over the years, many dissenters assigned the origin of thirst to a general state of the organism, e.g., dehydration of the body tissues. Still others held that the regulation of thirst was primarily, if not exclusively, a function of the central nervous system. Some of the earlier theories proposed, as we shall see, that more than one type of control mechanism might be involved in the regulation of something as complicated and important as the organism's fluid balance. Modern thought is tending more and more in this direction. It may be informative to follow the historical development of these ideas separately in our subsequent discussion.

"Local" Theories

Nearly all prescientific attempts to account for the urge to drink assumed that water intake and thirst were directly related to specific sensations. They differed with respect to the probable cause and locus of these sensations. Perhaps the oldest and certainly most persistent and popular notion is credited to Hippocrates (see Ludeman, 1745). According to this view, thirst refers directly to the sensations that arise from the mouth and throat when the buccal mucosa becomes dry and parched. This notion stirred up considerable interest in the seventeenth century (see Tancredi, 1607) and became widely accepted after it was restated by Haller (1747) and Jessen (1751). Because this "dry-mouth" theory has continued to enjoy great popularity (Bouffard, 1805; Blumenbach, 1820; Weber, 1846; Luciani, 1906; Cannon, 1911, 1912, 1918, 1919, 1929, 1933, 1934; Gregersen, 1932a, b), we might look at Haller's statement of this theory:

> Thirst is seated in the tongue, fauces, oesophagus, and stomach. For whenever these very sensible parts, which are constantly and naturally moistened by mucous and salival juices, grow dry from a deficiency of those or the like humors, or are irritated by a redundancy of muriatic or alkalescent salts here lodged, there

arises a sense much more intolerable than the former (hunger), as thirst is more dangerous; whose uneasy sense continues until the proportion of diluting water in the blood, being recruited, restores the necessary moisture and free secretion required in the parts before mentioned. From hence we learn, why thirst attends labour, which exhales a greater proportion of the water perspiration; and why it is a symptom of fevers where there is an obstruction of the exhaling vessels belonging to the tongue and fauces; why simple water is less efficacious in abating thirst, which yields nevertheless easily to some acid liquors, that not only moisten and render fluid, but also, by their mild irritation of the tongue and mouth, provoke forward the humours, and at the same time correct their putrid tendency. (See English translation, 1779.)

The earlier statements of this theory were based entirely on natural observation. Experimental interest in this problem arose around the middle of the nineteenth century, and a large number of relevant studies were soon conducted. Although the available research tools were crude by modern standards (a fact which has undoubtedly contributed to the often contradictory results), many ingenious techniques were developed by early experimenters to prove or disprove this hypothesis. It would be far beyond the scope of our discussion to treat this material in any detail, but it may be worthwhile to look at some of the studies whose results have largely determined the direction of more recent work.

Bidder and Schmidt (1852) argued that the moisture of the oral-pharyngeal mucosa was most directly influenced by the secretion of saliva and that an animal would drink continually if its salivary flow were interrupted. In a test of this hypothesis, the salivary ducts of dogs were tied off. It was found that animals became severely hyperdipsic when they were forced to breathe through the mouth. Fehr (1862), on the other hand, found that the complete removal of the salivary glands had no effect on total water intake. He attributed the earlier findings to an abnormal condition of the buccal mucosa which induced the animal to drink, not because it was thirsty but because the continuous ingestion of liquids removed the *painful* sensations of a parched throat.

Claude Bernard approached this problem in 1855 by dividing the parotid ducts of a hare and inserting parotid fistulae. Although the animal consumed more water than was normal, Bernard did not attribute this finding to local dryness of the mouth; rather, he suggested that the cause of hyperdipsia was a general loss of body water through the parotid fistulae. To prove his argument against a dry-mouth theory, Bernard prepared horses with esophageal fistulae so that water would pass through the mouth and throat but would never actually reach the stomach. He found that such animals drank incessantly and stopped only when exhausted. If the cannulae were closed off, allowing water to enter the digestive tract, the hyperdipsia vanished as soon as the animal had consumed a normal quantity of water. These results were replicated in dogs, and Bernard concluded that his findings could not be explained by a dry-mouth theory of thirst, for the oral and pharyngeal mucosa was almost continually bathed in water.

Schiff (1867) reached similar conclusions following the observation that only temporary relief from thirst was obtained by wetting the throat of a human subject. Although the mouth and throat were maintained in a moist state, thirst sensations returned and persisted. Schiff proposed that rinsing the mouth might merely relieve painful dryness and, hence, *seem* to alleviate thirst. Von Voit (1881) reported that wetting the mouth may relieve thirst at least temporarily in some situations but not in others. He consequently proposed that there may be two types of thirst, one relieved by local wetting and the other not. Lepidi-Chioti and Fubini (1885) found that brushing the back of the mouth with water had very little effect on thirst sensations in human subjects. They did report, however, that the application of cocaine (a local anesthetic which presumably prevented the elaboration of local sensory impulses) reliably relieved thirst for 15 to 35 min. Valenti (1909, 1910) replicated these experiments in dogs and found that the animals deprived of water for many days would temporarily refuse to drink following the local application of cocaine to their mouths.

The importance of sensory factors was questioned by Longet (1868), who sectioned the glossopharyngeal and lingual nerves in an attempt to reduce or eliminate the afferent connections from the oral cavity, pharynx, and esophagus. His dogs were found to consume normal amounts of water, and Longet concluded that these results could not be reconciled with a dry-mouth interpretation, even though some afferent innervation (the vagus and trigeminal nerves) remained intact in his preparation. Removal of a large proportion of the sensory feedback should, indeed, have at least reduced thirst and consequent water intake.

In spite of the predominantly negative results obtained in these early studies, there remained an almost religious belief in the importance of sensory mechanisms. Many investigators felt that their failure to obtain substantiating evidence was caused by faulty or insufficient experimental procedure or perhaps lack of control over some important variables. Few would admit that the sensations preceding water intake in man might not, in fact, be essential to the regulation of thirst.

Before we consider the historical development of the general and central theories of thirst, it should be mentioned that the specific "seat" of thirst has been assigned to many portions of the body by some of the earlier writers. Tancredi (1607) for instance, credits Aristotle with the notion that thirst sensations arise from the viscera; such a view was shared more recently by Kanter (1953) and Linazàsoro et al. (1954), who investigated the functions of the kidney. Galen hypothesized that thirst sensations might arise from the heart and lungs. Weber (1846) even suggested that one might feel thirst in the eyes if the conjunctives were not moistened by constant lachrymal secretion.

General Theories

We have already mentioned that until quite recently the vast majority of theoretical thought and experimental study was devoted to various sensory components of the dry-mouth theory of thirst. The idea that more general conditions of the organism might contribute to the regulation of water intake consequently gained little support; however, some of the great physiologists of the late eighteenth century proposed some interesting ideas.

Erasmus Darwin (1801) suggested that general dehydration of the body tends to thicken the blood, which then irritates special receptors in the mucosa of the mouth and throat and gives rise to the sensation of thirst. Dumas (1803) independently arrived at a similar hypothesis. He believed, however, that thick blood irritated some part of the central nervous system, which in turn was responsible for the dryness of the mouth and throat. Deneufbourg (1813) used Darwin's suggestions to draw a clear distinction between the "seat" and the "origin" of thirst. The urge to drink, he believed, was a direct correlate of sensations that arise from the mouth and throat. However, the origin of thirst was to be found in general body dehydration, which thickened the blood and, hence, irritated the sensory receptors of the buccal

cavity. He pointed out that under some conditions the sensory receptors of the mouth may become irritated even when there is no general dehydration. The effect of spicy foods would be a relevant example. Conversely, there are pathological conditions in which the desire to drink is not sufficient to maintain adequate hydration. Beaumont (1833) extended these notions by relating them to the general metabolic requirements of the body. He argued that food must be ingested to sustain the bodily processes that maintain life. Once ingested, the nutrients must be assimilated and distributed to every cell of the organism. This, Beaumont argued, can only be accomplished by the circulatory system. However, the blood can act as a carrier of nutrient substances only as long as it is itself fluid. Water deprivation decreases the amount of fluid available and increases the viscosity of the blood. When the concentration of solids becomes too great, sensory receptors in the mouth and throat are activated and then mediate the feeling or sensation of thirst, thus directing the organism toward water.

These ideas come quite close to some of our modern conceptions of the regulation of thirst and have been influential in determining the research interests of many workers of the present. Almost 100 years elapsed between Darwin's and Dumas' papers before serious and sustained interest was turned toward their notions. This lapse is surprising in view of the fact that at least some empirical confirmation of these hypotheses became available early in the nineteenth century. Rullier (1821) cites Orfilia's findings that blood serum concentration was decreased by water deprivation and that thirst could be relieved by intravenous injections of water. The antidipsic properties of intravenously injected water were well known to the physiologists and medical practitioners of the nineteenth century (Bernard, 1856; Ludwig, 1861; Schiff, 1867). We shall pursue these notions further in our discussion of modern general theories.

Central Theories

The physiological investigations of the eighteenth and nineteenth centuries are generally characterized by a heavy emphasis on the peripheral nervous system and particularly the sensory mechanisms. In no area of study was this emphasis more pronounced and stifling to theoretical thought than in research relating to thirst. Central mechanisms remained almost entirely neglected until the middle of this century. Theoretical proposals studiously avoided references to any central regulation of thirst. Even nonsensory peripheral mechanisms, as we have seen, were invoked only to relate the primary sensory factors to the needs of the organism. It is perhaps not remarkable, in view of this history, that significant advances have only recently been made. Before we leave this topic, mention should be made of a few "voices in the wilderness" who pointed out that some regulatory systems might be located in the central nervous system. We have already mentioned Dumas' (1803) theory which had allotted some mediary role to the brain. Callenfels (1824) discussed the possible role of the central nervous system in the perception of thirst, but he assigned to it only the role of a receiving area for the thirst sensations, which he believed to be generated in the mouth. Bonnier (1914) proposed that the olfactory lobe might contain a "hydrostatic" center, based on the clinical observation that edema disappeared following nasal cautery. We shall see later that until quite recently only few and purely speculative attempts suggested the possible locus of central nervous system integration.

PERIPHERAL-SENSORY THEORIES OF THIRST

Historically, the principal and most widely accepted theory of thirst attributed the regulation of water intake to a relative dryness of the mucosa of the mouth and throat. This notion dates back to the philosophers of ancient Greece and has not entirely lost its appeal even today. Many psychological theories of motivation still rely on variations in the intensity of sensory drive stimulation. Cannon's (1934) forceful restatement of this theory still graces most of our introductory texts. Regrettably, the texts omit mention of the well-established fact that the theory is almost certainly in error. It is one of the vagaries of scientific thought that such a notion should have survived at all, in view of the literally hundreds of research publications which have demonstrated its insufficiency. So as not to perpetuate this myth, it may be worthwhile to examine Cannon's proposal in some detail and to discuss some of the more recent and presumably better-controlled evidence which clearly demonstrates that local sensations are not essential to the regulation of thirst.

The Dry-Mouth Theory

Cannon (1918, 1919, 1929, 1933, 1934) stated that thirst is a specific *sensation* that arises from receptors located in the oral cavity and pharynx, especially in the root of the tongue. These receptors were believed to be sensitive to changes in the moisture content of the mucosa. According to this view, thirst is not a general sense. When the organism incurs a water deficit, the viscosity of the blood is kept constant by the withdrawal of fluid reserves from the tissues (notice the departure from earlier theories). The most important store of water are the salivary glands; saliva is over 97% water. When enough water has been withdrawn from these glands, they can no longer secrete enough saliva to maintain a comfortable level of moisture in the throat and oral cavity. The resultant dryness produces the sensation of burning; this is recognized as thirst and eventually leads to the search for and ingestion of water, thereby restoring the organism's water balance. Cannon suggested that man never complains of a general feeling of thirst or bodily dehydration but of a parched and burning throat. On a purely introspective level, this is probably quite true under normal circumstances. Interest in a dry-mouth theory has persisted largely because of this apparent face validity. When we look at the research literature, however, this eminently sensible explanation does not appear to be correct.

The Contribution of the Salivary Glands

It is quite true that the general fluid balance of the organism exerts a pronounced effect on the activity of the salivary glands. Gregersen (1931) found that dogs maintained in a hot environment pant almost continually and secrete large quantities of saliva. This tends to keep the buccal mucosa moist. Salivary flow begins to decrease soon, however, and is down to almost 50% of normal after a 24-hr period of water deprivation. The secretory activity of the salivary glands continues to drop when deprivation is continued and reaches about 20% of normal after 72 hr of deprivation. At this point the oral-pharyngeal mucosa begins to show signs of severe dryness. Still more directly in support of Cannon's theory is the finding that blood plasma volume correlates quite highly with the rate of salivary flow (Gregersen and Bullock, 1933). Holmes and Gregersen (1947) have demonstrated that intravenous injections of a 5% sodium chloride solution produce a significant increase in blood volume but a concomitant decrease in salivation. Intense thirst is also produced. These results are at variance with earlier findings (Smith, 1935) which had shown that the injection of sodium chloride solutions

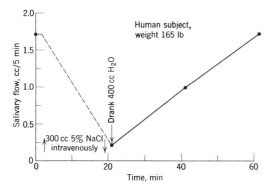

Fig. 7.5 Reduction of salivary flow after intravenous injection of 300 cc 5% NaCl and the return to control values after the drinking of water. (From Holmes and Gregersen, 1947.)

directly into the stomach did *not* induce consistent changes in salivary flow, although human subjects reported strong thirst sensations almost immediately after the treatment.

Adolph et al. (1947) carefully quantified the relation between salivary flow and relative water deficit in man and suggested that rate of salivation may be a useful objective measure of thirst. It was found that rate of salivary flow is a nearly linear function of general bodily fluid content. They reported a correlation of -0.74 between salivary flow and water deficit and demonstrated that a fluid deficit of approximately 8% of body weight causes a nearly complete cessation of salivation. Water deficits of 5% or less of total body weight invariably produce strong thirst sensations.

These and similar studies indicate that the secretion of saliva is in fact *correlated* with the organism's fluid balance and inversely related to its need for water. However, although rate of salivary flow may be a useful, if impractical, measure of thirst under normal conditions, this does not prove that thirst is *causally* related to salivary flow or the resultant dryness of the mouth. In fact, there is considerable evidence to question such an interpretation. Weir et al. reported as early as 1922 that intravenous injections of pilocarpine (a cholinomimetic agent that induces salivation) did not relieve thirst sensations in patients suffering from diabetes insipidus, in spite of the fact that salivary flow was greatly enhanced. Similar results have been obtained with normal subjects. Adolph et al. (1947) found that the administration of pilocarpine did not alleviate thirst sensations in severely dehydrated subjects. The desire to drink (and actual water

intake) appeared totally unaffected by the profuse salivation induced by pilocarpine treatment. The results of these carefully controlled experiments suggest that earlier studies (Pack, 1923) reporting a decreased water intake following the injection of pilocarpine may have failed to control for some of the many side effects that this drug is known to produce. Side effects may also account for such controversial findings as Kleitman's (1927) report of *increased* water consumption following the subcutaneous injection of pilocarpine in dogs.

That salivary flow is not an essential determinant of thirst and water intake is demonstrated still more convincingly in experiments concerned with the results of complete removal of the salivary glands. Montgomery (1931a, b) extirpated all six salivary glands and two orbital glands in dogs. No postoperative change in daily water consumption occurred. The animals reacted to pilocarpine precisely as before the operation. This observation suggests that the salivary glands do not play a necessary role in the regulation of the organism's fluid balance. Whatever effect pilocarpine might exert appears to be independent of the drug's action on the salivary glands.

The experiments were replicated by Gregersen and Cannon (1932); they argued that Montgomery's surgical techniques may have left some secretory organs intact, since she reported that the oral cavity of her animals did not dry out completely after the operation. In this replication the parotid duct was tied off, and the salivary and orbital glands were completely removed. Gregersen and Cannon found that this procedure did affect the total water consumption of dogs maintained in a warm environment. After several hours of panting, the operated animals consumed significantly more water than their unoperated controls, and the authors concluded that Montgomery's experiment had not been a fair test of Cannon's hypothesis. It seems more likely, however, that the shoe is on the other foot. Cannon's animals did not show an effect under normal conditions, a fact which in itself argues strongly against an essential contribution of this factor. Furthermore, the radical surgery of this replication may have increased general body temperature. Since heat loss in the dog is largely dependent on evaporation from the mucous membranes of the mouth and throat, the operated animals may actually have incurred a greater fluid loss than their controls, i.e., may have been rendered more thirsty.

Such an interpretation is supported by

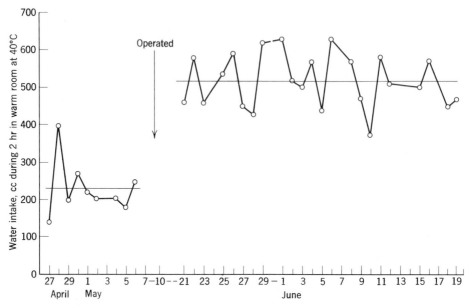

Fig. 7.6 Daily observations on a dog, showing the amount of water taken during 2 hr in a warm room (40°C) before and after exclusion of the salivary flow. (From Gregersen and Cannon, 1932.)

Steggerda (1939, 1941; Austin and Steggerda, 1936) in a report of the drinking habits of a human subject congenitally lacking all salivary glands. Although this person had learned to drink somewhat more frequently than normal controls (to relieve the dryness of his throat), there appeared to be no significant difference in total daily fluid intake. A similar case history has been reported by Zaus (1936). Further evidence against a local theory of thirst comes from experiments on the effect of partial or nearly complete deafferentation of the oral and pharyngeal tissue. Studies in this area have generally shown

little or no disturbance of water intake. Bellows and Van Wagenen (1939), for example, found that drinking behavior appeared totally unaffected by bilateral transections of the trigeminal nerve. The interruption of the glossopharyngeal and chorda tympani nerves was similarly without effect on water intake.

The Role of Local Sensory Receptors

Some of the more recent experiments leave little doubt that salivation does not play an essential role in the regulation of water intake. This fact, by itself, is not an adequate refutation of the

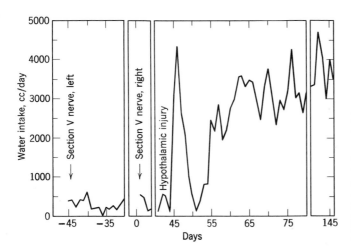

Fig. 7.7 Daily voluntary water intakes of a dog before and after bilateral division of the trigemini. On day 0 denervation was complete. On day 45 the tuber cinereum was cauterized. Typical diabetes insipidus followed: temporary phase, days 45 to 50 inclusive; remission; permanent phase, began day 53 and reached steady stage day 63. (From Bellows and Van Wagenen, 1939.)

dry-mouth theory, since the relative moisture of the mucous membranes of the mouth is not exclusively determined by the rate of salivary flow. However, the nonessential nature of the sensory factors is shown rather conclusively in experiments demonstrating continued thirst in spite of artificial wetting of the mouth and throat.

We have already mentioned several earlier investigations in this field (Bernard, 1856; Schiff, 1867; von Voit, 1881), which appeared to have settled this matter quite conclusively. Because the objection may be raised that these studies were performed almost a century ago and were probably lacking in experimental control and design, we might look briefly at some more recent replications of this work. Perhaps the most impressive of the early work was that of Bernard, who demonstrated that horses and dogs would drink almost incessantly when water was allowed to flow through the mouth and throat but not to reach the stomach. These experiments were replicated in principle by Bellows (1939), who obtained entirely comparable results and supported Bernard's conclusions. Several other experiments have found that moistening of the mouth does not appear to affect water intake. Bruce (1937) failed to observe any effects in the rat, and Andersson (1957) reports that drinking elicited by electrical stimulation of the hypothalamus in goats continues even when the mouth of the animal is continually bathed in water.

When we consider the enormous quantities of water that were sham-drunk in Bernard's and Bellow's studies, Cannon's interpretations of these findings do not appear very convincing. Cannon argued that the animals finally stopped drinking, not because they were exhausted but because they were actually satiated. Cannon believed that this satiation might be relatively brief because the persisting dehydration of the organism could cause a rapid withdrawal of water from the tissues of the mouth and throat, thereby reestablishing local dryness and thirst. Such an interpretation overlooks the fact that animals with esophageal fistulae drink much more than would normally be required to restore their fluid balance *before stopping for the first time.*

Still another group of findings fails to support the hypothesis that local sensory receptors may make essential contributions toward a regulation of thirst. Although some of the earlier experiments (Lepidi-Chioti and Fubini, 1885; Valenti, 1909, 1910) had suggested that anesthetization of the mouth and throat may significantly reduce or

temporarily inhibit thirst, later experiments and clinical studies have not replicated this finding. Leschke (1918) reports that novocainization of the throat does not alleviate or prevent the thirst which is elicited by intravenous injections of sodium chloride solutions. Rowntree (1922) found that the local application of cocaine fails to decrease the abnormal water intake of diabetes insipidus patients. Similar results have been published by Allison and Critchley (1943).

Adolph et al. (1954) reported that procainization of the mouth and throat slightly reduced the water intake of deprived rats, but also indicated that the animals continued to discriminate between water, sodium chloride solutions, and urea. The depression of water intake was temporary and not severe enough to support Cannon's theory. Wolf (1950) followed up Leschke's studies on the effects of intravenously administered sodium chloride solutions. He reported that his subjects complained of a dry throat long before thirst (i.e., the desire for water) became noticeable. The local sensation of dryness vanished almost immediately following the injection of glucose, but the desire for water persisted much longer. Wolf concluded that sensations of local dryness do not appear to be causally related to the desire to ingest water.

Cannon's dry-mouth theory is not tenable in view of the all but consistently negative research literature. His 1918 suggestion that organisms might learn to be thirsty even when the primary stimuli arising from the mouth and throat are not present does not seem to be a very useful one, although it would explain some of the negative literature. He proposed that all data derived from studies of salivary gland extirpation, drug effects on salivation, and moistening of the mouth did not disprove his hypothesis, since thirst might become conditioned to the presence of water. However, this suggestion overlooks the fact that animals on *ad libitum* watering schedules should, according to this theory, drink incessantly.

Conditioning has been invoked by other investigators in an effort to reconcile contradictory findings. One interesting suggestion was made by Wolf in 1950 and 1958. He proposed that the "osmoreceptors" of the body (i.e., tissues that may signal the organism's need for water) and the tissues of the mouth and throat undergo similar changes as the body dehydrates. Stimuli arising from these osmoreceptors might be considered unconditioned stimuli for thirst, whereas the concurrent sensations arising from the mouth and throat might be viewed as conditioned stimuli. The unconditioned response in this instance is the consumption of water. This scheme could explain why an organism ingests water, in the absence of general bodily dehydration or water need, as soon as the tissues of the mouth become dry or irritated.

Although this notion is largely speculative, it might resolve many of the difficulties encountered by traditional theories of thirst. For instance, all theories of thirst have found it difficult to explain why a relatively wet anchovy should induce thirst in an organism that is in perfect water balance. Neither local dryness nor general tissue dehydration can be invoked. However, one might assume that the local osmotic changes may act as a conditioned stimulus for thirst, since similar osmotic changes are normally associated with a parallel dehydration of the osmoreceptors. The rapid recovery from such thirst, even when no water is ingested, indicates the local nature of the stimulation (Wolf, 1958). This hypothesis could, of course, also account for drinking in the absence of local dryness or local sensations. Such intake would then simply be a manifestation of the unconditioned reflex. We must remember, however, that this notion is a purely *post hoc* explanation of troublesome data, and much remains to be done before we can legitimately invoke this hypothesis to bolster some other theory.

The Role of Muscular Contractions

Before we leave the discussion of peripheral factors in thirst, one last group of experiments should be mentioned. Cannon's local-dryness theory is conceptually related to the local-origin theories of hunger that were in vogue about the turn of the century. These theories suggested that hunger referred directly to sensations arising from the stomach during its periodic contractions.

Mueller (1919, 1920) was very much impressed with the evidence that seemed to relate hunger to such contractions and proposed a directly comparable theory of thirst. He succeeded in recording periodic contractions from the esophageal musculature in dogs, and suggested that thirst might be directly related to sensations arising from stretch receptors in the pharyngeal and esophageal muscles. This theory has never attracted much attention, partly, no doubt, because of the prevalent preoccupation with variations of the dry-mouth theory. It received its death blow in 1946 when Ladell demonstrated that the esophageal contractions recorded by Mueller were not

related to thirst, but rather seemed to be produced directly by irritation from the recording balloon. Ladell found that the contractions disappeared completely, even in thirsty subjects, if sufficient time was allowed for adaptation to the increased esophageal pressure. Even when contractions were present, there appeared to be no consistent correlation between thirst sensations (as reported by human subjects) and muscular activity.

Summary

The preceding sections are best summarized by the statement that the sensory correlates of thirst do not play a critical role in the regulation of water intake. It is safe to conclude from the evidence that local sensations contribute only in a limited fashion to the regulation of thirst under ordinary conditions.

Salivary flow seems to be positively correlated with general tissue dehydration and water need and may be useful as a measure of thirst under normal conditions. However, it is clear that thirst can exist when salivary flow is adequate. Experimental interference with salivation does not elicit thirst. Drugs that increase salivary flow do not reduce thirst reliably and significantly, and continual wetting of the mouth and throat provides little or no respite for the thirsty. Conversely, the congenital absence or surgical removal of the salivary apparatus does not appear to interfere with the normal regulation of water intake.

Anesthetization of the oral and pharyngeal mucosa appears to produce only minor effects on thirst. The contradictory results in this field suggest that the effects obtained with this technique may not be due to the elimination of sensory impulses from the mouth and throat, but, rather, to a more direct interference with muscular apparatus for swallowing. The nonessentiality of the sensory feedback from the mouth and throat is demonstrated convincingly in experiments showing that complete or partial deafferentation does not seem to interfere at all with the regulation of fluid intake.

Just what role the local sensations do play in the intact organism is not very clear. It is conceivable that Wolf's conditioning theory may help us to understand the function of this mechanism, but further data are needed before we can consider it to be more than an interesting suggestion.

As a comprehensive explanation of thirst, Cannon's dry-mouth theory is erroneous. More is involved in the regulation of the organism's fluid balance than merely sensory feedback from the mouth and throat.

GENERAL THEORIES

Just what constitutes a "general" theory of thirst has been the subject of much heated debate in the past 50 years (see Wolf, 1958). The problem is complicated. Many proponents of dry-mouth or central theories have acknowledged that local sensory or central neural mechanisms must in some fashion reflect a "general" state of the organism and must "regulate" thirst in accordance with the overall water needs of the body. Consequently, there is considerable overlap between some theoretical positions, and it is often difficult to classify a given hypothesis within the proposed framework of peripheral, general, and central notions. Under the heading of a general theory, notions relating the regulation of thirst *principally* to osmometric factors of the effects of general cellular dehydration will be discussed. It will become obvious in the course of this discussion that these general changes must influence thirst via central and/or peripheral nervous mechanisms. In themselves the general theories cannot explain thirst any better than the purely peripheral notions of Haller and Cannon.

Osmosis

A brief review of the fundamental mechanics of osmosis is necessary for much of the following discussion. The total body fluids can be divided into three main fluid systems: (1) *cellular fluid* refers to the water (plus solutes) found inside the cells of the body; (2) *interstitial fluid* is found between the cells of the body and serves as a nutrient medium for them; and (3) *blood* is confined to the vascular system. The fact that the blood contains blood cells, platelets, and other solid substances can be ignored here; attention will be restricted to its fluid part or plasma.

When we talk about the internal environment, or *milieu interne* of Claude Bernard, we are referring to the interstitial fluids that must be maintained in a stable, relatively constant state (or homeostasis) if the organism is to function normally and survive. Since there is a constant interchange among the fluid compartments of the body, the distinction between changes that affect one or the other portion of the total fluid volume is unnecessary. Compensatory adjustments take place in all of them. Generally, a distinction is made between *intracellular* fluids and *extracellular* fluids (interstitial water and serum). The cellular membrane provides a selectively permeable bar-

rier between these fluid compartments; the membrane generally allows water to pass freely in both directions, but may slow or prevent the passage of dissolved substances found either inside or outside the cell.

Whenever a semipermeable membrane separates two solutions of unequal concentrations, solvent will tend to move from the region of lower solute concentration into the region of higher solute concentration in an effort to establish an equilibrium between the two solutions. To visualize this situation, imagine a chamber separated into two compartments by a partition that allows water molecules to pass freely but does not permit the passage of some large molecules. If we now place pure water into one compartment and the same amount of water plus some salt into the other, the net result will be that water passes into the compartment containing the salt solution. When this system reaches equilibrium, the chambers will contain unequal volumes, and the pressure on the partition is the osmotic pressure of the solution.

Such transport of water can be demonstrated in the organism by injecting a sodium chloride solution of higher concentration than that found normally in the body (i.e., a hypertonic solution) into the abdominal cavity. Osmotic pressure gradients cause water to pass from the intracellular compartments into the abdominal cavity. If the abdominal cavity is drained after some delay, the recovered fluid will be considerably diluted (less concentrated) and greatly increased in volume.

Similar processes are constantly taking place throughout the organism in response to a constantly changing total water level. As water is lost through urinary excretion or perspiration, osmotic pressure gradients attempt to maintain equal concentrations of extra- and intracellular fluids. Unless water is added to the system (by drinking), the osmotic pressure increases, and eventually a point is reached where the osmotic transport system breaks down.

Before discussing how osmotic pressure differences, the resultant movement of water, or the consequent change in cell volume and size may affect the regulation of thirst, a careful distinction should be made between osmotic transport and active transport which involves the transport of ions against an electrochemical gradient. Some cells (for instance, muscle and nerve) are able to maintain a concentration of sodium ions much lower inside the cell membrane than outside. Only when such a cell is irritated does a movement of sodium ions take place. In order to recover excitability, the cell must re-establish the original distribution of ions within a very short time. This active transport of ions across a membrane and the maintenance of unequal concentrations in the face of osmotic pressure gradients require metabolic energy and must not be confused with the topic of our discussion.

Osmometric Theories

Some of the early theories of thirst (Darwin, 1801; Dumas, 1803; Deneufbourg, 1813; Beaumont, 1833) suggested that dehydration might increase the viscosity of the blood. This notion was designed to explain only why the primary stimulus for thirst (local dryness of the mouth) should reflect the organism's need for water; however, it provided the important suggestion that the relative concentration of some solute in the body fluids might be involved in the translation of water need to thirst.

This theory has become very influential in the past 50 years, and why its importance escaped notice for nearly a century is curious. When the nineteenth-century literature is scrutinized, it becomes obvious that early theorists had little or no experimental data to support such an idea; only indirect and circumstantial corroboration was available until the pioneering work of Mayer (1900a, b) and Wettendorff (1901) was published around the turn of the century.

Mayer (1900a, b) reported that water deprivation results in a pronounced increase in the osmotic pressure of the blood (suggesting a rise in electrolyte concentration), and that the osmotic pressure of venous blood, taken from the walls of the stomach, rose sharply after hypertonic solutions were injected into the stomach. Mayer concluded from these results that thirst may be directly related to variations in the osmotic pressure of the blood. According to this hypothesis, the blood becomes hypertonic as a result of general dehydration. The increased concentration of solutes irritates or stimulates receptors in the walls of the blood vessels. Mayer knew that the blood vessels are under the neural control of vasomotor centers in the bulbar brainstem. He proposed therefore that impulses from these receptors might be transmitted to the bulbar centers and thus produce vasodilatation and elevated blood pressure. These peripheral changes, in turn, were believed to excite receptors in the mouth and throat to give rise to the conscious sensation of thirst. In this hypothesis local sensory factors retain an essential role in translating bodily need

into "conscious awareness" and eventually behavior. The origin of thirst is here ascribed to general osmotic gradients which are directly related to the organism's water need.

Mayer's theoretical interpretations are the foundation of many recent experimental investigations and hypotheses which attempt to relate the regulation of thirst directly to variations in the concentration of some electrolyte. Wettendorff's (1901) studies, on the other hand, have given rise to a different interpretation. Wettendorff observed that the osmotic pressure of the blood did in fact change quite dramatically with prolonged water deprivation, but he reported that significant differences in osmotic pressure occurred only after 24 hr of deprivation. Since the body loses large quantities of water during the first day of deprivation, Wettendorff argued that the osmolarity of the blood must be maintained at the expense of intracellular fluids that osmose into the blood. Only when the stores of intracellular water become exhausted do we see a change in the osmolarity of the blood itself. Wettendorff argued that thirst cannot be regulated by osmotic pressure gradients of the blood, as Mayer had suggested, since nearly all animals and man replenish their water level (and, hence, may be said to be thirsty) long before the intracellular water stores are exhausted and noticeable differences in the osmolarity of the blood can be recorded. Wettendorff's findings have been replicated in recent experiments (Lifson, 1944; Wolf and Eddy, 1957; and Rubini et al., 1956), and one cannot argue that his results may have been influenced by inadequate recording techniques.

Wettendorff hypothesized that thirst might be directly related to progressive dehydration of cells that lose water and increase the concentration of solutes as the absolute water balance of the organism becomes negative. He further proposed that all cells might contain osmoreceptors which are sensitive to the resultant deflation of the cell and signal to some coordinating center in the brain that the organism is in need of water. According to this view, thirst is of general origin. Wettendorff suggested that all cells of the body contribute to this regulation, and that the local dryness of the mouth is merely one symptom of thirst.

Wettendorff's theory still plays an important role in our thinking, although one major modification has become necessary. According to his views, the intensity of thirst should be directly correlated with the neural feedback from all cells in the organism. One would have to predict, therefore, that the removal of part of this feedback should reduce or eliminate thirst. It was actually known at the time of Wettendorff's writing that this is not true. Lower animals and man survive and do not show a reduced desire for water when all sensory feedback from the entire body except the head, neck, and shoulders is eliminated. Furthermore, even the most refined anatomical and neurophysiological techniques have failed to suggest special end organs which might serve the role of Wettendorff's osmoreceptor. If cellular dehydration is, in fact, the critical event in the regulation of thirst, it must involve a special group of cells, and it is believed today that this osmoreceptor function may be served by some neural elements in the brain. (This matter will be discussed in more detail when central mechanisms are considered later.) The relative level of hydration of these cells presumably reflects general cellular water levels; it thus can serve as the metering device which either directly or indirectly (via other central nervous system mechanisms) regulates thirst and drinking behavior.

We shall see how influential the findings of Mayer and Wettendorff have been in determining the experimental and theoretical efforts of recent workers in this field. In fact, we still are not quite sure whether thirst is most directly related to cellular deformation produced by dehydration or to varying concentrations of some electrolyte in the extracellular or intracellular fluids.

In 1926, Nonnenbruch reported some interesting observations which suggested that cellular dehydration was not a sufficient stimulus for thirst, contrary to Wettendorff's theory. Nonnenbruch found that animals maintained on a salt-deficient diet did not react like normal animals to prolonged water deprivation. Few overt signs of thirst were displayed. Water intake was relatively low when the animals were returned to an *ad libitum* watering schedule, in spite of the fact that cellular dehydration certainly occurred. He concluded that thirst was regulated primarily by changing osmotic concentrations of body fluids, as Mayer had suggested earlier, and that the resultant dehydration of the cells had no essential regulatory function.

Nonnenbruch's findings gave impetus to several experimental investigations of the role of extracellular salts in the regulation of water intake and thirst. Perhaps the most frequently cited study is Arden's (1934) clinical study which showed that the oral administration of 20 grams of sodium chloride (diluted in 200 cc of water) pro-

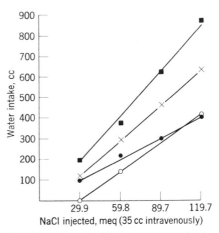

Fig. 7.8 Linear relationship between water intake and amount of NaCl (5, 10, 15, and 20% solution) injected in normal dogs. Note the individual variations in drinking response to the same amount of salt. (From Holmes and Gregersen, 1950a.)

duced intense thirst within 30 min. Thirst sensations increased over the following 2-hr period, salivation ceased entirely, and the mouth became parched and dry. The most interesting aspect of this study, however, is that thirst *disappeared* entirely after 7 hr although no water was consumed. Arden unfortunately neither performed urinalyses nor measured blood plasma osmolarity. We cannot be sure that the extracellular sodium concentrations returned to normal because of the influx of intracellular fluids; however, it seems rather certain that some degree of cellular dehydration persisted. Arden further reported that sodium bicarbonate solutions produced essentially the same effect, whereas potassium salts did not. Janssen (1936) replicated this study and observed that for potassium salts the resulting electrolyte imbalance was corrected primarily by renal excretion; sodium loads, on the other hand, produced excessive drinking. The findings have been corroborated by Elkinton and Taffel (1942) and Wolf and Eddy (1957) for extended periods of water deprivation. The urinary secretion of sodium and chloride decreases sharply as the urinary concentration of these ions falls. Potassium excretion appears unaffected by increased urinary concentration. The result is that over a period of prolonged deprivation plasma sodium and chloride increase, whereas potassium levels remain constant.

Although specific electrolytes appeared to be related to water intake in these studies, one cannot conclude that the regulation of thirst is directly and causally related to the plasma concentrations of sodium and chloride. This attractive hypothesis was clearly disproved by a series of studies conducted by Holmes and Gregersen. In 1947 these workers observed that intravenous injections of sodium chloride produced intense thirst sensations in man as well as a pronounced reduction in salivary flow and a sharp rise in serum chloride concentration. Both thirst and local dryness of the mouth were prevented if large amounts of water were consumed before the administration of sodium chloride. These results strongly supported the notion that thirst may be significantly correlated with serum electrolyte concentration; however, a subsequent investigation (Holmes and Gregersen, 1950) disproved this notion. It was found that intravenous injections of hypertonic sorbital solutions produced intense thirst sensations and drinking, in spite of the fact that the plasma concentrations of sodium and chloride are actually *reduced* by this treatment.

These results demonstrate only that the specific electrolytes used in these experiments are not directly related to the regulation of thirst, and considerable interest in osmometric mechanisms has remained. However, in the past 25 years, considerable evidence appears to favor an interpretation of thirst in terms of cellular dehydration *sui generis* rather than osmotic pressure per se.

Gilman (1937) has provided one of the most convincing demonstrations of the insufficiency of theoretical positions relying exclusively on osmotic pressure gradients. He compared the effects of intravenously administered sodium chloride with the effects of comparable injections of urea. Sodium chloride produces a pronounced decrease of cell volume because the NaCl ions do not readily pass through the cell membrane. Urea does enter the intracellular compartments without producing a significant shift of the fluid balance of the intracellular and extracellular compartments. Although the concentrations of the solutions were adjusted so that urea produced precisely the same increase in osmotic pressure (as measured by freezing point depression) as the hypertonic saline solution, the effects on water intake—and presumably thirst—were quite different. Following the injection of sodium chloride, dogs ingested large quantities of water until the serum concentration of this electrolyte returned to normal (i.e., preinjection) levels. Urea, on the other hand, elicited a much smaller water intake that did not restore the organism's water balance. Since the two injections had comparable effects on osmotic pressure,

Gilman argued that the pronounced difference in their elicitation of thirst could be explained only by the fact that urea fails to produce a difference in *effective* osmotic pressure and cellular dehydration.

A number of investigators (Bellows, 1939; Holmes and Gregersen, 1950; Adolph et al., 1954) have replicated these results. All studies have found that the effects of urea are smaller than those of isosmolar sodium chloride, and that urea produces effects that appear considerably delayed. This observation raises an uncomfortable question. Why does urea produce any effect at all if it does not affect cellular hydration, and if thirst is in fact independent of osmotic pressure changes as long as these do not force water out of the cells.

Zuidema et al. (1956) and Wolf (1958) have proposed that the effects of urea on water intake may be caused by an increase in the obligatory urine flow. As soon as the concentration of urea in the blood increases above normal levels, the organism attempts to remedy the situation by stepping up the excretion of urea via the kidneys. Such excretion requires greater than normal quantities of urine and produces a sizable water loss. This reaction may account for some of the delayed effects of urea injections which have repeatedly been noted; however, Bellows (1939) and Holmes and Gregersen (1950) reported drinking 5 to 15 min after the intravenous injection of urea. This interval is clearly too short for the operation of the postulated mechanism.

An alternative interpretation of the urea effects can be made in terms of osmotic transients. Although urea passes quite readily through the cellular membranes, some period of time is required before the sudden increase in the urea concentration of the extracellular fluid is balanced by a diffusion of urea into the cells. During this brief period there will be an effective osmotic pressure difference between the intra- and extracellular fluid compartments and a consequent movement of water out of the cells. This cellular dehydration is quite rapidly corrected by the influx of urea, and it is difficult to see how this mechanism alone can account for the often prolonged drinking which has been observed following urea injections. These osmotic transients may explain the early onset of the urea effect, and their duration might suffice to bridge the interval required for the appearance of the previously discussed water loss from increased obligatory urine flow. This matter has, unfortunately, not yet been settled by an appropriate experimental study of the precise

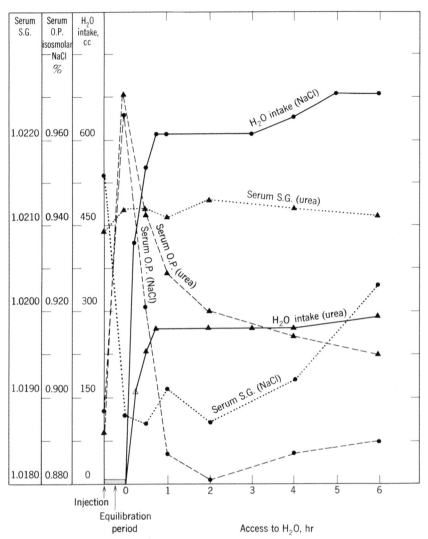

Fig. 7.9 Serum osmotic pressure, specific gravity changes, and voluntary water intake in dogs following the intravenous injection of 2.5 cc/kg isosmolar hypertonic NaCl (20%) and urea (40%). (From Gilman, 1937.)

duration of these osmotic gradients and of the onset of significant dehydration from increased urinary collection. We shall leave the argument open for the present time and look instead at another prediction that a cellular-dehydration theory provides.

We have already differentiated between *relative* and *absolute* dehydration or hydration. Relative dehydration can be produced by the injection of hypertonic sodium chloride solutions into the bloodstream. These solutions produce a relative hypertonicity of the extracellular fluid and a consequent movement of water out of the cell. If, on

the other hand, we *remove* extracellular salts, the *intra*cellular compartment becomes hypertonic with respect to the surrounding fluids; water then moves into the cell, producing relative cellular hydration and expansion of the cell. According to a cellular-dehydration theory of thirst, relative hydration should produce adipsia and prevent water intake. When we look at the experimental evidence for this prediction, a somewhat inconsistent picture emerges.

Darrow and Yannet (1935) partially depleted extracellular electrolytes by the following method. Isosmotic glucose was placed into the peritoneal cavity of dogs. Because of the peculiar diffusion pattern of glucose, extracellular electrolytes are drawn into the peritoneal cavity before glucose diffuses into the extracellular compartment. Darrow and Yannet made use of this phenomenon by withdrawing an amount of fluid, roughly equal to that previously injected, when the concentration of electrolytes was highest in the peritoneal cavity. This produced hypertonicity of the intracellular fluids (which had retained their normal concentration of salts) and a consequent movement of water into the cells. Although the total water balance of the organism remained constant, *relative* cellular hydration was produced. Darrow and Yannet reported that this procedure produced many of the physiological symptoms normally associated with cellular dehydration and thirst (severe dryness of the tongue and mucous membranes, loss of skin turgor, etc.) but no water intake.

A replication of this experiment by Remington et al. (1941) produced comparable results. During acute cellular dehydration no water intake occurred, and plasma concentrations of sodium and chloride were low. However, these workers report that the animals began to drink as cellular volume

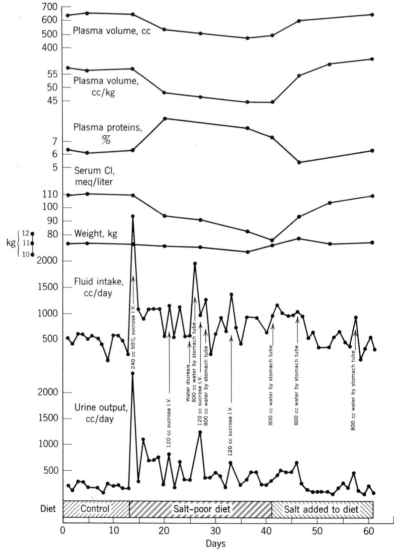

Fig. 7.10 Typical changes observed during a period of salt deficiency. Note especially the increase in water intake and urine output. I.V., intravenously. (From Holmes and Cizek, 1951.)

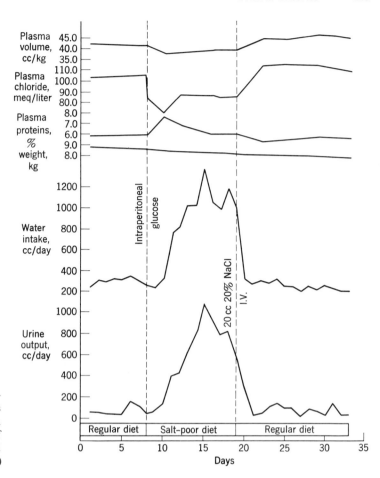

Fig. 7.11 Response of a salt-depleted animal when salt was restored by intravenous injection of an amount slightly in excess of that removed by intraperitoneal dialysis. (From Cizek et al., 1951.)

returned to normal. Nadal et al. (1941) have reported extensive clinical data which tend to confirm the hypothesis that severe water deficits, if produced by salt loss, do not elicit thirst sensations. These findings support a cellular-dehydration theory of thirst, although it is a bit puzzling why drinking should occur when the intracellular volume returns to normal.

On the other hand, we now have both clinical and experimental evidence which suggests that thirst may be elicited by cellular overhydration. No entirely satisfactory explanation of these data has been advanced. Holmes and Cizek (1951) and Cizek et al. (1951) have reported that the daily water consumption of dogs increases markedly when hyposalemia (a decrease of the salt concentration of the extracellular fluids) is produced by peritoneal extraction procedures (described above) in combination with a low salt diet. When sodium chloride was restored to the diet (and cellular hydration returned to normal levels), the water intake of these animals fell to pre-

experimental control levels. These studies confirm clinical reports (Schroeder, 1949; Soloff and Zatuchni, 1949; Elkinton and Squires, 1951; Strauss, 1957) of extreme thirst in hyposalemic patients; such thirst appears unrelieved by the ingestion of water (since this does not alleviate cellular hydration) but disappears immediately after an administration of sodium chloride draws water out of the cells. These reports quite clearly refer to intense thirst sensations, and it is unlikely that McCance's explanations of this phenomenon in terms of altered taste thresholds can account for the data. McCance (1936a, b; 1938) reported that the principal symptom of hyposalemia is a marked rise of taste thresholds and suggested that the frequently reported thirst sensations may be secondary to the sudden lack of taste.

Verney (1947) has proposed that osmoreceptors may show accommodation to prolonged changes in the effective osmotic pressure of body fluids. Elkinton and Squires (1951) have used a similar hypothesis to account for the thirst of hyposalemic patients. According to this notion, the receptor threshold adjusts in response to prolonged changes in the effective osmotic pressure; hyposalemic thirst might then be elicited by a small reduction of cellular volume such as the reduction that accompanies the eventual absorption of fluids from the peritoneal cavity. There is no evidence to discredit these notions and also no direct experimental support for them. They seem unlikely in view of the fact that a comparable accommodation to hypersalemia quite certainly does not seem to occur (Adolph, 1947a; Wolf, 1953).

Over 40 years ago, Adolph (1921) concluded from his studies of the effects of sodium chloride on diuresis that the important and essential event may not be osmotic pressure per se, but rather *changes* in osmotic pressure. The same reasoning might be applied to the proposed osmoreceptors, and one might argue that the critical factor in thirst may be a change in the effective osmotic pressure regardless of the direction of this change. Wolf (1950) has followed this line of thought and has suggested that the osmoreceptors might be sensitive, not to cellular dehydration or hypotonicity but to changes in cellular size. According to this theory, hydration results in cellular expansion which might stimulate the same neural elements as the cellular shrinkage produced by dehydration. If we assume, in accordance with Johannes Mueller's *doctrine of specific nerve energies* (or some variant of it), that the same information is carried by a nerve regardless of the nature of the stimulation, Wolf's "cellular-size" theory might account for both normal and hypotonic thirst. We must remember, however, that we do not have any relevant experimental data for such a notion, and that this interpretation depends on the operation of still unidentified receptors somewhere in the organism.

In this connection, it might be worthwhile to recall that we do not know whether the frequently postulated osmoreceptors are, in fact, afferent to the central nervous system mechanisms that regulate the organism's fluid balance. It is quite possible that central mechanisms may themselves perform the osmoreceptor function. This alternative may force some revisions in our theoretical thinking about the contributing peripheral mechanisms.

Before considering the central mechanisms that correlate the organism's water need with other behavior, we shall briefly review the status of the cellular-dehydration theory as formulated by Dill

(1938). In addition to the experimental evidence cited in favor of this notion, many other studies support the contention that thirst always results from dehydration of the cells of the organism. Dill himself reported (1938) that the intensity of thirst caused by sweating was a direct function of the salt concentration of the secreted fluids. When man is initially exposed to very high temperatures, little thirst results; the electrolyte concentration of the sweat is nearly as high as that of plasma, so that only little fluid moves into the extracellular compartment. In acclimated subjects sweating produces severe thirst, and the osmotic concentration of the sweat is reduced by nearly 65%. Huang (1955) has shown that acute depletion of sodium chloride in the rabbit produces a pronounced depression of water consumption that is fully compensated only after 6 to 8 days.

Although the phenomenon of hyposalemic thirst may restrict the generality of the conclusion, there is little doubt that a nearly perfect correlation exists between cellular dehydration and thirst. Furthermore, there are many instances in which cellular hydration, as required by this theory, was associated with adipsia or antidipsia. Rather than abandon the cellular-dehydration theory, we might look for *additional* mechanisms that may operate in some situations.

One persistent problem with this theory has been the lack of precise, quantitative experimen-

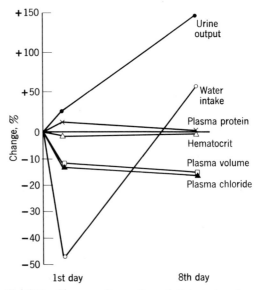

Fig. 7.12 Changes after peritoneal dialysis, based on the average of four experiments. (From Huang, 1955.)

tation. Both in the clinic and in the laboratory, only extreme hyperdipsia has been investigated because the available techniques for the assessment of plasma electrolytes allow only crude measures. Similarly inadequate are the methods for determining cellular water. Since these values are obtained by subtracting estimates of extracellular fluid from total body fluids, there are so many potential sources for cumulative error that the results are not reliable to below 1% of total as demanded by our theory. Wolf (1948, 1950) has developed a promising technique for estimating the amount of water loss by the cells for any combination of water load and sodium chloride concentration. Under the assumption that cells behave as perfect osmoreceptors, the following osmometric equation was developed:

$$V_e' = \frac{(W + L_{H_2O})(V_e A_{eop} + L_{eop})}{W A_{eop} + L_{eop}}$$

where V_e' is the final extracellular fluid volume after equilibration of a load of osmotically effective material; V_e is the initial extracellular volume (e.g., 20% of body weight); W is the initial water content of the body (e.g., 60% of body weight); L_{H_2O} is the net load of water; A_{eop} is the initial effective osmotic concentration of the plasma or extracellular fluid; and L_{eop} is the net effective osmotic load (adapted from Wolf, 1958).

Wolf (1958) has validated this equation by calculating the percentage of decrement in cellular water at the thirst threshold. In this study various degrees of hypertonicity (and thirst) were produced by slow intravenous infusions of salt water. Wolf found that the thirst threshold in man averaged 1.23% shrinkage of cell volume. This value correlates highly with osmotic thresholds computed by independent techniques (Verney, 1947) for the osmoreceptors of the antidiuretic hormone system (see the discussion of Verney's work under "Central Mechanisms"). Moreover, this theoretical value corresponds closely to values derived from the observation that man becomes thirsty when his water loss exceeds 0.5% of total body weight (Adolph, 1943b, 1947c).

Although this attempt at quantification is incomplete and may require adjustments and refinements as more information becomes available, it represents an important step in the right direction. As long as our predictions are of only qualitative nature, it will be difficult, if not impossible, to correct our theoretical views; improvements and modifications are sorely needed if we are to understand the complexities of the various factors that participate in the regulation of the organism's fluid balance and thirst.

Summary

Although some physiologists of the nineteenth century had suggested that osmotic mechanisms might be responsible for the translation of the organism's water need into conscious awareness or thirst, sustained experimental interest in osmotic factors dates back only to the pioneering studies of Mayer and Wettendorff published around the turn of the century.

Mayer's work suggested that thirst might be directly related to osmotic pressure gradients in the extracellular fluid compartment. This notion has been the starting point for a variety of investigations aimed at demonstrating the importance of plasma electrolyte concentrations.

Wettendorff adduced evidence indicating that osmotic factors were effective only if they resulted in a movement of water from the cells into the extracellular compartment, thus producing relative dehydration of the cells themselves. According to this notion, all cells (or some groups of cells) contain osmoreceptors that are sensitive to the decrease in cell volume.

Since the publication of these papers, much research has been devoted to various predictions deriving from these theories. Both hypotheses appear to be supported by a large body of evidence, and negative data are available which are not easily handled by either notion; however, it appears now that Wettendorff's cellular-dehydration theory, or some modification of it, may be the more fruitful approach to the problem of thirst. This is particularly true if it is assumed that the central mechanisms (which will be discussed in the following section) perform the hypothesized osmoreceptor function. The principal need in this area of research is to improve our techniques of measurement to allow a more quantitative assessment of the predictions that can be derived from the cellular-dehydration theory.

CENTRAL THEORIES

Throughout our discussion of the various peripheral mechanisms which may operate to meter the water needs of the organism and translate this physiological need into the "conscious perception of the urge to drink," we have almost invariably arrived at the conclusion that some integration of these mechanisms is

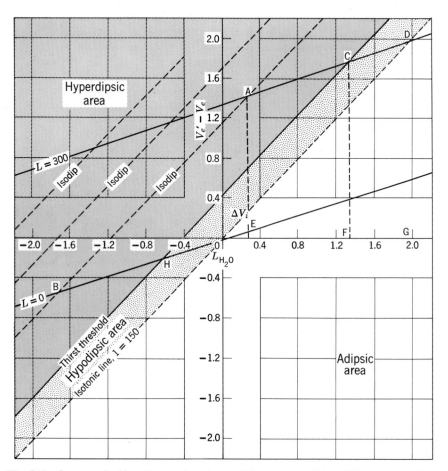

Fig. 7.13 Osmometric thirst diagram based on a 70-kg man containing 49 liters of total body water and 14 liters of extracellular fluid. Ordinate, change in extracellular volume in liters $(V_e' - V_e)$. Abscissa, load of water in liters (L_{H_2O}). The thirst threshold, separating the hyperdipsic area (densely stippled) from the hypodipsic area (sparsely stippled), is the heavy line, parallel to the isotonic line, which intersects the ordinate at ΔV_i. The value for ΔV_i was obtained by using the average T value (0.0123) found in human experiments. Thus, where the cellular water in a 70-kg man is 35 liters, $\Delta V_i = 0.0123 \times 35.000 = 0.431$ liter.

An isodip is a line (e.g., AB) which is the locus of all points (L_{Na}, L_{H_2O}) of equal thirst. For a hyperdipsic point, A, one measures the degree of thirst by passing a salt load line (in this case, $L = 300$) from A to the thirst threshold at C or to the isotonic line at D. The projections EF and EG measure, respectively, the volume of water required to move from the given hyperdipsia to hypodipsia, and from the given hyperdipsia to adipsia.

From the intersection of the thirst threshold and the salt load line $L = 0$, at H, the perpendicular to J may be erected. The abscissal distance from J to the origin represents the absolute water deficit, with no salt loss, which should just provoke thirst, according to the cellular-dehydration hypothesis. The value obtained here, namely -0.60 liter, represents a deficit of 0.86% of the body weight. Algebraically, this latter value is equal to $70T$ (total body water as percentage of body weight, multiplied by 0.0123). (From Wolf, 1950.)

needed before an effective influence on the gross behavior of the organism can result. Some early theories of thirst attempted to circumvent this problem by assigning specific sensory qualities to neural feedback from the mouth and throat; however, it soon became clear that this simple and attractive hypothesis could not account for the successful regulation of water intake.

The writers of the early nineteenth century began to postulate a drinking center somewhere in the brain which might correlate and coordinate information from various peripheral sources and translate these data into the psychological phenomenon of specific motivation. At first, only accessory functions were attributed to these central mechanisms; but the pendulum continued to swing farther and farther in the direction of increased emphasis on central functions. A tendency has developed in the past decade to disregard the contribution of peripheral factors almost entirely and to ascribe more and more regulatory functions to central nervous system mechanisms. This trend has carried us perhaps too far, and we might benefit from a re-evaluation of *all* available data. We have therefore devoted a greater than usual portion of our discussion to the peripheral mechanisms which might contribute to a regulation of water intake.

It should be remembered throughout the following discussion of central factors that these mechanisms cannot operate in a vacuum, but depend quite directly and immediately on information that must come from peripheral sources. The problem is not answered by the postulation or demonstration of central mechanisms. Thinking in terms of a little homunculus who lives somewhere in the brain and determines when an organism should be thirsty is thinking in error. Thirst (or, for that matter, any other form of motivation) may be elicited by stimulation of specific central sites or eliminated by their destruction; however, these central regulators represent merely "computers" which collect data from a variety of peripheral and central sources. Without this information the computer is useless.

This interdependence is perhaps most clearly demonstrated when we consider the problem of satiety. This topic is discussed last so that we shall be able to consider it in the light of information from all possible sources. However, the initiation of thirst also undoubtedly depends to some extent on peripheral factors, even if it can be demonstrated that the proposed osmometric metering device itself is located inside the central nervous system.

Vague references to a thirst center somewhere in the brain appeared over 150 years ago; only very recently has concrete evidence for such a mechanism been obtained. Less than 50 years ago Leschke (1918) attracted much serious attention with the hypothesis that an increase in plasma concentration of crystalloids might produce thirst because of an irritating action on the cortex. (This entire scheme was apparently based on the fact that intravenous injections of sodium chloride produce thirst.) Nor was this the last of the purely speculative central theories proposed in the absence of experimental evidence or even clinical observation. Brunn (1925), for some reason unable to replicate Leschke's findings, took issue with the cortical "seat" of thirst and suggested instead that "some vegetative center" in the brain might translate sensory information from the mouth and throat into thirst. A still more ambitious, if similarly fictional, attempt to integrate peripheral, osmometric, and central mechanisms was published by Oehme in 1922. According to this writer, increased salt concentrations of the extracellular fluids excite sensory receptors in the mouth and throat which then signal to diencephalic and cortical integrating mechanisms via sensory components of the vagus nerve. Although this theory appears reasonable in light of recent experimental evidence, little more than educated guesswork seems to have determined the choice of central mechanisms.

Although the attention of many research workers had previously been drawn to the hypothalamus because of its direct and important role in diabetes insipidus (the symptomatology of which includes polyuria and polydipsia), it was not until 1938 that the relevance of these findings to the regulation of thirst was formally accepted. In that year Bellows and Van Wagenen concluded from a detailed study of experimental diabetes insipidus that the hypothalamus may be directly and primarily involved in the regulation of water metabolism, of which the motivational aspect (thirst) is a component of greatest importance. Although clinical studies (Alajouanine and Thurel, 1946) showed conclusively that mechanical stimulation of the floor of the third ventricle produced strong subjective sensations of thirst in patients, matters unfortunately did not progress for nearly another decade. Occasional suggestions that the hypothalamus might be responsible for the regulation of thirst were made, but the attention of most research workers of that period was centered on the possible contribution of the cerebrum, particularly the frontal lobes (Allott, 1939; Luetscher and Blockman, 1943; MacCarty and Cooper, 1951).

Osmoreceptors in the Hypothalamus

Interest in the hypothalamic mechanisms was revived only when Verney published his provocative essay on the role of central osmometric factors in the release of antidiuretic hormone (ADH). Because Verney's work has had significant influence on the course of both theoretical and experimental work on thirst, we might discuss his findings is some detail, although the regulation of antidiuretic hormone secretion is only peripherally related to the problem of thirst.

Antidiuretic hormone is continually secreted. It serves to maintain a state of high permeability of the renal tubules so that water and electrolytes from filtered plasma are reabsorbed. Under normal circumstances approximately 99% of the renal filtrate is retained. The remaining 1% is excreted as a carrier for the various waste products that the organism must eliminate. When a negative water balance develops because of water deprivation, more ADH is secreted, and the concentration of the urine is consequently increased to conserve the water resources of the body. Conversely, antidiuretic hormone secretion is reduced when a positive water load develops, the permeability of the renal tubules is increased, and *more* of a less-concentrated urine is excreted.

Verney (1947) made the important observation that injections of hypertonic sodium chloride solutions into the carotid artery produce a rapid and marked increase in ADH secretion (i.e., the system responded as if a negative water balance had suddenly developed). Comparable injections of hypertonic sodium chloride into other arteries did not elicit this effect. Through a series of controlled observations, Verney established that the effective stimulus for increased secretion of antidiuretic hormone was a rise in the effective osmotic pressure of the arterial blood serving the diencephalic portion of the brain.

These findings led Verney to conclude that the hypothalamus must contain osmoreceptors that are sensitive to the osmotic pressure of the blood. He suggested further that these osmoreceptor cells become hydrated and increase in volume when the effective osmotic pressure of the extracellular fluid decreases as a result of water intake

or salt loss. This increase in cell size might be responsible for the decreased secretion of ADH which tends to correct the positive water load by allowing an increased secretion of fluids from the kidney. Conversely, a rise in extracellular osmotic pressure was believed to draw water out of these osmoreceptor cells and produce a decrease in cell size which stimulates the increased secretion of ADH. The antidiuretic hormone then causes a retention of body fluids by concentrating the urine.

If we remember the importance that most current theories of thirst place on the operation of osmoreceptors and cellular dehydration, it is not difficult to see why this work has had such profound effects on the entire field. Lest it be supposed that Verney's choice of the hypothalamus as the likely origin of the osmoreceptor mechanism was merely a lucky guess, we might briefly mention the classic research of Ranson et al. (1936); their work established beyond reasonable doubt that secretory cells in the supraoptic nuclei of the hypothalamus are the source of antidiuretic hormone. Furthermore, they demonstrated that the interruption of connections between this nucleus and the neurohypophysis results in loss of the reabsorptive capacity of the renal tubules.

Verney's findings have been confirmed and extended by a number of investigators. Since some of these findings may be relevant to the operation of similar osmometric centers in the regulation of thirst, we shall consider them briefly before proceeding with our discussion of subsequent investigations that were more directly concerned with the central factors of thirst.

Von Euler (1953) injected hypertonic saline or glucose solutions into the carotid artery and observed slow changes in the electrical activity recorded from the preoptic nuclei. Hypotonic solutions of tap water produced similar changes but of *opposite* electrical sign. Saywer and Gernandt (1956) replicated these results in another species (rabbits); they added the interesting observation that urea (which raises the osmotic pressure of the blood but fails to affect cellular size) did not evoke comparable results.

Verney's assumption that cellular expansion inhibits the secretion of antidiuretic hormone has been attacked (von Euler, 1953). However, it appears reasonable, not only because extracellular hypertonicity should, in fact, produce such cellular hydration (and increase the volume of the affected cells), but also because other reflexes in the body that are set off by the stretching of tissue

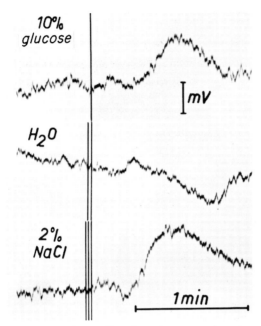

10%
glucose

$\int mV$

H_2O

2%
NaCl

1min

Fig. 7.14 EEG recordings from the supraoptic region, showing slow base line shifts in response to intracarotid injections of water, hypertonic saline, and hypertonic glucose solutions. (From von Euler, 1953.)

generally produce inhibition in response to stretch or pressure. For instance, the pressor receptors of the carotid react to increased arterial pressure by initiating an inhibition of the smooth muscles of the walls of the blood vessels; stretch receptors in the alveolar sacs inhibit inspiration, etc.

In view of the great popularity cellular-dehydration theories (based on changes in *effective* osmotic pressure) have enjoyed in the past decades, it is hardly surprising that Verney's demonstration of a specific osmoreceptor mechanism in the hypothalamus revolutionized the experimental approach to the study of thirst. Wolf's theory of thirst postulated explicitly that specific osmoreceptors of probably central origin rather than general tissue receptors provide the afferent link of the thirst reflex. Shortly thereafter, Bengt Andersson of Stockholm began to publish an extensive series of studies which have greatly contributed to our understanding of the regulation of water intake.

Stimulation Studies

Andersson was initially interested in the hormonal regulation of lactation. Previous experiments had demonstrated that electrical stimulation of a certain area of the hypothalamus elicits

lactation and a simultaneous rise in the specific gravity of the urine. Since the latter result did not seem to have a functional relationship to lactation, Andersson (1951) proceeded to stimulate various neighboring regions in an attempt to separate the two phenomena. Although he did not quite succeed in this, the experiment will be long remembered. Andersson observed rumination and licking in response to stimulation of the anterior portion of the lateral hypothalamus, and his findings led to a concentrated experimental attack on the role of these hypothalamic mechanisms in the regulation of thirst.

In 1952 Andersson published an extraordinary paper. He reasoned that the osmoreceptors which have played such an important role in our thinking about the thirst mechanism might be identical to those found by Verney. If this were true, direct contact of hypertonic solutions with these cells should produce cellular dehydration and elicit drinking. To test this hypothesis, Andersson injected 0.1 cc of hypertonic (1.5 to 2.0%) sodium chloride solution directly into the hypothalamus of unanesthetized goats. Nearly half of the animals tested began to drink in response to this treatment within 30 to 90 sec and consumed up to a gallon of water before the effects of the stimulation disappeared. Comparable injections of isotonic and hypotonic sodium chloride solutions had no effect on water intake. Histological verification of the intended placements demonstrated that hypertonic saline was an effective stimulus for thirst in only a relatively small portion of the hypothalamus, near the paraventricular nuclei of the medial diencephalon. Injections anterior to the optic chiasma or lateral and posterior to the paraventricular nuclei produced no effects (Andersson, 1952a, b).

Andersson concluded from these findings that Verney's osmoreceptor theory could provide an adequate explanation of thirst, although the same group of cells need not be involved in the regulation of both ADH release and water intake. He proposed that it was quite possible that different groups of osmoreceptors might be sensitive to an increased effective osmotic pressure of the extracellular fluids and independently elicit thirst and an increased renal retention of water. To test this hypothesis, Andersson (1953) repeated his earlier experiments demonstrating the elicitation of thirst by local saline injections and observed that renal functions were not affected by this procedure. He then placed comparable injections into the median eminence of the hypophyseal stalk and

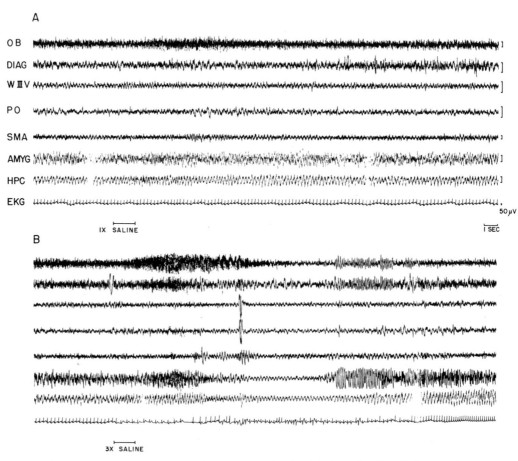

Fig. 7.15 Effects of intracarotid injections of 2 ml each of A, isotonic saline; B, hypertonic saline. OB, olfactory bulb; DIAG, diagonal band; WIIIV, wall of third ventricle above paraventricular nucleus; PO, preoptic area; AMYG, amygdaloid nucleus; SMA, supramammillary area; HPC, hippocampus; EKG, electrocardiogram. (From Sawyer and Gernandt, 1956.)

noticed a reduction of urinary flow (and increased urine concentration) but no drinking. Although both results appeared to be caused by the stimulation of osmoreceptors, the two mechanisms that cooperate in maintaining the organism's fluid balance constant were clearly anatomically distinct.

Andersson and McCann (1955a) attempted to localize more precisely the hypothalamic drinking center by means of microinjections of minute quantities of hypertonic saline solutions. (One of the persistent problems with the technique of injecting even small amounts of fluid directly into the brain is that the force of the injection tends to produce considerable spread of the injected substance.) In Andersson's study injections as small as 0.003 cc were found to induce drinking of large quantities of water. (The goat is a rumi-

nant which can take in relatively large amounts of fluid without becoming bloated.) Drinking began within 30 to 90 sec and persisted for 2 to 3 min. This response was elicited from a relatively small area, but Andersson and McCann were not satisfied with the precision of this localization.

In a subsequent study Andersson and McCann, (1955b) turned to electrical stimulation techniques (which themselves are subject to considerable spread of stimulation) for additional data. They found that electrical stimulation (0.5 to 1.3 volts, 50 cps) of the same region that had previously responded to osmotic stimulation reliably produced drinking, beginning only seconds after the onset of electrical stimulation and persisting without interruption as long as the current flow was maintained. Drinking stopped 3 to 4 sec after the cessation of electrical stimulation. Although it had often been difficult to replicate the results of osmotic stimulation in the same animal, frequently repeated electrical stimulations never failed to elicit drinking. Electrical stimulation apparently produced a more selective excitation in these experiments than the previous saline injections. Andersson and McCann were thus able to determine the boundaries of the hypothalamic drinking center more precisely. Pure drinking responses were obtained only from the caudal portion of the region previously believed responsible for thirst. More anteriorly placed electrodes elicited drinking in combination with ADH and oxytocin secretion which produced concomitant antidiuresis, urinary concentration, and lactation. Andersson suggested that stimulation of the anterior placements may have excited components of the paraventricular and supraoptic nuclei which regulate neurohypophyseal secretion of various hormones.

Lest it be thought that the hypothalamic drinking center is peculiar to goats or Andersson, let us briefly mention Greer's (1955) report of comparable results in the rat. In the course of experiments concerned principally with the role of the hypothalamus in various endocrine secretions, Greer observed that electrical stimulation produced vigorous licking in one of his animals. When this stimulation was repeated, the rat began to drink. Water intake continued as long as the stimulation was maintained, but ceased abruptly with the termination of current flow. During stimulation this animal drank even highly concentrated saline solutions which were ordinarily refused. This polydipsic behavior has also been observed by Andersson (1955), who reported that electrical stimulation of the drinking center in goats elicited "compulsive drinking." The animals even drank urea during stimulation if no water was available, although obvious signs of aversion were displayed. Greer's animal continued to respond for 5 days but finally stopped completely. Since direct currents were used in this experiment, this disappearance of the drinking response may have been due to a gradual polarization of the stimulating electrodes. Histological examination revealed that the electrodes were located in the area between the dorsomedial and the ventromedial nuclei. Greer argued that the drinking response could not have been mediated by relatively slow humoral processes because it occurred almost immediately after the onset of stimulation. More recently, Greer's findings have been replicated in Miller's laboratories at Yale University

(Miller, 1957, 1960). These studies have carefully mapped the drinking center in the rat and have contributed the important finding that at least in this species there appears to be partial, if not complete, overlap of the central mechanisms that regulate water and food intake. We shall return to this problem after a brief discussion of experiments investigating the hypothalamic regulation of thirst by means of ablation techniques.

Ablation Studies

Even before Andersson and his colleagues began to publish their reports of the effects of osmotic or electrical stimulation of the hypothalamus, Stevenson et al. (1950) observed that bilateral lesions of the ventral hypothalamus of rats produce a "chronic state of dehydration" characterized by delayed excretion of injected water loads and a sharp increase in urinary concentration. Witt et al. (1952) reported an interesting reversal of effects. Relatively small lesions placed near the median eminence of the hypothalamus resulted in a pronounced increase in water intake and urinary flow (diabetes insipidus). If these lesions were enlarged, however, to extend into the dorsal and lateral aspects of the anterior hypothalamus, complete adipsia occurred. This result was only temporary with smaller lesions but appeared to be permanent—the animals died of dehydration—when the lesions were large. Witt et al. managed to maintain these adipsic dogs for longer periods of time with pituitary extract administrations which controlled the diuresis resulting from the lack of ADH secretion. Although adipsic animals would not take water, they drank vigorously as soon as a slight amount of milk or meat extract was added to the water. These findings were all the more surprising because the animals also tended to show anorexia. Food or water alone did not induce feeding or drinking; as soon as food and water were mixed, ravenous consumption appeared. Similar results have been reported recently. We might postpone further discussion of Witt's findings until we have a more complete picture.

Teitelbaum and Stellar (1954) noticed that small bilateral lesions of the lateral hypothalamic area, at the level of the ventromedial nuclei, produced not only complete aphagia (as previously reported by Anand and Brobeck) but also complete adipsia. These effects persisted long enough to produce death unless remedial action was instituted. However, it was found that most animals eventually recovered if maintained by intragastric

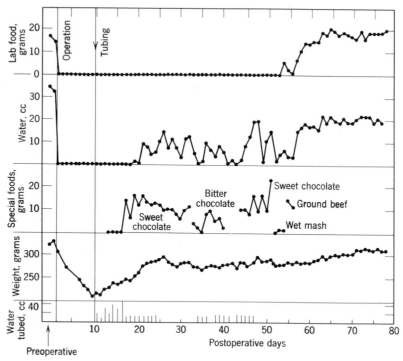

Fig. 7.16 The recovery of the eating of palatable ("special") foods in a rat with lateral hypothalamic aphagia and adipsia. Note the greatly delayed recovery of dry-food intake ("lab food"). (From Teitelbaum and Stellar, 1954, AAAS.)

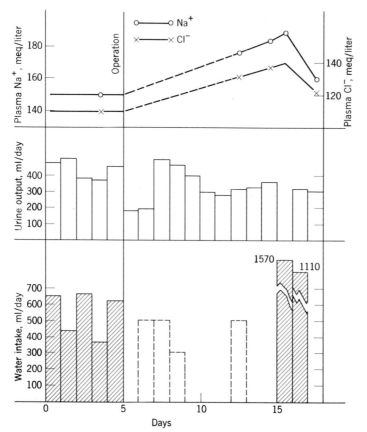

Fig. 7.17 The changes in water metabolism and plasma sodium chloride concentrations in a dog (preoperative weight, 24.5 kg) after a lesion in the hypothalamus. Dotted columns on the graph of water intake indicate the amount of milk and broth given as supplementary fluid. (From Andersson and McCann, 1956.)

feeding and watering. Andersson and McCann (1956) followed up earlier stimulation studies by demonstrating that electrolytic lesions of the area that responded to osmotic and electrical stimulation by the elicitation of drinking behavior produce partial or complete adipsia in dogs and goats. Depending on the size and precise location of the lesion, adipsia occurred with or without concurrent polyuria (diabetes insipidus) or disturbances of the sodium chloride metabolism. It is interesting to note that in goats there appears to be little or no anatomical overlap of the feeding and drinking mechanisms, for the adipsia in these experiments appeared to be accompanied by entirely normal appetites.

Montemurro and Stevenson (1957) attempted to unambiguously separate the two systems in the rat. They reported that lesions of the ventromedial nuclei of the hypothalamus reduced the water-food ratio (a measure previously used by Stevenson to assess impairments of the water regulation); however, this shift appeared to be primarily, if not exclusively, caused by a pronounced increase in food intake which was not matched by a comparable rise in water intake. Lesions of the lateral hypothalamus, on the other hand, seemed to produce pure adipsia in some animals. Three of their rats maintained a normal body weight (on a high fat diet) for as long as 55 days when adequate hydration was supplied by tube feeding.

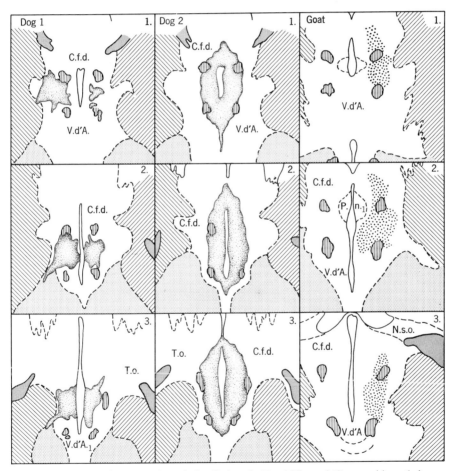

Fig. 7.18 Horizontal sections through the (1) dorsal, (2) middle, and (3) ventral hypothalamus of two dogs (the postoperative water intake of dog 2 is shown in Fig. 7.17) and of a goat. The black areas mark the extent of the hypothalamic lesions which caused temporary adipsia. The dotted areas on the sections of the goat mark the region of the hypothalamus where electrical stimulation produced polydipsia. C.f.d., columna fornicis descendens; N.s.o., nucleus supraopticus; P.n., nucleus paraventricularis; T.o., tractus opticus; V.d'A., tractus Vicq d'Azyr (mammillo-thalamic tract). (From Andersson and McCann, 1956.)

Without hydration, these animals ate less and began to lose weight rapidly. Montemurro and Stevenson concluded from their findings that the drinking center of the rat was located in the lateral hypothalamic region (which also contains the excitatory feeding mechanism). Many subsequent studies have supported this localization which is quite different from that of the drinking center in the goat.

Morrison and Mayer (1957) explored the lateral hypothalamus by means of small electrolytic lesions and reported that small lesions in an area extending from just rostral to the posterior hypothalamic nuclei to just caudal to the supraoptic nuclei produce adipsia always accompanied by aphagia. The authors suggested that both effects resulted directly from the ablation (i.e., were independent of each other), since neither complete food deprivation nor complete water deprivation succeeded in duplicating the effects of these lesions.

This conclusion is supported by reports of occasional exceptions to the rule that lateral hypothalamic damage always affects food and water intake concurrently. Smith and McCann (1962), for instance, observed a case of "pure" aphagia as well as aphagia accompanied by polydipsia.

One of Stevenson's earlier studies (1950) of the role of the ventromedial nuclei in the regulation of food intake had shown that bilateral destruction of these nuclei produces pronounced changes in food intake; such changes are not compensated by a comparable adjustment of the organism's water intake so that the food-water ratio, which is normally kept quite constant, is significantly lowered. Stevenson suggested that lesions affecting the ventromedial nuclei might also interfere with the operation of the drinking mechanism. Several authors have seriously considered the possibility that the aphagia commonly seen after lesions in the feeding center of the lateral hypothalamus might be secondary to the concurrent adipsia. (See discussion of this problem in Chapter 6 on hunger.) This problem has been analyzed in a number of recent publications (Grossman, 1960; Epstein, 1960; Teitelbaum, 1961; Teitelbaum and Epstein, 1962; Grossman, 1962a, b), and it appears clear today that adipsia and aphagia are two independent symptoms of lateral hypothalamic damage. The drinking mechanism appears to be more seriously affected by lateral lesions, for animals recover from aphagia relatively rapidly if proper hydration is supplied via stomach fistula. Adipsia, on the other hand, persists for many

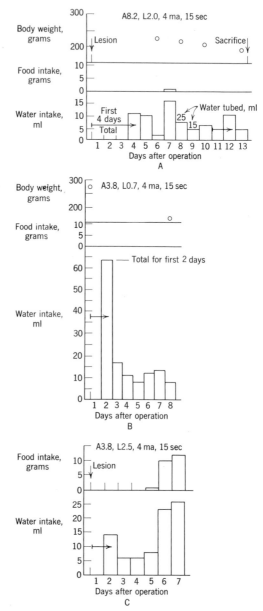

Fig. 7.19 A, food and water intake in a rat that manifested aphagia without adipsia. B, food and water intake in a rat that showed aphagia with relative polydipsia. C, food and water intake in a rat that, although initially manifesting aphagia without adipsia, recovered feeding behavior. (From Smith and McCann, 1962.)

months and is irreversible in some cases. Some impairment persists even in animals that appear to recover, for they will die of dehydration before accepting a quinine dilution of their water supply which is not aversive to normal animals.

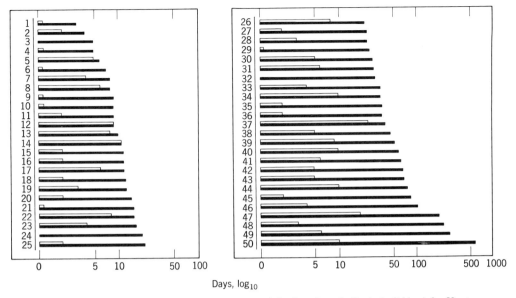

Fig. 7.20 The duration of aphagia (open bar) and the duration of adipsia (solid bar) for 50 rats with lateral hypothalamic damage, arranged in order of increasing adipsia. (From Epstein and Teitelbaum, 1964.)

Motivational Aspects of Central Regulation

The fact that the neural mechanisms that regulate feeding and drinking behavior at the level of the hypothalamus are biochemically separate mechanisms (in spite of the extensive anatomical overlap which apparently exists, at least in the rat) was demonstrated conclusively in a series of studies by Grossman (1960, 1962a, b). In these experiments minute amounts of crystalline chemicals were placed directly into specific points in the lateral hypothalamus by means of a double cannula which allowed repeated stimulation of the same site. Because the chemicals were used in crystalline form, the spread of these substances was minimized, and relatively precise localizations of the observed effects were possible. It was found that cholinergic substances elicit vigorous and prolonged drinking in sated animals when placed in an area of the lateral hypothalamus which corresponds quite well with the previously identified "feeding center." The stimulation appeared to have motivational properties, since animals worked (i.e., pressed a bar) to obtain water. The placement of adrenergic substances into the same points elicited vigorous feeding. The effects of central stimulation were reduced or eliminated by previous intraperitoneal injections of the appropriate cholinergic (atropine) or adrenergic (dibenzyline) blocking agents. Drinking in nor-

mally thirsty animals was inhibited by systemic injections or topical central applications of atropine. We may conclude from these results that the feeding and drinking mechanisms of the lateral hypothalamus are separate and distinct with respect to their neurochemical properties, even though extensive anatomical overlap was again demonstrated in these studies.

In these experiments specific chemical stimulation of the hypothalamus produced pronounced effects of an apparently motivational nature. Although the animals' efforts were only infrequently rewarded (VI-15 sec—i.e., a reinforcement is set up if at least one response is emitted during a variable interval [VI] the average length of which is 15 sec), sated animals worked to obtain water following the appropriate chemical stimulation. These results demonstrate that the stimulation of the hypothalamic drinking center does not merely elicit "drinking automatisms" devoid of motivational properties, as has sometimes been suggested. Andersson and Larsson (1956b) attempted earlier to answer these criticisms in a conditioning experiment that paired electrical stimulation of the hypothalamus with a previously neutral (conditioned) stimulus. After 110 pairings, there appeared to be no indication that any learning had taken place, and Andersson concluded that thirst elicited by electrical stimulation of the brain may not have all the motivational properties of normal thirst. However, a subsequent experiment (Andersson and Wyrwicka, 1957) succeeded in demonstrating that electrical stimulation can serve as the motivational component in a learning situation in which animals were trained to climb a short flight of stairs to reach water. Although considerable "shaping" of this response was required, all animals learned to go up the stairs as soon as electrical stimulation was applied to the hypothalamic drinking center. It appears rather certain at this point that such stimulation not only elicits appropriate motor sequences leading to the ingestion of water, but also induces thirst sensations sufficiently similar to normal thirst to motivate the performance of previously learned instrumental responses and the acquisition of new response sequences.

Stein and Seifter (1962) have reported that drinking can also be evoked by injections of muscarine (but not of nicotine) into the lateral hypothalamus of rats. The muscarine and carbachol effects were blocked by pretreatment with atropine, suggesting that the drinking effect may be due to an activation of muscarinic synapses in the lateral hypothalamus. A small drinking response was observed in these experiments when sodium chloride, nicotine bitartrate, and other salts were injected into the lateral hypothalamus. Since sucrose did not produce any drinking, this apparently nonspecific effect did not seem to be due to possible changes in osmolarity but rather to a general "salt" factor. Such an interpretation may account for the apparently paradoxical drinking effect which has occasionally been observed following intrahypothalamic injections of norepinephrine bitartrate (Miller, 1965; Myers, 1964).

The specificity of the cholinergic drinking effect has been further demonstrated in experiments showing that the injection of eserine (a drug which inhibits the enzyme cholinesterase and thus permits an accumulation of naturally occurring acetylcholine) into the lateral hypothalamus significantly increased the water consumption of slightly water deprived rats (Miller, 1965). These studies also showed interesting effects on diuretic mechanisms and body temperature. Carbachol injections into the lateral hypothalamus reduced the volume of urine and increased its concentration. A resulting change in osmolarity suggests that the decreased volume was due to reabsorption caused by the release of antidiuretic hormone from the pituitary rather than by a direct interference with kidney functions. These findings demonstrate that

the carbachol-induced drinking effect cannot be due to a primary diuresis. Cholinergic stimulation of the lateral hypothalamus also induced a marked drop in body temperature, an observation which is not easily reconcilable with Andersson and Larsson's (1961b) finding that cooling of the preoptic area inhibited drinking.

Thermoregulatory and Volumetric Influences of Extrahypothalamic Origin

A recent experiment by Andersson and Larsson (1961b) suggests that the regulation of food and water intake may be closely related as parts of a

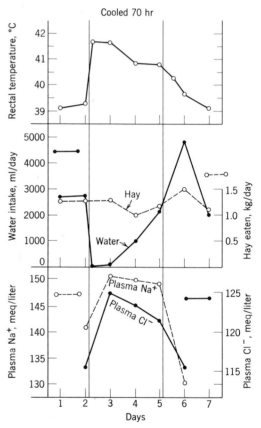

Fig. 7.21 Effects of chronic preoptic cooling on alimentation in a goat. During 70 hr of central cooling, water intake was totally abolished for the first 40 hr. Drinking remained reduced thereafter, the animal failing to make up its water deficit (as indicated by hyperconcentration of plasma electrolytes) until after preoptic cooling was stopped. During these periods of adipsia and hypodipsia, the animal continued to eat normal amounts of hay, despite the persistence of a marked core hyperthermia (40.8 to 41.5°C). (From Andersson et al., 1963.)

more general energy-regulating system. These workers found that cooling of the preoptic area of goats inhibited drinking in sated goats but induced feeding, whereas warming the same area induced drinking but inhibited feeding. Since the preoptic area contains the heat-loss mechanism of the organism, Andersson and Larsson suggested that Brobeck's (1948, 1960) thermoregulatory theory of hunger be extended to include the regulation of water intake. This suggestion was supported in a second experiment (Andersson and Larsson, 1961b) which demonstrated that inactivation of the preoptic heat-loss mechanism by proton irradiation produced complete adipsia in a goat (but surprisingly seemed to have no effect on food intake). These data suggest that the central regulation of thirst may in some way be affected by, or contribute to, the organism's thermal regulation, and that cellular dehydration may merely be one of several changes in the internal environment that affect water intake.

A finding by Epstein (1960) can be interpreted to question the osmoreceptor nature of the hypothalamic drinking mechanism, or at least question the relevance of Andersson's earlier demonstration that hypertonic solutions injected directly into the hypothalamus affect drinking behavior. Epstein observed that similar injections not only elicited drinking, but in some cases also elicited feeding in satiated rats. This suggests that the stimulating effect of hypertonic solutions may affect neural mechanisms in general rather than only osmoreceptors (unless we are willing to accept the unlikely conclusion that the hypothalamic feeding mechanism also depends on osmometric regulations).

Gilbert and Glaser (1961) have suggested that the hypothalamic control of water intake may not be the only central mechanism involved in the regulation of the organism's fluid balance and thirst. They pointed out that animals recover an almost normal regulation of water intake even after large hypothalamic lesions and suggested that other "receptor sites or effector circuits can compensate for the loss." Since thirst can result from a reduction of serum osmotic pressure (and a consequent overhydration of the cells), Gilbert and Glaser proposed that thirst under some conditions may occur because of a depletion of fluid *volume* in spite of serum hypo-osmolarity. Smith (1957) has suggested that the response to volume changes may be mediated by special receptors that are quite distinct from the osmoreceptors of the hypothalamus. Gilbert (1956) supported this

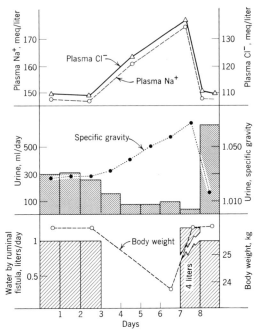

Fig. 7.22 The effects of withholding for 4 days the water otherwise given every day by ruminal fistula to a goat made permanently adipsic by proton irradiation of the preoptic region. The animal had free access to water but completely refused to drink in spite of the development of severe dehydration. Unlike a normal animal, however, it continued to eat its daily ration of food even on the fourth day of water depletion. (From Andersson et al., 1964.)

hypothesis with the observation that lesions of the subcommissural organ produced pronounced hypodipsia or even adipsia, whereas electrical stimulation of this small midbrain secretory structure increased water consumption. Gilbert (1957, 1960) suggested that the subcommissural organ may contain volume receptors which participate in the regulation of thirst, and that the same effector circuit may be activated by both osmotic and volume changes, since the posterior hypothalamus and the area of the subcommissural organ are linked by a number of major neural pathways (Nauta, 1958). Gilbert and Glaser (1961) have further suggested that this dual osmoreceptor–volume-receptor mechanism may similarly apply to the regulation of various hormone systems that directly or indirectly affect the organism's water or salt metabolism.

Other Extrahypothalamic Influences

Largely on the basis of the observation that complete and prolonged adipsia can be produced

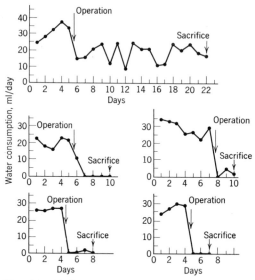

Fig. 7.23 Daily water consumption of five operated rats. Histological examination of the brains showed the subcommissural organ completely destroyed. (From G. J. Gilbert, *Anat. Rec,* 1956, **126**, 257.)

by small lesions in the lateral hypothalamus, it has been assumed that thirst may be regulated exclusively by a relatively autonomous center in this portion of the brain.

This interpretation began to be questioned when Gilbert (1956) reported hypodipsia and even adipsia following subcommissural lesions, and the doubts were solidified when Andersson and Larsson (1961b) obtained adipsia following proton irradiation of the preoptic area in goats. The initial chemical stimulation studies (Grossman, 1960, 1962a, b) supported the center notion in showing that the drinking response to cholinergic stimulation appeared to be specific to a small portion of the lateral hypothalamus. This localization has been verified by several investigators (Stein and Seifter, 1962; Miller et al., 1964). However, subsequent investigations of central structures which are functionally or anatomically related to the hypothalamus have shown that drinking may also be elicited or facilitated by cholinergic stimulation of a number of structures in the old cortex and related subcortical regions (Grossman, 1964a, b; Fisher and Coury, 1964; Miller et al., 1964; Wolf and Miller, 1964; Miller, 1965; Grossman, 1966).

In some instances the response to cholinergic stimulation of the extrahypothalamic areas seems to be identical to that seen after lateral hypothalamic stimulation, and sometimes it seems to be

even more pronounced. Grossman (1964b), for instance, reported that injections of carbachol into the medial septal area reliably elicited prolonged and intensive drinking in sated rats and that the water intake of animals deprived for 24 hr could be inhibited by injections of atropine into this portion of the brain. Fisher and Coury (1964) reported that cholinergic stimulation of the dorsomedial hippocampus, dentate gyrus, diagonal band of Broca, midline thalamus, and cingulate cortex elicited a more prolonged and intense drinking response than stimulation of the lateral hypothalamus and that significant water intake could also be elicited from the preoptic region, anterior thalamic nuclei, mammillary region, and medial midbrain.

Wolf and Miller (1964) demonstrated a most interesting relationship between the lateral hypothalamus and the preoptic area. Bilateral lesions in the lateral hypothalamus produced aphagia and adipsia and eliminated the drinking response to cholinergic stimulation of the preoptic area. *Ad libitum* water intake gradually returned to normal levels, but the effects of cholinergic stimulation did not reappear within the time limits of that experiment. Lesions in the preoptic area, on the other hand, did not modify *ad libitum* water intake and failed to inhibit the drinking response to cholinergic stimulaton of the lateral hypothalamus.

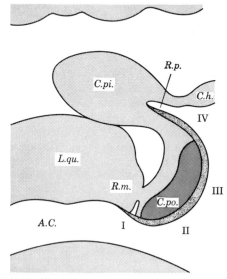

Fig. 7.24 The full extent of the subcommissural organ based upon selective staining methods. C.po., posterior commissure. (From G. J. Gilbert, *Anat. Rec,* 1956, **126**, 259.)

These observations suggest that at least some of the extrahypothalamic mechanisms which respond to cholinergic stimulation may influence drinking behavior indirectly, perhaps via the lateral hypothalamus. Grossman's investigations of the amygdaloid complex (Grossman, 1964a; Grossman and Grossman, 1963) have provided a more direct demonstration of such an interaction effect. Electrical stimulation of the anterior nuclei of the amygdala failed to elicit food or water intake in sated rats but inhibited food intake and increased water intake in food- and water-deprived animals. Both feeding and drinking responses were inhibited during and after electrical stimulation of the posterior amygdala. Very small lesions in the posterior amygdala resulted in hyperphagia and hyperdipsia, whereas lesions in the anterior amygdala induced mild hyperphagia accompanied by hypodipsia.

Chemical stimulation of these temporal lobe loci revealed the same neurochemical coding which characterized the hypothalamic centers. Chemical stimulation elicited neither feeding nor drinking in sated animals. However, bilateral injections of cholinergic substances into the ventral amygdala doubled the water intake of thirsty rats and reliably increased the animals' rate of lever pressing for water rewards. Injections of a cholinolytic substance (atropine) blocked the stimulation effect and reduced the water consumption of deprived animals. Norepinephrine injections into the same area did not reliably modify water intake but increased the food intake of deprived animals.

The lesion experiment reported by Grossman and Grossman (1963) suggests that inhibitory as well as excitatory influences may originate in the amygdala. Circumstantial support for such an interpretation was provided in the chemical stimulation experiment by the observation that injections of gamma-aminobutyric acid (GABA) into the amygdala produced effects on water intake which were similar to those seen after cholinergic stimulation. The two substances are chemically unrelated, and there is no reason to believe that GABA directly affects cholinergic pathways in the brain. However, some evidence is available which suggests that GABA may itself be a neural transmitter which selectively acts in certain inhibitory systems in the brain. The GABA injections may have stimulated a neural circuit which exerts inhibitory influences on the hypothalamic satiety mechanism, resulting in a net increase in drinking similar to that seen after cholinergic stimulation of a presumably excitatory influence on the lateral hypothalamic feeding center.

That still other portions of the brain may also contribute to the apparently diffuse and complex neural mechanism which helps to regulate water intake is implied by earlier findings of Andersson and Larsson (1956a). These workers observed that amphetamine, a well-known appetite depressant, inhibited the hyperdipsia that normally results from intravenous injections of hypertonic saline. The drug effect was abolished after prefrontal lobotomy, and the authors suggested that the prefrontal area of the cortex might influence thirst indirectly via some inhibitory action on the hypothalamic mechanisms.

The chemical stimulation experiments indicate that extrahypothalamic mechanisms may play a much more important role in the regulation of water intake and thirst than had previously been assumed. We do not, at present, have sufficient information about the exact nature of the contribution which the individual components of this complex regulatory system may make and cannot formulate a hypothesis regarding their interaction. It is clear, however, that we shall have to unravel these complex relationships if we are to understand the central regulation of thirst.

Summary

Although many of the early peripheral or general theories of thirst suggested that some central mechanism must exist to integrate the information from peripheral sources, relevant experimental data have only recently become available. Two developments are principally responsible for the advances in this field in the past fifteen years. Historically the first, though perhaps the less important, factor was the clinical and experimental demonstration that diabetes insipidus (a disease characterized by profuse urinary flow and hyperdipsia) was directly and causally related to a malfunction of the neurohypophyseal system, which is under the control of the paraventricular and supraoptic nuclei of the hypothalamus. Just before World War II, the possible relevance of these findings to a central regulation of thirst began to be appreciated. It was only after the turmoil of the war that the second major development occurred. In 1947 Verney published the now classic description of an osmoreceptor system in the hypothalamus which appeared to regulate neurohypophyseal function with respect to the secretion of antidiuretic hormone. He observed that a rise in the effective osmotic pressure of the extracellular

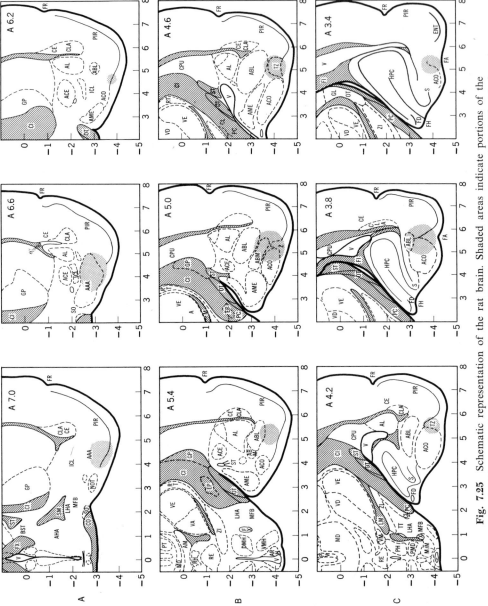

Fig. 7.25 Schematic representation of the rat brain. Shaded areas indicate portions of the amygdaloid complex from which modifications of food or water intake can be elicited. Electrical stimulation of the region shown in panel A inhibited feeding behavior but increased water intake in deprived rats. Small lesions in this area produced hyperphagia accompanied by hypodipsia. Electrical stimulation of the region shaded in panel B failed to affect food intake but increased water consumption. Small lesions produced the opposite effects. Stimulation of the region shaded in panel C inhibited both food and water intake. Small lesions in this area produced hyperphagia and hyperdipsia. (From Grossman and Grossman, 1963.)

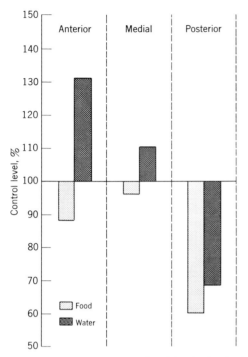

Fig. 7.26 Food and water intake of deprived animals during 1 hr of "chronic" electrical stimulation of the ventral amygdala. The data are expressed as a percentage of the average intake on control tests without the electrical stimulation. (From Grossman and Grossman, 1963.)

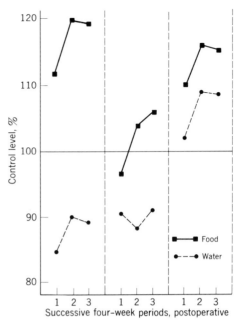

Fig. 7.27 Daily food and water intake following lesions in the ventral amygdala. The data are expressed as a percentage of the average intake during a six-week control period preceding the lesions. (From Grossman and Grossman, 1963.)

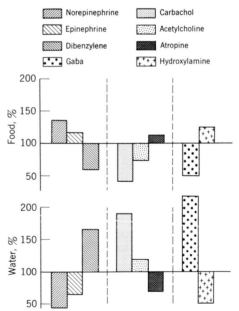

Fig. 7.28 Effects of adrenergic and cholinergic stimulation of the ventral amygdala on food and water intake (performance of food- and water-motivated instrumental responses) of deprived animals. The results are expressed as a percentage of the average performance on pre- and poststimulation control tests. (From Grossman and Grossman, 1963.)

fluid in the region of the diencephalon produced an inhibition of ADH secretion and a consequent retention of body fluids.

Similar central osmoreceptors had previously been postulated to account for the regulation of water intake, and Verney's findings triggered a concentrated effort which has greatly contributed to our understanding of thirst. Andersson reported that direct osmotic as well as electrical stimulation of a restricted region of the hypothalamus elicits drinking in sated goats; these findings have been replicated in a variety of other species. Several investigators have demonstrated that discrete electrolytic lesions in the same region produce adipsia which may or may not be accompanied by disturbances of the salt metabolism. Although the central thirst mechanism appears to be clearly differentiated in the goat, most other species that have been investigated (notably the rat) show a pronounced anatomical overlap of the hypothalamic mechanisms which regulate feeding and drinking behavior. The drinking center is located in the anterior portion of the goat hypothalamus but is nearly coexistent with the more posterior and lateral feeding center in the rat. Teitelbaum and his associates have been concerned with the consequent interaction of stimulation or ablation effects; it appears clear now that the two mechanisms are functionally as well as biochemically distinct and separate, although there seems to be considerable mutual interaction. Experiments by Andersson and by Grossman have shown that chemical as well as electrical stimulation of this hypothalamic drinking center produces effects which apparently have motivational properties similar at least to normal thirst.

The work of the past decades has greatly enhanced our understanding of the thirst mechanism by providing a precise anatomical localization of a central regulatory mechanism in the hypothalamus. What remains to be explored is the precise functional significance of this drinking center and its relation to the many other regions of the brain which recent research has shown to be involved in the regulation of water intake. What, for instance, is the role of possible volumetric influences of subcommissural origin and how does the regulation of the organism's fluid balance affect thermoregulatory or more general energy regulating mechanisms? The experimental observations of Gilbert and Andersson clearly suggest that these influences must be considered, but much remains to be learned before we can discuss the role of the hypothalamic drinking center in such a system of central factors. The picture is further complicated by the results of recent chemical stimulation studies indicating that thirst may be regulated by a complex and diffusely represented neural network which encompasses most, if not all, of the classical limbic system as well as such related subcortical structures as the amygdala, septal area, and even portions of the brainstem. Are some of these influences dependent on the integrity of the hypothalamic mechanisms as the experiments by Grossman and Miller suggest, and do we have to consider separate inhibitory and excitatory influences as indicated by the work on the amygdaloid complex? Can we attach any functional significance to the observation that food and water intake appear to be regulated by largely parallel and interwoven pathways which seem to maintain their functional identity, at least in part, by means of a neuropharmacological coding rather than purely anatomical mechanisms? Our understanding of the central regulation of thirst has come a long way in the past 20 years, but much work remains to be ac-

complished before we can hope to unravel the complex relationships uncovered by recent experiments.

SATIATION

We have seen that various peripheral mechanisms may contribute information to complex central systems which in some way translate this information into specific motivational forces that direct the organism's behavior toward a search for water and the consequent intake of water. But what causes the organism to stop drinking? How does it "know" that sufficient water has been ingested to return its fluid balance to zero? One might propose that the same peripheral and central mechanisms that initiate drinking are also responsible for satiation. However, even a cursory look at the experimental literature indicates that the temporal relationships in satiety cannot be explained by the peripheral mechanisms believed to be primarily responsible for the initiation of drinking. Dehydrated animals replace the accumulated water deficit rather precisely and stop drinking long before an appreciable amount of water has had an opportunity to be absorbed from the stomach. This rapid metering all but excludes osmometric or cellular hydration factors which seem to play such an important role in the initiation of thirst.

The truth of the matter is that we do not, at present, have a satisfactory explanation of satiation. We do not even have a separate central satiety mechanism comparable to the one that regulates the cessation of eating. This, of course, complicates matters; we do not know whether we should proceed under the assumption that such a satiety mechanism will someday be discovered, or whether we should attempt to account for the observed shut-off system by a direct inhibitory action on the excitatory drinking center of the hypothalamus. Worse yet, we may have to consider the possibility that some of the extrahypothalamic central structures which appear to influence drinking behavior (such as the amygdala or commissural organ) may exert their influence primarily, if not exclusively, by inhibiting the hypothalamic drinking center. At this time we do not have nearly enough information to suggest a coherent theory of satiation and shall have to be content to present some of the relevant experimental data without suggesting a conceptual framework for them.

Oral-Pharyngeal Factors

Many experimental and clinical studies of thirst have reported that dampening or wetting of the mouth may produce a temporary relief of thirst. However, you will remember that water which was allowed to wet the mouth and/or throat but not to reach the stomach did not provide adequate satiation. Bellows (1939) studied the drinking behavior of esophagostomized dogs, and some of his observations are relevant here. Bellows reported that his animals drank much larger quantities of water than would be required to restore their fluid balance, but he noticed that sham drinking did not proceed at a constant rate. The dogs drank for a while, stopped, and soon began to drink again. Bellows suggested that the brief stops might be due to a metering of the ingested fluids somewhere in the mouth or throat, rather than to the fatigue factor which previous investigators had invoked. Bellows explained the return to the water bucket by postulating an additional metering device below the fistula. Presumably, this metabolic metering device operates normally as a shut-off mechanism, but with such a long latency that it must be supplemented by a more immediate oral or pharyngeal mechanism. Bellows' hypothesis is open to relatively direct test, since one can determine the temporal parameters quite easily. This has not yet been done, but several studies (Adolph, 1939; Robinson and Adolph, 1943) provide some experimental support.

It was found that normal dogs rapidly drink an amount of water that returns their fluid balance to zero; no surplus water is ingested, and drinking stops before a significant effect on plasma osmolarity or cellular hydration can occur. Dogs with esophageal fistulae consume more water than would be required to stabilize their fluid balance before stopping, but the quantity ingested remains *proportional* to the actual water deficit. If an amount of water equal to the accumulated deficit is injected directly into the stomach of fistulated dogs and access to water is allowed immediately thereafter, sham drinking will match rather precisely the injected amount (and actual deficit). However, if access to water is not allowed until 20 min after the direct injection of water, the animals refuse to drink, although no water has passed through their presumably dry mouths.

Stomach Distension

Towbin (1949, 1955, 1964) has attempted to quantify these observations and obtain further evidence for the operation of the subpharyngeal metering device. After establishing a control level (the amount of water normally sham-drunk by a fistulated animal), he injected various percentages of this control level directly into the stomach. After a period of time calculated to allow complete absorption of the injected water into the extracellular fluid, Towbin offered water to these animals. The experiments showed that dogs are completely satiated when only 40% of the water that is sham-drunk is allowed to enter the stomach (i.e., sham drinking "overcompensated" by 250%). Towbin concluded that the proposed oral-pharyngeal mechanism cannot meter the ingested water accurately enough to provide for a shut-off mechanism that correlates with water need. Since satiation occurs too quickly to permit a direct effect on plasma osmolarity, Towbin argued that the subpharyngeal metering device might make use of gastric distension (i.e., the stretching of neural receptors in the walls of the stomach). To test this hypothesis, he introduced balloons into the stomach of his dogs via the lower esophageal opening. Following deprivation, these balloons were inflated with air or water to produce a volume displacement directly comparable to that caused by the amount of water previously found necessary to inhibit drinking. Drinking was inhibited by this manipulation, and there appeared to be no difference between balloons inflated with air and those filled with water. Towbin concluded from his observations that gastric distension was

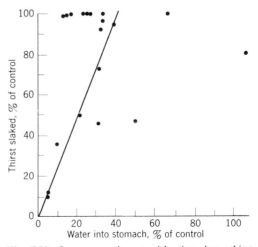

Fig. 7.29 In an experiment with nine dogs, thirst slacked 1 hr after water was put into the stomach. (From Towbin, 1949.)

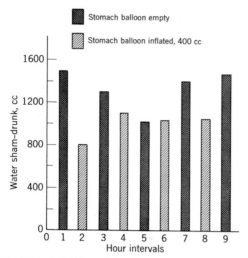

Fig. 7.30 Inhibition of sham drinking by the inflation of a stomach balloon. (From Towbin, 1949.)

one of the important subpharyngeal factors which affect satiation in the dog.

Montgomery and Holmes (1955) induced thirst by intravenous injections of hypertonic sodium chloride solutions. Stomach balloons were filled with water. It was found that maximum inhibition occurred only after the balloons had been inflated for 20 to 40 min, which corresponds rather nicely to the temporal factors in previous studies of the effects of intragastric water injections on sham drinking. The inhibition of drinking persisted for several minutes after the balloons had been deflated, and the effect was completely abolished by local anesthesia of the stomach. Although these results seem to support Towbin's hypothesis, we would like to point out that mechanical stomach distension might inhibit drinking not because thirst has actually been reduced but rather because noxious stimulation has been introduced. Miller (Kohn, 1951; Miller, 1952; Miller and Kessen, 1952; Berkun et al., 1952) has investigated the "reward value" of intragastric balloons with respect to hunger and has reported that hungry rats stop eating when a balloon is inflated; however, the rats also learned to *avoid* a response in a maze that was rewarded by such inflation of the stomach balloon. These results indicate that the mechanical distension of the stomach is aversive and that the negative qualities of this stimulation are stronger than any satiety value. Miller suggested that the apparent satiety effect of stomach distension may be accounted for entirely by the aversive properties of this stimulation.

Neural Feedback from the Stomach

That stomach distension may not be a factor in the regulation of satiety under normal conditions is further suggested by the finding that denervation of the stomach (vagotomy) almost entirely eliminates the inhibitory effect produced by inflating the stomach with a balloon (Towbin, 1949). Vagotomy seems to have no effect on the amount of water consumed in response to intravenous injections of hypertonic saline (Holmes and Gregersen, 1950) or normal thirst (Di Salvo, 1955a, b), in spite of the fact that more complete denervation (vagotomy plus spinal transection) was attempted in the latter studies.

Species Differences

A number of investigators have studied the role of gastric factors without attempting to distinguish between various possible neural or humoral mechanisms. An integration of these experiments is complicated by the fact that wide interspecies differences have been observed. Adolph (1950) noted, for instance, that drinking was inhibited immediately by intragastric injections of water in hamsters and guinea pigs, but little or no immediate effect was seen in dogs and rabbits. Miller et al. (1957) found that water injected directly into the stomach of rats immediately reduced thirst measured by consummatory activity as well as rate of performance of a previously acquired instrumental response. Miller found that the re-

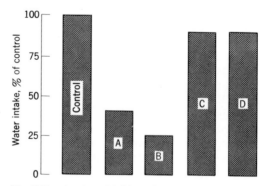

Fig. 7.31 Average drinking of eight dogs after intravenous injection of 20% NaCl (controls—100%) as compared with drinking after 20% NaCl and A, distension of balloon in the stomach 40 min before salt injection; B, introduction of water into the stomach 40 min before salt injection; C, procedure A preceded by cocainizing gastric mucosa; D, water introduced into the stomach at time of salt injection. (From Montgomery and Holmes, 1955.)

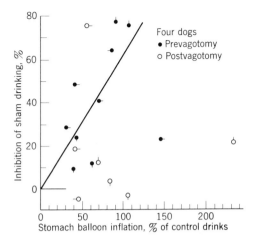

Fig. 7.32 Vagotomy, as it affects sensitivity to stomach balloon inflation. (From Towbin, 1949.)

corded inhibition of thirst never equaled that produced by normal drinking of the same quantities of water, and suggested that these findings indicate both an oral-pharngeal and a gastric mechanism.

Undoubtedly related to these differences is the fact that the rate and pattern of drinking differs greatly between species. Dogs, for instance, replenish the entire water deficit quite rapidly in one uninterrupted period of drinking (Adolph, 1950). Rats, on the other hand, drink slowly and intermittently even when quite thirsty, and longer pauses begin to appear as soon as a significant percentage of the accumulated water deficit is recovered (Adolph, 1947a). Man similarly replaces only 50 to 80% of his fluid deficit during the first half-hour after a prolonged period of deprivation.

It is quite possible that gastric distension operates as a limiting factor that comes into play earlier in some species than in others. The neural feedback from gastric distension does not appear to be *essential* under normal conditions but may, nevertheless, play a part in satiety. If the major regulation of satiety is gastric, as most investigations suggest, and if we can rule out neural feedback from pressor receptors (because of the demonstrated failure of stomach denervation), where then must we look for an answer? We have already eliminated osmometric factors as too slow, and there remain only unknown humoral mechanisms which have, to date, escaped detection.

Before we conclude our discussion of satiety, we might briefly mention Zotterman's work (Zotterman, 1949, 1956; Zotterman and Diamant, 1959) which may explain the oral-pharyngeal

metering system. His studies demonstrate that several species appear to have water receptors that respond selectively to distilled water. Other species have receptors that are inhibited by distilled water and to a lesser extent by hypotonic saline. These receptors increase their spontaneous firing when hypertonic saline is applied. Zotterman has suggested that the organism may have a specific "water taste" which depends on chemical (rather than osmotic) stimulation of specific receptors in the tongue. Although direct evidence has not yet become available, it is conceivable that the level of activity in these receptors might serve as the proposed oral metering device.

One other possibility deserves to be mentioned. Wolf (1958) has reported that some relief from thirst can be obtained by stimulation of "cold receptors" in the mouth, and an experiment by Hendry and Rasche (1961) provides some experimental support for this notion. Thirsty rats licked a tube from which a brief puff of cold air was delivered every time the rat's tongue came in contact with the tube. The "air drinking" was found to be rewarding only to thirsty animals; it reduced subsequent water intake in spite of the fact that such "cooling of the mouth" further decreased the water stores of the body because of evaporation of saliva.

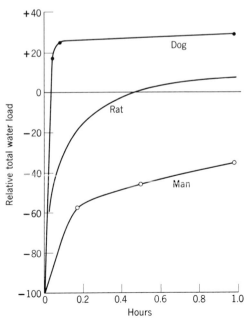

Fig. 7.33 Water intakes during the first hour of drinking in three species. (From Adolph, 1943b. Copyright 1943 by The Ronald Press Co.)

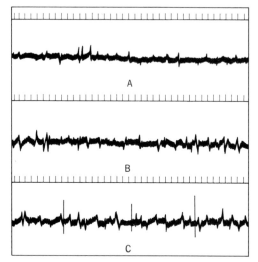

Fig. 7.34 Action potentials from the frog's glosso-pharyngeal nerve. A, control; B, after exposing the tongue to an extract of flies made with frog's saliva; and C, after exposing the tongue to an extract of flies made with distilled water. The records were made about 2 min after application of the extracts. Time marker, 50 cps. (From Zotterman, 1949.)

Summary

The best summary of our discussion of satiety mechanisms in thirst might be the statement that we do not know very much about them. We can list some factors that may contribute to a metering of the ingested liquid but do not seem to be *essential* to the shut-off system. We can also consider factors that do not enter into the regulation of satiety but appear of greatest importance to the *initiation* of drinking.

Osmometric changes (plasma osmolarity or cellular dehydration), for instance, do not seem to contribute to satiety, simply because the fluid deficit is recovered and drinking is stopped in many species long before an appreciable amount of water has been absorbed into the bloodstream.

Of the mechanisms which may normally contribute to satiation without being essential to it, we might mention two categories:

1. *Oral-pharyngeal factors* such as specific taste receptors, osmoreceptors, local cooling or wetting, and perhaps feedback from the pharyngeal musculature.

2. *Gastric factors* such as gastric distension or neural feedback from some other types of receptor mechanism in the gastric muscosa.

If we look at these categories, it appears certain

that the shut-off mechanism must depend on some form of humoral secretion from the stomach (what else is left?), but no such mechanism has been demonstrated to date.

THE RELATIONSHIP BETWEEN HUNGER AND THIRST

Although hunger and thirst appear to be quite distinct motivational forces, a pronounced interaction between dehydration and food deprivation can be observed. It is well known (and appears reasonable) that organisms reduce their food intake when deprived of water. A number of writers have commented upon this phenomenon and have demonstrated its operation in a variety of species (Adolph, 1947c; Asher and Hodes, 1939; Bing and Mendel, 1931; Cort, 1951; Kleitman, 1927). The converse also appears to be true, at least in some species. Less water is consumed (in spite of a negative water balance) during periods of food deprivation than when food is freely available (Calvin and Behan, 1954; Gregersen, 1932b; Robinson and Adolph, 1943). This is surprising, for most foods contain at least some water and many of the customary laboratory foods actually contain much. When water or food are restored, the organism appears to attempt to compensate for the voluntary deficit (Adolph, 1947c). The body, in addition to regulating food and water intake separately, apparently maintains a relatively constant food-water ratio; Stevenson (1949; Stevenson et al., 1950) has used this concept in his investigations of central mechanisms.

Adolph (1943b) demonstrated that rats lose weight about as rapidly during periods of water deprivation as they do when *both* food and water are unavailable. Only very little dry food

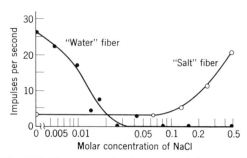

Fig. 7.35 Frequency of action potentials from a cat's single "water" fiber and a single "salt" fiber during the first second of stimulation by varying concentrations of NaCl. (From Cohen et al., 1955.)

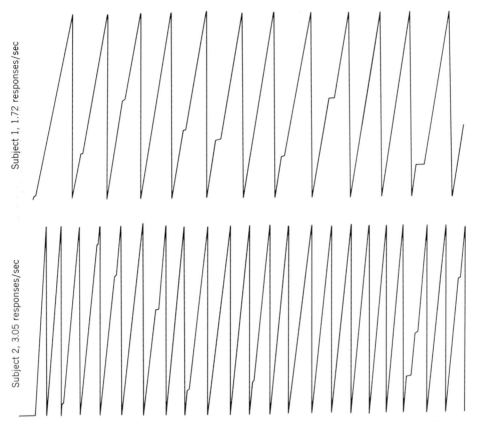

Fig. 7.36 Cumulative response curves for a 1-hr session of licking at the air tube. Records are after the fastest and slowest subjects on that particular day. The number given at the left is the average rate of responding for the hour. A single excursion of the pen requires 500 responses. (From Hendry and Rasche, 1961.)

is taken in the absence of adequate hydration. Rats deprived of food alone survive no longer than animals deprived of both food and water, and may, in fact, die sooner (Barker and Adolph, 1953; Wolf, 1958). Similar results have been reported for dogs (Howe et al., 1912).

Man and some species of animals tend to become thirsty during and after the ingestion of food, even when the diet itself contains a large amount of water. Kleitman (1927) found that dogs deprived of food drank only about 50% of their normal intake (which reduced their total water intake to about 10% since their diet contained a high percentage of water). Robinson and Adolph (1943) found that water intake was reduced even if food deprivation was maintained for only a single day. These results suggest that the decreased food intake is not caused by some long-term mechanism such as cumulative dehydration. Wolf (1958) has suggested that organisms use

endogenous water during periods of water deprivation to compensate for the reduced fluid intake. This theory is supported by the fact that up to 70% of the weight loss observed following a period of both food and water deprivation reflects a water loss (Elkinton and Taffel, 1942).

Lepkovsky et al. (1957) have proposed that the food-water interaction takes place in the digestive tract, since rats maintained a constant food-water ratio in the stomach (about 50% water) and in the intestinal tract (about 76% water) when shifted from *ad libitum* food and water to water deprivation. It was suggested that the sharply reduced food intake which resulted from the water deprivation occurred because only small amounts of water can be mobilized from the tissues. According to this notion, food can only be consumed in amounts that can be diluted to the appropriate food-water ratio by the available endogenous or exogenous water.

Central Factors

Strominger (1947) observed that bilateral destruction of the ventromedial nuclei of the hypothalamus produced not only hyperphagia in rats but also a comparable increase in water intake which was presumed to be secondary to the increased ingestion of dry food. Stevenson (1949; Stevenson et al., 1950), on the other hand, reported that similar lesions did not elicit sufficient compensatory drinking so that the food-water ratio was significantly increased. Whether these results can be interpreted to imply a direct central interaction between the feeding and drinking mechanisms is not entirely clear.

We have already mentioned that at least in the rat there appears to be almost complete anatomical overlap of the neural mechanisms that regulate food and water intake. Although recent experiments have shown that these systems are quite distinct functionally as well as biochemically, there appears to be an interesting reciprocal relationship (Grossman, 1960, 1962a, b) which might explain the observed interactions. Grossman observed that the specific chemical stimulation of the hypothalamus which elicited feeding decreased drinking, even in a testing situation that prevented a direct interference of the two responses. Chemical substances that elicited drinking reduced food intake. These findings suggest that the observed reduction in food intake during water deprivation (as well as the complementary reduction in water intake during food deprivation), may depend on central rather than peripheral interactions.

SUMMARY

In psychology thirst has generally been treated as one of the primary drives which presumably are characterized by a definite and simple physiological need. Because of this, thirst has been studied quite extensively as an example of a basic motivational force which is relatively uncomplicated by learning. Most psychological theories of motivation rely directly or indirectly on data from animal experiments on hunger or thirst. In view of this emphasis, it is perhaps surprising that no acceptable definition of this intervening variable has been worked out. Physiological need, as we have seen, does not seem to be a simple, unitary phenomenon which can be measured unambiguously with techniques now available. The regulation of thirst motivation is merely one aspect of the organism's fluid balance to which both secretory and excretory mechanisms contribute, and these are themselves subject to complex and inadequately understood humoral and neural regulation.

Moreover, it has been very difficult to establish just how and where the body's need of water is metered, and only very recently have some experimental data suggested possible neural systems that may be involved in the translation of the physiological need for water into specific psychological motivation to seek and ingest water. Subjective sensations of thirst (quite aside from being introspective and therefore useless for animal research and odious to the behavioral psychologist) are not dependable indices of physiological need, since they may occur when the body is, in fact, overhydrated, and since water deficits are not always reflected in thirst sensations.

For the purpose of animal experimentation, thirst has been defined operationally (i.e., an animal is thirsty whenever access to water has been denied for some period of time), and we have assumed from somewhat circular reasoning that animals are thirsty because we observe drinking. The complex physiological determination of thirst makes these definitions necessarily crude and often misleading, and much work remains to be done before we can hope to remedy this situation. The physiological psychologist cannot be content with these estimates, even though he may have to use them in his own research at the present time.

Prescientific interest in the physiological mechanisms of thirst can be traced back to the philosophers of ancient Greece, whose explanations persisted well into our century. Thirst, they believed, was a specific sensation, comparable to vision or audition, which originated in the mouth and throat whenever the buccal or pharyngeal mucosa became dry and parched. This theory was restated by Haller in the eighteenth century and enjoyed great popularity with the physiologists of the nineteenth century. Cannon made it the basis of his famous "dry-mouth theory of thirst" which was restated as recently as 1934; the theory continues to exert a dominant influence on psychological theories of motivation, in spite of excellent experimental evidence to the contrary. Perhaps most damaging to this hypothesis is the fact that sham drinking (where water is allowed to pass through the mouth and throat but not to enter the stomach) does not alleviate thirst, but many other types of data do not support the peripheral-sensory interpretation. Congenital or experimentally produced local dryness of the mouth (caused, in most cases, by partial or complete lack of salivation) does not seem to interfere with the regulation of water intake, and even local anesthesia of the sensory receptors or removal of their innervation appears to have a few deleterious effects. Although thirst sensations from the mouth undoubtedly are part of the total pattern under normal conditions (and may even be directly responsible for the thirst observed after the consumption of spicy foods), it seems rather certain that they are not an *essential* component of the thirst drive or the regulation of water intake. Even in satiation these local factors appear to play only a relatively minor role.

As the peripheral-sensory theories began to attract serious scientific consideration, it became obvious that some additional mechanism was required if the sensations from the mouth and throat were to reflect the organism's water need. Such considerations led some of the theorists of the nineteenth century to propose osmometric factors; these factors were presumed to be influenced by either the osmolarity of the blood plasma itself or the movement of water from the cells into the extracellular spaces of the body. Over the years these notions have gained considerable experimental support, and osmometric factors have been elevated to a position of dominance and independence from their initial position of subservience to the sensory mechanisms.

The pioneering work of Mayer (1900) and Wettendorff (1901) demonstrated that water deprivation does, in fact, produce pronounced changes in the osmotic pressure of the blood. Subsequent investigations suggested that the effective stimulus for thirst was not merely a rise of plasma osmotic pressure; rather, the stimulus involved a change in the *effective* osmotic pressure of the blood which causes water to move from the cells into the extracellular compartment. The resultant cellular dehydration appears to be an adequate and perhaps essential stimulus for thirst; what remains to be shown is how this general cellular change is translated into the specific motivation to seek and ingest water. There remain some additional questions about the effects of relative overhydration and expansion of the cells, but it seems rather certain that effective osmotic pressure or the consequent variation in cell volume are directly and causally related to thirst. But how does this affect the behavior of the orga-

nism? It is quite improbable that local sensory mechanisms in the mouth and throat transmit the required information in the form of specific sensations. It has been proposed that all cells (or some special group of cells) may act as osmoreceptors that signal to some central integrating mechanism whenever the effective osmotic pressure (or cell volume) deviates from normal. Since no general neural substrate for this mechanism has been observed, more and more interest has shifted to the possibility that this osmoreceptor function may be carried out by specific cells of possibly central origin.

Suggestions of a "central drinking mechanism" appeared in the literature over 150 years ago, but direct experimental evidence for such a drinking center has only recently become available. The recent advances were made possible by the demonstration that (1) diabetes insipidus (the symptomatology of which includes hyperdipsia) is a disturbance of hypothalamic origin; and (2) some cells in the hypothalamus appear to act as osmoreceptors and form part of the afferent link of the central mechanism determining antidiuretic hormone release. Following these crucial developments, Andersson, Grossman, and others have shown that osmotic, electrical, or chemical stimulation of a specific region of the hypothalamus induces vigorous drinking (and presumably thirst) in sated animals; Stellar, Teitelbaum, and others have demonstrated that bilateral destruction of this area produces at least temporary adipsia in a variety of species.

Not yet answered is the question whether this hypothalamic drinking center is itself the osmoreceptor system required by the osmometric theories, or whether it merely serves to integrate information from various peripheral sources and perhaps translates these data into specific motivation. Several other regions of the brain have been shown to affect drinking behavior, and we do not yet know how the various central and peripheral mechanisms interact. Thirst may also be affected by volumetric and thermoregulatory mechanisms, and much remains to be accomplished before we can provide a definite and complete explanation of thirst.

Perhaps the greatest obstacle to an unqualified acceptance of the osmometric theories has been the problem of satiation. Somehow the organism's water intake is metered quite precisely so that intake does not, under normal circumstances, exceed the cumulative deficit. This in itself presents no difficulties for osmometric theories, but it can be shown that this shut-off mechanism operates in many species long before a significant amount of water is absorbed from the stomach. Drinking stops although the osmotic conditions have not been materially affected. It has been demonstrated that this satiety mechanism depends largely on information from the gastrointestinal tract; however, it remains difficult to understand where and how this information is compared with the precise water needs of the organism, as it must if water intake is to match accurately the accumulated deficit. The problem is compounded by the fact that no satiety center has been demonstrated in the central nervous system and by the observation that neural feedback from the stomach does not seem to be an essential ingredient of the shut-off mechanism. These considerations suggest that we may have to look for a humoral messenger which originates in the gastrointestinal tract and affects either the hypothalamic drinking center or some as yet unknown satiety center.

Although our knowledge of water intake and thirst motivation has increased tremendously in the past decade, much research remains to be completed before we can hope to understand the complex interplay of factors that determine the organism's water exchange.

BIBLIOGRAPHY

Adolph, E. F. The regulation of the water content of the human organism. *J. Physiol. (London)*, 1921, **55**, 114–132.

Adolph, E. F. *The regulation of size as illustrated in unicellular organisms.* Springfield, Ill.: Thomas, 1931.

Adolph, E. F. The metabolism and distribution of water in body and tissues. *Physiol. Rev.*, 1933, **13**, 336–371.

Adolph, E. F. Measurements of water drinking in dogs. *Amer. J. Physiol.*, 1939, **125**, 75–86.

Adolph, E. F. Do rats thrive when drinking sea water? *Amer. J. Physiol.*, 1943a, **140**, 25–32.

Adolph, E. F. *Physiological regulations.* Lancaster, Pa.: Jacques Cattell Press, 1943b. Copyright 1943 by The Ronald Press Co.

Adolph, E. F. Exchanges of heat and tolerances to cold in men exposed to outdoor weather. *Amer. J. Physiol.*, 1946, **146**, 507–537.

Adolph, E. F. Urges to eat and drink in rats. *Amer. J. Physiol.*, 1947a, **151**, 110–125.

Adolph, E. F. Tolerance to heat and dehydration in several species of mammals. *Amer. J. Physiol.*, 1947b, **151**, 564–575.

Adolph, E. F. Water metabolism. *Ann. Rev. Physiol.*, 1947c, **9**, 381–408.

Adolph, E. F. Water ingestion and excretion in rats under some chemical influences. *Amer. J. Physiol.*, 1948, **155**, 309–316.

Adolph, E. F. Quantitative relations in the physiological constitutions of mammals. *Science*, 1949, **109**, 579–585.

Adolph, E. F. Thirst and its inhibition in the stomach. *Amer. J. Physiol.*, 1950, **161**, 374–386.

Adolph, E. F. Principles of water and salt balance. *Activities report, Res. Dev. Ass., Food & Container Inst., U.S. Army Forces*, 1951, **3**, 143–146.

Adolph, E. F. Ontogeny of physiological regulation in the rat. *Quart Rev. Biol.*, 1957, **32**, 89–137.

Adolph, E. F., & Dill, D. B. Observations on water metabolism in the desert. *Amer. J. Physiol.*, 1938, **123**, 369–378.

Adolph, E. F., & Northrop, J. P. Physiological adaptations to body-water excesses in rats. *Amer. J. Physiol.*, 1952, **168**, 320–334.

Adolph, E. F., & Parmington, S. L. Partial nephrectomy and the water exchange of rats. *Amer. J. Physiol.*, 1948, **155**, 317–326.

Adolph, E. F. et al. *Physiology of man in the desert.* New York: Interscience, 1947.

Adolph, E. F., Barker, J. P., & Hoy, P. A. Multiple factors in thirst. *Amer. J. Physiol.*, 1954, **178**, 538–562.

Alajouanine, T., & Thurel, R. Données cliniques, expérimentales et thérapeutiques sur la soif et la polyurie du diabete insipide. *Rev. neurol.*, 1946, **78**, 471.

Allison, R. S., & Critchley, M. Observations on thirst. *J. roy. nav. med. Serv.*, 1943, **29**, 258–266.

Allott, E. N. Sodium and chlorine retention without renal disease. *Lancet*, 1939, **1**, 1035–1037.

Andersson, B. The effect and localization of electrical stimulation of certain parts of the brainstem in sheep and goats. *Acta physiol. scand.*, 1951, **23**, 1–16.

Andersson, B. Polydipsia caused by intrahypothalamic injections of hypertonic NaCl-solutions. *Experientia*, 1952a, **8**, 157–158.

Andersson, B. Polydipsi som foeljd av injektioner av hypertonisk NaCl-loesning i hypothalamus. *Nord. Med.*, 1952b, **47**, 663–665.

Andersson, B. The effect of injections of hypertonic NaCl-solutions into different parts of the hypothalamus of goats. *Acta physiol. scand.*, 1953, **28**, 188–201.

Andersson, B. Observations on the water and electrolyte metabolism in the goat. *Acta physiol. scand.*, 1955, **33**, 50–65.

Andersson, B. Polydipsia, antidiuresis and milk ejection caused by hypothalamic stimulation. In *The neurohypophysis.* Proceedings of the Eighth Symposium of the Calston Research Society. H. Heller, Ed. New York: Academic Press, 1957.

Andersson, B., & Larsson, S. Water and food intake and the inhibitory effect of amphetamine on drinking and eating before and after "prefrontal lobotomy" in dogs. *Acta physiol. scand.*, 1956a, **38**, 22–30.

Andersson, B., & Larsson, S. An attempt to condition hypothalamic polydipsia. *Acta physiol. scand.*, 1956b, **36**, 377–382.

Andersson, B., & Larsson, S. Physiological and pharmacological aspects of the control of hunger and thirst. *Pharmacol. Rev.*, 1961a, **13**, 1–16.

Andersson, B., & Larsson, S. The influence of local temperature changes in the preoptic area and rostral hypothalamus on regulation of food and water intake. *Acta physiol. scand.*, 1961b, **52**, 75–89.

Andersson, B., & McCann, S. M. A further study of polydipsia evoked by hypothalamic stimulation in the goat. *Acta physiol. scand.*, 1955a, **33**, 333–346.

Andersson, B., & McCann, S. M. Drinking, antidiuresis and milk ejection from electrical stimulation within the hypothalamus of the goat. *Acta physiol. scand.*, 1955b, **35**, 191–201.

Andersson, B., & McCann, S. M. The effect of hypothalamic lesions on the water intake of the dog. *Acta physiol. scand.*, 1956, **35**, 312–320.

Andersson, B., & Wyrwicka, W. Elicitation of a drinking motor conditioned reaction by electrical stimulation of the hypothalamic "drinking area" in the goat. *Acta physiol. scand.*, 1957, **41**, 194.

Andersson, B., Gale, C., & Sundsten, J. W. In *Olfaction and taste*, Y. Zotterman, Ed. London: Pergamon Press, 1963.

Andersson, B., Gale, C., & Sundsten, J. W. Preoptic influences on water intake. In *Thirst, first international symposium on thirst in the regulation of body water*. M. J. Wayner, Ed. New York: Pergamon Press, 1964.

Arden, F. Experimental observations upon thirst and on potassium overdosage. *Aust. J. exp. Biol. med. Sci.*, 1934, **12**, 121–122.

Asher, D. W., & Hodes, H. L. Studies in experimental dehydration. *Amer. J. med. Technol.*, 1939, **5**, 216–234.

Austin, V. T., & Steggerda, F. R. Congenital dysfunction of the salivary glands with observations on the physiology of thirst. *Illinois med. J.*, 1936, **69**, 124–127.

Barker, J. P., & Adolph, E. F. Survival of rats without water and given sea water. *Amer. J. Physiol.*, 1953, **173**, 495–502.

Beaumont, W. *Experiments and observations on the gastric juice and physiology of digestion*. Plattsburgh, N. Y.: Allen, 1833. Facsimile of the original edition, Cambridge, Mass.: Harvard Univ. Press, 1929.

Bellows, R. T. Time factors in water drinking in dogs. *Amer. J. Physiol.*, 1939, **125**, 87–97.

Bellows, R. T., & Van Wagenen, W. P. The relationship of polydipsia and polyuria in diabetes insipidus. A study of experimental diabetes insipidus in dogs with and without esophageal fistulae. *J. nerv. ment. Dis.*, 1938, **88**, 417–473.

Bellows, R. T., & Van Wagenen, W. P. The effect of resection of the olfactory, gustatory and trigeminal nerves on water drinking in dogs without and with diabetes insipidus. *Amer. J. Physiol.*, 1939, **126**, 13–19.

Berkun, M. M., Kessen, M. L., & Miller, N. E. Hunger-reducing effects of food by stomach fistula versus food by mouth measured by a consummatory response. *J. comp. physiol. Psychol.*, 1952, **45**, 550.

Bernard, C. Leçons de physiologie expérimentale appliquée à la médecine. *Cours du semestre d'été, 1855. Vol. II*. Paris: Baillière, 1856, 49–52.

Bidder, F., & Schmidt, C. *Die Verdauungssaefte und der Stoffwechsel*. Mittau and Leipzig: Reyher, 1852.

Bing, F. C., & Mendel, L. B. The relationship between food and water intakes in mice. *Amer. J. Physiol.*, 1931, **98**, 169–179.

Blumenbach, J. F. *The institutions of physiology*. Trans. from Latin by John Elliotson. London: Burgess and Hill, 1820.

Bonnier, P. La soif et les centres hygrostatiques. *C. R. Soc. Biol. (Paris)*, 1914, **76**, 240–242.

Bouffard, M. A. Quelques considérations sur la soif. Paris: Université de Paris, thèse 437, 1805.

Brobeck, J. R. Food intake as a mechanism of temperature regulation. *Yale J. Biol. Med.*, 1948, **20**, 545.

Brobeck, J. R. Food and temperature. *Recent Progr. Hormone Res.*, 1960, **16**, 439–466.

Bruce, R. H. An experimental investigation of the thirst drive in rats with especial reference to the goal gradient hypothesis. *J. gen. Psychol.*, 1937, **17**, 49–62.

Brunn, F. The sensation of thirst. *J. Amer. med. Ass.*, 1925. **85**, 234–235.

Callenfels, G. T. *De fame et siti*. Gandavi: Univ. dissertation, 1824.

Calvin, A. D., & Behan, R. A. The effect of hunger upon drinking patterns in the rat. *Brit. J. Psychol.*, 1954, **45**, 294–298.

Cannon, W. B. A consideration of the nature of hunger. *Harvey Lect.*, 1911–1912, **7**, 130–152.

Cannon, W. B. The physiological basis of thirst. *Proc. roy. Soc. (London), B*, 1918, **90**, 283–301.

Cannon, W. B. Les bases physiologiques de la soif. *Rev. gén. Sci. pure. appl.* 1919, **30**, 69–79.

Cannon, W. B. *Bodily changes in pain, hunger, fear and rage* (2nd ed). New York: Appleton, 1929.

Cannon, W. B. Some modern extensions of Beaumont's studies on Alexis St. Martin. *J. Mich. med. Soc.*, 1933, **32**, 155–164.

Cannon, W. B. Hunger and thirst. In *A handbook of general experimental psychology*, Carl Murchison, Ed. Worcester, Mass.: Clark Univ. Press, 1934, 247–263.

Cizek, L. J., Semple, R. E., Huang, K. C., & Gregersen, M. I. Effect of extracellular electrolyte depletion on water intake in dogs. *Amer. J. Physiol.*, 1951, **164**, 415–422.

Cohen, M. J., Hagirara, S., & Zotterman, Y. The response spectrum of taste fibres in the cat. *Acta physiol. scand.*, 1955, **33**, 316–332.

Cort, R. L. The interrelationship of hunger and thirst in normal rats and rats with hypothalamic lesions. Yale University, School of Medicine, M.D. thesis, 1951.

Darrow, D. C., & Yannet, H. The changes in distribution of body water accompanying increase and decrease in extracellular electrolyte. *J. clin. Invest.*, 1935, **14**, 266–275.

Darwin, E. *Zoonomia, or, the laws of organic life.* London: Johnson, 1801.

Deneufbourg, E. F. Quelques considérations sur la soif. Paris: Université de Paris, Thèse 117, 1813.

Dill, D. B. *Life, heat and altitude.* Cambridge, Mass.: Harvard Univ. Press, 1938.

Di Salvo, N. A. Factors which alter drinking responses of dogs to intravenous injections of hypertonic sodium chloride solutions. *Amer. J. Physiol.*, 1955a, **180**, 139–145.

Di Salvo, N. A. Drinking responses to intravenous hypertonic sodium chloride solutions injected into unrestrained dogs. *Amer. J. Physiol.*, 1955b, **180**, 133–138.

Dumas, C. L. *Principes de physiologie. Vol. IV.* Paris: Déterville, 1803.

Elkinton, J. R., & Squires, R. D. The distribution of body fluids in congestive heart failure. I: Theoretic considerations. *Circulation*, 1951, **4**, 679–696.

Elkinton, J. R., & Taffel, M. Prolonged water deprivation in the dog. *J. clin. Invest.*, 1942, **21**, 787–794.

Epstein, A. N. Reciprocal changes in feeding behavior caused by intra-hypothalamic chemical injections. *Amer. J. Physiol.*, 1960, **199**, 969.

Epstein, A. N., & Teitelbaum, P. Severe and persistent deficits in thirst produced by lateral hypothalamic damage. In *Thirst, first international symposium on thirst in the regulation of body water.* M. J. Wayner, Ed. New York: Pergamon Press, 1964.

Fehr, C. Ueber die Extirpation saemmtlicher Speicheldruesen bei dem Hunde. *Arch. path. Anat.*, 1862, **25**, 186–188.

Fisher, A. E., & Coury, J. N.. Cholinergic tracing of a central neural circuit underlying the thirst drive. *Science*, 1962, **138**, 691–693.

Fisher, A. E., & Coury, J. N. Chemical tracing of neural pathways mediating the thirst drive. In *Thirst, first international symposium on thirst in the regulation of body water.* M. J. Wayner, Ed. New York: Pergamon Press, 1964.

Galen, C. *De locis affectis.* Trans. in E. R. Long, *Readings in pathology.* Springfield, Ill.: Thomas, 1929.

Gilbert, G. J. The subcommissural organ. *Anat. Rec.*, 1956, **126**, 253–265.

Gilbert, G. J. The subcommissural organ: a regulator of thirst. *Amer. J. Physiol.*, 1957, **191**, 243–247.

Gilbert, G. J. The subcommissural organ. *Neurology*, 1960, **10**, 138.

Gilbert, G. J., & Glaser, G. H. On the nervous system integration of water and salt metabolism. *Arch. Neurol. (Chicago)*, 1961, **5**, 179–196.

Gilman, A. The relation between blood osmotic pressure, fluid distribution and voluntary water intake. *Amer. J. Physiol.*, 1937, **120**, 323–328.

Greer, M. A. Suggestive evidence of a primary "drinking center" in hypothalamus of the rat. *Proc. Soc. exp. Biol. Med.*, 1955, **89**, 59–62.

Gregersen, M. I. A method for uniform stimulation of the salivary glands in the unanesthetized dog by exposure to a warm environment, with some observations on the quantitative changes in salivary flow during dehydration. *Amer. J. Physiol.*, 1931, **97**, 107–116.

Gregersen, M. I. The physiological mechanism of thirst. *Amer. J. Physiol.*, 1932a, **101**, 44–45.

Gregersen, M. I. Studies on the regulation of water intake. II: Conditions affecting the daily water intake of dogs as registered continuously by a photometer. *Amer. J. Physiol.*, 1932b, **102**, 344–349.

Gregersen, M. I., & Bullock, L. T. Observations on thirst in man in relation to changes in salivary flow and plasma volume. *Amer. J. Physiol.*, 1933, **105**, 39–40.

Gregersen, M. I., & Cannon, W. B. Studies on the regulation of water intake. I: The effect of extirpation of the salivary glands on the water intake of dogs while panting. *Amer. J. Physiol.*, 1932, **102**, 336–343.

Grossman, S. P. Eating or drinking elicited by direct adrenergic or cholinergic stimulation of hypothalamus. *Science*, 1960, **132**, 301–302.

Grossman, S. P. Direct adrenergic and cholinergic stimulation of hypothalamic mechanisms. *Amer. J. Physiol.*, 1962a, **202**, 872–882.

Grossman, S. P. Effects of adrenergic and cholinergic blocking agents on hypothalamic mechanisms. *Amer. J. Physiol.*, 1962b, **202**, 1230–1236.

Grossman, S. P. Behavioral effects of chemical stimulation of the ventral amygdala. *J. comp. physiol. Psychol.*, 1964a, **1**, 29–36.

Grossman, S. P. Effects of chemical stimulation of the septal area on motivation. *J. comp. physiol. Psychol.*, 1964b, **58**, 194–200.

Grossman, S. P. Behavioral effects of direct chemical stimulation of central nervous system structures. *Int. J. Neuropharmacol.*, 1964c, **3**, 45–58.

Grossman, S. P. The VMH: a center for affective reactions, satiety, or both? *Int. J. Physiol. Behav.*, 1966, **1**, 1–10.

Grossman, S. P., & Grossman, Lore. Food and water intake following lesions or electrical stimulation of the amygdala. *Amer. J. Physiol.*, 1963, **205**, 761–765.

Haller, A. *Primae lineae physiologiae.* Gottingae: Vandenhoeck, 1747, DLXXXIII, 314. Translation, Edinburgh: Elliot, 1779.

Hendry, D. P., & Rasche, R. H. Analysis of a new nonnutritive positive reinforcer based on thirst. *J. comp. physiol. Psychol.*, 1961, **54**, 477–483.

Holmes, J. H., & Cizek, L. J. Observations on sodium chloride depletion in the dog. *Amer. J. Physiol.*, 1951, **164**, 407–414.

Holmes, J. H., & Gregersen, M. I. Relation of the salivary flow to the thirst produced in man by intravenous injection of hypotonic salt solution. *Amer. J. Physiol.*, 1947, **151**, 252–257.

Holmes, J. H., & Gregersen, M. I. Observations on drinking induced by hypertonic solutions. *Amer. J. Physiol.*, 1950a, **162**, 326–337.

Holmes, J. H., & Gregersen, M. I. Role of sodium and

chloride in thirst. *Amer. J. Physiol.,* 1950b, **162,** 338–347.

Howe, P. E., Mattill, H. A., & Hawk, P. B. Fasting studies. VI: Distribution of nitrogen during a fast of one hundred and seventeen days. *J. biol. Chem.,* 1912, **11,** 103–127.

Huang, K. C. Effect of salt depletion and fasting on water exchange in the rabbit. *Amer. J. Physiol.,* 1955, **181,** 609–615.

Janssen, S. Pharmakologische Beeinflussung des Durstes. *Arch. exp. Path. Pharmakol.,* 1936, **181,** 126–127.

Jessen, P. C. De Siti. Jenae: Univ. dissertation, 1751.

Kanter, G. S. Heat and hydropenia; their effects on thirst and chloride regulation in dogs. *Amer. J. Physiol.,* 1953, **174,** 95–105.

Kleitman, N. The effect of starvation on the daily consumption of water by the dog. *Amer. J. Physiol.,* 1927, **81,** 336–340.

Kohn, M. Satiation of hunger from food injected directly into the stomach versus food ingested by mouth, *J. comp. physiol. Psychol.,* 1951, **44,** 412–422.

Kudo, T. Studies on the effects of thirst. I: Effects of thirst on the weights of the various organs and systems of adult albino rats. *Amer. J. Anat.,* 1921a, **28,** 399–430.

Kudo, T. Studies on the effects of thirst. II: Effects of thirst upon the growth of the body and of the various organs in young albino rats. *J. exp. Zool.,* 1921b, **33,** 435–461.

Ladell, W. S. S. Oesophageal activity in men during water privation. *J. Physiol. (London),* 1946, **104,** 43–44.

Lepidi-Chioti, G., & Fubini, A. Influenza delle penellazioni faringee di cloridrato di cocaina nella sensazione della sete e nella secrezione della saliva parotidea umana. *G. Accad. Med. Torino,* 1885, **33,** 905–906.

Lepkovsky, S., Lyman, R., Fleming, D., Nagumo, M., & Dimick, M. M. Gastorintestinal regulation of water and its effect on food intake and rate of digestion. *Amer. J. Physiol.,* 1957, **188,** 327–331.

Leschke, E. Ueber die Durstempfindung. *Arch. Psychiat,* 1918, **59,** 773–781.

Lifson, N. Note on the total osmotic activity of human plasma or serum. *J. biol. Chem.,* 1944, **152,** 659–663.

Linazàsoro, J. M., Jiménez Diaz, C., & Castro, Mendoza H. The kidney and thirst regulation. *Bull. Inst. med. Res. Malaya,* 1954, **7,** 53–61.

Longet, F. A. *Traité de physiologie. Vol. I.* Paris: Baillière, 1868, 21–38.

Luciani, L. Sulla genesi delle sensazioni della fame e della sete. *Arch. Fisiol.,* 1906, **3,** 541–546.

Ludeman, P. C. De Siti. Lugd. Bat: Luchtmans, Univ. dissertation, 1745.

Ludwig, C. *Lehrbuch der Physiologie des Menschen. Vol. II.* Leipzig and Heidelberg: Winter, 1861, 586.

Luetscher, J. A., Jr., & Blockman, S. S., Jr. Severe injury to kidneys and brain following sulfathiazole administration: high serum sodium and chloride

levels and persistent cerebral damage. *Ann. intern. Med.,* 1943, **18,** 741–756.

MacCarty, C. S., & Cooper, I. S. Neurologic and metabolic effects of bilateral ligation of the anterior cerebral arteries in man. *Proc. Mayo Clin.,* 1951, **26,** 185–190.

McCance, R. A. Experimental sodium chloride deficiency in man. *Proc. roy Soc. (London), B,* 1936a, **119,** 245–268.

McCance, R. A. Medical problems in mineral metabolism. III: Experimental human salt deficiency. *Lancet,* 1936b, **1,** 823–830.

McCance, R. A. The effect of salt deficiency in man on the volume of the extracellular fluids, and on the composition of sweat, saliva, gastric juice and cerebrospinal fluid. *J. Physiol. (London),* 1938, **92,** 208–218.

McClure, W. B., & Aldrich, C. A. Time required for disappearance of intradermally injected salt solutions. *J. Amer. med. Ass.* 1923, **81,** 293–294.

Magendie, F. *A summary of physiology.* John Revere, Trans. Baltimore: Coale, 1822.

Mayer, A. Note sur la soif d'origine gastrique. *C. R. Soc. Biol. (Paris),* 1900a, **52,** 523–524.

Mayer, A. Variations de la tension osmotique de sang chez les animaux privés de liquides. *C. R. Soc. Biol. (Paris),* 1900b, **52,** 153–155.

Mayer, A. *Essai sur la soif. Ses causes et son mécanisme. Travail du laboratoire de pathologie expérimentale et comparée de la Faculté de Médecine de Paris.* Paris: Félix Alcan, 1901.

Miller, N. E. Experiments on motivation. Studies combining psychological, physiological, and pharmacological techniques. *Science,* 1957, **126,** 1271–1278.

Miller, N. E. Motivational effects of brain stimulation and drugs. *Fed. Proc.,* 1960, **19,** 846–854.

Miller, N. E. Chemical coding of behavior in the brain. *Science,* 1965, **148,** 328–338.

Miller, N. E., & Kessen, M. L. Reward effects via stomach fistula compared with those of food via mouth. *J. comp. physiol. Psychol.,* 1952, **45,** 555.

Miller, N. E., Samlinger, R. I., & Woodrow, P. Thirst-reducing effects of water by stomach fistula vs. water by mouth measured by both a consummatory and an instrumental response. *J. comp. physiol. Psychol.,* 1957, **50,** 1–5.

Miller, N. E., Gottesman, Kay S., & Emery, Nona. Dose response to carbachol and norepinephrine in rat hypothalamus. *Amer. J. Physiol.,* 1964, **206,** 1384–1388.

Montemurro, D. G., & Stevenson, J. A. F. Localization of hypothalamic structures in the rat influencing water consumption. *Yale J. Biol. Med.,* 1955, **28,** 396.

Montemurro, D. G., & Stevenson, J. A. F. Adipsia produced by hypothalamic lesions. *Canad. J. Biochem.,* 1957, **35,** 31–37.

Montgomery, A. V., & Holmes, J. H. Gastric inhibition of the drinking response. *Amer. J. Physiol.,* 1955, **182,** 227–231.

Montgomery, M. F. The influence of atropine and pilocarpin on thirst (voluntary ingestion of water). *Amer. J. Physiol.,* 1931a, **98**, 35–41.

Montgomery, M. F. The role of the salivary glands in the thirst mechanism. *Amer. J. Physiol.,* 1931b, **96**, 221–227.

Morrison, S. D., & Mayer, J. Adipsia and aphagia in rats after lateral subthalamic lesions. *Amer. J. Physiol.,* 1957, **191**, 248–254.

Mueller, L. R. Ueber die Durstempfindung. *Neurol. Centralbl.,* 1919, **38**, 721–723.

Mueller, L. R. Ueber den Durst und ueber die Durstempfindung. *Dtsch. med. Wschr.,* 1920, **46**, 113–116.

Myers, R. D. Modification of drinking patterns by chronic intracranial chemical infusion. In *Thirst, first international symposium on thirst in the regulation of body water.* M. J. Wayner, Ed. New York: Pergamon Press, 1964.

Nadal, J. W., Pedersen, S., & Maddock, W. G. A comparison between dehydration from salt loss and from water deprivation. *J. clin. Invest.,* 1941, **20**, 691–703.

Nauta, W. J. H. Hippocampal projections and related neural pathways to the midbrain in the cat. *Brain,* 1958, **81**, 319.

Needham, J. Chemical heterogony and the ground-plan of animal growth. *Biol. Rev.,* 1934, **9**, 79–109.

Nonnenbruch, W. Pathologie und Pharmakologie des Wasserhaushaltes einschliesslich Oedem und Entzuendung. *Handbuch norm. path. Physiol.,* 1926, **17**, 223–286.

Oehme, C. Die Entstehung der Durstempfindung und die Regulation der Wasserzufuhr. *Dtsch. med. Wschr.,* 1922, **48**, 277.

Pack, G. T. New experiments on the nature of the sensation of thirst. *Amer. J. Physiol.,* 1923, **65**, 346–349.

Ranson, S. W., Fischer, C., & Ingram, W. R. The hypothalamico-hypophyseal mechanism in diabetes insipidus. Paper read before Association for Research in Nervous and Mental Diseases, Dec. 1936. In *The pituitary gland.* Baltimore: William and Wilkins, 1938.

Remington, J. W., Parkins, W. M., & Hays, H. W. Influence of electrolyte deprivation and final restoration on fluid intake, balance and distribution. *Proc. Soc. exp. Biol. Med.,* 1941, **47**, 183–187.

Robinson, E. A., & Adolph, E. F. Pattern of normal water drinking in dogs. *Amer. J. Physiol.,* 1943, **139**, 39–44.

Rowntree, L. G. The water balance of the body. *Physiol. Rev.,* 1922, **2**, 116–169.

Rubini, M. E., Wolf, A. V., & Meroney, W. H. Effects of sea water on the metabolism of men without food or sufficient water. Research Report WRAIR-190-56, Washington, D.C.: Walter Reed Army Medical Center, Nov. 1956.

Rullier, J. Soif. *Dict. Sci. méd.* (*Paris*), 1821, **51**, 448–490.

Sawyer, C. H., & Gernandt, B. E. Effects of intracarotid

and intraventricular injections of hypertonic solutions on electrical activity of the rabbit brain. *Amer. J. Physiol.,* 1956, **185**, 209–216.

Schiff, M. *Leçons sur la physiologie de la digestion, faites au muséum d'historie naturelle de Florence. Vol. I.* Emile Levier, Ed. Florence and Turin: Loescher, 1867, 41–42.

Schroeder, H. A. Renal failure associated with low extracellular sodium chloride. The low salt syndrome. *J. Amer. med. Ass.,* 1949, **141**, 117–124.

Shohl, A. T. *Mineral metabolism.* New York: Reinhold, 1939.

Smith, E. A. Salivary secretion during thirst. *Amer. J. Physiol.,* 1935, **113**, 123.

Smith, H. W. Salt and water volume receptors. *Amer. J. Med.,* 1957, **23**, 623.

Smith, R. W., & McCann, S. M. Alterations in food and water intake after hypothalamic lesions in the rat. *Amer. J. Physiol.,* 1962, **203**, 366–370.

Soloff, L. A., & Zatuchni, J. Syndrome of salt depletion induced by a regimen of sodium restriction and sodium diuresis. *J. Amer. med. Ass.,* 1949, **139**, 1136–1139.

Steggerda, F. R. The relation of dry mouth to thirst in the human. *Amer. J. Physiol.,* 1939, **126**, 635.

Steggerda, F. R. Observations on the water intake in an adult man with dysfunctioning salivary glands. *Amer. J. Physiol.,* 1941, **132**, 517–521.

Stein, L., & Seifter, J. Muscarinic synapses in the hypothalamus. *Amer. J. Physiol.,* 1962, **202**, 751–756.

Stevenson, J. A. F. Effects of hypothalamic lesions on water and energy metabolism in the rat. *Recent Progr. Hormone Res.,* 1949, **4**, 363–394.

Stevenson, J. A. F., Welt, L. G., & Orloff, J. Abnormalities of water and electrolyte metabolism in rats with hypothalamic lesions. *Amer. J. Physiol.,* 1950, **161**, 35–39.

Strauss, M. B. *Body water in man, the acquisition and maintenance of the body fluids.* Boston: Little, Brown, 1957.

Strominger, J. L. The relation between water intake and food intake in normal rats and in rats with hypothalamic hyperphagia. *Yale J. Biol. Med.,* 1947, **19**, 279–288.

Tancredi, L. De fame et siti. Lib. 3. Venetiis: Univ. dissertation, 1607.

Teitelbaum, P. Disturbances in feeding and drinking behavior after hypothalamic lesions. In *Nebraska symposium on motivation.* M. R. Jones, Ed. Lincoln: Univ. of Nebraska Press, 1961.

Teitelbaum, P., & Epstein, A. The lateral hypothalamic syndrome: recovery of feeding and drinking after lateral hypothalamic lesions. *Psychol. Rev.,* 1962, **69**, 74–90.

Teitelbaum, P., & Stellar, E. Recovery from the failure to eat, produced by hypothalamic lesions. *Science,* 1954, **120**, 894–895.

Towbin, E. J. Gastric distention as a factor in the satiation of thirst in esophagostomized dogs. *Amer. J.*

Physiol., 1949, **159**, 533–541.

Towbin, E. J. Thirst and hunger behavior in normal dogs and the effects of vagotomy and sympathectomy. *Amer. J. Physiol.*, 1955, **182**, 377–382.

Towbin, E. J. The role of the gastrointestinal tract in the regulation of water intake. In *Thirst, first international symposium on thirst in the regulation of body water.* M. J. Wayner, Ed. New York: Pergamon Press, 1964.

Valenti, A. Sulla, genesi delle sensazioni di fame e di sete. *Arch. Farmacol. sper.*, 1909, **8**, 285–296.

Valenti, A. Sur la genèse des sensations de faim et de soif. *Arch. ital. Biol.*, 1910, **53**, 94–104.

Verney, E. B. The antidiuretic hormone and the factors which determine its release. *Proc. roy. Soc. (London)*, B, 1947, **135**, 25–106.

Von Euler, C. A preliminary note on slow hypothalamic "osmopotentials." *Acta physiol. scand.*, 1953, **29**, 133–136.

Von Voit, C. Durstgefuehl. In *Hermann's Handbuch der Physiologie. Vol. VI.* Leipzig: Vogel, 1881, 566–568.

Weber, E. H. Der Tastsinn und das Gemeingefuehl. In *Wagner's Handwoerterbuch der Physiologie. Vol. 3.* Braunschweig: Vieweg, 1846, 586.

Weir, F. J., Larson, E. E., & Rowntree, L. G. Studies in diabetes insipidus, water balance, and water intoxication: Study I. *Arch. inter. Med.*, 1922, **29**, 306–330.

Wettendorff, H. Modifications du sang sous l'influence de la privation d'ear. Contribution a l'étude de la soif. Travaux du laboratoire de physiologie. *Instituts Solvay*, 1901, **4**, 353–384.

Witt, D. M., Keller, A. D., Batsel, H. L., & Lynch, J. R. Absence of thirst and resultant syndrome associated with anterior hypothalamectomy in the dog. *Amer. J. Physiol.*, 1952, **171**, 780.

Wolf, A. V. Estimation of changes in plasma and extra-cellular fluid volume following changes in body content of water and certain solutes, by means of an osmotic equation. *Amer. J. Physiol.*, 1948, **153**, 499–502.

Wolf, A. V. Osmometric analysis of thirst in man and dog. *Amer. J. Physiol.*, 1950, **161**, 75–86.

Wolf, A. V. Circulation and metabolic exchange. Renal function in electrolyte and water balance. *Symposium on circulation and homeostasis*, Oct. 1953. Also in *Med. Sci. Publ.*, 1953a, **3**, 79–89.

Wolf, A. V. Relative importance of load and distortion in renal excretion. *Fed. Proc.*, 1953b, **12**, 158.

Wolf, A. V. Some new perspectives in renal physiology. *J. Urol. (Baltimore)*, 1953c, **70**, 1–8.

Wolf, A. V. *Thirst: physiology of the urge to drink and problems of water lack.* Springfield, Ill.: Thomas, 1958.

Wolf, A. V., & Eddy, H. A. Effects of hypropenia and the ingestion of tap water and artificial sea waters in the fasting dog. Research Report WRAIR-90-57. Washington, D.C.: Walter Reed Army Medical Center, June 1957.

Wolf, G., & Miller, N. E. Lateral hypothalamic lesions: effects on drinking elicited by carbachol in preoptic area and posterior hypothalamus. *Science*, 1964, **143**, 585–587.

Zaus, E. A. Discussion of paper by Austin and Steggerda. *Illinois med. J.*, 1936, **69**, 127.

Zotterman, Y. The response of the frog's taste fibres to the application of pure water. *Acta physiol. scand.*, 1949, **18**, 181–189.

Zotterman, Y. Species differences in the water taste. *Acta physiol. scand.*, 1956, **37**, 60–70.

Zotterman, Y., & Diamant, H. Has water a specific taste? *Nature (London)*, 1959, **183**, 191–192.

Zuidema, G. D., Clarke, N. P., & Minton, M. F. Osmotic regulation of body fluids. *Amer. J. Physiol.*, 1956, **187**, 85–88.

CHAPTER EIGHT

Hormonal and Neural Mechanisms Contributing to the Regulation of Sexual Behavior

THE PHYSIOLOGY OF REPRODUCTION

Reproduction in the Female

The sexual motivation of the female is determined, at least in part, by rhythmic structural and functional changes of the ovaries. In most species three cycles of ovarian activity can be distinguished. The most basic cycle spans the life of the organism and proceeds from the initial development of the ovaries to the attainment of functional maturity and eventually senescence. Sexual behavior occurs only during the second stage of this cycle. During this period the ovaries undergo secondary rhythmic cycles because the maturation of ova is a discontinuous process. In primates, these are called *menstrual cycles*, defined as the interval from the onset of one period of uterine bleeding to the onset of the next one. In man, this cycle may range from 20 to 35 days with a median of approximately 28 days. The period of menstruation generally covers about 5 days. This period of endometrial degeneration is followed by the preovulatory stage which lasts 7 to 10 days. During this period straight uterine glands develop and the endometrium increases in thickness. This stage is terminated by ovulation. The final secretory or progestational stage covers the last 12 to 14 days of the menstrual cycle; during this time the uterine mucosa is modified to receive and implant a fertilized ovum.

These structural and functional developments are closely related to hormonal changes. Just before the onset of menstruation, the corpora lutea regress and stop elaborating progesterone. Because this hormone is necessary for the development and maintenance of the endometrium, rapid degeneration of this tissue and hemorrhage (i.e., menstruation) results. Following menstruation, follicles begin to grow and liberate estrogens.

Toward the end of the second stage, one follicle attains maturity and ovulates, it then becomes highly vascularized and forms a corpus luteum.

Subprimate mammalian species show a similar cycle of ovarian activity. The *estrous cycle* spans the interval between successive periods of estrus (a period of sexual excitement or "heat" during which the female is receptive to the male). The length of this estrous cycle varies considerably between species. Some seasonal breeders are in estrus only once or twice a year, but female receptivity continues for several weeks or months if copulation does not occur. Ovulation takes place during estrus, and the ovarian changes between ovulations are comparable to those discussed for the menstrual cycle.

The third cycle of ovarian activity, the *reproductive cycle*, is repeated with each gestation; its duration is roughly proportional to that of the menstrual or estrous cycle.

The endocrine functions of the ovaries. The ovary is surrounded by germinal epithelial cells from which ova arise and migrate into the ovary. In man, this process is complete at birth, and the ovaries contain several hundred thousand ova. Ova develop in large, fluid-filled follicles (liquor folliculi). Only 400 to 500 ova reach maturity during the normal life-span of man. Several ovarian hormones that appear to be essential to the menstrual and reproductive cycle have been isolated. One major group of ovarian hormones, the *estrogens*, is biologically active in producing vaginal cornification and other important structural changes. The three principal estrogens are *estriol*, *estrone*, and a partially reduced derivative of estrone called *estradiol*. A number of synthetic chemicals which have estrogenic actions have been developed. The most potent of these is diethylstilbene or *stilbestrol*, which is almost five

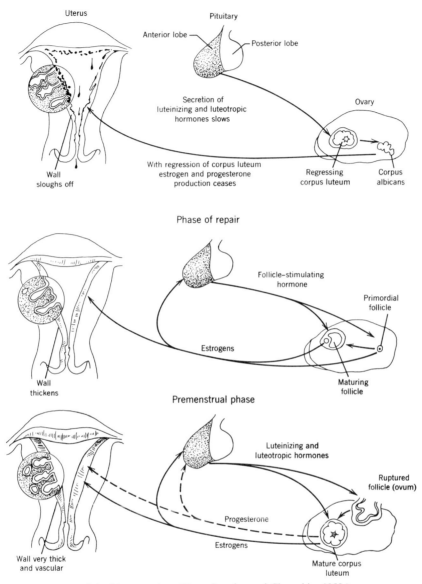

Destructive phase

Uterus

Pituitary

Anterior lobe

Posterior lobe

Secretion of
luteinizing and luteotropic
hormones slows

Ovary

With regression of corpus luteum
estrogen and progesterone
production ceases

Wall
sloughs off

Regressing
corpus luteum

Corpus
albicans

Phase of repair

Follicle–stimulating
hormone

Primordial
follicle

Estrogens

Wall
thickens

Maturing
follicle

Premenstrual phase

Luteinizing and
luteotropic hormones

Ruptured
follicle (ovum)

Progesterone

Estrogens

Wall very thick
and vascular

Mature corpus
luteum

Fig. 8.1 Menstruation. (From Langley and Cheraskin, 1958.)

times as active as estrone. A different ovarian hormone, *progesterone*, has been isolated from extracts of the corpora lutea. This hormone induces the formation of a progestational endometrium which is capable of implanting a fertilized ovum.

The endocrine functions of the ovary are directly under hypophyseal control. A reciprocating influence of ovarian hormones on pituitary secretion has also been demonstrated. Ovarian follicular growth is stimulated by a hypophyseal hormone appropriately called *follicle-stimulating hormone* (FSH). A second pituitary hormone induces follicular maturation, ovulation, and the formation of corpora lutea; this is called the *luteinizing hormone* (LH) or *interstitial-cell-stimulating hormone* (ICSH). Collectively, these two hormones are known as gonadotrophins. They act synergistically (i.e., a small amount of LH greatly augments the effects of FSH). Although the precise

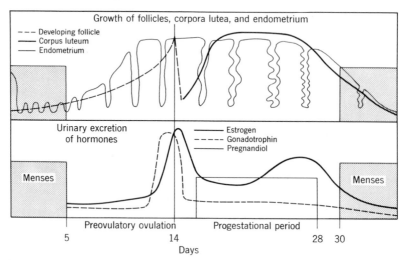

Fig. 8.2 Increased thickness of endometrium and changes in the shape of endometrial glands in relation to the size of ovarian follicles and corpora lutea and urinary excretion of sex hormones and gonadotrophins during a menstrual cycle. (From Howell, 1949.)

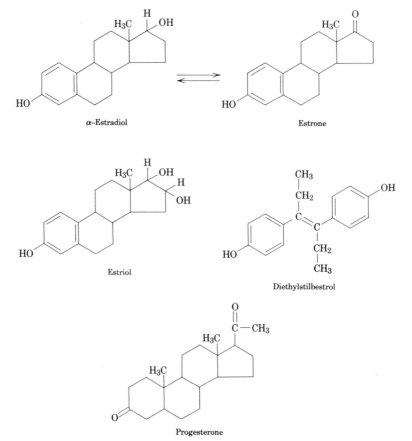

Fig. 8.3 The structural formulas of the female sex hormones. (From Langley and Cheraskin, 1958.)

448

interaction of hypophyseal and ovarian hormones is not known, the following sequence of events has been proposed by Gardner (see Fulton, 1950).

1. The pituitary secretes FSH and LH which promote follicular growth and stimulate the secretion of estrogen.
2. Estrogen acts on the pituitary to stimulate the formation of more LH and to inhibit the secretion of FSH. This produces ovulation and the formation of the corpora lutea.
3. Toward the end of the menstrual cycle, the corpora lutea regress, ovarian estrogen secretion is reduced, and the pituitary again steps up FSH secretion.

Before puberty there is little follicular growth in the ovaries and almost no endocrine activity. Moreover, little or no gonadotrophic hormones are secreted by the pituitary. Puberty is initiated by hypophyseal secretions of FSH and LH which stimulate follicular growth and ovarian hormone secretion. What stimulates the beginning of pituitary secretion is unknown. After 30 to 40 years of menstrual or estrous cycles, the ovaries are nearly completely depleted of follicles, and the production of ovarian hormones stops. The complete cessation of ovarian activity, the *menopause*, removes the regulatory effects of ovarian hormones on the pituitary gland and produces an excessive amount of gonadotrophic hormones (particularly FSH). Although the pituitary initiates ovarian function at puberty, it does not stop its gonadotrophic activity when the senility of the ovaries puts a halt to the organism's reproductive cycle.

Reproduction in the Male

Male sexual behavior, in contrast to that of the female, is not subject to cyclic variations. A period of sexual development and growth must precede maturity in the male as in the female.

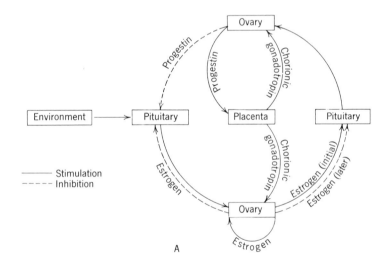

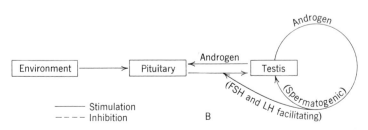

Fig. 8.4   A, the major endocrine influences operating during the normal reproductive cycle of the adult female mammal. B, the major endocrine influences operating during the normal reproductive cycle of the adult male mammal. (From Prosser, 1950.)

However, man's sexual responsiveness persists almost unchanged throughout his adult life and decreases only gradually as the general condition of the organism deteriorates in senescence. Male sexual motivation is nonetheless influenced by endocrine factors.

The male sexual hormones are collectively known as *androgens*. A variety of androgenic substances have been obtained from natural sources (particularly testicular tissue) or synthesized. The most active hormones are *testosterone* and *androsterone*. Closely related to the latter is a group of compounds known collectively as *17-ketosteroids* which are obtainable from human urine. Many, though not all, of these steroids are biologically active as androgens. It is generally believed that testosterone is the principal male sex hormone and that androsterone and at least some of the other androgenic compounds are metabolites of testosterone.

Testosterone is produced by gland cells in the intertubular connective tissue of the testes. The secretory activity of these interstitial cells of Leydig is under hypophyseal control. This function is exercised by the gonadotrophic substances FSH and LH (or ICSH). Although the FSH does not seem to exert a pronounced effect on the production and release of the testicular hormone (testosterone), it greatly potentiates the stimulating effects of the interstitial-cell-stimulating hormone (ICSH or LH). The testes, in turn, affect the release of gonadotrophins by the hypophysis. Androgenic substances are also produced at other sites, particularly the adrenal glands and the ovaries.

In man, the growth and function of the entire genital apparatus are directly controlled by androgenic hormones. If the androgen concentration falls below required levels during puberty, the scrotum remains small, the penis infantile, and the accessory glands of reproduction (seminal vesicles, prostate, bulbourethral glands) fail to develop. Androgens also control the development of secondary sex characteristics. Sex differences in extent and pattern of body hair, tonal quality of voice, muscular development, subcutaneous fat distribution, and skeletal structure are at least in part caused by differences in androgen levels. The androgenic hormones also affect physiological functions that are not obviously related to sexual behavior or reproduction; they influence the general metabolism by encouraging the retention of nitrogen, sodium, potassium, inorganic phosphorus, and chlorides.

The principal function of the male reproductive system is the production of spermatozoa and their delivery to the immediate proximity of the ovum maintained inside the female reproductive tract. The production of spermatozoa occurs in the testes under the control of the hypophysis. The hypophyseal regulation is exercised by the FSH which stimulates spermatogenesis even in the immature organism. Because this process is also sustained by high levels of testosterone, even in hypophysectomized animals, it has been suggested that the hypophyseal influence on spermatogenesis may be indirect. According to this hypothesis, the pituitary may stimulate the production of androgens by the testes, and the androgens induce spermatogenesis.

The number of spermatozoa in a single ejaculation has been estimated to be approximately 300 to 500 million. Mature spermatozoa are nonmotile and incapable of fertilization until they reach the epididymis. Here they acquire motility and a tolerance to temperatures higher than those of the testes—where temperatures are as low as 92°F (this tolerance is necessary if spermatozoa are to survive the high temperatures of the female genital tract). The activity of the spermatozoa in the epididymis is accompanied by the production of carbon dioxide, which renders the fluid acid and inhibits further movement until ejaculation. During ejaculation an orderly sequence of activity transports the spermatozoa from the epididymis and ductus deference through the excurrent ducts of the penis. First, the paraurethral and bulbourethral glands discharge a fluid that lubricates the urethra. Next, the prostate gland secretes a highly alkaline fluid which neutralizes the acid

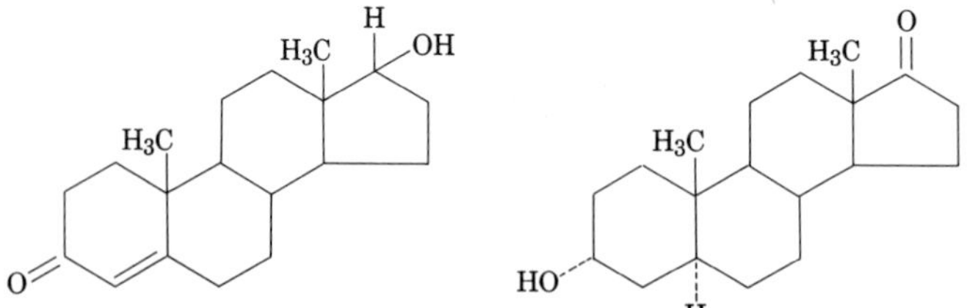

Fig. 8.5 The structural formulas of testosterone (left) and androsterone (right). (From Howell, 1949.)

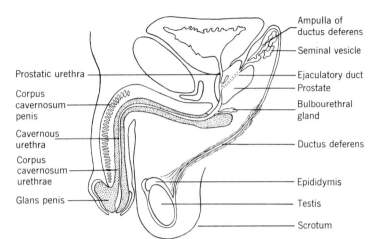

Prostatic urethra

Corpus cavernosum penis

Cavernous urethra

Corpus cavernosum urethrae

Glans penis

Ampulla of ductus deferens

Seminal vesicle

Ejaculatory duct

Prostate

Bulbourethral gland

Ductus deferens

Epididymis

Testis

Scrotum

Fig. 8.6   The male reproductive system. (From Howell, 1949.)

of the epididymal, urethral, and vaginal fluids to provide a neutral environment for the movement of the spermatozoa. These are then discharged from the ampulla of the ductus deference, followed by the bulky secretion of the seminal vesicles.

The process of ejaculation is a reflex phenomenon which has two separate components. The first of these, *emission*, refers to the sudden contraction of the smooth muscles of the internal genital organs which delivers the semen to the urethra. The second, *ejaculation proper*, refers to the contractions of skeletal muscles which expel the seminal fluid from the urethra. The afferent link of this reflex begins with sensory organs in the glands which send impulses over the pudendal nerves to the spinal cord. Emission is under the control of motor neurons traveling with the lumbar rami communicantes and hypogastric nerves. Ejaculation proper is controlled by parasympathetic neurons traveling with the internal pudendal nerves. Orgasm refers to sensations arising from the genital apparatus during the muscular contractions which produce emission and ejaculation. The precise origin and pathways of these sensory mechanisms are not known.

THE SEX DRIVE

Sexual motivation plays an important role in many psychological theories of behavior and has been accorded a position of eminence by being included in the list of primary drives. It is *not*, however, essential to the survival of the individual and is sufficiently different from other primary drives such as hunger or thirst to have led Beach (1956) to question the wisdom of a common classification. This argument is largely a semantic one,

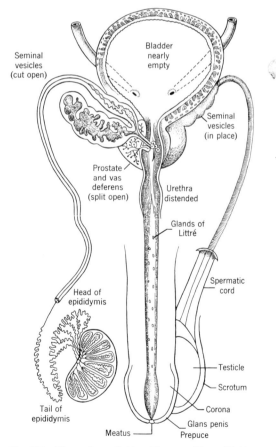

Seminal vesicles (cut open)

Bladder nearly empty

Seminal vesicles (in place)

Prostate and vas deferens (split open)

Urethra distended

Glands of Littré

Head of epididymis

Spermatic cord

Testicle

Scrotum

Tail of epididymis

Corona

Glans penis

Meatus

Prepuce

Fig. 8.7   The male genital tract in man. (From Dickinson, 1933.)

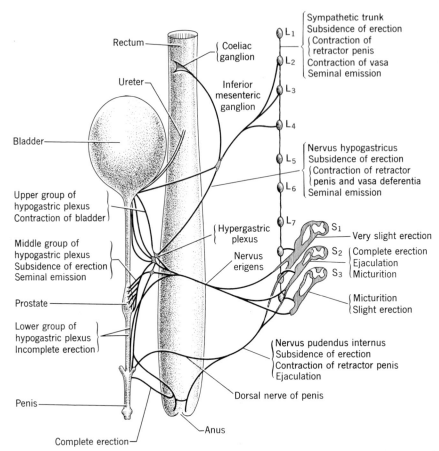

Fig. 8.8 Functional innervation of genital organs of the male cat. (From Semans and Langworthy, 1938.)

which need not concern us here; however, we do need to understand how sexual motivation may differ from the other drives because different physiological mechanisms may be involved.

Sexual motivation is not associated with a distinct biological need which develops over time and must be satisfied in order to maintain life. Gratification of sexual motivation may be desirable psychologically but is not essential or even important to the homeostatic balance and survival of the organism. This is quite different from hunger and thirst, which are directly related to biological needs and represent an integral part of the organism's homeostatic mechanism.

Additional important differences arise because sexual motivation is largely elicited by environmental cues, whereas hunger and thirst reflect internal changes which stimulate interoceptors. Although sexual behavior depends on hormonal conditions as well as influences of central origin,

these internal events merely set the stage so that specific stimuli of external origin can elicit or arouse sexual motivation. Animals reared and maintained in isolation typically do not show sexual behavior although the physiological basis of sexual responses is adequately developed. These facts suggest that the sex drive may itself be at least in part, learned, and that it must be acquired during specific stages of the individual's life. In man, this dependence on external stimulation may be obscured by his ability to recall and recombine previous stimuli, i.e., "imagination." Sexual motivation can be aroused by simulated sensory input which appears to be independent of direct external stimuli. This too is a product of learning and depends on previous experience.

The difference between sexual motivation and other primary drives is emphasized when satiation is considered. When a hungry or thirsty animal ingests a sufficient quantity of food or water to restore the energy or fluid balance of the organism, the physiological need is relieved and the organism returns to a state of homeostatic balance. Sexual activity depletes the organism's energy stores; the sex drive is sated only when fatigue and exhaustion *override* it, and it recurs when the body has replenished its energy stores.

It may be fruitful to consider the sex drive as more closely related to motivational forces of an emotional nature which are also aroused and sated by external stimulation. A clear biological basis exists for these drives, one which will become evident in subsequent discussions; however, the physiological mechanisms merely prime the organism to respond in specific ways to particular classes of environmental stimuli.

Little of this influence appears to be innate. Most, if not all, responses to sexual or emotional stimuli are learned, and our understanding of sexual and emotional motivation will be severely limited until we can unravel the details of this acquisition. Unfortunately, there has been little experimental interest in this important question. Many aspects of this complex problem remain to be explored before we can hope to understand what in turn motivates the acquisition of these responses.

The most illuminating studies of the acquisition of sexual behavior patterns are those of Harlow (see Harlow, 1962, for an instructive and entertaining review of this material). Harlow studied the effects of various degrees of "social deprivation" during infancy on adult behavior and found that monkeys reared without mothers or agemates fail to develop adequate sexual behavior. If paired, these monkeys live together "like brothers and sisters," showing only infantile and ineffective sexual play behavior. Only vicious and violent fighting resulted when male monkeys from this group were paired with sexually experienced normal females in heat. Socially deprived mature females in heat were paired with the "most experienced, patient and gentle" normal males in the colony, but successfully rebuffed all advances, cowered in a corner, or attacked the suitor.

Other aspects of the behavior of socially deprived monkeys appeared abnormal, and it is perhaps unfair to consider the effects on sexual adjustment in isolation. It seems clear, however, that the physiological basis of sexual behavior was perfectly intact in these animals and that the observed deficits of motivation were produced by the lack of appropriate experience during a crucial period of development. Harlow's studies have raised important questions about the role of external stimulation in the development of sexual behavior. We shall see in the course of our discussion of external stimulus situations that specific stimuli continue to play an important, and often essential, role in adult sexual motivation. Both human and infrahuman species do not mate indiscriminately, but show sexual motivation only when the environmental stimulus situation includes an "acceptable" partner. Just what makes a partner acceptable in each individual case remains to be elucidated.

Definition of Sexual Motivation

Sexual motivation is responsible for an almost infinite variety of behavioral responses, and it is difficult to arrive at an inclusive definition of sexual behavior which clearly distinguishes sexual from other social responses. Sexual behavior occurs only in real or imagined social situations, and most definitions refer directly or indirectly to the object of this behavior. When we attempt to define the motivation for such responses, matters are further complicated because we cannot employ our old standby, the operational definition. Time of deprivation is all but meaningless in this context; even a long list of experimental conditions, such as "female in heat," "sexually experienced male," both "deprived" and physiologically capable of "mating," do not guarantee that sexual behavior will ensue. Whether a given environmental condition will be sexually arousing depends on a host of factors over which the experimenter typically has inadequate control.

Because we have difficulties defining sexual responses, we often cannot be sure whether sexual motivation is present in a given situation. This problem is responsible for the fact that much less systematic research has been devoted to the study of sexual motivation than to any of the other basic motivations. Rarely has an attempt been made to define exactly what is meant by the term "sex drive"; most experimenters leave the matter of definition to the intuition of the reader. Somehow, one is expected to *know* what sexual behavior encompasses and what motivational forces are involved. This is not an acceptable situation, in spite of the fact that each of us can provide a subjectively accurate description; it assumes a priori that sexual motivation and behavior are constant and universal attributes. Such reliance on generalizations from introspective analyses has disappeared completely from other areas of experimental and physiological psychology and are intolerable when applied to sexual behavior.

One of the few attempts to define sexual motivation objectively (Stone, 1939b) suggests that the term sex drive denotes "aroused action tendencies in animals to respond to objects of their external environment that, in some measure, lead to the satisfaction or alleviation of dominant physiological 'urges' associated with reproduction." This definition is in general use today and has significantly influenced current theoretical thought. Unfortunately, it has led to the implicit assumption that "dominant physiological urges, associated with reproduction" somehow exist in the organism, and that these "urges" energize and direct behavior toward objects which satisfy or alleviate them. This is an erroneous interpretation of the research literature. Certain physiological (primarily hormonal) conditions provide a necessary condition for sexual motivation, but sexual arousal depends exclusively on external stimulation or a simulation of such input. Furthermore, there is considerable question whether sexual motivation is directly and causally related to the urge to reproduce. Although sexual behavior eventually serves the purpose of reproduction, this does not seem to provide the primary motivational component of sexual interactions in man. The urge to reproduce is satisfied or alleviated, not by sexual behavior per se but only by the long-delayed and uncertain consequences of the sexual act.

Where then does this leave us with respect to a definition of sexual motivation? For the purpose of our discussion, we might define our subject as *any combination of organismic (primarily hormonal) conditions and environmental stimuli that elicits a sequence of responses directly related to copulation.* We shall attempt to describe the organismic conditions and stimulus situations that fit this definition. Because our knowledge of these variables is incomplete at present, it may be best not to introduce bias into our definition by attempting greater specificity. A more serious problem with the definition may be the description of specific behavioral response categories. We shall attempt to clarify these by briefly discussing the types of response patterns that have been used as indices of sexual motivation.

Patterns of Sexual Behavior

Sexual behavior is difficult to analyze quantitatively because a variety of behavioral responses may be involved. Two basic approaches to this problem have been employed. Historically the first, and still the most prevalent, relies on the direct observation and recording of behavioral responses of a sexual nature. The second approach employs quantitative measures of instrumental responses not directly related to sexual behavior but presumably motivated sexually. We shall try to give some representative examples of both approaches and point out their advantages and problems.

Many classic experimental studies of sexual behavior relied on gross observations of overt sexual responses. If this technique is limited to the recording of actual copulatory behavior, an unambiguous but often not very enlightening picture emerges. Not only is much valuable information about other, potentially sexual responses lost, but it is impossible to obtain any measures of intensity or magnitude. If, on the other hand, an attempt is made to interpret the many behavioral sequences which may or may not lead to copulation, too much emphasis is placed on the empathic ability of the observer. Such subjective interpretations are open to experimenter bias; they typically lead to low interobserver correlations because the line between sexual and nonsexual behavior is not sufficiently clear.

Hemmingsen (1933) has distinguished twelve stages of sexual excitability in the female rat which are related to the hormonal changes of the estrous cycle and are defined by specific behavioral responses to standard stimuli. Much of this classification depends on the lordosis response (a specific body posture the female rat assumes to facilitate intromission). During the initial stage the female runs away or fights off the advances of the male. In subsequent stages increasing degrees of lordosis and presumably receptivity are displayed in the presence of a male. In the final stage (heat) some components of this response can be observed even when no sexual partner is available. As a first approximation to some objective measure of sexual motivation, this is not a bad scheme. However, it is extremely difficult to distinguish several degrees of the lordosis response, and other behavioral response patterns may need to be considered.

Ball (1937a) has attempted to provide more general criteria for the analysis of sexual motivation in the rat. Ball first demonstrated that different stimulus situations can be ranked empirically with respect to their effectiveness in eliciting sexual responses in female rats. Highest on this scale is an aggressive adult male, next a sexually "sluggish" male, then an immature rat, and finally manual stimulation just in front of the iliac crest. Ball next attempted to rate the intensity (rather than the type) of the female's response to each of these stimuli on a five-point scale. In subsequent experiments, ten- and thirteen-point rating scales were developed; attempts were made to validate these instruments by relating excitability scores to male responsiveness and anatomical changes occurring in the female progenital system during the estrous cycle. This technique has been used in many subsequent experiments as an index of female receptivity and sexual motivation, but the ratings tend to be subjective and do not provide a very reliable picture of the situation.

Grunt and Young (1952) have attempted to devise a quantitative measure of sex drive in the guinea pig. Their index is based on frequency scores of the following response patterns: nibbling, nuzzling, mounting, intromission, and ejaculation. The individual response categories are arbitrarily weighted in accordance with a postulated response hierarchy. Some measure of success was reported by these authors in differentiating the responses of normal, castrated, and testosterone-treated castrated animals. These ratings may be useful for relatively crude comparisons, but they seem to oversimplify the matter even at the primitive level of the guinea pig. With higher mammals such as monkeys, the success of similar devices has been minimal.

Other examples of simple, observational methods are the use of latency scores (i.e., the interval between the first meeting of sexual partners and the first clearly sexual response such as intromission) or the number of intromissions necessary to achieve ejaculation (Beach, 1956). Attempts have also been made to assess sexual motivation on the basis of the frequency of sexual responses to inappropriate stimuli of varying resemblance to the appropriate sexual partner. For instance, Beach (1942a, b, c) reported that injections of hormones increase the frequency of sexual responses of a male rat to animals other than a female rat; Tinbergen (1942) noted that wooden models of a female stickleback fish elicited sexual responses from sexually aggressive males.

Many other observational techniques have been devised by psychologists and physiologists attempting to measure the intensity of sexual motivation. In general, these efforts have produced few generally acceptable procedures, and widespread dissatisfaction with observational methods has prompted the development of more indirect, objective procedures. Denniston's (1954) point of view perhaps best illustrates the situation: "Sex responses are difficult to compare quantitatively. It seems doubtful, furthermore, that any one ejaculation is quantitatively equivalent to any other ejaculation, either within or between individuals" (p. 437).

Most of the investigations that have tried to obtain independent and objective measures of the intensity of sexual motivation have in some way pitted an aversive stimulus (such as electric shock) against the sex drive. One of the earliest studies on record in this area is that of Moss (1924), who recorded how often a male rat would cross an electrically charged grid to obtain access to a female in heat. Subsequent investigators have used the Columbia Obstructional Apparatus to obtain standardized measures of the intensity of aversive stimulation required to stop sexual behavior (Warner, 1927; Jenkins, 1928; Nissen, 1929). This apparatus consists of three compartments, separated by transparent doors. The animal is placed into the entrance compartment where he can observe an appropriate sexual partner in the "incentive compartment." In order to reach the partner, the animal must cross the electrified grid of the "obstruction compartment."

If we assume that a direct, uncomplicated correlation exists between intensity of sexual motivation and tolerance to aversive stimulation, this situation might provide a good index of sexual drive. Nissen (1929) found that castration decreased the frequency of grid crossing in the male, and Stone et al. (1935) reported some impressive correlations between frequency of grid crossing at a given level of electric shock and copulatory performance in rats. The correlation was only .33 when complete crossings were considered, but the value rose to .84 when both grid contacts and crossings were analyzed.

Beach et al. (see Beach, 1956) have reported an interesting variation of this idea. Low or high shock was applied whenever the male rat began to mount the female. Animals "punished" with the high-voltage shock stopped responding almost immediately and recovered only slowly if at all. The animals which received the low shock did not decrease the total number of successful intromissions, although the frequency of incomplete attempts increased.

Many investigators have objected to these procedures because sexual arousal may produce general sensitization to any form of sensory stimulation. Thus an objectively constant electric shock may not be comparable in its effect on dif-

Stage 1. No heat. The female defends herself against the male with one of her hindlegs.

Stage 1. No heat. The female defends herself against the male with one of her hindlegs.

Stage 1. No heat. The female rises on her hindlegs to prevent the male from mounting.

Stage 1. No heat. The female attempts to throw off the male.

Stage 2. No heat. The female allows the male to mount but does not flatten her back in lordosis to allow copulation.

Stage 3. Slight heat. The female flattens her back slightly when mounted.

Stage 4. Stronger heat. Pronounced lordosis during mounting.

Stage 9. Lordosis before mounting.

Fig. 8.9 Twelve stages of sexual arousal in the female rat as classified by Hemmingsen. (From Hemmingsen, 1933.)

Stage 10 (above). Vibrations of the ears are aroused by tickling with a finger.

Stage 10 (right). Vibrations of the ears between extreme positions $\frac{1}{2}$ to 1 cm apart.

Stage 11. Besides vibrations even lordosis is brought on by tickling with a finger.

Stage 12. When heat is intense, the lordosis persists for a while after each mounting. The male licks his genitals after an attempt at copulation.

Stage 11. When the heat is not very intense, the lordosis does not persist after mounting.

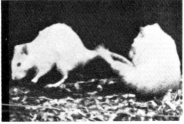

Sometimes the male rolls back on his hindquarters to lick his genitals after an attempt at copulation.

The successful introduction of the vaginal plug is characterized by the male rising hesitatingly on his hindquarters.

457

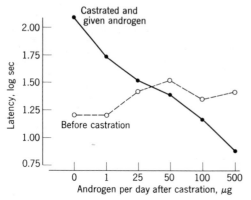

Fig. 8.10 Average delay preceding the first sexual mount in pre- and postoperative tests. (From Beach and Holz-Tucker, 1949.)

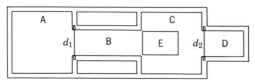

Fig. 8.11 Floor plan of the Columbia Obstructional Apparatus. A, entrance compartment; B, obstruction compartment; C, D, divided incentive compartment; E, release plate; d_1, manually operated door of entrance compartment; d_2, automatic door (operated by release plate) between two divisions of incentive compartment. (From Warner, 1927.)

ferent animals. Possible alternatives to the shock procedure have been proposed by several workers. Seward and Seward (1940) reported a small but statistically reliable correlation between time of sexual deprivation and the speed at which male guinea pigs crossed a hurdle to get to a receptive female. Denniston (1954) was less successful in demonstrating a reliable correlation between copulatory response latencies and simple instrumental wheel-turning responses. Beach and Jordan (1956) have reported a positive correlation between running speed in a straight alley and sexual responses to the female in the goal box. It was shown that animals under a particular experimental condition gave consistent running speeds which differed significantly from those of animals under other experimental conditions. These developments are promising, although the procedures are still time-consuming and tedious. An animal must have considerable experience with a particular incentive before his running speed in an alley stabilizes. Because different females appear to have widely varying "incentive value," Beach and Jordan's technique is not as simple as it may seem.

Before we terminate this discussion, we might briefly mention that general bodily activity seems to be quite highly related to sexual motivation in the female of many species. This relationship has been studied extensively in the running wheel. A female rat, for instance, runs the equivalent of 10 miles per day when in heat but less than 1 mile

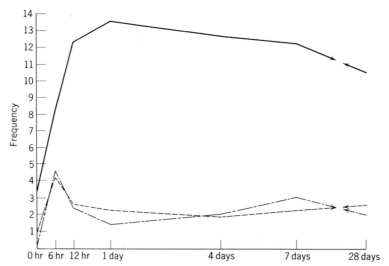

Fig. 8.12 Average number of crossings (———), contacts (— — —), and approaches (– – –) for each interval of sex deprivation in the male rat. (From Warner, 1927.)

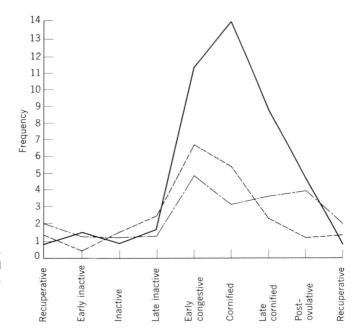

Fig. 8.13 Average number of crossings (——), contacts (——-—), and approaches (———) for the female. Grouping is based on the histological character of vaginal smears. (From Warner, 1927.)

per day during other stages of the estrous cycle. Conditions that affect sexual receptivity (ovariectomy, pregnancy, etc.) produce pronounced changes in this activity cycle, and activity measures can therefore be used as a rough index of sexual motivation.

Richter (1927) reported that similar activity cycles could be observed in the male rat and that variations in activity correlated with sexual arousal. Subsequent investigations have not been able to replicate these findings. The male rat does not seem to show systematic variations in activity, and several studies have shown that activity changes are not related to the strength of sexual motivation as measured by the latency of copulatory responses (Stone and Barker, 1934).

As a measure of sexual motivation, the activity cycle is not very satisfactory, even for the female of the species. All we can tell from the cyclical variations in activity is whether a female is in heat (i.e., receptive to the male). We cannot predict whether sexual motivation will be relatively high or low during successive periods of estrus, or whether the sexual drive of two females in heat will be similar or different.

In spite of the many developments in this field, the basic question unfortunately still has not been answered satisfactorily. What, precisely, is a sexual response and how does it differ from other response categories? This problem affects the observational techniques most directly, but it also

enters into the indirect measures because they require some measure of validation. If we cannot even agree on a definition of sexual behavior, how can we hope to use it as an index of sexual motivation? Many potentially sexual responses occur in nonsexual social situations, and we must know the incentive (i.e., the motivation) to be able to classify such a response. A complete tautology results if we then use the response to define the motive state.

It is surprising that results have been obtained in this field in spite of these problems, and it may be worthwhile to remember these difficulties when we attempt to interpret some apparently contra-

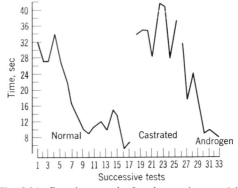

Fig. 8.14 Running speed of male rats in a straight alley leading to a goal box containing a female rat in heat. (From Beach and Jordan, 1956.)

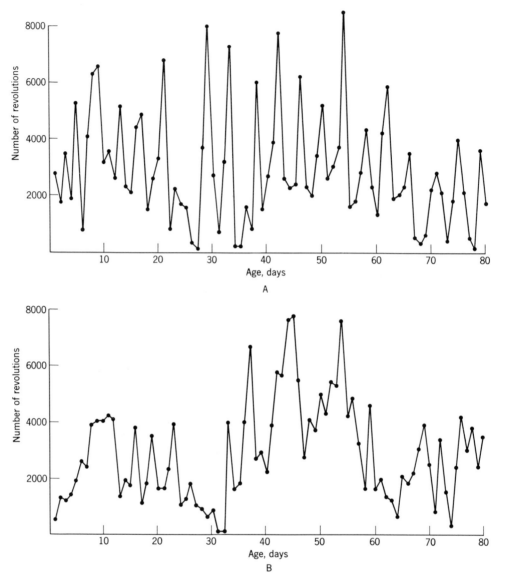

Fig. 8.15   A, typical activity curve of a female rat. B, the activity curve of a male rat. (From Wang, 1923–1925.)

dictory experimental findings. To make the transition to this material more pleasant, we might end this section with a brief mention of Anderson's (Anderson and Anderson, 1938) work; he demonstrated low but statistically reliable correlations among different measures of sexual behavior, including observational reports and performance measures on various interpolated tasks. Although the reported correlations are far from perfect, this work does suggest that a common factor may be measured more or less adequately by all the different techniques.

Summary

Sexual motivation departs from the pattern of the "primary drives" which we have so far considered. It is not based on an essential biological need, and its satiation tends to upset rather than restore the homeostatic balance of the organism. Whereas hunger and thirst are elicited by events in the internal environment, and hence do not depend on external stimuli, sexual motivation appears to be aroused directly by specific environmental stimulation. Complex neural and hormonal

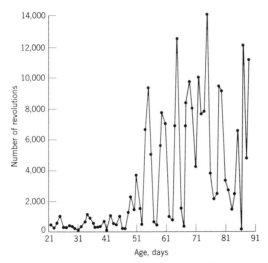

Fig. 8.16 Revolving drum record showing the burst of activity and the typical rhythms of activity at puberty. (From Stone, 1939b.)

mechanisms determine whether or not the organism will respond to potentially sexual stimuli, but these mechanisms cannot by themselves elicit sexual motivation. In this respect, the sex drive appears to be related to motivational variables of an emotional nature. In a further departure from the appetitive drives, learning seems to play a most important role, not only in sexual behavior but also in sexual motivation itself. Animals reared in isolation fail to develop sexual motivation and cannot, apparently, acquire it once a crucial developmental stage has passed.

The definition of sexual motivation and even sexual behavior poses a problem which has retarded experimental work in this field. Because there is no demonstrable biological need, "time of deprivation" becomes an all but meaningless variable, and operational definitions are difficult to construct. Such a variety of stimulus variables may affect sexual receptivity that it is difficult to select important aspects of the environment for manipulation or control. Moreover, there is no generally acceptable definition of sexual behavior itself, unless we restrict ourselves to actual copulatory responses. This is not a very sensitive measure and seems to be impossible to quantify.

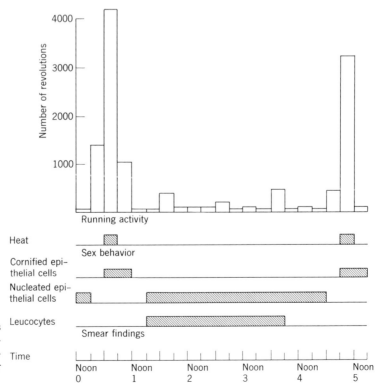

Fig. 8.17 Temporal relations between running activity, sexual receptivity, and the ovulation cycle established for 6-hr records. (From Stone, 1939b.)

The Role of Sensory Stimulation

We have emphasized in our introductory comments that sexual behavior—and presumably sexual motivation itself—is determined to a significant extent by external sensory stimulation. The most obvious and immediate source of such stimulation is the sexual partner. More subtle influences are exerted by a variety of environmental conditions which one does not necessarily associate with sexual behavior. Beach has provided a useful classification of environmental influences in an excellent review of this topic (Beach, 1951). The first category includes stimuli that do not directly elicit sexual behavior but are essential for the development of physiological conditions that make such behavior possible. Under this heading we shall consider only the effects of environmental temperature and illumination, although there are many other sensory influences that fit into this category.

Environmental temperatures have an indirect effect on sexual behavior because sexual maturity depends in many species on specific (usually warm) temperatures. A more direct temperature influence is responsible for the seasonal cycle of sexual responsiveness in many species. This influence may take the form of structural alterations, as in some species of fish which show marked gonadal regression when the water temperature rises (Burger, 1939), or may be mediated by hormonal

mechanisms that appear to be under the control of temperature fluctuations (Wells, 1935, 1936). More complexly related to hormonal mechanisms is the finding that the initiation of estrus (heat) tends to occur during the cooler portion of a day (Browman, 1943).

Seasonal and diurnal variations of illumination affect the sexual responsiveness of many species. The seasonal effects are apparently produced by functional changes in various endocrine mechanisms (see Marshall, 1942; Beach, 1948, for a summary of this material). Many investigations have shown that experimental increases of the daily exposure to light elicit mating behavior out of season in birds (Rowan, 1932; Witschi, 1935; Wolfson, 1940). Burger (1943) has demonstrated that specific wavelengths (between 580 and 680 mμ) are responsible for these effects in one avian species. Some seasonal breeders (sheep, goats, deer, cats, ferrets, etc.) copulate outside the normal mating season when the daily proportion of daylight is increased (Dawson, 1941; Rice, 1942; Hammond, 1944). At least in the ferret, this effect does not depend on specific wavelengths (Marshall and Bowden, 1934).

Endocrine secretions and consequent structural changes in the reproductive apparatus seem to be influenced, strange as it may seem, by social factors. Darling (1938) reported an interesting field study which indicated that reproductive success was correlated with the size of the breeding colony

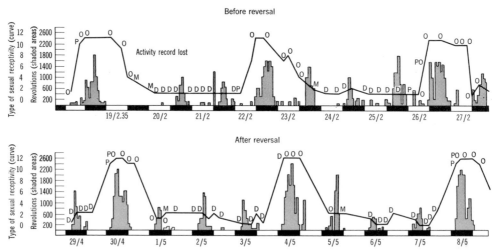

Fig. 8.18   The relation between the vaginal estrous stages, the degree of sexual receptivity, and the spontaneous muscular activity in a female rat before and after reversal of darkness and light. The unit of the abscissas is 3 hr. The black areas below the abscissas represent the dark periods. The adjacent letters represent the stage of the vaginal smear. D, dioestrus; P, pro-oestrus; O, oestrus; M, metoestrus. (From Hemmingsen and Krarup, 1937.)

in herring gulls. Some experimental studies of this problem have supported the thesis that social contacts may be necessary in some species to allow the development of physiological mechanisms necessary for sexual behavior and breeding (Mathews, 1939; see also Beach, 1951).

Beach's second category includes stimuli that do not directly elicit overt sexual behavior but "predispose the sexually ready organism to respond appropriately and completely to stimuli afforded by a potential mate" (Beach, 1951). This rather complex statement refers to the simple fact that many species will display courtship and mating behavior only in an accustomed environment (i.e., in the presence of specific stimuli). The environment must often contain special features before sexual behavior occurs. The toad and many species of aquatic birds mate only in the immediate vicinity of water (Noble, 1931; Schoolland, 1942), and some fish court and mate only if natural shelter or an appropriate nest is readily available (Breder, 1935). Males of some species stake out and defend a "sexual territory" outside of which they will not mate, although they readily cross these territorial boundaries for the purpose of seeking food or fighting. These territorial claims are generally respected by other males, and a female is no longer courted by other males once she enters into the sexual territory of a given male (Nice, 1941).

Beach's third and most important category comprises all the stimuli that derive directly from an animal of the opposite sex. These stimuli affect behavior directly and must be considered as an important component of sexual motivation itself. We attempt later to investigate the difficult question of how *essential* such stimuli are to the arousal and maintenance of sexual motivation. At this point we shall attempt merely to identify some of the stimuli and to describe their effect on sexual behavior.

The importance of specific sensory cues is apparently greatest in lower species. Many insects, for instance, depend exclusively on olfactory stimuli emitted by the scent glands of the female for the elicitation and direction of sexual responses (Lehman, 1932; Travis, 1939). An excellent demonstration of the importance of such chemical cues has been reported by Kellogg (1907), who found that male silkworm moths approached and attempted copulation with scent glands that had been dissected out of a female but paid absolutely no attention to the alive females from whom these glands had been removed. Other insects (such

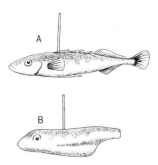

Fig. 8.19 Two models of a female *Gasterosteus*. A, model offering many characteristics, except the swollen abdomen. B, model which has extremely swollen abdomen but lacks most other characteristics. (From Tinbergen, 1942.)

as the cricket) attract sexual partners by auditory stimuli but completely disregard chemical cues.

Visual stimuli guide the sexual responses of many species of fish. One of the classic demonstrations has been reported by Breder and Coates (1935), who found that male guppies attempt to mate with the shadow of a swimming female. Tinbergen's (1942) well-known studies of the stickleback have shown that males will orient toward specific visual stimuli and attempt to mate with very crude cardboard models of the female of the species as long as the abdominal region is enlarged. Even very accurate models of female sticklebacks fail to elicit sexual response if the abdominal region is not bloated. Body colors and particular swimming movements are used by other species of fish to discriminate the sexes.

As we ascend the phylogenetic scale, more and more sensory modalities come into play, and stimuli from more than a single modality typically contribute to the elicitation and regulation of sexual responses. For instance, the initial approach of sexual partners depends exclusively on vision in some species of frogs. Once contact has been established, auditory and tactual stimuli determine whether or not sexual behavior will actually occur. Males and sexually unresponsive females utter a warning croak when a male frog establishes physical contact with them. These unresponsive animals are also slimmer than sexually responsive females bloated with unfertilized eggs. Male frogs indiscriminately clasp any other frog, but they attempt copulation only with fat animals which do not croak (Noble and Aronson, 1942). Tactile stimuli are also important in this species, for the ejaculation of sperm is triggered by tactile sensations that arise as a result of the spawning movements of the female. The spawning reaction in turn depends on tactile stimuli elicited by the male's clasp.

The sexual behavior of birds is elicited and directed primarily by visual and auditory stimuli. The female of many avian species is differentiated by often minor differences in coloring (the male, as a rule, is more colorful). Noble (1936) has reported an interesting example of this. Male flickers are characterized by a black "moustache." If such coloring is added to a female, she no longer elicits sexual responses from other males. The importance of visual stimuli was also nicely demonstrated in an earlier study by Noble and Vogt (1935), who observed that male pheasants attempted to copulate with the stuffed skin of a female but attacked the skin of males.

Mammals are generally less dependent on a single sensory modality. Yerkes and Elder (1936) have reported that sexual arousal and orientation toward the sexual partner depend primarily on visual and auditory cues in the primate. However, olfactory and tactile stimuli assume a predominant role in the maintenance of sexual arousal once bodily contact is established. That olfaction plays an important role in other mammals was shown by Beach and Gilmore (1949), who found that male dogs spent a significantly greater amount of time investigating the urine of receptive bitches than that of nonestrous bitches.

The role of tactile stimuli has been investigated in a variety of species and experimental situations. Ball (1937a) reports that female rats in heat can be sexually aroused by stroking of the ventral and lateral sides of the body. Similar responses to manual stimulation have been observed in the guinea pig (Young et al., 1938), hamster (Beach, 1950), sow (Altmann, 1941), and cat (Bard, 1939). Tactile stimulation plays an important role in the normal precoital play behavior of most species. Beach (1947) has observed that female hamsters, skunks, porcupines, and dogs assume coital positions when the male manipulates the vaginal region. Females initially resisting the male's attempts at coitus often invite such advances after some genital stimulation.

All these observations suggest that sensory stimulation plays an important role in the arousal and maintenance of sexual motivation. Many investigations have been undertaken to determine whether specific sensory mechanisms may be essential to sexual behavior. In our discussion of this material, we must be careful to distinguish between sensory deficits that make it physically impossible to mate and those that may have a more selective influence on sexual motivation without destroying the organism's ability to display sexual behavior.

Sexual Motivation in Animals Partially Deprived of Sensory Information

The preceding discussion showed that species lower on the phylogenetic scale depend more heavily on a single sensory modality than higher mammals. Interference with such sensory input should severely disrupt sexual behavior, but not affect sexual motivation itself. Beach (1951), for instance, reported that male wasps and silkworm moths fail to approach a receptive female after the olfactory apparatus has been destroyed. However, normal sexual behavior was displayed when bodily contact was made with a receptive female, suggesting that olfactory cues are not essential mechanisms for sexual arousal in this species. Kellogg (1907) has reported that the mating response of the male moth disappears completely after decapitation (presumably because it can no longer locate the female), but the sexual response of the female of this species remains unaffected by the operation.

Grosch (1947) made the interesting observation that male sexual motivation may be totally unaffected following complete removal of the reproductive organs. Male wasps whose posterior body segments had been removed approached the female and repeatedly attempted copulation. These findings suggest that tactile stimuli from the genitalia are not essential to sexual arousal at least in this species.

A similar situation is encountered when we consider fish. Although normal sexual behavior depends on visual cues in most species, they do not appear to be indispensable. Blinded females lay eggs in the presence of a male and eyeless males attempt to fertilize them, although the efficiency of the sexual responses is low (Noble and Curtis, 1939). Extensive cortical damage disrupts sexual responses (Noble and Borne, 1941) but apparently fails to interfere with sexual motivation. Even total decerebration (Aronson, 1948) does not dampen the ardor of male fishes, although the execution of the mating response is severely impaired.

Aronson and Noble's (1945) extensive studies of the mating behavior of frogs suggest that elementary components of the normal sexual behavior pattern can be elicited even after complete transection of the caudal medulla. Spinal frogs clasp a receptive female, assuming a typical, though often disoriented, mating posture. Other elements of normal mating behavior are apparently integrated at various higher levels of the brain. The survival of some sexual behavior after complete transection of the upper cord suggests that sexual behavior in this species is partly controlled by spinal reflexes which appear to be independent of higher influences. These data complicate the picture as far as sexual motivation (rather than behavior) is concerned. We may have to entertain the possibility that some sexual responses of other species may be reflexly controlled and hence cannot serve as indices of motivation as we have used the term.

So far, we have found little evidence for a specific neural substrate for sexual motivation. In lower species, even massive damage to the nervous system produces no deficits of a clearly motivational nature. Although the pattern of mating behavior is often disrupted, the deficits appear to be specific to particular response sequences and sensory-motor integrations rather than sexual motivation per se. Only one study of inframammalian species has suggested that specific brain damage may affect motivation rather than response mechanisms. Beach (1951) reports that subtotal forebrain lesions "reduced the male pigeon's responsiveness to the female without rendering him physically incapable of sexual performance." That the deficits observed in this experiment were indeed produced by changes in motivational factors is suggested by the finding that some males showed absolutely no interest in the female following extensive forebrain damage but copulated after androgen (the male hormone) treatment.

The neural mechanisms of sexual behavior and sexual motivation have been most extensively studied in subprimate mammals, particularly the rat, rabbit, guinea pig, and cat. Specific sensory modalities tend to be less crucial to the sexual arousal of mammals than they are in lower species. Progressive encephalization replaces many of the reflex mechanisms of lower animals by a more complex central nervous system integration, and motivational mechanisms become more clearly discernible. Nevertheless, fragmentary sexual responses that depend exclusively on spinal reflex mechanisms occur even in higher mammals. Male dogs and cats execute coital movements in response to manual stimulation of the genital apparatus, even when the spinal cord is completely transected above the lumbar segments (Schaefer, 1900; Dusser de Barenne and Koskoff, 1934).

Spinal cats continue to show some estrous reactions (Goltz, 1874) and assume a coital position in response to manual stimulation of the genital area when the spinal transection is made at a cervical level (Maes, 1939).

Sexual behavior is only slightly affected by complete sympathectomy. Although ejaculation is prevented, estrous behavior, penile erection, copulatory responses, and sexual motivation do not appear to be affected in a wide variety of mammalian species (Bacq, 1931; Bacq and Brouha, 1933; Brooks, 1937; Bard, 1939). Penile erection and ejaculation can be elicited by electrical stimulation of the sacral portion of the spinal cord in both normal and sympathectomized animals (Bacq and Brouha, 1933; Durfee et al., 1940).

Some aspects of estrous behavior in the female are surprisingly resistant to experimental manipulation. For instance, ovulation in the rabbit, which occurs only as a direct response to copulation, is totally unaffected by complete transection of the spinal cord at the lowest lumbar level. Ovulation persists even if this operation is supplemented by complete abdominal sympathectomy, hysterectomy, and extirpation of the proximal half of the vagina. Spinal females can be successfully impregnated and maintain a normal pregnancy that terminates with the delivery of normal litters (Goltz, 1874).

The various spinal reflex components of sexual behavior are not modified by changes in the organism's hormone balance. Dempsey and Rioch (1939) did not observe any change in the spinal reflexes of female guinea pigs following the injection of estrogen or progesterone. Bard (1939) has reported similar results for the spinal cat. Sawyer (1960) concluded from these observations that the partial behavioral patterns represented at the spinal level of either sex require integration from higher centers for normal differential hormonal activation.

Before we consider some of these higher centers, we must briefly discuss the role of specific sensory modalities in the sexual behavior of higher mammals. Perhaps the most surprising finding here is that afferent impulses from the genitalia do not seem to play an essential role in maintaining sexual arousal. In the female there is little or no change in sexual receptivity and actual copulatory behavior following anesthetization (Fee and Parks, 1930) or deafferentation (Brooks, 1937) of the vagina. Even complete surgical removal of the female genitalia (vagina and uterus) does not prevent mating in female rats and cats (Ball, 1934).

Female rabbits copulate in spite of local anesthesia of the genital apparatus and undergo normal ovulation, which in this species depends on a complex reflex chain involving the secretion of hormones from the pituitary (Fee and Parks, 1930). Even more striking is the fact that anesthesia of the perineum and penis (achieved by surgical removal of the lower spinal cord) does not impair sexual aggressiveness in the male cat (Bard, 1940). These animals show penile erection in the presence of a receptive female and attempt to copulate. Additional sympathectomy interferes with erection, but the copulatory behavior persists. Beach (1956) has found that removal of the os penis (penile bone) in the rat, either surgically or through early castration, interferes with the satisfactory completion of sexual behavior but not with attempts at copulation.

Brooks (1937) has investigated the role of specific sensory mechanisms in the arousal and execution of sexual behavior in the rabbit. Both male and female rabbits showed normal sexual activity following the removal of the olfactory bulbs. These results are surprising in view of the emphasis that has traditionally been placed on olfactory stimuli; such observations restrict the generality and functional significance of several olfactosexual phenomena (such as Le Magnen's 1952 finding that olfactory thresholds for synthetic musk and urinary steroids change as a function of sexual arousal).

Brooks also found that vision and audition do not seem to be any more essential to sexual behavior than olfactory stimulation. Enucleation of both eyes or destruction of the middle ear and labyrinth failed to produce any overt deficits in mating behavior. However, the typical laboratory situation does not provide a fair test of the normal function of distance receptors such as eyes and ears, because the animals are placed together in cramped quarters and cannot help but bump into one another. Vision and audition undoubtedly play a significant role in sexual behavior in wild animals, since initial contact depends almost exclusively on them. Sexual arousal itself apparently does not depend on these sensory modalities once contact with a receptive partner has been established. Sensory information from olfactory and tactile receptors can maintain sexual motivation in the absence of visual or auditory cues.

The nonessential nature of individual sensory modalities was demonstrated in a subsequent experiment by Brooks (1937) in which olfactory, auditory, and visual end organs were destroyed in

male and female rabbits. Normal sexual behavior was observed postoperatively, and Brooks concluded that these three sensory modalities are not essential for sexual arousal if the organism is otherwise intact. Beach (1942a, b) has replicated these experiments with albino rats and reports that the elimination of vision, audition, and olfaction does not interfere with sexual behavior in the experienced male as long as tactual sensations from the face are not interfered with. Inexperienced males failed to mate when any two of these modalities were eliminated. Beach concluded from these experiments that any sensory modality which permits the transmission of relevant information will sustain mating behavior.

Brooks (1937) arrived at a similar conclusion after discovering that olfactory bulb lesions *or* complete neodecortication did not affect sexual behavior of the rabbit. A combination of the two lesions completely abolished mating behavior in the male of this species. The olfactory input was not essential in the normal animal but was indispensable after the sensory input of other modalities had been severely impaired by neodecortication. Brooks also found that hemidecortication did not affect sexual behavior in either the male or the female of this species. The female appeared to be less dependent on cortical and sensory mechanisms than the male. Male rabbits refused to copulate following complete neodecortication combined with olfactory bulb removal, but the females continued to be sexually receptive. The additional removal of the remaining auditory and visual sensibility by extirpation of the end organs failed to suppress sexual arousal, receptivity, and ovulation. Even the additional ablation of rhinencephalic structures (amygdaloid complex, hippocampus, allocortical and juxtallocortical mantle) failed to eliminate sexual receptivity in these females; one questions just what sensory input, if any, may be essential.

The nonessential nature of specific sensory information has been noted in other species (see Bard, 1936). What is apparently indispensable is sufficient information about the environment to permit the conclusion that a sexually receptive partner is available. Whether this information is carried by visual, auditory, olfactory, or tactile nerves does not seem to be significant. The apparent contradiction between this conclusion and results obtained from lower species may be resolved if we consider the fact that many sensory systems exist in only very rudimentary form in these species. Other activities such as feeding or defense also relay almost exclusively on the same sensory modality that is found important in sexual behavior.

Summary

Sexual motivation depends directly as well as indirectly on external stimulation. According to Beach (1951), we can classify environmental conditions as follows.

1. STIMULI THAT DO NOT ELICIT SEXUAL BEHAVIOR BUT ARE ESSENTIAL TO THE DEVELOPMENT OF PHYSIOLOGICAL CONDITIONS WHICH MAKE SUCH BEHAVIOR POSSIBLE. Under this heading we have discussed the effects of temperature and illumination. Environmental temperatures determine sexual maturation and affect sexual motivation indirectly via hormonal mechanisms which regulate the seasonal cycle of sexual responsiveness in many species. Endocrine mechanisms are also responsible for the effects of seasonal or diurnal variations in illumination. In some species the specific wavelengths of light that elicit sexual receptivity have been determined.

2. STIMULI THAT PREDISPOSE A SEXUALLY READY ORGANISM TO RESPOND APPROPRIATELY TO STIMULI AFFORDED BY A POTENTIAL MATE. Many field studies have shown that most species fail to mate in an unaccustomed environment. Some even stake out a sexual territory, outside of which no sexual behavior can be observed. Other species mate only if specific environmental conditions are met, such as the presence of sufficient shelter, water, or nesting materials. It is difficult to decide whether these effects are due to a direct action on motivational variables, but the available evidence suggests that they may be.

3. STIMULI THAT DERIVE DIRECTLY FROM AN ANIMAL OF THE OPPOSITE SEX. Sexual motivation has been shown to depend very directly on stimuli of this category. If an animal is unaware of the presence of a potential mate, no sexual arousal can take place. Beyond that, however, we can ask whether specific sensory modalities (such as tactual sensations from the genitalia or olfactory cues) may play a more specific and perhaps essential role in sexual arousal. When we look at inframammalian species, it often appears that a single sensory modality may be indispensable to sexual arousal and mating behavior. As we ascend the phylogenetic scale, this dependence on particular sensations disappears. Instead, we find that sexual motivation and behavior persist as long as sufficient sensory information is available to inform the organism of the presence of a suitable partner. Males generally depend more heavily on sensory stimuli than females, but this may be true because the typically more active role of the male requires more differentiated sensory information. In mammals no specific sensory modality has been found essential to sexual motivation.

NEURAL REGULATION

Subcortical Mechanisms

It is difficult to obtain an accurate picture of the functional significance of lower brainstem mechanisms because this portion of the brain is not easily accessible. If one manages to get to it, one cannot rule out the possibility that the observed effects of lesions or stimulation may be due to afferent rather than efferent pathways. To circumvent this problem, physiologists have used the decerebrate preparation in which the brainstem is completely transected at a midcollicular level; thus the spinal cord, medulla, pons, and part of the midbrain are intact but are isolated from the higher influences. This preparation unfortunately shows a pronounced extensor rigidity which immobilizes the organism.

It is not very surprising that Dempsey and Rioch (1939) failed to observe estrous behavior in decerebrated female guinea pigs and that the many descriptions of the behavioral capabilities of this preparation have not included any sign of sexual behavior. Bard (1940) observed that the extensor rigidity of the decerebrated female cat was momentarily reversed by stimulation of the vagina with a glass rod. In response to such stimulation, estrous (as well as anestrous) females assumed a crouched mating posture which is typical of the species. Neither decerebrate bitches—which normally do not crouch when mating—nor male cats showed this effect. Since similar results have been obtained in spinal animals, this effect does not appear to depend on brainstem mechanisms. The specific contribution that this portion of the brain may make to the regulation of sexual behavior is still largely unknown.

The picture is quite different when we ascend to the diencephalic portion of the brainstem. Considerable evidence suggests that many, if not all, aspects of sexual motivation are integrated at the hypothalamic level. Neural and hormonal mechanisms appear to be regulated by specific hypothalamic centers, and a large research literature deals with these mechanisms in detail. Only a representative sample of this material can be given, the interested reader is directed to excellent reviews for further information (Beach, 1952; Sawyer, 1960).

Before attempting to delineate the areas of the hypothalamus that selectively serve essential functions with respect to the regulation of sexual behavior, we can narrow the field by briefly noting the portions of the diencephalon that certainly are not directly involved. The thalamus proper does not exert essential influences on sexual motivation. Bard (1939) reported that large thalamic lesions (superimposed on cortical damage) do not significantly affect sexual behavior in the cat; even complete bilateral removal of the thalamus (Dempsey and Morrison, discussed in Beach, 1952) fails to eliminate complete and appropriate mating behavior in this species in spite of obvious sensory deficits. Sawyer (1960) has reported that large thalamic lesions also fail to affect the sexual behavior of rabbits. The importance of the lower diencephalon is emphasized by the observation that the complete removal of the neocortex, rhinencephalon, striatum, and upper thalamus does not severely affect sexual behavior in the female cat and rabbit (Bard, 1940; Brooks, 1937).

One of the earliest experimental demonstrations of specific hypothalamic mechanisms was pro-vided by C. Fisher et al. (1938a, b). These workers observed that small electrolytic lesions in the supraoptic region of the anterior hypothalamus of cats completely eliminated all sexual behavior. The findings were replicated by Dey et al. (1940). Brookhart et al. (1940, 1941) demonstrated that guinea pigs with such lesions no longer react to estrogen treatment which normally induces sexual behavior in nonestrous females. These results, in combination with Ranson's (1934) observation that lesions behind the infundibulum do not affect mating behavior in cats, suggest that the essential mechanism may be located in the anterior hypothalamus.

Since the hypothalamus (particularly the supraoptic and paraventricular nuclei which are implicated in the anterior lesions) also controls some of the secretory functions of the hypophysis, the question has been raised whether these effects may be partly or completely determined by hormonal changes. If they are, the observed behavioral changes should be reversible with hormone substitution therapy, and some confusion has been created by conflicting reports about the effectiveness of this procedure. Brookhart et al. (1940, 1941) failed to restore estrous behavior in female guinea pigs with anterior hypothalamic lesions.

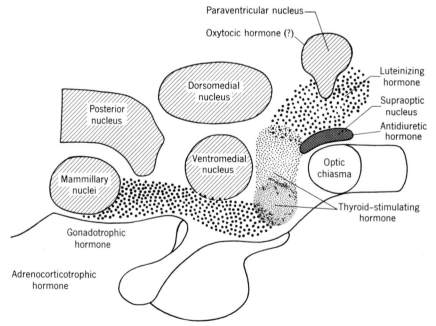

Fig. 8.20 A midline sagittal section through the hypothalamus and pituitary gland. The *stippled areas* indicate the sites where electrical stimulation or lesions have resulted in changes of pituitary secretion. (From Harris, 1955.)

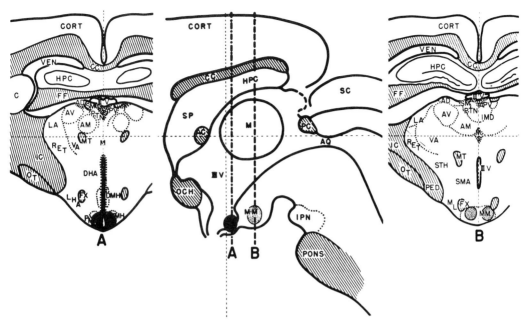

Fig. 8.21 Sites of hypothalamic lesions in the female rabbit brain. Mammillary lesions at B (stippled) abolished mating behavior in spite of therapy with exogenous estrogen but did not induce ovarian atrophy. Tuberal lesions at A (solid black) blocked copulation-induced ovulation or led to ovarian atrophy but did not diminish receptivity if extrinsic estrogen was supplied. (From Sawyer, 1957.)

Injections of ovarian hormones alone or in combination with pituitary hormones did not induce mating behavior. Brookhart and Dey (1941) showed that lesions between the optic chiasma and the stalk of the pituitary abolished or significantly reduced the sex drive of guinea pigs without damaging the testes. This suggests that gonadotrophic functions were not impaired, and the authors concluded that neural mechanisms essential to normal sexual arousal and behavior had been destroyed. Since Maes (1940a, b) found that estrogen treatment can sustain normal mating behavior in hypophysectomized animals, these results indicate that the hypothalamic mechanisms may be independent of hormonal mediation.

Neural and hormonal regulation may coexist and perhaps interact at the hypothalamic level. Sawyer and Robinson (1956) found that small electrolytic lesions in the anterior hypothalamus (rostral to the ventromedial nuclei and within or medial to the medial forebrain bundle) produced permanent anestrus and a complete disappearance of all sexual responses. The effect was not reversed by estrogen treatment. Hypophyseal functions were unimpaired, and ovulation was elicited by electrical stimulation of the ventromedial nuclei

of the hypothalamus. When the lesions were placed more medially and posteriorly (ventromedial nuclei, premammillary region, and mammillary bodies), the same behavioral results (complete anestrus) occurred, but the effects were reversible by estrogen treatment. In these animals ovarian atrophy occurred because of the lack of gonadotrophic activity of the pituitary.

The picture is unfortunately complicated by species differences. Sawyer (1956, 1957) has reported that small bilateral lesions of the mammillary region of the rabbit completely eliminated sexual behavior. This effect could not, as in the cat, be reversed by estrogen treatment, and the ovaries did not show anatomical or functional disturbances. Lesions of the ventromedial nuclei, on the other hand, duplicated rather precisely the results already observed in cats (anestrus and ovarian atrophy, the effects being reversible by estrogen treatment). Sawyer concluded on the basis of these findings that the basal tuberal area controls the release of pituitary gonadotrophins in both cats and rabbits but does not *directly* regulate mating behavior. He further suggested that a behavioral center may be located rostral to this area in the cat but caudal to it in the rabbit.

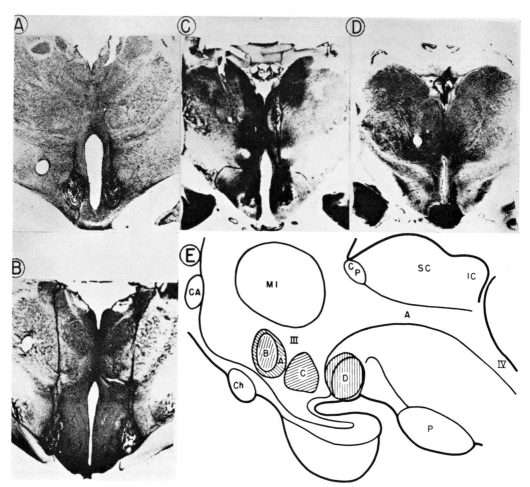

Fig. 8.22   A, B, anterior hypothalamic lesions which induced permanent anestrus in the female cat in spite of treatments with exogenous estrogen. C, ventromedial lesions which induced ovarian atrophy but did not abolish mating behavior if exogenous estrogen was supplied. B, mammillary lesions with the same effect as in C. E, midsagittal reconstruction showing anterior-posterior extent of lesions A to D. (From Sawyer, 1960.)

Similar dual mechanisms have been demonstrated in the rat by Rogers (see Goldstein, 1957). Premammillary lesions abolished or reduced sexual behavior, but the effect was reversible by hormone treatment. More anterior lesions produced permanent behavioral deficits which could not be compensated by androgen treatment.

The precise localization of these mechanisms in man has not yet been established. It has been shown, however, that sexual behavior is severely affected by hypothalamic damage either directly, or via hypophyseal (i.e., hormonal) malfunctions. Bauer (1954) reviewed 60 case histories of hypothalamic damage and reported that 43 showed marked modifications of sexual functions. The hypophysis was diagnosed as normal in the majority of these cases, and Bauer concluded that pronounced alterations of sexual behavior can occur in man as a result of hypothalamic pathology, even when the pituitary system remains unaffected.

Although our understanding of the hypothalamic control of sexual behavior has significantly improved in recent years, many experimental findings cannot yet be integrated in a coherent hypothesis. For instance, Dempsey and Rioch (1939) reported over 25 years ago that the sexual behavior of guinea pigs was entirely unaffected by brainstem transections rostral to the mammillary region but disappeared completely when the cut was made slightly behind the mammillary bodies. Bard (1940) obtained similar results in cats and suggested that the highest center of sex behavior may be found in the rostral mesencephalon or posterior hypothalamus. Reports of sexual precocity or facilitation following hypothalamic lesions have also been published. Bauer's survey of clinical material mentions sexual precocity from tumor growth in the hypothalamus. Hillarp et al. (1954) have reported that "compulsive male mating behavior" was observed in both male and female rats following preoptic lesions. Donovan and van der Werff ten Bosch (1956a, b) report a stimulating or facilitating effect of lesions in the anterior hypothalamus of ferrets. These animals are normally completely anestrous during the winter but were brought into heat by anterior hypothalamic lesions. The behavioral effects were accompanied and presumably caused by secretions of gonadotrophic hormones by the hypophysis. Lisk (1966) has recently reported that small lesions near the diencephalic-mesencephalic junction, in either the lateral or medial mammillary region, caused an increase of copulatory behavior in male rats. He suggested that the previously reported loss of sexual reactivity following posterior hypothalamic lesions might reflect a stimulating action of lesion-induced irritative foci.

The problem is not clarified when we turn to the results of experiments using electrical stimulation or recording procedures. Porter et al. (1957) obtained electroencephalographic recordings from various hypothalamic placements in estrous, estrogen-primed, and anestrous cats. Vaginal stimulation with a glass rod produced significant and reproducible EEG changes in the anterior and lateral hypothalamus. The region traversed by the medial forebrain bundle appeared to be particularly affected. Following stimulation, the EEG pattern was characterized by bursts of high-frequency, high-amplitude waves alternating with trains of high-amplitude slow waves. Estrous as well as estrogen-primed cats reliably showed these effects, but none was observed in anestrous females. Green (1954) previously observed less pronounced EEG changes in the anterior hypothalamus of unrestrained rabbits and reported that the electrical activity of this region was affected by sexual arousal during "love play" and castration. Similar changes were observed in the hippocampal EEG, and Green suggested that hypothalamic activity might be modified by a direct hippocampal influence.

Kawakami and Sawyer (see Sawyer, 1960) observed a generalized EEG reaction to vaginal stimulation of estrogen-primed rabbits in various cortical and subcortical structures. This reaction is characterized by an initial sleep-like record followed by "an unusually aroused pattern" believed to be indicative of pseudoarousal because the animal remains quiet throughout the period of electrical arousal. This EEG reaction can be elicited by low-frequency stimulation of the ventromedial nuclei of the hypothalamus.

Electrical stimulation of various regions within the hypothalamus elicits gonadotrophic secretions from the pituitary. Comparable stimulation of the hypophysis itself has no effect (Harris, 1937, 1948a, b). The technique of electrical stimulation is not well suited to the study of behavioral responses that require freedom of movement and are not completed in a short period of time. Isolated components of sexual behavior have been observed following electrical stimulation of a variety of hypothalamic as well as some extra-hypothalamic sites, but complete mating behavior has not been observed in any of these experiments.

Several investigators have reported long-lasting effects from direct chemical stimulation of the hypothalamic sites. A. Fisher (1956) found that male rats displayed sexual behavior after injections of testosterone into the lateral preoptic region. Similar injections into the medial preoptic area elicited maternal behavior. Harris (1958) reported that ovariectomized cats came into heat and displayed mating behavior following intrahypothalamic injections of estrogen in doses too small to have a direct effect on the uterus. These observations suggest that the neural mechanisms of the hypothalamus which regulate sexual behavior may be sensitive to the general hormone level. This chemical sensitivity may be the important link between hormonal and neural mechanisms that assures that sexual behavior correlates with the hormonal conditions of the organism.

Cortical and Rhinencephalic Mechanisms

The cerebrum does not appear to be essential to the regulation of sexual motivation. This is most obvious in the female, for sensory-motor deficits tend to influence the behavior of the male. The female cat continues to display mating behavior and sexual receptivity after the entire cerebrum has been removed (Bard, 1939). The female rabbit shows normal estrous behavior following complete decortication, even when the receptor organs for vision, audition, and olfaction

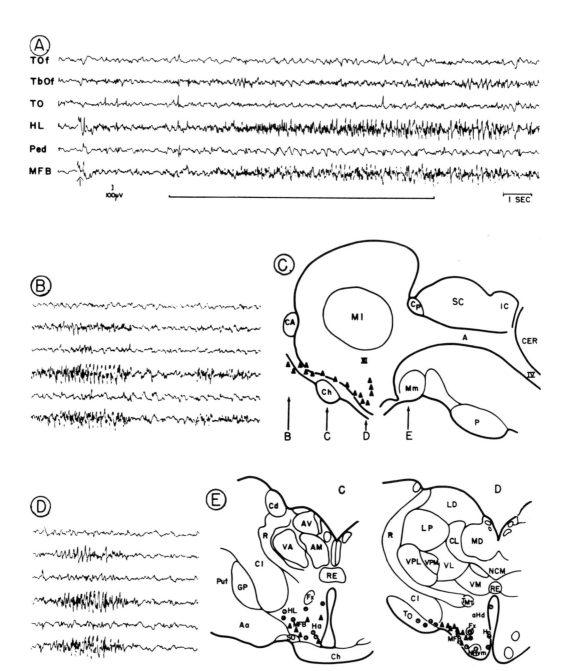

Fig. 8.23 A, selected EEG tracings during vaginal stimulation; B, D, afterreaction which lasted 3.3 min in an estrous cat. Dramatic changes are seen in lateral hypothalamic (HL) and medial forebrain bundle (MFB) channels. C and E are, respectively, a sagittal reconstruction and two cross sections of the cat brainstem showing areas from which altered electrical activity was recorded (solid triangles) and areas failing to show these changes (stippled circles). (From Sawyer, 1960.)

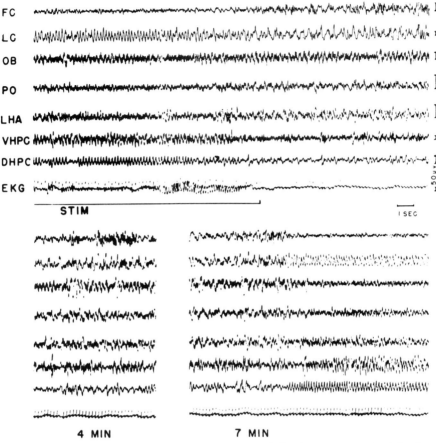

FC

LC

OB

PO

LHA

VHPC

DHPC

EKG

STIM   I SEC

4 MIN   7 MIN

Fig. 8.24 EEG tracings during and after vaginal stimulation in an estrogen-treated estrous rabbit. The afterreaction includes a sleep-like phase, which here lasted 7 min, and a phase of pseudoarousal characterized by high-amplitude slow waves (theta rhythm) in limbic cortical and hippocampal channels. FC, LC, frontal and limbic cortex; OB, olfactory bulb; PO, preoptic area; LHA, lateral hypothalamic area; VHPC and DHPC, ventral and dorsal hippocampus; EKG, electrocardiogram. (From Sawyer, 1960.)

are also ablated (Brooks, 1937). The female rat similarly continues to show normal estrous cycles, mating behavior, and pregnancy (Davis, 1939; Beach, 1951). Decorticate female rats lose the male-like mounting behavior which is frequently observed in normal animals, but female sexual responses remain intact (Beach, 1943).

The sexual behavior of the male is severely impaired or abolished by extensive cortical damage, but a survey of the literature suggests that these deficits may be due to sensory and motor defects rather than effects on sexual motivation. Such deficits are not equally reflected in the female because the female mating pattern is generally passive, requiring little sensory feedback and almost no precise motor coordination. These factors do enter into male mating behavior, and a

consequent loss of sexual behavior (as distinct from motivation) occurs. In the rat, Beach (1940) observed that small cortical lesions (up to 20%) had no effect on male sexual behavior. Progressively larger lesions reduced the percentage of males showing copulatory behavior, and no animal mated when more than 60% of the cortex was removed. The effects appeared to be independent of the localization of the lesion. In the male rabbit, sexual behavior survives the complete removal of the entire neocortex as long as the olfactory bulbs are intact (Brooks, 1937; Stone, 1939). Olfactory cues apparently suffice to direct the sexual behavior of this species even when the cortical projections of all other sensory modalities are removed. Large cortical lesions do not reduce sexual motivation in the male cat, although the

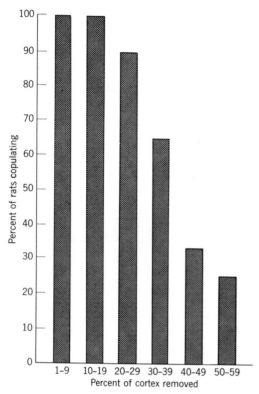

Percent of rats copulating

Percent of cortex removed

Fig. 8.25 Effects of partial decortication on sex behavior in male rats; percent of animals in each lesion group continuing to copulate after operation. (From Beach, 1940.)

execution of mating behavior is severely impaired. Beach (cited by Goldstein, 1957) has observed that male cats with large frontal lesions continue to attempt copulation with receptive females; however, most animals did not achieve intromission because of severe motor disturbances.

Because of the intimate anatomical relationship between the hypothalamus and various limbic structures, there has been considerable interest in the role of these rhinencephalic mechanisms in sexual behavior. Klüver and Bucy (1939) reported the now classic description of the effects of temporal pole lobectomy in the male monkey, which included marked hypersexuality. Schreiner and Kling (1953, 1954, 1956) have more recently demonstrated that comparable hypersexuality can be elicited in a variety of species by more restricted lesions of the amygdala and pyriform cortex. Green et al. (1957) localized the effect even more precisely in the cat. Sexual behavior remained unaffected by damage to the amygdaloid complex itself. Minute lesions in the pyriform cortex, un-

derneath the basolateral amygdaloid nuclei, produced pronounced hypersexuality. The effect was reduced following castration but reinstated by androgen or estrogen therapy. Sawa et al. (1954) and Terzian and Dalle Ore (1955) have observed similar changes in human sexual behavior following temporal lobe damage.

It is interesting to note that this allocortical mechanism does not appear to be involved in the regulation of female mating behavior. Neither Schreiner and Kling nor Green and his associates observed hypersexual responses in female animals, although the effects in males were clear and readily reproducible. Whether these results are attributable to a greater dependence of female sexuality on hormonal mechanisms is not yet clear. Gastaut (1952) has described estrous behavior in cats following various rhinencephalic lesions although the genital apparatus remained completely anestrous. The interaction between hormonal mechanisms and neural controls of rhinencephalic origin awaits further study.

MacLean (1955) has long maintained that the rhinencephalon subserves various visceral functions and has shown that isolated components of the male sexual pattern (such as penile erection and ejaculation) can be elicited by electrical or chemical stimulation of several regions of the hippocampal and amygdaloid gyri. Studies by Fauré (1956; Fauré and Gruner, 1956) also suggest that rhinencephalic structures participate in the regulation of sexual behavior. Various rhinencephalic and hypothalamic regions showed marked changes in electrical activity following intramuscular injections of adrenal steroids and gonadotrophins. Other portions of the brain did not respond differentially. Although we do not yet understand the functional significance of these electrophysiological changes, they may provide important leads for future research.

Summary

Several components of the response sequence that comprises normal mating behavior appear to be integrated at a spinal level in the form of simple reflex mechanisms. Lower animals especially tend to show surprisingly complete sexual response patterns following transection of the spinal cord. Only fractional responses of a clearly sexual nature survive such an operation in higher animals.

We have little conclusive evidence about the role of the lower brainstem (medulla, pons, and midbrain) in sexual behavior. The results of a few

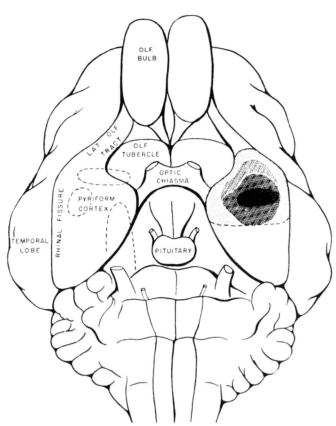

Fig. 8.26 Ventral aspect of the cat brain showing surface projection of areas where destruction caused specific behavioral changes. *Right*, concentric stippled circle showing quartile incidence of involvement in animals exhibiting hypersexuality. (From J. Green, C. D. Clemente, and J. de Groot, *J. comp. Neurol.*, 1957, **108**, 522.)

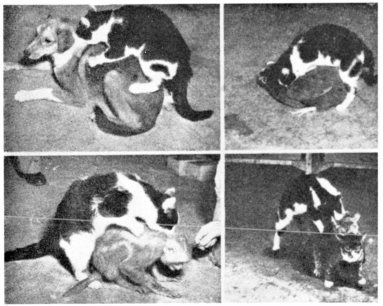

Fig. 8.27 Various phases of abnormal sexual activity displayed by male cats with lesions in the amygdala and pyriform cortex. The lower right photograph illustrates attempts at "tandem copulation" among four male preparations. (From Schreiner and Kling, 1953.)

475

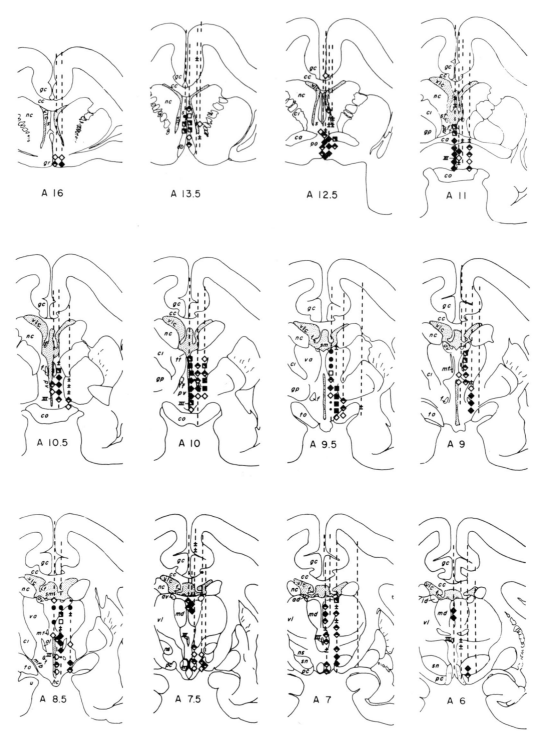

Fig. 8.28 Diamonds and squares in these cross sections through the squirrel monkey brain show loci at which electrical stimulation elicited penile erection. Squares indicate that stimulation was followed by electrical afterdischarges in the hippocampus. The open, half-filled, and solid symbols denote gradations from partial to full erection. Vertical dashes indicate points explored and found to be negative. (From MacLean and Ploog, 1962.)

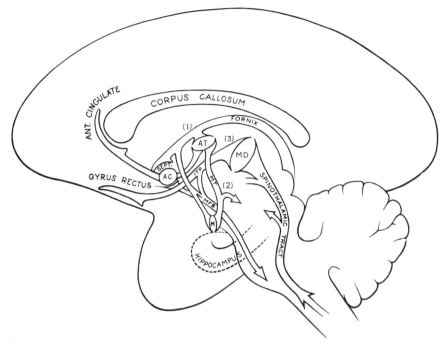

Fig. 8.29 Positive loci for penile erection are found in parts of three cortico-subcortical subdivisions of the limbic system, labeled 1, 2, and 3. The septum (SEPT) and medial part of the medial dorsal nucleus (MD) are nodal points with respect to erection. The medial forebrain bundle (MFB) and inferior thalamic peduncle (ITP) are important descending pathways. The drawing also schematizes connections of the spinothalamic pathway with the medial dorsal nucleus and intralaminar nuclei. Scratching of the genitals and/or ejaculation have been elicited by stimulation at various points along this pathway and regions of its termination in the foregoing structures. AC, anterior commissure; AT, anterior thalamus; M, mammillary bodies. (From MacLean, 1962.)

relevant studies suggest that no essential integration of neural or hormonal mechanisms takes place below the level of the diencephalon.

A major center of neural regulation apparently exists in the anterior hypothalamus. Lesions in the area of the preoptic and paraventricular nuclei completely abolish sexual motivation without affecting the hormonal balance of the organism. This effect is not reversed by hormone treatment. Injections of testosterone into the lateral aspect of this area elicit mating behavior, suggesting that this neural mechanism may be sensitive to the general hormone level of the organism and thus correlate sexual behavior with hormonal fluctuations. Pronounced EEG changes have been recorded from the entire region during vaginal stimulation or sexual arousal.

An additional center of hormonal regulation seems to exist in, or posterior to, the ventromedial nuclei of the hypothalamus. Lesions in the ventromedial nuclei or premammillary region abolish sexual behavior, but this effect can be reversed by hormone therapy. Whereas lesions in the anterior hypothalamus do not produce anatomical changes in the genitalia, pronounced gonadal atrophy (caused by a lack of gonadotrophic activity of the pituitary) is observed following premammillary lesions.

Several experiments have indicated that the specific location of these two mechanisms varies among species. It is probable that an additional inhibitory mechanism may be present in some species, since facilitation (i.e., hypersexuality) has been observed following hypothalamic lesions. There is no evidence that the thalamus proper may be specifically involved with sexual motivation.

When cortical functions are considered, species and sex differences become apparent. The male, as a rule, is much more sensitive to cortical damage than the female, which may reflect little more than the fact that his active role in copulation requires more detailed sensory feedback and motor coordination than the largely passive role of the female. A similar explanation may account for the observation that the effects of cortical damage are progressively more severe as we ascend the phylogenetic scale. Whereas both inframammalian species and lower mammals show little or no impairment following complete decortication, higher animals (especially the male of the species) are severely handicapped as soon as more than about 20% of the cerebrum is removed. Since other aspects of behavior show a similar progressive deficit, these findings may not indicate a greater encephalization of specific sexual functions.

There is some indication that the rhinencephalon may in some way be related to sexual behavior, at least in the male of the species. Early investigations of temporal lobe functions suggested that the amygdaloid complex may contain neural elements that participate in the regulation of sexual behavior; however, more recent studies have indicated that the observed effects may be due to an infringement on the underlying pyriform cortex. Isolated components of the male mating pattern (such as penile erection and ejaculation) have been elicited by electrical stimulation of various rhinencephalic structures, and lesions in this part of the brain often produce hypersexuality. However, this part of the cortex also serves other motivational mechanisms, and it is not clear that the observed effects are specific to sexual motivation. The rhinencephalon may represent a general integrative mechanism for motivational systems rather than a specific center for sexual motivation.

HORMONAL BASIS OF SEXUAL BEHAVIOR

Sexual behavior, arousal, and motivation occur only in special environmental situations which provide particular types of sensory stimulation; however, no amount of stimulation will arouse sexual motivation and behavior unless the organism is physically ready to mate. This physiological readiness to respond selectively to sexual stimuli is provided by hormonal changes which affect neural as well as non-neural mechanisms throughout the body.

In our brief description of the endocrine system and the physiological basis of reproduction in the male and female, we have already shown that sexual hormones of hypophyseal and gonadal origin influence the structural and functional readiness of the organism to respond appropriately to sexual stimulation. What remains to be explored is whether these hormonal influences are essential to sexual arousal and mating behavior. The material discussed in the following section has been reviewed in greater detail by Stone (1923a), Moore (1942a), Young (1941), and Beach (1948).

Hormonal Mechanisms as Determinants of Cyclical Sexual Arousal

Beach (1948) summarized data from a variety of experimental and observational studies indicating that sexual activity in seasonal breeders correlates highly with structural and functional changes of the gonads (ovaries or testes). In the female, sexual receptivity occurs when follicular development is near completion and estrogen production is high. The dependence on hormonal priming appears to be greatest in submammalian species but persists to some degree even in primates. The female of lower mammalian species does not permit coitus during anestrus or diestrus or during pregnancy when the ovarian cycle is interrupted. In primates, this intimate relationship no longer holds. The relatively primitive rhesus monkey displays more sexual behavior just before ovulation but can be induced to copulate any time on the insistence of an aggressive partner (Ball and Hartman, 1935; Carpenter, 1942). Female chimpanzees receive the male at any point during the estrous cycle (Yerkes and Elder, 1936). However, socially well-adjusted monkeys tend to concentrate their sexual activities during the portion of the estrous cycle that is characterized by a high estrogen level and follicular development (Allen et al., 1936). In man, the importance of hormonal factors further decreases, although several clinical reports (Davis, 1929; Dickinson, 1931) suggest that sexual receptivity in the human female is greatest just before and after menstruation. Greenblatt (1943) has even proposed that nymphomaniacal tendencies can be observed in many women just before menstruation.

That hormonal conditions and sexual arousal are in fact causally related has been demonstrated in experiments involving hormone administrations. Seasonal breeders (such as reptiles, opossums, and mares) can be brought into heat out of season by injections of gonadotrophic hormones (Hammond, 1938) or pituitary extract (Day, 1940). The resultant sexual activity is believed to be caused by the release of estrogens by the stimulated ovaries, since estrogen administrations are known to have comparable effects (Hammond, 1944; Hammond and Day, 1944). Animals that show cyclical estrous behavior respond similarly to hormone treatment. Anestrous cats (Friedgood, 1939) and bitches (Leathem, 1938) become sexually active in response to exogenous gonadotrophins. The behavioral effect is accompanied by follicular growth, uterine bleeding, and ovulation. Similar responses can be elicited by estrogen administration (Leathem, 1938). The role of specific hypophyseal hormones has been elucidated by Witschi and Pfeiffer (1935); chronic treatment with FSH produced anatomical changes in the vagina that are normally observed only during estrus. Sexual activity and ovulation, however, appeared only after additional injections of luteinizing hormone.

Hypophyseal and gonadal hormones not only affect the reproductive cycle but also influence sexual development in adolescence. Stone (1922) and Beach (1944) have studied the development of sexual activity in adolescent laboratory rats. Puberty was found to be influenced by dietary factors and occurred anywhere between 45 and 90 days of age (Stone, 1924a, b; 1925). Daily injections of testosterone propionate significantly advanced the age at which the first copulatory behavior was observed. Stone (1940) began testosterone treatments in male animals ranging from 22 to 26 days of age and observed that the experimental animals copulated 20 days sooner than untreated controls. Beach (1942d, e) extended Stone's work to the female of this species. Injections of gonadal hormones were begun when the animals were only 14 days old. In replication of Stone's findings, Beach observed that male rats copulated between 21 and 29 days of age, almost

one month before the normal appearance of sexual activity. Female rats displayed lordosis responses and sexual receptivity between 21 and 25 days of age.

The gradual decline of sexual motivation with age also appears to be caused by hormonal factors. Runge (1943) reported that the sexual vigor of aging stallions, bulls, and dogs can be restored by the transplantation of sexual glands from young animals. Steinach and Kun have reported that senile rats resume normal sexual activity following injections of anterior pituitary extract (1928) or gonadal hormones (1933). Minnick and Warden (1946) observed that injections of gonadal or pituitary hormones produce a marked rise in sexual activity in 24-month-old rats. The experimental animals copulated seven times as frequently as their untreated littermates. No difference between the gonadal and pituitary hormones was observed.

Several clinical reports (Steinach and Peczenik, 1936; Miller, 1938) suggest that old men respond to prolonged gonadal hormone treatment with increased sexual prowess and interest. Many clinical disorders of genital functions (retention of the testes in the abdomen, hypogenitalism, etc.) are accompanied by a complete lack of sexual motivation, although sexual behavior is physically possible. Sexual drive can be restored in these individuals by hormone treatment (Miller et al., 1938; Gordon and Fields, 1942).

Hormone injections have also been employed successfully to cure impotence in farm and domestic animals. Controlled laboratory studies of

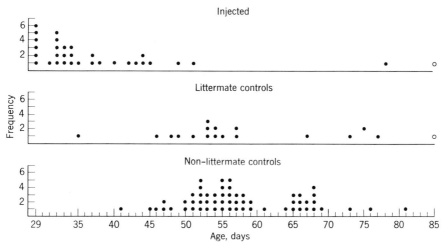

Fig. 8.30 Frequency distributions of the ages of first copulations of androgen-injected rats, their littermate controls, and a group of non-littermate controls similarly tested. (From Stone, 1940.)

this phenomenon have shown that nearly all cases of impotence respond to this treatment. Stone (1938a, b, c) observed that eighteen young but apparently completely impotent and disinterested male rats copulated vigorously after one or more injections of testosterone propionate. Although sexual motivation (as measured by the frequency of copulation) was not as high as in normal animals, some of the previously impotent rats sired healthy litters. Smith and Engle (1927) found that the transplantation of anterior pituitary tissue (which raises the level of gonadotrophic hormones and thus stimulates the secretion of abnormal quantities of gonadal hormones) produces hypersexuality in normal mice. These animals frequently mounted diestrous females and young males and ejaculated as a result of this contact. Beach (1942c) has also reported hypersexuality in rats following large injections of testosterone propionate. The animals attempted copulation with a variety of objects which do not elicit sexual behavior in normal males. Several investigators (C. D. Davis, 1939; Beach, 1940) have observed that sexual motivation may be restored by injections of androgens in animals that have been rendered totally unresponsive to sexual stimulation by extensive cortical damage. Beach suggests that the additional hormone supply may compensate for the loss of cortical function.

Castration and Hormone Replacement in the Male

Castration of the male (i.e., the removal of the gonadal glands or testes) does not in itself make it physically impossible to engage in mating behavior. However, the resultant hormonal deficiency produces anatomical and functional disturbances of the reproductive apparatus as well as a marked inhibition of sexual motivation. The severity of the postcastrational behavioral deficit is a function of species differences and age at castration.

In most lower vertebrate species, castration of the male results in the gradual decline and eventual loss of sexual motivation (fishes appear to be an exception to this rule; several workers have reported little or no deficit following the removal of the testes in various species). Most surprising perhaps is the fact that the decline of sexual motivation is very gradual. In amphibia, castration must occur well before the mating season if sexual behavior is to be affected (Edinger, 1913). Reptiles (Reynolds, 1943) and birds (Scott and Payne, 1934) tend to show more immediate, though less complete, inhibition.

In adult mammals, sexual behavior may persist for relatively long periods of time after castration. Steinach (1894b) reports that stallions and rats

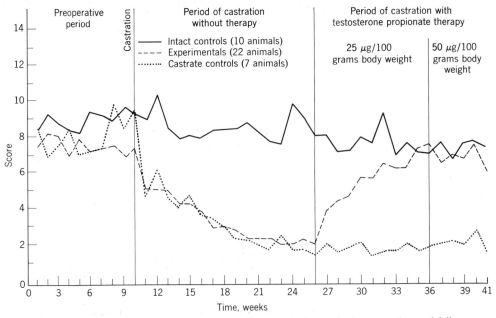

Fig. 8.31 Strength of the sex drive in male guinea pigs before and after castration and following therapy with testosterone propionate daily. (From Grunt and Young, 1952.)

continue to mate for many months following removal of the testes. Stone (1927) reported great individual differences in the delay of complete asexuality in the male rat. He removed the testes from 45 sexually mature (90 days old) rats and observed that sexual motivation (as measured by overt elements of the copulatory response) disappeared gradually and steadily. After six months, only 9% of the animals attempted to copulate with a receptive female. All rats continued to mate immediately after castration, but some dropped out rather quickly, whereas others persisted for many months. Sexual experience did not appear to be the determining factor in these experiments. Half of Stone's animals were allowed to copulate before castration, but this group did not show a statistically reliable advantage in postoperative sexual activity. In subsequent studies (Stone, 1937, 1939a) Stone replicated these findings using more refined quantitative measures of sexual behavior and observed that ejaculation was the first aspect of the sexual response sequence to be eliminated following castration. Nissen (1929) observed that castrated males cross an electrified grid less frequently than normal animals to reach a respective female. Postpuberal castration produces similar patterns of gradually declining sexual motivation in the rabbit (Stone, 1932) and rhesus monkey (Thorek, 1924).

Goldstein (1957) has reported interesting individual differences in the response to castration. He castrated male dogs after obtaining a measure of their normal level of sexual activity. All these animals showed an initial postoperative decline in sexual motivation, but very different recovery functions were subsequently observed. The sexual activity of three of these animals steadily declined and eventually all but disappeared. However, two animals showed only very minor and temporary disturbances of sexual activity, and the last two dogs performed *better* than before the operation following a brief postoperative drop. Goldstein observed that the level of postcastrational sexual activity was highly correlated ($r = .83$) with the number of preoperative copulation tests; he concluded that sexual experience before castration determines to a large extent the effectiveness of the operation in the dog. These correlations have not been observed in the rat (Stone, 1927).

In chimpanzees, there appears to be little or no decline of sexual motivation following castration, even when the gonadectomy is undertaken before puberty (Clark, 1945). Although ejaculation cannot be achieved, castrated chimpanzees continue to copulate.

At the human level, a variety of social factors vastly complicate the picture. Engle (1942) has published an extensive review of the clinical literature, concluding that prepuberal castration generally eliminates much if not all of the sexual drive in the human male, whereas postpuberal castration merely reduces sexual motivation. Nevertheless, many individual reports on record indicate that sexual motivation may not be impaired at all by castration (Feiner and Rothman, 1939; Rowe and Lawrence, 1928).

Prepuberal castration prevents the occurrence of copulatory behavior in most species. However, several investigators have noted that sexual *motivation* (as distinct from behavior) may not be completely inhibited. Beach (1942b) castrated male rats at the age of 21 days and observed their responses to receptive females 90 days after the operation. Although no actual copulatory behavior occurred, Beach noted "sex play" and several incomplete attempts at copulation. In prepuberally castrated guinea pigs, complete mating responses have been observed, although sexual activity tends to be less aggressive, shorter, and less intense (Seward, 1940; Sollenberger and Hamilton, 1939).

Beach and Holz-Tucker (1946) have obtained evidence which suggests that age at castration may not be as important a determinant of sexual motivation in the male rat as had previously been assumed. These workers castrated 50 male rats at ages ranging from 1 to 350 days of age and tested the animals several months after the operation. Although some incomplete copulatory responses were observed in some of the animals, the general finding was that all animals failed to respond appropriately to a receptive female, regardless of when the gonadectomy was performed.

The behavioral effects of gonadectomy are due to a resulting homonal imbalance rather than more immediate anatomical or neural deficits. This point becomes clear when we consider the effects of hormone substitution therapy in the male castrate.

Testicular implants or injections of androgens have been shown to elicit complete sexual behavior in amphibia (Edinger, 1913), reptiles (Reynolds, 1943), and birds (D. E. Davis and Domm, 1941, 1943). In mammals this restoration of sexual motivation has been studied in some detail. Steinach (1911) reported that prepuberally castrated male rats show normal mating behavior in adulthood following a testicular transplant. Shapiro (1937) castrated male rats before puberty and observed their responses to sexually receptive females after a nine-week period of isolation. When all animals failed to copulate, daily injections of testosterone propionate were begun. After 8 days of hormone treatment, the animals were retested and sexual play activity as well as several instances of copulation were recorded. Similar results have been reported by Stone (1938a).

Moore and Price (1938) found that rats castrated at age 30 days began to copulate almost immediately when testosterone was administered six months after the operation. Ejaculation returned after several weeks of hormone treatment. Stone (1939b) observed that individual components of the mating response tend to reappear in castrated animals in the inverse order in which they disappear following removal of the testes. When the hormone injections are stopped, a gradual loss of sexual behavior duplicates the sequence initially observed after castration.

Beach and Holz-Tucker (1946) have reported that daily injections of approximately 50 µg of testosterone propionate suffice to maintain normal sexual activity in the castrated male rat. The amount of exogenous hormone required to maintain normal sexual behavior was found to be unrelated to the age at castration. Beach and Holz-Tucker noted, however, that hormone substitution therapy was not as effective in animals castrated before 21 days of age; they suggested that very early castration may inhibit the development of the penis, an effect that cannot be compensated by hormone substitution therapy in adulthood. Beach and Holz-Tucker concluded from their ex-

periments that the development of normal patterns of sexual behavior does not depend on the integrity of the gonads or their secretion, for complete and appropriate patterns of responses were elicited in castrated animals following hormone therapy. The persisting impairment in animals castrated at a very early age was believed to be caused by mechanical rather than motivational problems.

In a subsequent study Beach and Holz-Tucker (1949) obtained evidence that suggests a direct relationship between gonadal hormone levels and intensity of sexual motivation. Fifty-two male rats were observed for six weeks to determine a base line level of sexual activity. The animals were then castrated and treated with daily androgen injections for an additional six weeks. The daily quantity of hormone was constant for a given animal but varied between groups of subjects from 1 to 500 µg. During the six-week test period, a significant positive relationship was observed between the amount of hormone injected and the percentage of animals that copulated during a 10-min exposure to a receptive female. Sexual behavior was maintained at preoperative levels by daily injections of 50 to 75 µg of androgen. Higher than normal scores were obtained by animals given larger doses of the hormone.

A subsequent replication of this experiment in the guinea pig (Grunt and Young, 1952) demonstrated that one must be careful in making interspecies generalizations. The sexual activity of castrated male guinea pigs could be maintained at preoperative levels by daily androgen injec-

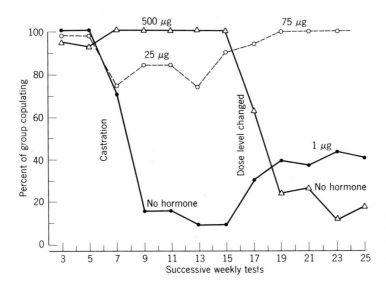

Fig. 8.32 Percentage of castrated male rats copulating after varying doses of androgens were administered. (From Beach and Holz-Tucker, 1949.)

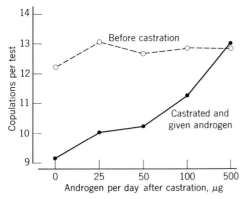

Fig. 8.33 Average frequency of copulations before and after castration. (From Beach and Holz-Tucker, 1949.)

tions, but no dose-response relationship could be observed in this species. Although a minimal dose of the hormone was necessary to maintain normal sexual behavior, larger doses failed to increase postcastrational sexual activity.

Beach and Jordan (1956) have attempted to assess the motivational effects of castration and hormone substitution therapy by a more indirect technique. In these experiments male rats were taught to run down a straight alley to a receptive female in the goal box. After running speeds had stabilized, the animals were castrated and placed into the runway. Running speeds were found to be significantly decreased following this operation, and this trend was reversed after injections of androgens. These results may be confounded with the fact that castration reduces the running behavior of the male rat (Heller, 1932); however, this explanation is not very likely, since the general level of activity and the animal's physical ability to run are not affected by gonadectomy (Campbell and Sheffield, 1953; Eayers, 1954).

In the human male castrate, prolonged androgen treatment is generally effective in restoring sexual motivation as well as penile erection, but the ability to ejaculate tends to remain defective, if not totally absent (Moehlig, 1940).

Some endocrinologists have suggested that androgens not only stimulate the development of male secondary sex characteristics and behavior, but also inhibit the establishment of female characteristics and behavior patterns. Conversely, the estrogens are believed to inhibit masculine responses and stimulate the development of female characteristics. The experimental evidence for this theory is interesting, though far from con-

clusive. Steinach (1911, 1912, 1913, 1940) has reported that castrated male rats and guinea pigs exhibit female mating behavior following the transplantation of ovarian tissues, and that such animals attract the sexual attention of normal males. Castrated female guinea pigs with testicular grafts were observed to display masculine patterns of sexual behavior. Moore (1919, 1920) and Sand (1919, 1920) have replicated and confirmed these observations. Ball (1939) reported that prepuberally castrated male rats show the typically female lordosis response following prolonged estrogen treatment. Beach (1942b), on the other hand, noted that male rats, castrated at the age of 21 days, show an *increase* of male sexual behavior following estrogen treatment. Kun (1933) has observed that normal male rats display both male and female behavior patterns following estrogen injections. Before we attempt to abstract some generalizations from these divergent findings, it may be worthwhile to consider the hormonal mechanisms of the female.

Castration and Hormone Replacement in the Female

The effects of castration have been less extensively studied in the female than in the male because the effects of ovariectomy (removal of the female gonadal glands or ovaries) are impressively consistent across many species. In contrast to the apparently more complex situation in the male, castration in the female always results in a *complete* cessation of all sexual activity and an apparently total lack of all sexual motivation. Whereas the castrated male continues to display sexual behavior for many weeks or months after the operation, the ovariectomized female *immediately* ceases to be receptive to the male and may vigorously resist any sexual advances. The age of castration seems to have no effect on subsequent sexual behavior, since absolutely none can be observed even when the ovaries are removed late in the female's life cycle.

These effects have been observed in amphibia (Weisman and Coates, 1944b), reptiles (Noble and Greenberg, 1941), fishes (Noble and Kumpf, 1936, 1937), and birds (Goodale, 1913). In mammals, we find a similar picture. Female mice (Wiesner and Mirskaia, 1930), rats (Nissen, 1929), guinea pigs (Hertz et al., 1937), and monkeys (Ball, 1936) completely refuse to copulate or even engage in sexual play activity following castration. Nissen (1929) has shown that ovariectomized rats cross an electrified grid much less frequently than normal females when the incentive for such behavior is a sexually aggressive male. He found that a normal female in estrus will cross the grid 13 to 14 times per 20-min test session, whereas castrated females cross only twice on the average. When hormone treatment was instituted, the mean number of crossings rose to 11.89.

Only in the human female do we find a deviation from this pattern. Although some deficits of sexual motivation have been reported (C. G. Heller et al., 1944a, b; Clauberg and Schultze, 1934), there are many clinical observations of little or no change. In a survey of 40 case histories, Filler and Drezner (1944) report that sexual motivation was not at all diminished in any of the patients, although anatomical and physiological indices of menopause were present in 85% of the cases.

Before we leave the topic of ovariectomy, we might briefly discuss a subject that appears to be intimately related to sexual receptivity in the female of some species. The female rat, for instance, displays marked fluctuations of general activity which appear to be intimately related to the anatomical and functional changes of the estrous cycle (Wang, 1923, 1924). Before puberty or during pregnancy, no regular rhythms of activity can be observed. However, during the sexually active portion of the rat's life-span, the female displays a very large increase in activity every fourth or

fifth day which correlates perfectly with estrus and sexual receptivity. Wang (1923) and Richter (1927) have shown that these activity cycles disappear completely following bilateral ovariectomy and that the general level of activity drops sharply. Subsequent experiments have demonstrated that partial removal of the ovaries has little effect on either the activity cycle or the total amount of general activity. Extensive ovarian damage interferes with the cyclical nature of activity, but complete ovariectomy is necessary to reduce the overall activity to that of normal animals in diestrus (Wang and Guttmacher, 1927). The transplantation of ovaries in castrated males produces a sharp rise in general activity as well as some cyclical fluctuations similar to those seen in the normal female (Wang et al., 1925).

Hormone treatments have a pronounced effect on the activity of ovariectomized females. Several investigators have reported a return of general activity to precastration levels following the injection of follicular extract (Richter, 1933). The specificity of this response was shown by Young and Fish (1945). These workers found that ovariectomized rats returned to normal activity levels following estrone injections, whereas comparable injections of progesterone had no effect. The amount of activity following replacement therapy appeared to be proportional to precastrational

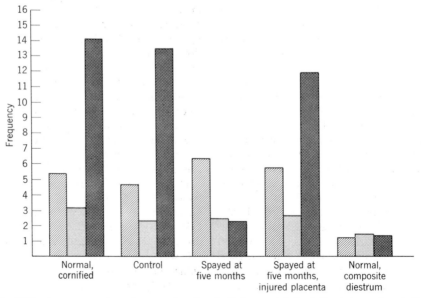

Fig. 8.34 Average number of approaches (hatched), contacts (stippled), and crossings (solid) for female rats in the Columbia Obstruction Test. The control group underwent sham ovariectomy. Data from Nissen, 1929. (From Stone, 1939b.)

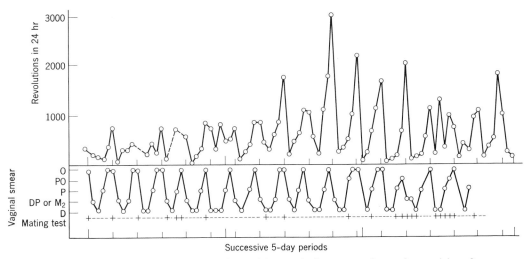

Fig. 8.35 Correlation between muscular activity, vaginal smear, and sexual receptivity of a normal female. O, oestrus; D, dioestrus; M, metoestrus; P, pro-oestrus; −, sexual responses of stages 1–2; +, sexual responses of stages 3–12 (as defined by Hemmingsen, 1933; see Fig. 8.9). (From Hemmingsen, 1933.)

levels rather than the amount of estrogen administered.

When we consider the effects of hormone treatment on sexual behavior itself, a similar picture emerges. Castrated female reptiles (Greenberg and Noble, 1944), fishes (Noble and Kumpf, 1936), and birds (D. E. Davis and Domm, 1941, 1943) display complete estrous and mating behavior following estrogen treatment. Dogs (Leathem, 1938), ferrets (Marshall and Hammond, 1945), and cats (Bard, 1936; Maes, 1939, 1940b), show comparable effects.

In the laboratory rat, the response of ovariectomized animals to hormone treatment has been studied in detail. Ball (1939) reports that prepuberally castrated females became sexually receptive in adulthood following estrogen treatment. The action of estrogen appears to be potentiated by subsequent injections of progesterone (Boling et al., 1938). Similar results have been obtained by Beach (1942c). He castrated virgin female rats which had been reared in isolation. Three weeks after ovariectomy, one group of animals received injections of estrogen while a second group received similar injections of estrogen followed by progesterone. The dosage of these hormone injections was systematically varied within each group. Eighteen hours after the hormone treatment was begun, each rat was placed into a cage with a sexually aggressive male. The following sexual responses were recorded: number of mountings permitted by the female, lordosis,

ear twitching, hopping, and back kicking. None of the animals that had received estrogen alone was very receptive to the advances of the male. However, the second group, which had received both estrogen and progesterone, demonstrated sexual receptivity levels that could not be differentiated either qualitatively or quantitatively from those of normal females. These experiments suggest that estrous behavior of normal intensity requires the synergistic action of estrogen and progesterone in the rat.

In a subsequent study Beach (1945b) had the good fortune to discover a female rat in which ovarian tissue was congenitally lacking. This animal was brought into heat by combined injections of estradiol and progesterone and was observed to display vigorous sexual behavior. The lordosis response was given as soon as a male attempted copulation, and the female continued to cooperate in repeated matings. During one 5-min period, the male was received fourteen times. Beach concluded that the hormonal mechanisms are not essential to the development of sexual behavior patterns in the female.

The results of these experiments suggest that estrogen may not be able to sustain sexual motivation in the castrated female and that progesterone may be an important and perhaps essential hormone. This conclusion is supported by several studies with other species. Boling and Blandau (1939) found that castrated female guinea pigs showed more intense sexual activity following combined injections of estrogen and progesterone than after comparable injections of estrogen alone, and Hertz et al. (1937) reported that copulatory behavior can be elicited in estrogen-primed female guinea pigs by injections of progesterone. Ring (1944) found that estrogen followed by progesterone injections elicited estrous behavior in a significantly higher percentage of ovariectomized mice than estrogen treatment alone.

Progesterone appears to have a clear facilitating effect on sexual behavior in these species, but this is not a universal finding. Progesterone has been reported to inhibit postcoital ovulation and induce a pronounced reduction in estrous receptivity in the female rabbit (Makepeace et al., 1937); progesterone inhibits estrus completely in the ferret (Marshall and Hammond, 1945). Estrogen-induced receptivity of ovariectomized rhesus monkeys also appears to be significantly reduced by progesterone injections (Ball, 1941a). These findings suggest once more that we must be careful in generalizing the results of experiments across species.

In primates, hormone substitution is an effective stimulus for sexual behavior in castrates (Elder, 1938; see also Beach, 1948). The female of the human species appears to react similarly to estrogen treatment, although it has been suggested that much of the observed effect may be caused by a placebo effect (C. G. Heller et al., 1944a, b). It is interesting to note that progesterone appears to have an inhibitory effect rather than a stimulating one in normal women (Greenblatt, 1944).

Reversal of Sexual Behavior

The importance of hormonal mechanisms is perhaps best illustrated by the behavioral effects of spontaneous or experimental gonadal alteration. The primary and secondary sexual characteristics of most species are not as invariant as one often supposes. There are many cases on record of animals that have shown a gradual reversal of these characteristics because of parasitism, dietary changes, or endocrinologic factors. (See reviews by Crew, 1921; Coe, 1940; Beach, 1948.) Most important, in the present context, is the fact that these reversals of morphology are almost invariably followed by appropriate changes in sexual motivation and behavior.

These relationships have been extensively studied in the laboratory rat, and there remains little doubt about the overriding importance of the sexual glands. Steinach (1911, 1912, 1913, 1940) has reported that castrated male rats and

guinea pigs exhibit female behavior patterns and attract normal males following the transplantation of ovaries. Moore (1919, 1920) observed that ovariectomized rats and guinea pigs display male sexual behavior after the implantation of testes. Moreover, bisexual behavior has been observed in hemicastrated animals which have one transplanted sexual gland from the opposite sex. Sand (1919, 1920) found that such animals display male sexual behavior if in contact with a female and female sexual responses to the advances of a normal male. Similar results have been reported by Steinach (1916).

The hormonal nature of these effects is emphasized by the finding that reversals of sexual response patterns can be induced by the administration of hormones of the opposite sex. Such results have been obtained in many submammalian species (see Beach, 1948) and are commonly observed in lower mammals. Ball (1937b) has reported male sexual responses in female rats following injections of testosterone propionate and female estrual responses following the administration of ovarian hormones. Similar results have been obtained in the rabbit (Hu and Frazier, 1940) and in dogs (Berg, 1944).

In man, estrogenic hormones have been reported to lower sexual motivation in the male but increase it in the female (Graller et al., 1941; Moore, 1942a, b; Foote, 1944). Androgenic hormones have variable effects on women. A reduction of sexual motivation has been observed in some patients (Greenblatt et al., 1942), but other workers have reported a restoration of responsiveness to sexual stimulation (see Abel, 1945).

The administration of hormones of the opposite sex frequently induces bisexual behavior, the direction of which is determined primarily by environmental stimuli. If androgen-treated females are in the company of normal females, they display male mating responses. However, they revert to a female behavior pattern if confronted by a sexually aggressive male (Ball, 1940; Cole et al., 1945). Estrogen-treated males similarly adjust their sexual role in accordance with the sex of the partner (Kun, 1933; Beach, 1941).

Bisexual behavior can be observed spontaneously in many mammalian species, and it is difficult to assess the role of hormonal factors in these instances. Although it is relatively rare that males display female mating patterns, the female of many species frequently shows incomplete masculine behavior. Several authors have suggested that the male sexual behavior pattern may be

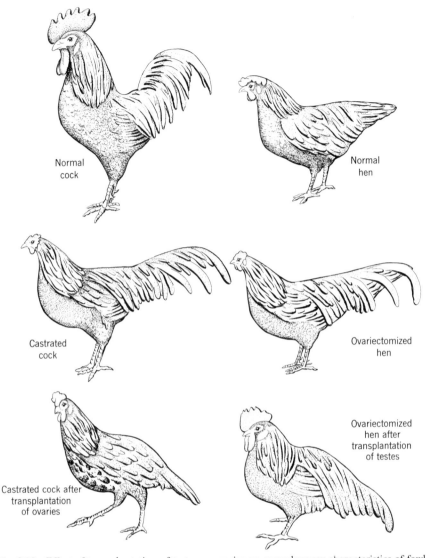

Fig. 8.36 Effect of transplantation of testes or ovaries on secondary sex characteristics of fowl.

part of the instinctive inheritance of the female. It has also been proposed that female animals displaying male sexual behavior may be reacting to some source of endogenous androgen (Hemmingsen, 1933). Since the male hormone is secreted (though normally in very small quantities) by a variety of endocrine glands, it has been difficult to test this hypothesis. Beach and Rasquin (1942) ruled out a gonadal origin of this hormone because the frequency of male sexual behavior in females was not reduced by pre- or postpuberal ovariectomy. In the male, female responses can occasionally be observed (Hamilton, 1914; Stone, 1924a; Beach, 1938). These

behavior patterns appear to be directly dependent on gonadal hormones, for castration abolishes them completely.

In man, bisexual behavior is a rather frequent occurrence in the male as well as the female of the species. In view of the apparent dependence of such behavior on hormonal mechanisms in lower species, it is tempting to conclude that bisexuality in man may be primarily caused by hormonal factors. This idea has been advanced and defended by a number of clinical investigators (Glass et al., 1940; Gordon, 1941), and several studies have provided some support for it. Glass et al. (1940) report that the androgen-estrogen ratio of male homosexuals was lower than normal. Reduction of homosexual tendencies following androgen treatment has been reported in the clinical literature (Lurie, 1944; Glass and Johnson, 1944). Other investigators have stressed the role of environmental or psychological factors in the development of bisexual or homosexual behavior (Engle, 1942), and Beach (1948) has eloquently pleaded the case for a joint consideration of physiological and environmental factors.

Summary

Sexual arousal depends most immediately on specific types of sensory stimulation. However, no amount of stimulation will elicit sexual motivation and mating behavior unless the organism is physically ready to mate. This important priming function is carried out by hormonal mechanisms. Although the endocrine system exerts a pervasive influence on sexual behavior, there are large species and sex differences with respect to the importance of hormonal mechanisms. Lower species, as a rule, are much more dependent on hormonal variables than are primates and man. The endocrine secretions are most constant in the male of most species, providing a stable level of sexual motivation which contrasts sharply with the cyclical nature of sexual receptivity in the female.

Hypophyseal and gonadal hormones determine sexual maturation as well as cyclical variations of sexual motivation during the reproductive phase of life. Removal of the gonadal glands in the male generally produces a gradual decline in sexual motivation which can be reversed by androgen-substitution therapy. Greater than normal amounts of hypophyseal or gonadal hormones produce hypersexuality, at least in some species. In the male, the effects of castration and hormone treatment vary considerably between species. In the female, more constant effects are observed; sexual motivation typically disappears completely and suddenly following ovariectomy in all species except man. An apparently complete restoration of sexual motivation and mating behavior is obtained by estrogen injections. (In some species these must be supplemented by progesterone.)

If the female hormones (estrogens) are injected into a male castrate, female sexual behavior patterns can be observed. Conversely, ovariectomized females display male mating behavior following the administration of androgens. Transplantations of gonadal tissue from the opposite sex have similar, though more permanent, effects. If both male and female sex glands are present in the same organism, bisexual behavior may be displayed.

SUMMARY

Sexual motivation is very closely related to various secretions of the endocrine system. Because the endocrine glands form a closely related and reciprocating system, we have presented a brief summary of the principal functions of the major glands. The following observations are most directly related to our topic.

The anterior lobe of the hypophysis elaborates several hormones that exert a trophic action on the sex and mammary glands; they also induce anatomical and functional changes in the genital apparatus which are essential determinants of sexual readiness as well as reproduction. The first of these gonadotrophins, follicle-stimulating hormone (FSH), induces the development of ovarian follicles in the female and the growth of the seminiferous tubules and maintenance of spermatogenesis in the male. As the follicle of the ovaries begins to grow, estrogen (the principal female sex hormone) is secreted. This hormone stimulates the production of the second gonadotrophic hormone, luteinizing hormone (LH) or interstitial-cell-stimulating hormone (ICSH). In the male, this hormone stimulates the development of the interstitial tissue of the testes and the secretion of androgen (the principal male sex hormone). In the female, LH regulates the final stages of follicular development and ovulation. It also stimulates the secretion of increased amounts of the gonadal hormones in both sexes which, in turn, affect pituitary mechanisms to secrete more LH and less FSH. The increased concentration of LH induces luteinization (the transformation of ovarian follicles into corpora lutea). Once the corpus luteum has reached a certain developmental level, it begins to secrete progesterone (the hormone of pregnancy) which cooperates with estrogen to ready the uterus for the implantation of ova during fertilization. Progesterone also stimulates the production of prolactin (or lactating hormone) by the anterior pituitary. Androgenic substances are also secreted by the adrenal cortex. The principal secretion of the adrenal medulla, epinephrine, stimulates the secretion of gonadotrophins by the anterior hypophysis. Other glands of the endocrine system have a more indirect effect on sexual behavior by affecting growth and various metabolic processes.

The hormonal mechanisms not only determine sexual maturity but also regulate sexual motivation during the reproductive phase of life. In the adult male, we normally see only minor fluctuations of hormone levels and a relatively constant level of sexual receptivity. The female of most species, on the other hand, is subject to pronounced periodic fluctuations of the hormone balance; we find a consequent variation of sexual motivation which appears to be most pronounced in lower species. In primates and man, social factors are at least partially able to compensate for these fluctuations.

The importance of hormonal mechanisms is best illustrated by the results of castration and hormone therapy. Removal of the testes results in a gradual decline of sexual motivation which tends to be complete after several weeks or months. Sexual behavior can be restored by injections of the male sex hormones. Considerable species differences have been observed with respect to the delay and severity of the castration effects as well as the effectiveness of hormone substitution in the male. As a rule, lower species seem to depend more exclusively on hormonal mechanisms. Ovariectomy produces complete and immediate cessation of all sexual activity in the female of all species except man. Estrogen treatment restores sexual motivation to precastrational levels in many species. In others, estrogen must be supplemented by progesterone if complete recovery is to be achieved.

Although the hormonal mechanisms are indispensable to sexual drive and behavior, they do not by themselves suffice to elicit sexual motivation; rather, they prime the organism to respond appropriately to certain classes of environmental stimuli. No sexual behavior can be observed unless specific environmental conditions are met. Given a physiologically ready organism, sexual motivation seems to be aroused very directly by stimuli that derive from the sexual partner. Although some of the lower species depend exclusively on information from a single sensory modality for this arousal, higher mammals are clearly able to dispense with any specific sensory input. Sexual arousal occurs as long as the animal can perceive the presence of a suitable sexual partner, even if such apparently important sensory information as tactual sensations from the genitalia has been eliminated.

In view of the nonspecificity of the sensory arousal mechanism, an investigation of the central neural integration of sexual motivation has been difficult. However, important advances have been made in the past 25 years, and a relatively complete picture of at least some aspects of these mechanisms is now available. Some isolated components of copulatory behavior appear to be integrated at the spinal level. These reflex mechanisms are particularly conspicuous in lower species. As we ascend the neuraxis, we find little evidence for essential neural integration in the medulla, pons, cerebellum, and mesencephalon. The diencephalon, on the other hand, contains a variety of neural centers which directly or indirectly regulate sexual motivation and behavior. The anterior hypothalamus contains neural elements which control sexual motivation relatively directly. Lesions in this area abolish sexual motivation completely without affecting the hormonal balance of the organism. Mating behavior can be elicited by direct injections of testosterone into this area (in intact animals), suggesting that this neural mechanism may be sensitive to the general hormone level. An anatomically as well as functionally distinct regulatory center has been located in the posteromedial hypothalamus. Lesions in this area abolish sexual motivation, but this effect is clearly mediated by hormonal (hypophyseal) mechanisms which are under hypothalamic control. Sexual motivation can be restored by the administration of gonadal or gonadotrophic hormones. The specific location of the neural and hormonal mechanisms varies somewhat between species. Additional inhibitory mechanisms may also be represented at the hypothalamic level, for several investigators have reported facilitation following hypothalamic damage.

Other subcortical structures have been investigated. The thalamus and basal ganglia almost certainly do not contribute specifically to the regulation of sexual behavior. The amygdaloid nuclei have been implicated in many studies, but some recent evidence suggests that the observed effects may be due to the involvement of neural elements of the underlying pyriform cortex.

It appears unlikely that the neocortex plays an important and specific role in sexual motivation. Partial or complete removal of the cortical mantle produces deficits in sexual behavior progressively more severe as we ascend the phylogenetic scale. However, this impairment seems to be caused primarily, if not exclusively, by an interference with sensory and motor functions rather than with mechanisms peculiar to sexual motivation.

Because their active role in copulatory behavior requires more sensory feedback and finer motor coordination than that of the inactive female, males tend to be more severely affected by cortical lesions.

Isolated components of male mating behavior have been elicited by electrical stimulation of rhinencephalic structures. However, the allocortical portion of the brain appears to play a role in a variety of motivational systems, and there is little evidence for a more selective influence on sexual behavior.

Sexual motivation is of particular interest to physiological psychology because it demonstrates very clearly the close interaction between environmental and organismic variables. Whereas some of the other primary drives seem all but independent of environmental factors, sensory mechanisms play a very essential role in sexual arousal. The field of sexual behavior is unusual in its emphasis on comparative investigation. In no other area of inquiry are data from so many divergent species available, and it is particularly engaging to follow the development of hormonal or neural mechanisms.

BIBLIOGRAPHY

Abel, S. Androgenic therapy in malignant disease of the female genitalia. *Amer. J. Obstet. Gynec.*, 1945, **49**, 327–342.

Allen, E., Diddle, A. W., Burford, T. H., & Elder, J. H. Analysis of urine of the chimpanzee for estrogenic content during various stages of the menstrual cycle. *Endocrinology*, 1936, **20**, 546–549.

Altmann, M. Interrelations of the sex cycle and the behavior of the sow. *J. comp. Psychol.*, 1941, **31**, 481–489.

Anderson, E. E., & Anderson, S. The relation between the weight of the endocrine glands and measures of sexual, emotional and exploratory behavior in the male albino rat. *J. comp. Psychol.*, 1938, **25–26**, 459–474.

Aronson, L. R. Problems in the behavior and physiology of a species of African mouthbreeding fish. *Trans. N.Y. Acad. Sci.*, 1948, **2**, 33–42.

Aronson, L. R., & Noble, G. K. The sexual behavior of Anura. II: Neural mechanisms controlling mating in the male leopard frog, *Rana pipiens*. *Bull. Amer. Mus. nat. Hist.*, 1945, **86**, 87–139.

Bacq, Z. M. Impotence of the male rodent after sympathetic denervation of the genital organs. *Amer. J. Physiol.*, 1931, **96**, 321.

Bacq, Z. M., & Brouha, L. Recherches sur la physiologie du système nerveux autonome. II: Le comportement des organs génitaux après énervation sympathetique. *Arch. int. Physiol.*, 1933, **35**, 250.

Ball, J. Normal sex behavior in the rat after total extirpation of the vasa deferentia. *Anat. Rec.*, 1934, **58**, 49.

Ball, J. Sexual responsivness in female monkeys after castration and subsequent estrin administration. *Psychol. Bull.*, 1936, **33**, 811.

Ball, J. A test for measuring sexual excitability in the female rat. *Comp. Psychol. Monogr.*, 1937a, **14**, 1–37.

Ball, J. The effect of male hormone on the sex behavior of female rats. *Psychol. Bull.*, 1937b, **34**, 725.

Ball, J. Male and female mating behavior in prepuberally castrated male rats receiving estrogens. *J. comp. Psychol.*, 1939, **28**, 273–283.

Ball, J. The effect of testosterone on the sex behavior of female rats. *J. comp. Psychol.*, 1940, **29**, 151–165.

Ball, J. Effect of progesterone upon sexual excitability in the female monkey. *Psychol. Bull.*, 1941, **38**, 533.

Ball, J., & Hartman, C. G. Sexual excitability as related to the menstrual cycle in the monkey. *Amer. J. Obstet. Gynec.*, 1935, **29**, 117–119.

Bard, P. Oestrual behavior in surviving decorticate cats. *Amer. J. Physiol.*, 1936, **116**, 4–5.

Bard, P. Central nervous mechanisms for emotional behavior patterns in animals. *Res. Publ., Ass. Res. nerv. ment. Dis.*, 1938–1939, **19**, 190–218.

Bard, P. *The hypothalamus and central levels of autonomic function.* Baltimore: Williams and Wilkins, 1940.

Bauer, D. Endocrine and other clinical manifestations of hypothalamic disease. *J. clin. Endocrinol.*, 1954, **14**, 13.

Beach, F. A. Sex reversals in the mating pattern of the rat. *J. genet. Psychol.*, 1938, **53**, 329–334.

Beach, F. A. Effects of cortical lesions upon the copulatory behavior of male rats. *J. comp. Psychol.*, 1940, **29**, 193–239.

Beach, F. A. Female mating behavior shown by male rats after administration of testosterone propionate. *Endocrinology*, 1941, **29**, 409–412.

Beach, F. A. Analysis of the stimuli adequate to elicit mating behavior in the sexually inexperienced male rat. *J. comp. Psychol.*, 1942a, **33**, 163–207.

Beach, F. A. Copulatory behavior in prepuberally castrated male rats and its modifications by estrogen administration. *Endocrinology*, 1942b, **31**, 679–683.

Beach, F. A. Effects of testosterone propionate upon the copulatory behavior of sexually inexperienced male rats. *J. comp. Psychol.*, 1942c, **33**, 227–247.

Beach, F. A. Importance of progesterone to induction of sexual receptivity in spayed female rats. *Proc. Soc. exp. Biol. Med.*, 1942d, **51**, 369–371.

Beach, F. A. Male and female mating behavior in prepuberally castrated female rats treated with androgens. *Endocrinology*, 1942e, **31**, 673–678.

Beach, F. A. Effects of injury to the cerebral cortex upon the display of masculine and feminine mating behavior by female rats. *J. comp. Psychol.*, 1943, **36**, 169–198.

Beach, F. A. Relative effects of androgen upon mating behavior in male rats subjected to castration or forebrain injury. *J. exp. Zool.*, 1944, **97**, 249–285.

Beach, F. A. Bisexual mating behavior in the male rat: effects of castration and hormone administration. *Physiol. Zool.,* 1945a, **18**, 390–402.

Beach, F. A. Hormonal induction of mating responses in a rat with congenital absence of gonadal tissue. *Anat. Rec.,* 1945b, **92**, 289–292.

Beach, F. A. A review of physiological and psychological studies of sexual behavior in mammals. *Physiol. Rev.,* 1947, **27**, 240–307.

Beach, F. A. *Hormones and behavior.* New York and London: Paul Hoeber, 1948.

Beach, F. A. Sexual behavior in animals and men. *The Harvey lectures, 1947–1948.* Springfield, Ill.: Thomas, 1950.

Beach, F. A. Instinctive behavior: reproductive activities. In *Handbook of experimental psychology,* S. S. Stevens, Ed. New York: Wiley, 1951.

Beach, F. A. Ciba foundation colloquium. *Endocrinology,* 1952, **3**, 209.

Beach, F. A. Characteristics of masculine "sex drive." In *Nebraska symposium on motivation,* M. R. Jones, Ed. Lincoln: Univ. of Nebraska Press, 1956.

Beach, F. A., & Gilmore, R. W. Response of male dogs to urine from females in heat. *J. Mammal.,* 1949, **30**, 391–392.

Beach, F. A., & Holz-Tucker, A. M. Mating behavior in male rats castrated at various ages and injected with androgen. *J. exp. Zool.,* 1946, **101**, 91–142.

Beach, F. A., & Holtz-Tucker, A. M. Effects of different concentrations of androgen upon sexual behavior in castrated male rats. *J. comp. physiol. Psychol.,* 1949, **42**, 433–453.

Beach, F. A., & Jordan, L. Effects of sexual reinforcement upon the performance of male rats in a straight runway. *J. comp. physiol. Psychol.,* 1956, **49**, 105–110.

Beach, F. A., & Rasquin, P. Masculine copulatory behavior in intact and castrated female rats. *Endocrinology,* 1942, **31**, 393–409.

Beach, F. A., Conovitz, M. W., Steinberg, F., & Goldstein, A. C. In *Nebraska symposium on motivation,* M. R. Jones, Ed. Lincoln: Univ. of Nebraska Press, 1956.

Berg, I. A. Development of behavior: the micturition pattern in the dog. *J. exp. Psychol.,* 1944, **34**, 343–368.

Boling, J. L., & Blandau, R. J. The estrogen-progesterone induction of mating responses in the spayed female rat. *Endocrinology,* 1939, **25**, 359–371.

Boling, J. L., Young, W. C., & Dempsey, E. W. Miscellaneous experiments on the estrogen-progesterone induction of heat in the spayed guinea pig. *Endocrinology,* 1938, **23**, 182–187.

Breder, C. M. The reproductive habits of the common catfish, *Ameriurus nebulosus* (Le Seuer), with a discussion of their significance in ontogeny and phylogeny. *Zoologica,* 1935, **19**, 143–185.

Breder, C. M., & Coates, C. W. Sex recognition in the guppy, *Lebistes reticulatus* (Peters). *Zoologica,* 1935, **19**, 187–207.

Brookhart, J. M., & Dey, F. L. Reduction of sexual behavior in male guinea pigs by hypothalamic lesions. *Amer. J. Physiol.,* 1941, **133**, 551.

Brookhart, J. M., Dey, F. L., & Ranson, S. W. Mating reactions, effect of ovarian hormones and hypothalamic lesions. *Proc. Soc. exp. Biol. Med.,* 1940, **44**, 61–64.

Brookhart, J. M., Dey, F. L., & Ranson, S. W. The abolition of mating behavior by hypothalamic lesions in guinea pigs. *Endocrinology,* 1941, **28**, 561–565.

Brooks, C. McC. The role of the cerebral cortex and of various sense organs in the excitation and execution of mating activity in the rabbit. *Amer. J. Physiol.,* 1937, **120**, 544–553.

Browman, L. G. The effect of controlled temperatures upon the spontaneous activity rhythms of the albino rat. *J. exp. Zool.,* 1943, **94**, 477–489.

Burger, J. W. Some further experiments on the relation of the external environment to the spermatogenetic cycle of *Fundulus heteroclitus. Anat. Rec.,* 1939, **75**, Suppl. 138.

Burger, J. W. Some effects of colored illumination on the sexual activation of the male starling. *J. exp. Zool.,* 1943, **94**, 161–168.

Campbell, B. A., & Sheffield, F. D. Relations of random activity to food deprivations. *J. comp. physiol. Psychol.,* 1953, **46**, 320–322.

Carpenter, C. R. Sexual behavior of free ranging rhesus monkeys (*Macaca mulatta*). I: Specimens, procedures and behavioral characteristics of estrus. II: Periodicity of estrus, homosexual, autoerotic and nonconformist behavior. *J. comp. Psychol.,* 1942, **33**, 113–162.

Clark, G. Prepubertal castration in the male chimpanzee, with some effects of replacement therapy. *Growth,* 1945, **9**, 327–339.

Clauberg, C., & Schultze, K. W. Die Folgen der Sterilisierung und der Kastration bei Mann und Frau. *Z. aerztl. Fortbild.,* 1934, **31**, 425.

Coe, W. R. Divergent pathways in sexual development. *Science,* 1940, **91**, 175–182.

Cole, H. H., Hart, G. H., & Miller, R. F. Studies on the hormonal control of estrous phenomena in the anestrous ewe. *Endocrinology,* 1945, **36**, 370–380.

Crew, F. A. E. Sex-reversal in frogs and toads. A review of the recorded cases of abnormality of the reproductive system and an account of a breeding experiment. *J. Genet.,* 1921, **11**, 141–181.

Darling, F. F. *Bird flocks and the breeding cycle.* Cambridge: Cambridge Univ. Press, 1938.

Davis, C. D. The effect of ablations of neocortex on mating, maternal behavior and the production of pseudo-pregnancy in the female rat and on copulatory activity in the male. *Amer. J. Physiol.,* 1939, **127**, 374–380.

Davis, D. E., & Domm, L. V. The sexual behavior of hormonally treated domestic fowl. *Proc. Soc. exp. Biol. Med.,* 1941, **48**, 667–669.

Davis, D. E., & Domm, L. V. The influence of hormones

on the sexual behavior of the fowl. In *Essays in biology*. Berkeley: Univ. of California Press, 1943.

Davis, K. B. *Factors in the sex life of twenty-two hundred women*. New York: Harper, 1929.

Dawson, A. B. Early estrus in the cat following increased illumination. *Endocrinology*, 1941, **28**, 907–910.

Day, F. T. Clinical and experimental observations on reproduction in the mare. *J. agric. Sci.*, 1940, **30**, 244–261.

Dempsey, E. W., & Rioch, D. McK. The localization in the brainstem of the oestrous responses of the female guinea pig. *J. Neurophysiol.*, 1939, **11**, 9–18.

Denniston, R. H. Qualification and comparison of sex drive under various conditions in terms of a learned response. *J. comp. physiol. Psychol.*, 1954, **47**, 437–440.

Dey, F. L., Fisher, C., Berry, C. M., & Ranson, S. W. Disturbances in reproductive functions caused by hypothalamic lesions in female guinea pigs. *Amer. J. Physiol.*, 1940, **129**, 39–46.

Dickinson, R. L. *A thousand marriages: a medical study of sex adjustment*. Baltimore: Williams and Wilkins, 1931.

Dickinson, R. L. *Human sex anatomy*. Baltimore: Williams and Wilkins, 1933.

Donovan, B. T., & van der Werff ten Bosch, J. J. Precocious puberty in rats with hypothalamic lesions. *Nature (London)*, 1956a, **178**, 745.

Donovan, B. T., & van der Werff ten Bosch, J. J. Oestrus in winter following hypothalamic lesions in the ferret. *J. Physiol. (London)*, 1956b, **132**, 57.

Durfee, T., Lerner, M. W., & Kaplan, N. The artificial production of seminal ejaculation. *Anat. Rec.*, 1940, Suppl. 76, 65–68.

Dusser de Barenne, J. G., & Koskoff, V. D. Further observations on the flexor rigidity in the hind legs of the spinal cat. *Amer. J. Physiol.*, 1934, **107**, 441–446.

Eayers, J. T. Spontaneous activity in the rat. *Brit. J. Anim. Behav.*, 1954, **2**, 25–30.

Edinger, F. Die Leistungen des Zentralnervensystems beim Frosch, dargestellt mit Ruecksicht auf die Lebensweise des Tieres. *Z. allg. Physiol.*, 1913, **15**, 15–64.

Elder, J. H. Effects of theelin injections in normal prepubescent chimpanzees. *Anat. Rec.*, 1938, **72**, 37–42.

Engle, E. T. The testis and hormones. In *Problems of ageing* (2nd ed.). E. V. Cowdry, Ed. Baltimore: Williams and Wilkins, 1942.

Fauré, J. De certains aspects du comportement en rapport avec des variations hormonales provoquées chez l'animal. *J. Physiol. (Paris)*, 1956, **48**, 529–531.

Fauré, J., & Gruner, J. Sur les modifications de l'activité bioélectrique du rhinencéphale et du thalamus recueillies sous l'influences des oestrogènes et des androgènes chez l'animal. *Rev. neurol.*, 1956, **94**, 161–168.

Fee, A. R., & Parks, A. S. Studies on ovulation; effect of vaginal anaesthesia on ovulation in rabbit. *J. Physiol. (London)*, 1930, **70**, 385–388.

Feiner, L., & Rothman, T. Study of a male castrate. *J. Amer. med. Ass.*, 1939, **113**, 2144–2146.

Filler, W., & Drezner, N. Results of surgical castration in women over forty. *Amer. J. Obstet. Gynec.*, 1944, **47**, 122–124.

Fisher, A. E. Maternal and sexual behavior induced by intracranial chemical stimulation. *Science*, 1956, **124**, 228.

Fisher, C., Ingram, W. R., & Ranson, S. W. *Diabetes insipidus and the neurohumoral control of water balance*. Ann Arbor, Mich.: Edward, 1938a.

Fisher, C., Magoun, H. W., & Ranson, S. W. Dystocia in diabetes insipidus. The relation of pituitary oxytocin to parturition. *Amer. J. Obstet. Gynec.*, 1938b, **36**, 1–9.

Foote, R. M. Diethylstilbestrol in the management of psychopathological states in males. *J. nerv. ment. Dis.*, 1944, **99**, 928–935.

Friedgood, H. B. Induction of estrous behavior in anestrous cats with the follicle-stimulating and luteinizing hormones of the anterior pituitary gland. *Amer. J. Physiol.*, 1939, **126**, 229–233.

Fulton, J. F., Ed. *A textbook of physiology*. Philadelphia: Saunders, 1950.

Gastaut, H. Corrélations entre le système nerveux végétatif et le systèmes de la vie de relation dans le rhinencéphale. *J. Physiol. Path. gén.*, 1952, **44**, 431–470.

Glass, S. J., & Johnson, R. W. Limitations and complications of organotherapy in male homosexuality. *J. clin. Endocrinol.*, 1944, **4**, 540–544.

Glass, S. J., Deuel, H. J., & Wright, C. A. Sex hormone studies in male homosexuality. *Endocrinology*, 1940, **26**, 590–594.

Goldstein, A. C. *Hormones, brain function, and behavior*. H. H. Hoagland, Ed. New York: Academic Press, 1957.

Goltz, F. L. Ueber den Einflus der Nerven auf vegetative Vorgaenge im Thierkoerper. *Dtsch. Natf. Tagebl.*, 1871, 147–148.

Goltz, F. L. Ueber den Einfluss des Nervensystems auf die Vorgänge während der Schwangerschaft und des Gebärakts. *Arch. ges. Physiol.*, 1874, **9**, 552.

Goodale, H. D. Castration in relation to the secondary sexual characters in brown leghorns. *Amer. Nat.*, 1913, **47**, 159–169.

Gordon, M. B. Endocrine consideration of genitourinary conditions in children. *Urol. Cutan. Rev.*, 1941, **45**, 3–7.

Gordon, M. B., & Fields, E. M. Comparative values of chorionic gonadotropic hormone and testosterone propionate in treatment of cryptorchidism and hypogenitalism. *J. clin. Endocrinol.*, 1942, **2**, 531–535.

Graller, D. L., Felson, H., & Schiff, L. Use of stilbestrol in males. *The association for the study of internal secretions. Program*. 25th annual meeting, 1941, 27.

Green, J. D. The comparative anatomy of the hypophysis with special reference to its blood supply and innervation. *Amer. J. Anat.*, 1951, **88**, 225–290.

Green, J. D. Electrical activity in the hypothalamus and hippocampus of conscious rabbits. *Anat. Rec.*, 1954, **118**, 304.

Green, J. D., Clemente, C. D., & de Groot, J. Rhinencephalic lesions and behavior in cats. *J. comp. Neurol.*, 1957, **108**, 505–545.

Greenberg, B., & Noble, G. K. Social behavior in the American chameleon (*Anolis carolinensis Voigt*). *Physiol. Zool.*, 1944, **17**, 392–439.

Greenblatt, R. B. Hormonal factors in libido. *J. clin. Endocrinol.*, 1943, **3**, 305–306.

Greenblatt, R. B. *Office endocrinology* (2nd ed.). Baltimore: Thomas, 1944.

Greenblatt, R. B., Mortara, F., & Torpin, R. Sexual libido in the female. *Amer. J. Obstet. Gynec.*, 1942, **44**, 658–663.

Grosch, D. S. The importance of antennae in mating reaction of male *Habrobracon. J. comp. physiol. Psychol.*, 1947, **40**, 23–39.

Grunt, J. A., & Young, W. C. Differential reactivity of individuals and the response of the male guinea pig to testosterone propionate. *Endocrinology*, 1952, **51**, 237–248.

Hamilton, G. V. A study of sexual tendencies in monkeys and baboons. *J. Anim. Behav.*, 1914, **4**, 295–319.

Hammond, J. Recent scientific research on horse breeding problems. *Yorkshire agric. Soc. J.*, 1938, 2–16.

Hammond, J. Control of ovulation in farm animals. *Nature* (*London*), 1944, **153**, 702.

Hammond, J., & Day, F. T. Oestrogen treatment of cattle: induced lactation and other effects. *J. Endocrinol.*, 1944, **4**, 53–82.

Harlow, H. F. The heterosexual affectional system in monkeys. *Amer. Psychol.*, 1962, **1**, 1–9.

Harris, G. W. The induction of ovulation in the rabbit by electrical stimulation of the hypothalamo-hypophysial mechanism. *Proc. roy. Soc.* (*London*), *B*, 1937, **122**, 374–394.

Harris, G. W. Stimulation of supraopticohypophysial tract in conscious rabbit with currents of different wave form. *J. Physiol.* (*London*), 1948a, **107**, 412–417.

Harris, G. W. Electrical stimulation of hypothalamus and mechanism of neural control of adenohypophysis. *J. Physiol.* (*London*), 1948b, **107**, 418–429.

Harris, G. W. Excretion of antidiuretic substance by kidney after electrical stimulaion of neurohypophysis in unanaesthetized rabbit. *J. Physiol.* (*London*), 1948c, **107**, 430–435.

Harris, G. W. Further evidence regarding endocrine status of neurohypophysic. *J. Physiol.* (*London*), 1948d, **107**, 436–448.

Harris, G. W. The function of the pituitary stalk. *Bull. Johns Hopk. Hosp.*, 1955, **97**, 358–375.

Harris, G. W. The reticular formation, stress and endocrine activity. In *The reticular formation of the brain,* H. H. Jasper, L. D. Proctor, R. S. Knighton, W. C. Noshay, & R. T. Costello, Eds. Boston: Little, Brown, 1958.

Harris, G. W. Central control of pituitary secretion. In *Handbook of physiology. Vol. II.* J. Field, H. W. Magoun, & V. E. Hall, Eds. Baltimore: Williams and Wilkins, 1960.

Heller, C. G., Chandler, R. E., & Myers, G. B. Effect of small and large doses of diethyl stilbestrol on menopausal symptoms, vaginal smear and urinary gonadotrophins in 23 oöphorectomized women. *J. clin. Endocrinol.*, 1944a, **4**, 109–116.

Heller, C. G., Farney, J. P., & Myers, G. B. Development and correlation of menopausal symptoms, vaginal smear and urinary gonadotrophin changes following castration in 27 women. *J. clin. Endocrinol.*, 1944b, **4**, 101–108.

Heller, R. E. Spontaneous activity in male rats in relation to testis hormone. *Endocrinology*, 1932, **16**, 626–632.

Hemmingsen, A. M. Studies on the oestrous-producing hormone (oestrin). *Skand. Arch. Physiol.*, 1933, **65**, 97–250.

Hemmingsen, A. M., & Krarup, N. B. The production of mating instincts in the rat with chemically well defined estrogenic compounds. *Kgl. Danske Vidensk. Selsk. Biol. Med.*, 1937, **13**, 1–10.

Hertz, R., Meyer, R. K., & Spielman, M. A. The specificity of progesterone in inducing receptivity in the ovariectomized guinea pig. *Endocrinology*, 1937, **21**, 533–535.

Hillarp, N.-Å., Olivercrona, H., & Silfverskiöld, W. Evidence for the participation of the preoptic area in male mating behavior. *Experientia*, 1954, **10**, 224.

Howell, W. H. *A textbook of physiology.* J. F. Fulton, Ed. Philadelphia: Saunders, 1949.

Hu, C. K., & Frazier, C. N. Masculinization of adult female rabbit following injection of testosterone propionate. *Proc. Soc. exp. Biol. Med.*, 1940, **42**, 820–823.

Jenkins, M. The effect of segregation of the sex behavior of the white rat as measured by the obstruction method. *Genet. Psychol. Monogr.*, 1928, **3**, 6.

Kellogg, V. Some silkworm moth reflexes. *Biol. Bull. Woods Hole*, 1907, **12**, 152–154.

Klüver, H., & Bucy, P. C. Preliminary analysis of functions of the temporal lobes in monkeys. *Arch. Neurol. Psychiat.* (*Chicago*), 1939, **42**, 979–1000.

Kun, H. Psychische Feminisierung und Hermaphrodisierung von Maennchen durch weibliches Sexualhormon. *Endocrinology*, 1933, **13**, 311–323.

Langley, L. L., & Cheraskin, E. *The physiology of man.* New York: McGraw-Hill, 1958.

Leathem, J. H. Experimental induction of estrus in the dog. *Endocrinology*, 1938, **22**, 559–567.

Lehman, R. S. Experiment to determine the attractivness of various aromatic compounds to adults of the wireworms. *J. econ. Entomol.*, 1932, **25**, 949–958.

Le Magnen, J. Les phénomènes olfacto-sexuels chez

l'homme. *Arch. Sci. physiol.*, 1952, **6**, 125–160.

Lisk, R. D. Inhibitory centers in sexual behavior in the male rat. *Science*, 1966, **152**, 669–670.

Lurie, L. A. The endocrine factor in homosexuality. Report of treatment of 4 cases with androgen hormone. *Amer. J. med. Sci.*, 1944, **208**, 176–184.

MacLean, P. D. The limbic system in relation to central grey and reticulum of the brainstem. *Psychosom. Med.*, 1955, **17**, 355.

MacLean, P. D. New findings relevant to the evolution of psychosexual functions of the brain. *J. nerv. ment. Dis.*, 1962, **135**, 289–301.

MacLean, P. D., & Ploog, D. W. Cerebral representation of penile erection. *J. Neurophysiol.*, 1962, **25**, 30–55.

MacLean, P. D., Denniston, R. H., & Dua, S. Further studies on cerebral representation of penile erection: caudal thalamus, midbrain, and pons. *J. Neurophysiol.*, 1963, **26**, 273–293.

Maes, J. P. Neural mechanism of sexual behavior in the female cat. *Nature (London)*, 1939, **144**, 598–599.

Maes, J. P. Hypophysectomie et comportement sexuel de la chatte. *C. R. Soc. Biol. (Paris)*, 1940a, **133**, 92–94.

Maes, J. P. Le mechanisme nerveux du comportement sexuel de la chatte. *C. R. Soc. Biol. (Paris)*, 1940b, **133**, 95–97.

Makepeace, A. W., Weinstein, G. L., & Friedman, M. H. The effect of progestin and progesterone on ovulation in the rabbit. *Amer. J. Physiol.*, 1937, **119**, 512–516.

Marshall, F. H. A. Exteroceptive factors in sexual periodicity. *Biol. Rev.*, 1942, **17**, 68–90.

Marshall, F. H. A., & Bowden, F. P. The effect of irradiation with different wave lengths on the oestrous cycle of the ferret, with remarks on the factors controlling sexual periodicity. *J. exp. Biol.*, 1934, **11**, 409–422.

Marshall, F. H. A., & Hammond, J. Experimental control by hormone action of the oestrous cycle in the ferret. *J. Endocrinol.*, 1945, **4**, 159–168.

Mathews, H. L. Visual stimulation and ovulation in pigeons. *Proc. roy. Soc. (London)*, B, 1939, **126**, 557–560.

Miller, N. E. Old minds rejuvenated by sex hormone. *Sci. News Letter*, Sept. 1938, **24**, 201.

Miller, N. E., Hubert, G., & Hamilton, J. B. Mental and behavioral changes following male hormone treatment of adult castration, hypogonadism and impotence. *Proc. Soc. exp. Biol. Med.*, 1938, **38**, 538–540.

Minnick, R. S., & Warden, C. J. The effects of sex hormones on the copulatory behavior of senile white rats. *Science*, 1946, **103**, 749–750.

Moehlig, R. C. Castration in the male. Notes on the hypothalamico-pituitary gonadal system. *Endocrinology*, 1940, **27**, 743–748.

Moore, C. R. On the physiological properties of the gonads as controllers of somatic and psychical characteristics I: The rat. *J. exp. Zool.*, 1919, **28**, 137–160.

Moore, C. R. Sex gland transplantation and the modifying effect in rats and guinea pigs. *Anat. Rec.*, 1920, **20**, 194.

Moore, C. R. The physiology of the testis and application of male sex hormone. *J. Urol. (Baltimore)*, 1942a, **47**, 31–44.

Moore, C. R. Comparative biology of testicular and ovarian hormones. *Biol. Symposia*, 1942b, **9**, 3–10.

Moore, C. R., & Price, D. Some effects of testosterone and testosterone propionate in the rat. *Anat. Rec.*, 1938, **71**, 59–78.

Moss, F. A. A study of animal drives. *J. exp. Psychol.*, 1924, **7**, 165–185.

Nice, M. M. The role of territory in bird life. *Amer. Midl. Nat.*, 1941, **26**, 441–487.

Nissen, H. W. The effects of gonadectomy, vasotomy, and injections of placental and orchic extracts on the sex behavior of the white rat. *Genet. Psychol. Monogr.*, 1929, **5**, 451–547.

Noble, G. K. *The biology of the amphibia.* New York: McGraw-Hill, 1931.

Noble, G. K. Courtship and sexual selection of the flicker (*Colaptes auratus luteus*). *Auk*, 1936, **53**, 269–282.

Noble, G. K., & Aronson, L. R. The sexual behavior of Anura. I: The normal mating pattern of *Rana pipiens. Bull. Amer. Mus. nat. Hist.*, 1942, **80**, 127–142.

Noble, G. K., & Borne, R. The effect of sex hormones on the social hierarchy of *Xiphophorus helleri. Anat. Rec.*, 1940, Suppl. 78, 147.

Noble, G. K., & Borne, R. The effect of forebrain lesions on the sexual and fighting behavior in *Betta splendens* and other fishes. *Anat. Rec.*, 1941, Suppl. 79, 49.

Noble, G. K., & Curtis, B. The social behavior of the jewel fish, *Hemicromis bimaculatus*, Gill. *Bull. Amer. Mus. nat. Hist.*, 1939, **76**, 1–46.

Noble, G. K., & Greenberg, B. Effects of seasons, castration and crystalline sex hormones upon the urogenital system and sexual behavior of the lizard (*Anolis carolinensis*). I: The adult female. *J. exp. Zool.*, 1941, **88**, 451–474.

Noble, G. K., & Kumpf, K. F. The sexual behavior and secondary sex characters of gonadectomized fish. *Anat. Rec.*, 1936–1937, **67**, 113.

Noble, G. K., & Vogt, W. An experimental study of sex recognition in birds. *Auk*, 1935, **52**, 278–286.

Porter, R. W., Cavanaugh, E. B., Critchlow, B. V., & Sawyer, C. H. Localized changes in electrical activity of the hypothalamus in estrous cats following vaginal stimulation. *Amer. J. Physiol.*. 1957, **189**, 145–151.

Prosser, C. L. *Comparative animal physiology.* Philadelphia: Saunders, 1950.

Ranson, S. W. The hypothalamus: its significance for visceral innervation and emotional expression (The Weir Mitchell oration). *Trans. Coll. Physns (Philadelphia)*, 1934, **2**, 222–242.

Rasmussen, A. T. Innervation of the hypophysis. *Endocrinology*, 1938, **23**, 263.

Reynolds, A. E. The normal seasonal reproductive cycle in the male *Eumeces fasciatus* together with some observations on the effects of castration and hormone administration. *J. Morph.*, 1943, **32**, 331–371.

Rice, V. A. *Breeding and improvement in farm animals* (3rd ed). New York: McGraw-Hill, 1942.

Richter, C. P. Animal behavior and internal drives. *Quart. Rev. Biol.*, 1927, **2**, 307–343.

Richter, C. P. The effect of early gonadectomy on the gross body activity of rats. *Endocrinology*, 1933, **17**, 445–450.

Ring, J. R. The estrogen-progesterone induction of sexual receptivity in the spayed female mouse. *Endocrinology*, 1944, **34**, 269–275.

Rowan, W. Experiments in bird migration. III: The effects of artificial light, castration and certain extracts on the autumn movements of the American crow (*Corvus brachyrhynchos*). *Proc. nat. Acad. Sci. (Washington)*, 1932, **18**, 639–654.

Rowe, A. W., & Lawrence, C. H. Studies of the endocrine glands. IV: The male and female gonads. *Endocrinology*, 1928, **12**, 591–662.

Runge, S. Testicular grafting in domestic animals. *Vet. J.*, 1943, **99**, 231–236; and *Biol. Abstr.*, 1944, **18**, 4482.

Sand, K. Experiments on the internal secretion of the sexual glands, especially on experimental hermaphroditism. *J. Physiol. (London)*, 1919–1920, **53**, 255–263.

Sawa, M., Yukiharu, U., Masaya, A., & Toshio, H. Preliminary report on the amygdaloidectomy on the psychotic patients, with interpretation of oral-emotional manifestations in schizophrenics. *Folia psychiat. neurol. jap.*, 1954, **7**, 309–316.

Sawyer, C. H. Effects of central nervous system lesions on ovulation in the rabbit. *Anat. Rev.*, 1956, **124**, 358.

Sawyer, C. H. Triggering of the pituitary by the central nervous system. In *Physiological triggers*. T. H. Bullock, Ed. Washington, D.C.: American Physiological Society, 1957.

Sawyer, C. H. Activation and blockade of the release of pituitary gonadotropin as influenced by the reticular formation. In *The reticular formation of the brain*, H. H. Jasper, L. D. Proctor, R. S. Knighton, W. C. Noshay, & R. T. Costello, Eds. Boston: Little, Brown, 1958.

Sawyer, C. H. Reproductive behavior. In *Handbook of Physiology Vol. II*. J. Field, H. W. Magoun, & V. E. Hall, Eds. Baltimore: Williams and Wilkins, 1960.

Sawyer, C. H. & Robinson, B. Separate hypothalamic areas controlling pituitary gonadothropic function and mating behavior in female cats and rabbits. *J. clin. Endocrinol.*, 1956, **16**, 914.

Schaefer, E. A. *Textbook of physiology. Vol. II.* New York: Macmillan, 1900.

Schoolland, J. B. Are there any innate behavior tendencies? *Genet. Psychol. Monogr.*, 1942, **25**, 219–287.

Schreiner, L. H., & Kling, A. Behavioral changes following rhinencephalic injury in cat. *J. Neurophysiol.*, 1953, **16**, 643.

Schreiner, L. H., & Kling, A. Effects of castration on hypersexual behavior induced by rhinencephalic injury in cat. *Arch. Neurol. Psychiat. (Chicago)*, 1954, **72**, 180.

Schreiner, L. H., & Kling, A. Rhinencephalon and behavior. *Amer. J. Physiol.*, 1956, **184**, 486.

Scott, H. M., & Payne, L. F. The effect of gonadectomy on the secondary sexual characters of the bronze turkey (*M. gallaparo*). *J. exp. Zool.*, 1934, **69**, 123–136.

Semans, J. H., & Langworthy, O. R. Observations on the neurophysiology of sexual function in the male cat. *J. Urol.*, 1938, **40**, 836–846.

Seward, J. P. Studies on the reproductive activities of the guinea pig. III: The effect of androgenic hormone on sex drive in males and females. *J. comp. Psychol.*, 1940, **30**, 435–449.

Seward, J. P., & Seward G. H. Studies on the reproductive activities of the guinea pig: I: Factors in maternal behavior. *J. comp. Psychol.*, 1940, **29**, 1–24.

Shapiro, H. A. Effect of testosterone propionate upon mating. *Nature (London)*, 1937, **139**, 588–589.

Smith, P. E., & Engle, E. T. Experimental evidence regarding the role of the anterior pituitary in the development and regulation of the genital system. *Amer. J. Anat.*, 1927, **40**, 159–217.

Sollenberger, R. T., & Hamilton, J. B. The effect of testosterone propionate upon the sexual behavior of castrated mal guinea pigs. *J. comp. Psychol.*, 1939, **28**, 81–92.

Steinach, E. Untersuchungen zur vergleichenden Physiologie der maennlichen Geschlechtsorgane. III: Ueber den Geschlechtstrieb der vor und nach der Pubertaet kastrierten Ratten, und ueber das Schicksal der akzessorischen Geschlechtsdrüsen in Folge der Kastration. *Pflüg. Arch. ges. Physiol.*, 1894, **56**, 304.

Steinach, E. Geschlechtstrieb und echt sekundare Geschlechtsmerkmale als Folge der innersekretorischen Funktion der Keimdruesen. III: Entwicklung der vollen Maennlichkeit in funktioneller und somatischer Beziehung bei Saeugern als Sonderwirkung des inneren Hodensekretes. *Zbl. Physiol.*, 1910, **24**, 551.

Steinach, E. Umstimmung des Geschlechtcharacters bei Saeugetieren durch Austausch der Pubertaetsdruesen. *Zbl. Physiol.*, 1911, **25**, 723–735.

Steinach, E. Willkuerliche Umwandlung von Saeugetiermaennchen in Tieren mit ausgepraegt weiblichen Geschlechtskarakteren und weiblicher Psyche. *Pflüg. Arch. ges. Physiol.*, 1912, **144**, 71–106.

Steinach, E. Feminierung von Maennchen und Maskulierung von Weibchen. *Zbl. Physiol.*, 1913, **27**, 717–723.

Steinach, E. Pubertaetsdruesen und Zwitterbildung. *Arch. Entwickl.-Mech. Org.*, 1916, **42**, 307.

Steinach, E. *Sex and life.* New York: Viking, 1940.

Steinach, E., & Kun, H. Die entwicklungsmechanische

Bedeutung der Hypophysis als Aktivator der Keim-drueseninkretion. *Med. Klin.,* 1928, **24,** 524.

Steinach, E., & Kun, H. Die Wirkungen des maennlichen Sexualhormons auf die psychischen und soma-tischen Geschlechtsmerkmale. *Akad. Anz. Ada. Wiss. (Wien),* 1933, No. 18.

Steinach, E., & Peczenik, O. Diagnostischer Test fuer hormonbedingte Stoerungen der maennlichen Sex-ualfunktion und seine klinische Anwendung. *Wien. klin. Wschr.,* 1936, **49,** 388.

Stone, C. P. The congenital sexual behavior of the young male albino rat. *J. comp. Psychol.,* 1922, **2,** 95–153.

Stone, C. P. Experimental studies of two important fac-tors underlying masculine sexual behavior: the nervous system and the internal secretion of the testis. *J. exp. Psychol.,* 1923, **6,** 84–106.

Stone, C. P. A note on "feminine" behavior in adult male rats. *Amer. J. Physiol.,* 1924a, **68,** 39–41.

Stone, C. P. The awakening of copulatory ability in the male albino rat. *Amer. J. Physiol.,* 1924b, **68,** 407–424.

Stone, C. P. Preliminary note on maternal behavior of rats living in parabiosis. *Endocrinology,* 1925, **9,** 505–512.

Stone, C. P. The retention of copulatory ability in male rats following castration. *J. comp. Psychol.,* 1927, **7,** 369–387.

Stone, C. P. The retention of copulatory ability in male rabbits following castration. *J. gen. Psychol.,* 1932, **40,** 296–305.

Stone, C. P. A quantitative study of copulatory frequency in male rats, following castration. *Psychol. Bull.,* 1937, **34,** 556.

Stone, C. P. Activation of impotent male rats by injec-tions of testosterone propionate. *J. comp. Psychol.,* 1938a, **24,** 445–450.

Stone, C. P. A quantitative study of sexual reactivation in castrated male rats. *Psychol. Bull.,* 1938b, **35,** 528–529.

Stone, C. P. Loss and restoration of copulatory activity in adult male rats following castration and subse-quent injections of testosterone propionate. *Endo-crinology,* 1938c, **23,** 529.

Stone, C. P. Copulatory activity in adult male rats fol-lowing castration and injections of testosterone propionate. *Endocrinology,* 1939a, **24,** 165–174.

Stone, C. P. Sex drive. In *Sex and internal secretions* (2nd ed.). Edgar Allen, Ed. Baltimore: Williams and Wilkins, 1939b.

Stone, C. P. Precocious copulatory activity induced in male rats by subcutaneous injections of testosterone propionate. *Endocrinology,* 1940, **26,** 511–515.

Stone, C. P., & Barker, R. G. Spontaneous activity, direct and indirect measures of sexual drive in adult male rats. *Proc. Soc. exp. Biol. Med.,* 1934, **32,** 195–199.

Stone, C. P., Barker, R. G., & Tomlin, M. I. Sexual drive in potent and impotent male rats as measured by the Columbia obstruction apparatus. *J. gen. Psy-chol.,* 1935, **47,** 33–48.

Terzian, H. & Dalle Ore, G. Syndrome of Kluever and Bucy reproduced in man bilateral removal of the temporal lobes. *Neurology* 1955, **5,** 373–380.

Thorek, M. Experimental investigation of the role of the Leydig, seminiferous and Sertoli cells and effects of testicular transplantation. *Endocrinology,* 1924, **8,** 61–90.

Tinbergen, N. An objectivistic study of the innate be-haviour of animals. *Bibl. biotheor.,* 1942, **1** (2), 39–98.

Travis, B. B. Habits of the june beetle *Phylophaga lanceo-lata* (Say) in Iowa. *J. econ. Entomal.,* 1939, **32,** 690–693.

Wang, G. H. Relation between "spontaneous" activity and oestrous cycle in the white rat. *Comp. Psychol. Monogr.,* 1923, **2,** 1–27.

Wang, G. H. A sexual activity rhythm in the female rat. *Amer. Nat.,* 1924, **58,** 36–42.

Wang, G. H., & Guttmacher, A. F. The effect of ovarian traumatization on the spontaneous activity and genital tract of the albino rat, correlated with a histological study of the ovaries. *Amer. J. Physiol.,* 1927, **82,** 335–349.

Wang, G. H., Richter, C. P., & Guttmacher, A. F. Ac-tivity studies of male castrated rats with ovarian transplants, and correlation of the activity within histology of the grafts. *Amer. J. Physiol.,* 1925, **73,** 581–598.

Warner, L. H. A study of sex behavior in the white rat by means of the obstruction method. *Comp. Psy-chol. Monogr.,* 1927, **4,** 1–68.

Weisman, A. I., & Coates, C. W. Failure of menopausal urine concentrates to induce egg extrusion in fe-male Xenopus frog test for pregnancy. *J. clin. Endo-crinol.,* 1944a, **4,** 35–36.

Weisman, A. I., & Coates, C. W. Frog test (*Xenopus laevis*) for pregnancy; report on 1000 tests over period of 4 years of study. *West. J. Surg.,* 1944b, **52,** 171–174.

Weisman, A. I., & Coates, C. W. The African frog (*Xenopus laevis*) in pregnancy diagnosis. *Res. Bull. N.Y. biol. Res. Found.,* 1944c.

Wells, L. J. Seasonal sexual rhythm and its experimental modification in the male of the thirteen-lined ground squirrel (*Citellus tridecemlineatus*). *Anat. Rec.,* 1935, **62,** 409–444.

Wells, L. J. Prolongation of breeding capacity in males of an annual breeding wild rodent (*Citellus tri-decemlineatus*) by constant low temperature. *Anat. Rec.,* 1936, Suppl. 64, 138.

Wiesner, B. P., & Mirskaia, L. On the endocrine basis of mating in the mouse. *Quart. J. exp. Physiol.,* 1930, **20,** 274–279.

Witschi, E. Seasonal sex characters in birds and their hormonal control. *Wilson Bull.,* 1935, **47,** 177–188.

Witschi, E., & Pfeiffer, C. A. The hormonal control of oestrus, ovulation and mating in the female rat. *Anat. Rec.*, 1935–1936, **64**, 85–99.

Wolfson, A. A preliminary report on some experiments on bird migration. *Condor*, 1940, **42**, 93–99.

Yerkes, R. M., & Elder, J. H. Oestrus, receptivity, and mating in chimpanzees. *Comp. Psychol. Monogr.*, 1936, **13**, 1–39.

Young, W. C. Observations and experiments on mating behavior in female mammals. *Quart. Rev. Biol.*, 1941, **16**, 135–156, 311–335.

Young, W. C., & Fish, W. R. The ovarian hormones and spontaneous running activity in the female rat. *Endocrinology*, 1945, **36**, 181–189.

Young, W. C., Dempsey, E. W., Myers, H. I., & Hagquist, C. W. The ovarian condition and sexual behavior in the female guinea pig. *Amer. J. Anat.*, 1938, **63**, 457–483.

CHAPTER NINE

Emotional Behavior

Attempts to treat the topic of emotion scientifically are hampered by the hypothetical nature of the concept and its elusiveness to satisfactory definition. This difficulty is particularly annoying to the psychologist; every layman can identify emotional events that are sufficiently distinct to be differentiated easily from each other yet share enough important characteristics to permit a common general classification. Every civilization has made a clear distinction between emotional and intellectual matters, although the exact language may have varied somewhat over the centuries. Individually, each of us is willing to acknowledge fellings of love, rage, fear, or frustration, and to assign them to a common class of nonrational phenomena. Moreover, we interpret the behavior of others in terms of these variables because we assume that motivational forces comparable to those affecting us must be operating to produce a particular behavioral reaction.

When we speak of "emotions" we refer to subjective feelings that occur in response to some external stimulus event. If a given stimulus were to arouse the same feeling with comparable intensity in every person, and if that feeling were to elicit a predictable behavioral reaction, we could study the relationship between classes of external stimuli and overt behavior and thus arrive at an operational definition of emotion. We could then disregard the subjective, experiential aspects of emotion and obtain an acceptable classification of emotional responses in terms of stimulus categories. Such definitions would still depend on subjective experience for the initial selection of stimuli to be investigated, and some rather tenuous assumptions would have to be made about the interspecies comparability of feelings; however, a reasonable basis for the experimental study of emotions would be provided.

Unfortunately, there are wide individual differences in the experiential effects of specific stimuli as well as the behavioral reactions to particular feelings because of the pervasive influence of learning. An individual's experiential and behavioral reaction to any situation are determined by such complex interactions of previously acquired response tendencies that it is impossible to predict his reaction to any but the simplest stimuli with any degree of confidence. Every clinician is concerned with abnormal emotional responses which do not conform to socially approved operational definitions, and we must remember that only the extreme instances of such nonconformity receive special attention.

Where then does this leave us with respect to the scientific treatment of emotion? Many behaviorists have concluded that emotions, much like "consciousness" and other "mentalistic" concepts, are not within the realm of scientific inquiry and should therefore be dropped from our vocabulary (Duffy, 1934, 1941; M. F. Meyer, 1933). Although it is desirable to rid psychology of inadequately defined and meaningless "explanatory concepts," we can justify such action only when dealing with phenomena of the theorist's own making. In the case of emotion, there may be some question with respect to specific classification, but there is no reason to doubt the reality of the phenomenon (Dunlap, 1932).

Most modern psychologists have assumed that it is entirely irrelevant whether operational definitions correspond directly to specific emotional phenomena as defined by subjective experience or common physiological mechanism, as long as the behavioral consequences of a stimulus are explained more satisfactorily than they would be if no emotion were assumed (Brown and Farber, 1951; Farber and West, 1960). Under the circum-

498

stances, this pragmatic approach is unquestionably of value, but it cannot be employed by the physiological psychologist who is interested in the physiological mechanisms that produce the behavioral manifestation of a particular emotion as well as the concomitant experience.

We are thus in the unfortunate position of trying to study the physiological basis of hypothetical concepts which are so poorly defined that we have no assurance of their correspondence to specific psychological or physiological functions. We do not, however, have much choice in the matter. In order to attack the problem at all on an experimental basis, we must depend on operational definitions or anthropomorphic interpretations of response categories. A survey of the literature suggests that such an approach can be fruitful if we are content to investigate specific and comparatively simple emotional phenomena which are least subject to modification by previously learned reaction tendencies. We must remember, however, that apparently contradictory results may exist because similar operational definitions of an emotional variable may not correspond to a common physiological function and because our semantic classifications of emotional phenomena may be misleading. A common physiological mechanism that is active in all emotional situations may exist; it is also possible that different physiological processes are responsible for each specific emotion, or that an interaction between specific and general mechanisms may determine each individual response.

It is not surprising, in view of these problems, that most psychology textbooks either avoid the treatment of emotion or concern themselves only with the measurement of physiological "correlates" of emotion such as changes in peripheral autonomic functions. This is an unsatisfactory approach because the autonomic responses tell us little or nothing about the physiological processes that are responsible for the emotional reaction; such responses merely supplement other behavioral measures of emotionality. A particular autonomic measure may show comparable changes in response to widely differing emotional and even nonemotional stimuli, and the correlation between specific autonomic changes and specific emotions is typically low.

Before we discuss the experimental literature, a final word of caution may be in order. Most research on the physiological basis of emotional behavior has been conducted with animals. Since we cannot ask an animal how he feels, this research has been restricted to emotions such as fear or rage which produce clearly interpretable behavioral reactions such as attack, defense, or flight responses. These emotions have the advantage of being relatively uncomplicated by previous learning; they are easily elicited in the course of experimentation and can be defined operationally in terms of specific stimulus situations and response categories. Much interesting and important research has been done within this limited portion of the spectrum of possible emotions, but the question remains whether we can generalize these findings to emotions in general, as has been attempted by some theorists. Such positive emotions as love, affection, or pleasure may not be integrated by the same physiological or anatomical mechanisms, and much research is needed before we can arrive at a satisfactory theory of emotion.

PERIPHERAL THEORIES OF EMOTION

James's Theory of Emotion

Emotional reactions are always accompanied by complex changes in a variety of physiological functions; such changes are integrated by the autonomic and somatic nervous systems as well as the endocrine glands. William James (1884, 1890) recognized this relationship in his now celebrated theory of emotions, which has influenced psychological thought since its formulation. His position is perhaps best summarized in his *Principles of Psychology* (1890), in which he stated:

> Our natural way of thinking about these coarser emotions (e.g., grief, fear, rage, love) is that the mental perception of some fact excites the mental affection called the emotion, and that this latter state of mind gives rise to the bodily sensations. My theory, on the contrary, is that *the bodily changes follow directly the perception of the exciting fact, and that our feeling of the same changes as they occur IS the emotion.*

Figure 9.1 reproduces a map of the neural pathways involved in this theory. Environmental stimuli excite sensory receptors (R) such as the eye and ear. Impulses from these receptors follow classical pathways to the sensory receiving areas of the cortex, whereupon the stimulus is perceived (path 1). Next, somatic as well as autonomic impulses initiated in the cortex excite skeletal muscles and viscera (path 2). This induces changes in such physiological functions as muscle tension, blood pressure, heart rate, pilomotor and sudo-

James-Lange

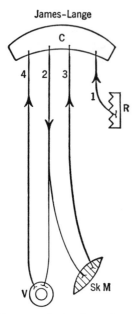

Fig. 9.1 Diagram of the James-Lange theory of emotion. R, receptor; C, cerebral cortex; V, viscus; Sk M, skeletal muscle; Th, thalamus. The connecting lines represent nerve paths; direction of impulses is indicated by arrows. (From Cannon, 1931.)

motor activity. These changes in turn excite interoceptors and initiate further impulses which return to the cortex via paths 3 and 4. The perception of these changes adds an emotional quality to the original perception of the stimulus.

Lange's Theory of Vascular Change

In 1885 Carl Lange independently proposed a peripheral-origin theory of emotion sufficiently similar to James's version to be combined with it in later years. The *James-Lange theory of emotion* that has played such an important role in psychology is essentially unchanged from James's original concept. Lange actually did not claim that the feelings of bodily change produced the emotions. He stated that:

Vasomotor disturbances, varied dilation of the blood vessels, and consequent excess of blood in the separate organs, are the real, primary effects of the affections, whereas the other phenomena—motor abnormalities, sensation paralysis, *subjective sensations*, disturbances of secretions and intelligence—are only secondary disturbances which have their cause in anomalies of vascular innervation (Lange, 1885; italics mine).

In other words, vasomotor changes *are* the emotions in Lange's theory.

Before considering some of the experimental evidence that has accumulated since the formulation of these notions, we shall take a closer look at the proposed mechanism to see whether it can explain the origin of emotions. Apart from the uselessness of referring any function to the cortex as a whole, it appears in the proposed circuit that *every* stimulus should initiate projections to the viscera and striped muscles and hence induce emotion. This is clearly not intended: we know that only some sensory impulses have this property, and therefore we must look for a "central screening mechanism" that determines which aspects of the total sensory input perform this arousal function. Since emotional reactions obviously can be learned, this selection cannot be explained simply on the basis of special anatomical pathways. We need a mechanism possessing the following properties: (1) it must be able to recognize stimuli that are innately emotion-producing; (2) it must be capable of comparing the present sensory input with the past history of the organism to determine whether an apparently neutral stimulus may have acquired emotional properties; and (3) it must be capable of exciting both somatic and autonomic motor centers.

This important aspect of the problem of emotion tends to be neglected by later theorists. For our present purpose, we might generously assume that such a provision could be added to James's theory and then consider other objections against the peripheral-origin theories.

Cannon's Objections to Peripheral-Origin Theories

W. B. Cannon (1927, 1931) has presented a critical analysis of the relevant clinical and experimental literature of the first decades of this century. He suggested five major areas of objection to the notion that the experience and expression of emotion is based on the perception of secondary sensations from the viscera. (James placed heavy emphasis on visceral responses but did not rely exclusively on them.)

1. TOTAL SEPARATION OF THE VISCERA FROM THE CENTRAL NERVOUS SYSTEM DOES NOT IMPAIR EMOTIONAL BEHAVIOR. Sir Charles Sherrington (1900) demonstrated that stimuli which normally elicited rage in dogs continued to do so following a complete transection of the spinal cord at a high cer-

vical level. Additional vagotomy failed to eliminate appropriate emotional reactions (snarling, growling, and biting) in response to painful stimulation of the animal's head. In these experiments the viscera and most of the skeletal musculature of the body were isolated from the brain. Since peripheral autonomic and somatomotor changes were no longer elicited, emotional responses, as defined by James, should have been eliminated.

Cannon (1927) reported that removal of the ganglia of the sympathetic chain did not impair the overt expression of emotion in cats, in spite of the reduction of visceral feedback. Neither Cannon's nor Sherrington's procedures entirely eliminated afferent or efferent connections with structures innervated by the autonomic nervous system. Cranial nerves carry afferent (VII and IX) as well as efferent (III, VII, and IX) fibers from portions of the autonomic system. Somatic sensations were not at all disturbed by Cannon's procedure and only partially interrupted in Sherrington's experiment (the head, neck, and shoulder remained unaffected by the spinal transection). It is nevertheless damaging to the peripheral-origin theories that neither Sherrington nor Cannon was able to detect the least impairment in the animal's ability to respond appropriately to stimuli that normally aroused anger, fear, disgust, or rage.

Hebb (1946a, 1949) has pointed out that James did not claim that the ability to *express* emotion depended on feedback from the viscera, but only that the *experience* of the emotional feeling would be lost if the circuit was interrupted. This is undoubtedly a valid criticism of Cannon's evaluation, but Dana (1921) has presented extensive clinical data which are not subject to this objection. The most convincing case history is that of a 40-year-old woman who fell from a horse and broke her neck at the level of C3 and C4. This produced complete quadriplegia and loss of cutaneous and deep sensations from the neck down. She lived for a year and reported emotions of grief, joy, displeasure, and affection that did not appear different from normal responses. No overt changes in personality or character were detectable, as one might have expected from a severe limiting of emotional experiences.

It can be argued that even these data do not represent conclusive evidence against a peripheral-origin theory of emotion if, as was suggested earlier, a central screening mechanism is provided. In such a system the experience of emo-

tion, although originally dependent on feedback from the viscera and skeletal musculature, could become conditioned to specific stimuli or even classes of stimuli. The subsequent presentation of such a stimulus would then elicit a "conditioned emotional reaction" independent of peripheral influences. The principal problem is that such a theory is essentially untestable. By the time an infant has acquired speech and can communicate his subjective emotional reactions, the presumably more primitive process of emotional conditioning would undoubtedly have been completed.

The appropriate conclusion is that Cannon's first objection is indeed valid. That the various peripheral concomitants of emotional behavior undoubtedly contribute to the experience of emotion must not be overlooked. All that has been demonstrated is that such visceral changes are *essential* neither to the experience nor to the expression of emotion. We shall return to this problem when we consider objective techniques for the assessment of emotional experience.

2. THE SAME VISCERAL CHANGES OCCUR IN DIVERSE EMOTIONAL STATES AND IN NONEMOTIONAL STATES. Much clinical and experimental evidence (see Cannon, 1927, for a summary of the early literature) has demonstrated that specific physiological functions such as heart rate or blood pressure may show similar, if not identical, changes in a variety of apparently diverse emotional situations and in such nonemotional states as physical exertion, rest, and exposure to heat or cold. By itself, this observation is not damaging to the peripheral-origin theories. James suggested that emotion was not dependent on particular responses in individual organs, but rather on the total feedback from peripheral structures. To refute this hypothesis, one would have to show that the total *pattern* of physiological change remained the same in different emotional reactions, and that this pattern was duplicated precisely in some clearly nonemotional situation. Such a demonstration has not been provided by Cannon or subsequent investigators. Recent studies of this problem have, in fact, raised some hopes that we may be able to distinguish different emotional situations on the basis of precisely these patterns of physiological change.

3. THE VISCERA ARE RELATIVELY INSENSITIVE STRUCTURES. Cannon correctly pointed out that visceral organs are relatively poorly supplied with nerves and that we are consequently unaware of normal physiological processes in these struc-

tures. However, this alone does not constitute adequate proof that the existing supply of nerves is incapable of performing the functions James assigned to them. We are well aware of changes in such autonomic processes as heart rate, vasomotor activity, or sudomotor activity, whether they occur in emotional or nonemotional situations. The viscera proper—the stomach, intestine, liver, pancreas, spleen, and kidneys—may actually have few or no fibers that mediate pain. There is ample evidence for stretch and pressure receptors as well as a sensitivity to temperature; all of us can testify to such concomitant sensations of emotional behavior as "a sinking stomach," "butterflies in the stomach," and "a lump in the throat."

4. VISCERAL CHANGES ARE TOO SLOW TO BE A DIRECT SOURCE OF EMOTIONAL FEELING. Smooth muscles have a comparatively long latency, to which must be added the time it takes for impulses to travel through the various stages suggested by James. Considerable additional time would have to elapse before sufficient muscular tension could be built up to produce a noticeable change from the prevailing state of rest. It is well established that the expression of emotion can follow appropriate stimulation after very brief intervals. The specific question with regard to the James-Lange theory is, however, whether the *feeling* of emotion occurs before the feedback from peripheral structures is complete. For an answer to this question, we must turn again to studies relying on verbal reports of affective feelings. We then encounter semantic problems with respect to what constitutes a complete emotion.

Newman et al. (1930) suggested that some kind of emotional experience appeared almost immediately upon the presentation of emotion-provoking stimuli; however, there seemed to be "an additional feature, a developing experience that comes *only from three to fifteen seconds after the exposure of the materials*" (Newman's italics). They concluded that a "complete emotional experience" develops only slowly because it depends on feedback from the viscera. It seems quite reasonable that emotional feelings should appear more complete after the development of physiological changes that one has learned to expect in similar situations. However, the fact that an appropriate emotional experience could be reported after intervals much too short to provide feedback from peripheral structures suggested that the role of these visceral changes may not be essential. Lehmann (1914) has presented an exhaustive summary of experimental studies which demonstrate

that specific autonomic changes always occurred *after* the reported emotion.

5. THE "ARTIFICIAL" INDUCTION OF VISCERAL CHANGES KNOWN TO OCCUR IN SPECIFIC EMOTIONS FAILS TO PRODUCE THESE EMOTIONS. Epinephrine acts as a humoral transmitter of neural impulses at most postganglionic sympathetic synapses. It also has a pronounced, direct effect on smooth muscles that are innervated by the sympathetic nervous system. Cannon argued, therefore, that the James-Lange theory would have to predict experience of emotion if epinephrine were injected—at least to the extent that the physiological response to epinephrine is comparable to responses occurring in a specific emotional situation. Such an analysis fails to take into account the total pattern of sympathetic, *parasympathetic,* and *somatic* responses which, according to James, may be operating to produce a particular emotion.

Parasympathetic and somatic functions are only slightly, if at all, affected by the injection of a sympathetic transmitter substance, and Cannon's objection loses much of its cogency. Moreover, he himself reported (1927, pp. 356-357) that subjects reacted to adrenaline injections with such statements as "I feel as if afraid"; he concluded that "in a small number of the affected cases, a real emotion develops, usually that of sorrow, with tears, sobs and sighings." Although it is fairly certain that these were not true emotions but rather conditioned emotional responses to the visceral changes, Cannon's main point does not seem supported.

Summary

Where do we stand, then, with respect to a peripheral-origin theory of emotion, such as that proposed by James or Lange? The last four of Cannon's objections, although well taken and in need of consideration, do not provide adequate evidence against such a theory. We shall see that there appears to be considerable covariation of emotion and peripheral autonomic and somatic events. The perception of peripheral stimuli undoubtedly contributes to the subjective experience of emotion. Cannon's first objection demonstrates fairly conclusively, however, that such feedback from peripheral sources is not an *essential* component either of the experience or of the expression of emotional responses.

PHYSIOLOGICAL CORRELATES OF EMOTION

We have seen in the previous discussion of the peripheral-origin theories of emotion that neither the subjective experience nor the expression of emotion is likely to be causally related to the accompanying autonomic or somatic changes. That these physiological "correlates" do not seem to be *essential* does not imply, however, that we should disregard them. Most research on emotion has been devoted to various physiological mechanisms that seem to be *affected* by the perception of emotion-producing stimuli. It was hoped that this concentration would provide objective criteria for classifying specific emotions as well as precise measures of their intensity. To date, no single measure that permits adequate differentiation and sensitivity has been found. To the extent, however, that feedback from peripheral sources contributes to the experiencing of specific emotions, we can expect that complex patterns of appropriate measures may provide the necessary information. Considerable research is continuing in this area.

A thorough coverage of the vast literature in this field would not fit into the limited scope of this discussion. We shall confine ourselves to a description of some of the more common measures and techniques, giving only illustrative

examples of the research findings. Dunbar's (1946) exhaustive treatment of bodily changes in emotion includes a more complete consideration of this area. An excellent monograph by Davis et al. (1957) contains a thorough treatment of autonomic and muscular responses to simple stimuli.

It should be remembered that the physiological changes that occur during emotion are under the immediate control of the autonomic nervous system but may be integrated by the somatic nervous system as well as by endocrine mechanisms. All are affected, directly or indirectly, by regulatory mechanisms of the central nervous system.

Electrical Properties of the Skin

The relationship between psychological phenomena and changes in skin resistance or skin conductance (*psychogalvanic reflex, galvanic skin response, palmar resistance or conduction, electrodermal response*) has intrigued psychologists and neurologists for well over a century. (See Landis and DeWick, 1929, for an excellent summary of the early literature.) The electrical changes of

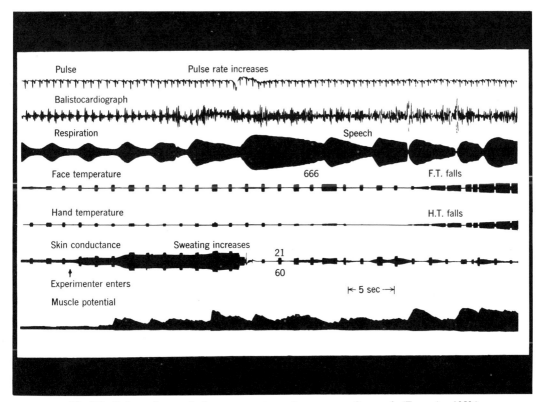

Fig. 9.2 Polygraph record of common autonomic measures of arousal. (From Ax, 1953.)

the skin are probably the most popular of the many measures of autonomic activity which have attracted the attention of psychologists.

Skin resistance refers to the electrical resistance of the skin to the flow of electromotive current and is measured in ohms. *Skin conductance* is measured in mhos (ohm spelled backward) and represents the reciprocal of resistance. It is customary to use conductance measures, since the reciprocal transformation tends to normalize the distribution of resistance changes. They are also more convenient because there appears to be an inverse relationship between activation and resistance.

The older terminology (PGR, GSR, etc.) is not acceptable; these electrical changes are no more psychological than other bodily functions, are not true reflexes in the classical sense, and certainly do not represent galvanic reactions, as these terms imply.

Skin conductance varies constantly. The absolute level of conductance at any point in time (*base line conductance*) represents a possible measure of general activation or arousal. It has not been used as frequently as the transitory increase in conductance which follows the sudden presentation of any strong or unusual stimulus. These rapid changes in skin conductance are superimposed on the base line and are generally expressed as a percentage change. For the purpose of such percentage conversions, the base line measure is usually taken during a brief period immediately preceding the presentation of the stimulus.

Two techniques are available for the assessment of these transitory changes, although it is not clear that they measure exactly the same thing. Féré (1888) is credited with pointing out the relationship between specific "affective variations" and changes in bodily resistance. His measuring technique, also called *exosomatic* or *resistance GSR*, relies on changes in skin resistance to a small current derived from an external source and passed through the subject by means of surface electrodes, usually placed on the palm and back of the hand. Tarchanoff (1890) independently developed an *endosomatic* technique; this does not require an external source of current because any two parts of the skin show a potential difference between them. This voltage shows a pronounced change following sensory stimulation. Whether this *voltage GSR* is actually caused by variations in conductivity is not entirely clear, but both techniques appear to measure the same underlying physiological process (Jeffress, 1928).

Recording techniques. Skin conductance is normally fairly low. Even large surface electrodes one-half inch or more in diameter usually show resistance in the order of 100,000 ohms. After the presentation of strong stimuli such as electric shock, skin resistance decreases by as much as 50%, a 100% increase in conductance. Even weak stimuli such as a barely audible click reliably produce measurable changes in resistance. Very small voltages are applied across the electrodes, so that the current that actually passes through the body is in the microampere range. Since the resistance changes are quite slow, standard galvanometers or microammeters can adequately measure both basic resistance levels and sudden changes in conductance. More refined techniques rely on the Wheatstone bridge circuit which allows a highly sensitive assessment of even the smallest changes in resistance. Permanent records of these data can be obtained with ink-writing instruments such as polygraphs.

The choice of measuring and amplifying systems must be considered carefully. Direct-current amplifiers have the advantage of providing measures of true skin conductance; however, skin resistance to direct current tends to decrease with time when the measuring voltage remains constant, and it shows a *relative* decrease as the voltage of the measuring current is increased (Gildemeister and Kaufold, 1920). Direct-current amplifiers are also more difficult to build and hence more expensive than alternating-current amplifiers. The latter measure only *impedance.* Impedance represents a combination of true ohmic resistance and capacitance and varies with the frequency of the alternating current applied to the skin. Basic resistance as well as the size of individual resistance changes therefore covary directly with frequency (Forbes and Landis, 1935). Alternating-current amplifiers have the advantage of being relatively free from electrode polarization, a major difficulty with direct-current circuits. Unidirectional current flow quickly deposits a thin layer of ions on one electrode, causing a marked rise in resistance. Although the use of nonpolarizing electrodes (such as combinations of manganese dioxide and zinc, or silver electrodes covered by a film of silver chloride) minimizes this problem, resistance changes occur even with the best electrodes and affect any direct-current measurement (Lykken, 1959).

The absolute level of skin resistance varies with electrode placement and is not comparable between subjects, or even within subjects when repeated measures are taken on different days. It is not obvious whether the absolute size of a resistance change independent of its base line or a relative measure or percentage change should be used. Since skin resistance to direct current varies systematically with time, a direct comparison of the magnitude of discrete resistance or conductance changes is not admissible, even if the recordings are obtained from the same subject with identical electrode placements. To compensate for this problem, Darrow (1934, 1937a) proposed a transformation in terms of log conductance which provides a relative measure. Haggard (1945, 1949) suggested still more complex mathematical transformations of the resistance data. A more thorough discussion of this problem can be found in Woodworth and Schlosberg's (1954) treatment of this subject.

Some general characteristics of the electrical responses of the skin should be mentioned. Resistance changes in response to discrete stimulation usually appear after 1 to 2 sec, although latencies as long as 15 to 20 sec have been reported (Abramovski, 1913; Peterson, 1907). There appears to be no direct relationship between the amplitude of the stimulus and the latency of the response; *stronger* stimuli elicit *greater* resistance changes but do not shorten the delay (Davis, 1930). Latency differences occur across stimulus modalities. The relationship between the intensity of the stimulus and the amplitude of the response has been described as a linear function by Hovland and Riesen (1940). The response amplitude decreases rapidly with successive stimulation when the intensity of the stimulus remains constant (Farmer and Chambers, 1925; Davis, 1930), the rate of adaptation being a function of the length of the intertrial interval (Coombs, 1938).

This habituation is reflected in a rise of the basic level of skin resistance and may represent a general relaxation of the subject. A similar change in skin resistance can be observed in experimental sessions when no stimuli are applied.

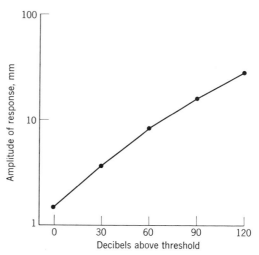

Fig. 9.4   Amplitude of galvanic response to varying intensities of tone. The ordinate scale is millimeters of response (spread logarithmically); the tone was 1000 cycles. (From Hovland and Riesen, 1940.)

Several experiments (Coombs, 1938; Porter, 1938) have shown that transfer of the effects of habituation occurs within and across sensory modalities but appears to be relatively small, becoming evident primarily in the shortened "extinction" of the response to the new stimulus.

A small, negative deflection usually precedes the principal response. Unless specific precautions are taken, muscular movement (Sommer, 1902–1903, 1905), pressure changes (Sommer, 1902–1903; Peterson, 1907), and temperature variations (Gildemeister and Ellinghaus, 1923) may influence the absolute levels of resistance and invalidate the results. Sudden respiratory movements may also produce transitory changes in skin resistance.

Waller (1918, 1919–1920) reported diurnal variations in conductivity, skin resistance being much higher in the morning following a period of rest than in the evening. This report confirms Mueller's (1904) observation that both physical and mental fatigue decrease the basic level of skin resistance and diminish transitory responses to stimulation. Wechsler (1925) found a nonmonotonic relationship between time of day and skin resistance. Palmar resistance was high in the morning and evening but low at noon. This function corresponds rather well to general temperature variations reported by Kleitman (1950) and may represent normal variations in sudomotor activity which occur as part of the heat-loss mechanism.

Theoretical considerations. Gildemeister (1915) suggested that variations in skin resistance might

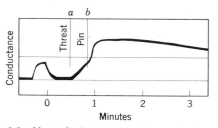

Fig. 9.3   Normal changes in skin conductance in response to *a*, the threat of a pinprick; *b*, a real pinprick. (From Waller, 1919–1920.)

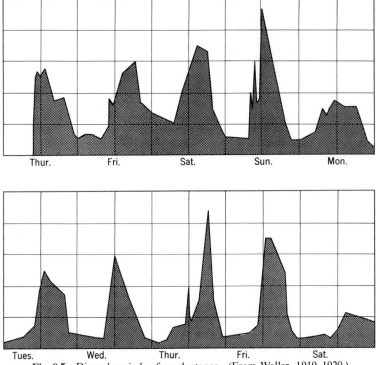

Fig. 9.5 Diurnal periods of conductance. (From Waller, 1919–1920.)

be due to changes in the amount or rate of polarization, and that variations in the electrical output of the skin, as measured by Tarchanoff's technique, could be explained on the basis of polarization. This view is generally accepted today and contrasts with earlier explanations in terms of electromotive forces of muscular origin (Tarchanoff, 1890; Sidis, 1910) or primary resistance changes (Féré, 1888; Piéron, 1910).

Although it is not entirely clear whether Féré's exosomatic method measures precisely the same phenomenon as Tarchanoff's endosomatic technique, both reflect the sudomotor activity of the sweat gland membranes. These are under the direct control of the sympathetic branch of the autonomic nervous system, in spite of the fact that acetylcholine rather than norepinephrine seems to be the neurohumoral transmitter. The central control of these sudomotor responses is exercised by reflex centers in the area of the *corpora quadrigemina* and the apex of the *calamus scrittorius* (Foa and Peserico, 1923). Although all sweat glands are innervated by sympathetic fibers, changes in resistance do not always occur in different parts of the organism. Richter (1924, 1926, 1929, 1931) has shown, for instance, that palmar

and plantar resistances rise during sleep, whereas those in other regions of the organism show a pronounced decline.

Sidis and Nelson (1910) noted that muscular contractions could elicit skin resistance changes and proposed that such changes might be caused by the summation of muscle potentials. This theory can account for both Féré's and Tarchanoff's observations but is disproved by Richter's (1929) experiments which demonstrated that skin resistance is reduced by a skin puncture under the electrodes.

Darrow (1927, 1934, 1936) demonstrated in a series of experiments that another potential explanation of skin resistance in terms of vascular changes is also not tenable. No consistent correlation between blood volume or blood pressure and skin resistance was observed. The latter did covary closely with an independent measure of sweat secretion; however, the lowered resistance cannot merely be the result of an enhancement of conduction by a low-resistance medium (sweat), since this effect would be long-lasting and cumulative. It is generally assumed today that electrophysiological processes that occur in the sudomotor cells before and during the secretion affect skin resistance. The exact nature of this relationship is still unknown.

Skin resistance changes occur in response not only to emotional stimuli but also to all novel, sudden, or intense stimuli. Unless we want to assume that all such stimuli give rise to specific emotional reactions, we are forced to agree with Woodworth and Schlosberg (1954), who believe that these changes reflect "general activation" rather than specific emotions per se. Correlations between the emotional intensity of stimuli and the magnitude of skin resistance changes are low (Wells and Forbes, 1911; Wechsler, 1925; Syz, 1926). Verbal reports of emotional reactions are not always accompanied by concomitant electrical changes. Resistance changes occur in response to stimuli that do not elicit a reportable emotion. Skin resistance changes are therefore not useful as an index of specific emotions. Even such crude divisions of affective behavior as pleasant versus unpleasant are not reliably distinguished. Comparable resistance changes have been reported in response to very pleasant and very unpleasant stimuli (Dysinger, 1931; Shock and Coombs, 1937).

In summary, we might say that skin resistance correlates quite highly with "arousal," "general activation," or even "attention," if we define these terms appropriately. Correlations with the emotional intensity of a stimulus are quite low and inconsistent, and the skin resistance measure cannot differentiate successfully between different types of emotions. Such measures may become more useful when combined with other indices of physiological change.

Circulatory Changes

Following Lange's (1885) theoretical emphasis on vasomotor changes, the relationship between emotional behavior and blood volume, blood pressure, or heart rate has been studied extensively. Every cell of the organism depends on an adequate blood supply for vital nutrients and oxygen as well as for the removal of waste products. When emergency demands are made in any given organ or organ system, blood volume must increase. Since the available supply of blood is constant, some other part of the body will then receive less than its normal supply.

Cardiac activity. Blood is distributed through the organism by an interaction of two principal mechanisms which may or may not act in concert. The first of these is the pumping activity of

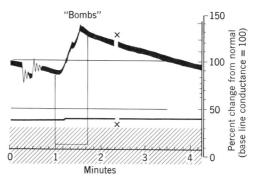

Fig. 9.6   Change in skin conductance in response to the suggested idea of an air raid. The brief interruption of light marked X was made for the purpose of testing the record for parallax. (From Waller, 1918.)

the heart itself. The amount of blood circulated through the organism per unit time is a direct function of the strength and rate of the heart's pumping action. When the heart muscle expands (*diastolic* phase), blood enters into it from the venous drainage. The duration of this expansion determines the amount of blood that is available for distribution during the next contraction (*systolic* phase). When the rate of this pumping action is low, circulatory exchange is at a minimum. When the heartbeat increases, blood flow is increased as long as the capacity of the pump is not exceeded. The duration of the systolic phases eventually becomes too short to admit enough blood to the heart, and the output per contraction becomes so small that total flow of blood actually decreases.

The pumping action of the heart can be monitored simply by amplifying the sound that is generated. The physician's stethoscope operates on this principle as do laboratory devices that amplify the heartbeat so it can drive a penmotor or counter of a *cardiotachometer* or be heard over a loudspeaker. Heartbeat per minute can be read directly from a *cardiochronograph* which draws successive lines the height of which are proportional to the duration of each complete cycle of the heart (Whitehorn et al., 1935; Whitehorn and Richter, 1937; Henry, 1938). A more sophisticated means of recording the detailed activity of the heart is the *electrocardiograph* (EKG) which provides a written record (electrocardiogram) of the electrical potentials generated by the heart muscle. This record is obtained from electrodes attached to the arms or legs with one electrode on each side of the heart.

The activity of the heart is complexly controlled

by the sympathetic and parasympathetic divisions of the autonomic nervous system and by subsidiary reflexes. It has been suggested that heart rate may be used as an index of balance between the two partially antagonistic portions of the autonomic nervous system; however, this index fails to consider the influence of a number of reflexive controls that are not directly dependent on either branch of the autonomic nervous system.

Sympathetic fibers reach the heart through the superior, middle, and inferior cardiac nerves, through direct fibers from the stellate ganglion, and probably through the vagus nerve. The action of these sympathetic impulses is mediated by epinephrine and norepinephrine. The heart is consequently subject to changes in the level of circulating catecholamines such as those occurring in "emergency" situations. Stimulation of sympathetic nerves accelerates and strengthens the heartbeat and decreases arteriovenous conduction time. Increased secretion of catecholamines by the adrenal medulla produces similar results, to the extent that the effects of a local increase of this transmitter substance are not canceled out by a concomitant reflex activation of the parasympathetic fibers in the vagus nerve.

Parasympathetic influences are carried primarily by the vagus (X) nerve, which exerts an inhibitory effect on heart rate and increases arteriovenous conduction time. These effects are mediated by the parasympathetic transmitter substance acetylcholine. The heart appears to remain under constant vagal tone or inhibition that is mediated primarily by the depressor reflexes of the arch of the aorta and the carotid sinus. With respect to the reflex regulation of cardiac activity, the sympathetic and parasympathetic nervous systems are reciprocally linked by central regulatory mechanisms. Thus, the heart can be slowed either through stimulation of parasympathetic vagal impulses or by inhibition of sympathetic tone.

Vascular factors. The second major factor that determines circulatory exchange is the relative dilation or constriction of the blood vessels through which the blood must travel to complete the arteriovenous cycle. When the activity of any organ in the body increases, local metabolic requirements necessitate an increased blood flow. This condition is produced by dilation of the arterioles in the vascular bed of the particular organ or organ system. To compensate for this demand, arterioles must constrict in inactive organs. The vascular changes are produced by the smooth muscles that make up the walls of the arteriole.

Vascular responses can be monitored crudely by inspection. Blanching by any portion of the body is an indication of vasoconstriction; flushing manifests vasodilation. Direct measures of blood flow in the venous drainage and relative measures of arteriovenous pressure differences have been used to assess vasomotor effects. With cardiac output remaining constant, an absolute decrease in venous blood flow implies an increase in arteriolar resistance (vasoconstriction). This produces a pressure *rise* in the arteries supplying the organ, accompanied by a pressure *fall* in its venous drainage. Other conditions being constant, vasodilation in an organ is accompanied by an increase in the organ's total blood supply.

These volumetric changes can be recorded by a *plethysmograph.* The organ is enclosed in a rigid container which is completely filled with air or water so that changes in the organ's volume can be recorded. More indirect measuring techniques rely on the fact that the photoelectric density of an organ is partially determined by its blood supply. The thin ear of the rabbit, for instance, contains large blood vessels. If a light is placed on one side of the ear and a photoelectric sensing device on the other, changes in the volume of blood in such a vessel can be recorded. Other techniques are based on the fact that vasoconstriction lowers the temperature of the affected region, whereas vasodilation produces a temperature rise. A measure of vasomotor change (not absolute level) can be obtained by recording the resistance change in a thermistor applied to the skin.

Vasomotor fibers are unmyelinated postganglionic sympathetic fibers which arise from cell bodies within the vertebral chain and prevertebral ganglia. Vasodilator impulses travel mainly over fibers of the parasympathetic division of the autonomic nervous system; they are also carried by fibers that leave the thoracolumbar region together with preganglionic constrictor fibers and by fibers that accompany somatic nerves to the extremities (Burn, 1938). These leave the spinal cord through the dorsal root, an interesting exception to the Bell-Magendie law which states that all ventral roots carry motor (efferent) impulses, and all dorsal roots sensory (afferent) impulses. Vasomotor activity is determined partly by direct segmental reflexes and partly by vasomotor centers located in the brainstem tegmentum, caudal to the midpoint of the pons. The central control mechanism responds to impulses arising from pressure receptors in the aortic arch and proximal portions of the carotid arteries, as well as in nuclei of the posterior and lateral hypothalamus.

The measurement of cardiovascular responses. The most common measure of circulatory exchange is blood pressure, which reflects both cardiac output and local vasomotor tone. As blood is forced through the vascular system, pressure gradients develop; these are a function of the *amount* of blood pumped by the heart per unit of time and the *diameters* of the vessels through which the blood must pass. The pressure gradients vary with the heart cycle. Minimum pressure (*diastolic pressure*) coincides with the diastole of the heart, maximum pressure (*systolic pressure*) with the systole. The useful work accomplished by a single heartbeat is measured by *pulse pressure*—the difference between systolic and diastolic pressure.

Blood pressure can be assessed directly by inserting a pressure gauge into an artery. In man, it is more convenient to measure blood pressure indirectly by applying a stethoscope or microphone to an artery below a pressure cuff. As long as the pressure in this cuff remains below that of the blood at diastole, no sound is heard. As the pressure increases, the pulse becomes audible because blood flows through the partially occluded artery only on systolic surges. The maximum pressure that can be applied before the heartbeat becomes clearly audible is regarded as an index of diastolic pressure. As the cuff pressure is further increased, the artery becomes totally occluded and the sound of the heartbeat again disappears. The maximum pressure that can be applied before the heartbeat becomes inaudible is a measure of systolic pressure.

This technique is not adequate for experimental purposes since it allows only intermittent recordings. Darrow (1937b), Stovkis (1938), and others have attempted to devise techniques for the continuous monitoring of systolic blood pressure. These methods are generally cumbersome and complicated, and most workers have compromised on a relative measure of pressure variations from a level somewhat above diastolic (*relative blood pressure*). This technique does not require the complete occlusion of an artery and thus permits continuous recording. The results reflect a complex interaction between blood pressure and total blood volume and must be evaluated with caution.

Now that we have an idea of what measures of circulatory phenomena are available, let us see how they correlate with other variables. A

number of studies (Shepard, 1906, 1914; Landis, 1925; Boas and Goldschmidt, 1932; Kleitman, 1939) have shown that sleep and relaxation are characterized by complex circulatory changes. The blood volume of the brain increases, producing a compensatory decrease in the rest of the body. This change is accompanied by peripheral vasodilation, lowered blood pressure, and a marked slowing of heart rate. Loud and sudden stimuli elicit an immediate but transitory increase in heart rate and blood pressure (Berg and Beebe-Center, 1941), as well as a temporary rise in peripheral blood volume, followed by a decrease.

Exercise produces a rise in systolic pressure, accompanied by a fall in diastolic pressure, thus exerting a concerted effect on pulse pressure. Heart rate is also increased. Mental activity does not affect circulatory functions unless the situation is stressful. The magnitude of the response to psychological stress varies between subjects (Landis and Gullette, 1925; Landis, 1926; Brown and Van Gelder, 1938). Although the correlations are often low, psychological stress tends to increase blood pressure by stimulating heart rate and inducing vasoconstriction. The latter is particularly pronounced in the intestinal organs (Barcroft and Florey, 1929; Drury et al., 1929). Ackner (1958) found evidence for a quantitative relationship between peripheral vasoconstriction and degree of anxiety.

Many experiments (Marston, 1917, 1924; Landis and Gullette, 1925; Landis, 1925) have shown that none of the measures of circulatory change

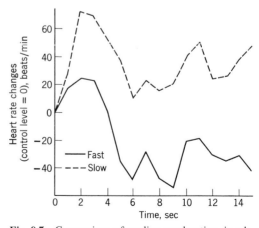

Fig. 9.7 Comparison of cardiac acceleration, in relation to the rate at the time of stimulation, for shots fired during fast and slow phases of the respiratory cardiac cycle. (From Berg and Beebe-Center, 1941.)

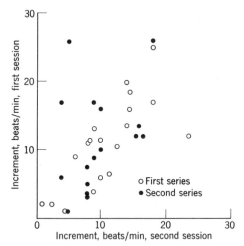

Fig. 9.8 Relation between cardiac startle responses of individuals on two different occasions. (From Berg and Beebe-Center, 1941.)

now available differentiates adequately between the various emotions. A clinical report (Wolf and Wolff, 1942, 1943) claimed to have distinguished reliably between anger and fear on the basis of vasomotor changes in the wall of the upper intestine.

Cardiovascular changes may reflect general arousal rather than specific emotional content. This conclusion is supported by a survey of clinical case histories by Boshes (1958). Although a variety of pathological cardiovascular conditions may be of psychosomatic origin, there is no indication that specific symptoms are related to particular emotional conditions.

Respiration

So far we have considered only visceral responses (in the sense that they are under principal control of the autonomic nervous system) that are not subject to voluntary regulation. This is a desirable feature of any physiological correlate of emotion, and only one physiological function that is partially under voluntary control has attracted sustained attention from workers in this field. The continued popularity of measures of respiratory movements is due in part to the relative simplicity of the recording devices and their sensitivity to a variety of psychological variables.

Respiration is essential to survival. A continuous supply of oxygen must be provided for various energy-yielding transformations, and waste products, especially carbon dioxide, must be speedily

removed from the tissues to avoid poisoning. The partial pressure of these two gases must at all times be maintained within narrow limits. All active processes within the organism require oxygen, and the rate and depth of breathing follow bodily requirements rather closely. Measures of respiratory functions therefore provide satisfactory indices of the organism's general level of activation or arousal. Respiratory responses are also part of all emotional reactions, but measures of respiration have not succeeded in distinguishing between different emotional situations, or between emotional and nonemotional reactions.

The measurement of respiration is relatively simple. The oldest and most direct technique relies on the *volume* of air exhaled. The subject breathes into a container equipped with pressure-sensing devices connected to a direct-current amplifier. The amplifier drives the motor of an ink-writer and provides separate records of the rate of respiratory cycles, the volume of air exhaled, and the relative duration of the exhalation. The technique is not generally useful for research in the psychophysiological laboratory because the attachment of the apparatus and the generally uncomfortable body position produce artifacts.

More practical are devices that rely on the physical expansion of the chest or abdomen, such as a flexible, air- or gas-filled tube stretched around the body with a strain gauge or diaphragm attached to the open end of the tube. The pressure changes resulting from respiratory movements are transcribed either directly on a kymograph or, after suitable amplification, on paper by an ink-writer. In spite of the comparative crudeness of this technique, it is useful if both thoracic (costal) and abdominal breathing movements are recorded simultaneously. Simultaneous recording is necessary because abdominal and costal breathing are delicately coordinated to meet the demands of specific situations and may vary independently. The principal criticism against much research in this field is that the relative contributions of these two mechanisms to changes in respiration are generally ignored.

A more recent development in this area is the recording of respiration by sensitive, miniature thermistors. These are taped to the nose so that the temperature-sensitive bead or disk is in the direct path of the airflow. Inhalation cools the thermistor and produces a recordable resistance change. Exhalation warms the thermistor because the air has acquired some of the body temperature. This technique can be quite useful if a thermistor with brief time constants and high temperature sensitivity is selected. The method is particularly suitable for animal research since it eliminates the need for bulky equipment and restraint.

No matter how respiratory change is measured, a knotty problem is presented by the complexity of the response. The respiratory cycle consists of three separate phases which may vary independently; however, it is sometimes difficult to obtain data that will show three clearly defined phases. The inhalation portion of the cycle is generally well defined. The beginning of the exhalation cycle is also obvious, but the point at which exhalation ends and the pause between cycles begins is often hard to define. This pause has unfortunately been included in the exhalation phase, a procedure which obscures valuable information.

Stoerring (1906) suggested the use of an inhalation-exhalation (I/E) ratio. This measure has been used widely with considerable success, although the inconsistent inclusion of the pause in the exhalation segment has made evaluation of some of the data difficult. Woodworth and Schlosberg (1954) objected to this measure because it presents statistical problems when widely different ratios are averaged. They recommended instead the use of the "I" fraction, obtained by dividing the duration of the inhalation phase by the duration of the whole cycle. They suggested that this measure might provide a direct index of the active, muscular phase of the respiratory cycle. It may very well do so, but the inclusion of the nonactive phase in the total duration creates problems that must be considered carefully before the measure is applied.

Respiration is regulated by chemical mechanisms that are sensitive to the metabolic and homeostatic demands of the organism and by nervous mechanisms providing reflexive control (the Hering-Breuer vagal reflex); some voluntary regulation also occurs. The central representation of respiratory functions is in the *medullary respiratory centers* which are located in the caudal third of the floor of the fourth ventricle, near the obex. Distinct mechanisms for the control of inhalation and exhalation can be identified. The neurons in these centers are sensitive to increases in the carbon dioxide and hydrogen ion concentration of the arterial blood, as well as to neural impulses from pressure receptors in the lungs which are carried primarily by the vagus nerve.

Under normal conditions the rhythm of breathing is determined by the periodic inhibition of inhalation by vagal impulses. Inflation of the lungs stimulates proprioceptive receptors in the walls of the respiratory bronchioles, alveolar ducts, and air sacs. Impulses from these receptors inhibit the inhalation center and play a major role in determining the respiratory cycle. Active contraction of exhalation muscles in deep breathing stimulates pulmonary deflation receptors which reflexively *stimulate* the inhalation center.

Another inhibitory system, the pneumotaxic center, is located in the tegmentum of the brainstem, rostral and lateral to the respiratory centers. Impulses from the inhalation center travel to this pneumotaxic center. When the input reaches a critical level, impulses from the pneumotaxic center trigger the inhalation mechanism. This breaks the pneumotaxic circuit, and a new cycle begins.

A series of early studies (see Ruckmick's 1936 review) demonstrated that respiratory rate increases following "pleasant" stimulation and decreases in response to "unpleasant" stimuli. Depth of breathing (i.e., the area under the curve) tended to show the opposite effect. Benussi (1914) claimed that the I/E ratio provided an exact measure of lying. He reported that this ratio was significantly greater three to five respiratory cycles before a truth-telling response than before lying, and smaller after telling the truth than after lying. Benussi's claims have never been verified, but measures of respiration are still used today in "lie detection." Burtt (1921) and Landis and Wiley (1926) have reported some success with the I/E fraction, but the diagnosis of lying was never more than 20% better than chance.

Respiratory changes are known to accompany most emotional reactions, but the evidence for specific and differential respiratory responses is not very convincing. Most of the initial enthusiasm can be traced to Feleky's (1914, 1916) work. Feleky reported impressive correlations between the magnitude of average I/E ratios and the imaginary experience of six primary emotions—pleasure, pain, anger, wonderment, fear, and disgust. Closer inspection of the data reveals that the exuberant conclusions are based on a single experimental session, one subject per emotion! Subsequent research has failed to replicate these results, although low correlations between various measures of respiratory change and various emotional situations have been reported. These correlations may be useful for the crude classification of group data but cannot serve as a diagnostic tool in the individual case.

Other Peripheral Measures

Many other physiological functions have, at some time or other, been measured and correlated with emotional reactions or general activation level.

Muscular tension. Skeletal muscles are generally arranged in pairs of antagonists, flexors and extensors. Both maintain a delicately balanced tension level which is lowest during relaxation and sleep and tends to increase as the organism alerts and prepares for action (Jacobson, 1938). When we talk about the tensions of a trying day, we refer, at least in part, to abnormally high levels of muscular tonus; somatic tension is a common symptom in anxiety.

A rough measure of muscular tonus can be obtained with a variety of mechanical recorders such as strain gauges. *Electromyographic* techniques are generally more convenient and allow a fairly precise measure of local muscle activity. The tonic contraction of postural adjustment as well as the rapid phasic contractions of voluntary movement produce large electrical potentials which can be picked up by either surface or needle electrodes. Following suitable amplification, these

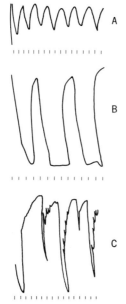

Fig. 9.9 Breathing curves during posed emotions. A, normal; B, pose for "wonder"; C, laughter. (From Feleky, 1916.)

impulses can be recorded directly, or the circuit can be arranged so that they can be averaged over several seconds. Jacobson (1951) has reviewed the various recording and data evaluation techniques in some detail. Muscle potentials are usually recorded from the forehead or neck and furnish a satisfactory record of general alertness (Travis and Lindsley, 1931; Lindsley, 1935; Kennedy and Travis, 1947, 1948; Travis and Kennedy, 1947, 1949). Even the intent to move, when there is no overt movement, produces a pronounced muscle discharge from the appropriate muscles (Jacobson, 1932, 1938, 1951; Max, 1934, 1935, 1937).

Skin temperature. The temperature of the skin is complexly determined by vasomotor activity, temperature of the blood, and general body temperature. It is recorded simply by applying a sensitive thermocouple or thermistor, depending on the available recording and amplification system, to the skin surface. These temperature-sensitive devices react to changes in temperature with pronounced variations in current flow which can be amplified and recorded by any ink-writing system. Mittelman and Wolff (1939, 1943) reported a pronounced fall in skin temperature during emotional reactions, and Ax (1953) has confirmed these results.

Gastrointestinal activity. Measures of gastrointestinal motility have not been used extensively in the psychophysiological laboratory. The recording procedure itself is sufficient to induce emotional reactions in all but the most hardened subjects. The subject must either swallow a balloon connected by an air tube to a pneumographic recording tambour or drink an opaque solution such as barium and then submit to a protracted X-ray or fluoroscopic examination. Neither procedure is very pleasant, and the latter may involve severe radiation hazards if used for prolonged experimental sessions.

Interest in the gastrointestinal measures was aroused by Cannon's (1915, 1929) report that normal digestive movements were inhibited after the presentation of a fear-arousing stimulus. Similar results were reported by Todd and Rowlands (1930) with fluoroscopic techniques. By using gastric, duodenal, and rectal balloons, Brunswick (1924) studied the gastrointestinal reactions of man to a great variety of emotional stimuli. He reported a loss of gastrointestinal tone during such different emotional reactions as fear, pain, envy, disappointment, irritation, and unpleasantness. Distress, surprise, and startle tended to augment gastric motility. A variety of apparently emotional stimuli failed to have any effect on the smooth muscle of the digestive tract.

Metabolic rate. Measures of metabolic rate generally depend on indices of oxygen consumption and carbon dioxide release. The nitrogen content of the urine as well as chemical analyses of other bodily waste products have been used in some studies. The basic procedure is quite forbidding. A rubber mask is placed on the lower half of the face, completely shutting off the normal air supply. The subject is then required to breathe a high-oxygen mixture from a tank similar to those used by skin divers.

Because this procedure frightens most subjects, a variety of indirect measures of metabolic rate have been proposed. Read (1924; Read and Barnett, 1934) noted that pulse rate (PR) and pulse pressure (PP) vary directly with oxygen consumption; the correlation between metabolic rate and those measures was reported to be .74 and .62 respectively. He suggested that an estimate of metabolic rate could be obtained by the following formula:

$$\text{Metabolic rate} = .75(\text{PR} + .74\text{PP}) - 72$$

A still more indirect measure of this function, through total heat output, can be obtained by the following formula:

$$\frac{\text{Calories/meter}^2/\text{hr}}{\text{(for men)}} = \frac{\text{PR} \times \text{PP}}{700} + 27$$

$$\frac{\text{Calories/meter}^2/\text{hr}}{\text{(for women)}} = \frac{3 \times \text{PR} \times \text{PP}}{700} + 24$$

Read and Barnett (1934) reported a correlation of .80 between metabolic rate and estimates obtained by these formulas.

Graff and Mayer (1923) suggested various emotional reactions to subjects under hypnosis and reported sizable increases in oxygen consumption following the suggestion of fear-inducing situations. Totten (1925) reported wide individual differences in subjects' reactions to emotional stimuli, some showing as much as a 20% increase in metabolic rate while others did not react at all. Ziegler and Levine (1925) reported a generally decreased metabolic rate in response to unpleasant stimuli. Landis (1925b, 1926) demonstrated in a carefully controlled experiment that the metabolic rate tended to rise during anticipation of an unpleasant stimulus (shock), but decreased rapidly when this stimulus was actually

presented. Rowles and Patrick (1934) reported that both verbal and sensory stimuli produced a rise in the metabolic rate, but they were unable to find appreciable correlations between emotional content and a change in metabolic rate.

Pilomotor responses. Perhaps the most frequently used observational index of emotional reactions in laboratory animals, particularly in cats, is the raising of body hair. This response, depending on smooth-muscle activity at the base of the hair, appears to be under sympathetic control. Because of technical measurement problems, the response has not been studied quantitatively although it is frequently reported in physiological experiments as an index of fear. Lindsley and Sassaman (1938) demonstrated that quantitative measures can be obtained, but little use has been made of this information. They employed motion pictures to obtain gross measurements of pilomotor activity and made bipolar recordings of muscle potentials at the base of the hair for more localized and precise records.

Biochemical measures. All neural processes are initiated and propagated by biochemical transformations. Considerable evidence exists for the hypothesis that different chemical events may be responsibe for the activity of different parts of the brain, and that grossly abnormal central processes may be reflected in grossly abnormal chemical reactions. These considerations have led to the intensive search for simple, chemical indices of emotional activity, either neurohumoral transmitter substances and their breakdown products or substances that appear to vary as a function of mental disease, emotional reactivity, or general arousal. A discussion of this material would lead us too far from the topic of this chapter, but a few representative examples may be of interest.

Ax (1953) reported that anger-provoking stimuli increase the secretion of norepinephrine by the adrenal medulla, whereas fear-provoking stimuli increase the secretion of epinephrine. Ström-Olsen and Weil-Malherbe (1958) reported that both of these catecholamines are excreted in urine in greater quantities during manic states than during periods of normal or depressive behavior. Variations in the emotional state of psychiatric patients have also been reported to be correlated with the excretion of norepinephrine (Elmadjian, 1959). Regan and Reilly (1958) have claimed to be able to distinguish emotional states on the basis of the epinephrine-norepinephrine ratio. Liddell and Weil-Malherbe (1953) did not find different catecholamine ratios in the cerebro-spinal fluids of schizophrenics and patients suspected of structural brain damage; however, the absolute concentration of both substances was lower in the schizophrenics.

Basowitz et al. (1955) measured the correlation between self-ratings of anxiety and the hippuric acid level of paratroopers in training. The relationship was negative, although previous studies (Persky et al., 1950) had suggested that the secretion of this substance by the kidney may be increased in patients with anxiety neuroses.

Another type of biochemical analysis has been attempted by Hoagland and his associates (Hoagland, 1957, 1961; Hoagland and Freeman, 1959). On the assumption that functional changes in the hypothalamus may affect not only emotional behavior but also the activity of the pituitary and adrenal glands, various indices of adrenocortical secretory activity have been analyzed. The response of schizophrenic patients to acute stress has been reported to be associated with a significant decrease in the excretion of 17-ketosteroids and uric acid, although the ACTH activity at rest was within normal limits. Other observers have reported that the mental state of schizophrenic patients appears to correlate with the rate of steroid excretion, high rates being associated with aggressive behavior and low secretion rates with quiet behavior (Batt et al., 1957). It is clear that the adrenocortical secretions are not causally related to the behavioral or emotional changes. However, they may reflect the activity of central mechanisms related to the control of emotional reactions and provide a promising, if indirect, measure of such activity. A more extensive *experimental* investigation of these secretory activities should be made.

Response patterns. A cursory survey of the vast research literature of the first half of the century leaves one with the impression that little of value can be abstracted from the low correlations that characterize the relationship between specific emotions and measurements of single autonomic responses. The high intersubject and intrasubject variability of these measures seems to hold little promise for all but the grossest group classification.

A new and perhaps more fruitful approach has been developed through the efforts of John Lacey (Lacey and Van Lehn, 1952; Lacey, 1956; Lacey and Lacey, 1958a, b). Lacey suggested that specific emotions might correlate with *patterns* of autonomic responses, and that these could be assessed through response profiles depicting the *relationship* between several autonomic measures. A further refinement of this technique is the application of lability measures; these are obtained by contrasting the spontaneous and induced response flutuations which are larger than some critical amplitude. In 1950 Lacey wrote:

> The evidence . . . seems to be in accordance with the hypotheses that "normal" individuals exhibit organized patterns of somatic reactions to stress which are reliable over a period of time extending to about 300 days. In the psychophysiological assay of individuals, patterning of somatic reaction is a variable as important as, possibly more important than, average reactivity itself. Both the degree to which two individuals are discriminating and the direction of that discrimination in terms of autonomic response systems may depend strikingly on the autonomic variable used.

Lacey (1950) demonstrated that response patterning occurred between various autonomic measures. During the past fifteen years, much research effort has been devoted to a search for specific relationships between such patterns of autonomic activity and particular emotional responses. This search has not yet been successful, possibly because the relationships are much more complex than we have naively assumed in the past.

We have already mentioned the use of autonomic response measurements in lie detection. The techniques have been refined in recent years in the direction suggested by Lacey's observations. Commercial lie detection polygraphs now generally contain at least three channels for the simultaneous measurement of respiration, skin resistance, and some cardiovascular response such as blood pressure. The resulting data are analyzed in terms of the total response pattern rather than the changes of amplitude in any one of the channels; they are said to be much more reliable than older, single-measure results.

Ellson et al. (1952) have studied the relative ability of a variety of autonomic measurements, taken singly or in combination, to detect deliberate lying on the part of voluntary subjects. He concluded that no single response measure allowed a significant prediction, but that a combination of several measures such as those used in commercial polygraphs provided acceptable results. Polygraph data have to be considered with caution, since they reflect only a general rise in emotionality which may or may not be caused by lying. An individual may have an emotional reaction to some question in spite of the fact that his answer is truthful.

THE EMERGENCY THEORY OF EMOTION

Changes in a variety of physiological functions occur during emotional stimulation but do not seem essential to either the experience or the expression of emotion. Similar if not identical changes occur in apparently emotionless situations, and widely different stimuli may produce comparable reactions. Particular autonomic and somatic responses are not characteristic of specific emotions but instead reflect a general increase in physiological activity.

Cannon (1932, 1939) suggested that the sympathetic division of the autonomic nervous system may discharge as a unit when bodily resources must suddenly be mobilized for vigorous muscular activity. He proposed that the sympathetic changes which accompany emotions "may reasonably be regarded as preparatory for struggle" (1939, p. 228). According to this hypothesis, the secretion of epinephrine cooperates with sympathetic nerve impulses to (1) free stores of glycogen from the liver for consumption by the muscles (as glucose), (2) aid in the conversion of lactic acid to glucose by stimulation of the respiratory mechanisms, and (3) redistribute blood from the viscera to the heart, brain, and extremities. The parasympathetic division conserves bodily resources by its ability to exert selective influences on single organs without producing corresponding effects on other regions of the body. The "emergency" theory of emotion suggests that by exciting the sympathetic nervous system and simultaneously inhibiting the parasympathetic system, emotion, "as exemplified by anger and fear," facilitates the body's general capacity to respond vigorously.

This theory explains why we should see the same physiological changes in various emotional and nonemotional situations; it is supported by the fact that animals without the sympathetic nervous system cannot endure very strong emotional stimulation and will "die of fright." However, Cannon's hypothesis is contradicted by several experimental observations. Epinephrine depletes liver glycogen but also decreases the glycogen stores of muscles, even when the concentration of epinephrine is too small to produce a rise in blood pressure (Major and Mann, 1932).

Somogyi (1951) has further shown that epinephrine tends to *inhibit* the utilization of glucose by slowing its transfer from the extracellular fluids to the tissue cells. Far from aiding the reconversion of lactic acid to glycogen, epinephrine seems to break down muscular glycogen and thus hinders rather than helps the emergency reaction. The cardiovascular effects of epinephrine are complex but similarly do not seem to be designed to "prepare the organism for struggle." Epinephrine decreases the blood flow in muscles at rest (Gellhorn, 1943), and in relatively large doses it seems to have similar effects on active muscles (Luco, 1939). That epinephrine accelerates the heart rate does not necessarily imply a significant improvement of circulation since stroke volume may decrease with abnormal acceleration.

THE EEG AND EMOTIONAL BEHAVIOR

Although the electrical activity of the brain hardly qualifies as a *peripheral* correlate of emotion, we shall discuss electroencephalographic (EEG) phenomena at this point because the EEG response represents, at present, merely another physiological measure of arousal.

Berger's (1929, 1933) original description of the electrical activity of the human brain characterized the behavioral state of rest and relaxation by fairly regular 10-sec waves (the *alpha rhythm*). This rhythm disappears immediately upon sensory stimulation. Subsequent experiments have confirmed this finding. (See Lindsley, 1951, for a more detailed discussion of this literature.) This blocking of the alpha rhythm depends on the novelty of the sensory stimulation; habituation develops very rapidly. Any frequently repeated sensory stimulus loses its ability to interrupt the alpha rhythm unless it is a conditioned stimulus for either positive or negative reinforcement. Apprehension and anxiety may act as nonspecific arousal stimuli and activate the electrical activity of the cortex (Williams, 1939; Thiesen, 1943; Harrison, 1946; Cohn, 1946; Darrow et al., 1946).

Electrical stimulation of the reticular formation of the brainstem elicits the cortical arousal response (Moruzzi and Magoun, 1949) as well as autonomic and somatic responses which commonly accompany emotional reactions (Ranson and Magoun, 1939). Lesions in the brainstem reticular formation abolish the activation pattern and produce high-amplitude, synchronized discharges near the alpha frequency. The effects of such lesions are lethargy, apathy, and somnolence, a behavior pattern which Lindsley (1951) has called the "antithesis of emotional excitement."

Lindsley's Arousal Theory of Emotion

These relationships led Lindsley (1951) to propose an *activation theory of emotion* (see Figure 9.13). This theory attempts to explain emotional reactions as well as motivation in general in terms of relative cortical arousal. It proposes that both visceral and somatic sensory impulses converge on the reticular formation of the lower brainstem. The impulses are then integrated and distributed to the hypothalamus where they stimulate the diencephalic waking center, and to the nonspecific projection nuclei of the thalamus through which they activate the cortex. When the input through this system is low, the organism is relaxed and the electrical activity of the brain resembles that of sleep. As this input increases, the organism alerts and orients itself toward the source of stimulation; the electrical pattern then becomes one of arousal, that is, of fast, low-voltage activity. Emotion as well as other motivational factors falls on an arousal continuum which extends from drowsiness and low emotional reactivity to strong emotions such as rage. Lindsley supported this interpretation by pointing out that rage, the "emotion par excellence," is always accompanied by alpha blocking, whereas sleep, the "antithesis of emotion," is characterized by slow, high-amplitude activity.

The widespread connections of the reticular formation and its diffuse cortical projections make it a tempting candidate for some functional role in the central regulation of emotional and motivational behavior. However, cortical arousal does not show the fine gradations required by Lindsley's theory, and we have no experimental evidence to suggest a correlation between specific emotional or motivational situations and cortical EEG. Cortical arousal may be a prerequisite for all behavior, but it does not in itself explain the variety of emotional behavior.

It has not yet been demonstrated that low-amplitude, high-frequency EEG patterns are necessarily an index of increased activity at the neuron level. Some central structures show large, slow waves during behavioral arousal; others remain entirely unaffected or show still different electrical responses. Gross behavioral changes do not affect the general cortical EEG once alpha blocking has occurred. Even stimuli that elicit violent rage reactions do not significantly alter the EEG if the animal is alert before the presentation of the stimulus.

Darrow's Concept of Sympathetic Overregulation

An interesting relationship between the electrical activity of the brain and emotional behavior has been suggested by Darrow (1947, 1950). He proposed that the pattern of cortical arousal

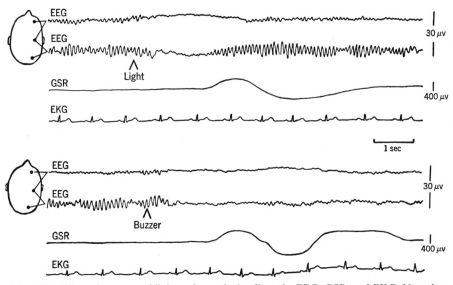

Fig. 9.10   Effect of unexpected light and sound stimuli on the EEG, GSR, and EKG. Note that both light and sound stimuli block the alpha rhythm of the EEG after a latency of about 0.4 sec; the GSR occurs after a latency of approximately 1 to 15 sec. (From Lindsley, 1950.)

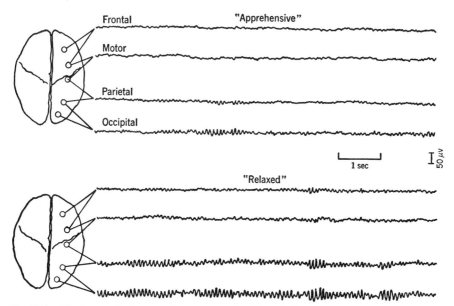

Fig. 9.11   Electroencephalograms from a normal subject during an initial apprehensive period and a later relaxed period. Note the reduction or suppression of alpha rhythm during apprehension. (From Lindsley, 1950.)

might represent an algebraic summation of potential differences which result from the nonsynchronized activity of many cortical neurons. The summation of such random activity tends to cancel most of the potential differences and thus gives rise to fast, low-amplitude activity typical of arousal. Darrow proposed that such

activity might be initiated by deficient sympathetic regulation but could become independent through neural feedback devices, resulting in a state of cortical tension or anxiety. All other emotions are thought to be characterized by slow, alpha-like patterns which arise from the *synchronized* activity of cortical neurons. The slow wave

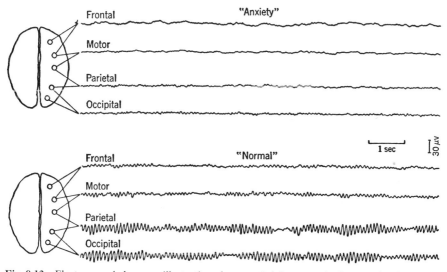

Fig. 9.12   Electroencephalograms illustrating absence of alpha waves in the records of a patient in an anxiety state and the well-regulated alpha rhythms of a normal subject. (The electroencephalograms of normal subjects and those of patients with anxiety cannot always be so readily differentiated.) (From Lindsley, 1950.)

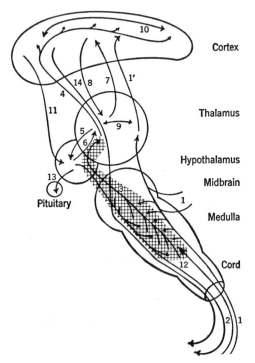

Cortex

Thalamus

Hypothalamus

Midbrain

Pituitary

Medulla

Cord

Fig. 9.13 Principal central nervous structures and probable pathways involved in emotional behavior. The diagram does not include the cerebellum and certain basal ganglia which may also participate. 1, somatic and cranial afferents; 1', direct thalamocortical projections; 2, visceral afferent pathways; 3, centripetal projections of reticular formation; 4, diffuse thalamocortical projections; 5 and 6, interconnections of hypothalamus and thalamus; 7 and 8, interconnections between thalamus and cortex; 9, intrathalamic connections; 10, intracortical connections; 11, corticohypothalamic pathways; 13, hypothalamo-hypophyseal tract; 14, corticospinal pathways. The cross-hatched area represents the reticular formation. (From Lindsley, 1951.)

pattern is believed to reflect an inhibition of cortical activity by cerebral vasoconstriction and a reduction of free acetylcholine. The alpha patterns presumably cannot be seen in experimental studies of emotion because all laboratory situations contain a prominent component of fear or anxiety.

Darrow's hypothesis is based almost entirely on general clinical evidence and contains some logical inconsistencies that need to be resolved. It is not clear, for instance, why fear or anxiety, which are often taken as the prototype of emotion, should be characterized by a pattern of cortical activity directly opposite that of other emotions.

It is also questionable why all emotions except anxiety should be accompanied by the same electrical pattern as that for sleep or relaxation. Darrow's dichotomous analysis of emotional responses does not correspond to subjective experience. It appears that speculations about the relationship between gross EEG changes and changes in emotionality may have to await further clarification of the functional significance of the electrocortical response itself.

THE ROLE OF SUBCORTICAL MECHANISMS IN THE REGULATION OF EMOTIONAL BEHAVIOR

Lower Portions of the Brainstem

Isolated sympathetic responses to noxious stimulation can be elicited in spinal animals. If both the medulla and spinal cord are intact, more coherent response patterns can be seen because many autonomic functions are integrated by bulbar centers. The contributions of the bulbar, pontine, and mesencephalic portions of the brainstem deserve more detailed description, for we begin to see integrated patterns of some emotional responses when these areas are intact.

Goltz (1892) provided the first scientific description of the emotional behavior of decerebrate animals. In these preparations the brainstem is transected by an intercollicular section which passes caudal to the posterior border of the diencephalon. Goltz's dog showed clear and coherent rage responses to stimuli which before surgery had never elicited such reactions. No other emotional reactions could be elicited during an eighteen-month period of survival. Woodworth and Sherrington (1904) replicated these results in cats and termed the behavior *pseudoaffective* since the responses to noxious stimulation were brief and stimulus-bound. A number of other researchers (Bazett and Penfield, 1922; Rothmann, 1923; Schaltenbrandt and Cobb, 1930; Keller, 1932) have reported similar results. Keller (1932) disagreed with Woodworth and Sherrington about the pseudoaffective nature of the responses. He stated that the emotional reaction to noxious stimuli in decerebrate animals seemed complete and could not, on the basis of objective criteria, be differentiated from that of normal animals. Bazett and Penfield (1922) and Schaltenbrandt and Cobb (1930) observed purring and pleasure reactions in decorticated cats and disagreed with earlier reports that only rage behavior could be elicited.

More recent studies (Macht and Bard, 1942; Kelly et al., 1946) have demonstrated that decerebrate animals will not show well-coordinated and directed attack behavior. Most of the somatic and autonomic changes that normally accompany rage behavior occur, but the attack reactions lack proper coordination, and isolated components of the response pattern often appear. Many *individual* responses that contribute to a complete emotional reaction may be regulated in the lower brainstem. These response patterns are intact in the decerebrate but are poorly coordinated because higher regulatory and integrative influences are absent. We must be careful, again, to distinguish between emotional *expression* as reported in these studies and subjective emotional *experience*. Dana (1921) summarized clinical evidence which indicated that apparently unchanged emotional feelings occurred in a patient whose spinal cord was severed at the cervical level, in spite of a complete elimination of feedback from the body below the neck.

Recent investigations of the role of the central gray of the mesencephalon have emphasized the importance of this region in emotional behavior (Hunsperger, 1956; Molina and Hunsperger, 1959; Hunsperger and Molina, 1958; Hunsperger, 1959). Electrical stimulation of the central gray elicits partial rage responses in cats. Small bilateral lesions of the same area produce a permanent and pronounced reduction of emotional responsiveness. Electrical stimulation of the hypothalamus or the amygdala which normally evokes rage fails to do so following such lesions of the midbrain. Amygdaloid or hypothalamic lesions have no effect on the rage behavior elicited by electrical stimulation of the mesencephalic gray. Hunsperger and his associates have concluded from these studies that the midbrain mechanism is not merely part of the efferent connections from the hypothalamus; it also represents a separate regulatory mechanism.

Diencephalic Mechanisms

That at least part of the integration of the various autonomic and somatic responses takes place at the hypothalamic, or perhaps thalamic, level is indicated by the results of decortication. Dusser de Barenne (1920) provided one of the earliest descriptions of the emotional behavior of such preparations, noting in particular that violent rage was often elicited by "trivial and irrelevant" stimuli. Cannon and Britton (1925, 1927) have described the emotional reactions of acutely decorticated cats to being tied down to a restraining device. These investigators coined the term "sham rage" to describe the fits of rage that occurred spontaneously every few minutes in these animals. In the intervening periods of quiet, rage could be elicited by the presentation of innocuous stimuli.

Bard and his co-workers (Bard, 1928, 1934a, b, 1939, 1950; Bard and Rioch, 1937; Bard and Mountcastle, 1948) have analyzed this sham rage response in considerable detail with acute as well as chronic preparations. They demonstrated by a series of successive surgical ablations that rage behavior persisted in spite of bilateral removal of the entire cortex and additional lesions of the striatum, pallidum, thalamus, and anterior and dorsal diencephalon. Transections below the level of the caudal hypothalamus abolished the rage responses.

The emotional reactions of the decorticate animals seemed to differ from those of normal animals primarily in being poorly directed with respect to the provoking stimulus. Bard suggested that the removal of forebrain influences may induce a marked emotional hypersensitivity and hyperexcitability since stimuli which the animals were indifferent to or even found pleasurable before the operation evoked violent rage responses.

This hyperexcitability may not be caused merely by a transient postoperative irritability of the remaining tissue as suggested by Lashley (1938). Bromiley (1948) reported that a decorticate dog survived for almost three years; throughout this time the animal showed rage reactions to such apparently neutral stimuli as cage manipulation and gentle handling.

A comparison of the effects of decerebration with those of decortication suggests that emotional behavior is partially integrated by diencephalic mechanisms. The contributions of specific hypothalamic centers has been studied in the past 25 years, and a relatively coherent picture of the functions of this "headganglion of the autonomic nervous system" (Peele, 1954) has emerged.

Electrical stimulation. Hess (1936, 1949, 1954) and his collaborators have mapped the behavioral responses to electrical stimulation of the entire diencephalic brainstem of cats. A variety of diverse emotional responses were elicited. Rage responses were evoked from anterior and lateral portions of the hypothalamus as well as from immediately adjacent telencephalic structures such as the preoptic area and basal septal nuclei.

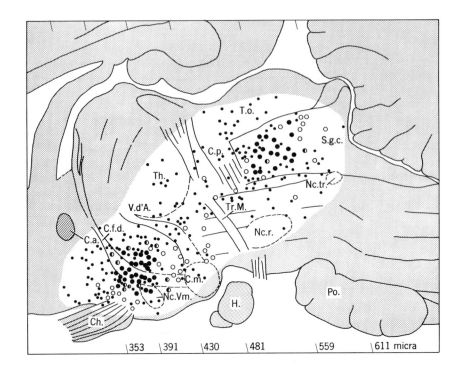

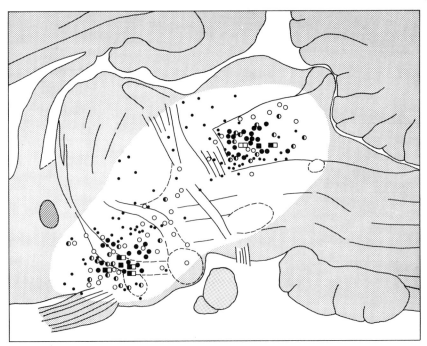

Fig. 9.14 Electrode placements in midbrain and hypothalamus from which affective reactions could be elicited. Defensive responses •, escape ○, escape with defensive movements ◐, attack ■, fright reactions or alternating attack and fright responses ◼◻. C.a., commissura anterior; C.f.d., columna fornicis descendens; C.m., corpus mammillare; C.p., commissura posterior; Ch., chiasma; H., hypophysis; Nc.om., nucleus oculomotorius; Nc.r., nucleus ruber; Nc.tr., nucleus trochlearis; Nc.vm., nucleus ventromedianus hypothalami; Po., pons; S.g.c., substantia grisea centralis mesencephali; T.o., tectum opticum; Th., thalamus; Tr.M., tractus Meynert; V.d'A., tractus Vicq d'Azyr. (From Hunsperger, 1956.)

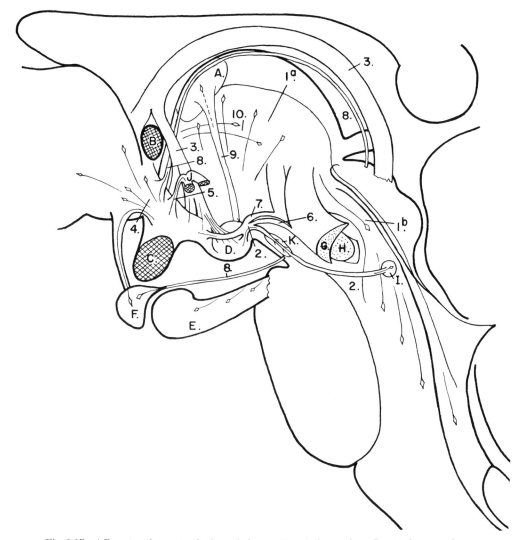

Fig. 9.15 Afferent pathways to the hypothalamus. A, anterior nucleus; B, anterior commissure; C, optic chiasma; D, mammillary body; E, hippocampus; F, amygdala; G, medial lemniscus; H, brachium conjunctivum; I, ventral tegmental nucleus, J, ansa lenticularis; K, ventral tegmental area. 1, periventricular system (*a*, thalamohypothalamic fibers; *b*, tegmentohypothalamic fibers); 2, mammillary peduncle; 3, fornix; 4, medial forebrain bundle; 5, pallidohypothalamic fibers; 6, lemniscal fibers to hypothalamus; 7, brachium fibers to hypothalamus; 8, terminal stria; 9, mammillothalamic tract; 10, inferior thalamic peduncle. (From Russell, 1961.)

Careful analysis of the data suggested that distinct systems to mediate attack, defense, and flight reactions may exist. The behavioral effects were accompanied by a variety of sympathetic responses common to normal emotional reactions (pilomotor and sudomotor activity, increased rate and depth of respiration, pupillary dilatation, and a rise in blood pressure, etc.). A number of reports (Ingram et al., 1936; Karplus, 1937; Ranson, 1939; Ranson and Magoun, 1939; Hinsey,

1940) have suggested that rage behavior can also be elicited from more posterior aspects of the hypothalamus.

Lesions. Electrical stimulation of the hypothalamus always elicits rage (i.e., attack, defense, or flight reactions). The destruction of hypothalamic tissue should therefore *decrease* emotional excitability. A number of experiments (Ingram et al., 1936; Ranson, 1939) have reported

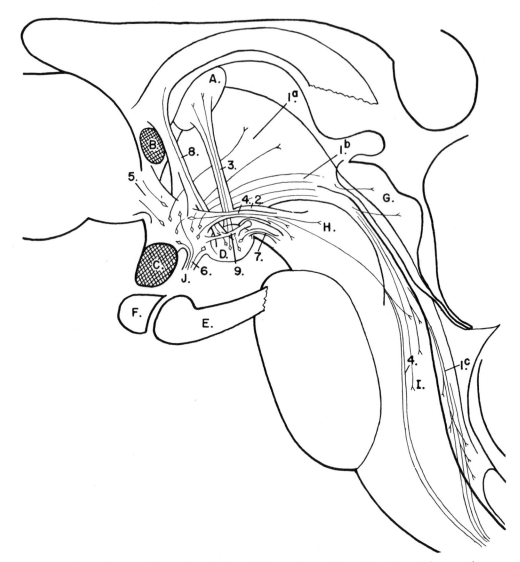

Fig. 9.16 Efferent pathways from the hypothalamus. A, anterior nucleus; B, anterior commissure; C, optic chiasma; D, mammillary body; E, hippocampus; F, amygdala; G, tectum; H, mesencephalic tegmentum; I, met- and myelencephalic tegmentum. 1, periventricular system (*a*, vertical fibers; *b*, horizontal fibers; *c*, dorsal longitudinal fasciculus); 2, mammillotegmental tract; 3, mammillothalamic tract; 4, diffuse hypothalamotegmental fibers; 5, medial forebrain bundle; 6, hypothalamo-hypophyseal tracts; 7, mammillary peduncle; 8, fornix; 9, supramammillary decussation. (From Russell, 1961.)

that hypothalamic lesions produced a marked reduction of emotional responsiveness as well as stolidity, drowsiness, and a general decrease of bodily activity sometimes leading to prolonged somnolence. However, integrated and well-directed rage responses could be elicited from these animals as long as they were not entirely somnolent (Kelly et al., 1946; Bard and Mountcastle, 1948). Masserman (1938) reported that the

emotional behavior of animals with hypothalamic lesions eventually returned to normal, provided metabolic and homeostatic functions recover sufficiently to restore the energy balance of the organism.

Kessler (1941) and Wheatley (1944), on the other hand, found that fairly small lesions in the ventromedial nuclei of the hypothalamus produced exactly the opposite results. Animals with bilateral lesions in or ventrolateral to the ventro-medial nuclei showed a pronounced and apparently permanent *increase* in emotional reactivity. Vicious rage responses, usually expressed in well-directed attack behavior, could be elicited by previously neutral stimuli. The emotional reactions of such animals appear to be similar to those of decorticates or of normal animals during electrical stimulation of other hypothalamic structures.

More evidence is needed to unravel the interrelationship between the individual hypothalamic mechanisms, but it appears certain that emotional reactions are at least partially integrated and controlled by these diencephalic centers. It is only when we inquire into the completeness of this subcortical regulation that serious problems are raised.

Hess (1936, 1949, 1954) and several others have been quite explicit in describing coordinated and well-directed affective responses to electrical stimulation. They suggest that the effects of electrical stimulation of the hypothalamus cannot be differentiated from emotional reactions to external noxious stimuli. Wheatley (1944) similarly stressed that the rage responses, which are so easily elicited from animals with ventromedial lesions, do not appear blind or senseless but are characterized by entirely appropriate attack or defense reactions as well as a complete set of autonomic responses.

White (1940), on the other hand, reported that

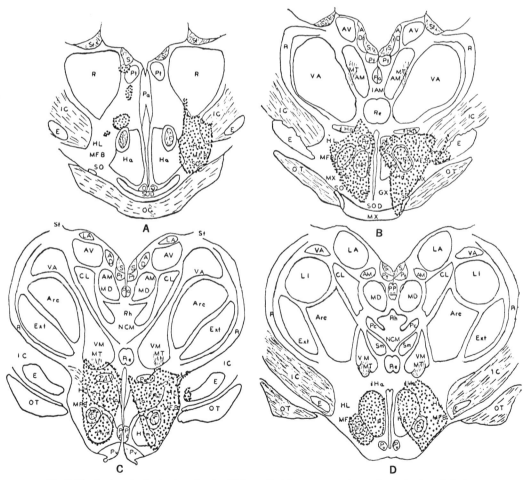

Fig. 9.17 Lesions in the brains of cats which resulted in savage postoperative behavior: A, lesions above the optic chiasma; B, lesions in the region of the dorsomedial hypothalamic nuclei; lesions in the region of the ventromedial hypothalamic nuclei; D, lesions in the posterior hypothalamic area. (From Wheatley, 1944.)

electrical stimulation of various hypothalamic structures of conscious human subjects failed to elicit unusual sensations or changes in subjective emotional experience, although a variety of sympathetic and parasympathetic responses were observed. Masserman (1941, 1942, 1943) called the emotional responses to electrical stimulation of the hypothalamus *pseudoaffective* and suggested that they differed significantly from true emotional reactions. In his own extensive research, Masserman found that electrical stimulation of the hypothalamus did not interfere with normal ongoing behavior. The animals continued to drink, groom themselves, and even displayed affective responses to petting (purring, head rubbing, etc.) unless the motor components of the rage response directly interfered with this behavior. The rage reactions were described as brief, stimulus-bound, stereotyped, and mechanical. Masserman failed to establish a conditioned emotional response to stimuli repeatedly presented together with electrical stimulation of the hypothalamus which evoked rage responses. This led him to conclude that such stimulation may not elicit a subjective experience of emotion and that the diencephalon may not act as "an afferent, experience-mediating organ, but as a way-station on efferent sympathetic and motor pathways." It has been suggested that the animals did begin to show some evidence of conditioning and that additional trials might have been needed to strengthen these reaction tendencies. The presence of an electrical field in the hypothalamus (produced by the unconditioned stimulus) may have interfered with the formation of a functional relationship between the conditioned stimulus and the effector circuit of the unconditioned response, and thus may have retarded learning. Successful conditioning has been reported in many recent experiments. This matter is further discussed in Chapter 10 which covers motivational properties of central stimulation.

Summary. Individual visceral components of emotional reactions depend on regulatory mechanisms in the lower brainstem. In the decerebrate animal only these mechanisms are functional, and peripheral rage responses can be elicited even by previously neutral or pleasant stimuli. These responses are stimulus-bound, lacking in direction and coordination, and must be considered subtotal. The lower brainstem centers do not seem to contribute to subjective experience.

When the hypothalamus is intact, these individual responses can be integrated into more complex behavior patterns which appear to have many of the attributes of emotional behavior in the normal animal. However, the capacity for emotional reaction seems to be limited to responses that have been classified as rage behavior (i.e., attack, defense, and flight reactions). Hypothalamic stimulation has occasionally been reported to elicit more positive emotional responses, or at least to enhance the reaction to pleasant stimuli; however, such behavior appears to require cortical integration because it does not occur when cortical influences are removed. The available evidence suggests that the subjective experience of emotion is not mediated by these hypothalamic mechanisms.

The Thalamus

Anatomically, the thalamus is ideally suited for the subcortical integration of afferent inputs to the organism. All sensory pathways, with the sole exception of olfactory connections, relay in the thalamic nuclei before they are distributed to the specific cortical projection areas (olfactory signals may reach the thalamus via less direct pathways). Interconnections exist between these specific relay nuclei. The intralaminar and midline nuclei of the thalamus receive nonspecific inputs from all sensory modalities via collaterals from the specific nuclei as well as the reticular formation of the brainstem. The nonspecific nuclei discharge profusely to all cortical areas. In the course of our discussion of the EEG correlates of emotional behavior, we have already mentioned the importance of this nonspecific input to the cortex. Destruction of the thalamic nuclei in this chain results in a comatose condition; the organism is totally unresponsive to the sensory information that continues to reach the cortical projection areas via the intact specific sensory systems.

Clinical evidence. The thalamic region is particularly prone to vascular disturbances. Early interest in the thalamic contribution to the regulation of emotional behavior dates back to clinical observations of patients with vascular infarcts or tumors in this area. Only a few samples of the vast clinical literature can be cited here. One of the earliest reports was that of Kirilzev (1891), who described a patient suffering from complete unilateral loss of the ability to express emotion but without detectable deterioration of voluntary motor functions. Autopsy showed a tumor near the center of the left thalamus. Similar case histories have been presented by Wilson (1924, 1929), who also found patients with directly opposite symptoms. Emotional situations continued to evoke appropriate facial expressions in a number of cases of complete paralysis, presumably because of a direct thalamic control of emotional responses. Head (1920) described a number of cases with various thalamic lesions and concluded that the characteristic symptom of such damage was "a tendency to react excessively to all potentially affective stimuli." Dana (1921) has summarized the case histories of patients with thalamic lesions or tumors who showed uncontrollable fits of laughter and weeping. These reactions did not appear to be related to specific stimulus situations and often occurred without subjective emotional experience. After surveying the clinical literature, Dana concluded that the thalamus was in fact the "seat of emotions," anticipating Cannon's well-known statement of the thalamic theory of emotion.

The Cannon-Bard thalamic theory of emotion. This theory was first presented by Cannon in 1927. It was revised and defended against early criticism in 1931 (Cannon, 1931) and extended by Bard in 1934. Since this theory is based primarily on early clinical data and the results of decortication, we shall discuss it before considering some of the more recent experimental evidence.

Cannon suggested that incoming sensory impulses receive "an emotional *quale*" in passing through the thalamus. In the normal state emotion is neither expressed nor experienced because of continuous inhibition of the thalamic mechanism by the cortex. Such inhibition can be removed by the arrival of emotion-provoking sensory impulses at the cortex. When this occurs, impulses are released by the thalamus and proceed caudally over somatic as well as autonomic motor nerves to give rise to emotional behavior. Simultaneously, the thalamus discharges impulses to the cortex to initiate the experience of emotion. A more detailed appreciation of the sequence of events can be gained from reference to Figure 9.18. A sensory receptor (R) is excited by an external stimulus and initiates impulses to the thalamic nuclei. Very strong stimuli may override cortical inhibition and directly activate thalamic mechanisms. These then discharge via hypothalamic viscera-motor centers in path 2 and send impulses that mediate an appreciation

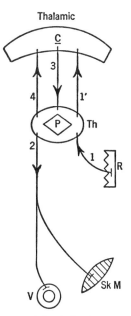

Fig. 9.18 Diagram of the thalamic theory of emotion. R, receptor; C, cerebral cortex; V, viscus; Sk M, skeletal muscle; Th, thalamus; P, pattern. The connecting lines represent nerve paths; the directions of impulses are indicated by arrows. Corticothalamic path 3 is inhibitory in function. (From Cannon, 1931.)

of this response to the cortex via path 4. This circuit is presumably involved in the startle reaction, which may be considered a primitive emotional reaction. Immediate and innate emotional reactions to external stimuli, such as the fear response of a naive monkey to a snake, also depend on this circuit. More commonly, sensory impulses cannot directly disinhibit the thalamic mechanisms, but travel on to the cortex via path 1'. Here they may invoke conditioned responses which release cortical inhibition of the thalamus via path 3 and give rise to thalamic discharge via paths 2 and 4.

The thalamic theory of emotion has generated considerable interest and received wide acceptance in psychological circles. The notion of a primitive, subcortical center for emotion, held in check by higher cortical functions, is an appealing idea which fits rather nicely with other psychological speculation. Because of this face validity, Cannon's theory remains the most prominent theory of emotion in spite of serious objections which have been raised against some of the basic assumptions.

The first of these objections concerns the emotional behavior of decorticate animals, which represents the principal experimental support for Cannon's theory. Far from corroborating the notion that the thalamus adds the "emotional quale" to sensory input, decortication studies demonstrate that complete removal of the thalamus proper has no effect on the rage reactions of the decorticate animal. Emotional responses disappear only when the posterior and ventral portions of the *hypothalamus* are removed. If we agree that this is the structure Cannon referred to when he talked about the thalamus, the proposed circuit can no longer be accepted. The hypothalamus has neither the specific sensory input nor the sensory projections to the cortex that the thalamic theory requires. (We shall see presently how Papez has endeavored to circumvent these problems in his own theoretical approach.)

Cannon's hypothesis also cannot answer a number of other questions. If rage behavior were elicited by the release of thalamic mechanisms from cortical inhibition, removal of the source of this inhibition in the decorticate animal should evoke a *permanent* and continuous rage reaction. There is some evidence that rage responses can be elicited by stimuli that were previously neutral, but clearly not all stimuli evoke emotional behavior. It has even been suggested that the experimental situations employed to test the decorticated animal's reaction to such "neutral" stimuli as restraint may evoke comparable responses in normal animals. There may be little hypersensitivity or hyperexcitability that cannot be explained by tissue irritation resulting from the severing of sensory pathways.

Rage responses have been elicited by electrical stimulation of the hypothalamus (Hess, 1949, 1954), the cerebral cortex (Kaada et al., 1953; Rothfield and Harman, 1954), and even the cerebellum (Zanchetti and Zoccolini, 1954). It is difficult to account for these results if rage is assumed to be caused by the release of cortical inhibition.

Thalamic or hypothalamic lesions typically produce a change in the organism's emotional responsiveness, but Cannon's interpretations of these data have been criticized. Lashley (1938) suggested that these "changes in affectivity" may reflect changes in the intensity or quality of *sensation* produced by the irritation of sensory neurons anywhere along the classical sensory pathways; other workers have pointed out that almost all sensory, motor, and integrative pathways of the central nervous system relay in the thalamus, so that a behavioral response to lesions

or stimulations of this area is all but impossible to interpret. Cannon's hypothesis has nevertheless served an important function in drawing attention to this portion of the central nervous system. Later theories of emotional behavior, although they rely heavily on cortical integration and control, have continued to assign important *partial* regulatory functions to the diencephalic portion of the brainstem.

Experimental evidence. We have already considered the hypothalamic contribution to emotional behavior and shall now investigate the functions of specific thalamic nuclei. This problem is difficult because of the extensive sensory and motor projections of the thalamus. Lesions are rarely, if ever, confined to a specific nucleus, and we must always consider the possibility that neighboring areas may have been invaded. The problem is even worse when we consider the effects of electrical stimulation, for we have but incomplete knowledge about the parameters that determine spread of excitation. With these cautions in mind, some representative examples of the clinical and experimental literature may now be discussed.

Spiegel et al. (1940, 1951) have reported that lesions in the dorsomedial nuclei of the thalamus reduce the emotional hypersensitivity of some mental patients. Normal animals similarly show a general, though transitory, reduction of emotional reactivity following comparable lesions.

Masserman's study of neurotic behavior in animals suggests that the role of these nuclei is not as simple as Spiegel's results indicate. Masserman reported that lesions restricted to the dorsomedial nuclei may produce directly opposite results. That is, they increase irritability and aggressive behavior (Schreiner et al., 1953), although neurotic tendencies seem reduced or eliminated (Pechtel et al., 1955; Masserman and Pechtel, 1956).

A more or less pronounced and permanent reduction of emotional sensitivity following lesions in the anterior and intralaminar nuclei has been reported, but electrical stimulation of these structures does not seem to evoke a comparable increase in reactivity (Baird et al., 1951; Schreiner et al., 1953; Masserman and Pechtel, 1956). Electrical stimulation of the posterior nuclei, on the other hand, has been reported to evoke conditioned anxiety as well as offensive and defensive behavioral responses in both cats and monkeys (Delgado, 1955).

One of the persistent problems plaguing all experimental investigations of the role of thalamic mechanisms in emotion is the fact that the thalamus has important sensory functions. It is very difficult to identify behavioral effects that are specific to changes in the emotional capacity of the organism rather than a modification of sensory factors. Any decrease in emotional reactivity following thalamic ablations may be due to a specific or general change in sensory perception, even in the few cases when a direct effect on the thalamic mechanisms that mediate thalamic pain

(Bowsher, 1957) can be ruled out. Electrical stimulation may simulate excessive sensory input and give rise to rage behavior without any actual involvement of mechanisms specific to emotion.

THE ROLE OF THE CORTEX IN EMOTION

The early theories of emotion emphasized subcortical centers of integration, relegating to the cortex as a whole only sensory (James-Lange) or associative (Cannon-Bard) functions not peculiar to emotion. During the past 25 years it has

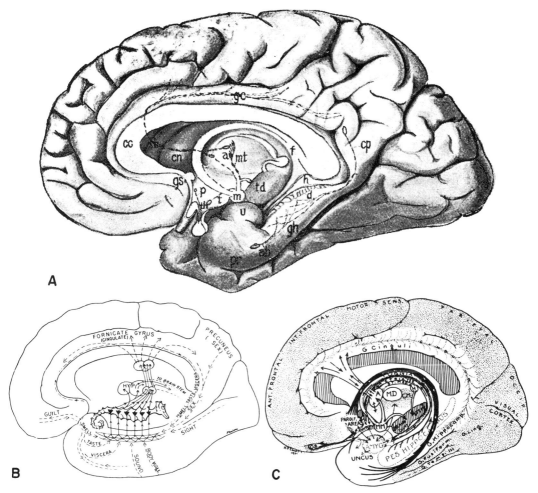

Fig. 9.19 The principal connections of the limbic system. A, according to the original proposal of Papez, 1937. *a*, anterior nucleus; *ab*, angular bundle; *cc*, corpus callosum; *cn*, caudate nucleus; *cp*, posterior cingulum; *d*, dentate gyrus; *f*, fornix; *gc*, cingulate gyrus; *gh*, hippocampal gyrus; *gs*, subcallosal gyrus; *h*, hippocampus nudus; *m*, mammillary body; *mt*, mammillothalamic tract; *p*, pars optica of the hypothalamus; *pr*, pyriform area; *sub*, subcallosal bundle; *t*, tuber cinereum; *td*, mammillotegmental tract; *th*, hypophyseal tract; *u*, uncus. B, according to MacLean, 1949. C, according to Penfield and Jasper, 1954. (From Russell, 1961.)

become increasingly evident that such concepts cannot account for the complexities of emotional behavior. Theoretical and research interest has shifted to cortical structures.

The subcortical mechanisms uncovered by previous research almost certainly *participate* in the regulation of emotion. It is logical, therefore, to begin the study of cortical functions with the areas of the cerebrum that have well-defined anatomical connections with such subcortical regulatory mechanisms. Precisely this reasoning led Papez (1937, 1939) to propose a mechanism of emotion that involved the hypothalamus, anterior thalamic nuclei, gyrus cinguli, hippocampus, and their interconnections. Before we consider this theory in some detail, it may be useful to review the anatomy and physiology of the cortical regions which appear most directly related to the regulation of emotional behavior. Pribram and Kruger's 1954 review of the "olfactory brain" presents a more thorough discussion of this material.

The Anatomy and Physiology of the Limbic System

On the basis of developmental and cytoarchitectonic considerations, the cortex has three relatively distinct subdivisions. Phylogenetically the youngest and cytoarchitecturally most complex portion is known as *isocortex* or *neocortex* (also *ectopallium* or *neopallium*). The neocortex is characterized by six distinct neuronal layers. It comprises most of the lateral and dorsal aspects of the cerebral hemispheres and appears to be concerned with associative as well as sensory and motor functions. Although undoubtedly involved in every emotional response, these functions are not peculiar to emotion and will not directly concern us here.

Next, the *juxtallocortex* (*mesocortex* or *paleopallium*) is phylogenetically older and structurally less complex (four to five layers). Included in this classification are the cingulate, retrosplenial, and hippocampal gyri, the island of Reil, the operculum, and the portion of the subcallosal and frontotemporal cortex that does not meet the criteria for neocortex.

The oldest and most primitive cortex contains only three layers; it is found in the olfactory bulb and tubercle, the area of the diagonal band of Broca, the septal area, the prepyriform and periamygdaloid complex, and the hippocampal formation (hippocampus, dentate gyrus, and hippocampal rudiment). It is called *allocortex* (*archipallium*).

Most allocortical and juxtallocortical structures are covered by neocortex and are not easily accessible. We therefore know a great deal about the functions of the latter but are only beginning to explore the older portions of the cerebral cortex. Most allocortical and some juxtallocortical structures have direct or indirect connections to the olfactory bulb. Until recently, this part of the brain was believed to serve only olfactory functions and was referred to as the "olfactory brain" or "rhinencephalon."

MacLean (1949) has suggested the term "visceral brain" in recognition of the fact that the cortical representations of autonomic responses are located in allo- and juxtallocortical structures rather than in the neocortex.

Some confusion is created by the lack of agreement about the precise limits of these conceptual units. Various cortical and subcortical structures have at one time or another been included on the basis of anatomical or functional connections, and these terms are all but meaningless unless a detailed list of structures is supplied to define the concept.

It may be profitable to avoid terminology based on speculations about common functional properties; instead, we shall return to Broca's (1878) nomenclature which is based entirely on anatomical considerations. Broca suggested the term *grand lobe limbique* (or *limbic lobe*) for the region of the brain that surrounds the hilus of the hemisphere (*le limbe de l'hémisphère*). The original definition of this term included (1) the olfactory tubercle (anterior perforated substance in primates), (2) the prepyriform cortex (uncus in man), (3) the diagonal band of Broca, (4) the cortical portion of the septal region, (5) the hippocampal rudiment and hippocampus, including the subiculum and fascia dentata, (6) the subcallosal gyrus, and (7) the cingulate and retrosplenial area.

More recently, the definition of the *limbic system* has been extended to include frontal granular and entorhinal cortex and now essentially encompasses all allocortical and juxtallocortical portions of the cerebrum. Various subcortical structures that do not meet the criteria for cortex (caudate, hypothalamic, and thalamic areas) have also at times been included largely on the basis of extensive reciprocal connections. These extensions of the definition tend to confuse the picture, and we shall restrict the limbic system to cortical structures for the purpose of our discussion.

Anatomical and functional considerations suggest one important exception to this rule. The amygdaloid complex does not meet the criteria for cortex. However, this group of nuclei, commonly divided into a basolateral and a corticomedial group, is located in the temporal lobe of the cerebrum and has afferent connections primarily with other portions of the limbic cortex. It will be convenient to treat the amygdala as part of the limbic system rather than as a separate, subcortical entity.

Now that we have arrived at a working definition of the structures to be included in our discussion, let us return to functional considerations. Until recently, most of the limbic system was believed to be concerned primarily with olfaction. This assumption rested on known anatomical connections with the olfactory bulb but derived most of its conviction from studies of comparative and ontogenetic morphology. These studies demonstrated that in primitive, macrosmatic vertebrates most or all of the cerebrum consists of allocortex or juxtallocortex, and that the sense of smell is of much greater importance in these species than it is in higher vertebrates. Recent investigations have shown, however, that the olfactory functions are not nearly so widely represented as had previously been assumed and that the olfactory projections may involve many regulatory functions in addition to the simple sensation of olfactory stimuli.

On the basis of extensive data from the fields of experimental and ontogenetic histology as well as electrographic and axonographic anatomy, Pribram and Kruger (1954) suggested a classification of the structures which we have included in our definition of the limbic system into three distinct systems.

The first of these receives direct afferent connections from the olfactory bulb and includes the olfactory tubercle, area of the diagonal band, prepyriform cortex, and corticomedial nuclei of the amygdala. At least some of the functions of this system presumably relate to olfaction.

The second system is defined by the fact that it receives direct connections from the first (but not from the olfactory bulb); it includes subcallosal and frontotemporal juxtallocortex, the septal region, and the basolateral nuclei of the amygdala.

The third system receives afferent connections from the second (but not from the first or the olfactory bulb). It contains entorhinal cortex, the retrosplenial and cingulate gyri, and the hippocampal formation (including the subiculum and fascia dentata).

Each of these systems is abundantly interconnected, and the second and third have extensive connections with the anterior and midline nuclei of the thalamus and with many hypothalamic regions.

On the afferent side, evoked potentials can be recorded from each of these systems following the presentation of an olfactory stimulus. However, some structures in each of the three systems also respond to gustatory, tactile, visual, and auditory stimuli (Gerard et al., 1936; Robinson and Lennox, 1951; MacLean et al., 1952), suggesting that these projections may serve other than primary sensory functions.

On the efferent side, various autonomic responses and many diffuse somatic motor reactions have been elicited from each of the three systems (Smith, 1945; Kremer, 1947; Kaada, 1951; Gastaut, 1952). In contrast to the discrete organization and somatotopic localization of isocortical efferent functions, the allocortical and juxtallocortical control of both smooth and striated muscle is diffuse and poorly localized.

Electrical stimulation spreads excitation to extensive portions of the limbic system and, with stronger stimuli, even to the rest of the cerebral cortex (Jung, 1949; Kaada, 1951). Such far-ranging spread of the effects of local stimulation is almost never observed in the neocortex and may be an important clue to the functional organization of the limbic system. Also of interest is the fact that recruiting responses can be observed in the intralaminal and midline nuclei of the thalamus following electrical stimulation of many limbic system structures (Morison and Dempsey, 1942; Jasper, 1949; Jasper and Ajmone-Marsan, 1950; French and Magoun, 1952; Starzl and Whitlock, 1952).

Behavioral evidence confirms the impression gained from these anatomical and neurophysiological studies. Much of the olfactory brain does not seem to be essential to olfaction. Swann (1934, 1935), for instance, found that olfactory discrimination was essentially unaffected by lesions of the medial and lateral olfactory stria, the septal region, the prepyriform cortex, the hippocampal formation, or the amygdaloid nuclei. Only resection of the olfactory bulb itself or damage to the intermediate olfactory stria impaired discrimination behavior signficantly. Brown and Ghiselli (1938) similarly reported that large lesions of subcortical structures which are associated with the limbic system failed to affect olfactory discrimination habits. Comparable results were obtained by Lashley and Sperry (1943) following resection of the radiations of the anterior thalamic nuclei to the cingulate cortex.

Allen (1940, 1941) has reported that massive lesions of the amygdala, pyriform cortex, or hippocampal formation did not affect a simple olfactory discrimination or a complex conditioned avoidance response to olfactory stimuli. Only a negative conditioned response (i.e., *not* to respond to a particular stimulus) was impaired by these lesions, and this result might be due to a variety of effects on other than olfactory functions.

The results of these experiments do not support the contention that any structure other than the olfactory bulb itself is *essential* to olfaction. Other parts of the limbic system may, however, contribute to olfactory function in the normal animal. In other sensory modalities the primary cortical projection areas must be destroyed *completely* before deficits in sensory discrimination can be demonstrated (Harlow, 1939; Ruch et al., 1938; Evarts, 1942; Bagshaw and Pribram, 1953). Even the first system of the olfactory brain has not been completely destroyed in any of these studies.

Papez's Theory of Emotion

The first cortical theories of emotion were based primarily on the intimate anatomical relationship between thalamic and hypothalamic centers which seem to be involved in the regulation of emotional behavior and certain cortical structures. Little experimental evidence for a direct relationship between structures and emotion was available. It seems appropriate, therefore, to consider Papez's contribution (as well as MacLean's more recent extension of it) in the light of these data and postpone a discussion of the more recent experimental work which relates to it.

Papez's theory (1937, 1939) deserves special attention because it represents the first organized attempt to delineate *specific* cortical mechanisms which may participate in the regulation of emotion. Herrick had suggested in 1933 that the limbic system might influence "the internal apparatus of general bodily attitude, disposition, and affective tone," but this rather nonspecific suggestion can hardly be called a theory of emotion. Papez was greatly influenced by Bard's experiments demonstrating the importance of hypothalamic mechanisms in rage behavior, and he was convinced that the *expression* of emotion depended entirely on the integrative action of the hypothalamus. He suggested, however, that emotional *expression* and emotional *experience* may be dis-

sociated phenomena, and that the subjective experience of emotion requires participation of the cortex.

The heart of Papez's theory can best be stated in his own words:

> The cortex of the cingular gyrus may be looked upon as the receptive region for the experiencing of emotion as the result of impulses coming from the hypothalamic region, in the same way as the *area striata* is considered the receptive cortex for photic excitations coming from the retina. Radiation of the emotive process from the *gyrus cinguli* to other regions in the cerebral cortex would add emotional coloring to psychic processes occurring elsewhere.

Reference to Figure 9.20 will clarify the proposed circuit. Papez suggested that there are primitive sensory centers in the subthalamus (pars ventralis of the lateral and medial geniculate body, the nucleus praegeniculatus, the reticular nucleus, and the nucleus of the mammillary peduncle).

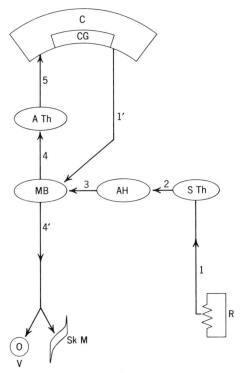

Fig. 9.20 Diagram of the Papez cortical theory of emotion. R, sensory receptor; S Th, subthalamic sensory receiving centers; AH, anterior and medial hypothalamus; MB, mammillary bodies; A Th, anterior nuclei of thalamus; CG, cingulate gyrus; C, cortex; V, viscera; Sk M, skeletal muscles.

These relay stations are believed to receive afferents from the optic tract, the acoustic nerve, the spinothalamic and trigeminothalamic tracts, and the medial lemniscus. Papez believed that from these nuclei the sensory information may be relayed via diffuse fiber connections to the anterior and medial portions of the hypothalamus which "regulate visceral activities and emotional expression." From here, the information is projected to the mammillary bodies which also gather additional afferent input from the cortex via the medial forebrain bundle, the fornix, and the mammillary peduncle. This cortical input (path l') allows for the excitation of hypothalamic mechanisms by "psychic activity" ("imagination," "memory," and "thought") which is believed to originate in the hippocampal formation. The composite pattern of hypothalamic activity is then transferred from the mammillary bodies via the mammillothalamic tract to the anterior nuclei of the thalamus; these nuclei relay the impulses via the medial thalamocortical radiations to the cortex of the cingulate gyrus which gives rise to the appropriate emotional experience.

Papez further suggested that additional afferent impulses may reach the cortex (lateral and dorsal isocortex) via the internal capsule (the "stream of perceiving"). A third system is thought to relay impulses of "a more global nature" from the dorsomedial nuclei of the thalamus to the frontal lobes and to serve "the global organization of the processes of thinking and comprehending" which are presumably part of any subjective emotional reaction. Papez (1939) emphasized that these three systems must "be combined in the cortex to yield integral psychological products."

Papez's theory has not received much attention in psychological circles, partly because his interesting speculations were not supported by behavioral data. The role of the hippocampus, for instance, was inferred from the fact that the tissue deformation (Negri bodies) which accompanies rabies or hydrophobia (the symptomatology of which includes severe emotional upset), is found only in the hippocampus and cerebellum. The cingulate gyrus owed its position of eminence to clinical reports from patients suffering with tumors of the corpus callosum believed to encroach upon the cingulate gyrus. (The list of clinical symptoms also includes memory defects, drowsiness, delirium, and disorientation in time and space—to name only a few—and it is difficult for the layman to see why emotional disturbances in particular should be referred to the cingulate

region. Additional damage to either frontal or parietal lobes or both was present in all the cases cited, making it even more doubtful that any specific assignment of function can be derived from these data.)

Similarly inadequate is the behavioral evidence used to relate the mammillary bodies and anterior thalamic nuclei to emotional behavior. Papez referred to experiments (Ranson, 1934) which demonstrated that lesions in the region of the mammillary bodies produce drowsiness and somnolence and that animals with such lesions tend to be particularly "tame and tractable." The role of the anterior nuclei of the thalamus is inferred from clinical evidence of spontaneous laughter and weeping following tumor growth or vascular damage.

Most of the suggested anatomical connections exist and may, in fact, be functionally related to the central regulation of emotional behavior. The most important aspect of Papez's theory (and a crucial point in the hypotheses of Cannon and Bard) has, however, not been supported by recent anatomical and electrophysiological studies. The subthalamic nuclei may receive some sensory fibers from some classical pathways, but it appears unlikely that all sensory modalities feed into this subthalamic system; it is improbable that sufficient information could be carried by the few collaterals that have been demonstrated to satisfy Papez's theory, which requires a complete and detailed interpretation of the total sensory input at this level. A major sensory receiving area certainly does not exist in this part of the brain.

We cannot accept the details of Papez's theory, but we are greatly indebted to him for originating a valuable and fruitful approach. His ideas stirred up theoretical as well as experimental interest and controversy in neurophysiological and neurological circles and is responsible for much of the subsequent investigation of the limbic system. In 1949, Paul MacLean re-examined Papez's notions on the basis of more recent anatomical, physiological, and behavioral evidence and proposed a number of important revisions.

MacLean's Theory of Emotion

MacLean agreed with Papez's basic premise that the hypothalamus may be the effector mechanism of emotional expression and that "only the cerebral cortex is capable of appreciating all the various affective qualities of experience and combining them into such states of feeling as fear, anger, love, and hate" (Papez, 1937). MacLean

(1949) argued that these integrative processes must take place in the primitive allocortical and juxtallocortical portions of the cerebrum, not only because these have, as Papez pointed out, intimate reciprocal connections with subcortical systems known to participate in the regulation of emotional behavior, but also because they alone contain the cortical representation of visceral functions which are an integral part of the normal expression of emotion. Vasomotor, sudomotor, cardiac, and respiratory functions have little or no neocortical representation. They are, however, affected by stimulation or ablation of large portions of the limbic system (or "visceral brain" as this part of the cerebrum is called by MacLean for obvious reasons).

In primitive organisms much of the limbic system is concerned with olfaction. MacLean suggested that olfaction may be a "visceral sense" of supreme importance to primitive animals and may contribute to the regulation of all basic motivational needs. The sense of smell is essential in such diverse behaviors as obtaining food and detecting enemies or sexual partners. The more complex affective behavior of higher organisms may continue to be integrated by the same olfactory mechanisms, although the sense of smell no longer contributes proportionally. Support for this notion is found in the fact that many limbic system structures are proportionally larger in microsmatic and even anosmatic higher species than they are in more primitive macrosmatic organisms, although they no longer seem to serve the sense of smell.

MacLean emphasized in his hypothesis the role of the hippocampal formation and its close association with the amygdala. He suggested that the dentate and hippocampal gyri may have primarily sensory functions, receiving direct afferents from olfactory, gustatory, and visceral sources as well as projections from the classical sensory receiving areas of the lateral neocortex. The dentate gyrus is known to discharge directly to the motor components of the hippocampus proper. The hippocampal gyrus relays first in the subiculum and is also intimately associated with the amygdala.

MacLean suggested that the afferent connections of the amygdala may be predominantly parasympathetic and subserve such functions as feeding, digestion, elimination, and sleep. The hippocampal outflow, on the other hand, is thought to be predominantly sympathetic and to participate in the regulation of fight, flight, and arousal. As a whole, the hippocampal formation is believed to "provide the kind of analyzer that can derive universals from the particulars of experience and relate them symbolically in the experience of emotion."

MacLean departs from the views of Papez primarily in de-emphasizing the role of the cingulate gyrus. He stated that "in the light of subsequent experimental findings, Papez's delimination of this region in the experiencing of emotion strikes one today as a considerable *tour de force.*" In MacLean's own theory, it is the hippocampus, aided by the amygdaloid complex, that is most directly concerned with the subjective experience of emotion. He suggested that "the hippocampal gyrus may serve as affectoceptor cortex and the hippocampus as affectomotor cortex, somewhat analogous to the somatic sensory and motor gyri of the neocortex." The role of the cingulate gyrus in this theory appears to be that of a visceromotor center which integrates various autonomic and somatic motor responses and emotional experience. These mechanisms, MacLean writes, "suggest a possible explanation of how intense emotion could paralyze both thought and action."

MacLean's revision lacks the elegance and completeness of Papez's original theory. No attempt is made to follow explicitly the course of events from the reception of an emotion-provoking stimulus to the expression and experience of emotion, but this is in line with the experimental evidence that has accumulated since the late 1930's. The cortical mechanisms that participate in the regulation of emotion appear to be much more complex than Papez's theory suggested.

Subsequent developments have further complicated the problem. Apparently identical effects can result from the ablation or stimulation of very different areas of the limbic system, including many anatomically distinct structures. Although emotional disturbances can be demonstrated following resection of the hippocampal or amygdaloid connections, these deficits are certainly not so complete and general as one might expect from MacLean's theory. The same is true for the cingulate gyrus and other portions of the limbic system.

It appears today that most, if not all, of the allocortical and juxtallocortical structures are involved in the regulation of emotional behavior, and no single mechanism which mediates a particular class of responses such as rage or fear can be pointed out. Anatomically distinct structures in the cortex may contribute selective aspects of a general regulatory function which integrates specific subcortical mechanisms; this notion is elaborated in our discussion of more general theories of motivation.

Experimental Evidence for Cortical Mechanisms

Much experimental and clinical evidence for the participation of various limbic system structures in the regulation of emotion has accumulated over the past two decades. However, the influx of information has only emphasized the complexity of the problem; much remains to be done before we can begin to unravel the relationship between the numerous cortical mechanisms which appear to contribute to the cortical regulation of emotional behavior. Only some of the extensive and ever-growing literature in this field can be reviewed at the present time, and no theoretical scheme able to fit all data into a well-organized and comprehensive picture can be offered.

Lateral aspects of the limbic system. *Temporal lobe lesions.* One of the earliest and most influential investigations of the functional significance of the limbic system is the series of experiments which Klüver and Bucy (1937, 1938, 1939) reported almost 30 years ago. In these studies large portions of the temporal aspects of the cerebral hemispheres (involving the hippocampal formation, amygdala, and pyriform and frontotemporal cortex) were ablated. A bewildering variety of behavioral changes which appeared to be based on disturbances of an emotional or motivational nature were reported.

Normally aggressive and intractable rhesus monkeys became tame and friendly, showing neither fear nor anger. They seemed constantly active and compulsively mouthed everything in sight, including such objects as dirt, feces, nails, a burning match, or a hissing snake. The animals were markedly hypersexual and approached male and female monkeys indiscriminately. They masturbated constantly and attempted copulation with a variety of other species (cats, dogs, etc.). Klüver and Bucy (1939, p. 988) concluded that these animals behaved as if "certain properties of the objects, their being 'dangerous,' 'inedible,' or 'indifferent,' have suddenly become ineffective in determining visually guided actions."

Such sweeping changes in a variety of apparently unrelated emotional or motivational factors contrast sharply with the apparently specific regulation of these functions in a subcortical center. It might be argued that a discrete localization of specific functions may exist *within* the rather large areas affected by these lesions, but this does not seem to be a totally satisfactory explanation of the observed deficits. Such an interpretation is supported by the fact that different classes of motivational variables were differentially affected in these experiments. Sexual and appetitive behaviors appeared released or *increased,* but negative emotional responses (fear or rage) were strongly *reduced* or absent. Although much recent research has been devoted to this problem, the matter seems to be more complicated than the early investigators assumed.

Bard and Mountcastle (1948) and Bard (1950) investigated the cortical control of emotional behavior by means of successive ablations. First, all neocortical structures were removed, leaving allocortical and juxtallocortical portions of the cerebrum (i.e., the limbic system) and their subcortical connections intact. Such neodecorticated animals appeared remarkably tame, placid, and emotionally unresponsive. Even strong noxious stimulation failed to elicit attack, defense, or flight reactions. Additional removal of the amygdaloid complex or cingulate gyrus, or both, produced a striking increase in emotional reactivity. The authors suggested that these structures may normally exert a restraining influence on subcortical mechanisms, and that the effects of this inhibition may be particularly evident after excitatory influences from the neocortex are removed.

Rothfield and Harman (1954) confirmed the results of neodecortication and demonstrated that the hippocampal system may also participate in this inhibition of subcortical emotional mechanisms. Transection of the fornix (the major efferent outflow from the hippocampus) *after neodecortication* increased emotional reactivity much like extirpation of the amygdala or the cingulate gyrus. An interpretation of these results is complicated because discrete hippocampal lesions *in the intact animal* do not seem to have comparable effects. Bard and Mountcastle (1948) reported that such lesions appeared not to affect rage or anger, although they produced a slight increase in the response to pleasant stimuli.

The amygdaloid complex. Klüver and Bucy's results stimulated much interest in the lateral aspects of the limbic system; their studies were quickly followed by a number of investigations attempting to elucidate the contribution of restricted portions of the temporal lobe. Spiegel et al. (1940) reported that discrete lesions of the amygdaloid nuclei in the intact animal produced rage responses and a general increase in emotional reactivity. These results resemble those obtained with amygdaloid ablation in the neocorticate animal, but they are directly opposite those seen in the normal animal after larger lesions involving the amygdala.

Bard and Mountcastle (1948) and Bard (1950) reported a similar increase in emotional reactivity in cats after bilateral removal of the pyriform lobe

and amygdala. Six to eight weeks *after* the operation, these animals developed an increasing hypersensitivity to all stimulation and displayed vicious rage responses to previously neutral stimuli. It was suggested that the behavior of these animals may be identical to the sham rage of decorticate animals and may be related to a release of hypothalamic mechanisms from inhibitory influences which originate in the cingulate gyrus, hippocampal formation, and amygdala.

Bard and Mountcastle were unable to replicate

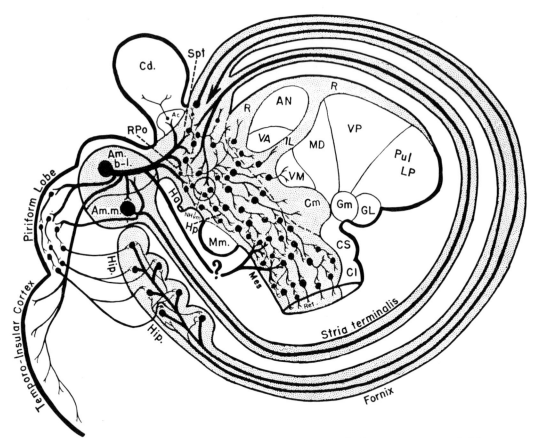

Fig. 9.21 The neuronal organization of the amygdaloid projection system as revealed by electrophysiological studies. The stippled area indicates subcortical integrative structures regulating "global" somato-autonomic responses, diffuse projection mechanisms, and limbic structures projecting into this subcortical system. Ac, anterior commissure; Am. b-1, basolateral subdivision of the amygdala; Am. m, corticomedial subdivision of the amygdala; AN, anterior thalamic nuclei; Cd, caudate nucleus; Cl, inferior colliculus; Cm, center median thalamic nucleus; CS, superior colliculus; GL, lateral geniculate body; Gm, medial geniculate body; Ha, anterior hypothalamus; Hip, hippocampus; Hp, posterior hypothalamus; IL, intralaminar thalamic nuclei; LP, lateral posterior thalamic nucleus; MD, medial dorsal thalamic nucleus; Mes, mesencephalon; Mm, mammillary body; NHvm, ventromedial hypothalamic nucleus; Pul, pulvinar; R, reticular thalamic nucleus; Ret, reticular formation; Rpo, preoptic area; Spt, septal region; VA, ventral anterior thalamic nucleus; VM, ventromedial thalamic nucleus; VP, ventral posterior thalamic nucleus. (From Gloor, 1955.)

these effects in monkeys, and Fuller et al. (1957; see also Fulton, 1951, p. 80) failed to obtain comparable results in dogs. Although one dog showed a conspicuous lowering of the rage threshold immediately after the operation, this behavior vanished after a few weeks. Six other dogs with similar lesions appeared to have *higher* thresholds for emotion-provoking stimuli and were generally indifferent and unresponsive. Socially dominant animals became submissive, presumably because the threshold for aggressive or defensive behavior was raised. Rosvold et al. (1954) observed similar changes in the social pecking order of monkeys following amygdalectomy, but stressed the fact that these animals appeared *more* aggressive in the single-cage situation. More recent experiments (Clemente et al., 1957; Pribram, 1962) have also suggested that damage to the amygdaloid complex may modify aggressiveness in "social" situations.

A number of investigations have failed to show increased emotional reactivity following amygdaloid and periamygdaloid lesions (Gastaut, 1952; Morin et al., 1952a, b; Schreiner and Kling, 1953, 1956). Some or all of the components of the "Klüver-Bucy syndrome" have generally been reported in these studies, but the symptoms were often much less pronounced and sometimes quite temporary.

The apparently contradictory results may be due to slight variations in the ablation procedure; these variations determine the differential involvement of specific aspects of the amygdaloid complex or surrounding entorhinal area. Within this region we may expect to find both inhibitory and excitatory mechanisms which coordinate their functions under normal circumstances but may be differentially affected by various lesions. Such an interpretation is supported by the fact that specific components of the Klüver-Bucy syndrome seem to depend on the precise nature of the lesion.

It is also possible that the rage behavior that may develop postsurgically after several days or even weeks may reflect a stimulating effect of irritative scar tissues. That the amygdaloid complex may be peculiarly susceptible to such irritations is suggested by the results of recent experiments (Grossman, 1963); these showed that a *single* injection of a cholinergic substance into the basal nuclei of the amygdaloid complex produced epileptiform seizures and striking behavioral and electrophysiological changes which persisted for months. Following the stimulation, the cats were vicious and hypersensitive to any form of stimulation. The animals attacked other cats and human handlers without apparent provocation or concern for safety. The electrophysiological response of the amygdaloid complex included seizure and spike activity as late as six months after the single cholinergic stimulation, and the behavioral changes persisted until the animals were sacrificed.

That these results are related to a stimulating effect on the amygdaloid mechanisms is suggested by the results of studies which observe the effects of electrical stimulation of the amygdala (Ursin, 1960). Rage and attack behavior as well as some defensive "fear-like" responses have been elicited from a variety of amygdaloid placements, supporting the hypothesis that the amygdala may normally exert a facilitatory influence on emotional behavior rather than an inhibitory one. Yet Egger and Flynn (1962) succeeded in suppressing the attack reactions normally elicited through hypothalamic stimulation by concurrently stimulating the amygdaloid area. Unless we assume that the amygdaloid stimulation may have set up a seizure focus and thus acted as a functional lesion, these results suggest that at least some aspects of the amygdaloid complex may exert inhibitory influences on the hypothalamic centers which integrate rage behavior.

An intimate relation between the effects of amygdaloid lesions and the activity of subcortical mechanisms was demonstarted by Schreiner and Kling. The placidity and tameness that resulted from bilateral amygdalectomy in their experiments disappeared abruptly after additional destruction of the ventromedial nuclei of the hypothalamus (Schreiner and Kling, 1953; Kling et al., 1960).

Anand and Brobeck (1951), on the other hand, reported that rats were highly aggressive and vicious following primary lesions of the ventromedial nuclei, and that this hyperreactivity disappeared completely after additional ablation of the amygdala. Brady (1958a) cites reports from C. T. Morgan's laboratory which indicate that secondary amygdala lesions have comparable effects on emotional hypersensitivity caused by primary septal lesions.

The hypersexual behavior characteristic of the Klüver-Bucy syndrome disappears following castration but can be restored by hormone substitution therapy, suggesting that hypothalamic mechanisms may also be involved in this phenomenon (Schreiner and Kling, 1954).

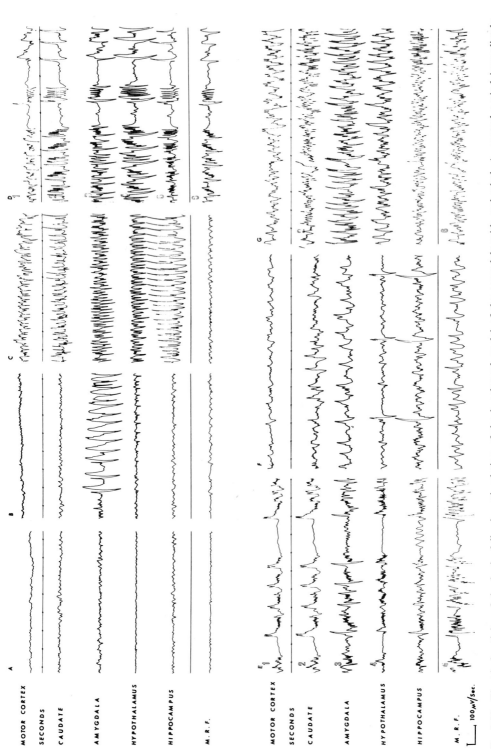

Fig. 9.22 Electrical activity of the brain following stimulation of the basolateral nuclei of the amygdala with carbachol. A, control period immediately preceding central stimulation; B, onset of spike discharges in the amygdaloid area, 3 min after bilateral administration of carbachol; C, records obtained during brief quiet period between overt motor seizures, 40 min after bilateral stimulation; D, electrical activity 4 hr after stimulation (no overt seizure activity); E, spike discharges alternating with brief periods of low electrical activity, 24 hr after stimulation (no overt seizure activity); F, EEG pattern five months after stimulation (animal vicious but otherwise normal); G, spike pattern, recorded within minutes after overt motor seizures, five months after amygdaloid stimulation. (From Grossman, 1963, © AAAS.)

A similarly close relation to hypothalamic mechanisms may be responsible for the amygdaloid influence on food and water intake. Small lesions or electrical or chemical stimulation of the amygdaloid complex markedly modify food and water intake in deprived animals (where the hypothalamic feeding and drinking centers are presumably active) but fail to elicit feeding or drinking in sated rats (Grossman and Grossman, 1963; Grossman, 1964a).

Changes in emotional reactivity have been studied in several formal behavioral test situations. Some of the earlier studies (Brady et al., 1954; Weiskrantz, 1956) suggested that amygdaloid lesions significantly retarded the acquisition of active avoidance responses but did not affect the performance of previously learned avoidance behavior. Horvath (1963) reported more recently that the retention as well as the acquisition of active avoidance responses were significantly impaired by small lesions in the basolateral portion of the amygdaloid complex. He noted that relatively simple one-way avoidance tasks which minimize the influence of competing response tendencies were less severely affected than the more customary two-way shuttle box type of response. Passive avoidance responses (i.e., the withholding of previously reinforced reactions) were least influenced by amygdaloid damage. Ursin (1965) subsequently demonstrated that the active avoidance deficit which results from amygdaloid lesions may be masked in the one-way avoidance situation by the apparently rewarding effects of handling. Marked deficits became apparent when the apparatus was modified to permit mechanical rearrangement of the compartments. Ursin also demonstrated an interesting difference between lateral and medial lesions. Laterally placed lesions in the amygdaloid complex interfered specifically with active avoidance responses; more medially placed lesions or damage to the efferents from the medial amygdala (the stria terminalis) produced apparently selective effects on passive avoidance.

Schwartzbaum and associates (Schwartzbaum, 1960, 1965; Thompson and Schwartzbaum, 1964; Schwartzbaum et al., 1964; Kellicutt and Schwartzbaum, 1963) have shown that amygdaloid lesions do not interfere with the acquisition or performance of simple discrimination behavior but block the formation of a conditioned emotional response and interfere with response suppression under nonreinforced conditions. Amygdalectomized animals also responded only very sluggishly and incompletely to changes in the reinforcement conditions, an effect which may reflect a deficit in the affective response to both positive and negative reinforcement. Possibly related to the reported impairment on passive avoidance behavior is the observation that even simple discrimination responses break down following amygdalectomy if the testing paradigm involves go/no-go conditions which require response inhibition on no-go trials (Brutkowski et al., 1960; Schwartzbaum et al., 1964).

King and Meyer (1958) demonstrated that amygdalectomy reduced the excessive rage responses of animals with previously placed septal lesions. Schwartzbaum and Gay (1966) have replicated these observations but found that the abnormal response perseveration of the septal animal was not affected by amygdalectomy.

The amygdala-hippocampal region. Smith (1950) found that lesions involving the hippocampal formation in addition to the amygdaloid complex produced tameness and docility in monkeys without necessarily eliciting other components of the Klüver-Bucy syndrome. Subsequent investigations of the hippocampal-amygdaloid region (Thompson and Walker, 1951; Walker et al., 1953) have confirmed the findings of Smith. Bilateral lesions of these structures in the monkey produce a temporary (five to six months) lowering of emotional reactivity. Although animals maintain the ability to respond appropriately to rage or fear-provoking stimuli, the intensity of stimulation has to be significantly greater than normal to elicit overt signs of rage or fear. These monkeys showed no other detectable deficit except a slight *decrease* in sexual activity, a sharp contrast to the *hyper*sexuality normally observed with amygdaloid lesions. One possible explanation of this result may be the fact that drowsiness and apathy are often seen in animals with temporal lobe lesions (Poirier, 1952). These effects may have been superimposed on other components of the temporal lobe syndrome.

Mishkin (1954) and Mishkin and Pribram (1954) report that bilateral lesions of the rostral portions of the temporal lobe (including the amygdala and rostral portion of the hippocampus) in baboons and monkeys produce many, if not all, of the symptoms characteristic of the Klüver-Bucy syndrome; however, the effects appeared less pronounced and were quite temporary in some cases.

The hippocampus. Electrical and chemical stimulation of various portions of the hippo-

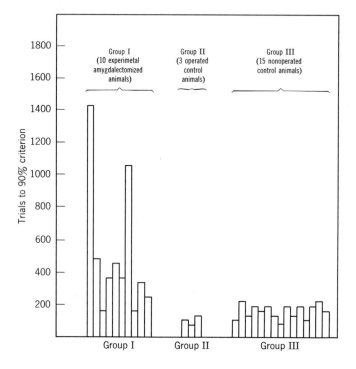

Fig. 9.23 The effect of rhinencephalic injury on the acquisition of a conditioned avoidance response. (From Brady et al., 1954.)

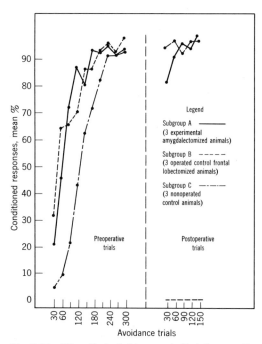

Fig. 9.24 The effect of rhinencephalic injury on the retention of a conditioned avoidance response. (From Brady et al., 1954.)

campus appears to facilitate or elicit "emotional" responses as well as individual autonomic reactions similar to those commonly seen in normal emotional behavior. MacLean (1954, 1957) has reported pleasure reactions in cats following chemical or electrical stimulation of the hippocampus. This effect may be the result of stimulation-induced seizure activity and may reflect the effects of a functional lesion. This interpretation is supported by Bard and Mountcastle's observation of similar enhanced pleasure reactions following bilateral hippocampal ablations; more recent stimulation studies have generally demonstrated aversive effects. MacLean and Delgado (1953) earlier observed that cholinergic stimulation of the rostral hippocampus facilitated attack responses to mildly noxious stimulation and that electrical stimulation elicited such emotional reactions as growling and defensive pawing. Similar observations have been reported by Kaada et al. (1953) following electrical stimulation of the hippocampus, fimbria, and hippocampal gyrus. Naquet (1954) has reported fully developed rage reactions to stimulation of the anterior (but not posterior) hippocampus.

MacLean and Delgado (1953) also observed such autonomic reactions as respiratory slowing, pupillary dilatation, and salivation during and immediately after hippocampal stimulation. Similar observations have been reported by Kaada et al. (1953) and others.

The hippocampus also exerts important influences on hormonal mechanisms which may affect emotional behavior. Fendler et al. (1961) have reported a large (up to 300%) increase in ACTH secretion following hippocampal lesions, and Endroczi et al. (1959) reported that electrical stimulation of the hippocampus reduced the ACTH level in spite of concurrent application of stressor stimuli.

The effects of hippocampal lesions on emotional behavior have been studied extensively in various experimental situations. On the purely observational level, Rothfield and Harman (1954) reported excessive emotional reactions to normal handling following transection of the fornix (which carries many of the efferents from the hippocampus), even in animals that were almost totally unresponsive to noxious stimulation as a result of neocortical damage. These earlier observations receive some support from the Orbach et al. (1960) report of marked and chronic ferocity in a monkey with bilateral hippocampal lesions; however, there is no scarcity of conflicting evidence. For instance, Fuller et al. (1957) reported that hippocampal lesions produced a loss of social dominance in the dog, whereas Mirsky (1960) could detect no change in social ranking in the monkey, although the animals appeared to be less fearful of man after hippocampal damage.

The results of more formal behavioral experiments can best be discussed under two headings: experiments dealing with active avoidance responses which require some overt response from the animal if it is to avoid or escape electric shock, and experiments dealing with passive avoidance (or approach-avoidance conflict behavior) which requires that the animal withhold a food-rewarded response in order to avoid punishment. (The response suppression reported during the conditioned emotional response experiment fits into neither of these categories since it does not avoid the unconditioned stimulus.)

Pribram and Weiskrantz (1957) reported that hippocampal lesions which invaded the entorhinal area produced a significant decrement in the performance of a preoperatively acquired active avoidance response; such lesions prolonged the retraining required to reach the preoperative criterion but had no effect on experimental extinction. Thomas and Otis (1958a) similarly reported that rats with dorsal hippocampal lesions that invaded the cingulate area required reliably more

trials than normals or operated animals with neocortical damage to reach criterion performance in a shuttle box avoidance situation. However, Brady et al. (1954) reported that cats with hippocampal or cingulate lesions acquired a shuttle box avoidance habit as rapidly as controls; this finding has more recently been replicated by Hunt and Diamond (1957). The issue is further complicated by the report (Isaacson et al.,1961) that rats with hippocampal lesions acquired an active avoidance response (shuttle box) *faster* and showed more resistance to extinction than normal controls. Although it is possible that these results reflect the stimulating effects of an irritative lesion, the size of some of Isaacson's lesions (up to 90%) suggests that this explanation may not be very probable.

Electrical stimulation of the hippocampus has been reported to interfere with the performance of avoidance responses (Delgado et al., 1956), but recent studies by Flynn and Wasman suggest that this interference may be the result of motor rather than motivational or associative deficits (Flynn and Wasman, 1960).

The situation is apparently simpler when we turn to a discussion of the effects of hippocampal lesions on passive avoidance or approach-avoidance conflict behavior, although a number of problems remain to be clarified. Kimura (1958) reported that posterior hippocampal lesions produce faster postoperative extinction and interfere with the acquisition of passive avoidance responses. Isaacson and Wickelgren (1962) similarly found that animals with large hippocampal lesions could not learn to avoid a punished response. Teitelbaum and Milner (1963) have reported that rats with dorsal hippocampal lesions could not refrain from leaving a "safe" platform in the center of an electrified grid. Snyder and Isaacson (1965) have also reported selective passive avoidance deficits. Bureš et al. (1962) found impaired learning and complete loss of preoperatively acquired passive avoidance responses in still another test situation following the intraperitoneal injection of physostigmine; the injection was assumed, largely on the basis of electrophysiological evidence, to act on the hippocampus. Some discordant notes have been sounded in this apparent concert of opinion. Kimble (1963) reported that rats with posterior hippocampal lesions show the expected deficits in passive avoidance behavior, but he also noted that animals with comparable neocortical damage show a similar impairment.

Brady (1958a; Brady and Hunt, 1955) has reported that hippocampal lesions virtually eliminated a preoperatively acquired conditioned emotional response and made it "difficult, if not impossible" (1958, p. 217) to recondition the response. Thomas and Otis (1958) reported that rats with relatively large hippocampal lesions which invaded the cingulate cortex acquired a conditioned emotional response as readily as normal controls.

An interpretation of these effects is complicated by the fact that hippocampal lesions and stimulation also produce a variety of sensory, motor, motivational, and possibly associative effects which may influence the results observed in these tests. The effects of hippocampal damage on passive avoidance behavior, for instance, may be confounded by the sharp increase in locomotor activity which has been reported in a number of studies (Kimble, 1963; Karmos and Grastyan, 1962; Teitelbaum and Milner, 1963), or by an apparently increased motivation for food and water (Ehrlich, 1963; Fuller et al., 1957; Peretz, 1963). The latter factor may, of course, also influence the animals' behavior in the conditioned emotional response situation. All the behavioral experiments are subject to a possibly confounding effect of hippocampal lesions on associative mechanisms. There are numerous clinical observations of a marked loss of recent memory in man following hippocampal injury (Penfield and Milner, 1958; Victor et al., 1961). Possibly related deficits have been seen in animals, particularly in delayed-response situations which may depend most heavily on recent memory functions (Stepien et al., 1960; Karmos and Grastyán, 1962; Pribram et al., 1962; Roberts et al., 1962). Finally, the extensive anatomical and functional connections between the hippocampus and the midbrain and thalamic reticular formation, as well as some recent observations (Grossman and Mountford, 1964) of general depressive effects of chemical interference with hippocampal functions, suggest that nonspecific motivational influences must also be considered. Much more selective techniques of stimulation and ablation are needed before we can hope to unravel this complicated matter.

The behavioral effects of at least some types of hippocampal lesions may be related to the apparently excessive tendency of hippocampal animals to perseverate in previously rewarded behavior after the experimental situation has been changed to nonreward. Response perseveration has been demonstrated under several reinforcement conditions (Ellen and Wilson, 1963; Clark

and Isaacson, 1965; Jarrard, 1965; Schmaltz and Isaacson, 1966) and may account for the inhibitory effect of hippocampal lesions on position reversal habits (Lash, 1964) and alternation habits (Pribram et al., 1962; Mahut and Cordeau, 1963).

An interpretation of the role of hippocampal mechanisms in the regulation of emotional behavior is complicated by the fact that few experiments have succeeded in restricting the lesions to the hippocampus proper. Significant damage to neighboring structures has been reported in most of the studies, and this raises the possibility of confounding influences. Some or all of the behavioral deficits seen after hippocampal damage may be related to (1) an interruption of the stria terminalis (Ursin, 1965, has shown that stria lesions result in passive avoidance deficits and response perseveration); (2) damage to the tail of the caudate nucleus (Fox et al., 1964, demonstrated deficits in passive avoidance behavior following lesions in the head of the caudate nucleus); or (3) lesions in the insular cortex (Kaada et al., 1962, and Paré and Dumas, 1965, have shown passive avoidance deficits and response perseveration following even limited damage to this portion of the cortex).

The frontotemporal cortex. Fulton and his associates (Fulton et al., 1949; Fulton, 1951; Pribram et al., 1952; Pribram and Bagshaw, 1953) have studied the role of the frontotemporal juxtallocortex in some detail. Bilateral ablation of this region produced many of the emotional disturbances characteristic of the Klüver-Bucy syndrome; the resultant tameness, docility, and general lowering of the animals' emotional responsiveness were particularly pronounced. Abnormal oral tendencies were less frequently encountered. Hypersexuality was never seen and may represent the only purely amygdaloid contribution to this syndrome.

Summary. In spite of some remaining contradictions, the majority of the available evidence suggests that restricted lesions within a rather large portion of the lateral limbic system (i.e., pyriform cortex, amygdaloid complex, and hippocampal formation) reduce emotional reactivity, especially with respect to fear and rage.

These observations have prompted a clinical application to cases of extreme hyperemotionality (Obrador, 1947; Oldham, 1953; Sawa et al., 1954; Terzian and Dalle Ore, 1955). None of these subjects has, so far, come to autopsy, so we cannot evaluate the extent of the damage to critical struc-

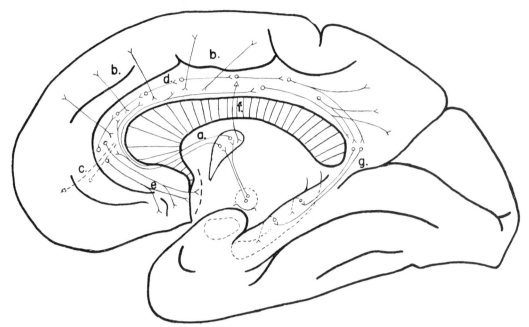

Fig. 9.25 Afferent and efferent connections of the cingulate cortex. *a*, anterior thalamic radiations to areas 24 and 23; *b*, intracortical connections between area 24 and areas 6, 8, and 9; *c*, projection of the granular prefrontal cortex into *d*, the anterior cingulum; *e*, projection to septal and orbital regions from the precallosal cingulate cortex; *f*, projection from the middle supracallosal cingulate cortex to the anterior nucleus; *g*, posterior cingulum from the retrosplenial cingulate cortex to the presubiculum. (From Russell, 1961.)

tures; nevertheless, the results have been far from encouraging. "Emotional indifference" of various extents has been reported in all cases, but some of the other effects observed in the laboratory also appear. Patients with such lesions tend to show pronounced hypersexuality, memory deficits, and voracious appetites. Their general condition can hardly be said to have improved.

The cingulate gyrus. Removal of the cingulate gyrus in the neodecorticate animal produces a rise in emotional responsiveness which is similar to that seen after ablation of the amygdala and hippocampus. Amygdalectomy sharply *lowers* the rage or fear threshold in normal animals; cingulectomy produces similar results, although there may be important differences between the specific behavioral deficits that warrant some discussion.

Smith (1944) first described a loss of fear and aggressiveness in cingulectomized animals. Ward (1948) confirmed this finding and suggested that the animals appeared to have lost their "social conscience." He described the behavior of his cingulectomized monkeys as follows:

Such an animal shows no grooming behavior or acts of affection toward its companions. In fact, it treats them as it treats all inanimate objects and will walk on them, bump into them if they happen to be in the way and will even sit on them. It will openly eat food in the hand of a companion without being prepared to do battle and appears surprised when it is rebuffed. Such an animal never shows actual hostility to its fellows. It never fights nor tries to escape when removed from a cage (Ward, 1948, p. 440).

A comparable reduction of emotional responsiveness has been reported by Bard and Mountcastle (1948).

Subsequent investigators (Glees et al., 1950; Pribram and Fulton, 1954) have reported that these behavioral changes tend to be short-lived, disappearing within six weeks to three months. Fulton (1951) reports that cingulectomized animals show no detectable intellectual deficits or abnormal sexual behavior. Animals trained in a visual discrimination habit continued to perform the response as before the operation. However, if the food reward was snatched from under the animal's nose after a correct response, it showed much less frustrational behavior than normal monkeys and willingly returned to the test situation immediately after the frustrating experience.

Many investigations of the effects of restricted cingulate lesions on emotional behavior (Kennard, 1955; Pechtel et al., 1955) have reported an immediate and often transient increase in emotionality following bilateral damage. The animals tend to be very aggressive and vicious immediately after the operation, presumably because of the removal of some inhibitory influence on hypothalamic mechanisms (Brutkowski, 1964).

Because the side effects of cingulate lesions are apparently much less undesirable than those accompanying amygdalectomies, the former procedure has been employed frequently in clinical cases of anxiety neuroses and obsessions (Le Beau and Pecker, 1950, Cairns, 1950, and Livingston, 1951, as cited by Fulton, 1951). Fulton has recommended this operation on the basis of over 100 case histories which indicated improvement without severe intellectual deficit (Fulton, 1951).

It must be remembered, however, that the surgical approach to these structures is difficult. The size and the precise location of cingulate lesions are often poorly controlled and can be assessed only when histological data become available. This information has not been acquired in most instances, and final evaluation of most clinical case histories must be deferred. We should also bear in mind that the behavioral testing procedures commonly employed in clinical situations are inadequate. Tests of emotional responsiveness are especially crude and unreliable and may be influenced by the expectations of the tester. Case histories may nevertheless be a source of valuable information, because changes in complex intellectual functions that go unnoticed in animal experiments may be observed; however, it is important to keep the limitations of this information in mind.

The exact nature of the behavioral deficits which result from discrete lesions in the cingulate gyrus has become the focus of much experimental effort since Kaada reported in 1951 that electrical stimulation of the cingulate gyrus resulted in a general response facilitation whereas stimulation of the subcallosal septal area produced a general inhibitory effect on behavior.

McCleary (1961) and Lubar (1964) subsequently demonstrated that animals with cingular lesions perform a passive avoidance response reliably *better* than normals, although their behavior in an active avoidance situation is clearly impaired. At least some of the facilitatory effects of cingular lesions are duplicated by damage to the cingulum bundle or mammillothalamic tract which are afferent to the facilitatory area of the cingulate gyrus proper (Thomas and Slotnick, 1962; Thomas et al., 1963; Krieckhaus, 1964).

Dahl et al. (1962) and Ploog and MacLean (1963) have failed to observe active avoidance deficits following mammillothalamic tract lesions. Krieckhaus (1964) has suggested that this failure may be the result of procedural differences (the two-way avoidance situations may, in fact, have appeared as one-way tests to the subjects). Mammillothalamic lesions produce behavioral deficits which may not be identical to those seen after cingulate gyrus damage. Cats with bilateral lesions transecting the mammillothalamic tracts show a performance impairment in two-way active avoidance situations that seems identical to the impairment seen after cingulate damage. However, whereas cingulectomized animals clearly demonstrate this deficit during postoperative acquisition, the animals with mammillothalamic tract lesions show little or no impairment when trained after surgery (Moore, 1964; Thomas et al., 1963; Krieckhaus, 1964).

A recent experiment by Lubar and associates (1966) indicates that still other influences may be important for the response facilitation seen after cingulate lesions. Lubar et al. demonstrated that the most effective lesions were those that infringed on the white matter underneath the cingulate gyrus, and that marked active avoidance deficits could be produced by lesions limited to the posterolateral gyrus. An earlier study by Lubar (1964) demonstrated another peculiar feature of the cingulate lesion effect. Lubar found that even large cingulate lesions failed to affect the acquisition and performance of one-way active avoidance responses. Subsequent work by Lubar and Perachio (1965) has confirmed this finding; cingulectomized animals were markedly impaired on two-way (shuttle box) active avoidance but quite normal on a one-way active-avoidance task.

An interesting exception was reported by Peretz (1960) who found that moderately large cingulate lesions produced reliable active avoidance deficits even in a one-way avoidance situation. It is possible that this apparently contradictory finding was the result of handling. Unlike subsequent investigators, Peretz transferred his subjects manually from the safe to the shocked compartment between trials, thus possibly introducing an approach-avoidance conflict component which might have produced the unusual results.

Lubar's (1964) study also demonstrated that animals with combined lesions in the septal inhibitory and cingulate facilitatory area act essentially normal in passive avoidance situations suggesting an algebraic interaction of the two mechanisms.

Thomas and his associates (Thomas and Slotnick, 1962, 1963; Thomas et al., 1963; Krieckhaus, 1964) have interpreted the changes in avoidance behavior which result from damage to the cingulate gyrus or related structures as suggesting a more specific effect on an unconditioned crouching response to the painful shock which is used as the aversive stimulus in all the avoidance situations. Such "freezing" behavior is a common reaction to shock, and the response failure of the cingulectomized animal is, in fact, typically accompanied by increased crouching. We should not lose sight of the fact, however, that the crouching response may itself reflect a more general change in emotional reactivity or even a general response inhibition as McCleary (1961) suggests.

The septal region. It is difficult to distinguish between the portion of the "septal area" that meets the requirements for cortex and the nuclei that must be assigned to subcortical systems. A functional differentiation between cortical and subcortical mechanisms in this area of gradual transition has not yet been achieved. It appears more appropriate, therefore, to consider the contribution of the septal *region* without attempting to differentiate artificially between cortical and subcortical areas.

A number of workers (Fulton and Ingraham, 1929; Spiegel et al., 1940; Wheatley, 1944) have reported that lesions in the ventral portion of the septal area produce emotional hypersensitivity, viciousness, and exaggerated rage responses to normal handling. This phenomenon has been studied in detail by Brady and Nauta (1953, 1955; see also Brady, 1958a, b, 1960), and the results suggest (1) a significant increase in the magnitude of the rat's startle response to a loud auditory stimulus following septal (but neither habenular nor hippocampal) lesions, and (2) a significant increase in emotional reactivity as measured on a seven-point rating scale (resistance to handling or capture, urination and defecation, squealing, etc.).

Although a few investigators (Harrison and Lyon, 1957) have failed to replicate the septal

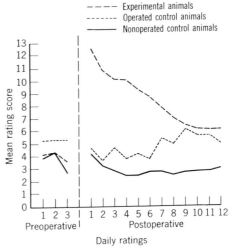

Fig. 9.26 Changes in emotional reactivity following septal lesions. (From Brady and Nauta, 1953.)

rage effect, most studies have agreed that bilateral septal lesions produce at least temporary viciousness and excessive reactivity to any form of stimulation (King, 1958; Hunt, 1957). It seems that the postoperative irritability disappears gradually with continued handling, so that the septal animal may be indistinguishable from normals only a few weeks after surgery. A study by Moore (1964) indicates that cats may be less prone to show overt changes in emotional reactivity than rats. Only about half of the lesioned cats in this study showed any sign of postoperative irritability.

Formal behavioral investigations of the effects of septal lesions have shown complex impairments which persist indefinitely and may affect behavior long after overt signs of septal rage have disappeared. Although some contradictory evidence must be taken into consideration, the basic pattern of behavioral changes is clear. Septal lesions improve performance during the acquisition of active avoidance behavior, interfere with the performance of preoperatively acquired active avoidance responses, and impair performance in all test situations in which appetitive responding must be suppressed.

Brady and Nauta (1953) reported a postoperative impairment in the performance of a conditioned emotional response in an operant (bar-pressing) situation but failed to find a comparable deficit in postoperative acquisition of the response suppression. Brady and Nauta (1955) could not confirm the earlier observations, but other investigators (Harvey et al., 1961) have replicated the

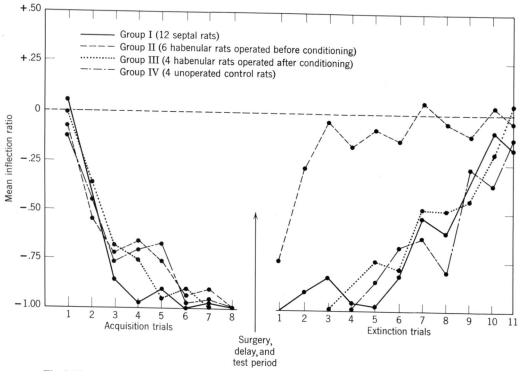

Fig. 9.27 Acquisition and extinction of the conditioned emotional response following septal or habenular lesions. (From Brady and Nauta, 1955.)

postoperative impairment in conditioned emotional response performance and have also reported marked inhibitory effects on the *acquisition* of conditioned emotional responses and the suppression of appetitive behavior by direct punishment. The apparent reduction of the effects of punishment has also been reported by Simmons and Thomas (1961).

Perseveration of appetitive behavior is seen in passive avoidance (or approach-avoidance conflict) situations in which the animal is asked to withhold a previously rewarded but now punished response. McCleary first demonstrated that cats with septal lesions have significant difficulty with this simple avoidance response. Several investigators have subsequently confirmed these observations (Kaada et al., 1962; Lubar, 1964; Zucker and McCleary, 1964).

The effects of septal lesions on active avoidance are complex and difficult to interpret. Tracy and Harrison (1956) reported that rats with septal lesions perform a preoperatively learned active avoidance response more poorly than normals. Similar postoperative deficits have been noted by McCleary et al. (1965), Rich and Thompson

(1965), and Moore (1964) in both cats and rats. Several investigators (Rich and Thompson, 1965; Moore, 1964) have also reported that septal animals were retarded in postoperative *acquisition* of active, two-way avoidance responses, but this appears to be an atypical finding which may be related to the size and/or location of the lesions in these studies. More commonly, it is reported that septal lesions facilitate the acquisition of two-way active avoidance habits (King, 1958; Fox et al., 1964). Septal damage seems to facilitate active avoidance behavior when the lesions are placed before the initial training but impairs the performance of the same avoidance response if the lesions are placed after training has been completed. The retention deficit may be related to an interference with associative mechanisms rather than motivational mechanisms. This hypothesis receives some circumstantial support from the rich interconnections of the septal region with hippocampal and thalamic projection systems that have been implicated in learning and retention processes. Experimental evidence for the suggested dual effects of septal lesions is not yet available.

The matter is further complicated by the fact that the performance of some types of active avoidance responses may be impaired following septal lesions even during acquisition. The most notable examples of such an apparent reversal of effects have been observed in one-way avoidance situations which require that an animal respond to a conditioned stimulus by jumping from a start compartment (which acquires conditioned stimulus properties) into a distinct safe compartment (which acquires secondary reward properties) (Kenyon, 1962; Vanderwolf, 1964; Kenyon and Krieckhaus, 1965a, b). Zucker (1965) has suggested that this impairment may be related to the septal animals' aversion to the handling required between trials in the typical one-way avoidance experiment. He found that septal lesions *improved* performance during the acquisition of a one-way avoidance habit if the apparatus was modified to avoid handling between trials.

Nielson et al. (1965) have reported that septal lesions interfered with the acquisition of still another type of avoidance habit (shock avoidance in a T-maze), but this finding might have been influenced by a procedural detail which is typical of the T-maze situation. The animals were rewarded for selecting the initially nonpreferred side of the maze; Zucker and McCleary (1964) have already shown that the position habit reversal required in this situation is itself impaired by septal damage.

Chemical stimulation studies (Grossman, 1964b) have shown that rats receiving cholinergic stimulation of the medial septal area before each daily training session failed to acquire a simple two-way avoidance response, although they promptly learned to perform the jumping response required to escape from the shock unconditioned stimulus. All experimental animals failed to respond to the conditioned stimulus in 240 trials, indicating a total inability to learn an emotional response to the conditioned stimulus. The same cholinergic stimulation interfered only slightly with a *previously acquired* lever-pressing avoidance response. Atropine (a cholinergic blocking agent which should mimic the effects of electrolytic lesions) improved the performance of the lever-pressing avoidance response. Cholinergic stimulation of the septal area also elicited drinking in sated animals and increased the water intake of deprived rats.

Although some of the details of the septal influence on behavior in aversive situations remain to be worked out, it seems certain that significant regulatory influences are disturbed by stimulation or damage to this portion of the brain. Not as clear is the nature of this influence. It has been assumed that the changes in avoidance behavior are related to the apparent emotional hypersensitivity which characterizes the septal animals at least for a few weeks after surgery (King, 1958), but this interpretation has been questioned by a number of observations. Marked changes in avoidance behavior can be recorded in animals that do not show any overt sign of postoperative irritability or septal rage. Furthermore, most investigations have continued behavioral testing for a sufficient postoperative interval to assure that overt signs of emotional hyperreactivity have worn off; yet the effects on avoidance behavior remain (Kenyon, 1962; Krieckhaus et al., 1964; Moore, 1964).

A related hypothesis suggests that the impaired performance of passive avoidance responses as well as the improvement in active avoidance habits may be due to a weakening of the crouching reflex to the electric shock (Krieckhaus et al., 1964; Kenyon and Krieckhaus, 1965a;b;). It seems unlikely that the septal area should be an integrative center for crouching reflexes per se. Crouching may, however, be a more sensitive index of emotional reactivity than gross inspection of an animals response to handling and may therefore correlate better with changes in avoidance behavior which are typical of the septal animal.

This hypothesis removes one of the objections to interpreting the septal lesion effects in terms of increased emotionality, but other questions remain. The performance deficits seen when septal lesions are placed after training may be caused by an interference with associate mechanisms. However, septal lesions also interfere with behavior in a characteristic fashion in a variety of appetitive test situations. Septal rats have significant difficulty learning an appropriate pattern of responding in various operant situations, the deficit always being in the direction of overresponding. The septal animals take longer to learn to distribute responses appropriately on fixed-interval schedules of reinforcement; they consistently overrespond on DRL (differential reinforcement of low rates of responding) schedules which reinforce only responses that follow a previous reward by some minimum interval (Ellen and Powell, 1962a, b; Ellen et al., 1964). Schwartzbaum et al. (1964) reported that septal lesions increased the rate of responding during nonreinforced conditions in a discriminated operant situation and retarded extinction of bar-pressing behavior. Septal lesions also increased the number of perseverative errors during acquisition of a simultaneous brightness discrimination. Zucker and McCleary (1964) similarly found that septal cats were deficient in reversing a simple position habit in a Wisconsin General Test Apparatus. Normal cats ceased responding when the choice of the previously correct side was suddenly non-reinforced; animals with septal lesions continued to respond to the incorrect side. It may be noteworthy that this deficit disappeared on subsequent reversals. On the basis of these and related observations, McCleary (McCleary, 1961; Zucker and McCleary, 1964; McCleary et al., 1965) suggested that the septal syndrome may reflect an increased tendency to perseverate because the mechanism which normally inhibits overt responses to nonreinforced or punished stimuli has been lost.

Still another hypothesis is suggested by the observation that septal lesions and chemical stimulation affect food and water intake and presumably modify the level of appetitive motivation in tests of passive avoidance or schedule-related timing behavior (Simmons and Thomas, 1961; Grossman, 1964b; Harvey and Hunt, 1965; Harvey et al., 1965). This hypothesis suggests that the septal area, like other aspects of the limbic system, may contain portions of regulatory mechanisms for most if not all motivational functions, and that the individual systems are not sufficiently distinct anatomically to permit selective damage by gross lesions. Although changes in appetitive drive states must be taken into consideration, several observations indicate that this interpretation cannot account for all the behavioral changes already reported. Zucker (1965) did not find an increase in daily food intake following septal lesions which reliably modified passive avoidance behavior. Kasper (1964, 1965) observed that continuous electrical stimulation of the septal area increased perseverative errors on a passive-avoidance task and interfered with the reversal of a position habit but did not change water intake. The chemical stimlation studies of Grossman (1964b) also argue against such an interpretation. Cholinergic stimulation interfered with active avoidance behavior but increased water consumption. Cholinergic blockade reduced water consumption but facilitated avoidance behavior.

Response perseveration appears to be the common element in most of the behavioral changes seen after septal damage, suggesting a change in the effectiveness of nonreinforcement and punishment. This interpretation accounts for the effects of septal lesions on passive avoidance, reversal learning, timing in operant conditioning situations, and the depression in active avoidance responding which has been seen in a number of experimental situations. It does not adequately account for the apparent facilitation of active avoidance learning which has been reported in some two-way situations.

I do not favor an interpretation of the reward-aversion effects elicited by electrical stimulation of the septal area (and other subcortical and cortical limbic system structures) in terms of general emotional changes such as pleasure, aversion, or general negative or positive affective reactions. However, the self-stimulation data can be so interpreted; the reader is referred to Chapter 10 for a more detailed discussion of these experiments.

The frontal lobes. The frontal lobes are made up primarily of neocortex (although frontal lobotomies and lobectomies almost invariably damage juxtallocortical structures) and hence cannot be considered an integral part of the limbic system as we have defined it. Experimental research and clinical data suggest, however, that at least some portions of the neocortex in this area may be in much closer anatomical and functional relation with the limbic system (as well as subcortical structures implicated in the regulation of emotional behavior) than with the more posterior aspects of the isocortical mantle. The frontal, granular portion of the cerebrum does not appear to have definite sensory or motor functions. The somewhat vague "association cortex" label found in most textbooks does little but conveniently hide our ignorance of the functional significance of the frontal lobes in behavior. The granular cortex of the frontal lobes receives a major part of the hypothalamic outflow to the cerebrum (via the periventricular fiber system, dorsomedial nuclei of the thalamus, and anterior thalamic radiations); it thus meets the principal criterion that has been used to assign a major role in the regulation of emotion to such limbic system structures as the cingulate gyrus.

Ferrier (1875) first described the effects of orbitofrontal ablations in monkeys. He reported that the removal of a rather large part of the brain seemed to have no effect on the organism's sensory or motor abilities, but that a decided change was produced in "the animals' character and disposition," in the direction of increased tameness and docility. Bianchi (1922) confirmed these findings and added the important observation that such lesions also seemed to interfere with memory. After extensive frontal ablations his monkeys appeared incapable of performing responses that were acquired postoperatively or of learning new ones. A more detailed analysis of these memory deficits suggests that the acquisition and retention of simple manipulatory or discriminatory habits may not be measurably affected by frontal lobe damage. More complex learned behavior patterns such as delayed reactions or tasks involving a temporal sequence of responses are significantly impaired.

Fulton and Jacobsen's (1935a, b) important observations gave rise to the use of frontal lobotomy in clinical practice. These workers reported that the frustrational responses of normal chimpanzees to nonreward (extinction) in a test situation disappeared completely after frontal lobe ablation. "Temper tantrums and anxiety behavior" vanished, and the animals appeared to forget quickly any reason for anger or disappointment. Fulton later reported that "the most ferocious specimens have been reduced to a state of friendly docility" (Fulton, 1949, 1951).

Moniz (1936) argued that the behavioral changes observed by Fulton and Jacobsen were precisely those needed to cure or alleviate many mental diseases characterized by irrational fears, anxiety states, and obsessional behavior. He proceeded to interrupt the frontal projections in 20 patients and published an enthusiastic report of his findings. These favorable results led to the rapid acceptance of this procedure, and 20,000 patients were subjected to frontal lobotomies of varying extent during the next 15 years.

During this period valuable clinical information on the long-term effects of such lesions has become available. It now seems that the glowing reports of Moniz and other early workers were premature and misleading. Although a percentage of cases (often given at 50% or more) may have benefited from these operations with respect to their anxiety symptoms, most have also shown severe intellectual deficits often worse than the original problem (Rylander, 1939, 1948). Only some types of mental diseases benefit significantly from frontal lobe damage. Moreover, small lesions restricted to some aspects of the frontal cortex may be much more beneficial than the radical procedures employed by earlier workers. Clinical studies of the effects of such limited damage have contributed to our understanding of the functional organization of this portion of the brain, and it may be worthwhile to discuss briefly some of the relevant findings.

Scoville (1948, 1949) argued that the beneficial effects of frontal lobe damage may derive from an interruption of connections from either the hypothalamus, the anterior cingulate gyrus, or the lateral surfaces (areas 9 and 10 of Brodmann). He

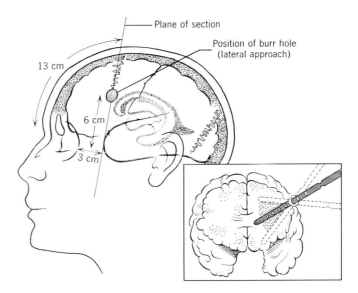

Fig. 9.28 Technique of leucotomy as performed by Freeman and Watts. (A leucotomy is guided by bone rather than by cerebral landmarks.) (From Elliott et al., 1948.)

devised and applied three separate undercutting procedures in an attempt to decide among these alternatives. On the basis of a large number of cases, Scoville came to the reluctant conclusion that there appeared to be no significant difference between the effectiveness of these three procedures.

Meyer and McLardy (1949) concluded, on the basis of the data from 95 leucotomy cases, that ablation of the medial aspects of the frontal lobes may be most effective with emotional disorders, since it is least likely to incur pronounced intellectual deficits. Mettler (1949), however, recommends ablation of the lateral surfaces (areas 9 and 10) for alleviation of anxiety without severe intellectual deficits. Fulton (1951) reports considerable success with this operation, but he also emphasizes the importance of the ensuing memory deficits.

Another line of attack has been opened by Reitman and associates (Reitman, 1946; Dax et al., 1948) with the argument that specific lesions may be appropriate only for particular mental diseases. Hyperactivity is conspicuous in monkeys following orbital ablations, and this procedure is suggested for the relief of chronic depressions. A number of workers have reported favorable results from this operation (Egan, 1949; Fleming and Phillips, 1949). Patients with primarily manic symptoms seem to benefit more from restricted lesions of the lateral surface (areas 9 and 10). Most of these patients show severe intellectual deficits which may offset the benefits of the remission of other symptoms (Dax et al., 1948; Penfield 1948; Malmo and Shagass, 1950; Fulton, 1951).

With the recent advance of a variety of psychotropic drugs which provide at least a temporary remission of fear, anxiety, and depression, the use of surgical treatments has declined in the past decade. There has been a proportional decline of interest in the detailed functional organization of the frontal cortex. The evidence we do have suggests that at least certain aspects participate in the regulation of emotion, but opinions are divided about the specific nature of this contribution. It has been suggested (Arnold, 1950) that the frontal lobes may be concerned only with sympathetic aspects of emotions (and hence participate in the regulation of fear and anxiety). Most workers have assumed that the frontal neocortex is important primarily as a relay station which interconnects neocortical and limbic system structures and provides for the integration and distribution of important hypothalamic and thalamic afferent inputs to the cerebrum.

It may be important for our understanding of frontal lobe functions to point out that not all frontal lesions result in a lowering of emotional responsiveness, although a superficial review of the experimental and clinical literature tends to give this impression.

Kennard (1955) reported, for instance, that removal of the frontal pole or more discrete portions of the orbitofrontal cortex of monkeys resulted in rage behavior and viciousness. Similar observations have been reported for prefrontal dogs (Auleytner and Brutkowski, 1960) and cats (Bond et al., 1957). Smaller lesions in the premotor cortex have also been reported to facilitate rather than inhibit emotional responsiveness (Aleksandrov, 1949; Bykov, 1957). Even the mesial surface of the frontal lobe may contribute to this excitatory mechanism, as is suggested by Brutkowski's recent observation of violent rage reactions following lesions in the genual and subgenual gyri of the dog cortex (Brutkowski et al., 1961). This apparent release phenomenon has been studied in some detail in the framework of classical and instrumental learning situations (Brutkowski et al., 1960, 1963; Brutkowski and Mempel, 1961; Brutkowski and Dabrowska, 1963). The details of this research are too complex to be presented here, and the interested reader is referred to Brutkowski's (1964) summary for a more detailed discussion. The basic finding can be conveyed, however, by the simple statement that frontal lesions produced disinhibition in all experimental situations. That is, the frontal animals responded postoperatively to stimuli that previously had acquired negative properties from nonreinforcement, punishment, or other experimental techniques.

Before we leave the topic of emotion and at-

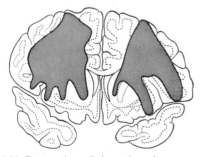

Fig. 9.29 Destruction of tissue in a leucotomy. The extent of destruction is inevitably uncertain. (From Freeman and Watts, 1948.)

tempt to integrate the complex picture presented by motivational variables, we shall briefly discuss Arnold's (1950) excitatory theory of emotion.

Arnold's Excitatory Theory of Emotion

Arnold attempts to trace the sequence of events in an emotion-arousing situation from the perception of an external stimulus to the *experience* and *expression* of the consequent emotion. This theoretical framework has recently (Arnold, 1960) been modified and expanded to cover all motivational events, but the extension had become unnecessarily speculative and will not be discussed here. We shall be concerned only with the earlier and more modest theory of emotion.

According to Arnold, any response presupposes the focusing of the "autogenic activity" of the cortex on the stimuli that elicit it in a process of attention. This focusing occurs by means of the activation of transcortical or corticothalamic fibers. These fibers modify the sensory input at either the cortical or thalamic level in accordance with our "expectations." (Arnold states that "this fusion of expectancy and sensation represents a psychological evaluation of the situation. . . .") The resulting emotional attitude (anger, fear, disgust, etc.) then initiates nerve impulses from the cortex to centers in the thalamus-hypothalamus; these impulses touch off the appropriate pattern of emotional expression as well as the corresponding peripheral changes. The autonomic effects thus produced (changes in muscle tone, blood pressure, heart rate, etc.) are then reported back to the cortex via afferent sensory pathways. This cortical perception of organic changes may again be evaluated as to "how it affects me." A complete emotional experience includes the whole sequence: "evaluation, emotional attitude (or feeling) resulting in emotional expression, autonomic changes, and their cortical perception and re-evaluation."

Arnold suggests that the physiological reactions to various emotions may be mediated by different cortical systems. She proposes that fear and anxiety may be characterized by sympathetic stimulation which is regulated by centers in the posterior part of the hypothalamus and that these emotions are under the *excitatory* control of mechanisms located in the frontal lobes (via the dorsomedial nuclei of the thalamus). Excitement (including "affection" and "interest") is accompanied in this scheme by *moderate* parasympathetic stimulation. Anger or rage is on the same continuum but represents intense parasympathetic

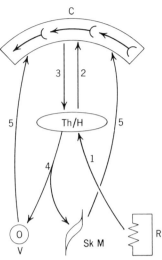

Fig. 9.30 Diagram of Arnold's excitatory theory of emotion. R, sensory receptor; Th/H, thalamus-hypothalamus; C, cortex; V, viscera; Sk M, skeletal muscles.

discharge. Arnold suggests that the parasympathetic division of the autonomic nervous system may be regulated by centers in the anterior hypothalamus. These are under cortical *excitatory* control which is exercised by the cingulate gyrus (via the anterior nuclei of the thalamus) and hippocampus (via the fornix).

Shorn of its peculiar language, this theory provides a compromise between earlier notions. The James-Lange theory unmistakably contributes the need for an evaluation of the feedback from the autonomic nervous system. The conceptualization of thalamic-hypothalamic centers under cortical control as well as the differentiation of sympathetic and parasympathetic "emotions" has been proposed by Cannon. Arnold's contributions are the proposal that the cortical control is excitatory rather than inhibitory as conjectured by Cannon, and the postulation that specific cortical areas regulate particular types of emotions.

We have already considered the evidence in defense or attack of these notions, and it appears unnecessary to discuss this theory at great length. There is little experimental evidence for the proposed classification of emotional responses in terms of sympathetic-parasympathetic components, although the notion continues to elicit support. Autonomic changes are essential to neither the experience nor the expression of emotion, and it appears unlikely that such changes might determine the site of cortical representation, as proposed by Arnold and others. Sympathetic responses are not solely or even primarily integrated in the frontal cortex, and parasympathetic control is not peculiar to the cingulate-hippocampal complex. Furthermore, the cortical control of subcortical centers which may be involved in the regulation of emotional behavior is neither totally excitatory nor exclusively inhibitory, as proposed by Arnold and Cannon respectively. Instead, some cortical areas exert a regulatory influence on a particular emotional variable which may be excitatory with respect to some targets and inhibitory with respect to others. This point will be treated more fully in our discussion of general motivational theories.

SUMMARY

The concept of "emotion" has, to date, eluded all attempts at satisfactory definition. Emotional reactions consist of two separable and not necessarily corresponding aspects: the *expression* of emotion in terms of overt somatic as well as autonomic responses, and the *experience* of emotion in terms of less molar responses of the central nervous system. Emotional experiences have not yet been measured directly and can be inferred only from subjective feelings. We can define the behavioral (expressional) aspect of emotion operationally, but this may not correspond to subjective experience. Emotional experience can be assessed only in terms of voluntary verbal reports; these may be influenced by other motivational aspects of the testing situation and must be accepted with caution.

The physiological basis of emotional behavior has been the subject of experimental and theoretical consideration for almost 100 years. As early as 1884 William James proposed a psychophysiological theory of emotion which suggested that the subjective experience of emotion is nothing more than the perception of autonomic and somatic responses to the emotion-provoking stimulus. Lange (1885) proposed a similar theory which stated that the experience of emotion derives from the perception of vascular changes that occur as a direct consequence of emotional stimulation. These theories fail to consider the possibility of overt responses that may be in direct contrast to the emotional experience (i.e., one may attack an enemy though mortally afraid of him) and do not explain why certain stimuli elicit emotional responses while others do not.

W. B. Cannon (1927) attacked the *peripheral theories of emotion* of James and Lange, on the more technical grounds that (1) total separation of the viscera from the central nervous system does not impair emotional behavior; (2) the same visceral responses occur in very different emotional as well as nonemotional situations; (3) the viscera are relatively insensitive structures; (4) visceral changes are too slow to be a direct source of emotional feeling; and (5) the artificial induction of visceral changes known to occur in specific emotions fail to produce them.

Although the evidence for many of these points is not entirely convincing, the James-Lange theory of emotion, as it has been called collectively, cannot explain the complexities of emotional behavior.

Subsequent experimental studies have shown that "physiological correlates" of emotional responses such as cardiovascular changes, pilomotor and sudomotor activity, and respiration do not seem *essential* to either the experience or the expression of emotion. Pronounced autonomic changes accompany most emotional reactions, but we have been unable to show that specific changes are peculiar to specific emotions, or that emotions depend in any way on the occurrence of such autonomic responses. Research on this problem is continuing in the expectation that certain *patterns* of autonomic discharge may be characteristic of particular emotions and hence may serve as objective indices of emotional arousal.

The role of the central nervous system in the regulation of emotional behavior is complex and poorly understood. Although we are beginning to accumulate many individual pieces of the puzzle, we have not been able to assemble them into a coherent picture.

Isolated sympathetic responses to noxious stimulation (similar at least to those occurring during emotional arousal in the normal animal) can be elicited in the spinal preparation. If both the medulla and the spinal cord are intact, more complete autonomic response patterns can be observed since many of these functions are partially integrated in bulbar centers. If pontine and mesencephalic connections are also intact, the organism's response to noxious stimulation becomes more coordinated and directed. However, the behavior remains "subtotal" in nature because the autonomic and somatic responses are not appropriately coordinated. In decerebrate animals (which have all connections above the mesencephalon severed), a hypersensitivity to noxious stimulation may appear so that previously neutral stimuli elicit partial rage reactions.

A considerably different pattern emerges when the posterior and ventral portions of the diencephalon are intact. The hyperreactivity to noxious stimulation remains, but we now find well-coordinated and well-executed rage behavior in response to previously neutral stimuli. The rage responses of these *decorticate* animals are complete and can be distinguished from those of normal animals only by the fact that they are stimulus-bound and may lack direction.

Electrical stimulation of hypothalamic mechanisms in the intact animal elicits well-coordinated and well-directed attack, defense, or flight reactions, depending on the precise locus of stimulation. Lesions of these structures produce varying degrees of emotional unresponsiveness and stupor, although lesions of the ventromedial nuclei have been shown to elicit precisely opposite results.

Both sympathetic and parasympathetic responses are integrated at the level of the hypothalamus, and it has been proposed that the efferent control of emotional behavior may be regulated by these mechanisms. This concept of a general hypothalamic motor center for all emotions must be viewed with caution, since there is little evidence for the hypothalamic regulation of emotional behavior other than that elicited by noxious stimulation (attack, defense, or flight).

W. B. Cannon proposed in 1927 that the emotional aspects of behavior may be regulated by thalamic mechanisms that are normally inhibited by unspecified cortical controls. He suggested that sudden and intense stimuli may supersede this inhibition directly at the thalamic level and induce impulses which travel from the thalamus to (1) peripheral motor units (presumably via the hypothalamic motor relays) to give rise to both autonomic and somatic emotional responses, and (2) cortical regions which give rise to the subjective experience of emotion. This mechanism presumably accounts for the effect of innately emotion-provoking stimuli. More commonly, sensory impulses are transmitted from peripheral sensory organs *through* the thalamus (which does not respond to them because of cortical inhibition) to the cortex. At the cortex conditioned responses that release the cortical inhibition of thalamic mechanisms are elicited; this produces the thalamic discharge to peripheral and corti-

cal structures that evokes the expression and experience of emotion. Cannon's theory has remained influential in psychological circles in spite of the accumulation of experimental evidence which demonstrates that the thalamus itself is not essential to emotion, and that cortical control of subcortical mechanisms of emotion is both inhibitory and excitatory.

The role of the cortex in emotion has been investigated during the past two decades. The impetus for most of this interest in specific cortical mechanisms derives from Papez's (1937) theory of emotion; he proposed that the expression of emotion depended entirely on the integrative action of the hypothalamus, but that emotional experience required cortical mechanisms. In view of the close interdependence of these two aspects of emotional reactions, Papez suggested that emotional experience might be a function of the cingulate gyrus which has extensive reciprocal connections with the hypothalamus. He proposed that the hypothalamic centers may be activated by afferent input from primitive sensory centers in the subthalamus. These centers then discharge simultaneously to peripheral motor units and the cingulate gyrus; thus the expressional and experiential aspects of emotion occur in close temporal contiguity. MacLean (1949) agreed with Papez's basic reasoning but suggested that the hippocampal formation rather than the cingulate gyrus may be the cortical structure responsible for the experience of emotion.

At the time of their proposal, neither of these theories was supported by an impressive body of experimental evidence, although clinical case histories provided some inferential support for them. Considerable research effort has been concentrated on these and other portions of the limbic system in the past 20 years, and the results suggest that the cortical control of emotion may be more complex than these early theories implied.

The entire limbic system (i.e., all allo- and juxtallocortical portions of the cerebrum as well as the amygdaloid complex) may be involved in the regulation of emotional or motivational variables. It is not yet clear whether the control of specific emotions can be assigned to particular structures. Certain aspects of the isocortex (particularly some portions of the frontal lobes) seem to exert an influence on these limbic system structures, since both neodecortication and restricted frontal lobe lesions affect emotional behavior.

A variety of emotional responses have been enhanced or reduced by ablation or stimulation of amygdaloid, hippocampal, cingulate, septal, or orbitofrontal regions. It is clear that these mechanisms play an important part in the regulation of emotional behavior, but we cannot discern a clear functional interrelationship between the individual mechanisms or suggest a common circuit for emotional reactions. Much remains to be accomplished before we can begin to understand the specific contributions of the many aspects of cortical control.

BIBLIOGRAPHY

Abramovski, E. Recherches experimentales sur la volontée., *J. de Psychol.,* 1913, **10,** 491–508.

Ackner, B. Discussion on physiological measurements of "emotional tension." *Proc. roy. Soc. Med.,* 1958, **51,** 76–78.

Aleksandrov, I. S. On the relationship between the cerebral cortex and the diencephalon. Uczenye zapiski Lenigradkogo pedagogiceskogo instituta im. A. I. Hercena, 1949, **83,** 141–230.

Allen, W. F. Effect of ablating the frontal lobes, hippocampi, and occipito-parieto-temporal (excepting pyriform areas) lobes on positive and negative olfactory conditioned reflexes. *Amer. J. Physiol.,* 1940, **128,** 754–771.

Allen, W. F. Effect of ablating the pyriform-amygdaloid area and hippocampi on positive and negative olfactory conditioned reflexes and on conditioned olfactory differentiation. *Amer. J. Physiol.,* 1941, **132,** 81–92.

Anand, B. K., & Brobeck, J. R. Hypothalamic control of food intake in rats and cats. *Yale J. Biol. Med.,* 1951, **24,** 123–140.

Arnold, Magda B. An excitatory theory of emotion. In *The second international symposium on feelings and emotions.* M. L. Reymert, Ed. New York: McGraw-Hill, 1950.

Arnold, Magda B. *Emotion and personality. Vol. II. Neurological and physiological aspects.* New York: Columbia Univ. Press, 1960.

Auleytner, B., & Brutkowski, S. Effects of bilateral prefrontal lobectomy on the classical (type I) defensive conditioned reflexes and some other responses related to defensive behavior in dogs. *Acta Biol. exp.* (*Warsaw*), 1960, **20,** 243–262.

Ax, A. F. The physiological differentiation of fear and anger in humans. *Psychosom. Med.,* 1953, **15,** 433–442.

Bagshaw, M. H., & Pribram, K. H. Cortical organization in gustation. *J. Neurophysiol.,* 1953, **16,** 499.

Baird, H. N., Gudetti, B., Reyes, V., Wycis, H. T., & Spiegel, E. G. Stimulation of anterior thalamic nuclei in man and cat. *Fed. Proc.,* 1951, **10,** 8.

Barcroft, J., & Florey, H. The effects of exercise on the vascular conditions in the spleen and the colon. *J. Physiol.* (*London*), 1929, **68,** 181–189.

Bard, P. A diencephalic mechanism for the expression of rage with special reference to the sympathetic nervous system. *Amer. J. Physiol.,* 1928, **84,** 490–515.

Bard, P. Emotion. I: The neuro-humoral basis of emotional reactions. In *Handbook of general experimental psychology.* C. Murchison, Ed. Worcester, Mass.: Clark Univ. Press, 1934a.

Bard, P. On emotional expression after decortication with some remarks on certain theoretical views, parts I and II. *Psychol. Rev.,* 1934b, **41,** 309–329, 424–449.

Bard, P. Central nervous mechanisms for emotional behavior patterns in animals. *Res. Publ., Ass. Res. nerv. ment. Dis.,* 1939, **19,** 190–218.

Bard, P. Central nervous mechanisms for the expression of anger in animals. In *The second international symposium on feelings and emotions.* M. L. Reymert, Ed. New York: McGraw-Hill, 1950.

Bard, P., & Mountcastle, V. B. Some forebrain mechanisms involved in expression of rage with special reference to suppression of angry behavior. *Res. Publ., Ass. Res. nerv. ment. Dis.,* 1948, **27,** 362–404.

Bard, P., & Rioch, D. McK. A study of four cats deprived of neocortex and additional portions of the forebrain. *Bull. Johns Hopk. Hosp.,* 1937, **60,** 73–147.

Basowitz, H., Persky H., Korchin, S. J., & Grinker, R. R. *Anxiety and stress.* New York: McGraw-Hill, 1955.

Batt, J. C., Kay, W. W., Reiss, M., & Sands, D. E. Endocrine concomitants of schizophrenia. *J. ment. Sci.,* 1957, **103,** 240–256.

Bazett, H. C., & Penfield, W. G. A study of the Sherrington decerebrate animal in the chronic as well as the acute condition. *Brain,* 1922, **45,** 185–265.

Benussi, V. Die Atmungssymptome der Luege. *Arch. ges. Psychol.,* 1914, **31,** 244–273.

Berg, R. L., & Beebe-Center, J. G. Cardiac startle in man. *J. exp. Psychol.,* 1941, **28,** 262–279.

Berger, H. Ueber das Elektrenkephalogramm des Menschen. *Arch. Psychiat. Nervenkr.,* 1929, **87,** 527–570.

Berger, H. Ueber das Elektrenkephalogramm des Menschen, VI. *Arch. Psychiat. Nervenkr.,* 1933, **99,** 555–574.

Bianchi, L. *The mechanism of the brain and the function of the frontal lobes.* J. H. Macdonald, Trans. New York: Wm. Wood, 1922.

Boas, E. P., & Goldschmidt, E. F. *The heart-rate.* Springfield; Ill.: Thomas, 1932.

Bond, D. D., Randt, C. T., Bidder, T. G., & Rowland, V. Posterior septal, fornical and anterior thalamic lesions in the cat. *Arch. Neurol. Psychiat.* (*Chicago*), 1957, **78,** 143–162.

Boshes, B. Emotions, hypothalamus and the cardiovascular system. *Amer. J. Cardiol.,* 1958, **1,** 212–223.

Bowsher, D. Termination of the central pain pathway in man: the conscious appreciation of pain. *Brain,* 1957, **80,** 606–622.

Brady, J. V. *Biological and biochemical bases of behavior.* H. F. Harlow & C. Woolsey, Eds. Madison: Univ. of Wisconsin Press, 1958a.

Brady, J. V. *Experimental psychopathology.* H. H. Jasper, L. D. Proctor, R. S. Knighton, W. C. Noshay, & R. T. Costello, Eds. Boston: Little, Brown, 1958b.

Brady, J. V. Emotional behavior. In *Handbook of physiology. Vol. III.* J. Field, H. W. Magoun, & V. E. Hall, Eds. Baltimore: Williams and Wilkins, 1960.

Brady, J. V., & Hunt, H. F. An experimental approach to the analysis of emotional behavior. *J. Psychol.,* 1955, **40**, 313–324.

Brady, J. V., & Nauta, W. J. H. Subcortical mechanisms in emotional behavior: affective changes following septal forebrain lesions in the albino rat. *J. comp. physiol. Psychol.,* 1953, **46**, 339–346.

Brady, J. V., & Nauta, W. J. H. Subcortical mechanisms in emotional behavior: the duration of affective changes following septal and habenular lesions in the albino rat. *J. comp. physiol. Psychol.,* 1955, **48**, 412–420.

Brady, J. V., Schreiner, L., Geller, I., & Kling, A. Subcortical mechanisms in emotional behavior: the effect of rhinencephalic injury upon the acquisition and retention of a conditioned avoidance response in cats. *J. comp. physiol. Psychol.,* 1954, **49**, 179–186.

Broca, P. Anatomie comparée des circonvolutions cerebrales. Le grand lobe limbique et la scissure limbique dans la série des mammifères. *Rev. Anthropol.,* 1878, **1**, 385–498.

Bromiley, R. B. Conditioned responses in a dog after removal of neocortex. *J. comp. physiol. Psychol.,* 1948, **41**, 102–110.

Brown, C. H., & Van Gelder, D. Emotional reactions before examinations. I: Physiological changes. *J. Psychol.,* 1938, **5**, 1–9.

Brown, C. W., & Ghiselli, E. E. Subcortical mechanisms in learning. IV: Olfactory discrimination. *J. comp. Psychol.,* 1938, **26**, 109.

Brown, J. S., & Farber, I. E. Emotions conceptualized as intervening variables—with suggestions toward a theory of frustration. *Psychol. Bull.,* 1951, **48**, 465–495.

Brunswick, D. The effect of emotional stimuli on the gastro-intestinal tone. *J. comp. Psychol.,* 1924, **4**, 19–79.

Brutkowski, S. Prefrontal cortex and drive inhibition. In *The frontal granular cortex and behavior.* J. M. Warren & K. Akert, Eds. New York: McGraw-Hill, 1964.

Brutkowski, S., & Dabrowska, J. Disinhibition after prefrontal lesions as a function of duration of intertrial intervals. *Science,* 1963, **139**, 505–506.

Brutkowski, S., & Mempel, E. Disinhibition of inhibitory conditioned responses following selective brain lesions in dogs. *Science,* 1961, **134**, 2040–2041.

Brutkowski, S., Fonberg, E., & Mempel, E. Elementary type II (instrumental) conditioned reflexes in amygdala dogs. *Acta Biol. exp.* (*Warsaw*), 1960, **20**, 263–271.

Brutkowski, S., Fonberg, E., & Mempel, E. Angry behaviour in dogs following bilateral lesions in the genual portion of the rostral cingulate gyrus. *Acta Biol. exp.* (*Warsaw*), 1961, **21**, 199–205.

Brutkowski, S., Mishkin, M., & Rosvold, H. E. Positive and inhibitory motor conditioned reflexes in monkeys after ablation of orbital or dorsolateral surface of the frontal cortex. In *Proceedings of the conference on central and peripheral mechanisms of motor functions,* E. Gutmann & P. Hnik, Eds. Prague: Czechoslovakian Academy of Science, 1963.

Bureš, J. Z., Bohdanecky, Z., & Weiss, T. Physostigmine induced hippocampal theta activity and learning in rats. *Psychopharmacologia,* 1962, **3**, 254–263.

Burn, J. H. Sympathetic vasodilators. *Physiol. Rev.* 1938, **18**, 137–153.

Burtt, H. E. The inspiration-expiration ratios during truth and falsehood. *J. exp. Psychol.,* 1921, **4**, 1–23,

Butter, C. M., Mishkin, M., & Rosvold, H. E. Conditioning and extinction of a food-rewarded response after selective ablations of frontal cortex in rhesus monkeys. *Exp. Neurol.,* 1963, **7**, 65–75.

Bykov, K. M. *The cerebral cortex and the internal organs.* W. H. Gantt, Trans. New York: Chemical Publishing Co., 1957.

Cannon, W. B. *Bodily changes in pain, hunger, fear and rage.* New York: Appleton, 1915.

Cannon, W. B. The James-Lange theory of emotions: a critical examination and an alternation. *Amer. J. Psychol.,* 1927, **39**, 106–124.

Cannon, W. B. *Bodily changes in pain, hunger, fear and rage* (2nd ed.). New York: Appleton, 1929.

Cannon, W. B. Again the James-Lange and the thalamic theories of emotion. *Psychol. Rev.,* 1931, **38**, 281–295.

Cannon, W. B. *The wisdom of the body.* New York: Norton, 1932.

Cannon, W. B. *Bodily changes in pain, hunger, fear and rage* (3rd ed.). New York: Appleton-Century, 1936.

Cannon, W. B. *The wisdom of the body* (2nd ed.). New York: Norton, 1939.

Cannon, W. B., & Britton, S. W. Pseudoaffective medulliadrenal secretion. *Amer. J. Physiol.,* 1925, **72**, 283–294.

Cannon, W. B., & Britton, S. W. The influence of emotion on medulliadrenal secretion. *Amer. J. Physiol.,* 1927, **79**, 433–465.

Clark, C. V. H., & Isaacson, R. L. Effect of bilateral hippocampal ablation on DRL performance. *J. comp. physiol. Psychol.,* 1965, **59**, 137–140.

Clemente, C. D., Green, J. D., & de Groot, J. Studies on behavior following rhinencephalic lesions in adult cats. *Anat. Rec.,* 1957, **127**, 279.

Cohn, R. The influence of emotion on the human electroencephalogram. *J. nerv. ment. Dis.,* 1946, **104**, 351–357.

Coombs, C. H. Adaptation of the galvanic response to auditory stimuli. *J. exp. Psychol.,* 1938, **22**, 244–268.

Cornwell, P. R. Orbital and proreal lesions in cats. *J. comp. physiol. Psychol.* (in press).

Dahl, D., Ingram, W. R., & Knott, J. R. Diencephalic lesions and avoidance learning in cats. *Arch. Neurol. (Chicago)* 1962, **7**, 314–319.

Dana, C. L. The anatomic seat of the emotions: a discussion of the James-Lange Theory. *Arch. Neurol. Psychiat. (Chicago)*, 1921, **6**, 634–639.

Darrow, C. W. Sensory, secretory and electrical changes in the skin following bodily excitation. *J. exp. Psychol.*, 1927, **10**, 197–226.

Darrow, C. W. The significance of skin resistance in the light of its relation to the amount of perspiration. *J. gen. Psychol.*, 1934, **11**, 451–452.

Darrow, C. W. The galvanic skin reflex (sweating) and blood-pressure as preparatory and facilitative functions. *Psychol. Bull.*, 1936, **33**, 73–94.

Darrow, C. W. Neural mechanisms controlling the palmar galvanic skin reflex and palmar sweating. *Arch. Neurol. Psychiat. (Chicago)*, 1937a, **37**, 641–663.

Darrow, C. W. Continuous records of systolic and diastolic blood pressure. *Arch. Neurol. Psychiat. (Chicago)*, 1937b, **38**, 365–370.

Darrow, C. W. Psychological and psychophysiological significance of the electroencephalogram. *Psychol. Rev.*, 1947, **54**, 157–168.

Darrow, C. W. Neurophysiological effect of emotion on the brain. In *The second international symposium on feelings and emotions*. M. L. Reymert, Ed. New York: McGraw-Hill, 1950.

Darrow, C. W., Pathman, J., & Kronenberg, G. Level of autonomic activity and electroencephalogram. *J. exp. Psychol.*, 1946, **36**, 355–365.

Davis, R. C. Factors affecting the galvanic reflex. *Arch. Psychol. (N.Y.)*, 1930, **115**, 1–64.

Davis, R. C. Response patterns. *Trans. N.Y. Acad. Sci.*, 1957, **19**, 731–739.

Davis, R. C., & Buchwald, A. M. An exploration of somatic response patterns: stimulus and sex differences. *J. comp. physiol. Psychol.*, 1957, **50**, 44–52.

Davis, R. C., Buchwald, A. M., & Frankmann, R. W. Autonomic and muscular responses and their relation to simple stimuli. *Psychol. Monogr.*, 1955, **69**, 1–71.

Davis, R. C., Lundervold, A., & Miller, J. D. The pattern of somatic response during a repetitive motor task and its modification by visual stimuli. *J. comp. physiol. Psychol.*, 1957, **50**, 53–60.

Dax, E., Cunningham, F., & Radley-Smith, E. J. Discussion: prefrontal leucotomy with reference to indications and results. Section of Psychiatry. *Proc. roy. Soc. Med.*, 1945–1946, **39**, 448–449.

Dax, E., Cunningham, F., Reitman, B., & Radley-Smith, E. J. Prefrontal leucotomy: 1. Investigations into clinical problems. 2. Vertical and horizontal incisions of the frontal lobes. 3. Physiological aspects. Summary of three papers presented at the International Congress of Psychosurgery, Lisbon, 1948. *Dig. Neurol. Psychiat.*, 1948, **16**, 533.

Delgado, J. M. R. Cerebral structures involved in transmission and elaboration of noxious stimulation. *J. Neurophysiol.*, 1955, **18**, 261–275.

Delgado, J. M. R., Rosvold, H. E., & Looney, E. Evoking conditioned fear by electrical stimulation of subcortical structures in the monkey brain. *J. comp. physiol. Psychol.*, 1956, **49**, 373.

Drury, A. N., Florey, H., & Florey, M. E. The vascular reaction of the colonic mucosa of the dog to fright. *J. Physiol. (London)*, 1929, **68**, 173–180.

Duffy, E. Emotion: an example of the need for reorientation in psychology. *Psychol. Rev.*, 1934, **41**, 184–198.

Duffy, E. An explanation of "emotional" phenomena without the use of the concept "emotion." *J. gen. Psychol.*, 1941, **25**, 283–293.

Dunbar, H. F. *Emotions and bodily changes: a survey of literature on psychosomatic interrelationships, 1910–1945.* New York: Columbia Univ. Press, 1946.

Dunlap, K. Are emotions teleological constructs? *Amer. J. Psychol.*, 1932, **44**, 146–162.

Dusser de Barenne, J. G. Récherches expérimentales sur les fonctions du système nerveux central, faites en particulier sur deux chats donc le neopallium a été enlevé. *Arch. Neurol. Physiol.*, 1920, **4**, 31–123.

Dysinger, D. W. A comparative study of affective responses by means of the impressive and expressive methods. *Psychol. Monogr.*, 1931, **187** (monograph).

Egan, G. Results of isolation of the orbital lobes in leucotomy. *J. ment. Sci.*, 1949, **95**, 115–123.

Egger, M. D., & Flynn, J. P. Amygdaloid suppression of hypothalamically elicited attack behavior. *Science*, 1962, **136**, 43–44.

Ehrlich, A. Effects of tegmental lesions on motivated behavior in rats. *J. comp. physiol. Psychol.*, 1963, **56**, 390–396.

Ellen, P., & Powell, E. W. Temporal discrimination in rats with rhinencephalic lesions. *Exp. Neurol.*, 1962a, **6**, 538–547.

Ellen, P., & Powell, E. W. Effects of septal lesions on behavior generated by positive reinforcement. *Exp. Neurol.*, 1962b, **6**, 1–11.

Ellen, P., & Wilson, A. S. Perseveration in the rat following hippocampal lesions. *Exp. Neurol.*, 1963, **8**, 310–317.

Ellen, P., Wilson, A. S., & Powell, E. W. Septal inhibition and timing behavior in the rat. *Exp. Neurol.*, 1964, **10**, 120–132.

Elliott, H., Albert, S., & Bremmer, W. A program for prefrontal lobotomy with report of the effect on intractable pain. *Treatment Serv. Bull.*, 1948, **3**, 26–35.

Ellson, D. G., Davis, R. C., Saltzman, I. J., & Burke, C. J. Report of research on detection of deception. Contract N6nr-18011, Office of Naval Research, 1952.

Elmadjian, F. *Molecules and mental health.* F. A. Gibbs, Ed. Philadelphia: Lippincott, 1959.

Endroczi, E., Lissak, K., Bohus, B., & Kovacs, S. The inhibitory influence of archicortical structures on pituitary-adrenal function. *Acta physiol. Acad. Sci.*

hung., 1959, **16**, 17–22.

Evarts, E. V. Effects of auditory cortex ablation on frequency discrimination in monkey. *J. Neurophysiol.,* 1952, **15**, 443.

Farber, I. E., & West, L. J. Conceptual problems of research on emotions. *Psychiat. Res. Rep. Amer. psychiat. Ass.,* 1960, **12**, 1–7.

Farmer, E., & Chambers, E. G. Concerning the use of psychogalvanic reflex in psychological experiments. *Brit. J. Psychol.,* 1925, **15**, 237–254.

Feleky, A. M. The expression of emotion. *Psychol. Rev.,* 1914, **21**, 33–41.

Feleky, A. M. The influence of emotions on respiration. *J. exp. Psychol.,* 1916, **1**, 218–241.

Fendler, K., Karmos, G., & Telegdy, G. The effect of hippocampal lesions on pituitary-adrenal function. *Acta physiol. Acad. Sci. hung.,* 1961, **20**, 293–297.

Féré, C. Note sur des modifications de la tension electrique dans le corps humain. *C. R. Soc. Biol. (Paris),* 1888, **5**, 28–33.

Ferrier, D. The Croonian Lecture. Experiments on the brain of monkeys (second series). *Phil. Trans.,* 1875, **165**, 433–488.

Fischer, A. E., & Coury, J. N. Cholinergic tracing of a central neural circuit underlying the thirst drive. *Science,* 1962, **138**, 691–693.

Fleming, G. W., & Phillips, D. G. Transorbital leucotomy. *J. ment. Sci.,* 1949, **50**, 197–202.

Flynn, J. P., & Wasman, M. Learning and cortically evoked movement during propagated hippocampal afterdischarges. *Science,* 1960, **131**, 1607–1608.

Foa, C., & Peserico, E. Le vie del riflesso neurogalvanico. *Arch. Fisiol.,* 1923, **21**, 119–130.

Forbes, T. W., & Landis, C. The limiting A. C. frequency for the exhibition of the galvanic skin ("psychogalvanic") response. *J. gen. Psychol.,* 1935, **13**, 188–193.

Fox, S. S., Kimble, D. P., & Lickey, M. E. Comparison of caudate nucleus and septal area lesions on two types of avoidance behavior. *J. comp. physiol. Psychol.,* 1964, **58**, 380–386.

Freeman, W., & Watts, J. W. The thalamic projection to the frontal lobe. *Res. Publ., Ass. Res. nerv. ment. Dis.,* 1948, **27**, 200–209.

French, J. D., & Magoun, H. W. Effects of chronic lesions in central cephalic brainstem of monkeys. *A.M.A. Arch. Neurol. Psychiat.,* 1952, **68**, 591.

Fuller, J. L., Rosvold, H. E., & Pribram, K. H. The effect on affective and cognitive behavior in the dog of lesions of the pyriform-amygdala hippocampal complex. *J. comp. physiol. Psychol.,* 1957, **50**, 89–96.

Fulton, J. F. *Physiology of the nervous system.* New York: Oxford Univ. Press, 1949.

Fulton, J. F. *Frontal lobotomy and affective behavior. A neurophysiological analysis.* New York: Norton, 1951.

Fulton, J. F., & Ingraham, F. D. Emotional disturbances following experimental lesions of the base of the brain. *J. Physiol. (London),* 1929, **67**, 27–28.

Fulton, J. F., & Jacobsen, C. F. The functions of the frontal lobes, a comparative study in monkeys, chimpanzees and man. *Advanc. mod. Biol. (Moscow),* 1935, **4**, 113–23. *Abstracts from the second international neurological congress, London,* 1935, pp. 70–71.

Fulton, J. F., Pribram, K. H., Stevenson, J. A. F., & Wall P. D. Interrelations between orbital gyrus, insula, temporal tip, and anterior cingulate. *Trans. Amer. neurol. Ass.,* 1949, **74**, 175–179.

Gastaut, H. Corrélations entre le système nerveux végétatif et le système de la vie de relation dans le rhinencéphale. *J. Physiol. Path. gén.,* 1952, **44**, 431–470.

Gault, F. P. Autonomic and muscular responses in a simple reaction situation and a discrimination reaction. Indiana Univ., Ph.D. thesis, 1959.

Gellhorn, E. *Autonomic regulations.* New York: Interscience, 1943.

Gerard, R. W., Marshall, W. H., & Saul, L. J. Electrical activity of the cat's brain. *A.M.A. Arch. Neurol. Psychiat.,* 1936, **36**, 675.

Gildemeister, M. Der sogenannte psychogalvanische Reflex und seine physikalischchemische Deutung. *Pflüg. Arch. ges. Physiol.,* 1915, **162**, 489–506.

Gildemeister, M., & Ellinghaus, J. Zur Physiologie der menschlichen Haut. III: Ueber die Abhaengigkeit des galvanischen Hautreflexes von der Temperatur der Haut. *Pflüg. Arch. ges. Physiol.,* 1923, **200**, 262–277.

Gildemeister, M., & Kaufold, R. Ueber das electrische Leitungsvermoegen der ueberlebenden menschlichen Haut. *Pflüg. Arch. ges. Physiol.,* 1920, **179**, 154–158.

Glees, P., Cole, J., Whitty, C. W. M., & Cairns, H. The effects of lesions in the cingular gyrus and adjacent areas in monkeys. *J. Neurol. Psychiat.,* 1950, **13**, 178–190.

Gloor, P. Electrophysiological studies on the connections on the amygdaloid nucleus in the cat. I: The neuronal organization of the amygdaloid projection system. *EEG clin. Neurophysiol.,* 1955, **7**, 223–242.

Golla, F. L., & Antonovitch, S. The respiratory rhythm in its relation to the mechanisms of thought. *Brain,* 1929, **25**, 491–509.

Goltz, F., Der Hund ohne Grosshirn. *Pflüg. Arch. ges. Physiol.,* 1892, **51**, 570–614.

Graff, E., & Mayer, L. Ueber den Einfluss der Affekte auf den Gesamtstoffwechsel. *Z. ges. Neurol. Psychiat.,* 1923, **86**, 245–253.

Grossman, S. P. Chemically induced epileptiform seizures in the cat. *Science,* 1963, **142**, 409–411.

Grossman, S. P. Behavioral effects of chemical stimulation of the ventral amygdala. *J. comp. physiol. Psychol.,* 1964a, **57**, 29–36.

Grossman, S. P. Effect of chemical stimulation of the septal area on motivation. *J. comp. physiol. Psychol.,* 1964b, **58**, 194–200.

Grossman, S. P., & Grossman, Lore. Food and water intake following lesions or electrical stimulation of the amygdala. *Amer. J. Physiol.,* 1963, **205**, 761–765.

Grossman, S. P., & Mountford, Helen. Effects of chemical stimulation of the dorsal hippocampus on learning and performance. *Amer. J. Physiol.,* 1964, **207,** 1387–1393.

Haggard, E. A. Experimental studies in affective processes. II: On the quantification and evaluation of "measured" changes in skin resistance. *J. exp. Psychol.,* 1945, **35,** 46–56.

Haggard, E. A. On the application of analysis of variance to GSR data. I: The selection of an appropriate measure. II: Some effects of the use of inappropriate measures. *J. exp. Psychol.,* 1949, **39,** 378–392.

Harlow, H. F. Recovery of pattern discrimination in monkeys following unilateral occipital lobectomy. *J. comp. Psychol.,* 1939, **27,** 467.

Harrison, J. M. An examination of the varying effects of certain stimuli upon the alpha-rhythm of a single normal individual. *Brit. J. Psychol.,* 1946, **37,** 20–29.

Harrison, J. M., & Lyon, M. The role of the septal nuclei and components of the fornix in the behavior of the rat. *J. comp. Neurol.,* 1957, **108,** 121–137.

Harvey, J. A., & Hunt, H. F. Effect of septal lesions on thirst in the rat as indicated by water consumption and operant responding for water reward. *J. comp. physiol. Psychol.,* 1965, **59,** 49–56.

Harvey, J. A., Jacobson, L. E., & Hunt, H. F. Long-term effects of lesions in the peptal forebrain on acquisition and retention of conditioned fear. *Amer. Psychologist,* 1961, **16,** 449.

Harvey, J. A., Lints, C. E., Jacobson, L. E., & Hunt, H. F. Effects of lesions in the septal area on conditioned fear and discriminated instrumental punishment in the albino rat. *J. comp. physiol. Psychol.,* 1965, **59,** 37–48.

Head, H. *Studies in neurology.* London: Oxford Univ. Press, 1920.

Hebb, D. O. Emotion in man and animal: an analysis of the intuitive processes of recognition. *Psychol. Bull.,* 1946a, **53,** 88–106.

Hebb, D. O. On the nature of fear. *Psychol. Bull.,* 1946b, **53,** 259–276.

Hebb, D. O. *Organization of behavior: a neuropsychological theory.* New York: Wiley, 1949.

Henry, F. A direct reading cardio-chronoscope. *J. exp. Psychol.,* 1938, **22,** 598–601.

Herrick, C. J. The functions of the olfactory parts of the cortex. *Proc. nat. Acad. Sci. (Washington),* 1933, **19,** 7.

Hess, W. R. Hypothalamus und die Zentren des autonomen Nervensystems: Physiologie. *Arch. Psychiat. Nervenkr.,* 1936, **104,** 548–557.

Hess, W. R. *Das Zeischenhirn: Syndrome, Lokalizationen, Funktionen.* Basel: Schwabe, 1949.

Hess, W. R. *Diencephalon: autonomic and extrapyramidal functions.* New York: Grune and Stratton, 1954.

Hess, W. R., & Akert, K. Experimental data on role of hypothalamus in mechanism of emotional behavior. *A.M.A. Arch. Neurol. Psychiat.,* 1955, **73,** 127–129.

Hinsey, J. C. The hypothalamus and somatic responses. *Res. Publ., Ass. Res. nerv. ment. Dis.,* 1940, **20,** 657–688.

Hoagland, H. *Hormones, brain function and behavior.* New York: Academic Press, 1957.

Hoagland, H. Some endocrine stress responses in man. In *The physiology of emotions.* A. Simon, Ed. Springfield, Ill.: Thomas, 1961.

Hoagland, H., & Freeman, H. Some neuroendocrine considerations. *Res. Publ., Ass. Res. nerv. ment. Dis.,* 1959, **37,** 183–203.

Hoff, H. E. Cardiac output: regulation and estimation. In *A textbook of physiology.* J. F. Fulton, Ed. Philadelphia: Saunders, 1950.

Horvath, F. E. Effects of basolateral amygdalectomy on three types of avoidance behavior. *J. comp. physiol. Psychol.,* 1963, **56,** 380–389.

Hovland, C. I., & Riesen, A. H. Magnitude of galvanic and vasomotor response as a function of stimulus intensity. *J. gen. Psychol.,* 1940, **23,** 103–121.

Hunsperger, R. W. Affektreaktionen auf elektrische Reizung im Hirnstamm der Katze. *Helv. physiol. Acta,* 1956, **14,** 70–92.

Hunsperger, R. W. Les représentations centrales des réactions affectives dans le cerveau antérieur et dans le tranc cérébral. *Neuro-chirurgie.,* 1959, **5,** 207–233.

Hunsperger, R. W., & Molina, F. A. de. Ein System fuer Affektreaktionen im Mantelgebiet der Ventrikelhoehlen von Vorderhirn und Hirnstamm. *Pflüg. Arch. ges. Physiol.,* 1958, **268,** 32–33.

Hunt, H. F. Some effects of meprobamate on conditioned fear and emotional behavior. *Ann. N.Y. Acad. Sci.,* 1957, **67,** 712–722.

Hunt, H. F., & Diamond, I. T. Some effects of hippocampal lesions on conditioned avoidance behavior in the cat. *Proceedings of the fifteenth international psychological congress, Brussels,* 1957.

Ingram, W. R., Barris, R. W, & Ranson, S. W. Catalepsy: an experimental study. *Arch. Neurol. Psychiat. (Chicago),* 1936, **35,** 1175–1197.

Isaacson, R. L., & Wickelgren, W. D. Hippocampal ablation and passive avoidance, *Science,* 1962, **138,** 1104–1106.

Isaacson, R. L., Douglas, R. J., & Moore, R. Y. The effect of radical hippocampal ablation on acquisition of avoidance responses. *J. comp. physiol. Psychol.,* 1961, **54,** 625–628.

Jacobsen, C. F. A study of cerebral function in learning. The frontal lobes. *J. comp. Neurol.,* 1931, **52,** 271–340.

Jacobsen, C. F. Functions of frontal association areas in primates. *Arch. Neurol. Psychiat. (Chicago),* 1935, **33,** 558–569.

Jacobson, E. The electrophysiology of mental activities. *Amer. J. Psychol.,* 1932, **44,** 677–694.

Jacobson, E. *Progressive relaxation.* Chicago: Univ. of Chicago Press, 1938.

Jacobson, E. Muscular tension and the estimation of effort. *Amer. J. Psychol.,* 1951, **64,** 112–117.

James, W. What is emotion? *Mind,* 1884, **9,** 188–205.

James, W. *The principles of psychology. Vol. II.* New York: Henry Holt, 1890.

Jansen, J., Jr., Andersen, P., & Kaada, B. R. Subcortical

mechanisms in the "searching" or "attention" response elicited by prefrontal cortical stimulation in unanesthetized cats. *Yale J. Biol. Med.,* 1955–1956, **28**, 331–341.

Jarrard, L. E. Hippocampal ablation and operant behavior in the rat. *Psychonom. Sci.,* 1965, **2**, 115–116.

Jasper, H. H. Diffuse projection systems: the integrative action of the thalamic reticular system. *EEG clin. Neurophysiol.,* 1949, **1**, 305.

Jasper, H. H., & Ajmone-Marsan, C. Thalamocortical integrating mechanisms. *Res. Pub., Ass. Res. nerv. ment. Dis.,* 1950, **30**, 493.

Jeffress, L. A. Galvanic phenomena of the skin. *J. exp. Psychol.,* 1928, **11**, 130–144.

Jung, R. Hirnelektrische Untersuchungen ueber den Elektrokrampf: die Erregungsabläufe in corticalen und subcorticalen Hirnregionen bei Katze und Hund. *Arch. Psychiat.,* 1949, **183**, 206–244.

Kaada, B. R. Somato-motor, autonomic and electrocorticographic responses to electrical stimulation of "rhinencephalic" and other forebrain structures in primates, cat and dog. *Acta physiol. scand.,* 1951, **24**, Suppl. 83, 1–285.

Kaada, B. R. Cingulate, posterior orbital, anterior insular and temporal pole cortex. In *Handbook of physiology. Vol. II.* J. Field, H. W. Magoun, & V. E. Hall, Eds. Baltimore: Williams and Wilkins, 1960.

Kaada, B. R., Jansen, J., Jr., & Andersen, P. Stimulation of the hippocampus and medial cortical areas in unanesthetized cats. *Neurology,* 1953, **3**, 844–857.

Kaada, B. R., Rasmussen, E. W., & Kveim, O. Impaired acquisition of passive avoidance behavior by subcallosal, septal, hypothalamic, and insular lesions in rats. *J. comp. physiol. Psychol.,* 1962, **55**, 661–670.

Karmos, G., & Grastyán, E. Influence of hippocampal lesions on simple and delayed conditional reflexes. *Acta physiol. Acad. Sci. hung.,* 1962, **21**, 215–224.

Karplus, J. P. Die Physiologie der vegetativen Zentren. Auf Grund experimenteller Erfahrungen. In *Handbuch der Neurologie.* O. Bumke & O. Foerster, Eds. Berlin: Springer, 1937.

Kasper, P. Attenuation of passive avoidance by continuous septal stimulation. *Psychonom. Sci.,* 1964, **1**, 219–220.

Kasper, P. Disruption of positive habit reversal by septal stimulation. *Psychonom. Sci.,* 1965, **3**, 111–112.

Keller, A. D. Autonomic discharges elicited by physiological stimuli in mid-brain preparations. *Amer. J. Physiol.,* 1932, **100**, 576–586.

Kellicutt, M. H., & Schwartzbaum, J. S. Formation of a conditioned emotional response (CER) following lesions of the amygdaloid complex in rats. *Psychol. Rep.,* 1963, **12**, 351–358.

Kelly, A. H., Beaton, L. E., & Magoun, H. W. A midbrain mechanism for facio-vocal activity. *J. Neurophysiol.,* 1946, **9**, 181–189.

Kennard, Margaret A. Effect of bilateral ablation of cingulate area on behavior of cats. *J. Neurophysiol.,* 1955, **18**, 159–169.

Kennedy, J. L., & Travis, R. C. Prediction of speed of performance by muscle action potentials. *Science,* 1947, **106**, 410–411.

Kennedy, J. L., & Travis, R. C. Prediction and control of alertness. II: Continuous tracking. *J. comp. physiol. Psychol.,* 1948, **41**, 203–210.

Kenyon, J. The effect of septal lesions upon motivated behavior in the rat. McGill University, doctoral dissertation, 1962.

Kenyon, J., & Krieckhaus, E. E. Enhanced avoidance behavior following septal lesions in the rat as a function of lesion size and spontaneous activity. *J. comp. physiol. Psychol.,* 1965a, **59**, 466–469.

Kenyon, J., & Krieckhaus, E. E. Decrements in one-way avoidance learning following septal lesions. *Psychonom. Sci.,* 1965b, **3**, 113–114.

Kessler, M. M. Spontaneous and reflex emotional responses differentiated by lesions in diencephalon. *Proc. Soc. exp. Biol. Med.,* 1941, **47**, 225–227.

Kimble, D. P. The effects of bilateral hippocampal lesions in rats. *J. comp. physiol. Psychol.,* 1963, **56**, 273–283.

Kimura, D. Effects of selective hippocampal damage on avoidance behavior in the rat. *Canad. J. Psychol.,* 1958, **12**, 213–218.

King, F. A. Effects of septal and amygdaloid lesions on emotional behavior and conditioned avoidance responses in the rat. *J. nerv. ment. Dis.,* 1958, **126**, 57–63.

King, F. A., & Meyer, P. M. Effects of amygdaloid lesions upon septal hyperemotionality in the rat. *Science,* 1958, **128**, 655–656.

Kirilzev, S. Cases of affection of the optic thalamus. *Neurol. Zbl.,* 1891, **10**, 310.

Kleitman, N. *Sleep and wakefulness.* Chicago: Univ. of Chicago Press, 1939.

Kleitman, N. The sleep-wakefulness cycle. In *Problems of consciousness.* H. A. Abramson, Ed. New York: Josiah Macy, Jr. Foundation, 1950.

Kling, A., Orbach, J., Schwartz, N. B., & Towne, J. C. Injury to the limbic system and associated structures in cats. *Arch. gen. Psychiat.,* 1960, **3**, 391–420.

Klüver, H., & Bucy, P. C. "Psychic blindness" and other symptoms following bilateral temporal lobectomy in rhesus monkeys. *Amer. J. Physiol.,* 1937, **119**, 352–353.

Klüver, H., & Bucy, P. C. An analysis of certain effects of bilateral temporal lobectomy in the rhesus monkey, with special reference to "psychic blindness." *J. Psychol.,* 1938, **5**, 33–54.

Klüver, H., & Bucy, P. C. Preliminary analysis of functions of the temporal lobes in monkeys. *Arch. Neurol. Psychiat. (Chicago),* 1939, **42**, 979–1000.

Kremer, F. Autonomic and somatic relations induced by stimulation of the cingular gyrus in dogs. *J. Neurophysiol.,* 1947, **10**, 371.

Krieckhaus, E. E. Decrements in avoidance behavior following mammillothalamic tractotomy in cats. *J. Neurophysiol.,* 1964, **27**, 753–767

Krieckhaus, E. E. Decrements in avoidance behavior

following mammillothalamic tractotomy in rats and subsequent recovery with D-amphetamine. *J. comp. physiol. Psychol.,* 1965, **60,** 31–35.

Krieckhaus, E. E., Simmons, H. J., Thomas, G. J., & Kenyon, J. Septal lesions enhance shock avoidance behavior in the rat. *Exp. Neurol.,* 1964, **9,** 107–113.

Lacey, J. I. Consistency of patterns of somatic response to stress. *Amer. Psychologist.,* 1949, **4,** 232–233.

Lacey, J. I. Individual differences in somatic response patterns. *J. comp. physiol. Psychol.,* 1950, **43,** 338–350.

Lacey, J. I. The evaluation of autonomic responses: toward a general solution. *Ann. N.Y. Acad. Sci.,* 1956, **67,** 123–163.

Lacey, J. I., & Lacey, B. C. The relationship of resting autonomic cyclic activity to motor impulsivity. *Res. Publ., Ass. Res. nerv. ment. Dis.,* 1958a, **36,** 144–209.

Lacey, J. I., & Lacey, B. C. Verification and extension of the principle of autonomic response sterotypy. *Amer. J. Psychol.,* 1958b, **71,** 50–73.

Lacey, J. I., & Lacey, B. C. The relationship of resting autonomic cyclic activity to motor impulsivity. *Res. Publ., Ass. Res. nerv. ment. Dis.,* 1958c, **36,** 144–209.

Lacey, J. I., & Van Lehn, R. Differential emphasis in somatic response to stress: an experimental study. *Psychosom. Med.,* 1952, **14,** 71–81.

Lacey, J. I., Bateman, D. E., & Van Lehn, R. Autonomic response specificity. An experimental study. *Psychosom. Med.,* 1953, **15,** 8–21.

Lacey, J. I., Smith, R. L., & Green, A. Use of conditioned autonomic responses in the study of anxiety. *Psychosom. Med.,* 1955, **17,** 208–217.

Lacey, O. L. An analysis of the appropriate unit for use in the measurement of level of galvanic skin resistance. *J. exp. Psychol.,* 1947, **37,** 449–457.

Lacey, O. L., & Siegel, P. S. An analysis of the unit of measurement of the galvanic skin response. *J. exp. Psychol.,* 1949, **39,** 122–127.

Landis, C. Changes in blood-pressure during sleep as determined by the Erlanger method. *Amer. J. Physiol.,* 1925a, **73,** 551–555.

Landis, C. Studies of emotional reactions. IV: Metabolic rate. *Amer. J. Physiol.,* 1925b, **74,** 188–203.

Landis, C. Studies of emotional reactions. V: Severe emotional upset. *J. comp. Psychol.,* 1926, **6,** 221–242.

Landis, C., & DeWick, H. N. The electrical phenomena of the skin (psychogalvanic reflex). *Psychol. Bull.,* 1929, **26,** 64–119.

Landis, C., & Gullette, R. Studies of emotional reactions. III: Systolic blood-pressure and inspiration-expiration ratios. *J. comp. Psychol.,* 1925, **5,** 221–253.

Landis, C., & Wiley, L. E. Changes in blood pressure during deception. *J. comp. Psychol.,* 1926, **6,** 1–19.

Lange, C. G. *Om Sindsbevaegelser. et psyko. fysiolog. studie.* Copenhagen: Krønar, 1885.

Lash, L. Response discriminability and the hippocampus. *J. comp. physiol. Psychol.,* 1964, **57,** 251–256.

Lashley, K. S. The thalamus and emotion. *Psychol. Rev.,* 1938, **45,** 42–61.

Lashley, K. S., & Sperry, R. W. Olfactory discrimination after destruction of the anterior thalamic nuclei. *Amer. J. Physiol.,* 1943, **139,** 446.

Lehmann, A. *Hauptgesetze des menschlichen Gefuehlslebens.* Leipzig: Reisland, 1914.

Liddell, D. W., & Weil-Malherbe, H. The effects of methedrine and of lysergic acid diethylamide on mental processes and on the blood adrenaline level. *J. Neurol. Neurosurg. Psychiat.,* 1953, **16,** 7–13.

Lindsley, D. B. Electrical activity of human motor units during voluntary contraction. *Amer. J. Physiol.,* 1935, **114,** 90–99.

Lindsley, D. B. Emotions and the EEG. In *The second international symposium on feelings and emotions.* M. L. Reymert, Ed. New York: McGraw-Hill, 1950.

Lindsley, D. B. Emotion. *Handbook of experimental psychology.* S. S. Stevens, Ed. New York: Wiley, 1951.

Lindsley, D. B., & Sassaman, W. H. Autonomic activity and brain potentials associated with "voluntary" control of the pilomotors (MM a rectores pilorum). *J. Neurophysiol.,* 1938, **1,** 342–349.

Lubar, J. F. Effects of medial cortical lesions on the avoidance behavior of the cat. *J. comp. physiol. Psychol.,* 1964, **58,** 38–46.

Lubar, J. F., & Perachio, A. A. One-way and two-way learning and transfer of an active avoidance response in normal and cingulectomized cats. *J. comp. physiol. Psychol.,* 1965, **60,** 46–52.

Lubar, J. F., Perachio, A. A., & Kavanagh, A. J. Deficits in active avoidance behavior following lesions of the lateral and posterolateral gyrus of the cat. *J. comp. physiol. Psychol.,* 1966 (in press).

Luco, L. V. The defatiguing effect of adrenaline. *Amer. J. Physiol.,* 1939, **125,** 197–203.

Lykken, D. T. Properties of electrodes used in electrodermal measurements. *J. comp. physiol. Psychol.,* 1959, **52,** 629–634.

McCleary, R. A. Response specificity in the behavioral effects of limbic system lesions in the cat. *J. comp. physiol. Psychol.,* 1961, **54,** 605–613.

McCleary, R. A., Jones, C., & Ursin, H. Avoidance and retention deficits in septal cats. *Psychonom. Sci.,* 1965, **2,** 85–86.

McCulloch, W. S. *The precentral motor cortex.* P. C. Bucy, Ed. Urbana: Univ. of Illinois Press, 1944.

Macht, M. B., & Bard, P. Studies on decerebrate cats in the chronic state. *Fed. Proc.,* 1942, **1,** 55–56.

MacLean, P. D. Psychosomatic disease and the "visceral brain." *Psychosom. Med.,* 1949, **11,** 338–353.

MacLean, P. D. The limbic system and its hippocampal formation: studies in animals and their possible application to man. *J. Neurosurg.,* 1954, **11,** 29–44.

MacLean, P. D. Chemical and electrical stimulation of hippocampus in unrestrained animals. II: Behavioral findings. *Arch. Neurol. Psychiat. (Chicago),* 1957, **78,** 128–142.

MacLean, P. D., & Delgado, J. M. R. Electrical and chemical stimulation of frontotemporal portion of limbic system in the waking animal. *EEG clin. Neurophysiol.,* 1953, **5**, 91–100.

MacLean, P. D., Horwitz, N. H., & Robinson, F. Olfactory-like responses in pyriform area to non-olfactory stimulation. *Yale. J. Biol. Med.,* 1952, **25**, 159.

Mahut, H., & Cordeau, J. P. Spatial reversal deficits in monkeys with amydalahippocampal ablations. *Exp. Neurol.,* 1963, **7**, 426–434.

Major, S. G., & Mann, F. C. Glycogenolytic effect of epinephrine on skeletal muscle. *Amer. J. Physiol.,* 1932, **101**, 462–468.

Malmo, R. B., & Shagass, C. Behavioral and physiologic changes under stress after operations on the frontal lobes. *Arch. Neurol. Psychiat. (Chicago),* 1950, **63**, 113–124.

Malmo, R. B., Shagass, C., & Davis, J. Specificity of bodily reaction under stress. A physiological study of somatic symptom mechanisms in psychiatric patients. *Res. Publ., Ass. Res. nerv. ment. Dis.,* 1950, **29**, 231–261.

Marston, W. M. Systolic blood-pressure symptoms of deception. *J. exp. Psychol.,* 1917, **2**, 117–163.

Marston, W. M. A theory of emotions and affection based upon systolic blood pressure studies. *Amer. J. Psychol.,* 1924, **35**, 469–506.

Masserman, J. H. Destruction of the hypothalamus in cats. *Arch. Neurol. Psychiat. (Chicago),* 1938, **39**, 1250–1271.

Masserman, J. H. Is the hypothalamus a center of emotion? *Psychosom. Med.,* 1941, **3**, 3–25.

Masserman, J. H. Hypothalamus in psychiatry. *Amer. J. Psychiat.,* 1942, **98**, 633–637.

Masserman, J. H. *Behavior and neurosis.* Chicago: Univ. of Chicago Press, 1943.

Masserman, J. H., & Pechtel, C. How brain lesions affect normal and neurotic behavior (an experimental approach). *Amer. J. Psychiat.,* 1956, **112**, 865–872.

Max, L. W. An experimental study of the motor theory of consciousness. I: Critique of earlier studies.*J. gen. Psychol.,* 1934, **11**, 112–125.

Max, L. W. An experimental study of the motor theory of consciousness. III: Action-current responses in deaf-mutes during sleep. *J. comp. Psychol.,* 1935, **19**, 469–486.

Max, L. W. An experimental study of the motor theory of consciousness. IV: Action-current responses of the deaf during awakening, kinesthetic imagery and abstract thinking. *J. comp. Psychol.,* 1937, **24**, 301–344.

Mettler, F. A., Ed. (The Columbia-Greystone Associates). *Selective partial ablation of the frontal cortex. A correlative study of its effects on human psychotic subjects.* New York: Paul Hoeber, 1949, Chapter 14.

Meyer, A., & McLardy, T. Clinicoanatomical studies of frontal lobe function based on leucotomy material. *J. ment. Sci.,* 1949, **95**, 403–417.

Meyer, M. F. That whale among the fishes—the theory of emotions. *Psychol. Rev.* 1933, **40**, 292–300.

Milner, Brenda, & Penfield, W. The effect of hippocampal lesions on recent memory. *Trans. Amer. neurol. Ass.,* 1955, **80**, 42–48.

Mirsky, A. F. Studies of the effects of brain lesions on social behavior in *Macaca mulatta:* methodological and theoretical consideration. *Ann. N.Y. Acad. Sci.,* 1960, **85**, 785–794.

Mishkin, M. Visual discrimination performance following partial ablations of the temporal lobe. II: Ventral surface vs. hippocampus. *J. comp. physiol. Psychol.,* 1954, **47**, 187–193.

Mishkin, M. Perseveration of central sets after frontal lesions in monkeys. In *The frontal granular cortex and behavior.* J. M. Warren & K. Akert, Eds. New York: McGraw-Hill, 1964.

Mishkin, M., & Pribram, K. H. Visual discrimination performance following partial ablations of temporal lobe: ventral vs. lateral. *J. comp. physiol. Psychol.,* 1954, **47**, 14–20.

Mittelman, B., & Wolff, H. G. Affective states and skin temperature: experimental study of subjects with "cold hands" and Raynaud's syndrome. *Psychosom. Med.,* 1939, **71**, 257–266.

Mittelman, B., & Wolff, H. G. Emotions and skin temperature: observations on patients during psychotherapeutic (psychoanalytic) interviews. *Psychosom. Med.,* 1943, **5**, 211–31.

Molina, F. A. de, & Hunsperger, R. W. Relaciones foncionales de la amygdala, hipotalamo, substancia gris central del mesencefalo. *Actas Soc. exp. C. Fisiol.,* 1958, **4**, 165–166.

Molina, F. A. de, & Hunsperger, R. W. Central representation of affective reactions in forebrain and brainstem: electrical stimulation of amygdala, stria terminalis, and adjacent structures. *J. Physiol. (London),* 1959, **145**, 265–281.

Molina, F. A. de, & Hunsperger, R. W. Organization of the subcortical system governing defense and flight reactions in the cat. *J. Physiol. (London),* 1962, **160**, 200–213.

Moniz, E. *Tentatives opératoires dans le traitement de certaines psychoses.* Paris: Masson, 1936.

Moore, R. Y. Effects of some rhinencephalic lesions on retention of conditioned avoidance behavior in cats. *J. comp. physiol. Psychol.,* 1964, **57**, 65–71.

Morgan, C. T., & Stellar, E. *Physiological psychology.* New York: McGraw-Hill, 1950.

Morin, G., Gastaut, H., Naquet, H., & Roger, A. Variations du cycle d'excitabilite des aires receptrices visuelles du chat, sous l'effet d'agents pharmacodynamiques. *J. Physiol. (Paris),* 1951, **43**, 820–824.

Morin, G., Gastaut, H., Vigouroux, R., & Roger, A. Comportement émotionnel et lésions experimentales du rhinencephale chez la chat. *C. R. Soc. Biol. (Paris),* 1952a, **146**, 1959–1961.

Morin, G., Naquet, H., & Badier, M. Stimulation electrique de la region amygdalienne et pression artérielle chez la chat. *J. Physiol. (Paris),* 1952b, **44**, 303–305.

Morison, R. S., & Dempsey, E. W. A study of thalamocortical relations. *Amer. J. Physiol.*, 1942, **135**, 281.

Moruzzi, G., & Magoun, H. W. Brain stem reticular formation and activation of the EEG. *EEG clin. Neurophysiol.*, 1949, **1**, 455–473.

Mueller, E. K. Über Einfluss psychischer und physiologischer Vorgänge auf das electrische Vermoegen des Koerpers. *Physik. Med. Mschr.*, 1904–1905, **1**, 212–214.

Naquet, R. Effects of stimulation of the rhinencephalon in the waking cat. *EEG clin. Neurophysiol.*, 1954, **6**, 711–712.

Newman, E. B., Perkins, F. T., & Wheeler, R. H. Cannon's theory of emotion: a critique. *Psychol. Rev.*, 1930, **37**, 305–326.

Nielson, H. C., McIver, A. H., & Boswell, R. S. Effect of septal lesions on learning, emotionality, activity and exploratory behavior in rats. *Exp. Neurol.*, 1965, **11**, 147–157.

Obrador, A. S. Temporal lobotomy. *J. Neuropath. exp. Neurol.*, 1947, **6**, 185–193.

Oldham, A. J. Effects of temporal lobe lesions on behavior in paranoid states. *J. ment. Sci.*, 1953, **99**, 580–587.

Orbach, J., Milner, B., & Rasmussen, T. Learning and retention in monkeys after amygdalahippocampal resection. *Arch Neurol.* (*Chicago*), 1960, **3**, 230–251.

Papez, J. W. A proposed mechanism of emotion. *Arch. Neurol. Psychiat.* (*Chicago*), 1937, **38**, 725–743.

Papez, J. W. Cerebral mechanisms. *Res. Publ., Ass. Res. nerv. ment. Dis.*, 1939, **89**, 145–159.

Paré, W. P., & Dumas, J. S. The effects of insular neocortical lesions on passive and active avoidance behavior in the rat. *Psychonom. Sci.*, 1965, **2**, 87–88.

Pechtel, C., Masserman, J. H., Schreiner, L., & Levitt, M. Differential effects of lesions of the medio-dorsal nuclei of the thalamus on normal and neurotic behavior in the cat. *J. nerv. ment. Dis.*, 1955, **121**, 26–33.

Peele, T. L. *The neuroanatomical basis for clinical neurology.* New York: McGraw-Hill, 1954.

Penfield, W. Symposium on gyrectomy. I: Bilateral frontal gyrectomy and postoperative intelligence. *Res. Publ., Ass. Res. nerv. ment. Dis.*, 1948, **27**, 519–534.

Penfield, W., & Milner, Brenda. Memory deficit produced by bilateral lesions in the hippocampal zone. *A.M.A. Arch. Neurol. Psychiat.*, 1958, **79**, 475–497.

Peretz, E. The effects of lesions of the anterior cingulate cortex on the behavior of the rat. *J. comp. physiol. Psychol.*, 1960, **53**, 540–548.

Peretz, E. The effect of hippocampal ablation on the strength of food-obtaining responses. *Amer. Psychologist*, 1963, **18**, 464.

Persky, H., Grinker, R. R., & Mirsky, M. Excretion of hippuric acid in subjects with free anxiety. *J. clin. Invest.*, 1950, **29**, 110–114.

Peterson, F. The galvanometer as a measure of emotions. *Brit. med. J.*, 1907, **2**, 804–806.

Piéron, H. Les variations physio-galvaniques comme phénomène d'expression des émotions. *Rev. Psychiat.*, 1910, **14**, 486–506.

Ploog, D. W., & MacLean, P. D. On functions of the mammillary bodies in the squirrel monkey. *Exp. Neurol.*, 1963, **7**, 76–85.

Poirier, L. J. Anatomical and experimental studies on the temporal pole of the macaque. *J. comp. Neurol.*, 1952, **96**, 209–248.

Porter, J. M., Jr. Adaptation of the galvanic skin response. *J. exp. Psychol.*, 1938, **23**, 553–557.

Pribram, K. H. Interrelations of psychology and the neurological disciplines. In *Psychology: a study of a science.* S. Koch, Ed. New York: McGraw-Hill, 1962.

Pribram, K. H., & Bagshaw, M. Further analysis of the temporal lobe syndrome utilizing frontotemporal ablations. *J. comp. Neurol.*, 1953, **99**, 347–375.

Pribram, K. H., & Fulton, J. F. An experimental critique of the effects of anterior cingulate ablations in monkey. *Brain*, 1954, **77**, 34–44.

Pribram, K. H., & Kruger, L. Functions of the "olfactory brain." *Ann. N.Y. Acad. Sci.*, 1954, **58**, 109–38.

Pribram, K. H., & Weiskrantz, L. A comparison of the effects of medial and lateral cerebral resections on conditioned avoidance behavior of monkeys. *J. comp. physiol. Psychol.*, 1957, **50**, 74–80.

Pribram, K. H., Mishkin, M., Rosvold, H. E., & Kaplan, S. J. Effects on delayed-response performance of lesions of dorsolateral and ventromedial frontal cortex of baboons. *J. comp. physiol. Psychol.*, 1952, **45**, 565–575.

Pribram, K. H., Wilson, W. A., Jr., & Connors, J. Effects of lesions of the medial forebrain on alternation behavior of rhesus monkeys. *Exp. Neurol.*, 1962, **6**, 36–47.

Ranson, S. W. The hypothalamus: its significance for visceral innervation and emotional expression. *Trans. Coll. Physns* (*Philadelphia*), 1934, **2**, 222–242.

Ranson, S. W. Somnolence caused by hypothalamic lesions in the monkey. *Arch. Neurol. Psychiat.* (*Chicago*), 1939, **41**, 1–23.

Ranson, S. W., & Magoun, H. W. The hypothalamus. *Ergebn. Physiol.*, 1939, **41**, 56–163.

Read, J. M. Basal pulse rate and pulse pressure changes accompanying variations in basal metabolic rate. *Arch. intern. Med.*, 1924, **34**, 553–565.

Read, J. M., & Barnett, C. W. New formulae for prediction of basal metabolism from pulse rate and pulse pressure. *Proc. Soc. exp. Biol. Med.*, 1934, **31**, 723–725.

Regan, P. F., & Reilly, J. Circulating epinephrine and norepinephrine in changing emotional states. *J. nerv. ment. Dis.*, 1958, **127**, 12–16.

Reitman, F. Orbital cortex syndrome following leucotomy. *Amer. J. Psychiat.*, 1946, **103**, 238–241.

Rich, I., & Thompson, R. Role of the hippocampo-septal system, thalamus and hypothalamus in avoidance conditioning. *J. comp. physiol. Psychol.*, 1965, **59**, 66–72.

Richter, C. P. The sweat glands studied by the electrical resistance method. *Amer. J. Physiol.*, 1924, **68**, 147.

Richter, C. P. The significance of changes in the electrical resistance of the body during sleep. *Proc. Nat. Acad. Sci. (Washington)*, 1926, **12**, 214–222.

Richter, C. P. Pathological sleep and similar conditions studied by electrical skin resistance method. *Arch. Neurol. Psychiat. (Chicago)*, 1929, **21**, 363–375.

Richter, C. P. Sleep produced by hypnotics studied by the electrical skin resistance method. *J. Pharmacol. exp. Therap.*, 1931, **42**, 471–486.

Roberts, W. W., Dember, W. N., & Brodwick, M. Alternation and exploration in rats with hippocampal lesions. *J. comp. physiol. Psychol.*, 1962, **55**, 695–700.

Robinson, F., & Lennox, M. A. Sensory mechanisms in hippocampus, cingulate gyrus and cerebellum of the cat. *Fed. Proc.*, 1951, **10**, 110.

Rosvold, H. E., Mirski, A. F., & Pribram, K. H. Influence of amygdalectomy on social behavior in monkeys. *J. comp. physiol. Psychol.*, 1954, **47**, 173–178.

Rothfield, L., & Harman, P. On the relation of the hippocampal-fornix system to the control of rage responses in cats. *J. comp. Neurol.*, 1954, **101**, 265–282.

Rothmann, H. Zusammenfassender Bericht ueber den Rothmannschen grosshirnlosen Hund nach klinischer und anatomischer Untersuchung. *Zschr. ges. Neurol. Psychiat.*, 1923, **87**, 247–313.

Rowles, E., & Patrick, J. R. The effect of various stimuli on the basal metabolic rate, the blood-pressure and the galvanic reflex in man. *J. exp. Psychol.*, 1934, **17**, 847–861.

Ruch, T. C., Fulton, J. F., & German, W. J. Sensory discrimination in monkey, chimpanzee and man after lesions of the parietal lobe. *Arch. Neurol. Psychiat. (Chicago)*, 1938, **39**, 919.

Ruckmick, C. A. *The psychology of feeling and emotion.* New York: McGraw-Hill, 1936.

Russell, G. V. Interrelationships within the limbic and centrencephalic systems. In *Electrical stimulation of the brain.* D. E. Sheer, Ed. Austin: Univ. of Texas Press, 1961.

Rylander, G. *Personality changes after operations on the frontal lobes. A clinical study of 32 cases.* Copenhagen: Munksgaard, 1939.

Rylander, G. Personality analysis before and after frontal lobotomy. *Res. Publ., Ass. Res. nerv. ment. Dis.*, 1948, **27**, 691–705.

Sawa, M., Yukiharu, U., Masaya, A., & Toshio, H. Preliminary report on the amygdaloidectomy on the psychotic patients, with interpretation of oral-emotional manifestations in schizophrenics. *Folia psychiat. neurol. jap.*, 1954, **7**, 309–316.

Schaltenbrandt, G., & Cobb, S. Clinical and anatomical studies on two cats without neocortex. *Brain,* 1930, **53**, 449.

Schlosberg, H. Three dimensions of emotion. *Psychol Rev.*, 1954, **61**, 81–88.

Schlosberg, H., & Stanly, W. C. A simple test of the normality of twenty-four distributions of electrical skin conductance. *Science,* 1953, **117**, 35–37.

Schmaltz, L. W., & Isaacson, R. L. The effects of preliminary training conditions upon DRL 20 performance in the hippocampectomized rat. *J. Physiol. Behav.*, 1966 **1**, 175–182.

Schreiner, L. H., & Kling, A. Behavioral changes following rhinencephalic injury in cat. *J. Neurophysiol.*, 1953, **16**, 643–659.

Schreiner, L. H., & Kling, A. Effects of castration on hypersexual behavior induced by rhinencephalic injury in cat. *Arch. Neurol. Psychiat. (Chicago)*, 1954, **72**, 180–186.

Schreiner, L. H., & Kling, A. Rhinencephalon and behavior. *Amer. J. Physiol.*, 1956, **184**, 486–490.

Schreiner, L. H., Rioch, D. McK., Pechtel, C., & Masserman, J. H. Behavioral changes following thalamic injury in the cat. *J. Neurophysiol.*, 1953, **16**, 254.

Schwartzbaum, J. S. Changes in reinforcing properties of stimuli following ablation of the amygdaloid complex in monkeys. *J. comp. physiol. Psychol.*, 1960, **53**, 388–395.

Schwartzbaum, J. S. Discrimination behavior after amygdalectomy in monkeys: visual and somesthetic learning and perceptual capacity. *J. comp. physiol. Psychol.*, 1965, **60**, 314–319.

Schwartzbaum, J. S., & Gay, Patricia E. Interacting effects of septal and amygdaloid lesions in the rat. *J. comp. physiol. Psychol.*, 1966, **61**, 59–65.

Schwartzbaum, J. S., Thompson, J. B., & Kellicutt, M. H. Auditory frequency discrimination and generalization following lesions of the amygdaloid area in rats. *J. comp. physiol. Psychol.*, 1964, **57**, 257–266.

Scoville, W. B. Proposed methods of cortical undercutting of certain areas of the frontal lobes as a substitute for prefrontal lobotomy. A. Orbital surface. B. Areas 9 and 10 of Brodmann. C. Cingular gyrus. Preliminary report of 9 operative cases. *Dig. Neurol. Psychiat.*, 1948, **16**, 533.

Scoville, W. B. Selective cortical undercutting as a means of modifying and studying frontal lobe function in man. Preliminary report of 43 operative cases. *J. Neurosurg.*, 1949, **6**, 65–73; and Selective cortical undercutting. *Proc. roy. Soc. Med. Suppl.*, 1949, **42**, 3–8.

Scoville, W. B., & Milner, Brenda. Loss of recent memory after bilateral hippocampal lesions. *J. Neurol. Neurosurg. Psychiat.*, 1957, **20**, 11–21.

Shephard, J. F. Organic changes and feeling. *Amer. J. Psychol.*, 1906, **17**, 522–584.

Shephard, J. F. *The circulation and sleep, with atlas.* New York: Macmillan, 1914.

Sherrington, C. S. Experiments on the value of vascular and visceral factors for the genesis of emotion. *Proc. roy. Soc. (London),* B, 1900, **66**, 390–403.

Shock, N. W., & Coombs, C. H. Changes in skin resistance and affective tone. *Amer. J. Psychol.*, 1937, **49**, 611–620.

Sidis, B. The nature and cause of the galvanic phenomenon. *J. abnorm. Psychol.*, 1910, **5**, 69–74.

Sidis, B., & Nelson, L. The nature and causation of the galvanic phenomenon. I: The nature of the galvanic phenomenon. *Psychol. Rev.*, 1910, **17**, 98–146.

Simmons, H. J., & Thomas, G. J. Septal lesions reduce the inhibitory effects of punishment. Paper read at 33rd annual meeting of the Midwestern Psychological Association, Chicago, 1961.

Smith, W. K. The results of ablation of the cingular region of the cerebral cortex. *Fed. Proc.*, 1944, **3**, 42–43.

Smith, W. K. The functional significance of the rostral cingular cortex as revealed by its responses to electrical excitation. *J. Neurophysiol.*, 1945, **8**, 241.

Smith, W. K. Non-olfactory functions of the pyriform-amygdaloid-hippocampal complex. *Fed. Proc.*, 1950, **9**, 118.

Snyder, D. R., & Isaacson, R. L. Effects of large and small bilateral hippocampal lesions on two types of passive-avoidance responses. *Psychol. Rep.*, 1965, **16**, 1277–1290.

Sommer, R. Zur Messung der Motorischen Begleiterscheinungen psychischer Zustaende. *Beitr. Psychiat. Klinic (Wien)*, 1902–1903, **1**, 143–164.

Sommer, R. Die Natur der electrischen Vorgaenge an der Haut, besonders der Finger. *Münch. med. Wschr.*, 1905, **52** (2), 2493–2495.

Somogyi, M. Mechanisms of epinephrine-hyperglycemia. *Endocrinology*, 1951, **49**, 774–781.

Spiegel, E. A., Miller, H. R., & Oppenheimer, M. J. Forebrain and rage reactions. *J. Neurophysiol.*, 1940, **3**, 538–548.

Spiegel, E. A., Wycis, H. T., Marks, M., & Lee, A. J. Stereotaxic apparatus for operations on the human brain. *Science*, 1947, **106**, 349.

Spiegel, E. A., Wycis, H. T., Freed, H., & Orchinik, C. The central mechanism of the emotions. *Amer. J. Psychiat.*, 1951, **108**, 426.

Starzl, T. E., & Whitlock, D. G. Diffuse thalamic projection system in monkey. *J. Neurophysiol.*, 1952, **15**, 449.

Stepien, L. S., Cordeau, J. P., & Rasmussen, T. The effect of temporal lobe and hippocampal lesions on auditory and visual recent memory in monkeys. *Brain*, 1960, **83**, 470–489.

Stoerring, G. Experimentelle Beitraege zur Lehre vom Gefuehl. *Arch. ges. Psychol.*, 1906, **6**, 316–356.

Stovkis, B. A method for the uninterrupted registering of blood pressure as a psychophysiological research-technique for the study of psychic stimuli on the blood pressure. *J. exp. Psychol.*, 1938, **22**, 365–376.

Ström-Olsen, R., & Weil-Malherbe, H. Humoral changes in manic depressive psychosis with particular reference to the excretion of catecholamines in urine. *J. ment. Sci.*, 1958, **104**, 696–704.

Swann, H. G. The function of the brain in olfaction. II: The results of destruction of olfactory and other nervous structures upon the discrimination of odors. *J. comp. Neurol.*, 1934, **59**, 175.

Swann, H. G. The function of the brain in olfaction. III: Effects of large cortical lesions on olfactory discrimination. *Amer. J. Physiol.*, 1935, **111**, 257.

Syz, H. C. Observations on the unreliability of subjective reports of emotional reactions. *Brit. J. Psychol.*, 1926, **17**, 119–126.

Tarchanoff, J. Ueber die galvanischen Erscheinungen an der Haut des Menschen bei Reizung der Sinnesorgane und bei verschiedenen Formen der psychischen Taetigkeit. *Pflüg. Arch. ges Physiol.*, 1890, **46**, 46–55.

Teitelbaum, H., & Milner, P. Activity changes following partial hippocampal lesions in rats. *J. comp. physiol. Psychol.*, 1963, **56**, 284–289.

Terzian, H., & Dalle Ore, G. Syndrome of Kluever and Bucy reproduced in man by bilateral removal of the temporal lobes. *Neurology*, 1955, **5**, 373–380.

Thiesen, J. W. Effects of certain forms of emotion on the normal electroencephalogram. *Arch. Psychol. (N.Y.)*, 1943, **265** (monograph).

Thomas, G. J., & Otis, L. S. Effects of rhinencephalic lesions on conditioning of avoidance responses in the rat. *J. comp. physiol. Psychol.*, 1958a, **51**, 130–134.

Thomas, G. J., & Otis, L. S. Effects of rhinencephalic lesions on maze learning in rats. *J. comp. physiol. Psychol.*, 1958b, **51**, 161–166.

Thomas, G. J., & Slotnick, B. Effects of lesions in the cingulum on maze learning and avoidance conditioning in the rat. *J. comp. physiol. Psychol.*, 1962, **55**, 1085–1091.

Thomas, G. J., & Slotnick, B. Impairment of avoidance responding by lesions in cingulate cortex in rats depends on food drive. *J. comp. physiol. Psychol.*, 1963, **56**, 959–964.

Thomas, G. J., Fry, W. J., Fry, F. J., Slotnick, B., & Krieckhaus, E. E. Behavioral effects of mammillo-thalamic tractotomy in cats. *J. Neurophysiol.*, 1963, **26**, 857–876.

Thompson, A. F., & Walker, A. E. Behavioral alterations following lesions of the medial surface of the temporal lobe. *Arch. Neurol. Psychiat. (Chicago)*, 1951, **65**, 251–252.

Thompson, J. B., & Schwartzbaum, J. S. Discrimination behavior and conditioned suppression (CER) following localized lesions in the amygdala and putamen. *Psychol. Rep.*, 1964, **15**, 587–606.

Todd, T. W., & Rowlands, M. E. Studies in the alimentary canal of man. VI: Emotional interference in gastric behavior patterns. *J. comp. Psychol.*, 1930, **10**, 167–188.

Totten, E. Oxygen consumption during emotional stimulation. *Comp. Psychol. Monogr.*, 1925, **3**, 13.

Tracy, W. H., & Harrison, J. M. Aversive behavior following lesions of the septal region of the forebrain in the rat. *Amer. J. Psychol.*, 1956, **69**, 443–447.

Travis, L. E., & Lindsley, D. B. The relation of frequency and extent of action currents to intensity of muscular contraction. *J. exp. Psychol.*, 1931, **14**, 359–381.

Travis, R. C., & Kennedy, J. L. Prediction and automatic

control of alertness. I: Control of look-out alertness. *J. comp. physiol. Psychol.,* 1947, **40**, 457–461.

Travis, R. C., & Kennedy, J. L. Prediction and control of alertness. III: Calibration of the alertness indicator and further results. *J. comp. physiol. Psychol.,* 1949, **42**, 45–57.

Ursin, H. The temporal lobe substrate of fear and anger. *Acta psychiat. neurol. scand., Kbh.,* 1960, **35**, 378–396.

Ursin, H. Effect of amygdaloid lesions on avoidance behavior and visual discrimination in cats. *Exp. Neurol.,* 1965, **11**, 298–317.

Vanderwolf, C. H. Effect of combined medial thalamic and septal lesions on active-avoidance behavior. *J. comp. physiol. Psychol.,* 1964, **58**, 31–37.

Victor, M., Angevine, J. B., Mancall, E. L., & Fisher, C. M. Memory loss with lesions of hippocampal formation. *Arch. Neurol. (Chicago),* 1961, **5**, 244–263.

Walker, A. E., Thompson, A. F., & McQueen, J. D. Behavior and the temporal rhinencephalon in the monkey. *Bull. Johns Hopk. Hosp.,* 1953, **93**, 65–93.

Waller, A. D. The galvanometric measurement of "emotive" physiological changes. *Proc. roy. Soc. (London),* B, 1918, **90**, 214–217.

Waller, A. D. Concerning emotive phenomena. II: Periodic variations of conductance of the palm of the human hand. *Proc. roy. Soc. (London),* B, 1919–1920, **91**, 17–32.

Ward, A. A., Jr. The anterior cingular gyrus and personality. *Res. Publ., Ass. Res. nerv. ment. Dis.,* 1948, **27**, 438–445.

Wechsler, D. The measurement of emotional reaction. *Arch. Psychol. (N.Y.),* 1925, **76** (monograph).

Weiskrantz, L. Behavioral changes associated with ablations of the amygdaloid complex in monkey. *J. comp. physiol. Psychol.,* 1956, **49**, 381–391.

Wells, F. L., & Forbes, A. On certain electrical processes in the human body and their relations to emotional reactions. *Arch. Psychol. (N.Y.),* 1911, **16** (monograph).

Wheatley, M. D. The hypothalamus and affective behavior in cats: a study of the effects of experimental lesions, with anatomic correlations. *Arch. Neurol. Psychiat. (Chicago),* 1944, **52**, 296–316.

White, J. C. Autonomic discharge from stimulation of the hypothalamus in man. *Res. Publ., Ass. Res. nerv. ment. Dis.,* 1940, **20**, 854–863.

Whitehorn, J. C., & Richter, H. Unsteadiness of the heart rate in psychotic and neurotic states. *Arch. Neurol. Psychiat. (Chicago),* 1937, **38**, 62–70.

Whitehorn, J. C., Kaufman, M. R., & Thomas, J. M. Heart rate in relation to emotional disturbances. *Arch. Neurol. Psychiat. (Chicago),* 1935, **33**, 712–731.

Williams, A. C., Jr. Some psychological correlates of the electroencephalogram. *Arch. Psychol. (N.Y.),* 1939, **240** (monograph).

Wilson, S. A. K. Pathological laughing and crying. *J. Neurol. Psychopath.,* 1924, **4**, 299–333.

Wilson, S. A. K. *Modern problems in neurology.* New York: Wm. Wood, 1929.

Wolf, S., & Wolff, H. G. Evidence on the genesis of peptic ulcers in man. *J. Amer. med. Ass.,* 1942, **120**, 670–675.

Wolf, S., & Wolff, H. G. *Human gastric function.* New York: Oxford Univ. Press, 1943.

Woodworth, R. S., & Schlosberg, H. *Experimental psychology.* New York: Henry Holt, 1954.

Woodworth, R. S., & Sherrington, C. S. A pseudoaffective reflex and its spinal path. *J. Physiol. (London),* 1904, **31**, 234–243.

Wycis, H. T., & Spiegel, E. A. Thalamotomy—neurosurgical aspects. *Proc. roy. Soc. Med. Suppl.,* 1949, **42**, 84.

Zanchetti, A., & Zoccolini, A. Autonomic hypothalamic outbursts elicited by cerebellar stimulation. *J. Neurophysiol.,* 1954, **17**, 475–483.

Ziegler, L. H., & Levine, B. S. The influence of emotional reactions on basal metabolism. *Amer. J. med. Sci.,* 1925, **169**, 68–76.

Zucker, I. Effect of lesions of the septal-limbic area on the behavior of cats. *J. comp. physiol. Psychol.,* 1965, **60**, 344–352.

Zucker, I., & McCleary, R. A. Perseveration in septal cats. *Psychonom. Sci.,* 1964, **1**, 387–388.

CHAPTER TEN

Rewarding and Aversive Effects of Central Stimulation

Before attempting to integrate the empirical data and theoretical proposals of the previous chapters into a coherent theory of motivation, some recent experimental observations and their implications must be discussed. In 1954 Olds and Milner noticed that some animals appeared to "enjoy" electrical stimulation of certain areas of the brain and learned an instrumental response to obtain such stimulation. At about the same time Neal Miller and his associates (1953, 1954) observed that stimulation of certain hypothalamic points appeared to be sufficiently "aversive" to serve as the motivational component of an instrumental learning situation. Since then, the "reward-aversion" phenomena have been investigated in some detail, and considerable theoretical debate has been engendered by the implications of such a dual mechanism for a hedonistic theory of motivation (see Olds, 1955).

Historically, motivation has always been subsumed under the hedonistic principle that the organism responds to its environment in order to maximize pleasure and minimize pain. With the rise of behaviorism, subjective explanatory concepts such as pleasure and pain became unacceptable. The hedonistic theory was largely replaced by the more parsimonious and objective hypothesis that motivation is based on a general tendency of the organism to minimize all types of stimulation. Such a notion is implied in most recent theories of motivation and has been stated explicitly by Neal E. Miller (see Miller, 1959, for a discussion of this hypothesis).

Before considering specific experimental results, it may be worthwhile to discuss the basic experimental paradigm. The self-stimulation procedure allows animals to deliver brief (typically less than 0.5 sec) electrical shocks to specific points in the brain by means of permanently implanted electrodes. The animal is often first trained to perform some instrumental response (such as bar pressing) for a reward such as food or escape from painful grid shock. Brain stimulation is then delivered whenever the animal presses the bar, and the conventional reward is gradually omitted. The reward property of central stimulation is not, however, a secondary phenomenon, as Brobeck (1963) has suggested. Instrumental responses can be acquired even when no other incentive is used (Miller, 1961a, b; Schnitzer et al., 1965).

If the stimulating electrode is placed into a reward region, the animals respond regularly for long periods of time, delivering several thousand shocks per hour to their brain. If the electrode is in an "aversive" region, the animals perform instrumental responses to terminate (i.e., escape) such stimulation whenever it is presented. This aversion appears not to be merely centrally elicited pain, since the aversion regions are not in or near the classical sensory pathways.

A variety of stimulus parameters have been used in self-stimulation experiments, but the most common technique relies on 60-cycle sine waves (alternating current) delivered through sufficient resistance to produce a current flow of 10 to 300 μa (in the rat).

Frequently repeated applications of such stimulation do not produce significant tissue damage. Many experimenters have reported long-term observations on animals that self-stimulated for several hours per day for weeks or months. A good illustration of this unusual persistence of instrumental behavior has been published by Valenstein and Beer (1964). Rats given continuous access to a lever that provided intracranial stimulation worked almost continually throughout a 20-day observation period, *averaging* 29.2 responses per minute overall, a truly remarkable effect. Olds (1961) has reported that the threshold for reward stimulation may even decline in the course of an experiment. Given a choice between operating a lever to obtain electrical stimulation of a rewarding area of the brain and receiving the same number of stimulations at random intervals without having to work for them, rats do not show a reliable preference unless the stimulating current is very high. At near-seizure intensities, most rats prefer to control the interstimulation interval by operating a lever (Meyers and Valenstein, 1964). The electrical current does not merely disrupt all normal brain activity as was suggested in some of the earlier discussions. A good demonstration of this has been reported by Beer and Valenstein (1960) who found that rats can perform difficult auditory discriminations during electrical stimulation of reward areas.

Several workers (Olds, 1958d; Stein, 1958; Reynolds, 1958) have demonstrated that current intensity is an important variable in the self-stimulation experiment. Once an animal has learned to procure electrical stimulation, the response rate for stimulation from a given electrode remains surprisingly constant for a particular current intensity. If the subject is tested daily, little or no fluctuation in response rate can be observed, either within a test period or over days.

At some electrode sites there is little evidence of satiation, even when the individual test periods are prolonged. For electrical stimulation of at least some areas of the brain rats (Olds, 1958c) and monkeys (Lilly, 1958) work until exhausted.

Clinical observations (Heath, 1954; Sem-Jacobson, 1959; Delgado and Hamlin, 1960) suggest that apparently pleasurable sensations can be elicited by electrical stimulation of several upper brainstem regions in human patients undergoing neurosurgery. The verbal reports of these psychiatric patients are, however, often confused and do not permit a confident conclusion about the nature of the observed effects. However, Sem-Jacobson and Torkildsen (1960) reported that patients can be taught to administer such stimulation to their own brains and will operate a lever for hours when no other rewards are given. Recent experiments reported by Bishop and his associates (1963) indicated that the brain of man may contain a clearly defined reward system which encompasses the head of the caudate nucleus, the amygdala, septal area, medial and posterior hypothalamus, the midbrain tegmentum, and the intralaminar nuclei of the thalamus.

Schizophrenic patients lever-pressed at a steady rate for stimulation of any of these areas and appeared to find the effects pleasurable. The stimulation was reported to have "temporary therapeutic effects." Several aversive areas were also demonstrated in these experiments, primarily in the caudate nucleus and parts of the medial thalamus.

EFFECTS OF CHANGES IN THE PARAMETERS OF STIMULATION

Changes in current intensity affect self-stimulation rates at most electrode placements, but the direction of the effects is variable. In the rat, self-stimulation typically starts with current intensities of about 10 to 20 μa. Response rates rise monotonically at some electrode sites (notably the posterior hypothalamus and anterior forebrain) as the current of the stimulation is increased. Asymtote is reached only when overt motor seizures begin to interfere with the response sequence. Other electrode placements do not show this simple correlation between current intensity and response frequency. At some sites a rise in current intensity may produce no effect on response rate (diagonal band of Broca) or may actually decrease it (medial hypothalamus). When an increase in stimulus intensity lowers the response rate, further increments in current intensity often produce the opposite effect, establishing a nonmonotonic relationship between response rate and current intensity (see Olds, 1958c, d, 1960a, b).

It has been proposed (Olds, 1961) that the differential effects of current intensity may be due to the spread of stimulation to neural elements which may be part of the reward mechanism (producing an increased response rate), neutral (having no effect), or part of the aversion system (producing a decline in response rate). This hypothesis accounts for the nonmonotonic functions obtained from some hypothalamic placements by postulating alternating "lamina" of neural elements responsible for reward and aversion effects.

This interpretation is supported by the observation that nonmonotonic relationships between current and rate of responding are found only in areas of the brain where the reward and aversion systems seem to overlap or adjoin so closely that a spread of excitation to the opposite area is likely, particularly at higher current values. Reynolds (1958), for instance, reported that the

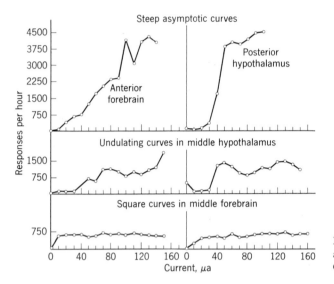

Fig. 10.1 Self-stimulation response rates as a function of current intensity. (From Olds, 1958d, AAAS.)

rate of self-stimulation in the ventromedial nuclei of the hypothalamus rises to a maximal value with initial increases in current intensity but drops sharply as further increases elicit a spread of excitation to adjacent aversive regions. Steiner and D'Amato (1964) reported that low-current stimulation of the amygdaloid complex produced aversive effects, whereas an *increase* in stimulus intensity elicited rewarding effects. This apparent paradox finds a simple explanation in the fact that the amygdaloid complex contains two distinct motivational areas. The central and medial nuclei of the corticomedial division of the amygdala are part of the reward system, and animals will self-stimulate at very high rates at electrode sites in this area. The lateral and basolateral nuclei of the basolateral division, on the other hand, seem to be part of a pure aversion system. Most of the intervening portions of the amygdaloid complex seem to be ambivalent, and the effect of stimulation is determined largely by the extent to which the current spreads to the positive and negative areas (Wurtz and Olds, 1963). A similar overlap of the reward and aversion systems may account for the observation that electrical stimulation of other portions of the brain often appears initially aversive but acquires rewarding properties with continued experience (Schnitzer et al., 1965).

A complication was pointed out some years ago (Olds, 1958a) but tends—only too often—to be forgotten. We cannot judge the dispersion of neural elements that are functionally part of the reward system purely by the relation between stimulus intensity and response rate: electrical stimu-

lation of almost any part of the brain produces not only rewarding or aversive effects but also many sensory, motor, motivational, or emotional effects which may facilitate or, more commonly, interfere with the reward effect or the performance of the instrumental response itself.

Response rate is, under most circumstances, a useful measure of the rewarding properties of central stimulation, but a number of observations (Valenstein, 1964) indicate that the rate measure must be interpreted with caution. Hodos and Valenstein (1960), for instance, showed that rats, given a choice of several electrode sites or stimulus intensities, often do not select the combination that supports the highest rate of responding.

An excellent demonstration of the importance of current intensity has been reported by Valenstein and Beer (1962). They investigated the relative strength of the reward effect of intracranial stimulation in approach-approach conflict situations which pitted water rewards or a chance to avoid electric shock against the intracranial stimulation. Rate of choice of self-stimulation for each one of the electrode sites was quite clearly determined by the intensity of the electrical stimulation, suggesting a relation between current and magnitude of reward.

Uyeda and Gengerelli (1959) reported that the frequency and shape of the stimulating pulse appeared to be important determinants of response rate. Sine waves produced higher rates of responding than square waves and frequencies between 35 and 100 cps produced better results than either lower or higher repetition rates.

More complex relationships between some of the parameters of electrical stimulation and the intensity of the reward effect have been reported in recent experiments. Keesey (1964a) has reported a parametric analysis of the relation between pulse train duration and the reward properties of hypothalamic stimulation. When rats were permitted to regulate the duration of central stimulation under varying conditions of pulse frequency and stimulus intensity, the preferred duration was found to be a decreasing function of both frequency and intensity of stimulation. An examination of response rate on an aperiodic (variable interval) schedule of reinforcement showed, however, that maximal rates were maintained by stimulus durations which significantly exceeded the apparently preferred duration in the self-selection experiment. These observations suggest that duration of stimulation may determine the effectiveness of electrical stimulation but may not contribute measurably to a spread of current to neighboring, and possibly aversive, regions. Work and Elder (1964) have also reported that the relation between "optimal" stimulus duration and stimulus frequency is described by a decreasing, negatively accelerated function.

Deutsch (1964) has reported an interesting relation between the interpulse interval of intracranial stimulation and the intensity of its apparent reward effects. He observed that rate of responding jumped suddenly when the interval between the two pulses of a compound stimulus was gradually increased. McIntire and Wright (1965) have suggested on the basis of extensive observations of 112 pairings of duration and intensity parameters, that the magnitude of the reward effect may be best described in terms of the total electrical charge on the tissues (i.e., microcoulombs). They also replicated earlier observations which suggested that the optimal stimulus duration increases on aperiodic schedules of reinforcement (Keesey, 1964).

RELATIONSHIP BETWEEN REWARD AND AVERSION SYSTEMS

Bower and Miller (1958) have shown that electrical stimulation of the same hypothalamic site can initially be rewarding but quickly become aversive if maintained for several seconds. Animals with electrodes in the medial forebrain bundle learned to press a bar to obtain electrical stimulation. The rate of bar pressing was found to be an inverse function of stimulus duration. If pressing a lever started a continuous stimulus, the animals learned a second response (wheel turning) to terminate the electrical current and subsequently alternated between start and stop responses (see also Miller, 1961a, b). The animals that pressed the lever to obtain electrical stimulation also learned to escape from prolonged exposures to the stimulus by running to the nonpreferred side of a T-maze. Similar results have been observed in cats (Roberts, 1958b).

Valenstein and Valenstein (1964) and Hodos (1965) have shown that repetitive on-off responses for central stimulation rewards can be obtained not only from the hypothalamic and tegmental areas but also from the hippocampus, the amygdala, and the septal area; this finding suggests a much more diffuse distribution of the apparently aversive effects than had previously been assumed. Hodos (1965) showed that the latency of stimulus initiation and stimulus termination was a decreasing function of stimulus intensity, a peculiar observation since it suggests that the intense stimuli did not produce more punishing effects than weaker ones.

It seems that both the termination and onset of intracranial stimulation may be rewarding. This result is puzzling unless we assume that current from the same electrode stimulates both rewarding and aversive systems. If the electrode is placed nearer the reward system (or if the two mechanisms have different response latencies or recruitment rates), we would expect to see an initial reward effect which is then superseded by a stronger aversive reaction. Such an interpretation is supported by the observation that animals which show both reward and aversion effects do not learn to avoid electrical stimulation, although they quickly acquire an instrumental response to escape (i.e., terminate) it (Bower and Miller, 1958; Roberts, 1958a, b).

A different explanation has been advanced by Brown and Cohen (1959). These workers elicited hypothalamic rage by stimulating points in the lateral hypothalamus, and they showed that cats can learn to escape this stimulation by crossing a barrier. After repeated pairings of an auditory conditioned stimulus with such hypothalamic stimulation, the animals avoided the stimulation by responding to the buzzer. The same animals were then placed into a straight runway. If they traversed the alley in less than 100 sec, brief hypothalamic stimulation was applied in the goal box. If they failed to run in this time, they were led through the apparatus and given electrical stimulation during the intertrial interval. The animals that previously escaped or avoided hypothalamic stimulation now traversed the runway *faster* than control animals. Brown and Cohen concluded from these observations that hypothalamic stimulation may produce general arousal which nonspecifically energizes whatever behavior is appropriate to the experimental situation. It is difficult to apply this explanation to the basic reward-aversion phenomenon, for animals in operant conditioning situations certainly can perform a variety of responses other than bar pressing. Moreover, it is not quite clear why only the responses that lead to the goal box (and self-stimulation) should be energized in a maze-type experiment.

An alternative explanation of Brown and Cohen's data might be that electrical stimulation produces a pure aversion effect (hence the avoidance learning) but no reward effect at all. The animals traverse the runway faster than their controls because they are subsequently removed from the threatening situation. According to this view, the alley itself becomes the conditioned stimulus for aversive hypothalamic stimulation, and the animals perform escape responses. That the situation allows avoidance of the stimulation by not responding may have been difficult for subjects to learn under the experimental conditions.

Stein (1965) has reported a related observation. He trained rats in a shuttle box to avoid punishing midbrain stimulation until they reached a low but stable level of performance. Subsequently, brief periods of intracranial stimulation at rewarding or neutral points were given before each trial in the shuttle box. Stein observed a marked facilitation of the avoidance behavior following stimulation of highly reinforcing electrode sites in the medial forebrain bundle, but stimulation of neutral sites had no effect. Since amphetamine also produced facilitatory effects, the facilitation may have been the result of a general increase in arousal or responsiveness.

Such an interpretation cannot account, however, for earlier observations (Olds and Olds, 1961a; Stein and Hearst, 1958) that noncontingent rewarding stimulation interfered with the performance of food-rewarded responses and that the number of trials required to reach criterion on a shuttle box avoidance task were doubled when the conditioned stimulus was rewarding intracranial stimulation (Mogenson and Morrison, 1962).

Olds has defended the notion that separate reward and aversion systems exist; he suggests that the combined effects are obtainable only from specific areas that are separate from the larger system of motivational areas from which discrete reward or aversion effects can be obtained. He suggests that the combined effects may be caused by the stimulation of areas of anatomical overlap between the two systems, as Miller suggests, or a third motivational system which responds positively to brief and mild stimulation but negatively to prolonged or intense activation. It appears more parsimonious at present to accept the first of these alternatives.

Stein and Ray (1959) have devised an interesting experimental procedure which permits the animal to regulate the intensity of stimulation. The animals are tested in a two-lever operant conditioning box. The levers are connected to the stimulation source so that a response at lever A increases the current intensity by a small amount whereas a response at lever B decreases it. A constant current can be maintained by alternating responses between the two bars. Current levels were continuously recorded. Animals with electrodes in the rostral reward system (cingulate gyrus) stepped up the current intensity until severe motor seizures interfered with the bar-pressing behavior. Stein and Ray suggest that there is no negative feedback from these placements since there is no known aversive mechanism in the vicinity. Animals with more ventral electrodes generally achieved a fairly precise regulation of current intensity at levels well above the reward threshold but much below the intensity selected for the more dorsal placements.

A somewhat similar determination of aversive thresholds has been reported by Boren and Malis (1961). These workers subjected monkeys to electrical stimulation of gradually increasing intensity. The animals learned to maintain the current at threshold level by pressing a lever which reduced the current intensity by a small fraction. This study has additional theoretical implications since it showed that the threshold of aversive stimulation could be raised by an analgesic drug (anileridine). It was also observed that for long periods of time the animals tolerated current levels that usually evoked escape responses, if the current was applied discretely. The authors interpret these data as indicating that lower current levels can serve as warning signals in the normal experimental paradigm when the relation between current levels and rate of responding is under investigation.

Poschel and Ninteman (1965) have used a different and somewhat unusual approach to this problem. They selected electrode placements in the medial hypothalamus which showed a clear rewarding effect when the stimulus duration was brief and an equally clear aversive effect when the duration of the intracranial stimulation exceeded some maximal value. When stimulation was continuously applied to such an electrode site, the animals rapidly learned to regulate the intensity of the intracranial stimulus, permitting an estimate of the animals' thresholds for aversive stimulation of a mixed, reward-aversion area. The threshold values were found to be highly resistant to adaptation or fatigue caused by prolonged stimulation and seemed stable over repeated days of testing.

ANATOMICAL DISTRIBUTION OF REWARD-AVERSION

Following the initial demonstration of the reward and aversion phenomena, Olds and his co-workers (Olds, 1960b; Olds et al., 1960) have mapped the distribution of the reward and aversion system in the rat brain. Lilly (1958) has attempted a similar correlation in the monkey.

On the basis of over 200 electrode placements, Olds (1961) concluded that a large portion of the brain (60% of all placements) is motivationally inert. The entire neocortex and most of the thalamus belong into this category. A surprisingly large number of sites (35% of the attempted placements) appeared to be involved in the reward mechanism. This system included most of the rhinencephalon, the hypothalamus, and some aspects of the thalamus and tegmentum. By far the highest response rates are obtained from placements in the posterior hypothalamus and medial tegmentum (80 responses per minute), the preoptic and septal area, and some placements in the posterior rhinencephalon (50 to 60 responses per minute). Stimulation of the anterior hypothalamus and anterior telencephalon are much less effective (5 to 15 responses per minute).

Aversive effects are observed from only a very small number of electrode sites (approximately 5% of the attempted placements) in the posterior and lateral diencephalon and lateral tegmental regions. These observations indicate that the aversive system is located in the immediate vicinity of the most effective reward points, and recent investigations have suggested that both systems may be affected by electrical stimulation of the

posterior hypothalamus. Olds (1958d) has observed that continuous access to self-stimulation (48 hr) produces satiation (i.e., a sharp response decrement) in animals with electrodes in various forebrain locations, but merely a gradual slowing (attributable perhaps to general fatigue) in animals with hypothalamic electrodes. These differences may indicate a functional division within the reward system.

Olds and Olds (1963) have recently reinvestigated the anatomical distribution of the reward-aversion systems in the brain. An analysis of 96 electrodes placements showed that (1) all of the hypothalamus appeared to be involved in the reward system, (2) the strongest approach reactions were elicited from the medial forebrain bundle, (3) avoidance responses were elicited from the hypothalamus only when very intense or prolonged stimulation was employed, and (4) the aversion system did not seem to be as clearly defined as the reward system. Pure negative reinforcement was elicited at points diffusely scattered through the thalamus, dorsal tegmentum, and periventricular area of the midbrain.

Olds and Olds emphasized that fibers which yielded apparently opposite behavioral effects seemed to be in close synaptic relationship and that nuclei throughout the brainstem tended to yield ambivalent effects. They suggested that the effects of the main afferent tracts might be inhibitory rather than excitatory, and that this arrangement might mediate a system of reciprocal inhibitions between positive and negative reinforcement processes.

These as well as related anatomical observations (Olds, 1961) have suggested to many workers that the reward effects might be mediated by the medial forebrain bundle (MFB) and that the distribution of reward areas may correspond to the distribution field of this tract. The evidence for this interpretation is, at present, conflicting.

Schiff (1964) reported that lesions in the ventral tegmentum attenuated or completely inhibited the rewarding effects of septal stimulation, whereas lesions in the dorsal tegmentum had no effect. Lorens (1965), on the other hand, found that lesions in the medial forebrain bundle in the lateral hypothalamus (i.e., at the site of its greatest concentration) did not reliably and significantly interfere with the rewarding effects of other hypothalamic, septal, or midbrain sites. McIntire and Wright (1965) have reported that the response rate for stimulation of the septal area was consistently lower for 112 different combinations of

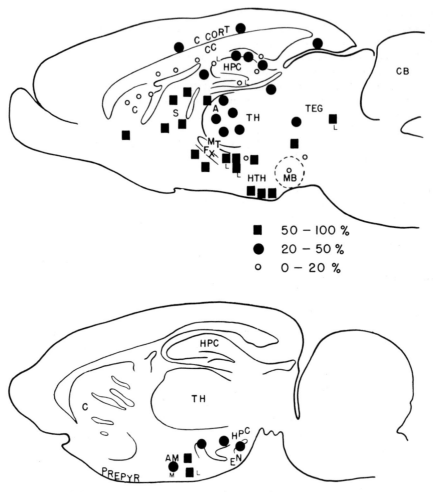

Fig. 10.2   Medial and lateral sagittal sections of the rat brain showing loci of rewarding effects with self-stimulation. The squares and circles indicate the percentage of bar pressing produced during a 6-hr test period. A, anterior thalamus; AM, amygdala; C, caudate nucleus; CB, cerebellum; CC, corpus callosum; C CORT, cingulate cortex; EN, entorhinal cortex; FX, fornix; HPC, hippocampus; HTH, hypothalamus; MB, mammillary body; MT, mammillothalamic tract; PREPYR, prepyriform cortex; S, septal region; TEG, tegmentum; TH, thalamus. The medial section (upper) is near the midline; the lateral section (lower) is 2 to 3 mm more lateral. The letters M (medial) and L (lateral) near a given locus indicate that it is about 2 mm medial or lateral to the plane shown. (From Olds, 1956b.)

stimulus duration and amplitude than for comparable stimulation of the medial forebrain bundle.

Ward (1960) reported that large lesions in the septal area did not interfere with self-stimulation at electrode sites in the midbrain tegmentum. Complete destruction of the amygdaloid complex produced similar, negative results (Ward, 1961). Olds and Hogberg (1964) reported that lesions in the anterior hypothalamus, the olfactory tubercle, and anterior amygdala decreased but did not abolish self-stimulation at electrode sites in the posterior hypothalamus. Wilkinson and Peele (1963) similarly found that lesions in the amygdala and hippocampal formation did not abolish self-stimulation in the midbrain tegmentum, lateral hypothalamus, and basal telencephalon. Morgane (1961a, b) disclosed more drastic effects. Medial forebrain bundle lesions anterior and posterior to the lateral hypothalamic feeding center significantly depressed self-stimulation in the feeding center.

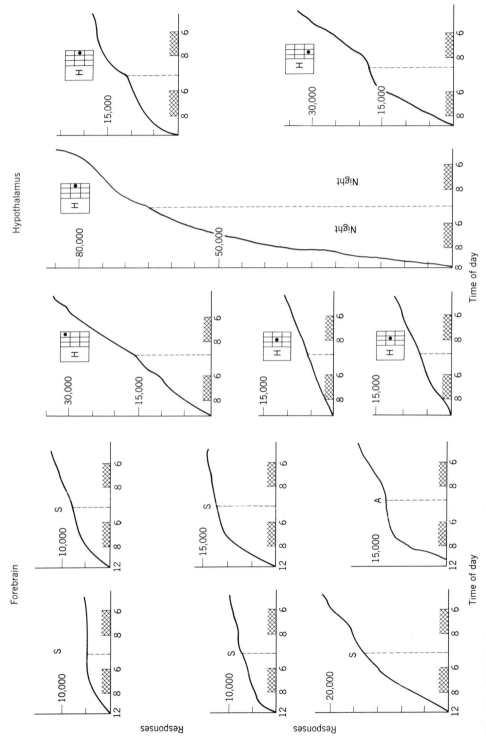

Fig. 10.3 Self-stimulation response rates of animals with electrodes implanted in the forebrain and hypothalamic areas in a continuous 48-hr test period. S, septal region; A, amygdala; H, hypothalamus. The boxes marked H indicate the electrode positions in the hypothalamus as medial to lateral (left to right) and anterior posterior (top to bottom). The dotted lines represent the end of the first 24-hr period. The shaded areas on the abscissa represent the period of darkness from 8 p.m. to 6 a.m. The animals with hypothalamic electrodes produced self-stimulation rates in the same order of magnitude on the second day as on the first, which was not true of most of the animals with electrodes in the forebrain. (From Olds, 1958d, AAAS.)

571

Self-stimulation or escape from central stimulation has been observed in cats (Roberts, 1958a, b), monkeys (Bursten and Delgado, 1958; Lilly, 1959a, b; Brady, 1957, 1958a, b), teleosts (Boyd and Gardner, 1962), and man (Bishop et al., 1963). However, not enough histological information is yet available to decide whether the distribution of the reward or avoidance mechanisms in these species is comparable to that observed in the rat.

COMPARABILITY OF SELF-STIMULATION REWARDS TO CONVENTIONAL REINFORCEMENTS

Following the initial demonstration of the self-stimulation phenomenon by Olds and Milner, there has been much theoretical and experimental interest in the apparently nonspecific reward mechanism. Olds and his associates (Olds, 1956a, b, c, 1958a, b, c, d, 1959, 1960a, b) attempted to show that electrical stimulation of a reward region follows the same laws as any other reward. We have already mentioned that variations in current intensity affect response rates in most areas of the reward system, although the relationship is not always described by a monotonic function. It is very doubtful that we can draw a clear analogy between current intensity and "amount of reward"; higher intensities of stimulation do not produce more stimulation of the same neural units but merely induce a greater spread of effective stimulation, thereby exciting a larger number of neural elements which may or may not be part of the reward system. Even when the additional units do belong to the reward system, one still must assume that magnitude of reward somehow correlates directly with the number of reward units stimulated.

One of Olds's earlier experiments (1956c) established that lever pressing for central stimulation is not merely a compulsive response automatism as some critics have suggested. Two groups of animals were run in a simple maze, one to food reward, the other to a lever allowing self-stimulation. Both groups had been deprived of food. The results of this experiment are unambiguous and can be summarized as follows. Running time decreased rapidly for both groups and reached asymptote after approximately 20 trials; there was no reliable difference between groups. During extinction, running time increased equally for both groups. Both showed a marked improvement on the first run of each of the three acquisition days, suggesting that no priming is required to start self-stimulation. We should note here that Seward et al. (1959, 1960) have reached a different conclusion, based on the observation that massed practice seems to produce faster running and more intrasession improvement (and slower extinction) than spaced trials. Seward suggests that the superiority of massed reinforcements indicates a "warming up" effect of electrical stimulation on performance.

Olds (1956c) has also compared the strength of the drive for self-stimulation with that produced by 24 hr of food deprivation. In a straight runway, rats ran slightly faster for self-stimulation than for food; comparable results were obtained in an obstruction box experiment. The animals were allowed to obtain three self-stimulations (or three bits of food) at one end of the box and then had to cross an electrically charged grid to obtain three more on the other side. The intensity of the grid shock was gradually increased until each animal was stopped from further crossings. Although it is gratuitous to assume that the magnitude of the food reward was in any way comparable to that obtained from self-stimulation, most animals of the food reward group were stopped by as little as 50 to 60 μa of grid shock, whereas the rats running to self-stimulation crossed much higher current intensities. The higher the current of the central stimulation, the higher the electrical shock the animals were willing to tolerate.

Falk (1961) reported that water-deprived rats trained to press one lever for water rewards and another for brain stimulation preferred to self-stimulate except under extreme deprivation conditions. Bishop et al. (1963) noted similarly that human subjects disregarded an attractive tray of food when permitted to self-stimulate, even though they had been without nourishment for 7 hr. Routtenberg and Lindy (1965) reported that rats, permitted to self-stimulate at certain lateral hypothalamic sites during their daily 1-hr period of access to food, starved rather than interrupt their stimulation-rewarded lever-pressing behavior. Animals that were permitted to self-stimulate at other electrode sites took enough time to eat and maintained normal body weights. Spies (1965) similarly found that rats, given a choice between food and brain stimulation rewards in a T-maze, preferred the brain stimulation at all food deprivation levels between 2 hr and 10 days, when hypothalamic electrodes were tested. At all other electrode sites, a similar preference existed for brief periods of deprivation, but all animals reliably

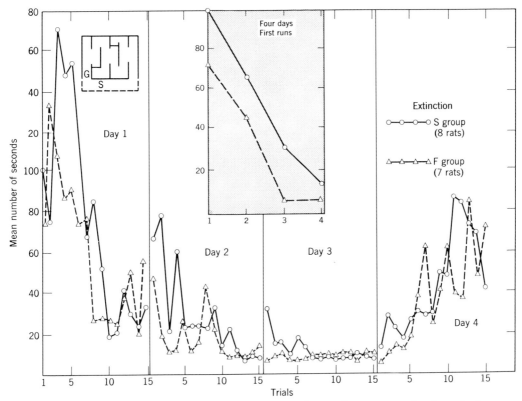

Fig. 10.4 Comparison of time scores in a maze experiment of a group running for a food reward (– – –) with another group running for a stimulation reward (——). In the maze (upper left) the animal runs from the starting position S, through the maze, to the goal position G. At G it finds a pedal, steps on it, and stimulates its brain. After the stimulation the pedal is swung back, and the goal box becomes the start box as the animal runs the maze again. Both the food reward and stimulation reward groups were under 24-hr food deprivation. The marked day-to-day improvement shown in the first runs on the 3 days following the first day is given in the stippled insert. The stimulation reward group ran as fast as the food reward group at the end of the test period and learned almost as quickly. (From Olds, 1956c.)

selected the food reward when the deprivation was extended to 48 hr or longer.

Kling and Matsumiya (1962) have demonstrated that electrical stimulation of certain hypothalamic placements can be used as an effective reward in a brightness discrimination learning experiment. Keesey (1964b) has extended this work to demonstrate that delay of reward influences rate of stimulation-rewarded learning in much the same way that more conventional reinforcers operate.

There is little uncertainty about the primary reinforcing properties of electrical brain stimulation. However, an important question remains to be answered about its ability to impart this reinforcing property to neutral stimuli through conditioning. Stein (1958) demonstrated in a classical

conditioning paradigm that secondary reinforcing powers can be acquired by stimuli that are repeatedly associated with rewarding brain stimulation. Seward et al. (1959), on the other hand, failed to demonstrate secondary reinforcement effects with a light that was frequently paired with rewarding electrical stimulation; Mogenson (1965) has reported similar negative effects.

EFFECTS OF SCHEDULES OF REINFORCEMENT

Several investigators (Sidman et al., 1955; Brady, 1957, 1958a, b) have demonstrated that the response rate of rats and cats in a lever-pressing situation is a function of the reward schedule. In this respect, self-stimulation appears to act very

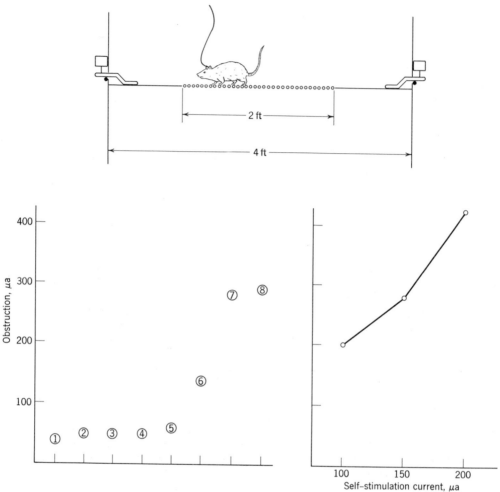

Fig. 10.5 Comparison of food reward and stimulation reward in an obstruction box experiment. *Top,* obstruction box. An animal receives electrical self-stimulation on one side, then must cross a shock grid to get more. *Bottom left,* circled numbers represent eight rats under 24-hr food deprivation running for a food reward. The position of each circled number indicates the amount of electric current (in microamperes) required to stop the rat. *Bottom right,* a rat running for self-stimulation only. The animals withstood more foot shock to obtain the self-stimulation reward than they did for the food reward. (From Olds, 1961.)

much like conventional rewards such as food or water. Each type of reward schedule (i.e., aperiodic or ratio reinforcement) produces a specific response pattern which is maintained over many months with no reinforcement other than electrical stimulation.

Sidman et al. (1955) found that the rate of responding on aperiodic schedules is negatively correlated with the average duration of the inter-reward interval and that fixed-ratio schedules are extremely sensitive to small changes in the intensity of stimulation. Several other investigators

(Brady and Conrad, 1960; Brady, 1960; Brodie et al., 1960) have successfully employed various schedules of reinforcement, although it has recently been suggested (Gallistel, 1964) that animals may self-stimulate only when the reward schedule is relatively "good." The evidence for this suggestion is only spotty. Sidman et al. (1955) did not extend the schedules beyond VI 16″ and FR 7. Brodie et al. reported that some monkeys would not respond on a schedule higher than FR 20. However, these findings may be peculiar to some electrode sites: one animal in the Brodie

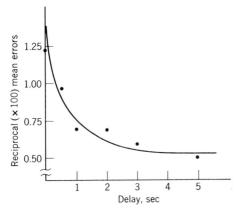

Fig. 10.6 Rate of learning as a function of the delay of reward. The reciprocal, times 100, of the mean number of errors in 500 trials is plotted against the delay interval. The curve has been visually fitted to the data points. (From Keesey, 1964b, © AAAS.)

et al. study continued to work on a FR 150, and Brady (1960) reported success with FR 50 also in monkeys. Relatively "poor" VI schedules (with 1- and 2-min means) have been used by Brady and Conrad (1960).

RELATIONSHIP TO OTHER DRIVE MECHANISMS

Perhaps the most important question about the reward-aversion phenomena concerns their independence from other primary drives. Olds has advanced and defended the notion that the observed effects are caused by the stimulation of separate neural systems which in some general fashion provide reward or aversion per se. From this follows a general hedonistic theory of motivation which divides motivational stimuli into two categories: "stimuli which the organism has mechanisms to minimize (i.e., painful things) and stimuli which the organism has mechanisms to maximize (i.e., pleasant things)" (Olds, 1961, p. 350).

We might assume, on the other hand, that electrical stimulation elicits or reduces specific drive stimulation and is rewarding or aversive because of this effect. Hunger, thirst, sexual arousal, and various emotional drives can be elicited or inhibited by electrical stimulation of just those regions that appear to be most directly implicated in the reward and aversion phenomena. To help clarify this situation, several investigators have attempted to study the relationship between self-stimulation and a variety of other motivational variables.

Olds (1958a, c) has provided one of the best demonstrations of the covariance between specific primary drives and the effectiveness of self-stimulation at various points in the brain. For these experiments 22 animals were trained to bar-press for electrical stimulation of reward points; their feeding schedule alternated 24 hr of *ad libitum* access to food with 24 hr of deprivation. The animals were allowed to self-stimulate for 80 min per day. Fourteen days after the response rates had stabilized, all animals were castrated. Daily self-stimulation tests continued for the next two weeks of gradually declining androgen levels. Next, 2 mg of testosterone propionate were administered and produced a 7-day rise in androgen levels followed by a gradual decline over the next 7-day period.

The results of this experiment are complex, but the following generalizations can be abstracted: (1) for medial electrode placements in the hypothalamus and the forebrain, the rate of self-stimulation correlated positively with hunger and negatively with sexual arousal; (2) slightly lateral placements showed a positive correlation with both food deprivation and androgen levels; (3) far-lateral placements showed a positive cor-

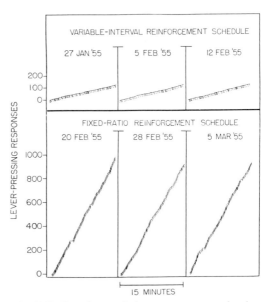

Fig. 10.7 Sample cumulative response curves showing stable lever-pressing rates for variable-interval (mean of 16 sec) and fixed-ratio (7 to 1) intracranial electrical stimulation rewards. Oblique "pips" indicate reinforcements. (From Sidman et al., 1955, AAAS.)

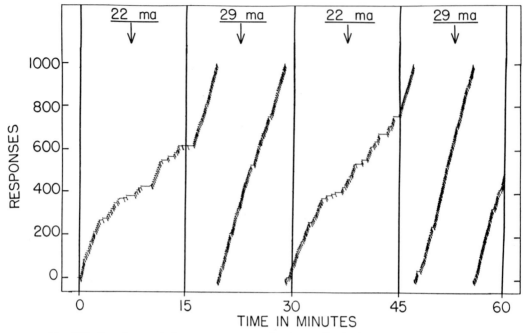

Fig. 10.8 Sample cumulative response curves showing a 60-min lever-pressing session for a fixed-ratio (8 to 1) intracranial stimulation reinforcement. The intensity of the electrical reward stimulus was varied as indicated during alternate 15-min periods. Oblique "pips" indicate reinforcements. (From Sidman et al., 1955, AAAS.)

relation with sexual arousal but no covariance with hunger; and (4) the effects of food deprivation and androgen administration correlated −.72. Olds concluded that "these experiments clearly suggest anatomical differentiation between the hunger-reward system and the androgen-reward system."

The relationship between sexual arousal and the effect of central stimulation is not so simple as these results seem to suggest. Hodos and Valenstein (1960) found that estrus, which produces pronounced variations in the estrogen levels and the sexual receptivity in the female rat, does not influence the rate of responding for central brain stimulation. The same authors found that food deprivation increased self-stimulation in the animals that did not react to estrous variations. This may indicate that the electrodes were located in the part of the reward system that is affected by hunger but not by sexual arousal. Food deprivation did not produce greater than normal effects during periods of heat. Prescott (1966) has more recently reported a very close correlation between the estrous cycle and the rate of self-stimulation at hypothalamic electrodes. The highest rates were observed during the period of vaginal

cornification. The changes in stimulation rate did not appear to be caused by the increase in general activity which accompanies estrus in the rat since response rates during extinction did not show estrus-related fluctuations.

The intimate relationship between the hypothalamic mechanisms which regulate food intake and those responsible for the reward effect, if they are indeed separate, is further demonstrated by subsequent experiments by Olds (1961). In these studies electrical stimulation was applied to the posteroventral hypothalamus for 0.5 sec every 10 sec during a 1-hr test session per day. This procedure was observed to increase the daily *ad libitum* food intake significantly. Olds notes that very high rates of self-stimulation can be obtained from the same points. Other electrode placements in the same area showed very low rates of self-stimulation and no effect on food intake. Margules and Olds (1962) reported that all electrode sites from which feeding could be elicited by electrical stimulation also showed high rates of self-stimulation.

Hoebel and Teitelbaum (1962) have reported that stimulation of the ventromedial nuclei of the hypothalamus (the satiety center for hunger) reduced food intake and inhibited self-stimulation at electrode sites in the lateral hypothalamus (the feeding center). Lesions in the area of the ventro-medial nuclei increased food intake and lateral hypothalamic self-stimulation. Furthermore, hungry animals self-stimulated more frequently than sated rats. The authors concluded that "within

the medial and lateral hypothalamus, the feeding systems control self-stimulation in a manner analogous to their control of feeding. . . . It may be that the pleasure of lateral hypothalamic self-stimulation is similar to the gratification obtained by eating." Hoebel (1965) has recently shown that radio-frequency lesions in the ventromedial

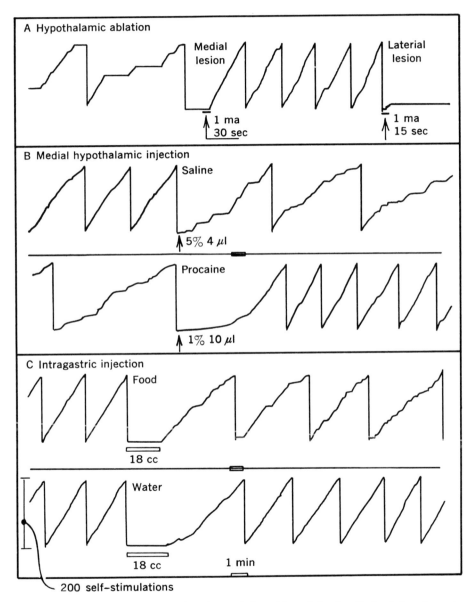

Fig. 10.9 Cumulative records showing changes in lateral hypothalamic self-stimulation. A, acceleration of self-stimulation caused by destruction of both ventromedial regions. B, inhibition of self-stimulation by chemical excitation of both ventromedial regions, and subsequent disinhibition of self-stimulation by anesthetization of these regions. C, prolonged inhibition of self-stimulation by tube-feeding a liquid diet (top) but only transient inhibition by tube-feeding an equal volume of water (bottom). (From Hoebel and Teitelbaum, 1962, © AAAS.)

nucleus also increase the rate of lateral hypothalamic self-stimulation after food satiation had depressed it.

Although these findings seem to argue against
a general reward mechanism, they do not support
a drive reduction theory of reinforcement. We
shall leave this question open and return to it
after discussing several additional studies which
have suggested a close relationship between self-
stimulation and specific drives. Miller and his
collaborators (see Miller, 1961a, b) have observed
a positive relation between electrical stimulation
of the hypothalamus which elicits ejaculation and
reward effects. Of 128 electrode placements that
did not produce ejaculation, only 43% were found
rewarding. However, 89% of the 18 placements

from which ejaculation could be elicited were
also rewarding.

Brady (1957, 1958a, b) found that the rate of
self-stimulation increased markedly with food
deprivation in both rats and cats. Most interesting,
however, is the additional observation that there
was a very close temporal relationship between
the rate of self-stimulation and thirst. In this
experiment a thirsty rat with a septal electrode
was placed into a two-lever operant conditioning
apparatus and allowed to work for water on one
bar and for self-stimulation on the other. In one
part of this study, both water and the self-stimulation rewards were on continuous reinforcement
schedules. In this condition the rat pressed initially for both water and brain stimulation.

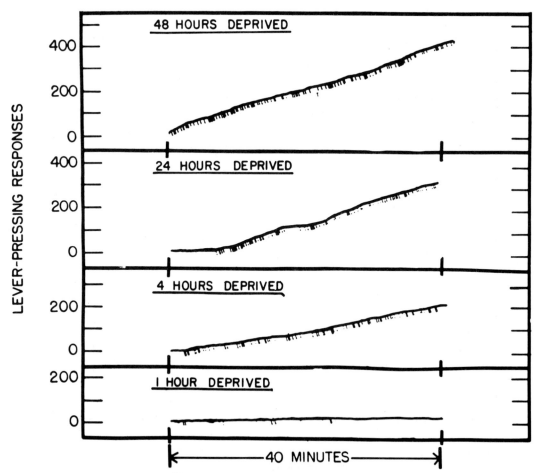

Fig. 10.10 Cumulative response curves showing lever-pressing rates for a variable-interval
(mean of 16 sec) intracranial electrical stimulation reward during four separate 40-min experimental sessions following 1, 4, 24, and 48 hr of deprivation, respectively. Oblique "pips" indicate
reinforcements. (From Brady et al., 1957.)

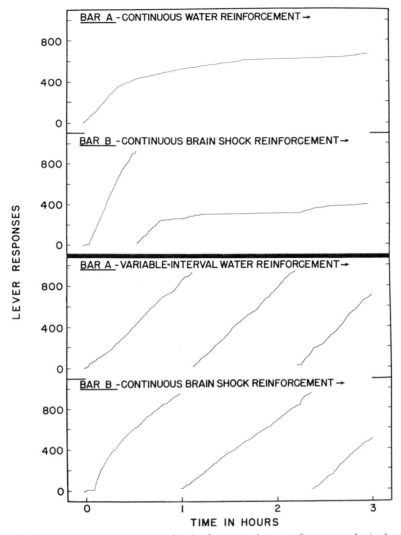

Fig. 10.11 Cumulative response curves showing lever-pressing rates for water or brain shock on continuous- and variable-interval schedules of reinforcement. The animal has access to two bars; bar A is reinforced with water, bar B with brain shock. (From Brady, 1961.)

Within 1 hr, however, the thirst was satiated, and the animal stopped responding on the water bar. Instead of now concentrating his efforts on the self-stimulation lever, as might have been expected, he completely stopped responding on both bars.

When this experiment was repeated with the water reward on an aperiodic reinforcement schedule (but with self-stimulation remaining on 100% reinforcement), rapid satiation was prevented, and the animal continued to press for several hours for both water and electrical stimulation. These observations are important, not only because they demonstrate a covariance be-

tween self-stimulation and still another drive, but also because they suggest that the reward properties of the electrical stimulation were entirely dependent on the biological drive that was active in this situation. Wilkinson and Peele (1962) have demonstrated the specificity of the relation between hunger and self-stimulation. Food deprivation and feeding affected response rates only for stimulation at lateral hypothalamic electrodes. All other implant sites failed to show any correlation.

The specificity of the relationship between particular drives and the effectiveness of self-stimulation are emphasized by the fact that specific electrode placements appear to be selectively affected by variations in one particular drive but not by variations in others. This fact undoubtedly explains such negative results as those reported by Reynolds (1958), who failed to observe a consistent correlation between food deprivation and rate of self-stimulation, and by Newman (1961), who did not observe reliable changes in self-stimulation following castration.

THE ROLE OF EMOTIONALITY

The reward-aversion mechanisms appear to be widely distributed in a portion of the central nervous system which has been implicated in the regulation of emotional behavior. This coincidence raises the question whether there are demonstrable relationships between the reward-aversion effect and emotionality.

This question has been investigated by Brady (1957, 1958a, b, 1961) in a conditioned emotional response (CER) paradigm. This procedure requires that animals be trained to bar-press for some reward which is delivered on an aperiodic or ratio schedule of reinforcement. Once a stable level of performance has been acquired, a conditioned stimulus (CS) is introduced which terminates contiguously with a brief, but strong and painful, grid shock. Typically, this procedure leads rather rapidly to the formation of a conditioned response to the CS onset which takes the form of a complete suppression of bar pressing during the CS interval (typically several minutes);

such signs of emotionality as urination, defecation, vocalization, and crouching are observed.

Brady (1957) applied this procedure to two groups of rats, one trained to bar-press for brain stimulation, the other for water reward *or* brain stimulation. Following the attainment of stable response rates (on a VI 16-sec schedule of reinforcement), a clicking noise was presented for 3 min during the bar-pressing tests. The 3-min CS terminated with a painful grid shock. On the eighth presentation of this CS-UCS combination, all animals that worked for water reward showed perfect acquisition of the CER (i.e., the lever pressing stopped as soon as the CS was presented). None of the animals that bar-pressed for brain stimulation showed any signs of conditioning (i.e., the response rate appeared unaffected by the CS, and anxiety responses were not observed).

That this effect is due to motivational rather than associative factors was demonstrated when the reward conditions were reversed. Animals that previously had shown a CER while working for water rewards failed to do so when switched to self-stimulation. Conversely, animals that previously had shown no CER while working for brain stimulation readily acquired it when switched to water rewards.

Brady reports data from an animal which was switched repeatedly between the reward conditions; the animal showed a clear suppression of bar pressing during the CS interval while working for water but showed absolutely no effect during

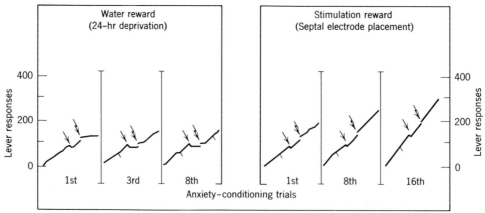

Fig. 10.12 Sample cumulative response curves showing acquisition trials for the conditioned anxiety response superimposed upon lever pressing for a variable-interval (mean of 16 sec) water and intracranial electrical stimulation reward. The unbroken arrows indicate the onset of the conditioned auditory stimulus; the broken arrows indicate the termination of the CS contiguously with the brief unconditioned grid shock stimulus to the feet during each trial. (From Brady, 1957.)

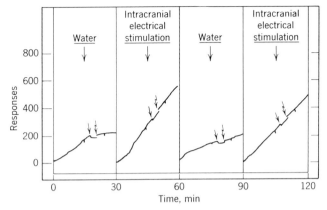

Fig. 10.13 Sample cumulative response curves showing the differential effect of the conditioned-anxiety procedure during a 2-hr experimental session with alternate 30-min periods of a variable-interval (mean of 16 sec) water and intracranial electrical stimulation reward. The oblique unbroken arrows indicate the onset of the conditioned auditory stimulus; the oblique broken arrows indicate the termination of the CS contiguously with the brief unconditioned grid shock stimulus to the feet during each of the alternate 30-min periods. (From Brady, 1957.)

self-stimulation sessions. This paradox was also evident during extinction of the CER (CS presented without the UCS). On alternating days, the extinction procedure was carried out while the animals pressed the bar for water or for electrical brain stimulation. Throughout the 10-day extinction experiment, conditioned emotional responses continued to be made on the days when the animals were working for water rewards but were never made when the animals were self-stimulating.

An interpretation of these results is complicated by several factors. (1) Conditioned emotional responses can be established in some rats even while they work for brain stimulation rewards. Brady (1957) suggests that this may be true particularly for anterior electrode placements. (2) In cats, no differential effects can be observed, although the electrodes are placed in a posteroventral position.

Experiments on monkeys (Brady, 1958) have shown that the development of the CER may depend very directly on the magnitude of the competing reward. Monkeys that bar-pressed for a 20-μa stimulation quickly acquired a CER and stopped pressing the lever during the CS interval. When the stimulus intensity was raised to 30 μa, the CER was eliminated. The initial rates of responding were roughly comparable for a food reward which permitted the acquisition and per-

formance of a CER and the 20-μa self-stimulation condition which did not. The 30-μa condition produced a much higher rate of responding than the food reward, and the two conditions should not be compared. A subsequent experiment suggests that the differential effects of the CER procedure are not entirely due to the difference in the initial rate of responding. Animals working for food on a fixed-ratio schedule performed as well as animals working for brain stimulation on a similar schedule. Nevertheless, conditioned emotional responses appeared during the food reward sessions but not during the self-stimulation experiment. A residual question remains here with respect to the sensitivity of a high fixed-ratio reinforcement schedule to motivational variables, but the experiment demonstrates that conditioned emotional responses can be obtained in situations which elicit near-maximal rates of responding.

Deutsch and Howarth (1962) demonstrated an interesting relationship between emotional variables and the reinforcing properties of electrical brain stimulation. Rats trained to press a lever for brain stimulation rewards continued to do so in extinction when a fear-inducing CS was presented. This disinhibitory effect was greatest for tegmental electrodes and smallest for hypothalamic and septal electrodes.

That electrical stimulation of reward areas may not produce results comparable in all respects to those obtained with conventional rewards, in spite of the many apparent similarities, was shown by Brady in 1958. We have previously noted that schedules of reinforcement appear to have all but identical effects on behavior whether the reward is food, water, or brain stimulation. Brady's investigation has pointed out an interesting exception to this rule. Monkeys normally adapt quite readily to an experimental procedure that rewards slow rates of responding. In the study under discussion, monkeys working for food reward learned to adjust to a reinforcement schedule that rewarded only responses occurring at least 20 sec apart. Following some training in this procedure, the animals showed a slow, steady rate of responding which reflected the temporal characteristics of the schedule quite accurately (i.e., the animals maximized rewards). When brain stimulation was substituted for the food reward, this adjustment broke down completely. The rate of responding increased nearly four-fold, and the number of reinforcements consequently dropped sharply. The differential effect remained even when the animals were allowed to work for food on alternating days. On food reward days performance dropped and rewards were maximized, but a much less optimal adjustment was achieved with the intervening self-stimulation tests.

Brady (1961) has reported an interesting observation which sharply contrasts the effects of peripheral and central electrical stimulation. In the typical CER experiment the CS is terminated contiguously with painful peripheral shock, and ongoing behavior is suppressed (at least when conventional rewards are used). Brady found that substitution of a single brain shock to a reward area for the grid shock produces precisely the opposite effect. A rat trained to work for water rewards on a poor variable-interval schedule (120 sec) responded to the CS by markedly increasing the rate of lever pressing, after the termination of the CS had repeatedly been paired with a single 5-sec shock to the septal area. This effect extinguished rapidly after several presentations of the CS alone.

EXTINCTION

One other interesting difference between the rewarding effects of central stimulation and those produced by more conventional reinforcements should be noted. Several experiments (Seward et al., 1959, 1960) have shown that instrumental

responses rewarded only by central stimulation tend to extinguish very rapidly when the reinforcements are discontinued. Normal extinction curves have been obtained only in experiments on hungry or thirsty animals (Olds, 1956a, b), and the possibility cannot be discounted that the extinction performance may be related to the irrelevant drive conditions. Animals even tend to show considerable extinction between successive days of an experiment (Olds, 1956b), so that the performance on the first trial of each day is significantly lower than that of the last trial of the preceding day. This peculiar phenomenon disappears if food- or water-deprived animals are tested (Olds, 1958a, b, c).

Deutsch (1960, 1963) has suggested a theory of intracranial self-stimulation which is based, to a large measure, on the apparently peculiar response to experimental extinction and the perhaps analogous difficulty with poor aperiodic reinforcement schedules. Deutsch proposed that electrical stimulation rewards the response that produced it and simultaneously *motivates* further instances of that response. According to this hypothesis, no innate or acquired drive for central self-stimulation exists, but the stimulation provides its own motivation. This theory leads to a number of interesting predictions, the principal one being that the time which has elapsed since the most recent central stimulation should be the only determinant of extinction and should significantly influence performance when the reinforcements are presented aperiodically.

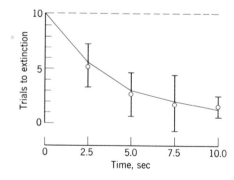

Fig. 10.14   The average effect of lever withdrawal on five animals. The solid line shows the prediction from Deutsch's hypothesis. The dashed line shows the prediction from the hypothesis that extinction is a function of the number of unreinforced trials. The circles indicate the experimentally observed effects of lever withdrawal. (From Howarth and Deutsch, 1962, © AAAS.)

Howarth and Deutsch (1962) tested this prediction by withdrawing the self-stimulation lever from the experimental apparatus at the beginning of extinction and reinserting it after variable periods of enforced nonresponding. In agreement with the prediction, they found that the number of trials required to complete extinction appeared to be a simple function of the amount of time the lever was not present at the beginning of the extinction procedure. These observations are particularly remarkable since the intervals used for the lever withdrawal ranged only from 1 to 10 sec.

Deutsch et al. (1964) tested the prediction in another experimental situation. Rats were trained to run in a T-maze with water rewards in one arm and rewarding brain stimulation in the other. It was found that the animals preferred the intracranial stimulation to the water rewards; however, the probability of choice of the electrical stimulation over the water decreased with the delay since the last brain stimulus and with the intensity of the thirst.

Deutsch (Deutsch and Howarth, 1963; see also Gallistel, 1964) concluded from these experiments that the tendency to perform learned habits for brain stimulation reward is a simple function of the time since the previous reward and that the motivational and reinforcing properties of electrical stimulation appear to be due to different physiological mechanisms.

This interpretation has recently been criticized by a number of workers, largely because the relationships reported by Deutsch and his associates seem to be characteristic, not of intracranial brain stimulation per se but of some of the peculiarities of the typical self-stimulation experiment or the effects of stimulation of specific electrode sites. Although it is common to see a decrement in the rate of responding between the end of one session and the beginning of the next, complete extinction (as predicted by Deutsch's theory) is seen very rarely. Animals may be kept out of the self-stimulation situation for several months without requiring a priming stimulus when returned to the apparatus (Kent and Grossman, unpublished observations).

Pliskoff and Hawkins (1963) essentially confirmed the effects of bar withdrawal on extinction performance and observed that free reward stimuli presented during the period of lever withdrawal increased the number of nonreinforced responses during the subsequent extinction session. However, when the training schedule was modified slightly to give the animals experience with the test apparatus that lacked the lever, this effect disappeared; this observation suggests that the results reported by Howarth and Deutsch are not independent with respect to the training procedure, as they should be if Deutsch's hypothesis is correct.

Stutz et al. (1965) have observed that animals can be trained to wait for periods up to 20 min between short bouts of intracranial self-stimulation, seriously questioning the adequacy of the drive decay concept.

Pliskoff et al. (1965) reported recently that fixed-interval, fixed-ratio, DRL (differential reinforcement of low rates of responding), and variable-interval schedules of reinforcement could support stable performance levels on a lever when the reinforcement consisted of introducing a second lever which produced rewarding brain stimulation for a fixed number of responses before being withdrawn again. Pliskoff showed typical schedule performance and concluded that there are, in fact, no important differences between the central stimulation and more conventional reinforcers.

An interesting observation has been reported by Gibson et al. (1965). They suggest that the apparent differences between intracranial reinforcements and other rewards may be artifacts of the reward procedure, rather than the result of dual central effects or other physiological differences. In these experiments rats were trained in an operant situation, with two variations of the common reward procedure. The first required the subject to press a lever for water or brain stimulation rewards which were both delivered at a dipper cup located some distance from the lever—the typical arrangement in conventional reward situations. The other procedure placed both the conventional water reward and the brain stimulation on an immediate reinforcement schedule more typical of the self-stimulation procedure. The animals received water (or brain stimulation) rewards immediately upon licking a tube. The results showed that the animals' performances were significantly affected by a change in the nature of the instrumental response, but the type of reinforcement had no effect at all.

These observations need to be followed up in other experimental situations using different experimental paradigms, but the results suggest that central stimulation may affect behavior precisely as other rewards do, provided the delay of reinforcement and nature of the response are equated. These results also have interesting implications for theoretical interpretations of the nature of conventional rewards.

DRUG STUDIES

Experiments by Olds and his associates (Olds et al., 1956) provide some indirect evidence for a relation between emotional variables and the reward phenomenon. For this investigation animals were trained to bar-press for central stimulation until stable and reproducible rates were obtained. The animals were then tested after intraperitoneal injections of reserpine (1 mg/kg), chlorpromazine (2.5 mg/kg), or pentobarbital (10 mg/kg).

Reserpine had the most pronounced effect. It at first appears that the rate of self-stimulation was generally depressed, and the explanation comes to mind that this effect may be due to a nonspecific depressive action of reserpine. However, self-stimulation rates at electrodes posterior and lateral to the anterior commissure were more severely affected than those at electrodes in front of the commissure; Olds suggested that this difference may indicate a selective action of the drug. The rather neat scheme for reserpine seems to break down when we consider the effects of the other drugs.

Chlorpromazine also produced a marked depression, but only in some animals. The inhibitory effects were obtained both at anterior and posterior electrode placements. Little or no effect of the drug was seen at some placements. Pentobarbital had no effect on self-stimulation except at some tegmental sites which tended to show inhibition.

Olds et al. (1957) essentially replicated this early study and observed some interesting relationships. Chlorpromazine (2 mg/kg) produced a marked inhibitory effect in 81% of the animals, morphine (7 mg/kg) in only 68% of the animals, and meprobamate (80 mg/kg) and pentobarbital (10 mg/kg) in only 32% and 12% of the cases respectively.

Meprobamate, morphine, and pentobarbital also produced opposite effects (response facilitation) in a significant number of animals. The authors suggested that the effectiveness of chlorpromazine seemed high for most animals that self-stimulated at high initial rates and significantly lower when the initial response rate was low.

The differences in the direction of some of the drug effects were at least to some extent corre-

lated with placement. Stimulation of septal electrodes tended to be inhibited by all drugs, and tegmental placements showed primarily facilitatory effects. Hypothalamic electrodes showed little or no drug effect.

A word of caution might be in order here. Although some efforts were made in this study to investigate crude dose-response relationships and equate the sedative effects of the various substances, it is not clear what importance can be assigned to the observed differential affects. We know too little about the central action of some of these substances to attempt seriously to equate their effects on something as complex and poorly understood as the reward effect.

A subsequent experiment (Olds, 1961) showed that the inhibitory effects of reserpine and chlorpromazine appear only at relatively high current levels, suggesting that the interaction of drugs and central stimulation may cause seizure activity. A second investigation localized the inhibitory effect of chlorpromazine. A marked depression of self-stimulation was observed at all electrode sites in the posterior hypothalamus and anterior septal region. A smaller effect appeared at placements in the medial hypothalamus, and no inhibition was seen at electrodes in the anterior hypothalamus.

Lysergic acid diethylamide (LSD) was also found to reduce the rate of self-stimulation. This effect was reversed for some electrode placements in the septal region (but not for others in the forebrain) by pretreatment with serotonin.

Similar inhibitory effects of chlorpromazine and reserpine on self-stimulation behavior as well as facilitatory effects of amphetamine and methyl phenidate have been reported by several investigators (Cook and Weidley, 1957; Stein, 1964a, b). These observations are interesting but it is difficult at present to abstract from them any hypothesis which would help us to understand the self-stimulation phenomenon itself. Particularly in view of the large number of drugs that produce essentially comparable effects (i.e., inhibition) on self-stimulation, it seems doubtful that this line of investigation will be fruitful in the future (see also Olds et al., 1957).

A possible exception to these pessimistic statements may be developing in an area of psychopharmacology which is not primarily concerned with the study of reward-aversion mechanisms in the brain but uses changes in self-stimulation rate as an index of central drug effects.

A recent example may illustrate this approach.

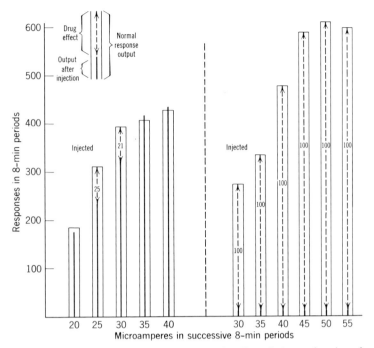

Fig. 10.15 Differential effects of chlorpromazine (2 mg/kg) as a function of electrode placement. *Left,* animal with an electrode in the middle hypothalamus. *Right,* animal with an electrode in the posteroventral hypothalamus. *Bars,* normal self-stimulation rates at different current intensities; *solid lines,* self-stimulation rates after drug injection; *dashed lines,* difference in self-stimulation rates due to the drug injection. The numbers within the bars indicate the percentage decrease in self-stimulation rates. (From Olds, 1961.)

Poschel and Ninteman (1963, 1964) trained rats to bar-press for stimulation of the posterolateral hypothalamus. After the response rate had stabilized, several monoamine oxidase (MAO) inhibitors [pargyline, parnate, iproniazid, etryptamine, alpha-methyl metatyrosine (α-mmt)] were injected intraperitoneally 1.5 hr after the start of a 6-hr self-stimulation test. All the drugs markedly facilitated self-stimulation behavior, but the peak effects were delayed 1 to 2 hr, the time presumably associated with the inhibition of brain MAO. In view of earlier observations which suggested that norepinephrine may serve excitatory functions in the reward system, Poschel and Ninteman concluded that the observed facilitation might be related to a high level of this amine rather than serotonin or dopa which are, of course, also affected by the monoamine oxidase inhibitors.

A somewhat different approach has been taken by Olds and Olds (1958). In this experiment rats were trained to lever-press for electrical stimulation of the brain until stable response rates

had been obtained. Microinjections of various pharmacological substances were then substituted for the electrical stimulus. The results of this experiment are ambiguous, but it was found that acetylcholine and serotonin (both possible neural transmitter substances) had no reward effect. Adenosine triphosphate (ATP), an energy-rich phosphate which represents the major energy source for cellular metabolism, and norepinephrine (another neurohumor) produced some effects at high concentrations. Marsilid, a compound which appears to inhibit the metabolism of several centrally active substances, produced the best effects. The animals self-stimulated at moderate rates (300 per hour) which appeared to be higher in the posterior hypothalamus and dorsal preoptic region than in other placements.

More recently, Olds et al. (1964) recorded the rate of self-injection of a variety of chemicals into the lateral hypothalamus and found that carbachol (a parasympathomimetic) produced significant self-injection rates. Substances that chelate calcium produced even higher rates of responding. The apparently rewarding effects of the chelating agents were inhibited when epinephrine, norepinephrine, or serotonin was added to the injections. These observations are particularly interesting because injections of carbachol into this portion of the brainstem have been shown to elicit thirst, whereas injections of catecholamines elicit feeding behavior (Grossman, 1960, 1962).

"It is unfortunately not clear that the effects of carbachol or catecholamines are specific to the reward-aversion mechanism. Microinjections of cholinergic substances into the hypothalamus of rats produces hyperactivity and hyperreactivity to sensory inputs and injections of catecholamines into the same regions evoke drowsiness, sleep or coma (Grossman, 1962). In the absence of appropriate control tests, one cannot be sure that rats receiving intrahypothalamic injections of these

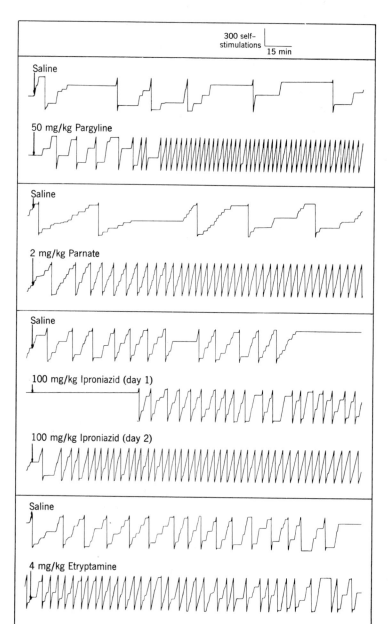

Fig. 10.16 Cumulative records of self-stimulation from four rats under saline and drug conditions. Arrows indicate the time of intraperitoneal drug injections. Records read from left to right and are 4.5 hr long. Each reset of the recorder pen equals 550 self-stimulations. (From Poschel and Ninteman, 1964.)

drugs would not increase or decrease their operant level of bar-pressing independent of any specific effect on the reward-aversion system.

The central reward-aversion mechanism can also be investigated by combining microinjection and electrical stimulation techniques. Preliminary observations from my laboratory indicate that the reinforcing properties of electrical stimulation can be modified significantly by microinjections of various centrally active drugs at the site of stimulation as well as at related sites in the limbic system."

LONG-TERM OBSERVATIONS

We have considered only the most obvious and objective results of central stimulation—its ability to motivate some instrumental response which either provides or terminates such stimulation. Lilly's (1958) more clinical descriptions of the behavior of animals during and after such stimulation may therefore be of interest.

Lilly made long-term observations on three monkeys, each of which had systems of "roving" electrodes implanted so that several hundred electrode placements could be investigated in a single animal. This method provides a much more complete picture of the reactions of the same subject to electrical stimulation of various brain areas than the customary procedure. We must not forget, however, that Lilly's results may be affected by lesions made by other electrode tracts.

In Lilly's studies electrical stimulation was successively applied to each one of several hundred placements. He observed that the monkey showed overt signs of pleasure (contentment, increased interest, reduction of anxiety, improved cooperation with the observer, improved appetite, etc.) following electrical stimulation of many placements below the corpus callosum. If presented with a lever, the animals quickly learned to self-stimulate at these points. Stimulation at other (generally more ́ventral) placements produced pupillary dilatation, hyperventilation, piloerection, defecation, and biting, or, as Lilly suggests, "a fright syndrome." The monkeys learned rapidly to terminate such stimulation by pressing levers and made every effort to prevent the experimenter from turning on such stimulation.

Lilly observed that stronger reward effects are obtained from some regions than from others and that animals exposed to stimulation in a highly rewarding area subsequently self-stimulate at significantly reduced rates in less rewarding areas. (This "little pig" effect has also been observed by Brady, 1961.)

When given continuous access to the self-stimulation lever, Lilly's monkeys initially pressed until exhausted (after as many as 200,000 responses). Eventually, however, a regular rhythm of 16 hr of "work" and 8 hr of sleep emerged; the pattern tended to remain relatively constant over prolonged periods. In Lilly's experiments self-stimulation has been used as the sole motivational variable in rather complex learning situations involving alternation between two levers, delayed alternation, and "quasi-counting" with two triggers.

The most interesting observation relates to the long-term effects of central stimulation. Lilly reports that animals allowed to self-stimulate reward areas are "remarkably easy to work with; few, if any, bites or scratches occur during or after such periods. The animals are less jittery, more tractable, more interested in the observer's activities and develop a more affectionate attitude to the observer such as grooming the observer's hand instead of scratching, etc." Stimulation here also reverses the aftereffects of previous stimulation of aversive areas. It can also eliminate the depressed behavior characteristic of a monkey left alone for a long period of time; the animals's liveliness and interest are increased by stimulation.

ELECTRICAL STIMULATION OF SUBCORTICAL STRUCTURES AS THE UNCONDITIONED STIMULUS IN ESCAPE-AVOIDANCE SITUATIONS

That electrical stimulation of the brain may have aversive properties has been known ever since brain stimulation techniques were first used. This effect was long believed to be caused by the central stimulation of pain pathways or neural structures directly or indirectly related to pain. However, Hess and his collaborators (Hess, 1938, 1932, 1954, 1957) showed clearly that specific emotional responses (attack, defense, and flight reactions) can be elicited by electrical stimulation of central structures that do not appear to be part of the pain pathways. Many investigators (Miller et al., 1953, 1954; Delgado et al., 1954; Olds, 1960a; Lilly, 1958) have more recently studied the motivational aspects of these responses.

Miller and his associates (1953, 1954) have shown that electrical stimulation of various electrode placements in the midbrain and diencephalon elicits "alarm" responses and is sufficiently aversive to serve as the UCS in an instrumental escape learning situation. In the initial experiment cats were trained to escape painful grid shock by turning a little paddle wheel. When central stimulation of alarm points was substituted for the peripheral shock, the animals either immediately turned the wheel to terminate the central stimulus or quickly learned to do so. Cats lacking previous experience with the experimental task could also be taught to turn the wheel to terminate central stimulation. Control stimulation in other regions of the brain (which did not elicit the alarm reaction) failed to produce learning but could be used as a CS in an avoidance situation. Since the animals learned to avoid stimulation of the alarm points when the CS was electrical stimulation at neighboring sites, the possibility was ruled out that the control stimuli (which were presented at a higher intensity than the stimulation of the alarm points) failed to be effective unconditioned stimuli because of localized seizure activity. A peripheral stimulus could also serve as the CS in the avoidance situation.

In a subsequent experiment Miller et al. showed that the centrally elicited alarm reaction can be used to condition an emotional response to the test apparatus. Cats that were repeatedly stimulated in a distinctive compartment learned to escape from that compartment during trials without further stimulation. Control animals that received high-intensity stimulation of sensory-motor areas failed to learn the escape response.

The aversive properties of central stimulation were demonstrated in still another experimental paradigm which pitted approach motivation (hunger) against the aversion produced by electrical stimulation of the hypothalamic alarm region. In this experiment hungry cats received central stimulation only while feeding. A violent withdrawal from the food dish was produced by electrical stimulation of the hypothalamus and various sensory-motor areas. However, whereas one or two stimulations of the hypothalamic placements sufficed to keep the hungry animals from approaching the feeding dish for many subsequent trials, stimulation of the sensory-motor cortex failed to produce any learning. Although the overt response to stimulation was similar in both areas, the cats returned to the feeding dish as soon as cortical stimulation was terminated, but they avoided the food for many trials following hypothalamic stimulation. This experiment indicates quite convincingly that the hypothalamic

stimulation has motivational properties that are not shared by the cortical stimulation.

Miller (1961b) has summarized the evidence from these experiments as follows:

> the foregoing experiments have shown step by step that electrical stimulation of the cat's brain eliciting "alarm" reactions has all the functional properties of externally elicited pain and fear: (1) Its administration can motivate and its termination reinforce trial-and-error learning; (2) it can be used to establish a conditioned response; (3) it can be used to condition an emotional disturbance to a distinctive compartment, and after this, during trials without any further stimulation, the cats will learn to escape from that compartment; (4) it can serve as a punishment to teach hungry cats to avoid food.

Clearly different results were obtained from an animal with an electrode in the posterior hypothalamic nucleus. Stimulation at this site produced the classical "flight" response first described by Hess (1954, 1957). This animal rapidly learned to escape such stimulation by choosing the correct arm of a T-maze but failed to acquire a simple avoidance response even after more than 200 trials.

Roberts (1958a) followed up the initial observations with a series of experiments designed to compare the effects of electrical stimulation of flight and alarm points with those produced by peripherally elicited pain. Cats were trained to run down a straight alley to escape stimulation. The intensities were selected so that the flight motivation (as measured by the strength of pull against a restraining device) was strongest and the drive elicited by the peripherally induced pain (shock to rib cage) weakest. With these parameters all three types of stimulation produced rapid and approximately equal escape learning. Only stimulation of the alarm points and peripheral pain produced any avoidance learning, in agreement with Miller's earlier observations.

Roberts (1958b) demonstrated further that stimulation of flight points appears to have an initially positive component, since animals learned an instrumental response to obtain such stimulation. However, prolonged or intense stimulation at these sites appeared to be aversive, as shown by the fact that the same animals learned another response to terminate such stimulation. These combined reward-aversion effects have also been observed in rats (Bower and Miller, 1958) and suggest a partial overlap of the reward and aversion mechanisms, at least at some sites in the posterior hypothalamus.

Bower (1959) found that the latency of the escape response in these approach-avoidance situations decreased as the intensity or frequency of the brain stimulation was increased. Stein (1962) and Keesey and Lindsley (1962) have reported similar observations. Valenstein and Valenstein (1963) and Hodos (1965) have reported that the latency of approach responses also decreases as the intensity of the brain stimulation is increased, an observation which is at variance with the suggested interpretation of the alternation behavior. Hodos (1965) also reported that rats that work to turn stimulation on and off repeatedly will work harder to obtain longer trains of stimulation. This indicates that maintained stimulation of a reward-aversion area may not be aversive. Hodos suggested that the termination of the stimulation may be rewarding because it provides relief from noxious peripheral effects which result from the excitation of some brain area even though this excitation is not, itself, noxious.

THEORETICAL IMPLICATIONS

The empirical findings of the last decade leave no doubt that electrical stimulation of many areas in the brain may be rewarding or aversive. It is not nearly so clear how these effects should be interpreted or how they relate to current theories of motivation or emotion. The reward-aversion effects can be obtained only from structures that are intimately related to the limbic system or the rhinencephalon; this finding has been interpreted to support the contention that motivation somehow is a property of limbic mechanisms. Few would quarrel with this basic statement, but the fact that the limbic system encompasses many anatomically distinct areas of the brain must not be overlooked.

On a more behavioral level, there arises the question whether the reward-aversion phenomena are, in fact, independent of *specific* drive mechanisms. Must we, as Olds suggests, think of autonomous reward and aversion mechanisms and return to the hedonistic dualism that was so popular around the turn of the century? Or should we subsume the empirical facts of reward and aversion under a drive reduction hypothesis which proposes that the arousal of specific drives through external or internal stimulation is aversive whereas the reduction of such drives is rewarding?

Olds has suggested that the demonstrated re-

ward effect following stimulation of central structures precludes the latter interpretation. This exception is well taken if we insist on a very literal interpretation of Miller's "stimulus reduction hypothesis of reinforcement." It assumes that the excitation of neural elements must invariably produce an increment in drive stimulation, and it is at this point that we would like to take issue with the objection. It is well known that the central nervous system contains many neural systems which exert an inhibitory function when activated normally or via electrical stimulation, and there is considerable evidence that such inhibitory mechanisms play an important role in motivation.

The situation is perhaps clearest when we consider hunger motivation, for which a distinct inhibitory mechanism has been isolated at the very heart of the reward system (the ventromedial nuclei of the hypothalamus). Additional inhibitory influences on food intake have been localized in the amygdaloid complex, which is also part of the reward system. Similar inhibitory mechanisms exist in the limbic system for sexual arousal, general activity, and thirst. Although specific inhibitory effects have been obtained from more localized areas than those producing the reward effect, it is becoming increasingly clear that the entire limbic system participates in the regulation of specific drives (see Grossman, 1964a, b). It seems reasonable to propose that the reward effect, which appears to be so widely distributed throughout the limbic system, may in fact represent several specific effects which relate to the reduction of particular drives.

This hypothesis is supported by the observation that the rate of self-stimulation in *specific areas* is affected by variations in *specific drives*. The correlation between self-stimulation and specific drives is much too general a phenomenon to be fortuitous. Aversive effects may be caused by the central elicitation of pain and/or the stimulation of *excitatory* mechanisms which elicit other drive stimulation. The major portion of the aversion system is located in areas which, when stimulated, give rise to hunger, thirst, or sexual motivation; termination of stimulation in these areas might be expected to be reinforcing because it produces instantaneous satiation.

We do not wish to suggest that *all* reinforcement must be produced by drive stimulus reduction. Drive reduction may account for reinforcement in a majority of situations where drive stimulation is not only subjectively aversive but also detrimental to the organism if maintained for longer periods of time. However, there are several conditions (such as sexual arousal or exploratory behavior) in which an increase in drive stimulation appears to be rewarding. The proposed interpretation of the reward-aversion phenomena can account for these situations if we assume that the stimulation of excitatory mechanisms may also be rewarding.

Further evidence for a functional relation between variations in specific drives and the reward phenomenon is the observation that self-stimulation, at least at some electrode sites, is not subject to satiation. This, of course, should be true if the reward effect is due to a pseudosatiation of a biological drive which continues to build up while the animal is busy at the self-stimulation lever. That hungry animals prefer to work for self-stimulation rather than food, at least for the first 24 or 48 hr of deprivation, may be due to the fact that the satiation effect is much more immediate (and possibly more complete) following direct central stimulation. The animal may have to learn that the temporary gratification from self-stimulation does not, in the long run, correct the organism's energy balance.

Although introspective analyses do not generally contribute materially to scientific argument, we might point out that generalized feelings of pleasantness or unpleasantness do not seem to occur unless specific motivations are involved.

Advocates of the hedonistic interpretation of the reward-aversion effect have pointed out that sated animals will self-stimulate at electrode placements which are affected by food deprivation, suggesting that the reward effect is at least partially independent of hunger. This argument is not compelling unless it can be demonstrated that completely sated animals continue to work for electrical stimulation of electrode sites that are not related to any other drive mechanism. So far, neither of these conditions has been met. It appears unlikely that this proof will be forthcoming, in view of the extensive anatomical overlap of the central systems which regulate food and water intake as well as sexual motivation and emotional behavior.

Several other hypothesis have been advanced to account for the apparently nonspecific motivational effect of electrical brain stimulation. Malmo (1961) observed cardiac deceleration during septal stimulation and suggested that the rewarding effects of septal stimulation might be related to this "parasympathetic or quieting effect." A priori, this hypothesis does not appear very likely, in view of the wide distribution of the reward system in portions of the brainstem from which sympathetic and parasympathetic excitation can be elicited. However, several investigators have attempted to elucidate the possible role of cardiac slowing in the reward-aversion effect, and a brief look at some of the evidence may be worthwhile. Peretz-Cruet et al. (1963) replicated Malmo's observation that septal self-stimulation produced deceleration of the heart rate, but he also noted a marked acceleration when the animals self-stimulated at hypothalamic sites. Meyers et al. (1963) reported that the cardiac response to both hypothalamic and septal stimulation is polyphasic, the first component being acceleration, the second deceleration. Only the acceleration can be observed when the interstimulus interval is reduced. These observations do not support the hypothesis that the rewarding property of central electrical stimulation is in any way related to concurrent effects on heart rate.

Early electrophysiological observations suggested that the rewarding effect of intracranial stimulation might be unnatural and result directly from seizure activity in limbic or midbrain structures (Nielson et al., 1958; Porter et al., 1958). Newman and Feldman (1964) renewed interest in this possibility by reporting that "seizure-like" afterdischarges promptly appeared in cortical and subcortical locations during self-stimulation of basomedial forebrain structures. That these EEG effects are not causally related to the reward effect is suggested by the finding (Reid et al., 1964) that anticonvulsant drugs *facilitated* lever-pressing behavior which was reinforced by hypothalamic stimulation. The rate of lever pressing for septal and hypothalamic stimulation was markedly increased by phenobarbital. Mogenson (1964a) reported that many animals show a small decrease in rate of responding for central stimulation rewards following large doses of pentobarbital; he also noted that animals which convulsed in response to the rewarding stimulus no longer show any seizure activity and respond much more frequently to the lever than before.

SUMMARY

Electrical stimulation of widely scattered points in the limbic system (including such subcortical regions as the hypothalamus and amygdaloid complex) appears to have rewarding and/or aversive properties. The majority of electrode placements in this system of nuclei and fiber tracts permit rewarding stimulation. Animals of a variety of species (rats, cats, monkeys, and man) learn and perform a variety of instrumental responses to obtain electrical stimulation of these points.

Relatively few placements, particularly those in the posterolateral hypothalamus, thalamus, and tegmentum, show a negative (i.e., aversive) effect. Animals learn and perform instrumental responses to escape and/or avoid such stimulation. From some electrode placements, particularly in the posterior hypothalamus, amygdala, hippocampus, and septal area, both rewarding and aversive effects can be obtained. Animals work to obtain brief trains of electrical pulses, but also to terminate (i.e., escape) prolonged or intense stimulation of the same electrode sites. In contrast to purely aversive placements, no avoidance learning can be established with stimulation of the combined reward-aversion sites. It is believed that the combined effects may be due to a partial anatomical overlap of mechanisms which mediate rewarding and aversive effects.

Self-stimulation rates are a function of reward schedule and current intensities. At some central sites self-stimulation increases monotonically with current intensity, suggesting a progressive recruitment of neural elements which are part of the reward system. Other stimulation sites show a nonmonotonic relationship between current intensity and rate of self-stimulation, which suggests that current spreads to neural elements which are either neutral or part of the aversive system. The rate of self-stimulation also varies as a function of deprivation with most if not all primary drives. The available evidence indicates that the rate of self-stimulation at a specific electrode site correlates positively with only one particular drive, suggesting a close functional relation between specific drives and the reward effect.

Self-stimulation, at least at some electrode sites, is not subject to satiation, which suggests a pseudosatiation effect on biological drives which continue to build up. Brady's observation that conditioned emotional responses (i.e., a suppression of ongoing behavior) cannot be established while the animal is working for central stimulation indicates that the pseudosatiation elicited by central stimulation may have more pronounced effects than conventional rewards, perhaps because of the immediacy or the intensity of the reward. This point is also made in studies showing that hungry animals prefer to work for self-stimulation at certain electrode sites rather than for food.

Attempts to modify self-stimulation behavior

pharmacologically (by either central or peripheral administration of various chemicals) have been effective, but the results have not yet been sufficiently specific to permit a meaningful interpretation of the data.

The reward-aversion phenomena are frequently interpreted to suggest nonspecific motivational systems which, when stimulated, mediate pleasure or aversion. Such an interpretation supports theoretical positions that subsume all motivational phenomena under a hedonistic dualism of pleasure and pain. An alternative explanation of the reward-aversion effect which might be closer to the theoretical climate of our days has been advanced. According to this view, the reward effect is caused by the excitation of inhibitory (and in some cases excitatory) mechanisms which contribute to the central regulation of *specific* drives. Self-stimulation is thought to provide pseudosatiation of a prevailing drive (or, in some cases, excitation of specific drives).

BIBLIOGRAPHY

Beer, B., & Valenstein, E. S. Discrimination of tones during reinforcing brain stimulation. *Science,* 1960, **132,** 297.

Bishop, M. P., Elder, S. T., & Heath, R. G. Intracranial self-stimulation in man. *Science,* 1963, **140,** 394–395.

Boren, J. J., & Malis, J. L. Determining thresholds of aversive brain stimulation. *Amer. J. Physiol.,* 1961, **3,** 429–433.

Bower, G. H. Response latency as a function of brain stimulation variables. *J. comp. physiol. Psychol.,* 1959, **52,** 533–535.

Bower, G. H., & Miller, N. E. Rewarding and punishing effects from stimulating the same place in the rat's brain. *J. comp. physiol. Psychol.,* 1958, **51,** 669–678.

Boyd, E., & Gardner, L. Positive and negative reinforcement from intracranial self-stimulation in teleosts. *Science,* 1962, **136,** 648.

Brady, J. V. A comparative approach to the experimental analysis of emotional behavior. In *Experimental psychopathology.* P. H. Hoch & J. Zubin, Eds. New York: Grune and Stratton, 1957.

Brady, J. V. Temporal and emotional factors related to electrical self-stimulation of the limbic system. In *The reticular formation of the brain.* H. H. Jasper, L. D. Proctor, R. S. Knighton, W. C. Noshay, & R. T. Costello, Eds. Boston: Little, Brown, 1958a.

Brady, J. V. The paleocortex and behavioral motivation. In *Biological and biochemical bases of behavior.* H. F. Harlow & C. N. Woolsey, Eds. Madison: Univ. of Wisconsin Press, 1958b.

Brady, J. V. Temporal and emotional effects related to intracranial electrical self-stimulation. In *Electrical studies on the unanesthetized brain*. E. R. Ramey & D. S. O'Doherty, Eds. New York: Paul Hoeber, 1960.

Brady, J. V. Motivational-emotional factors and intracranial self-stimulation. In *Electrical stimulation of the brain*. D. E. Sheer, Ed. Austin: Univ. of Texas Press, 1961.

Brady, J. V., & Conrad, D. G. Some effects of limbic system self-stimulation upon conditioned emotional behavior. *J. comp. physiol. Psychol.*, 1960, **53**, 128–137.

Brady, J. V., Boren, J. J., Conrad, D. G., & Sidman, M. The effect of food and water deprivation upon intracranial self-stimulation. *J. comp. physiol. Psychol.*, 1957, **50**, 134–137.

Brobeck, J. R. Self-stimulation experiments. Letter in *Science*, 1963, **140**, 218–219.

Brodie, D., Moreno, O. M., Malis, J. L., & Boren, J. J. Nonreversibility of the appetitive characteristics of intracranial stimulation. *Amer. J. Physiol.*, 1960, **199**, 707–709.

Brown, G. W., & Cohen, B. D. Avoidance and approach learning motivated by stimulation of identical hypothalamic loci. *Amer. J. Physiol.*, 1959, **197**, 153–157.

Bursten, B., & Delgado, J. M. R. Positive reinforcement induced by intracerebral stimulation in the monkey. *J. comp. physiol. Psychol.*, 1958, **51**, 6–10.

Cook, L., & Weidley, E. Behavioral effects of some psychopharmacological agents. *Ann. N.Y. Acad. Sci.*, 1957, **66**, 740–752.

Davis, J. D., & Miller, N. E. Fear and pain: their effect on self-injection of amobarbitol sodium by rats. *Science*, 1963, **141**, 1286.

Delgado, J. M. R., & Hamlin, H. In *Electrical studies on the unanesthetized brain*. E. R. Ramey & D. S. O'Doherty, Eds. New York: Paul Hoeber, 1960.

Delgado, J. M. R., Roberts, W. W., & Miller, N. E. Learning motivated by electrical stimulation of the brain. *Amer. J. Physiol.*, 1954, **179**, 587–593.

Deutsch, J. A. *The structural basis of behavior*. Chicago: Univ. of Chicago Press, 1960.

Deutsch, J. A. Learning and electrical self-stimulation of the brain. *J. theoret. Biol.*, 1963, **4**, 193–214.

Deutsch, J. A. Behavioral measurement of the neural refractory period and its application to intracranial self-stimulation. *J. comp. physiol. Psychol.*, 1964, **58**, 1–9.

Deutsch, J. A., & Howarth, C. I. Evocation by fear of a habit learned for electrical stimulation of the brain. *Science*, 1962, **136**, 3521.

Deutsch, J. A., & Howarth, C. I. Some tests of a theory of intracranial self-stimulation. *Psychol. Rev.*, 1963, **70**, 444–460.

Deutsch, J. A., Adams, D. W., & Metzner, R. J. Choice of intracranial stimulation as a function of delay between stimulations and strength of competing drive. *J. comp. physiol. Psychol.*, 1964, **57**, 241–243.

Falk, J. Septal stimulation as a reinforcer of and an alternative to consummatory behavior. *J. exp. Anal. Behav.*, 1961, **4**, 213–215.

Gallistel, C. R. Electrical self-stimulation and its theoretical implications. *Psychol. Bull.*, 1964, **61**, 23–34.

Gibson, W. E., Reid, L. D., Sokai, M., & Porter, P. B. Intracranial reinforcement compared with sugar-water reinforcement. *Science*, 1965, **148**, 1357–1358.

Grossman, S. P. Eating or drinking elicited by direct adrenergic or cholinergic stimulation of hypothalamus. *Science*, 1960, **132**, 301–302.

Grossman, S. P. Direct adrenergic and cholinergic stimulation of hypothalamic mechanisms. *Amer. J. Physiol.*, 1962, **202**, 1230–1236.

Grossman, S. P. Behavioral effects of chemical stimulation of the ventral amygdala. *J. comp. physiol. Psychol.*, 1964a, **57**, 29–36.

Grossman, S. P. Effect of chemical stimulation of the septal area on motivation. *J. comp. physiol. Psychol.*, 1964b, **58**, 194–200.

Grossman, S. P., & Grossman, Lore. Food and water intake following lesions or electrical stimulation of the amygdala. *Amer. J. Physiol.*, 1963, **205**, 761–765.

Hawkins, T. D., & Pliskoff, S. S. Brain stimulus intensity, rate of self-stimulation and reinforcing strength: an analysis through chaining. *J. exp. Anal. Behav.*, 1964, **7**, 285–288.

Heath, R. G., Ed. *Studies in schizophrenia*. Cambridge, Mass.: Harvard Univ. Press, 1954.

Hess, W. R. *Beitraege zur Physiologie des Hirnstammes. I: Die Methodik der lokalisierten Reizung und Ausschaltung subkortikaler Hirnabschnitte*. Leipzig: Thieme, 1932.

Hess, W. R. *Beitraege zur Physiologie des Hirnstammes. II: Das Zwischenhirn und die Regulation von Kreislauf und Atmung*. Leipzig: Thieme, 1938.

Hess, W. R. *Das Zwischenhirn: Syndrome, Lokalisationen, Funktionen* (2nd ed.). Basel: Schwabe, 1954.

Hess, W. R. *Functional organization of the diencephalon*. New York: Grune and Stratton, 1957.

Hodos, W. Motivational properties of long durations of rewarding brain stimulation. *J. comp. physiol. Psychol.*, 1965, **59**, 219–224.

Hodos, W., & Valenstein, E. S. Motivational variables affecting the rate of behavior maintained by intracranial stimulation. *J. comp. physiol. Psychol.*, 1960, **53**, 502–508.

Hoebel, B. G. Hunger and satiety in hypothalamic regulation of self-stimulation. *Dissert. Abstr.*, 1963, **23**, 4753–4754.

Hoebel, B. G. Hypothalamic lesions by electrocauterization: disinhibition of feeding and self-stimulation. *Science*, 1965, **149**, 452–453.

Hoebel, B. G., & Teitelbaum, P. Hypothalamic control of feeding and self-stimulation. *Science*, 1962, **135**, 375–377.

Howarth, C. I., & Deutsch, J. A. Drive decay: the cause of fast "extinction" of habits learned for brain stimulation. *Science,* 1962, **137**, 35–36.

Keesey, R. E. Duration of stimulation and the reward properties of hypothalamic stimulation. *J. comp. physiol. Psychol.,* 1964a, **58**, 201–207.

Keesey, R. E. Intracranial reward delay and the acquisition rate of a brightness discrimination. *Science,* 1964b, **143**, 702–703.

Keesey, R. E., & Lindsley, D. B. Duration of stimulation and the reinforcing properties of hypothalamic stimulation. *Amer. Psychologist,* 1962, **17**, 375 (abstract).

Kling, J. W., & Matsumiya, Y. Relative reinforcement values of food and intracranial stimulation. *Science,* 1962, **135**, 668–670.

Lilly, J. C. Learning motivated by subcortical stimulation: the start and stop patterns of behavior. In *The reticular formation of the brain.* H. H. Jasper, L. D. Proctor, R. S. Knighton, W. C. Noshay, & R. T. Costello, Eds. Boston: Little, Brown, 1958.

Lilly, J. C. Rewarding and punishing systems in the brain. In *The central nervous system and behavior.* M. A. B. Brazier, Ed. New York: Josiah Macy, Jr. Foundation, 1959a.

Lilly, J. C. "Stop" and "start" systems. In *Neuropharmacology.* H. A. Abramson, Ed. New York: Josiah Macy, Jr. Foundation, 1959b.

Lorens, S. The effect of lesions in the central nervous system on self-stimulation in the rat. Univ. of Chicago, unpublished doctoral dissertation, 1965.

McIntire, R. W., & Wright, J. E. Parameters related to response rate for septal and medial forebrain bundle stimulation. *J. comp. physiol. Psychol.,* 1965, **59**, 131–134.

Malmo, R. Slowing of heart rate after septal self-stimulation in rats. *Science,* 1961, **133**, 1128–1130.

Margules, D. L., & Olds, J. Identical "feeding" and "rewarding" systems in the lateral hypothalamus of rats. *Science,* 1962, **135**, 374–375.

Meyers, W. J., & Valenstein, E. S. Animal preference for method of obtaining reinforcing brain stimulation. *J. comp. physiol. Psychol.,* 1964, **51**, 675–678.

Meyers, W. J., Valenstein, E. S., & Lacey, J. I. Heart rate changes after reinforcing brain stimulation in rats. *Science,* 1963, **140**, 1233–1235.

Miller, N. E. Liberalization of basic S-R concepts: extensions to conflict behavior, motivation, and social learning. In *Psychology: a study of a science. Vol. II.* S. Koch, Ed. New York: McGraw-Hill, 1959.

Miller, N. E. Implications for theories of reinforcement. In *Electrical stimulation of the brain.* D. E. Sheer, Ed. Austin: Univ. of Texas Press, 1961a.

Miller, N. E. Learning and performance motivated by direct stimulation of the brain. In *Electrical stimulation of the brain.* D. E. Sheer, Ed. Austin: Univ. of Texas Press, 1961b.

Miller, N. E., Roberts, W. W., & Delgado, J. M. R. *Learning motivated by electrical stimulation of the brain.* Motion picture shown at the experimental division of the American Psychology Association., Sept. 1953, and the International Congress of Psychology, Montreal, June 1954.

Miller, N. E., Richter, M. L., Baily, C. J., & Southwick, J. B. "Thirst" induced or reduced, respectively, by minute injections of hypertonic NaCl or water into the ventricles of cats. Paper read at meeting of Eastern Psychology Association, New York, 1955.

Miller, N. E., Richter, M. L., Lacy, G. M., & Jensen, D. D. The effect of ventricular injections of hypertonic saline and of water on an instrumental-response measure of thirst. Paper read at meeting of Eastern Psychology Association, Atlantic City, March 1956.

Mogenson, G. J. Effects of sodium pentobarbitol on brain self-stimulation. *J. comp. physiol. Psychol.,* 1964a, **58**, 461–462.

Mogenson, G. J. Avoidance responses to rewarding brain stimulation: replication and extension. *J. comp. physiol. Psychol.,* 1964b, **58**, 465–467.

Mogenson, G. J. An attempt to establish secondary reinforcement with rewarding brain self-stimulation. *Psychol. Rep.,* 1965, **16**, 163–167.

Mogenson, G. J., & Morrison, M. J. Avoidance responses to "reward" stimulation of the brain. *J. comp. physiol. Psychol.,* 1962, **55**, 691–694.

Morgane, P. J. Electrophysiological studies of feeding and satiety centers in the rat. *Amer. J. Physiol.,* 1961a, **201**, 838–844.

Morgane, P. J. Medial forebrain bundle and "feeding centers" of the hypothalamus. *J. comp. Neurol.,* 1961b, **117**, 1–26.

Newman, B. L. Behavioral effects of self-stimulation of the septal area and related structures. *J. comp. physiol. Psychol.,* 1961, **54**, 340–345.

Newman, B. L., & Feldman, S. M. Electrophysiological activity accompanying intracranial self-stimulation. *J. comp. physiol. Psychol.,* 1964, **57**, 244–247.

Nielson, H. C., Doty, R. W., & Rutledge, L. T. Motivational and perceptual aspects of subcortical stimulation in cats. *Amer. J. Physiol.,* 1958, **194**, 427–432.

Olds, J. Physiological mechanisms of reward. In *Nebraska symposium on motivation.* M. R. Jones, Ed. Lincoln: Univ. of Nebraska Press, 1955.

Olds, J. A preliminary mapping of electrical reinforcing effects in the rat brain. *J. comp. physiol. Psychol.,* 1956a, **49**, 281–285.

Olds, J. Neurophysiology of drive. *Psychiat. Res. Rep. Amer. psychiat. Ass.,* 1956b, **6**, 15–20.

Olds, J. Runaway and maze behavior controlled by basomedial forebrain stimulation in the rat. *J. comp. physiol. Psychol.,* 1956c, **49**, 507–512.

Olds, J. Adaptive functions of the paleocortex. In *Biological and biochemical bases of behavior.* H. Harlow & C. Woolsey, Eds. Madison: Univ. of Wisconsin Press, 1958a.

Olds, J. Effects of hunger and male sex hormones on self-stimulation of the brain. *J. comp. physiol. Psychol.,* 1958b, **51**, 320–324.

Olds, J. Satiation effects in self-stimulation of the brain. *J. comp. physiol. Psychol.,* 1958c, **51**, 675–678.

Olds, J. Self-stimulation of the brain. *Science,* 1958d, **127**, 315–324.

Olds, J. Studies of neuropharmacologicals by electrical and chemical manipulation of the brain in animals with chronically implanted electrodes. In *Neuropsychopharmacology.* B. P. Bradley, P. Deniker, & C. Radouco-Thomas, Eds. Amsterdam: Elsevier, 1959.

Olds, J. Approach-avoidance dissociations in rat brain. *Amer. J. Physiol.,* 1960a, **199**, 965–968.

Olds, J. Differentiation of reward systems in the brain by self-stimulation techniques. In *Electrical studies on the unanesthetized brain.* E. R. Ramsey & D. S. O'Doherty, Eds. New York: Paul Hoeber, 1960b.

Olds, J. Differential effects of drive and drugs on self-stimulation at different brain sites. In *Electrical stimulation of the brain.* D. E. Sheer, Ed. Austin: Univ. of Texas Press, 1961.

Olds, J., & Milner, P. Positive reinforcement produced by electrical stimulation of the septal area and other regions of the rat brain. *J. comp. physiol. Psychol.,* 1954, **47**, 419–427.

Olds, J., & Olds, M. E. Positive reinforcement produced by stimulating hypothalamus with iproniazid and other compounds. *Science,* 1958, **127**, 1175–1176.

Olds, J., & Olds, M. E. Interference and learning in paleocortical systems. In *Brain mechanisms and learning.* J. E. Delafresnaye, A. Fessard, R. W. Gerard, & J. Konorski, Eds. Oxford: Blackwell Scientific, 1961a.

Olds, J., & Peretz, B. A motivational analysis of the reticular activating system. *EEG clin. Neurophysiol.,* 1960, **12**, 445–454.

Olds, J., Killam, K. F., & Bach-y-Rita, P. Self-stimulation of the brain used as a screening method for tranquilizing drugs. *Science,* 1956, **124**, 265–266.

Olds, J., Killam, K. F., & Eiduson, S. Effects of tranquilizers on self-stimulation of the brain. In *Psychotropic drugs.* S. Garattini & V. Ghetti, Eds. Amsterdam: Elsevier, 1957.

Olds, J., Travis, R. P., & Schwing, R. C. Topographic organization of hypothalamic self-stimulation functions. *J. comp. physiol. Psychol.,* 1960, **53**, 23–32.

Olds, J., Yuwiler, A., Olds, M. E., & Yun, C. Neurohumors in hypothalamic substrates of reward. *Amer. J. Physiol.,* 1964, **207**, 242–254.

Olds, M. E., & Hogberg, D. Subcortical lesions and mass retention in the rat. *Exp. Neurol.,* 1964, **10**, 296–304.

Olds, M. E., & Olds, J. Emotional and associative mechanisms in rat brain. *J. comp. physiol. Psychol.,* 1961b, **54**, 120–126.

Olds, M. E., & Olds, J. Approach-escape interaction in rat brain. *Amer. J. Physiol.,* 1962, **203**, 803–810.

Olds, M. E., & Olds, J. Approach-avoidance analysis of rat diencephalon. *J. comp. Neurol.,* 1963, **120**, 259–295.

Peretz-Cruet, J., Black, W. C., & Brady, J. V. Heart rate: differential effects of hypothalamic and septal self-stimulation. *Science,* 1963, **140**, 1235–1236.

Pliskoff, S. S., & Hawkins, T. D. Test of Deutsch's drive-decay theory of rewarding self-stimulation of the brain. *Science,* 1963, **141**, 823–824.

Pliskoff, S. S., Wright, J. E., & Hawkins, D. T. Brain stimulation as a reinforcer: intermittent schedules. *J. exp. Anal. Behav.,* 1965, **8**, 75–88.

Porter, R. W., Conrad, D., & Brady, J. V. Some electroencephalographic patterns induced by self-stimulation in monkeys. *Fed. Proc.,* 1958, **17**, 125.

Poschel, B. P. H., & Ninteman, F. W. Norepinephrine: a possible excitatory neurohormone of the reward system. *Life Sci.,* 1963, **10**, 782–788.

Poschel, B. P. H., & Ninteman, F. W. Excitatory (antidepressant?) effects of monoamine oxidase inhibitors on the reward system of the brain. *Life Sci.,* 1964, **3**, 903–910.

Poschel, B. P. H., & Ninteman, F. W. Self-determined aversive thresholds from the medial hypothalamus of the rat. *Psychol. Rep.,* 1965, **16**, 585–591.

Prescott, R. G. W., Estrous cycle in the rat: effects on self-stimulation behavior. *Science,* 1966, **152**, 796–797.

Reid, L. D., Gibson, W. E., Gledhill, S. M., & Porter, P. B. Anticonvulsant drugs and self-stimulating behavior. *J. comp. physiol. Psychol.,* 1964, **57**, 353–356.

Reynolds, R. W. The relationship between stimulation voltage and hypothalamic self-stimulation in the rat. *J. comp. physiol. Psychol.,* 1958, **51**, 193–198.

Roberts, W. W. Rapid escape learning without avoidance learning motivated by hypothalamic stimulations in cats. *J. comp. physiol. Psychol.,* 1958a, **51**, 391–399.

Roberts, W. W. Both rewarding and punishing effects from stimulation of posterior hypothalamus of cat with same electrode at same intensity. *J. comp. physiol. Psychol.,* 1958b, **51**, 400–407.

Routtenberg, A., & Lindy, J. Effects of the availability of rewarding septal and hypothalamic stimulation on barpressing for food under conditions of deprivation. *J. comp. physiol. Psychol.,* 1965, **60**, 158–161.

Sandler, J. A. A brief overview of the research program on "Puzzling Punishment Effects" at Coral Gables VAH. *Newsletter Res. psychol.,* 1964, **6**, 10–13.

Schiff, B. B. The effects of tegmental lesions on the reward properties of septal stimulation. *Psychonom. Sci.,* 1964, **1**, 397–398.

Schnitzer, S. B., Reid, L. D., & Porter, P. B. Electrical intracranial stimulation as a primary reinforcer for cats. *Psychol. Rep.,* 1965, **16**, 335–338.

Sem-Jacobson, C. W. Effects of electrical stimulation on the human brain. *EEG clin. Neurophysiol.,* 1959, **11**, 379.

Sem-Jacobson, C. W., & Torkildsen, A. In *Electrical studies on the unanesthetized brain.* E. R. Ramey & D. S. O'Doherty, Eds. New York: Paul Hoeber, 1960.

Seward, J. P., Uyeda, A. A., & Olds, J. Resistance to

extinction following cranial self-stimulation. *J. comp. physiol. Psychol.*, 1959, **52**, 294–299.

Seward, J. P., Uyeda, A. A., & Olds, J. Reinforcing effect of brain stimulation on run-way performance as a function of interval between trials. *J. comp. physiol. Psychol.*, 1960, **53**, 224–227.

Sidman, M., Brady, J. V., Conrad, D. G., & Schulman, A. Reward schedules and behavior maintained by intracranial self-stimulation. *Science*, 1955, **122**, 830–831.

Spies, G. Food versus intracranial self-stimulation reinforcement in food-deprived rats. *J. comp. physiol. Psychol.*, 1965, **60**, 153–157.

Stein, L. Secondary reinforcement established with subcortical stimulation. *Science*, 1958, **127**, 466–467.

Stein, L. An analysis of stimulus-duration preferences in self-stimulation of the brain. *J. comp. physiol. Psychol.*, 1962, **55**, 405–414.

Stein, L. Amphetamine and neural reward mechanisms. In *Ciba foundation symposium on animal behavior and drug action.* H. Steinberg, A. V. S. DeReuk, & J. Knight, Eds. London: Churchill, 1964a.

Stein, L. Reciprocal action of reward and punishment mechanisms. In *The role of pleasure in behavior.* R. G. Heath, Ed. New York: Paul Hoeber, 1964b.

Stein, L. Facilitation of avoidance behavior by positive brain stimulation. *J. comp. psysiol. Psychol.*, 1965, **60**, 9–19.

Stein, L., & Hearst, E. Inhibitory effect of positively reinforcing brain stimulation on learning. *Amer. Psychologist*, 1958, **13**, 408.

Stein, L., & Ray, O. S. Self-regulation of brain stimulating current intensity in the rat. *Science*, 1959, **130**, 570–572.

Steiner, S. S., & D'Amato, M. R. Rewarding and aversive effects of amygdaloid self-stimulation as a function of current intensity. *Psychonom. Sci.*, 1964, **1**, 27–28.

Stutz, R. M., Lewin, I., & Rocklin, K. W. Generality of "drive-decay" as an explanatory concept. *Psychonom. Sci.*, 1965, **2**, 127–128.

Uyeda, A., & Gengerelli, J. Influence of rectangular pulses and sine waves of varying frequency on brain self-stimulation in the rat. *Psychol. Rep.*, 1959, **5**, 641–647.

Valenstein, E. S. Problems of measurement and interpretation with reinforcing brain stimulation. *Psychol. Rev.*, 1964, **71**, 415–437.

Valenstein, E. S., & Beer, B. Reinforcing brain stimulation in competition with water reward and shock avoidance. *Science*, 1962, **137**, 1052–1054.

Valenstein, E. S., & Beer, B. Continuous opportunity for reinforcing brain stimulation. *J. exp. Anal. Behav.*, 1964, **7**, 183–184.

Valenstein, E. S., & Meyers, W. J. Rate-independent tests of reinforcing consequences of brain stimulation. *J. comp. physiol. Psychol.*, 1964, **57**, 52–60.

Valenstein, E. S., & Valenstein, Thelma. When does reinforcing brain stimulation become punishing? *Amer. Psychologist*, 1963, **18**, 436 (abstract).

Valenstein, E. S., & Valenstein, Thelma. Interaction of positive and negative reinforcing neural systems. *Science*, 1964, **145**, 1456–1457.

Wadson, R. E., Ried, L. D., & Porter, P. B. Overnight performance decrement with intracranial reinforcement. *Psychol. Rep.*, 1965, **16**, 653–658.

Ward, H. P. Basal tegmental self-stimulation after septal ablation. *A.M.A. Arch. Neurol.*, 1960, **3**, 158–162.

Ward, H. P. Tegmental self-stimulation after amygdaloid ablation. *A.M.A. Arch. Neurol.*, 1961, **4**, 657–659.

Wetzel, M. C. The contribution of self-stimulation to straight alley performance in the rat. *Dissert. Abstr.*, 1963, **23**, 3001–3002.

Wilkinson, H. A., & Peele, T. L. Modification of intracranial self-stimulation by hunger and satiety. *Amer. J. Physiol.*, 1962, **203**, 537–741.

Wilkinson, H. A., & Peele, T. L. Intracranial self-stimulation in cats. *J. comp. Neurol.*, 1963, **121**, 425–440.

Work, M. S., & Elder, T. S. Self-determined stimulus train duration of intracranial self-stimulation as a function of pulse frequency in the rat. *Psychol. Rep.*, 1964, **15**, 83–90.

Wurtz, R. H., & Olds, J. Amygdaloid stimulation and operant reinforcement in the rat. *J. comp. physiol. Psychol.*, 1963, **56**, 941–949.

CHAPTER ELEVEN

Psychophysiological Theories of Motivation

The basic concern of all fields of scientific inquiry is the study of specific cause-effect relationships. In psychology, the cause of all behavior (except some reflexly determined responses of individual organs) is a complex interaction of external and internal stimuli with constantly changing organismic conditions. Psychophysical and neurophysiological investigations have shown that the definition of external stimuli in terms of their effects on the organism is far from simple. However, we can specify the stimulus situation with a precision that is more than adequate (in relation to our ignorance of some of the other factors that must interact with the effects of these stimuli) to provide a satisfactory degree of control over this aspect of the experimental situation. The psychologist's description of the effects of such stimulation in terms of gross motor responses, although crude perhaps to the neurophysiologist, similarly seems to be amply precise for most present needs.

The third and most important link in the cause-effect sequence has until recently received little experimental attention. The complex organismic conditions that determine the organism's response to peripheral stimuli have commonly been considered only in terms of intervening variables or hypothetical constructs to be held constant or defined operationally for the purpose of psychological investigations. Such concepts as learning, motivation, or emotion form the very cornerstones of psychological thought, but the psychologist has conveniently argued that the experimental investigation of organismic variables is properly within the domain of physiological rather than psychological research. This theory leaves the psychologist in the rather peculiar position of having to depend on the whims of another science for a description of the very processes which on the experimental level determine the outcome of every psychological experiment and on the theoretical level underlie the principal explanatory concepts used in the description and prediction of behavior. This situation has led to a proliferation of ill-defined concepts, such as "drives," "needs," "urges," "instincts," "desires," "habits," "incentives," and "sets." These terms may or may not refer to some hypothetical condition of the organism and are generally of insufficient specificity to allow more than indirect and partial control and manipulation.

It is often argued by hard-headed behaviorists that the operational definition of an intervening variable is entirely adequate for the experimental investigation of such basic processes as motivation or learning. This position overlooks a problem to which the behaviorist should be particularly sensitive. How did the hypothetical construct originate, and does it in fact describe a real phenomenon in the sense that corresponding physiological processes occur? To assume that these questions are irrelevant as long as the use of such a hypothetical construct permits some degree of success in predicting behavior is simply not a scientific attitude. Scientific inquiry not only serves the pragmatic purpose of prediction but also attempts to *understand* the phenomena under investigation. The use of intervening variables is justified if there is reason to believe that the theoretical concepts represent an approximation of a process that is potentially demonstrable. In psychology this justification does not always prevail. Most of the intervening variables originate from the introspective feeling of the theorist; there exists considerable doubt, in some instances, whether there are physiological processes that correspond even roughly to the psychological concept as operationally defined. The use of these hypothetical constructs is a perfectly acceptable way to substitute temporarily for missing knowledge, but they should never become so firmly established that one ceases looking for the missing member in the cause-effect chain.

The inadequacy of operational definitions of simple intervening variables such as hunger or thirst can be easily demonstrated. The common practice of defining these motivational factors in terms of hours of food or water deprivation demonstrably does not result in the same degree of motivation in different subjects or, for that matter, in the same subject from day to day. Such factors as nutrient reserves, metabolic rate, activity, environmental temperature, etc., can be as important determinants of hunger and thirst motivation as time of deprivation. When such motivational factors as sexual arousal or emotionality are considered, operational definitions are even less useful. Time of deprivation is not an important determinant of sexual or emotional arousal, and the influence of prior learning is so pervasive that it becomes all but impossible to maintain effective control over the many potentially relevant aspects of the environment.

The previous chapters have reviewed the experimental and theoretical literature attempting to relate physiological processes to specific drives or motives. It was found that even such basic motivational factors as hunger, thirst, sexual motivation, or emotion were difficult to define. Operational definitions in terms of hours of deprivation, intensity of noxious stimulation, or injections of hormonal substances have enabled us to proceed with experimental investigations, but the results of these studies may be incomplete and even misleading.

A simple correspondence between the physiological needs of the organism, a "conscious awareness" of the physiological conditions that arouse and maintain a drive to some particuliar action, and the overt action itself may not exist. Most basic motivational forces arise from some physiological need state (the clearest examples are the organism's energy and fluid balances, which are usually maintained within rather narrow limits); however, some organic needs such as vitamin deficiencies seem to elicit neither the drive to corrective action nor the required action itself. Conversely, some compelling drives (such as sexual motivation) cannot be traced to specific needs or deficiencies and may not be expressed in overt behavior, depending on a variety of other conditions. In the case of emotion, it is clear that the effectiveness of a particular environmental stimulus depends on the past history of the organism. The experience of an emotion may, furthermore, not give rise to an appropriate behavioral reaction, or it may evoke an apparently contradictory response.

If physiological need does not reliably elicit a conscious drive to corrective action, and if the presence of such a drive to action does not necessarily evoke the appropriate overt behavior, how can motivation be defined? To argue for the simple omission of the concept of motivation from scientific consideration because of these conceptual difficulties solves no problem. All overt behavior is motivated and cannot be investigated without allowance for this fact. To disregard the physiological basis of motivation and define it only in terms of overt stimulus-response relationships (i.e., the animal is hungry because he eats) has immediate pragmatic value and may even improve the predictive powers of behavioral theories, but this practice is of little help when attempting to determine the causes of behavior.

The physiological psychologist must be aware that the immediate concern is not to improve the predictive powers of some behavioral theory, but rather to understand the complex chain of stimulus-response relationships that intervene between an external stimulus and the organism's overt response to it. This overt reaction is determined largely by the associative history of the organism and by the *balance* of motivational forces or drives operating at the time. Unless one has a thorough understanding of the neural and chemical events that occur in response to external or internal stimulation, one cannot hope to understand the causation of behavior or predict it with accuracy.

The physiological psychologist must isolate the exteral and internal stimuli that arouse a motivational condition and determine the neural and/or chemical processes that translate these environmental changes into activity in the central mechanisms directly responsible for the drive to action. For such drives as hunger, thirst, elimination, sleep, temperature, and regulation, studies must be made of the homeostatic mechanisms of the organism and of the physiological processes that translate homeostatic needs (defined as deviations from some optimal balance) into neural activity in specific central regulatory systems or centers. Specifically, we must find what mechanical, chemical, or neural changes may be elicited by temporary deviations from the homeostatic "zero"; how these events are transformed into excitatory or inhibitory signals to specific portions of the central nervous system; and how the activity of various central regulatory mechanisms may be integrated and translated into a single and specific drive state.

With other motivational forces, such as sexual or emotional arousal, the problem is further complicated by the pervasive influence of learning. In higher forms, at least, very few stimuli innately elicit emotional reactions. Necessary, therefore, is a search for the neural mechanisms involved in assigning motivational potency to stimuli and screening the stimuli which must be rerouted to specific centers. At a more reduced level of analysis, the neurochemical mechanisms that determine the organism's responsiveness to stimuli of learned sexual or emotional value must be accounted for.

Once we begin to understand the complex physiological mechanisms that contribute to the level of excitation in individual motivational systems, a thorough study of the interaction of different drive mechanisms must be undertaken, since overt behavior under normal circumstances is complexly determined. This interaction may have peripheral components. (Thirst or emotional arousal may cause dryness of the mouth which interferes with feeding behavior.) However, it is becoming increasingly clear that there are central interconnections that permit a more direct and perhaps less "conscious" interaction among all motivational mechanisms.

Finally, we must attempt to study the processes by which the activity of the motivational mechanisms is translated into overt behavior. Is a response to a distinct sensation of hunger, thirst, sexual arousal, or emotion made by emitting reaction sequences which in the past have led to the reduction of such drive stimulation? Or are these sensations nonessential concomitants of central processes which somehow direct the overt behavior of the organism? To put this question on a different level, we might ask whether the activity of the central motivational mechanisms directly controls the efferent motor pathways, serving primarily as a releaser of pre-established motor acts, or whether it somehow influences transmission in afferent sensory systems, producing distinct sensations which then serve as the unconditioned stimuli for the overt responses.

Considerable experimental and theoretical advances have been made in the past decades for the first of these problems. Although much remains to be accomplished, we are beginning to discern specific central regulatory centers for many different types of motivational forces and are gaining at least a partial understanding of the chemical and neural events that influence the activity of these central mechanisms. We have learned that these centers may consist of rather complex neural circuits which involve many parts of the brain and receive afferent inputs from many different peripheral and central sources. Precisely how the separate parts of these systems interrelate is not yet clear, but one begins to see some order in the chaos and much progress should be made in the next few years. As yet, there is little concrete information about the interaction between different drive systems, aside from occasional experiments which suggest that extensive central interaction does in fact take place. The last and perhaps most important aspect of the problem of motivation has been neglected by experimenters as well as theorists, partly because the question of conscious awareness of motivation cannot be attacked in the animal laboratory. Our empirical knowledge is confined to the realm of specific centers or, at best, neural systems. Few theorists have ventured a guess about the integration and transformation of neural activity in these neural mechanisms into awareness and eventually overt behavior.

RECENT THEORETICAL INTERPRETATIONS

Local Theories

Most modern psychological theories of motivation are based on the "local" theories of motivation or drive stimulation proposed by Cannon (1934) and earlier workers. One of the more explicit examples of such an approach is Hull's (1943) suggestion that the survival of the individual and of the species requires the maintenance of optimal environment conditions and that specific and persistent "drive stimulation" (S_d) arises when a deviation from these optimal conditions produces a "need." Such needs are believed to stimulate specific sensory receptors and elicit afferent, neural impulses toward central ganglia; these ganglia act as a kind of automatic switchboard, directing the impulses to the muscles or glands whose action is necessary to reduce the particular need. Satiation or drive reduction, in this system, depends exclusively on the cessation of drive stimulation and is presumably brought about by the restoration of optimal conditions in the external or internal environment.

The simplicity of such hypotheses is appealing, but experimental evidence indicates that the notion of specific drive stimulation may be an oversimplification of a complex problem. The most telling argument against specific drive stimulation derives from experiments showing that (1) denervation or removal of the stomach fails to interfere with hunger motivation or the regulation of food intake; (2) removal of the genital organs does not eliminate sexual motivation; and (3) artificial induction of specific drive stimulation (such as dryness of the mouth and throat) fails to elicit motivation. All these experiments may have failed to deal with the appropriate source of afferent signals (drive stimulation may arise from the *lower* portion of the gastrointestinal tract rather than from the *stomach* in the case of hunger). Additional research is needed to clarify the role of specific peripheral neural mechanisms. However, it is doubtful that we will discover a *single* neural system which is essential to either the elicitation or the cessation of motivation.

The psychologist's reluctance to give up this simple notion is quite understandable if we look at the alternatives that recent neurophysiological research has suggested. Instead of a simple stimulus-response relationship which does not require the postulation of complex mechanisms beyond sensory systems similar, if not identical, to the classical sensory modalities, we are forced to contemplate separate excitory and inhibitory centers in subcortical structures; their excitation or inhibition by neural as well as chemical messengers; the need for cortical integration and elaboration of their activity; and, finally, the translation of the total subcortical and cortical activity into sensations and/or overt behavior. Moreover, many of the pieces of this puzzle are still missing, so that any theoretical approach must be either very incomplete or highly speculative. We can no longer gloss over the subjective, experiential aspects of motivation by glibly referring such functions to the cortex as a whole.

According to the convenient notions of early theorists in this field, motivated or emotional behavior simply occurred as a direct consequence of drive stimulation, and the subjective aspects of motivation were regarded as nonessential byproducts of this process. Nobody was greatly concerned about the need for integrating these motivational influences with other, ongoing processes in the central nervous system beyond assigning such functions to the cortex. We have become much too sophisticated to accept such notions

at face value. That this awareness is presently a mixed blessing will become obvious in the discussion of some of the current theoretical schemes, which are characterized by complexity and confusion.

Lashley

Lashley (1938) opened a new era in physiological psychology with the proposal that motivation, far from representing a simple sensory reaction to specific peripheral drive stimuli, must instead be the end product of a complex integration of neural and humoral factors which contribute to the activity of central regulatory mechanisms. Lashley did not elaborate the neuroanatomical or physiological aspects of this multifactor theory, but his thoughtful description of the functional properties of such central mechanisms has greatly influenced all subsequent theories.

Perhaps the most important contribution of Lashley's suggestion is the clear implication that the central regulation of motivation cannot depend on a single sensory input or simple, stereotyped motor acts or response sequences. Lashley admitted that a single stimulus may, in some rather artificial situations, suffice to elicit motivated responses; he insisted, however, that under normal conditions sensory stimuli of most sensory modalities interact with humoral conditions in the internal environment to produce a level of motivation that reflects all of these factors. Similarly, he pointed out that motivational forces are not necessarily or even typically related to specific acts or response mechanisms, although the limitations of laboratory experiments have sometimes created this impression. It is safe to predict that a thirsty animal will ingest water if it is available, but the specific responses to water will depend on the particular stimulus situation and appear stereotyped only if the environment is constant.

Beach

Beach's (1942a, b, 1944, 1947a, b) work on sexual motivation has supported Lashley's hypothesis in showing that sexual arousal is a function of the total amount of nonspecific sensory input interacting with hormal mechanisms and associative factors. Beach and others further demonstrated that several different areas of the brain contribute to the regulation of sexual behavior, but that only one subcortical (hypothalamic) center of integration appears to be essential to sexual arousal and behavior. Similar findings characterize the current literature in the areas of hunger, thirst, and emotional behavior, and there appears to be little quarrel with Lashley's basic hypothesis.

Morgan's Central Theory of Motivation

Although the outlines of a general central theory of motivation were discernible in Lashley's (1938) provocative review of the problem of instinctive behavior, the first formal statement of such a notion must be credited to Morgan. In his *Physiological Psychology* (1943) Morgan proposed a "central theory of drive" which has remained unchanged save for minor additions and deletions (Morgan and Stellar, 1950; Morgan, 1956; Morgan, 1957).

Disillusioned with local theories by quickly accumulating negative evidence, he suggested that a drive should be regarded as a state of nervous activity in a system of centers and pathways in the central nervous system. Each system is concerned primarily with one particular kind of motivation, although there may be considerable overlap between the neural systems subserving different drives. Such a *central motive state* (CMS) can be aroused by external or internal stimuli as well as by chemical and hormonal changes in the blood. The latter are often, if not always, the primary conditions that either affect central mechanisms directly or initiate peripheral sensory stimuli which then stimulate the neural centers. Once a central motive state is set up, it is expected to persist without additional support by a process of reverberation of neural circuits or of tonus supplied by other centers which are in constant activity.

This central motive state "predisposes the organism to react in certain ways to particular stimuli and not to react to others." It primes the organism to approach or withdraw from stimuli having certain characteristics, or as Morgan put it: "the CMS functions as a selective valve or switch for certain S-R relationships and not others." The CMS may further *emit* certain random patterns of behavior such as the general bodily activity which precedes and accompanies more specific forms of motivated behavior; it may also emit particular patterns of behavior which occur in the absence of the appropriate environmental conditions, such as sexual behavior patterns emitted in the absence of a partner.

The satisfaction or reduction of a central motive state may occur in a number of ways. Elimination of the peripheral drive stimulus or humoral motive factor (HMF) which originally aroused the central motive state can reduce it. Alternatively, some humoral messenger different from the humoral factors which aroused the CMS may directly reduce it. Another possibility is that "stimulation in the course of drive-instigated behavior" may reduce the CMS, "or that behavior resulting from central motive states may itself reduce these states."

More recently, Morgan suggested that the reverberating activity of the reticular formation of the brainstem may be the most general kind of central motive state. Such a general drive state can determine the predisposition of the organism to react to its environment and perhaps to develop more selective central motive states. He further suggested that central motive states can be aroused by the lack of sensory stimulation as well as by an increase in such stimulation, thus explaining the existence of the so-called sensory drives which are apparently reduced by an increase in sensory stimulation. This notion rests on the demonstration that the nervous system is far from inactive during sleep or bodily inactivity and maintains a constant level of neural activity which, according to Morgan, may build up a tendency for action which is released by any sensory stimulation.

Morgan has suggested that central motive states may be complexly regulated by "elaborate mechanisms involving much of the forebrain and the brainstem." The hypothalamic centers, which have been shown to participate in the regulation of almost all physiological drives, are believed to function as "volume controls" for these complex integrative systems.

Stellar's Multifactor Theory of Motivation

Elaborating on the theoretical proposals of Lashley, Beach, and Morgan, Stellar (1954, 1960) has developed a multifactor theory of motivation. This theory provides a specific anatomical locus for Morgan's "central motive state" as well as Lashley's "integrative mechanism" and has led to a great deal of fruitful research in the past decade.

The central hypothesis is that "*The amount of motivated behavior is a direct function of the amount of activity in certain excitatory centers of the hypothalamus*," and that

> The activity of these excitatory centers, in turn, is determined by a large number of factors which can be grouped in four general classes: (*a*) *inhibitory centers* which serve only to depress the activity of the excitatory centers, (*b*) *sensory*

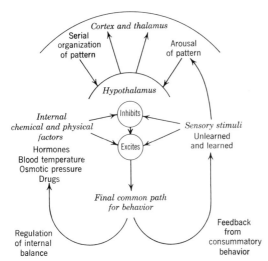

Fig. 11.1 Schematic diagram of the physiological factors contributing to the control of motivated behavior. (From Stellar, 1954.)

stimuli which control hypothalamic activity through the afferent impulses they can set up, (*c*) *the internal environment* which can influence the hypothalamus through its rich vascular supply and the cerebrospinal fluid, and (*d*) *cortical and thalamic centers* which can exert excitatory and inhibitory influences on the hypothalamus (Stellar, 1954, p. 6)

Stellar explains the choice of the hypothalamus as the central regulatory mechanism by pointing to experimental evidence which indicates that motivated behavior is severely affected by small lesions in the hypothalamus, and that specific drives such as hunger, thirst, sexual motivation, or emotion appear to be selectively affected by restricted damage to specific portions of the hypothalamus. Stellar admits that individual drive mechanisms can be affected by lesions in other areas of the central nervous system, but he points out that the effects of extrahypothalamic lesions are rarely as pronounced as those of hypothalamic damage; he suggests that secondary mechanisms, which in turn affect the hypothalamic centers, may be responsible for these effects.

There is little quarrel with the experimental evidence cited in support of this contention, but Stellar's interpretation may not be as irrefutable as it might at first seem. One might argue, for instance, that the hypothalamus merely serves as a funnel for motivational mechanisms which are integrated at higher levels of the brain, such as the limbic system, and that the apparent primacy of the hypothalamic centers may be largely an artifact of the anatomical structure of this system. The currently available evidence does not favor one of these alternatives, and it may be best to maintain an open mind with respect to the specific anatomical localization of the central regulatory mechanism.

One of the most interesting aspects of Stellar's theory is the postulation of inhibitory centers which are believed to depress the activity of the excitatory mechanisms rather than affect behavior in a more direct fashion. The influence of these inhibitory mechanisms is suggested to represent the primary neural mechanism for the regulation of satiation, which thus becomes subject to a separate central regulation. Logically, the postulation of distinct satiety mechanisms is very desirable for any theory of motivation; almost all the available evidence suggests that the physiological processes which presumably give rise to motivation cannot be directly affected by consummatory behavior in the relatively brief time often required for complete or partial satiation.

The experimental evidence for distinct inhibitory centers in the hypothalamus (or any other portion of the brain) remains spotty, however, in spite of extensive investigative effort. The evidence consists primarily of the results of investigations of feeding behavior and emotionality which show an increase following lesions in the area of the ventromedial nuclei of the hypothalamus. The theory receives some support from the demonstration of separate hypothalamic centers for the regulation of sleep and wakefulness. The uniqueness of the hypothalamic inhibitory influence is questionable, however, since lesions in several other portions of the brain produce an apparent increase in emotional reactivity. Recent investigations of feeding and drinking behavior suggest that inhibitory influences may also be represented in several regions of the limbic circuit. Although it is clear that the central regulation of motivation requires inhibitory as well as excitatory influences, these may not be specifically localized in the hypothalamus and may, in fact, influence behavior directly rather than via a braking action on the excitatory mechanisms.

Stellar's interpretation of the role of sensory stimuli, which presumably originate in the internal as well as the external environment, is quite direct and simple. In agreement with Beach's findings on the expendability of specific sensory modalities, Stellar suggests that no single sensory input is indispensable to the arousal of motivated behavior. Instead, motivated behavior is determined by the sum of afferent inputs to the excitatory centers of the hypothalamus. Although afferent impulses are generally believed to have an additive effect on the arousal of motivation, additional inhibitory afferents to the hypothalamus are postulated; these excite the inhibitory centers and thus produce a negative effect on the activity of the excitatory centers.

Stellar thought that learned stimuli may affect the activity of the hypothalamic centers (a process which presumably requires integration of the afferent signals at higher levels of the brain). However, his discussion of sensory factors relies for the most part on direct collaterals from the primary sensory pathways and suggests a direct sensory control of hypothalamic functions reminiscent of reflex connections which do not depend on a perception of the sensory input. This may be an important aspect of Stellar's theory, for it implies that the regulation of motivated behavior is essentially independent of a conscious perception of the drive stimulation. Although not explicitly stated, this assumption implies the conclusion that the sensation of hunger, thirst, sexual arousal, or emotionality is a nonessential correlate of the activity of the hypothalamic centers, and that motivated behavior could, at least under special conditions, continue in the absence of such sensations.

The internal environment exerts an important influence on the excitatory and inhibitory centers of the hypothalamus, primarily via hormonal (chemical) changes which affect the neural tissue of the hypothalamus directly via the blood supply of the diencephalon or via the ventricular fluids. Stellar, like Morgan, believes that the hormonal changes affect motivation by changing the excitability of the hypothalamic centers. The experimental support for this suggestion derives primarily from the demonstration that hypothalamic lesions prevent the excitatory action of sex hormones and that osmotic stimulation of certain aspects of the hypothalamus elicits drinking in sated animals. Stellar summarizes the contributions of the internal environment as follows:

(*a*) A variety of kinds of changes in the internal environment can play a role in the regulation of motivation: variations in the concentration of certain chemicals, especially hormones, changes in osmotic pressure, and changes in blood temperature. (*b*) The best hypothesis at present is that these internal changes operate by contributing to the activity of the excitatory hypothalamic centers controlling motivation.

(*c*) An equally important, but less well-supported, hypothesis is that internal changes, normally produced by consummatory behavior, operate in the production of satiation by depressing excitatory centers or arousing inhibitory centers of the hypothalamus (Stellar, 1954, pp. 12-13).

There is very little quarrel with this aspect of Stellar's theory, although one might add the provision that chemical changes may exert an indirect effect on the hypothalamic mechanisms by changing the excitability of other neural centers which, in turn, affect the hypothalamus. An interesting question arises, however, with respect to the proposed mechanism for this influence. Although a change in the excitability or threshold of specific neural mechanisms appears quite plausible, it appears possible, and in some instances even likely, that chemical changes in the blood or tissue fluids might have a more direct stimulating action and might suffice to trigger neural activity in the absence of other inputs to the system. Perhaps the clearest example of such a direct action is the effect of local injections of hypertonic solutions into the hypothalamus. Such osmotic stimulation of the anterior hypothalamus has been shown to elicit drinking in *sated* animals presumably characterized by minimal excitatory input to the hypothalamic drinking center. Both types of mechanisms may, in fact, exist.

This theory postulates cortical and thalamic centers which may exert excitatory as well as inhibitory influences on the hypothalamic mechanisms. Stellar even suggests that the hypothalamus may be "under the direct control of a number of different cortical and thalamic centers" which are not further specified.

Stellar's treatment of the mechanisms by which the excitatory centers of the hypothalamus affect overt behavior is scanty. Admitting that very little is known about the effector mechanisms, he suggests that the hypothalamic centers exert "some kind of 'priming' effect" on the effector pathways controlled by other parts of the nervous system. This neglect of the effector system is common to all theories of motivation and represents an area in which research and theoretical inquiry is badly needed.

Other Multifactor Hypotheses

On the basis of very different experimental observations and theoretical considerations, European ethologists have independently arrived at similar multifactor theories. Much less explicit about specific physiological and anatomical mechanisms, the ethological theories of Lorenz (1950) and Tinbergen (1951) propose essentially that some center in the brain is "charged" by many neural and hormonal inputs until a threshold is reached. In the presence of appropriate environmental stimuli (and sometimes even in the absence of such releasers), the stored energy is then discharged or released through efferent pathways; the energy thus gives rise to consummatory activity which is directly proportional to the charge of the center. Satiation occurs automatically as the charge of the central mechanism is reduced and eventually falls below the threshold. These theories, aside from being unnecessarily vague about physiological and anatomical details, are contradicted by experiments which demonstrate that hunger (as defined by consummatory behavior or the organisms' willingness to work for food) can be completely sated by injections of food directly into the stomach (Kohn, 1951; Berkun et al., 1952; Miller and Kessen, 1952).

Deutsch (1960) has recently suggested, in the context of a more ambitious theory of behavior, that (1) specific neural "elements" or "primary links" in the central nervous system may be selectively sensitive to chemical changes in the fluids surrounding them; (2) excitation of these central elements produces an indirect excitation of specific portions of the motor system, causing the organism to "persist in a certain type of activity"; and (3) this motor activity produces a "receptor discharge" from an "analyzer" element which then transmits back to the central elements and increases their threshold to stimulation by the chemical state.

Deutsch suggests that each of the primary links may be innately connected to receptoral structures which can "turn off" the activity in the element. As examples, Deutsch cites receptors in

the mouth and throat which are believed to inhibit the central element sensitive to cellular dehydration; the taste receptors believed to suppress the central elements responsible for special appetites (as well as hunger in general); and receptors in the stomach which presumably inhibit the hunger element. Deutsch cites in support of this purely local theory of satiation some experiments which indicate that direct central stimulation can produce inhibitory effects on specific drives such as hunger. He unfortunately does not attempt to explain how this theory accounts for the research literature which indicates that satiation and motivation are not dependent on specific neural feedback.

Lindsley's Activation Theory

Lindsley's (1951, 1957, 1960) theoretical position differs in its basic orientation from the views of Morgan, Stellar, and Beach. All the theories discussed so far have been concerned primarily with the neural and/or chemical mechanisms which translate external or internal stimulus changes into neural activity in specific motivational centers or systems in the brain and thus give rise to the motivational states that presumably energize and direct behavior. Lindsley, on the other hand, appears to be concerned more immediately with the neural mechanisms which then translate these motivational states into appropriate behavior (i.e., the motivational effector mechanism). This is a very important problem, and Lindsley's suggestions deserve far more attention than they have received in the past.

Lindsley (1957) suggests that the process of motivation can be visualized as having two distinct aspects: (1) *a general arousal and alerting function* (to a need or want) which "may give rise to attention and/or increased activity of a generalized sort," and (2) *specific alerting functions*

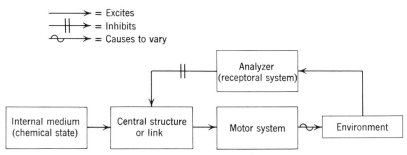

Fig. 11.2 The suggested mechanism of need. (From Deutsch, 1960.)

which result in "a focusing of this activity upon stimulus cues associated with a goal or the satisfaction of a need or want."

Both of these functions require some measure of control over afferent, efferent, and central pathways, and Lindsley proposed that the reticular formation of the brainstem and thalamus, perhaps in combination with certain limbic mechanisms, may provide the necessary integration of these functions. This important suggestion is based on experimental literature demonstrating the following:

1. The brainstem reticular formation appears to contain excitatory as well as inhibitory mechanisms which affect spinal motor neurons and the activity of the muscles they control (Magoun and Rhines, 1948; Lindsley et al., 1949b). Interference with the anatomically distinct inhibitory mechanism increases tonicity, hyperreflexia, and spasticity, whereas destruction of the facilitatory system supresses "involuntary" (spinal reflex) and voluntary (cortically induced) movements.

2. The reticular formation contains sensory afferents which appear to be responsible for the maintenance of arousal in cortical functions. Electrical stimulation of this arousal mechanism (Moruzzi and Magoun, 1949) produces desynchronization and activation of the cortical EEG and behavioral arousal; destruction of this aspect

of the reticular formation (Lindsley et al., 1949a, 1950) produces electrophysiological and behavioral "sleep" or somnolence, even though the sensory input to the cortex (by means of the classical sensory pathways) is not interrupted. Elimination of the primary sensory pathways, on the other hand, does not result in somnolence, suggesting that the effects of reticular lesions are independent of the resulting reduction of sensory stimulation per se. The arousal function of the reticular formation appears itself to be influenced by cortical functions (French et al., 1955), for electrical stimulation of various cortical sites produces noticeable changes in the electrical activity of the midbrain reticular formation.

3. All sensory modalities appear to be subject to a centrifugal regulation of afferent input (Granit and Kaada, 1952; Granit, 1955; Hagbarth and Kerr, 1954). This inhibitory, or in some instances facilitatory, influence appears to be, at least in part, a function of reticular mechanisms, both in the brainstem and thalamus. Afferent input may be affected at the first synaptic junction in the sensory pathways, by collaterals to and from the reticular formation, and by corticothalamic and corticoreticular feedback systems. The cortical influence on sensory afferents may be related to the rhythm of cortical activity (Bishop, 1933; Bartley and Bishop, 1933); stimulation of classical sensory pathways produces cortical

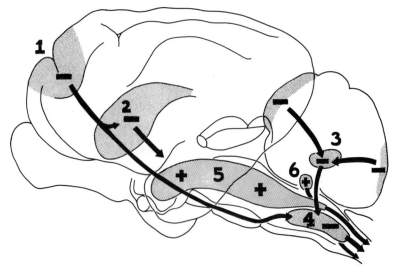

Fig. 11.3 Inhibitory (minus) and facilitatory (plus) pathways influencing spinal motor activity. Inhibitory or suppressor pathways: 1, corticobulboreticular; 2, caudatospinal; 3, cerebellobulboreticular; 4, reticulospinal. Facilitatory pathways: 5, reticulospinal; 6, vestibulospinal. (From Lindsley et al., 1949b.)

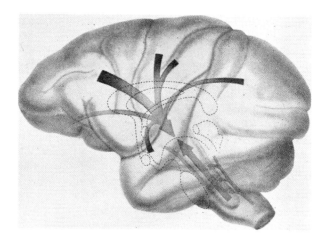

Fig. 11.4   Schema projected on the monkey brain showing the corticoreticular influence on the reticular formation and the ARAS. Cortical stimulation produces potential changes in the reticular formation; thus cortical events can presumably influence the cortex via the ARAS as well as lower centers. (From French et al., 1955.)

evoked potentials only if the arrival of the sensory input at the cortex is synchronized with the spontaneous electrical activity of the brain.

On the basis of these and related findings, Lindsley proposed the following hypothesis.

1. The general arousal and alerting aspect of motivation may be subserved by the ascending reticular formation of the midbrain. The rostral projections of this system may primarily take an extrathalamic route to the cortex, although the diffuse thalamic projections may also participate in this function.

2. The specific alerting aspects of motivation may be related to the activity of the diffuse thalamocortical projection system or some combination of it and the thalamocortical (semispecific) projections to the secondary sensory areas of the cortex.

3. The limbic system (Lindsley is rather careful in assigning specific functions to this portion of the brain) presumably contains mechanisms concerned with homeostatic as well as associative and integrative functions; if we may extrapolate from Lindsley's writings, these mechanisms may influence both cortical and reticular functions and modify general and specific arousal properties of the sensory stimuli.

Lindsley's theory, as it stands today, provides the mechanism by which other as yet unspecified central processes can determine the arousal or drive value of sensory stimuli from both external and internal receptor systems. The theory is particularly appealing because it provides clearly distinct anatomical and physiological substrates for the energizing and the cue properties of drive stimulation. However, it requires extensive elaboration and integration with theoretical proposals more directly concerned with the development of specific drives.

A CONTEMPORARY TWO-FACTOR THEORY OF MOTIVATION

Following this brief review of the psychophysiological theories of motivation which have influenced the field during the past 25 years, an integration of recent experimental findings into a rather speculative theoretical proposal will be attempted; I shall try to provide a more complete picture of the complex pattern of peripheral and central mechanisms which contribute to the regulation of motivational processes. This hypothesis borrows freely from the theories of Morgan, Stellar, and Lindsley but departs from them at several important points in accordance with recent empirical findings. In order to present a clear picture of the theoretical issues, only cursory reference will be made to supporting data. A detailed review of the relevant literature can be found in the preceding chapters.

Perhaps the most radical departure from earlier theories is a distinction between homeostatic and nonhomeostatic drive mechanisms. Although the central regulation of all motivational processes appears to be very similar, there are many physiological and psychological differences between homeostatic drives (such as hunger, thirst, sleep, and elimination) which are elicited and reduced directly by changes in the *internal* environment and nonhomeostatic drives (such as sexual or emotional arousal, and perhaps, activity itself) which appear to be elicited and reduced by changes in the *external* environment of the organism. The earlier theories of Morgan and Stellar are based primarily on evidence relevant to homeostatic drive mechanisms (i.e., hunger and thirst) and have encountered serious difficulties when applied to such problems as sexual or emotional arousal. Lindsley's approach, on the other hand, applies quite well to emotional and sexual arousal but cannot by itself handle the homeostatic regulation characteristic of such primary drives as hunger and thirst.

Before discussing the two-factor theory of motivation, it may be useful to enumerate some of the major differences between homeostatic and nonhomeostatic drives. Perhaps the most obvious of these is that homeostatic drives develop apparently automatically under all environmental conditions that permit survival. Although extreme changes in the external milieu (such as heat, cold) have a *modulating* effect on this development, these influences are normally minor and do not affect the basic process. Nonhomeostatic drives, on the other hand, are typically elicited by specific changes in the external environment, although the threshold of excitation depends to a significant degree on hormonal and neural events in the internal milieu. These internal changes normally prime the organism to respond preferentially to particular classes of external stimuli; they do not under normal circumstances elicit the motivational state.

A related difference has significant implications for a psychophysiological theory of motivation: the elicitation of homeostatic drives appears to be independent of learning, whereas prior experience and memory contribute importantly to the arousal of nonhomeostatic drives. Such learned associations as "time of day" or "odor of food" modulate basic homeostatic drive processes. Some innate responses to emotional or sexual stimuli must exist to provide a basis for the conditioning which seems so essential to the elicitation of nonhomeostatic drive states. However, homeostatic drives are *essentially* independent of such associations, and nonhomeostatic drives, at least in the mature organism, are regulated by a stimulus input whose effectiveness is almost totally determined by learning.

The basic difference between these two classes of motivational variables becomes even clearer when we consider the problem of drive reduction or satiation. Homeostatic drives are elicited by internal stimuli which arise from a physiological need state (i.e., the development of an imbalance of essential homeostatic processes). Drive reduc-

tion, in the final analysis, can occur only when the behavior of the organism has resulted in a physiological or biochemical process which re-establishes the homeostatic balance. Some learned or unlearned signals may *temporarily* terminate the drive-instigated behavior. Such intermediary satiety mechanisms may be essential to bridge the time lag between remedial action and its final physiological effect. However, re-establishment of the homeostatic balance and a consequent cessation of the internal stimulation which originally elicited the drive state appear absolutely essential to satiation or drive reduction.

Although the same requirements (i.e., cessation of drive stimulation) apply to the nonhomeostatic drives, the basic processes are quite different. Since nonhomeostatic drives are elicited by specific external stimuli, drive reduction becomes a relatively simple and direct problem of removing the source of stimulation. No complex intermediary mechanisms are required, for the cessation of the external stimulation produces immediate and direct effects on the central drive state. This simple and direct relation between external stimuli and arousal of nonhomeostatic drive states may be complicated by the apparently extremely rapid conditioning of emotional responses to stimuli that occur in the presence of events which innately, or on the basis of previous learning, arouse nonhomeostatic drives. This conditioning may account for the apparent persistence of nonhomeostatic drives after the cessation of stimuli that initially aroused them, but it does not materially alter the simple and direct relation between external events and drive induction or reduction.

Many other differences between homeostatic and nonhomeostatic drive mechanisms could be listed; it is surprising that the basic central regulatory mechanisms may, in fact, be as similar as they appear on the basis of presently available information. The two classes of motivational events will be treated separately in the following discussion to stimulate opposition and research, although it may be possible to reduce the two-factor theory, at least with respect to the important central components of the system, to a simpler single-factor approach.

Homeostatic Drives

Homeostatic drives are believed to arise as a direct consequence of internal stimulation that results when an essential physiological process deviates from some optimal level of functioning.

Homeostatic processes maintain vital physiological or biochemical functions (such as the organism's energy or fluid balance) within rather narrow limits. If this balance is disturbed by increased output or insufficient input, neural and/or chemical changes occur; these stimulate specific central regulatory mechanisms and exert a facilitatory effect on nonspecific reticular mechanisms. Afferent input from exteroceptors may facilitate the central regulatory functions but cannot by itself produce sufficient stimulation to elicit a homeostatic drive in the absence of a related physiological "need." The primary indicators of homeostatic functions may be chemical events such as changes in blood sugar, the concentration of other chemicals in the extracellular fluids, or osmotic pressure gradients. Presently known indicators may themselves be the by-product of more primary metabolic processes and may therefore correlate imperfectly or only belatedly, with basic physiological imbalances.

The chemical events affect the central regulatory mechanism and related aspects of the nonspecific reticular system (1) *directly*, by a stimulating or facilitating action on specific subcortical or cortical neurons—such a direct effect is suggested by the central effects of osmotic stimulation or goldthioglucose injections; (2) *indirectly*, via a stimulating or inhibiting effect on peripheral interoceptors which, in turn, control the activity of the central regulatory mechanisms; or (3) *directly or indirectly*, by stimulating other central neural functions which contribute to the excitation or inhibition of the specific regulatory mechanism.

Although homeostatic drives are related specifically and exclusively to a single physiological need (i.e., imbalance), a number of physiological and biochemical processes may contribute to, or be affected by, a particular homeostatic mechanism. It is probable, therefore, that several messenger systems may contribute relevant information to the central regulatory mechanisms, and that direct as well as indirect pathways are used by different messengers. If we may generalize from the overdetermination of other vital physiological functions, it appears likely that no individual messenger system is essential to the regulation of motivational processes.

The activity of the central mechanisms does not appear to be a simple additive function of all facilitating and inhibiting inputs (a position which predicts quantitative changes following the elimination or stimulation of a single input). Instead,

the various chemical and neural messenger systems may be carriers of essentially the same information, so that one or more of them can be eliminated without materially affecting the central regulation. Artificial stimulation of a single messenger system, as in central osmotic stimulation, may nevertheless produce marked effects on the central regulatory mechanism, because a single input may suffice to control the activity of the central regulator.

The specific central regulatory mechanisms are composed of complex, interacting systems of nuclei and pathways which are diffusely represented in rhinencephalic (cortical) and related subcortical structures (primarily the amygdala, septal area, and hypothalamus). We can no longer agree with the attractively simple view of Stellar (1954) that the central regulation of motivation is performed exclusively by pairs of excitatory and inhibitory centers or nuclei in the hypothalamus. It appears impossible, on purely anatomical grounds, that the hypothalamic nuclei possess sufficiently extensive afferent and efferent connections to (1) collect and integrate essential information from a variety of messenger systems as well as related central regulatory functions; (2) directly or indirectly mediate the subjective sensations which, at least in man, provide a possibly essential component of drive stimulation; and (3) selectively and specifically facilitate or initiate complex motor responses which translate the activity of the regulatory mechanism into overt behavior. This argument is all the more compelling because the destruction of any of the major neural pathways to and from the hypothalamus (such as the fornix, medial forebrain bundle, and mammillothalamic tract) does not interfere significantly with any of the homeostatic drive mechanisms.

A more diffuse representation of the central regulatory functions is also suggested by the recent experimental finding that such homeostatic drives as hunger or thirst (as well as emotional and sexual behavior) appear to be significantly affected by lesions and/or stimulation of a variety of rhinencephalic and related subcortical regions. Since lesions and stimulation of specific hypothalamic areas typically produce more drastic effects, it can still be argued that the extrahypothalamic mechanisms merely contribute information to the hypothalamic regulatory centers; thus, the effects of rhinencephalic lesions or stimulation may be the result of adding or subtracting excitatory or inhibitory influences. I would like to propose the alternative hypothesis that the hypothalamus is merely part of a complex system of interacting nuclei and pathways and that the apparently unique effects of hypothalamic damage or stimulation may be a "geographic" artifact. Such results would be expected if essential components of the afferent or efferent connections of the central regulatory mechanism originated, relayed, or terminated in the hypothalamic centers, or even if the hypothalamus, because of its anatomical structure, represented the most constricted, i.e., densely populated, portion of the complex circuit.

According to this hypothesis, every drive state is diffusely represented in all portions of this complex circuit. The interrelation between individual components of this system and the nature of their specific contribution is not yet understood. It is suggested, however, that information, rather than being passed on to a single center, may be processed in a closed circuit to which all the individual components contribute. Although we do not yet have sufficient experimental information to suggest a specific assignment of function, it is proposed that most, if not all, neural afferents to the system as well as to its major efferent connections, occur via cortical or reticular connections. The hypothalamic centers may serve as specialized sensory receptor organs which selectively respond to changes in the chemical environment.

The overall level of activity or the efferent output in this circuit, rather than the activity of any individual component, is related to the intensity of motivation. Even the output from the central regulatory mechanism may not perfectly correlate with consummatory behavior or other behavioral indices of motivation because several drive states may interact and compete at any point in time.

The interaction of drive states occurs peripherally as well as centrally and requires a central integrative mechanism which also controls the "final common path" (i.e., determines which one of a number of concurrently active drive states can, at any point in time, command the organism's motor facilities). Since these functional requirements demand extensive anatomical cross-connections among the various central regulatory mechanisms for specific drives, it is suggested that the central integrator, although functionally distinct, may be part of the same rhinencephalic-subcortical circuit which contains the individual regulatory mechanisms.

Finally, I propose a rather specific functional role for some aspects of the nonspecific midbrain and thalamic reticular formation. This system may respond to a variety of neural inputs and perhaps chemical changes by modulating the general level of reactivity or arousal of central regulatory mechanisms—thereby providing what psychologists have called the "generalized" or "energizing" aspect of motivation. In accordance with Lindsley's suggestions, this nonspecific function may be related to reticular components of the midbrain which are stimulated or facilitated by the chemical or neural messengers released whenever a homeostatic imbalance develops, neural afferents from related extereoceptors or interoceptors, and afferents from the central regulatory mechanisms and the central integrator itself.

Other more rostral components of the reticular formation are believed to respond to neural afferents from the rhinencephalic-subcortical circuit by preferentially processing sensory information relevant to the dominant drive states and selectively facilitating gross effector mechanisms such as muscles and glands.

Experimental evidence has accumulated rapidly in the past fifteen years which shows rather unequivocally that some aspects of the reticular formation modulate EEG as well as behavior arousal, transmission in sensory systems, and the tonic activity level in striated and smooth muscles. The proposed relation between specific motivational processes and reticular functions is speculative at present.

Drive reduction or satiety has posed a major problem to all psychophysiological theories of motivation, largely because consummatory behavior often ceases before the ingested substances could possibly have affected the homeostatic balance that presumably elicited the drive state. We can attempt to circumvent this problem by postulating neural and/or chemical feedback from the consummatory response or from some upper portion of the gastrointestinal tract; however, feedback fails to explain how the organism's intake could be so closely regulated as to meet precisely its momentary needs. It seems impossible to escape the conclusion that a dual satiety mechanism must be present which consists of (1) a humoral or neural messenger system triggered either by the consummatory response itself or by the initial effects of the ingested substances on some rostral portion of the gastrointestinal tract; and (2) neural and/or chemical feedback from the homeostatic mechanism itself.

The initial satiety messenger system is believed to exercise a graduated but relatively rapid inhibitory effect directly on the central regulatory mechanisms; it acts as soon as consummatory responses bring the organism (i.e., some receptor system in the mouth, throat, stomach, or upper intestine) into direct contact with substances that are potentially capable of restoring the organism's homeostatic balance. This messenger can transmit information relevant to the presence and quantity (i.e., duration of contact) of particular substances and provide a short-term regulation of consummatory activity. However, since this messenger system operates independently of the homeostatic processes that elicit the drive state and determine its strength, it cannot regulate intake in accordance with the organism's needs. The effect of such a system is short-lived.

Once the ingested substances have been assimilated and metabolized sufficiently to affect the original physiological imbalance directly, the drive state is reduced (not merely inhibited as in the case of the temporary satiety messengers) by a gradual reversal of the chemical changes that initially excited the central regulatory mechanism. If the satiety messengers inhibited the central regulatory mechanisms (and consummatory activity) before sufficient food or water was ingested to restore the organism's energy or fluid balance, consummatory activity would be resumed because the temporary inhibition of the initial satiety messengers dissipates rapidly, and the central regulatory mechanisms would continue to receive excitatory inputs from the homeostatic imbalance.

Satiety or drive reduction thus may be a biphasic process, consisting of (1) an initial inhibitory action on the central regulatory mechanisms which is short-lived and related only to the presence and absolute magnitude of substances potentially capable of restoring the homeostatic balance, and (2) a delayed reduction of excitatory inputs to the central regulatory mechanisms from the physiological processes that initially aroused the drive state. The effects of the first phase dissipate rapidly (in a matter of minutes or, at most, hours), allowing the regulatory influence of the second phase to control long-term behavior.

Nonhomeostatic Drives

Nonhomeostatic drives (such as sexual or emotional arousal) are elicited by sensory afferents that arise as the direct consequence of changes in the external environment. All stimuli that evoke a distinct sensation are potentially capable of stimulating nonhomeostatic drive mechanisms. Anatomical connections exist so that some en-

vironmental stimuli *reflexly* facilitate or stimulate specific central regulatory mechanisms concerned with nonhomeostatic drive states. At least some of these innate connections appear to originate cortically or at relatively high levels of perceptual integration, for the innate releaser properties of sensory inputs often depend on the perception of complex stimulus compounds (i.e., monkeys respond to the presentation of snakes with a specific emotional reaction). These innate connections do not play a major role in the mature organism, but they are essential as a basis for establishing *conditioned* connections which are responsible for the motivational effects of most stimulus events.

On the basis of innate or conditioned anatomical connections, sensory afferents are capable of exerting a *direct* facilitatory or stimulating effect on specific regulatory mechanisms which are diffusely represented in the same rhinencephalic-subcortical circuit previously described for homeostatic drive states. The central regulatory mechanisms for nonhomeostatic drives interact with each other as well as with the central regulatory mechanisms for *homeostatic* drive states via the central integrator described previously. The motivational basis of behavior must be regarded, at any point in time, as the end result of a complex interaction of often opposing forces. It is the function of the integrator mechanisms to provide the anatomical connections essential for this interaction and to act as a selective switch which permits the selection of behavioral responses in accordance with the momentarily dominant drive state.

Afferent input to the central regulatory mechanisms for nonhomeostatic drives does not automatically elicit a drive state. The effectiveness of sensory stimuli is determined, at least in part, by chemical factors (such as the level of circulating sex hormones or the local concentration of such substances as catecholamines). These chemical factors control the excitability or threshold of the central regulatory mechanisms and produce a selective facilitation or inhibition of related sensory and motor pathways through a tonic effect on specific portions of the midbrain reticular formation and/or nonspecific thalamic projection nuclei.

These hormonal factors cannot under normal circumstances *elicit* a drive state but merely facilitate specific central mechanisms and related sensory and motor functions. However, this facilitation can be so extreme under some conditions that previously ineffective or neutral inputs suffice to elicit motivational effects. The level of these chemical catalysts is determined by specific homeostatic processes such as those determining the estrous cycle; direct sensory input from exteroceptors; and activity of related central motivational mechanisms.

Nonhomeostatic drives are not based on specific physiological needs, and no satiety mechanism per se exists. The drive states are elicited directly by specific environmental stimuli and persist until the behavioral responses have terminated the stimulation or removed the organism from the environment. If neither of these alternatives is available, other drive mechanisms are activated or strengthened, either as a direct consequence of the persisting behavioral reaction to the nonhomeostatic drive stimulation or because homeostatic needs develop which elicit competing drives. Eventually, these incompatible drive states become sufficiently strong to determine the direction of behavior and thus terminate the organism's reaction to the original drive state. In addition, mechanisms analogous to the process of habituation tend to reduce the effectiveness of prolonged sensory stimulation on both specific and nonspecific (reticular) mechanisms. This habituation effect, though not specific to drive stimulation, contributes to the eventual reduction of nonhomeostatic drives.

MAJOR PROBLEMS

A number of important problems remain to be solved before a clear picture of the physiological basis of motivation can emerge. In the case of homeostatic drives we know that motivation correlates all but perfectly with specific homeostatic processes which control such essential physiological functions as the organism's energy and fluid balance. We also know that certain parts of the brain appear to be intimately and directly related to motivational processes of a homeostatic (and nonhomeostatic) nature. But how is the close correlation between physiological need and psychological drive state accomplished?

The past 50 years of intensive experimental investigation have suggested several chemical messenger systems which may relay essential information to the brain. However, we cannot yet be sure that these hormonal correlates are in fact *causally* related to motivational events or *uniquely* responsible for the transmission of essential information to the brain. It appears likely that each motivational process may be affected by several messengers,

and it is essential to determine whether the individual components of this complex messenger system carry unique information about different physiological processes or whether a partial or complete duplication of function may exist, as proposed in the present theory. The latter alternative is suggested by the consistent experimental finding that regulation does not appear to be completely, or even severely, affected by a drastic interference with one of the presently known messengers. These messengers may, of course, be merely nonessential by-products of more basic processes which are not affected by our experimental manipulations. Further work is badly needed in this area before we can decide between the alternatives.

Also in need of study are the central regulatory mechanisms that must respond to the messengers by somehow generating motivational forces which eventually become strong enough to direct the organism's behavior in such a way as to insure a re-establishment of the homeostatic balance. Recent findings indicate that most if not all of the limbic system may be directly related to the regulation of motivational functions. It would seem likely that different anatomical structures within this complex system exercise specific and unique functions, and one of the major problems in the area of motivation is to discover the specific functional role of the individual components. This is particularly important if, as we have suggested, the limbic circuit acts as a unit to determine the level of specific homeostatic and nonhomeostatic drive states. However, the same answers are needed if we assume that the cortical components of this circuit merely contribute to the excitation or inhibition of hypothalamic centers. Such information is essential if we are ever to decide between these alternatives.

The nature and locus of interaction between individual drive states represent another closely related problem. Most motivational mechanisms are active at any point in time. Behavior, on the other hand, can be directed only toward the satisfaction or reduction of one of the opposing motivational states. Complex integrative mechanisms are required to permit a direct interaction between the individual drive states and a selection of the momentarily dominant motivational force. Conceptually, this integrator function is obviously of great significance to any theory of motivation, yet we have no directly relevant experimental evidence to guide our thinking about this important problem.

Finally, there remains the long-neglected question: *How* is the activity of this integrator (or of the individual regulatory mechanisms) translated into overt behavior? Is this accomplished (1) by a direct releasing of efferent motor pathways, as the ethologists seem to suggest when they propose that specific motor acts are emitted by the organism under the appropriate motivational conditions, or (2) by an unconditioned or conditioned response to specific sensations, as was first suggested by the local theorists of ancient Greece? Alternatively, are we perhaps responding to sensory signals that do not reach conscious awareness? This problem will have to be solved before we can understand the complex relationship between motivation and overt behavior.

DISCUSSION

The experimental evidence that supports the proposed theoretical model has been discussed in detail in the preceding chapters. It may be useful, however, to recall the nature of the evidence that suggested the principal deviations from earlier theories and to discuss some of the changes in the general conceptual framework.

The distinction between homeostatic and nonhomeostatic drives is proposed on logical and pragmatic grounds rather than on compelling experimental proof. The theoretical models of Morgan, Stellar, and Lindsley demonstrate how difficult it is to conceptualize a common physiological basis of motivation in a way that accounts for (1) the precise regulation of continually variable physiological processes which interact to give rise to what we have called a homeostatic drive; and (2) the instantaneous arousal of motivational responses by environmental stimulus changes whose motivational significance is largely learned and hence peculiar to the individual. It is possible that all motivational processes can be regulated by common central, if not peripheral, mechanisms. However, to describe such mechanisms on the basis of information now available results in such complex and unwieldy concepts that it seems useful to study separately what may be two sides of the same coin.

We need not dwell on the well-documented relationship between such basic homeostatic mechanisms as the organism's energy or fluid balance and motivational processes, except to emphasize the diversity and complexity of the physiological events that contribute to a single homeostatic function. We have only recently come to appreciate the implications of this complexity in terms of the diversity of signals that must affect the

regulation of a drive state; we have not yet drawn the necessary conclusions about the probable nature of the related central regulatory functions. Some of the earlier multifactor theories of motivation suggested that different neural and/or chemical messengers might affect a particular central regulatory mechanism but failed to propose a sufficiently complex central representation to permit an analysis and integration of this heterogenous input. It seems unlikely, on purely anatomical grounds, that a single nucleus or center could have the extensive afferent and efferent connections to carry out the multitude of functions that we must assign to such a central regulatory mechanism. Moreover, we are beginning to accumulate experimental evidence suggesting that each drive state may be diffusely represented in many different areas of the brain.

This diffuse representation has been demonstrated most clearly perhaps for nonhomeostatic drive states related to emotional behavior; we have a large and well-documented body of evidence indicating that neocortical (primarily frontal), allocortical, and juxtallocortical (hippocampal, septal, and cingulate) mechanisms collaborate with subcortical nuclei of the amygdala, septal area, and hypothalamus in the control of emotional arousal (see Brady, 1960, for a recent review of the literature).

With sexual motivation and such homeostatic drives as hunger and thirst, the diffuse nature of the central regulatory mechanisms is only gradually becoming evident. At first glance, these drive states seem to be controlled by discrete hypothalamic centers. The literature suggests that these mechanisms continue to function even when all other portions of the proposed circuit for central regulatory functions are destroyed, and that a severe impairment of regulatory processes invariably results when the hypothalamic centers are damaged in otherwise intact animals.

These observations form the basis for Stellar's hypothalamic theory of motivation which holds that motivation is a direct function of the activity of specific hypothalamic centers. This approach has been very fruitful, but the evidence for an exclusively hypothalamic control of motivational processes is not compelling; recent findings suggest a more active participation of extrahypothalamic mechanisms. The present model has attempted to broaden the conceptual basis of motivational functions, and it may be appropriate to attempt briefly a justification of this departure from earlier views.

First, the evidence for motivational processes

in the decerebrate animal is not as clear as is generally assumed. Severe sensory-motor deficits permit only rudimentary reflex responses to the environment, and an assessment of the motivational makeup of such a preparation is difficult. We have been overly impressed by the evidence for some remnant of motivational control in these animals and have tended to overlook obvious deficits.

Second, the severe deficits following discrete hypothalamic damage do not necessarily imply that essential centers must be located in this portion of the brain. It is equally reasonable to assume that the hypothalamus may be part of a larger system of regulatory mechanisms and contain greater concentrations of neurons subserving a particular regulatory function than other portions of the system, so that lesions or stimulation can affect a greater percentage of the total population of relevant neural elements. Such a hypothesis is reasonable in view of the fact that the hypothalamus, because of its peculiar anatomical configuration, seems to act as a funnel for most afferent and efferent impulses to and from the cortex.

The funnel analogy provides another potential explanation of the hypothalamic lesion or stimulation effects. At least some of the behavioral deficits may be caused by an interruption of fibers which merely pass *through* the hypothalamus and carry essential afferent or efferent information to and from higher portions of the brain. Some generally unsuccessful attempts have been made to test this hypothesis by damaging or stimulating areas above or below the hypothalamic centers. The largely negative results of these studies are no more embarrassing to the proposed model than to the notion of hypothalamic centers which, after all, must receive information and exert their effects on behavior via neural pathways.

The potential importance of extrahypothalamic mechanisms has been emphasized in the past ten years by experimental observations indicating that the effects of even large hypothalamic lesions are not irreversible. Teitelbaum and Stellar (1954) first observed that the aphagia and adipsia caused by bilateral hypothalamic damage gradually disappear if the animals are maintained by force-feeding until the recovery is complete. Teitelbaum and Epstein (Teitelbaum, 1961; Teitelbaum and Epstein, 1962) have investigated this recovery phenomenon in detail and concluded that the gross impairment of feeding and drinking behavior which results from lateral hypothalamic damage is always reversible, regardless of the size

and location of the lesion. A similar recovery of function has been described by Masserman (1938) for the regulation of emotional reactivity which is temporarily disturbed by certain hypothalamic lesions.

It seems unlikely that the hypothalamic tissue surrounding the lesion could be responsible for this apparent recovery of function, in view of the fact that even the largest lesions do not produce irreversible effects. The size and location of the lesion do not seem to correlate with the duration of the impairment. Instead, it seems that extrahypothalamic mechanisms that normally collaborate with the hypothalamic nuclei to regulate motivational processes can carry out these functions even when the hypothalamic contribution is totally absent. It may be interesting, in this connection, to mention Teitelbaum's (1961) observation that animals which have recovered from the effects of hypothalamic damage continue to be extremely sensitive to the taste of solid foods and liquids and cannot effect a satisfactory regulation of intake when the access to food and water is limited. These residual deficits may reflect the only unique contribution of the hypothalamic mechanisms.

Specific extrahypothalamic mechanisms have recently been shown to contribute to the regulation of feeding and drinking behavior. Disturbances in food intake have repeatedly been observed following damage to the temporal lobe or, more specifically, to the amygdaloid complex (Green et al., 1957; Wood, 1958; Morgane and Kosman, 1959). Detailed investigations of this phenomenon have obtained evidence of both inhibitory and excitatory mechanisms in specific portions of the amygdala and have suggested that these nuclei may also contribute to the regulation of water intake (Grossman and Grossman, 1963; Grossman, 1964a).

Other experiments have shown that drinking behavior (and presumably thirst) can be elicited by chemical stimulation of nearly all portions of the limbic system (Fisher and Coury, 1962; Grossman, 1964b). Additional extrahypothalamic mechanisms have been described by Gilbert (1956; 1957), who found that lesions or stimulation in the area of the subcommissural organ markedly affected water intake.

A similar distribution of the feeding system is suggested by reports of drastic changes in food intake following lesions or stimulation of portions of the frontal and frontotemporal cortex (Ruch and Shenkin, 1943; Schaltenbrandt and Cobb, 1931), thalamus (Ruch et al., 1941), hippocampus

(Ehrlich, 1963; Fuller et al., 1957), the preoptic area (Andersson and Larsson, 1961), and the midbrain reticular formation (Collins, 1954). Morgane (1961a, b, c) has recently reported aphagia and adipsia following lesions lateral and dorsal to the hypothalamic feeding and drinking centers. The regulation of food and water intake appeared most severely affected by damage to the tip of the globus pallidus.

The central representation of sexual motivation has not received much experimental interest in recent years, and we do not have as much evidence for extrahypothalamic mechanisms as we do for hunger or thirst. It is clear, however, that sexual receptivity is affected by lesions or stimulation of many portions of the brain and that the concept of a discrete hypothalamic regulatory center may be as inadequate here as it is for the other drive states.

Particularly, the male of the species shows marked hypersexuality following damage to the temporal lobes (Klüver and Bucy, 1939) or more restricted lesions in the amygdaloid complex (Schreiner and Kling, 1953; 1954) or hippocampus (Kim, 1960). Gastaut (1952) has described the estrous behavior in cats following a variety of rhinencephalic lesions, and MacLean and his associates (MacLean, 1955; MacLean and Ploog, 1962; MacLean et al., 1963) have shown that specific sexual responses such as penile erection or ejaculation can be elicited by electrical stimulation of the hippocampus and its projections into the septum and anterior and midline thalamic nuclei; the mammillary bodies, mammillary tract, anterior thalamus, and cingulate gyrus; and the medial dorsal nucleus of the thalamus and the inferior thalamic peduncle.

Electrophysiological studies generally confirm the impression that sexual arousal may be widely and diffusely represented throughout the limbic system and thalamus. Fauré and his associates (Fauré, 1956; Fauré and Gruner, 1956), for instance, have reported that the intramuscular injection of gonadotrophins and adrenal steroids produces marked changes in the electrical activity of many rhinencephalic areas. Green (1954) observed that castration as well as sexual arousal during "love play" altered the electrical activity of the hippocampus and anterior hypothalamus. He suggested, on the basis of anatomical considerations, that the modification of hypothalamic activity might be secondary to hippocampal influences. Kawakami and Sawyer (see Sawyer, 1960) have recently recorded a specific EEG patterns (an initially "sleep-like" record followed by

"an unusually aroused pattern") from a variety of rhinencephalic placements during vaginal stimulation.

It is clear that many extrahypothalamic mechanisms contribute to the regulation of probably all drive states. What remains to be established is the nature of the individual contributions and the locus and *modus operandi* of the integrator of the diverse influences. At least two distinct levels of integration appear to be necessary: the many different signals that affect the overall regulation of a specific drive state must be analyzed, interpreted, and somehow integrated into a single motivational force; and the many temporally coexistent drive states must similarly be analyzed to permit the elaboration of coherent and goal-directed behavior.

I have suggested that the integration of the diverse signals that contribute to the regulation of a single drive state may be a continuing process within the complex neural circuits which subserve the central regulating functions; I also proposed that extensive interconnections between the individual neural networks may account for the interaction between drive states. All integrative functions are assigned to the same anatomical mechanisms as the basic regulatory processes, because no anatomically distinct integrative mechanism has yet been demonstrated and because the central regulatory mechanisms for individual drive states appear to be so extensively intertwined that they are almost coexistent in many portions of the brain.

The extensive anatomical overlap of motivational functions has been demonstrated in many different experimental situations. In view of the importance of this interrelationship to the proposed model, a few examples may be useful. Perhaps the clearest example is the ventromedial nucleus of the hypothalamus, which has been accused of being a center for feeding behavior (i.e., satiety) (Hetherington, 1944); sexual motivation (Sawyer, 1960), and emotional arousal (Wheatley, 1944). The story is not very different when we look at components of the limbic system. The amygdala, for instance, has been shown to contribute to the regulation of feeding and drinking behavior (Grossman and Grossman, 1963; Grossman, 1964); sexual motivation (Schreiner and Kling, 1953; 1954); emotional arousal; and related autonomic reactions (Bard and Mountcastle, 1948).

The inadequacy of the concept of a motivational center has been demonstrated in recent experiments. Robinson (1964) observed behavioral resposes of a motivational nature (feeding, drinking, penile erection, aggression) to electrical stimulation of many different and noncontiguous areas of the brain (including the amygdala, cingulate gyrus, septal area, hypothalamus, and tegmentum). Robinson noted that very different responses could be obtained from closely adjacent stimulation sites and even from the same electrode placement. Applying a stochastic analysis to behavioral data from 5885 different stimulation points, Robinson concluded that the substrate for alimentary reactions did not appear to be "anatomically circumscribed" and that the essential lack of purity of the response to electrical stimulation argued against the center concept.

Little can be said about the postulated non-specific regulatory functions at this point. The principal experimental support for this mechanism unfortunately consists largely of electrophysiological data which may not be simply and directly related to such concepts as Brown's (1961) "general activator" function or Hull's (1943) "non-directive drive." The past decade has shown that wishful thinking cannot bridge the gap between electrophysiological arousal and the nonspecific energizing aspect of motivation as defined behaviorally. Some attempts are currently being made to investigate this matter experimentally (Grossman et al., 1965), but additional information is needed before we can do more than reason by analogy to electrophysiological events.

Our model reflects this uncertainty in suggesting primarily second-order functions. We know that all sensory afferents to the brain have collaterals to the reticular formation of the brainstem and thalamus, and that variations in a number of chemical constituents of the blood affect its activity. Efferent influences from the reticular formation modulate the electrical activity of both subcortical and cortical neurons and selectively inhibit or facilitate conduction in specific sensory or motor pathways (see Jasper et al., 1958, for a review of the reticular formation). An attempt has been made to incorporate these functions, as they apply specifically to motivational processes, without trying to achieve a perfect match between the suggested physiological mechanisms and psychological concepts. In view of the present lack of behavioral data, this approach appears to be justified.

Finally, a few words may be in order about the suggested satiety mechanisms. For nonhomeostatic drives satiety refers simply to the reduction or removal of the external stimulation that evoked the drive. For homeostatic drives a conceptual problem arises because consummatory behavior typically stops before the ingested substances could possibly affect the physiological processes thought to be responsible for the elicitation of the drive. Logically, this observation requires the postulation of an independent satiety mechanism which regulates consummatory behavior by metering intake, but how could such a mechanism adjust behavior in accordance with the organism's needs? A closer look at the experimental literature suggests that consummatory activity typically stops before the organism's requirements are met and that the remaining deficit is corrected only after a delay sufficient to permit feedback from basic physiological processes. This process suggests the operation of more than one satiety mechanism, and the simplest of available alternatives has been suggested.

Historically, all drive states were believed to be simply and directly related to peripheral sensory stimulation. We know now that this is not true, but we may have overreacted to the negative evidence. It appears likely that many of the sensory mechanisms that have been shown to be *nonessential* to the regulation of the organism's overall food or water balance (taste, dryness of the mouth and throat, muscular contractions, distension, or other feedback from the stomach, etc.) may contribute important signals for the initiation or cessation of intake and be responsible for short-term regulation (i.e., "meal size" rather than total daily intake). A few examples of the many observations that support such an interpretation may suffice. Esophagostomized animals consume more water than necessary to restore their fluid balance, but they do not drink constantly, they adjust their intake to be *proportional* to their fluid deficit, and they reduce sham drinking in response to mechanical distension of the stomach (Bellows, 1939; Adolph, 1939; Towbin, 1949). Water intake in intact animals is reduced following the local application of anesthetics to the mouth and throat (Adolph et al., 1954). Similar observations have been reported in the literature on food intake.

BIBLIOGRAPHY

Adolph, E. F. Measurements of water drinking in dogs. *Amer. J. Physiol.*, 1939, **125**, 75–86.

Adolph, E. F., Barker, J. P., & Hoy, P. A. Multiple factors in thirst. *Amer. J. Physiol.*, 1954, **178**, 538–562.

Andersson, B., & Larsson, S. The influence of local temperature changes in the preoptic area and rostral hypothalamus on regulation of food and water intake. *Acta physiol. scand.,* 1961, **52,** 75–89.

Bard, P., & Mountcastle, V. B. Some forebrain mechanisms involved in expression of rage with specific reference to suppression of angry behavior. *Res. Publ., Ass. Res. nerv. ment. Dis.,* 1948, **27,** 362–404.

Bartley, S. H., & Bishop, G. H. The cortical response to stimulation of the optic nerve in the rabbit. *Amer. J. Physiol.,* 1933, **103,** 159–72.

Beach, F. A. Analysis of factors involved in the arousal, maintenance, and manifestation of sexual excitement in male animals. *Psychosom. Med.,* 1942a, **4,** 173–198.

Beach, F. A. Central nervous mechanisms involved in the reproductive behavior of vertebrates. *Psychol. Bull.,* 1942b, **39,** 200–206.

Beach, F. A. Relative effect of androgen upon the mating behavior of male rats subjected to forebrain injury or castration. *J. exp. Zool.,* 1944, **97,** 249–295.

Beach, F. A. A review of physiological and psychological studies of sexual behavior in mammals. *Physiol. Rev.,* 1947a, **27,** 240–307.

Beach, F. A. Evolutionary changes in the physiological contol of mating behavior in mammals. *Psychol. Rev.,* 1947b, **54,** 297–315.

Bellows, R. T. Time factors in water drinking in dogs. *Amer. J. Physiol.,* 1939, **125,** 87–97.

Berkun, M. M., Kessen, M. L., & Miller, N. E. Hunger-reducing effects of food by stomach fistula versus food by mouth measured by a consummatory response. *J. comp. physiol. Psychol.,* 1952, **45,** 550.

Bishop, G. H. Cyclic changes in excitability of the optic pathway of the rabbit. *Amer. J. Physiol.,* 1933, 103, 213–224.

Brady, J. V. Emotional behavior. In J. Field, H. W. Magoun & V. E. Hall, Eds. *Handbook of physiology. Vol. III.* Baltimore: Williams and Wilkins, 1960.

Brown, J. S. *The motivation of behavior.* New York: McGraw-Hill, 1961.

Cannon, W. B. Hunger and thirst. In *Handbook of general experimental psychology.* C. Murchison, Ed. Worcester, Mass.: Clark Univ. Press, 1934a.

Cannon, W. B. The significance of the emotional level. *J. Missouri med. Ass.,* 1934b, **31,** 177–184.

Child, C. M. *Physiological foundations of behavior.* New York: Henry Holt, 1924.

Collins, E. Localization of an experimental hypothalamic and midbrain syndrome simulating sleep. *J. comp. Neurol.,* 1954, **100,** 661–697.

Deutsch, J. A. *The structural basis of behavior.* Chicago: Univ. of Chicago Press, 1960.

Ehrlich, A. Effects of tegmental lesions on motivated behavior in rats. *J. comp. physiol. Psychol.,* 1963, **56,** 390–396.

Fauré, J. De certains aspects du comportement en rapport avec des variations hormonales provoqueés chez l'animal. *J. Physiol. (Paris),* 1956, **48,** 529–531.

Fauré, J., & Gruner, J. Sur les modifications de l'activité bioélectrique du rhinencéphale et du thalamus recueillies sous l'influence des oestrogènes et des androgènes chez l'animal. *Rev. neurol.,* 1956, **94,** 161–168.

Fisher, A. E., & Coury, J. N. Cholinergic tracing of a central neural circuit underlying the thirst drive. *Science,* 1962, **138,** 691–693.

French, J. D., Hérnández-Peón, R., & Livingston, R. B. Projections from cortex to cephalic brainstem (reticular formation) in monkey. *J. Neurophysiol.,* 1955, **18,** 74–95.

Fuller, J. L., Rosvold, H. E., & Pribram, K. H. The effect on affective and cognitive behavior in the dog of lesions of the pyriform-amygdala-hippocampal complex. *J. comp. physiol. Psychol.,* 1957, **50,** 89–96.

Gastaut, H. Corrélations entre le système nerveux végétif et le système de la view de relation dans le rhinencéphale. *J. Physiol. Path. gén.,* 1952, **44,** 431–470.

Gilbert, G. J. The subcommissural organ. *Anat. Rec.,* 1956, **126,** 253–265.

Gilbert, G. J. The subcommissural organ: a regulator of thirst. *Amer. J. Physiol.,* 1957, **191,** 243–247.

Granit, R. Centrifugal and antidromic effects on ganglion cells of retina. *J. Neurophysiol.,* 1955, **18,** 388–411.

Granit, R. *Receptors and sensory perception.* New Haven, Conn.: Yale Univ. Press, 1955b.

Granit, R., & Kaada, B. R. Influence of stimulation of central nervous structures on muscle spindles in cat. *Acta physiol. scand.,* 1952, **27,** 130–160.

Green, J. Electrical activity in the hypothalamus and hippocampus of conscious rabbits. *Anat. Rec.,* 1954, **118,** 304.

Green, J. D., Clemente, C. D., & de Groot, J. Rhinencephalic lesions and behavior in cats. *J. comp. Neurol.,* 1957, **108,** 505–546.

Grossman, S. P. Behavioral effects of chemical stimulation of the ventral amygdala. *J. comp. physiol. Psychol.,* 1964a, **57,** 29–36.

Grossman, S. P. Effects of chemical stimulation of the septal area on motivation. *J. comp. physiol. Psychol.,* 1964b, **58,** 194–200.

Grossman, S. P., & Grossman, Lore. Food and water intake following lesions or electrical stimulation of the amygdala. *Amer. J. Physiol.,* 1963, **205,** 761–765.

Grossman, S. P., Peters, R. H., Freedman, P. E., & Willer, H. I. Behavioral effects of cholinergic stimulation of the thalamic reticular formation. *J. comp. physiol. Psychol.,* 1965, **59,** 57–65.

Hagbarth, K. E., & Kerr, D. I. B. Central influences on spinal afferent conduction. *J. Neurophysiol.,* 1954, **17,** 295–307.

Herrick, C. J. *Neurological foundations of animal behavior.* New York: Henry Holt, 1924.

Hetherington, A. W. Non-production of hypothalamic obesity in the rat by lesions rostral or dorsal to the ventro-medial hypothalamic nuclei. *J. comp. Neurol.,* 1944, **80,** 33.

Hull, C. L. *Principles of behavior.* New York: Appleton-Century, 1943.

Jasper, H. H., Proctor, L. D., Knighton, R. S., Noshay, W. C., & Costello, R. T., Eds. *The reticular formation of the brain.* Boston: Little, Brown, 1958.

Kim, C. Sexual activity of male rats following ablation of hippocampus. *J. comp. physiol. Psychol.,* 1960, **53,** 553–557.

Klüver, H., & Bucy, P. C. Preliminary analysis of functions of the temporal lobes in monkeys. *Arch. Neurol. Psychiat. (Chicago),* 1939, **42,** 979–1000.

Kohn, M. Satiation of hunger from food injected directly into the stomach versus food ingested by mouth. *J. comp. physiol. Psychol.,* 1951, **44,** 412–422.

Lashley, K. S. Experimental analysis of instinctive behavior. *Psychol. Rev.,* 1938, **45,** 445–471.

Lindsley, D. B. Emotion. In *Handbook of experimental psychology.* S. S. Stevens, Ed. New York: Wiley, 1951.

Lindsley, D. B. Psychophysiology and motivation. In *Nebraska symposium on motivation.* M. R. Jones, Ed. Lincoln: Univ. of Nebraska Press, 1957.

Lindsley, D. B. Attention, consciousness, sleep and wakefulness. In *Handbook of physiology. Vol. III.* J. Field, H. W. Magoun, & V. E. Hall, Eds. Baltimore: Williams and Wilkins, 1960.

Lindsley, D. B., Bowden, J., & Magoun, H. W. Effect upon the EEG of acute injury to the brain stem activating system. *EEG clin. Neurophysiol.,* 1949a, **1,** 475–486.

Lindsley, D. B., Schreiner, L. H., & Magoun, H. W. An electromyographic study of spasticity. *J. Neurophysiol.,* 1949b, **12,** 197–205.

Lindsley, D. B., Schreiner, L. H., Knowles, W. B., & Magoun, H. W. Behavioral and EEG changes following chronic brainstem lesions in the cat. *EEG clin. Neurophysiol.,* 1950, **2,** 483–498.

Lorenz, K. C. Die vergleichende Methode zum Studium angeborener Verhaltensweisen (Besprechung), *Z. Tierpsychol.,* 1950a, **7,** 465–468.

Lorenz, K. C. The comparative method in studying innate behavior patterns. *Sympos. soc. exp. Biol.,* 1950b, **4,** 221–268.

MacLean, P. D. The limbic system in relation to central grey and reticulum of the brainstem. *Psychosom. Med.,* 1955, **17,** 355.

MacLean, P. D., & Ploog, D. W. Cerebral representation of penile erection. *J. Neurophysiol.,* 1962, **25,** 30–55.

MacLean, P. D., Denniston, R. H., & Dua, S. Further studies on cerebral representation of penile erection: caudal thalamus, midbrain, and pons. *J. Neurophysiol.,* 1963, **26,** 273–293.

Magoun, H. W., & Rhines, Ruth. *Spasticity: the stretch reflex and extrapyramidal systems.* Springfield, Ill.: Thomas, 1948.

Masserman, J. H. Destruction of the hypothalamus in cats. *Arch. Neurol. Psychiat. (Chicago),* 1938, **39,** 1250–1271.

Miller, N. E. Experiments on motivation. *Science,* 1957, **126,** 1271–1278.

Miller, N. E., & Kessen, M. L. Reward effects via stomach fistula compared with those of food via mouth. *J. comp. physiol. Psychol.,* 1952, **45,** 555.

Morgan, C. T. *Physiological psychology.* New York: McGraw-Hill, 1943.

Morgan, C. T. *Introduction to psychology.* New York: McGraw-Hill, 1956.

Morgan, C. T. Physiological mechanisms of motivation. In *Nebraska symposium on motivation.* M. R. Jones, Ed. Lincoln: Univ. of Nebraska Press, 1957.

Morgan, C. T. Physiological theory of drive. In *Psychology: a study of a science. Vol I.* S. Koch, Ed. New York: McGraw-Hill, 1959.

Morgan, C. T., & Stellar, E. *Physiological psychology* (rev. ed.). New York: McGraw-Hill, 1950.

Morgane, P. J. Electrophysiological studies of feeding and satiety centers in the rat. *Amer. J. Physiol.,* 1961a, **201,** 838–844.

Morgane, P. J. Evidence of a "hunger motivational" system in the lateral hypothalamus of the rat. *Nature (London),* 1961b, **191,** 672–674.

Morgane, P. J. Medial forebrain bundle and "feeding centers" of the hypothalamus. *J. comp. Neurol.,* 1961c, **117,** 1–26.

Morgane, P. J., & Kosman, A. J. A rhinencephalic feeding center in the cat. *Amer. J. Physiol.,* 1959, **197,** 158–162.

Moruzzi, G., & Magoun, H. W. Brainstem reticular formation and activation of the EEG. *EEG clin. Neurophysiol.,* 1949, **1,** 455–473.

Robinson, B. W. Forebrain alimentary responses: some organizational principles. In *Thirst, first international symposium on thirst in the regulation of body water.* M. J. Wayner, Ed. New York: Pergamon Press, 1964.

Ruch, T. C., & Shenkin, H. A. The relation of area 13 on orbital surface of frontal lobes to hyperactivity and hyperphagia in monkeys. *J. Neurophysiol.,* 1943, **6,** 349–360.

Ruch, T. C., Blum, M., & Brobeck, J. R. Taste disturbances from thalamic lesions in monkeys. *Amer. J. Physiol.,* 1941, **133,** 433.

Sawyer, C. H. Reproductive behavior. In *Handbook of physiology. Vol. II.* J. Field, H. W. Magoun, & V. E. Hall, Eds. Baltimore: Williams and Wilkins, 1960.

Schaltenbrandt, G., & Cobb, S. Clinical and anatomical studies of two cats without neocortex. *Brain,* 1931, **53,** 449–488.

Schreiner, L. H., & Kling, A. Behavioral changes following rhinencephalic injury in cat. *J. Neurophysiol.,* 1953, **16,** 643.

Schreiner, L. H., & Kling, A. Effects of castration on hypersexual behavior induced by rhinencephalic injury in cat. *Arch. Neurol. Psychiat. (Chicago),* 1954, **72,** 180.

Stellar, E. The physiology of motivation. *Psychol. Rev.,* 1954, **61,** 5–22.

Stellar, E. Drive and motivation. In *Handbook of physiology. Vol. III.* J. Field, H. W. Magoun, & V. E. Hall, Eds. Baltimore: Williams and Wilkins, 1960.

Teitelbaum, P. Disturbances in feeding and drinking behavior after hypothalamic lesions. In *Nebraska symposium on motivation.* M. R. Jones, Ed., Lincoln: Univ. of Nebraska Press, 1961.

Teitelbaum, P., & Epstein, A. N. Recovery of feeding and drinking after lateral hypothalamic lesions. *Psychol. Rev.,* 1962, **69**, 74–90.

Teitelbaum, P., & Stellar, E. Recovery from the failure to eat, produced by hypothalamic lesions. *Science,* 1954, **120**, 894–895.

Tinbergen, N. *The study of instinct.* London: Oxford Univ. Press, 1951.

Towbin, E. J. Gastric distension as a factor in the satiation of thirst in esophagostomized dogs. *Amer. J. Physiol.,* 1949, **159**, 533–541.

Wood, D. C. Behavioral changes following discrete lesions of temporal lobe structures. *Neurology,* 1958, **8**, 215–220.

Wheatley, M. D. The hypothalamus and affective behavior in cats: a study of the effects of experimental lesions with anatomic correlations. *Arch. Neurol. Psychiat. (Chicago),* 1944, **52**, 296–316.

PART FOUR

CHAPTER TWELVE

Electrophysiological Correlates of Learning

In Part Three, behavior was viewed as partly determined by basic motivational variables which energize and direct the organism's responses to changes in the environment in a way that maintains optimal physiological conditions. Being hungry, thirsty, or sexually or emotionally aroused does not suffice, however, to produce *appropriate* responses. Although the organism is endowed with a basic reflex repertoire which is functional soon after birth, this limited variety of responses cannot maintain life, except for some very primitive species. More complex organisms develop such complicated mechanisms for the maintenance of basic physiological processes under widely varying environmental conditions that a stereotyped genetic coding of responses to specific environmental stimuli becomes impractical. As we proceed upward on the phylogenetic scale, we observe a decreasing dependence on innate reflex behavior and a concurrent increase in the importance of acquired response patterns. In higher mammalian species this development reaches a point at which the organism is totally unable to survive unless carefully tutored for a significant part of its life cycle. Furthermore, most higher species would be extinct if the acquisition of adaptive response patterns, beginning at or soon after birth, did not continue throughout the life of the organism. The influence of learning on behavior is so pronounced in man and most higher mammals that it is difficult to demonstrate more than a handful of unlearned reflex responses in the adult organism.

To understand behavior, one must study the neural and biochemical processes that are affected when an organism learns. The first question one might reasonably ask is whether a common mechanism or sequence of physiological events may characterize all learning, regardless of the en-vironmental and internal conditions that initiate the process. Psychologists have studied the acquisition of new behavioral responses in a variety of apparently distinct situations. There is as yet little agreement whether a common psychological (and by inference, physiological) process is measured in the different experimental paradigms. Can appetitive and defensive classical conditioning in which innate reflex responses are transferred to novel stimuli be placed on the same continuum with instrumental learning in which previously acquired responses are combined in novel and complex response sequences? Does concept formation on the human level represent merely a more complex interaction of the same basic processes responsible for salivary conditioning? Although these questions seem to invade the domain of the behavioral learning psychologists, they are of greatest importance to the physiological psychologist in guiding the search for physiological or biochemical mechanisms. So far, we have tended to search for *the* anatomical site or physiological process which may be responsible for learning without paying much attention to the possibility that essentially different mechanisms may be involved in different learning situations. This approach may, at least in part, account for the diversity of experimental findings which will become apparent in the following discussion. The Russian workers, for example, have followed the Pavlovian tradition of working with simple reflex responses, whereas American psychologists and physiologists have generally used much more complex learning situations such as avoidance learning or appetitive operant conditioning. Very simple learning tasks (such as straight alleys) have been used by some behavioral psychologists; this technique has not found much acceptance among physiological workers, largely because the response measure (running speed) has only an inferential relationship with learning when we define it as the acquisition of new responses or response patterns.

The experimental study of learning is further complicated by the fact that the acquisition of new responses is markedly affected by motivational, sensory, and motor variables which only too frequently go uncontrolled in learning experiments. Although the precise nature of the interaction is not yet clear from a physiological point of view, ample evidence suggests that an organism will learn little or nothing unless specifically and adequately motivated to do so. Whether this is a direct effect on the learning process or merely an indirect effect on performance need not concern us here. The fact remains that it is often difficult to decide whether an improvement or impairment of learning after some experimental manipulation can be attributed to an effect on the learning process per se. Many studies of the effects of central nervous system lesions or stimulation are woefully inadequate and inconclusive because this question has not been answered.

The situation is similar when we consider sensory factors. Even the simplest learning situations require a discrimination between the relevant stimulus or stimulus compound and the incidental stimuli of the environment. The difficulty of a learning task is directly proportional to the complexity of these purely sensory discriminations, and one might well expect to observe a deficit in learning following experimental manipulations which in some way interfere with sensory processes. Even an improvement in learning ability is potentially possible if the sensory input can be altered so that the relevant aspects of the stimulus situation achieve greater prominence. None of this, however, bears a necessary and direct relationship to the learning process itself, and we must be careful to assess possible sensory effects before concluding that the process of acquisition or retention has been affected. Motor disturbances are potentially easier to rule out as a contaminating influence, but very few workers have actually bothered to demonstrate that we can do so with confidence in any particular learning experiment.

Less obvious, and consequently much more difficult to assess, is the possible involvement of such complex and poorly understood phenomena as attention and emotion. Central nervous system lesions may primarily affect the organism's ability to pay attention or concentrate on the relevant aspects of the stimulus situation. There is evidence to suggest that this variable may enter into most, if not all, of our standard learning situations. Emotionality is another motivational variable that may confound the results of learning experiments. We have abundant evidence that many central nervous system mechanisms are in some way involved in the control of an organism's emotional responsiveness. If the same or closely related structures are then implicated as a part of the central system which may regulate the acquisition of new responses or response sequences, we must ask whether this relationship may not again be very indirect. Would we not expect an animal to learn faster if the experimental manipulation had lowered the general emotional effect of the learning situation? Conversely, a marked increase in emotional reactivity, such as has frequently been reported after limbic system lesions, might be expected to interfere with learning. These effects must be regarded as secondary and not causally related to the physiological mechanisms underlying learning itself.

We shall return to these problems in the course of our discussion whenever an experiment provides a particularly clear example of some uncontrolled influence. The reader should keep in mind, however, that these problems are to some extent inherent in most experimental designs and that caution must be used in interpreting all experimental data.

Before turning to the discussion of the experimental and theoretical literature in the field of learning, some general statements about the area may be in order. The neurophysiological basis of learning has been a very popular subject since Pavlov's important work on conditioning was published in the first decades of this century. The advent of refined anatomical, electrophysiological, and behavioral techniques in the past 20 years has provided many of the tools needed to attack the problem in the laboratory. The volume of research in this field is so large that a detailed presentation is not within the scope of this book. Only representative examples of current and historically important work will be discussed. The reader is referred to the *Annual Review of Physiology,* the *Quarterly Review of Physiology,* and the *Annual Review of Psychology* which contain review articles on the subject. Of the many recent symposia, the *Moscow Colloquium on Electroencephalography* contains many relevant papers and may be particularly instructive.

ELECTROENCEPHALOGRAPHIC CORRELATES OF LEARNING

It seems appropriate to begin the treatment of learning with a discussion of the physiological changes observed during the acquisition of new behavior patterns. Only when the parts of the organism (and particularly the nervous system) specifically involved in learning are elucidated can we begin to investigate the particular functional role of each anatomical structure. Although the relation between some of the electrophysiological variables and functional modifications remains quite tenuous at present, a vast research literature has accumulated in the past decades. This literature is difficult to interpret, for widely different experimental situations and physiological techniques have been applied without any attempt at standardization. The situation is complicated because we do not yet know precisely how the electrophysiological activity which can be recorded from all portions of the nervous system relates to neural activity. Particularly refractory to interpretation are EEG changes, for these rhythmic oscillations are not simply and directly related to the activity of single nerve cells. If one finds that the frequency or amplitude of EEG recordings from a particular area of the brain is altered after a particular experimental manipulation, all that can be known is that this part of the nervous system may play some role in a neural process which occurs under these circumstances. To show that this process is uniquely related to learning, it would have to be demonstrated that the same electrophysiological changes do not occur in any other situation that does not involve learning. To suggest, furthermore, that the functional change mirrored in the EEG tracings is in fact a component of the learning process *sine qua non* requires the additional proof that the same electrophysiological changes can be observed in *all* learning situations. Neither of these conditions has yet been met for any of the electrophysiological phenomena to be reported. The reader should keep these reservations in mind throughout the following discussion.

The Orienting, Alerting, or Arousal Response

Behavioral orienting. The first time a novel stimulus is presented to an animal or the intensity of a constantly present stimulus is noticeably changed, a sequence of behavioral responses can be observed which indicates that the animal is attending to the change in the environment. The animal turns its head, pricks up its ears, and may get up to approach and investigate the source of stimulation (Grastyán et al., 1959; Voronin and Sokolov, 1960). Pavlov (1927) noted that the first few presentations of a to-be-conditioned stimulus always elicited this behavior and suggested that this "orienting reflex" constituted an important initial phase of the conditioning process. Russian physiologists and psychologists have carefully investigated the behavioral and autonomic components of this response. Western workers paid little attention to this work until it was demonstrated that distinctive electrophysiological changes accompany the alerting response in all types of learning situations. Most Western investigators use the terms "orienting response," "alerting response," or "arousal response" interchangeably to refer to the electrophysiological changes elicited by a novel stimulus. Although some work has been done on the behavioral and autonomic aspects of the orienting response, most interest has been focused on the EEG changes that precede and accompany behavioral arousal. Before treating this subject at length, it might be useful to discuss some general properties of the orienting response as defined behaviorally.

The orienting response seems to be nonspecific. It is elicited by stimuli or by changes in the intensity of normally present stimuli of all sensory modalities. Even very weak stimuli initially elicit the response, although more pronounced effects are observed following intense and sudden stimulation. The orienting response gradually disappears with repeated nonreinforced stimulus presentations. This reaction is called *habituation* and will be discussed in greater detail in the next section. Man and most species of infrahuman animals show marked individual differences with respect to the intensity of the orienting response. Some individuals show EEG, autonomic, and behavioral responses to even minimal changes in sensory stimulation, whereas relatively intense stimuli are required to elicit at least some components (usually EEG and GSR changes) of the orienting response in others. Even subjects who initially show a marked or *generalized* orienting response (EEG changes particularly of the sensory and motor cortices, cardiovascular, sudomotor, and respiratory responses, as well as an increase in general muscle tension and overt behavioral responses such as eye and head movements toward the source of stimulation) habituate rather rapidly. Eventually, only a *localized* response remains in the form of a brief alteration of the spontaneous EEG rhythm of the specific sensory receiving area for the stimulus modality.

In the chapter on emotion, some of the research that relates various autonomic measures to arousal or activation was reviewed. Although most of the earlier studies attempted to show a more specific relationship to particular emotions, it appears today that autonomic responses represent little more than one aspect of the generalized orienting response. Several studies of orienting behavior have observed such autonomic changes as a rise in blood pressure (Darrow, 1936), heart rate, and sudomotor activity (Morrell and Jasper, 1956; Voronin and Sokolov, 1960). Jasper and Cruikshank (1937) noted that the pupillary response to light appeared to have response latencies identical to those of the alpha block. Autonomic responses constitute an important part of the "generalized orienting response" as described by some of the Russian workers in this field (Voronin and Sokolov, 1960).

Electrophysiological responses to novel stimuli. When an organism is sleeping, resting, or merely inattentive, fairly regular electrical potentials can be recorded from the brain. These 8- to 12-cps waves have been called *alpha waves* by Hans Berger, who discovered in 1929 that they can be recorded from the scalp of human subjects. Berger also observed that the slow, high-amplitude pattern changes immediately after the presentation of a novel stimulus to a fast, low-amplitude discharge which is much more asynchronous than the alpha waves. This *blocking* of the alpha rhythm (see Figure 12.1) is typically associated with behavioral arousal and orienting. Rheinberger and Jasper (1937) coined the term "activation pattern" to describe the EEG response to novel stimulation. Other terms (such as beta rhythm, arousal reaction, and desynchronization) have been employed by later workers and are generally used interchangeably today. Most of the early studies of the activation pattern were carried out on human subjects because stereotaxic procedures permitting precise localizations of the recording electrodes in animal brains had not yet been perfected. Since 1940 the emphasis has shifted to animal research and the exploration of subcortical structures by means of depth electrodes permanently implanted in the brain.

After Adrian (Adrian and Matthews, 1934) confirmed Berger's findings, many early researchers concentrated on variables affecting the arousal reaction. They soon found that the electrophysiological response to novel stimulation occurred after much shorter response latencies than overt behavioral reactions (0.16 sec as compared with 0.35 sec for pressing a key to the same stimulus), and that the response did not terminate with the cessation of stimulation (Adrian and Matthews, 1934; Rheinberger and Jasper, 1937). The relatively long duration of the activation pattern has given rise to the speculation that the release of some chemical substances may be responsible for the protracted EEG change (Rheinberger and Jasper, 1937; Darrow, 1947). Little direct evidence is as yet available for this suggestion (see Figure 12.2).

Another early discovery was that the intensity and duration of the arousal reaction are modality-dependent. Almost all the early work in this field was done with visual stimuli, and it was suggested in the 1930's that the activation pattern might represent "the attempt to see" (Loomis et al., 1936). This theory was based on the observation (Adrian and Matthews, 1934) that merely having the eyes open in a uniform field did not elicit EEG changes and that hypnotic suggestions to "see" or "not see" a stimulus could alternately elicit or suppress the arousal reaction (Loomis et al., 1936). Subsequent studies (Jasper et al., 1935; Rheinberger and Jasper, 1937) showed that stimuli of other sensory modalities can elicit the activation pattern, although the intensity and duration of this response tend to be smaller than in the visual system. Since some animals (such as the cat) show maximal responses to stimulation in other sensory modalities, it has been suggested that the modality differences may reflect the importance of specific sensory mechanisms (Jasper and Cruikshank, 1937). Thus, in man, the visual system may be dominant (i.e., carry the most information) and therefore be able to arouse the cortical EEG preferentially, whereas the auditory system may be of greater importance to the cat (see Figure 12.3).

The results of several studies (Adrian and Matthews, 1934; Bagchi, 1937; Jasper and Cruikshank, 1937) suggest that the arousal value or meaning of a stimulus may be a more important determinant of the magnitude of the activation response than intensity per se. An unexpected soft light produces more prolonged desynchronization than a bright but expected light (Rheinberger and Jasper, 1937); the subject's name evokes a more pronounced arousal response than neutral words (Bagchi, 1937); and the squeal of a mouse is perhaps not surprisingly the most effective stimulus

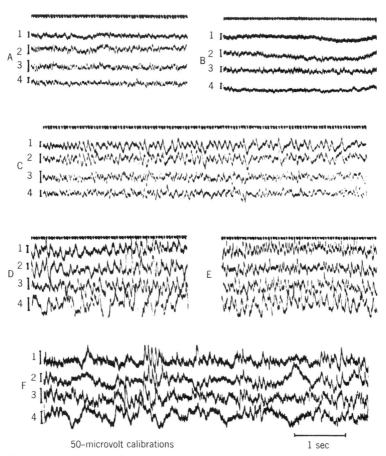

50-microvolt calibrations   1 sec

Fig. 12.1 Variations in general activation as represented by cortical electrograms. All records were obtained with monopolar leads from 1, the motor areas; 2, the sensory areas; 3, the auditory areas; and 4, the visual areas. Negativity on the cortex is represented by an upward deflection.

A, B, activation records obtained during (A) moderate and (B) intense excitement. C, activity obtained with subsequent relaxation of the same animal as in A. D, E, 24 hr after Dial anesthesia. E follows D by 90 sec, during which time visual and auditory stimuli were administered. Note the increased frequency in all areas in E. F, same animal as D and E completely relaxed (asleep) 48 hr after Dial anesthesia. (From Rheinberger and Jasper, 1937.)

for EEG arousal in the cat (Travis and Milisen, 1936). Because of this interaction with the dimension of meaning, it is all but impossible to predict the duration of the arousal response to any specific stimulus.

Jasper and Cruikshank (1936) suggested in one of the early studies that a lawful (logarithmic) relationship exists between the duration of a visual stimulus and the duration of the activation pattern (as well as between the intensity of the stimulus and the latency of the activation pattern). Subsequent experiments, however, have generally failed to observe a predictable relationship between these parameters.

With the advent of stereotaxic procedures, it became possible to record the electrical activity of more restricted areas of the brain, and this technological advance has greatly enhanced our understanding of the activation pattern in the past fifteen years. One of the most interesting developments has been the discovery that cortical arousal can be specific to the sensory cortex directly related to the modality of the stimulus. One of the earlier studies (Rheinberger and Jasper, 1937) had shown that the activation pattern is restricted to the specific sensory receiving area under Dial anesthesia, and that a generalized arousal reaction rapidly disappears with repeated nonrein-

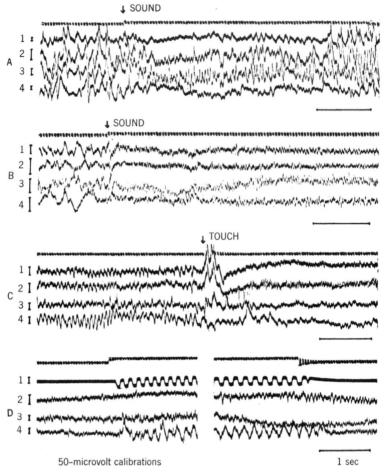

Fig. 12.2 Effects of stimuli on the electrograms of anesthetized and unanesthetized cats. A, 24 hr after Dial anesthesia. Sound stimulus causes increased frequency in the auditory region with blocking in the other regions. 1, motor areas; 2, sensory areas; 3, auditory areas; 4, visual areas. Monopolar recording. B, same animal 9 days postoperatively. Note the similarity of response of all regions to the same intensity of sound as used in A. 1,2,3,4, same. Bipolar recording. C, tactual stimulus to the left foreleg. 1, left motor; 2, right motor; 3, left sensory; 4, right sensory. Monopolar recording. D, introduction and cessation of a flickering light stimulus at 5.2 cps. Note the following of the flicker frequency by the potentials of the occipital region. 1, photocell record; 2, sensory areas; 3, auditory areas; 4, visual areas. C, D, same animal, 8 and 6 days postoperatively. (From Rheinberger and Jasper, 1937.)

forced presentations of the stimulus. The response of the sensory cortex, on the other hand, tended to extinguish much more gradually. More recent studies (Green and Arduini, 1954; Grastyán et al., 1959; Adey et al., 1960; Voronin and Sokolov, 1960) have found that the initial presentation of most stimuli produces a general desynchronization response in all areas of the neocortex as well as presumably related changes in the electrical activity of the midbrain and thalamic reticular

formation. This generalized response disappears with repeated presentations of the same stimulus, and alpha blocking remains only in the sensory projection area of the stimulus modality. Gastaut et al. (1957) have observed that some stimuli fail to produce a generalized arousal response but always elicit alpha blocking in the specific cortical projection area.

Another interesting development is the demonstration that the EEG arousal response can be

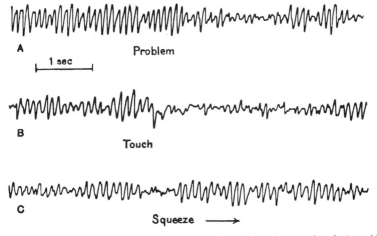

Fig. 12.3 Abolition of the alpha rhythm by nonvisual activities. A, eyes closed. A problem in mental arithmetic is given at the signal. B, eyes closed. The nose is touched with cotton wool. C, persistence of rhythm in spite of muscular effort. With the eyes closed, pliers are squeezed as tightly as possible. (From Adrian and Matthews, 1934.)

elicited during sleep without concomitant behavioral activation (Jouvet, 1961). This dissociation of electrophysiological and behavioral arousal can only be obtained under special conditions. Generally, EEG arousal is seen only when the animal also shows overt behavioral signs of attention.

Much of the work of the past fifteen years has been devoted to the anatomical and physiological mechanisms responsible for the arousal response. The crucial development in this field is the demonstration by Moruzzi and Magoun (1949) that electrical stimulation of the midbrain reticular formation elicits a generalized activation pattern at the cortex which is essentially indistinguishable from that evoked by sensory stimulation. The nonspecific thalamic nuclei responded similarly to midbrain stimulation and, when stimulated, elicited generalized cortical arousal. Since the reticular formation receives collaterals from all sensory pathways, Moruzzi and Magoun suggested that cortical arousal was mediated by this nonspecific projection mechanism.

Lindsley et al. (1949, 1950) have supported this interpretation by showing that the arousal response to sensory stimuli is abolished by destruction of the midbrain reticular formation but can be elicited by electrical stimulation rostral to the lesion site. Animals with midbrain reticular formation lesions were found to be comatose and completely unresponsive to sensory stimulation, in spite of the fact that the classical sensory pathways were not affected by the lesion.

The importance of the midbrain and thalamic reticular formation has been demonstrated in many later studies. Jansen et al. (1955–1956) found that bilateral lesions in the intralaminar nuclei of the thalamus diminished or abolished the cortical arousal response; the animals, however, did not appear totally unresponsive to sensory stimulation but merely showed a correlated reduction in attention. That these effects are not merely caused by the removal of relatively large areas of neural tissue was shown in this study by control lesions (cingulum, fornix, anterior, dorsomedial and center median nuclei of the thalamus, habenula, stria medullaris, caudate nucleus, and portions of the hypothalamus) that did not affect the cortical arousal response (see Figure 12.4).

It has been suggested that the generalized alpha blocking typically observed after the first few stimulus presentations may be mediated by the midbrain reticular formation (Lindsley et al., 1949, 1950), whereas the modality-specific local responses of the sensory projection areas may represent an influence of the thalamic portion of the reticular formation (Jasper et al., 1955; Gastaut, 1958a). Gastaut et al. (1957) have further suggested that the lower brainstem may be more rapidly inhibited by repetitive stimulation and that this inhibition, in turn, facilitates the thalamo-cortical influences that are responsible for the localized desynchronization.

Between 1950 and 1960 many experimental studies which supported the early findings were

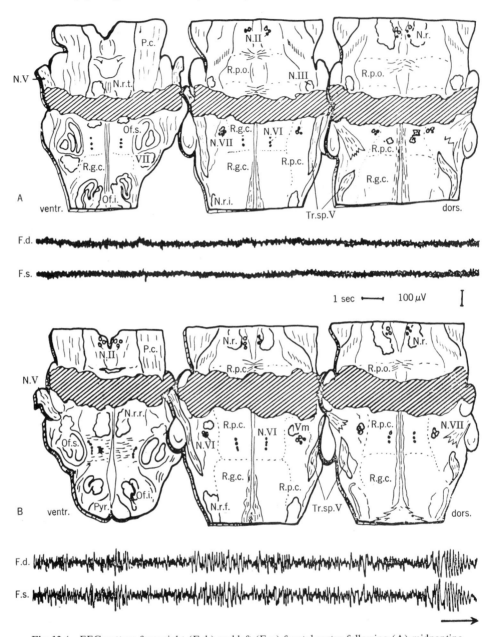

Fig. 12.4   EEG pattern from right (F.d.) and left (F.s.) frontal cortex following (A) midpontine and (B) rostropontine transection. (From Batini et al., 1959.)

published, and the notion became quite generally accepted that general activation, arousal, or even drive might be directly related to the reticular formation. This interpretation has been questioned by several recent studies which show that massive damage to the midbrain or thalamic reticular formation fails to abolish behavioral and EEG arousal if the lesions are inflicted in multiple stages to minimize surgical shock (Adametz, 1959; Chow et al., 1959; Lourie et al., 1960). This finding suggests that other areas of the brain may be involved in the arousal reaction, and several limbic system sites have been implicated in recent studies.

Green and Arduini (1954), for instance, observed that neocortical desynchronization was always accompanied by the appearance of high-

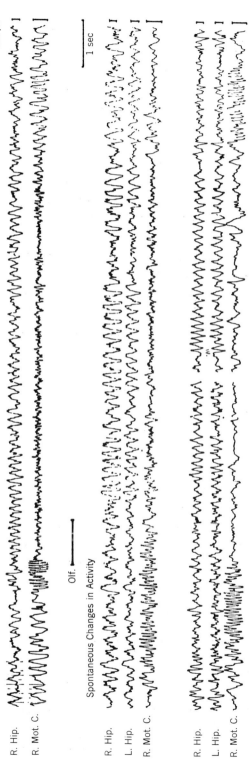

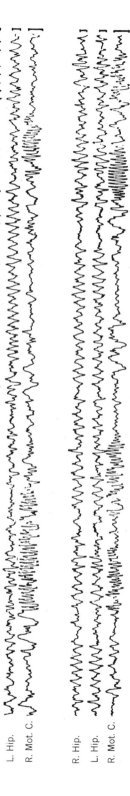

R. Hip.

R. Mot. C.

Spontaneous Changes in Activity

Olf.

R. Hip.

L. Hip.

R. Mot. C.

R. Hip.

L. Hip.

R. Mot. C.

R. Hip.

L. Hip.

R. Mot. C.

R. Hip.

L. Hip.

R. Mot. C.

100 μV

1 sec

Fig. 12.5 Induced and spontaneous hippocampal and cortical activity in an acute rabbit preparation. R. Hip., right hippocampus; R. Mot. C., right motor cortex; L. Hip., left hippocampus. The first pair of records shows the effect of an olfactory stimulus (Olf.). Examples of inverse relationships between neocortex and paleocortex are seen in the second, third, and fourth groups of records. The fifth group shows the absence of an inverse relationship. (From Green and Arduini, 1954.)

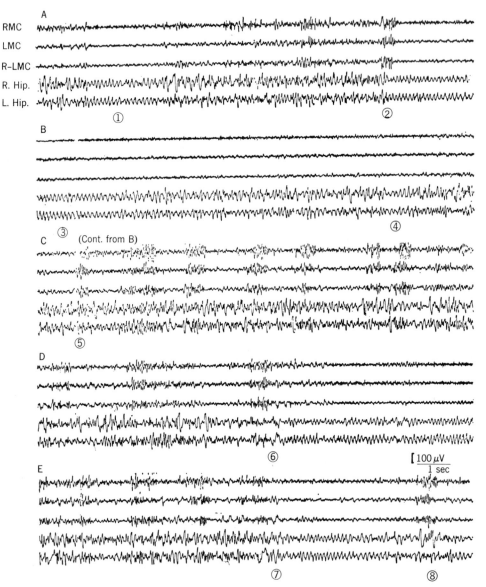

RMC
LMC
R-LMC
R. Hip.
L. Hip.

Fig. 12.6 Cortical and hippocampal EEG activity during sleep and arousal. RMC and LMC, right and left motor cortices; R. Hip. and L. Hip., right and left hippocampi. The records are from an unanesthetized rabbit. In A the animal is drowsy. A transition is seen between 1 and 2. At 2 the animal nodded and apparently woke up. In B and C the animal changed in behavior from alertness to drowsiness or light sleep. Note the gradual desynchronization of the hippocampus between 3 and 4 and the abrupt appearance of regular spindles in the cortical record at 5. In D, while the animal was drowsing, a cat was brought into the room. Up to 6 the cat was on a EEG console out of sight of the rabbit. At 6 the cat placed its forepaws on the ledge of a cable input window and stared at the rabbit. The following arousal lasted for about 30 sec, although the cat immediately returned to the console. Record E shows a response in the same animal, three weeks later, to similar exposure to a cat. Note the brevity in this case. The cat was in view at 7 and spindles returned at 8. Note the varying patterns of cortical and hippocampal activity in alertness and drowsiness. (From Green and Arduini, 1954.)

amplitude slow waves (4 to 6 cps) in the hippo-campus, even when cortical arousal was induced by direct electrical stimulation of the reticular formation. This inverse relationship between hippocampal and cortical activity was maintained during rest or sleep. As soon as the cortex began to show the large, slow waves characteristic of this state, fast, low-voltage activity appeared in the hippocampus. Green and Arduini proposed that the hippocampal slow waves might represent a "specialized paleocortical arousal reaction whose unusual pattern is somehow correlated with distinctive morphological or functional properties of this part of the brain" (see Figures 12.5 to 12.8).

A very different interpretation of the same electrophysiological phenomenon has been advanced by Grastyán and his collaborators (1959, 1961). Grastyán noted that cats stopped all ongoing behavior and oriented toward a moving object during electrical stimulation of the hippocampal-fornix system. As soon as the stimulation was terminated, the animals "lost interest" in the moving object and continued the previously ongoing behavior. Grastyán observed in a subsequent study that electrical stimulation of the hippocampus alone interrupted any ongoing behavior, even when no specific sensory stimuli were presented to distract the animal, and suggested that the hippocampus might serve inhibitory function (see Figures 12.9, 12.10, 12.11).

Grastyán et al. (1959) further investigated the role of the hippocampal formation in a series of conditioning studies involving instrumental approach and avoidance learning. In view of Green

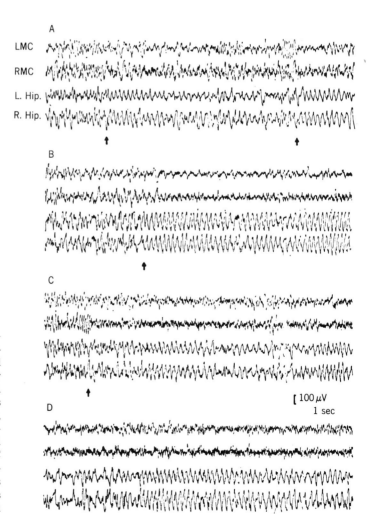

Fig. 12.7 Variations in time relationships of hippocampal and cortical arousal to various natural stimuli. All stimuli were auditory and are indicated by arrows. In A a stimulus arouses the hippocampus but not the cortex. Following this, a louder sound produces a simultaneous arousal. In B hippocampal arousal precedes cortical. In C cortical arousal precedes hippocampal. In D the hippocampus is aroused in a rabbit whose cortex is already alerted. (From Green and Arduini, 1954.)

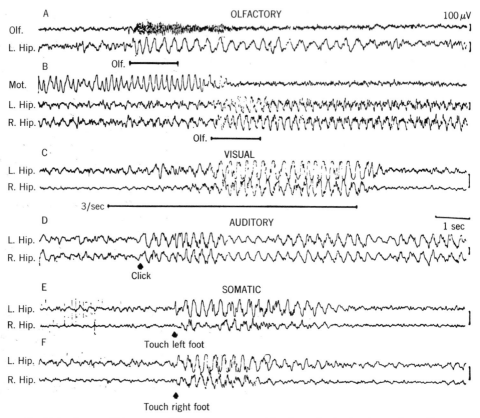

Fig. 12.8   Acute rabbit preparations under curare and local anesthetic, showing various afferent responses. Olf., olfactory bulb; Mot., motor cortex; L. and R. Hip., left and right hippocampi. Note the characteristic hippocampal response to various modalities of stimulation. (From Green and Arduini, 1954.)

and Arduini's earlier finding that a reciprocal relationship seemed to exist between cortical and hippocampal activity, Grastyán predicted that the initial presentation of the CS would elicit cortical desynchronization and hippocampal slow waves.

Only part of this prediction was borne out. During the first few presentations of the CS and UCS, alpha blocking was recorded from all neocortical leads as expected; however, the hippocampus continued to show the same low-amplitude, high-frequency pattern that seems to be characteristic of this structure during the resting state. Several CS-UCS pairings were required before the hippocampal slow waves and the reciprocal relationship between cortical and hippocampal activity began to appear. The hippocampal slow waves were in evidence throughout the subsequent training period but diminished as conditioned responses to the CS began to be made;

the waves disappeared completely after the learned response had been firmly established.

When the EEG data were compared with motion pictures of the animals' behavior during training, it became obvious that the hippocampal slow waves were always associated with overt, behavioral orientation toward the source of stimulation. Overt orienting responses were not made during the initial CS presentations, presumably because the relatively low-intensity stimulus had not yet acquired special significance for the animals. Only when the role of the CS as a cue for the impending presentation of the UCS began to be appreciated did behavioral orienting and hippocampal slow-wave activity appear. As the animals learned to perform the required responses to the CS (such as mounting a platform to obtain food or hopping a barrier to avoid painful shock), the behavioral orienting response to the CS diminished and finally disappeared; the disappearance of the behavioral response was almost perfectly correlated with the cessation of hippocampal slow waves. When the conditioned response (CR) was firmly established, both cortex and hippocampus showed desynchronized, fast activity, and the animals responded to the CS without orienting noticeably toward the source of the light or tone. Grastyán reported that this relation between the behavioral orienting response and the hippocampal slow-wave pattern was perfect and invariant. Whenever behavioral orienting responses occurred (even in late training), hippocampal slow waves could be recorded, and the slow-wave pattern never appeared without clear behavioral orienting.

It is possible to interpret these results in accordance with Green and Arduini's suggestion that the hippocampal slow waves may represent a specialized arousal reaction of paleocortical structures if we assume that behavioral orienting depends directly on the arousal of these mechanisms. Grastyán, however, has suggested that it may not be necessary to propose that the same electrophysiological pattern (high-amplitude slow waves) represents inhibition in one portion of the brain (the neocortex) but excitation or arousal in another (the paleocortex), as Green and Arduini's interpretation requires. Instead, Grastyán argues that slow-wave activity may represent a depressed or relatively inactive state in the hippocampus as well as the neocortex. Because his previous studies

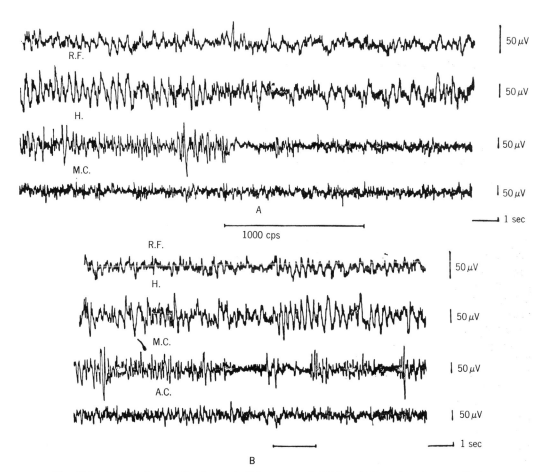

Fig. 12.9   A, at its first application an indifferent sound (1000 cps) desynchronizes equally the activities of the neocortex and hippocampus. B, a familiar calling sound (puss, shoo) elicits rhythmic slow waves in the hippocampus. R.F., reticular formation; H., hippocampus; M. C., motor cortex; A. C., auditory cortex. (From Lissak and Grastyán, 1960.)

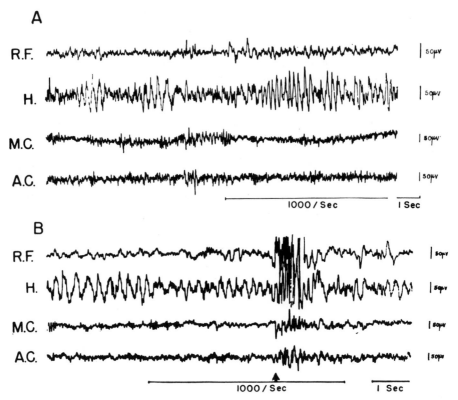

Fig. 12.10 A, a few associations of the formerly indifferent sound stimulus with an electric shock evoke a vigorous orienting reaction and slow potentials in the hippocampus. B, at the appearance of the CR (arrow), the stimulus begins to desynchronize hippocampal activity again. R.F., reticular formation; H., hippocampus; M.C., motor cortex; A.C., auditory cortex. (From Grastyán et al., 1959.)

suggested that the hippocampus might serve inhibitory functions, Grastyán proposed that the normal function of the hippocampus may be to prevent the occurrence of orienting responses to insignificant sensory stimulation, and that this inhibitory function may be suppressed during the initial phase of learning.

Although Grastyán's interpretation is very appealing and accounts for the experimental findings with the parsimonious assumption that a particular electrophysiological pattern represents the same functional state regardless of its point of origin in the nervous system, some caution is necessary. Recent studies by Holmes and Adey (1960) have shown that high-amplitude slow waves can be recorded from the entorhinal cortex immediately adjacent to the hippocampus, even after a CR is firmly established. In a delayed-response situation, cats were trained to choose one of two elevated pathways leading to goal boxes which were alternately baited in the pres-

ence of the animal (see Figure 12.12). Even before training, slow, 4- to 6-cps waves were recorded from the entorhinal cortex whenever the cats appeared alert or attentive. This pattern continued on all learning trials and persisted throughout subsequent performance and extinction trials. Holmes and Adey reported that the slow-wave pattern tended to appear just before the animals began to walk toward one of the goal boxes. They suggested that the 4- to 6-cps activity of the entorhinal cortex and hippocampus might indicate "a readiness to act" since it "accompanies an alert state found in goal-directed motor activity and appears without gross movement, both spontaneously and during extinction of the approach habit" (see Figures 12.13 and 12.14).

It is difficult to evaluate these conflicting results for several reasons. In spite of the close anatomical relation between the entorhinal cortex and the hippocampus, it is dangerous to assume functional equality. It is also possible that the nature

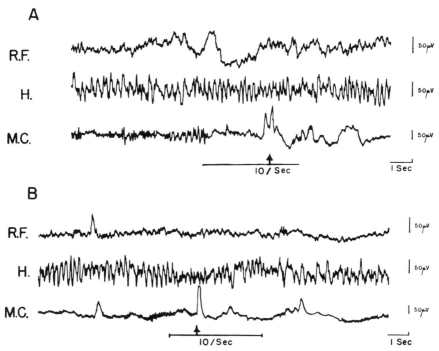

Fig. 12.11 A, alimentary CR. At the early stage of the development of the CR, the stage of the orienting reaction, the CS elicits a series of rhythmic slow waves in the hippocampus. B, at the stabilization of the CR, the former CS desynchronizes the activity of the hippocampus. (From Grastyán, 1959.)

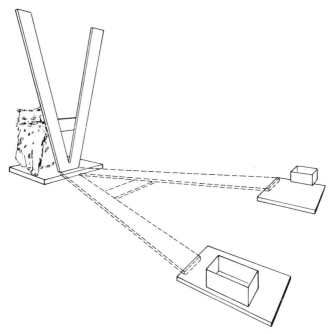

Fig. 12.12 Training apparatus for the delayed-response test used by Holmes and Adey, 1960. A cat is placed on the starting platform with the bridge walkways raised as shown. The animal's attention is then drawn to a food container, while food is placed in one of the two pans on the right. After a 5- to 10-sec delay the bridge is lowered and the animal walks to one of the goal boxes. Boxes are placed so that the animal cannot see the reward until he reaches it. (From Holmes and Adey, 1960.)

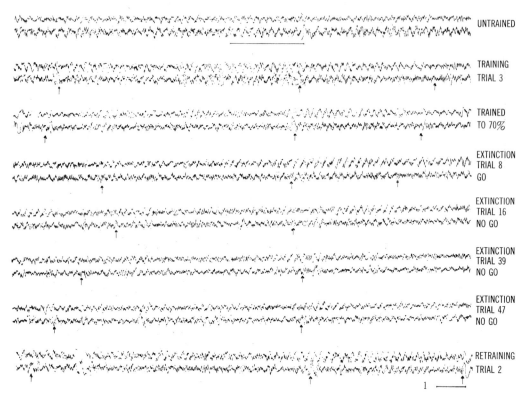

Fig. 12.13 EEG tracings obtained during the training and extinction of a delayed-response problem. Left entorhinal area above, right below. The first record shows the animal untrained (slow waves during spontaneous walking are underlined). The next record shows the time at which food was shown to the animal (first arrow), the bridge was lowered (second arrow), and the animal reached the goal box (third arrow). In the third record the slow rhythm is largely confined to the approach phase after the bridge is lowered. Subsequent tracings show the gradual decrease in slow rhythm with extinction and its return with retraining. Standardization, μV, 1 sec. (From Holmes and Adey, 1960.)

of the task (a delayed response requiring prolonged attention to the stimulus situation) necessitated behavioral orienting even after the response sequence was well learned. This would account for the persistence of the slow-wave activity, and since Holmes and Adey reported that 4- to 6-cps waves were seen before training only when the animals appeared "alert" and "attended to extraneous stimuli," one is inclined to favor Grastyán's suggestion that behavioral orienting may be directly related to the hippocampal slow waves.

Eidelberg et al. (1959) have reported that the slow waves which characterize the electrical activity of the dorsal hippocampus during some phases of neocortical arousal were abolished by septal lesions or partial destruction of the thalamic midline nuclei, whereas lesions of other thalamic

nuclei had no effect (see Figure 12.15). Adey et al. (1962) have replicated these results and observed that entorhinal destruction did not interfere with the development of the hippocampal slow-wave response; however, the dorsal hippocampus and entorhinal area showed synchronous slow-wave activity. Several recent studies (Eidelberg et al., 1959; Grastyán, 1959; Novikova and Farber, 1959) have shown that low-voltage, fast activity is typically superimposed on the hippocampal slow waves during periods of neocortical arousal, suggesting that desynchronization may, after all, characterize the response of the allocortical structures.

Kaada and his collaborators (Kaada et al., 1953; Kaada and Johannessen, 1960; Fangel and Kaada, 1960) have shown that a cortical activation pattern accompanied by behavioral arousal or attention

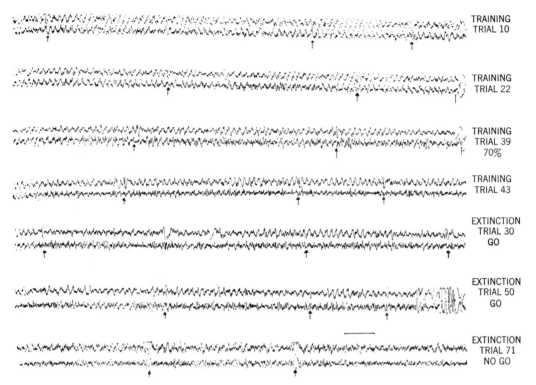

Fig. 12.14 EEG tracings obtained during training and extinction of a delayed-response problem. Left entorhinal area above, left hippocampus below. Note that the hippocampal slow-wave response drops out as the animal reaches a standard of 70% correct and does not return with extinction as the entorhinal response decreases. (From Holmes and Adey, 1960.)

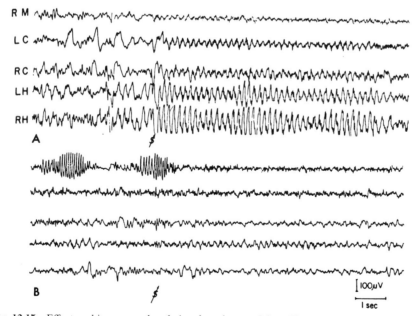

Fig. 12.15 Effect on hippocampal and cingulate theta activity of large, bilateral lesions involving the nucleus of the center median and the dorsomedial nucleus. A, control; B, after lesion. RM, right motor; LC; left cingulate; RC, right cingulate; LH and RH, left and right hippocampus. (From Eidelberg et al., 1959.)

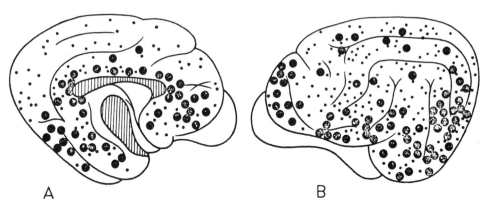

Fig. 12.16   A, medial, and B, lateral view of the cat's hemisphere indicating points (●) from which a generalized electrocortical activation was obtained by electrical stimulation and other points (·) from which there were no such effects. (From Kaada and Johannessen, 1960.)

can be elicited by hippocampal and medial cortex stimulation (see Figures 12.16 and 12.17). Whether these effects are mediated by the thalamic reticular formation remains to be seen; the widespread cortical connections of the hippocampus suggest a direct arousal effect may be possible. Because recent theories of motivation have placed heavy emphasis on the hippocampal formation and the limbic system as a whole, one might ask whether the arousal function of this system is comparable to that presumably exercised by the reticular formation. It is possible that the limbic system mediates arousal responses to internal drive stimulation which is simulated by electrical stimulation, whereas the reticular formation mediates an arousal response to external stimulation. A direct interaction between these two mechanisms, which might explain the complete inhibition of the arousal response following massive reticular formation lesions as well as the paradoxical effects of multistage lesions, has not yet been demonstrated. An experimental investigation of this question is complicated by the fact that the potential anatomical connections between the reticular formation and the limbic system are so numerous and diffuse that it is practically impossible to eliminate even a major portion of them.

Before we leave the topic of EEG arousal, we might ask what this electrophysiological change indicates about the functional properties of the brain. It is generally assumed that desynchronization or fast, low-amplitude waves represent "excitation" of neural mechanisms, whereas the slow, high-amplitude alpha rhythm is a sign of relative inhibition. Recent studies using microelectrode techniques to assess the electrical activity of single

units (or at most a few neurons) have questioned this concept (see Figures 12.18 and 12.19).

Ricci et al. (1957) report that the discharge frequency of single neurons may increase, decrease, or remain unaffected during cortical desynchronization or arousal, as measured by the EEG; they suggested that the electrocorticogram may not provide a reliable index of excitation or inhibition of cortical cells.

These findings correspond nicely with the previous demonstration by Machne et al. (1955) that novel stimulation produces widely different response patterns in individual neurons of the midbrain reticular formation. Three main groups of reactions were observed: (1) cells that had been firing before the presentation of the stimulus stopped briefly and then continued with bursts of afterdischarges after the stimulus had arrived at the cortex; (2) neurons that had been silent before the stimulus presentation began to fire; and (3) some cells that had been active during stimulation stopped and remained silent for some time after the cessation of the stimulus. Prolonged stimulation increased the rate of firing of most cells, but some were observed to slow or even stop firing.

Kogan (1960) has measured the threshold of excitability of cortical neurons before and during EEG desynchronization (produced by the presentation of an auditory CS which had previously been paired with a shock UCS and elicited generalized cortical activation). He reports that the primary sensory receiving area showed a decreased threshold for neural excitability during the period of cortical desynchronization. However, other cortical areas showed an increase, in

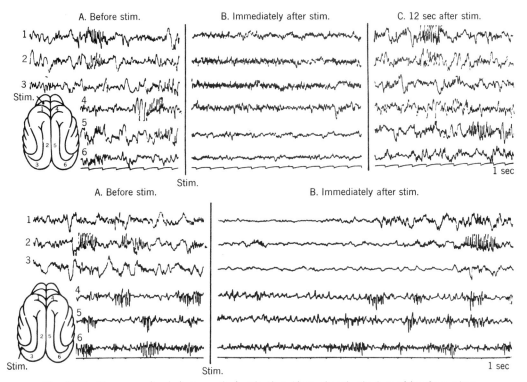

A. Before stim.   B. Immediately after stim.   C. 12 sec after stim.

Stim.

1
2
3
4
5
6

Stim.

1 sec

A. Before stim.   B. Immediately after stim.

1
2
3
4
5
6

Stim.   Stim.   1 sec

Fig. 12.17 *Top,* generalized electrocortical activation (desynchronization) resulting from stimulation of the frontal cortex as indicated by the arrow on the inset. Stimulus parameters, 40 cps, 4 msec, 3 volts, 5 sec. Light Nembutal-chloralose anesthesia. *Bottom,* electrocortical activation resulting from stimulation of the posterior suprasylvian gyrus. Note the disappearance of intermittent (6 to 8 cps) bursts and slow waves with no increase of low-voltage fast activity. Stimulus parameters, 40 cps, 8 msec, 4 volts, 6 sec. Light Nembutal-chloralose anesthesia. (From Kaada and Johannessen, 1960.)

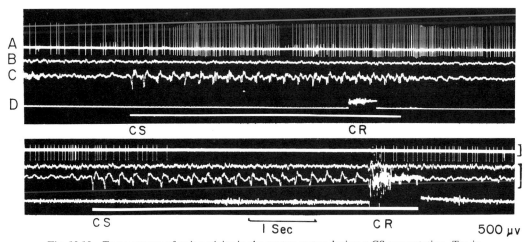

A
B
C
D

C S   C R

C S   I Sec   C R   500 μv

Fig. 12.18 Two patterns of unit activity in the motor cortex during a CS presentation. *Top,* increased firing during CS and response. *Bottom,* inhibition of unit during CS. A, microelectrode in motor cortex; B, EEG record from motor area; C, EEG record from occipital area; D, EMG. (From Jasper et al., 1958.)

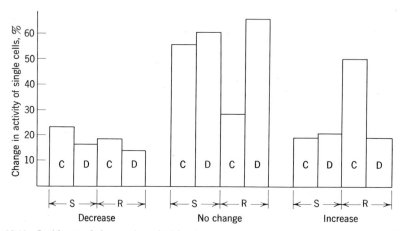

Fig. 12.19   Incidence of changes in unit firing in motor cortex (expressed as percentages) during CR and during differential stimulus without response. S, stimulus interval; R, response interval; C, conditioning trial; D, differential trial. (From Jasper et al., 1958.)

spite of the fact that the gross EEG activation pattern was identical in all areas. Other workers have found that the sensory cortex shows a *decreased* unit activity during cortical desynchronization associated with awakening, and the presence of a tonic inhibitory influence on many cortical neurons has been suggested (Hubel, 1959; Evarts, 1960). Some investigators have even proposed that the low-amplitude fast EEG pattern (cortical desynchronization) may represent the activation of inhibitory neurons and relate more directly to inhibitory than excitatory processes (Purpura, 1958; Russek, 1959).

Much more work is needed, particularly in unanesthetized animals, before we can hope to understand these complex findings. It seems clear, however, that the cortical arousal or activation pattern is not descriptive of a general rise in excitability or even neural activity, as has been widely believed in the past. It appears that cortical desynchronization may be associated with a complex organization of neural activity which may represent inhibitory as well as excitatory processes.

It is very difficult to interpret the results of microelectrode studies because we do not yet know whether an increase in the activity of a specific neuron represents an excitatory or an inhibitory influence. With the rapid advance in technological knowledge, many more investigators will hopefully be able to make use of microelectrode techniques. Some experimenters (see Morrell, 1961) have suggested that the overall behavior of a large population of neurons (as measured by macroelectrodes) may provide a better index of func-

tional changes than detailed records from a few individual units. This position, however, presupposes that we can interpret the cumulative changes obtained by the EEG, and embarrassingly little progress has been made in this direction during the past 30 years.

Summary. The presentation of any novel stimulus (or stimulus change) produces a sudden alteration in the electrical activity of the cortex. The slow, synchronous activity (alpha rhythm) typical of the resting organism gives way to fast, low-amplitude discharges which typically outlast the stimulus. This activation pattern is elicited by stimuli of all sensory modalities but generally appears more prominent in a specific modality (vision in man, audition in the cat). The intensity and duration of the cortical arousal response are a function of stimulus intensity and duration, but other variables such as arousal value or meaning of the stimulus can significantly affect this relationship. The activation pattern is at least partly determined by reticular mechanisms. Lesions in the midbrain or thalamic reticular formation abolish all arousal reactions, at least when the lesions are made in a single stage. Electrical stimulation of these areas produces cortical activation which is indistinguishable from that elicited by sensory stimulation. Other areas of the brain (particularly the limbic system) may play an important role in the regulation of cortical arousal. Recent microelectrode studies have suggested that the cortical arousal response may not be representative of a simple increase in cortical activity, as had been assumed in the past. Both excitatory and inhibitory influences may be reflected in the desynchronization of the gross EEG pattern. Further work is needed to elucidate the functional significance of the cortical activation pattern.

Habituation

In our discussion of the orienting response and the cortical arousal pattern we noted that these responses disappear rapidly with repeated non-reinforced presentations of the initially effective stimulus or stimulus change. The phenomenon of behavioral habituation was first observed by Pavlov (1927) and has received considerable attention from the experimental psychologists (Dodge, 1923; King, 1926) and physiologists (Voronin and Sokolov, 1960). The gradual disappearance of EEG arousal was observed by many of the early workers (Ectors, 1936; Jasper, 1937; Rheinberger and Jasper, 1937; Clark and Ward, 1945); however, little systematic research was undertaken to study this interesting phenom-

enon in detail until the developments of the 1950's made it imperative to know more about the physiological mechanisms responsible for habituation.

Habituation must be clearly differentiated from adaptation. The latter occurs after prolonged and continuous stimulation of a sensory receptor or sensory pathway and represents exhaustion or fatigue of the neural mechanism. Habituation, on the other hand, occurs with widely spaced presentations of even very weak stimuli and does not represent a breakdown of receptor or transmitter function. Rather, the sensory mechanisms seem to be actively inhibited by some central process which is itself subject to extinction or "disinhibition." The organism appears to learn not to respond or not to transmit sensory information which has been without significance or consequence in the past. This aspect of habituation makes it particularly interesting in the present context: habituation may represent a simple learning process that may serve as a model for more complex situations (see Figure 12.20).

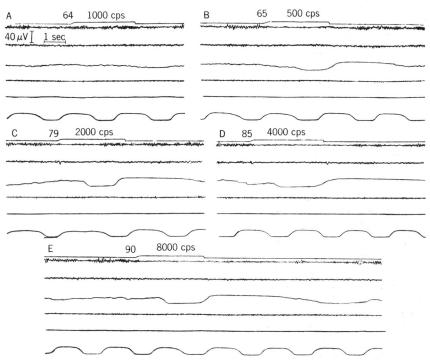

Fig. 12.20 Selective habituation of different components of the orienting response to sound (70 db). In A to E, from top to bottom: signal for sound, occipital EEG, EEG of motor region, SGR, EMG, eye movements, and respiration. The first number is the number of stimulations; the second is the frequency of tone. A, habituated to 1000 cps; no orienting reflex. B, same intensity but the change to 500 cps produces generalized orienting in the form of EEG depression and SGR. C, 2000 cps produces a slight orienting reaction. D, 4000 cps evokes prolonged EEG depression and SGR. E, 8000 cps gives prolonged generalized orienting reaction (EEG depression, SGR, and change of respiration). (From Sokolov, 1960.)

Habituation of the gross orienting response is selective and specific. A stimulus differing only slightly from one that has previously been habituated elicits a complete orienting response (Sharpless and Jasper, 1956; Roger et al., 1958). The effects of habituation generalize to the extent that fewer trials are required to habituate the orienting response to the second stimulus (Beck et al., 1958). As mentioned earlier, stimuli of some sensory modalities produce more intense and prolonged orienting responses. This "preferential arousal value" is also reflected in the resistance of these responses to extinction or habituation. In man, it is difficult, if not impossible, to achieve complete habituation of the EEG response to visual stimuli; other species tend to show similar, selective resistance to habituation, although other sensory modalities may be involved. The dimension of meaning plays a very important role in habituation, for the response to stimuli that serve as conditioned stimuli does not habituate so long as reinforcement is provided. Several studies have shown that the orienting response shows greater resistance to extinction after withdrawal of the reinforcement than the overt CR itself. We shall return to this subject in our discussion of the electrophysiological correlates of habituation.

Habituation of electrophysiological responses. The alpha block. The desynchronization of the cortical EEG produced by the initial presentations of a novel stimulus tends to shorten and gradually disappear completely with repeated nonreinforced stimulus presentations. The disappearance is most rapid in sensory modalities that show only partial arousal responses. There is some controversy in the literature about the completeness of the habituation that can be obtained in such primary modalities as vision in man and audition in the cat. Several investigators (Morrell, 1958; Morrell and Morrell, 1960; Voronin and Sokolov, 1960) have been unable to observe habituation of the localized (occipital) components of the desynchronization response to light in man. Morrell (1958) has suggested that specific sensory modalities may be particularly resistant to habituation for phylogenetic reasons. Others (Gastaut et al., 1957; Rusinov and Smirnov, 1957b) have reported complete habituation of the EEG response to light, although many more trials were needed than with stimuli of other modalities.

The rapidity and completeness of habituation appear to be, at least in part, a function of stimulus complexity. Whereas the alpha block to single-click stimuli disappears rapidly (within six trials in one experiment), many more trials (about 40 in the same study) are needed to habituate the generalized desynchronization response to a pure tone, and a complex stimulus compound such as a rapidly changing tone requires even more stimulus presentations (Sharpless and Jasper, 1956; Garcia-Austt et al., 1961). An orderly process can be observed which includes a gradual shortening of the desynchronization response accompanied by an increase in the response latency from about 0.2 to 20.0 sec. The effects of habituation generalize much like overt responses to sensory stimuli. Sharpless and Jasper (1956), for instance, found that a 600-cps tone failed to elicit desynchronization responses following the habituation of a 500-cps stimulus, but tones of 100 or 1000 cps continued to produce behavioral orienting as well as alpha blocking. The effects of previous habituation were noticeable, however, in the form of increased response latencies and a deceased duration of the alpha block.

The generalization of habituation has been studied in greater detail by Apelbaum et al. (1960). In these studies cats were completely habituated to a 200-cps tone at 92 db. The generalization gradient of habituation was assessed by measuring the resistance to habituation of responses to test stimuli ranging from 202 to 500 cps. Cats that had not previously been habituated to the 200-cps stimulus habituated to the sequence of test tones in a random order. Fewer trials were needed to habituate the experimental animals, and the arousal response disappeared most rapidly to stimuli similar to the 200-cps tone. The effect diminished in a lawful fashion with increasing distance from the habituated stimulus (see Figures 12.21 and 12.22).

A very interesting example of generalization has been reported by Rusinov and Smirnov (1957a, b). These workers habituated the cortical arousal response to a group of words that had similar meanings but different sounds. When words of different meaning were subsequently introduced, complete and generalized cortical desynchronization and no evidence of habituation were observed. This apparently selective generalization along the dimension of meaning was interpreted to suggest corticofugal influences on the habituation process. We shall return to this problem in a moment.

An interesting variation of the generalization experiment has been reported by Sokolov (1955). In these studies a pinpoint light was focused on

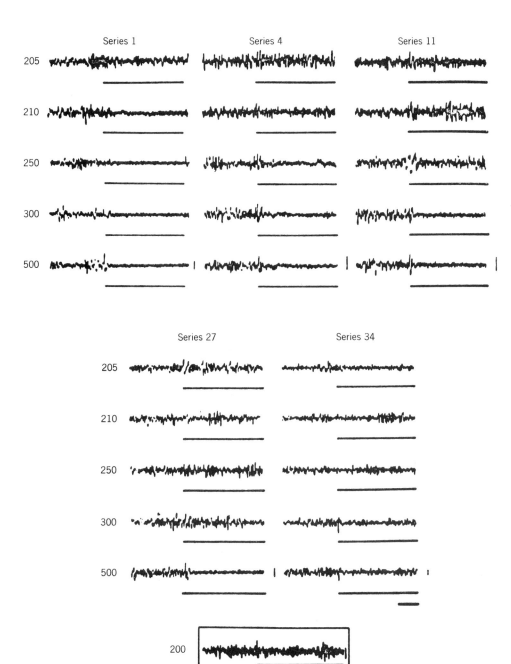

Fig. 12.21 Discrimination of EEG arousal. The animal was habituated to a basic (200-cps) tone. As successive series were applied in the course of secondary habituation, the borderline tone (separating negative from positive pitches) passed from its initial value at 210 (series 1) through 250 (series 4), 300 (series 11), and 500 cps (series 27); eventually total ineffectiveness was achieved (series 34). (From Apelbaum et al., 1960.)

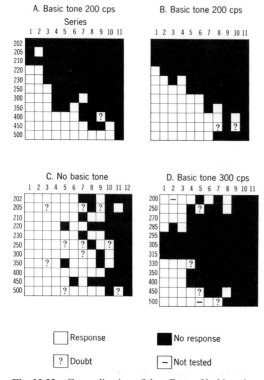

Response ☐   No response ■

? Doubt   — Not tested

Fig. 12.22 Generalization of the effects of habituation. Distribution of EEG arousal responses to auditory test stimuli differing only slightly from a basic tone which no longer elicited an arousal response. Vertical scales represent the frequency (cps) of the test stimuli. Horizontal scales represent repeated tests. (From Apelbaum et al., 1960.)

a spot on the subject's retina. The arousal response to this stimulus was habituated. Sokolov demonstrated a lawful gradient of spatial generalization by showing that the likelihood of an arousal response increased directly as a function of the distance from the previously stimulated spot. At 5° from the original point of stimulation, complete generalization was observed. Stimulation of a spot 10° from the first point produced intermittent and weak activation responses. Little or no generalization was found at a point 15° from the test spot.

Several recent studies have shown that habituation of the cortical arousal reaction is highly selective with respect to stimulus patterns as well as frequency and amplitude. John and Killam (1960a) reported that the habituation to a flashing light was specific to the flicker frequency. Glickman and Feldman (1960) found that the habituation of the cortical arousal response to

repetitive electrical stimulation of the midbrain reticular formation was specific to the frequency of the central stimulus.

The effects of habituation are prolonged, although apparently not permanent. Depending on the number of nonreinforced stimulus presentations, some localized desynchronization usually returns within hours of the habituation experiment. Complete, generalized alpha blocking reappears typically within days of the last trial.

It has been suggested that two components of the cortical response to novel stimuli that may respond differentially to habituation can be distinguished. Sharpless and Jasper (1956) differentiate between a short (a few seconds at most) "phasic" response which occurs during and immediately after the presentation of a stimulus and tends to be very resistant to habituation and a more prolonged tonic reaction which may last several minutes and habituates rapidly. The phasic response reappears after brief rest periods, whereas habituation of the tonic responses tends to be more permanent. Sokolov (1960) has discussed a related observation. When an intermittent light flickering at 18 cps was first presented, the expected alpha blocking and photic driving of the occipital rhythm were observed. The frequency-specific response habituated rapidly and disappeared completely long before alpha blocking was habituated.

Sharpless and Jasper (1956) suggested that the phasic response may represent an activation of the nonspecific thalamic projection system which is closely related to the classical sensory pathways; the tonic response, on the other hand, may represent a more general influence of the midbrain reticular formation. To test this hypothesis, they cut the brachia of the inferior colliculi in three cats before the habituation experiment. This procedure eliminates the auditory pathways to the cortex but does not affect the sensory input to the reticular formation. The animals showed, as predicted, no phasic response to auditory stimuli. Moreover, very intense sounds were needed to elicit any cortical response at all, and habituation, once achieved, tended to be more general than in normal cats. These animals also showed a very interesting, although difficult to interpret, "summation" phenomenon. When the stimuli were repeated every 30 sec, no cortical arousal could be observed on the first or second presentation, but every third or fourth stimulus presentation elicited generalized cortical arousal.

Sharpless and Jasper proposed that the disappearance of the phasic response in these animals indicated that either the cortex or the non-specific thalamic projection systems are responsible for this response. A further experiment was devised to distinguish between these alternatives. In several cats the auditory cortex was removed bilaterally before habituation, and complete phasic and tonic responses were observed post-operatively. These findings support the author's hypothesis; however, the experiments are perhaps not as conclusive as we might wish because it is extremely difficult to remove all the auditory cortex in the cat.

Other experimenters (Caspers et al., 1958) reported that the thalamic and upper mesencephalic reticular formation did not show recordable EEG changes during habituation, whereas a clear decrease in amplitude was observed in the lower mesencephalic portion of this system. The criterion of habituation in these experiments (disappearance of the generalized cortical activation response to a simple tone) unfortunately does not permit conclusions about the proposed participation of the thalamic mechanisms in the phasic portion of the arousal response.

Caspers' findings conflict with the report of Sharpless and Jasper (1956) that electrophysiological arousal responses could be recorded from the thalamic as well as the mesencephalic reticular formation, although the amplitude of these responses was much smaller than that of cortical arousal reactions. It is tempting to try to analyze the activation pattern into functionally and anatomically distinct components, but there is little direct evidence at present to suggest a clear dichotomy of response categories. It may be worthwhile to maintain an open mind with respect to the possible role of the thalamic and mesencephalic reticular formation.

One other interesting aspect of the habituated arousal response must be mentioned before we discuss evoked potential changes. We have pointed out that habituation of the orienting response must be carefully distinguished from receptor adaptation or fatigue. Perhaps the clearest argument for this distinction is the fact that disinhibition of habituation (but not of adaptation) can be demonstrated. For instance, when a puff of air is presented together with a previously habituated tone, a complete arousal reaction to the auditory stimulus returns (Sharpless and Jasper, 1956). Moreover, either an increase or decrease in the intensity of a previously habituated stimulus will again evoke the activation

pattern (Danilova, 1958; Mihalevskaya, 1958; Sokolov, 1958), ruling out a potential explanation of the disinhibition in terms of an increased excitation of reticular pathways.

Habituation must be distinguished from the response decrement which can be produced by a number of other experimental manipulations. Providing a warning signal (tone) immediately before the presentation of a stimulus (light) of another modality sharply reduces the magnitude and duration of the localized desynchronization response to the first stimulus (Wells, 1959). Requiring an immediate behavioral response also seems to interfere with the development of clear alpha blocking, at least in some situations. Gastaut et al. (1957) report, for instance, that a visual stimulus fails to produce the characteristic blocking of the occipital alpha pattern if the subject is instructed to clench his fist whenever the light appears.

Before we turn to the subject of evoked potentials, we might briefly mention that EEG responses other than alpha blocking seem to be subject to habituation. John and Killam (1959) report that photic driving of the EEG in response to the presentation of intermittent light stimuli disappears gradually from the midbrain reticular formation and hippocampal formation with repeated stimulus presentations. This loss of the photic-driving response seems to occur more rapidly in man than in other species (Jus and Jus, 1959), in spite of the fact that desynchronization responses to light are more difficult to habituate.

Evoked potentials. The use of evoked potentials as a means of assessing cortical and subcortical excitability changes has vastly increased now that sophisticated "averaging" devices have been developed; these can sample several hundred evoked responses and cancel out the nonsystematic components of the electrical waveform so that even very small (but consistent) potentials can be clearly observed.

Averaging can be achieved in a variety of ways, ranging from the simple superposition of oscilloscope traces to the use of modern computers which algebraically add several hundred oscilloscope traces and arrive at a single composite picture which can be displayed graphically or converted into digital values. The sensitivity of the different techniques varies so widely that "complete disappearance" of the evoked response as measured by one technique may be comparable to "a significant reduction in size" as measured by another. Furthermore, an evoked potential can be analyzed into several distinct components. Several workers have reported results that are applicable only to particular components of this response. With these precautions in mind, we can look at some of the experimental work that has been done with this response.

Whenever a novel sensory stimulus is presented to an organism, a marked and clear evoked potential can be recorded from the specific sensory projection area of the stimulus modality. Smaller potential changes can be recorded from all other areas of the brain, but we shall be concerned mostly with the primary potential recorded from the sensory cortex and the classical sensory pathways. The amplitude of the evoked potential is proportional to the intensity of the stimulus, at least up to some maximum limit. The evoked response to stimuli of moderate intensity tends to decrease with repeated nonreinforced presentations of the stimulus. First to disappear is the generalized potential which can initially be recorded from all areas of the brain. Additional trials reduce the amplitude of the potential, even in the specific sensory pathways, to the extent that sophisticated averaging devices are needed to demonstrate its continued presence.

A study by Garcia-Austt et al. (1961) demonstrates a typical situation. These workers presented a flickering light to human subjects and recorded evoked potentials with monopolar leads at C_4, T_2, and O_2 (using the international "10-20" system) with the reference electrode on the nose or mastoid. Fifteen-minute trials (2000 to 4000 flashes per trial) were presented and the responses were averaged. After 300 to 500 trials, a pronounced waxing and waning of the evoked potential and a marked decrease in response amplitude were observed. With progressing habituation, slow afterdischarges which tended to follow the frequency of the stimulus were seen. Eventually, the response disappeared from all leads except O_2, where a complex, low-amplitude waveform persisted. No habituation could be observed when very intense stimuli which elicited a maximal potential change were used. The waxing and waning of the evoked potential during habituation has been reported by several other investigators, and Morrell and Morrell (1960) have suggested that these oscillations in response amplitude follow a predictable pattern which may represent gradually changing central influences.

The progressive diminution and eventual disappearance of the response of the primary sensory mechanisms to environmental stimulation have attracted a good deal of interest, for they suggest that central mechanisms can in some way control the sensory input to the brain. The first explanation to come to mind is that these effects are nothing more than simple receptor or conductor exhaustion or fatigue, but this does not seem to be the answer. Habituation of the evoked potential can be obtained with widely spaced stimulus presentations which should have no cumulative effect on the receptor mechanism. Furthermore, disinhibition of the habituated response can be demonstrated when the intensity of the stimulus is changed slightly or when a second stimulus is added (Galambos et al., 1956). This again suggests that some mechanism actively suppresses the sensory input after nonreinforced presentations of the stimulus. A large literature has accumulated around some central questions: What portion of the brain exerts this all-important function? Where along the sensory pathways does the blocking of the sensory information take place? And, perhaps most importantly, how does this gradual inhibition develop? The answer to the last question is particularly intriguing because the inhibition may be "learned."

The work of Hernández-Peón and his collaborators as well as some recent Russian studies (Gershuni et al., 1960; Voronin and Sokolov, 1960) demonstrated conclusively that evoked responses to stimuli of all sensory modalities show habituation at all levels of the classical sensory pathways. These findings suggest (Hernández-Peón, 1960, 1961) that sensory input may be primarily inhibited at the level of the first afferent synapse. This interpretation contrasts with the position of most Russian workers (see Voronin and Sokolov, 1960), who suggest instead that sensory input can be modified at each synaptic junction (see Figure 12.23).

The theoretical positions about the origin of this inhibitory effect are similarly divergent. Most Western workers agree, on the basis of findings from electrical stimulation and lesioning experiments, that habituation and related phenomena such as facilitation depend on subcortical influences primarily from the reticular formation. The Russians, on the other hand, point out that the selectivity of habituation is often based on complex learned distinctions which cannot be made without the neocortex and insist on a predominantly cortical origin of habituation. Our present knowledge does not permit an unqualified deci-

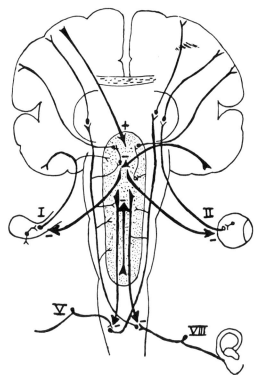

Granit (1955a) found that the electrical activity of retinal ganglion cells can be increased or decreased by electrical stimulation of the midbrain reticular formation and that similar effects can be obtained by stimulation of the visual pathway itself (at the level of the inferior colliculi) presumably because of antidromic conduction.

Galambos (1956) found that electrical stimulation of the olivocochlear bundle near the fourth ventricle, completely suppressed the auditory evoked potentials recorded from the round window of the cochlea. Because it was found that stimulation of the floor of the fourth ventricle also produced a contraction of the muscles of the inner

Fig. 12.23 Schematic representation of plastic inhibitory influences involved in habituation and extinction. Centrifugal inhibition from the upper part of the brainstem reticular system blocks afferent transmission at the olfactory bulb (I), at the retina (II), at the spinal trigeminal sensory nucleus (V), and at the cochlear nucleus (VIII). The arrows terminating in the rostral portion of the arousal system represent possible inhibitory influences coming from the limbic system and from lower levels of the reticular system itself. (From Hernández-Peón, 1960.)

sion between these alternatives. Instead, we might discuss some of the experimental results that have become available in the past decade and postpone judgment on the theoretical issues until some inconsistencies can be resolved.

The fact that the reticular formation affects sensory input is beyond doubt. One of the earliest studies in this area was the demonstration by Hagbarth and Kerr (1954) that electrical stimulation of the bulbar and midbrain reticular formation reduces the amplitude of evoked potentials throughout the somatosensory pathways. These findings have been replicated and extended (Hernández-Peón and Hagbarth, 1955; Hagbarth and Fex, 1959), and the generality of this effect has been demonstrated in many subsequent experiments.

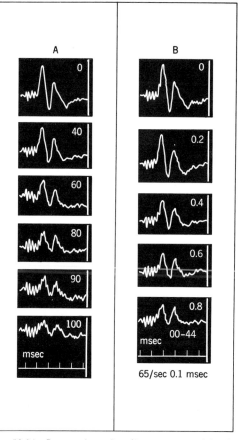

Fig. 12.24 Suppression of auditory nerve activity by shocks to the medulla. A, effect of shock frequency. (The higher the shock rates, indicated in the upper right of each trace, the greater the suppression; 100/sec is the optimum.) B, effect of shock strength. (At fixed frequency, 65/sec, the higher the shock voltage, indicated in the right corner, the greater the suppression.) (From Galambos, 1956.)

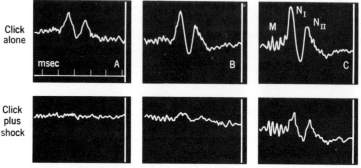

Tensor and stapedius cut; curarized; stapes disarticulated

Fig. 12.25 Suppression of auditory nerve response by shocks to the medulla. *Top*, auditory nerve activity (N_I and N_{II} in C) evoked by (A) weak and (B, C) progressively stronger clicks is abolished or reduced (bottom) when 100/sec shocks are applied to the medulla. The hair cell response (M in C) is unaffected. (From Galambos, 1956.)

ear, these experiments were repeated in curarized animals following removal of these muscles. The evoked potentials continued to be suppressed, and Galambos concluded that stimulation of the olivocochlear bundle produces a direct centrifugal inhibition of the receptor function or transmission at the first synapse; this reaction might also be responsible for the phenomenon of habituation (see Figures 12.24, 12.25, 12.26).

A subsequent experiment by Hugelin et al. (1960) suggests that the muscles of the inner ear do in fact play some role in the control of auditory input. These workers replicated Galambos' basic finding that electrical stimulation of the midbrain reduces the amplitude of auditory evoked poten-

tials at the round window, the dorsal cochlear nucleus, and geniculate bodies. However, the cochlear output was reduced only very little when the inner-ear muscles were removed, and no change in the evoked responses of the dorsal cochlear nucleus or the geniculate bodies could be seen. When the muscles of only one ear were removed, bilateral reticular stimulation reduced the evoked potentials at the intact ear but had little or no effect on the electrical activity of the other. Hugelin et al. concluded that the inhibition or reduction of the evoked potential was caused primarily, if not exclusively, by the action of the inner-ear muscles.

This interpretation does not seem to apply to

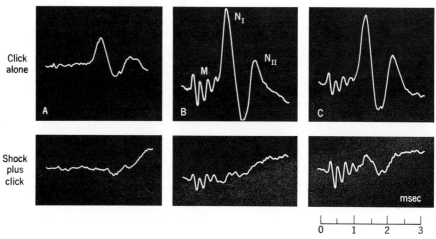

Fig. 12.26 Suppression of auditory nerve activity by single shocks to the medulla. The N_I and N_{II} components are abolished (bottom) when shock precedes click by 8 msec. When the stapedius muscle is cut, the effect disappears. (From Galambos, 1956.)

the phenomenon of habituation, for Moushegian et al. (1961) found that curarized animals show habituation in spite of complete bilateral transection of the inner-ear muscles. Disinhibition of the evoked potentials could also be obtained in these animals by pairing the auditory stimulus with a puff of air to the face.

Covian et al. (1961) found that the cortical evoked response to tactile stimulation disappeared completely when the sensory stimulus was preceded by relatively strong electrical stimulation of the midbrain reticular formation. The negative component of the evoked potential disappeared when the intensity of the reticular stimulation was much lower.

These experiments should not be interpreted to suggest that the reticular influence is necessarily inhibitory or that the reticular formation as a whole is responsible for habituation. Hernández-Peón et al. (1957a, 1958, 1960a, c) report that electrical stimulation of the midbrain reticular formation produces a reappearance of previously habituated evoked responses in the olfactory bulb. Fuster (1957) has reported behavioral data which suggest that reticular stimulation may produce facilitatory effects with respect to sensory perception. Monkeys were trained to discriminate between two solid objects; speed of choice was not a factor. After the animals reached criterion, the situation was changed so that the objects were visible for only a fraction of a second. Performance fell to near-chance levels. The percentage of correct responses increased significantly when the mesencephalic reticular formation was electrically stimulated just before the presentation of the objects.

Very interesting differential effects have also been observed following lesions in the reticular formation. Hernández-Peón and his associates (1957c) found that previously habituated responses to auditory stimuli reappeared at the dorsal cochlear nucleus following lesions in the mesencephalic tegmentum. Brust-Carmona (1958) similarly found that the habituation of post-rotatory nystagmus was reversed by lesions in the pontine reticular formation and could not be re-established postoperatively. However, Hernández-Peón et al. (1958) observed that similar lesions neither abolished nor prevented the habituation of evoked responses to olfactory stimuli and suggested (1960c) that different levels of the reticular formation might control different sensory modalities.

Such a conclusion is generally supported by more drastic ablation studies. Palestini and Lifschitz (1961) reported that transections of the brainstem at the midpontine level produced continuous cortical activation, a facilitation of visual and auditory evoked potentials, and a reappearance of previously habituated evoked responses. When the brainstem was transected at a slightly more rostral level, the animals appeared somnolent and showed reduced evoked responses that habituated almost immediately. Transections below the midpontine level had no effect on the course of habituation (see Figures 12.27 and 12.28).

A particularly interesting experiment has been reported by Hernández-Peón and Brust-Carmona (1961). Using electrical stimulation of the belly, these workers found that the evoked responses from upper thoracic segments of the spinal cord habituated in decorticated, decerebrated, and even spinal (transection at C2) animals. These results confirm an earlier report (Prosser and Hunter,

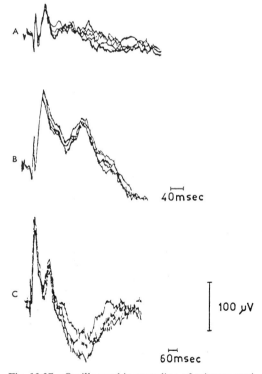

Fig. 12.27 Oscillographic recording of primary cortical photic responses. Stimulus: flash 1/sec. Five responses in each trace. A, cat unanesthetized and dark-adapted; B, the same cat after midpontine section (amplification and sweep rate as in A); C, same condition as in B, but with the sweep rate slowed to show the last deflection. (From Palestini and Lifschitz, 1961.)

Habituation

Normal Cat
1st flashes

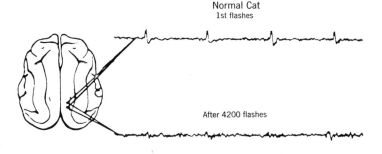

After 4200 flashes

Pretrigeminal Cat
1st flashes

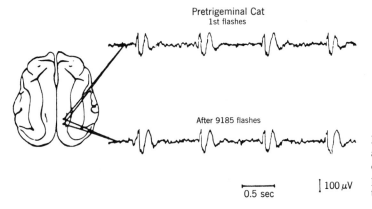

After 9185 flashes

0.5 sec

] 100 µV

Fig. 12.28 Lack of habituation and potentiation of the primary cortical evoked potential after midpontine transection. (From Palestini and Lifschitz, 1961.)

1936) that spinal flexor reflexes gradually disappear with repeated elicitations, and suggest that even the lowest portions of the reticular formation can exert an inhibitory effect on sensory transmission. If habituation is, in fact, a simple form of learned behavior, these findings may indicate that learning can take place in the spinal animal.

We have established that transmission in all sensory systems is affected by the reticular formation, and that different levels of this nonspecific system affect different sensory modalities. The topic of our discussion, habituation, is presumably directly related to these inhibitory influences, but it remains to be seen just where the reticular formation inhibits the sensory input. It has already been mentioned that evoked potentials gradually disappear from all levels of the classical sensory pathways, and it should be added that the evoked responses decrease or disappear first at the cortex, then at the next lower sensory relay nucleus, and finally at the sensory receptor itself.

Hernández-Peón et al. (1956a, 1958) found, for

example, that the evoked responses to photic stimulation diminished markedly at the cortical projection area and thalamic relay nuclei, whereas there was absolutely no change in the evoked potential from the optic tract. Lifschitz (1960) similarly reported that the evoked responses to auditory stimuli disappeared from the cortex before diminishing at the cochlear nuclei. Gershuni et al. (1960) found that in the course of habituation evoked responses to clicks disappeared completely from the cortical leads, were greatly diminished at the mesencephalic leads, and showed least habituation at the round window. Hernández-Peón and his co-workers (1958) have reported a similar sequence for the evoked responses to tactile stimulation. These findings have been interpreted to suggest that the reticular formation may exert inhibitory effects at all levels of the sensory system and that higher levels show the cumulative effects of inhibitory influences at several synapses (see Figure 12.29).

If the reticular formation is causally related to the control of sensory input, we might expect to

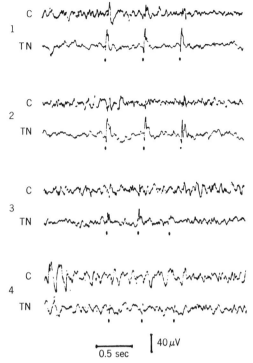

	40 μV
0.5 sec	

Fig. 12.29 Potentials evoked by tactile stimuli (weak electrical pulses 0.1 msec duration) applied to the face of a freely moving cat. Simultaneous records from the sensory-motor cortex (C) and from the spinal fifth sensory nucleus (TN). The cortical potentials (1) disappeared earlier (2) than the bulbar potentials. (3). Habituation at the bulbar and cortical levels persisted during physiological sleep (4). (From Hernández-Peón, 1960.)

see noticeable changes in the electrical activity of this system in the course of habituation. This, unfortunately, has not yet been demonstrated. Lifschitz (1960) reported that evoked potentials can be recorded from the reticular formation following long latencies, but these responses habituated much more rapidly (often within four to six stimulus presentations) than those recorded from the classical sensory pathways. The potentials evoked from the reticular formation were pharmacologically distinct from those of the sensory system; the former are facilitated by chloralose and inhibited by barbiturates.

Huttenlocher (1960) described a very different reticular response pattern which takes the form of slow waves of 50- to 100-msec duration and apparently fails to habituate. Huttenlocher's results are, unfortunately, difficult to interpret because he obtained only incomplete habituation at the cortical level.

We can be fairly certain at this time that habituation is related to inhibitory influences from the reticular formation. Not so clear is whether this inhibitory effect develops in the reticular formation itself merely as a function of repeated nonreinforced stimulation or whether the reticular formation is, in turn, controlled by cortical influences. The Russian workers (see Voronin and Sokolov, 1960) argue cogently that the selective inhibition of nonreinforced sensory input can occur only if each stimulus presentation leaves a trace somewhere in the nervous system; such a "trace" is somehow strengthened by repeated presentations of the same stimulus until it is strong enough to completely inhibit the specific sensory input.

In many situations this selectivity requires very difficult discriminations, for different receptors may be stimulated on different occasions. Thus, the response to a small black dot may habituate rapidly, although the same retinal receptors are never stimulated more than once, suggesting that something like concept formation may be involved in this apparently simple case of habituation. Similarly, we can imagine situations in which a particular stimulus occurs as part of a complex stimulus compound. The response to such a stimulus could presumably be habituated selectively, so that a complete response would again be elicited if the stimulus occurred out of context.

We can argue that habituation indicates that an organism has learned not to respond to a nonreinforced stimulus; this would seem to be a direct analog to the conventional learning situation in which the organism learns to respond to a specific stimulus because it is reinforced in some manner. This possibility raises interesting problems for the psychologist, who assumes that a memory trace is established because of the effects of reinforcement. It does not by itself require the participation of cortical mechanisms, since it is well known that relatively complex tasks can be learned by decorticated animals. However, when we return to the problem of selectivity, some cortical guidance of the reticular influence appears almost inescapable.

Most American workers have argued against a *necessary* contribution of neocortical mechanisms to habituation (as well as to other learning phenomena) on the grounds that habituation can be obtained quite readily in decorticated, decerebrated, and even spinal animals (Hernández-Peón et al., 1958, 1960a, b, c; Hernández-Peón and Brust-Carmona, 1961). This conservative position is probably correct, but it tells us nothing about a possible contribution of the cortical mechanisms in the intact animal.

That the neocortex normally regulates some aspects of the reticular formation is suggested by a number of experiments. Rusinov and Smirnov (1957a) reported that human subjects showed complete habituation to words with similar meanings (but different sounds), but exhibited immediate and complete disinhibition as soon as a word with different meaning (but similar sound) was presented. Voronin and Sokolov (1960) habituated the generalized and localized orienting response to a complex stimulus compound consisting of tactile, visual, and auditory stimuli; subsequent presentations of only one of the three stimuli produced electrophysiological changes in the cortical projection areas of the missing stimuli. Jouvet (1961) found that cortical, mesencephalic, and cochlear evoked potentials persisted undiminished after the EEG arousal pattern had completely habituated, and that complete habituation was not obtainable in neodecorticated animals. Jouvet concluded that habituation represents an inhibitory effect on the reticular formation by the cortex. Similar hypotheses have been advanced by most Russian workers, in spite of the fact that this position cannot account for the persistence of habituation, at least with respect to evoked potentials, in the decorticated animal. Unless we assume that the habituation of the EEG responses to novel stimulation depends on basically different neural mechanisms than those responsible for the habituation of the evoked potential response, this view appears untenable at present.

Before we leave the interesting topic of habituation, two closely related phenomena should be mentioned. The first of these, dishabituation, refers to a return of the previously habituated evoked response following certain changes in the environment. Several investigators have reported that evoked responses show something like spontaneous recovery after prolonged periods of rest. Previously habituated evoked responses reappear, but they tend to rehabituate rapidly unless reinforcement is introduced. This spontaneous recovery has been demonstrated in the auditory (Hernández-Peón et al., 1957a) and olfactory systems (Hernández-Peón et al., 1957b, 1958). A stimulus that no longer elicits evoked responses immediately reacquires this ability if it is preceded by a novel stimulus (Hernández-Peón et al., 1956a, b, 1957a, b, 1958) or if it is followed by a noxious UCS (Galambos, 1956; Hernández-Peón

et al., 1957b, 1958). Dishabituation can also be obtained by barbiturate anesthesia (Hernández-Peón et al., 1957a, b, 1958; Hernández-Peón and Burst-Carmona, 1961) and by lesions in the mesencephalic tegmentum (Hernández-Peón et al., 1957a, b, 1958). A particularly interesting example of dishabituation has been reported by Hagbarth and Kugelberg (1958), who found that a previously habituated abdominal skin reflex to tactile stimulation could again be elicited by stimulation of neighboring skin receptors. Adaptation of the receptors can presumably be ruled out in these experiments because relatively long intertrial intervals were used; Hagbarth and Kugelberg concluded that habituation may take place in the internuncial neurons of the spinal cord (see Figure 12.30).

Closely related to habituation is the phenomenon of "attention" and "distraction." Electrophysiologically, this phenomenon refers to a reduction or disappearance of evoked responses to one stimulus while the animal reorients or shifts his attention to a novel stimulus. This suppression of the evoked response occurs only during EEG arousal and tends to be very short-lived unless the novel stimulus serves as a cue (CS) for noxious or appetitive stimulation. Thus, if one records evoked responses to click stimuli from any level of the auditory pathways of a cat and then suddenly presents a mouse, the auditory evoked potentials diminish or disappear while the cat watches the mouse. Evoked potentials reappear in the auditory system as soon as the distracting stimulus is removed.

The classic experiment in this area was done by Hernández-Peón et al. (1956b), who reported that evoked responses to click stimuli disappeared during the presentation of visual, olfactory, or tactile stimuli. The generality of this temporary inhibition has been established in many subsequent studies which have extended the initial findings to the visual (Hernández-Peón et al., 1957b) and olfactory (Palestini et al., 1959) systems, as well as to the skin senses (Brust-Carmona and Hernández-Peón, 1959; Palestini et al., 1959; Hernández-Peón et al., 1961a, b, c).

In all these experiments the disappearance of the evoked potential is assumed to be in some way related to the fact that the animal is paying attention to the novel stimulus and ignoring the other. Some experiments with human subjects support this interpretation. Hernández-Peón and Donoso (1959) recorded evoked potentials to brief flashes of light from the visual cortex of human subjects.

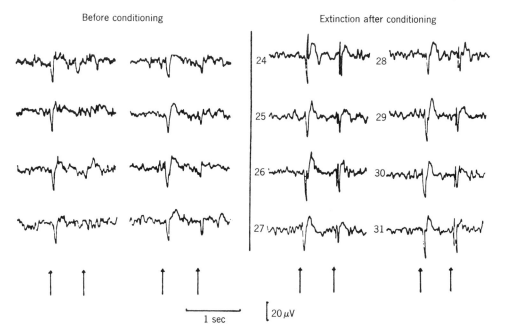

Fig. 12.30 Auditory potentials from the mesencephalic reticular formation evoked by paired clicks. The potentials on the left column were obtained before associating the clicks with unavoidable electric shock. The potentials on the right column were obtained after conditioning and during an experimental stage of nonreinforcement. The numbers correspond to the trials after the last electric shock. (From Hernández-Peón, 1960.)

The evoked potentials were greatly reduced when the subjects were distracted by arithmetic problems, and the inhibition was stronger with more difficult problems. Garcia-Austt et al. (1961) used a similar situation to study this phenomenon in greater detail. Evoked responses to visual stimulation increased when the subjects were asked to pay attention to the light source or to count the number of flashes per second. A marked reduction (particularly in cortical areas other than the visual cortex) was observed when the subjects were asked to perform other tasks during the stimulation. Although some of the observed inhibition may have occurred because the sensory receptors were less exposed to the stimulation during the performance of the distracting tasks, this cannot be the whole explanation.

Perhaps the most interesting aspect of this temporary inhibition of the evoked response is that it does not seem to depend on cortical mechanisms. Hernández-Peón (1961) found that the introduction of novel stimuli produced a marked diminution of subcortically recorded evoked potentials in decorticated cats, and that destruction of the specific auditory pathways at the mesencephalic level similarly did not interfere with the inhibitory

effect. Galambos and Sheatz (1962) have observed similar results in cats and monkeys whose auditory pathways were transected just rostral to the inferior colliculi. The animals were curarized before the experiment to rule out a direct muscular effect. These findings suggest that the inhibitory effects of novel stimulation (i.e., the attention phenomenon) may be mediated, like habituation itself, by aspects of the reticular formation.

Summary. Behavioral and electroencephalographic orienting responses as well as the evoked potentials of the specific sensory pathways and cortical projection areas gradually diminish and eventually disappear with repeated nonreinforced presentations of all but very strong or noxious stimuli. This process of habituation represents an active inhibition of specific sensory input rather than a breakdown of receptor or transmitter function. Habituation tends to be highly specific, although some generalization to similar stimuli can be demonstrated.

Habituation of the cortical arousal response follows a lawful pattern. Relatively few stimulus presentations are required to produce a disappearance of the generalized desynchronization response. The remaining response of the specific cortical projection areas then shortens, and its latency increases. The rapidity and completeness of habituation is a function of sensory modality, stimulus intensity, and stimulus complexity. The effects of habituation are prolonged but not permanent. The localized desynchronization response consists of a brief phasic component which is very resistant to habituation and may reflect activation of the nonspecific thalamic projection system, and a more prolonged tonic reaction which habituates readily and may represent an influence of the midbrain reticular formation.

The evoked response to sensory stimuli of moderate intensity tends to decrease and eventually disappear with repeated nonreinforced stimulus presentations. First to disappear is the generalized potential which can initially be recorded from all parts of the brain. Next, the response of the specific cortical projection area diminishes, followed by the evoked responses of the higher relay nuclei of the sensory pathways. The evoked potentials remain longest and strongest at the receptor or the first synapse.

This gradual inhibition of the sensory mechanisms is not caused by receptor adaptation but seems to represent an active suppression of the sensory pathways. Although the question is not yet completely resolved, it appears that the inhibitory influences originate in the reticular formation of the brainstem and affect sensory pathways at all levels of the brain. Some information suggests that different portions of the reticular formation may serve this suppressive function for different sensory modalities, and that even the spinal portion of this system can affect somatosensory input.

The reticular influences have been demonstrated in decorticated, decerebrated, and even spinal animals, suggesting that cortical regulation is not essential. Many experiments have, however, indicated that the cortex, when present, may influence and control the course of habituation, presumably via a direct corticofugal influence on the various components of the reticular formation. This cortical influence is perhaps clearest for such phenomena as generalization of habituation along a continuum of meaning in man; cortical influences are also indicated by the fact that stimuli which serve as cues (CS) for appetitive or noxious events (UCS) do not seem to lose their ability to elicit full evoked responses (as well as behavioral and EEG orienting) in spite of repeated and even massed presentations.

The effects of habituation are prolonged but not permanent. Dishabituation (i.e., a reappearance of the evoked responses at all levels of the sensory pathways and cortical areas) has been observed following (1) a period of rest, (2) the presentation of a novel stimulus, (3) repeated pairings with a noxious unconditioned stimulus, (4) lesions in the mesencephalic tegmentum, and (5) barbiturate anesthesia.

If the animal's attention is distracted by the simultaneous presentation of a novel stimulus, a temporary diminution or disappearance of the evoked response to most simple sensory stimuli can be observed. Although we have only inferential evidence for this conclusion, it is generally assumed that the momentary suppression of specific sensory input is closely related to the phenomenon of habituation.

Electrophysiological Changes during Conditioning

EEG changes. If the electrical activity of the brain as recorded by the electroencephalogram bears some lawful relationship to neural processes, specific local EEG changes should occur during the process of connection formation or learning.

Many electrophysiological studies (Chow, 1961; Chow et al., 1957; Gastaut, 1957, 1958a, b; Gastaut et al., 1957; Jouvet et al., 1956a, b; Jouvet and Hernández-Peón, 1957; Morrell and Jasper, 1956; Yoshii, 1957) have observed that the previously habituated cortical desynchronization response to the CS is disinhibited as soon as the stimulus is paired with a noxious or appetitive UCS. Conditioned cortical desynchronization appears before overt conditioned responses can be observed and extinguishes less rapidly than peripheral responses when the reinforcement is withheld (Iwama, 1950; Iwama and Abe, 1953; Motokawa, 1949; Motokawa and Huzimori, 1949; Segundo et al., 1959). The CS elicits generalized desynchronization in all areas of the cortex during the initial stages of conditioning. This response becomes localized in the motor cortex as conditioning proceeds and as overt conditioned responses begin to appear. Roger et al. (1958) found that conditioning was retarded when the electrocortical response to the CS was thoroughly habituated before the beginning of conditioning (see Figures 12.31 and 12.32).

Rabinovitch (1958) analyzed the activity of individual cortical layers in the motor cortex and the sensory projection area of the CS during conditioning. He reported that the initial CS-UCS

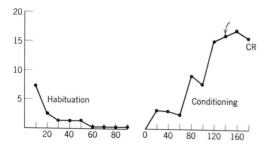

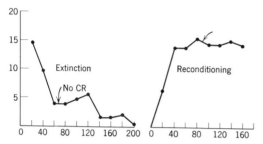

Fig. 12.31 Number of EEG arousal reactions (ordinate) to a tonal CS per block of 10 to 20 presentations (abscissa) for a cat. The first appearance of a flexion CR in the course of training and retraining, or its full disappearance during extinction, is noted by the arrows. (From Doty, 1958.)

pairings increased the amplitude and frequency of the electrical activity of all cortical layers in the motor and sensory cortices. As the overt motor response began to appear, these electrophysiological responses became briefer and tended to occur only in layer four of the auditory cortex and layer five of the motor cortex. During the execution of the motor response itself, slow (2 to 3 cps) potentials were observed in layer two of the motor cortex. These potentials were interpreted as being directly related to some inhibitory process, since CS presentations during the presence of such slow waves failed to produce conditioned responses even in well-trained animals.

We cannot conclude from these findings that the correlation between cortical desynchronization and specific phases of the learning process is descriptive of a causal relationship. Several investigators (Key and Bradley, 1959; Beck et al., 1958) have shown that behavioral conditioning can be elaborated in atropine- or bulbocapnine-treated animals which do not show the characteristic desynchronization response to the CS. Several studies (Milstein and Stevens, 1961; Johnson et al., 1960) have reported that highly abnormal EEG discharges induced in epileptic patients by the presentation of flickering lights failed to interfere with the acquisition or retention of verbal materials. Morrell (1961) has concluded from these observations that the gross EEG response "may not be taken as a sign of information proc-

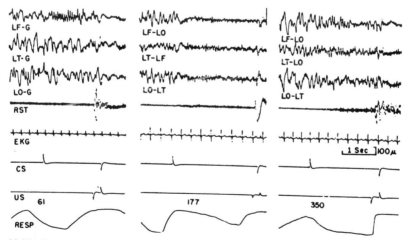

Fig. 12.32 EEG records at different stages of training. Trial 61, no evidence of conditioning. Trial 177, the fully conditioned state with both electrocortical and flexion responses (RST is the electromyogram of the right semitendinosus muscle). Trial 350, flexion CR beginning during moderately high-amplitude EEG. LF, left frontal cortex; LT, left temporal cortex; LO, left occipital cortex; G, reference electrode. (From Doty, 1958.)

essing, nor may its localization indicate the site (if it exists) of memory recording or storage" (p. 466).

In view of these considerations, we shall dispense with a detailed discussion of the many studies that have been concerned primarily with the desynchronization response. Instead, we shall briefly consider related investigations that have attempted to demonstrate a correlation between the conditioning process and other electrophysiological changes which may bear a more direct and essential relationship to the neural processes that underly learning.

Before discussing cortical slow-wave activity during conditioning, we might briefly mention Lesse's (1957a, b) frequently cited report of characteristic 40- to 50-cps discharges from the amygdaloid area of cats during avoidance learning. Lesse trained animals to avoid painful grid shock by moving from one compartment of the test apparatus to another whenever a buzzer sounded. He observed that 40- to 50-cps activity appeared in the amygdala whenever the UCS was presented and that these bursts of high-frequency, high-amplitude discharges became conditioned to the auditory CS. Since other stimuli that produced alerting and cortical arousal did not elicit similar EEG changes, Lesse concluded that the 40- to 50-cps activity might be directly related to emotional arousal which eventually becomes conditioned to the CS. A recent report by Gault and Leaton (1963) linking the 40-cps activity of the

amygdala specifically to olfactory activity has questioned this interpretation (see Figures 12.33 and 12.34).

Slow-wave activity. Many of the earlier EEG studies (Livanov and Poliakov, 1945; Motokawa, 1949; Motokawa and Huzimori, 1949; Iwama, 1950; Iwama and Abe, 1953; Morrell and Ross, 1953) noted that hypersynchronous slow waves often appeared during the CS-UCS interval, and this phenomenon has recently received considerable attention. With long CS-UCS intervals the CS initially elicits cortical as well as subcortical desynchronization which persists until the UCS has been terminated. As conditioning progresses, this desynchronization response tends to shorten and eventually give way to a brief blocking response to the CS, followed by hypersynchronous slow waves. These remain until just before the onset of the UCS, when a second brief desynchronization can be observed. The slow waves that appear during the CS-UCS interval tend to be larger and more synchronous than the alpha activity of the intertrial intervals (see Figures 12.35 and 12.36).

Several workers (see Gastaut, 1957, for a review of this position) have suggested that this EEG pattern may represent a process analogous to Pavlov's "internal inhibition." This hypothesis receives support from the observations that (1) differential stimuli (DS) that are never followed by the UCS tend to elicit slow, hypersynchronous

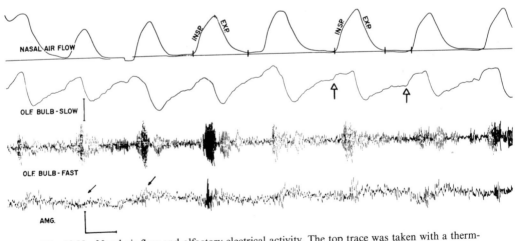

Fig. 12.33 Nasal air flow and olfactory electrical activity. The top trace was taken with a thermistor in the nare. The olfactory bulb slow record was taken with filters set to reject activity slower than 5 cps. The two solid arrows indicate points at which amygdala 40-cps activity did not accompany olfactory bulb fast activity. The open arrows indicate the portion of the olfactory slow wave which corresponds to the beginning of inspiration. Time, 1 sec; amplitude, 200 μV for Olf. Bulb-Fast and Amg., 600 μV for Olf. Bulb-Slow. (From Gault and Leaton, 1963.)

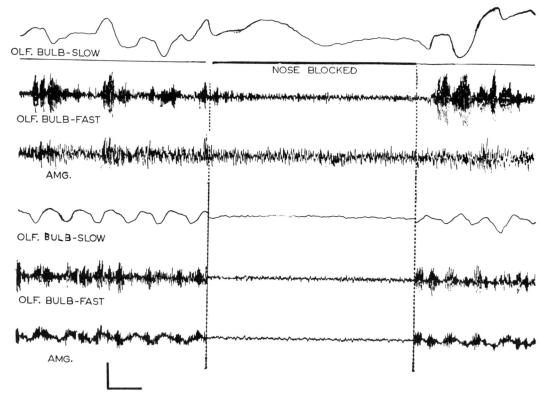

Fig. 12.34 EEG activity pattern obtained while the nose was blocked. Time, 1 sec; amplitude, 200 µV for Olf. Bulb-Fast and Amg., 600 µV for Olf. Bulb-Slow. (From Gault and Leaton, 1963.)

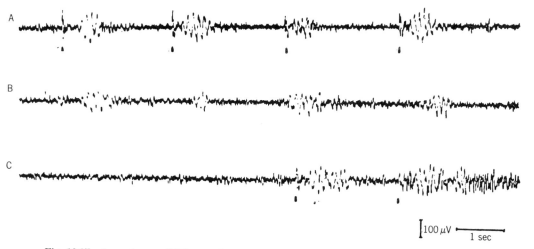

Fig. 12.35 A continuous EEG record from the visual cortex. After monotonous presentation of a great number of flashes of light at regular intervals, the evoked potentials were followed by (A) bursts of slow waves which persisted at approximately the same intervals for a few seconds immediately after interrupting (B) the photic stimulation. When the photic stimuli were presented again (C), the spindle bursts reappeared. (From Hernández-Peón, 1960.)

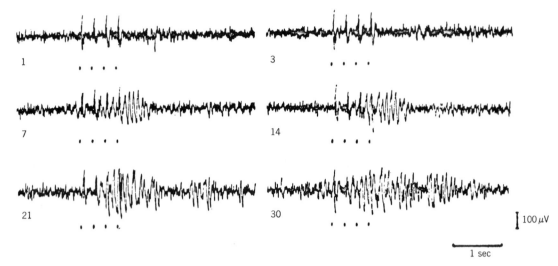

Fig. 12.36 Electrical activity from the visual cortex of a cat previously conditioned to flashes of light (four flashes at a rate of 1/sec) associated with an electric shock delivered to a leg. The numbers correspond to trials without reinforcement. During extinction the photic stimuli progressively triggered bursts of slow waves. (From Hernández-Peón, 1960.)

discharges in the differential conditioning situation; (2) the CS itself elicits a similar EEG pattern following extinction; and (3) slow waves can be recorded from many cortical areas during the final stages of conditioning when the desynchronization response to the CS has become localized in the motor areas or the specific projection areas of the UCS modality. In view of the theoretical emphasis that some workers have placed on the hypersynchronous activity, it may be worthwhile to discuss a typical experiment in some detail.

Rowland and Gluck (1960) paired an auditory CS with unavoidable shock and gradually lengthened the CS duration from 5 to 120 sec as training progressed. When a 2-min CS-UCS interval was reached, a brief cortical desynchronization was elicited at the onset of the CS; this was followed by hypersynchronous slow waves which gave way to a second desynchronization just before the onset of the UCS. An auditory DS that was never reinforced elicited only a brief desynchronization response to the stimulus onset and was followed by continuous slow-wave activity. Synchronous slow waves also appeared immediately when the DS (signaling "no shock") was presented during the desynchronization response to the CS.

Kogan (1959, 1960) has observed similar hypersynchronous responses during differential conditioning and found that cortical excitability was depressed whenever these slow waves were present. Rabinovitch (1958) has reported that synchro-

nous slow waves temporarily appear in the motor cortex during late phases of the conditioning process and that the CS fails to elicit a CR when these waves are present. Hypersynchronous slow waves also occurred occasionally in the well-trained animal and were always associated with a response failure. Morrell (1960) has shown that hypersynchrony of the outer cortical layer tends to be associated with a decrease in single-unit discharge.

All these observations support the hypothesis that inhibitory processes may be reflected in this EEG pattern. Rowland and Gluck (1960), however, have presented some interesting control data which suggest that we must be careful in generalizing from these observations. When the same stimuli that had previously been used in the defensive classical conditioning experiment were employed in appetitive conditioning, very different results were obtained. In the latter situation the CS served as a signal for "food" in a lever-pressing task and the DS indicated "no food." Here the negative stimulus reliably elicited *desynchronization* rather than the hypersynchronous slow waves seen in the classical defensive learning paradigm. These findings suggest that hypersynchrony may not be generally related to inhibitory processes as Gastaut (1957) suggests but perhaps reflects the emotional reaction to a stimulus which signals that the noxious stimulation normally presented will not occur.

A rather puzzling report has been published by

Guselnikov and Drozhennikov (1959). Using a differential conditioning paradigm, these workers found that the DS elicited hypersynchronous slow waves only during the acquisition of the differential response. Once the discrimination was well established, the DS no longer elicited the characteristic EEG pattern.

An interpretation of cortical hypersynchrony is complicated by the frequently reported (Green and Arduini, 1954; Yoshii, 1957; Grastyán, 1959; Adey et al., 1960) slow-wave activity of hippocampal origin which can be recorded from many subcortical as well as cortical leads during some phases of conditioning. The slow waves that appear in cortical leads during long CS-UCS intervals, extinction, or differential conditioning may in some fashion be related to this hippocampal activity rather than to some independent cortical process.

Although the hippocampal slow waves were originally considered to be part of the arousal response, a number of recent reports have emphasized the persistence of this EEG pattern in conditioning. Yoshii et al. (1957a) monitored the electrical activity of a large number of subcortical and cortical regions during simple and trace conditioning. A variety of auditory (buzzer, bell) or visual (steady lights) stimuli were used as a signal for foot shock. Early in conditioning desynchronization or an increase in the high-frequency activity was observed from all cortical and subcortical leads. As conditioning progressed, however, slow (5-cps) waves began to dominate the electrical activity of many subcortical leads, and this activity tended to persist throughout the conditioning experiment.

Grastyán et al. (1959) observed similar slow waves in the hippocampus and midbrain reticular formation during both appetitive (the animals were trained to climb to a platform to obtain food from a feeder) and defensive (shuttle box avoidance) learning. Both the hippocampus and reticular formation showed a marked desynchronization during the early stages of conditioning. The slow waves appeared only when behavioral conditioned responses began to be made. No correlation between successful performance and the presence of the EEG response was reported, and the slow waves diminished again and eventually disappeared completely as the behavioral response became well established. Slow waves occurred again during differential conditioning (the negative stimulus continued to elicit this pattern

even after the differential learning was well established) and extinction.

Adey et al. (1960) observed 5.5- to 6.5-cps slow waves in the entorhinal cortex and dorsal hippocampus during the acquisition of a T-maze habit which appeared to be related to the performance of the approach response. As soon as the animal left the start box, slow waves appeared, reached a maximum at the goal, and subsided rapidly once the animal had been reinforced. In a subsequent study Adey et al. recorded hippocampal activity during delayed-approach learning. The animals were allowed to watch while food was being placed under a can, but they could not reach the food until a small bridge between them and the reward was lowered. During the delay period, 3.5- to 4.5-cps activity appeared in the hippocampus which gave way to 5- to 6-cps waves during the approach response. When reward was withheld (extinction), the hippocampal activity slowed to 3 to 4 cps, even during approaches to the goal. A cross-correlational analysis showed that the hippocampal activity led that of the entorhinal cortex during acquisition, but this phase relationship was reversed when the behavioral response was well established.

Responses to repetitive stimuli. Many recent studies have used repetitive conditioned stimuli in order to identify anatomical structures that respond to conditioned stimuli during different phases of the learning process.

One of the earliest studies to use periodic stimuli as tracers of neural activity was reported by Livanov and Poliakov (1945). The UCS in their experiment was repetitive electrical stimulation of the skin, and the CS was a light which flickered at the same rate (3 cps) as the UCS. It was noted that 3-cps driving of the cortical EEG appeared after only a few CS-UCS pairings during the CS presentation as well as during the intertrial intervals. When the behavioral CR (leg flexion) became well established, the spontaneous repetitive rhythms disappeared from the intertrial periods but occurred reliably when the CS was presented. Perhaps the most interesting aspect of this study is the observation that frequency-specific activity was most pronounced in the visual cortex during the early stages of conditioning but later became localized primarily in the motor cortex which had shown little or no photic driving during the initial CS-UCS presentations. Majkowski (1959) has reported similar findings.

Livanov et al. (1951) extended the earlier findings by demonstrating that comparable results could be obtained by pairing a visual CS with direct electrical stimulation of the motor cortex. A flickering CS that was paired repeatedly with isorhythmic electrical stimulation of the motor cortex came to elicit the same motor response (leg flexion) as the UCS. Jasper and Majkowski (cited by Morrell, 1961) have replicated these observations, noting that the CR tends to be repeated at or near the CS frequency.

Chow et al. (1957) reported an interesting combination of conventional learning and electrocortical (sensory-sensory) conditioning. They established unilateral epileptogenic foci in the occipital cortex by spraying ethyl chloride through a small opening in the skull to facilitate the development of frequency-specific responses in the visual projection areas. The animals were then trained on a shuttle box avoidance task to a criterion of 90% correct responses. The CS in this study was a flashing light, and photic driving at the CS frequency nearly always preceded the avoidance response (see Figure 12.37).

In the second stage of the experiment, the animals were exposed to repeated pairings of the flickering visual stimulus with a previously neutral tone until the tone by itself elicited localized desynchronization or frequency-specific discharges from the occipital cortex. The cats were then returned to the avoidance situation, and the tone was used as the CS for shock. Although it elicited photic driving at or near the frequency of the visual stimulus (which had previously been the CS for the avoidance task) on a significant number of trials (24 out of 35), the tone never elicited a behavioral avoidance response. A retest with the visual CS produced correct responses on 86% of the trials (see Figure 12.38).

These findings are frequently cited as evidence against the hypothesis that frequency-specific repetitive responses carry information essential to the conditioning process. However, Chow's findings demonstrate only that the presence of frequency-specific activity is not a sufficient condition for learning or the performance of a learned response; they do not show that such activity may not be an essential aspect of the learning process. Chow et al. (1957) unfortunately did not test the interesting prediction that acquisition of the behavioral CR to the tone might be improved by the tone's previous association with the flickering light.

Majkowski (1958) has suggested that the frequency-specific response to a repetitive CS undergoes an orderly sequence of changes during conditioning. With a photic CS, driving is at first localized in the occipital region. It then "generalizes" to other portions of the cortex during the early phases of acquisition. As conditioned motor responses begin to appear, photic driving becomes again localized, but this time occurs in the contralateral sensory-motor area. The frequency-specific responses of the motor cortex disappear as soon as a motor CR is made, and Majkowski has presented evidence suggesting that the photic-driving response may be inhibited by proprioceptive feedback from the overt CR.

This sequence of events has been investigated in great detail in a series of studies which has become a classic in the field. John and Killam (1959, 1960a) used a 10-cps flickering light as the signal (CS) for electric shock in a shuttle box avoidance situation. The electrical activity of a large number of cortical and subcortical regions was recorded throughout the conditioning process. Before the conditioning experiment, the frequency-specific EEG response to the CS was habituated by presenting twenty 15-sec exposures to the flickering light daily for 20 days. Photic driving was initially recorded from the visual cortex, lateral geniculate body, superior colliculi, hippocampus, and occasionally from the medial forebrain bundle and fornix. The repetitive responses habituated completely within 19 to 20 days except for occasional driving at the occipital cortex (see Figures 12.39 and 12.40).

Frequency-specific responses reappeared at all recording sites (visual and auditory cortex, lateral geniculate bodies, superior colliculi, midbrain reticular formation and nucleus ventralis anterior of the thalamus, fornix, septum, hippocampus, and amygdaloid area) during the initial CS-UCS pairings. However, such responses began to decrease in amplitude and gradually disappeared with continued conditioning trials from all leads except the visual cortex, hippocampus, and midbrain reticular formation. When the first avoidance responses appeared, the repetitive responses were reduced in the hippocampus and reticular formation, and the cortical responses shifted to a "superior harmonic" (20 to 30 cps) of the CS frequency. Occasional repetitive responses were observed in the fornix, septum, and lateral geniculate bodies. As the avoidance response approached the 100% level of performance, 40- to 50-cps high-amplitude bursts began to appear in the amygdaloid complex. Frequency-specific re-

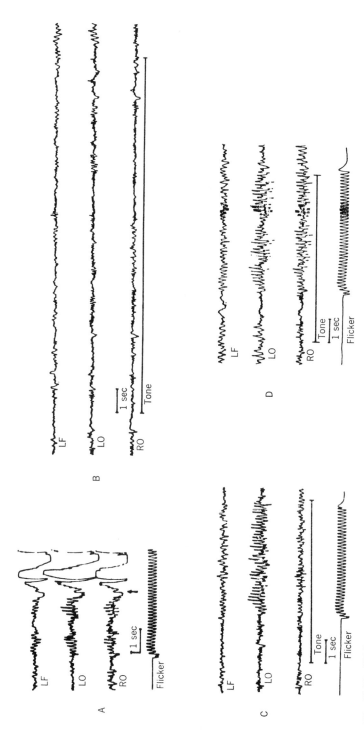

Fig. 12.37 EEG responses to peripheral stimuli after avoidance conditioning. LF, left frontal; LO, left occipital; RF, right frontal; RO, right occipital. A, response in double-grill box to flicker after avoidance training and before cortical conditioning. B, response in double-grill box to tone alone after avoidance training to flicker and before cortical conditioning. The arrow indicates onset of overt avoidance response. C, response to tone plus subsequent flicker. Note the conditioned generalized desynchronization. (From Chow et al., 1957.)

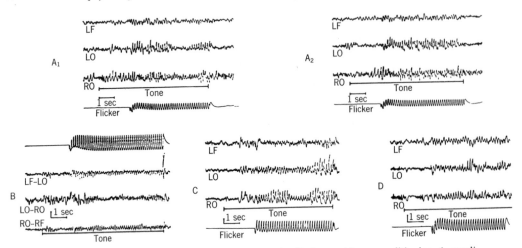

Fig. 12.38 EEG responses to visual and auditory stimuli after avoidance conditioning. A, conditioned repetitive discharge to tone alone. B, conditioned repetitive discharge to tone after cortical conditioning. Note the onset of discharge before presentation of flicker. C, bilateral conditioned repetitive discharge to tone alone before presentation of flicker. D, conditioned localized desynchronization in occipital region on presentation of tone alone. (From Chow et al., 1957.)

sponses disappeared completely from the fornix, septum, and hippocampus but increased in the nucleus ventralis anterior of the thalamus.

When the animals had reached criterion on the avoidance task, differential conditioning was begun; a 6.8-cps flickering light was used as the differential stimulus (DS). The initial presentations of the DS elicited avoidance responses, and 10-cps activity was recorded from the visual cortex. The EEG response rate gradually changed to 7 cps as the behavioral responses to the DS were extinguished. When the 10-cps CS was then reintroduced into the experiment, 7-cps driving appeared in the EEG, and the effects of extinction generalized so that no avoidance responses occurred to the CS. With additional training the CS again elicited the avoidance response, and the 10-cps activity returned to the EEG.

John and Killam argued that these electrical changes must be significantly related to the learning process because the frequency-specific responses disappeared when the behavioral avoidance response was extinguished or blocked by reserpine. The authors suggested that repetitive responses appear in the classical sensory pathways during the early stages of conditioning, then shift to the extralemniscal system, and finally return to the visual pathways. During extinction or gradual blockade of the behavioral CR, this sequence appeared to be reversed.

John and Killam (1960b) reported an interesting extension of these studies. In addition to con-

ditioning an avoidance response to a 6-cps flickering light, they trained the cats to bar-press for milk when a 10-cps flickering light was presented. During early approach training there was a marked increase in frequency-specific activity in the reticular formation and hippocampus. The repetitive discharges diminished at all levels except the visual cortex as the bar-pressing response became well established. However, when bar pressing began to be reinforced only during the CS presentation, a sharp rise occurred in frequency-specific activity in the reticular formation, hippocampus, medial and posterior suprasylvian gyri, visual cortex, lateral geniculate body, and fornix. This increase was most pronounced in the visual cortex, fornix, and reticular formation; repetitive discharges persisted in these areas throughout the experiment. This observation presents an interesting contrast to the earlier finding that frequency-specific responses decrease and eventually disappear as avoidance learning reaches criterion (see Figure 12.41).

After the animals had learned to associate the 10-cps stimulus with food reinforcement, differential conditioning was begun by presenting the 6-cps light without reinforcement. When lever pressing occurred in response to the negative (6-cps) stimulus, a marked depression of 6-cps activity could be observed in all leads. Conversely, when lever pressing did not occur in response to the positive (10-cps) stimulus, a similar decrease in 10-cps activity was noted. John and

Start of experiment

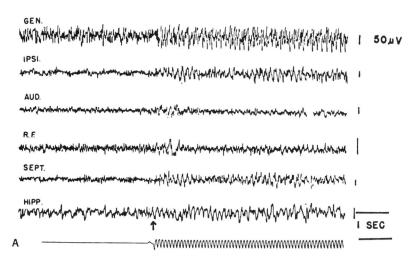

Habituation

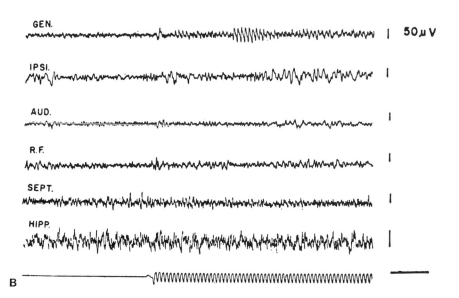

Fig. 12.39 This figure and Fig. 12.40 show records of the electrical activity of the brain of the cat at successive stages in the establishment of the conditioned avoidance response. In each figure the channels record the lateral geniculate nucleus (Gen.), visual cortex (IPSI.), auditory cortex (AUD.), midbrain tegmentum (R.F.), septum (SEPT.), and hippocampus (HIPP.). A, the responses to initial presentation of 10/sec photic stimulation (signal). B, records obtained 20 days after those above; photic stimulation was presented daily without reinforcement. (From John and Killam, 1959.)

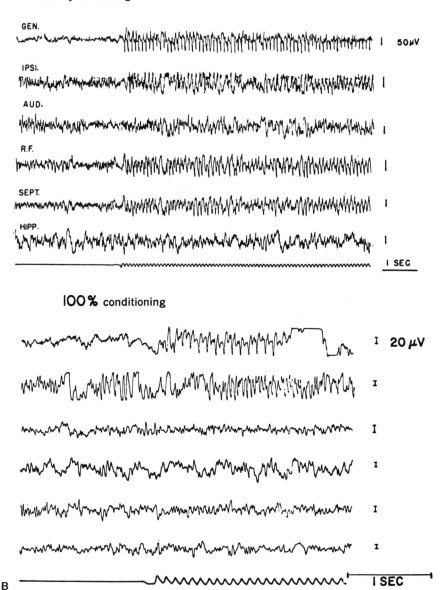

Fig. 12.40 A, EEG records obtained on the first day of reinforcement, consisting of shocks to the feet during the last second of photic stimulation, 1 day after the stimulation recorded in part B of Figure 12.39. B, records obtained 20 days after those above, with avoidance responses fully established after daily training. Note the faster paper speed. (From John and Killam, 1959.)

Killam also reported that some structures, particularly the visual cortex and fornix, showed a frequency shift during inappropriate behavioral responses (i.e., bar pressing to the 6-cps light or not pressing when the 10-cps light was presented) toward the frequency that would be compatible with the behavioral response. Thus, if the animal

pressed the lever erroneously during the presentation of the 6-cps negative stimulus, 10-cps discharges could be recorded from the visual cortex. Six-cps activity appeared whenever the animal failed to bar-press in response to the 10-cps light. When the response to the 10-cps CS was inhibited, hypersynchronous slow discharges in the dorsal hippocampus also appeared (see Figures 12.42 and 12.43).

Finally, the animals were trained to perform avoidance responses when the 6-cps stimulus was presented but to bar-press for food whenever the 10-cps light appeared. During this differential approach-avoidance learning, a marked increase in frequency-specific activity *to both* stimuli was observed, particularly in the amygdaloid area, hippocampus, and visual cortex. A slight decrease of repetitive responses from the midbrain reticular formation was also recorded (see Figure 12.44).

John and Killam concluded from their observations that a memory trace of the temporal pattern of stimulation may have been established in the nonspecific extralemniscal pathways and that such a trace permitted a comparison of new sensory stimulation with a "reference standard"

which was reflected in the repetitive discharges from these systems. The classical sensory pathways, on the other hand, are believed to be stimulus-bound, so that behavior is appropriate when the activity of the two systems coincides. This interpretation has been criticized by many workers in the field, largely because it cannot logically account for the discrimination of frequencies beyond the range of the normal EEG rhythm. It has been suggested that the adventitious use of stimulus frequencies at or near the normal rhythm of the hippocampus or other subcortical structures may be directly responsible for the reported findings. Although there have been some relevant studies within the past few years, the crucial experiment has not yet been reported.

Liberson and Ellen (1960), for instance, suggested that the 6-cps differential stimulus employed by John and Killam produced frequency-

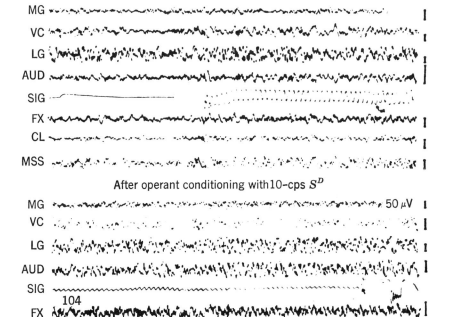

Fig. 12.41 *Top*, EEG records obtained after operant conditioning. (The cats were steadily pressing the lever, on introduction of a 10-cps flicker; the arrow indicates lever presses.) *Bottom*, EEG records obtained after the lever-pressing response was brought under control of the 10-cps flicker. (The arrow indicates lever presses.) MG, medial geniculate body; VC, visual cortex; LG, lateral geniculate body; AUD, auditory cortex; SIG, record of CS and CR; FX, fornix; CL, centralis lateralis; MSS, medial suprasylvian gyrus; VH, ventral hippocampus. (From John and Killam, 1960b.)

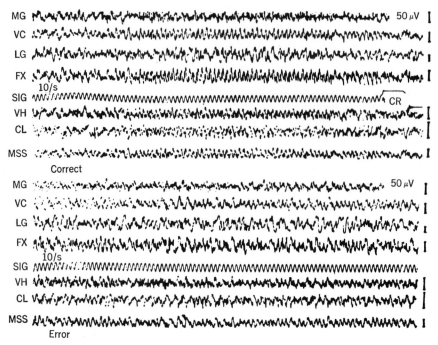

Fig. 12.42 EEG records obtained during differential conditioning with a 10-cps positive stimulus and a 6-cps negative stimulus. *Top,* correct response to 10-cps flicker (arrow indicates lever press). *Bottom,* error of omission to 10-cps flicker. Key to the labels is given in Figure 12.41. (From John and Killam, 1960b.)

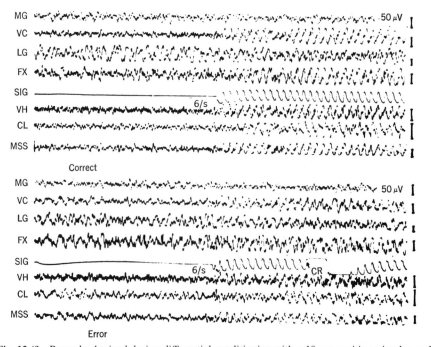

Fig. 12.43 Records obtained during differential conditioning with a 10-cps positive stimulus and a 6-cps negative stimulus. *Top,* correct responses to 6-cps flicker. *Bottom,* error of commission to 6-cps flicker (arrow indicates lever press). Key to the labels is given in Figure 12.41. (From John and Killam, 1960b.)

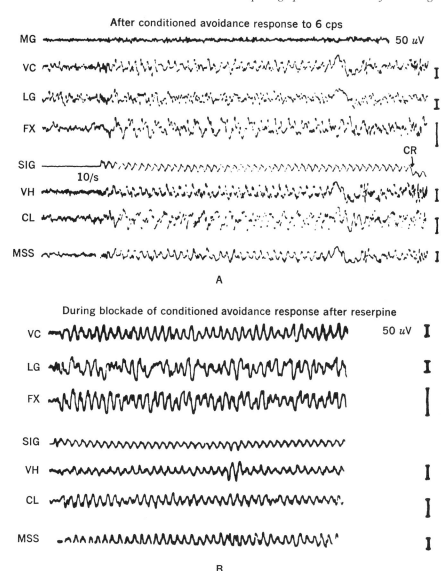

Fig. 12.44 A, EEG records obtained during lever press to 50-cps flicker after conditioning to the 6-cps flicker (arrow indicates lever press). *Bottom,* EEG records obtained on presentation of the 10-cps flicker after performance of the conditioned avoidance response to the 6-cps flicker was blocked by injection of reserpine (100 μg/kg). Key to the labels is given in Figure 12.41. (From John and Killam, 1960b.)

specific responses which could not be separated from hippocampal slow waves; they reported that the elegant findings could not be fully replicated when a 3-cps CS was used. They trained rats to avoid an electric shock by pressing a lever within a 5-sec CS interval; frequency-specific responses were recorded from the visual cortex and occasionally from the hippocampus during acquisition. Photic driving also occurred in the intertrial intervals during the early stages of learning, but this spontaneous activity disappeared as the appropriate behavioral responses began to be made. Frequency-specific discharges continued to be recorded from the cortex and hippocampus when the behavioral CR was well established, but the authors could not find a correlation between the occurrence of this pattern and successful performance on individual trials. The experiment of Liberson et al. is unfortunately not comparable to John and Killam's procedure in so many important aspects (species differences, recording sites, testing procedure) that the results are difficult to evaluate.

Other investigators have similarly departed from John and Killam's experimental paradigm, and a direct comparison of the results should not be attempted. Stern et al. (1960) used classical trace conditioning (5- to 10-sec CS-UCS interval) to analyze the appearance of frequency-specific responses. The CS was a flashing light of a frequency that was individually adjusted to produce maximal photic driving. All frequencies were between 3 and 33 cps. The UCS was electric shock to the right foreleg. EEG recordings from the visual and motor areas were analyzed with a Walker-type frequency analyzer. Stern et al. noted three different patterns of repetitive responses in different animals. Four dogs showed a "temporally localized frequency-specific response" during the delay period between the CS offset and the UCS onset. This response appeared within the first ten trials and disappeared as the behavioral CR stabilized. One animal showed a "temporally generalized frequency-specific response" on the contralateral occipital and motor cortices; this appeared as soon as the animal was placed into the testing apparatus. Other dogs showed a "temporally localized non-frequency-specific response" to the CS; this response appeared during the delay period and was restricted to a specific frequency not directly related to that of the CS. None of these EEG patterns showed clear changes on trials when the animals failed to respond appropriately to the CS.

Chow (1960) used an interesting variation of the tracer technique to investigate the electrocortical events during the acquisition of successive visual discriminations in monkeys. The relevant stimuli in this experiment were pairs of visual patterns (red versus green squares, black triangles versus black circles, etc.) which were presented individually. The animals learned to push the stimulus panel within 5 sec after the presentation of a correct stimulus or to withhold this response for 5 sec after the presentation of the negative stimulus. A continuous light was presented during the intertrial interval and began to flicker at 5- to 10-cps just before each trial. The intermittent stimulus did not carry any information about the relevant stimuli but merely served as a signal and background for the stimulus presentations. One would not expect to see significant changes in frequency-specific activity. Chow reported no systematic alterations in the repetitive responses of the visual and temporal cortex, but he observed a reliable decrease in the amplitude of the activity of the middle and inferior temporal gyri on negative trials. (Since the animals had learned during pretraining to push the stimulus panel whenever it was presented, learning to inhibit this response was undoubtedly the crucial aspect of this task.)

These results provide a convenient comparison for the next study, in which the flicker frequency takes on significance as the crucial stimulus difference determining the appropriateness of the behavioral response. The same visual stimuli were presented as before; however, the problem was reversed repeatedly, the signal for the reversal being a change in the flicker frequency of the background illumination. For instance, a 4-cps light was presented during the initial experiment when the animals learned to respond to a triangle and not to respond to a circle. After the animals had mastered this problem, the flicker frequency was increased to 10 cps and the previously negative stimulus became positive. Four such reversals were carried to a criterion of fourteen out of fifteen responses. Photic driving increased markedly at the beginning of each reversal but decreased rapidly during the next few trials. Chow did not report any correlation between correct or incorrect responses and specific frequencies of the cortical rhythm, although the situation would seem to allow such differences to show up clearly.

Chow dismisses the increase of frequency-specific discharges at the beginning of each reversal as alerting responses to a changed stimulus situation. It seems only fair to point out that the frequency-specific discharges occurred reliably whenever the frequency of the stimulus became an important aspect of the stimulus situation. We might mention here Kooi's hypothesis that the frequency-specific responses to a flickering background light should be *attenuated* in cerebral areas directly involved in learning, as a result of local desynchronization and what Kooi calls "competition between the photic stimulus and mental processes for dendritic elements" (see Kooi et al., 1960). Chow's results can certainly be interpreted to support such a hypothesis.

McAdam et al. (1961) have reported temporarily increased frequency-specific driving in the hippocampus and reticular formation during the early trials of classical conditioning; this driving disappeared during later stages of learning.

Jasper et al. (1958, 1960) have obtained micro-electrode recordings during the acquisition and performance of an avoidance response to a flickering light CS in monkeys. Unit responses to the CS were found in the frontal, motor, sensory, and parietal cortex even before conditioning, showing that the cortical response to this stimulus was not restricted to the specific projection areas. Unit discharges at the flash frequency were seen only at the motor cortex. During acquisition, driving increased in the parietal cortex, although some units in all cortical areas showed frequency-specific responses. Other units, however, showed no change or increased or decreased unit firing whenever the CS appeared. Jasper et al. concluded that the formation of temporary connections does not involve rigid pathways from sensory to motor centers.

Evoked potentials. We have already discussed the gradual disappearance of evoked responses during habituation and the rapid reappearance of high-amplitude potentials when the stimulus is paired with a noxious or appetitive UCS. Beyond that, several studies (Artemyev and Bozladnova, 1952; Hernández-Peón et al., 1956a, b) suggest that the amplitude of the evoked responses to the CS correlates highly with the appearance of behavioral responses. These studies also indicate that evoked potentials appear in the motor cortex at about the same time that the first overt conditioned responses occur (Jouvet and Hernández-Peón, 1957). The relevance of these observations to the conditioning process itself is, however, doubtful. The amplitude of the evoked potential tends to decrease markedly when the behavioral CR is well established (Hearst et al., 1960; Roitbak, 1959, 1960), and motor activity per se seems to influence the amplitude of evoked responses (Worden, 1959). Furthermore, there are some puzzling differences between conditioning paradigms. Majkowski (cited by Morrell, 1961), for instance, reported that the evoked responses to the CS attenuated rapidly in an instrumental avoidance situation; however, the same stimulus continued to elicit high-amplitude evoked potentials when used as the CS signaling unavoidable shock in a classical defensive conditioning experiment (see Figure 12.45).

Summary. A number of electrophysiological changes occur during some phases of the conditioning process, but it seems that none of them bears an essential relationship to the learning process itself. As soon as a neutral stimulus is

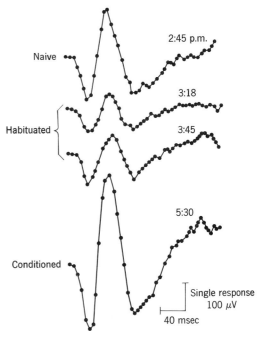

Fig. 12.45 Click-evoked responses, averaged by computer, recorded bipolarly from the cortex of the inferior bank of the superior temporal gyrus in the monkey. (From Galambos and Sheatz, 1962.)

paired with a noxious or appetitive UCS, it begins to elicit generalized cortical desynchronization in all areas of the cortex. This response becomes localized in the motor areas as conditioning progresses. Learning is retarded when the cortical desynchronization response to the CS is thoroughly habituated before the beginning of training. However, several studies have shown that conditioning can be elaborated although the cortical arousal response is pharmacologically blocked or distorted by the elicitation of epileptiform seizure discharges.

We know little more about the significance of the slow waves recorded from cortical and subcortical regions during various phases of conditioning. Hypersynchronous slow waves often appear when long CS-UCS intervals are used. The CS onset produces a brief desynchronization response which is followed by marked slow-wave activity until just before the onset of the UCS. Since these slow waves are particularly prominent during extinction and during the presentation of a negative stimulus in differential conditioning, they have been interpreted as a sign of internal inhibition. However, differential stimuli do not always elicit such EEG patterns, and there is some question about possible confusion of these slow waves with discharges of hippocampal origin.

Attempts to use repetitive stimuli as tracers of the neural processes that occur during conditioning have produced some very interesting, although not totally consistent, findings. A repetitive CS elicits photic driving in the specific sensory projection areas during the early stages of learning. This activity tends to generalize to all cortical areas during later stages of conditioning and becomes localized in the motor cortex when behavioral responses to the CS begin to appear. Frequency-specific responses can also be seen in subcortical areas. John and Killam have shown that photic driving appears first in the classical sensory pathways, shifts next to the extralemniscal system, and eventually returns to the specific pathways when the CR has become well established. These authors argue that the frequency-specific responses must be specifically related to the learning process because they disappear (in the inverse order of appearance) during extinction or pharmacological blocking. Although frequency-specific driving has been observed by many other workers, John and Killam's theoretical interpretation of its significance is not generally accepted. Frequency-specific responses are only seen in the rather narrow frequency range of the normal EEG, and the theory does not offer a logical explanation for the selective storage of frequencies outside this range.

The amplitude of evoked potentials has been observed to increase during conditioning, particularly in the motor areas of the cortex at the time when behavioral responses to the CS begin to appear. However, this does not seem to be an invariant and essential part of the conditioning process, and little theoretical emphasis has been placed on this modification.

Although the many EEG studies of the past 25 years have provided much provocative and interesting information, no clear relation between specific electrophysiological response patterns and the conditioning process has become evident. Learning does not, as we shall see later, seem to be an exclusive or even primary property of any single part of the central nervous system. We should, therefore, not be surprised to find that no specific anatomical area shows electrophysiological changes uniquely related to learning. Perhaps our recording techniques are not yet sophisticated enough to permit us to observe important functional changes in neural activity that occur during conditioning.

ATTEMPTS TO CONDITION ELECTROPHYSIOLOGICAL RESPONSES

Conditioning of the Electroencephalographic Arousal Response

Durup and Fessard (1935) discovered, during one of the earliest investigations of the EEG desynchronization response to simple visual stimuli, that this electrophysiological response could be conditioned much like overt motor responses. The EEG response to visual stimuli was projected on the screen of a cathode-ray oscilloscope, and permanent records were obtained by photographing this screen. The camera was set to take a picture automatically whenever the stimulus source was activated. When an apparatus failure occurred, no visual stimuli were presented but the camera continued to operate. Durup and Fessard noted that the click of the camera elicited the same localized desynchronization of the visual cortex that had previously been evoked by the light stimulus. When the camera noise was repeatedly presented alone, this response diminished and finally disappeared completely. Since the click did not evoke occipital alpha blocking before it was paired with the visual stimulus, Durup and Fessard concluded that the auditory stimulus had acquired the ability to alter the occipital rhythm as a result of its association with the visual stimulus. They suggested that this acquisition and the extinction that followed the omission of the light appeared identical to the conditioning and extinction of overt motor responses.

This interesting observation was quickly confirmed by a number of investigators and opened an area of research which has provided many provocative results. Loomis et al. (1936) replicated Durup and Fessard's findings in a more formal investigation and found that a weak auditory stimulus which produced little cortical desynchronization before the experiment came to do so rather rapidly after it was paired repeatedly with a visual stimulus. Cruikshank (1937) observed that an auditory stimulus which preceded a visual stimulus by a constant interval acquired the ability to elicit the EEG response to light when the visual stimulus was omitted. Since the response occurred after the normal CS-UCS interval, Cruikshank suggested that trace conditioning had been established. Similar results have been reported by Jasper and Cruikshank (1937).

In spite of these encouraging replications of Durup and Fessard's findings, considerable doubt remained about the comparability of this *sensory-sensory* conditioning of an electrophysiological response and normal learning. Evidence for conditioning accumulated rapidly, but it was soon pointed out that even prolonged experiments, using many hundreds of conditioning trials, never succeeded in producing more than 30 to 50% conditioned responses and that extinction following the omission of the UCS was always very rapid.

An experiment by Travis and Egan (1938) will illustrate these objections (Table 12.1). These workers used a 750-msec auditory stimulus as the CS and a 250-msec visual stimulus which ended contiguously with the tone as the UCS. Before conditioning the tone alone produced cortical desynchronization on 11% of the stimulus presentations. After many CS-UCS pairings this proportion rose to only 34% and returned to the preconditioning level after only three or four nonreinforced presentations of the conditioned stimulus.

Knott and Henry (1941) observed that the acquisition of the conditioned alpha-block response was very rapid, reaching maximal levels within about one-fifth the number of trials normally needed to establish an overt CR. They suggested that the presentation of a novel stimulus complex (the CS-UCS compound) might produce sensitization rather than conditioning, and this possibility has remained a problem in spite of many subsequent attempts to control for pseudoconditioning. According to this interpretation, cortical excitability is increased by the presentation of the novel stimulus complex, and the observed cortical desynchronization represents an unconditioned response rather than a conditioned one. Knott and Henry attempted to distinguish between these alternatives by using a 4-sec CS-UCS interval (the auditory CS was presented for 5 sec, and the 1-sec visual UCS ended contiguously with the tone); such an interval minimized the effects of sensitization and allowed sufficient time for the alpha rhythm to recover from any CS-induced alterations. The authors reported only inconsistent and highly unstable conditioning and concluded that the anticipatory responses to the CS occurred because of sensitization rather than conditioning. The results are unfortunately not as conclusive as one might wish, since a 4-sec CS-UCS interval fails to produce conditioning of many behavioral responses. More recent investigations have confirmed the relative instability of the conditioned alpha-block response, but the phenomenon is generally considered to be true conditioning, although sensitization may play a role in the development of the response.

Jasper and Shagass (1941a) studied the conditioning of the alpha-block response in man, using a variety of classical conditioning paradigms (see Figures 12.46 to 12.50). They obtained evidence for simple, cyclic, delayed, trace, differential, differential-delayed, and backward conditioning which seemed to rule out the possibility of sensitization as an essential provision. The differential conditioning experiment provides a particularly convincing argument against pseudoconditioning. Jasper and Shagass, for instance, reported that a tone which differed by only 100 cps from the CS failed to elicit any conditioned responses, but the CS continued to do so reliably. Even in these experiments, it is possible that sensitization may have contributed to the observed effects, since the differential stimulus was never paired with the

TABLE 12.1

Relative effectiveness of a tone presented alone (preconditioning) and with a light (sensory-sensory conditioning) in depressing the alpha rhythm

	Individual Subjects																Subjects Grouped	
	I		II		III		IV		V		VI		VII		VIII			
	% Eff.	N	% Eff.	N	% Eff.	N	% Eff.	N	% Eff.	N	% Eff.	N	% Eff.	N	% Eff.	N	% Eff.	N
Tone alone (pre-conditioning)	8	112	13	98	6	55	13	87	10	83	12	60	6	36	14	112	11	643
Tone with light	42	154	40	162	26	171	22	144	34	243	35	225	38	110	41	176	35	1385
Difference	34		27		20		9		24		23		32		27		24	
Conditioned responses	7.7		5.4		5.9		1.3		5.3		4.4		5.2		5.4		12.0	

From Travis and Egan, 1938.

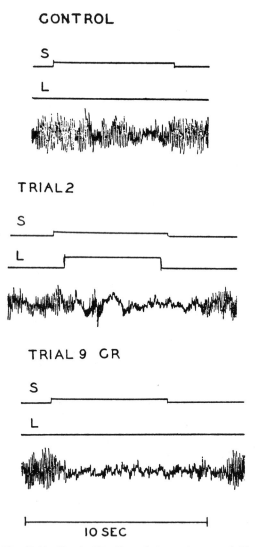

Fig. 12.46 Simple CR. Control shows that sound (S) without light (L) had no effect on alpha waves. (The short depression of the alpha in this sample was similar to spontaneous changes throughout the record in this subject.) Trial 2 was the second conditioning trial. Trial 9 shows blocking of alpha rhythm as the CR to sound. (From Jasper and Shagass, 1941a.)

visual UCS and may therefore have habituated rapidly before a stable differential response was established. Differential conditioning has been reported in other experiments (Morrell and Jasper, 1956), but the possibility of habituation was again not adequately controlled. Jasper and Shagass (1941b) observed in a subsequent experiment that the alpha-block response to time intervals in delayed, trace, and cyclical conditioning experi-

ments tended to be more accurate than the subjects' verbally reported estimates of these time intervals, indicating that the conditioned desynchronization response is not related to a conscious "anticipatory set" as suggested by Loomis et al. (1936).

The course of sensory-sensory conditioning has been studied in some detail, and some interesting observations have been reported. Iwama (1950), using long CS-UCS intervals, found that after conditioning the first response to the CS may be an enhancement of the prevailing alpha rhythm; this gives way to the conditioned desynchronization only toward the end of the CS-UCS interval. Motokawa and Huzimori (1949) found that more than one desynchronization response may be elicited by a single CS, provided the CS-UCS interval is sufficiently long. The 10-sec CS (bell) elicited a brief alpha-block response immediately after its onset and a second desynchronization response just before the onset of the UCS. It seems likely that the initial response may have been due to sensitization in these experiments, whereas the second alpha block, occurring without a change in the stimulus situation, seems to represent a true anticipatory response.

Rowland and Gluck (1960) have recently reported a related observation. Using a 2-min auditory CS (a train of clicks), these workers found that sleeping cats showed a brief EEG arousal immediately after the onset of the CS; this pattern was rapidly replaced by a return to the synchronous waves which characterized the relaxed state before the CS application. Just before the termination of the CS (and the onset of the shock UCS), a second desynchronization occurred. During differential conditioning a negative CS (i.e., one never followed by shock) came to reliably elicit synchronous slow waves or enhance the alpha rhythm of a resting animal.

Ádám and his collaborators have shown that conditioned EEG arousal can be obtained when either the CS or the UCS are interoceptive stimuli. Ádám and Mészáros (1960) reported that stimulation of the renal pelvis via a fistula caused EEG arousal which could be conditioned to an exteroceptive CS. Ádám et al. (1960) found that the cortical desynchronization response to electrical stimulation of the reticular formation could be conditioned to an interoceptive CS applied via intestinal fistulae.

Gastaut et al. (1957) reported an interesting comparison of sensory-sensory conditioning in human subjects using visual (continuous or in-

CONTROL

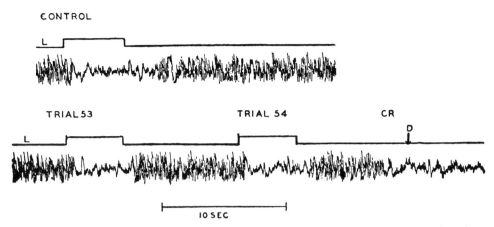

Fig. 12.47   Cyclic CR. Control with single light (L) shows no tendency for cyclic repetition of the alpha response. After 54 repetitions of light at a constant interval (9.4 sec), one stimulus was omitted at D following anticipatory blocking of the alpha rhythm which did not return for 90 sec. (From Jasper and Shagass, 1941a.)

termittent light) and somesthetic (passive displacement of the hand or voluntary clenching of the fist) unconditioned stimuli. The CS in both cases was a pure tone. Repeated CS-UCS pairings resulted in bilateral occipital alpha blocking (with the visual UCS) or contralateral blocking of the Rolandic rhythm (with the somatic UCS) to the CS. When both the visual and somatic uncondi-

tioned stimuli were presented at the same time (the subjects were instructed to clench the fist as soon as the light was presented), bilateral blocking of the alpha rhythm was observed in both Rolandic and occipital regions. When this compound UCS was paired with an auditory CS, anticipatory responses which initially resembled the unconditioned response were made to the CS. The

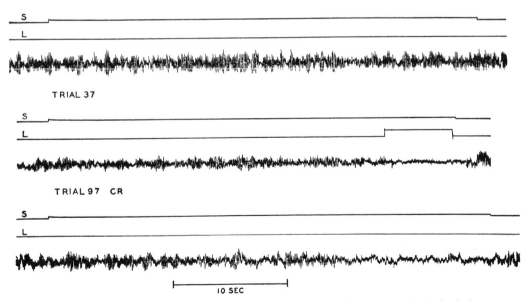

Fig. 12.48   Delayed CR. Control shows no effect of a long continuous sound stimulus before conditioning. Trial 37 shows conditioning with a delay of 30 sec. Trial 97 was a test trial showing delayed conditioned blocking of the alpha rhythm; it was anticipatory. (From Jasper and Shagass, 1941a.)

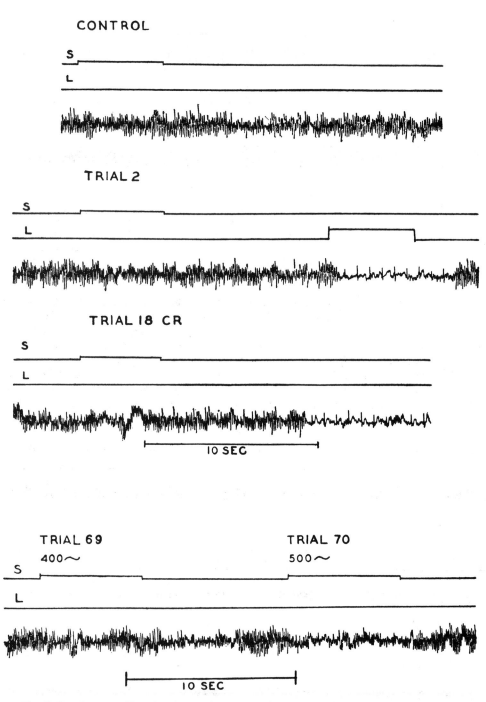

Fig. 12.49 *Top,* trace CR. After the usual control, trial 2 shows conditioning with an interval of 9.4 sec between the end of sound (S) and the beginning of light (L). Trial 18 shows an anticipatory CR to sound after a delay of 8.4 sec. *Bottom,* differential CR. Simple and differential CR to 500-cps tone has been established. Trial 69 shows differential conditioning (the absence of response to 400 cps followed by a response to 500 cps in trial 70).

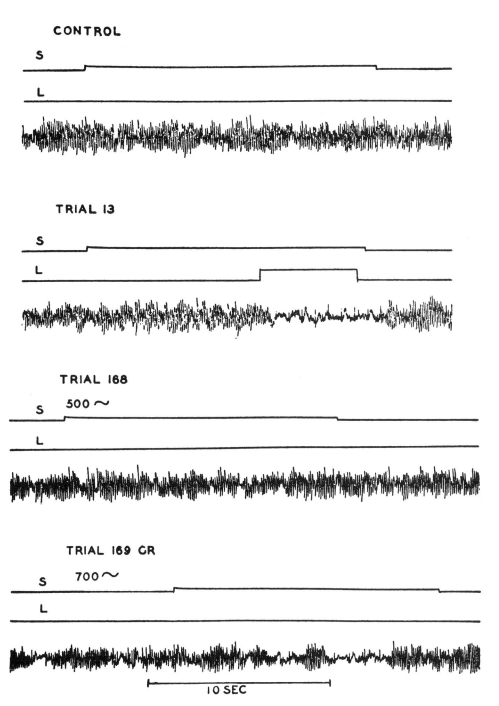

Fig. 12.49 (continued)   Differential delayed CR. A control and delayed conditioning trial (trial 13) is similar to those at the left except that 700 is then reinforced by light and 500 is never paired with light. Test trial 168 with 500 cps then caused no change in alpha waves (it did before differential conditioning), whereas 700 cps in trial 169 caused delayed blocking of alpha waves. (From Jasper and Shagass, 1941a.)

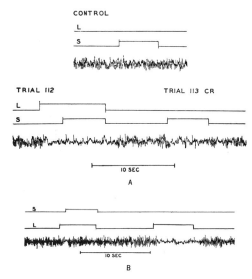

Fig. 12.50 A, backward CR [light (L) preceding sound (S) by 3.7 sec in conditioning trial 112]. Test trial 113 shows conditioned blocking of the alpha rhythm to sound after backward conditioning. B, sound (S) presented during a light stimulus (L) after backward conditioning caused a prompt return of the alpha rhythm. The succeeding light presented alone caused the usual blocking response. (From Jasper and Shagass, 1941a.)

desynchronization response of the visual cortex disappeared completely, however, after a few additional CS-UCS pairings, and the conditioned alpha-block response to the compound stimulus became sharply localized in the contralateral Rolandic region. Gastaut suggested that this response persisted because it represented an anticipatory facilitation of a cortical region involved in the elaboration of the motor response (fist clenching) to the visual stimulus.

Morrell and Jasper's (1956) studies suggest that the conditioned cortical response to the CS is a direct function of the parameters of the unconditioned response. A flickering light of various flash frequencies was used as the UCS, and tactile, auditory, and visual stimuli were used as the CS. Morrell and Jasper discovered that, depending on the frequency of the UCS flicker, the CR was either (1) a localized blocking of the occipital alpha rhythm, (2) a facilitation of the prevailing occipital rhythm, or (3) photic driving at or near the flicker frequency of the UCS. Stimuli of different sensory modalities appeared to be differentially effective as conditioned stimuli in the sensory-sensory paradigm. Conditioned alpha blocking reached a criterion of four consecutive anticipa-

tory responses most rapidly with a tactile stimulus (9.5 trials on the average) and least rapidly with the visual CS (13.2 trials on the average). No effort was made to control for intensity differences in these experiments, which may account for the differential effects (see Figures 12.51 to 12.54).

Morrell and Jasper also reported some evidence for surprisingly rapid differential conditioning of tones of 200 and 500 cps. A relatively severe criterion of nine out of ten correct responses was met in about three times the number of trials required to establish the original CR (11.1 trials).

Very different conditioned responses were observed when a UCS was used that produced synchronization and augmentation of the occipital rhythm (at 12 to 14 cps) instead of the usually observed alpha blocking. Following repeated pairings of such a UCS with an auditory CS, conditioned responses that seemed identical to the unconditioned response appeared in the visual cortex. The fact that the CS elicited this augmentation response rather than the alpha blocking it evoked before habituation constitutes perhaps the best argument against pseudoconditioning or sensitization.

Several studies have shown that the conditioned desynchronization response is selectively affected by irritative cortical lesions or seizure foci. Morrell et al. (1956) reported, for instance, that unilateral implants of aluminum hydroxide cream into frontal, auditory, somatosensory, or visual areas of the cortex produced a marked impairment of the conditioned alpha block to the CS of the particular sensory modality. Conditioning to stimuli of other modalities seemed unaffected by such lesions. Monkeys with seizure foci in the auditory cortex showed a marked deficit in conditioning to an auditory CS but not to a tactual CS, and animals with lesions in the postcentral "leg" area showed a deficit to touch but not to sound. If the CS-UCS pairings were presented only during periods when the seizure focus was quiescent, conditioning could be observed even to stimuli of the sensory modality that was directly affected by the lesions. However, the CR could never be elicited, even after many trials, during a period of seizure discharge from the sensory cortex. The epileptiform disturbances did not, however, seem to interfere with memory of previous learning, since conditioned alpha blocking could be elicited almost immediately after a cortical seizure discharge (see Figures 12.55 and 12.56).

Perhaps the most interesting aspect of these results is the observation that surgical removal of

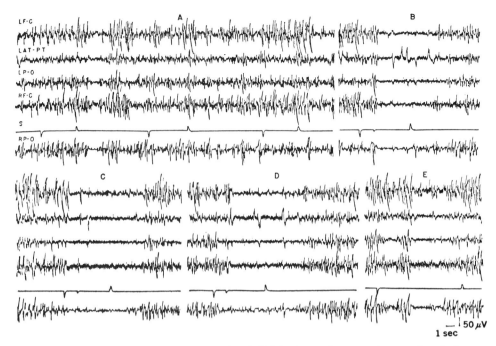

Fig. 12.51 EEG records obtained in a relaxed slightly drowsy but not asleep monkey during conditioning. The records are from the left frontocentral (LF-C), left anterior-posterior temporal (LAT-PT), left parieto-occipital LP-O), right frontocentral (RF-C), and right parieto-occipital areas (RP-O). S is the signal marker. A, the absence of response to the CS, following repeated, nonreinforced habituation trials. B, the first conditioning trial. A generalized activation response has been conditioned to the tone (first pip) in C. It appears in the occipital region after further conditioning in D. When the tone was presented alone, after conditioning, a biphasic activation response was obtained as shown in E, the first being the simple CR to the tone, the second a response to the previous time interval between tone and light. (From Morrell and Jasper, 1956.)

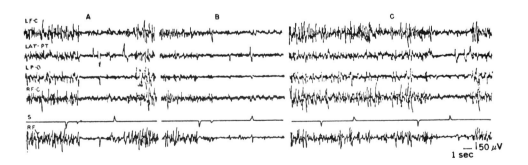

Fig. 12.52 EEG records obtained during conditioning. A, the first conditioning trial showing a response to a 500-cps flicker UCS but none to the touch CS. B, fully developed CR to touch with blocking localized to occipital regions. C, differential response to touch after conditioning. (From Morrell and Jasper, 1956.)

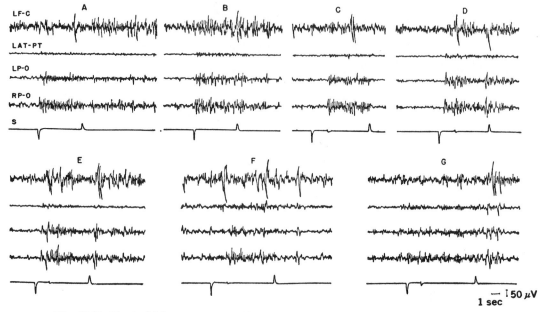

Fig. 12.53 Photic-driving response to flicker stimuli within the range of the normal EEG rhythm (6 to 12 cps). A,B, unconditioned responses to 6-cps flicker stimuli. C, first conditioning trial showing a response to the 6-cps flicker UCS but no response to the 500-cps tone CS. D,E,F,G, varieties of conditioned photic driving. (From Morrell and Jasper, 1956.)

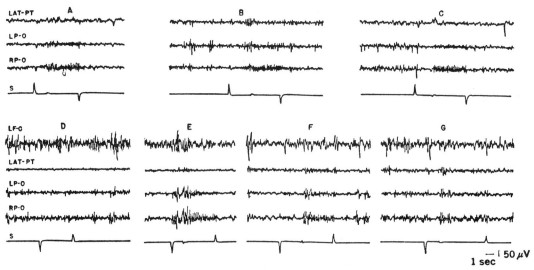

Fig. 12.54 Examples of conditioned photic driving. A,B, frequency-specific (6 cps in A and 8 cps in B) repetitive discharge beginning before the onset of the flicker UCS and gradually increasing in voltage to the point when flicker appears (a tone of 500 cps is the CS). C, a localized desynchronization in the occipital regions, the most stable form of the conditioned EEG response. D, background light (CS) alone before conditioning. E, conditioned repetitive response to background light (flicker at 6 cps is the UCS). F, a mixed response showing a low-voltage frequency-specific component and a brief localized desynchronization. G, a typical conditioned desynchronization of the localized variety but with background light rather than tone as the CS. (From Morrell and Jasper, 1956.)

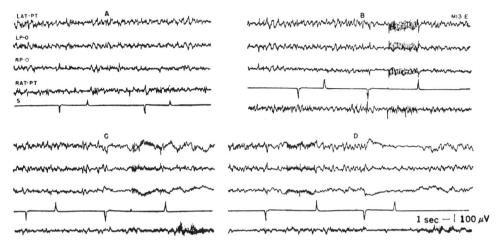

Fig. 12.55 EEG tracings obtained during conditioning from a monkey with an epileptogenic lesion in the left postcentral region. A, no response to stimulation of the left leg before conditioning. B, a differential CR to a 500-cps tone (CS), preceded by no response to a 200-cps tone which had not been reinforced by the visual stimulus (flicker). C, a differential CR to a visual CS (the first deflection of the signal marker indicates the presentation of a neutral visual stimulus). D, a CR to a somatic stimulus to the left leg, followed by another response to stimulation of the right leg which had never been reinforced by the flicker UCS. (From Morrell et al., 1956.)

the seizure focus greatly *improved* an animal's performance on subsequent tests, suggesting that the contralateral tissues may be affected by the abnormal activity of the irritative focus. When Morrell et al. placed similar irritative lesions into the amygdala-hippocampal region of the temporal lobe, a more general impairment of cortical conditioning, involving conditioned responses to stimuli of all sensory modalities, was observed. This impairment may be related to the general, short-term memory deficits reported in human subjects with epileptic seizure activity in the tem-

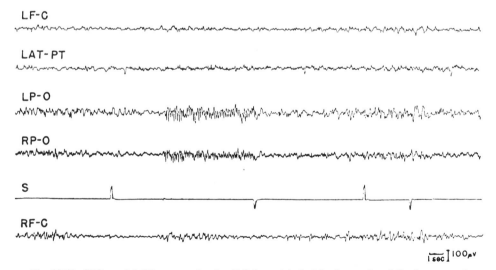

Fig. 12.56 Differential CR to somatic stimuli (left or right leg) in the monkey following removal of the epileptogenic lesion in the left postcentral region. The first stimulus is the positively conditioned response to stimulation of the left leg reinforced by flicker; the second stimulus is the negatively conditioned stimulus to the right leg. (From Morrell et al., 1956.)

poral lobe (Penfield, 1952; Milner and Penfield, 1955; Penfield et al., 1952). However, Morrell (1954, 1956) found that conditioned desynchronization can be obtained quite readily in patients with localized temporal lobe seizure foci. Conditioning to a tactile CS appeared essentially unimpaired, but auditory stimuli were found to be less effective in these patients than in normal subjects, presumably because the auditory projection areas are located in the immediate vicinity of the seizure foci. This differential effect is particularly intriguing in view of the finding that the reaction time for overt motor responses to tactile and auditory stimuli did not differ.

Photic Driving

The report by Morrell and Jasper (1956) also contains information on the conditioning of still another unconditioned EEG response which has received considerable attention in recent years. When a flashing light at flicker frequencies of 6 to 12 cps was used as the UCS (see Figures 12.53 and 12.54), relatively high-amplitude slow waves which followed the frequency of the UCS were observed in the visual cortex. When an auditory CS was first paired with this UCS, generalized cortical desynchronization was observed during the CS-UCS interval. With repeated pairings this generalized response disappeared, and the CS elicited a driving response in the occipital cortex which tended to approximate the frequency of the UCS. This frequency-specific CR was not always present and oscillated considerably in form and latency. As conditioning proceeded, the CR tended to occur progressively earlier and approximated the frequency of the UCS better and better. The frequency-specific CR was present only at the occipital cortex. It showed no tendency to generalize and disappeared rapidly with continuing reinforced conditioning trials. The photic-driving CR usually appeared early in conditioning (between the sixth and tenth trials) and disappeared between the thirteenth and twenty-eighth trials. While present, the frequency-specific CR appeared to be highly specific, being elicited neither by novel stimuli (light or touch) nor by an auditory stimulus which differed only in frequency from the CS.

Morrell and Jasper suggested that these findings rule out an explanation in terms of nonspecific sensitization or "setting" of the occipital rhythm which might be triggered by any stimulus. Photic driving did, however, appear spontaneously during the intertrial intervals, and the authors unfortunately failed to present sufficient information to permit a statistical comparison of the frequency of photic-driving responses during the CS-UCS interval and the intertrial periods. Morrell and Jasper proposed that the diffuse cortical desynchronization which characterizes the response to the initial nonreinforced presentation of the to-be-conditioned stimulus may represent a general orienting response; such a response may habituate with repeated stimulus presentations and reappear during the first conditioning trials when the CS acquires meaning. This generalized alerting response in turn habituates, as the specific significance of the CS begins to be appreciated, and gives way to localized facilitation or alerting in the cortical projection area of the UCS; this localized alerting remains as long as reinforcement is provided. Morrell and Jasper further suggest that the transitory frequency-specific conditioned responses which appeared between these two stages may be an objective trace in the cortical activity of a conditioned temporary connection. They proposed that this trace may continue to be present in the later stages of learning, although buried under the fast, low-amplitude activity of the alpha-block response.

The phenomenon of photic driving and its elicitation by previously neutral conditioned stimuli has been replicated in many later experiments; however, there is considerable difference of opinion about the accuracy of the frequency matching. Morrell and Jasper's early interpretation of the phenomenon as a necessary and information-carrying aspect of the conditioning process is widely disputed, primarily because the frequency-specific CR can be observed only with unconditioned stimuli of a rather narrow band of frequencies which are common in the normal cortical EEG.

Morrell et al. (1957) replicated the original findings in cats and rabbits and observed an oscillation between the generalized and localized conditioned desynchronization responses after the conditioned frequency-specific discharges had disappeared from the occipital cortex. Conditioned driving of the occipital rhythm was briefly but clearly observed with unconditioned stimuli of relatively low flicker frequencies which were well within the normal frequency range of the occipital EEG. At higher frequencies complex response patterns were observed; Morrell et al. have interpreted these as "harmonics" of the UCS frequency. Since the occipital rhythm rarely, if ever, matches precisely even these harmonics, it becomes difficult to assess these results. Almost any frequency can be interpreted as approaching some harmonic of a given UCS frequency. Careful computer analysis of these data is needed before we can conclude with any degree of confidence that the rhythmic responses to the CS are in fact related to the UCS frequency. It becomes difficult to understand the usefulness of these harmonics as "information-carrying traces of temporary connections" if a given frequency can represent harmonics of different UCS frequencies.

Yoshii et al. (1957) report an interesting investigation of subcortical changes during sensory-sensory conditioning. The UCS in these experiments was a flashing light, flickering at 5 cps and the CS was a 5- or 10-sec tone. In agreement with Morrell and Jasper, Yoshii and his associates observed a relatively brief period of generalized conditioned cortical arousal. This was rapidly re-placed by localized hypersynchronous discharges in the occipital cortex which tended to approximate the frequency of the UCS. Although this frequency-specific response was very unstable, no clear third phase of localized alpha blocking was observed. The frequency-specific driving appeared much earlier and tended to be more pronounced in the mesencephalic reticular formation than in the occipital leads, beginning immediately after the onset of the CS and continuing long after the tone had terminated. Frequency-specific driving of the reticular formation began to be seen as soon as the animal was placed into the experimental apparatus. It disappeared when the animal was transferred to a neutral environment, suggesting that the test apparatus had itself become a CS. Yoshii suggested that there may be a reciprocal interaction between the cortex and the reticular formation during the establishment of conditioned

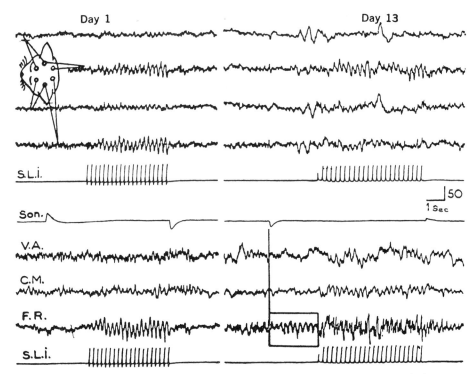

Fig. 12.57 Cortical EEG activity in frontotemporal and temporo-occipital regions during conditioning (first four lines). Records of the UCS (rhythmic light flashes, S.L.i.) and of the CS (continuous sound, Son.) are shown in the next two lines. The next three lines are records from the nucleus ventralis anterior of the thalamus (V.A.), the center median (C.M.), and the mesencephalic reticular formation (F.R.). The last tracing (S.L.i.) again records the photic UCS. On the first day of the experiment, the sound (CS) is without effect. Only the unconditioned driving of the occipital and reticular activity at a frequency of the light flashes can be seen. On the thirteenth day the sound produces a clear CR at the same frequency as the rhythmic light flashes. (From Yoshii et al., 1957a.)

cortical responses; such a relationship is reflected in the gradual transition from generalized desynchronization (representing reticular activation) to regularly recurring discharges (representing reticular inhibition) (see Figure 12.57).

Yoshii and Hockaday (1958) followed up these findings in subsequent studies which used the CS and UCS parameters originally employed by Morrell and Jasper (1956). The initial response to the CS (generalized alpha blocking and evoked potentials) was habituated in 20 to 50 trials. During the initial phase of conditioning, the CS again elicited generalized desynchronization and widespread evoked potentials which increased in amplitude and duration as conditioning continued. Gradually, these responses diminished, and slow waves began to appear in all cortical and subcortical (amygdala, hippocampus, reticular formation) leads; the waves became frequency-specific (approaching the frequency of the 7.5-cps UCS) with continued training. Eventually, all subcortical leads returned to asynchronous, nonspecific activity, but the cortex continued to show conditioned driving at or near the frequency of the UCS. Frequency-specific responses appeared initially when the 5- to 7-cps arousal response first began to be seen in the hippocampus, but persisted after the hippocampal activity had returned to high-frequency, low-amplitude patterns. In the well-conditioned animal frequency-specific responses appeared in cortical leads during the intertrial interval. These spontaneous rhythms were particularly prevalent just before the onset of the CS, and Yoshii and Hockaday suggested that temporal conditioning might account for these responses (see Figures 12.58, 12.59, 12.60).

In an effort to obtain some information about the role of the thalamic portion of the reticular formation in the development of these frequency-specific responses, Yoshii and Hockaday lesioned the nonspecific thalamic projection nuclei of three animals before conditioning. Two of these animals failed to show any impairment, but the third —with extensive damage to the center median nucleus—did not develop any frequency-specific responses in spite of continued conditioning trials. This result, unfortunately, is less conclusive than one might wish, for frequency-specific conditioned responses cannot be established in all normal animals. Yoshii and Hockaday, for instance, reported successful conditioning in only nine out of eleven animals in the original study.

The authors suggested that the mesencephalic reticular formation may be involved in the initial phase of cortical conditioning which is characterized by generalized conditioned desynchronization. The second phase, characterized by frequency-specific responses, is believed to reflect a suppression of these nonspecific reticular influences by the amygdaloid-hippocampal system.

Morrell et al. (1960) have attempted to obtain more detailed information about the frequency-specific conditioned responses by means of a computer analysis of electroencephalographic recordings; these can identify specific frequencies even when the amplitude of the responses is equal to or smaller than the "background noise." Such an analysis yields a more precise picture of the EEG frequencies than can be obtained by visual inspection. The procedure allows a test of Morrell's earlier (1956) hypothesis that frequency-specific discharges may not merely disappear during the later stages of conditioning, but rather may be submerged under the localized desynchronization response which typically follows the period of photic driving. If the frequency-specific discharges do represent a neural memory trace of the UCS which is used during conditioning to determine the response to the CS (Morrell and Jasper, 1956; John and Killam, 1959), Morrell's hypothesis should be verified.

Morrell et al. found that conditioned frequency-specific driving which appeared about the twentieth trial disappeared completely after about twenty additional CS-UCS pairings when localized desynchronization first appeared in the occipital cortex. No evidence of a persisting rhythm was obtained. However, when an extraneous

Fig. 12.58   A, EEG records obtained during the first day of conditioning of a cat. Waves at a frequency of about 7 cps are seen in the anterior parietal (aP) and posterior temporal (pT) lead just before the onset of the CS. Generalized evoked potentials and desynchronization are seen during the CS. B, EEG records obtained during the second day of conditioning. Waves at a frequency of 7.5 cps are seen in the posterior temporal lead during the CS. C, first reinforcement on the third day of conditioning. Waves at a frequency of 7.5 cps appeared spontaneously in all leads, those in the anterior temporal and parietal leads being the most conspicuous. P, parietal; F, frontal; T, temporal; p, posterior; a, anterior; Hippo, hippocampus; RF, reticular formation. (From Yoshii and Hockaday, 1958.)

F - T

pP - aT

aP - pT

Hippo

RF

CS   UCS

A

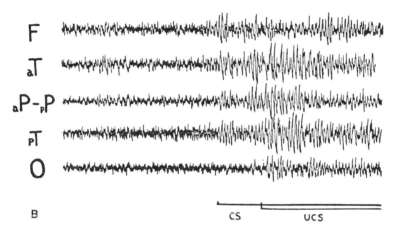

F

aT

aP - pP

pT

O

CS   UCS

B

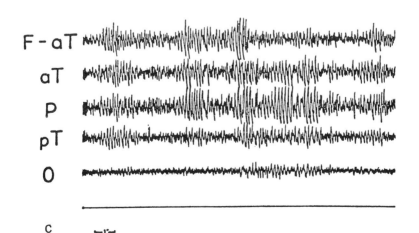

F - aT

aT

P

pT

O

C   1

683

novel stimulus was presented during the third stage of conditioning, an immediate, though temporary, return of the frequency-specific driving response was observed on the subsequent trials. This is particularly interesting in view of Grastyán's (1959) observation that the hippocampal arousal response (slow waves at 5 to 7 cps), which habituated during the early stages of conditioning, reappeared under similar circumstances.

Since frequency-specific conditioned responses generally appear only in the frequency range which characterized the arousal response of the limbic cortex, Morrell et al. suggested the interesting possibility that slow repetitive responses to the CS may be related to the arousal of hippocampal mechanisms which seems to follow a comparable time course during conditioning. This suggestion is quite plausible because of the proximity of the cortical recording electrodes to the limbic cortex; it gains additional support from the

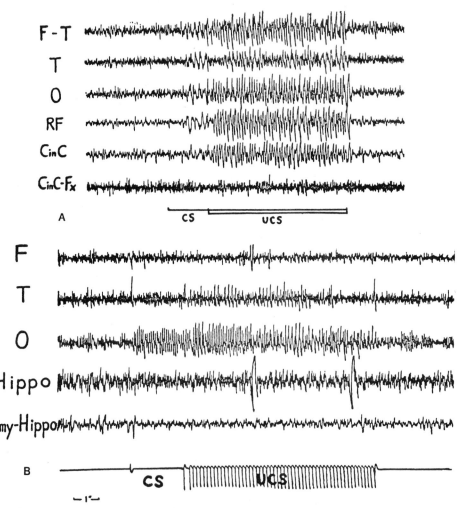

Fig. 12.59 A, eighth reinforcement on the first day of conditioning of a cat. The CS is a 450-cps tone, the UCS a 7.5-cps flicker. Generalized evoked potentials and desynchronization followed by slow waves at 3 to 4 cps appeared in the frontal (F), temporal (T), and occipital (O) cortices and in the midbrain reticular formation (RF) during the CS. (Cin C, cingulate cortex; Fx, fornix.) B, fourth reinforcement on the fifth day of conditioning of a cat. The CS and UCS are the same as in A; 15-cps waves (harmonics) are seen in the occipital lead and are facilitated during the CS and UCS. These waves concentrated in the occipital cortex after 5 days of conditioning. (Hippo, hippocampus; Amy, amygdala.) (From Yoshii and Hockaday, 1958.)

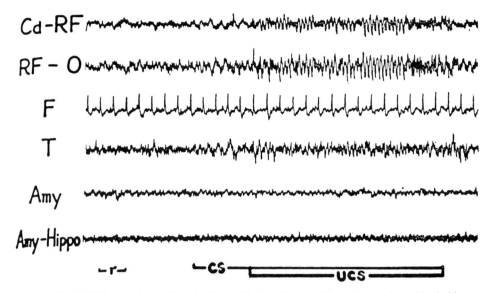

Fig. 12.60 EEG records showing photic conditioning in a cat. The center median of both sides, the nucleus medialis dorsalis of the right thalamus, and the nucleus ventralis lateralis and ventralis medialis of the left thalamus were destroyed. The EEG was recorded from the left side. Note the marked slow potentials from the caudate nucleus, reticular formation, and temporal cortex during the CS. At no time were any frequency-characteristic waves seen during the CS in this preparation. Cd, caudate nucleus; other abbreviations as in Figure 12.59. (From Yoshii and Hockaday, 1958.)

observation that the frequency-specific conditioned responses do not behave, at least in some respects, as other conditioned responses do. The latency of the response, for instance, does not show a progressive decrement with increasing practice as one might expect. The response disappears completely in spite of continued reinforcement. These considerations suggest that the CS may merely reacquire the ability to elicit hippocampal arousal responses which habituate as the animal learns to deal effectively with the situation.

A second important finding of Morrell's study was that the frequency-specific responses of the second stage of conditioning were not as specific as had previously been assumed. He observed complex patterns of electrophysiological responses which matched the frequency of the UCS only part of the time. When the frequency of the UCS was changed in successive experiments on the same animals, correlated changes in the CR could be observed which did not, however, seem to be directly and linearly related to the change in the UCS frequency. For example, one animal developed a CR at 6 cps when the UCS frequency was 3 cps, but showed conditioned driving at 3 cps when the UCS frequency was changed to 4 cps in a subsequent experiment. When a 6-cps UCS was used in a third experiment, conditioned driving occurred at or very close to 6 cps. The latter rate appeared to be frequency-specific. The most interesting aspect of these results is that the same CR (i.e., driving at 6 cps) occurred when the UCS was a 3-cps or a 6-cps stimulus.

These and related considerations have led Morrell (1959) to suggest that the repetitive discharge which occurs during conditioning may not carry information or represent part of the memory mechanism. Morrell points out that the conditioned responses seldom match the frequency of the UCS precisely, although the repetitive discharges tend to approach the frequency of the UCS as conditioning proceeds. He suggested that the CR may be influenced, but not determined, by the UCS; furthermore, this influence may take the form of selective augmentation of the components of the normal electrical activity of the cortex that are most closely related to the UCS flicker frequency. This transient facilitation of cortical activity may be preparatory and perhaps necessary to the development of the final localized desynchronization CR, but it should not be confused with a memory trace as such.

A sharply contrasting position is taken by other workers in the field who hold that the slow rhythms

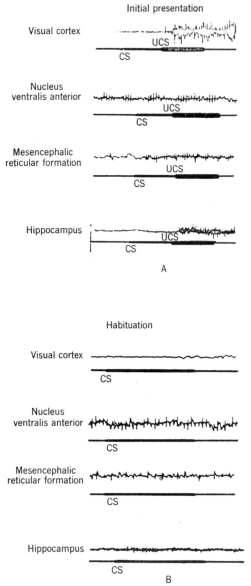

Fig. 12.61 A, microelectrode records from cortical and subcortical regions in a cat with a chronic epileptogenic lesion in the visual cortex. Initial presentation of the signal stimuli. Onset of the CS (500-cps tone) is indicated by the first widening of the signal channel. Onset of the UCS (intermittent light 10 cps) is indicated by the second widening of the signal channel. B, pattern of response after habituation. (From Morrell, 1960.)

of the second stage of conditioning may be a necessary part of the memory storage mechanism. John et al. (1961), for instance, write:

A mechanism of this sort would appear to provide means for storage of a representation of a temporal sequence of events, lasting be-

yond the duration of the events themselves. Such a mechanism for internal representation of past events seems, on logical basis, to be essential to enable an animal to perform two differentiated responses to two similar stimuli, either of which may be presented in a given experimental situation. This is particularly true if the two conditioned stimuli are, for example, two frequencies of flickering light, which cannot be discriminated on the basis of the characteristics of a single constituent flash. To account for differential performance in response to two such similar stimuli differing only with respect to their temporal sequence, we must evoke some facility for storage of a representation of the temporal sequence of previously-experienced events in order to permit comparison with a present input, thus making identification possible (p. 1161).

Some investigators have attempted to reconcile these opposing positions by suggesting that both kinds of responses may, in fact, be present at different phases of the conditioning process. Yoshii et al. (1960), for example, distinguish between non-frequency-specific slow waves of hippocampal origin which appear during the early phases of conditioning in subcortical as well as cortical leads, and "true" frequency-specific waves which are seen only in cortical leads and persist after the hippocampal arousal response has habituated. Yoshii suggested that the adventitious use of UCS frequencies approximating the characteristic pattern of the hippocampal arousal response may easily lead to a confusion of these superficially similar, but basically different, phenomena. This interesting distinction is unfortunately not easily made, since UCS frequencies that are sufficiently distinct from the hippocampal activity typically do not produce true frequency-specific driving, but only rhythmic waves which appear to be at some harmonic of the UCS frequency.

Before leaving this controversial area, we shall discuss Morrell's (1960) microelectrode study of the behavior of single units in the visual cortex, reticular formation, dorsal hippocampus, and nucleus ventralis anterior of the thalamus during sensory-sensory conditioning. Morrell found, much in agreement with previous microelectrode studies, that the individual cells of a given brain area do not seem to act in concert so that it is impossible to state whether the activity of an area increased or decreased. Instead, Morrell employed a statistical criterion to define changes in the neural activity of a given brain region; he considered the activity of an area increased or decreased whenever more than 50% of the units sampled showed an increase or decrease in firing at a given stage of conditioning (see Figures 12.61 and 12.62).

During the initial individual presentations of the CS or UCS, the units of the visual cortex appeared to respond only to the UCS. The mesencephalic reticular formation was activated by both the CS and the UCS, and the units of the nucleus ventralis anterior responded to neither. The majority of the hippocampal neurons increased their rate of firing in response to the UCS but showed no significant response to the CS. In the course of habituation of the CS, all brain areas gradually ceased responding to the CS.

The first phase of conditioning, generalized cor-

tical desynchronization to the CS, was characterized by increased unit activity in the visual cortex, dorsal hippocampus, and midbrain reticular formation. During the second phase (frequency-specific repetitive responses to the CS in the visual cortex), the presentation of the CS was followed by an inhibition of unit activity in the visual cortex and reticular formation and an increase of activity in the dorsal hippocampus. The final stage of conditioning (localized EEG desynchronization in the visual cortex) was characterized by increased unit activity in the visual cortex and nucleus ventralis anterior and a complete absence of responses from the reticular formation and dorsal hippocampus (see Table 12.2).

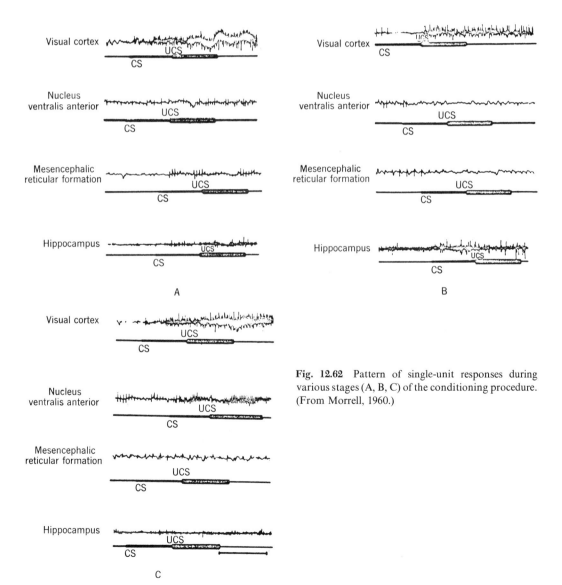

Fig. 12.62 Pattern of single-unit responses during various stages (A, B, C) of the conditioning procedure. (From Morrell, 1960.)

TABLE 12.2

Pattern of unit discharge during development of conditioned electrical response

	CS		UCS
		Response to	
Initial presentation	0	Visual cortex	↑
	0	Vent. ant.	0
	↑	Mes. retic.	↑
	0	Hippocampus	↑
Habituation*	0	Visual cortex	
	0	Vent. ant.	
	0	Mes. retic.	
	0	Hippocampus	
Stage I (Trial 32)	↑	Visual cortex	↑
	0	Vent. ant.	↑
	↑	Mes. retic.	↑
	↑	Hippocampus	↑
Stage II (Trial 39)	↓	Visual cortex	↑
	↓	Vent. ant.	↓
	↓	Mes. retic.	↓
	↑	Hippocampus	↑
Stage III (Trial 78)	↑	Visual cortex	↑
	↑	Vent. ant.	↑
	0	Mes. retic.	0
	0	Hippocampus	0

* Relay nuclei in auditory system not monitored.
↑ > 50% increased firing
↓ > 50% decreased firing
0—No change
From Morrell, 1960.

Morrell interpreted these results as supporting earlier proposals by Gastaut (1958a, b) and Yoshii et al. (1957a) that the initial phase of sensory-sensory conditioning (generalized desynchronization) reflects, in some way, the activity of the mesencephalic reticular formation, whereas the final, localized alpha-block response requires the participation of the thalamocortical mechanisms. The increased activity of the dorsal hippocampus during the second stage of conditioning supports Morrell's suggestion that the repetitive discharges which characterize the EEG during this stage may represent limbic influences. Frequency-specific responses were recorded only from units at or near the cortical surface in these experiments, but not from electrodes placed 2.0 mm below the surface. This suggests that the synaptic membrane of the apical dendrites may be directly involved in these responses.

We have seen that the alpha-block CR is mark-

edly impaired by chronic epileptogenic lesions in the cortical projection area of the CS modality. We might expect a comparable effect on the conditioned repetitive slow waves which occur during the second phase of cortical conditioning when the UCS is a flickering light. Some recent experiments have shown, however, that these driving responses seem to be augmented and facilitated, rather than inhibited, by such lesions.

Morrell (1958) reported that the unilateral placement of aluminum hydroxide cream (alumina) into the visual projection area augmented the conditioned repetitive response, particularly in the directly affected hemisphere. The initial CS presentations produced generalized desynchronization as seen in normal animals. However, the conditioned repetitive responses appeared earlier than usual and persisted for as many as 100 trials. Moreover, the affected portion of the occipital cortex never developed the conditioned and localized desynchronization response which normally appears during the last phase of cortical conditioning. Localized alpha blocking did appear after the usual number of trials in the hemisphere contralateral to the irritative focus.

Morrell and Chow (see Morrell, 1958) have shown a similar persistence of the normally quite short-lived conditioned repetitive responses after nonirritative lesions in the rostral portion of the reticular formation. Bilateral coagulation lesions which involved the nucleus reticularis, nucleus ventralis anterior, and the anterior portion of the internal capsule were made in five cats. After recuperation cortical conditioning was attempted, using an auditory CS and a low-frequency intermittent light for the UCS. Generalized conditioned desynchronization was seen in the first few CS-UCS pairings. Repetitive responses to the CS appeared as early as the fifth or sixth trial and persisted for as many as 80 trials. The localized desynchronization response of the occipital cortex never fully developed in these animals, suggesting that the localized activation pattern depends on the thalamic reticular formation.

Morrell suggests that the marked facilitation of the conditioned repetitive responses may reflect a release of the cortical mechanisms from inhibitory influences of the rostral reticular formation. The repetitive slow waves represent, according to this view, a predominantly cortical influence which in normal subjects is suppressed during later stages of conditioning by centripetal thalamic influences.

Before we leave the area of electrocortical con-

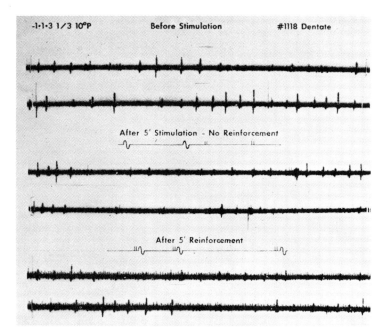

Fig. 12.63 Single-unit responses recorded from the dentate gyrus. The small unit responses occur at a rate of approximately 1/sec before stimulation; the rate is not greatly increased by uncorrelated stimulation of a reward area. When stimulation is correlated as reinforcement for the unit response, continuous firing (at a rate of about 30/sec) ensues. (From Olds and Olds, 1961.)

ditioning, experiments by Olds and Olds (1961) should be discussed, although extensive control tests are needed before we can interpret the fascinating findings of these studies. Olds and Olds first implanted electrodes in the medial forebrain bundle of rats and tested for reward effects at these placements. Animals that showed a high rate of self-stimulation were then maintained under meprobamate sedation (which does not alter the effects of self-stimulation) while microelectrodes were gradually lowered into their brain until unit responses showing a resting frequency of one to two responses per second were recorded. Electrical stimulation was then applied to the medial forebrain bundle through the self-stimulation electrode. If this stimulation did not change the unit activity under the microelectrode, instrumental operant conditioning of the unit discharge was then begun: each unit discharge was reinforced with a brief reward stimulus to the medial forebrain bundle. (see Figures 12.63 and 12.64).

The results of this procedure are remarkable. Units in the dentate gyrus, fimbria, and mammillothalamic tract region showed conditioned responses after as few as 10 or 20 reinforcements.

Units that had previously fired only once or twice per second began to respond continuously at discharge rates of up to 30 per second. These bursts of activity often lasted for several minutes, and the response amplitude decreased in a lawful fashion. Other units in the same areas responded by bursts which were much slower and did not show a tendency to decrease in amplitude.

Neocortical units showed little, if any, conditioning, whereas many subcortical units conditioned extremely rapidly. Some cells at the base of the neocortical mantle showed evidence of conditioning when the spontaneous discharges were reinforced for long periods of time; however, the time course of this gradual augmentation of response rate varied enough from that observed with subcortical units to suggest very different mechanisms.

Although it is perhaps premature to agree with Old's suggestion that the conditioning of subcortical unit responses may be the basic mechanism of instrumental conditioning, these interesting results, suggest that each neuron may be a negative feedback system as originally proposed by Ashby (1952). One should note, however, that

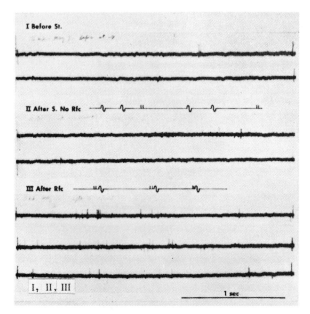

Fig. 12.64 Single-unit responses recorded from the anterior rhinencephalon. I, control record. II, after noncontingent stimulation of a reward area. III, after contingent stimulation. IV, after waiting for the unit to slow down (about 5 min), the reinforcement procedure is undertaken a second time; the large lattice-type artifact indicates a 60-cps sine wave reward stimulus. V, after another wait an unsuccessful attempt is made to correlate the stimulation with pauses. (From Olds and Olds, 1961.)

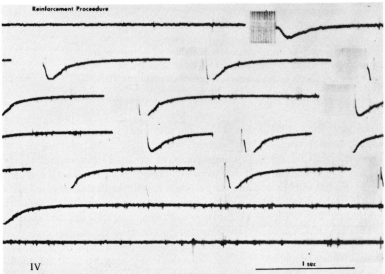

Old's findings do not require the assumption that conditioning occurred within a single neuron, for many different neurons at different levels of the brain may have increased their rate of firing in response to the reinforcement. The fact that only one of these cells was monitored in the experiments should not be interpreted to imply that conditioning occurred only within this cell.

Summary

Durup and Fessard's (1935) serendipidous observation of conditioned EEG arousal stimulated considerable experimental and speculative interest in sensory-sensory conditioning of electrophysiological responses. The basic observations of Durup and Fessard's experiment have been replicated, and some investigators have reported evidence for cyclic, delayed, trace, differential, differential-delayed, and even backward conditioning of the EEG arousal response (Jasper and Shagass, 1941a). Serious questions have nevertheless been raised by experiments demonstrating that the conditioning of the arousal response rarely reaches more than 30% conditioned responses and that extinction, following omission of the

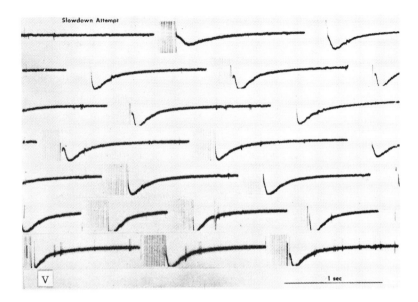

Slowdown Attempt

V   1 sec

UCS, is always very rapid (Travis and Egan, 1938; Knott and Henry, 1941). Pseudoconditioning (sensitization, differential habituation) has not been convincingly ruled out as a potential explanation of the observed EEG changes.

In spite of these problems, a number of investigations have attempted to study the development of the conditioned arousal response in some detail. It has been reported that the CS onset produces a brief conditioned desynchronization response followed by hypersynchronous discharges which are terminated by a second, brief desynchronization response just before the onset of the UCS (Motokawa and Huzimori, 1949; Rowland and Gluck, 1960). The conditioned desynchronization response may be specific to some regions of the cortex and may appear in the cortical projection areas of the CS, UCS, and UCR at different stages of the conditioning process (Gastaut et al., 1957; Morrell and Jasper, 1956). Irritative lesions in the sensory projection areas of the cortex interfere with the development of conditioned desynchronization responses, and subsequent ablation of the seizure focus improves an animal's performance on additional tests (Morrell et al., 1956).

Other unconditioned electrophysiological response patterns have been studied in this context. Frequency-specific driving can be recorded from primary sensory projection areas when intermittent stimuli are presented. Morrell and Jasper (1956) first demonstrated that the rhythmic response of the occipital EEG to a visual stimulus

flickering at 6 cps could be conditioned to a previously ineffective tone. Subsequent studies have shown that this CR is rarely truely frequency-specific but tends to approximate the frequency (or one of its harmonics) of the UCS (Morrell et al., 1957; Yoshii et al., 1957a). Morrell and associates (1960) have shown that the frequency-specific responses appear in different portions of the cortex at different times in the conditioning process. Microelectrode studies have demonstrated a very complex relation between the repetitive responses in the gross EEG and single-unit activity (Morrell, 1960).

Olds and Olds (1961) have developed a new technique which may shed some light on the activity of single cells during the conditioning process. Using electrical brain stimulation as rewards, these workers demonstrated that the activity of single neurons could be conditioned in an operant conditioning paradigm. Technical difficulties have prevented more extensive use of this interesting technique in the past, but more detailed studies should soon be forthcoming.

BIBLIOGRAPHY

Ádám, G., & Mészáros, I. Conditioned and unconditioned cerebral cortical activation to renal pelvic stimulation. *Acta physiol. Acad. Sci. hung.,* 1960, **18,** 137–141.

Ádám, G., Mészáros, I., Lehotzky, K., Nagy, A., & Rajk, A. On the role of the brainstem activation system in the conditioning to visceral stimulation. *Acta physiol. Acad. Sci. hung.,* 1960, **18,** 143–147.

Adametz, J. H. Rate of recovery of functioning in cats with rostral reticular lesions. *J. Neurosurg.,* 1959, **16,** 85–97.

Adey, W. R., Dunlop, C. W., & Hendrix, C. E. Hippocampal slow waves. *Arch. Neurol. (Chicago),* 1960, **3,** 74–90.

Adey, W. R., Walter, D. O., & Lindsley, D. F. Subthalamic lesions. Effects on learned behavior and correlated hippocampal and sub-cortical slow-wave activity. *Arch. Neurol. (Chicago),* 1962, **6,** 194–207.

Adrian, E. D., & Matthews, B. H. C. The Berger rhythm: potential changes from the occipital lobes of man. *Brain,* 1934, **57,** 355–384.

Apelbaum, J., Silva, E. E., Frick, O., & Segundo, J. P. Specificity and biasing of arousal reaction habituation. *EEG clin. Neurophysiol.,* 1960, **12,** 829–840.

Artemyev, V. V., & Bozladnova, N. I. Electrical reaction of the auditory area of the cortex of the cerebral hemispheres during the formation of a conditioned defense reflex. *Tr. Inst. Fiziol. (Moskow),* 1952, **1,** 228.

Ashby, W. R. *Design for a brain.* New York: Wiley, 1952.

Bagchi, B. K. The adaption and variability of response of the human brain rhythm. *J. Psychol.,* 1937, **3,** 463–485.

Batini, C., Moruzzi, G., Palestini, M., Rossi, G. F., & Zanchetti, A. Effects of complete pontine transections on the sleep-wakefulness rhythm: the midpontine pretrigminal preparation. *Arch. ital. Biol.,* 1959, **97,** 1–12.

Beck, E. C., & Doty, R. W. Conditioned flexion reflexes acquired during combined catalepsy and de-efferentation. *J. comp. physiol. Psychol.,* 1957, **50,** 211.

Beck, E. C., Doty, R. W., & Kooi, K. A. Electrocortical reactions associated with conditioned flexion reflexes. *EEG clin. Neurophysiol.,* 1958, **10,** 279–289.

Berger, H. Über das Elektrenkephalogramm des Menschen. I. *Arch. Psychiat. Nervenkr.,* 1929, **87,** 527–570.

Brust-Carmona, H. Mechanismos subcorticales del aprendzaje. Habituación del nistagmo post rotatorio. University of Mexico, unpublished M.A. dissertation, 1958.

Brust-Carmona, H., & Hernández-Peón, R. Sensory transmission in the spinal cord during attention and tactile habituation. *Proceedings of the 21st international physiological congress, Buenos Aires,* 1959, 44.

Caspers, H., Lerche, E., & Grueter, H. Adaptionserscheinungen der akustisch ausgelösten Weckreaktion bei Reizung mit definierten Tonimpulsen. *Pflüg. Arch. ges. Physiol.,* 1958, **267,** 128–141.

Chow, K. L. Brain waves and visual discrimination learning in monkey. In *Recent advances in biological psychiatry.* J. Wortis, Ed. New York: Grune and Stratton, 1960.

Chow, K. L. Changes of brain electropotentials during visual discrimination learning in monkey. *J. Neurophysiol.,* 1961, **24,** 377–390.

Chow, K. L., Dement, W. C., & John, E. R. Conditioned electrocorticographic potentials and behavioral avoidance response in cat. *J. Neurophysiol.,* 1957, **20,** 482–493.

Chow, K. L., Dement, W. C., & Mitchell, S. A., Jr. Effects of lesions of the rostral thalamus on brain waves and behavior in cats. *EEG clin. Neurophysiol.,* 1959, **11,** 107–120.

Clark, S. L., & Ward, J. W. Electroencephalograms of different cortical regions of normal and anesthetized cats. *J. Neurophysiol.,* 1945, **8,** 99–112.

Covian, M. R., Timo-Iaria, C., & Marseillan, R. F. Changes in cortical evoked potentials by previous reticular stimulation. In *Brain mechanisms and learning.* J. F. Delafresnaye, A. Fessard, R. W. Gerard, & J. Konorski, Eds. Oxford: Blackwell Scientific, 1961.

Cruikshank, R. M. Human occipital brain potentials as affected by intensity-duration variables of visual stimulation. *J. exp. Psychol.,* 1937, **21,** 625–641.

Danilova, N. N. Changes in the EEG response to a rhythmic visual stimulus following the orienting reflex. In *The orienting reflex and investigatory behavior.* Moscow: Pavlov Institute, 1958 (Russian).

Darrow, C. W. The galvanic skin response (sweating) and blood pressure as preparatory and facilitative functions. *Psychol. Bull.,* 1936, **33,** 73–94.

Darrow, C. W. Psychological and psychophysiological significance of the electroencephalogram. *Psychol. Rev.,* 1947, **54,** 137–168.

Dodge, R. Habituation to rotation. *J. exp. Psychol.,* 1923, **6,** 1–36.

Doty, R. W. Discussion of Gastaut's paper. In *The reticular formation of the brain.* H. H. Jasper, L. D. Proctor, R. S. Knighton, W. C. Noshay, & R. T. Costello, Eds., Boston: Little, Brown, 1958.

Durup, G., & Fessard, A. L'électroencéphalogramme de l'homme. *Année psychol.,* 1935, **36,** 1–32.

Ectors, L. Etude le l'activité électrique du cortex cérébral chez le lapin non-narcotisé ni curarisé. *Arch. int. Physiol.,* 1936, **43,** 267–298.

Eidelberg, E., White, J. C., & Brazier, Mary A. B. The hippocampal arousal pattern in rabbits. *Exp. Neurol.,* 1959, **1,** 483.

Evarts, E. V. Spontaneous and evoked activity of single units in visual cortex of cat during sleep and waking. *Fed. Proc.,* 1960, **19,** 290.

Fangel, C., & Kaada, B. R. Behavior "attention" and fear induced by cortical stimulation in the cat. *EEG clin. Neurophysiol.,* 1960, **12,** 575–588.

Fuster, J. M. Tachistoscopic perception in monkeys. *Fed. Proc.,* 1957, **16,** 43.

Galambos, R. Suppression of auditory nerve activity by stimulation of efferent fibers to the cochlea. *J. Neurophysiol.,* 1956, **19,** 424–437.

Galambos, R., & Sheatz, G. S. An electroencephalograph study of classical conditioning. *Amer. J. Physiol.,* 1962, **203,** 173–184.

Galambos, R., Sheatz, G., & Vernier, V. G. Electrophysiological correlates of a conditioned response in cats. *Science,* 1956, **123,** 376–377.

García-Austt, E., Bogacz, J., & Vanzulli, A. Significance of the photic stimulus on the evoked responses in man. In *Brain mechanisms and learning.* J. F. Delafresnaye, A. Fessard, R. W. Gerard, & J. Konorski, Eds. Oxford: Blackwell Scientific, 1961.

Gastaut, H. État actuel des connaissances sur l'électroencéphalographie du conditionment. Colleque de Marseille. *EEG clin. Neurophysiol.,* 1957, Suppl. 6, 133.

Gastaut, H. Some aspects of the neurophysiological basis of conditioned reflexes and behavior. In *Neurological basis of behavior.* G. E. W. Wolstenholme & C. M. O'Connor, Eds. Boston: Little, Brown, 1958a.

Gastaut, H. The role of the reticular formation in establishing conditioned reactions. In *The reticular formation of the brain.* H. H. Jasper, L. C. Proctor, R. S. Knighton, W. C. Noshay, & R. T. Costello, Eds. Boston: Little, Brown, 1958b.

Gastaut, H., Jus, A., Jus, C., Morrell, F., Storm Van Leeuwen, W., Dongier, S., Naquet, R., Regis, H., Roger, A., Bekkering, D., Kamp, A., & Werre, J. Étude topographique des réactions électroencéphalographiques conditionées chez l'homme. *EEG clin. Neurophysiol.,* 1957, **9**, 1–34.

Gault, F. P., & Leaton, R. N. Electrical activity of the olfactory system. *EEG clin. Neurophysiol.,* 1963, **15**, 299–304.

Gershuni, G. V., Kozhevnikov, V. A., Maruseva, A. M., Avakyan, R. V., Radionova, E. A., Altoman, J. A., & Soroko, V. I. Modifications in electrical responses of the auditory system in different states of the higher nervous activity. In *The Moscow colloquium on electroencephalography of higher nervous activity.* H. H. Jasper & G. D. Smirnov, Eds. *EEG clin. Neurophysiol.,* 1960, Suppl. 13, 115–123.

Glickman, S. E., & Feldman, S. M. Habituation to direct stimulation of the reticular formation. *Fed. Proc.,* 1960, **19**, 288.

Granit, R. Centrifugal and antidromic effects on ganglion cells of retina. *J. Neurophysiol.,* 1955a, **18**, 388–411.

Granit, R. *Receptors and sensory perception.* New Haven, Conn.: Yale Univ. Press, 1955b.

Grastyán, E. The hippocampus and higher nervous activity. In *The central nervous system and behavior.* M. A. B. Brazier, Ed. New York: Josiah Macy, Jr. Foundation, 1959.

Grastyán, E. The significance of the earliest manifestations of conditioning in the mechanism of learning. In *Brain mechanisms and learning.* J. F. Delafresnaye, A. Fessard, R. W. Gerard, & J. Konorski, Eds. Oxford: Blackwell Scientific, 1961.

Grastyán, E., & Karmos, G. A study of possible "dreaming" mechanisms in the cat. *Acta physiol. Acad. Sci. hung.,* 1961, **20**, 41–50.

Grastyán, E., Lissak, K., Madarasz, I., & Donhoffer, H. Hippocampal electrical activity during the development of conditioned reflexes. *EEG clin. Neurophysiol.,* 1959, **11**, 409–430.

Green, J. D., & Arduini, A. Hippocampal electrical activity in arousal. *J. Neurophysiol.,* 1954, **17**, 533–557.

Guselnikov, V. I., & Drozhennikov, V. A. Reflection of orienting and CR activity in the potentials of the cerebral hemispheres in pigeons. *Pavlov J. higher nerv. Activ.,* 1959, **9**, 844–852.

Hagbarth, K. E., & Fex, J. Centrifugal influences on single unit activity in spinal sensory paths. *J. Neurophysiol.,* 1959, **22**, 329–338.

Hagbarth, K. E., & Kerr, D. I. B. Central influences on spinal afferent conduction. *J. Neurophysiol.,* 1954, **18**, 388–411.

Hagbarth, K. E., & Kugelberg, E. Plasticity of the human abdominal skin reflex. *Brain,* 1958, **81**, 305–318.

Hearst, E., Beer, B., Sheatz, G., & Galambos, R. Some electrophysiological correlates of conditioning in the monkey. *EEG clin. Neurophysiol.,* 1960, **12**, 137.

Hernández-Peón, R. Central mechanisms controlling conduction along central sensory pathways. *Acta neurol. lat.-amer.,* 1955a, **1**, 256–264.

Hernández-Peón, R. Mechanismes neurophysiologiques concernant l'habituation, l'attention et le conditionement. Colloque de Marseilles. Paris: Masson, 1955b.

Hernández-Peón, R. Centrifugal control of sensory inflow to the brain and sensory perception. *Acta neurol. lat.-amer.,* 1959, **5**, 279–298.

Hernández-Peón, R. Neurophysiological correlates of habituation and other manifestations of plastic inhibition (internal inhibition). In *The Moscow colloquium on electroencephalography of higher nervous activity.* H. H. Jasper & G. D. Smirnov, Eds. *EEG clin. Neurophysiol.,* 1960, Suppl. 13, 101–114.

Hernández-Peón, R. Reticular mechanisms of sensory control. In *Sensory communication.* W. A. Rosenblith, Ed. Cambridge, Mass.: M.I.T. Press, 1961.

Hernández-Peón, R., & Brust-Carmona, H. Functional role of subcortical structures in habituation and conditioning. In *Brain mechanisms and learning.* J. F. Delafresnaye, A. Fessard, R. W. Gerard, & J. Konorski, Eds. Oxford: Blackwell Scientific, 1961.

Hernández-Peón, R., & Donoso, M. Influence of attention and suggestion upon subcortical evoked electrical activity in the human brain. *Proceedings of the first international congress of neurological sciences, Brussels, 1957. Vol. III. EEG clinical neurophysiology and epilepsy.* London: Pergamon Press, 1959.

Hernández-Peón, R., & Hagbarth, K. E. Interaction between afferent and cortically induced reticular responses. *J. Neurophysiol.,* 1955, **18**, 44–55.

Hernández-Peón, R., & Scherrer, H. "Habituation" to acoustic stimuli in cochlear nucleus. *Fed. Proc.,* 1955, **14**, 71.

Hernández-Peón, R., Guzmán-Flores, C., Alcaraz, M., & Fernández-Guardiola, A. Photic potentials in the visual pathway during attention and photic habituation. *Fed. Proc.,* 1956a, **15**, 91–92.

Hernández-Peón, R., Scherrer, H., & Jouvet, M. Modification of electric activity in cochlear nucleus during "attention" in unanesthesized cats. *Science,* 1956b, **123,** 331–332.

Hernández-Peón, R., Scherrer, H., & Valasco, M. Central influences on afferent conduction in the somatic and visual pathways. *Acta neurol. lat.-amer.,* 1956c, **2,** 8–22.

Hernández-Peón, R., Alcocer-Cuarón, C., Lavín, A., & Santibañez, G. Regulación centrífuga de la actividad eléctrica del bulbo olfatorio. *I. Reun. Cient. Cienc. Fisiol. Montevideo,* 1957a, 192–193.

Hernández-Peón, R., Guzmán-Flores, C., Alcaraz, M., & Fernández-Guardiola, A. Sensory transmission in visual pathway during "attention" in unanesthetized cats. *Acta neurol. lat.-amer.,* 1957b, 3, 1–8.

Hernández-Peón, R., Jouvet, M., & Scherrer, H. Auditory potentials at the cochlear nucleus during acoustic habituation. *Acta neurol. lat.-amer.,* 1957c, 3, 144–156.

Hernández-Peón, R., Guzmán-Flores, C., Alcaraz, M., & Fernández-Guardiola, A. Habituation in the visual pathway. *Acta neurol. lat.-amer.,* 1958, 4, 121–129.

Hernández-Peón, R., Alcocer-Cuarón, C., Lavín, A., & Santibañez, G. Centrifugal suppression of induced activity in the olfactory bulb during distraction and olfactory habituation. Reported in Hernández-Peón, R. Neurophysiological correlates of habituation and other manifestations of plastic habituation (internal inhibition). In *The Moscow colloquium on electroencephalography of higher nervous activity.* H. H. Jasper & G. D. Smirnov, Eds. *EEG clin. Neurophysiol.,* 1960a, Suppl. 13, 101–114.

Hernández-Peón, R., Davidovitch, A., & Miranda, H. Habituation to tactile stimuli in the spinal trigeminal sensory nucleus. Reported in Hernández-Peón, R. Neurophysiological correlates of habituation and other manifestations of plastic inhibition (internal inhibition). In *The Moscow colloquium on electroencephalography of higher nervous activity.* H. H. Jasper & G. D. Smirnov, Eds. *EEG clin. Neurophysiol.,* 1960b, Suppl. 13, 104–114.

Hernández-Peón, R., Lavín, A., Alcocer-Cuarón, C., & Marcelin, J. P. Electrical activity of the olfactory bulb during wakefulness and sleep. *EEG clin. Neurophysiol.,* 1960c, **12,** 41–58.

Holmes, J. E., & Adey, W. R. Electrical activity of the entorhinal cortex during conditioned behavior. *Amer. J. Physiol.,* 1960, **199,** 741–744.

Hubel, D. H. Single unit activity in striate cortex of unrestrained cats. *J. Physiol. (London),* 1959, **147,** 226–238.

Hugelin, A., Dumont, S., & Pailes, N. Formation reticulaire et transmission des informations auditives au niveau de l'oreille moyenne et des voies acoustiques centrales. *EEG clin. Neurophysiol.,* 1960, **12,** 797–818.

Huttenlocher, P. R. Effects of state of arousal on click

responses in the mesencephalic reticular formation. *EEG clin. Neurophysiol.,* 1960, **12,** 819–827.

Iwama, K. Delayed conditioned reflex in man and brain waves. *Tohoku J. exp. Med.,* 1950, **52,** 53–62.

Iwama, K., & Abe, M. Conditioned galvanic skin reflex and electroencephalogram. *Tohoku J. exp. Med.,* 1953, **57,** 327–335.

Jansen, J., Jr., Andersen, P., & Kaada, B. R. Subcortical mechanisms involved in the "searching" or "attention" response elicited by prefrontal cortical stimulation in unanesthetized cats. *Yale J. Biol. Med.,* 1955–1956, **28,** 331–341.

Jasper, H. H. Electrical signs of cortical activity. *Psychol. Bull.,* 1937, **34,** 411–481.

Jasper, H. H., & Cruikshank, R. M. Variations in blocking time of occipital potentials in man as affected by intensity and duration of light stimulation. *Psychol. Bull.,* 1936, **33,** 770–771.

Jasper, H. H., & Cruikshank, R. M. Electroencephalography. II: Visual stimulation and the after image as affecting the occipital alpha rhythm. *J. gen. Psychol.,* 1937, **17,** 29–48.

Jasper, H. H., & Shagass, C. Conditioning the occipital alpha rhythm in man. *J. exp. Psychol.,* 1941a, **28,** 373–388.

Jasper, H. H., & Shagass, C. Conscious time judgments related to conditioned time intervals and voluntary control of the alpha rhythm. *J. exp. Psychol.,* 1941b, **28,** 503–508.

Jasper, H. H., Cruikshank, R. M., & Howard, H. Action currents from the occipital regions of the brain in man as affected by variables of attention and external stimulation. *Psychol. Bull.,* 1935, **32,** 565.

Jasper, H. H., Naquet, R., & King, E. E. Thalamocortical recruiting responses in sensory receiving areas in the cat. *EEG clin. Neurophysiol.,* 1955, **7,** 99–114.

Jasper, H. H., Ricci, G. F., & Doane, B. Patterns of cortical neuronal discharge during conditioned responses in monkeys. In *Neurological basis of behavior.* G. E. W. Wolestenholme & C. M. O'Connor, Eds. Boston: Little, Brown, 1958.

Jasper, H. H., Ricci, H. G., & Doane, B. Microelectrode analysis of cortical cell discharge during avoidance conditioning in the monkey. In *The Moscow colloquium on electroencephalography of higher nervous activity.* H. H. Jasper & G. D. Smirnov, Eds. *EEG clin. Neurophysiol.,* 1960, Suppl. 13.

John, E. R., & Killam, K. F. Electrophysiological correlates of avoidance conditioning in the cat. *J. Pharmacol. exp. Therap.,* 1959, **125,** 252–274.

John, E. R., & Killam, K. F. Studies of electrical activity of brain during differential conditioning in cats. In *Recent advances in biological psychiatry.* J. Wortis, Ed. New York: Grune and Stratton, 1960a.

John, E. R., & Killam, K. F. Electrophysiological correlates of differential approach-avoidance conditioning in cats. *J. nerv. ment. Dis.,* 1960b, **136,** 183–201.

John, E. R., Leiman, A. L., & Sachs, E. An exploration

of the functional relationship between electroencephalographic potentials and differential inhibition. *Ann. N.Y. Acad. Sci.,* 1961, **92**, 1160–1182.

Johnson, L. C., Ulett, G. A., Sines, J. O., & Stern, J. A. Cortical activity and cognitive functioning. *EEG clin. Neurophysiol.,* 1960, **12**, 861–874.

Jouvet, M. Recherches sur les mécanismes neurophysiologiques du sommeil et de l'apprentissage négatif. In *Brain mechanisms and learning.* J. F. Delafresnaye, A. Fessard, R. W. Gerhard, & J. Konorski, Eds. Oxford: Blackwell Scientific, 1961.

Jouvet, M., & Hernández-Peón, R. The neurophysiological mechanisms concerning habituation, attention and conditioning. In *EEG clin. Neurophysiol.,* 1957, Suppl. 6, 39–49.

Jouvet, M., Benoit, O., & Courjon, J. Aspects EEG de la formation de liasions temporaires dans le cerveau. *Communication XXe congrès international de physiologie, Bruxelles,* 1956a, 475–476.

Jouvet, M., Benoit, O., & Courjon, J. The influence of experimental produced by cortical stimulation upon responses of the specific and unspecific systems to auditory signals. *EEG clin. Neurophysiol.,* 1956b, **8**, 732.

Jus, A., & Jus, C. Studies on photic driving conditioning in man. *EEG clin. Neurophysiol.,* 1959, **11**, 178.

Kaada, B. R., & Johannessen, N. B. Generalized electrocortical activation by cortical stimulation in the cat. *EEG clin. Neurophysiol.,* 1960, **12**, 567–573.

Kaada, B. R., Jansen, J., Jr., & Andersen, P. Stimulation of the hippocampus and medial cortical areas in unanesthetized cats. *Neurology,* 1953, **3**, 844–857.

Key, B. J., & Bradley, P. B. The effect of drugs on conditioned arousal responses. *EEG clin. Neurophysiol.,* 1959, **11**, 841.

King, B. C. The influence of repeated rotation on decerebrate and on blinded squabs. *J. comp. Psychol.,* 1926, **6**, 399–421.

Knott, J. R., & Henry, C. E. The conditioning of the blocking of the alpha rhythm of the human electroencephalogram. *J. exp. Psychol.,* 1941, **28**, 134–144.

Kogan, A. B. Physiological meaning of the brain potentials desynchronisation and hypersynchronisation. *Proceedings of the 21st international physiological congress, Buenos Aires,* 1959, 147.

Kogan, A. B. The manifestations of processes of higher nervous activity in the electrical potentials of the cortex during free behavior of animals. In *The Moscow colloquium on electroencephalography of higher nervous activity.* H. H. Jasper & G. D. Smirnov, Eds. *EEG clin. Neurophysiol.,* 1960, Suppl. 13, 51–64.

Kooi, K. A., Thomas, M. H., & Mortenson, F. N. Photoconvulsive and photomyoclonic responses in adults. *Neurology,* 1960, **10**, 1051–1058.

Lesse, H. Amygdaloid electrical activity during a conditioned response. Fifth International Congress on EEG and Clinical Neurophysiology, Brussels. *Abstract of reports.* 1957a, 99.

Lesse, H. Electrographic recordings of amygdaloid activity during a conditioned response. *Fed. Proc.,* 1957b, **16**, 79.

Lesse, H. Rhinencephalic electrophysiological activity during "emotional behavior" in cats. *Psychiat. Res. Rep. Amer. psychiat. Ass.,* 1960, **12**, 224–237.

Liberson, W. T., & Ellen, P. Conditioning of the driven brain wave rhythm in the cortex and the hippocampus of the rat. In *Recent advances in biological psychiatry.* J. Wortis, Ed. New York: Grune and Stratton, 1960.

Lifschitz, W. Auditory evoked potentials in the central nervous system during acoustic habituation. Reported in Hernández-Peón, R. Neurophysiological correlates of habituation and other manifestations of plastic inhibition (internal inhibition). In *The Moscow colloquium on electroencephalography of higher nervous activity.* H. H. Jasper & G. D. Smirnov, Eds. *EEG clin. Neurophysiol.,* 1960, Suppl. 13, 101–114.

Lindsley, D. B., Bowden, J. W., & Magoun, H. W. Effect upon the EEG of acute injury to the brainstem activating system. *EEG clin. Neurophysiol.,* 1949, **1**, 475–486.

Lindsley, D. B., Schreiner, L. H., Knowles, W. B., & Magoun, H. W. Behavioral and EEG changes following chronic brainstem lesions in the cat. *EEG clin. Neurophysiol.,* 1950, **2**, 483–498.

Lissak, K., & Grastyán, E. The changes of hippocampal electrical activity during conditioning. In *The Moscow colloquium on electroencephalography of higher nervous activity.* H. H. Jasper & G. D. Smirnov, Eds. *EEG clin. Neurophysiol.,* 1960, Suppl. 13, 271–280.

Livanov, M. N., & Poliakov, K. L. The electrical reactions of the cerebral cortex of a rabbit during the formation of a conditioned defense reflex by means of rhythmic stimulation. *Bull. Acad. Sci. U.S.S.R. biol. Ser.,* 1945, **3**, 286.

Livanov, M. N., Korolkova, T. A., & Frenkel, G. M. Electrophysiological studies of higher nervous activity. *Zh. vyssh. nerv. Deyat. Pavlova,* 1951, **1**, 521.

Loomis, A. L., Harvey, E. N., & Hobart, G. A. Electrical potentials of the human brain. *J. exp. Psychol.,* 1936, **19**, 249–279.

Lourie, H., Vanasupa, P., & O'Leary, J. L. Experimental observations upon chronic progressive lesions of the brainstem tegmentum and midline thalamus. *Surg. Forum,* 1960, **10**, 756–760.

McAdam, D., Snodgrass, L., Knott, J. R., & Ingram, W. R. Some preliminary observations of electrical changes in deep brain structures during acquisition of a classical conditioned response. *EEG clin. Neurophysiol.,* 1961, **13**, 146 (abstract).

Machne, X., Calma, I., & Magoun, H. W. Unit activity of central cephalic brainstem in EEG arousal. *J. Neurophysiol.,* 1955, **18**, 547–558.

Majkowski, J. The encephalogram and electromyogram of motor conditioned reflexes after paralysis with curare. *Acta physiol. pol.,* 1958, **9**, 565–581; and *EEG clin. Neurophysiol.,* 1958, **10**, 503–514.

Majkowski, J. The influence of kinesthetic stimuli on conditioned cortical rhythms in EEG and EMG examinations in rabbit. *EEG clin. Neurophysiol.,* 1959, **11**, 178.

Mihalevskaya, M. B. The relationship between the orienting reflex and motor responses in man during the determination of visual threshold. In *The orienting reflex and investigatory behavior.* Moscow: Pavlov Institute, 1958 (Russian).

Milner, Brenda, & Penfield, W. Effect of hippocampal lesions on recent memory. Paper read at American Neurological Association meeting, Chicago, June 1955.

Milstein, V., & Stevens, J. R. Verbal and conditioned avoidance learning during abnormal EEG discharge. *J. nerv. ment. Dis.,* 1961, **132**, 50–60.

Morrell, F. Conditioned alpha response in patients with seizures of focal cortical and of centrencephalic origin. *EEG clin. Neurophysiol.,* 1954, **6**, 694–695.

Morrell, F. Interseizure disturbances in focal epilepsy. *Neurology,* 1956, **6**, 327–333.

Morrell, F. Some electrical events involved in the formation of temporary connections. In *The reticular formation of the brain.* H. H. Jasper, L. D. Proctor, R. S. Knighton, W. C. Noshay, & R. T. Costello, Eds. Boston: Little, Brown, 1958.

Morrell, F. Electroencephalographic studies of conditioned learning. In *The central nervous system and behavior* (2nd conference). M. A. B. Brazier, Ed. New York: Josiah Macy, Jr. Foundation, 1959.

Morrell, F. Microelectrode and steady potential studies suggesting a dendritic locus of closure. In *The Moscow colloquium on electroencephalography of higher nervous activity.* H. H. Jasper & G. D. Smirnov, Eds. *EEG clin. Neurophysiol.,* 1960, Suppl. 13, 65–80.

Morrell, F. Electrophysiological contributions to the neural basis of learning. *Physiol. Rev.,* 1961, **41**, 493–494.

Morrell, F., & Jasper, H. H. Electrographic studies of the formation of temporary connections in the brain. *EEG clin. Neurophysiol.,* 1956, **8**, 201–215.

Morrell, F., & Ross, M. Central inhibition in cortical conditioned reflexes. *A.M.A. Arch. Neurol. Psychiat.,* 1953, **70**, 611.

Morrell, F., Roberts, L., & Jasper, H. H. Effect of focal epileptogenic lesions and their ablation upon conditioned electrical responses of the brain in the monkey. *EEG clin. Neurophysiol.,* 1956, **8**, 217–235.

Morrell, F., Naquet, R., & Gastaut, H. Evolution of some electrical signs of conditioning. I: Normal cat and rabbit. *J. Neurophysiol.,* 1957, **20**, 574–587.

Morrell, F., Barlow, J., & Brazier, Mary A. B. Analysis of conditioned repetitive response by means of the average response computer. In *Recent advances in biological psychiatry.* J. Wortis, Ed. New York: Grune and Stratton, 1960.

Morrell, L., & Morrell, F. Periodic oscillation in the habituation curve of electrographic activation. *EEG clin. Neurophysiol.,* 1960, **12**, 757.

Moruzzi, G., & Magoun, H. W. Brainstem reticular formation and activation of the EEG. *EEG clin. Neurophysiol.,* 1949, **1**, 455–473.

Motokawa, K. Electroencephalograms of man in the generalization and differentiation of conditioned reflexes. *Tohoku J. exp. Med.,* 1949, **50**, 225–234.

Motokawa, K., & Huzimori, B. Electroencephalograms and conditioned reflexes. *Tohoku J. exp. Med.,* 1949, **50**, 215–223.

Moushegian, G., Rupert, A., Marsh, J. T., & Galambos, R. Evoked cortical potentials in the absence of middle ear muscles. *Science,* 1961, **133**, 582.

Novikova, L. A., & Farber, L. A. Synchronized rhythms in the cortex and reticular formation of the rabbit brain during orienting reactions. *Sechenov physiol. J. U.S.S.R.,* 1959, **45** (11), 1–13.

Olds, J., & Olds, Marianne E. Interference and learning in paleocortical systems. In *Brain mechanisms and learning.* J. F. Delafresnaye, A. Fessard, R. W. Gerard, & J. Konorski, Eds. Oxford: Blackwell Scientific, 1961.

Palestini, M., & Lifschitz, W. Functions of bulbopontine reticular formation and plastic phenomena in the central nervous system. In *Brain mechanisms and learning.* J. F. Delafresnaye, A. Fessard, R. W. Gerard, & J. Konorski, Eds. Oxford: Blackwell Scientific, 1961.

Palestini, M., Davidovitch, A., & Hernández-Peón, R. Functional significance of centrifugal influences upon the retina. *Acta neurol. lat.-amer.,* 1959, **5**, 113–131.

Pavlov, I. *Conditioned reflexes. An investigation of the physiological activity of the cerebral cortex.* New York: Oxford Univ. Press, 1927.

Penfield, W. Memory mechanisms. *Arch. Neurol. Psychiat. (Chicago),* 1952, **67**, 178–191.

Penfield, W., Jasper, H. H., & Feindel, W. Temporal lobe automatism. Stimulation and electrographic studies. *EEG clin. Neurophysiol.,* 1952, **4**, 369.

Prosser, C. L., & Hunter, W. S. The extinction of startle responses and spinal reflexes in the white rat. *Amer. J. Physiol.,* 1936, **117**, 609–618.

Purpura, D. P. Discussion. In *The central nervous system and behavior* (1st conference). M. A. B. Brazier, Ed. New York: Josiah Macy, Jr. Foundation, 1958.

Rabinovitch, M. Y. The electrical activity in different layers of the cortex of the motor and acoustic analysers during the elaboration of conditioned defensive reflexes. *Zh. vyssh. nerv. Deyat. Pavlova,* 1958, **8**, 546.

Rheinberger, M., & Jasper, H. H. The electrical activity of the cerebral cortex in the unanesthetized cat. *Amer. J. Physiol.,* 1937, **119**, 186–196.

Ricci, G. F., Doane, B., & Jasper, H. H. Microelectrode studies of conditioning: technique and preliminary results. *Proceedings of the first international congress of neurological sciences, Brussels*, 1957, 401–415.

Roger, A., Voronin, L. G., & Sokolov, E. N. An EEG investigation of temporary connections during extinction of the orienting reflex in man. *Pavlov J. higher Nerv. Activ.* 1958, **1**, 1–16 (Russian).

Roitbak, A. I. Primary responses of the cerebral cortex to sound clicks and electrical stimulation of the medial geniculate nucleus; their changes during unconditioned stimulation. *Proceedings of the 21st international physiological congress, Buenos Aires*, 1959, 234.

Roitbak, A. I. Electrical phenomena in the cerebral cortex during extinction of the orienting and conditioned reflexes. *EEG clin. Neurophysiol.*, 1960, Suppl. 13, 91–100.

Rowland, V., & Gluck, H. Electrographic arousal and its inhibition as studied by auditory conditioning. In *Recent advances in biological psychiatry*. J. Wortis, Ed. New York: Grune and Stratton, 1960.

Rusinov, V. S., & Rabinovitch, M. Y. Electroencephalographic researches in the laboratories and clinics of the Soviet Union. *EEG clin. Neurophysiol.*, 1958, Suppl. 8, 1–36.

Rusinov, V. S., & Smirnov, G. D. Electroencephalographic investigation of conditioned reflexes in man. Fourth International Congress on EEG and Clinical Neurophysiology, Brussels. *Congress proceedings*, 1957a.

Rusinov, V. S., & Smirnov, G. D. Quelque données sur l'étude électroencéphalographique de l'activité nerveuse supérieure. *EEG clin. Neurophysiol.*, 1957b, Suppl. 6, 9–23.

Russek, M. On the mechanism of "external inhibition." *Acta physiol. lat.-amer.*, 1959, **9**, 133–137.

Segundo, J. P., Roig, J. A., & Sommer-Smith, J. A. Conditioning of reticular formation stimulation effects. *EEG clin. Neurophysiol.*, 1959, **11**, 471–484.

Sharpless, S., & Jasper, H. H. Habituation of the arousal reaction. *Brain*, 1956, **79**, 655–680.

Sokolov, E. N. Higher nervous activity and perception. In *Psychological problems*. Moscow: Pavlov Institute, 1955 (Russian).

Sokolov, E. N. Perception and conditioned reflexes. *Bull. Moscow Univ.*, 1958 (Russian, monograph).

Sokolov, E. N. Neuronal models and the orienting reflex. In *The central nervous system and behavior* (3rd conference). M. A. B. Brazier, Ed. New York: Josiah Macy, Jr. Foundation, 1960.

Stern, J. A., Ulett, G. A., & Sines, J. O. Electrocortical changes during conditioning. In *Recent advances in biological psychiatry*. J. Wortis, Ed. New York: Grune and Stratton, 1960.

Thompson, R., & Massopust, L. C., Jr. The effect of subcortical lesions on retention of a brightness discrimination in rats. *J. comp. physiol. Psychol.*, 1960, **53**, 488–496.

Travis, L. E., & Egan, J. P. Conditioning of the electrical response of the cortex. *J. exp. Psychol.*, 1938, **22**, 524–531.

Travis, L. E., & Milisen, R. L. Brain potentials from the rat. *J. gen. Psychol.*, 1936, **49**, 405–409.

Voronin, L. G., & Sokolov, E. N. Cortical mechanisms of the orienting reflex and its relation to the conditioned reflex. In *The Moscow colloquium on electroencephalography of higher nervous activity*. H. H. Jasper & G. D. Smirnov, Eds. *EEG clin. Neurophysiol.*, 1960, Suppl. 13, 335–346.

Wells, C. E. Modification of alpha-wave responsiveness to light by juxtaposition of auditory stimuli. *A.M.A. Arch. Neurol.*, 1959, **1**, 689–694.

Worden, F. G. Discussion. In *The central nervous system and behavior* (2nd conference). M. A. B. Brazier, Ed. New York: Josiah Macy, Jr. Foundation, 1959.

Yoshii, N. Principes méthodologiques de l'investigation électroencéphalographique du comportement conditionné. Colloque de Marseille. *EEG clin. Neurophysiol.*, 1957, Suppl. 6, 75.

Yoshii, N., & Hockaday, W. J. Conditioning of frequency-characteristic repetitive electroencephalographic response with intermittent photic stimulation. *EEG clin. Neurophysiol.*, 1958, **10**, 487–502.

Yoshii, N., Pruvot, P., & Gastaut, H. Electrographic activity of the mesencephalic reticular formation during conditioning in the cat. *EEG clin. Neurophysiol.*, 1957a, **9**, 595–608.

Yoshii, N., Matsumoto, J., Ogura, H., Shimokochi, M., alographic study on conditioned reflex in animals. *Proceedings of the first international congress of neurological sciences, Brussels*, 1957b.

Yoshii, N., Matsumoto, J., Ogura, H., Shimokochi, M., Yamaguchi, Y., & Yamasaki, H. Conditioned reflex and electroencephalography. In *The Moscow colloquium on electroencephalography of higher nervous activity*. H. H. Jasper & G. D. Smirnov, Eds. *EEG clin. Neurophysiol.*, 1960, Suppl. 13, 199–210.

CHAPTER THIRTEEN

The Effects of Central Nervous System Stimulation and Lesions on Acquisition and Retention

Before we can investigate the physiological or biochemical events that occur during learning, we must know *where* in the organism to look for them. Learning modifies the organism's response to specific sensory stimuli and can occur only in structures that permit a direct interaction between the sensory and motor systems. This fact restricts our search to the central nervous system, but it tells us little about where in this vastly complicated network of neurons we should begin to look.

The answer to our problem appears quite simple at first: We might selectively destroy specific portions of the central nervous system and then test for a deficit in retention or in the ability to learn new relationships. This approach has been used by many investigators, and we shall discuss their findings in some detail. We must remember, however, that the behavior of a brain-damaged organism is determined by the portion of the central nervous system that remains intact.

If we do not observe a deficit in learning or retention, we cannot conclude that the destroyed portion of the brain does not under normal circumstances participate in the acquisition of new behavior. It is possible that learning functions are impaired even though our crude measuring devices fail to register the deficit. The neural mechanism responsible for learning may contain "elements in parallel," so that the destruction of one of them does not necessarily eliminate or impair the entire system.

On the other hand, if we observe a deficit in learning or retention, we cannot conclude that these functions are necessarily exercised by the destroyed area of the brain. Much of the central nervous system is composed of "series networks" which can be interrupted at many different levels. If, for instance, we cut the optic nerve and test

for a deficit in the acquisition or retention of a task involving visual discriminations, we should not be surprised when a deficit develops. It is clear that the deficit is not one of learning or memory, but rather one of sensory input, for we know that the visual system depends on the integrity of the optic nerve.

The answer is much less conclusive when we observe learning or retention deficits following damage to areas of the brain which are not, as far as we know, a direct and essential part of the sensory or motor systems. It is dangerous to conclude that such an area is specifically related to learning when all we have established is that the *performance* of a learned response appears impaired. Even if we can eliminate the possibility that the behavioral deficit may be caused by a change in motivational factors, we know only that the destroyed area of the brain is necessary for the performance of a learned response. It may be necessary because the area contains neurons which facilitate or inhibit neural mechanisms in other parts of the central nervous system; because pathways happen to pass through the affected area on their way to other portions of the brain; or because mechanisms that are essential to the integration of the motor response itself are affected. There are many other possibilities and the interested reader is referred to Gregory's (1961) discussion of this problem for further detail.

In spite of these objections, we shall now look at some of the many studies that have used ablation techniques. Although our conclusions must be tempered with caution, the investigations have suggested several interesting findings which have been tested in sufficient detail to make it seem likely that we are on the right path. Probably the most interesting of these is the observation that

698

learning does not seem to be the exclusive property of any single part of the central nervous system, but may be a functional attribute of many or all neural mechanisms. This observation is clearest, perhaps, when we consider the evidence of learning in very simple organisms lacking a complex nervous system, but it is amply supported by the findings of lesioning studies in higher animals.

Another potentially fruitful approach to the general problem of localization has been the electrical or chemical stimulation experiment. Stimulation techniques have been applied in studies of learning and retention, but some peculiar conceptual problems often make it difficult to interpret their results. If we assume that a particular neural mechanism is normally active in the course of acquisition, it is difficult to see how additional and nonspecific stimulation of this neural pathway could produce anything but interference with learning. Similarly, if we crudely and nonselectively stimulate a storage mechanism at the very moment that highly specific processes must occur to produce a particular response, confusion and a consequent memory deficit should be expected. Interference rather than facilitation appears to be the logical result of any stimulation procedure, and comparable effects might be expected after stimulation and ablation. Such apparently contradictory results have, in fact, been observed in many studies and have created needless confusion and disagreement in the literature.

Acquisition or retention can be improved by electrical or chemical stimulation only if (1) the motivational mechanisms which are activated affect the performance of the conditioned response rather than its acquisition or retention; (2) normally inhibitory systems are disrupted; or (3) the neural systems which are activated do not normally participate in the acquisition or retention of the particular stimulus response relationships under investigation, but produce direct or indirect facilitation under the particular conditions of the experiment. The latter would appear to be an exceptional condition which is rarely met in the laboratory, and we have therefore included the stimulation studies in our discussion of ablation effects. Many stimulation studies are difficult to interpret, moreover, because functional lesions of unknown extent are often produced by the elicitation of seizure activity at the site of stimulation which may spread to distant portions of the brain. In view of these problems, we shall only mention a sampling of the available literature.

THE ROLE OF CORTICAL MECHANISMS

The ability of man and higher animals to acquire complex habits correlates well with the phylogenetic development of the cerebral cortex, and many psychologists and physiologists have attempted to detect a causal relationship in this correlation. The neocortical mantle has attracted particular attention because of its disproportionately greater development in primates and man. Many investigators have tried to localize specific "association areas" in the frontal and temporal lobes of the cerebrum since Pavlov (1927) suggested that conditioning might depend on cortical mechanism.

Decortication

Fishes without a true cortex (Schiller, 1948) as well as insects and invertebrates without any brain at all (Maier and Schneirla, 1935) are quite capable of learning simple stimulus-response relationships. Cortical mechanisms are therefore not indispensable, but a question remains about the function of the cortex when it is well developed.

Zeliony (see Poltyrew and Zeliony, 1930) reported in 1911 that a dog deprived of all neocortex could not be conditioned. However, Zeliony and Poltyrew (1930) replicated this experiment after casual observations suggested that decorticated animals seemed to be able to remember preoperatively acquired habits. They succeeded in demonstrating defensive conditioning in neodecorticated dogs even when a rather complicated differential-conditioning paradigm was employed. Some animals learned to lift one forepaw when a whistle was blown and the other paw when the experimenter knocked on wood.

Because Zeliony and Poltyrew did not publish any histological verification of the completeness of their ablations, the experiment was repeated by a number of American workers. Using auditory, thermal, or tactile stimuli as the CS for avoidable shock, Girden et al. (1936) obtained clear evidence of conditioning in a neodecorticated dog (see Figure 13.1), and Bromiley (1948) later reported similar results. Girden and his associates suggested that the conditioned responses of neodecorticated animals differed from those of the normal dog in being more "diffuse" (i.e., responses never lost the emotional components normally seen only during the initial stages of defensive conditioning). However, Bromiley (1948) reported that the disturbing effect of the emotional hypersensitivity of the neodecorticated animal could be

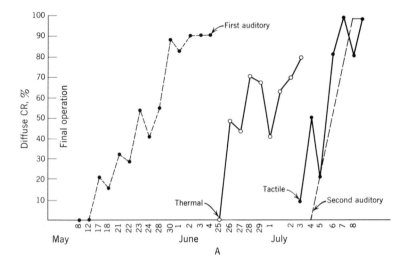

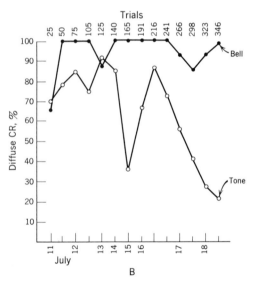

Fig. 13.1   A, rate of conditioning to acoustic, thermal, and tactile stimuli following complete decortication. B, auditory discrimination following complete decortication. Response to the bell was always reinforced with shock. The CR to the tone was extinguished by the omission of shock. (From Girden et al., 1936.)

minimized by careful handling during the experiment and that even differential conditioning (responding to a light but not to a tone) could be obtained. Conditioning in neodecorticated animals is naturally limited by the sensory and motor impairments of this preparation, but there is no clear evidence to suggest that the learning process itself is affected.

Several experiments of the late 1930's suggested that two independent mechanisms for conditioning may exist, one in the cortex, the other in the subcortex. Girden and Culler (1937) dissected the semitendinous muscle out of the leg of a dog and, keeping its blood and nerve supply intact, observed that this isolated muscle could be conditioned to contract even though gross flexor responses were inhibited by curare. The conditioned responses disappeared completely when the curare was allowed to wear off, and conditioning established in the normal animal disappeared after the administration of curare.

Curariform drugs have been used by a number

of investigators, and it may be useful to discuss their action briefly. Curare is the generic term for various South American arrow poisons which may contain several different alkaloids. The first of these to be successfully isolated and synthesized in the laboratory was *d*-tubocurarine. Curariform drugs selectively block the transmission of nerve impulses at the neuromuscular junction and in autonomic ganglia. They specifically interfere with the nicotinic action of acetylcholine and have been used as sympathetic blocking agents. Curariform drugs are used in physiological experiments whenever it is desirable to immobilize an animal without interfering with sensory or central nervous system functions. In most modern studies a curariform drug called *gallamine* (flaxedil) is used in preference to tubocurarine.

The dissociation of skeletal conditioning under curare has been replicated (Culler et al., 1939; Girden, 1940), and similar results have been obtained with autonomic responses (Girden, 1942b, c). Culler et al. (1939) found that curare significantly depressed excitability of the cortex (as measured by the latency of an overt response to direct cortical stimulation), whereas the excitability of neuromuscular junction (as measured by the latency of overt responses to direct stimulation of the motor roots of the spinal cord) appeared unchanged. The authors interpreted these findings to suggest that conditioning in the normal animal might involve cortical mechanisms which are depressed by curare, whereas conditioning in the curarized animal depends on alternate subcortical mechanisms which are normally inhibited by the cortex and thus cease to function when the curare wears off.

This extrapolation seems to go far beyond the experimental facts, but Girden (1940, 1942b, c) presented some evidence that lends support to Culler's hypothesis. Girden removed the auditory cortex before attempting to condition normal and curarized animals to an auditory CS, and found that there was no dissociation between the normal and the drugged states. Conditioning established under curare persisted after the drug had worn off, and animals that had been conditioned before being curarized responded to the CS when paralyzed. It can be argued that these findings support Culler's hypothesis because conditioning may have involved subcortical mechanisms in the lesioned as well as the curarized animals. The results may not be as conclusive as Girden suggested because recent studies have shown that several auditory receiving areas exist, some of which may not have been affected by the ablation.

The experimental use of curare in learning experiments has more recently received renewed attention in investigations of the role of proprioceptive feedback in conditioning (Black and Lang, 1964; K. V. Smith, 1964; Solomon and Turner, 1962; Black et al., 1962). Although this topic is not directly relevant to our present discussion, some pertinent observations were recorded in these studies. Perhaps the most interesting finding is the demonstration that classical conditioning of autonomic responses (cardiac, exophthalmic, and pupillary) is possible in curarized animals and seems to persist with little or no decrement after the drug has worn off.

Classically conditioned somatomotor responses, on the other hand, seem to "dissociate" under curare. Black and Lang (1964) reported that avoidance (leg flexion) responses conditioned in the normal state disappeared under curare and reappeared when the drug wore off. K. V. Smith (1964) questions these results; he suggests that skeletal muscles are not totally paralyzed by either curare or tubocurarine and that conditioning might persist if a sufficiently sensitive measure could be developed. This is an important question, but it does not explain the loss of conditioned responses acquired under curare once the drug effect wears off.

Separate subcortical mechanisms have been demonstrated by several experimenters, as we shall see in the next section of this chapter, and some evidence suggests that more than one subcortical mechanism may be available to the neodecorticated animal. Ghiselli (1938b), for example, found that the bilateral removal of the superior colliculi did not impair the ability of a normal animal to learn or remember a brightness discrimination habit. The same operation produced complete amnesia when the visual cortex had been removed before the original learning. The discrimination could be relearned by animals possessing neither visual cortices nor superior colliculi. These findings suggest that the superior colliculi can mediate learning when the cortical projection areas are removed, and that some other subcortical mechanisms can take over following additional destruction of the superior colliculi. These findings, however, are in need of replication.

Ablation or Stimulation of the Cortical Projection Area of the CS

The visual cortex. Removal of the visual projection area does not affect the retention of a previously learned response to a visual stimulus, nor does it interfere with the acquisition of new habits. This fact had already been suggested by the results of complete neodecortication, but several experiments have established it in greater detail.

Marquis and Hilgard (1936), in a classical conditioning situation, paired a flash of light (CS) with a puff of air to the eyeball (UCS); they demonstrated that dogs without the occipital cortex (1) acquire the conditioned eyeblink response as rapidly as normal animals and (2) show perfect retention of the preoperatively acquired habit.

Very similar results have been obtained in more complex instrumental learning situations. Wing and Smith (1942) found that dogs lacking area 17 were perfectly capable of learning to lift a foreleg to avoid electric shock when the CS was a visual stimulus. Wing (1946) reported that these animals could even learn to respond to slight differences in the general level of illumination. Even after massive damage to the occipital lobe, dogs could be trained to respond to a change in the general level of illumination, and preoperatively acquired intensity discriminations appeared completely unaffected by the cortical lesion.

Wing (1947) extended his findings by showing that comparable results could be obtained in an appetitive conditioning situation in which animals were rewarded with food for lifting the foreleg. An interesting deficit became apparent when the animals were trained preoperatively to respond to a change in light intensity only when the change was in one direction (i.e., always to respond to an increase in illumination but not to a decrease, or vice versa). After removal of the striate area, the animals appeared unable to discriminate between the correct and incorrect direction of change and responded indiscriminately to all changes in the level of illumination. The CR was retained without impairment but seemed to have lost its specificity. Wing presented additional evidence suggesting that the differential habit could be partially restored by retraining, but complete recovery was not observed. He concluded that the striate area plays an essential role in the acquisition and retention of differential conditioning but not of simple conditioned responses to intensity differences.

Although the acquisition and retention of simple visual habits appear unaffected by striate lesions, a very interesting deficit can be observed when the animals are required to discriminate between two or more visual stimuli. Simple brightness discriminations are readily acquired by animals with occipital cortical lesions, but a partial

or complete loss of memory occurs if the same lesions are made after an animal has mastered the task (Klüver, 1936; Lashley, 1929, 1935b, 1939; K. V. Smith, 1937).

The performance decrement does not seem to be merely the result of a sensory deficit, because the animals can relearn the discrimination habit in about as many trials as were required for the preoperative acquisition of the habit. (Lashley, 1929). Nor is it caused by the loss of detail vision which follows destruction of area 17. Animals blinded before the original training by destruction of the lens of the eye show the same memory loss when the occipital cortex is destroyed (Lashley, 1929).

R. Thompson (1960c) reopened this area of investigation by studying the retention of brightness discriminations after multistage lesions. Thompson trained rats in an avoidance situation to make a simple brightness discrimination and tested for retention after unilateral and bilateral striate lesions. The rats showed little or no deficit after unilateral ablations of the visual cortex and continued to exhibit near-perfect retention when the remaining occipital area was subsequently removed. However, retention was severely impaired when the rats were maintained in dark cages and not given experience with the discrimination task in the interim between the two operations.

Experiments by Gunin (1960) indicate that both the postoperative acquisition and the retention of intensity discrimination habits may be impaired. He ablated the visual area of neonatal (7 to 10 days of age) rats and allowed them to recuperate for six to eight months before beginning to train them in a differential intensity discrimination habit. All animals showed a significant impairment when visual stimuli were used, but no deficit on a comparable auditory discrimination task.

Lashley (1929, 1943) found little impairment in original learning when rats without occipital cortices were required to solve a complicated maze on the basis of brightness differences. Although the animals made more errors in the early part of training than their normal controls, the total number of trials to criterion showed only a small, though statistically reliable, difference. Krechevsky's well-known studies of spatial and visual "hypotheses" in rats suggest that animals may abandon visual "hypotheses" after destruction of the striate cortex, even though they are presumably able to learn the maze on the basis of brightness cues.

Although retention and, to a lesser extent, acquisition of a brightness discrimination are impaired by total removal of the occipital cortex, only a very small remnant of the visual projection area seems to be needed to perform these functions. Lashley (1929, 1935a, b) made partial lesions of the striate area and found that retention is unaffected until nearly all the visual cortex is removed.

Movement discriminations, which depend primarily on brightness differences, show similar deficits following removal of the striate cortex. There is little or no postoperative retention of such a discrimination, but relearning is possible; however, many more trials are needed to reach criterion than before the cortical damage (Kennedy, 1939).

The visual cortex is essential for the perception of detail and color, and it is not surprising that no amount of training will succeed in establishing a color or form discrimination after removal of area 17 (Lashley, 1931). Such habits can be established and retained when only a small remnant of striate cortex is intact (Lashley, 1939; Settlage, 1939). Some retraining is needed, particularly when a large portion of the visual area is removed after the original learning. This requirement, however, seems to be due to a problem of reorientation and fixation rather than of memory: animals gradually recover the discrimination habit without additional training if they are maintained in a normal environment, but not when they are kept in the dark (Harlow, 1939; Settlage, 1939).

Similar explanations account for the effects of partial or complete interruptions of the visual pathway itself. Complete destruction abolishes all detail vision, and partial transections of the optic nerve or partial destruction of the lateral geniculate bodies produces marked impairment of learning and retention of form and pattern discriminations (Brown and Ghiselli, 1938c). Of interest is Ghiselli's (1938b) report that removal of the superior colliculi did not impair the acquisition of form discrimination habits, whereas damage to the pretectal nuclei (Brown and Ghiselli, 1938c) produced a reliable deficit. These findings disagree with the generally accepted theory that the colliculi form a major way station of the visual pathways, whereas the pretectal nuclei are active primarily as reflex centers for occulomotor reactions. A replication of the findings is badly needed.

The visual association areas. Although they are not directly part of the cortical projection area of the CS, we might briefly inquire into the effects of lesions in the adjacent visual association areas

(areas 18 and 19 of Brodmann). The role of these areas in learning and retention is unfortunately not as clear as we might wish, in spite of considerable research effort.

Ades (1946) trained monkeys to criterion on three different discrimination tasks involving color, size, and form. He then removed areas 18 and 19 and tested for retention after a period of postoperative recuperation. The animals remembered absolutely nothing, but they relearned all discriminations in about the same number of trials required for the original acquisition (see Figure 13.2). Lashley (1948) performed essentially the same experiment and found no postoperative impairment except with one monkey in whom the lesion infringed on the striate area itself. Since Ades did not present histological confirmation of the extent of his lesions, it is possible that the conflicting results may simply be due to a differential involvement of the striate cortex. However, several subsequent investigations have reported an impairment of retention following damage to the visual association areas when the striate cortex was apparently not involved.

Ades and Raab (1949), for instance, reported that the bilateral removal of areas 18 and 19 produced complete amnesia for a pattern discrimination if the operation was performed in one stage. No impairment was noted after a multistage operation which permitted a period of rest between the removal of these areas on each hemisphere. Animals that had lost the discrimination habit after a single-stage operation could be restrained in about as many trials as had been required for the original learning, provided the temporal cortex was left intact. Bilateral removal of the temporal lobes did not affect retention of the discrimination habit when the cortical association areas were intact. However, when areas 18 and 19 *and* the temporal lobes were removed, the habit was lost completely and could not be re-established by retraining. Since relearning was possible when only the association areas were destroyed, Ades and Raab suggested that some part of the temporal lobe can substitute for the visual association cortex, at least with respect to the acquisition and retention of pattern discrimination (see Figure 13.3).

Riopelle and Ades (1953) subsequently reported that the impairment of acquisition and retention of visual form and pattern discrimination habits is directly related to the amount of damage to the visual association areas. Partial lesions of areas 18 and 19 produced only minor deficits, but memory

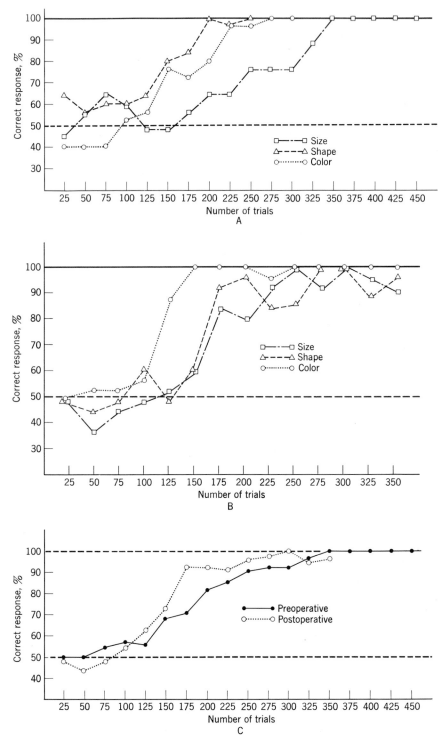

Fig. 13.2 A, preoperative learning curves on three discriminations. B, learning curves on the same three discriminations as represented in A, but after bilateral, one-stage extirpation of areas 18 and 19. C, average results on three types of discrimination before and after bilateral, one-stage extirpation of areas 18 and 19. (From Ades, 1946.)

was lost completely and reacquisition was impossible when areas 18 and 19 and large portions of the temporal lobe were removed. Bates and Ettlinger (1960) have reported a postoperative impairment of visual form discrimination after inferotemporal lesions.

The evidence from all these studies must be considered with caution, for several investigations have shown that temporal lobe lesions produce deficits in sensory capacity which are quite similar to those seen after destruction of area 17. Wilson and Mishkin (1959), for instance, reported that inferotemporal lesions reduced visual acuity as much as destruction of area 17; they concluded that both areas independently serve primary visual functions. Pasik et al. (1960) found that inferotemporal lesions produced greater impairment of a simultaneous discrimination habit when the stimuli were small (1 in.) than when they were large (3 in.), suggesting again a primary sensory deficit. They also noted, however, that a "go/no-go" *successive* discrimination habit seemed impaired only on "no-go" trials. The authors suggested that the animals' inability to inhibit responses on nonrewarded trials may be attributed to the increased tendency to manipulate objects which is such a prominent symptom of the temporal lobe syndrome as described by Klüver and Bucy (1939).

An interpretation of the role of the inferotemporal mechanisms is further complicated by a report by Orbach and Fantz (1958). They found that inferotemporal lesions greatly impaired retention of a visual discrimination habit, but that prolonged overtraining on the original task protected the animals against the effects of this lesion. It is difficult to see why overtraining should affect performance if only sensory mechanisms were impaired by the lesion.

Area 18 does not by itself seem to be essential to discrimination learning. Lashley's studies on partial lesions showed only small effects, and Evarts (1952a, b) has reported no deficit either in retention or in postoperative acquisition of a rather complex discrimination habit which required the subjects to select a green stimulus when a buzzer was sounded but a red stimulus when the auditory signal was omitted.

Destruction of the striate cortex does not reduce an animal's ability to generalize a previously learned discrimination habit to a new set of stimulus conditions. Hebb (1938), for instance, trained rats to discriminate between two panels of different intensities; he then tested for the generalization of this habit to a different set of panels of different absolute intensities but constant brightness differences. He found that rats with their striate cortices destroyed performed as well as normal animals and concluded that generalization of intensity discriminations did not depend on the striate cortex (see Figure 13.4). Lashley (1948) observed that destruction of the visual association areas similarly failed to impair a monkey's performance on tests of intensity generalizations.

Several studies have established that animals trained to discriminate more complex stimuli show more generalization after striate lesions, presumably because their ability to discriminate form and pattern is impaired (Maier, 1941; Wapner, 1944). This may not, however, be the sole reason, because similar results can be obtained with cortical lesions that do not involve area 17. Maier (1941) reported that the extent of generalization appeared to be a function of the size rather than the location of the cortical lesion; however, subsequent experiments (Wapner, 1944) have failed to replicate this aspect of Maier's findings.

Before leaving the topic of visual learning, we should briefly discuss the specificity of the sensory input to the visual projection areas of the two hemispheres. J. Levine (1945a, b) reported that visual discriminations of animals trained with one eye blindfolded were retained perfectly when the blindfold was switched to the other eye (interocular transfer), even when the crossed fibers of the optic chiasma were cut (see Figure 13.5).

This observation suggests than an interchange of information can take place between the two hemispheres, presumably via the corpus callosum. Lashley (1929) found that transections of the posterior portion of the bridge between the hemispheres did not impair interocular transfer, but more recent experiments (Myers, 1955, 1956; Sperry et al., 1956) have demonstrated that this structure is essential when the sensory input to each hemisphere from the contralateral eye is destroyed by a transection of the optic chiasma in the midsagittal plane. Animals trained to discriminate between various visual stimuli showed absolutely no interocular transfer; they even learned and retained directly conflicting habits when trained and tested first with one eye and then with the other. These findings suggest that the process of connection formation which underlies learning may be lateralized, at least for the sensory components of the cortical mechanism, even though the CR itself may require bilateral integra-

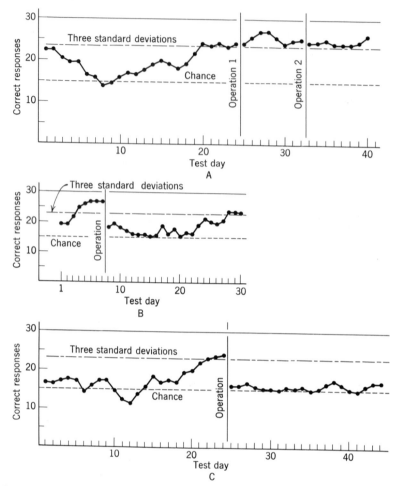

Fig. 13.3 A, smoothed curve of performance before, between, and after unilateral extirpations of areas 18 and 19. B, smoothed curve of performance before and after bilateral extirpation of areas 18 and 19. C, smoothed curve of performance after bitemporal decortication and subsequent bilateral extirpation of areas 18 and 19.

tion. This, of course, indicates that stimulus-response connections may not be made by a direct transcortical route, but rather via subcortical mechanisms which can affect both hemispheres in spite of the callosal transection. We shall return to this interesting problem later in our discussion.

The auditory cortex. A consideration of the role of the auditory cortex is complicated by the rather diffuse cortical projections of the auditory system which are only gradually being uncovered. Although an area of the temporal lobe has long been identified as the "auditory cortex," as many as two or three additional regions that appear to be intimately related to audition have been found. It is not yet perfectly clear whether these areas par-

ticipate in basic sensory functions or serve merely as association areas analogous to areas 18 and 19 of the visual system (see Figure 13.6).

It is difficult to interpret the earlier ablation studies because some of the secondary areas have only recently been discovered; the anatomical information presented in some of the studies to be discussed is insufficient to decide the extent of the damage. These problems are undoubtedly responsible for some of the contradictions that will become apparent in our discussion.

The primary auditory cortex seems to be essential for the retention of even the simplest auditory habits, although no sensory deficit in simple intensity (loudness) discrimination can be demonstrated.

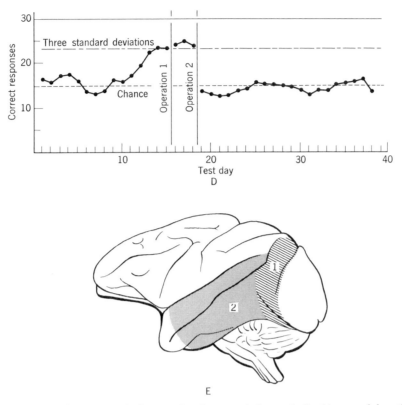

E

Fig. 13.3 (continued)   D, smoothed curve of performance before and after bitemporal decortication and after subsequent bilateral extirpation of areas 18 and 19. E, lateral view of macaque brain showing (1) area of preoccipital cortex and (2) area of temporal cortex removed. (From Ades and Raab, 1949.)

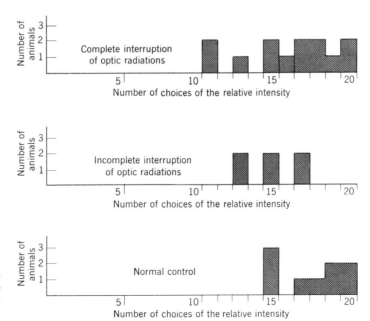

Fig. 13.4   Histograms showing the number of choices of the relative intensity in 20 critical trials. (From Hebb, 1938.)

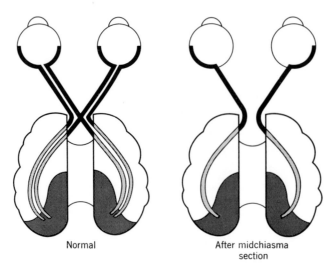

Normal   After midchiasma
                          section

Fig. 13.5 Optic chiasma section results in unilateral restriction of retinal stimulation. (From Myers, 1961.)

Raab and Ades (1946), for instance, found that dogs and cats can learn a simple response such as leg flexion when the CS is a tone or a change in the intensity of a background noise even after the primary auditory area has been removed bilaterally. A preoperatively acquired response is totally lost following such ablations, and little or no savings can be demonstrated in the relearning of the same habit. Similar results have been obtained in the rat, although several studies have suggested that the effects of auditory cortex lesions on retention may be less severe in this species than in the cat and dog. (Wiley, 1932, 1937; Pennington, 1937, 1941). These species differences may be produced solely by a differential involvement of the secondary auditory areas, but insufficient anatomical detail has been presented by the authors of these studies to be sure of this conclusion.

Allen (1945) differentiated between auditory areas I, II, and III and found that the removal of any *one* of these regions did not effect a simple conditioned auditory discrimination habit. When areas I and II were destroyed together, the classical dissociation between acquisition and retention occurred. The animal completely forgot a preoperatively learned discrimination but could be retrained in about the same number of trials required for the original learning. The most puzzling aspect of Allen's findings was the animals' complete inability to relearn the discrimination after larger lesions involving all three auditory areas. The animals showed complete amnesia for a preoperatively acquired habit and showed no sign of relearning after more than 1000 additional trials. Although Allen's learning situation was considerably more complex than those used in

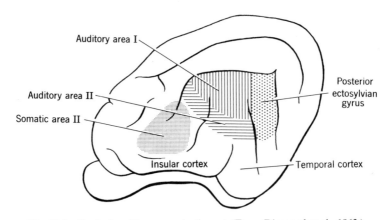

Auditory area I

Auditory area II

Somatic area II

Insular cortex

Posterior
ectosylvian
gyrus

Temporal cortex

Fig. 13.6 Cortical auditory areas in the cat. (From Diamond et al., 1962.)

most of the earlier studies, the task could have been mastered on the basis of a simple discrimination; the failure of his animals to relearn remains an interesting problem.

Several studies have used differential-conditioning paradigms to examine the role of the individual auditory areas in greater detail. D. R. Meyer and Woolsey (1952) investigated the response to frequency (pitch) differences in animals deprived of varying amounts of auditory cortex. Using a Brogden-Culler rotary conditioning apparatus, the investigators trained animals to avoid electric shock by (1) responding to a variable sequence of 3 to 12 tones that were identical except for the last, which was of a slightly higher frequency than the others (CS+); or by (2) not responding to a sequence of 3 to 12 tones which were all of the same frequency as the first tones of the positive stimulus compound.

The results of these studies are complex, and only a brief summary of the principal findings can be presented here (see Figure 13.7 for further details). The most interesting aspect of Meyer and Woolsey's results is that this rather complex frequency discrimination was completely unaffected when either auditory area I or auditory area II were bilaterally removed, even when the posterior ectosylvian gyrus and somatic area II, which may serve as auditory association areas, were also destroyed. Complete amnesia resulted when both auditory areas and the posterior ectosylvian gyrus were destroyed, but the CR could be reacquired. Although the frequency discrimination could not be relearned when the lesion extended into somatic area II, an avoidance response could still be conditioned to a simple tone. Even this disappeared and could not be reacquired when massive lesions which completely destroyed all cortical projections of the auditory system were made.

These findings replicate Allen's earlier observation that conditioned responses to even the simplest auditory stimuli cannot be acquired when all the auditory cortex is removed; they suggest that this inability may represent an impairment of sensory capacity rather than learning capacity. Whether the frequency discrimination deficit can be explained in this fashion is unfortunately not clear. Animals can learn to respond to a single tone when both auditory areas, the posterior ectosylvian gyrus, and somatic area II are destroyed. None of these areas individually appears to be essential to the acquisition of a complex frequency discrimination habit, but any one of them apparently must be present if the CR is to be retained.

Rather than speculate on the implications of these results here, we shall return to this problem after discussing some recent studies in the area.

Diamond and Neff (1957) compared the effects of cortical lesions on frequency and pattern discriminations in an avoidance (shuttle box) situation. Three combinations of positive and negative stimuli were used. For the frequency discrimination test the negative stimulus consisted of three groups of three 800-cps tones, and the positive CS was composed of three groups of three tones, the first and third were identical to those used in the negative CS (800 cps), but the second was a 1000-cps tone. For the pattern discrimination tests both the negative and the positive stimuli contained tones of 800 and 1000 cps and were discriminable only on the basis of patterning. All animals were trained to a stringent criterion (ten out of ten consecutive avoidance responses) before various portions of the auditory cortex were removed (see Figure 13.8).

Diamond and Neff found little or no deficit in retention when auditory area I was removed bilaterally. Pattern discrimination habits were lost completely (but could be reacquired) when the lesions extended into auditory areas I and II as well as into the posterior ectosylvian gyrus. Massive lesions that destroyed "all of the auditory cortex" produced complete amnesia for the pattern discrimination habit, and retraining was completely unsuccessful. The authors reported, however, that the frequency discrimination could be learned even after complete extirpation of the auditory cortex. If we compare these findings with the earlier results of Meyer and Woolsey, it seems probable that Diamond and Neff may not have succeeded in removing all the auditory projection areas. It is nonetheless of considerable interest that the animals could acquire a complex frequency discrimination habit even after a pattern discrimination had apparently become impossible. We are again tempted to suggest that the observed deficits may be sensory rather than associative. However, it is possible that the pattern discrimination habit required a very different and perhaps more complex neural integration than a CR to frequency differences.

Diamond et al. (1962) extended these studies, using an essentially comparable experimental paradigm (see Figure 13.9). However, they chose a new stimulus pattern containing a positive CS of a single frequency and a negative CS of tones of two frequencies. All animals again were trained before both auditory areas and the posterior ecto-

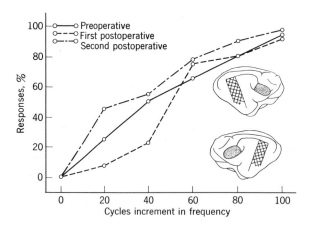

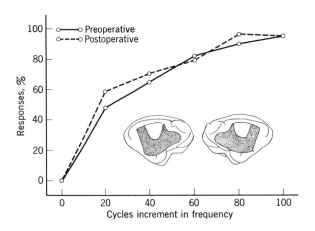

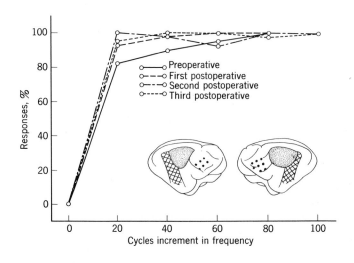

Fig. 13.7(A)   *Top,* sequential destruction of somatic area II and the posterior ectosylvian gyrus. Neither operation has an important effect upon discrimination of frequency. *Middle,* removal of auditory area II, the posterior ectosylvian gyrus, and somatic area II. With auditory area I intact, postoperative discrimination of frequency is normal. *Bottom,* sequential destruction of auditory area I, the posterial ectosylvian gyrus, and somatic area II. None of these operations changes the capacity for frequency discrimination. (From D. R. Meyer and Woolsey, 1952.)

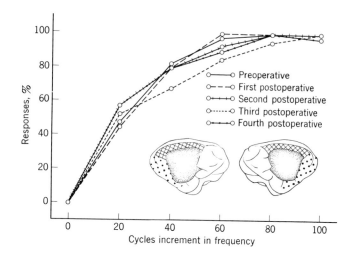

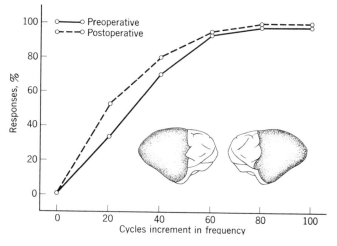

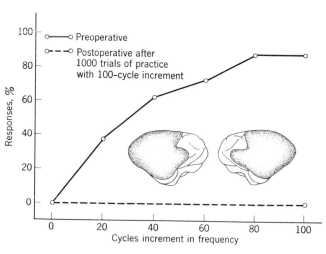

Fig. 13.7(B) *Top,* destruction first of auditory areas I and II and the posterior ectosylvian gyrus. Subsequent sequential removal of the cerebellar tuber vermis, the suprasylvian gyrus, and the temporal cortex as shown. All operations are without effect. *Middle,* massive extirpation of the posterior cerebral cortex, sparing somatic area II. The capacity for frequency discrimination is retained, but extensive retraining is required. *Bottom,* massive extirpation of the posterior cerebral cortex, including the auditory region. Postoperatively there is no evidence for frequency discrimination within 50 sessions or 1000 trials, or for simple conditioning to a pure tone within 40 sessions or 800 trials. (From D. R. Meyer and Woolsey, 1952.)

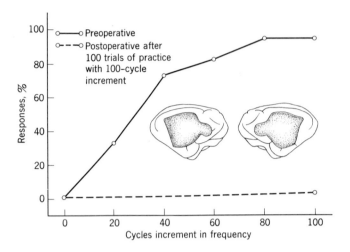

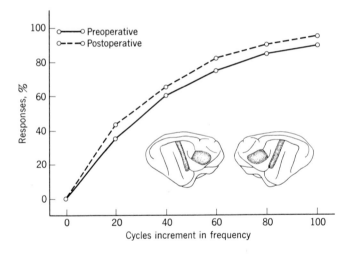

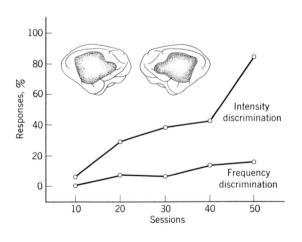

Fig. 13.7(C) *Top,* removal of auditory areas I and II, the posterior ectosylvian gyrus, and somatic area II. Postoperative discrimination of frequency is negligible, but simple conditioning to a pure tone is rapidly established and changes of 6-db intensity are discriminated. *Middle,* removal of somatic area II and the middle-frequency portion of auditory areas I and II. Postoperative discrimination of frequency is normal. *Bottom,* removal of auditory areas I and II, the posterior ectosylvian gyrus, and somatic area II. Discrimination of a 100-cycle change lags far behind discrimination of a 4-db change as postoperative practice proceeds. (From D. R. Meyer and Woolsey, 1952.)

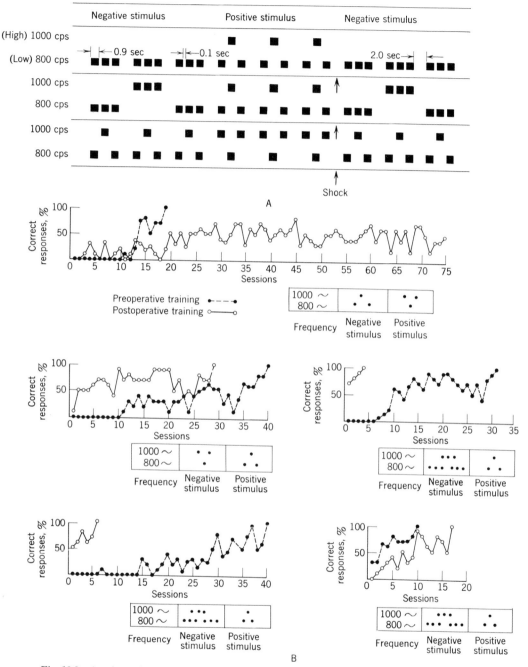

Fig. 13.8 A, schematic representation of the patterns of tones used by Diamond and Neff, 1957. A positive group of three tones is presented three times, or for a duration of approximately 15 sec, and is followed by shock. The duration of the negative stimulus varies from trial to trial but is always longer than the diagram indicates. Time constants shown in the top patterns apply to both positive and negative stimuli. B, Pre- and postoperative learning curves for five experimental animals. The pattern used for each animal is symbolized below the record of training. (From Diamond and Neff, 1957.)

sylvian gyrus were removed. Postoperatively, all animals showed complete amnesia, and three of the subjects failed to relearn the pattern discrimination problem. Two of them reacquired the frequency discrimination habit, but one failed to do so in spite of considerable retraining. These findings seem to contradict Diamond and Neff's earlier observation that relearning of a pattern discrimination was possible following lesions of the auditory area and the posterior ectosylvian gyrus. The authors suggest that this discrepancy may be due to incomplete removal of these areas in the earlier study.

Butler et al. (1957) noted the remarkable persistence of frequency discrimination habits in the early studies; they reopened the question by training six cats in a shuttle box avoidance situation to respond to very small differences in the frequency of a continuously present intermittent auditory signal. Butler and his associates found that the animals could relearn the frequency discrimination habit even when both auditory areas, the posterior ectosylvian gyrus, and somatic area II were bilaterally removed. Their results contradict the earlier report by Meyer and Woolsey that these areas seem to be essential to the acquisition of frequency discriminations; it is tempting to explain this discrepancy in terms of a differential involvement of sensory mechanisms. However, the two experiments are not quite comparable. Meyer and Woolsey gave only one comparison stimulus before the UCS and punished responses to the negative CS, so that the animals had to learn to respond to one frequency but to inhibit responses to another. Butler's group, on the other hand, presented several comparison stimuli and did not punish responses to the negative CS.

R. F. Thompson (1960) has compared these two paradigms, holding the size of the lesions constant. One group of animals was trained according to the experimental design employed by Butler et al., although a rotary conditioning apparatus rather than the shuttle box was used. After extirpation of both auditory areas, the posterior ectosylvian gyrus, and somatic area II, these animals showed complete amnesia for the discrimination but reacquired it rapidly in approximately half the number of trials required for the original learning. The second group of animals was trained according to the paradigm of Meyer and Woolsey, but punishment of the negative CS was omitted. After comparable lesions, these animals had complete amnesia for the discrimination and were unable to relearn it even after 1500 trials. How-

ever, when the animals were switched to the Butler procedure, relearning occurred rapidly, suggesting that the previously observed deficit might not be caused by a sensory impairment. When the same animals were then switched back to the training procedure of Meyer and Woolsey, no evidence of differential learning could be obtained; the animals responded to both positive and negative stimuli. As a last measure, countershock (i.e., punishment of responses to the negative stimulus) was introduced, but the animals merely ceased responding to either the positive or the negative stimulus. Since the animals had shown their ability to make the necessary frequency discrimination when tested with the Butler paradigm, these findings suggest that the auditory cortex or some portion thereof may perform a function that is an essential component of one learning situation but not of the other. Just what this essential difference between the two procedures might be is not clear.

R. Thompson (1962) has reported another interesting study of the role of the auditory cortex in frequency discrimination learning. He removed the auditory cortex (i.e. auditory areas I and II, the posterior ectosylvian gyrus, and somatic area II) in twelve animals and trained them (as well as 24 unoperated controls) on an avoidance task which used a 250-cps tone as the CS. All animals learned the response to criterion, although the operated animals required almost three times as many trials as the controls. Additional deficits became apparent when the operated and control subjects were extinguished with different CS frequencies. Although the operated animals extinguished faster than the control group when the CS frequency was identical or similar (500 cps) to that used during training, this relationship was reversed when very dissimilar tones were used. Whereas the control group responded only once or twice to tones of 2000, 4000, or 5000 cps (showing little generalization beyond 1000 cps), the operated animals required as many trials to extinction when a 5000-cps tone was used as when the 250-cps CS itself was employed (see Figure 13.10).

This completely flat generalization gradient seems to indicate that the cortical lesions may have drastically interfered with the animals' ability to discriminate frequencies, but how does this interpretation account for the earlier findings just reviewed? We might speculate that massive lesions of the auditory cortex may produce a sensory deficit which makes it very difficult, but not impossible, for the animal to discriminate frequen-

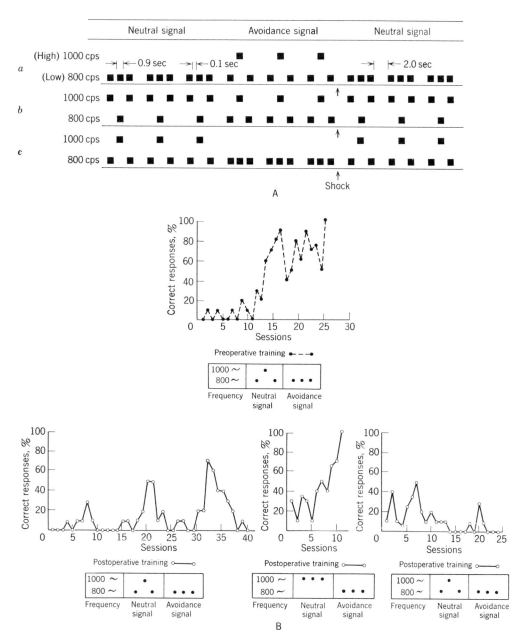

Fig. 13.9 A, schematic representation of the patterns of tones used by Diamond et al., 1962. The avoidance signal is presented three times, or for a duration of approximately 15 sec, and is followed by shock. The number of times a neutral signal is presented is varied from trial to trial but is always longer than the diagram shows. Time constants shown in the top patterns apply to both neutral and avoidance signals. *a*, frequency discrimination; *b*, pattern discrimination; *c*, discrimination in which the neutral signal consists of tones of two frequencies and the avoidance signal consists of tones of only one of the frequencies. B, an animal learned neutral signal versus avoidance signal discrimination before an operation (upper curve) but was unable to relearn the problem after the operation (lower left record). After learning a neutral signal versus avoidance signal habit (lower middle curve), the animal still failed to relearn the original problem (lower right record). (Diamond et al., 1962.)

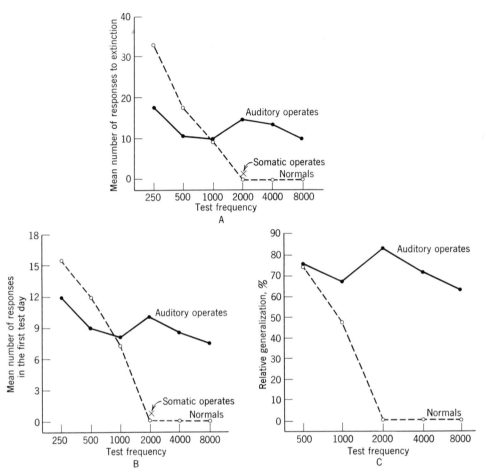

Fig. 13.10 A, amount of absolute stimulus generalization measured by the total number of responses to extinction as a function of test frequency. B, amount of absolute stimulus generalization measured by the number of responses in the first test day as a function of test frequency. C, amount of relative generalization for the number of responses in the first test day measured as a function of test frequency. Note that although both normals and auditory operates have the same amount of relative generalization to the 500-cps tone, the normals decline rapidly for higher test frequencies but the operates remain at approximately the same level for all test frequencies. (From R. Thompson, 1962.)

cies. In the acquisition phase of an avoidance response, where incorrect responses and the absence of correct responses are punished severely, animals may be able to make the discrimination, particularly when several comparison stimuli are presented and the CS-UCS interval is relatively long, as in the Butler et al. paradigm. Such a sensory deficit may be reflected in Thompson's finding that animals with massive cortical damage learned the avoidance response to a simple tone CS much more slowly and extinguished much more rapidly than normal controls. The flat generalization gradient may also reflect this deficit,

since the motivation for a precise discrimination is relatively small in the extinction situation.

Still another type of learning situation has been employed in studies concerned with the functions of the auditory projection and association areas. Early experiments on sound localization in the rat (Wiley, 1937) suggested that animals preoperatively trained to go to that one of two compartments from which a sound emanated would lose this habit after bilateral removal of the auditory cortex but could reacquire it in about the same number of trials needed for the original learning. Subsequent experiments with cats generally showed that the performance of learned responses based on the ability to localize sound appeared to be permanently lost after massive auditory cortex lesions. Moreover, relearning seemed to be impossible, particularly when the correct and incorrect goal boxes were in close proximity (Neff et al., 1950; Arnott and Neff, 1950; Neff and Diamond, 1958; Neff et al., 1956). Some evidence for relearning has been obtained when the goal boxes were separated by 180° (Rosner and Neff, 1949). Although it is possible that species differences account for the discrepancy between some of the earlier studies and those reported in the past 20 years, it seems likely that the latter experimenters removed more cortical tissue and may simply have been more successful in removing most or all of the auditory projection areas (see Figure 13.11).

Neff and Diamond (1958) have hypothesized that temporal discrimination may be one of the functions of the auditory cortex. In support of this notion, they pointed out that auditory pattern discrimination and sound localization (which depends on a discrimination of the temporal differences in the arrival of sound at the two ears) are permanently abolished by ablations of the auditory cortex, whereas frequency and intensity discriminations can be reacquired. In view of the recent studies which have suggested that the ability to perform simple intensity and frequency discriminations may also be impaired, though perhaps not totally abolished, by cortical damage, this distinction may represent a quantitative difference rather than a qualitative one. Nonetheless, it is not clear to what extent destruction of any part of the cortical projection or association areas for audition affects learning or retention per se.

Somatosensory cortex. Relatively little work has been reported with somesthetic conditioned stimuli, largely because it is quite difficult to control the intensity parameter of the stimulation. Ruch (1935) reported that lesions in the posterior portion of the parietal lobe produced some memory loss of a roughness discrimination habit in chimpanzees and monkeys. Relearning was possible in fewer trials than were required to establish the habit preoperatively. Bilateral destruction of the entire parietal lobe produced almost complete amnesia for the discrimination habit; retraining was again possible, although many more trials were required. To what extent simple sensory deficits may be responsible for these results is

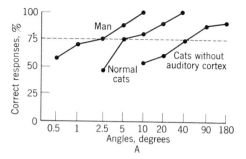

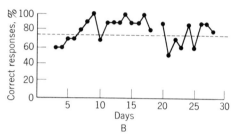

Fig. 13.11 A, angles discriminated correctly in sound localization by man, normal cats, and cats with the auditory cortex ablated. The dashed line indicates the 75% correct level. B, curve showing postoperative performance in a sound localization situation. The angle between food boxes and, thus, between successive positions of the buzzer was 180°. (From Neff and Diamond, 1958. Reproduced with permission of the copyright owners, the Regents of the University of Wisconsin.)

not clear, but it seems certain that removal of the parietal lobe produces severe deficits. D. E. Smith (1939) investigated the effects of various cortical lesions on roughness discriminations in a Y-maze and concluded that the habit was remarkably insensitive to massive lesions of the postcentral cortex. Only four of his rats failed to perform the discrimination postoperatively, and histological examination of the brains of these animals showed such massive damage to motor and premotor areas (as well as other parts of the frontal lobe) that it seems doubtful whether the observed impairment was specific to the roughness discrimination task.

Zubeck (1951, 1952) has reported that roughness discriminations were completely forgotten after bilateral removal of somatic areas I and II; tactile form discrimination habits were only slightly affected. The roughness discrimination could be relearned in about the same number of trials required for the preoperative acquisition of the habit. Kruger and Porter (1958) have found that similar ablations produce some impairment of form discrimination in monkeys, but performance returns to preoperative levels with very little retraining. There is some doubt about the generality of these findings, for Zubeck (1952b) has reported that a cat with lesions in somatic areas I and II was unable to relearn a roughness discrimination habit in spite of prolonged retraining, and Allen (1946, 1947) observed a similar persistence of impairment in the dog. Allen trained his animals to respond to a positive tactile stimulus (stroking the back with the grain) and to withhold responses to a negative stimulus (stroking the back against the grain). He found that the CR (leg flexion) to the positive CS was retained after the operation, but that the animals appeared unable to inhibit the response when the negative CS was presented. The results of Zubeck's studies on the rat suggest that Allen may have observed an impairment because the learning situation employed was much more complex and may have provided a more sensitive test of the effects of the lesions. However, Allen's description of his histological material also suggests that his ablations may have been larger than those made by other investigators, thus contributing to the contradictory results.

Ruch (Ruch, 1935; Ruch et al., 1937, 1938, 1940) has shown that the memory of a kinesthetic discrimination problem is impaired by removal of either the precentral, postcentral, or posterior parietal cortex, but the habit can be restored by some retraining. The deficit was most marked after posterior parietal lesions, and the importance of this area to somesthetic discriminations has been demonstrated in a variety of learning situations (J. S. Blum et al., 1950; R. A. Blum, 1952; Helen Pribram and Barry, 1956). J. S. Blum et al. (1950) have even suggested that the posterior parietal lobe may be quite specifically concerned with somesthetic discrimination learning.

Before leaving this discussion, we should like to mention that the sensory input to the somatosensory projection areas appears to be quite distinctly lateralized. This is shown most clearly in an experiment by Stamm and Sperry (1957). These investigators trained cats to perform roughness and form discriminations with one paw. Normal animals readily transferred this habit to the contralateral forepaw, but animals with complete callosal transections had to relearn all problems and did not show any effects of the previous acquisition. Comparable results have been reported for tactile discriminations in monkeys (Glickstein and Sperry, 1960; Ebner and Myers, 1960).

Glickstein and Sperry (1960) found that somesthetic discriminations learned with one paw would transfer quite readily to the other paw, even when the corpus collosum was cut, provided the somesthetic projection area corresponding to the first paw was destroyed. This finding suggests that the same cortical hemisphere can mediate learning for both sides of the body if the other hemisphere is destroyed. Since Glickstein and Sperry used animals with complete callosal sections, there must exist some subcortical pathway which is normally inhibited by the presence of both somatosensory projection areas.

Electrical stimulation of the cortical projection areas of the CS or UCS. Very few reports are available that relate electrical stimulation of primary sensory receiving areas to acquisition or retention, because an impairment of these functions following stimulation of the sensory pathways of the CS or UCS cannot easily be related to associative mechanisms. One interesting example of such work may suffice to illustrate the problem. Zuckermann (1959) reported a series of studies on the effects of cortical and reticular stimulation on a simple classically conditioned eyeblink response (see Figure 13.12). The CS was an intermittent click, the UCS a puff of air to the cornea. The intensity of the 5-sec electrical stimulation of the brain was sufficient to induce seizure activity. The first experiment showed that stimulation-induced seizures of the sensory-motor cortex produced a 5- to 15-sec period of absolute inhibition during which no conditioned responses could be elicited, even in well-trained animals. When testing was continued, responses reappeared briefly, followed by a second and more prolonged (5- to 20-min) period of inhibition. In the second experiment Zuckermann localized the seizure activity to the projection area of the UCS and found that normal responses to the CS continued to be made as soon as the 5-sec stimulation of the sensory areas was terminated. No evidence for a persisting inhibition was obtained. However, when the seizure activity was localized in the projection area of the CS (auditory cortex), a 15- to 60-sec period of inhibition was observed. Previous studies (Chow and Obrist, 1954; Henry and Pribram, 1954) showed that permanent irritative foci in the projection area of the CS (visual cortex) did not interfere with the retention of a visual discrimination habit, although epileptiform spike discharges dominated the EEG record. Kraft et al. (1960)

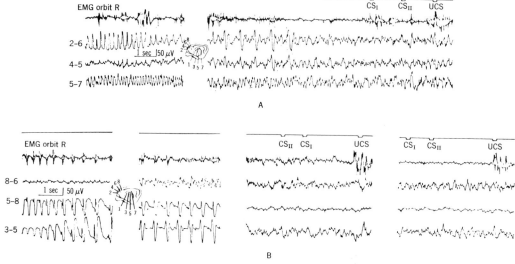

Fig. 13.12 A, effect of focal cortical discharge (sensory-motor area) on a corneal CR. Top line, CS_{II}, continuous tone (second-order conditioned stimulus); CS_I, metronone; UCS, air puff to cornea. Remaining traces are as indicated. Note the appearance of an orbicularis CR immediately on cessation of paroxysmal EGG discharges in the cortical area to which the UCS projects and the absence of evoked responses which are normally present in the acoustic area. B, effect of focal cortical discharge (acoustic area) on a corneal CR. Tracings are as in A. The corneal CR here cannot be elicited long after paroxysmal discharges have ceased in the cortical area to which the CS projects. (From Zuckermann, 1959.)

found that such irritative foci in the visual cortex significantly impaired the acquisition of visual discrimination problems, whereas spatial alternation tasks were readily learned.

Similar deficits have been reported following lesions in the primary cortical projection areas, and it appears likely that the results of both types of studies are due to a direct interference with sensory rather than associative functions.

Ablations or Stimulation of the Association Areas

A discussion of the cortical projection areas of the UCS is inappropriate in the present context since the effects of unconditioned stimuli are rarely modality-specific and fit better into the category of motivational variables discussed in previous chapters. We shall therefore now briefly review the role of the cortical association areas.

The term association area implies that learning and other higher mental processes should occur in these regions, but the areas have received this fanciful label largely because of our ignorance about their functional properties. They are almost certainly not directly concerned with simple sensory or motor processes, although numerous fibers from the thalamic nuclei project into them; but their function as a cortical association area is still only poorly understood. Before we proceed with our discussion, it may be useful to review briefly the anatomical boundaries of these areas.

The most prominent of the association areas is the *prefrontal granular cortex*. This portion includes areas 9, 10, 11, and 12, which occupy the dorsal and lateral surface of the frontal lobe from the frontal pole to the transitional area 8, and areas 13 and 14 of the orbital surface. These regions receive projections from the nucleus dorsomedialis of the thalamus. Two small association areas are found in the posterior part of the cortex, the *parieto-occipito-temporal* region (i.e., the area common to the three sensory lobes of the cortex) and the *anterior temporal* region which occupies the tip of the temporal lobe. The first of these seems to be related quite directly to sensory functions, receiving cortical inputs from all sensory areas as well as projections from the pulvinar nucleus of the thalamus. The anterior temporal region is without known thalamic projections and may be concerned primarily with emotional

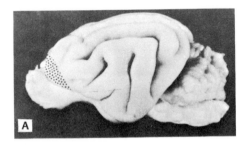

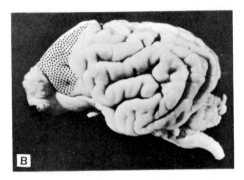

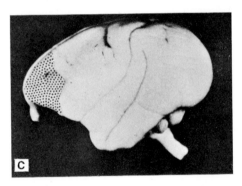

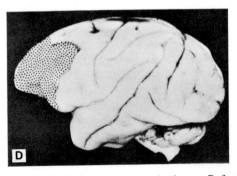

Fig. 13.13 A, frontal granular area in the cat; B, frontal granular area in the dog; C, frontal granular area in the squirrel monkey; D, frontal granular area in the rhesus monkey. The pictures are not made to scale. (From Akert, 1964.)

behavior. Only the orbitofrontal cortex has been clearly linked experimentally with learning and retention, and we shall confine our discussion to this area.

A vast and often contradictory literature which attempts to analyze the functional contributions of the association areas, particularly those of the prefrontal granular cortex, has accumulated in the past 20 years. Much of the confusion arises from the inappropriate assumption that the frontal lobe, or at least its nonmotor portions, can be treated as a homogeneous unit. A brief survey of the anatomy of this part of the brain suggests that this is untrue (see Figure 13.13).

The grossest functional division separates the frontal lobe into a motor region from which overt muscular responses can be elicited by electrical stimulation and a nonmotor area which appears to be inexcitable. The two portions meet in the posterior half of the frontal lobe, area 6 of Brodmann being the disputed "no-man's land" between them. In primates and man, this distinction roughly parallels a cytoarchitectonic division of the frontal lobe into granular and agranual cortex. The cytoarchitectonic boundaries are much less distinct in carnivores and rodents, and this may explain important functional species differences. A further anatomic parallel to the gross divisions of the frontal lobe into motor and nonmotor areas is provided by differential thalamacortical projections. The motor areas receive afferents from the lateral and medial portions of the ventrolateral nucleus, whereas the prefrontal cortex (Brodmann areas 8 through 12) receives inputs from the dorsomedial nucleus as well as afferents from the intralaminar nuclei.

Degeneration studies by Akert (1964) have shown that the dorsomedial frontal granular cortex does not receive any direct thalamacortical projections; similar athalamic cortex has been demonstrated in the association areas of the temporal lobe. The projections from the dorsomedial nucleus to the frontal cortex were found to follow a specific pattern so that the *pars paralamellaris* of the nucleus projects selectively to area 8, the *pars parvocellularis* to area 9, and the *pars magnocellularis* to the orbitofrontal cortex.

The frontal granular cortex projects afferents through the cingulum bundle to the presubiculum and entorhinal area which, in turn, project to the hippocampus proper. Most of the fibers in this limbic projection arise from area 9, dorsal to the sulcus principalis, and from cells within the folds of that sulcus.

Important frontotemporal projections via the uncinate fasciculus arise from most parts of the prefrontal granular cortex, although the area ventral to the sulcus principalis appears to participate most heavily in this projection. Fibers from the dorsal surface (area 9) are rare. The frontotemporal projections provide important connections to the amygdaloid area and hippocampus; these areas complete a feedback circuit via hypothalamic projections (see Figure 13.14).

The subcortical projections of the prefrontal cortex travel mainly through the internal capsule, although some extracapsular pathways through the ventral forebrain have been described. Direct efferents from the dorsal surface of the frontal lobe reach the head of the caudate nucleus, whereas those from the ventral and orbitofrontal regions project to the putamen. Virtually all the granular cortex projects to the lateral hypothalamus and preoptic area as well as to the adjoining subthalamic regions. Specific frontohypothalamic projections to the ventromedial nuclei (M. Meyer, 1950) and mammillary bodies (M. Meyer, 1949) have also been reported.

The frontothalamic projections roughly reverse the pattern established by the thalamacortical projections from the dorsomedial nuclei. Extensive projections to the intralaminar nuclei have also been observed. (For a detailed discussion of the efferent projections of the frontal lobe, see Nauta, 1964.)

Extensive damage to the orbitofrontal cortex does not affect learning or retention of simple conditioned responses. A deficit becomes noticeable primarily when experimental paradigms demand that the subject respond to sensory information which was presented at some previous moment but is not available at the time of the response. Perhaps the simplest example of such a task is the delayed-alternation experiment in multiple mazes. Here the animal is trained to make alternate right and left turns at successive choice points and can only solve the problem by remembering, without the aid of external cues, which way it turned on the last choice point. A delay is introduced between one response and the next by extending the length of the runway between choice points. If normal rats are required

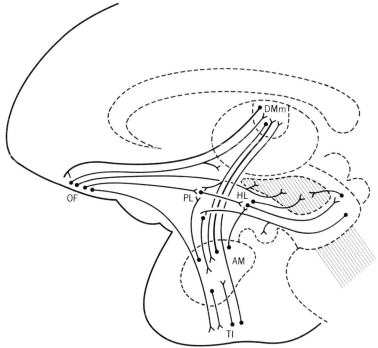

Fig. 13.14 Connections between the amygdaloid complex (AM), the medial part of the dorsomedial thalamic nucleus (DMm), the caudal orbitofrontal cortex (OF), and ventral regions of the temporal lobe (TI). All except the TI project directly to the lateral preopticohypothalamic region (PL and HL), which in turn has efferent connections with the mesencephalic reticular formation. (From Nauta, 1962.)

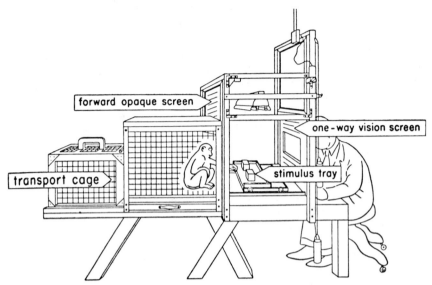

Fig. 13.15 Delayed-response trial using the Wisconsin General Test Apparatus. (From Harlow, 1958a. Reproduced with permission of the copyright owners, the Regents of the University of Wisconsin.)

to learn such a maze, prolonged training is needed, but all animals will eventually reach a nearly perfect performance level. Rats with frontal lobe lesions take much longer to acquire even moderate levels of proficiency in this test and are often totally unable to master the problem (Loucks, 1931; Morgan and Wood, 1943; Leary et al., 1952; Mishkin and Pribram, 1956).

An even clearer example of this type of learning problem is the delayed-reaction test in which the subject is allowed to watch the reward being placed under one of two stimulus objects. An opaque door is then lowered between the subject and the stimuli for the duration of a predetermined delay of several seconds. When this door is removed, the subject is allowed one choice between the stimulus objects. This has long been regarded as a test of short-term memory, but recent experiments have indicated that a number of other variables must be considered (see Figure 13.15).

Normal animals can learn such a delayed response quite easily, even when a minute or more intervenes between the initial exposure of the stimuli and the response itself. Monkeys with bilateral prefrontal lesions, on the other hand, cannot solve such a problem, even when the delay is short. This was first demonstrated by Jacobsen and his associates (Jacobsen et al., 1935; Jacobsen, 1936, 1939), who believed the impairment to be caused by a short-term memory deficit

(see Figures 13.16 and 13.17). Jacobsen showed that the failure on the delayed-reaction test could not be attributed to a general impairment of intelligence or of the ability to learn. The same animals learned or retained a visual discrimination problem as competently as normal animals; they even succeeded in a highly complex "stick and platform" problem which required the use of several tools (sticks). Only when this problem was changed to require short-term memory (i.e., the sticks were not presented together as before but in different places) did the animals with prefrontal lesions fail the test. Finan (1939) obtained very similar results in various learning situations which require that the animals remember a stimulus for several seconds. Although monkeys with prefrontal lesions could not solve delayed-response problems even when the delays were short, they showed little or no deficit in learning a temporal maze in which one path was shorter than the other; they also learned to avoid electric shock in a shuttle box by moving from one grill to the other some seconds after a CS was presented. Finan concluded that the deficits observed in the delayed-response experiments could not be caused simply by an impairment of short-term memory.

Jacobsen et al. (1935) reported that the capacity for delayed-response learning appeared to be an exclusive property of a relatively small portion of frontal cortex, for extensive damage to

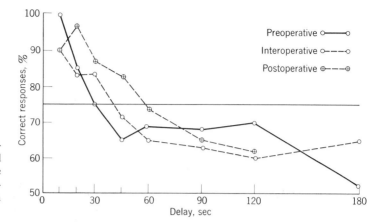

Fig. 13.16 Preoperative, interoperative (unilateral temporal lobectomy), and postoperative (bilateral) tests for delayed response in the monkey. (From Jacobsen and Elder, 1936.)

the motor, premotor, or sensory projection areas did not produce a comparable deficit in spite of marked motor and sensory impairments. Lashley (1938), on the other hand, observed a deficit in delayed-response learning following lesions designed to destroy the visual association areas 18 and 19. These lesions undoubtedly encroached on the parieto-occipito-temporal association area, and it is possible that the impairment of delayed reactions may be common to damage to all association areas.

Jacobsen's results have been confirmed in several laboratories (J. S. Blum et al., 1951; Harlow et al., 1952; D. R. Meyer et al., 1951; Miles and Bloomquist, 1960; Bättig et al., 1960; French, 1964) (see Figure 13.18). However, some of the more recent studies have shown that animals with frontal lesions can master the delayed-response problem under certain circumstances and may show small but consistent impairments in discrimination learning situations (Harlow, 1958a, b; Riopelle and Churukian, 1958; Orbach and Fischer, 1959).

The first observations of the behavior of animals with frontal lobe damage (Ferrier, 1886; Bianchi, 1895) describe a marked rise in spontaneous locomotor activity. The hypothesis has been advanced that this tendency may be responsible for some or all of the behavioral impairments seen in learning situations. The hyperactivity may specifically interfere with the delayed response because during the delay period the animal engages in "extracurricular" activities which compete and interfere either directly with the execution of the learned response itself (Richter and Hines, 1934; French, 1959a, b, c) or with the acquisition of mnemonic devices such as postural adjustments or spatial orientations which might

help bridge the delay interval (Orbach and Fischer, 1959). Mettler (1944) extended this notion by arguing that the frontal monkey may be not only hyperactive but, more generally, hyper*reactive* to all sensory inputs and thus more easily distracted during the delay period.

A similar position has been taken by Finan (1942), who suggested that delayed-response learning might be impaired by the inattentiveness of the animal during the time the correct stimulus is presented. To test this hypothesis, Finan allowed monkeys to obtain food from the correct receptacle *before* imposing the delay and found that all animals with frontal lesions were able to solve the problem under these conditions. One of his animals even performed satisfactorily on

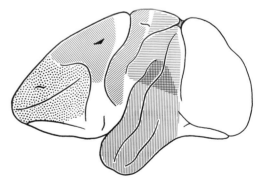

Fig. 13.17 Summary of the effects of cortical ablations on the capacity for delayed response in the monkey. Extirpation of the hatched regions—parietal, postcentral convolutions, temporal lobes, and motor-premotor areas —causes no impairment of ability. Ablation of the stippled area was followed by permanent impairment of the capacity for delayed response. The essential region for delayed response is restricted to a small area about the frontal sulcus. (From Jacobsen, 1936.)

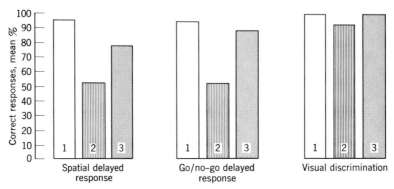

Fig. 13.18 Average performance of four chimpanzees on spatial and go/no-go delayed responses and on a visual pattern discrimination. The first column in each set represents the average performance during the week preceding frontal lobotomy, the second column the performance during the third week after this operation, and the third column the performance during the thirteenth week after the operation. (From Rosvold et al., 1961.)

Jacobsen's original problem after some training with the predelay reinforcement. This experiment has been replicated by Spaet and Harlow (1943) in a slightly modified situation. Animals were allowed to find food under a single object. After a delay period of several seconds, two dissimilar objects were presented, one of which was the same object that had been used before. Monkeys with prefrontal lesions learned to select the correct object, presumably because they were forced to pay attention to it when it was first presented.

Malmo (1942) has also obtained evidence suggesting that animals with prefrontal lesions may fail the delayed-response test because they are distracted during the delay period or because they fail to pay attention to the stimulus situation. He found that prefrontal monkeys could learn the task as well as control animals if all lights were turned off during the delay interval.

Malmo suggested that this inability to concentrate on a problem should affect performance in other learning situations, and a number of experiments have reported such deficits. Harlow and Dagnan (1943) found that animals with prefrontal lesions can learn a variety of visual discriminations but make many more errors than their normal controls before reaching criterion. These animals also have great difficulties adjusting to a change in the problem, such as a reversal of the correct and incorrect stimuli. Prefrontal monkeys also show much slower reaction times than normal animals, and this deficit has been interpreted as being caused by inattentiveness (Harlow and Johnson, 1943). The attentiveness factor has also been invoked to explain the very interesting finding that monkeys with frontal lesions can

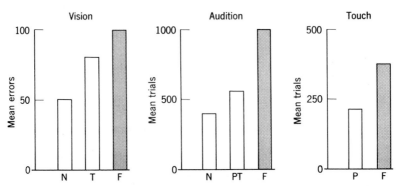

Fig. 13.19 Effects of frontal lesions on visual, auditory, and tactual discrimination learning. T, temporal; P, parietal; F, frontal; N, normal; PT, parietotemporal. (From Rosvold and Mishkin, 1961.)

learn the delayed-response problem even when Jacobson's procedure is used without any modifications, provided they are trained under a light Nembutal or Dial sedation (Wade, 1947).

Gross (1963a, b, c) obtained quantitative measures of the basic lesion effect on locomotor activity. He found that lesions confined to the sulcus principalis and those involving all the lateral-frontal cortex increased locomotor activity in the presence of light but not in darkness. Novel stimuli depressed the activity of the lesioned animals more than that of normals in the dark as well as in the light. This finding suggests hyperreactivity rather than simple hyperactivity and confirms the earlier observations of Mettler (1944). Gross also observed, however, that the locomotor changes were not correlated with the severity of the concurrent deficits in delayed-response problems. This agrees with the results of previous investigations (Ruch and Shenkin, 1943; K. H. Pribram, 1950; Miles and Bloomquist, 1960), which indicated that hyperactivity is not a sufficient condition for deficits in delayed-response situations. The two effects appear to be independent, although common physiological mechanisms may contribute to both.

Several investigators (Campbell and Harlow, 1945; Moss and Harlow, 1948; R. A. Blum, 1952) have reported that monkeys and chimpanzees with extensive frontal lesions can solve delayed-response problems even without the aid of predelay reinforcement or sedation. If prolonged periods of postoperative recuperation are allowed and intensive training on a variety of learning problems is given before the test of delayed responses, some, though not all, animals will learn this task as well as normal animals. The studies that have shown this most clearly have made minor changes in procedure which may help the animal focus its attention on the appropriate stimuli.

Stamm (1963) has reported some interesting observations which suggest that timing behavior is not, per se, affected by frontal lobe damage. Normal monkeys and animals with cingulate gyrus or frontal lobe lesions were trained in an operant (lever-pressing) situation to emit successive responses only after some delay (a DRL schedule that provides differential reinforcement for low rates of responding). The frontal monkeys were noticeably poorer in withholding responses early in the training regimen, but they gradually adjusted their performance to the reward schedule. In fact, with a very long and difficult delay of 70 sec, more frontal animals adjusted to the schedule and showed optimal timing behavior than cingulate-lesioned animals or normals. By establishing an arbitrary criterion of at least 50% rewarded responses, Stamm was able to show that the longest delays on which criterion performance was obtained differed significantly for his groups (65 sec for the frontal animals, 47.5 sec for the normals, and 35 sec for the cingulate-lesioned animals). An analysis of the interresponse times (IRT's) showed clear-cut patterns of timing behavior for the frontal monkeys even at the longer delays, suggesting that the frontal lesions did not interfere with this form of behavioral adjustment.

A subsequent analysis of the delayed-alternation performance of lobectomized monkeys (see Stamm, 1964) indicated a complete postoperative loss of retention but a reacquisition of the problem with retraining. The postoperative rate of improvement initially paralleled the preoperative curves, but flattened out near 70 to 75% correct performance. It took about 800 trials to produce the improvement required to go from 70 to 90% correct.

Frontal lobe damage generally, though not always, results in performance deficits in behavioral test situations which do not require a delayed response to stimulation. Visual and auditory discriminations have been reported affected to varying degrees by frontal ablations. The question has been raised whether these sensory deficits might be attributable to a general inability to withhold nonrewarded responses to negative stimuli, as reported by several investigators (French, 1964; Mishkin et al., 1962; Brush et al., 1961).

Other studies (R. A. Blum, 1952; Weiskrantz and Mishkin, 1958; Rosvold and Mishkin, 1961) have shown more marked and apparently modality-specific deficits in discrimination situations. Recent investigations of this problem suggest that the deficits may be related to functional impairments represented in specific portions of the frontal lobe (see Figure 13.19).

Gross and Weiskrantz (1962) showed that lesions confined to the banks and depths of the sulcus principalis produced a significantly greater impairment on delayed-response problems; however, such lesions caused significantly less inhibition of simultaneous and successive visual and auditory discriminations than did lateral-frontal lesions which spared the sulcus (see Figure 13.20).

A subsequent analysis of the effects of lesions

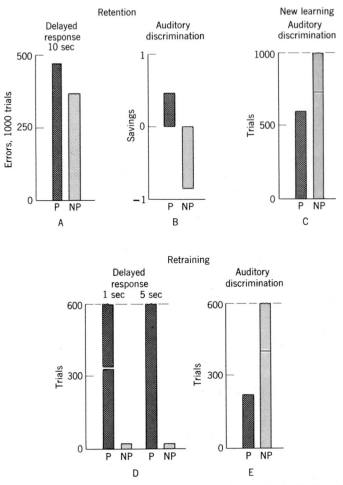

Fig. 13.20 Performances of monkeys with lesions in the principalis (P) and nonprincipalis (NP) portions of the frontal cortex. Dashed lines indicate the points at which testing was terminated. The bars broken at their upper ends indicate that one or more monkeys failed to reach criterion by this point; the scores of the remaining members of the group are indicated by a horizontal line within the broken bar. Criterion in all cases was 90 correct out of 100 trials. A, total errors in 1000 trials of postoperative testing of the retention of a 10-sec delayed response. B, savings scores on postoperative testing of the retention of a go/no-go auditory discrimination (white noise versus 1000-cps tone). C, trials to criterion on the postoperative acquisition of a new go/no-go auditory discrimination (chimes versus buzzer). D, trials to criterion on postoperative retraining on delayed response with delays of 1 and 5 sec. E, retraining on the auditory discrimination acquired before and reacquired after operation. (From Gross and Weiskrantz, 1964.)

in the lateral-prefrontal area (Gross, 1963a) compared the effects of total ablation of the area (T group) with those obtained by lesioning only the sulcus principalis (P group) or all the lateral cortex except the sulcus principalis (NP group). The results are summarized in Figure 13.21. The data suggest that the auditory discrimination deficit may be independent of the delayed-response impairment.

The precise nature of the auditory impairment is still uncertain. The deficit appears to be independent of possible general influences on test performance, for visual discrimination problems that demanded essentially comparable behavioral responses were often not affected by the same lesions which all but destroyed the auditory discrimination. It has been suggested that the lack of spatial contiguity between the auditory stimuli and the response (and reward) may be a factor, but observations reported by Bättig et al. (1960) argue against such an interpretation. In these experiments frontal monkeys performed a visual discrimination based on diffuse or nonspatial cues as successfully as normals.

This finding suggests that modality-specific effects may be a contributing factor in the delayed-response situation. The results of some of the earlier studies (Denny-Brown, 1951) suggested that the delayed response to visual cues may be particularly affected by frontal lesions. However, a sequence of studies by K. H. Pribram and his associates indicates that the frontal deficits cannot be attributed to specific sensory difficulties. Frontal monkeys were found to have as much difficulty with object as with spatial alternations (Pribram and Mishkin, 1956; Pribram, 1961).

Impressed with the apparent specificity of the delayed-response deficit, K. H. Pribram and his associates analyzed several potentially important aspects of the problem in some detail. Some of the earlier observations (Pribram, 1950) showed that food deprivation was an important variable. Monkeys performed measurably better on the delayed-response problem when very hungry, which suggests that the motivational properties of the reward conditions may be affected directly

by the frontal lesions. The frontal animals also persisted longer in a previously correct response following a reversal of the reinforcement conditions (Pribram, 1961), suggesting a similar inappropriate tendency to persist and relative lack of effect of nonreinforcement. (See the discussion of Fulton's observation of reduced "frustrational" responses to removal of reinforcement in Chapter 9.)

A similar perseveration of set had been reported earlier by Harlow and Settlage (1948) and has been used by Mishkin and his associates to explain the frontal animals' persistent response to novelty in discrimination experiments (Brush et al., 1961; Mishkin et al., 1962).

K. H. Pribram et al. (1964) reported related observations. They found frontal-lesioned animals required significantly more trials to extinction in a multiple-choice situation even after the first correct choice had been made. The optimal solution for the multiple-choice problem (which reinforced five successive correct responses before changing the task) consisted of an alternation, AABBAA fashion, of two strategies: (1) moving each of the test objects until the reinforcement was found (searching), and (2) selecting the object that was rewarded on the preceding trial. The first strategy is appropriate in the first trial of each novel problem, the second for all trials within a problem following initial reinforcement. The data reproduced in Figure 13.22 show that the frontal monkeys tended to persist in the previously rein-

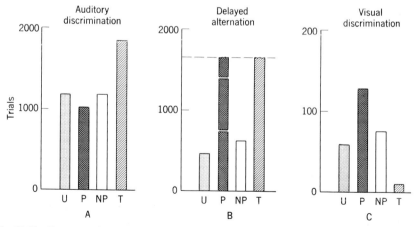

Fig. 13.21 Postoperative trials to criterion of unoperated monkeys (U) and of animals with lesions in the principalis (P), nonprincipalis (NP), and entire (T) frontal cortex on acquisition of A, go/no-go auditory discrimination (white noise versus 1000-cps tone); B, 3-sec delayed alternation; and C, go/no-go object discrimination. See also the legend for Figure 13.20. (From Gross and Weiskrantz, 1964.)

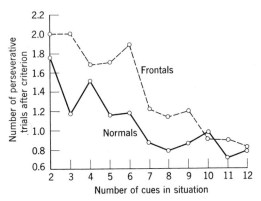

Fig. 13.22 Average number of perseverative responses in normal and frontal monkeys. (From K. H. Pribram et al., 1964.)

forced response and failed to shift to a search strategy when the conditions of reinforcement were altered. In confirmation of previous observations, Pribram found that the frontal animals made *fewer* perseverative responses than normals whenever a *novel*, positive cue was presented (see Figure 13.23).

A replication of the study with schizophrenic lobotomized patients (K. H. Pribram, 1961) duplicated the earlier results. A subsequent experiment used a similar multiple-choice design but reinforced all but perseverative responses. On the initial 150 trials of this peculiar problem, the frontal lobe monkeys made significantly *fewer* errors than normals (see Figure 13.24), demonstrating a strong

tendency to *shift* to novel cues. A detailed analysis of the data showed that (1) there were no significant differences between the frontal and control groups in position habits, and (2) the frontal animals sampled a greater variety of cues and repeated the same choice fewer times than normals.

This observation leaves us with the paradox that the frontal animals perseverate longer in previously reinforced habits in some conditions but display a significantly greater tendency to shift to novel cues in others. Pribram suggested that the nature of the impairment may be related to differences in the reinforcement conditions. Perseveration occurred in all situations in which a perseverative response was repeatedly reinforced. Switching occurred in a situation that *never* reinforced perseverative responses but always rewarded switching. This finding reduces the problem of frontal lobe effects, or at least part of it, to an increased sensitivity to the reward properties of stimuli; the generality and limits of this interesting concept must be established carefully in future studies.

Mishkin and his associates have also attempted to describe the effects of frontal lesions in terms of the perseveration of "central sets" or, more recently, the perseveration of central "mediating processes" which presumably are not specific to a particular type of set. The experimental support for this hypothesis has been summarized by Mishkin (1964).

It is possible to view the difficulty of the frontal-lesioned animal as a simple inability to withhold

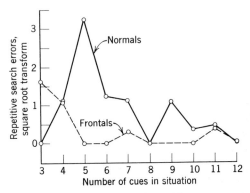

Fig. 13.23 Average number of repetitive errors made in a multiple-object experiment during search trials in which the novel cue is first added. A repetitive error is made by a monkey when, during a succession of trials, he moves more than once an object other than the one under which the peanut is placed. (From K. H. Pribram et al., 1964.)

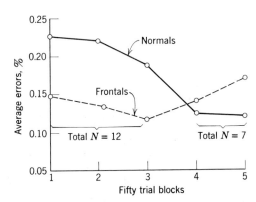

Fig. 13.24 Average number of errors in an eight-choice game. All objects were rewarded except the one selected on the previous trial. Six normal and six frontally lesioned monkeys were tested during the first 150 trials, and three normal and four frontally lesioned monkeys during the final 100 trials. (From K. H. Pribram et al., 1964.)

previously reinforced responses when they are punished or not reinforced in a novel experimental situation. Several investigators (K. H. Pribram and Mishkin, 1956; Weiskrantz and Mishkin, 1958; Bättig et al., 1960) have pointed out that frontal animals tend to have difficulty with sensory discriminations only when the problem is of the "go/no-go" variety which requires that the animal withhold responses to the negative stimulus. The passive avoidance deficits seen after septal lesions have been interpreted as the result of interruption of fibers from the mesiofrontal cortex (McCleary, 1961).

This apparent lack of response to nonreinforcement and even punishment may be reflected in a variety of situations. Mishkin (1964) demonstrated, for instance, that frontal animals may perform more poorly than normals in a sequence of learning set experiments (see Figure 13.25) which alternated two conditions of reinforcement.

A closer look at these data reveals that the animals performed as well as normals on all problems that required a choice of the object which was baited in full view of the animal on the first trial of each experiment. They performed consistently worse than normals only on problems that required a choice of the object which was *not* baited on the first trial. Mishkin interpreted these results in terms of an increased response perseveration tendency (see Figure 13.26).

This line of reasoning has been followed up in an unusual experiment (Brush et al., 1961) which consisted of the repeated presentation of an object that was either always baited (and responses to it reinforced) or always unbaited. The investigators reasoned that this procedure might impart negative and positive qualities to specific objects

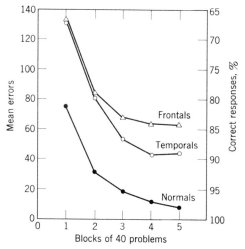

Fig. 13.25 Mean errors on learning set. Each block represents 40 problems or 400 trials. Each group consisted of four animals. Based on Brush et al., 1961. (From Mishkin, 1964.)

and that the frontal monkeys would persist in reacting to these qualities in novel experimental situations. Each "attractive" and "aversive" stimulus was subsequently paired with an "indifferent" stimulus object. On some tests the animals were rewarded for persisting in the previously acquired preference (i.e., they responded to the previously reinforced stimuli or the novel stimulus when it was paired with a previously negative object). On other trials switching was rewarded. The results of these experiments (see Figure 13.27) indicate that the frontal animals performed about as well as normals when allowed to respond according to previously acquired preferences; however, performance was significantly impaired when the

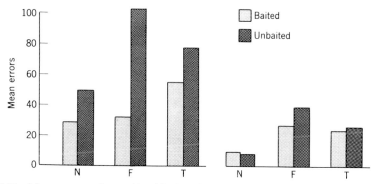

Fig. 13.26 Mean errors on first and last blocks of learning set. Each block represents 20 "baited" and 20 "unbaited" problems: N, normal; F, lateral frontal; T, inferotemporal. Based on Brush et al., 1961. (From Mishkin, 1964.)

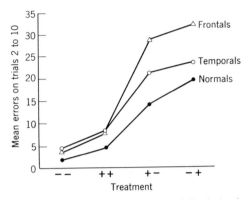

Fig. 13.27 Mean errors on two forms of discrimination reversal (+ −, − +) and two forms of nonreversal (− −, + +). Errors on the first (informing) trial have been excluded. (From Brush et al., 1961.)

rewarded response contradicted these preferences.

An interesting reversal of effects occurred when the problem was modified slightly so that objects (a "neutral" and a "positive" or "negative" stimulus) were paired only once rather than repeatedly as before (Mishkin et al., 1962). In this one-trial paradigm, all pairings with positive stimuli were presented in succession, followed or preceded by all the pairings with negative stimuli. The animal could solve the problems by acquiring the principle of always (or never) matching the stimulus which was baited before the delay period. In this type of problem, the frontal animals

selected the novel stimulus more frequently than the controls and performed more poorly because of *switching* rather than perseveration errors (see Figure 13.28).

The concept of perseverative response or stimulus interference does not explain the switching tendency of the frontal animals in the one-trial situation. Mishkin and his associates therefore suggested that all deficits might be due to the perseveration of central mediating processes. The frontal animals differ from normals, according to this hypothesis, not in the type of set initially developed in a learning situation, but in their perseveration in this set under changed experimental conditions which make it clearly inappropriate.

Subsequent studies by Mishkin and Rosvold (see Mishkin, 1964) showed that this hypothesis predicted the deficit of frontal animals on spatial and object reversal tests. The frontals performed poorly on the reversal tests because they had a strong tendency to perseverate in the previously correct response (see Figure 13.29).

Mishkin and associates have published some additional observations which suggest that the frontal lobe deficit may not, after all, be explainable in terms of a single mechanism such as perseveration of central mediating processes or set. (Brutkowski et al., 1963; Mishkin, 1964). A comparison of the effects of lateral-frontal and orbitofrontal lesions demonstrated some important differences and suggested the operation of at least two distinct factors. The orbitofrontal animals

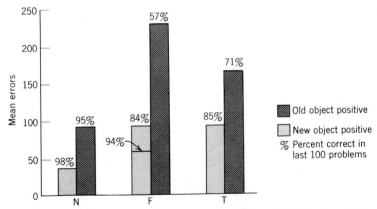

Fig. 13.28 Mean errors on 400 matching-from-sample problems (old object positive) and 400 nonmatching-from-sample problems (new object positive). Each animal served as its own control, having received 400 problems of each type: N, normal; F, frontal; T, temporal. Line and percentage figures within the bar graph for frontal animals indicate performance levels for three of the four animals in the group. (From Mishkin et al., 1962.)

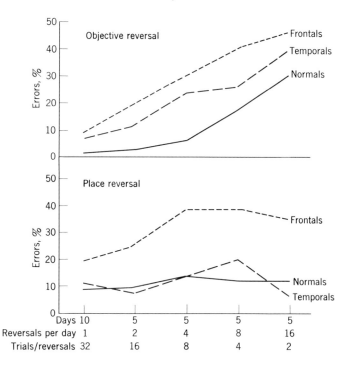

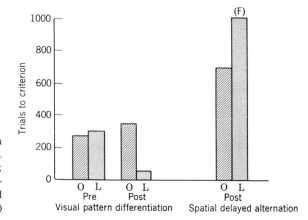

Fig. 13.29 Mean percentage of errors on object and place discrimination reversal. Errors on the first (informing) trial have been excluded. (From Mishkin, 1964.)

were significantly *less* impaired than the lateral-frontal animals on tests of spatial-delayed alternation, but they required many more trials to relearn a visual discrimination response (see Figure 13.30).

Subsequent experiments showed that the orbitofrontal animals also exhibited a greater impairment in experiments on learning sets, apparently because of strong and persevering spontaneous and acquired object preferences. They also performed more poorly in experiments using the one-trial paradigm, apparently because they had a greater tendency to shift responses to novel

stimuli. The orbitofrontal lesions seemed to produce a more severe deficit in all but the delayed-response situation, suggesting that at least two factors may be involved in the overall deficit of the frontal-lesioned animal.

A review of the literature suggests that several distinct functional processes may be represented even within the lateral cortex of the frontal lobe. For instance, lesions confined to the area of the sulcus principalis produce a severe and permanent impairment which appears to be specific to delayed-response problems (R. A. Blum, 1952; Mishkin, 1957; Gross and Weiskrantz, 1962).

Fig. 13.30 Mean errors preceding criterion on visual differentiation and delayed alternation. Each group consisted of four animals: O, orbital; L, lateral. All lateral animals failed to learn delayed alternation withing 1000 trials (F). Based on Brutkowski et al., 1963. (From Mishkin, 1964.)

Lesions in other parts of the lateral cortex result in milder temporary deficits on delayed-response problems, but typically in a more extensive interference with the performance of sensory discriminations (K. H. Pribram et al., 1952; K. H. Pribram, 1955a, b; Gross and Weiskrantz, 1962). However, total destruction of the lateral cortex produces an impairment on tests of delayed alternations that is more severe than the impairment seen after principal sulcus lesions.

Most of the work on frontal lobe functions has been done in primates, partly because the agranular cortex is best developed in primates and man; moreover, the higher functions that we have assigned to the frontal lobe have a priori seemed to be more characteristic of the complex primate.

An interesting exception to this rule is the work of Warren (see his 1964 review) with cats. Warren found that in cats frontal lobe lesions of varying extent (ranging from localized destruction of the area surrounding the *gyrus proreus* to ablation of most of the cortex anterior to the *cruciate sulcus*) significantly affected the retention of a double alternation (RRLLRRLL) problem; however, all cats eventually relearned the problem to the preoperative criterion. A second retest for recall 37 months after the operation failed to show any differences between the normal and frontal groups. In some studies prefrontal-lesioned monkeys have shown a similar pattern of deficit and postoperative rehabilitation (see Warren et al., 1957; Leary et al., 1952).

Significantly fewer frontal than normal animals were capable of acquiring a simple delayed-response habit, but the surprising aspect of these results is that some of the frontal cats *did* learn the problem even when a 10-sec delay was introduced. The frontal animals failed only when an opaque screen obscured the stimuli during the long delay period. Similar, relatively mild deficits have been reported by Warren (Warren and Akert, 1960) after orbitofrontal lesions and by Lawicka and Konorski (1961) after more extensive prefrontal damage.

A number of visual discrimination problems were learned and retained without apparent difficulty by the frontal lobe cats (Warren et al., 1962; Warren, 1964). A more detailed analysis of the animals' performance on discrimination problems showed that the frontal cats displayed little impairment on successive discrimination problems as long as different cues were used in consecutive tests. They were reliably poorer than controls in spatial as well as nonspatial reversal

problems, but their locomotor activity did not appear to be impaired (Lawicka and Konorski, 1961; Warren, 1964).

Konorski's laboratory has supplied some interesting information about the behavior of dogs with frontal lesions. Lawicka and Konorski (1959) showed that frontal dogs can learn delayed-response problems as competently as normals, as long as they are permitted to assume a bodily orientation to the correct stimulus during the delay period. When this postural mnemonic was removed, little or no evidence of delayed responding remained. In a more recent paper Lawicka and Konorski (1961) suggested that the impairment of delayed-response performance may be much more severe in dogs than in cats. Konorski (1961b) also reported that frontal dogs show some initial deficits in all discrimination situations but return to normal performance levels with some retraining. Frontal dogs did not show the hyperactivity that is so characteristic of the monkey (Lawicka and Konorski, 1959, 1961). This may be an important observation, for it suggests that hyperactivity cannot be the principal cause of other performance deficits observed in frontal animals.

Work with new-world (squirrel) monkeys (Miles, 1964) has demonstrated that this species also does not show the hyperactivity normally seen in prefrontal-lesioned monkeys. However, a severe and persistent inability to learn or perform simple delayed responses occurs. Simple object discrimination habits were retained almost perfectly. The latency of avoidance responses was reliably increased, supporting earlier observations that suggested a reduced effect of punishment (K. H. Pribram and Weiskrantz, 1957).

An interesting analysis of the effects of frontal lesions on reversal and avoidance behavior in the rat has been provided by R. Thompson (1964). Damage to the orbitofrontal cortex or its thalamic projection nucleus depressed avoidance performance but did not interfere with the performance on simple habit-reversal problems.

Harlow (1959) has shown that the solution of delayed-response problems develops as a function of age in the rhesus monkey. The effects of prefrontal lesions in infant monkeys consequently also vary with age (Harlow et al., 1964). Animals that were operated at age 5 days (when the delayed-response ability is still totally absent) or at age 150 days (when the ability is only poorly developed) showed little or no deficits on simple visual discriminations (see Figure 13.31) or

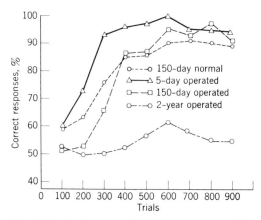

Fig. 13.31 Performance of operated groups and the 150-day normal group on 900 zero-sec delayed-response trials. (From Harlow et al., 1964.)

delayed-response tasks (see Figure 13.32). However, animals that received the same treatment at age two years showed the typical pattern of impairment. These interesting findings parallel earlier observations of sparing of sensory or motor functions when the relevant cortical areas were destroyed in early infancy (Kennard, 1938; Benjamin and Thompson, 1959). They may indicate that the nervous system of the newborn is sufficiently plastic to permit a transfer of function to intact portions of the brain.

Electrical stimulation of the association areas. Weiskrantz et al. (1960) have reported that electrical stimulation of the area of the sulcus principalis severely impaired the learning of a delayed-alternation response in monkeys. The effects appeared to be task-specific, for the same stimulation procedure neither affected the acquisition of an auditory discrimination habit nor evoked any other overt behavioral changes. Stamm and Pribram (1960) observed that the establishment of irritative foci on the lateral-frontal cortex of monkeys impaired the acquisition of delayed-alternation habits without interfering with the establishment of a visual discrimination response. The retention of preoperatively acquired delayed-alternation or visual discrimination habits was not measurably affected. These results confirm Rosvold and Delgado's (1956) earlier report that electrical stimulation of the frontal cortex does not affect the performance (i.e., retention) of previously acquired delayed-alternation or visual discrimination responses. Experiments by Stamm (1961) have shown that electrical stimulation of the frontal cortex sig-

nificantly reduced the performance of monkeys during the acquisition phase of an alternation habit, the severity of the deficit being a function of the degree of prior learning. Stimulation reduced the performance to chance levels only during the early phases of learning, and little or no effect remained at the asymptote.

A subsequent experiment (Stamm and Mahoney, 1962) showed that facilitatory as well as inhibitory effects could be obtained by stimulating the frontal lobe. Monkeys with unilateral frontal lesions tended to respond better during low-amplitude electrical stimulation of the remaining frontal lobe throughout the acquisition phase of an alternation habit. The rate of improvement for even the poorest of the stimulated animals was significantly higher than that for the best unoperated control. Perhaps the most surprising aspect of these results is that the stimulation appeared to produce long-lasting facilitatory effects on acquisition or retention, as suggested by the fact that the total number of trials to a criterion of 85% correct responses was significantly smaller for the experimental group than for the control group. Recent observations indicate that the facilitatory effects of frontal stimulation are independent of the unilateral ablation. Similar effects have been seen in unlesioned monkeys (Stamm, 1964). Electrical stimulation of the frontal cortex also appears to facilitate the acquisition of a single-position reversal habit (Stamm, 1964).

Stamm's procedure, unfortunately, does not permit an analysis of the current flow in these experiments, but it seems possible that the facilitatory effects may be related to the establishment

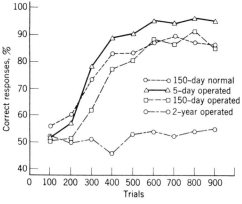

Fig. 13.32 Performance of the operated groups and the 150-day normal group on 900 5-sec delayed-response trials. (From Harlow et al., 1964.)

of a "dominant focus," as described by Rusinov (1956) and Morrell (1961), rather than to stimulation in the usual sense. The higher-amplitude inhibitory effects may well reflect true stimulation, although the similarity between lesion and stimulation effects suggests that the electrical current may have interfered with rather than stimulated the local neural activity.

Burns and Mogenson (Burns, 1958; Mogenson, 1958; Burns and Mogenson, 1958, 1961) have reported a significant impairment of learned behavior (bar pressing for food) during intermittent electrical stimulation of frontopolar, cingulate, and mesial occipital areas. Animals receiving a burst of stimulation whenever a reward was presented failed to acquire the bar-pressing behavior at all. Animals receiving electrical stimulation of the mesial occipital cortex before and during training in a multiple-unit maze made significantly more errors than normal controls, but sensory or motor deficits cannot be ruled out as contributing factors. It is, however, not clear that Burns and Mogenson's results can be interpreted as related to associative functions. The observed results may have been caused by a punishing effect of the stimulation, an inhibition of motivation (the animals often refused to eat the reward pellets), or motor effects that may have interfered with the response sequence.

Temporary Depression of Cortical Functions

Before we leave the subject of cortical factors, some recent experiments which have attempted to study the role of the cortex by temporarily inactivating all cortical functions should be discussed. Such a depression can be produced in a number of ways; it is worthwhile to discuss some of these techniques briefly at this point, since such "reversible lesions" may become a versatile research tool.

Dusser de Barenne and McCulloch (1941) first observed that stimuli applied directly to the cortical surface often elicited a peculiar depression of the local electrical activity which tended to spread from the point of stimulation and inhibited cortical responses to other stimuli. Leão (1944, 1947) investigated this phenomenon extensively and discovered the following relationships. Strong electrical stimulation, certain chemical substances, or even mechanical deformation or prolonged exposure of the cortical surface produce a slow, high-amplitude direct-current shift; this shift is characterized by an initial negative component followed after several minutes by a weaker positive potential. These direct-current changes spread gradually from the point of stimulation, traveling with a velocity of approximately 3 to 6 mm/sec. The negative component of this shift typically attains an amplitude of 5 to 10 mV. All normal EEG activity is inhibited during and immediately following the passage of such a direct-current wave. Several such direct-current shifts may be produced by a single stimulation, and a depression of cortical activity that lasts for 3 to 5 hr can be observed (Bureš and Burešova, 1956).

The gradual spread of the direct-current shift and the accompanying depression of EEG activity

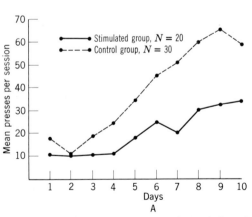

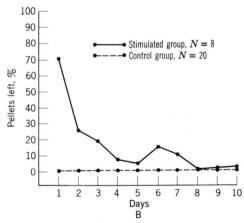

Fig. 13.33 Effects of electrical stimulation of frontopolar, cingulate, and mesial occipital cortical areas on operant behavior. A, mean number of responses per day. B, percent of pellets left on each of the testing days. (From Burns and Mogenson, 1961.)

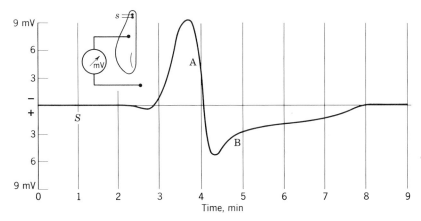

Fig. 13.34 Slow-voltage potential accompanying the spreading depression of Leão. The voltage readings are taken at 5-sec intervals. An upward deflection denotes negativity of the cortex with respect to the extracortical reference electrode. Electrodes are arranged as shown in the inset (*s*, stimulating electrodes). Stimulation (5 sec of "tetanizing" current from an induction coil) was delivered at the time marked *S*. (From Leão, 1947.)

do not seem to involve synaptic mechanisms, since anoxia (Leão and Morison, 1945) and anesthesia (Sloan and Jasper, 1950) have no marked effect. Some of the earlier investigators (Marshall and Essig, 1951; Marshall, 1950) suggested that Leão's depression might be a pathological condition brought on by extensive craniotomy, drying, cooling, or other nonphysiological factors which did not play a functional role in the intact organism. It was soon demonstrated, however, that the spreading depression passes across areas of fully protected cortical tissue with no change in velocity (Harreveld and Stamm,

1951; Ross and Magun, 1954). Bures (1954) observed that a prolonged depression could be produced by polarization of the cortex even when the skull was not subjected to surgical procedures. Other early theories (Harreveld and Stamm, 1953b) suggested that vasomotor disturbances might be responsible for the relatively large potential shifts. However, studies of neuropharmacological factors (Grafstein, 1956) have indicated that changes in the potassium transfer of cortical neurons may be directly related to the spreading depression.

Grafstein (1956) has proposed that the initiation

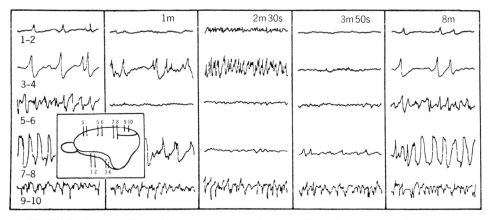

Fig. 13.35 Spread of depression to various cortical regions. Electrodes are arranged as shown in the inset. *s*, stimulating electrodes; first strip, control; subsequent strips at times after stimulation noted in upper right corner. Note the spread of depression to all areas except the retrosplenial gyrus (sampled by electrodes 9 and 10) and the episode of spike activity during depression of the olfactory cortex. (From Leão and Morison, 1945.)

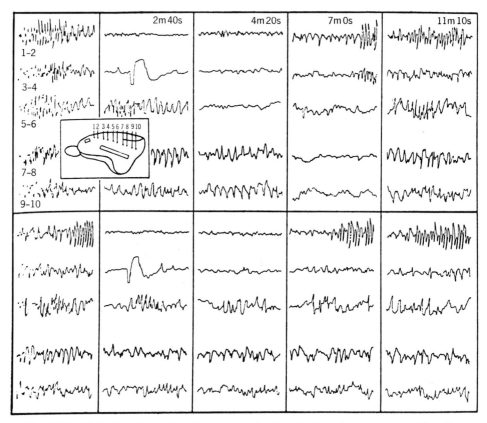

Fig. 13.36 Elicitation of spreading depression by local application of potassium, and the effect of cocaine on the spread when this drug is applied on the lateral aspect of the hemisphere. Electrodes are arranged as shown in the inset. *Upper records:* The first strip shows spontaneous activity, and the subsequent ones the spread of the depression and recovery. The depression was elicited by application of a small piece of filter paper (shown in the inset, frontal to electrode 1) soaked in 1% KCl. The times in the strips indicate the intervals from the application of this filter paper.

Lower records: The first strip, taken 7 min after the last one in the upper row, shows spontaneous activity, 5 min after a long piece of filter paper, soaked in 10% cocaine hydrochloride, was applied on the lateral aspect of the hemisphere, not directly on the path of the spread of the depression (see inset). The subsequent records show the limited spread of the depression, elicited by a second application of potassium made in exactly the same manner as the previous one. The strips were taken at the same intervals, after the second application of KCl, as indicated in the corresponding strips of the upper row. There was no appreciable change in the spontaneous activity after the application of cocaine. (From Leão and Morison, 1945.)

and propagation of spreading depression depend on the liberation of relatively large quantities of potassium which depolarize neighboring neurons and thus establish a chain reaction. Grafstein based her proposal primarily on the following observations. (1) A brief phase of intense neuronal excitation (as measured by microelectrodes) precedes the initial negative component of the direct-current shift. (2) The spread of the direct-current potential can be arrested by applying strong repetitive electrical stimulation to the cortex shortly before the spreading depression is elicited in neighboring areas. This suggests that cellular stores of some substance (presumably potassium) essential to the propagation of the direct-current potential may be gradually depleted. (3) During a series of successive depressions, the amplitude of the negative potential decreases but can be restored by topical applications of potassium cloride or further reduced by the administration of calcium chloride. (4) Polarizing currents applied to the surface of the cortex increase the conduction velocity and amplitude of the direct-current shift, provided the applied potential has a positive-negative relation to the direction of the spread of the depression. Negative-to-positive potential gradients reduce the velocity of the spreading depression and decrease its amplitude, suggesting that the propagation of the direct-current shift depends on a positively charged particle. (5) The duration of spreading depression can be increased by interruption of the cerebral blood flow or inhalation of nitrogen, indicating that oxidative processes may be essential to the recovery from Leão's depression.

Grafstein's proposal has received some direct experimental support. Brinley et al. (1960a, b) devised an ingenious apparatus which permitted the assessment of potassium ion output by cortical cells. During spreading depression, they recorded a marked rise in potassium output which correlated almost perfectly with the time course of the initial negative component of the direct-current shift. Brinley's tracer technique does not provide a direct measure of absolute potassium output, but the authors estimated the potassium loss to be approximately 600×10^{-12} mole/mm^2 of cortical surface during the passage of spreading depression. This value represents approximately seven to eight times the normal concentration of extracellular potassium and agrees fairly well with the observation that spreading depression can be initiated by applying directly to the cortical surface potassium solutions of about fifteen times the normal concentration.

On the basis of these findings, Brinley and his co-workers concur with Grafstein's hypothesis that the depression is initiated by processes which make the cell membrane more permeable to potassium and increase the extracellular concentration of this ion. The propagation of the depression presumably depends on a depolarization of immediately adjacent cells, and this might account for the fact that the spread of the depression occurs only in areas of the brain characterized by a very high cell density.

Most of the investigations reporting reliable effects have been concerned with cortical tissue that clearly meets this criterion, and it is generally reported that sulci tend to retard and even stop the spread of the direct-current shift. The only subcortical structure that has been shown to be susceptible to a spreading depression is the hippocampal formation (Liberson and Cadilhac, 1953;

Liberson and Akert, 1955; Weiss and Fifkova, 1960). However, a spreading depression of cortical origin has never been observed to cross over into hippocampal tissue, and hippocampal disturbances apparently do not affect cortical functions. This selectivity is perhaps one of the most useful properties of the spreading depression. Although Leão (1944) reported that tetanic callosal stimulation can set up a spreading depression in the homologous region of the contralateral cortex (see also Marshall, 1959), this transcallosal mechanism is apparently not activated by spreading depression itself. Thus, it is possible to confine the functional ablation to one of the hemispheres.

Bureš and his collaborators (see Bureš and Burešova, 1960a, b for a review of this work) attempted to study the behavioral correlates of the spreading depression in some detail and applied this technique to an investigation of the role of cortical mechanisms in simple conditioning and learning. Unfortunately, practical considerations did not permit simultaneous recording of electrophysiological and behavioral measures in these studies so that we must infer the presence of cortical inhibition from behavioral data. This tautological design is far from ideal, but some of Bureš's results are important and warrant closer scrutiny, even though careful replications of this work are badly needed.

Before discussing some of the findings that relate directly to learning, a brief review of the effects on unconditioned behavior may be useful. Simple postural reflexes do not seem to be impaired by bilateral cortical spreading depression. More elaborate postural responses such as righting reflexes and balancing on a small stand are severely depressed. General locomotor activity and reactivity to sensory stimuli are decreased, and many subcortical regulatory mechanisms such as water metabolism, thermoregulation, and sleep and wakefulness cycles are affected (Bureš and Burešova, 1956; Burešova, 1957a, b, c; Bureš and Burešova, 1960a). Weiss and Bureš have discussed some evidence suggesting that the spreading depression may selectively remove some inhibitory influences on the reticular arousal mechanisms of the brainstem; however, general reflex inhibition, as defined by these workers, seemed increased (see also Bureš and Burešova, 1956).

None of these impairments accounts for the radical modification of recently learned behavior which Bureš and his collaborators have observed in a number of studies.

In the first of these, Bureš and Burešova (1960a)

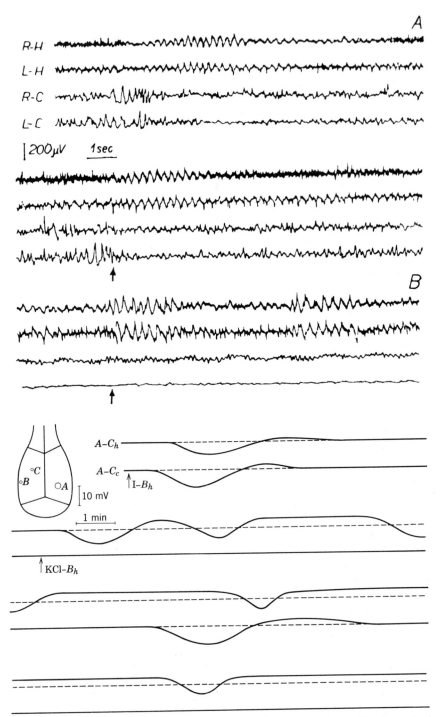

Fig. 13.37 *Top,* hippocampal arousal before and during bilateral cortical spreading depression in a curarized rat. R-H, L-H, bipolar leads from right and left hippocampus; R-C, L-C, bipolar leads from right and left parietal cortex. A, control recording of spontaneous arousal (above) and arousal evoked by tactile stimulation (below). B, hippocampal arousal during bilateral spreading depression in the cortex. *Bottom,* steady potential changes elicited in the hippocampus of a curarized rat by KCl application. *A, B,* and *C* are trephine openings. *A,* surface reference electrode. *B,* point of insertion of the hippocampal pipette; C_h, hippocampal capillary electrode, 3 mm deep; C_c, surface wick electrode on the overlying cortex; I-B_h, introduction of the pipette into the hippocampus; KCl-B_h, introduction of a small KCl crystal into the hippocampus. (From Bureš, 1959.)

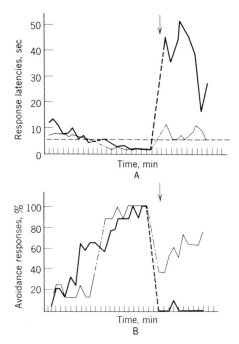

Fig. 13.38 Elaboration of a simple avoidance reaction in rats. The effect of bilateral cortical spreading depression is shown by the thin line (eight rats). The effect of hippocampal spreading depression is shown by the heavy line (nine rats). A, mean latencies of the avoidance or escape reaction. The broken horizontal line indicates the avoidance latency. B, percentage of avoidance reactions. The arrow in each chart indicates application of KCl. (From Bureš, 1959.)

trained one group of rats to obtain food by rearing up on their hindlegs in response to an auditory CS. Another group of animals were trained to avoid or escape electric shock by jumping onto the mesh walls of the apparatus whenever the same stimulus was presented. After the animals had reached criterion on these tasks (90% correct), small trephine holes were made in the skull, and filter papers soaked in either saline (the control condition) or 2% or 25% KCl were bilaterally applied to the cortical surface before testing the animals in the approach or avoidance situation.

No changes were observed following the control application of saline, but all animals stopped responding to the CS within one-half to 1 min after the application of potassium chloride. The animals failed to respond to the tone in both the appetitive and the aversive situations, although they displayed apparently emotional behavior in response to the UCS. When the shock appeared across the grid floor, all animals ran around, squealed, and "hopped up and down," but failed to perform the simple escape response of jumping onto the mesh of the walls. As the spreading depression dissipated, the escape responses reappeared long before the first avoidance reactions began to be made; full recovery (i.e., a return to the 90% performance level) did not appear until 3 to 5 hr after the topical application of potassium chloride. In an attempt to obtain evidence on the contribution of more restricted components of the cortical mantle, Bureš analyzed the performance data from animals with potassium chloride applications to occipital, temporal, or frontal portions of the cerebrum. No clear-cut differences were observed, presumably because the depression (as measured by its inhibition of normal EEG activity) spread to the entire cortical mantle within 1 to 2 min.

Bureš's findings are particularly interesting in view of the fact that unconditioned responses to the electric shock appeared little affected, whereas even very primitive learned responses, such as escaping from the shock by jumping onto the wiremesh walls of the apparatus, were completely suppressed during the depression. This observation suggests a degree of selectivity with respect to acquired behavior that has not been observed with other techniques.

One further detail of this first study is worth mentioning. Conditioned responses in both appetitive and aversive conditioning situations did not reappear until the normal EEG activity of the cortex had fully recovered, although the large negative slow waves typically disappeared 1 to 2 hr earlier. This indicates that cortical functions may be inhibited by the depletion of potassium even after the primary disturbances have subsided and suggests that attempted correlations between electrophysiological and behavioral effects must take this gradual recovery into account.

In subsequent studies Bureš (Bureš and Burešova, 1960a, b) found that rats cannot acquire a complex visual discrimination habit when trained during spreading depression of even one hemisphere. Furthermore, conflicting information can be stored in each hemisphere, in spite of non-lateralized sensory input, when unilateral spreading depression is employed during the learning of the conflicting habits.

In a simple discrimination learning situation, rats were trained to escape from electric shock by choosing the right (or left) of two alternative pathways. Twenty-four hr after the attainment of a stringent criterion of performance on this task, the discrimination was reversed during unilateral

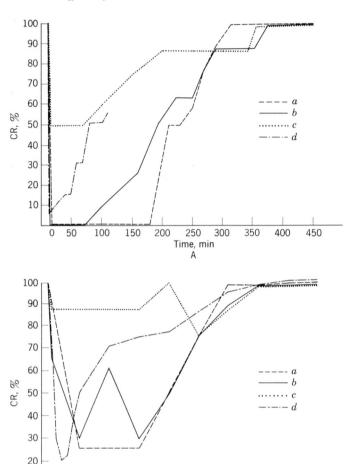

Fig. 13.39 A, effect of spreading depression from application of 25% KCl to the occipital region of both hemispheres. Ordinate, percent of (*a*) alimentary and (*b*) defensive conditioned responses, (*c*) percent of jumps onto the mesh in response to electrical stimulation, and (*d*) EEG amplitude in percent of original amplitude. Abscissa, time from the moment of KCl application in minutes. B, effect of spreading depression evoked by applying 2% KCl on the occipital region of both hemispheres. Markings are as in A. (From Bureš and Burešova, 1960a.)

spreading depression. Finally, the animals were tested under control conditions (no spreading depression), spreading depression of the same hemisphere as during the reversal training, or spreading depression on the contralateral hemisphere. The control animals as well as those with contralateral depression chose the initially correct side, disregarding the intervening reversal training. Animals with ipsilateral depression selected the side that had been correct during the reversal learning.

Bureš and Burešova (1960a) reported some additional findings which are relevant to the problem of interhemispheric transfer. In one study a simple avoidance response was elaborated while the animals were subjected to unilateral spreading depression. Five to ten trials were then given after the animals had recovered from the depression, and a final test was administered during spreading depression of the contralateral hemisphere. The experimental animals were found to perform significantly better than a control group which had not received the initial training under unilateral depression. Other animals, trained under unilateral spreading depression and tested during a depression of the contralateral side, did not show any evidence of transfer. Bureš suggested that these results may indicate that the presence of a well-established memory trace in one hemisphere facilitates the development of a corresponding CR in the other hemisphere if training is presented while both sides are intact. This

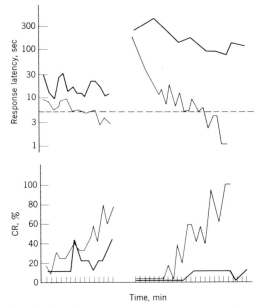

Fig. 13.40 Elaboration of two types of avoidance responses in control rats (thin line, twelve animals) and in rats with bilateral cortical spreading depression evoked by 25% KCl (heavy line, eight animals). (From Bureš, 1959.)

The incompleteness of the protection in these studies may indicate that cortical areas essential to the performance of the learned response were not entirely exempt from the effects of spreading depression. We do not yet know, however, whether lack of protection can be ascribed to an incomplete diffusion of the cations over the intended area, or whether other cortical mechanisms may be involved. Much remains to be learned about the effects of spreading depression and the means of arresting it at some desired point. However, the technique of producing what amounts to a massive functional lesion which apparently is readily reversible holds great promise for future research; we may expect additional work in this area.

THE LIMBIC SYSTEM

The limbic system appears to be primarily concerned with the regulation of motivational functions which influence behavior in all learning situations but are not an integral part of the learning process itself. It is, however, often difficult to interpret the behavioral effects of limbic system lesions or stimulation in terms of distinct motivational mechanisms, and we have at least some

memory does not seem to transfer passively to the other hemisphere when spreading depression inactivates the original response mechanism.

A still more selective application of the technique has been reported by Beran (1960). In these studies an attempt was made to spare certain regions of the cortex by the topical application of such cations as Ca^{++} or Mg^{++} which are known to arrest the propagation of the depression. These experiments were plagued by methodological difficulties which made it difficult to predict the extent and completeness of the protection, but some interesting—if preliminary—data are available.

One experiment found that the application of Mg^{++} to the sensory-motor cortex on the dominant hemisphere protected a learned response from the normally drastic effects of spreading depression in that hemisphere. Other experiments demonstrated a considerable shortening of the KCl-produced inhibition (though not complete protection) following topical applications of magnesium chloride to the occipital cortex when the behavioral task involved a complex visual discrimination. A comparable protection of the frontotemporal cortex had no effect on the length or intensity of the behavioral depression.

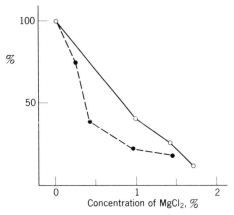

Fig. 13.41 Protection of food-rewarded operant behavior from the effect of spreading depression by applying $MgCl_2$ solutions to the sensory-motor cortical area contralateral to the preferred forelimb (solid line). Spreading depression was produced by 2% KCl 20 min after the $MgCl_2$ application (dashed line). Ordinate for solid line, duration of the impairment of conditional responses in the $MgCl_2$-treated animals with respect to control experiments (control duration, 100%). Ordinate for dashed line, amplitude of the slow potential wave penetrating into the $MgCl_2$-treated area with respect to control values (without $MgCl_2$, 100%). (From Bureš, 1959.)

evidence which suggests that individual components of this complex circuit may be specifically concerned with acquisition, memory storage, and recall. The hippocampus and associated structures in particular have been implicated by clinical as well as experimental observations. We shall discuss this material in some detail before briefly summarizing the behavioral changes seen after lesions or stimulation in other limbic structures.

The Hippocampus

Evidence for a direct participation of hippocampal mechanisms in associative processes was first contributed by clinical observations which indicated that bilateral damage to the hippocampal formation from tumor growth or vascular disturbances resulted in severe deficits of recent memory. These effects appeared to be specific to a short-term memory mechanism, for general intelligence and long-term memory were not affected. These observations have led to the suggestion (Penfield and Milner, 1958) that the initial recording of memory traces may be accomplished by hippocampal mechanisms. Much recent research interest has been devoted to this problem.

Although many investigations have shown that acquisition, retention (performance), or extinction may be affected by hippocampal damage or stimulation, motivational effects have generally not been adequately controlled. It is therefore often not clear whether motivational or associative mechanisms were affected in these studies. We have included this material in our discussion of learning primarily because the severity of the effects of hippocampal lesions or stimulation seems to increase dramatically with the complexity of the learning problem. This suggests that associative functions may be affected at least concurrently with motivational mechanisms.

When we look at simple, appetitive learning situations, it is almost impossible to demonstrate effects of either stimulation or extirpation. Correll (1957), for instance, stimulated the ventral hippocampus of cats during either the acquisition or the extinction (or both) of a simple response sequence which consisted of running down a straight alley and pressing a lever mounted in the goal box of the apparatus. Animals stimulated during acquisition ran somewhat more slowly than their normal controls but showed no other deficits in either speed of learning or performance. A more significant effect of electrical stimulation was observed during extinction. The experimental ani-

mals continued to perform the nonrewarded responses much longer than their unstimulated controls. It seems rather certain that motivational disturbances were responsible for these results.

Ehrlich (1963) reported that rats with lesions in the rostral hippocampus ran faster in a straight alley to food reward than normal animals. The acquisition of this simple response is not described.

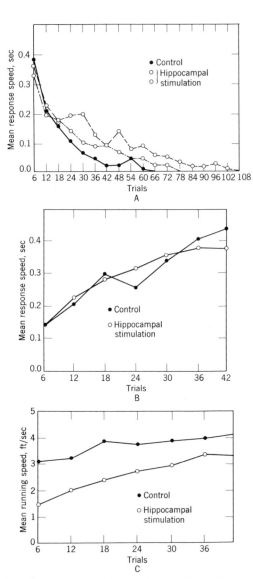

Fig. 13.42 Effects of electrical stimulation of the ventral hippocampus on appetitive learning (running through a straight alley in a goal box containing a food-rewarded lever). A, extinction curves as measured by response speed. B, total response speeds during learning. C, running speed in the alley during learning. (From Correll, 1957.)

Asymptotic differences in running speed presumably relate to motivational, rather than associative, factors. Several other investigators (Karmos and Grastyán, 1962) have reported that cats with hippocampal lesions learn simple conditioned responses as readily as normal controls, and we must conclude that the hippocampal formation does not seem to be essential to the acquisition or retention of simple response sequences.

This conclusion is supported when we consider simple discrimination learning studies. Hippocampal lesions do not impair the acquisition or performance of simple olfactory (Swann, 1934, 1935; Allen, 1940, 1941) or visual (Kimble, 1963) discriminations. Auditory as well as visual discrimination learning also appears unaffected by hippocampal seizures induced by strong electrical stimulation (Weiskrantz et al., 1962).

When successive rather than simultaneous discriminations are required for a successful solution of the problem, very different results have been observed. Kimble (1963) set up a conditional problem (turn right in response to white and left to black) which appeared very sensitive to hippocampal damage. Animals with hippocampal lesions did not learn this problem as readily as operated (neocortical lesions) or unoperated control subjects and continued to show some performance decrements long after the control groups had reached criterion. Similar results were obtained in another conditioning learning situation. K. H. Pribram et al. (1962) found that monkeys with bilateral lesions in the ventral hippocampus and entorhinal cortex were markedly deficient in learning a simple alternation task. An interpretation of these results is complicated by the recent observation that spontaneous alternation tendencies may also be affected (i.e., reduced) by lesions in the rostral hippocampus (Roberts et al., 1962).

When we consider the evidence from still more complex learning situations, there emerges a somewhat inconsistent picture which indicates that learning deficits following hippocampal damage may be observable under some experimental conditions but not under others. Many studies have shown a marked impairment of acquisition or retention, but sufficient negative evidence is available to suggest that these deficits may be very specifically related to particular aspects of the training or testing situation rather than learning ability per se.

In delayed-response learning we find, for instance, Stepien's (Stepien et al., 1960) report of large and significant decrements in acquisition following lesions in the ventral hippocampus and amygdala. Karmos and Grastyán (1962) observed that relatively small hippocampal lesions prevented the acquisition of a multiple-choice response when a 5-sec delay was interposed between the presentation of the stimuli and the response itself. On the other side of the ledger, we find Mishkin's (1954) report of no effects of hippocampal lesions on the performance of a delayed response and the Orbach et al. (1960) demonstration of no impairment of delayed-response learning following lesions in the ventral hippocampus and amygdala, even when the animals were distracted during the intertrial interval.

The effects of hippocampal lesions on acquisition are most clearly shown in complex learning situations such as multiple-unit mazes of the Lashley or Hebb-Williams type. One of the earliest studies of hippocampal lesions (Lashley, 1943) failed to observe a difference between animals with hippocampal lesions and control animals with massive cortical ablations. However, more recent investigations have generally reported marked effects, and it seems likely that the crude surgical lesions of the earlier studies may have been inadequate.

Thomas and Otis (1958) destroyed the rostral tip of the hippocampal formation in rats before training them in a complex maze and found that the experimental animals learned the problem significantly more slowly than controls with neocortical lesions. Kaada et al. (1961) have found very similar results, and Kimble (1963) has reported that rats with lesions in the posterior hippocampus make more errors in simple as well as complex Hebb-Williams mazes than control animals with neocortical lesions.

Hippocampal lesions seem to effect acquisition only in learning situations that require short-term memory of stimuli, as in the delayed-response problem, or of responses in single- or double-alternation situations. It has therefore been suggested that the deficit may be specifically related to neural mechanisms, such as reverberatory circuits, which serve the temporary storage of information rather than the relatively permanent retention of repeatedly presented information. The first of these mechanisms might be illustrated by the temporary recall of a telephone number which one looks up, dials, and immediately forgets. The second might be involved in the gradual learning of this number if one finds it necessary to use it frequently. We can attempt

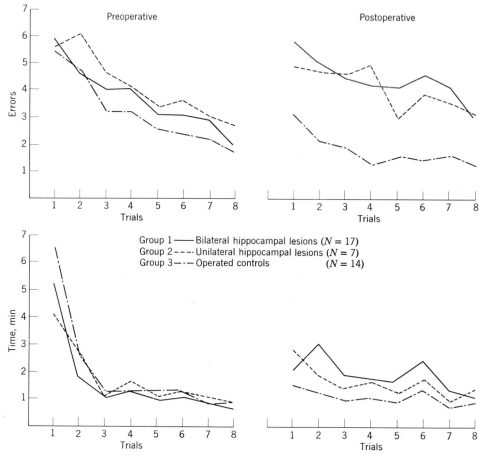

Fig. 13.43 Effects of hippocampal lesions on acquisition and retention. Learning curves based on mean forward errors (top) and on median time (bottom) in preoperative training (left) and postoperative retraining (right). (From Kaada et al., 1961.)

to differentiate between these alternatives by comparing the effects of hippocampal lesions on the acquisition of a new response with those observed when the lesion is made after the problem has been mastered. If a long-term storage mechanism is affected, we can expect to observe a marked deficit in retention when hippocampal lesions are made after a response is well learned. If the lesion interrupts short-term storage mechanisms, we can predict a deficit in retention only to the extent that the performance of the well-trained response is dependent on immediate recall. Although the available evidence does not yet permit a definite selection of these alternatives, it appears that clear retention deficits can be observed only under conditions that require short-term memory (i.e., those that also show an impairment during acquisition). It may be tentatively suggested that the

hippocampal formation does not represent the anatomical substrate for memory, as some recent workers have supposed, but rather serves quite specifically the function of *temporary* information storage. It may be useful to discuss briefly some of the recent experimental evidence on this point.

K. H. Pribram and Weiskrantz (1957) observed no performance decrement following bilateral lesions in the ventral hippocampus and entorhinal cortex in a simple active avoidance situation. Karmos and Grastyán (1962) reported that cats showed no performance decrements in a simple classical conditioning situation following hippocampal lesions, and R. Thompson and Massopust (1960) found no significant decrement in the postoperative performance of a simple black-white discrimination. K. H. Pribram et al. (1962) found that the performance of an alternation task was markedly affected by lesions in the ventral hippocampus. Dorsal hippocampal damage also impaired performance on a delayed-alternation task (K. H. Pribram et al., 1962). These findings as well as clinical case histories (Penfield and Milner, 1958; Victor et al., 1961) support the hypothesis clearly, but some data do not fit as nicely.

Brady and Hunt (1955), for instance, have reported that lesions in the anterior hippocampus interfere with the retention of a simple CER, and Kimura (1958) found that lesions in the posterior hippocampus lead to faster extinction of a passive avoidance response. It is not obvious that these tasks involve short-term memory mechanisms after the task has been learned, and therefore these findings appear to contradict our hypothesis. Both studies report, however, that postoperative acquisition or relearning was severely affected in these animals, supporting the contention that only those experimental situations that also present a clear impairment of acquisition show memory deficits.

Other studies have shown that performance decrements can be observed in active avoidance situations following various hippocampal lesions (Hunt and Diamond, 1957) or chemical stimulation (Bureš et al., 1962) if the animals are tested soon after they have attained criterion performance. Both studies agree in demonstrating that prolonged overtraining can protect the animals from the effects of hippocampal lesions or stimulation, suggesting that some short-term memory which may not yet have been consolidated into a permanent storage system has been affected in these studies.

Avoidance learning appears to be peculiarly sensitive to the effects of hippocampal damage, and the possibility that motivational rather than associative factors may be responsible for this affinity should be explored. It is quite possible that the motivational responses to painful shock or other noxious stimulation may be reduced by hippocampal lesions, thus leading to poorer performance during acquisition and retention. The effects of overtraining may then reflect little more than the well-known fact that overlearned responses can be elicited under motivational conditions that are not sufficient to elicit a less well-established response sequence.

That the hippocampal formation is related to many motivational mechanisms is well established. Electrical stimulation of various hippocampal placements has been shown to (1) have positive reward properties (Delgado et al., 1954;

Bursten and Delgado, 1958), (2) improve performance on food-motivated tasks (Correll, 1957), (3) produce enhanced "pleasure" reactions (MacLean, 1954, 1957), or (4) elicit rage or attack behavior (MacLean and Delgado, 1953; Naquet, 1954). Lesions in the hippocampus have been reported to (1) increase food intake and performance of food-motivated instrumental responses (H. Teitelbaum, 1960; Ehrlich, 1963), (2) enhance pleasure reactions (Bard and Mountcastle, 1948), (3) increase sexual aggressiveness (Kim, 1960), and (4) reduce fear of human observers (Weiskrantz, 1956).

The effect of motivational variables is most difficult to assess in learning situations involving noxious stimulation, and it may be worthwhile to examine some of the experimental evidence in this area.

Most interesting and consistent is the behavior of animals with hippocampal lesions on passive-avoidance tasks which require that the animals withhold a previously reinforced response in order to avoid electric shock. Normal animals learn this "response" of not responding very rapidly, often requiring only a single shock reinforcement. Animals with hippocampal lesions, on the other hand, appear incapable of withholding the punished response and continue to perform the appetitive responses in spite of numerous and intense punishments. Kimura (1958), for instance, reported that rats with bilateral lesions in the posterior hippocampus did not learn to avoid a goal box that contained food, even when the floor of the compartment was electrified with a very high shock. Other workers (Isaacson and Wicklegren, 1962; Kimble, 1963) have reported similar results following more massive damage to the hippocampal formation. H. Teitelbaum and Milner (1963) found that rats with dorsal hippocampal lesions could not inhibit unconditioned locomotor activity and would repeatedly leave a safe platform placed in the center of an electrified grid.

Less clear-cut are the effects of hippocampal damage on active avoidance behavior. Several workers (K. H. Pribram and Weiskrantz, 1957; Thomas and Otis, 1958) reported deficits in the acquisition or retention of avoidance responses in a shuttle box situation. Others (Brady et al., 1954; Hunt and Diamond, 1957) observed no significant impairment in similar situations, and Isaacson et al. (1961) reported that rats with large hippocampal lesions learn a shuttle box avoidance response faster than normal controls.

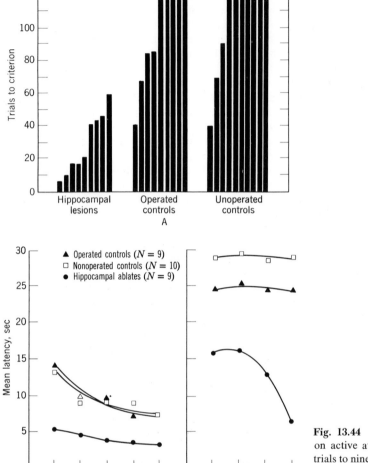

Fig. 13.44 Effects of hippocampal lesions on active avoidance learning in the rat. A, trials to nine avoidance responses in ten trials (learning criterion) for all groups. B, mean latencies for all groups during conditioning (left) and extinction trials (right). (From Isaacson et al., 1961.)

Flynn and Wasman (1960) found that classical defense conditioning could not be elaborated during hippocampal afterdischarges. This result seemed to be due to an inhibition of the response mechanism rather than an impairment of acquisition, for the animals performed conditioned responses as soon as the seizure activity terminated.

It is clear from these reports that we do not yet understand the contribution of the hippocampal mechanisms to avoidance motivation. One reason for our rather spectacular lack of success in this area may be the tacit assumption that there is only *one* hippocampal system or mechanism. The available evidence suggests in-

stead that there may be several distinct, and even functionally incompatible or opposed, mechanisms within the hippocampal formation which may not be anatomically distinct enough to permit selective activation or inhibition with our crude techniques. Until we have much more information on this matter, it appears pointless to attempt a consistent interpretation of the various effects of hippocampal lesions on acquisition or retention of avoidance responses.

The situation is fortunately clearer when we consider appetitive learning. Here we find little or no evidence for a hippocampal participation in simple approach learning; rather, we find consistent reports of an involvement in complex learning which requires the short-term storage of changing or new information on every trial. Delayed-response tasks or complex mazes most clearly show this effect. We have hypothesized on the basis of these data that the hippocampal formation may not be related to memory per se, but rather may subserve only short-term storage functions. We must point out, however, that hippocampal damage produces general hyperactivity (Karmos and Grastyán, 1962; Roberts et al., 1962; Kimble, 1963; H. Teitelbaum and Milner, 1963) which may interfere directly with delayed-response tasks by making it difficult for the subject to maintain a postural orientation or may indirectly affect this as well as other complex learning behavior by distracting the animal.

Electrical Stimulation of the Hippocampus

A group of studies by Knott and his associates (Knott et al., 1956, 1960b; Knott and Ingram, 1961) have shown that low-intensity electrical stimulation of various electrode placements in the hippocampus, which presumably did not evoke seizure activity, failed to affect the performance of a learned bar-pressing response.

A suppression of performance can be demonstrated when hippocampal seizures are induced by means of either chemical or electrical stimulation. MacLean et al. (1955–1956) found, for example, that cats and monkeys failed to perform a previously acquired avoidance response when hippocampal seizures were induced by local applications of carbachol. The impairment seemed to be independent of possible motor effects, for the animals responded appropriately to the UCS. In a second experiment similar results were obtained in a classical trace-conditioning paradigm involving autonomic (cardiac and respiratory) responses.

Flynn et al. (1961) have reported that classically conditioned leg flexion responses were completely blocked by electrically induced hippocampal seizures that did not spread to cortical areas. They again ruled out motor deficits by demonstrating normal responses to the UCS. Most interesting, perhaps, is a report by Flynn and Wasman (1960) about the effects of localized hippocampal seizures on the acquisition of avoidance responses. They found that cats trained only during hippocampal afterdischarges showed little evidence of learning during 100 trials. However, when hippocampal stimulation was then discontinued, the animals learned the avoidance response significantly faster than control animals

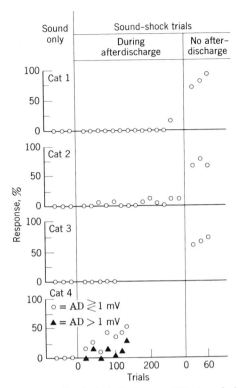

Fig. 13.45 Classical defensive conditioning during stimulation-induced afterdischarges in the hippocampal formation, in the relative absence of performance (cats 1, 2, and 3). Performance may take place if afterdischarges are not intense and occasionally even during intense afterdischarges (cat 4). (From Flynn and Wasman, 1960, © AAAS.)

that had not been exposed to the training under hippocampal stimulation. These findings suggest that the observed results of hippocampal seizures may not be due to an effect on mechanisms essential for learning or retention. Flynn and Wasman further demonstrated that the latency of forepaw movements elicited by direct stimulation of the motor cortex is significantly increased and that their magnitude is significantly depressed during hippocampal seizure activity. They suggested that the frequently reported memory deficits may be at least partially explained by a motor depression.

The Amygdaloid Complex

The amygdala has been shown to participate in the central regulation of emotional behavior. This may explain most, if not all, of the reported effects of amygdalectomy on acquisition or retention. We have, however, no definite proof of this hypothesis and shall present some representative examples from the recent research literature to illustrate the problem.

Destruction of all or part of the amygdaloid complex almost inevitably retards the acquisition of active avoidance responses. Brady et al. (1954) reported, for instance, that bilateral amygdaloid lesions significantly impaired the acquisition of avoidance responses in cats, although all animals finally learned the problem to criterion. Animals operated after the completion of training showed no performance decrements, suggesting that memory was not itself affected by these lesions. Brady's description of the behavior of his animals indicates that the observed impairment was of a motivational rather than associative nature. Whereas all control animals showed marked emotional reactions to the CS (defecation, urination, vocalization, and piloerection), particularly during the earlier stages of training, such responses were only rarely observed in the experimental animals.

Weiskrantz (1956) employed two different testing situations to assess the effects of amygdalectomy (combined with resection of the medial temporal pole) in monkeys. Active avoidance learning was measured in a standard shuttle box apparatus, and the conditioned emotional responses were assessed by the suppression of behavior in a food-rewarded panel-pressing situation. The amygdalectomized animals learned both problems more slowly than did their operated or normal controls, but they eventually reached comparable performance levels. When the lesions were made after acquisition had been completed, no clear decrement in performance appeared, but both avoidance and conditioned emotional responses were extinguished more quickly when the shock reinforcement was withheld. Associative factors seem to be implicated both in this and in Brady's study, for the operated animals eventually performed as well as the control group; however, we have evidence for a marked change in emotional behavior which might be directly responsible for the observed impairment. Weiskrantz emphasized the pronounced tameness of the amygdalectomized animals. They approached and even reached for observers. They permitted petting and handling without showing overt signs of excitement and seemed little disturbed by the electric shocks in the training apparatus. Anyone who has ever worked with *Macacca mulatta* monkeys will testify that this behavior is very atypical for this

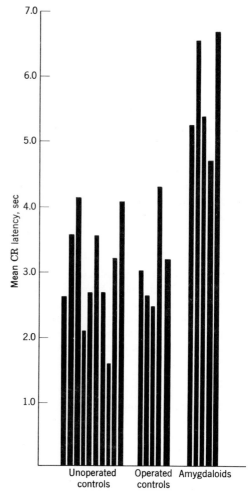

Fig. 13.46 Mean latency of conditioned avoidance responses for unoperated controls, operated controls, and animals with amygdaloid lesions. (From King, 1958.)

species. A subsequent experiment (Weiskrantz and Wilson, 1958) showed comparable results in still another aversive learning situation which required the animals to learn to press a lever at least once every 10 sec (Sidman avoidance schedule) to avoid shock.

The impairment of avoidance learning can be predicted rather easily from our hypothesis. Not as obvious is an explanation of other learning deficits that have been reported. Fuller et al. (1957), for example, found that animals with large temporal lobe lesions showed a significant postoperative performance decrement on simple discrimination and delayed-response problems. It is possible that these deficits were caused by the destruction of neural tissue not belonging to the amygdaloid complex, but some recent results indicate that even restricted amygdaloid damage may produce performance decrements that may not be directly related to motivational mechanisms.

Schwartzbaum and Pribram (1960) found that amygdalectomized monkeys showed no significant impairment on a simple brightness discrimination problem. However, they failed completely to generalize the learned information on tests of transposition requiring a response to relative rather than absolute stimulus differences. A similar lack of generalization had previously been reported (Schwartzbaum, 1960a, b) in a simple bar-pressing situation, and these findings may indicate that the amygdaloid mechanisms are involved in a process that contributes to acquisition in at least some learning situations. More information is needed about this interesting topic before definitive remarks can be made.

The Septal Area

The influence of motivational or emotional factors is clearest when we consider the septal area. Yet even here we find some experimental results that may indicate a more complex interaction of effects than had previously been assumed. Brady and Nauta (1953, 1955) reported that septal lesions produced an immediate and pronounced increase in emotional reactivity (ex-

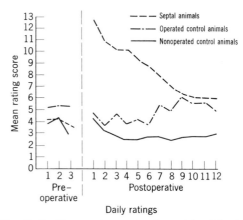

Fig. 13.47 Changes in emotional reactivity following experimental septal lesions. (From Brady and Nauta, 1953.)

plosive startle reactions, vicious attack responses to normal handling, etc.) but significantly impaired the performance of a preoperatively acquired CER. Tracy and Harrison (1956) similarly found that the performance of instrumental escape responses (bar pressing to terminate noxious noise) was markedly impaired following septal lesions, although sensory thresholds were not affected in the UCS modality. These findings are striking in view of the large body of evidence that shows a marked increase in

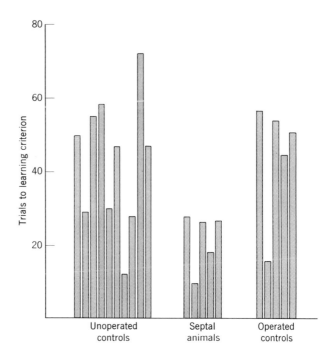

Fig. 13.48 Rate of avoidance conditioning in unoperated controls, animals with septal lesions, and operated controls. (From King, 1958.)

emotionality following septal lesions. An interpretation of these results is complicated by subsequent reports (King, 1958) which indicate that animals with septal lesions may learn avoidance responses more rapidly than their normal controls.

This problem has recently been pursued further by McCleary (1961), who demonstrated that animals with subcallosal lesions are almost completely incapable of performing a previously acquired passive avoidance response (i.e., withholding a food-reinforced response that is punished) but perform as well as or better than their normal controls on postoperative tests of active avoidance behavior in a shuttle box. Whether this inhibitory mechanism is involved in other than aversive situations is not yet clear. Thomas et al. (1959) found that septal lesions had very little effect on the acquisition or retention of non-emotional food-reinforced habits in a Lashley type III maze. Only those animals that showed marked postoperative changes in emotional behavior and strenuously objected to handling showed an impairment in the acquisition of the maze problem. Incidental observations suggested that excessive and persistent exploratory tendencies may have contributed to this effect.

Ingram (1958) has reported that cats trained to bar-press for food stopped responding during low-intensity electrical stimulation of the septal area and returned only reluctantly to the lever after the stimulation was terminated. Several animals displayed emotional behavior during the stimulation. It appears likely that the observed interference with learned behavior may be caused by the punishing effect of the electrical stimulation or by direct interference of the emotional responses that were observed. These results have been replicated by Knott et al. (1960b).

The Cingulate Gyrus

The mesial cortex appears to be a part of the limbic circuit which contributes to the regulation of emotional and perhaps general motivational functions. It is not surprising to find that massive cingulate lesions affect the acquisition or performance of avoidance responses, as reported by several investigators. Although these results are frequently cited as evidence for an important, if highly specific, role of this area in conditioning, it seems rather certain that the observed deficits are of a motivational nature. Some examples will suffice to demonstrate this fact.

Thomas (1959) reported that lesions in the thalamocingulate projections retarded the acquisition of avoidance responses but had no effect on appetitive maze learning. Peretz (1960) found that lesions in the anterior cingulate cortex impaired avoidance learning but increased the rate of performance of a food-reinforced habit. Thomas and Slotnick (1960) reported that lesions of the anterior portion of the mesial cortex produce a significant decrement in the performance of passive avoidance responses.

McCleary (1961) has explored this problem in some detail and found that lesions in the anterior mesial cortex very markedly impaired passive avoidance responses when food was the reward but had no effect on the acquisition or performance of an active avoidance response in a shuttle box. More posterior lesions in the cingulate gyrus, on the other hand, did not affect passive avoidance behavior but significantly retarded the acquisition of an active avoidance response. These interesting findings suggest that the central regulation of emotional behavior may be related to complex mechanisms which are, at least in part, represented in the cingulate area. There seems but little reason to believe that associative rather than motivational functions were affected in these studies. (A more extensive discussion of the overt effects of lesions in various parts of the limbic system can be found in Chapter 9.)

DIENCEPHALIC MECHANISMS

The Thalamus

Four anatomically and functionally distinct groups of thalamic nuclei must be distinguished.

The first of these receives specific sensory impulses from the ascending sensory pathways (spinothalamics, lemniscal systems, quintothalamics, optic, and auditory systems, etc.) and projects specifically and directly to the primary and secondary sensory areas of the cortex. Prominent nuclei in this group are (1) posteromedial ventral nuclei (trigeminal lemnisci, taste pathways), (2) posterolateral ventral nuclei (spinothalamics, medial lemnisci), and (3) medial (audition) and lateral (vision) geniculate bodies.

The second group of thalamic nuclei serves as a relay station between other central mechanisms. Most prominent in this group are the lateral and anterior ventral nuclei which receive impulses from the cerebellum, red nucleus, and striatum and project to the motor areas of the precentral gyrus. Also part of this group are the anterior

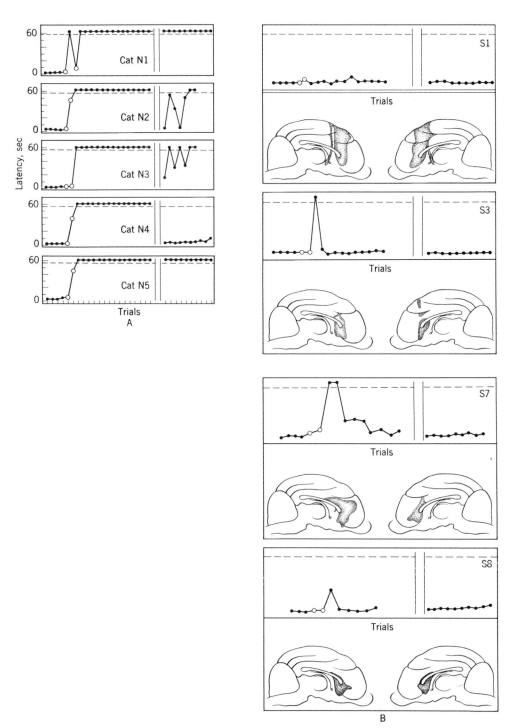

Fig. 13.49 Approach latencies of (A) normal and (B) operated cats in a passive-avoidance test. (Lesions are indicated on the insets.) Open circles represent trials on which a shock was received at the food trough. Since the animals were allowed only 60 sec on each trial, points above the dashed line represent trials during which a subject did not enter the feeding cubicle. The performance on shock day is shown to the left of the two parallel vertical lines; to the right are shown the first ten trials of the following day. Compare with Figure 13.50 which gives effects on active-avoidance tests. (From McCleary, 1961.)

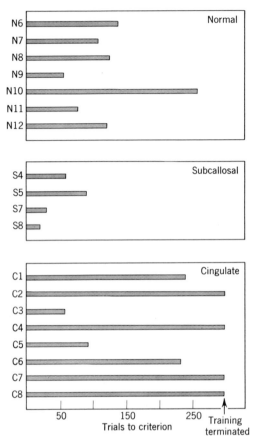

Fig. 13.50   Trials to criterion on an active-avoidance test for normal controls and animals with cingulate or septal lesions. (From McCleary, 1961.)

and dorsomedial nuclei. They receive impulses from the hypothalamus and project to the cingulate gyrus and frontal cortex respectively.

A third group of nuclei (the association nuclei) receives impulses primarily from other thalamic nuclei and projects to the association areas of the cortex. This group includes much of the dorsomedial aspect of the thalamus which projects to the prefrontal cortex; the lateral posterior and lateral dorsal nuclei which project to the posterior parietal area; and the pulvinar nucleus which projects to the visual association areas and the posterior temporal lobe.

A fourth group of nuclei (the nonspecific nuclei) projects nonspecifically to all areas of the cortex, providing a thalamocortical extension of the reticular mechanisms of the lower brainstem. Stimulation of these nuclei produces general cortical arousal, and lesions greatly reduce or abolish alertness. Included in this group are the

medial (paracentral, central lateral, centrum medianum, rhomboid, central medial) and reticular nuclei of the thalamus.

A brief review of the anatomical connections of the thalamic nuclei has been provided at this point because a thorough understanding of the functional role of specific thalamic nuclei is essential to an interpretation of the often-confusing literature. For example, lesions that infringe on specific sensory nuclei may well appear to impair acquisition or retention when, in fact, they affect only sensory mechanisms. Damage to the second group of nuclei may affect learning and retention by interrupting fiber tracts which interconnect central mechanisms; such tracts may or may not be directly related to associative functions. Lesions in the nonspecific thalamic nuclei may produce changes in the general level of cortical activation which may influence performance during tests of acquisition or retention, although motivational mechanisms may be primarily affected. We do not yet know enough about the role of the third (association) group of nuclei to interpret definitively any changes in learning or retention that may result from lesions within this part of the thalamus. However, these nuclei do not appear to have specific sensory or relay functions and are only indirectly related to the thalamic reticular formation. It is possible, therefore, that associative functions may be represented in some of or all the nuclei of this third group. We shall confine our discussion to some studies of these association nuclei and refer the reader to our discussion of reticular mechanisms (Chapter 5) for related findings. It must be remembered, however, that the topographical organization of the thalamus makes it very difficult to destroy some of these nuclei selectively. The possibility of direct or indirect (degeneration) damage to neighboring sensory, relay, or reticular nuclei has not been ruled out in most of the studies to be reported.

One of the earliest studies of the thalamic contribution to the acquisition or retention of complex behavior sequences was reported by Brown and Ghiselli (1938a). These workers found that lesions in the anterior nuclei had little or no effect on acquisition, whereas damage to almost all other areas of the thalamus retarded learning significantly; the severity of the deficits correlated with the size rather than the specific location of the lesion. Since almost all lesions infringed considerably on sensory or relay nuclei, these findings were not unexpected.

Later investigations have been more successful

in restricting the extent of direct damage to the association and relay nuclei. Schreiner et al. (1953), for example, destroyed the dorsomedial nuclei of the thalamus in cats after the animals had mastered several discrimination and manipulation tasks. Postoperative performance was found to be impaired in all tests and even prolonged retraining failed to re-establish preoperative performance levels. These are unambiguous deficits, but it is not at all clear that they represent an associative impairment. Schreiner et al. report that the lesions produced hyperirritability, viciousness, and increased reactivity to both noxious and non-noxious stimuli. Since some of the dorsomedial nuclei relay impulses from the hypothalamus to the cingulate gyrus and frontal cortex, the observed impairment of "retention" may have been due to a change in affective rather than associative functions.

Chow (1954) has reported a comprehensive study of the effects of lesions in the dorsomedial and pulvinar nuclei on the performance of monkeys in various behavioral test situations. Chow found that incomplete bilateral destruction of these association nuclei did not significantly affect performance of preoperatively learned visual or tactile discriminations, audiovisual conditioned responses, or delayed-response problems. Some animals showed a postoperative impairment, but neither the extent nor the exact location of the lesions appeared to correlate with the severity of the behavioral deficits.

Peters et al. (1956) have further explored the possible role of the dorsomedial nuclei in more complex learning situations, suggesting that delayed-response learning may be particularly affected by damage to the thalamocortical projections to frontal cortical areas known to be involved in the performance of delayed responses (Jacobsen, 1936; Harlow et al., 1952; R. A. Blum, 1952). They found that large, bilateral lesions of the dorsomedial nuclei, although they temporarily impaired postoperative performance, did not retard the acquisition of delayed-response and delayed-alternation habits.

Rosvold et al. (1958) have reported that lesions in the medial thalamus significantly impaired performance on a single alternation task, and Schreiner et al. (1953) observed that dorsomedial lesions produced a temporary amnesia and persisting performance decrements on a simple lever-pressing task. These findings may be related to changes in emotional behavior which have been noted in the later studies. Such an interpretation is

supported by Pechtel's (1955) finding that cats with dorsomedial lesions showed a postoperative amnesia for conditioned emotional responses that were established just before the lesion. That these deficits involved motivational rather than memory functions is suggested by the finding that all lesioned animals showed a marked impairment in the postoperative learning of a similar emotional response.

Knott et al. (1960a) have reported a significant impairment of postoperative performance of a simple lever-pressing task following dorsomedial but not centrum medianum lesions. No changes in emotional behavior were reported in this study. A report by Warren and Akert (1960) suggests that associative deficits may result from dorsomedial lesions that are perhaps independent of the frequently reported changes in emotional responsiveness. Warren and Akert trained cats on a complex conditioned visual discrimination problem in a Wisconsin General Test Apparatus (WGTA) and tested for retention following large bilateral lesions in the dorsomedial nuclei. The animals did not show overt signs of irritability or emotional hypersensitivity, but they were significantly poorer on the discrimination problem than before the operation. R. Thompson and Massopust (1960) similarly failed to report overt changes in emotional behavior following bilateral damage to the dorsomedial nuclei which produced a significant performance decrement on a simple black-white discrimination problem. Retention deficits following lesions in more posterior portions of the thalamus were also observed in this study. A possible involvement of emotional factors cannot be entirely ruled out because objective tests of emotionality were not reported.

The possible effects of thalamic lesions on learning and performance in emotional situations has been investigated more specifically by Brady and Nauta (1955). These workers found that lesions in the habenular complex of the thalamus did not significantly impair the acquisition or retention of a CER (suppression of bar pressing for food during the CS for shock). However, animals with habenular lesions extinguished reliably faster than normal subjects, the rapidity of extinction being related to the extent of the habenular damage. Whether these effects can be attributed to an effect on associative mechanisms is not clear at this time. Dahl and his associates (1962) have reported that large lesions in the anterior thalamus did not affect the performance of simple avoidance responses in a shuttle box situation.

R. Thompson (1960a, b; Thompson et al., 1961) found that lesions in the posteroventral nuclei of the thalamus produced a severe deficit in retention of a kinesthetic habit, whereas lesions medial to the lateral geniculate bodies had no effect on this response. Damage to the habenular nuclei or the subthalamus similarly failed to affect postoperative performance. Thompson and his collaborators also noted that posteromedial lesions significantly impaired retention of an active avoidance response to a visual CS. Cardo (1960) found complete amnesia of a preoperatively acquired avoidance response following lesions in the medial thalamus, and Adey and Lindsley (1959) reported a similar impairment in postoperative retention of avoidance behavior following subthalamic damage.

The possible role of thalamic mechanisms in acquisition and retention requires further study in situations which minimize the possible contribution of affective changes. Until such information becomes available, we must conclude that a participation of thalamic circuits in associative functions is possible but has not yet been demonstrated.

Electrical and chemical stimulation of thalamic nuclei. Endroczi et al. (1959) trained dogs to obtain food by pushing a door when a bell was presented and to withhold this response when another auditory stimulus was given. After the animals reached criterion on this difficult conditional discrimination task (300 to 350 training trials were required), electrical stimulation was applied to either lateral or medial thalamic nuclei. Stimulation of the lateral nuclei produced a 40- to 50-sec inhibition of the conditioned door-pushing response, but sensory or emotional mechanisms may have been responsible for this effect. The authors noted that the animals exhibited marked fear and attempted to escape when the intensity of the electrical stimulation was slightly increased. Electrical stimulation of the center median nucleus appeared to facilitate the CR and even elicit it spontaneously when no CS was presented. The animals were observed to display pleasure reactions during this stimulation and appeared excited and friendly.

Very different results were obtained by Grossman et al. (1965) using chemical stimulation techniques. Cholinergic stimulation of the thalamic midline nuclei of rats produced a significant impairment of performance during the acquisition of a simple shuttle box avoidance response. Asymptotic performance was not reliably affected by the stimulation or by a change to nonstimulation conditions. An analysis of the response latencies indicated that all animals learned the instrumental escape response as rapidly as the unoperated controls. These findings suggest that sensory-motor deficits as well as motivational factors can be ruled out; the observed effects may

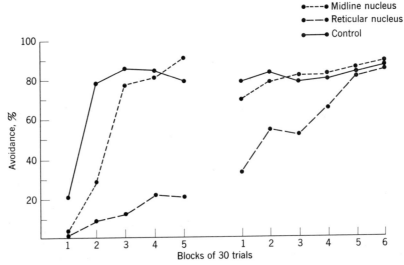

Fig. 13.51 Avoidance performance in a shuttle box following cholinergic stimulation of the thalamic reticular formation (left) and sham stimulation (right). (From Grossman et al., 1965.)

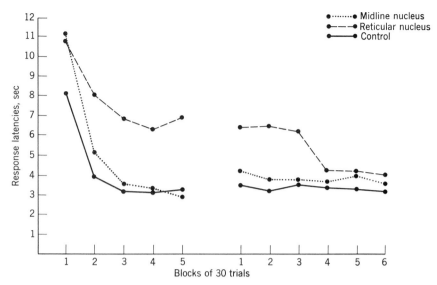

Fig. 13.52 Response latencies in a shuttle box following cholinergic stimulation of the thalamic reticular formation (left) and after sham stimulation (right). (From Grossman et al., 1965.)

be due to an interference with mechanisms essential to the acquisition but not to the performance of the avoidance response.

Cholinergic stimulation of the reticular nuclei of the thalamus produced a significant depression of asymptotic performance as well as rate of acquisition. When cholinergic stimulation was discontinued after 150 trials, a gradual improvement occurred, and group performance reached an asymptote after 165 trials which was comparable to that of the control group. All stimulated animals acquired the instrumental response during the first 60 trials of the stimulation experiment and escaped rapidly and efficiently whenever the UCS was presented.

Grossman and Peters (1966) have shown that the application of a cholinergic blocking agent (atropine) to the reticular nuclei of the thalamus produces a marked performance deficit during acquisition as well as at the asymptote of performance in appetitive (black-white discrimination in a T-maze) and aversive (avoidance behavior in a shuttle box) training situations. This pattern of results (similar behavioral effects of chemical stimulation or inhibition) suggests that the reticular nuclei may provide an essential link in the pathways responsible for learning and/or retention.

Application of the cholinergic blocking agent to the midline nuclei, on the other hand, produced reliable facilitatory effects on behavior in both appetitive and aversive test situations, suggesting a possible relationship to inhibitory motivational processes rather than to mechanisms specifically related to learning.

The Hypothalamus

The hypothalamic portion of the diencephalon, small as it may be, has been implicated in a great variety of functions. The hypothalamus is strategically located, so that corticofugal and corticipetal reticular influences and most of the efferents from the rhinencephalon must pass through it. Specific regulatory mechanisms for most of the homeostatic functions that give rise to primary motivation have been localized near the third ventricle, and several authors have considered this region to be the headganglion of the autonomic nervous system (see Peele, 1954). It has been noted that far more functions per millimeter of tissue have been imputed to the hypothalamus than to any other portion of the nervous system. That basic memory mechanisms should also be represented is unlikely.

It should not be surprising that hypothalamic lesions affect the performance of learned responses during both acquisition and retention. For instance, if hunger or thirst is impaired or abolished by lateral hypothalamic lesions, a marked decrement in the rate of acquisition or performance of food-motivated or water-motivated responses might be expected. Similarly, an impair-

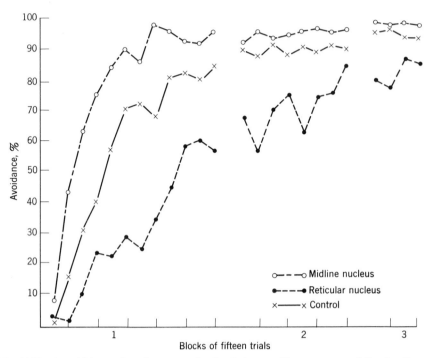

Fig. 13.53 Acquisition and performance of a shuttle box avoidance response following the application of atropine (sections 1 and 3) or sham stimulation (section 2) to the thalamic reticular formation. (From Grossman and Peters, 1966.)

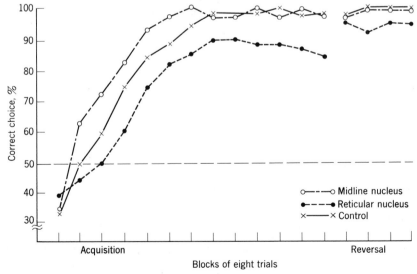

Fig. 13.54 Acquisition and performance of a black-white discrimination response in a T-maze. The experimental animals received atropine injections in the thalamic reticular formation before each daily test during the acquisition phase. (From Grossman and Peters, 1966.)

ment, or even an improvement of performance in an avoidance situation might be predicted following damage to the ventromedial nuclei or the rhinencephalic efferents which course through the lateral portion of the hypothalamus. In our discussion of motivation, we have cited many such findings and we shall not reiterate them here. Several recent findings require discussion because their relation to motivational changes is not immediately obvious.

One interesting example is provided by studies demonstrating an impairment of acquisition or retention of a food-motivated (bar-pressing) response following bilateral lesions in the ventromedial nuclei of the hypothalamus. These lesions are known to produce overeating and obesity in free-feeding situations, and one might predict a consequent improvement of performance on food-motivated tasks. Miller et al. (1950) demonstrated that the opposite is, in fact, true. Animals with such lesions work *less* for food than normal animals do, although they consume more food when it is available *ad libitum*.

Similar observations have been reported by Ingram (1958). One group of cats was trained to bar-press for food before bilateral lesions were made in the ventromedial hypothalamus; another group was operated on before training was attempted. Ingram observed that animals trained to criterion before the operation either failed to respond at all or showed lower response rates on the first postoperative test. After 10 days of re-training, all animals bar-pressed again, but the rate of responding remained very low. Three of the animals that were operated on before the initial training did not learn to bar-press although a 72-hr deprivation regimen was imposed; the remaining animals were significantly retarded throughout acquisition and never reached performance levels comparable to those of normal animals. Knott et al. (1960a) have reported directly comparable results.

Since the animals ate voraciously when given free access to food in these studies, it has been suggested that the observed deficits in acquisition or retention may be related to associative mechanisms. Miller et al. (1950), on the other hand, suggested that ventromedial lesions may increase an animal's food intake through a disturbance of the satiety mechanisms which may determine how soon an animal *stops* eating without necessarily influencing hunger or appetite. An actual lowering of hunger motivation (accompanied by marked hyperphagia and obesity) has also been observed in other studies. P. Teitelbaum (1955) reported, for instance, that hyperphagic animals show a much greater decrease in food intake than normal animals when the diet is made less palatable by the addition of cellulose or quinine. Observations by P. Teitelbaum and Campbell (1958) suggest further that the increased food intake of these animals may be due to a greater meal size rather than more frequent intake. These findings support Miller's hypothesis and suggest that the

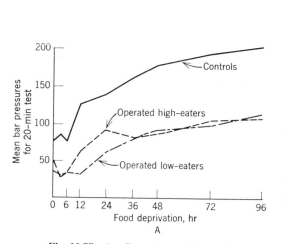
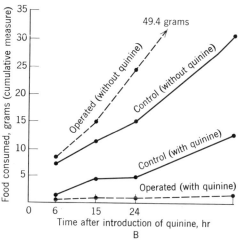

Fig. 13.55 A, effect of hypothalamic lesions on the rate of bar pressing for food rewards after various intervals of food deprivation. B, effect of a bitter taste on the food intake of animals with hypothalamic lesions. (From Miller et al., 1950, AAAS.)

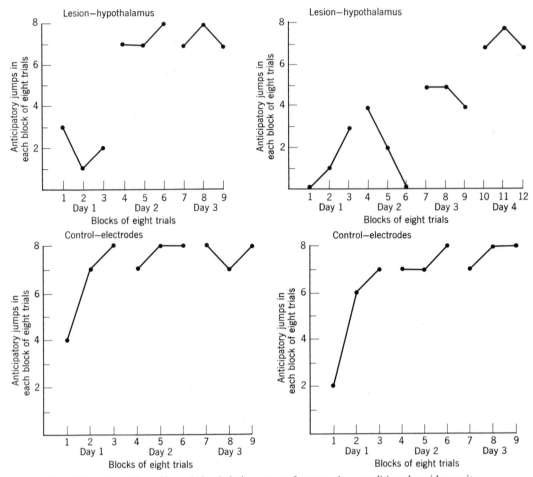

Fig. 13.56   *Top,* effect of hypothalamic lesions on performance in a conditioned avoidance situation. *Bottom,* the performance of control animals. (From Knott and Ingram, 1961.)

observed impairment of acquisition and retention of food-motivated behavior are related to motivational rather than associative mechanisms.

Several studies have shown an impairment or improvement in the acquisition or performance of escape and avoidance responses following various hypothalamic lesions. Most of these findings can be explained on the basis of motivational changes. S. Levine and Soliday (1960), for example, reported that rats with lesions in the median eminence learned an instrumental avoidance response significantly faster than normal or sham-operated controls. Such results would be expected if the lesions increased the animals' sensitivity to electric shock or lowered the threshold of emotional responses. We have already discussed several studies which indicate that such changes can be expected following lesions in various hypothalamic areas.

R. Thompson and his collaborators (Thompson and Hawkins, 1961; Thompson and Massopust, 1960), on the other hand, found that lesions lateral to the mammillary bodies impaired the retention (i.e., performance) of escape as well as avoidance behavior and retarded the acquisition of a brightness discrimination which also involved shock motivation. It is not necessary to assume deficits in associative mechanisms or memory to account for these results. Either a marked increase or decrease in emotional reactivity (depending on the intensity of the UCS) would produce comparable effects, and hypothalamic lesions are known to produce such changes.

Less obvious is an explanation of Thomas's finding (Thomas et al., 1959a, b) that bilateral interruption of the mammillothalamic tract impaired retention of avoidance responses and significantly increased the number of relearning trials necessary to reacquire criterion on this task. Although the mammillothalamic tract represents the major hypothalamocortical connection, no clear changes in emotional responsiveness have been demonstrated following bilateral destruction of this tract, and none was observed in Thomas's experiment. Furthermore, the animals did eventually reach criterion performance postoperatively, so that the effect cannot simply be interpreted as a performance decrement. It is possible that a small effect on emotional mechanisms might be reflected during the acquisition, but not during the performance, of an overtrained response. However, associative factors cannot be eliminated. It may be worthwhile to consider the possibility that some fibers that course through the hypothalamus on their way to more caudal relay stations are more directly involved in learning and retention than has previously been assumed.

Electrical stimulation of hypothalamic mechanisms. Knott and associates (Knott et al., 1956, 1960b; Ingram, 1958; Knott and Ingram, 1961) have reported several studies which indicate that electrical stimulation of various hypothalamic areas inhibits or reduces the performance of previously acquired instrumental responses (bar pressing) for food reward. In view of the importance of this area in the central regulation of feeding behavior and emotional responsiveness, these results may not be caused by an interference with associative mechanisms; however, the authors observed free feeding during electrical stimulation of the hypothalamus and reported only isolated cases of conditioned anxiety.

Because many experimenters have observed aversive properties of hypothalamic stimulation, various alternative interpretations of these results must be considered. Chemical activation or inhibition of specific hypothalamic mechanisms has been shown selectively to enhance or inhibit the performance of food- or water-motivated responses (Grossman, 1960, 1962a, b), but these effects appeared to be the result of changes in specific motivational rather than associative mechanisms. The results of most other studies of the effects of chemical or electrical stimulation of the hypothalamus seem best explained on the basis of motivational rather than associative functions, and we shall not discuss them at this point.

Similar interpretations may be appropriate for the frequently cited experiments reported by Grastyán et al. (1956). However, their results have generally been discussed in the framework

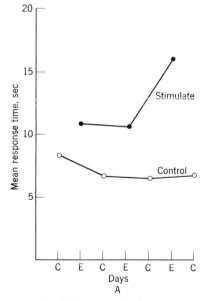

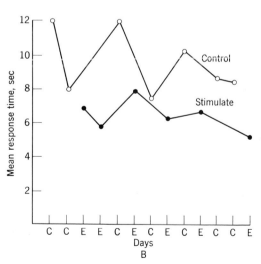

Fig. 13.57 A, inhibition of appetitive behavior (lever pressing) by hypothalamic stimulation. B, facilitation of appetitive behavior (lever pressing) by hypothalamic stimulation. On control (C) days ten trials are given without stimulation; on experimental (E) days stimulation is given throughout the period of testing. The mean time for ten trials is plotted. (From Knott et al., 1960b.)

of associative mechanisms, and we shall briefly describe the principal observations. Grastyán et al. reported that electrical stimulation of the dorsolateral hypothalamus of cats facilitated—and even elicited—a simple food-reinforced instrumental response, whereas similar stimulation of the posteromedial hypothalamus and more posterior aspects of the mesencephalic reticular formation inhibited the appetitive response. This relationship appeared to be reversed when stimulation was applied during the presentation of a CS for a simple escape-avoidance response. Stimulation of the dorsolateral hypothalamus inhibited the defensive responses; stimulation of the posteromedial hypothalamus and mesencephalon facilitated them. The authors suggested that these effects may be caused by a stimulation of specific portions of the reticular formation

that are involved in learning and memory. However, we must remember that electrical stimulation of the lateral hypothalamus elicits feeding behavior in sated animals, whereas stimulation of the medial aspects of the hypothalamus inhibits food intake in deprived animals. The complementary effects on emotional behavior are open to a similar analysis, although the anatomical relationships are not as clear.

THE BASAL GANGLIA

The basal ganglia are known to be part of the organism's response mechanism; this may account for the obvious lack of interest that physiological psychologists have shown in these nuclei. Buchwald's (1961a, b, c) observations of the effects of electrical stimulation of the caudate nuclei have

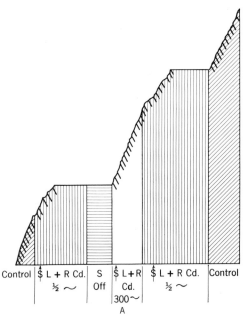

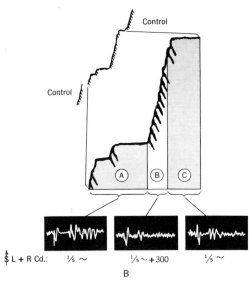

Fig. 13.58 A, effect of high- and low-frequency stimulation of the caudate nucleus on rate of bar pressing for a food reward (ratio of reinforcement, 1 unit of food per 12 presses). Slope of the curve is proportional to the rate of response. Control: responses for food reward before caudate stimulation. $L + R$ Cd($\frac{1}{2}\sim$): bilateral stimulation of the caudate nuclei at a rate of 1 p/2 sec first slows and then stops pressing. Stimulation parameters (suprathreshold for spindle production): 0.1-msec pulse duration, 50 volts. Off: caudate stimulation is stopped; the cat still does not respond. $L + R$ Cd(300$\sim$): bilateral high-frequency stimulation of the caudate nuclei (300 p/sec, 0.01-msec pulse duration, 70 volts) causes immediate return to the control rate of bar pressing.

B, effect of simultaneous low- and high-frequency stimulation of the caudate nuclei on a bar-pressing response. (A), oscilloscope tracing on the left shows evoked potential and caudate spindle elicited by low-frequency (1 p/5 sec) stimulation. The response rate during this stimulation falls to zero. (B), the middle trace shows abolition of spindling by simultaneous low- and high-frequency (300 p/sec) stimulation of the caudate nuclei. The response rate returns to control values. (C), the trace on the right shows the recurrence of the caudate spindle when the high-frequency stimulation is discontinued. Bar pressing is again inhibited.

reopened the question, and we may soon expect to see further work in this field. Only a few recent studies relating the caudate nucleus to associative processes are available at this time. All agree that this structure does not seem to be involved in simple learning and retention but may play an important role in complex problems. Although some interesting exceptions have been reported, the typical result of caudate damage is an impairment in the acquisition or retention of delayed-response problems which appears similar to that produced by frontal cortex lesions.

Rosvold and Delgado (1956) reported, for example, that the postoperative performance of a single-alternation task was significantly impaired by small lesions in the head of the caudate as well as by lesions in the medial portion of the thalamus. Their findings suggested that the observed effects might be due to an extensive caudatothalamocortical system which is, in some fashion, essential to the successful solution of this type of learning problem.

Rosvold et al. (1958) pursued this notion in a study which demonstrated that visual discrimination learning was not affected by lesions in the head of the caudate nucleus, whereas the performance of single-alternation responses was severely impaired. R. Thompson (1959) reported that small caudate lesions did not affect the performance of an avoidance response but facilitated the extinction of this behavior when the reinforcement was withheld. Larger lesions similarly failed to affect postoperative performance of a previously acquired response; however, an even more marked effect on extinction was noted, and relearning was found to be significantly retarded. Knott et al. (1960a) reported a temporary performance decrement in a food-reinforced bar-pressing response during the first weeks after lesions in the head or body of the caudate nucleus, but they observed no permanent effects.

Bättig et al. (1960) investigated the relation between caudate and frontal cortex mechanisms by comparing the effects of lesions in these struc-

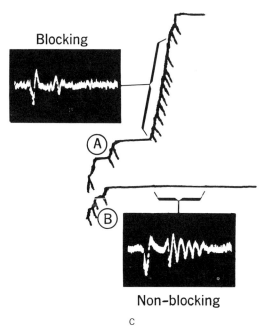

Non-blocking

C

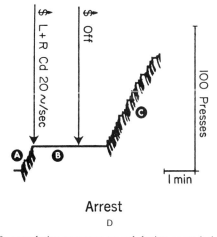

Arrest

D

Fig. 13.58 (continued) C, effects on the response rate of adding 300 p/sec to present continuously 1 p/5 sec bilateral stimulation of the caudate nuclei. (A), restoration of bar pressing with a spindle-blocking 300-p/sec bilateral caudate stimulus. (B), failure to restore bar pressing with a nonblocking 300-p/sec stimulus. Electrical recording from anterior sigmoid gyrus. Stimulation parameters: 1 p/5 sec, 0.01-msec pulse duration; (A), 80 volts; (B), 50 volts.

D, cumulative response record during arrest induced by bilateral caudate stimulation; 0.1-msec pulse duration, 30 volts, 20 p/sec (20 cps). (A), control rate of bar pressing; (B), bar pressing stops during stimulation; (C), bar pressing resumed after discontinuation of stimulation. (From Buchwald et al., 1961c.)

tures. Frontal and caudate nucleus lesions were found to have no effect on performance in a visual discrimination situation, but both alternation and delayed-response problems showed a marked postoperative impairment. Animals with caudate lesions appeared less severely affected than those with frontal lesions and seemed to have significantly less trouble with delayed-response problems than with tests involving alternation behavior. However, Bättig et al. suggested that these quantitative differences may have been caused by differences in the extent rather than in the location of the lesion or by a lack of strict correspondence between the testing situations.

Bättig et al. (1960) have contributed additional information about these mechanisms in a study comparing the effects of caudate and frontal lesions on complex visual and auditory discrimination learning. Under the conditions of the Bättig experiment, both frontal and caudate lesions significantly impaired the acquisition of auditory as well as visual (color and pattern) discrimination habits; the frontal lesions again produced a slightly greater deficit. These results suggest that the caudate nucleus may play an integral role in the acquisition or performance of some complex behavior sequences; however, we must remember that such factors as distractibility or attentiveness have been implicated in studies of the effects of frontal lesions and may account for the deficits seen after caudate damage as well. Basic associative or memory mechanisms are not likely to be found in this area of the brain.

THE BRAINSTEM

The effects of brainstem lesions or electrical stimulation have not yet been investigated thoroughly, and the few existing data are difficult to interpret. Lesions in this portion of the brain may produce severe sensory or motor deficits because of a direct involvement of the primary afferent pathways. Lesions may also reduce or abolish general, nonspecific motivation to the point where little or no behavior can be observed—for example, by affecting the nonspecific reticular pathways. It is difficult enough to assess the possible role of sensory or motor deficits in learning experiments; it is practically impossible to determine whether a response failure is caused by a direct involvement of memory mechanisms or by a concurrent impairment of general motivation.

The motivational mechanisms of the brainstem reticular formation (the ascending arousal system) are general rather than specific. Their partial or complete destruction, therefore, produces performance deficits that appear almost indistinguishable from those expected after an impairment of memory mechanisms. Only carefully controlled experiments which provide a clear picture of possible differences in the performance decrement during acquisition and long-term retention can provide some answers to this problem. Such investigations are scarce in the literature.

Hernández-Peón et al. (1956) reported that small lesions in the mesencephalic reticular forma-

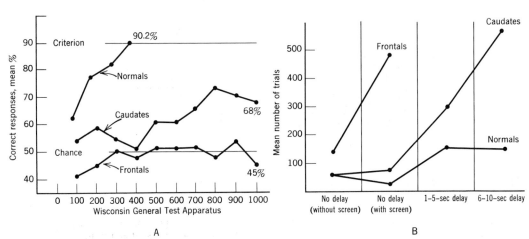

Fig. 13.59 Effects of caudate nucleus and frontal cortex lesions on A, a single delayed alternation in the Wisconsin General Test Apparatus (average learning curves); B, a delayed response in the WGTA (number of trials to learn including criterion). (From Bättig et al., 1960.)

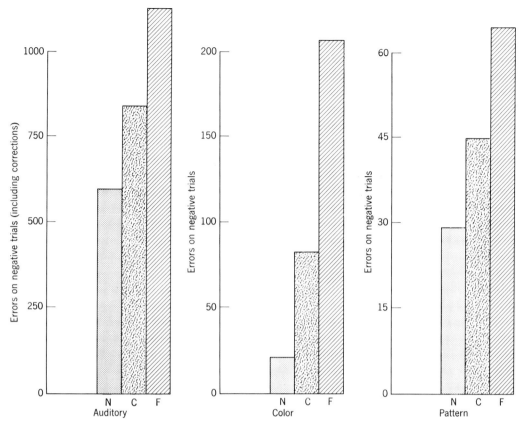

Fig. 13.60 Effects of caudate nucleus and frontal cortex lesions on visual (color and pattern) and auditory discrimination learning. For the auditory test errors are shown only for the first 500 trials including corrections. For the visual tests the scores are errors to criterion. The ordinates of the three graphs are drawn to different scales to emphasize the similarity of the relative differences among the groups. N, normals; C, caudate lesions; F, frontal lesions. (From Bättig et al., 1962.)

tion produced complete amnesia for a simple conditioned salivary response, although no marked impairment of general activity or the unconditioned salivary response was observed. Since the classically conditioned salivary response was not affected by lesions in the specific or nonspecific thalamic projection nuclei, the hippocampus, or the amygdala, and even survived complete decortication, the authors hypothesized that this type of learning may be mediated by neuronal mechanisms of the mesencephalic reticular formation. We must point out, however, that similar results would be expected if the lesions produced a general lowering of motivation or arousal, and this possibility is not ruled out by the casual observation of normalcy.

Doty et al. (1959) produced lesions of varying extent in the mesencephalic reticular formation of cats and reported some interesting individual case histories. One animal acquired a simple respiratory CR after massive lesions (100 mm³) in the upper portion of the central brainstem. The cat was completely somnolent after the operation, but recuperated sufficiently within the first postoperative week to begin training on the CR problem. Another animal relearned a previously acquired leg flexion response within 9 days of postoperative training following large (79 mm³) lesions in the central mesencephalic gray. The animal was lethargic and showed marked motor uncoordination and postural deficits, but reacquired the CR and showed complete extinction 80 trials after the reinforcement was discontinued. Other animals with slightly different lesions remained cataleptic throughout the postoperative survival period and failed to demonstrate any sign of learning or retention. These results suggest that some aspects of the reticular formation are not essential to the formation of simple conditioned responses.

Kreindler et al. (1959) have reported data supporting this hypothesis. They found that more complex associations, although temporarily affected, can be relearned after mesencephalic injury. Dogs were trained to give a leg flexion response to a bell and to withhold the response when a buzzer sounded. Following relatively large lesions in the pontomesencephalic tegmentum, the animals were spastic, somnolent, and hyporeactive to any form of sensory stimulation. However, within three weeks these symptoms abated sufficiently to allow a relearning of the conditioned responses to criterion. The experimental procedure did not permit the assumption that this retraining was essential.

R. Thompson and Massopust (1960) reported a marked and apparently permanent postoperative deficit in the retention of an avoidance response to visual stimuli following lesions in and posterior to the mammillary bodies. In a subsequent experiment Thompson (Thompson and Hawkins, 1961) demonstrated that this effect appeared to be caused by damage to an area posterior to the habenulopeduncular tract which contains the interpeduncular nucleus. Thompson (1960a, b; Thompson et al., 1961) reported, in addition, that lesions restricted to the interpeduncular nucleus impaired the retention of visual discrimination habits based on food or avoidance motivation; the postoperative retention of kinesthetic and auditory habits also seemed to be affected. The extent of the damage to the interpeduncular nucleus was correlated with the severity of the behavioral deficit. Lesions of the midbrain tegmentum or red nucleus had no effect on retention. Thompson concluded that the interpeduncular nucleus may play a significant role in retention, for deficits could be demonstrated although different motivational conditions and sensory modalities were involved in the various experiments.

Earlier workers (Bailey and Davis, 1942) had suggested that memory deficits following lesions in the interpeduncular nucleus might be due to a temporary general sensory or motor deficit. R. Thompson and Rich (1961) argued that if this were the cause of the observed deficits, a progressive reduction of the postoperative impairment with increased recovery periods before the test of retention could be expected. To test this hypothesis Thompson and Rich trained animals on visual discrimination or avoidance tasks and tested for postoperative retention one or three weeks after interpeduncular damage. Retention was significantly impaired one week after the operation, but no reliable effects remained after three weeks of recuperation. These findings were interpreted to support the Bailey and Davis hypothesis, although it is not immediately obvious why preference should be given to a temporary sensory or motor deficit rather than to a temporary impairment of associative or motivational mechanisms.

Grossman (unpublished observations) has observed that chemical stimulation or functional ablation of the interpeduncular nucleus does not reliably affect learning in a simple visual discrimination problem, although response latencies appear to be affected.

We have already mentioned the study by Grastyán et al. (1956) which demonstrated that electrical stimulation of the midbrain reticular formation inhibited a simple alimentary CR, but appeared to facilitate and even elicit a defensive CR. Similar effects were obtained from hypothalamic structures, and we suggested that motivational rather than associative mechanisms may be responsible for this effect. Such an interpretation is obvious when we consider the response to hypothalamic stimulation, but it is not as clearly applicable to midbrain mechanisms.

Zuckermann (1959) has reported that stimulation-induced seizure activity in the midbrain reticular formation produced an initial period of inhibition during which classically conditioned eyeblink responses could not be elicited. However, a prolonged facilitation was recorded after this period of subnormality. It is possible that the differential effects that Grastyán et al. have reported may be due to the different temporal conditions of their alimentary and defensive conditioning experiments. Zuckermann also reported that stimulation of the midbrain reticular formation during the early stages of conditioning (trials 8 through 16) produced conditioned responses if the CS was presented during or immediately after electrical stimulation, although no overt signs of learning had been displayed before the stimulation trial.

Zuckermann followed up these observations by testing the conditioned responses of well-trained animals when the intertrial interval was progressively shortened. Control animals stopped re-

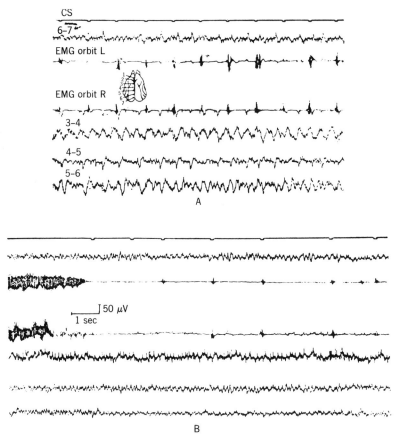

Fig. 13.61   Effect of reticular seizures on the blink reflex A, termination of seizure; B, 60 sec later. Note that the blink reflex, elicited here about every 2 sec, is absent only during the first few seconds and persists for minutes despite intense cortical desynchronization. (From Zuckermann, 1959.)

sponding to the CS when the intertrial interval was reduced from 4 to 2 min. However, when reticular formation stimulation was applied 10 sec before each trial, animals continued to respond, even when the intertrial interval was reduced to 10 sec. These results may not reflect an effect on associative mechanisms per se, but they are of interest in the present context because a facilitatory effect which may have entered into other investigations in this area, was observed.

Fuster (1957), for instance, has reported that electrical stimulation of the midbrain reticular formation improved the performance of monkeys on a tachistoscopic recognition-discrimination task. The animals were first trained to discriminate between two visual stimuli which were presented simultaneously for the duration of each trial. The same stimuli were then presented tachistoscopically for only a fraction of a second, and Fuster

observed that the animals required extensive retraining. If midbrain reticular formation stimulation was given just before the tachistoscopic presentation of the visual stimuli, performance was significantly improved. Fuster suggested that the perceptual responses of the animal had been facilitated by the stimulation; this appears to be a more reasonable hypothesis than subsequently advanced proposals that associative functions may have been affected.

The possible contribution of the mesencephalic reticular formation to learning, retention, or memory has been investigated in a number of studies using chemical means of stimulation and inhibition. Encouraged by the apparently selective effects of chemical stimulation and ablation in the reticular formation of the thalamus (Grossman et al., 1965; Grossman and Peters, 1966), Grossman and associates conducted a series of experiments to determine the response of the midbrain reticular formation to cholinergic and adrenergic stimulation and blockade.

The initial experiments (Grossman, 1966a) showed that small, implant-produced bilateral lesions in the midbrain reticular formation significantly reduced the avoidance behavior of rats without affecting their response to the UCS. Cholinergic stimulation of the same site produced a complex behavioral response. The initial application of a cholinergic drug to the midbrain resulted in a marked depression of avoidance behavior and even reduced the animal's response to the UCS. However, when repeated treatments were given before each daily training period, the behavioral results were reversed. The animals performed reliably better in the avoidance situation and responded more promptly to the UCS on the infrequent occasions when the avoidance response did not appear.

The implant-produced lesions reliably facilitated the acquisition and performance of simple appetitive habits in maze and operant conditioning situations. Cholinergic stimulation, on the other hand, impaired performance in all appetitive situations, even when frequently repeated (Grossman and Grossman, 1966).

It is possible that these effects represent the result of a temporary facilitation or interference with associative mechanisms, but it seems more likely that here, as well as in most (if not all) of the studies discussed in this section, a nonspecific motivational deficit may be the cause of the behavioral changes. The midbrain reticular formation may be the anatomical substrate for motivational processes (as well as other sensory, motor, or integrative and associative functions) which are sufficiently general to affect behavior in a variety of test situations but are appropriate only to some experimental conditions and are even interfering in others. The nonspecific arousal mechanism postulated by Lindsley (1960) and others fits the requirements of such a system admirably, but other mechanisms, concerned with emotionality or general reactivity, may be substituted in the present context.

If the preceding interpretation is correct, a simple explanation of the apparently paradoxical results of the chemical stimulation studies becomes possible. Arousal is the directly appropriate or relevant drive in the avoidance situation. Partial inhibition or lowering of this drive state produced by damage or seizure activity in the reticular formation would be expected to reduce performance in the avoidance situation. The same lowering of emotionality or nonspecific arousal would be

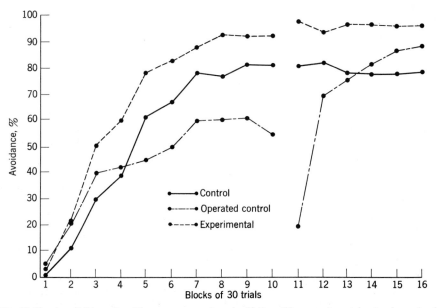

Fig. 13.62 Acquisition of avoidance responses in a shuttle box. The experimental animals received cholinergic stimulations of the midbrain reticular formation during the 300-trial acquisition period. The operated controls were sham-stimulated during this period but received cholinergic stimulation during the reversal period. (From Grossman, 1966b.)

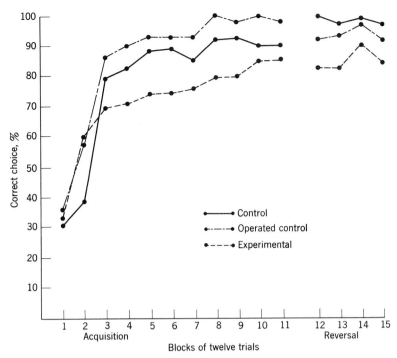

Fig. 13.63 Acquisition and performance of a brightness discrimination habit in a T-maze apparatus. The experimental animals received cholinergic stimulation in the midbrain reticular formation before each daily test session. The operated controls received cholinergic drugs during the reversal period. (From Grossman and Grossman, 1966.)

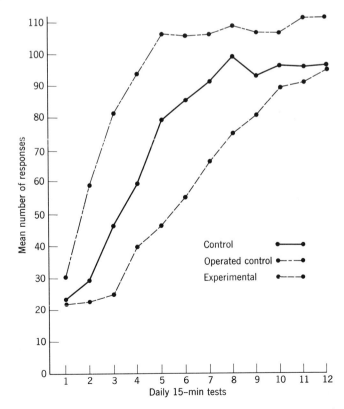

Fig. 13.64 Acquisition of a lever-pressing habit beginning with the first session during which each subject reached a "minimal criterion" of ten responses each 15 min. The experimental animals received cholinergic stimulation in the midbrain reticular formation immediately before each daily test. (From Grossman and Grossman, 1966.)

expected to improve performance in appetitive situations where arousal beyond a minimal threshold is irrelevant or even disruptive. Conversely, the stimulation-based increase in arousal should interfere with behavior in the appetitive situations because it energizes competing behavior rather than the appropriate goal-directed activity recorded in these experiments. On the other hand, the stimulation-caused increase in arousal should summate with the task-related arousal and produce better performance in the avoidance situation. An interpretation of the behavioral effects in terms of motivational rather than associative mechanisms is supported by the observation that cholinergic stimulation of the midbrain reticular formation reliably produced electrophysiological arousal responses as well as a marked increase in locomotor activity.

SPINAL CORD

It is clear, on the basis of recent studies of lower organisms, that conditioning can be observed in very simple species which do not possess a complex nervous system. We cannot, however, generalize this information to more complex organisms, for it is conceivable that the functional specialization (differentiation of specific tissues) which characterizes higher phyla may significantly alter the situation. Whether a rat, dog, or monkey can learn even the simplest conditioned responses after the brain is entirely severed from the spinal cord has been a hotly contested issue for many years.

Following some suggestive reports by Culler (Culler and Mettler, 1934; Culler et al., 1939) and Prosser and Hunter (1936), two groups of investigators have studied learning in spinal animals and have consistently reported conflicting results.

Shurrager and his colleagues (Shurrager and Culler, 1938, 1941; Shurrager and Shurrager, 1941, 1946) have used the response of the isolated semitendinosus muscle to weak electric shock or manual pressure of the tail (CS) as a measure of conditioning. The UCS in these experiments was electric shock to the foot. Shurrager obtained evidence of conditioning in at least some of his animals (98 of 219 dogs in one group of experiments) and reported that typical learning and extinction curves could be obtained from the animals which responded to the CS. Shurrager also found that conditioning and extinction occurred more and more rapidly when the animals were subjected to repeated cycles of acquisition and extinction, a finding which is, of course, typical for almost all learning situations.

Kellogg and his associates (Kellogg, 1947; Kellogg et al., 1946, 1947) have presented evidence which suggests that the conditioned responses observed by Shurrager may be due to sensitization rather than conditioning. In Kellogg's experiments the CR consisted of an overt flexor response of the hindleg to a weak electric shock (CS) delivered to the opposite hindlimb. Kellogg consistently failed to obtain any evidence of learning in his animals and concluded that Shurrager's results might be caused by factors other than conditioning.

Kellogg's case, however, is not as clear as one might wish, since his experimental procedure stacked the cards against Shurrager and against a demonstration of conditioning. Shock to the opposite hindleg (the CS in these studies) may produce a crossed-extensor reflex reaction that is precisely the opposite of the conditioned response. This reaction might account for Shurrager's finding (conditioning in an isolated flexor muscle) and suggests that a more sensitive technique should, in fact, demonstrate the learning of an overt motor response.

A more recent experiment by Dykman and Shurrager (1956) supports this interpretation but suggests that other variables may enter into the problem. In this experiment an overt leg flexion was conditioned to a tactile stimulus to the back of the animals. Clear evidence of conditioning was obtained in twelve kittens and one puppy. The animals gave positive results in repeated cycles of conditioning and extinction when the CS was applied ipsilateral to the UCS. Six cats also gave positive results in successive cycles of contralateral conditioning and extinction. In addition, these animals learned a CR when the tactile stimulus was applied to the tail. Conditioning was most clearly established in animals subjected to the spinal transection at a very early age, suggesting that the plasticity of the immature nervous system may be a contributing factor to the positive results. Unfortunately, we cannot dismiss the possibility that regeneration of some neural pathways may have influenced the findings of Dykman and Shurrager.

ELECTRICAL STIMULATION OF THE BRAIN AS THE CONDITIONED OR UNCONDITIONED STIMULUS

We have seen in previous sections that no specific portion of the brain or spinal cord appears to be essential to simple conditioning or to the retention of previously acquired behavior pat-

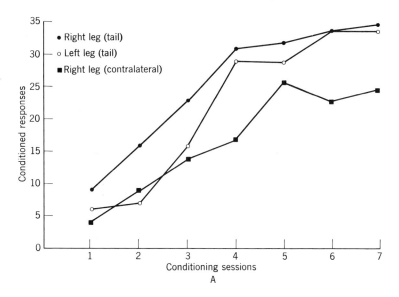

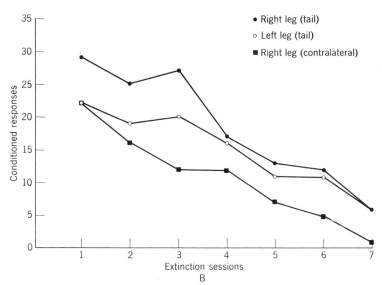

Fig. 13.65 Conditioned leg flexion responses in spinal kittens. A, mean number of conditioned responses in seven consecutive conditioning sessions of 40 trials each. B, mean number of conditioned responses in seven consecutive extinction sessions of 40 trials each. (From Dykman and Shurrager, 1956.)

terns. The electrical activity of many areas of the brain changes during some phases of the conditioning process, but learning can occur without these electrophysiological correlates; very similar, if not identical, EEG changes can be observed in situations that do not require the acquisition of new stimulus-response relationships. Before we outline the theoretical proposals that have attempted to interpret these largely negative find-

ings, we shall briefly discuss experiments that were designed to investigate the problem of localization by substituting direct stimulation of central structures for either the CS or the UCS. This approach seems ideally suited to the problem, for portions of the pathways that are traveled by the conditioned or unconditioned stimuli can be selectively bypassed. If, as is commonly assumed, learning involves a direct interaction between the

CS and the UCS, this technique may indicate where the essential interaction between the two neural systems takes place, or at least which portions of the system are not essential.

Electrical Stimulation as the Unconditioned Stimulus

Considerable confusion has been created in the literature by the indiscriminate use of the term "unconditioned stimulus." Originally, this term was applied only to stimuli that elicited a stereotyped and involuntary or reflex response such as salivation or leg flexion in appetitive or defensive classical conditioning experiments. When used in this fashion, the term unconditioned stimulus refers to an essential component of the learning process and cannot be confused with motivation or drive. However, when a direct analogy between classical and instrumental learning is attempted, this distinction breaks down, and "UCS" becomes merely another word for drive stimulation or motivation. The UCS no longer elicits a stereotyped, reflex reaction, but rather energizes a great variety of often totally unrelated behavioral responses. These unconditioned responses occur because the existing motivational conditions have, in the past, been alleviated by these or related responses, not because innate anatomical or physiological conditions necessitate them.

A large number of studies have been concerned with the effectiveness of central stimulation as the UCS (or, more properly, as the motivational component) in appetitive or defensive instrumental conditioning situations. These have been described in some detail in the chapters on motivation and will not be repeated here. We might briefly recall, however, that both electrical and chemical stimulation of certain hypothalamic, septal, and amygdaloid areas elicits feeding or drinking behavior and learned instrumental responses. Hypothalamic stimulation also elicits learned escape and avoidance responses and can serve as the UCS in avoidance learning situations. Although motivational functions are undoubtedly relevant to any discussion of learning, it is reasonable that the central regulation of primary motivational processes should be independent of the neural processes that underlie conditioning; we have therefore attempted to treat the two subjects separately.

Classical studies of Loucks, Gantt, and Brogden. One of the first problems to be investigated when

electrical stimulation techniques became available to the physiological psychologist was the role of sensory pathways in classical conditioning. The initial experiments were reported by Loucks in 1933 and 1935. Using an induction coil technique, Loucks (1934) produced a leg flexion response (UCR) by direct electrical stimulation of the sigmoid gyrus of dogs (UCS). He then attempted to condition this response by pairing a 1-sec buzzer (CS) with the electrical stimulation so that the 0.1-sec UCS ended contiguously with the CS. Twenty conditioning trials were given per day for a period of about two months. At irregular intervals the CS-UCS interval was extended to test for the development of a CR to the buzzer. The intertrial interval varied between 30 and 120 sec. Three dogs failed to show any sign of conditioning in spite of prolonged training, and Loucks concluded that direct electrical stimulation of the motor cortex could not serve as the UCS, probably because the UCR lacked an emotional component.

Two other dogs received exactly the same training but were rewarded by food at the end of each trial. Both animals learned the conditioned leg flexion response and extinguished when the UCS was omitted and food rewards were given at irregular intervals. Since the first group of dogs (which failed to show any evidence of conditioning) had received the same amount of food rewards at irregular intervals during the training session, Loucks argued that conditioning to the central UCS was possible only because "an opportunity [existed] for a backward association to be set up between the sensory experience (resulting from the proprioceptive feedback of the limb movement) and the eating of food" (p. 17). It is doubtful that the concept of backward conditioning can, in fact, explain these findings; a more likely interpretation of Loucks's results has been suggested by more recent workers (Doty, 1961). We shall return to this matter after discussing some of the earlier studies that have attempted to clarify this problem.

Several experiments (Gantt, 1937; Gantt and Loucks, 1938; Loucks and Gantt, 1938) demonstrated that electrical stimulation of spinal nerves or nerve roots which elicited unconditioned responses could successfully serve as the UCS in classical conditioning experiments. However, the intensity of the electrical stimulation had to be very high, and the results have been attributed to a spread of stimulation to sensory pathways.

Brogden and Gantt (1942) reported successful

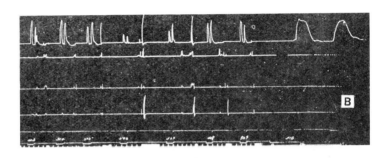

Fig. 13.66 Early attempts to condition a cortically elicited leg flexion response. A, final eleven trials of training without food reinforcement, showing no conditioned responses in the right hindleg. B, first phase of training in which the dog was fed crackers between each trial. Definite conditioned movements in the right hindleg occurred at each buzzer signal. The CR was a sustained movement, whereas the UCR to cortical shock was a relatively brief swing of short latency. (From Loucks, 1935.)

conditioning when electrical stimulation of the cerebellum was substituted for foot shock in a classical defensive-conditioning paradigm. Since the conditioned responses appeared very similar to those elicited directly by cerebellar stimulation, Brogden and Gantt suggested that central conditioning had been demonstrated in the absence of motivational factors. Although there is little argument with the conclusion that conditioning to a central UCS was obtained in these studies, there is considerable doubt whether sensory factors were, in fact, ruled out. Recent anatomical work has demonstrated extensive, somatotopically organized sensory representations in the cerebellum, and it appears likely, in view of the rather crude techniques used in these early studies, that the stimulation involved large areas of the cerebellum; thus, sensory as well as motor effects may have been produced by the UCS. An unambiguous interpretation of these findings would require a replication of Brogden and Gantt's study.

The possibility that classical conditioning might be established on the basis of direct stimulation of the motor system has intrigued many subsequent investigators because a successful demonstration of such a phenomenon would have important implications for theories attempting to deal with the relationship between motivation and learning. To the extent that sensory factors can be ruled out, conditioning without apparent motivation might be demonstrable in this fashion;

this could clarify the role of motivational factors in learning and permit a study of associative processes, uncomplicated by motivational variables. A great number of studies were undertaken during the 1940's and early 1950's; these have for the most part remained unpublished because the results were ambiguous or clearly negative, confirming Loucks's earlier findings.

The stalemate was finally broken when Giurgea (1953a 1953b, 1955) reported a series of experiments which appeared to have succeeded where others failed. Giurgea reported rapid conditioning (often within 50 trials) of leg flexion or head-turning responses elicited by direct electrical stimulation of the sigmoid gyrus (motor cortex) in dogs. The CS in these experiments was also centrally administered (electrical stimulation of the occipital cortex). Six to ten trials were administered per day with an intertrial interval of 3 to 5 min.

This direct contradiction of Loucks's earlier findings appears to be due to a very slight procedural difference. Giurgea found that the conditioned responses of even very well-trained animals extinguished when the intertrial interval was reduced to 2 min. (Loucks had used intervals ranging from 30 to 120 sec, the most frequent interval being 30 or 60 sec). Although the reasons for the apparent influence of the intertrial interval are not obvious (peripherally administered conditioned stimuli certainly produce adequate conditioning even at the shorter intervals), it seems

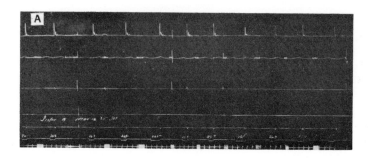

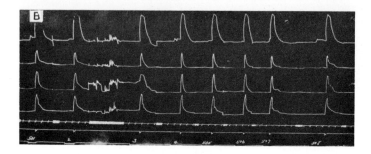

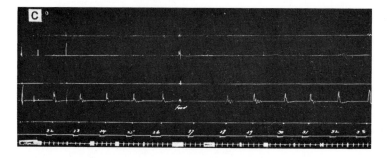

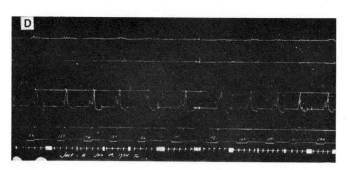

Fig. 13.67 Classical conditioning of a leg flexion response evoked by electrical stimulation of the spinal cord. A, lines from top to bottom: right hindleg, right foreleg, left hindleg, UCS (shock at right fasciculus gracilis), conditioned signal (buzzer), time in seconds. This record is for the fourteenth day of training but shows only 11 of 20 trials given on that day. The record is typical of the first 21 days of training (trials 1 to 420) in which the right hindleg moved only when the reinforcing stimulus was applied to the cord, indicating an absence of conditioning. B, lines as in the first record, except for the position of the time line (twenty-sixth day of training). The tracings for the right hindlimb indicates an anticipatory movement at every trial except one. C, lines as in the first record, except that reinforcing shocks were applied to the left sixth dorsal spinal root (second day of training). D, lines as in C (seventh day of training). All but two trials exhibit clear-cut conditioned responses in the left hindleg. (From Loucks and Gantt, 1938.)

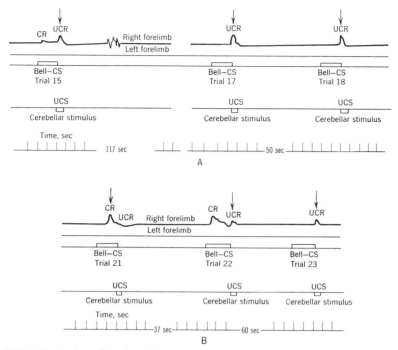

Fig. 13.68 Classical conditioning of leg flexion responses evoked by cerebellar stimulation. A, early stage. B, late stage. (From Brogden and Gantt, 1942.)

rather certain that the negative results of earlier workers are at least in part due to this variable. In fact, Loucks's positive results with the animals that received food after each trial may be due to a prolongation of the intertrial interval rather than backward associations or motivational factors, as has been suggested by others.

Recent positive evidence from the laboratories of Giurgea and Doty. After the initial demonstration of central-central conditioning, Giurgea and his collaborators investigated this phenomenon in some detail. Attempting to answer some critics who suggested that leakage of the stimulating current to the meninges might produce pain (and thereby provide the motivational component of the conditioning process), Raiciulescu et al. (1956) demonstrated that conditioning of centrally elicited movements was possible after destruction of the Gasserian ganglion (an operation that presumably denervates the meninges). Giurgea and Raiciulescu (1957) further demonstrated that the UCS (electrical stimulation of the sigmoid gyrus) did not produce seizure activity in the motor cortex which might spread to neighboring sensory areas.

The connections between the conditioned and

unconditioned stimuli can apparently be established along subcortical pathways. Conditioning occurred in animals with histologically confirmed transections of the corpus callosum when the CS and UCS were delivered to opposite hemispheres (Raiciulescu and Giurgea, 1957; Giurgea and Raiciulescu, 1957). The importance of subcortical connections has been stressed by Doty and Rutledge (1959), who found that undercutting of the stimulated area of the cortex produced much more severe deficits than circumsection.

Nikolaeva (1957) has reported successful defensive conditioning in cats with electrical stimulation of the motor cortex as the UCS.

Doty and Giurgea (1961) have replicated the basic findings in monkeys, cats, and dogs and concluded that "in the usual sense of the word, there is no motivation involved in the formation of conditioned responses by coupling cortical stimulation" (p. 145). Before we take issue with this rather categorical statement, a few words must be said about some recent experiments which have used subcortical stimulation as the UCS.

Segundo et al. (1959) used electrical stimulation of the rostral (center median nucleus of the thalamus) or midbrain reticular formation as the UCS in a series of conditioning experiments. The intensity of stimulation was individually adjusted for each of seven cats to produce a stereotyped head-turning or cowering response. The CS was repeatedly presented alone until all behavioral orienting responses and EEG arousal reactions had become completely habituated. The CS-UCS pairings were then presented until the CS elicited a clear motor response 100% of the time. The number of trials required to reach criterion performance varied from 60 to 600.

External inhibition was demonstrated (a novel stimulus, presented just before the CS, inhibited the CR), and generalization to tones of frequencies similar to that of the CS was observed. The animals then learned to respond to sounds of one frequency and not to respond to other frequencies (differential conditioning) or to withhold responses when the CS was preceded by another auditory stimulus (conditioned inhibition). When

tested during sleep, the animals showed electrophysiological and behavioral arousal and performed the CR as the CS was presented. Differential stimuli failed to produce behavioral arousal or conditioned reactions, although EEG arousal was observed. The conditioned responses extinguished completely following repeated nonreinforced presentations of the CS. Disinhibition was obtained when the CS was preceded by a novel stimulus. Small lesions at the electrode sites used for the UCS stimulation failed to abolish the conditioned reaction in six out of seven animals. These findings are interesting, but difficult to evaluate in view of the sensory, motor, and motivational functions of the reticular formation. Although motor responses were clearly elicited by the UCS, we have no evidence that sensory or motivational mechanisms may not have been excited at the same time. Furthermore, it is con-

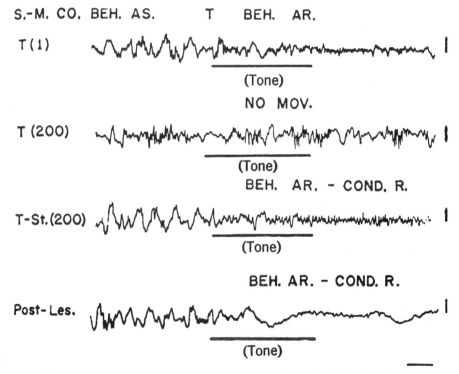

Fig. 13.69 Classical conditioning of an EEG (arousal) and behavioral (head-turning) response evoked by electrical stimulation of the midbrain reticular formation (records from right sensory-motor cortex). T(1), first presentation of the tone CS produces EEG and behavioral arousal. T(200), after 200 applications of the CS no behavioral or EEG effect occurs. T-St.(200), after 200 CS-UCS pairings, the tone alone produces EEG and behavioral arousal and the CR (head movement). Post-Les., after electrolytic destruction of the area surrounding the electrode (midbrain reticular formation), the effect of the tone persists. BEH. AR., behaviorally aroused; BEH. AS., behaviorally asleep; Post-Les., postlesion. (From Segundo et al., 1959.)

Control   Tone

R

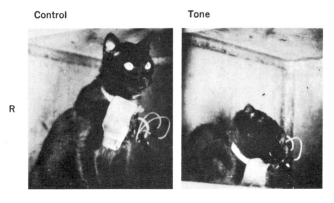

Control   Buzzer   Tone

NON-R

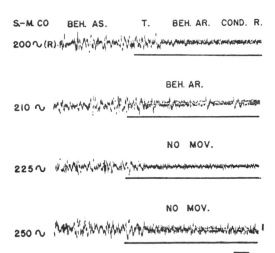

Fig. 13.70 Conditioned inhibition of a behavioral CR which is based on a UCR to electrical stimulation of the midbrain reticular formation. *Top line,* conditioned cowering response to CR (tone) when applied alone. *Bottom line,* no response to the nonreinforced buzzer tone association. NON-R, nonreinforced; R, reinforced. (From Segundo et al., 1959.)

ceivable that the general arousal or activation which presumably results from reticular stimulation may itself have sensory properties.

A closer look at the literature indicates that the conditioning of responses elicited by direct stimulation of the motor cortex is a fragile phenomenon. The animals must receive prolonged pretraining to avoid emotional reactions to the conditioning situation; long intertrial intervals must be used, and extraneous stimulation must be kept to an absolute minimum. If these provisions are met, conditioned reactions develop, apparently quite rapidly, and stable performance levels can be obtained. We have no reason at present to question the phenomenon itself, but there is considerable doubt about the theoretical interpretations that have been derived from it.

Doty (1961), as mentioned, believes that sensory factors are clearly ruled out in these experiments and discusses the findings under the heading "Formation of Conditioned Reflexes Independent of Motivation." This interpretation has recently become accepted by a number of workers, but it seems that some caution is indicated. Although meningeal stimulation appears to be eliminated as a contributing sensory factor, one wonders about the possibility of the stimulation or excitation

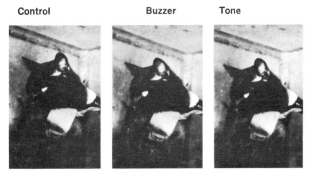

Fig. 13.71 Frequency discrimination of an auditory CS which elicits behavioral (cowering) and EEG (arousal) responses initially evoked by electrical stimulation of the midbrain reticular formation. EEG (records from right sensory-motor cortex) effects of positive (200 cps) and negative (210, 225, and 250 cps) tones. Key is given in Figure 13.69. (From Segundo et al., 1959.)

spreading to neighboring areas of the cortex which may have sensory functions. Sensory representations have been demonstrated even within the motor cortex itself, and these may, at least in part, be responsible for the observed effects.

A perhaps more serious objection must be raised with respect to the sensory feedback from the movement itself and possible emotional reactions to such movements. The execution of the UCR undoubtedly produces proprioceptive feedback which may induce rather disturbing emotional responses. There is, in fact, some experimental evidence for this suggestion. Loucks (1933, 1935), for instance, reported that electrical stimulation of the sigmoid gyrus which elicited a clear motor response could be used as the CS in a leg flexion experiment, although attempts were made to eliminate the proprioceptive feedback from the response itself. Additional controls indicated that the auditory and vibratory cues from the induction coil used to produce the electrical stimulus did not serve as extraneous cues in the experiment. Loucks concluded that stimulation of the motor cortex produced a direct sensory experience which can be used as the CS in conditioning experiments. Similar effects were reported by Gantt (1937) following electrical stimulation of the motor cortex or cerebellum. These findings are in need of replication, in view of the primitive techniques then available, but sensory factors can certainly not be discounted, a priori, even in the most modern studies.

Whether conditioning depends on these sensory or emotional consequences of the UCR is open to debate because of the peculiar temporal relationships, but the problem requires much additional study before we can agree with Doty's categorical statements. It might be possible, for instance, to sever the afferents from the part of the body that is to be involved in the CR, either before or after conditioning, and to observe the development or extinction of the CR. Since postural corrections are necessary in almost all parts of the body when a limb is raised, it may be necessary to search for a UCR that does not require extensive postural adjustments. Whether motivation is an essential component of *all* learning situations is a sufficiently important question to warrant further research with this interesting preparation.

Electrical Stimulation as the Conditioned Stimulus

In view of the fact that learning can take place when the cortical projection areas of the CS (or even the entire neocortex) are destroyed, many investigators have suggested that the essential interaction between the CS and the UCS modalities may take place somewhere along the sensory pathways, perhaps by means of the diffuse reticular formation which receives collaterals from all sensory systems. It is quite possible that such a mechanism exists and, in fact, accounts for the conditioning of decerebrate animals. However, in the intact animal conditioning does not apparently depend on this direct interaction, for electrical stimulation of sensory areas of the cortex (which presumably does not produce a direct feedback to the reticular formation) can serve as the CS in appetitive as well as defensive classical conditioning.

Early studies of the motor system. The first experimental demonstration of the effectiveness of centrally applied stimuli (Loucks, 1933; 1935) suggested that electrical stimulation of even extrasensory areas (the motor cortex) produced sufficiently distinct sensory effects to serve as the CS. Because the induction coil technique used in these experiments may produce considerably more spread of excitation than modern stimulation procedures, it is not certain that the results were obtained from the motor areas.

Subsequent studies in Loucks's laboratory (Loucks, 1938) demonstrated that electrical stimulation of the visual cortex could serve as the CS for salivary as well as leg flexion responses. A series of control experiments suggested that cortical stimulation rather than some artifact of the stimulation procedure provided the essential stimulus.

Loucks (1938) also reported that a well-established conditioned (salivary) response could not be elicited while the subject was asleep, although the intensity of the cortical stimulation was increased gradually until overt epileptiform seizures were elicited.

Loucks's initial findings created considerable interest. The basic results were rapidly replicated in several laboratories. Gantt (1937) reported that electrical stimulation of the dorsal roots, occipital cortex, motor cortex, or cerebellum could serve as the UCS in classical conditioning experiments and suggested the somewhat misleading term "intraneural" to describe this procedure.

Later studies of sensory systems and subcortical mechanisms. The next major group of studies in this field were reported by Giurgea (1953a; 1953b; 1955). Successful conditioning was obtained when

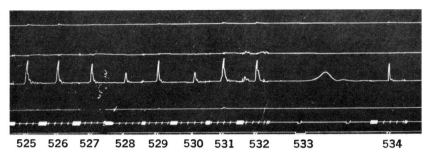

Fig. 13.72   Classical conditioning of a leg flexion response evoked by shock to the left foreleg. Electrical stimulation of the cortex is used as the CS. Lines from top to bottom: right hindleg, right foreleg, left foreleg, left hindleg, time in seconds, cortical and cutaneous shock on same tracing. The major excursions in trials 525, 526, 527, 529, 531, 532, and 534 represent the unconditional lifting of the left foreleg at cutaneous shock. In trials 528, 530, and 533 the cutaneous shock (UCS) is omitted and a conditional movement occurs. (From Loucks, 1935.)

both CS and UCS were delivered directly to the cortex. The CS in these experiments was a train of electrical pulses delivered to the occipital cortex.

Doty et al. (1956) pointed out that electrical stimulation of the cortex has been shown to elicit painful sensations in man (Penfield, 1935; Ray and Wolff, 1940) and attempted to control for this factor in a series of experiments. In an instrumental learning paradigm cats were trained to avoid a painful peripheral shock by responding to the cortically applied CS. Exploring a large portion of the brain (marginal, posterolateral, middle, and posterior ectosylvian gyrus), Doty et al. found that almost all cortical placements as well as stimulation of the dura could be used to establish a CR in about as many trials as are required for the development of conditioned responses to peripheral auditory or visual stimuli. Once established, the conditioned reactions appeared stable (one

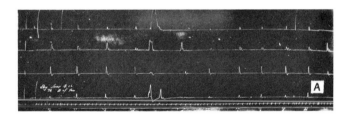

Fig. 13.73   Electrical stimulation of the right lateral gyrus as the CS for limb withdrawal based on cutaneous shock to the left foreleg (UCS). A, lines from top to bottom: right hindleg, right foreleg, left foreleg, left hindleg, time in seconds, cortical shock and cutaneous shock at left foreleg both on last line. Lifting of limbs at the second of two marks on the bottom line indicates absence of conditioning. B, lines as in the first record. Spontaneous lifting of the right hindleg and right foreleg. Left foreleg (receiving shock) shows little spontaneous movement. C, lines as in the first record. Anticipatory conditioned movement in the left foreleg. (From Loucks, 1938.)

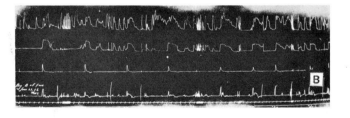

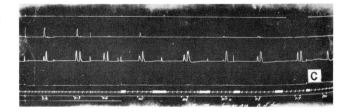

animal responded at a high level three months after training had been discontinued) and specific to a particular locus of stimulation (the animals rapidly learned to respond to stimulation of one cortical point and not to respond to stimulation of others). Some of the animals even learned to discriminate between the frequency of electrical stimulation of the same area of the brain.

Doty and his collaborators further attempted to demonstrate that these results are due to cortical stimulation rather than to a spread of excitation to sensory neurons in the meninges. Relying on earlier investigations which showed that stimulation of the meningeal tissue produces marked galvanic skin responses (Spiegel and Hunsicker, 1936; M. Levine and Wolff, 1932), whereas stimulation of the cortex (except for the motor areas) does not (Langworthy and Richter, 1930), Doty et al. measured the GSR of all animals to the cortical CS. An attempt was also made to denervate the meninges in the animals that failed to give a GSR to either cortical or meningeal stimulation. The results of these control experiments indicate that animals which do not show a GSR to cortical stimulation can be conditioned to give a behavioral response to the cortical stimulus. Conditioning was not affected by denervation of the meninges, and Doty concluded that the CR appeared to be made in response to the stimulation of cortical neurons rather than some peripheral, sensory receptors.

Doty and Rutledge (1959) replicated these findings in a series of experiments which attempted to investigate the properties of the central CS in some detail. They found that the threshold of effective stimulation did not vary systematically from one area of the cortex to another and that the rate of acquisition did not appear to be related to the site of central stimulation. Rate of acquisition (i.e., the number of trials to a criterion of 60% avoidance) was roughly comparable for visual, auditory, or central conditioned stimuli. Perhaps the most interesting result of this group of studies is that animals trained to respond to auditory or visual stimuli generalized this response readily to cortical stimulation of most areas, whereas little or no generalization was observed when the training stimulus was centrally applied and the test stimuli were administered peripherally. This finding conflicts with the observation, reported by Giurgea and Raiciulescu (1957), that conditioned responses to electrical stimulation of the parieto-occipital area generalized readily to peripheral photic as well as auditory stimuli.

Doty and Rutledge (1959) also observed generalization between central stimulation of homotopic areas of the cortex; this generalization persisted even when the cortical area originally stimulated during the acquisition of the CR was extirpated before the stimulation of the homotopic cortex. Generalization to homotopic areas was demonstrable even when the hippocampal commissure and posterior three-fourths of the corpus callosum were transected before the initial conditioning trials. Little evidence for generalization was obtained between heterotopic cortical areas.

These results are intriguing but should be considered with some caution, for Doty and Rutledge's experimental situation appears to have invited generalization, as defined rather generously by these authors. Generalization was said to have occurred if the animals made some conditioned responses to the test stimuli during the first test session and attained criterion (60% avoidance) in about one-fourth of the number of trials required for the original learning. With this "transfer of training" definition, generalization even occurred from peripheral photic to peripheral auditory stimuli, and one is left to wonder how much of this may be due to sensitization rather than generalization, as commonly defined. Doty and Rutledge suggested that the very extensive generalization supports Sperry's (1955) proposal that conditioning may involve only a shift in the facilitatory set of the effector system rather than the formation of new pathways from sensory to motor circuits.

An interesting difference between peripherally and centrally applied conditioned stimuli has been reported by Rutledge and Doty (1955). Chlorpromazine appears to suppress conditioned responses to peripheral stimuli at dosage levels which have little effect on the animal's response to centrally applied conditioned stimuli. Since it is impossible to equate the intensity parameter of peripheral and central stimulation, these findings may represent little more than a difference in the arousal value of the stimuli. However, the implications of a possible pharamacological distinction are sufficiently important to warrant discussion of these findings and further research.

Doty and Rutledge (1959) have provided some information which suggests that the effects of cortical stimulation may be mediated by subcortical structures. After a CER to electrical stimulation of the marginal gyrus had been established, the stimulated cortex was partially isolated by either undercutting at a depth of 3 to 5 mm (for a distance of 9 to 15 mm) or by a semicircular incision, 5 mm deep and 8 mm in diameter. All animals showed a marked postoperative deficit (requiring from 100 to 400 retraining trials to reach preoperative performance levels), but undercutting produced significantly greater impairments than the circumsection.

Mogenson (1959) attempted to replicate some of the earlier findings in the rat, using electrical stimulation of areas 17 (visual), 18 (visual association), or 4 (motor) as the CS for an avoidance response. Only 3 of the 17 animals tested reached Mogenson's criterion of 25 avoidance responses in 30 consecutive trials (note that this is a much more severe criterion than that employed by Doty and his colleagues), although the experimental procedure (eight to ten trials per day, 3- to 5-min intertrial interval) appeared to be comparable to that used in earlier studies. Mogenson noted, however, that all his animals exhibited a conditioned "anxiety" response to the CS and suggested that the central stimulus was providing information relevant to the UCS.

In view of the observed conditioning of anxiety responses to the central CS, Mogenson trained rats to lever-press for food reward in an operant conditioning situation and then attempted to establish a CER to a centrally applied CS. Seven of the animals received pretraining in the previous experiment in which the central stimulation served as the cue for avoidable grid shock; five additional animals received shock for the first time in the bar-pressing experiment. Conditioning—as measured by a partial suppression of lever pressing during the CS interval—was achieved in all thirteen animals, and Mogenson suggested that cortical stimulation might interfere with the development of complex conditioned responses (such as those required in the avoidance experiments). He also suggested that the effectiveness of central stimulation as the CS in conditioning experiments may depend on the nature of the CR.

In a recent paper Mogenson (1962) reports an interesting finding which indicates that experience with peripheral stimuli of a particular sensory modality is not essential to the establishment of conditioned responses to electrical stimulation of the cortical projection area of that modality. He enucleated one group of rats just before they opened their eyes (13 days of age) and another group at the age of 65 to 70 days. All animals (and a normal control group) were later trained to press a lever for water rewards in an operant conditioning apparatus. Electrical stimulation of the visual cortex was then used as the CS for unavoid-

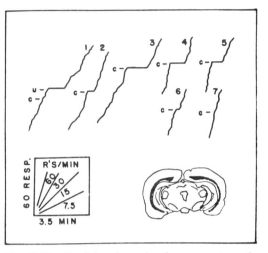

Fig. 13.74 Conditioned emotional responses to cortical stimulation (CS). Cumulative bar-pressing records: *c*, cortical stimulation; *u*, shock; 1, second reinforced trial—no CR; 2, test trial after five reinforcements; 3, test trial after seven reinforcements; 4-7, records for extinction showing second, sixth, ninth, and tenth extinction trials. (From Mogenson, 1959.)

able grid shock in the bar-pressing situation. Both groups of peripherally blinded rats acquired a CER (suppression of bar pressing during the CS interval) to the central CS. No significant difference was observed between the two groups of blinded animals. The control animals, however, acquired the CER more rapidly than the experimental groups, suggesting that degenerative changes in the visual cortex may have taken place and interfered to some extent with conditioning.

Nielson et al. (1958) report that electrical stimulation of the caudate nucleus of cats can be used as the CS in an avoidance paradigm. Cats were trained to lever-press for food in a standard operant conditioning situation, and stimulation was applied to the caudate nucleus while the animals were working for food rewards. The authors suggested that the stimulation appeared to be motivationally neutral because it did not affect the rate of bar pressing. In a different experimental environment, caudatal stimulation was repeatedly paired with painful peripheral shock in a classical defensive–conditioning paradigm. The animals were subsequently returned to the lever-pressing apparatus which had been modified so that each bar press produced both caudate stimulation and food rewards. All but two of the animals promptly stopped responding, suggesting that a passive avoidance response had been conditioned to the caudate stimulation.

The results of these experiments must be evaluated with some caution, in view of the observation by Buchwald et al. (1961a, b, c) that at least some types of caudate stimulation interfere with learned instrumental behavior such as bar pressing for food. The neutrality of the motivational effects of caudatal stimulation is also open to some question; several studies have reported positive as well as negative (aversive) effects, and Nielson et al. found two animals that lever-pressed to obtain the caudatal stimulation which had previously been paired with painful grid shock.

Nielson et al. (1962) have extended this work to other subcortical structures. Electrode placements in the caudate, center median nucleus of the thalamus, hippocampus, and midbrain reticular formation permitted the establishment of conditioned avoidance responses. Only stimulation of the nucleus ventralis anterior of the thalamus consistently failed to produce reliable conditioning. Throughout the training period three tests for generalization were randomly interspersed in each group of 25 daily training trials. It was found that the conditioned responses did not generalize to peripheral stimuli such as light or sound or to electrical stimulation of subcortical regions other than that stimulated during training. Two exceptions were noted: (1) total generalization occurred when the test stimulus was applied to different levels of the same fiber tract (medial lemniscus)

and (2) partial generalization occurred when the test stimulus was applied to the same electrode site, but at frequencies differing from those used during training, or when a test stimulus with the same frequency as that of training stimuli to the superior colliculi or center median nucleus was applied to the mesencephalic reticular formation. These findings appear to conflict with the ready generalization between cortical and peripheral stimulation, as reported by Doty and Rutledge. However, this discrepancy is primarily a semantic one, as additional studies demonstrated.

After criterion performance (60% avoidance) had been attained, Nielson et al. tested for transfer of training (using the definition of generalization employed by Doty and Rutledge in earlier studies) by recording the number of trials required to establish the same avoidance response to electrical stimulation of a different subcortical electrode site. Transfer of training was demonstrated in all experiments. The amount of savings did not vary systematically with electrode placements, and similar effects were observed when the frequency of stimulation of the same electrode site was varied.

Although interesting, these results should not be interpreted as necessarily representing a selective transfer of training effect as the term is used in behavioral research. No controls were employed, in order to demonstrate that the previous training

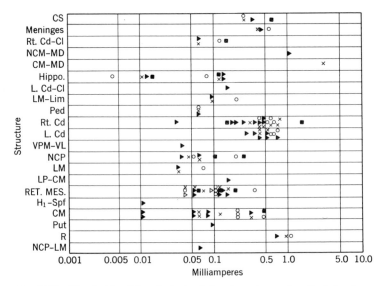

Fig. 13.75 Thresholds of electrical stimulation to various subcortical structures which elicit conditioned avoidance responses. Symbols indicate stimulus frequencies in pulses per second: triangles, 300 p/sec; crosses, 150 p/sec; circles, 30 p/sec; squares, 3 p/sec. (From Nielson et al., 1962.)

rather than prior stimulation of the brain per se was responsible for the improvement, and one wonders whether the animals might not have shown similar "savings" on a totally unrelated task. A simple way to control for such sensitization might be the uncorrelated presentation of the CS and UCS for the same number of trials used for the original training experiment.

Mogenson and Morrison (1962) have reported that electrical stimulation of hypothalamic areas which appears to be rewarding can also serve as the CS for an avoidance response. Rats trained earlier to lever-press for brain stimulation rewards were trained to perform an instrumental avoidance response whenever the central stimulation was applied. All animals reached criterion on this task and subsequently showed greatly reduced performance rates when returned to the self-stimulation situation.

SUMMARY

What, if any, portion of the central nervous system may be uniquely and essentially related to learning and retention? This has been the central question of the past chapters. We have previously seen that electrophysiological experiments have not yet succeeded in demonstrating EEG or evoked-potential changes within any area of the brain which may be uniquely related to conditioning or recall. In this chapter we have discussed experiments that have attempted to investigate the problem of localization by selectively destroying or stimulating specific portions of the nervous system. The answers have again been far from convincing, and we begin to wonder whether the neurophysiological and/or biochemical changes that provide the basis for learning and memory may perhaps not be unique to any specific portion of the brain. This hypothesis might account for the observation that although specific types of learning or memory appear to be affected by lesions in particular portions of the central nervous system, a complete inhibition of associative functions has never been demonstrated.

We began our discussion by examining the effects of decortication and noted that conditioning can be demonstrated in animals deprived of all cortical tissue, and that separate cortical and subcortical mechanisms may be available. Although simple conditioned responses can be established in decorticated animals, the resultant severe retention deficits suggest that cortical mechanisms may normally participate in the neural processes underlying acquisition. This differ-

ential effect had been noted in many of the earlier ablation studies, but it has received special attention in recent experiments concerned with the effects of reversible, functional ablations of the neocortex. It was found that rats do not perform even very simple learned appetitive or escape responses during a spreading depression that selectively involves the neocortex. Unconditioned reactions such as simple postural reflexes do not appear to be affected by the neocortical depression, suggesting that an interference with the integrative processes essential to recall may be responsible for the observed results. There is some indication that sensory functions may be impaired by the cortical depression, but this effect does not appear to be severe enough to account for the total absence of simple conditioned reactions. The animals displayed apparently emotional behavior in response to the shock UCS but failed to perform the simple escape responses. Recent extensions of this interesting work show that conflicting habits can be stored in the two hemispheres if training is provided under unilateral cortical depression. This is a most remarkable finding, in view of the fact that the sensory input to the hemispheres is not lateralized.

When more selective ablations of the cortical projection areas of the CS are attempted, conditioning can be demonstrated, even in some relatively complex instrumental learning paradigms, as long as the CS or its essential features are not obscured by sensory deficits. Ablations of the visual projection area produce impairments which cannot be explained on the basis of sensory deficits, and it is possible that some integrative functions are normally executed by this portion of the brain. Visual discriminations that are learned before the destruction of cortical tissue appear to be completely forgotten. The discrimination responses can be relearned in about as many trials as were required for the original acquisition, and animals deprived of the visual areas before the learning experiment show little or no deficit.

Although some negative results have been reported, the available evidence suggests that a similar situation may exist with respect to the visual association areas. Lesions in areas 18 and 19 have been reported to destroy all memory of a previously acquired discrimination, but they do not appear to interfere with the acquisition of the same conditioned responses. There is at least some indication that a second sensory area in the inferotemporal region may be one of the mechanisms that apparently can assume at least some of the functions of the visual areas.

The selective impairment of memory has been demonstrated even more clearly in the auditory modality. Our understanding of the role of cortical mechanisms in audition has been hampered by the fact that more than one primary auditory area may exist. It seems clear, however, that the retention of even the simplest conditioned responses to auditory stimuli is lost following cortical lesions that do not apparently affect sensory capabilities or the acquisition of the same conditioned responses. Very complex auditory habits cannot even be acquired after massive cortical damage. However, we have no evidence that this deficit may not be partly or totally due to a primary sensory impairment rather than to a selective effect on associative mechanisms.

Our knowledge of somatosensory areas is relatively meager, but the available data suggest that lesions in this portion of the brain do not interfere with simple conditioning (to tactile stimuli) unless primary sensory deficits make a discrimination of the CS impossible. Again, some information indicates that the recall of preoperatively acquired habits may be more severely affected.

Before we leave this provocative subject, it should be pointed out that the apparently differential effects of cortical lesions on memory may be the result of sensory deficits. If an animal has learned to respond to some particular aspect of the CS or stimulus complex, and if the cortical lesions specifically interfere with the perception of that aspect of the stimulus, an apparent memory deficit should be expected. Unless the sensory capabilities of the organism are totally destroyed, one should not be surprised if the animal subsequently learns to respond to some other aspect of the stimulus situation in about as many trials as were required for the initial learning. Sensory deficits in experimental animals can, unfortunately, be assessed only in discrimination experiments that require memory. It is therefore difficult, if not impossible, to distinguish partial sensory impairments which require a reorientation to other stimulus aspects from a memory deficit.

The situation is no less complex for other areas of the cortex. Frontal lobe lesions produce apparent intellectual deficits in man which suggest that basic memory functions may be affected. A detailed analysis of the frontal lobe syndrome in animals has so far produced an ambiguous picture. Animals with frontal lesions do poorly on delayed-response problems and on certain discrimination tasks which require the inhibition of responses to prominent aspects of the stimulus situation. The

deficits have been explained on the basis of perseverative tendencies, and it is not immediately clear to what extent we can consider them to be directly related to an interference with processes that are primarily and directly related to acquisition, memory, or recall. Since the frontal animals can apparently function almost normally in all test situations in which the influence of potentially distracting stimuli is minimized, it has been suggested that the basic deficit may be related to the animal's ability to concentrate or pay attention rather than to an associative impairment. This interpretation appears to account adequately for the results of most animal studies, but some question remains about the apparently more severe intellectual deficits which have been described in man. It is possible that these can also be reduced to a problem of attention or concentration, but most neurologists in the field appear unwilling to accept this interpretation.

A similar divergence of experimental findings and theoretical thought is apparent with respect to the functional role of other areas of the brain (notably the hippocampus). It seems possible that progressive encephalization, combined with an increasing complexity of integrative processes, may have resulted in a different anatomical distribution of associative functions in man. Much more experimental and clinical evidence is needed before this question can be answered.

Throughout our discussion of cortical factors in learning, it has been difficult, if not impossible, to rule out the effects of sensory deficits. When we turn to subcortical mechanisms, sensory factors assume a much less prominent position, but motivational processes must be taken into account; this is at least as difficult, as evidenced by the many investigations of limbic functions and the often confusing interpretations of the effects of lesions or stimulation in this area of the brain.

The limbic system appears to be concerned primarily with motivational functions which affect performance in learning experiments or tests of retention but are not a unique component of the conditioning process. Stimulation or lesions almost anywhere in this complex circuit severely affect performance in both appetitive and defensive conditioning situations. These deficits do not, however, appear to be unique to learned responses, as a test of unconditioned reactions demonstrates.

Many investigators continue to emphasize the potential role of the limbic system in learning and retention because it is often difficult to observe clearly unlearned responses in the adult animal. However, the behavioral deficits that can be seen after destruction of most, if not all, aspects of the limbic system are most clearly related to motivational impairments and are not sufficiently general to necessitate the postulation of associative deficits.

A possible exception to this rule is the hippocampal formation. This structure shows electrophysiological changes during conditioning and extinction which may be related to associative functions and appear to be related to memory in man. Penfield and his colleagues report severe memory deficits in patients with hippocampal damage and spontaneous recall of long-forgotten events during electrical stimulation of certain aspects of this structure.

Animal experiments have generally not supported Penfield's contention that the hippocampus may contain the primary recording center for memory. Simple appetitive and defensive conditioning situations do not, as a rule, show any impairment in either learning or retention. Even relatively complex discrimination problems typically do not appear to be affected by hippocampal damage. Only when the test situation requires responses to stimuli that are not present at the time the response must be made do we see a clear impairment. This apparent difficulty with delayed-response problems is quite similar to that observed after frontal lobe damage, and we would like to suggest that the interpretation of the behavioral impairment may also be similar.

That the hippocampus may be concerned with attention rather than learning is suggested by electrophysiological studies which indicate that the modifications of the hippocampal EEG observed during acquisition and extinction may be related to arousal or attention rather than learning per se. Investigations of the motivational effects of hippocampal lesions have, furthermore, demonstrated changes in appetitive and emotional processes which undoubtedly contribute to performance in all learning situations. The modifications of motivational functions may not be severe enough to interfere with the performance of very simple or overtrained behavioral responses, but they may disrupt more complex response sequences such as those required in the delayed-response test.

An analysis of thalamic functions is complicated by the fact that this central core of the brain contains nuclei that serve widely divergent functions. Sensory processes must again be taken into account, for it is difficult to produce lesions in some portions of the thalamus without causing direct or indirect damage to sensory nuclei or pathways. Additional problems are created by the fact that many of the thalamic nuclei appear to serve as relay stations, often between very distant portions of the central nervous system, whereas other nuclei appear to integrate intrathalamic processes or participate in reticular functions. Lesions presumably restricted to nonsensory components of the thalamus have been reported to interfere selectively with the acquisition or performance of learned responses. The effects are typically sizable, but it is not clear that motivational effects can be eliminated. Emotional changes such as increased viciousness and hyperirritability are often reported, and a change in affective rather than associative functions must be considered. Since some aspects of the thalamus represent the rostral extensions of the arousal system of the midbrain reticular formation, nonspecific motivational factors can also not be ignored. Several recent studies have suggested that partial destruction of the nonspecific projection system of the thalamus produces performance deficits that may not be related to associative mechanisms; rather, they may represent nonspecific effects of a reduced general level of arousal or motivation.

The hypothalamus is so densely populated with neural systems which appear to be an essential part of most, if not all, primary motivational functions that it is impossible to destroy or stimulate any portion without producing extensive motivational changes. These motivational processes predictably affect performance in learning experiments or retention tests, but the resultant deficits cannot be ascribed to associative processes. Some investigators have demonstrated effects on acquired behavior such as bar pressing for food in the absence of a noticeable impairment of such unconditioned (or at least very extensively overlearned) behavior as free feeding. However, recently acquired instrumental responses are undoubtedly more severely affected by motivational changes than overtrained responses, and it is questionable whether these results can be interpreted to suggest a direct effect on associative functions.

The basal ganglia are part of the organism's response mechanism and have not, until recently, received much attention from investigators concerned with learning and retention. The available literature suggests that the basal ganglia are not involved in simple learning or retention, but some deficits have been reported on delayed-response problems following lesions in the caudate nucleus. These impairments appear to be very similar to those recorded following frontal lobe damage, and it has been suggested that the effects may be due to an interruption or interference with a caudatothalamocortical fiber system. Recent experiments using electrical stimulation of the caudate nucleus report an apparently nonspecific inhibition of learned responses combined with cortical EEG reactions (the caudate spindle). The extent to which associative functions are specifically involved in this phenomenon is not yet clear.

The effects of lesions or stimulation of the brainstem are difficult to interpret. Almost all classical sensory and motor pathways pass through this bottleneck, and the reticular arousal system, which contributes to both sensory and motor functions, makes up a large portion of the brainstem. Several investigators have suggested that some portion of the reticular formation may also play an important role in conditioning, and at least some experimental evidence can be interpreted to support this contention.

The principal problem here, as in other parts of the central nervous system, is the experimental isolation of associative mechanisms. Large lesions in the brainstem are known to produce complete stupor, presumably because they interfere with the reticular arousal mechanisms. Smaller lesions as well as electrical stimulation of the same areas have been shown to inhibit recently acquired responses without, in some instances, affecting the relevant unconditioned reactions. However, this reaction may be due to a partial destruction or inhibition of the arousal mechanism rather than associative functions (i.e., the animal may remember perfectly well what to do but may be too lethargic to do it).

The anatomy of the reticular formation appears ideally suited for the complex interchanges that must take place between the pathways of the conditioned and unconditioned stimuli during learning, and its influence on sensory and motor processes could be an important aspect of the conditioning process. Because of this, much theoretical and experimental interest continues to be directed toward this part of the brain, in spite of the fact that clear experimental support for an essential role in learning is still lacking.

The reticular formation extends into the rostral half of the spinal cord, and we might expect to observe learning in spinal animals if reticular mechanisms represented a necessary and sufficient substrate for conditioning. The experimental evidence for spinal conditioning is, however, not totally convincing. One group of experimenters has obtained evidence for simple conditioning in spinal cats and dogs, but the experimental procedure does not clearly rule out alternative explanations of the observed behavioral modifications in terms of sensitization. Other workers have not been successful in demonstrating spinal conditioning, but this negative evidence may be due, at least in part, to the selection of relatively insensitive measures of the conditioning process. The problem of learning in spinal animals must be reinvestigated before a clear picture can emerge.

Are the afferent pathways of the conditioned and unconditioned stimuli indispensible to the acquisition of learned behavior? The findings discussed in this chapter suggest that a direct interaction between the afferent CS and UCS systems (either in the form of connections between the primary sensory pathways or via collaterals in the reticular formation) does not appear to be required in the intact animal. Electrical stimulation of cortical sensory and extrasensory areas has been successfully used as the CS in both classical and instrumental learning experiments. Stimulation of subcortical areas which do not appear to be directly related to sensory pathways has also been effective in various conditioning situations. Although this matter deserves further attention, available evidence indicates that these results are not related to the stimulation of peripheral sensory receptors in the meninges, but rather to the direct excitation of cortical or subcortical neurons.

Cortical stimulation might produce a characteristic feedback to the afferent pathways, but this interpretation does not seem very likely in view of the apparent specificity of the central stimulation effects. Animals can be trained to respond differentially to electrical stimulation of closely adjacent cortical areas or even to frequency differences in the stimulation of the same area. Although it is possible that corticofugal projections may be sufficiently distinct to handle a differential feedback system, such selectivity has not been demonstrated.

One peculiar finding in this area of research has been the apparently very extensive generalization or transfer of training between cortical conditioned stimuli and between cortical and peripheral stimuli. The extent of this effect suggests that stringent controls for possible sensitization phenomena must be used before these experimental results can be interpreted.

A final question must be raised: What, specifically, is the animal responding to? With cortical and, perhaps, cerebellar stimulation, it appears likely that the artificial excitation of sensory projection neurons may actually give rise directly to some sensory perception which may be peculiar to the locus or frequency of stimulation. An explanation of the effects of stimulation of extra-sensory cortical and subcortical regions is less obvious. Stimulation of the motor cortex or motor pathways may produce a secondary effect owing to proprioceptive feedback which results from the elicitation of overt movements. Where such movement is absent, distinct, afferent feedback may be produced by a noticeable change in motor tonus or autonomic motor functions. The latter may be particularly important when hypothalamic stimulation is used as the CS, although it is conceivable that other effects of the stimulation (such as the sudden elicitation of hunger, thirst, sexual arousal, or emotional responses) may themselves have sensory components that are sufficiently distinct to serve as the CS.

Perhaps even more interesting is the question whether centrally elicited motor responses can be conditioned to peripherally or centrally applied conditioned stimuli. Although some confusion has been created in the literature by early reports of negative findings, it seems rather certain today that electrical stimulation of cortical or cerebellar motor areas can, in fact, serve as the UCS in classical defensive conditioning. What remains to be clarified is whether sensory factors can indeed be ruled out, as has been suggested by some recent experimenters.

This issue is of considerable interest in view of the importance which such findings may hold for theoreticians concerned with the role of motivation in learning. If it were possible to rule out sensory factors completely in the experiments of Giurgea and Doty, we would have to conclude that motivation (i.e., the sensory aspect of the UCS) is not essential to learning. This finding, aside from clarifying a long-standing issue in experimental psychology, would permit investigations of learning processes uncomplicated by motivational variables which have been a source of frustration in this field. Such an expectation is still utopian, in spite of some of the exuberant claims that have been made. Some form of pro-

prioceptive feedback may be an essential result of the central UCS, and this complex problem deserves much more attention than it has received in the past. The matter is not settled by demonstrating that conditioning can occur even when the limb directly involved in the UCR to the central stimulation is denervated, because complex postural adjustments which can produce extensive sensory feedback may, nonetheless, be performed. We have also suggested that an emotional reaction to the *involuntary* movement of a limb may occur and may well serve motivational functions in this situation. It is inconceivable that the involuntary movement of a limb should not be startling and even noxious to the animal. After some training the animal may therefore prefer to perform the movement in anticipation of the central stimulus. There are ways to control for at least some of these possibilities, and it is to be hoped that interest in this important problem will continue.

BIBLIOGRAPHY

Ades, H. W. Effects of extirpation of parastriate cortex on learned discrimination in monkeys. *J. Neuropath. exp. Neurol.,* 1946, **5**, 60.

Ades, H. W., & Raab, D. H. Effects of preoccipital and temporal decortication on learned visual discrimination in monkeys. *J. Neurophysiol.,* 1949, **12**, 101–108.

Adey, W. R., & Lindsley, D. F. On the role of subthalamic areas in maintenance of brainstem reticular excitability. *Exp. Neurol.,* 1959, **1**, 305–321.

Akert, K. Comparative anatomy of the frontal cortex and thalamocortical connections. In *The frontal granular cortex and behavior.* J. M. Warren & K. Akert, Eds. New York: McGraw-Hill, 1964.

Akert, K., Orth, O. S., Harlow, H. F., & Schultz, K. A. Learned behavior of rhesus monkeys following neonatal bilateral prefrontal lobotomy. *Science,* 1960, **132**, 1944–1945.

Allen, W. F. Effect of ablating the frontal lobe, hippocampus and occipito-parieto-temporal (excepting pyriform areas) lobes on positive and negative olfactory conditioned reflexes. *Amer. J. Physiol.,* 1940, **128**, 754–771.

Allen, W. F. Effect of ablating the pyriform-amygdaloid areas and hippocampi on positive and negative olfactory conditioned reflexes and on conditioned olfactory differentiation. *Amer. J. Physiol.,* 1941, **132**, 81–92.

Allen, W. F. Effects of destroying three localized cerebral cortical areas for sound on correct conditioned differential responses of the dog's foreleg. *Amer. J. Physiol.,* 1945, **144**, 415–428.

Allen, W. F. Effect of bilateral destruction of three lateral cerebral cortical areas on correct conditioned differential responses from general cutaneous stimulation. *Amer. J. Physiol.,* 1946, **147,** 454–461.

Allen, W. F. Effect of partial and complete destruction of the tactile cerebral cortex on correct conditioned differential foreleg responses from cutaneous stimulation. *Amer. J. Physiol.,* 1947, **151,** 325–337.

Arnott, G. P., & Neff, W. D. The function of the auditory cortex: the control of learned responses to sound cues. *Amer. Psychol.,* 1950, **5,** 270.

Bailey, P., & Davis, E. S. The syndrome of obstinate progression in the cat. *Proc. Soc. exp. Biol. Med.,* 1942, **51,** 307.

Bard, P., & Mountcastle, V. B. Some forebrain mechanisms involved in expression of rage with special reference to suppression of angry behavior. *Res. Publ., Ass. Res. nerv. ment. Dis.,* 1948, **27,** 362–404.

Bates, J. A. V., & Ettlinger, G. Posterior biparietal ablations in the monkey. *Arch. Neurol. (Chicago),* 1960, **3,** 177–192.

Bättig, K., Rosvold, H. E., & Mishkin, M. Comparison of the effects of frontal and caudate lesions on delayed response and alternation in monkeys. *J. comp. physiol. Psychol.,* 1960, **53,** 400–404.

Bättig, K., Rosvold, H. E., & Mishkin, M. Comparison of the effects of frontal and caudate lesions on discrimination learning in monkeys. *J comp. physiol. Psychol.,* 1962, **55,** 458–463.

Benjamin, R. M., & Thompson, R. F. Differential effects of cortical lesions in infant and adult cats on roughness descrimination. *Exp. Neurol.,* 1959, **1,** 305–321.

Beran, V. Unpublished data reported by J. Bureš & O. Burešova. In *The Moscow colloquium on electro-encephalography of higher nervous activity.* H. H. Jasper & G. D. Smirnov, Eds. *EEG clin. Neurophysiol.,* 1960, Suppl. 13, 359–376.

Bianchi, L. The functions of the frontal lobes. *Brain,* 1895, **18,** 497–530.

Black, A. H., & Lang, W. M. Cardiac conditioning and skeletal responding in curarized dogs. *Psychol. Rev.,* 1964, **71**(1), 80–85.

Black, A. H., Carlson, N. J., & Solomon, R. L. Exploratory studies of the conditioning of autonomic responses in curarized dogs. *Psychol. Monogr.,* 1962, **76,** 1–31.

Blum, J. S., Chow, K. L., & Pribram, K. H. A behavioral analysis of the organization of the pareito-temporo-preoccipital cortex. *J. comp. Neurol.,* 1950, **93,** 53–100.

Blum, J. S., Chow, K. L., & Blum, R. A. Delayed response performance of monkeys with frontal removals after excitant and sedative drugs. *J. Neurophysiol.,* 1951, **14,** 197–202.

Blum, R. A. Effects of subtotal lesions of frontal granular cortex on delayed reaction in monkeys. *Arch. Neurol. Psychiat. (Chicago),* 1952, **67,** 375–386.

Brady, J. V., & Hunt, H. F. An experimental approach to the analysis of emotional behavior. *J. Psychol.,* 1955, **40,** 313–324.

Brady, J. V., & Nauta, W. J. H. Subcortical mechanisms in emotional behavior: affective changes following septal forebrain lesions in the albino rat. *J. comp. physiol. Psychol.,* 1953, **46,** 339–346.

Brady, J. V., & Nauta, W. J. H. Subcortical mechanisms in emotional behavior: the duration of affective changes following septal and habenular lesions in the albino rat. *J. comp. physiol. Psychol.,* 1955, **43,** 412.

Brady, J. V., Schreiner, L., Geller, I., & Kling, A. Subcortical mechanisms in emotional behavior: the effect of rhinencephalic injury upon the acquisition and retention of a conditioned avoidance response in cats. *J. comp. physiol. Psychol.,* 1954, **49,** 179–186.

Brinley, G., Kardel, A., & Marshall, W. H. Effects of GABA on K^{42} outflux from the rabbit cortex. *J. Neurophysiol.,* 1960a, **23,** 236–245.

Brinley, G., Kardel, A., & Marshall, W. Potassium outflux from the rabbit cortex during spreading depression. *J. Neurophysiol.,* 1960b, **23,** 246–256.

Brogden, W. J., & Gantt, W. H. Intraneural conditioning: cerebellar conditioned reflexes. *Arch. Neurol. Psychiat. (Chicago),* 1942, **48,** 437–455.

Bromiley, R. B. Conditioned response in a dog after removal of neocortex. *J. comp. physiol. Psychol.,* 1948, **41,** 102–110.

Brown, C. W., & Ghiselli, E. E. Subcortical mechanisms in learning. II: The maze. *J. comp. Psychol.,* 1938a, **26,** 27–44.

Brown, C. W., & Ghiselli, E. E. Subcortical mechanisms in learning. IV: Olfactory discrimination. *J. comp. Psychol.,* 1938b, **26,** 109–120.

Brown, C. W., & Ghiselli, E. E. Subcortical mechanisms in learning. VI: Pattern vision discrimination. *J. comp. Psychol.,* 1938c, **26,** 287–300.

Brush, E. S., Mishkin, M., & Rosvold, H. E. Effects of object preferences and aversions on discrimination learning in monkeys with frontal lesions. *J. comp. physiol. Psychol.,* 1961, **54,** 319–325.

Brutkowski, S., Mishkin, M., & Rosvold, H. E. Positive and inhibitory motor CRs in monkeys after ablation of orbital or dorsolateral surface of the frontal cortex. In *Central and peripheral mechanisms of motor functions.* E. Gutman, Ed. Praha: Czechoslovakia Academy of Science, 1963.

Buchwald, N. A., Wyers, E. J., Okuma, T., & Heuser, G. The "caudate-spindle." I: Electrophysiological properties. *EEG clin. Neurophysiol.,* 1961a, **13,** 509–518.

Buchwald, N. A., Heuser, G., Wyers, E. J., & Lauprecht, C. W. The "caudate-spindle." III: Inhibition by high frequency stimulation of subcortical structures. *EEG clin. Neurophysiol.,* 1961b, **13,** 525–530.

Buchwald, N. A., Wyers, E. J., Lauprecht, C. W., & Heuser, G. The "caudate-spindle." IV: A behavioral index of caudate-induced inhibition. *EEG clin. Neurophysiol.*, 1961c, **13**, 531–537.

Bureš, J. Electrotonic mechanisms in activity of the central nervous system. Production of spreading depression of EEG activity by electrotonus. *Physiol. bohemoslov.*, 1954, **3**, 272–286.

Bureš, J. Reversible decortication and behavior. In *The central nervous system and behavior.* M. A. B. Brazier, Ed. New York: Josiah Macy, Jr. Foundation, 1959, 207–248.

Bureš, J., & Burešova, O. Metabolic nature and physiological manifestations of spreading EEG depression of Leão. *Physiol. bohemoslov.*, 1956, Suppl. 4–6.

Bureš, J., & Burešova, O. The use of Leão's spreading cortical depression in research on conditioned reflexes. In *The Moscow colloquium on electroencephalography of higher nervous activity.* H. H. Jasper & G. D. Smirnov, Eds. *EEG clin. Neurophysiol.*, 1960a, Suppl. 13, 359–376.

Bureš, J., & Burešova, O. The use of Leão's spreading depression in the study of inter-hemispheric transfer of memory traces. *J. comp. physiol. Psychol.*, 1960b, **53**, 558–565.

Bureš, J., Burešova, O., & Beran, V. A contribution to the problem of the "dominant" hemisphere in rats. *Physiol. bohemoslov.*, 1958, **7**, 29–37.

Bureš, J., Bohdanecky, Z., & Weiss, T. Physostigmine induced hippocampal theta activity and learning in rats. *Psychopharmacologia*, 1962, **3**, 254–263.

Burešova, O. Changes in cerebral circulation in rats during spreading EEG depression. *Physiol. bohemoslov.*, 1957a, **6**, 1–11.

Burešova, O. Disturbances in thermoregulation and metabolism as a result of prolonged EEG depression. *Physiol. bohemoslov.*, 1957b, **6**, 369.

Burešova, O. Influencing water metabolism by spreading EEG depression. *Physiol. bohemoslov.*, 1957c, **6**, 12–20.

Burns, N. M. Effects of cortical stimulation on learning. McGill Univ., unpublished doctoral dissertation, 1958.

Burns, N. M., & Mogenson, G. J. Effects of cortical stimulation on habit acquisition. *Canad. J. Psychol.*, 1958, **12**, 77–82.

Burns, N. M., & Mogenson, G. J. Interference and improvement in performance produced by cortical stimulation. In *Electrical stimulation of the brain.* D. E. Sheer, Ed. Austin: Texas Univ. Press, 1961.

Bursten, B., & Delgado, J. M. R. Positive reinforcement induced by intracerebral stimulation in the monkey. *J. comp. physiol. Psychol.*, 1958, **51**, 6–10.

Butler, R. A., Diamond, I. T., & Neff, W. D. Role of auditory cortex in discrimination of changes in frequency. *J Neurophysiol.*, 1957, **20**, 108–120.

Campbell, R. J., & Harlow, H. F. Problem solution by monkeys following bilateral removal of the prefrontal areas. V: Spatial delayed reactions. *J. exp. Psychol.*, 1945, **35**, 110.

Cardo, B. Action de lésions thalamiques et hypothala-

miques sur le conditionnement de fuite et la différenciation tonale chez le rat. *J. Physiol. (Paris)*, 1960, **52**, 537–553.

Chow, K. L. Lack of behavioral effects following destruction of some thalamic association nuclei. *Arch. Neurol. Psychiat. (Chicago)*, 1954, **71**, 762.

Chow, K. L., & Obrist, W. D. EEG and behavioral changes on application of $Al(OH)_3$ cream on preoccipital cortex of monkeys. *Arch. Neurol. Psychiat. (Chicago)*, 1954, **72**, 80–87.

Correll, R. E. The effect of bilateral hippocampal stimulation on the acquisition and extinction of an instrumental response. *J. comp. physiol. Psychol.*, 1957, **50**, 624–629.

Culler, E. A., & Mettler, F. A. Conditioned behavior in a decorticate dog. *J. comp. Psychol.*, 1934, **18**, 291–303.

Culler, E. A., Coakley, J. D., Shurrager, P. S., & Ades, H. W. Differential effects of curare upon higher and lower levels of the central nervous system. *Amer. J. Psychol.*, 1939, **52**, 266–273.

Dahl, D., Ingram, W. R., & Knott, J. R. Diencephalic lesions and avoidance learning in cats. *Arch. Neurol. (Chicago)*, 1962, **7**, 314.

Delgado, J. M. R., Roberts, W. W., & Miller, N. E. Learning motivated by electrical stimulation of the brain. *Amer. J. Physiol.*, 1954, **179**, 587–593.

Denny-Brown, D. The frontal lobes and their functions. In *Modern trends in neurology.* A. Feiling, Ed. New York: Paul Hoeber, 1951.

Diamond, I. T., & Neff, W. D. Ablation of temporal cortex and discrimination of auditory patterns. *J. Neurophysiol.*, 1957, **20**, 300–315.

Diamond, I. T., Goldberg, J. M., & Neff, W. D. Tonal discrimination after ablation of auditory cortex. *J. Neurophysiol.*, 1962, **25**, 223–285.

Doty, R. W. Conditioned reflexes formed and evoked by brain stimulation. In *Electrical stimulation of the brain.* D. E. Sheer, Ed. Austin: Univ. of Texas Press, 1961.

Doty, R. W., & Giurgea, C. Conditioned reflexes established by coupling electrical excitation of two cortical areas. In *Brain mechanisms and learning.* J. F. Delafresnaye, A. Fessard, R. W. Gerard, & J. Konorski, Eds. Oxford: Blackwell Scientific, 1961.

Doty, R. W., & Rutledge, L. T. "Generalization" between cortically and peripherally applied stimuli eliciting conditioned reflexes. *J. Neurophysiol.*, 1959, **22**, 428–435.

Doty, R. W., Rutledge, L. T., & Larson, R. M. Conditioned reflexes established to electrical stimulation of cat cerebral cortex. *J. Neurophysiol.*, 1956, **19**, 401–415.

Doty, R. W., Beck, E. C., & Kooi, K. A. Effect of brainstem lesions on conditioned responses of cats. *Exp. Neurol.*, 1959, **1**, 360.

Dusser de Barrene, J. C., & McCulloch, W. S. Suppression of a motor response obtained from area 4 by stimulation of area 4S. *J. Neurophysiol.,* 1941, **4,** 311–323.

Dykman, R. A., & Shurrager, P. S. Successive and maintained conditioning in spinal cornivores. *J. comp. physiol. Psychol.,* 1956, **49,** 27–35.

Ebner, F. F., & Myers, R. E. Inter- and intra-hemispheric transmission of tactile gnosis in normal and corpus-callosum sectioned monkey. *Fed. Proc.,* 1960, **19,** 292 (abstract).

Ehrlich, A. Effects of tegmental lesions on motivated behavior in rats. *J. comp. physiol. Psychol.,* 1963, **56,** 390–396.

Endroczi, E., Yang, T. L., Lissak, K., & Medgyesi, P. The effect of stimulation of the brainstem on conditioned reflex activity and on behavior. *Acta physiol. Acad. Sci. hung.,* 1959, **16,** 291–297.

Evarts, E. V. Effects of ablation of prestriate cortex on auditory-visual association in monkeys. *J. Neurophysiol.,* 1952a, **15,** 191–200.

Evarts, E. V. Effects of auditory cortex ablation on auditory-visual association in monkeys. *J. Neurophysiol.,* 1952b, **15,** 435–441.

Ferrier, D. *Functions of the brain.* London: Smith and Elder, 1886.

Finan, J. L. Effects of frontal lobe lesions on temporally organized behavior in monkeys. *J. Neurophysiol.,* 1939, **2,** 208–226.

Finan, J. L. Delayed response with pre-delay reinforcement in monkeys after the removal of the frontal lobe. *Amer. J. Psychol.,* 1942, **55,** 202.

Flynn, J. P., & Wasman, M. Learning and cortically evoked movement during propagated hippocampal afterdischarges. *Science,* 1960, **131,** 1607–1608.

Flynn, J. P., MacLean, P. D., & Kim, C. Effects of hippocampal afterdischarges on conditioned responses. In *Electrical stimulation of the brain.* D. E. Sheer, Ed. Austin: Univ. of Texas Press, 1961.

French, G. M. Locomotor effects of regional ablations of frontal cortex in rhesus monkeys. *J. comp. physiol. Psychol.,* 1959a, **52,** 18–24.

French, G. M. Performance of squirrel monkeys on variants of delayed response. *J comp. physiol. Psychol.,* 1959b, **52,** 741–745.

French, G. M. A deficit associated with hypermotility in monkeys with lesions of the dorsolateral frontal granular cortex. *J. comp. physiol. Psychol.,* 1959c, **52,** 25–28.

French, G. M. The frontal lobes and association. In *The frontal granular cortex and behavior.* J. M. Warren & K. Akert, Eds. New York: McGraw-Hill, 1964.

Fuller, J. L., Rosvold, H. E., & Pribram, K. H. The effect on affective and cognitive behavior in the dog of lesions of the pyriform-amygdala-hippocampal complex. *J. comp. physiol. Psychol.,* 1957, **50,** 89–96.

Fulton, J. F. *The frontal lobes and human behaviour.* The Sherrington Lectures. Liverpool: Univ. of Liverpool Press, 1952.

Fuster, J. M. Tachistoscopic perception in monkeys. *Fed. Proc.,* 1957, **16,** 43.

Gantt, W. H. Contributions to the physiology of the conditioned reflex. *Arch. Neurol. Psychiat. (Chicago),* 1937, **37,** 848–858.

Gantt, W. H., & Loucks, R. B. Posterior nerve function as tested by the conditioned reflex method. *Amer. J. Physiol.,* 1938, **112,** 74.

Ghiselli, E. E. Mass action and equipotentiality of the cerebral cortex in brightness discrimination. *J. comp. Psychol.,* 1938a, **25,** 273–290.

Ghiselli, E. E. The relationship between the superior colliculus and the striate area in brightness discrimination. *J. gen. Psychol.,* 1938b, **52,** 151–157.

Girden, E. Cerebral mechanisms in conditioning under curare. *Amer. J. Psychol.,* 1940, **53,** 397–406.

Girden, E. The acoustic mechanism of the cerebral cortex. *Amer. J. Psychol.,* 1942a, **55,** 518–527.

Girden, E. The dissociation of blood pressure conditioned responses under erythrodine. *J. exp. Psychol.,* 1942b, **31,** 219–231.

Girden, E. The dissociation of pupillary conditioned reflexes under erythrodine and curare. *J. exp. Psychol.,* 1942c, **31,** 322–332.

Girden, E., & Culler, E. Conditioned responses in curarized striate muscle in dogs. *J. comp. Psychol.,* 1937, **23,** 261–274.

Girden, E., Mettler, F. A., Finch, G., & Culler, E. Conditioned responses in a decorticate dog to acoustic, thermal, and tactile stimulation. *J. comp. Psychol.,* 1936, **21,** 367–385.

Giurgea, C. *Eleboraea reflexului conditional prin excitarea directa a scoartei cerebrale.* Bucharest: Editura Academiei Rep. Pop. Romane, 1953a.

Giurgea, C. Dinamica elaborarii conexiunii temporare, prin excitarea directa a scoartei cerebrale. *Stud. Cercet. Fiziol.,* 1953b, **4,** 41–73.

Giurgea, C. Die Dynamik der Ausarbeitung einer zeitlichen Beziehung durch direkte Reizung der Hirnrinde. *Berl. ges. Physiol.,* 1955, **175,** 80.

Giurgea, C., & Raiciulescu, N. Nai date asupra reflexului conditionat prin ercitarea directa a cortexului cerebral. *Rev. Fiziol. norm. Pat.,* 1957, **4,** 218–225.

Glickstein, M., & Sperry, R. W. Intermanual somesthetic transfer in split brain rhesus monkey. *J. comp. physiol. Psychol.,* 1960, **53,** 322–327.

Grafstein, B. Locus of propagation of spreading cortical depression. *J. Neurophysiol.,* 1956, **19,** 308–315.

Grastyán, E., Lissak, K., & Kikesi, F. Facilitation and inhibition of conditioned alimentary and defensive reflexes by stimulation of the hypothalamus and the reticular formation. *Acta physiol. Acad. Sci. hung.,* 1956, **9,** 133–151.

Gregory, R. L. The brain as an engineering problem. In *Current problems in animal behavior.* W. H. Thorpe & O. L. Zangwill, Eds. Cambridge: Cambridge Univ. Press, 1961.

Gross, C. G. Comparison of the effects of partial and total lateral frontal lesions on test performance by monkeys. *J. comp. physiol. Psychol.,* 1963a, **56,** 41–47.

Gross, C. G. Effect of food deprivation on performance of delayed response and delayed alternation by normal and brain operated monkeys. *J. comp. physiol. Psychol.,* 1963b, 56, 48–51.

Gross, C. G. Locomotor activity under various stimulus conditions following partial lateral frontal cortical lesions in monkeys. *J. comp. physiol. Psychol.,* 1963c, **56,** 232–236.

Gross, C. G., & Weiskrantz, L. Evidence for dissociation between impairment on auditory discrimination and delayed response in frontal monkeys. *Exp. Neurol.,* 1962, **5,** 453–476.

Gross, C. G., & Weiskrantz, L. Some changes in behavior produced by lateral lesions in the macaque. In *The frontal granular cortex and behavior.* J. M. Warren & K. Akert, Eds. New York: McGraw-Hill, 1964.

Grossman, S. P. Eating or drinking elicited by direct adrenergic or cholinergic stimulation of hypothalamus. *Science,* 1960, **132,** 301–302.

Grossman, S. P. Direct adrenergic and cholinergic stimulation of hypothalamic mechanisms. *Amer. J. Physiol.,* 1962a, **202,** 872–882.

Grossman, S. P. Effects of adrenergic and cholinergic blocking agents on hypothalamic mechanisms. *Amer. J. Physiol.,* 1962b, **202,** 1230–1236.

Grossman, S. P. The VHM: a center for affective reactions, satiety or both? *Int. J. Physiol. Behav.,* 1966a, **1,** 1–10.

Grossman, S. P. Acquisition and performance of avoidance responses during chemical stimulation of the midbrain reticular formation. *J. comp. physiol. Psychol.,* 1966b, **61,** 42–49.

Grossman, S. P., & Grossman, Lore. Effects of chemical stimulation of the midbrain reticular formation on appetitive behavior. *J. comp. physiol. Psychol.,* 1966, **61,** 333–338.

Grossman, S. P., & Peters, R. Acquisition of appetitive and avoidance habits following atropine-induced blocking of the thalamic reticular formation. *J. comp. physiol. Psychol.,* 1966, **61,** 325–332.

Grossman, S. P., Peters, R. H., Freedman, P. E., & Willer, H. I. Behavioral effects of cholinergic stimulation of the thalamic reticular formation. *J. comp. physiol. Psychol.,* 1965, **59,** 57–65.

Gunin, V. I. Changes in the higher nervous activity of albino rats resulting from extirpation of the cortical termination of the visual analyser in early life. *Pavlov J. higher nerv. Activ.,* 1960, **10,** 486–491.

Harlow, H. F. Recovery of pattern discrimination in monkeys following unilateral occipital lobectomy. *J. comp. Psychol.,* 1939, **27,** 467–489.

Harlow, H. F. Behavioral contributions to interdisciplinary research. In *Biological and biochemical bases of behavior.* H. F. Harlow & C. N. Woolsey, Eds. Madison: Univ. of Wisconsin Press, 1958a.

Harlow, H. F. Learning set and error factor theory. In *Psychology: study of a science. Vol. II.* S. Koch, Ed.

New York: McGraw-Hill, 1958b.

Harlow, H. F. The development of learning in the rhesus monkey. *Amer. Scientist,* 1959, **47,** 459–479.

Harlow, H. F., & Dagnan, J. Problem solution by monkeys following bilateral removal of the prefrontal areas. I: The discrimination and discrimination-reversal problems. *J. exp. Psychol.,* 1943, **32,** 351.

Harlow, H. F., & Johnson, T. Problem solution by monkeys following bilateral removal of the prefrontal areas. II: Test of initiation of behavior. *J. exp. Psychol.,* 1943, **32,** 495.

Harlow, H. F., & Settlage, P. Effect of extirpation of frontal areas upon learning performance of monkeys. *Res. Publ., Ass. Res. nerv. ment. Dis.,* 1948, **27,** 446–459.

Harlow, H. F., Davis, R. T., Settlage, P. H., & Meyer, D. R. Analysis of frontal and posterior association syndromes in brain-damaged monkeys. *J. comp. physiol. Psychol.,* 1952, **45,** 419–437.

Harlow, H. F., Akert, K., & Schiltz, K. A. The effects of bilateral prefrontal lesions on learned behavior of neonatal infant and preadolescent monkeys. In *The frontal granular cortex and behavior.* J. M. Warren & K. Akert, Eds. New York: McGraw-Hill, 1964.

Harreveld, A. van, & Stamm, J. S. On conditions for recording of Leão's spreading depression. *EEG clin. Neurophysiol.,* 1951, **3,** 323–328.

Harreveld, A. van, & Stamm, J. S. Effect of pentobarbital and ether on spreading cortical depression. *Amer. J. Physiol.,* 1953a, **173,** 164–170.

Harreveld, A. van, & Stamm, J. S. Spreading cortical convulsions and depressions. *J. Neurophysiol.,* 1953b, **16,** 352–366.

Hebb, D. O. The innate organization of visual activity. III: Discrimination of brightness after removal of the striate cortex in the rat. *J. comp. Psychol.,* 1938, **25,** 427–437.

Henry, C. E., & Pribram, K. H. Effect of aluminum hydroxide cream implantation in cortex of monkey on EEG and behavior performance. *EEG clin. Neurophysiol.,* 1954, **6,** 693–694 (abstract).

Hernández-Peón, R., Brust-Carmona, H., Eckhaus, E., Lopez-Mendoza, E., & Alcocer-Cuarón, C. Functional role of brainstem reticular systems in a salivary conditioned response. *Fed. Proc.,* 1956, **15,** 91.

Heuser, G., Buchwald, N. A., & Wyers, E. J. The "caudate-spindle." II: Facilitatory and inhibitory caudate-cortical pathways. *EEG clin. Neurophysiol.,* 1961, **13,** 519–524.

Hunt, H. F., & Diamond, I. T. Some effects of hippocampal lesions on conditioned avoidance behavior in the cat. In *Proceedings of the fifteenth international congress of psychology, Brussels,* 1957, 203–204.

Ingram, W. R. Modification of learning by lesions and stimulation in the diencephalon and related structures. In *The reticular formation of the brain.* H. H. Jasper, L. D. Proctor, R. S. Knighton, W. C. Noshay,

& R. T. Costello, Eds. Boston: Little, Brown, 1958.

Isaacson, R. L., & Wickelgren, W. D. Hippocampal ablation and passive avoidance. *Science,* 1962, **138,** 1104–1106.

Isaacson, R. L., Douglas, R. J., & Moore, R. Y. The effect of radical hippocampal ablation on acquisition of avoidance responses. *J. comp. physiol. Psychol.,* 1961, **54,** 625–628.

Jacobsen, C. F. Studies of cerebral function in primates. *Comp. Psychol. Monogr.,* 1936, **13**(3), 1–68.

Jacobsen, C. F. The effects of extirpations on higher brain processes. *Physiol. Rev.,* 1939, **19,** 303.

Jacobsen, C. F., & Elder, J. H. The effect of temporal lobe lesions on delayed response in monkeys. *Comp. Psychol. Monogr.,* 1936, **13,** 61.

Jacobsen, C. F., Wolfe, J. B., & Jackson, T. A. An experimental analysis of the functions of the frontal association areas in primates. *J. nerv. ment. Dis.,* 1935, **82,** 1–14.

Kaada, B. R., Rasmussen, E. W., & Kveim, O. Effects of hippocampal lesions on maze learning and retention in rats. *Exp. Neurol.,* 1961, **3,** 333.

Karmos, G., & Grastyán, E. Influence of hippocampal lesions on simple and delayed conditional reflexes. *Acta physiol. Acad. Sci. hung.,* 1962, **21,** 215–224.

Kellogg, W. N. Is "spinal conditioning" conditioning? *J. exp. Psychol.,* 1947, **37,** 263–265.

Kellogg, W. N., Deese, J., & Pronko, N. H. On the behavior of the lumbospinal dog. *J. exp. Psychol.,* 1946, **36,** 503–511.

Kellogg, W. N., Deese, J., Pronko, N. H., & Feinberg, M. An attempt to condition the chronic spinal dog. *J. exp. Psychol.,* 1947, **37,** 99–117.

Kennard, Margaret A. Reorganization of motor function in the cerebral cortex of monkeys deprived of motor and premotor areas in infancy. *J. Neurophysiol.,* 1938, **1,** 477–496.

Kennedy, J. L. The effects of complete and partial occipital lobectomy upon the thresholds of visual real movement in the cat. *J. genet. Psychol.,* 1939, **54,** 119–149.

Kim, C. Sexual activity of male rats following ablation of hippocampus. *J. comp. physiol. Psychol.,* 1960, **53,** 553–557.

Kimble, D. P. The effects of bilateral hippocampal lesions in rats. *J. comp. physiol. Psychol.,* 1963, **56,** 273–283.

Kimura, D. Effects of selective hippocampal damage on avoidance behavior in the rat. *Canad. J. Psychol.,* 1958, **12,** 213–218.

King, F. A. Effects of septal and amygdaloid lesions on emotional behavior and conditioned avoidance responses in the rat. *J. nerv. ment. Dis.,* 1958, **126,** 57–63.

Klüver, H. An analysis of the effects of the removal of the occipital lobes in monkeys. *J. Psychol.,* 1936, **2,** 49.

Klüver, H., & Bucy, P. C. Preliminary analysis of functions of the temporal lobes in monkeys. *Arch. Neurol. Psychiat. (Chicago),* 1939, **42,** 979–1000.

Knott, J. R., & Ingram, W. R. Diencephalic influences on learning and performance. In *Electrical stimulation of the brain.* D. E. Sheer, Ed. Austin: Univ. of Texas Press, 1961.

Knott, J. R., Ingram, W. R., & Correll, R. E. Diencephalic influences on performance. *EEG clin. Neurophysiol.,* 1956, **8,** 524.

Knott, J. R., Ingram, W. R., & Correll, R. E. Effects of certain subcortical lesions on learning and performance in the cat. *A.M.A. Arch. Neurol. Psychiat.,* 1960a, **2,** 247.

Knott, J. R., Ingram, W. R., & Correll, R. E. Some effects of subcortical stimulation on the bar press response. *A.M.A. Arch. Neurol. Psychiat.* 1960b, **2,** 476–484.

Konorski, J. The physiological approach to the problem of recent memory. In *Brain mechanisms and learning.* J. F. Delafresnaye, A. Fessard, R. W. Gerard, & J. Konorski, Eds. Oxford: Blackwell Scientific, 1961a.

Konorski, J. Disinhibition of inhibitory CRs after prefrontal lesions in dogs. In *Brain mechanisms and learning.* J. F. Delafresnaye, A. Fessard, R. W. Gerard, & J. Konorski, Eds. Oxford: Blackwell Scientific, 1961b.

Kraft, M. S., Obrist, W. D., & Pribram, K. H. The effect of irritative lesions of the striate cortex on learning of visual discriminations in monkeys. *J. comp. physiol. Psychol.,* 1960, **53,** 17–22.

Kreindler, A., Ungher, I., & Volanskii, D. Effect of a circumscribed lesion of the reticular formation in the brainstem on the higher nervous activity of dogs. *Sechenov physiol. J. U.S.S.R.,* 1959, **45,** 247.

Kruger, L., & Porter, P. B. A behavioral study of the functions of the rolandic cortex in the monkey. *J. comp. Neurol.,* 1958, **109,** 439–467.

Langworthy, O. R., & Richter, C. P. The influence of efferent cerebral pathways upon the sympathetic nervous system. *Brain,* 1930, **53,** 178–193.

Lashley, K. S. The human salivary reflex and its use in psychology. *Psychol. Rev.,* 1916, **23,** 446–464.

Lashley, K. S. The retention of habits by the rat after destruction of the frontal portion of the cerebrum. *Psychobiology,* 1917, **1,** 3.

Lashley, K. S. Studies of cerebral function in learning. II: The effects of long continued practice upon cerebral localization. *J. comp. Psychol.,* 1921a, **1,** 453–468.

Lashley, K. S. Studies of cerebral function in learning. III: The motor areas. *Brain,* 1921b, **44,** 256–286.

Lashley, K. S. Studies of cerebral function in learning. IV: Vicarious function after destruction of the visual areas. *Amer. J. Physiol.,* 1922, **59,** 44–71.

Lashley, K. S. Studies of cerebral function in learning. V: The retention of motor habits after destruction of the so-called motor areas in primates. *Arch. Neurol. Psychiat. (Chicago),* 1924, **12,** 249–276.

Lashley, K. S. *Brain mechanisms and intelligence.* Chicago: Univ. of Chicago Press, 1929.

Lashley, K. S. The mechanisms of vision. IV: The cerebral areas necessary for pattern vision in the rat. *J. comp. Neurol.*, 1931, **53**, 417.

Lashley, K. S. The mechanisms of vision. V: The structure and image forming power of the rat's eye. *J. comp. Psychol.*, 1932, **13**, 173–200.

Lashley, K. S. Studies of cerebral function in learning. XI: The behavior of the rat in latch-box situations. *Comp. Psychol. Monogr.*, 1935a, **11**, 1–42.

Lashley, K. S. The mechanisms of vision. XII: Nervous structures concerned in the acquisition and retention of habits based on reactions to light. *Comp. Psychol. Monogr.*, 1935b, **11**, 43–79.

Lashley, K. S. The mechanisms of vision. XV: Preliminary studies of the rat's capacity for detail vision. *J. genet. Psychol.*, 1938, **18**, 123–193.

Lashley, K. S. The mechanisms of vision. XVI: The functioning of small remnants of the visual cortex. *J. comp. Neurol.*, 1939, **70**, 45–67.

Lashley, K. S. Thalamo-cortical connections of the rat's brain. *J. comp. Neurol.*, 1941, **75**, 67–121.

Lashley, K. S. The mechanisms of vision. XVII: Autonomy of the visual cortex. *J. genet. Psychol.*, 1942a, **60**, 197–221.

Lashley, K. S. The problem of cerebral organization in vision. *Biol. Symposia*, 1942b, **7**, 301–322.

Lashley, K. S. Studies of cerebral function in learning. XII: Loss of the maze habit after occipital lesions in blind rats. *J. comp. Neurol.*, 1943, **79**, 431–462.

Lashley, K. S. Studies of cerebral function in learning. XIII: Apparent absence of transcortical association in maze learning. *J. comp. Neurol.*, 1944, **80**, 257–281.

Lashley, K. S. The mechanisms of vision. XVIII: Effects of destroying the visual 'associative areas' of the monkey. *Genet. Psychol. Monogr.*, 1948, **37**, 107–166.

Lashley, K. S. In search of the engram. *Proc. Soc. exp. Biol. Med.* 1950, Symposium 4, 454–482.

Lashley, K. S. The problem of serial order in behavior. *Hixon symposium on cerebral mechanisms in behavior. Vol. XIV.* New York: Wiley, 1951.

Lashley, K. S., & McCarthy, D. A. The survival of the maze habit after cerebellar injuries. *J. comp. Psychol.*, 1926, **6**, 423–433.

Lashley, K. S., & Wiley, L. E. Studies of cerebral function in learning. IX: Mass action in relation to the number of elements in the problem to be learned. *J. comp. Neurol.*, 1933, **57**, 3–55.

Lawicka, W., & Konorski, J. The physiological mechanism of delayed reactions. III: The effect of prefrontal ablations on delayed reactions in dogs. *Acta Biol. exp. (Warsaw)*, 1959, **19**, 221–231.

Lawicka, W., & Konorski, J. The effects of prefrontal lobectomies on the delayed responses in cats. *Acta Biol. exp. (Warsaw)*, 1961, **21**, 141–156.

Leão, A. A. P. Spreading depression of activity in the cerebral cortex. *J. Neurophysiol.*, 1944, **7**, 359–390.

Leão, A. A. P. Further observations on spreading depression of activity in the cerebral cortex. *J. Neurophysiol.*, 1947, **10**, 409–414.

Leão, A. A. P., & Morison, R. S. Propagation of spreading cortical depression. *J. Neurophysiol.*, 1945, **8**, 33–45.

Leary, R. W., Harlow, H. F., Settlage, P. H., & Greenwood, D. D. Performance on double-alternation problems by normal and brain-injured monkeys. *J. comp. physiol. Psychol.*, 1952, **45**, 576–584.

Levine, J. Studies in the interrelations of central nervous structures in binocular vision, I. *J. genet. Psychol.*, 1945a, **67**, 105–129.

Levine, J. Studies in the interrelations of central nervous structures in binocular vision, II. *J. genet. Psychol.*, 1945b, **67**, 131–142.

Levine, M., & Wolff, H. G. Cerebral circulation. Afferent impulses from the blood vessels of the pia. *Arch. Neurol. Psychiat. (Chicago)*, 1932, **28**, 140–150.

Levine, S., & Soliday, S. The effects of hypothalamic lesions on conditioned avoidance learning. *J. comp. physiol. Psychol.*, 1960, **53**, 497–501.

Liberson, W. T., & Akert, K. Hippocampal seizure states in guinea pigs. *EEG clin. Neurophysiol.*, 1955, **7**, 211–222.

Liberson, W. T., & Cadilhac, S. G. Further studies of hippocampal seizure states. *EEG clin. Neurophysiol.*, 1953, Suppl. 3, 42.

Lindsley, D. B. Attention, consciousness, sleep and wakefulness. In *Handbook of physiology. Vol. III.* J. Field, H. W. Magoun, & V. E. Hall, Eds. Baltimore: Williams and Wilkins, 1960.

Loucks, R. B. The efficacy of the rat's motor cortex in delayed alternation. *J. comp. Neurol.*, 1931, **53**, 511–567.

Loucks, R. B. Preliminary report of a technique for stimulation or destruction of tissues beneath the integument and the establishing of conditioned reactions with faradization of the cerebral cortex. *J. comp. Psychol.*, 1933, **16**, 439–444.

Loucks, R. B. A technique for faradic stimulation of tissues beneath the integument in the absence of conductors penetrating the skin. *J. comp. Psychol.*, 1934, **18**, 305–313.

Loucks, R. B. The experimental delimitation of neural structures essential for learning: the attempt to condition striped muscle responses with faradization of the sigmoid gyri. *J. Psychol.*, 1935, **1**, 5–44.

Loucks, R. B. Studies of neural structures essential for learning. II: The conditioning of salivary and striped muscle responses to faradization of cortical sensory elements and action of sleep upon such mechanisms. *J. comp. Psychol.*, 1938, **25**, 315–332.

Loucks, R. B., & Gantt, W. H. The conditioning of striped muscle responses based upon faradic stimulation of dorsal roots and dorsal columns of the spinal cord. *J. comp. Psychol.*, 1938, **25**, 415–426.

McCleary, R. A. Response specificity in the behavioral effects of limbic system lesions in the cat. *J. comp. physiol. Psychol.*, 1961, **54**, 605–613.

MacLean, P. D. The limbic system and its hippocampal formation: studies in animals and their possible application to man. *J. Neurosurg.,* 1954, **11,** 29–44.

MacLean, P. D. Chemical and electrical stimulation of hippocampus in unrestrained animals. II: Behavioral findings. *Arch. Neurol. Psychiat. (Chicago),* 1957, **78,** 128–142.

MacLean, P. D., & Delgado, J. M. R. Electrical and chemical stimulation of frontotemporal portion of limbic system in the waking animal. *EEG clin. Neurophysiol.,* 1953, **5,** 91–100.

MacLean, P. D., Flanigan, S., Flynn, J. P., Kim, C., & Stevens, J. R. Hippocampal function: tentative correlations of conditioning, EEG, drug, and radioautographic studies. *Yale J. Biol. Med.,* 1955–1956, **28,** 380–395.

Maier, N. R. F. The effect of cortical injury on equivalence reactions in rats. *J. comp. Psychol.,* 1941, **32,** 165–189.

Maier, N. R. F., & Schneirla, T. C. *Principles of psychology.* New York: McGraw-Hill, 1935.

Malmo, R. B. Interference factors in delayed response in monkeys after removal of frontal lobes. *J. Neurophysiol.,* 1942, **5,** 295–308.

Marquis, D. G., & Hilgard, E. R. Conditioned lid responses to light in dogs after removal of the visual cortex. *J. comp. Psychol.,* 1936, **22,** 157.

Marshall, W. H. Relation of dehydration of brain to spreading depression of Leão. *EEG clin. Neurophysiol.,* 1950, **2,** 177–185.

Marshall, W. H. Spreading cortical depression of Leão. *Physiol. Rev.,* 1959, **39,** 239–279.

Marshall, W. H., & Essig, C. F. Relationship of air exposure of cortex to spreading depression of Leão. *J. Neurophysiol.,* 1951, **14,** 265–273.

Mettler, F. A. Physiologic effects of bilateral simultaneous frontal lesions in the primate. *J. comp. Neurol.,* 1944, **81,** 105–136.

Meyer, D. R., & Woolsey, C. N. Effects of localized cortical destruction on auditory discriminative conditioning in cat. *J. Neurophysiol.,* 1952, **15,** 149–162.

Meyer, D. R., Harlow, H. F., & Settlage, P. H. A survey of delayed response performance by normal and brain-damaged monkeys. *J. comp. physiol. Psychol.,* 1951, **44,** 17–25.

Meyer, M. A study of efferent connections of the frontal lobe in the human brain after leucotomy. *Brain,* 1949, **72,** 265–269.

Meyer, M. *Fifth international anatomical congress, Oxford.* New York: Cambridge Univ. Press, 1950.

Miles, R. C. Learning by squirrel monkeys with frontal lesions. In *The frontal granular cortex and behavior.* J. M. Warren & K. Akert, Eds. New York: McGraw-Hill, 1964.

Miles, R. C., & Bloomquist, A. J. Frontal lesions and behavioral deficits in monkey. *J. Neurophysiol.,* 1960, **23,** 471–484.

Miller, N. E., Bailey, C. J., & Stevenson, J. A. F. Decreased "hunger" but increased food intake resulting from hypothalamic lesions. *Science,* 1950, **112,** 256–259.

Mishkin, M. Visual discrimination performance following partial ablations of the temporal lobe. II: Ventral surface vs. hippocampus. *J. comp. physiol. Psychol.,* 1954, **47,** 187–193.

Mishkin, M. Effects of small frontal lesions on delayed alternation in monkeys. *J. Neurophysiol.,* 1957, **20,** 615–622.

Mishkin, M. Perseveration of central sets after frontal lesions in monkeys. In *The frontal granular cortex and behavior.* J. M. Warren & K. Akert, Eds. New York: McGraw-Hill, 1964.

Mishkin, M., & Pribram, K. H. Analysis of the effects of frontal lesions in monkey. II: Object alternation. *J. comp. physiol. Psychol.,* 1956, **49,** 41–45.

Mishkin, M., Prockop, E. S., & Rosvold, H. E. One-trial object-discrimination learning in monkeys with frontal lesions. *J. comp. physiol. Psychol.,* 1962, **55,** 178–181.

Mogenson, G. J. Conditioned responses to cortical stimulation. McGill Univ., Ph.D. dissertation, 1958.

Mogenson, G. J. Conditioned responses to cortical stimulation with the use of two different instrumental techniques. *J. comp. physiol. Psychol.,* 1959, **52,** 497–500.

Mogenson, G. J. Electrical stimulation of the visual cortex as the conditioned stimulus in peripherally blind rats. *J. comp. physiol. Psychol.,* 1962, **55,** 492–494.

Mogenson, G. J., & Morrison, M. J. Avoidance responses to "reward" stimulation of the brain. *J. comp. physiol. Psychol.,* 1962, **55,** 691–694.

Morgan, C. T., & Wood, W. M. Cortical localization of symbolic processes in the rat. II: Effect of cortical lesions upon delayed alternation. *J. Neurophysiol.,* 1943, **6,** 173–180.

Morrell, F. Effect of anodal polarization on the firing pattern of single cortical cells. *Ann. N.Y. Acad. Sci.,* 1961, **92,** 860–876.

Moss, E., & Harlow, H. F. Problem solution by monkeys following extensive unilateral decortication and pre-frontal lobotomy of contralateral side. *J. Psychol.,* 1948, **25,** 223–226.

Myers, R. E. Interocular transfer of pattern discrimination in cats following section of crossed optic fibers. *J. comp. physiol. Psychol.,* 1955, **48,** 470–473.

Myers, R. E. Function of corpus callosum in interocular transfer. *Brain,* 1956, **79,** 358.

Myers, R. E. Corpus callosum and visual gnosis. In *Brain mechanisms and learning.* J. F. Delafresnaye, A. Fessard, R. W. Gerard, & J. Konorski, Eds. Oxford: Blackwell Scientific, 1961.

Myers, R. E., & Henson, C. O. Role of corpus callosum in transfer of tactuokinesthetic learning in chimpanzee. *Arch. Neurol. (Chicago),* 1960, **3,** 404–409.

Naquet, R. Effects of stimulation of the rhinencephalon in the waking cat. *EEG clin. Neurophysiol.*, 1954, **6**, 711–712.

Nauta, W. J. H. Neural associations of the amygdaloid complex in the monkey. *Brain*, 1962, **85**, 505–520.

Nauta, W. J. H. Some efferent connections of the prefrontal cortex in the monkey. In *The frontal granular cortex and behavior*. J. M. Warren & K. Akert, Eds. New York: McGraw-Hill, 1964.

Neff, W. D., & Diamond, I. T. The neural basis of auditory discrimination. In *Biological and biochemical bases of behavior*. H. F. Harlow & C. N. Woolsey, Eds. Madison: Univ. of Wisconsin Press, 1958.

Neff, W. D., Arnott, G. P., & Fisher, J. D. Function of the auditory cortex: localization of sound in space. *Amer. J. Physiol.*, 1950, **163**, 738 (abstract).

Neff, W. D., Fisher, J. F., Diamond, I. T., & Yella, M. Role of auditory cortex in discrimination requiring localization of sound in space. *J. Neurophysiol.*, 1956, **19**, 500.

Nielson, H. C., Doty, R. W., & Rutledge, L. T. Motivational and perceptual aspects of subcortical stimulation in cats. *Amer. J. Physiol.*, 1958, **194**, 427–432.

Nielson, H. C., Knight, J. M., & Porter, P. B. Subcortical conditioning, generalization and transfer. *J. comp. physiol. Psychol.*, 1962, **55**, 168–173.

Nikolaeva, N. I. Summation of stimuli in the cerebral cortex. *Sechenov. physiol. J. U.S.S.R.*, 1957, **43**, 27–34.

Orbach, J., & Fischer, G. J. Bilateral resections of frontal granular cortex. *Arch. Neurol. (Chicago)*, 1959, **1**, 78–86.

Orbach, J., & Fantz, R. L. Differential effects of neocortical resections on overtrained and non-overtrained visual habits in monkeys. *J. comp. physiol. Psychol.*, 1958, **51**, 126.

Orbach, J., Milner, B., & Rasmussen, T. Learning and retention in monkeys after amygdala-hippocampal resection. *Arch. Neurol. (Chicago)*, 1960, **3**, 230.

Pasik, T., Pasik, P., Battersby, W. S., & Bender, M. B. Factors influencing visual behavior of monkeys with bilateral temporal lobe lesions. *J. comp. Neurol.*, 1960, **115**, 89–102.

Pavlov, I. *Conditioned reflexes. An investigation of the physiological activity of the cerebral cortex*. New York: Oxford Univ. Press, 1927.

Pechtel, C., Masserman, J. H., Schreiner, L., & Levitt, M. Differential effects of lesions of mediodorsal nuclei of thalamus on normal and neurotic behavior in cat. *J. nerv. ment. Dis.*, 1955, **121**, 26–33.

Peele, T. L. *The neuroanatomic basis of clinical neurology*. New York: McGraw-Hill, 1954.

Penfield, W. A contribution to the mechanism of intracranial pain. *Res. Publ., Ass. Res. nerv. ment. Dis.*, 1935, **15**, 399–416.

Penfield, W., & Milner, Brenda. Memory deficit produced by bilateral lesions in the hippocampal zone. *A.M.A. Arch. Neurol. Psychiat.*, 1958, **79**, 475–497.

Pennington, L. A. The function of the brain in auditory localization. II: The effect of cortical operation upon original learning. *J. comp. Neurol.*, 1937, **66**, 415.

Pennington, L. A. The effects of cortical destruction upon responses to tones. *J. comp. Neurol.*, 1941, **74**, 169.

Peretz, E. The effects of lesions of the anterior cingulate cortex on the behavior of the rat. *J. comp. physiol. Psychol.*, 1960, **53**, 540–548.

Peters, R. H., Rosvold, H. E., & Mirsky, A. F. The effect of thalamic lesions upon delayed response-type test in the rhesus monkey. *J. comp. physiol. Psychol.*, 1956, **49**, 111–116.

Poltyrew, S. S., & Zeliony, G. P. Grosshirnrinde und Assoziations-funktion. *Z. Biol.*, 1930, **90**, 157–160.

Pribram, Helen B., & Barry, J. Further behavioral analysis of parieto-temporo-preoccipital cortex. *J. Neurophysiol.*, 1956, **19**, 99–106.

Pribram, K. H. Some physical and pharmacological factors affecting delayed response performance of baboons following frontal lobotomy. *J. Neurophysiol.*, 1950, **13**, 373–382.

Pribram, K. H. Lesions of "frontal eye fields" and delayed response of baboons. *J. Neurophysiol.*, 1955a, **18**, 105–112.

Pribram, K. H. Toward a science of neuropsychology. In *Current trends in psychology and the behavioral sciences*. Pittsburgh: Univ. of Pittsburgh Press, 1955b.

Pribram, K. H. A further experimental analysis of the behavioral deficit that follows injury to the primate frontal cortex. *Exp. Neurol.*, 1961, **3**, 432–466.

Pribram, K. H., & Mishkin, M. Analysis of the effects of frontal lesions in monkey. III: Object alternation. *J. comp. physiol. Psychol.*, 1956, **49**, 41–45.

Pribram, K. H., & Weiskrantz, L. A comparison of the effects of medial and lateral cerebral resections on conditioned avoidance behavior of monkeys. *J. comp. physiol. Psychol.*, 1957, **50**, 74–80.

Pribram, K. H., Mishkin, M., Rosvold, H. E., & Kaplan, S. J. Effects on delayed response performance of lesions of dorsolateral and ventromedial frontal cortex of baboons. *J. comp. physiol. Psychol.*, 1952, **45**, 565–575.

Pribram, K. H., Wilson, W. A., Jr., & Connors, J. Effects of lesions of the medial forebrain on alternation behavior of rhesus monkeys. *Exp. Neurol.*, 1962, **6**, 36–47.

Pribram, K. H., Ahumada, A., Hartog, J., & Ross, L. A progress report on the neurological processes disturbed by frontal lesions in primates. In *The frontal granular cortex and behavior*. J. M. Warren & K. Akert, Eds. New York: McGraw-Hill, 1964.

Prosser, C. L., & Hunter, W. S. The extinction of startle responses and spinal reflexes in the white rat. *Amer. J. Physiol.*, 1936, **117**, 609–618.

Raab, D. H., & Ades, H. W. Cortical and midbrain

mediation of a conditioned discrimination of acoustic intensities. *Amer. J. Psychol.,* 1946, **59**, 59.

Raiciulescu, N., & Giurgea, C. Reflex conditionat interemisferic prin exciterea electrica directa a scoartei cerebrale dupa sectionarea corpului calos. *Rev. Fiziol. norm. Pat.,* 1957, **4**, 336–339.

Raiciulescu, N., Giurgea, C., & Savescu, C. Reflex conditionat la exciterea directa a cortexului cerebral dupa distrugerea ganglionului lui Gasser. *Rev. Fiziol. norm. Pat.,* 1956, **3**, 304–308.

Ray, B. S., & Wolff, H. G. Experimental studies on headache. Pain-sensitive structures of the head and their significance in headache. *Arch. Surg.,* 1940, **41**, 813–856.

Richter, C. P., & Hines, M. The production of the "grasp reflex" in adult macaques by experimental frontal lobe lesions. *Res. Publ., Ass. Res. nerv. ment. Dis.,* 1934, **13**, 211–224.

Riopelle, A. J., & Ades, H. W. Visual discrimination performance in rhesus monkeys following extirpation of prestriate and temporal cortex. *J. genet. Psychol.,* 1953, **83**, 63.

Riopelle, A. J., & Churukian, G. A. The effect of varying the intertrial interval in discrimination learning by normal and brain-operated monkeys. *J. comp. physiol. Psychol.,* 1958, **51**, 119–125.

Roberts, W. W., Dember, W. N., & Bordwich, M. Alternation and exploration in rats with hippocampal lesions. *J. comp. physiol. Psychol.,* 1962, **55**, 695–700.

Rosner, B. S., & Neff, W. D. Function of the auditory cortex: acquisition and retention of an approach response to a sound stimulus. *Amer. Psychologist,* 1949, **4**, 235 (abstract).

Ross, J., & Magun, R. Comparison between the spread of seizure discharges and of spreading depression. *EEG clin. Neurophysiol.,* 1954, **6**, 518.

Rosvold, H. E., & Delgado, J. M. R. The effect on delayed-alternation test performance of stimulating or destroying electrically structures within the frontal lobes of the monkey's brain. *J. comp. physiol. Psychol.,* 1956, **49**, 365–372.

Rosvold, H. E., & Mishkin, M. Non-sensory effects of frontal lesions on discrimination learning and performance. In *Brain mechanisms and learning.* J. F. Delafresnaye, A. Fessard, R. W. Gerard, & J. Konorski, Eds. Oxford: Blackwell Scientific, 1961.

Rosvold, H. E., Mishkin, M., & Szwarcbart, M. K. Effects of subcortical lesions in monkeys on visual-discrimination and single-alternation performance. *J. comp. physiol. Psychol.,* 1958, **51**, 437–444.

Rosvold, H. E., Szwarcbart, M. K., Mirsky, A. F., & Mishkin, M. The effect of frontal-lobe damage on delayed response performance in chimpanzees. *J. comp. physiol. Psychol.,* 1961, **54**, 368–374.

Ruch, T. C. Cortical localization of somatic sensibility. The effect of precentral, postcentral, and posterior parietal lesions upon the performance of monkeys trained to discriminate weights. *Res. Publ., Ass. Res. nerv. ment. Dis.,* 1935, **15**, 289–330.

Ruch, T. C., & Shenkin, H. A. The relation of area 13 on the orbital surface of the frontal lobes to hyperactivity and hyperphagia in monkeys. *J. Neurophysiol.,* 1943, **6**, 349–360.

Ruch, T. C., Fulton, J. F., & Kasdon, S. Further experiments on the somato-sensory functions of the cerebral cortex in the monkey and chimpanzee. *Amer. J. Physiol.,* 1937, **119**, 394–395.

Ruch, T. C., Fulton, J. F., & German, W. J. Sensory discrimination in the monkey, chimpanzee, and man after lesions of the parietal lobe. *Arch. Neurol. Psychiat. (Chicago),* 1938, **39**, 919–937.

Ruch, T. C., Kasdon, S., & Fulton, J. F. Late recovery of sensory discriminative ability after parietal lesions in the chimpanzee. *Amer. J. Physiol.,* 1940, **129**, 453.

Rusinov, V. S. Electrophysiological research in the dominant area in the higher parts of the central nervous system. *Abstracts from the twentieth international physiological congress, Brussels,* 1956.

Rutledge, L. T., Jr., & Doty, R. W. Differential action of chloropromazine on conditioned responses to peripheral versus direct cortical stimuli. *Fed. Proc.,* 1955, **14**, 126.

Schiller, P. H. Delayed response in the minnow. *J. comp. physiol. Psychol.,* 1948, **41**, 233–238.

Schreiner, L. H., Rioch, D. McK., Pechtel, C., & Masserman, J. H. Behavioral changes following thalamic injury in cat. *J. Neurophysiol.,* 1953, **16**, 234–246.

Schwartzbaum, J. S. Changes in reinforcing properties of stimuli following ablation of the amygdaloid complex in monkeys. *J. comp. physiol. Psychol.,* 1960a, **53**, 388–395.

Schwartzbaum, J. S. Response to changes in reinforcing conditions of bar pressing after ablation of the amygdaloid complex in monkeys. *Psychol. Rep.,* 1960b, **6**, 215–221.

Schwartzbaum, J. S., & Pribram, K. H. The effects of amygdalectomy in monkeys on transposition along a brightness continuum. *J. comp. physiol. Psychol.,* 1960, **53**, 396–399.

Segundo, J. P., Roig, J. A., & Sommer-Smith, J. A. Conditioning of reticular formation stimulation effects. *EEG clin. Neurophysiol.,* 1959, **11**, 471–484.

Settlage, P. H. The effect of occipital lesions on visually-guided behavior in the monkey. I: Influence of the lesions on final capacities in a variety of problem situations. *J. comp. Psychol.,* 1939, **27**, 93–131.

Shurrager, P. S., & Culler, E. A. Phenomena allied to conditioning in the spinal dog. *Amer. J. Physiol.,* 1938, **123**, 186–187.

Shurrager, P. S., & Culler, E. Conditioned extinction of a reflex in a spinal dog. *J. exp. Psychol.,* 1941, **28**, 287–303.

Shurrager, P. S., & Shurrager, Harriet C. Converting a spinal CR into a reflex. *J. exp. Psychol.,* 1941, **29**, 217–224.

Shurrager, P. S., & Shurrager, Harriet C. The rate of

learning measured at a single synapse. *J. exp. Psychol.*, 1946, **36**, 347–354.

Sloan, N., & Jasper, H. H. Studies on the regulatory functions of the limbic cortex. *EEG clin. Neurophysiol.*, 1950, **2**, 317–327.

Smith, D. E. Cerebral localization in somaesthetic discrimination in the rat. *J. comp. Psychol.*, 1939, **28**, 161–188.

Smith, K. V. Visual discrimination in the cat. V: The postoperative effects of removal of the striate cortex upon intensity discrimination. *J. genet. Psychol.*, 1937, **51**, 329.

Smith, K. V. Curare drugs and total paralysis. *Psychol. Rev.*, 1964, **71**, 77–79.

Solomon, R. L., & Turner, L. H. Discriminative classical conditioning in dogs paralyzed by curare can later control discriminative avoidance responses in the normal state. *Psychol. Rev.*, 1962, **69**, 202–219.

Spaet, T., & Harlow, H. F. Problem solution by monkeys following bilateral removal of the prefrontal areas. II: Delayed-reaction problems involving use of the matching-from-sample method. *J. exp. Psychol.*, 1943, **32**, 424–434.

Sperry, R. W. On the neural basis of the conditioned response. *Brit. J. Anim. Behav.*, 1955, **3**, 41–44.

Sperry, R. W., Stamm, J. S., & Miner, N. Relearning tests for interocular transfer following division of optic chiasma and corpus callosum in cats. *J. comp. physiol. Psychol.*, 1956, **49**, 529.

Spiegel, E. A., & Hunsicker, W. C. The conduction of cortical impulses to the autonomic system. *J. nerv. ment. Dis.*, 1936, **83**, 249–273.

Stamm, J. S. Electrical stimulation of frontal cortex in monkeys during learning of an alternation task. *J. Neurophysiol.*, 1961, **24**, 414–426.

Stamm, J. S. Function of prefrontal cortex in timing behavior of monkeys. *Exp. Neurol.*, 1963, **7**, 87–97.

Stamm, J. S. Retardation and facilitation in learning by stimulation of frontal cortex in monkeys. *The frontal granular cortex and behavior.* J. M. Warren & K. Akert, Eds. New York: McGraw-Hill, 1964.

Stamm, J. S., & Mahoney, W. A. Facilitation in learning by electrical excitation of frontal cortex of monkeys. *Fed. Proc.*, 1962, **21**, 358.

Stamm, J. S., & Pribram, K. H. Effects of epileptogenic lesions in frontal cortex on learning and retention in monkeys. *J. Neurophysiol.*, 1960, **23**, 552–563.

Stamm, J. S., & Sperry, R. W. Function of corpus callosum in contralateral transfer of somesthetic discrimination in cats. *J. comp. physiol. Psychol.*, 1957, **50**, 138.

Stepien, L. S., Cordeau, J. P., & Rasmussen, T. The effect of temporal lobe and hippocampal lesions on auditory and visual recent memory in monkeys. *Brain*, 1960, **83**, 470–489.

Swann, H. G. The function of the brain in olfaction. II: The results of destruction of olfactory and other nervous structures upon the discrimination of odors. *J. comp. Neurol.*, 1934, **59**, 175–201.

Swann, H. G. The function of the brain in olfaction. The effects of large cortical lesions on olfactory discrimination. *Amer. J. Physiol.*, 1935, **111**, 257–262.

Teitelbaum, H. The effect of hippocampal lesions on extinction of an operant response. Paper read at the annual meeting of the Canadian Psychological Association, 1960.

Teitelbaum, H., & Milner, P. Activity changes following partial hippocampal lesions in rats. *J. comp. physiol. Psychol.*, 1963, **56**, 284–289.

Teitelbaum, P. Sensory control of hypothalamic hyperphagia. *J. comp. physiol. Psychol.*, 1955, **48**, 158–163.

Teitelbaum, P., & Campbell, B. A. Ingestion patterns in hyperphagic and normal rats. *J. comp. physiol. Psychol.*, 1958, **51**, 135–141.

Thomas, G. J. *Behavioral effects of interruption of Papez's circuit in rat and cat.* Paper read at the 126th annual meeting of the American Association for the Advancement of Science, Chicago, Dec. 26–30, 1959.

Thomas, G. J., & Otis, L. S. Effects of rhinencephalic lesions on conditioning of avoidance responses in the rat. *J. comp. Physiol.*, 1958, **51**, 130–134.

Thomas, G. J., & Slotnick, B. Behavioral alterations in rats following lesions in the anterior limbic cortex. Paper read at the first annual meeting of the Psychonomics Society, Chicago, Sept. 2–3, 1960.

Thomas, G. J., Fry, F. J., Fry, W. J., Slotnick, B. Behavioral alterations in cats following mammillothalamic tractotomy. *Physiologist*, 1959a, **2**, 114–115.

Thomas, G. J., Moore, R. Y., Harvey, J. A., & Hunt, H. F. Relation between the behavioral syndrome produced by lesions in the septal region of the forebrain and maze learning of the rat. *J. comp. physiol. Psychol.*, 1959b, **52**, 527–532.

Thompson, R. Effects of lesions in the caudate nuclei and dorsofrontal cortex on conditioned avoidance behavior in cats. *J. comp. physiol. Psychol.*, 1959, **52**, 650–659.

Thompson, R. Interpeduncular nucleus and avoidance conditioning. *Science*, 1960a, **132**, 1551–1553.

Thompson, R. The effect of damage to the interpeduncular nucleus on retention of a kinesthetic habit in rats. *Amer. Psychologist*, 1960b, **15**, 482 (abstract).

Thompson, R. Retention of a brightness discrimination following neocortical damage in the rat. *J. comp. physiol. Psychol.*, 1960c, **53**, 212–215.

Thompson, R. The role of cerebral cortex in stimulus generalization. *J. comp. physiol. Psychol.*, 1962, **55**, 279–287.

Thompson, R. A note on cortical and subcortical injuries and avoidance learning by rats. In *The frontal granular cortex and behavior.* J. M. Warren & K. Akert, Eds. New York: McGraw-Hill, 1964.

Thompson, R., & Hawkins, W. F. Memory unaffected by mamillary body lesions in the rat. *Exp. Neurol.*, 1961, **3**, 189.

Thompson, R., & Massopust, L. C., Jr. The effect of subcortical lesions on retention of a brightness discrimination in rats. *J. comp. physiol. Psychol.,* 1960, **53,** 488–496.

Thompson, R., & Rich, I. Transitory behavioral effects of interpeduncular nucleus damage. *Exp. Neurol.,* 1961, **4,** 310.

Thompson, R., Malin, C. F., Jr., & Hawkins, W. F. Effects of subcortical lesions on retention of a kinesthetic discrimination habit. *Exp. Neurol.,* 1961, **3,** 367.

Thompson, R. F. Function of auditory cortex of cat in frequency discrimination. *J. Neurophysiol.,* 1960, **23,** 321–324.

Tracy, W. H., & Harrison, J. M. Aversive behavior following lesions of the septal region of the forebrain in the rat. *Amer. J. Psychol.,* 1956, **69,** 443.

Victor, M., Angevine, J. B., Mancall, E. L., & Fisher, C. M. Memory loss with lesions of hippocampal formation. *Arch. Neurol. (Chicago),* 1961, **5,** 244–263.

Wade, Marjorie. The effect of sedatives upon delayed responses in monkeys following removal of the prefrontal lobes. *J. Neurophysiol.,* 1947, **10,** 57–61.

Wapner, S. The differential effects of cortical injury and retesting on equivalence reactions in the rat. *Psychol. Monogr.,* 1944, **57,** 1–59.

Warren, J. M. The behavior of carnivores and primates with lesions in the prefrontal cortex. In *The frontal granular cortex and behavior.* J. M. Warren & K. Akert, Eds. New York: McGraw-Hill, 1964.

Warren, J. M., & Akert, K. Impaired problem solving by cats with thalamic lesions. *J. comp. physiol. Psychol.,* 1960, **53,** 207–211.

Warren, J. M., & Harlow, H. F. Learned discrimination performance by monkeys after prolonged postoperative recovery from large cortical lesions. *J. comp. physiol. Psychol.,* 1952a, **45,** 119–126.

Warren, J. M., & Harlow, H. F. Discrimination learning by normal and brain operated monkeys. *J. genet. Psychol.,* 1952b, **81,** 45–52.

Warren, J. M., Leary, R. W., Harlow, H. F., & French, G. M. Function of association cortex in monkeys. *Brit. J. Anim. Behav.,* 1957, **5,** 131–138.

Warren, J. M., Warren, H., & Akert, K. Orbitofrontal cortical lesions and learning in cats. *J. comp. Neurol.,* 1962, **118,** 17–41.

Weiskrantz, L. Behavioral changes associated with ablation of the amygdaloid complex in monkeys. *J. comp. physiol. Psychol.,* 1956, **49,** 381–391.

Weiskrantz, L., & Mishkin, M. Effects of temporal and frontal cortical lesions on auditory discrimination in monkeys. *Brain,* 1958, **81,** 406–414.

Weiskrantz, L., & Wilson, W. A., Jr. The effect of ventral rhinencephalic lesions on avoidance thresholds in monkeys. *J. comp. physiol. Psychol.,* 1958, **51,** 167–171.

Weiskrantz, L., Mihailovic, L., & Gross, C. G. Stimulation of frontal cortex and delayed alternation performance. *Science,* 1960, **131,** 1443–1444.

Weiskrantz, L., Mihailovic, L., & Gross, C. G. Effects of stimulation of frontal cortex and hippocampus on behavior in the monkey. *Brain,* 1962, **85,** 487–504.

Weiss, T., & Fifkova, E. The use of spreading EEG depression for analyzing the mutual relationships between the cortex and the hippocampus. *EEG clin. Neurophysiol.,* 1960, **12,** 841–850.

Wiley, L. E. The function of the brain in audition. *J. comp. Neurol.,* 1932, **54,** 109–141.

Wiley, L. E. A further investigation of auditory cerebral mechanisms. *J. comp. Neurol.,* 1937, **66,** 327–331.

Wilson, W. A., Jr., & Mishkin, M. Comparison of the effects of the inferotemporal and lateral occipital lesions on visually guided behavior in monkeys. *J. comp. physiol. Psychol.,* 1959, **52,** 10–17.

Wing, K. G. The role of the optic cortex of the dog in the retention of learned responses to light: conditioning with light and shock. *Amer. J. Psychol.,* 1946, **59,** 583.

Wing, K. G. The role of the optic cortex of the dog in the retention of learned responses to light: conditioning with light and food. *Amer. J. Psychol.,* 1947, **60,** 30.

Wing, K. G., & Smith, K. V. The role of the optic cortex in the dog in the determination of the functional properties of conditioned reactions to light. *J. exp. Psychol.,* 1942, **31,** 78.

Zubeck, J. P. Sudies in somesthesis. I: Role of the somesthetic cortex in roughness discrimination in the rat. *J. comp. physiol. Psychol.,* 1951, **44,** 339–353.

Zubeck, J. P. Studies in somesthetics. II: Role of somatic sensory areas I and II in roughness discrimination in cat. *J. Neurophysiol.,* 1952, **15,** 401–408.

Zuckermann, E. Effect of cortical and reticular stimulation on conditioned reflex activity. *J. Neurophysiol.,* 1959, **22,** 633–643.

CHAPTER FOURTEEN

Consolidation

Most physiological theories of learning and retention make use of the notion that the acquisition process initially produces reversible changes in the central nervous system, changes that serve as the basis of short-term recall but do not themselves constitute permanent or long-term memory traces. A variety of physiological mechanisms have been postulated to account for these reversible, functional changes. Most hypotheses assume a temporary facilitation of synaptic transmission between the central representations of the conditioned and unconditioned stimuli and share the conviction that these are *functional* modifications which decay rapidly and leave little or no permanent trace in the central nervous system. Only when a particular combination of stimuli is repeatedly presented in such a fashion that the same central pathways are subjected to recurrent or continual facilitation does a second process begin to take place; this process in some way translates the pattern of temporary or lowered synaptic resistance into permanent or at least long-term memory traces. These permanent memories would seem to depend on nearly irreversible biochemical and/or anatomical changes which develop only slowly and represent *structural* modifications in the central nervous system. There is currently little agreement about the precise nature of permanent memory traces and the biological mechanisms that produce them. Most physiological theories imply the existence of a transition from temporary functional facilitation to permanent structural modification, but few have bothered to detail the mechanism.

There is neither physiological nor biochemical evidence for a dualistic memory mechanism; however, clinical observations of amnesia induced by concussion, electroconvulsive shock (ECS), or drug (Metrazol, insulin) treatment suggest a differential effect on recent memory. A large and often contradictory body of experimental evidence, accumulated in the past fifteen years, suggests that long- and short-term recall may be functionally distinct processes which are differentially affected by a variety of experimental manipulations. This supposition has given rise to the purely hypothetical concept of "consolidation," designed to describe a process by which short-term memory is transferred into permanent memory traces.

The concept of consolidation was first used by Müller and Pilzecker (1900) around the turn of the century to describe the memory "fixation" that appeared to take place during verbal learning. DeCamp (1915) introduced consolidation to American psychology and suggested a broader interpretation, but it was not until recently that the phenomenon and its physiological implications were studied in the animal laboratory. Except for the use of such physiological manipulations as electroconvulsive shock or drug-induced seizure states, these investigations have rarely strayed from a purely behavioral analysis of the consolidation process. They are concerned with the differential effects on long- and short-term memory rather than with the physiological, anatomical, or biochemical mechanisms involved. Therefore the literature is not directly related to our present concern; however, the problem of consolidation has such important implications for physiological theories of learning that it is useful to present at least an abbreviated review of the experimental literature.

Experiments concerned with the consolidation process have been reported for 25 years or more.

797

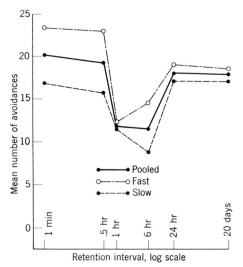

Fig. 14.1 Mean number of avoidance responses as a function of retention interval. Data are plotted separately for fast learners and for slow learners and for all subjects pooled. (From Kamin, 1963.)

They have always been concerned with demonstrating the effects of some interfering manipulation on retention and only indirectly on the hypothesized consolidation process.

A more direct demonstration of behavioral changes which may be related to something like the proposed consolidation process has been reported by Kamin (1963). He trained "maze-bright" and "maze-dull" rats to a lenient criterion of three consecutive avoidance responses in a shuttle box apparatus and tested for retention at various intervals after the last training trial. Both groups of animals showed good retention and little or no systematic performance decrements when tested after 1 min, 30 min, or 24 hr and 20 days. All animals showed a sharp drop in performance 1 and 6 hr after the last training trial. Because Kamin did not present data for the period between 6 and 24 hr, it cannot be known when the animals' performance did, in fact, recover.

It has been suggested that the temporary interference with the performance of the learned response may correlate with the transfer of memory traces from short- to long-term storage mechanisms and thus reflect consolidation processes. Although these findings do not present compelling proof of such a fixation mechanism, the hypothesis appears better supported by Kamin's studies than by some earlier ones which are open to other interpretations.

CLINICAL AND EXPERIMENTAL BACKGROUND

The initial experimental interest in the problem of consolidation dates back to the late 1930's and early 1940's, when clinical studies of the effects of ECS and Metrazol and insulin treatments revealed rather peculiar effects on "recent" memory. Like concussion-induced amnesias, these effects appeared to be most severe for memories of events close in time to the shock. Recall was found to return gradually and become available in a definite temporal pattern, i.e., the more recent the memory the longer it took for recall to become possible. The subjective importance of the memory did not seem to affect ease of recall. Instead, there appeared to be a *total* and *permanent* loss of memory for events immediately preceding the ECS or drug treatment. The temporal parameters of the amnesia were such that some theorists suggested that short-term memory may be totally obliterated by any convulsive activity of the brain (presumably because these memories depend on functional changes in neural processes that do not survive sudden and violent seizure activity). Long-term memory, on the other hand, is affected only temporarily, if at all, since it is probably based on structural modifications, either within or between neurons, that are not significantly altered by brief functional disturbances.

Before we discuss some of the experimental literature surrounding these problems, we should mention another distinction which was first made in the early clinical studies and has generally been confirmed in the animal laboratory. Electroconvulsive shock or drug-induced seizure states affect recall but do not seem to reduce the organism's ability to learn (Zubin and Barrera, 1941). This finding is particularly important in the present context because it supports the contention that the convulsive activity interrupts functional memory traces (such as reverberatory circuits) without physically damaging neural mechanisms essential to learning or memory. With ECS no evidence of persistent physical damage has been observed. It is generally assumed that the observed behavioral changes (including temporary loss of consciousness) are due solely to the momentary disruption of ongoing neuronal activity. Similar assumptions are frequently made about the effects of chemically induced seizure states, although drugs like Metrazol have been shown to produce neuronal damage (Speidel, 1940) which appears to be cumulative and eventually irreversible (Ziskind et al., 1941) if repeated treatments are given.

EARLY DRUG STUDIES

Most of the recent work on consolidation has employed ECS. However, some drug studies have demonstrated interesting effects which have often been ignored. It may be instructive to discuss these briefly before turning to the effects of ECS itself.

A single dose of Metrazol (a drug that produces electrophysiological and, in higher dosages, behavioral seizures), administered immediately after animals reach criterion performance on some instrumental habit, significantly interferes with performance on retention tests given long after the convulsive effects of the drug have worn off. The animals appear capable of relearning the same task and show no deficit when required to learn a novel problem. Since there is no evidence of persisting sensory, motor, or motivational deficits, these observations have been interpreted as being related to a selective effect on memory storage or consolidation (Loken, 1941; Heron and Carlson, 1941). It has even been suggested that the Metrazol-induced impairment of memory may be greater than that commonly seen after ECS (Kessler and Gellhorn, 1943), but thorough parametric comparisons of shock intensity and drug dosage effects have not been reported.

Insulin shock, induced shortly after the completion of acquisition, produces effects apparently similar to those seen after Metrazol treatment, the severity of the effect being related to the recency of the memory and the difficulty of the problem (Ries and Berman, 1944). Other techniques have occasionally been used to produce generalized seizure states in studies of acquisition and retention, but the mechanism of action of most of the agents is too obscure to warrant discussion at this point. A few examples may suffice. Hunt et al. (1953a) treated animals with carbon disulfide gas and observed effects on retention performance that were similar, though less severe, than those seen after electroconvulsive or Metrazol shock. Brady et al. (1953) studied the effects of audiogenic seizures on CER and reported a pronounced and often complete loss of performance.

Presumably related, though not typically discussed with this material, are studies concerned with the effects of localized epileptogenic lesions on learning and/or retention (Chow and Obrist, 1954; Henry and Pribram, 1954; Morrell et al., 1956; Kraft et al., 1960; Stamm and Pribram,

1960; Chow, 1961). These studies have generally shown that the acquisition of instrumental habits is retarded or even impossible if seizure foci are established in the association or primary projection areas of sensory modalities that are relevant to the solution of the problem. However, most of these studies also show that the same foci do not significantly interfere with the recall of habits learned before the discharging foci were set up. The apparent lack of effect on memory may not be significant in the present context, since none of the studies has induced the local seizure activity soon enough after the completion of acquisition to interfere with either short-term memory, as that term is customarily used, or the consolidation process itself.

An interesting and perhaps more immediately relevant group of studies has been reported on the effects of anesthesia or *lowered* neuronal activity on retention and/or memory. Although we do not fully understand the physiological mechanisms by which anesthetics and other sedative drugs achieve their obvious behavioral effects, it is generally assumed that they must somehow reduce transmission effectiveness in some essential portions of the brain, particularly in the reticular formation of the brainstem. It may be instructive to discuss some of the findings briefly.

To the extent that short-term memory and consolidation depend on reverberatory activity in neural circuits involving portions of the brain affected by these chemicals, we might expect a total loss of recall when anesthesia is applied before permanent memory traces can be established. Clinical observations do, in fact, indicate such an effect, although further information is sorely needed from more closely controlled studies. Artusio (1955), for instance, reported that patients under very light ether anesthesia showed no impairment of memory, successfully solved a variety of logic problems, and conversed freely and coherently; however, they could not recall these events when tested after the anesthesia had completely worn off. Unfortunately, it is not clear that these interesting observations are related to a basic interference with a primary consolidation process or memory fixation, since it has been reported (Orkin et al., 1956; Reiff and Scheerer, 1959) that events occurring under deep anesthesia can subsequently be recalled if the subject is placed under hypnosis. We must consider the possibility that learning (and retention) may take place at several levels of the nervous system and that barbiturates and other anesthetics may interfere with only one of these mechanisms; thus, the organism is forced to make use of facilities that are not available under ordinary circumstances.

Pearlman et al. (1961) compared the effects of Metrazol, pentobarbital, and ether on memory in an approach-avoidance situation. Rats were trained to bar-press for water and then given a single painful, but nonconvulsive, shock through the manipulandum. Ether anesthesia interfered with the memory of the punishment (i.e., bar pressing increased on a subsequent recall test) if given within 10 sec of the shock trial but not if delayed until 10 min later. This effect was small (only 30% of the animals bar-pressed on a recall test 24 hr after the shock) compared with that of the other two drugs. Three-fourths of the animals given pentobarbital within 10 sec of the shock trial returned to the lever on the retention test, and all animals bar-pressed if given Metrazol. Almost none of the pentobarbital-treated animals returned to the lever when the drug was given 10 min after the shock; however, a significant percentage of animals given Metrazol after the same delay worked the lever on the retention test. Abt et al. (1961) have reported a more profound and long-lasting effect of ether anesthesia on simple avoidance behavior in the mouse.

The effects of barbiturates and other depressant drugs on memory are difficult to interpret, particularly in view of the repeatedly reported observation that anesthetics may protect memory traces from the normally disruptive effects of electroconvulsive shock. Several investigators have reported that ECS does not significantly impair subsequent recall if given while the subject is under ether (Porter and Stone, 1947; Stone and Walker, 1949; Hunt et al., 1953a, b) or Nembutal anesthesia (Siegel et al., 1949). McGaugh and Alpern (1966) have, however, reported that ether anesthesia which prevented the convulsive reaction to ECS did not protect the memory of a single punishment from its disruptive effects.

McGaugh and Alpern's data require further study of this problem, but the same drugs which interfere with recall under some circumstances appear able to protect the organism against the disruptive effects of ECS at least in some situations. The situation is complicated by reports (Ziskind et al., 1941) of a significant *enhancement* of the ECS effect on memory by various barbiturates. Other studies (Rabe and Gerard, 1959) have suggested that barbiturates may slow the consolidation process (i.e., increase the duration of the interval during which memories are affected by ECS or Metrazol), whereas psychomimetics such as meprobamate retard acquisition but seem to protect established memories from the disruptive effects of ECS. The latter effect may merely reflect the longer period of training (and consolidation) required to attain criterion under meprobamate. For readers who like to puzzle about inconsistencies, it might be mentioned that hypnotic drugs (Putnam and Merritt, 1937; Shipley and McGregor, 1940) and alcohol (Page, 1941) seem to raise the threshold for electroshock-induced seizures and even provide a measure of protection against the behavioral effects of electrophysiological seizures. We shall have to defer further discussion of these interesting effects until more information about the basic mode of action of these drugs becomes available.

Still other means of disrupting the pattern of neural activity have been used to study the role of consolidation processes in memory trace formation. Otis and Cerf (1958) induced heat narcosis in goldfish, 0, 15, 60, or 240 min after the animals had reached criterion on a simple avoidance habit. Recall on subsequent retention tests was almost completely destroyed in all animals heated immediately after the completion of training. Significant impairments were seen in animals narcotized as late as 15 min after the last training trial, but not in fish receiving the same treatment 1 or 4 hr after the end of the acquisition period.

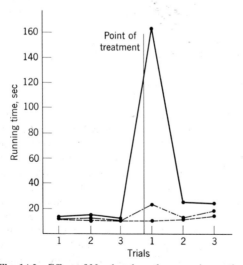

Fig. 14.2 Effect of Nembutal on the amnesic reaction to ECS: animals given a saline placebo after the ECS treatment (•——•), animals receiving Nembutal but no ECS (•—·—·—•), animals given Nembutal after the ECS treatment (•– – – –•). (From Siegel et al., 1949.)

THE HYPOTHERMIA ARGUMENT

A favorite argument for an essential contribution of reverberatory activity to short-term memory and consolidation processes (Gerard, 1955) has been based on clinical observations first reported 25 years ago. Experimenting with hypothermia in patients, Fay and Smith (1941) observed that man continued to function rationally when cooled below 92°F. The subjects were capable of carrying on a meaningful conversation but showed an apparently complete amnesia for everything that transpired in the hypothermic state when they were returned to normal body temperatures.

Ransmeier (Ransmeier, 1954; Ransmeier and Gerard, 1954) has reported that hamsters cooled to 15°C, 1 min after each training trial in a maze-learning situation, required reliably longer to reach criterion performance than normal hamsters or than animals cooled to the same body temperature 5 min after each trial. He also demonstrated, however, that a variety of experimental manipulations similarly interfered with acquisition performance if presented within the first minute or two after each trial. Moreover, several findings suggest that Ransmeier's observations may not be specifically related to hypothermia or even to the consequent disruption of neural activity.

Jones (1943) earlier reported that hypothermia does not seem to interfere with learning or retention in rats. A number of experiments have replicated and extended these early observations. Mrosovsky (1963) cooled rats to an even lower body temperature (2°C) immediately after the animals reached criterion on a shuttle box avoidance task. He found that EEG activity ceased completely at approximately 18°C, and that even cardiac activity and respiration were temporarily suspended at 10 to 15°C. However, when he tested the animals after they had returned to normal body temperatures and recuperated from the experimental procedure for 13 days, no significant effects on retention were noticeable. Similar negative results have been reported by Andjus et al. (1956) and by Sudak and Essman (1961). These findings represent some of the most impressive evidence against the hypothesis that reverberatory neural activity may be essential to the formation of memory traces.

We must point out a technical flaw in the hypothermia experiments which tempers the conclusiveness of these findings. We cannot "flash-freeze" animals like vegetables and expect them to recover. All hypothermia experiments have used a gradual cooling procedure which requires several hours to reduce body temperature to the point where the electrical activity of the brain disappears. It is thus possible that reverberatory activity may have continued for a sufficient period of time to result in structural modifications and consolidation of the memory trace before the hypothermia disrupted the relevant pattern of neural activity. These experiments need to be replicated when techniques for more rapid, yet safe, cooling become available. They do, however, demonstrate rather conclusively that the consolidation process, if it exists, must either be independent of reverberatory activity or be complete within a much shorter period of time (a maximum of about 2 hr) than had previously been assumed. The hypothermia experiments also show quite clearly that any memory persisting longer than a few hours cannot be based on reverberatory activity in any portion of the central nervous system.

EARLY CLINICAL AND EXPERIMENTAL USES OF ECS

The typical consolidation experiment uses ECS rather than drug treatments or temperature changes to disrupt ongoing neural activity. The basic procedure, as developed in psychiatric clinics, consists of placing surface electrodes on opposite sides of the subject's head and passing a brief (0.1 to 0.2 sec) and relatively high (upward of 500 ma in man) current. This produces temporary seizure activity in almost all parts of the brain and results in a momentary loss of consciousness often, though not always, accompanied by overt motor seizures. Electroconvulsive shock has been employed in the treatment of psychiatric patients who do not respond to normal psychotherapeutic approaches. The extent of the benefits to be derived has been questioned in recent years, and the treatment lost much of its initial popularity after the development of tranquilizing drugs, which serve the same purpose without producing some of the undesirable side effects of ECS.

The mode of action of ECS is essentially a mystery, but it is generally assumed that it produces whatever effects it may have by momentarily interrupting neural activity related to the psychiatric disorder. The patient has no recall of the shock treatment and shows a more or less complete amnesia for the events immediately preceding the shock treatment. It is this aspect of ECS that suggested its use in experiments on consolidation. Clinical estimates of the temporal parameters of the amnesia vary from a few minutes to several days, but even the more conservative estimates suggest that short-term memory mechanisms or consolidation processes may be differentially affected.

Some of the earliest experimental studies of the effects of ECS on associative processes, undertaken by Gellhorn and his associates, were concerned with extinction rather than acquisition. Gellhorn et al. (1942) trained rats in a simple double-grill avoidance situation and extinguished the learned response completely before applying ECS or Metrazol shock. He found that all animals again showed avoidance after the shock treatment and that this reversal of the extinction effects could be repeatedly demonstrated in the same animals. An interesting effect of ECS and insulin shock was reported by Gellhorn (1945). He trained animals in an avoidance situation to respond successively to several distinct conditioned stimuli by shaping a response to the first CS and then extinguishing the conditioned reaction while developing the same CR to a different CS. After several acquisition-extinction cycles, Gellhorn applied ECS or insulin shock and found that the animals now responded to all conditioned stimuli. If we view extinction simply as a process of learning not to respond to a previously reinforced stimulus, these results are difficult to comprehend; unless a differential impairment of motivational mechanisms is assumed, a selective effect on extinction rather than recent memory per se is implied. These results are of interest because they suggest that the ECS effect may not be independent of the motivational situation, as has been assumed in most ECS studies. It is reasonable to suggest that Gellhorn may have observed selective effects on extinction because the motivation for responding to a CS that signals painful shock is considerably greater than the motivation to avoid unnecessary exertion by not responding to a cue that may turn out to be harmless. It is unfortunate that this line of inquiry has not been continued.

Duncan (1945, 1948, 1949) demonstrated in one of the earlier series of studies that the effectiveness of ECS in suppressing retention performance varied as a function of the time interval between the learning experience and the convulsive shock. He trained rats in a multiple T-maze apparatus, giving one trial per day followed after some fixed time interval by ECS. He found that animals receiving the ECS treatment within the first 20 to 30 min after each learning trial performed much more poorly than either control animals not receiving ECS treatments or animals given electroconvulsive shocks more than 1 hr after each daily trial. There was no significant difference between the latter groups. Applying painful shocks to the hindlegs at any time after each training trial did not significantly reduce the animals' performance.

The exact temporal parameters of the ECS effect on retention performance have been the subject of a number of more recent experiments. The information from these studies is potentially important, for it may help us define short-term or long-term memory and assist in the study of the consolidation process which presumably intervenes between the two.

R. Thompson and Dean (1955) introduced a

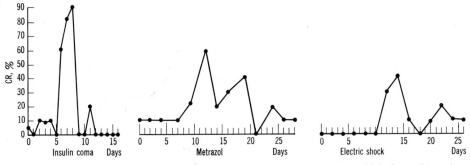

Fig. 14.3 Effect of insulin coma, Metrazol, and ECS on previously inhibited conditioned responses. Inhibited conditioned responses are restored by insulin coma (5 units insulin/kg intraperitoneally and 5 units subcutaneously), Metrazol convulsions (45 mg/kg), and intense electric shock applied to the head. (From Gellhorn et al., 1942.)

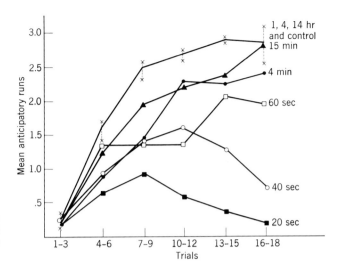

Fig. 14.4 Effect of ECS on acquisition. ECS was given 20 sec, 40 sec, 1 min, 4 min, 15 min, or 1, 4, and 14 hr after the learning trial. (From Duncan, 1949.)

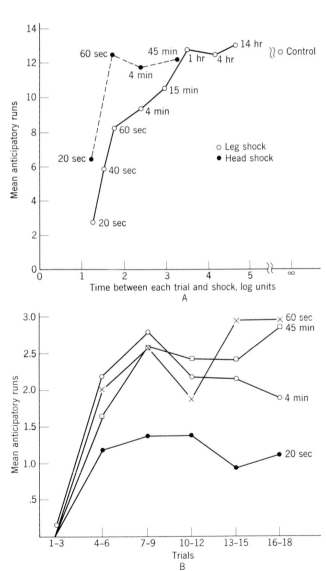

Fig. 14.5 Effects of peripheral shock on acquisition. Mean anticipatory runs (A) and learning curves (B) for animals shocked through the legs after each trial. (From Duncan, 1949.)

procedural refinement (massed trials) which permitted the completion of acquisition in a single, relatively short training session and gave only a single ECS treatment. The results showed that (1) the most severe effects were obtained after the shortest delays (10 and 120 sec), (2) significant impairments could be observed when the ECS treatment was presented 1 hr after the last trial, and (3) no effects could be obtained when the shock treatment was delayed by 4 hr.

Leukel (1957) gave ECS treatments 1, 5, 30, or 120 min after each of the first ten acquisition trials in a water maze. None of the ECS groups showed a significant impairment (of either speed or error scores) during the ten-trial ECS treatment period, but they took reliably longer to reach criterion after the electroshock was discontinued. It is difficult to interpret these findings because memory deficits may have been difficult to detect in the initial stages of acquisition. However, Carson (1957) has reported that ECS treatments given during later stages of acquisition did not produce reliable performance deficits in subsequent learning or retention trials. The same number of electroconvulsive shocks, given after the completion of training, produced a reliable decrement of performance on subsequent retention tests. More interesting, in the present context, is the fact that in Leukel's study there were no

marked differences between the long- and short-delay groups. Significant effects could be obtained even when the ECS treatment was given 2 hr after the last training trial.

Several investigators (Pearlman et al., 1961; Heriot and Coleman, 1962; Bureš and Burešova, 1963) have reported marked effects of ECS on the retention of passive avoidance responses even when the ECS treatment was given several hours after the punishment. Chorover and Schiller (1965) and Quartermain et al. (1965), on the other hand, could observe ECS effects in similar avoidance situations only when the treatment was administered within a few seconds after the punished response.

Chorover and Schiller (1966) in an attempt to reconcile these apparently paradoxical findings, have suggested that the training paradigm employed in the studies reporting effects of delayed ECS may have produced a generalized CER to the apparatus. This CER may have produced motor inhibition and thus reduced exploratory behavior and the probability that an animal enters the shocked compartment. Electroconvulsive shock may have suppressed this inhibitory effect of the CER, thus increasing locomotor activity and the probability that the animal enters the shock compartment. The apparent memory impairment perhaps reflects merely an increase in exploratory behavior.

In support of this hypothesis, Chorover and Schiller demonstrated that prolonged ECS effects could be obtained in the passive-avoidance paradigm used by Bureš and Burešova (1963) but not in a similar paradigm which allowed escape from the punishing shock and reduced the CER. They also found that ECS-treated animals urinated and defecated as much as normals, although they entered the shock compartment more frequently, suggesting at least some retention of the effects of noxious stimulation in the apparatus. Exploratory activity was found to be reduced by the training procedure used in the experimental paradigm which had shown the delayed ECS effects. This inhibitory effect was, as predicted, significantly reduced by ECS treatments. Chorover and Schiller (1966) concluded from their observations that retrograde amnesia may be responsible for the impaired performance in passive avoidance situations only when the ECS treatment is given within a few seconds after the learning trial, and that behavioral effects seen when the treatment delay is longer may be artifacts of the training or or testing procedure.

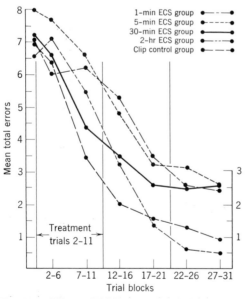

Fig. 14.6 Effects of ECS, given after each of the first ten trials in a water maze, on the total number of errors to criterion. (From Leukel, 1957.)

ECS EFFECTS ON EMOTIONAL BEHAVIOR

Masserman and Jacques (1948) opened a very interesting area of investigation by studying the effects of ECS on emotional behavior. They found that cats made experimentally "neurotic" by various techniques returned to more adaptive and normal response patterns after a few ECS treatments, suggesting a possibly selective effect on recently acquired emotional reactions. They also observed, however, that the ECS-treated animals performed poorly on complex behavioral tasks and that control animals which were not "neurotic" but received ECS treatments showed similar deficits. No histological damage which might account for the behavioral changes was found.

Brady and his associates have continued this line of investigation, using the CER technique. In one of these experiments (Hunt and Brady, 1951), rats were trained to lever-press for water rewards in an operant conditioning apparatus. When stable performance levels were obtained, a CER was established in a different apparatus and this emotional response transferred to the lever-pressing situation (i.e., the animals stopped lever pressing during the CS for unavoidable grid shock). After six ECS treatments, given at the rate of one per day, none of the experimental animals showed any evidence of retaining the CER, either in the original training situation or in the operant conditioning apparatus. All rats readily reacquired the CER and showed perfect retention after 60 days, suggesting a temporary interference with memory mechanisms rather than a basic effect on associative capabilities. Perhaps the most interesting aspect of Hunt and Brady's results is that bar-pressing performance did not appear to be at all affected by the ECS treatment, suggesting a selective effect on the CER mechanism. This selective effect may be due simply to the overtraining of the lever-pressing habit or to the recency of the memory of the CER; however, the rather clear-cut differential effects suggest that other factors may have to be considered.

Brady (1951) also reported that conditioned emotional responses which are "lost" after repeated ECS treatments spontaneously reappear after approximately 30 days. A residual effect of the ECS treatment remains, however, in the form of a greater susceptibility to extinction. In a subsequent experiment Brady (1952) established a CER and waited 30, 60, or 90 days before applying 21 ECS treatments (three per day). In agreement

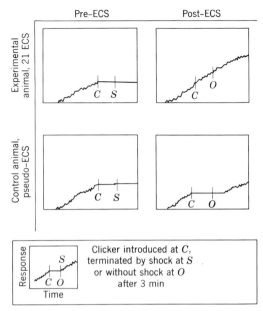

Fig. 14.7   Effect of ECS on CER. Typical cumulative curves for two rats. (From Hunt and Brady, 1951.)

with earlier findings on the effects of ECS on the retention of appetitive habits, Brady found that the ECS treatments did not affect performance when given after any of these long delays. Similar results have been reported by Hunt et al. (1952).

INTERACTION EFFECTS

Electroconvulsive shock appears to disrupt physiological processes that are not related to memory storage. Rosvold (1949), for example, reported that ECS may interrupt gestation and interfere markedly with maternal behaviors which are presumably instinctive rather than acquired. R. Thompson et al. (1958) found that ECS effects on retention performance were more severe in young (30 to 40 days of age) than in old (60 to 200 days of age) rats. Since myelinization in the rat is not complete until about age 50 days, the authors suggested that the ECS effect may be related primarily to unmyelinated fibers.

Saul and Feld (1961) have recently reported data suggesting that ECS-induced seizure activity may originate in the hippocampus, gradually involve other portions of the limbic system, and finally spread to the neocortical mantle. It is not clear whether this sequence of events has any functional significance.

C. W. Thompson et al. (1961) hypothesized that "bright" animals derived from the Tryon

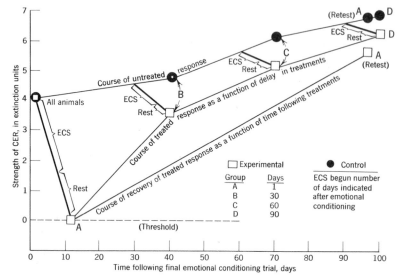

Fig. 14.8   Changes in the strength of the CER as a function of ECS treatments and elapsed time. (From Brady, 1952.)

"maze-bright" strain might have faster consolidation rates than normal or "maze-dull" animals; they supported this contention with the observation that ECS treatments produced a greater impairment of performance in maze-dull animals. This finding is of some interest in view of the Woolley et al. (1960) observation that maze-bright rats seem to have significantly lower thresholds for ECS-induced seizures. We should point out, however, that the severity of the ECS effect appears to be influenced by a number of variables and that it may be premature to generalize from isolated observations.

A fine illustration of such interaction effects has recently been reported by R. Thompson and Pennington (1958) who found that the intertrial interval during acquisition significantly affected the severity of ECS-induced performance deficits. They reported that animals trained with very short (45 sec) or relatively long (5 or 6 min) intertrial intervals showed significantly greater performance deficits than rats trained with intermediate (4 to 5 min) intervals.

Some controversy has centered around the possibility that at least some of the ECS effects may be related to an interference with neural processes not specifically related to acquisition, retention, or recall. McGinnies (1947), for instance, reported that repeated ECS treatments, given after rats had learned to run a complex elevated T-maze, did not seem to affect memory (the num-

ber of errors in the maze did not increase reliably) but markedly slowed down the animals. Horowitz and Stone (1947), on the other hand, observed a significant increase in errors but no effect on speed measures in a very similar multiple-unit T-maze apparatus. Further confusion has been created by reports (Hunt et al., 1953b) suggesting that ECS may *improve* performance of learned responses under some testing conditions.

THE "FEAR" HYPOTHESIS

The initial experimental studies of the effects of ECS on retention in animals (Gellhorn et al., 1942; Siegel, 1943; Duncan, 1945) demonstrated that the treatment, administered immediately after a learning experience, significantly interferes with the performance of learned responses on subsequent retention tests. However, these studies also suggested that the observed impairment of performance might be the result of a variety of physiological and psychological effects of ECS which are not directly related to a disruption of ongoing neural activity and might have nothing to do with memory mechanisms or consolidation processes. Some of the alternative explanations suggested at this time were quickly discarded. Others have remained the subject of intensive investigation and debate and are still problems of importance.

Perhaps the most elusive of these possibilities

is the suggestion that the ECS experience, although not subject to voluntary recall, may somehow induce anxiety or fear. This reaction may become conditioned to the test situation and thus establish an approach-avoidance conflict which reduces the net approach tendencies and interferes with performance on the retention tests by changing motivational factors rather than associative factors.

Such an interpretation is supported by clinical reports of patients who develop a profound aversion to ECS treatment although neither pain nor even discomfort is ever consciously experienced during the shock treatment. Human subjects often report a disquieting disorganization in time and space *after* ECS, which might account for the gradually developing aversion observed in both man and animals (Gallinek, 1956).

One of the first animal studies of ECS effects on retention suggested that a gradually increasing fear of the electroshock rather than a memory deficit may be responsible for the performance decrements observed on retention tests. Siegel (1943) studied the effects of ECS on running speed in a straight alley and observed that after repeated electroconvulsive shocks performance dropped significantly when the animals were merely connected to the shock apparatus without actually receiving the electric current.

Hayes (1948) further tested the hypothesis that the ECS-induced impairment of performance on retention tests may be related to fear rather than to mechanisms peculiar to memory. He found that rats given ECS in the goal box of his apparatus showed marked fear reactions to the test situation; lower shock levels (which induced only *petit-mal*-like responses and probably did not seriously interfere with consciousness) produced more severe fear effects than very high-intensity shocks which induced *grand-mal*-like seizures.

Duncan (1948, 1949) discredited the fear hypothesis at least temporarily when he reported that the ECS effects on retention performance could not be duplicated by applying the same shock to the hindfeet rather than to the head. Animals receiving the painful but nonconvulsive foot shock within 20 sec of the learning experience showed an impairment of performance on subsequent retention tests, suggesting that conditioned fear may, in fact, have contributed to Duncan's results. However, foot shock appeared to have no reliable effects on performance when given at longer intervals (60 sec) which still permitted a clear ECS effect. Duncan used this difference in the tem-

poral gradients to argue that the ECS effects must be independent of the fear that might be produced by the shock treatment. This is not, however, a totally convincing argument, particularly in view of the fact that Duncan shocked the *hindfeet* of his rats and thus may have encouraged rather than punished running behavior.

Coons and Miller (1960) replicated Duncan's study and reported essentially comparable findings. They did not, however, agree with Duncan's interpretation of the results and performed additional experiments which seem to support the fear or conflict hypothesis.

In the first experiment Coons and Miller trained rats to run down a straight alley to food reward. After this response was well established, painful grid shock was given at the food cup, followed 20 sec, 1 min, or 60 min later by ECS administered in the home cage. The consolidation hypothesis predicts that the animals receiving the ECS treatment soon after the grid shock experience should persist longest in running to the goal compartment. The results of the experiment supported the fear hypothesis; the animals receiving ECS immediately after the grid shock learned most rapidly to avoid the food cup and to stop running in the alley. Though not statistically reliable, these findings are noteworthy because their direction is clearly opposite that predicted by the consolidation hypothesis.

In a second experiment Coons and Miller trained rats to avoid painful electric shock by running from a light to a dark compartment in a shuttle box apparatus. After the animals had learned this task, the procedure was modified by (1) presenting the shock in the previously safe (dark) compartment and (2) giving ECS in the home cage 20 sec, 1 min, or 60 min after each daily learning trial. According to the consolidation hypothesis, the animals that received the ECS treatment immediately after being shocked in the previously safe compartment should have difficulty in remembering this experience and therefore persist longest in the previously acquired, but now punished, avoidance response. However, animals receiving ECS after only 20 sec adjusted to the change in procedure most rapidly and showed the fewest persisting avoidance responses. This time the results met criteria of statistical significance, and Coons and Miller suggested that fear of the ECS treatment may have intensified or summated with the fear of the grid shock to produce the apparent enhancement of performance.

Several studies of the effects of ECS on per-

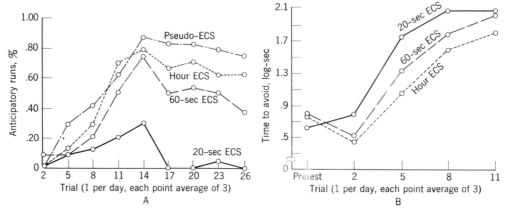

Fig. 14.9 Effects of ECS on performance in a shuttle box apparatus. A, when either amnesia or conflict would hinder learning to make anticipatory runs, learning is poorer the shorter the interval between each training trial and the ECS. B, when the effects of conflict would help and amnesia would hinder learning to stop the avoidance response, learning is better (as indicated by longer avoidance times) the shorter the interval between each training trial and the ECS. (From Coons and Miller, 1960.)

formance in avoidance situations have failed to support this hypothesis. Madsen and McGaugh (1961) used a simple, one-trial learning situation to investigate the effects of ECS on retention performance. Rats were placed on a platform surrounded by a grid floor. Painful foot shock was delivered as soon as the animals stepped off the platform to investigate the apparatus. Half of the subjects were then given ECS 5 sec after the foot shock. The other half served as a control group. According to a fear interpretation, ECS should elicit fear responses that summate with the effects of the grid shock. The ECS group should therefore stay on the safe platform longer than the controls during subsequent retention tests. Madsen and McGaugh's experiments showed that significantly *fewer* animals from the ECS group remained on the platform longer than 15 sec on a retention test given 24 hr after the acquisition trial.

Heriot and Coleman (1962) have reported similar results, using an approach-avoidance situation. Rats trained to lever-press for food received a single painful shock through the manipulandum before receiving ECS 1, 7, 26, 50, or 180 min later. On subsequent retention tests all the ECS-treated animals, except those of the 180-min delay group, returned to the lever without hesitation; this finding suggests that the ECS experience may have interfered with retention rather than increased emotionality or fear.

Hudspeth et al. (1964) have suggested that

ECS may have both amnesic and aversive effects, and that the apparent contradiction between the findings from different laboratories may be related to procedural differences which emphasize one or the other effect. They pointed out that the recent studies which have failed to observe aversive effects of ECS have almost always employed single electroshock treatments. Hudspeth tested this hypothesis in a rather complicated study, using essentially the same apparatus and procedure as Madsen and McGaugh (1961) but recording the effects of repeated ECS treatments on nonshocked as well as shocked animals.

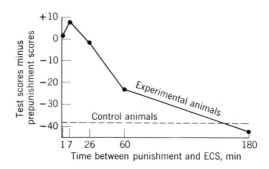

Fig. 14.10 Effect of ECS on retention as a function of the time interval between original learning and ECS. Control data extended from 1 min for ease of comparison. The rise for the 7-min experimental group fails to reach significance at the 0.10 level. (From Heriot and Coleman, 1962.)

In agreement with earlier findings of Madsen and McGaugh, the results of these experiments showed that the animals which received ECS shortly after each daily trial in the avoidance situation learned the avoidance response more slowly than control subjects. This observation supports the hypothesis that the ECS effects may be due to an interference with the consolidation process. However, Hudspeth also found that rats which did not receive any foot shock punishment for leaving the safety platform also seemed to learn the passive avoidance response if given ECS after each daily trial. Control animals that received neither the foot shock nor the ECS treatment did not show this gradually developing preference for the platform, suggesting that the effects observed in the ECS group may be due to an aversive property of the treatment. The investigators suggested that the animals receiving repeated ECS treatment may gradually have learned to associate the aversive effects with the apparatus cues; conditioned seizure activity or conditioned fear or anxiety responses may thus have been elicited by previously neutral stimuli.

McGaugh and Madsen (1964) have recently reported similar results in a T-maze experiment. Rats learned to avoid the arm in the maze in which repeated ECS treatments were administered. However, a single ECS treatment, given immediately after the animals received a painful grid shock in one arm of the maze, seemed to interfere with the recall of the punishment and resulted in a greater percentage of nonavoidance responses.

It is not entirely clear, at present, just what role the possibly aversive properties of ECS play in other experimental situations. Hudspeth's hypothesis is interesting but does not explain the effects of ECS treatments that are given in the home cage.

Closely related to the fear interpretation is the "competing response" hypothesis recently discussed by Adams and Lewis (1962a, b; Lewis and Adams, 1963). They suggested that electrophysiological and behavioral seizure activity or other aversive effects of the ECS treatments may become conditioned to cues that are repeatedly associated with the shock experience. This notion differs from the fear hypothesis in being less specific about what effects of ECS become conditioned to the apparatus cues. It implies only that the ECS may act as a UCS for a variety of behavioral responses which interfere with the response sequence appropriate to the testing situation.

In support of this hypothesis, Adams and Lewis (1962a, b) reported that repeated electroconvulsive shocks given 15 min (note the long intervals) after each learning experience in a shuttle box significantly retarded the acquisition of the avoidance response if and only if the ECS treatments were given in the same apparatus. In this experiment identical shock treatments in the home cage did not interfere with acquisition. The acquisition of the avoidance response was retarded even when the electroconvulsive shocks were given in the shuttle box *before* the first avoidance training trial.

In a subsequent experiment (Lewis and Adams, 1963) the rats received three trials per day in the shuttle box apparatus; these were followed after 5 min by ECS administration (1) in the black "shock" compartment of the shuttle box, (2) in the white "safe" compartment, or (3) on a white workbench not previously associated with the experiment. Four such treatments were followed by fifteen trials with ECS. In agreement with their predictions, Lewis and Adams found that the animals receiving the ECS treatments outside the apparatus performed best and that those shocked in the shock compartment of the shuttle box made the fewest avoidance responses.

These findings are consistent with the conditioning hypothesis, but subsequent investigations have obtained contradictory results which seriously question the generality of this notion. Leonard and Zavala (1964), for instance, could find no support for a competing response interpretation in an active-avoidance experiment. All animals showed marked memory deficits when ECS was given soon after five massed training trials, and there was no difference between animals treated inside or outside the training apparatus.

Quartermain et al. (1965) similarly demonstrated ECS effects which seemed to be entirely independent of the location of the rat at the time of the treatment. Quartermain's results further suggest that the ECS effect is not merely due to a reduction in the time available for learning or rehearsal because of the rapid removal of the subject from the stimulus situation. Animals thrown into a black bag within 2 sec after the training trial did not show any memory deficits, whereas animals given ECS in the apparatus (or in the black bag) after the same delay demonstrated a severe impairment.

Procedural variations may account for some of these inconsistencies, but the very fact that such differences can be obtained suggests that a simple explanation of the ECS effects either in terms of acquired fear or competing responses may not be adequate.

RELATIONSHIP TO CEREBRAL ANOXIA

A very interesting and perhaps theoretically important question can be raised about the physiological processes that are affected by ECS and the various drug treatments that have been used in consolidation studies. We do have electrophysiological evidence of extreme seizure activity during and following electroconvulsive and drug treatments, but it is not clear precisely how these disruptive effects are initiated and maintained. One of the earlier and most persistent explanations of the ECS effects on neural activity has attempted to relate the momentary functional disturbances to anoxia of the central nervous system. If this interpretation were correct, similar if not identical effects on memory would be expected from temporary anoxia and from ECS treatments.

The experimental evidence for this hypothesis is not entirely conclusive. Sola et al. (1948) reported

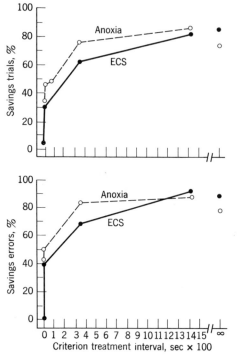

Fig. 14.11 Percentage savings (in trials and errors) as a function of the criterion treatment (anoxia or ECS) interval. (From R. Thompson and Pryer, 1956.)

almost 20 years ago that guinea pigs exposed for 400 hr to environmental conditions designed to simulate those found at an altitude of 23,000 ft did not show any noticeable behavioral effects. However, Jensen et al. (1948), working in the same laboratory, observed significant memory deficits (and some physical brain damage) when animals were exposed for 250 hr to an environmental condition designed to simulate an altitude of 30,000 ft. Hayes (1953) reported that anoxia produced by compression of the animal's chest caused a significant decrement in maze performance which appeared similar to that seen after ECS treatments. These results are difficult to interpret, for both the anoxia and the ECS treatments were given 1 hr after the learning experience, a delay which in most other studies has shown little or no significant effect of ECS.

R. Thompson and Pryer (1956) devised an interesting parametric study of the effects of anoxia given after various time intervals since the last learning trial. Their study suggests that the exposure to environmental conditions simulating 20,000 ft may have effects similar to those seen after ECS. They observed significant retention deficits when the anoxia treatments were given 30 or 120 sec after the completion of the training trial, but not after delays of 15 min, 1 hr, or 4 hr. These temporal relationships were almost identical to those found when ECS treatments were given instead of the anoxia, but the magnitude of the ECS effect was reliably greater at each of the delays.

R. Thompson (1957) has reported another study which compared the effects of two levels of anoxia (20,000- and 30,000-ft simulated altitude) and single or repeated ECS treatments. In this experiment no reliable differences were observed between any of these treatments, but all experimental groups differed significantly from control animals. Thompson concluded that anoxia may produce effects comparable to those seen after ECS treatments and that a single exposure to either treatment seemed sufficient to erase the memory trace.

Unfortunately, it is not entirely clear that these effects are directly related to the activity of central nervous system mechanisms, for Nielson et al. (1963) have shown that a brief arrest of cerebral circulation does not interfere with retention. Up to 6 min of circulatory arrest had no noticeable effect on recall or learning ability in dogs. Longer periods of anoxia (8 min) seemed to interfere with the animals' ability to learn novel problems (and may have produced serious structural damage in the brain) but did not, surprisingly, seem to affect retention of previously acquired habits.

SUMMARY

Most physiological theories of learning and retention have postulated two distinct memory mechanisms: one, based on reversible, functional changes in the central nervous system, to account for short-term memory; the other, based on more permanent anatomical modifications, to account for long-term storage. The assumption is made that all information is initially stored by short-term memory mechanisms and then is gradually transferred to more permanent storage. An alternative view holds that the memory traces gradually "harden" or become "fixed." This purely hypothetical process of fixation or transfer has been called memory consolidation. Several experimental procedures have been devised to interfere selectively with this mechanism and thus permit an investigation of basic memory processes.

Basically, these techniques rely on electrical or pharmacological means to disrupt momentarily the activity of the central nervous system and thereby interfere with functional memory traces. The earlier experiments typically recorded the effects of insulin or Metrazol shock on behavior. It was noted that following such treatments animals showed a marked retention deficit which appeared similar to the amnesic reactions observed in human subjects. The hypothesis was advanced that a selective effect on short-term memory may be responsible for the performance changes observed in experimental and clinical situations. It was soon discovered that patients responded to ECS with a similar amnesic reaction, and most recent experimental studies of the consolidation process have used this technique. Electroconvulsive shock permits more adequate control over important parameters than the drug studies do.

There is little doubt that electroshock or drug treatments can severely impair an animal's performance on retention tests of recently acquired instrumental or emotional responses. But does this tell us anything about consolidation or memory? There is now considerable evidence that the observed performance decrements may be due in part or entirely to the elicitation of fear or related emotional reactions to ECS rather than to a direct interference with memory. More generally, it is not clear that an interpretation of the ECS effect

in terms of "competing response tendencies" can be ruled out.

Even if some or all of the ECS-induced performance decrement is found to be related to changes in associative processes, important questions remain. We know little or nothing about the physiological effects of ECS, Metrazol shock, or insulin shock, and we can only guess about the nature of the resultant disturbance in central nervous functions. It has been suggested that the ECS effect on memory and related disturbances may be caused by cerebral anoxia, but the evidence for this interpretation is contradictory. The complex interaction between ECS and barbiturates indicates that other physiological and chemical events may need to be considered before we can explain the behavioral effects of ECS.

The empirical findings reported during the past two decades are provocative and deserve further attention and study, but they should not be used indiscriminately as evidence for dual memory mechanisms, consolidation processes, or the lability of recent memory.

BIBLIOGRAPHY

Abt, J. P., Essman, W. B., & Jarvik, M. E. Ether-induced retrograde amnesia for one-trial conditioning in mice. *Science*, 1961, **133**, 1477–1478.

Adams, H. E., & Lewis, D. J. Electroconvulsive shock, retrograde amnesia, and competing responses. *J. comp. physiol. Psychol.*, 1962a, **55**, 299–301.

Adams, H. E., & Lewis, D. J. Retrograde amnesia and competing responses. *J. comp. physiol. Psychol.*, 1962b, **55**, 302–305.

Andjus, R. K., Knöpfelmacher, F., Russell, R. W., & Smith, A. U. Some effects of severe hypothermia on learning retention. *Quart. J. exp. Psychol.*, 1956, **8**, 15–23.

Artusio, J. F. Ether analgesia during major surgery. *J. Amer. med. Ass.*, 1955, **157**, 33–36.

Brady, J. V. The effect of electroconvulsive shock on a conditioned emotional response: the permanence of the effect. *J. comp. physiol. Psychol.*, 1951, **44**, 507–511.

Brady, J. V. The effect of electroconvulsive shock on a conditioned emotional response: the significance of the interval between the emotional conditioning and the electroconvulsive shock. *J. comp. physiol. Psychol.*, 1952, **45**, 9–13.

Brady, J. V., Stebbins. W. C., & Galambos, R. The effect of audiogenic convulsions on a conditioned emotional response. *J. comp. physiol. Psychol.*, 1953, **46**, 363–367.

Braun, H. W., Russell, R. W., & Patton, R. A. Duration of decrements in learning and retention following electroshock convulsions in the white rat. *J. comp. physiol. Psychol.,* 1949, **42,** 87–106.

Bureš, J., & Burešova, O. Cortical spreading depression as a memory disturbing factor. *J. comp. physiol. Psychol.,* 1963, **56,** 268–272.

Carson, R. C. The effect of electroconvulsive shock on a learned avoidance response. *J. comp. physiol. Psychol.,* 1957, **50,** 125–129.

Chorover, S. L., & Schiller, P. H. Short-term retrograde amnesia (RA) in rats. *J. comp. physiol. Psychol.,* 1965, **59,** 73–78.

Chorover, S. L., & Schiller, P. H. Reexamination of prolonged retrograde amnesia in one-trial learning. *J. comp. physiol. Psychol.,* 1966, **61,** 34–41.

Chow, K. L. Effect of local electrographic after-discharges on visual learning and retention in monkey. *J. Neurophysiol.,* 1961, **24,** 391–400.

Chow, K. L., & Obrist, W. D. EEG and behavioral changes on application of Al(OH)$_3$ cream on pre-occipital cortex of monkeys. *Arch. Neurol. Psychiat. (Chicago),* 1954, **72,** 80–87.

Coons, E. E., & Miller, N. E. Conflict versus consolidation of memory traces to explain "retrograde amnesia" produced by ECS. *J. comp. physiol. Psychol.,* 1960, **53,** 524–531.

DeCamp, J. E. A study of retroactive inhibition. *Psychol. Monogr.,* 1915, **19,** 84.

Duncan, C. P. The effect of electroshock convulsions on the maze habit in the white rat. *J. exp. Psychol.,* 1945, **35,** 267–278.

Duncan, C. P. Habit reversal induced by electroshock in the rat. *J. comp. physiol. Psychol.,* 1948, **41,** 11–16.

Duncan, C. P. The retroactive effect of electroshock on learning. *J. comp. physiol. Psychol.,* 1949, **42,** 32–44.

Fay, T., & Smith, L. W. Observations on reflex responses during prolonged periods of human refrigeration. *Arch. Neurol. Psychiat. (Chicago),* 1941, **45,** 215–222.

Gallinek, A. Fear and anxiety in the course of electroshock therapy. *Amer. J. Psychiat.,* 1956, **113,** 428–434.

Gellhorn, E. Further investigations on the recovery of inhibited conditioned reactions. *Proc. Soc. exp. Biol. Med.,* 1945, **59,** 155–161.

Gellhorn, E., Kessler, M. M., & Minatoya, H. Influence of metrazol, insulin, hypoglycemia, and electrically induced convulsions on re-establishment of inhibited conditioned reflexes. *Proc. Soc. exp. Biol. Med.,* 1942, **50,** 260–262.

Gerard, R. W. Biological roots of psychiatry. *Science,* 1955, **122,** 225–230.

Hayes, K. J. Cognitive and emotional effects of electroconvulsive shock in rats. *J. comp. physiol. Psychol.,* 1948, **41,** 40–61.

Hayes, K. J. Anoxic and convulsive amnesia in rats. *J. comp. physiol. Psychol.,* 1953, **46,** 216–217.

Henry, C. E., & Pribram, K. H. Effect of aluminum hydroxide cream implantation in cortex of monkey on EEG and behavior performance. *EEG clin. Neurophysiol.,* 1954, **6,** 693–694 (abstract).

Heriot, J. T., & Coleman, P. D. The effect of electroconvulsive shock on retention of a modified "one-trial" conditioned avoidance. *J. comp. physiol. Psychol.,* 1962, **55,** 1082–1084.

Heron, W. T., & Carlson, W. S. The effects of metrazol shock on retention of the maze habit. *J. comp. Psychol.,* 1941, **32,** 307–309.

Horowitz, M. W., & Stone, C. P. The disorganizing effects of electroconvulsive shock on a light discrimination in albino rats. *J. comp. physiol. Psychol.,* 1947, **40,** 15–21.

Hudspeth, W. J., McGaugh, J. L., & Thompson, C. W. Aversive and amnesic effects of electroconvulsive shock. *J. comp. physiol. Psychol.,* 1964, **57,** 61–64.

Hunt, H. F., & Brady, J. V. Some effects of electro-convulsive shock on a conditioned emotional response ("anxiety"). *J. comp. physiol. Psychol.,* 1951, **44,** 88–98.

Hunt, H. F., Jernberg, P., & Brady, J. V. The effect of electro-convulsive shock on a conditioned emotional response: the effect of post-ECS extinction on the reappearance of the response. *J. comp. physiol. Psychol.,* 1952, **45,** 589–599.

Hunt, H. F., Jernberg, P., & Otis, L. S. The effect of carbon disulphide convulsions on a conditioned emotional response. *J. comp. physiol. Psychol.,* 1953a, **46,** 465–469.

Hunt, H. F., Jernberg, P., & Lawlor, W. G. The effect of electroconvulsive shock on a conditioned emotional response: the effect of electroconvulsive shock under ether anesthesia. *J. comp. physiol. Psychol.,* 1953b, **46,** 64–68.

Jensen, A. V., Becker, R. F., & Windle, W. F. Alterations in brain structure and memory after intermittent exposure to 30,000 feet simulated altitude. *Arch. Neurol. Psychiat. (Chicago),* 1948, **60,** 221–239.

Jones, M. R. The effect of hypothermia on retention. *J. comp. physiol. Psychol.,* 1943, **35,** 311–316.

Kamin, L. J. Retention of an incompletely learned avoidance response: some further analysis. *J. comp. physiol. Psychol.,* 1963, **56,** 713–718.

Kessler, M. M., & Gellhorn, E. The effect of electrically and chemically induced convulsions on conditioned reflexes. *Amer. J. Psychiat.,* 1943, **99,** 687–691.

Kraft, M. S., Obrist, W. D., & Pribram, K. H. The effect of irritative lesions of the striate cortex on learning of visual discriminations in monkeys. *J. comp. physiol. Psychol.,* 1960, **53,** 17–22.

Leonard, D. J., & Zavala, A. Electroconvulsive shock, retroactive amnesia, and the single-shock method. *Science,* 1964, **146,** 1073–1074.

Leukel, F. A comparison of the effects of ECS and anesthesia on acquisition of the maze habit. *J. comp. physiol. Psychol.,* 1957, **50,** 300–306.

Lewis, D. J., & Adams, H. E. Retrograde amnesia from

conditioned competing responses. *Science,* 1963, **141**, 516–517.

Loken, R. D. Metrazol and maze behavior. *J. comp. Psychol.,* 1941, **32**, 11–16.

McGaugh, J. L. & Alpern, H. P. Effects of electroshock on memory: amnesia without convulsions. *Science,* 1966, **152**, 665–666.

McGaugh, J. L., & Madsen, M. C. Amnesic and punishing effects of electroconvulsive shock. *Science,* 1964, **144**, 182–183.

McGinnies, E. Changes in the performance of albino rats subjected to electroshock convulsions. *J. comp. physiol. Psychol.,* 1947, **40**, 31–36.

Madsen, M. C., & McGaugh, J. L. The effect of ECS on one-trial avoidance learning. *J. comp. physiol. Psychol.,* 1961, **54**, 522–523.

Masserman, J. H., & Jacques, M. G. The effects of cerebral electroshock on experimental neuroses in cats. *Amer. J. Psychiat.,* 1948, **104**, 92–99.

Morrell, F., Roberts, L., & Jasper, H. H. Effect of focal epileptogenic lesions and their ablation upon conditioned electrical responses of the brain in the monkey. *EEG clin. Neurophysiol.,* 1956, **8**, 217–286.

Mrosovsky, N. Retention and reversal of conditioned avoidance following severe hypothermia. *J. comp. physiol. Psychol.,* 1963, **56**, 811–813.

Müller, G. E., & Pilzecker, A. Experimentelle Beiträge zur Lehre vom Gedächtnis. *Z. Psychol.,* 1900, Suppl. 1.

Nielson, H. C., Zimmerman, J. M., & Colliver, J. C. Effect of complete arrest of cerebral circulation on learning and retention in dogs. *J. comp. physiol. Psychol.,* 1963, **56**, 974–978.

Orkin, L., Bergman, P. S., & Nathanson, M. Effect of atropine, scopolamine, and meperidine on man. *Anesthesiology,* 1956, **17**, 30–37.

Otis, L. S., & Cerf, J. A. The effect of heat narcosis on the retention of a conditioned avoidance response in goldfish. *Amer. Psychologist,* 1958, **13**, 419 (abstract).

Page, J. D. Studies in electrically-induced convulsions in animals. *J. comp. Psychol.,* 1941, **31**, 181–194.

Pearlman, C. H., Sharpless, S. K., & Jarvik, M. E. Retrograde amnesia produced leg anesthetic and convuliant agents. *J. comp. physiol. Psychol.,* 1961, **54**, 109–112.

Porter, P. B., & Stone, C. P. Electroconvulsive shock in rats under ether anesthesia. *J. comp. physiol. Psychol.,* 1947, **40**, 441–456.

Putnam, T. J., & Merritt, H. H. Experimental determination of the anticonvulsant properties of some phenyl derivatives. *Science,* 1937, **85**, 525–526.

Quartermain, D., Paolino, R. M., & Miller, N. E. A brief temporal gradient of retrograde amnesia independent of situational change. *Science,* 1965, **149**, 1116–1118.

Rabe, A., & Gerard, R. W. The influence of drugs on

memory fixation time. *Amer. Psychologist,* 1959, **14**, 423 (abstract).

Ransmeier, R. E. The effects of convulsion, hypoxia, hypothermia and anesthesia on retention in the hamster. Univ. of Chicago, unpublished Ph.D. thesis, 1954.

Ransmeier, R. E., & Gerard, R. W. Effects of temperature, convulsion and metabolic factors on rodent memory and EEG. *Amer. J. Physiol.,* 1954, **179**, 663–664.

Reiff, R., & Scheerer, M. *Memory and hypnotic age regression.* New York: International Universities Press, 1959.

Ries, B. F., & Berman, L. The mechanism of the insulin effect on abnormal behavior. *Amer. J. Psychiat.,* 1944, **100**, 674–680.

Rosvold, H. E. Effects of electro-convulsive shock on gestation and maternal behavior. *J. comp. physiol. Psychol.,* 1949, **42**, 118–136.

Saul, G. D., & Feld, M. The limbic system and EST seizures. In *Recent advances in biological psychiatry. Vol. III.* J. Wortis, Ed. New York: Grune and Stratton, 1961.

Shipley, W. H., & McGregor, J. S. The clinical applications of electrically induced convulsions. *Proc. roy. Soc. Med.,* 1940, **33**, 267–274.

Siegel, P. S. The effect of electroshock convulsions on the acquisition of a simple running response in the rat. *J. comp. Psychol.,* 1943, **36**, 61–65.

Siegel, P. S., McGinnies, E. M., & Box, J. C. The runway performance of rats subjected to electroconvulsive shock following nembutal anesthesia. *J. comp. physiol. Psychol.,* 1949, **42**, 417–421.

Sola, A. E., Becker, R. F., & Windle, W. F. Effects of chronic decompression anoxia on retention in guinea pigs: special considerations at 23,000 feet. *J. comp. physiol. Psychol.,* 1948, **41**, 196–202.

Speidel, C. C. Studies of living nerves. VI: Effects of metrazol on tissues of frog tadpoles with special reference to the injury and recovery of individual nerve fibers. *Proc. Amer. phil. Soc.,* 1940, **83**, 349–378.

Stamm, J. S., & Pribram, K. H. Effects of epileptogenic lesions in frontal cortex on learning and retention in monkeys. *J. Neurophysiol.,* 1960, **23**, 552–563.

Stone, C. P., & Walker, H. H. A note on modification of the effects of electro-convulsive shock on maternal behavior by ether anesthesia. *J. comp. physiol. Psychol.,* 1949, **42**, 429–432.

Sudak, F. N., & Essman, W. B. Memory and problem solving after reanimation from deep hypothermia. *Amer. Zool.,* 1961, **1**, 392 (abstract).

Thompson, C. W., McGaugh, J. C., Smith, C. E., Hudspeth, W. J., & Westbrook, W. H. Strain differences in the retroactive effects of electroconvulsive shock on mass learning. *Canad. J. Psychol.,* 1961, **15**, 67–74.

Thompson, R. The comparative effects of ECS and

anoxia on memory. *J. comp. physiol. Psychol.,* 1957, **50,** 397–400.

Thompson, R., & Dean, W. A further study on the retroactive effect of ECS. *J. comp. physiol. Psychol.,* 1955, **48,** 488–491.

Thompson, R., & Pennington, D. F. Memory decrement produced by ECS as a function of distribution in original learning. *J. comp. physiol. Psychol.,* 1958, **50,** 401–404.

Thompson, R., & Pryer, R. S. The effect of anoxia on the retention of a discrimination habit. *J. comp. physiol. Psychol.,* 1956, **49,** 297–300.

Thompson, R., Haravey, F., Pennington, D. F., Smith,

J., Jr., Gannon, D., & Stockwell, F. An analysis of the differential effects of ECS on memory in young and adult rats. *Canad. J. Psychol.,* 1958, **12,** 83–96.

Woolley, D. E., Rosenzweig, M. R., Krech, D., Bennett, E. L., & Timiras, P. S. Strain and sex differences in threshold and pattern of electroshock convulsion in rats. *Physiologist,* 1960, **3,** 182.

Ziskind, E., Loken, R. D., & Gengerelli, J. A. Effect of metrazol on recent learning. *Proc. Soc. exp. Biol. Med.,* 1941, **43,** 64–65.

Zubin, J., & Barrera, S. E. Effect of convulsive therapy on memory. *Proc. Soc. exp. Biol. Med.,* 1941, **48,** 596–597.

CHAPTER FIFTEEN

Physiological Theories of Learning

We cannot hope to interpret the behavior of even the simplest organism without an understanding of the complex influences that its past history exerts on present response tendencies. Behavior is partly determined by learning, and the physical processes that underlie the functional changes we call learning have presented an important challenge to behavioral scientists. What precisely happens when an organism is in the process of learning? The past 50 years of concentrated research effort have produced much empirical evidence about the *environmental* conditions that promote learning, and rather elegant theories have been developed to describe the interaction between some of the variables that influence the formation of new stimulus-response relationships. However, until recently little has been known about the physical changes that must take place inside the organism when it modifies its response to some stimulus or stimulus compound.

A variety of physiological, anatomical, and biochemical hypotheses have been advanced in recent years to describe the physical events that must occur when we observe learning on the behavioral level. The next two chapters discuss these interpretations and the supporting evidence in some detail. Before we begin, however, we should point out a few problems that are not adequately resolved by any of the theories available at present.

Although individual theories differ about the level at which novel *functional* connections between the pathways of the conditioned and unconditioned stimuli are established, all agree that this interaction is the fundamental event in learning. The theories also differ about the nature of the physical change that eventually causes the presentation of the CS to evoke sufficient activity

in the pathways of the UCS to elicit the behavioral response previously evoked only by the UCS. However, all assume explicitly or implicitly that the *initial* interaction between the central CS and UCS representations occurs as a direct result of temporal contiguity.

This assumption raises all sorts of problems, for the empirical "laws" that have been worked out to describe the temporal relationship between conditioned and unconditioned stimuli do not seem to agree with this basic assumption. Unless we assume radically different transmission properties and latencies in the CS and UCS pathways (an assumption not supported by the fact that stimuli of the same sensory modality may serve as conditioned or unconditioned stimuli), we would predict that perfect temporal contiguity of the CS and UCS should provide the ideal paradigm for learning, and that acquisition should improve when the UCS precedes the CS because the latter is presumably attracted in some fashion by the intense activity in the UCS pathways. The empirical facts could not disagree more thoroughly. Perfect contiguity of the conditioned and unconditioned stimuli produces little or no acquisition, and "backward" conditioning is significantly less effective than the conventional procedure of presenting the CS a fraction of a second or more before the UCS. No adequate explanations have been offered for these temporal relationships, and major modifications in all current theories may be required to accommodate the empirical facts.

Another problem occasioned by these considerations is that all physiological, anatomical, and biochemical approaches attempt to explain the physical basis of the establishment of novel connections (or facilitation of previously nonfunctional connections) by proposing that "use" or activation of a synaptic connection at least temporarily lowers its threshold. Most theories are concerned with the mechanisms by which this facilitation can occur and eventually become permanent. These are perfectly legitimate questions but seem to be related more to the problem of memory or information storage than to the process of learning itself. Memory, presumably, is the relatively permanent end product of the learning process and may, in fact, be constructed of the cumulative effects of repetitive facilitations of particular neural pathways, as is suggested in these theories. Learning, on the other hand, is the process that *initiates* this facilitatory effect, and this aspect of the problem is either totally neglected or glossed over in the available physiological theories of "learning."

One might argue that once a synaptic connection has been used and thereby facilitated, learning has taken place and that subsequent excitations of the same pathway merely serve to consolidate the memory, thus adding some measure of permanence. It is, of course, possible to maintain that this gradual strengthening of the conditioned connection represents a part of the learning process itself; this interpretation permits us to title the present chapter "Physiological Theories of Learning." However, we should remember that the crucial event which affords the development of these memory traces is the *initial* excitation of previously nonfunctional synaptic connections. More attention must be paid to the causation of this initial link in the complex chain of events which take place during the establishment of a memory trace if we are to understand the problem of learning rather than merely the consolidation of learning into permanent storage.

Other conceptual and often purely semantic issues have clouded the important problems in this field. What, for instance, is a memory? Strictly speaking, memory refers to the recall of a single event in time or space and represents a distinct bit of information. When the clinician tests memory in man, he investigates ability to recall; when we study learning and retention in the animal laboratory, we typically ask a very different kind of question—one that may not be directly related to the problem. We are generally concerned with the animal's ability to combine a number of temporally or spatially related memories in a process that is analogous to reasoning in man rather than to simple recall. Reasoning, presumably, cannot take place without recall of essential bits of information, but it would seem to encompass a more complex integration of neural events than simple memory.

A closely related distinction, which we would like to propose for the sake of clarity, relates to the semantic confusion between the terms "learning" and "conditioning." We cannot assume on an a priori basis that the two concepts can be used interchangeably, even though some behavioral evidence suggests, at our present, crude level of understanding, that at least a few of the same laws may apply to them. Conditioning refers to the *involuntary* acquisition of simple response tendencies which may never acquire the status of a conscious memory. The end product of conditioning is similar at least to the simple memory as we have defined it. The concept of learning, on the other hand, should be restricted to the *voluntary* acquisition of relatively complex chains of instrumental responses which lead to reinforcement or reward. Here we clearly are not dealing with a single memory trace but with a complexly interacting set of memories which must be combined in a specific temporal sequence.

Several approaches have been used, singly or in combination, to explain the formation of memory traces. Functional physiological changes or more permanent anatomical alternations have been proposed as the physical basis of memory. Recent extensions of these traditional views have frequently used a combination of factors, attributing learning and short-term memory to reversible and temporary physiological processes and long-term or relatively permanent memory to anatomical, structural alterations.

In the past decade biochemical explanations that attempt to account for both long- and short-term memory on the basis of intracellular biochemical processes have been advanced. These may provide a basis for the functional changes proposed in the physiological theories and are not necessarily incompatible with the anatomical alterations that have been suggested to account for long-term memory. Biochemical theories attempt to deal with the problem of learning at a different level of discourse than the traditional physiological or anatomical theories. We should not, then, try to choose between physiological and anatomical theories on the one hand and biochemical explanations on the other, but rather search for the commonality between the different approaches that may someday permit us to explain psychological events on the basis of physiological and anatomical events which are, in turn, the reflection of known biochemical processes.

A BRIEF HISTORY

Man has always been fascinated by the problem of how the past history of an organism can influence its present behavior, and some of the earliest known writings of Greek philosophers contain speculations about the physical changes that must somehow be responsible for learning, memory, and forgetting. Parmenides (sixth century B.C.) postulated, for example, that stimuli produced particular mixtures of light and dark in the body and that a memory of the stimulus event persisted as long as the mixture obtained. Diogenes (fifth century B.C.) proposed that memory might be related to the distribution of air in the body, and Plato suggested, nearly 2400 years ago, that the mind of man might be analogous to a block of wax on which sensory experiences can be impressed "as from the seal of a ring," and that differences in the ability to remember might be related to differences in the size, hardness, or purity of this wax block. Zeno (340–265 B.C.) continued this line of thought, proposing that the mind starts as a *tabula rasa* on which sensations and experiences engrave memory traces which then determine the behavior of the organism.

The first physiological theory of memory dates back to Aristotle (384–322 B.C.), who suggested that sensory impressions might somehow be transmitted to the heart by movements of the blood. These movements were thought to persist after the environmental stimuli had ceased and were thought to be responsible for memory. Erasistratus (310–250 B.C.) carried out the first dissection of the human brain and concluded that the "animal spirits" or physical mediators of mental processes must be located in the brain. Galen (138–201 A.D.) extended this hypothesis by suggesting that sensations are recorded in the ventricles of the brain. This view remained dogma for nearly 1500 years, and only minor modifications of Galen's memory theory were attempted until Descartes (1596–1650) reassigned the "seat of mental activity" to the pineal gland. Specific movements within this gland were thought to send "animal spirits" through the "pores of the brain" until they came upon the part containing traces of the object to be recalled. Once certain pores had been used, passage of subsequent "spirits" was facilitated so that a memory trace could be more easily located. Thomas Willis (1621–1675) disagreed with Descartes about the location of memory traces, holding that the vital animal spirits are generated in the cerebral (voluntary activities) and cerebellar (involuntary activities) cortices and that the cerebral convolutions are the store of memories.

In the following century David Hartley (1705–1757) presented an interesting extension of Newton's theory of vibrating particles to the physiology of memory. He suggested that vibrations originating in the white medullary substance of the brain constitute the physical basis of memory. According to the theory, sensations modulate the natural vibrations of the medullary particles. On the first presentation of a stimulus, the vibrations return rapidly to their normal rhythm; however, the return to normal activity is more and more retarded if the sensation occurs repeatedly, until the modified vibrations permanently replace the natural rhythm and thereby establish a memory trace. According to this interesting hypothesis, memories differ from normal sensations only in producing a less intense vibration; no separate "memory center" need exist because memory consists of sensations.

The first theory to refer memory to changes in electrical forces and magnetic fields was proposed by Zanotti (1693–1777), although it is not clear from his writings whether the theory merely proposed an analogy to electrical events or actually anticipated the discovery of bioelectrical currents in the nervous system.

The notion that repeated use of a neural pathway could facilitate its subsequent excitation appeared again in the writings of Charles Bonnét (1720–1793), who suggested that nerves "vibrate" more readily when repeatedly activated and that the feeling accompanying this increase in "suppleness" or mobility might constitute memory. The notion of vibration as a physical basis of memory was generally accepted among the scientific and philosophical writers of the eighteenth century (including such well-known scientists as Erasmus Darwin), and only one minor modification of direct interest must be mentioned before we proceed to more modern concepts of learning and retention. Georges Cabanis (1757–1808) essentially agreed with his contemporaries but introduced the important idea that the nervous system might be divided into functional levels; thus, reflex acts might be carried out independently by the spinal cord, "semi-conscious" activities by an intermediary level, and all complicated functions such as "thought, volition and memory," by higher centers in the cerebrum.

Very specific localizations of various memory functions were attempted early in the nineteenth century by such phrenologists as Gall (1758–1828) and Spurzheim (1776–1832) (see Gall and Spurzheim, 1810–1819), but their views never gained wide acceptance in the scientific community. Flourens (1794–1867) carried out a number of animal experiments to disprove the precise localizations suggested by the phrenologists and showed in a series of studies remarkably similar to the later work of Lashley (1950) that the cerebrum appeared to be "equipotential" with respect to learning and retention. He concluded that the cerebrum functions as a whole and that it is incorrect to assign memory to any specific portion of it.

Perhaps the first anatomical theory of learning was proposed by Alexander Bain (1818–1903) in a provocative volume published in 1855. Bain suggested that "for every act of memory, every exercise of bodily aptitude, every habit, recollection, train of ideas, there is a specific grouping or co-ordination of sensations and movements by virtue of specific growths in the cell-junctions" (p. 91). He believed that the "renewed feelings" or memories must occupy the same parts of the brain as the original sensations, and that memory, therefore, did not have a separate location in the central nervous system but merely represented a persisting activity in the sensory-motor pathways.

An entirely novel concept of "organismic" memory was introduced by Jessen (1793–1875) in a little-noticed publication of 1855. The theory was popularized and extended by Ewald Hering (1834–1918) in a famous report to the Viennese Academy of Sciences (1870). According to this view, memory is characteristic of all "organized matter" rather than being confined to certain portions of the nervous system. Heredity is itself merely memory that is passed on via the germ cell, and the total memory of an organism includes inherited as well as acquired habits. Hering suggested that memory is a largely "unconscious" process of all matter which can exist in muscles (which he thought to be specifically strengthened by use) as well as brain tissue. We are only aware of the memory functions of the brain because the recall of sensory impressions requires "consciousness," whereas motor memories can be recalled without reaching conscious awareness. Hering's theory of organic memory was accepted by such influential physiologists as Samuel Butler (1835–1902) and T. A. Ribot (1839–1916), al-

though Ribot suggested that rearrangements in the molecular structure of the cell rather than Hering's vibrations might be the memory trace. Ribot's theory is provocative in view of recent interest in biochemical theories. He suggested, more specifically, that the passage of nervous currents rearranged the molecular structure of the cell and that a repetition of the same neural current somehow prevented the molecule from returning to its original state, thereby setting up a permanent memory trace.

The idea that learning and memory may be a general property of all cells is reflected in a number of theories which proposed that the memory trace might be stored in any portion of the nervous system. Broca (1824–1880), for instance, suggested that specific types of memory might be stored in particular portions of the cerebrum, and Hitzig (1838–1907) extended this idea by proposing that "the store of ideas is to be sought in all parts of the cortex, or rather, all parts of the brain." Adolf Horwicz (1831–1894) went still further in advancing the notion that memory was a function of all parts of the nervous system (although he also held the peculiar view that a concentration of memory traces could be found in the "great commissures of the brain"). Adolf Kussmaul (1822–1902) concurred with this, for he believed that the numerous interconnections in the nervous system precluded the possibility that any area of the brain could be active independently of other parts of the central nervous system. He specifically rejected the notion that there might be a "special storehouse in the brain where images and ideas lie together, arranged in separate compartments."

With the development of experimental surgical techniques, investigators concentrated their research efforts on easily accessible cortical regions. This research led to the conclusion that memory functions are diffusely represented in all portions of the brain or at least all portions of the cortex, so that the degree of impairment is directly proportional to the percentage of brain tissue damaged. This theory of "equipotentiality," which influenced the later writing of Karl Lashley (1950), was clearly stated by Goltz (1834–1902), Ferrier (1834–1928), and many others of that period.

Still another concept, that of the interaction between two simultaneously active neural centers, was proposed before Waldeyer's neuron theory established that the nervous system is not composed of a continuous gelatinous mass. William

James (1842–1910), for example, explained learning in a fashion very much like Pavlov's interpretation which still dominates the thinking of most Russian writers. James proposed that the concurrent activity of two neural centers might cause the formation of a pathway between them because they tend to "drain" into each other. Once such a pathway is formed, excitation of one of the centers automatically elicits excitation in the other. The temporal CS-UCS relationship is explained, according to James, by the assumption that when one area is excited immediately after another, the energy flow from the first to the second is greater than vice versa.

Undoubtedly the most revolutionary influence on theories of learning and retention was Waldeyer's (1836–1912) histological demonstration that nerve cells are not anatomically connected. He hypothesized "junction points" (subsequently called *synapses*, plural of *synapsis*, by Sir Charles Sherrington) which conduct nerve impulses from one neuron to the next, and this notion profoundly influenced all subsequent theories of learning. The problem became one of explaining the mechanisms by which the synaptic "resistance" (not necessarily used in its strict electrical sense) between specific cells or neural centers could be lowered by use or simultaneous excitation. Three major classes of explanatory concepts have been offered in the past 60 years: (1) theories that rely partly or exclusively on a facilitation of synaptic transmission by electrophysiological events; (2) theories that propose a lowering of synaptic resistance as a result of permanent anatomical changes; and (3) theories that hold intracellular biochemical changes responsible for preferential synaptic transmission of particular stimulus patterns. Although several theorists have crossed these arbitrary lines to suggest theories of memory that make use of physiological as well as anatomical changes, we shall treat these three groups of notions separately in an attempt to keep the central issues clear.

BASIC ANATOMICAL AND PHYSIOLOGICAL PROCESSES

Theories postulating specific anatomical changes to account for lowered synaptic resistance between the pathways of the CS and UCS can take a variety of forms, as we shall see in later sections of our discussion. However, all theories are subject to the paradoxical requirement that the central nervous system of the adult organism must simultaneously be (1) capable of continuous, structural change or growth to permit the establishment of novel connections and (2) sufficiently static or constant to account for the persistence of memories over the lifetime of the organism. (See Gerard, 1953, for a more extensive treatment of this issue.)

The second requirement presents few problems since we have ample evidence that the CNS of most species is, in fact, static after maturation, at least with respect to its gross morphology. This constancy accounts nicely for the permanence of memory but makes it difficult to explain learning and the establishment of memory traces. To circumvent this annoying problem, most anatomical theories of learning or retention have attempted to demonstrate that the CNS is not totally static after maturation. Direct evidence for this proposition is not plentiful. The principal support for anatomical theories of learning derives from perhaps unwarranted extrapolations of data from experiments on embryonic development (neurogenesis) and regeneration of peripheral neural tissue (neurohistopathology).

It is quite clear that neuronal growth occurs in the central and peripheral nervous systems of the developing organism and that the potential for growth of peripheral nerves and their processes remains in the mature animal. However, there is little direct evidence for continuing development or regeneration in the CNS of the mature organism (Ramón y Cajal, 1928; Ranson and Clark, 1959), and this has been the major problem of all anatomical theories of learning. Since this issue is so central to our topic, we shall briefly review (1) nerve growth in the embryological state; (2) regeneration of neural tissue in the peripheral and central portions of the nervous system; and (3) evidence for continuous neural growth or movement in the mature CNS.

Neuronal Growth in the Embryonic State

Developing neurons establish axonal processes bearing amoeboid tips which project pseudopodia into the interstitial spaces of the tissue through which the fiber is growing. There is considerable disagreement about the influences that determine the direction of growth. Hereditary factors are believed to play a role because the nervous system shows few intraspecies differences, but specific evidence for such an inherited guidance mechanism is totally lacking. The exact course of individual fibers appears to be partly determined by the terrain through which they are growing, but this factor is not a major determinant of the overall direction of axonal growth. Developing axons exhibit stereotropic properties (i.e., the direction of growth is partly determined by the presence of solid objects such as blood vessels, nerve bundles, or connective tissue), and it is thought that this property may account for the formation of distinct nerve bundles. Additional mechanisms must be operating to direct neuronal growth to specific organs and structures. The same factors presumably operate to determine the connection of regenerating axons in the peripheral nervous system. We shall discuss this material in the framework of regeneration studies which have provided most of the experimental evidence for these mechanisms.

Regeneration of Peripheral Nerves

Neural tissue, at least in the peripheral nervous system, maintains some capability to regenerate following injury. If the axon of a peripheral motor neuron is severed relatively close to its termination, degenerative processes occur in the cell body, followed by a regrowth of the distal portion of the axon and its terminations. Regeneration does not occur under all conditions; e.g., the cell may degenerate and die if the cut is too close to the cell body.

The mechanisms that stimulate and maintain neural growth after injury have been subject to much debate. One school of thought holds that neurons constantly assimilate protoplasmic material which they incorporate into the architectural plan of the cell and its processes, producing a continuous tendency to grow. Although the evidence for such a growth potential is spotty, many of the current anatomical theories of learning are based on the assumption of continuous growth independent of external influences, and we shall present some of the arguments and evidence for this notion.

Other investigators (see Ramón y Cajal, 1928 for a summary of the early literature) have suggested that such environmental influences as bioelectrical attractions (Kappers, 1917, 1919, 1929, 1932; Child, 1921, 1924) chemical reactions (Ramón y Cajal, 1899, 1905, 1911, 1928; Sperry, 1951, 1958), metabolic gradients (Child, 1924), and stereotropic factors (Harrison, 1910, 1914; Haidenhain, 1911) may determine not only neuronal growth itself but also the direction and pattern of development. Most anatomical theories of learning and retention represent a direct extension of the notion that neuronal growth may be

stimulated and directed by external influences which are the result of activity in other neural pathways or centers.

Before we discuss these theories, it might be profitable to examine the experimental and theoretical literature that is more directly concerned with the proposed mechanisms for growth in the mature organism. Three types of explanations have been offered: (1) neurogenetic theories propose that the direction of growth may be determined by pre-established pathways; (2) mechanical theories assume that the direction of growth follows essentially a random pattern which is determined by paths of least resistance; and (3) neurotropic theories propose that neural growth may be stimulated and directed by chemical, metabolic, or electrical gradients.

Neurogenetic theories. One of the earliest and most influential hypotheses in this area was proposed by His (1889) nearly 80 years ago. He suggested that in the developing embryo the growth and orientation of axonal processes (and hence the development of the central and peripheral nervous systems) are governed by two related principles: (1) that growth is the result of the continuous "impulsion" of protoplasm, and (2) that the direction of growth is determined by pre-existing pathways in the mesoderm.

Held (1905) extended these principles to regeneration in the mature organism on the basis of experimental observation of the regeneration of crushed peripheral nerves. He found that regenerating nerve fibers tended to enter the neurilemmal sheath of the degenerated axon, thereby re-establishing connections with the originally innervated organ. This observation led to the hypothesis that the direction of growth in the embryo as well as in the mature organism may be determined by a system of "conducting" cells through which the neurofibrils grow "with no possible deviation."

A related theory has been advanced by Dustin (1910), who suggested that the course of neuronal growth, at least in regeneration, may be determined by the location of connective scar tissue. Growth, according to this theory, is the direct result of "axonal turgescence" and does not depend on external stimulation.

The neurogenetic theories have not received general acceptance, largely because they fail to explain why the embryonic tissues should arrange themselves in such a fashion as to provide the most convenient pathways for the developing neurofibrils and for the reconnection of regenerating neurons in the mature organism. They have been discussed briefly because the concept of *predetermined* pathways for neural growth has been used to critize anatomical theories of learning. Flexibility is an unconditioned requirement of anatomical theories. It is interesting to note that all early theories agree in postulating a continuous growth potential which is somehow inherent to the neuron and develops in the absence of external stimulation.

Mechanical theories of neuronal growth. The mechanical theories of Harrison (1910) and Haidenhain (1911) represent important modifications of the neurogenetic hypothesis of His, Held, and Dustin. The somewhat teleological argument that the direction of growth is determined by pre-existing pathways gives way to the hypothesis that stereotropic forces which were thought to operate in an essentially random fashion determine the geography of the nervous system. The amoeboid tip of growing neurons was believed to develop "exploratory" processes which guide neuronal growth along a path of least resistance. Order is introduced into this chaotic system by the suggestion that the initial direction of growth may be determined by the orientation of neuroblasts and by an innate tendency to reach specific peripheral organs by the shortest possible route.

The modern reader may frown at the teleological implications of the latter postulates, but the approach led to the introduction of the concept of stereotropism into neurology. The notion of guidance of neuronal growth by random mechanical factors has recurred in many later theories in spite of the fact that fairly good negative evidence had been published even before Harris and Haidenhain proposed stereotropic influences. Frossman (1898), for instance, reported that the introduction of resinous materials had little or no effect on neuronal development in the embryo and that many neurons choose paths *through* the foreign matter rather than readily available paths of less resistance around it. Ramón y Cajal (1928) has indicated that the scar tissue, which appears to attract regenerating neurons, is more densely populated by connective cells than normal tissue and should therefore offer more rather than less resistance to the developing neuron. Mechanical factors may, at least under some circumstances, contribute to the direction of neuronal growth in the embryo as well as in the mature organism. However, it is generally accepted today that other

mechanisms must operate to explain the specificity and lack of intraspecies differences of neural patterns.

Neurotropic theories. *Chemotropism.* One of the earliest and most influential theories of neuronal growth to posit an active influence of environmental factors was advanced by Ramón y Cajal in 1898 (see also Ramón y Cajal , 1911, 1928, for modifications of this hypothesis). Cajal agreed with the then generally accepted concepts of continuous protoplasmic growth, development of exploratory processes on the tip of the growing neuron, and growth along paths of least resistance (stereotropism), but he argued that these principles did not suffice to explain the specificity of neural connections. He proposed that the amoeboid qualities of the developing axon are caused by the attracting or neurotropic properties of chemical substances which may be secreted by cells in the environment of the growing neuron. He postulated that these chemical substances may exert an attractive force on specific neurons,

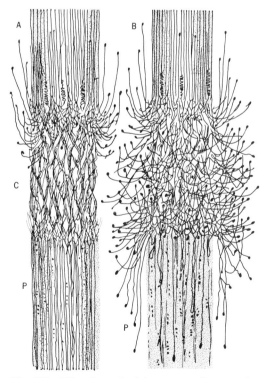

Fig. 15.1 What the path of the sprouts of regenerating axons would be if only mechanical factors were involved. B, central stump; C, area of transection; P, peripheral stump; A, the actual disposition. (From Ramón y Cajal, 1928.)

thereby determining the final orientation and direction of growth.

Some early support for the suggested chemotropism was reported by Frossman (1898), who found that point-to-point regeneration occurred even when pieces of collodion were inserted into the path of the regenerating axons. He further observed that regenerative growth occurred in the direction of isolated brain tissue but not in the direction of parenchymas from the liver and spleen. In accordance with an earlier suggestion by Cajal, Frossman concluded that the direction of neural regeneration was determined by soluble substances, produced by the degeneration of myelin sheaths, which exert a neurotropic effect on specific neural tissues.

Ramón y Cajal (1928) replicated these experiments and noted that neural tissue appears to lose its attractive properties when treated in such a way that all Schwann cells are destroyed. Regeneration was successful when even a few of these cells were left intact. A concentration of regenerating neurons in the immediate vicinity of the remaining Schwann cells was observed. Other research on this problem (Ramón y Cajal, 1905–1906; Merzbacher, 1905) convinced Cajal that specific attracting or chemotropic substances must be secreted both by the organ to be innervated and by the distal stump of the severed axon, and that the final direction and destination of neural growth are determined by these chemotropic influences.

According to Cajal, the primary secreting agents are the Schwann cells of the distal nerve stump; such cells were thought to secrete a catalytic agent which stimulates a receiving system in the developing axon. This stimulation was believed to lead to the assimilation of protoplasmic material by "neurobiones" which have the capacity to "reproduce by equal division and to form linear chains and colonies" and "migrate by changing neurofibrils." The theory suggests that two distinct chemical forces may be acting: (1) a general excitatory force promotes growth in the direction of the organ to be innervated, and (2) a more selective stimulant attracts specifically those fibers that are to have a particular relationship to the secreting region.

Cajal's theory of chemotropism has recently received renewed interest and support. Speidel (1936, 1940, 1942) observed, for example, that neuronal growth in nerve explants from living tadpoles appeared to be affected by a variety of chemical substances such as alcohol, Metrazol,

and Chloretone. Geiger (1958, 1959) reported that lysergic acid diethylamide (LSD-25) inhibited the growth of brain tissue *in vitro*. Very small doses of serotonin appeared to have a facilitatory effect. Perhaps more directly relevant to Cajal's theory are observations of the amphibian motor system reported by Weiss (1929, 1936), Sperry (1947, 1950, 1955, 1958), and Sperry and Deupree (1956).

The initial studies by Weiss showed that disturbances of the nerve-muscle connections in the limbs of larval amphibians failed to produce the expected functional disorders, even when the experimental paradigm precluded relearning or reflex adjustment. Sperry and his collaborators (Sperry, 1947, 1950; Sperry and Deupree, 1956) replicated these observations and suggested that an alteration of the peripheral connections of a motor neuron might somehow lead to a compensatory switch in its synaptic relations with motor centers (Sperry, 1955).

Sperry (1958) has expanded this hypothesis by suggesting that the apparent influence of muscle fibers on specific motor neurons may be due to a selective tolerance for specific types of neuronal end feet. The theory proposes that neurons and their target organs undergo chemical differentiation during embryological development and that each neuron or neuron system achieves a specific chemical affinity to guide its development. Selective interconnections between systems of neurons are explained on the basis of the same system of chemical affinities. Sperry further suggested that evolutionary selection may be the cause of the development and perpetuation of common chemical affinities within a species. Direct supporting evidence for this proposal is largely lacking at present, but Sperry thinks that chemical differentiation, although at a cruder level than that suggested for the patterning of synaptic relationships, may be indicated by the selectivity of staining reactions in the central nervous system, the selectivity of drug effects and toxicity reactions, and the preferential effects of bacterial and viral infections.

Bioelectrical influences. It has always been tempting to ascribe the direction of neuronal growth and development to external influences which arise as the result of cellular activity either in neighboring neurons or in the organ to be innervated. As soon as the electrical events that characterize neuronal activity began to be appreciated, a number of theories were advanced; these subordinated the direction of neural growth to

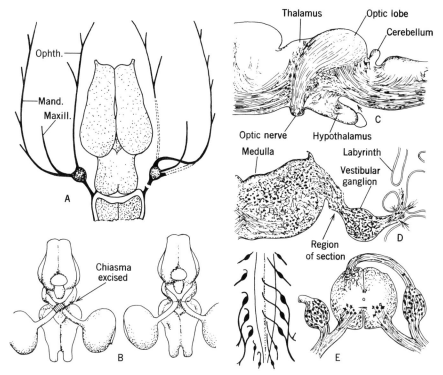

Fig. 15.2   Regeneration of central synaptic connections is found to effect an orderly re-establishment of reflex functions in most nonmammalian species. A, regeneration of divided trigeminal nerve root, with peripheral cross union of ophthalamic and mandibular nerves; B, regeneration of divided optic nerves into the wrong side of the brain; C, regeneration of sectioned mesencephalic fiber tracts with eyes rotated 180°; D, regeneration of divided vestibular nerve root with the optic nerve resected; E, regeneration of crossed sensory roots of the hindlimb. (From Sperry, 1958b. Reproduced with permission of the copyright owners, the Regents of the University of Wisconsin.)

magnetic fields believed to be generated by intense neural activity. Although the earlier theories of embryological development have not survived the gradual accumulation of negative evidence, some of the basic concepts continue to be used in modern anatomical theories of learning, as we shall see in a later section of this discussion. Diverting attention from this aspect of the problem for a moment, it is instructive that one of the earliest theories to explain the specificity of embryological development on the basis of electrical attracting forces (Kappers, 1917) suggested that the basic process might "offer an analogy to the law of association in psychology."

Bok (1915a, b, 1917) first suggested that neuronal activity might itself be the stimulus for growth in neighboring areas. He proposed that the growth of a myelinated nerve fiber might stimulate adjacent cells in a process called "stimu-logenous fibrillation" to send out axons or axon sprouts perpendicular to the stimulating fiber.

Kappers (1917, 1919, 1920, 1929, 1932, 1933) formulated a theory of "neurobiotaxis" which profoundly influenced subsequent anatomical theories of learning. He proposed that the anatomical relationship between neurons is determined by electrical currents emanating from active neural elements. According to this theory, neurons are electrically polarized and generate magnetic fields which influence the direction of growth of axonal as well as dendritic processes and induce the migration of nerve cells in the direction of the electrical force. Activity in a neural center, Kappers maintained, generates a state of electrical negativity which attracts processes of other neurons. More specifically, positive charges are produced inside the neuron or neuron pool as a consequence of activity; the activity sets up a strong compensatory field of negativity on the outside of the cell or the center. Neurons in the vicinity of such a region are then believed to extend dendritic processes toward the negative field or even to shift totally toward the active center. (The concept of neuronal movement was first suggested by Ramón y Cajal in 1899 and remained influential during the early decades of this century. A summary of the experimental evidence for neuronal movement was published by Hamburger and Levi-Montalcini in 1950.)

Kappers' original theory implied a random process of attraction whereby frequently active centers or fibers attract neural processes from other parts of the nervous system. To circumvent the problem of specificity, Kappers appended the proviso that the bioelectric gradients could be effective only with respect to "functionally related

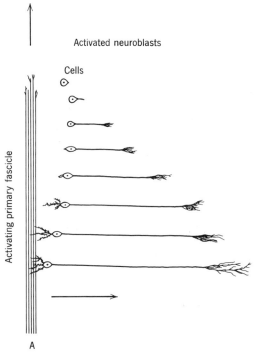

Fig. 15.3 Schematic conceptualization of "neurobiotaxic" influences as illustrated by the activation of adjacent neuroblasts by an unmyelinated (growing) fascicle. The vertical arrow indicates the direction of growth of the activating bundle and the direction of its nerve current, which starts at A. The horizontal arrow indicates the course of the irradiating influence (current) perpendicularly to the activating bundle. Notice that the proximal cells are sooner activated (and have moved further) than the more distant ones. (From C. U. A. Kappers, *J. comp. Neurol,* 1917, **27**, 268, Figure 4.)

neurons." He unfortunately did not indicate how this selectivity could be achieved, although one could assume that concurrent activity leading to common connections is typically a sign of functional relationship. Kappers also proposed that temporary anatomical connections similar to those ostensibly established during conditioning might be formed because neurobiotaxic attractions exist betweeen two concurrently active neural centers. This mechanism might apply to the "near-simultaneity" of excitation which exists in the pathways of the CS and UCS and has served as a model for subsequent theories of learning.

Kappers' theory was based primarily on experimental observations indicating that the movement or growth of living tissue could be affected by strong external currents. One of the first demonstrations of the phenomenon was reported by Müller-Hettlingen (1883); he observed that if the sprouting seed of a bean was exposed to constant current, the tips of the roots turned up and grew toward the negative pole of the stimulus source. Bancroft (1904) reported that the tentacles and manubria of a medusa oriented toward the cathode during exposure to a constant current, and Verworn (1889) found that one-celled organisms develop processes and eventually may shift toward the cathodal pole of strong direct-current flow.

More recent investigations have generally failed to support Kappers' theory. Marsh and Beams (1946) have presented photomicrographic evidence which suggests that a direct current of sufficient density may affect fiber growth in an explant of nerve cells from the medulla; however, only inhibitory effects were observed, and these do not fit Kappers' theory. Anodal stimulation suppressed fiber growth, but no compensatory facilitation was observed at the cathode. No evidence indicating that the direction of fiber growth proceeded along the lines of force between the two poles, as Kappers' theory suggests, was obtained.

Other investigations have been even less gracious to the theory of neurobiotaxis. Goodman (1932) obtained evidence suggesting that stimulation (and hence cellular activity) is not an essential condition for the development of appropriate retinocortical projections, and Speidel (1933) found electrical stimulation to have no effect on cone growth. Speidel also noted that fibers of common origin may grow in opposite directions, a finding that contradicts Kappers' theory, even if the nebulous "functional specificity" clause is accepted.

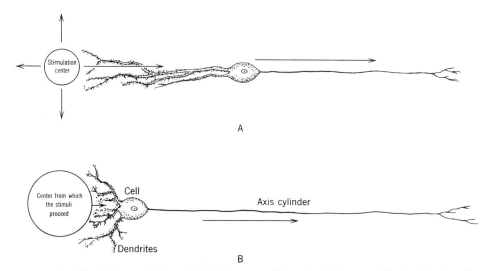

A

B

Fig. 15.4   The influence of "neurobiotaxic" currents. The axis cylinder runs with the dierction of the nervous current, whereas the dendritic outgrowth and the final shifting of the cell body occur against the nervous current. A, giant dendrites have grown out toward the center of stimulation. B, the cell body (perikaryon) has shifted toward the center of stimulation; the axis cylinder is consequently elongated. (From C. U. A. Kappers, *J. comp. Neurol*, 1917, **27**, 266, Figure 3.)

This brief summary of evidence and theory related to peripheral nerve growth in embryo and mature organism has been presented because such material is used extensively and often inappropriately as support for many of the more recent anatomical theories of learning. The next section deals with the modicum of evidence that *is* relevant to central neural regeneration and movement.

Regeneration in the Central Nervous System

Standard neuroanatomy text books (i.e., Ranson and Clark, 1959) generally conclude that regeneration beyond some rather rudimentary developments does not occur in the central nervous system. If proved, this conclusion would meet head-on the neuroanatomical theories of learning that depend, in some fashion, on the actual formation of new or larger synaptic connections as a result of use or activation. However, circumstantial evidence indicates a limited amount of regeneration and, by analogy, growth of the intact neuron. Rather than review the vast literature which shows that little or no growth occurs in the mature brain, we shall concentrate in this section on the few bits of evidence that permit the theorists to continue using the concept of anatomical growth.

Bielschowsky (1905, 1911) observed that fibers of apparently neural origin invaded the area of lesion in the cerebral cortex and spinal cord, and

he suggested that these fibers might be recently developed processes of regenerating neurons. This interpretation was questioned by Herxheimer and Gierlich (1907); they thought Bielschowsky's observations were perhaps attributable to staining artifacts or to fibers which failed to degenerate as a result of the lesioning procedure. Ramón y Cajal (1928) had observed that the axons of posterior root fibers and cells within the spinal cord do show a degree of regeneration, although the extent of neuronal growth is generally insufficient to produce even partial restoration of function. Cajal believed that the incompleteness of central regeneration might be due to a lack of essential hemotropic substances which, according to his theory, are secreted by the Schwann cells of the peripheral myelin sheath. He cites for support Tello (1911), who reported that vigorous regenerative growth could be induced in the central nervous system by the placement of Schwann cells into the vicinity of the lesion.

Windle (1955) reported some regeneration in the spinal cord of young animals, and Liu and Chambers (1955) suggested that vigorous regeneration of dorsal root fibers can be observed if the regenerating fibers are isolated from neighboring neural tissue. By far the most convincing evidence for central regeneration has been obtained in lower vertebrates such as fishes and amphibia. Piatt (1955), for instance, reported regeneration in the completely severed spinal cord of fishes and amphibia, and Sperry and his colleagues (Sperry, 1941, 1947, 1948, 1950, 1951a, b, 1955, 1958a, b; Sperry and Deupree, 1956) have observed extensive regeneration in a variety of lower vertebrates. Optic, vestibular, trigeminal, and spinal sensory nerves, as well as tectospinal and other central pathways, apparently regenerate in these species to the point that little or no loss of function is detectable.

A group of studies by Rose et al. (1959) and Malis et al. (1960) suggests that regeneration may be quite extensive, even in the brain of higher vertebrates. Rose and his collaborators used irradiation techniques to produce highly selective cortical lesions which apparently completely destroy neural tissue in specific laminae of the cortex. They reported that examination of the irradiated lamina shortly after the lesion showed the target area to be completely devoid of any neural cell bodies or processes. However, extensive fiber growth of presumably neural origin was observed when the sections were taken seven weeks after the irradiation. On the basis of the peculiar pattern formed by these regenerating neural processes, Rose concluded that they must be newly developed fibers which invade the lesioned area from neighboring tissue rather than neurons which recovered from the effects of irradiation.

The potential theoretical implications of these observations are so important that we must be doubly careful in searching for a possible source of artifact in Rose's procedures before accepting the generality of his results. It should be recalled that earlier workers had not been able to observe significant central regeneration except under what Cajal called "quite unusual pathological conditions." Since irradiation is known to stimulate genetic mutations and abnormal tissue growth, it is possible that the conditions of Rose's experiments were, in fact, "unusual and pathological." Rose himself recognizes these problems, but favors an alternative interpretation of his results —that cortical neurons do possess a capacity for continuous growth under normal conditions and that his procedure served to "expose the normal growing process by providing a clear stage, so to speak, for the growth to be observed." He speculates that all synaptic terminals may be only temporary structures which are continually being depleted and reconstituted as needed. Such a system would provide the plasticity demanded by anatomical theories of learning, but fails to suggest a mechanism for the well-known permanence of memory.

Central regeneration and growth appear to be possible, although the likelihood seems to decrease as one ascends the phylogenetic scale. It can be argued that most anatomical theories of learning do not require growth over an appreciable distance and that even the evidence for limited regeneration and growth in the higher vertebrates may be sufficient to provide a possible basis for memory. A perhaps more serious shortcoming of the evidence we have just discussed is that none of it may apply to the intact animal. Even if regeneration occurs in the central nervous system, this does not constitute proof that neuronal growth can and does occur in the absence of neural damage. This, however, is precisely the requirement of a learning theory, and we must be careful to remember this distinction.

Growth or Movement in the Normal, Mature Nervous System

Until quite recently there was little or no evidence in direct support of the notion that neural tissue may be in a state of continuous change or development in the central nervous system. However, the concept has been kept alive by an idea first proposed by Coghill in 1919 as part of a more ambitious theory of reflex development. Because Coghill's proposal has been the cornerstone of many subsequent theories of learning, we shall present this theory in some detail before discussing the recent evidence which can be interpreted to support it.

The heart of Coghill's theory is the proposition that the development of neural tissue slows but does not stop at maturity. Accordingly, neuronal growth continues throughout the life-span of the organism and produces an excess of potential synaptic connections which is the essential factor in the plasticity or adaptiveness of behavior. The organism's capacity for learning, according to this theory, is limited only to the extent of this neural "overgrowth." Lower species have little provision for the continuing development of new synaptic connections and are therefore unable to profit extensively from experience, whereas the brain of man and other higher mammals is characterized by such extensive overgrowth that a "limitless" number of potential connections is available.

The experience of the organism (i.e., specific environmental stimuli) does not determine the amount or direction of neuronal growth but turns potential synaptic connections into functional pathways in a process called "consolidation." The pattern of stimulation imparts a specificity or selective sensitivity to the growing dendritic extensions of those cells so that the synaptic connections formed during the stimulation have a permanently lowered threshold for that particular pattern of excitation. Since neuronal growth is a continuous process, a single neuron can, in this fashion, acquire a selective sensitivity to a large number and variety of stimuli; this, presumably, is the basis of learning and retention. Coghill suggested that "conditioning processes are registered in structural counterparts in the sense that neural mechanisms acquire functional specificity with reference to experience, of the mode of excitation." According to this theory, learning is no more than the development of specific sensitivity to a pattern of stimulation which was present when a synaptic connection was formed due to continuous and entirely independent growth tendencies.

Coghill's interesting views have influenced many more recent theoretical formulations. Particularly important is the concept of growth as an independent, innate, and essentially random process which determines the number and type of *potential* synaptic connections that are available for conditioning but does not, itself, represent acquisition or memory. This concept contrasts quite sharply with the theories of Kappers and Cajal suggesting that neural growth and its direction are determined by external attractive forces which are themselves the result of stimulation.

Learning, according to Coghill, is the result of external stimulation; it requires a constantly developing nervous system, but only because the process of growth permits the functional coding of distinct synaptic junctions whereby the threshold of excitation is preferentially lowered for particular patterns of stimulation. The postulation of extensive neuronal overgrowth of potential synaptic junctions has been used widely to explain how a few pairings of conditioned and unconditioned stimuli can possibly result in the establishment of novel functional connections between distant regions of the brain.

The concept of continuous growth, useful as it may be in other respects, has raised important questions about the perseverance of learned connections. Are we to assume that potential synaptic junctions, once they are used, persist indefinitely in spite of this innate tendency for continuous growth? It would seem that Coghill's theory should predict rapid forgetting, and this, of course, does not agree with the literature on memory. Other problems cannot readily be explained

by Coghill's concept of learning (such as the demonstrable resistance of memory to damage in the central nervous system), but his ideas have stimulated much experimentation and thought and must be considered among the cornerstones of modern theories of learning.

At the time of Coghill's writings and for a considerable time thereafter, continuous neural growth in the central nervous system was little more than an elegant speculation. Some evidence has accumulated recently, however, which lends empirical support at least to the notion of limited growth. Dynamic properties are suggested by the recent observation of Schadé and his collaborators (Schadé, 1959a, b; Schadé and Baxter, 1960) that the number of basal and apical dendrites in the rabbit cortex increases significantly during the first year of life. Schadé reported that the surface area of cell bodies per unit cortex decreased during the first 5 days of life and that the surface area of apical and basal dendrites showed a marked tendency to increase after the first 5 days. This increase appeared to be particularly marked during the second and third postnatal week and continued, though at a decelerating rate, until age 300 days. In a discussion of these findings, Schadé (1963) suggested that growth of dendritic processes may continue in man until about age 40. This notion of a continuously developing nervous system agrees well with Rose's interpretation of his regeneration studies, and one might hope for further histological evidence in this promising area of investigation.

Continuous neuronal growth in the mature organism has been postulated by another group of investigators who observed that axoplasmic materials appear to be continuously transported from the soma of the neuron to their active axonal extensions. Young (1945) observed a swelling immediately behind a temporary constriction of nerve fibers, and Hydén (1947) noted a movement of nucleoproteins from the soma to all cellular processes under conditions of continuous cellular activity. Gerard (1950) reported that cytoplasmic material can migrate even *in vitro*, the implication being that the apparent movement may be due to forces arising within the cell itself. Axoplasmic movement and growth in peripheral nerve fibers have been observed in a number of investigations (Cook and Gerard, 1931; Weiss and Hiscoe, 1948; A. J. Samuels et al., 1951; Parker and Paine, 1934), but it is unfortunately not clear whether we can generalize these findings to the central nervous system.

Neuronal growth is an essential condition for

permanent or long-term memory according to all anatomical theories of learning; however, growth even over relatively short distances must be a very slow process, and this has been a major problem for such a theory. It seems doubtful that any of the suggested physiological mechanisms of facilitation could possibly bridge the time interval required for axonal or dendritic growth, and several theorists have attempted to circumvent the problem by postulating some form of movement which may not depend on physical growth itself.

Some evidence for this relatively rapid type of change has been obtained in a number of time-lapse photographic studies of brain tissue cultures (Canti et al., 1935; Pomerat, 1951; Lumsden and Pomerat, 1951; Geiger, 1958, 1959, 1963). These investigations have shown that neural as well as glial tissue *in vitro* maintains a pulsating activity which appears to follow rhythmic cycles averaging about 6 to 8 hr for neuronal tissue, but only 5 min for glia cells. (The latter finding may be important in connection with Galambos' 1961 suggestion that learning is a function of glia-neuron interaction.)

Geiger (1959) reported that this pulsating movement appeared to be selectively affected by changes in the chemical composition of the cell environment. A marked slowing of the axonic and dendritic movement was observed after small amounts of lysergic acid diethylamide (LSD-25) were added to the cell medium, and serotonin produced rhythmic contractions of the cell soma which imparted an exaggerated pulsating movement to the processes of the cell. During these movements cytoplasmic materials appeared to be pumped into and along the axons, producing a swelling of the axon cylinder. These findings suggest that chemical substrates in the environment of neural and glial tissue may produce marked changes in nerve activity and thus may affect the formation of temporary synaptic connections during conditioning. Although these speculations require much additional investigation, some support for them can be abstracted from Geiger's observation that synaptic connections appeared to be formed (and broken) by the movement of cellular processes *in vitro*. Particularly interesting in this connection is Geiger's report that some of the newly formed synaptic junctions persisted for weeks and even months, suggesting a possible mechanism for even long-term memory.

Another provocative fact is the observation by Pomerat and others (Pomerat, 1951; Canti

et al., 1935) that glia cells also exhibit definite movement, at least in tissue cultures. *In vitro*, glia and neurons appear to interact physically in a very interesting fashion. Oligodendroglial satellite cells showed in the presence of neurons a pulsating movement which resulted in the extrusion of some materials from the glia cells, a movement around neurons and axonal processes, and even a spider-like climbing of glia around neuronal tissue. These observations are particularly interesting because glia tend to be relatively inactive in the absence of neuronal tissue and respond to some chemical substances by markedly increasing their contact with neurons and accelerating the rate of transfer of chemical substances from the glial cells to the neurons.

These findings may be relevant to the problem of learning in view of the proposal that all neural functions and particularly the functional changes which occur during learning may be the result of an interaction between glia cells and neurons. In the human brain glia cells outnumber neurons nearly 10:1, and it has been suggested that these cells may do more than provide structural support for the neural components of the brain, as is commonly indicated in textbooks. It has long been suspected that the glia cells may control essential metabolic processes in nerve cells by determining the supply of important nutrients and enzymes. This, in turn, may indicate, as Galambos (1961) has suggested, that the glia cells act as the programming computer of neural function and that learning as well as retention may essentially depend on glial rather than neuronal processes.

That the glia may be the "seat of intelligence" was suggested 80 years ago (Nansen, 1886), and the idea has persisted in such theories as Schleich's attempt (1930, cited by Klüver, 1958) to reduce all "psychological" activity (such as "thinking, remembering, forgetting, imagination and action") to neuroglial activity. Klüver (1958) has suggested facetiously that "psychoneurology" may well develop an important subdivision called "psychogliology," and Galambos (1961) has published a speculative hypothesis that glia cells may be quite directly and essentially involved in learning and memory. He suggested that glia cells may act "in some unknown way" to organize neurons and provide a basis for the "fields" and cell assemblies which have been proposed in recent theories of learning. He believes that glia cells may receive afferent impulses and permit efferent discharges from the neurons only after some kind of organization is imposed on the neuronal activity. Glia cells are, according to this hypothesis, capable of instructing the neural centers; they can act themselves as a kind of genetic memory which may be based on changes in the nucleic acids, as proposed by recent biochemical theories.

In view of the very speculative nature of this hypothesis, it may be permissible to go a step further and attempt to integrate the recent finding on glia motility into Galambos' proposal. The suggested neuron-glial interaction might, for example, consist of an actual movement of glial processes in and out of synaptic junctions, thus altering the amount of non-neural, resistive tissue at the synapse. This movement, in turn, might affect the conduction of impulses in the neural pathways by permitting a greater or smaller area of contact between conducting axonal processes and postsynaptic membranes. Particularly when combined with the notion of neuronal movement, this purely anatomical mechanism might account for the phenomenon of learning.

It is also possible to suggest more chemically oriented hypotheses to account for a neuron-glial interaction. The glia might determine the metabolic activity of the nerve cell by regulating the production of essential enzymatic substrates and thereby affect its reactivity either directly or by regulating the growth or movement of axonal and dendritic processes. These hypotheses are highly speculative, and much more experimental evidence is needed to conclude that glia cells perform any essential functions specifically related to learning and/or memory. It may be worthwhile to remember that a large number of cells in the central nervous system are, in fact, of non-neural origin and that these tissues may contribute more than structural support to neural functions.

Before discussing some of the theoretical speculations that have used the concept of anatomical growth or development as a possible basis for long-term memory, we shall briefly discuss some rather circumstantial evidence which has been cited in support of the related assumption that prolonged neural activity is an essential and sufficient stimulus for such structural change. There is little direct experimental support for this contention, but several workers (Detweiler, 1936; Fernard and Young, 1951) have shown that the size of neurons (cell bodies as well as axons) seems to be a function of the number of afferent inputs to it. This anatomical correlation does not prove the intended causal relationship (it seems, in fact, equally reasonable to suggest that the number of afferent terminals on a cell may be determined by the availability of synaptic membrane). However, other investigators (Weiss and Taylor, 1944; Sauders and Young, 1946; Aitken et al., 1947; Evans and Vizoso, 1951) have shown a significant decrease in cell size following a reduction or elimination of the neuron's afferent or efferent connections, indicating that activity may be a determinant of overall cell size. Whether this relationship should be generalized to support the contention that activity *induces* directional growth at specific axon terminals is, of course, a very different matter.

THEORIES OF LEARNING

Many of the classical theories of learning and memory postulated physical changes in the central nervous system. However, anatomical theories in the modern sense of the word became possible only after Waldeyer's (1891) postulation of the neuron doctrine; this stated for the first time that the individual neuron is the structural and functional unit of the nervous system. The subsequent demonstration of synaptic junctions between individual neurons rapidly led to the conclusion that the process of learning must be related to a change in the resistance of synaptic junctions to the transmission of neural impulses. The term "resistance" here is not used only in the contemporary sense of electrical resistance, but generally refers to the fact that greater spatial separation between two neurons must make an interaction or transmission of excitation more difficult. The course of neural impulses in the central nervous system was conceived to follow a "path of least resistance" (or *most intimate anatomical connections*). The redirection of neural events that presumably takes place during learning was believed to be the result of physical changes at the synapse which selectively lowered the resistance of particular pathways between the central representations of the conditioned and unconditioned stimuli. Any event that caused two neurons to draw together more closely or to increase an already existing area of contact was thought to decrease the resistance to nerve impulses. Most of the earlier physiological theories of learning (as well as some recent ones) were concerned primarily with the postulation of mechanisms which could rapidly produce such a decrease in intercellular resistance and maintain novel anatomical arrangements sufficiently long to account for the known persistence of memory traces.

Tanzi

One of the first and most influential anatomical theories of learning was proposed by Tanzi in 1893. His hypothesis has provided the basis for the writings of Ramón y Cajal (1911), Toennies (1949), Hebb (1949), Eccles (1953), McIntyre (1953), and Thorpe (1956), and has received considerable support from recent histological findings. The hypothesis, in fact, sounds astonishingly modern if we "translate" some of the old-fashioned language into current terminology, and it may be as close an approximation to the "truth" as is presently available.

Tanzi argued that changes taking place within a single neuron may be analogous to those observed in the unicellular amoeba and that the axonal and dendritic processes of nerve cells react to intracellular metabolic changes in much the same fashion as pseudopodia. He postulated that the passage of nerve impulses through a neuron cause metabolic changes which increase the volume of the cell and elongate its "rudimentary protoplasmic filaments." Repeated activation of the cell then causes its axonal and dendritic processes to approach closer and closer to adjoining neurons, thereby decreasing synaptic resistance and facilitating the conduction of subsequent impulses. Finally, a firm "associative bond" which represents the physical basis of memory is formed.

Child

Child's (1921, 1924) anatomical theory of learning is so intimately tied to his more general concept of neural development that it may be useful to follow his reasoning by starting at the embryological level. Following Kappers' suggestion of neurobiotaxis, Child proposed that "gradients of attraction" arise as a direct result of metabolic activity during the initial development of the neuron as well as during subsequent excitation from stimulation. Combinations of these metabolic gradients, according to Child's theory, produce attractive or repulsive forces analogous to those produced by magnetic fields. Increased metabolic activity within a neuron polarizes the cell so that the interior becomes strongly positive and its exterior compensatorily negative.

During embroylogical development this negativity of the exterior of active neurons attracts growth processes from inactive or less active neurons that are comparatively positive in charge. Most important to his learning theory is the postulation that large areas of the brain may acquire attractive properties simply by being more active (and hence more negative) than neighboring areas. As a result of these attractive forces, the processes of two cells eventually join to form a single functional unit. This notion is so similar to Kappers' theory of neurobiotaxis that it is difficult to detect an essential difference between the two proposals, except that Child explicitly extends this theory of embryological development to the problem of learning.

According to this theory, the concurrent activation of pathways by the conditioned and unconditioned stimuli produces metabolic gradients so that axonal processes of neurons in the CS pathway become attracted to the strong negativity which presumably surrounds the highly active UCS pathways. Each repetition of the CS-UCS combination produces some amount of anatomical growth; this brings fibers of the CS pathway into closer contact with neurons that are active during the presentation of the UCS until they finally "form a functional unit" so that excitations of the CS pathways become capable of stimulating activity in the pathways of the UCS. Child does not attempt to explain how forgetting could occur in this rather rigid structural system, but one might charitably assume that anatomical connections can be severed when simultaneous excitation of the CS pathways and other areas of the brain sets up novel "gradients of metabolic activity."

A more serious shortcoming of Child's theory is unfortunately inherent in his basic assumptions about the development of these gradients of attraction. The metabolic gradients are presumably strongest between areas of maximum and minimum neural activity. In the conditioning situation the pathways of the UCS are very active and therefore exert an attractive force. However, the pathways of the CS are presumably more active than any other "irrelevant" neural system, and its neurons should be least attracted by the negativity that surrounds the UCS pathways. Although we may be reading into Child's theory, it seems to propose that *all stimuli except those present during the presentation of the UCS* should form anatomical connections with the UCS pathways, an interpretation that clearly was not intended by its author. Charitable critics might point out that only the CS is *repeatedly* paired with the UCS so that small but cumulative effects account for the learning process; however, this interpretation overlooks the obvious fact that, at least in simple learning situations, a single CS-UCS pairing can be sufficient to produce what appear to be fairly permanent connections.

Holt

Holt (1931) approached the problems of learning in a similar manner by applying Kappers' notion of neurobiotaxis directly to the problem of learning. He does, in fact, go considerably further than necessary in proposing that learning is not merely an extension of processes active during embryological development but that the initial development of the nervous system is, in effect, based on learning. Taking issue with contemporary theories of embryological development, Holt suggests that the nervous system may be initially composed of an essentially random network of individual neurons which do not have innate tendencies to form specific connections. Instead, neurons exhibit an innate potential of reacting to guiding stimulation which determines their connections in embryological development as well as during postnatal life by facilitating growth in specific directions on the basis of bioelectrical gradients of attraction and repulsion. He argued more specifically that a "reflex connection," whether we call it innate or learned, is formed on the basis of Kappers' principle that simultaneously active neurons exert an attractive force on each other. Kappers' theory is supplemented by the interesting proposal that synaptic resistance *randomly* changes in the nervous system so that the initial pathway of a stimulus is determined only by chance.

Before discussing Holt's theory of learning, it may be instructive to see briefly how this notion applies to embryological development. The basic assumption is that the central nervous system develops in an essentially random fashion. No permanent, *functional* interconnections exist between individual nerve cells until excitation of certain portions of the nervous system sets up metabolic gradients which exert attractive influences on neighboring neurons. In the early stages of embryological development, the nervous system consists essentially of (1) afferent fibers that are connected to peripheral sensory receptors but lack functional connections to central pathways or centers; (2) central neurons that are not yet connected at either end; and (3) efferent neurons that originate randomly at almost any point in the central nervous system but are connected to specific groups of effectors. When the sensory receptors are initially stimulated, impulses are transmitted to the central nervous system where they follow random paths of momentarily lowered synaptic resistance. This excitation will eventually spread to some efferent neurons which then produce an overt response to the stimulus that is totally random with respect to the eliciting stimulation.

In the fetus any stimulus is as likely as any other to elicit a particular motor response because permanent synaptic connections do not yet exist and because motor responses depend on randomly occurring facilitation between afferent and efferent pathways. Once a motor response has occurred, kinesthetic afferent impulses are initiated; these return to the central nervous system and are passed on to the previously active efferent fibers because these fibers presumably retain a measure of facilitation from the preceding excitation. This feedback in turn sets up a cycle of afferent-efferent stimulation which produces neurobiotaxic growth and establishes a reflex connection. Some inhibitory effect presumably develops gradually and eventually terminates the cycle of excitation until renewed sensory stimulation occurs.

Holt suggested that this chain of events may explain not only innate reflex connections but also those formed on the basis of conditioning. He wrote:

> Inasmuch as every afferent impulse spreads more or less widely as it traverses the central nervous system, the afferent impulse which is to be conditioned will somewhere come to a synaptic region which forms a part of the sensorimotor tract along which the unconditioned impulses are traveling to a muscle. At this point of conjunction, the conditions requisite for neurobiotaxic growth are realized, and the dendrites on the motor side of the synapse of the junction will be stimulated to grow contracurrently, toward the terminal arborizations of the neurons on which the to-be-conditioned impulses are arriving. This dendritic growth will tend to reduce the extent of non-nervous, and more resistant, tissue across which subsequent nerve impulses arriving on the same to-be-conditioned path must pass in order to reach the motor side (the dendrites) of this synaptic region. Thus will be reduced the resistance which this synapse interposes between the to-be-conditioned impulses and the already established motor outlines of the unconditioned impulse.

Holt illustrated this hypothesis by applying it it to the problem of avoidance learning. Assuming that an organism has an innate tendency to approach all stimuli, he suggested that aversive stimuli are not originally noxious but merely set up very intense activity in some parts of the brain. This intense excitation then is thought to spread randomly throughout the nervous system and initiate a variety of uncoordinated motor responses such as "crying, howling, wriggling and writhing," which are not originally indicative of emotional reactions. (Motivation, apparently, does not even enter into the problem of learning, except insofar as unconditioned stimuli may set up strong and widespread central excitation.) Eventually, movements that remove the organism from the noxious stimulation and thus terminate the widespread central excitation will occur. This, in turn, facilitates the connections between the efferent neurons active in the escape movements and those activated directly by the noxious stimulation. These connections then have a selectively reduced resistance to the specific afferent input and are more likely to be activated if the original stimulation recurs.

This notion explains rather elegantly why crying and random startle movements should be a part of the organism's response to all types of noxious stimulation. However, it seems to provide a rather weak explanation of the specific strengthening of the escape movements or, for that matter, of the subjective experience which, at least in man, accompanies or precedes the escape or avoidance responses. Holt does not specifically illustrate how this hypothesis might apply to appetitive learning but suggests that the same principles apply. His hypothesis has exerted a considerable influence on later anatomical theories of learning, although the basic mechanism of facilitation of neuronal growth—neurobiotaxis—had little experimental support, even when Holt first published his ideas.

The experimental literature which suggests that neurobiotaxic influences on neuronal growth do not seem to operate as proposed by Kappers and Holt has already been discussed. However, other difficulties with Holt's theory apparently have not been appreciated by some of the subsequent writers in this field. As a theory of development, the postulation of essentially random initial connections creates more problems than it solves when we consider the apparent intraspecies and even interspecies similarities of neural connections. As a theory of learning, Holt's hypothesis creates conceptual difficulties about the optimal CS-UCS interval in all behavioral conditioning paradigms. It would seem that backward conditioning, where the UCS precedes the CS and thus

might have an opportunity to establish the bioelectric gradients of attraction, should be the most efficient temporal arrangement. This supposition is contradicted by behavioral studies which show that even contiguity is not the most efficient design.

Young

One of the earlier examples of a dualistic theory of long- and short-term memory has been presented by Young (1938, 1951). Working on a behavioral analysis of the effects of central lesions in some rather unusual subjects (cuttlefish and octopi), Young found that memory functions appeared to be localized only in those relatively small portions of the brains of these primitive animals that did not seem to be related to the sensorymotor apparatus. These "association" areas appeared to be cytoarchitecturally much more complex than the rest of the brain, presenting the appearance of an intricate "feltwork" of complex, multiple interconnections.

Young originally hypothesized, in accordance with some of Lashley's observations, that specific neural interconnections may not be an essential prerequisite for learning or memory. He suggested that recall may be represented simply by continually active reverberatory circuits which are established in a feltwork of random connections purely on the basis of chance fluctuations in synaptic thresholds. In his more recent writings Young (1951) modified this position by suggesting that reverberatory activity may account only for short-term memory and that the permanent storage of memory traces may be due to a structural modification of the synaptic terminals in the reverberatory circuit, presumably as a direct result of frequent and prolonged excitation. Young suggested that the synaptic resistance may be permanently lowered either by a growth of additional end feet or by an enlargement of existing synaptic terminals. In this fashion the temporary facilitation, which originally resulted from the activity of reverberatory circuits, is presumably consolidated into permanent memory traces. Essentially similar ideas have been proposed by Hebb and Eccles; their theories will be discussed at greater length because they have provided more details of the proposed physiological and anatomical mechanisms.

Hebb-Milner

An interesting extension of Holt's ideas has been proposed by Hebb (1949, 1959, 1961) in a two-factor theory which attempts to salvage the advantages of neural growth without using Kappers' improbable notion of bioelectric attraction. Hebb proposed that the neurons of the sensory projection areas may be randomly connected to a large number of cells in the association areas and that the pattern of excitation which results from stimulation of any cell in the sensory cortex is determined by random variations in the threshold of association neurons. Stimulation of a cell in the sensory cortex sets up a pattern of propagated excitation in the association areas which involves a complex network of neurons and eventually (purely by chance) returns the impulse to the cell that originated it. Hebb postulates that use of a neural pathway results in temporary synaptic facilitation so that the impulse, when it arrives at the original neuron, finds a path of least resistance or lowered thresholds which correspond to the circuit just traversed. The impulse is thus induced to retrace the same circuit; this circuit acquires cumulative facilitation with each passage and establishes a reverberating activity, although the primary input to the circuit no longer exists. In this fashion, a reverberating circuit or, as Hebb calls it, "cell assembly" is established; this circuit remains active until anatomical changes which lay down a permanent memory trace can take place.

According to this theory, the recognition of simple stimuli or patterns of stimulation (such as

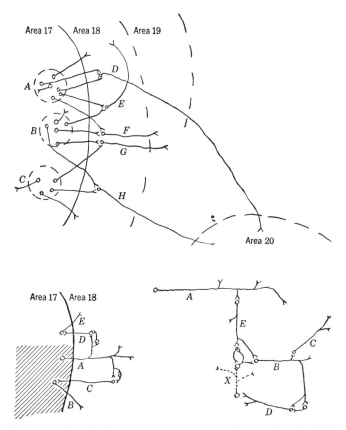

Fig. 15.5 Examples of "random" connections of cortical cells, postulated by Hebb, to account for the formation of reverberating circuits. *Top*, convergence of cells in Brodmann's area 17 upon cells in area 18, these cells in turn leading to other areas. A, B, C, three grossly distinct regions in area 17; D, E, F, G, H, cells in area 18. *Bottom left*, cells in A and B lie in a region of area 17 (shown by hatching) which is massively excited by an afferent stimulation. C is a cell in area 18 which leads back into 17. E is in area 17 but lies outside the region of activity. *Bottom right*, A, B, and C are cells in area 18 which are excited by converging fibers (not shown) leading from a specific pattern of activity in area 17. D, E, and X are among the many cells with which A, B, and C have connections that would contribute to an integration of their activity. (From Hebb, 1949.)

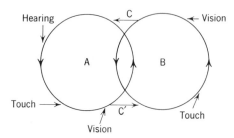

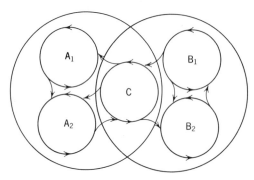

Fig. 15.6 Interaction of cell assemblies and phase sequences, as postulated by Hebb. *Top*, A and B represent two conceptual avtivities, C and C' possible connections between A and B. These are not simple closed neural circuits, or even the more complex assemblies, but phase cycles. They are systems of assemblies whose several activities are temporally integrated and tend to recur in an irregular cycle. A was originally organized by auditory, tactual, and visual stimulation (that is, it involves assemblies in each of these modes), B by visual and tactual stimulation. When these cycles are well organized, their activity may be initated by part of the original stimulation—A, for example, by hearing, touch, or vision. When A and B are simultaneously active, they may acquire an interfacilitation which is diagrammatically represented by C and C'. The learning is independent of any particular stimulation; the association might be set up by two visual stimulations but be manifest later when A is aroused by hearing or B by touch. *Bottom*, to illustrate the possibility that a subsystem C may act as a link between two systems (conceptual complexes). One concept is represented by A_1, A_2, and C, the second by B_1, B_2, and C. The two systems have a subsystem C in common to provide a basis of prompt association. (From Hebb, 1949.)

a straight line) depends on the facilitation of individual cell assemblies. More complex memories (such as a square constructed of four straight lines) are stored in the form of "phase sequences" made up of a number of cell assemblies which are interconnected so that a sequential order of excitation occurs. The initial formation of such phase sequences is again due to temporary facilitation in a

random network that is self-exciting and thus acts as a reverberating circuit. Anatomical changes (to be discussed later) eventually occur as a result of the continuous activity and establish a permanent memory trace in the form of particular patterns of synaptic facilitation.

This aspect of Hebb's hypothesis has been criticized, primarily on the grounds that the proposed system is inherently unstable. Stimulation of a single cell or cell assembly should eventually lead to the continual firing of all neurons of the nervous system. In a circuit where every element is at least potentially connected with every other element and where chance or use alone determine synaptic thresholds, it is indeed difficult to see why excitation should ever be confined to specific neural networks and how neural activity could ever diminish and eventually cease.

Milner (1957) has recently modified Hebb's hypothesis in an attempt to circumvent some of these problems. Hebb had not used the concept of inhibition in his writings, for there was little experimental support for such a notion in 1949. At the time of Milner's revision, definite inhibitory functions had been assigned to the Golgi type II neurons of the spinal cord (Eccles et al., 1956), permitting the assumption that these neurons might exert similar inhibitory effects in the association areas of the cortex, where they appear to be quite prominent (Lorenté de Nó, 1949).

Without presenting the details of Milner's proposal, the following essential points can be summarized: (1) the input to cells of the association area can be inhibitory as well as excitatory; and (2) intensive and repeated activation of a neural network tends to inhibit neighboring cells. Milner's hypothesis thus limits the spread of excitation by postulating inhibitory influences which develop as the result of a specific pattern of excitation. The inhibitory influences also explain the eventual cessation of activity in a reverberatory circuit. When neurons have been active for some time, adaptation develops, gradually decreases the cell's rate of firing, and thus reduces its inhibitory effects on neighboring neurons. These neurons are then free to fire and thus to inhibit some member of the cell assembly. When this occurs, the reverberatory circuit is broken and remains quiescent until the next stimulus is presented.

According to this modification, sensory inputs to the cortical receiving areas set up in the association areas specific patterns of excitation (cell assemblies, phase sequences) which remain active for a finite period of time. When two such patterns are active simultaneously or contiguously, as in conditioning, a facilitation of transmission is assumed to occur in overlapping fringe areas of the two cell assemblies. This facilitation gradually reduces synaptic resistance until excitation in cell assembly A (representing the CS) can induce excitation in cell assembly B (representing the UCS).

This modification adds considerably to Hebb's hypothesis which goes on to suggest that the reverberatory activity in cell assemblies and phase sequences serves to (1) initiate and maintain metabolic processes which result in permanent anatomical changes and thus provide the physical bases for permanent facilitation between the CS and UCS systems, and (2) preserve the memory until the essential structural alterations, which presumably require some time to develop, can be completed.

In general terms, Hebb suggests that "when an axon of cell A is near enough to excite cell B and repeatedly or persistently takes part in firing it, some growth process or metabolic change takes place in one or both such that A's efficiency as one of the cells firing B is increased." This is perhaps the most general statement of an anatomical learning theory and can hardly be challenged on logical or experimental grounds. Hebb proceeds, however, to suggest a specific mechanism for this gradually developing facilitation by proposing that "when one cell repeatedly assists in firing another, the axon of the first cell develops synaptic knobs (or enlarges them if they already exist) in contact with the soma of the second cell." This postulated growth or enlargement of terminal end feet presumably reduces synaptic resistance by increasing the area of contact and by decreasing the amount of non-neural tissue between the two neurons.

In support of this interpretation, Hebb cites Lorenté de Nó's observation that it generally takes afferent impulses from more than one source to obtain a sufficient electrotonic change in the postsynaptic membrane for an impulse to pass across a synapse. Hebb suggests that the enlargement of existing end feet or the growth of additional ones might account for the transformation of nonfunctional junctions into a low-resistance pathway. This aspect of his theory is interesting because it does not require the assumption of extensive anatomical growth from one area of the brain to another as some interpretations demand, but merely the facilitation of existing connections. This facilitation requires only that all afferent and efferent pathways are potentially connected and that simultaneous or contiguous excitation or activation produces anatomical changes which transform the existing nonfunctional connections into active low-resistance pathways.

The weakest point in Hebb's theory (as well as in related hypotheses) is not the proposed anatomical development itself but rather the physiological mechanism that is assumed to stimulate the necessary anatomical growth. Even if reverberatory circuits could maintain repetitive activity long enough to permit substantial anatomical development, it is not at all clear how sufficient specificity could possibly be attained to account for the selective association between conditioned and unconditioned stimuli.

Eccles

Eccles and his associates (Eccles and McIntyre, 1951; Eccles, 1953, 1957, 1964; McIntyre, 1953) have suggested a theory of learning based on synaptic facilitation which is in most aspects similar to Hebb's proposal. Like Hebb, Eccles holds that the selective lowering of synaptic resistance between the "central representations" of the conditioned and unconditioned stimuli is the essential functional change that must occur during learning. Furthermore, some structural, anatomical alteration must develop to produce the long-term effects that account for the permanent storage of memory traces. Eccles does, however, go a step further than Hebb in proposing complex physiological processes to account for the anatomical development. The details of this theory have been revised frequently during the past 20 years to remain consonant with his theory of synaptic transmission, but the framework has remained essentially unchanged and will be presented here. The reader is referred to Eccles (1946, 1947, 1964) for a review of the changing emphasis on electrical and chemical transmission mechanisms and brief statements of how this information may be incorporated into the basic theory of learning.

Eccles' theory of synaptic facilitation relies heavily on evidence obtained in studies of the facilitatory effect of tetanic stimulation. This effect was first observed by Lloyd (1949), who reported that rapid (about 300 pulses/sec) stimulation of dorsal root fibers enhanced the response of related ventral root fibers to subsequent test stimuli. The facilitatory effect persisted, though with gradually diminishing amplitude, for several minutes. Lloyd reported that the potentiation

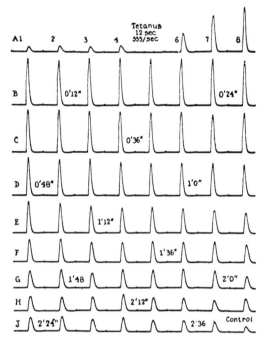

Fig. 15.7 Posttetanic potentiation. Monosynaptic reflex spikes discharged from gastrocnemius motor neurons in response to a maximum group I afferent volley from the gastrocnemius nerve. After the first four control responses, the gastrocnemius nerve is tetanized as shown. Subsequent tests at 2.4-sec intervals reveal the slow development and subsidence of a large posttetanic potentiation. (From Lloyd, 1949.)

seemed to be of presynaptic origin because antidromic stimulation of the motor neurons did not produce comparable effects; he suggested that the effect might be due to temporary hyperpolarization since its time course appeared to be strikingly similar to that of the positive afterpotential. Eccles and Rall (1951) observed that the increased reactivity of the ventral root fibers did not seem to be linearly related to the frequency of tetanizing or "conditioning" shocks and that the size of the postsynaptic potential did not, during the early phases of posttetanic potentiation (PTP), correlate with the amplitude of the presynaptic spike. They concluded that the facilitatory effect of tetanic stimulation must be caused by a change in the spatial relationship between cellular membranes.

In his earlier writings Eccles (Eccles and McIntyre, 1951; Eccles, 1953) suggested that repetitive stimulation of a neuron might produce sufficient swelling of the presynaptic end feet

to increase significantly the area of contact between two neurons and thus provide a low-resistance pathway for subsequent impulses. This interpretation was based primarily on the observation, reported by Hill and associates (Hill, 1949, 1950a, b; Hill and Keynes, 1949), that the opacity of a crustacean nerve trunk was significantly increased following repeated tetanic stimulation. Hill suggested that this change in opacity might be due to an enlargement of the fiber volume which could result from osmolarity changes in its interior. According to this hypothesis, fiber volume (the swelling postulated by Eccles) increases because an inflow of water re-establishes normal osmotic pressure relationships between the intra- and extracellular spaces. The transmission of neural impulses produces a movement of sodium ions into the cell and a compensatory expulsion of potassium ions, resulting in an increased osmotic pressure of the intracellular fluids. Hill suggested that an additional mechanism may operate during rapid, tetanic stimulation. Because of the rapidly increasing concentration of potassium outside the nerve fiber, some may diffuse into the axon, thus adding to the ionic imbalance caused by the high intracellular concentration of sodium.

The magnitude of the swelling reported by Hill and associates is not very large, but Eccles suggested that a greater change could be expected in the presynaptic end feet because a relatively higher surface-to-volume ratio is characteristic of small-diameter neural processes. He further proposed that the synaptic knobs may have a sufficiently greater radius of curvature than the axon itself to swell more readily and extensively.

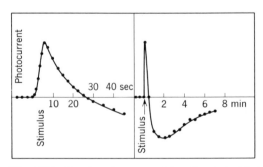

Fig. 15.8 Opacity change resulting from electrical stimulation of a nerve fiber at 50/sec for 5 sec. The positive direction represents an increase in opacity. The early phase (left) was recorded photographically. Temperature, 15°C. (From Hill and Keynes, 1949.)

The ionic swelling may also be supported or facilitated by movements of axoplasmic materials from the soma to the end feet. Such movements have been observed in stimulated giant axons (Weiss, 1941; Cook and Gerard, 1931) under rather artificial conditions (the axis cylinder was mechanically constricted). However, it is not yet clear to what extent this mechanism might even temporarily increase the diameter of end feet.

There is little argument with the basic proposition that use (or at least tetanic stimulation) of a pathway may produce temporary facilitation. However, the suggested explanation of this facilitatory effect in terms of a swelling of presynaptic terminals appears to be in need of re-examination. This aspect of the theory rests primarily on Lorenté de Nó's suggestion that two or more end feet must terminate on a postsynaptic fiber in order to effectively produce sufficient stimulation to permit propagation of an impulse across synaptic junctions. Eccles (as well as Hebb and others) seems to assume that an increase in the surface area of a single end foot can produce as much facilitation as two smaller axon terminals. However, the proposed swelling does not, per se, increase the size or number of the vesicles containing the humoral transmitter substance which presumably is responsible for the propagation of impulses across the synapse. It is difficult to see how a mere increase in nonactive tissue could be responsible for the proposed facilitation. If, on the other hand, it is suggested that the observed movements of axoplasmic materials increase the concentration of transmitter substances at the synapse, the facilitation would appear to be the result of intracellular biochemical events rather than the anatomical growth. We shall return to this problem in a later section of this chapter.

Even if we accept Eccles' hypothesis of the anatomical basis of synaptic facilitation, serious difficulties arise when we extend this notion to the problem of learning and retention. Hill's data indicate that only a very small swelling can be produced by the rapid administration of 500 tetanic impulses and that changes of the order of magnitude assumed in Eccles' theory can be seen only after 10,000 stimulations. Learning, on the other hand, often requires only a single CS-UCS pairing which presumably does not elicit such intense and prolonged neural activity.

Ström (1951) has pointed out that normal neurons do not propagate impulses of sufficient amplitude to generate posttetanic potentiation. We might add that normal neuronal activity rarely reaches the high repetition rates which seem necessary for the demonstration of facilitation in the laboratory. Eccles and his colleagues (Eccles, 1957; Eccles et al., 1959) have argued that the frequency and amplitude of rapidly and persistently firing neurons (such as might be found in a reverberatory circuit) could, in fact, produce effects sufficiently like posttetanic potentiation to account for short-term memory.

McIntyre (1953) has pointed out that very brief tetanic stimulation of some presynaptic fibers can produce a detectable lowering of synaptic resistance (i.e., enhance the response to single test stimuli); this lowered resistance persists for several minutes and decays only gradually in an approximately exponential function. McIntyre conceded that even short-term memory might not depend directly on the primary effects of posttetanic potentiation. He suggested that some structural changes might result from repeated activation of a synaptic junction which, in turn, could be responsible for the gradual development of more specific and permanent memory traces.

Several experimental observations support the contention that normal neural activity may produce facilitatory effects similar at least to those seen after tetanic stimulation. Granit (1956), for instance, reported that stretching of a muscle produced a marked increase in the firing rate of stretch receptors which eventually led to a significant enhancement of activity in the related motor neurons. Eccles and Westerman (1959) have reported the related observation that increased use of a pathway, produced by continual stretch of extensor muscles, resulted in a markedly enhanced facilitatory response to tetanic stimulation of the ventral root fibers.

What at present appears to be a greater problem is the persisting question whether the temporal properties of posttetanic potentiation do not, in fact, preclude a significant contribution to learning. The facilitatory effects themselves may be too short-lived to account even for short-term recall; they certainly cannot account for the consolidation process which is responsible for the anatomical developments that presumably form the physical basis of long-term memory storage. The problem may be circumvented by the postulation of long-lasting reverberatory activity or the assumption that posttetanic effects stimulate anatomical changes which in some fashion continue after the cessation of the facilitation itself. Neither of these assumptions appears very likely at the present time, but even more

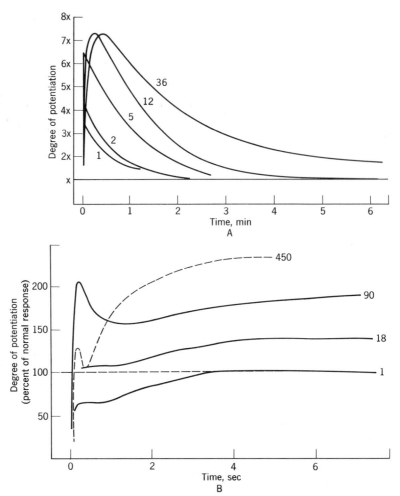

Fig. 15.9 A, time courses of posttetanic potentiations after conditioning tetani of various durations (marked in seconds on the curves) at a constant frequency of about 500/sec. Note the progressive slowing of posttetanic potentiation as the conditioning tetanus is made more severe. (From Lloyd, 1949.)

B, plotting as in A, but after less severe conditioning tetani and over a much briefer time scale in order to show, after a moderate tetanus (90 volleys), the separation of the early brief potentiation from the later; after 450 volleys the early potentiation is negligible, and in the 18-volley record there is a transition to the depression observed after 1 volley. All tetani are at 300/sec. The horizontal broken line shows the potential of the control reflex spike. (From Eccles and Rall, 1953.)

serious problems arise from the explicit prediction that disuse of a neural pathway should lead to a gradual disappearance of the anatomical swelling and thus produce rapid forgetting.

Disuse brought about by unilateral deafferentation of some segments of the spinal cord does seem to reduce the response to tetanic stimulation (Eccles et al., 1959), but it is not at all clear that this increased threshold can be related either to

memory or to the postulated reduction in structural contact between neurons. The observed decrease may be due to scar tissue formation or other degenerative changes, and it appears implausible that the survival of memory over long periods of disuse as demonstrated in retention tests could be explained on this basis. Moreover, experimental as well as clinical observations suggest that forgetting may be due to interference

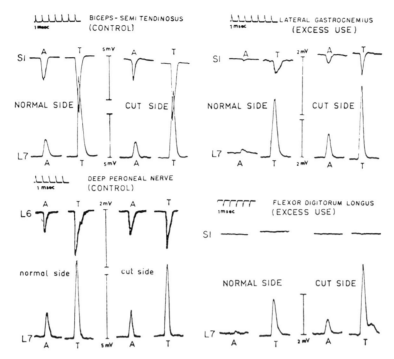

Fig. 15.10 Monosynaptic reflexes recorded in the L_6, L_7, or S_1 ventral roots in response to maximum group Ia afferent volleys from the four muscles as specified. *Left*, the response of normal biceps semitendinosus and deep peroneal muscles before (A) and during (T) maximum posttetanic potentiation. *Right*, monosynaptic reflex responses from muscles which had been subjected to excess use. (From Eccles and Westerman, 1959.)

rather than to an obliteration of the memory trace itself.

Eccles attempts to answer some of these criticisms by suggesting that repeated use of a pathway might produce successive and somehow additive effects on the anatomical structure of the synapse and perhaps result in permanent structural modifications which are progressively less affected by disuse; however, there appears to be absolutely no empirical evidence for this suggestion. The geography of the nervous system would not seem to permit the physical expansion which presumably results from such a continuous increase in the number of synaptic connections.

Eccles has recently (1957, 1964) relied more extensively on chemical transmission mechanisms and the fact that increased use of a synapse may stimulate the production and release of the chemical transmitter substances. This circumvents some of the criticisms that have been mentioned, but we shall not at this point pursue the suggestion further because there is little or no empirical evidence for the proposed mechanisms

(see the discussion of enzyme induction systems in Chapter 16).

On a more molar level, Eccles has made use of the physiological and anatomical mechanisms we have just discussed in a theory of learning and memory which appears surprisingly naive from a psychological point of view. According to this hypothesis, the cortex consists of one or more random nerve nets which are functionally interconnected so that it takes a simultaneous input from at least two parallel neurons to achieve transmission at the next synaptic junction. Conditioning, in this system, consists essentially of a repeated confluence of impulses from the CS and UCS modalities in a convergence center in which a particular spatiotemporal pattern of excitation is generated.

Repeated activation of this pattern of excitation establishes a specific pathway through the random nerve net which eventually terminates at a receiving center and triggers the conditioned response. Presumably because of differences in intensity, the UCS alone is initially capable of

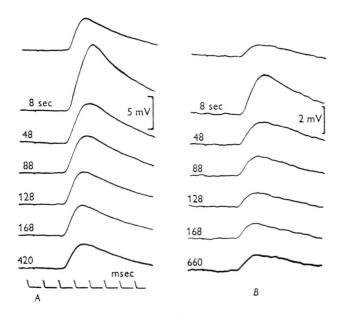

Fig. 15.11 Intracellular EPSPs evoked in a motor neuron by maximum group Ia volleys in the flexor hallucis longus nerve (A), and in the flexor digitorum longus nerve (B) which had been severed 15 days previously. Top records in A and B were taken before the conditioning tetanus (400 cps, for 10 sec). Subsequent records were taken at the indicated intervals after the tetanus. The same time scale was applied throughout, but there were different voltage scales for the two series as indicated. (From Eccles et al., 1959.)

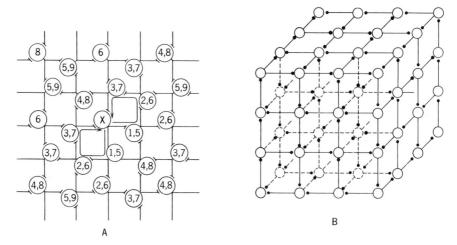

Fig. 15.12 A, the simplest type of neuronal network that will give indefinite outward spread from an excited focus and also provide closed self-re-exciting chains of all degrees of complexity. Each neuron is assumed to have only two synaptic knobs on its surface and in turn to have an axon which has only two knobs on other neurons. This net could be extended in any direction, and there would be virtual radial symmetry from any point. (The numerals on each neuron give the number of synapses traversed in leading to its first, and second, activation in spread from neuron X.) The two simplest closed chains (four-neuron arcs) are shown by arrows. The next simplest are six eight-neuron arcs, then twelve-neuron arcs, etc. (From Eccles, 1951.)

B, diagram of a neuronal network with each neuron receiving and giving three synaptic contacts (conventions as in A). Because of the complexity of the diagram, it has been impossible to draw the full connections for more than a very few neurons. Only the surface neurons of the deeper layers 3 and 4 are shown. Connections and cells in the depth of the cube are indicated by broken lines. In any plane the adjacent transmission lines alternate in direction. (From Eccles, 1953.)

traversing this pathway to the receiving center (and thus elicits the UCR), but the CS is not. Several CS-UCS pairings are needed to establish sufficient facilitation at the synaptic junctions of the convergence center (which are common to the CS and UCS pathways) to permit passage of the CS signal. The facilitation eventually produces anatomical changes which establish a permanent path of lowered resistance between the CS pathways and the receiving center.

Activation of the UCS pathway, according to this theory, produces effects similar to those of posttetanic potentiation, i.e., facilitation of the interneurons which connect the CS and UCS pathways at the convergence center. Eccles hypothesizes that the strong stimulation, which presumably characterizes all unconditioned stimuli, sets up reverberatory activity that persists long enough to produce facilitatory effects like PTP. He points out that the neurons of the cerebral cortex may be more plastic than those of the spinal cord, so that fewer and less intense volleys of stimulation may be needed to achieve some measure of synaptic facilitation. This argument is supported by such experiments as Clare and Bishop's (1955), who reported that there are more dendritic terminations in the cortical association areas than in other portions of the brain. (Since the latent period at axodendritic junctions in only 1 msec as compared with 15 to 20 msec at axosomatic junctions, a greater amount of integration would be expected in areas where dendritic terminals predominate.) Extinction, according to Eccles, occurs because the omission of the UCS leads to a shrinking of some of the end feet in the CS-UCS convergence center until the functional connection between the CS pathways and the receiving center is finally broken.

Stated in these relatively concrete terms, many aspects of Eccles' theory of learning and memory appear to be in disagreement with well-established behavioral observations. Serious difficulties remain even if we concede the main points of his theory of synaptic facilitation, namely that (1) reverberatory activity, which might be set up by a single stimulus presentation, produces effects sufficiently similar to those of tetanic stimulation to result in a temporary facilitation of transmission; and (2) this facilitation, under some circumstances, stimulates anatomical or chemical processes, such as swelling of axon terminals or an increase in the manufacture and release of transmitter substances, which serve as long-term memory traces. Except for the suggestion that

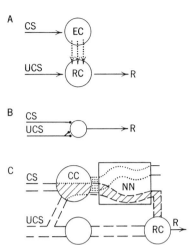

Fig. 15.13 Schematic representation of the neural mechanisms involved in Eccles' (1953) "molar" theory of learning. In A the arrows indicate nervous pathways; B is a redrawing of a simplified model which shows converging synaptic connections of the CS and UCS lines. In C nervous pathways are drawn as broad bands along which conduction occurs, particularly in the neuronal network NN. The interruptions in the bands indicate synaptic relays. Nerve centers containing large populations of neurons are indicated by circles. The neuronal network NN is an extremely complex neuronal system (for example, an area or areas of the cerebral cortex). CC, convergence center; EC, emitting center; RC, response center. (From Eccles, 1953.)

facilitatory effects similar to PTP may be the first step in this sequence, these notions are not drastically different from those proposed by others in the field and may, in fact, account for synaptic facilitation. To the extent that facilitation becomes an essential or important aspect of the physiological changes that take place during learning, this is a noteworthy development.

The proposed "molar" theory of learning and memory requires assumptions that are difficult to maintain in view of the available literature. Although some of these difficulties may be primarily semantic, questions must be raised about the notion of a convergence center of at least implicitly cortical origin, an efferent receiving center, and the randomness of the suggested cortical connections. Moreover, the UCS is assumed to cause the facilitatory effects that permit the transmission of impulses from the CS pathway to the UCR receiving center. Unless the unlikely assumption is made that the facilitatory effects of a UCS presentation are effective only on the *next* CS input (unlikely because learning has been demonstrated with exceedingly long intertrial intervals), the temporal sequence in this system would appear to be wrong. Conditioning does not occur (or at least is very inefficient) if the UCS precedes the CS or even occurs simultaneously with it. Conditioning is most effective when the CS *precedes* the UCS by at least 0.5 sec, suggesting a sequence of events directly opposite to that implied by Eccles' theory.

It has already been mentioned that the proposed mechanism of forgetting does not seem to agree with behavioral observations (disuse does not lead to a disappearance of the memory). Other problems (such as the effects of reinforcement in more complex learning tasks and the conceptual difficulties that arise when one considers cyclical- or trace-conditioning paradigms) exist, and extensive modifications will have to be made before Eccles' theory can be fruitfully applied to the problem of learning. It has been treated in some detail because it is considered by many to be the most influential and current theory of learning and because it presents a detailed account of the proposed mechanisms. The latter is, perhaps, the source of the difficulties we have encountered.

Fessard

Fessard's (1954, 1961; Fessard and Szabo, 1961) hypothesis of learning, although based primarily on electronic models of neural processes, is quite similar in most essential respects to Eccles' notion. Fessard pointed out that the neurons of the central nervous system are continually active, even in the absence of specific stimulation, and that this intermittent activity of resting cells may be essential for the maintenance of a minimal level of synaptic facilitation or transmittive effectiveness.

Stimulation of a cell, according to Fessard, increases its firing rate and produces a temporary increase in transmittive effectiveness, the magnitude of which is ostensibly proportional to the intensity and duration of stimulation. He proposed that conditioning requires an interaction of the CS and UCS signals in the "heterogeneous pathways" of the reticular formation. Learning is thought to take place when impulses, originating in the UCS pathways, arrive at interneurons in the midbrain reticular formation; these neurons still retain some of the facilitation which resulted from the previous passage of impulses originating in the CS pathways.

Fessard does not further describe the events that may alter the synaptic resistance at these points of confluence so that the CS signals eventually suffice to penetrate the "neural network" of the reticular formation. He does, however, suggest that the memory traces produced by this interaction of the CS and UCS signals may be stored by hippocampal mechanisms which are activated (for the purpose of recall) by cortical as well as reticular projections.

Konorski

Konorski (1948, 1950, 1961) has proposed a theory of memory which, in most essential respects, is similar to those of Hebb and Milner. This coincidence deserves special consideration because Konorski's theory, unlike that of his colleagues, is derived from Pavlovian dogma rather than recent neurophysiological findings. Like Hebb, Konorski comes to the somewhat unusual conclusion that memory traces are stored in the association areas of the cortex or, more specifically, in the association areas that are closest to the primary projection area of the CS. Short-term recall, according to this theory, is based on reverberatory activity in these association areas. The perseverating activity also stimulates structural changes at existing synaptic junctions and thus converts potential connections between the CS and UCS "analyzers" into low-resistance pathways which represent the structural basis of long-term memory.

The details of this consolidation process and the exact nature of the proposed structural changes are not described, at least in his English-language publications. However, an interesting analysis of the results of recent microelectrode studies, presented in Konorski's more recent (1961) writings, suggests that the memory function of reverberatory circuits depends on "steady-ON" neurons. Since long-term recall is presumably related to structural changes which result from such reverberatory activity, it seems that Konorski has assigned all memory functions to these neurons. This conclusion is qualified, however, by the further suggestion that ON and OFF neurons are essential to the discrimination between stimuli of the same sensory modality.

In view of the rather extensive and reasonably sound evidence indicating that cortical mechanisms are essential neither to learning nor to retention, it seems surprising that both Hebb and Konorski should localize memory in the association cortex. This may be an unessential or even unimportant aspect of Hebb's theory, which is originally and primarily concerned with the problems of perception rather than those of memory itself. Konorski, on the other hand, quite explicitly supports the Pavlovian tradition which maintains that learning requires a direct *cortical* association between the projection areas of the conditioned and unconditioned stimuli.

A number of experiments have reported a deficit in retention (although not typically in learning ability) following damage of the primary sensory cortex as well as the related association areas. We have discussed these studies in Chapter 13 and no further detail will be presented here. In his recent writings Konorski (1961) particularly emphasized a group of discrimination studies which Chorazyna, Stepien, and others performed in his laboratories at Warsaw. Using complex stimuli (pairs of "like" or "unlike" lights or tones), these studies indicated that the destruction of cortical association areas produces modality-specific decrements in discrimination performance which Konorski interprets as related to memory deficits. Although some of these experiments demonstrate that the experimental animals appear to be capable of other, simpler discriminations, it is not at all clear from the often meager description of the methodology and results how complex sensory deficits could be ruled out as a possible and perhaps even most probable explanation of the observed results. Observations on decorticate animals indicate that cortical connections cannot be an essential element of primitive memory mechanisms. It is possible that more complex patterns of recognition, particularly those requiring difficult sensory discrimination or a temporal integration of many components, may require cortical connections. However, it seems improbable that the process of connection formation should be something uniquely or even predominantly related to the association areas.

Some physiological theories of learning have been concerned primarily with the "where" rather than the "how" of conditioning. We have already discussed the extensive research literature which suggests that learning and retention may not be the exclusive property of any one aspect of the central nervous system. It may nonetheless be instructive to look at some of these theoretical proposals since the suggested central connections may be uniquely related, though not essential, to learning alone or to learning and storage of memory traces.

Penfield

Penfield (1952, 1954, 1958) coined the term "centrencephalic system" to describe the central portion of the nervous system which he believed to be specifically concerned with thought, memory, and learning. The system, as described in the more recent papers, includes (1) sensory pathways, (2) the diffuse reticular projection systems of the midbrain and thalamus, and (3) portions of the rhinencephalon and temporal neocortex. Penfield suggested, in effect, that sensory inputs may require integration and analysis by complexly interconnected neural networks which operate at several levels of the reticular formation. The results of this preliminary "digestion" are then thought to be distributed to cortical mechanisms for storage and subsequent recall. Memory functions are specifically related to the hippocampal gyrus, periamgdaloid area, and hippocampus proper.

This rather precise localization of the memory trace and recall mechanisms is based on clinical observations which show, apparently unambiguously, that clear and distinct memories of often long-forgotten events can be evoked in man by electrical stimulation of these portions of the brain (Penfield and Milner, 1958). There is also some corroborating evidence of memory deficits following tumor growth or surgical damage to the hippocampus and hippocampal gyrus (Scoville and Milner, 1957; Milner, 1958). Others report temporary amnesia for recent events following electrical stimulation of temporal lobe structures; the electrical stimulation may have elicited seizure activity in this very sensitive region of the brain (Bickford et al., 1958). Animal experiments (see Chapter 13), on the other hand, typically do not show significant effects on retention or learning ability following stimulation or lesions of the hippocampus and related temporal lobe structures unless very complex behavioral testing situations are employed. This finding suggests that these portions of the brain may not be essential to basic memory functions. The clinical effects reported by Penfield and his associates may be due to a stimulation or disturbance of "higher-order" integration or reasoning processes not essentially involved in simple conditioning.

Russell

Russell (1959) has suggested a theory of memory, based on clinical observations, which attempts to relate classical Pavlovian concepts and modern neurological observations. Russell proposed that memories peculiar to the sensory modalities involved in the learning task may be stored in the related cortical association areas and that the hippocampal formation may in some fashion determine what is stored in these locations and when and how it can be retrieved. The process of learning, according to this hypothesis, involves a facilitation of specific pathways through "complex neural networks" which presumably terminate in the hippocampal formation.

Gastaut

As a counterthought to these cortically oriented hypotheses, we briefly mention Gastaut (1958a, b), who has valiantly defended his contention that subcortical rather than cortical mechanisms must be involved in conditioning, retention, and recall because even relatively complex learning can be demonstrated in decorticated animals. He admits that the learned behavior repertoire of the decorticated animal may be more severely restricted than might be predicted on the basis of sensory and motor deficits and acknowledges that cortical mechanisms, particularly those located in the association areas, may normally contribute to the "full elaboration" of conditioned responses. However, the actual "connection formation" or "closure" between the CS and UCS pathways, which he believes to be the essential event underlying learning, is assumed to take place in the nonspecific projection nuclei of the thalamus.

Gastaut suggested that this rostral extension of the midbrain reticular formation may be uniquely suited anatomically for this purpose, for it receives direct inputs from all sensory pathways (I. Samuels, 1959) as well as corticofugal projections from all sensory and association areas (Eccles, 1953).

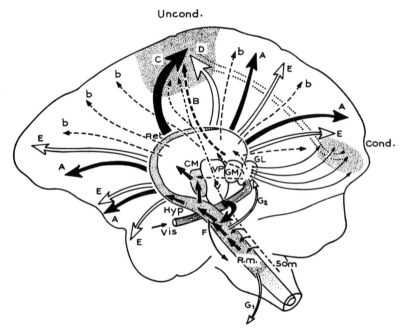

Uncond.

Vis: visual projection by way of the lateral geniculate (GL) to the striate area. (Conditioned area, Cond.)

Som: somesthetic projection by way of the ventroposterior (VP) nucleus to the sensory motor cortex. (Unconditioned area, Uncond.)

Parallel dotted lines: hypothetical cortico-cortical link

Fig. 15.14 The conceptual nervous system of Gastaut (1958). Visual and somesthetic collaterals to the mesencephalic reticular system (R.m.) connect with the hypothalamus (Hyp), the reticular nucleus (Ret), and the center median of the thalamus (CM). *Interpretation of arrows:* A, concomitant generalized activation of the orientation reaction or, to a minor degree, of a generalized excitation of the reticular substance of the mesencephalon. B, the conditioned evoked potential, resulting from facilitation by "reiterated association," of a sector of secondary irradiated projections (*b*). C, localized activation, issued either from a restricted sector of the diffuse thalamic system or from a secondary action produced by the irradiated projection itself. D, localized internal inhibition, reproduced by the intervention of a diffuse thalamic sector. E, generalized internal inhibition, by liberation of this same diffuse system as a whole. (From Gastaut, 1958b.)

His choice of the rostral reticular formation as the site of closure is based primarily on electroencephalographic evidence which indicates that, once conditioning has taken place, the CS produces a purely local desynchronization in the cortical projection area of the UCS rather than the general alpha blocking which characterizes the response to novel stimuli. This limited cortical response can be elicited by electrical stimulation of the thalamic reticular formation and, as far as we know, from no other portion of the brain.

Because Gastaut believes that the localized desynchronization response is importantly related to the elaboration of conditioned responses, he suggested that it might be indicative of thalamic closure between the CS and UCS systems. He has been much less explicit with respect to the more molecular events which presumably produce this functional closure, and has suggested such esoteric processes as "heterogenic summation" or "remanence" as a possible basis for short-term memory and "structural modifications in the macromolecular build-up of the protein constituents of the synapses" as a basis for long-term storage.

SUMMARY

Physiological theories of learning or memory have existed for over 2000 years. The basic concepts have changed remarkably little over the centuries, even though significant advances have been made, particularly in the course of the past 50 years. Physiological or, more precisely, anatomical theories of learning have always assumed that learning consists of the selective facilitation of neural pathways through use or concurrent activity in adjacent neural systems. It has generally been further assumed that this facilitation must be the result of anatomical growth or movement which somehow reduces the resistance of synaptic junctions. Experimental evidence for the suggested mechanisms is far from satisfactory.

The first of the modern physiological theories was proposed by Tanzi (1893) almost 75 years ago. He suggested that the passage of nerve impulses may produce metabolic changes which increase the volume of the conducting cell and cause its processes to approach neighboring cells more closely, thereby establishing an "associative bond."

Child (1921, 1924) elaborated this notion by applying Kappers' theory of neurobiotaxis to the learning process. He suggested that "gradients of attraction" might arise from a cell during the passage of bioelectrical patterns of excitation. These gradients could then induce attractive or repulsive forces, similar to magnetic fields, and guide the growth of neural processes in the direction of stimulation. Child's hypothesis is of particular interest because he attempted to subsume embryological development and the physical basis of learning and memory under the same anatomical and physiological mechanisms.

Holt (1931) has been the most recent proponent of an essentially neurobiotaxic theory of learning. Following Child's proposal that embryological development and learning must somehow represent similar if not identical changes in the central nervous system, Holt proposed that the nervous system may initially be composed of a random network of individual neurons totally lacking in functional organization. Use or excitation of a particular random sequence of neurons in this system produces "guiding forces" or specific facilitation which establish innate as well as acquired "reflex connections."

Neurobiotaxic gradients of attraction or repulsion have not been accepted in the past 30 years. Their place in anatomical theories of learning has been taken by "reverberatory activity" in neural pathways. This is thought somehow to provide sufficiently intense and persisting metabolic activity to lower synaptic resistance and eventually induce anatomical growth or movement.

Young (1945), one of the earlier theorists to use this concept, suggested initially that memory traces might consist simply of specific patterns of recurrent activity in continually active reverberatory circuits. These patterns of neural firing are thought to be set up by repeated stimulation of a pathway in the central nervous system. In his more recent writings Young (1951) has modified this hypothesis by proposing that only short-term memory may depend directly on such reverberatory activity, whereas permanent memory storage may require structural modifications in the synaptic junctions of the reverberatory circuit.

Very similar hypotheses have been advanced by Hebb (1949), Milner (1957), and Eccles (1953), to name only some of the more influential writers in this field. Although the details of these hypotheses may vary, common basic concepts are easily discernible. It is assumed that individual neurons are essentially randomly connected, at least in the relevant portions of the central nervous system; use or excitation of a neuron can, under some circumstances, set up reverberatory activity which outlasts the stimulus by minutes, hours, or even days. It is further suggested that persistent, concurrent activity in contiguous neural circuits (and almost all portions of the CNS are assumed to be contiguous by means of some connection or another) produces synaptic facilitation at points where the two systems meet, so that subsequent stimulation of one will induce excitation in the other.

There is some evidence that the response of the nervous system may outlast the stimulation, but it is questionable whether this reverberatory activity can persist long enough to account for either short-term memory or the suggested anatomical modifications. Recent studies of posttetanic potentiation have suggested that repeated and very intense use of a neural pathway may produce temporary facilitation at the synaptic junction. We cannot be sure, however, that the magnitude and duration of this effect are even remotely sufficient to account for the establishment of memory traces. Finally, there is little evidence for the anatomical growth or movement which is assumed to result from repeated activation of a neural circuit. This idea has existed for a long time, but its durability does not constitute proof of its validity. Some experiments have shown a certain amount of plasticity in the nervous system, but it is not at all clear how this may be related to bioelectrical activity or memory.

Since the time of Aristotle, it has been a favorite pastime of philosophers and scientists to speculate about the "seat of memory." As more and more experimental evidence was collected, particularly from selective lesioning studies, it became abundantly clear that learning or memory could not be the exclusive property of any single portion of the central nervous system. This does not mean, of course, that some areas of the brain may not normally contribute specifically and importantly to the establishment, storage, and recall of memories. A number of interesting speculations appear to have some measure of experimental support and should therefore be mentioned briefly.

Primarily on the basis of ablation studies, Konorski (1948), Hebb (1949), and others have suggested that the association areas of the cortex may be specifically related to learning, memory, or recall. Electroencephalographic studies, on the other hand, have implicated the reticular formation of the midbrain and thalamus and suggested that important information may reach higher centers through these nonspecific sensory systems. Gastaut (1958a, b) and others used this evidence to construct models of the learning process which assumed that closure between the CS-UCS pathways may be exclusively a subcortical phenomenon. Penfield (1952) emphasized the role of the hippocampal system, but he tried to integrate current experimental evidence by proposing a "centrencephalic" mechanism which includes the specific sensory projection system as well as the ascending reticular formation and portions of the rhinencephalon and temporal neocortex.

BIBLIOGRAPHY

Aitken, J. T., Sharman, M., & Young, J. Z. Maturation of regenerating nerve fibres with various peripheral connections. *J. Anat.*, 1947, **81**, 1–22.

Aristotle. *De Memoria et Reminiscentia.* I. Bekker, Ed. London: Oxford Univ. Press, 1837.

Bain, A. *The senses and the intellect.* London: J. W. Parker, 1855.

Bain, A. *Mind and body: the theories of their relation.* London: Henry S. King, 1872.

Bancroft, F. W. Note on the galvanotropic reaction of the medusa polorchis penicillata, *A. Agassiz. J. exp. Zool.*, 1904, **1**, 289–292.

Bickford, R. G., Mulder, D. W., Dodge, H. W., Svien, H. J., & Rome, H. P. Changes in memory functions produced by electrical stimulation of the temporal lobe in man. *Res. Publ., Ass. Res. nerv. ment. Dis.*, 1958, **36**, 227–243.

Bielschowsky, M. Ueber das Verhalten der Achsencylinder in Geschwulsten des Nervensystems. *J. Psychol. Neurol.*, 1905–1906, **14**, 28–29.

Bielschowsky, M. Zur Kenntniss der Alzheimerischen Krankheit. *J. Psychol. Neurol.*, 1911, **18**, 69–73.

Bok, S. T. Stimulogenous fibrillation, the cause of the structure in the nervous system. *Psychiat. Neurol. Bladen (Amsterdam)*, 1915a, **19**, 393–400.

Bok, S. T. Die Entwicklung der Hirnnerven und ihrer Zentralen Bahnen. Die Stimulogene Fibrillation. *Folia neurobiol.*, 1915b, **9**, 14–35.

Bok, S. T. The development of reflexes and reflex tracts. *Psychiat. Neurol. Bladen (Amsterdam)*, 1917, **21**, 281–303.

Bonnét, C. *Essai de psychologie.* Paris: Sorbonne, 1754.

Bonnét, C. *Analyse abrégée de l'essai analytique sur les facultés de l'âme.* Paris: Sorbonne, 1769.

Broca, P. Remarques sur le siège de la faculté du langage articulé, suivies d'une observation d'aphémie. *Bull. Soc. Anat. (Paris)*, 1861, **6**, 330–357.

Butler, S. *Unconscious memory.* London: David Bogue, 1880.

Cabanis, P. J. G. *Rapports du physique et du moral de l'homme.* Paris: Sorbonne, 1799.

Canti, R. G., Bland, J. W., & Russell, D. S. Tissue culture of glomata, cinematograph demonstration. *Res. Publ., Ass. Res. nerv. ment. Dis.* 1935, **16**, 1.

Child, C. M. *The origin and development of the nervous system.* Chicago: Univ. of Chicago Press, 1921.

Child, C. M. *Physiological foundations of behavior.* New York: Henry Holt, 1924.

Clare, M. H., & Bishop, G. H. Dendritic circuits: the properties of cortical paths involving dendrites. *Amer. J. Psychiat.*, 1955, **111**, 818–825.

Coghill, G. E. *Anatomy and the problem of behavior.* New York: Macmillan and Cambridge Univ. Press, 1919.

Cook, D. D., & Gerard, R. W. The effects of stimulation on the degeneration of severed peripheral nerve. *Amer. J. Physiol.*, 1931, **97**, 412–425.

Darwin, E. *Zoönomia: or the laws of organic life.* London: Johnson, 1794.

Descartes, R. *Traité des passions de l'âme.* Amsterdam: Elsevier, 1650.

Detweiler, S. R. *Neuroembryology: an experimental study.* New York: Macmillan, 1936.

Dustin, P. Le rôle des trophismes et de l'odogenesis dans la regeneration du systéme nerveux. *Arch. Biol.*, 1910, **25**, 16–37.

Eccles, J. C. An electrical hypothesis of synaptic and neuro-muscular transmission. *Ann. N.Y. Acad. Sci.*, 1946, **47**, 429–455.

Eccles, J. C. Acetylcholine and synaptic transmission in the spinal cord. *J. Neurophysiol.*, 1947, **10**, 197–204.

Eccles, J. C. Hypotheses relating to the mind-brain problem. *Nature*, 1951, **167**, 53–57.

Eccles, J. C. *The neurophysiological basis of mind.* Oxford: Clarendon Press, 1953.

Eccles, J. C. *The physiology of nerve cells.* Baltimore: Johns Hopkins Press, 1957.

Eccles, J. C. The effects of use and disuse on synaptic function. In *Brain mechanisms and learning.* J. F. Delafresnaye, A. Fessard, R. W. Gerard, & J. Konorski, Eds. Oxford: Blackwell Scientific, 1961.

Eccles, J. C. *The physiology of synapses.* New York: Academic Press, 1964.

Eccles, J. C., & McIntyre, A. K. Plasticity of mammalian monosynaptic reflexes. *Nature (London)*, 1951, **167**, 466–468.

Eccles, J. C., & Rall, W. Effects induced in a monosynaptic reflex path by its activation. *J. Neurophysiol.*, 1951, **14**, 353–376.

Eccles, J. C., Fatt, P., & Landgren, S. Central pathways for direct inhibitory action of impulses in largest afferent nerve fibres to muscle. *J. Neurophysiol.*, 1956, **19**, 75–98.

Eccles, J. C., Krujevic, K., & Miledi, R. Delayed effects of peripheral severance of afferent nerve fibres on the efficacy of their central synapses. *J. Physiol. (London)*, 1959, **145**, 204–220.

Eccles, R. M., & Westerman, R. A. Enhanced synaptic function due to excess use. *Nature (London)*, 1959, **184**, 460–461.

Evans, D. H. L., & Vizoso, A. D. Observations on the mode of growth of motor nerve fibers in rabbits during post-natal development. *J. comp. Neurol.*, 1951, **95**, 429–461.

Fernard, V. S. V., & Young, J. Z. The sizes of the nerve fibres of muscle nerves. *Proc. roy. Soc. (London)*, B, 1951, **139**, 38–58.

Ferrier, D. *The functions of the brain.* London: Smith, Elder, 1886.

Fessard, A. Mechanisms of nervous integration and conscious experience. In *Brain mechanisms and consciousness.* E. D. Adrian, F. Brenner, H. H. Jasper, & J. F. Delafresnaye, Eds. Springfield, Ill.: Thomas, 1954.

Fessard, A. The role of neuronal networks in sensory communications within the brain. In *Sensory communication.* W. A. Rosenblith, Ed. Cambridge, Mass.: M. I. T. Press, 1961.

Fessard, A., & Szabo, T. Possibilité d'un transfert de la facilitation post-tétanique dans une chaîne disynaptique. *J. Physiol. (Paris)*, 1959, **51**, 465–466.

Fessard, A., & Szabo, T. La facilitation de postactivation comme facteur de plasticité dans l'establissement des liasions temporaires. In *Brain mechanisms and learning.* J. F. Delafresnaye, A. Fessard, R. W. Gerard, & J. Konorski, Eds. Oxford: Blackwell Scientific, 1961.

Flourens, M. J. P. *Recherches expérimentales sur les propriétés et les fonctions du système nerveaux dans les animaux vertébrés.* Paris: Crevot, 1824.

Frossman, P. Ueber die Ursachen welche die Wachtstrumsrichtung der peripheren Nervenfasern bei der Regeneration bestimen. *Zieglers Beiträge*, 1898, **24** (monograph).

Galambos, R. A glia-neural theory of brain function. *Proc. nat. Acad. Sci. (Washington)*, 1961, **57**, 129–136.

Galen, C. *On the uses of the parts of the human body.* Paris: Ballière, 1854.

Gall, F. J., & Spurzheim, J. G. *Anatomie et physiologie du système nerveux en général et du cerveau en particulier, avec des observations sur la possibilité de reconnôitre plusieurs dispositions intellectuelles et morales de l'homme et des animaux par la configuration de leurs têtes.* Paris: Sorbonne, 1810–1819. 4 vols.

Gastaut, H. Some aspects of the neurophysiological basis of conditioned reflexes and behavior. In *Ciba foundation symposium on the neurological basis of behavior.* London: Churchill, 1958a.

Gastaut, H. The role of the reticular formation in establishing conditioned reactions. In *The reticular formation of the brain.* H. H. Jasper, L. D. Proctor, R. S. Knighton, W. C. Noshay, & R. T. Costello, Eds. Boston: Little, Brown, 1958b.

Geiger, R. S. Subcultures of adult mammalian brain cortex. *Exp. Cell Res.*, 1958, **14**, 541–566.

Geiger, R. S. Effects of LSD-25, serotonin and sera from schizophrenic patients on adult mammalian brain cultures. *J. Neuropsychiat.*, 1959, **1**, 185–190.

Geiger, R. S. The behavior of adult mammalian brain cells in culture. In *International review of neurobiology.* C. C. Pfeiffer & J. R. Smythies, Eds., 1963, **5**, 1–51.

Gerard, R. W. Some aspects of neural growth, regeneration and function. In *Genetic neurology. Conference of the international union of biological science.* P. Weiss, Ed. Chicago: Univ. of Chicago Press, 1950.

Gerard, R. W. What is memory? *Scient. American*, 1953, **189**(3), 118–126.

Goltz, F. Ueber die Verrichtungen des Grosshirns. *Arch. ges. Physiol.*, 1881, **26**, 1–49.

Goodman, L. Effect of total absence of function on the optic system of rabbits. *Amer. J. Physiol.*, 1932, **100**, 46–63.

Granit, R. Reflex rebound by post-tetanic potentiation. Temporal summation—spasticity. *J. Physiol. (London)*, 1956, **131**, 32–51.

Haidenhain, R. *Plasma und Zelle*, 1911, **2**, 587.

Hamburger, V., & Levi-Montalcini, R. Some aspects of neuroembryology. In *Genetic neurology. Conference of the international union of biological science.* P. Weiss, Ed. Chicago: Univ. of Chicago Press, 1950.

Harrison, R. G. The outgrowth of the nerve fibers as a mode of protoplasmic movement. *J. exp. Zool.*, 1910, **9**, 787–848.

Harrison, R. G. The reaction of embryonic cells of solid surfaces. *J. exp. Zool.*, 1914, **17**, 521–544.

Hartley, D. *Observations on man, his frame, his duty and his expectations.* London: S. Richardson, 1749.

Hebb, D. O. *The organization of behavior: a neuropsychological theory.* New York: Wiley, 1949.

Hebb, D. O. A neuropsychological theory. In *Psychology: a study of a science. Vol. I.* S. Koch, Ed. New York: McGraw-Hill, 1959.

Hebb, D. O. Distinctive features of learning in the higher animals. In *Brain mechanisms and learning.* J. F. Delafresnaye, A. Fessard, R. W. Gerard, & J. Konorski, Eds. Oxford: Blackwell Scientific, 1961.

Held, J. Die Entstehung der Neurofibrillen. *Neurol. Centralbl.*, 1905, 8 (monograph).

Hering, E. Ueber das Gedächtniss als eine allgemeine Funktion der organisierten Materie. *Almanach Kaiserl. Akad. Wiss. (Wien)*, 1870, **20**, 253–278.

Herxheimer, G., & Gierlich, N. Studien ueber die Neurofibrillen im Zentralnervensystem. Entwickelung und normales Verhalten. *Veränderungen unter pathologischen Bedingungen*, Wiesbaden: J. F. Bergmann, 1907.

Hill, D. K. The effect of stimulation on the opacity of a crustacean nerve trunk and its relation to fiber diameter. *J. Physiol. (London)*, 1950a, **111**, 283–303.

Hill, D. K. The volume changes resulting from stimulation of a giant nerve fibre. *J. Physiol. (London)*, 1950b, **111**, 304–327.

Hill, D. K., & Keynes, R. D. Opacity changes in stimulated nerve. *J. Physiol. (London)*, 1949, **108**, 278–281.

His, W. Neuroblasten und deren Entstehung in embryonalen Mark. *Abhand, Math. Phys. Klass. Königl. Gesellsch. Wiss.*, 1889–1890, **15** (monograph).

Hitzig, E. *Untersuchungen ueber das Gehirn.* Berlin: Hirschwald, 1874.

Holt, E. B. *Animal drive and the learning process.* New York: Henry Holt, 1931.

Horwicz, A. *Psychologische Analysen auf physiologischer Grundlage.* Halle and Magdeburg: Faber, 1872–1878.

Hydén, H. Protein and nucleotide metabolism in the nerve cell under different functional conditions. *Nucleic acids: symposium of the society for experimental biology. Vol. I.* 1947, 152–161.

James, W. What is an emotion? *Mind*, 1884, **9**, 188–205.

James, W. *Principles of psychology*, New York: Henry Holt, 1890.

Jessen, P. W. *Versuch einer wissenschaftlichen Begründung der Psychologie.* Kiel: I. Alberti, 1855.

Kappers, C. U. A. Further contributions on neurobiotaxis. *J. comp. Neurol.*, 1917, **27**, 261–298.

Kappers, C. U. A. The logetic character of growth. *J. comp. Neurol.*, 1919, **31**, 51–67.

Kappers, C. U. A. On structural laws in the nervous system: the principles of neurobiotaxis. *Brain*, 1920, **43**, 125–149.

Kappers, C. U. A. *The evolution of the nervous system in invertebrates, vertebrates and man.* Haarlem: F. Bohn, 1929.

Kappers, C. U. A. Principles of development of the nervous system. In *Cytology and cellular pathology of the nervous system.* W. Penfield, Ed. New York: Paul Hoeber, 1932.

Kappers, C. U. A. Phenomenon of neurobiotaxis in the central nervous system. *Section of anatomy and embryology. Seventeenth international congress of medicine, London.* 1933, Section 1, pt. 11, 109.

Klüver, H. Cerebral organization and behavior. In *The brain and human behavior.* H. C. Solomon, S. Cobb, & W. Penfield, Eds. Baltimore: Williams and Wilkins, 1958.

Konorski, J. *Conditioned reflexes and neuron organization.* Cambridge: Cambridge Univ. Press, 1948.

Konorski, J. Mechanisms of learning. *Sympos. Soc. exp. Biol.*, 1950, **4**, 409–431.

Konorski, J. The physiological approach to the problem of recent memory. In *Brain mechanisms and learning.* J. F. Delafresnaye, A. Fessard, R. W. Gerard, & J. Konorski, Eds. Oxford: Blackwell Scientific, 1961.

Kussmaul, A. Die Stöhrungen der Sprache. In *Ziemssen's Handbuch der speziellen Pathologie und Therapie.* Leipzig: Anhang, 1877.

Lashley, K. S. In search of the engram. *Sympos. Soc. exp. Biol.*, 1950, **4**, 454–482.

Liu, C. N., & Chambers, W. W. Intraspinal sprouting

elicited from intact spinal sensory neurons by adjacent posterior root section. *Amer. J. Physiol.*, 1955, **183**, 640.

Lloyd, D. P. C. Post-tetanic potentiation of response in monosynaptic reflex pathways of the spinal cord. *J. gen. Physiol.*, 1949, **33**, 147–170.

Lorenté de Nó, R. Cerebral cortex: architecture. In *Physiology of the nervous system* (3rd ed.). J. F. Fulton, Ed. New York: Oxford Univ. Press, 1949.

Lumsden, C. E., & Pomerat, C. M. Normal oligdendrocytes in tissue culture. *J. exp. cell. Res.*, 1951, **2**, 103.

McIntyre, A. K. Synaptic function and learning. *Proceedings of the nineteenth international physiological congress, Montreal.* 1953, 107–114.

Malis, L. I., Baker, C. P., Kruger, L., & Rose, J. E. Effects of heavy ionizing monoenergetic particles on the cerebral cortex. II: Histological appearances of laminar lesions and growth of nerve fibers after laminar destruction. *J. comp. Neurol.*, 1960, **115**, 243–297.

Marsh, G., & Beams, H. W. In vitro control of growing chick nerve fibers by applied electrical currents. *J. cell. comp. Physiol.*, 1946, **27**, 139–158.

Merzbacher, C. Zur Biologie der Nervendegeneration. Ergebnisse von Transplantationsversuche. *Neurol. Centralbl.*, 1905 (monograph).

Milner, Brenda. Psychological deficits produced by temporal lobe excision. *Res. Publ., Ass. Res. nerv. ment. Dis.*, 1958, **36**, 244–257.

Milner, P. M. The cell assembly: Mark II. *Psychol. Rev.*, 1957, **64**, 242–252.

Müller-Hettlingen, A. Ueber galvanishe Erscheinungen an Keimenden Samen. *Pflüg. Arch. ges. Physiol.*, 1883, **31**, 192.

Nansen, F. The structure and combination of the histological elements of the central nervous system. Bergen: Bergens Museum Aarbs, 1886. Cited by P. Glees in *Neuroglia. morphology and function.* Springfield, Ill.: Thomas, 1955.

Parker, G. H., & Paine, V. L. Progressive nerve degeneration and its rate in the lateral line nerve of the catfish. *Amer. J. Anat.*, 1934, **54**, 1–25.

Penfield, W. Memory mechanisms. *Arch. Neurol. Psychiat. (Chicago)*, 1952, **67**, 178–191.

Penfield, W. Studies of the cerebral cortex of man. A review and an interpretation. In *Brain mechanisms and consciousness.* E. D. Adrian, F. Bremer, H. H. Jasper, & J. F. Delafresnaye, Ed. Springfield, Ill.: Thomas, 1954.

Penfield, W. Centrencephalic integrating system. *Brain*, 1958, **81**, 231–234.

Penfield, W., & Milner, Brenda. The memory deficit produced by bilateral lesions in the hippocampal zone. *Arch. Neurol. Psychiat. (Chicago)*, 1958, **79**, 475–497.

Piatt, J. Regeneration of the spinal cord in the salamander. *J. exp. Zool.*, 1955, **129**, 177–207.

Pomerat, G. M. Pulsative activity of cells from the human brain in tissue. *J. nerv. ment. Dis.*, 1951, **114**, 430–449.

Ramón y Cajal, S. *Textura del sistema nervioso del hombre y de los vertebrados. Vol. I,* 1899; *Vol. II,* 1904. Madrid: La paz.

Ramón y Cajal, S. Mecanismo de la regeneracion de los nervios. *Trab. Lab. Invest. biol.,* 1905–1906, **4** (monograph).

Ramón y Cajal, S. *Histologie du systeme nerveux de l'homme et des vertébres. Vol. II.* Paris: Maloine, 1911.

Ramón y Cajal, S. *Degeneration and regeneration of the nervous system.* London: Oxford Univ. Press, 1928.

Ranson, S. W., & Clark, S. *The anatomy of the nervous system* (10th ed.). Philadelphia: Saunders, 1959.

Ribot, T. A. *Les maladies de la mémoire.* Paris: Baillière, 1881.

Rose, J. E., Malis, L. I., & Baker, C. P. Neural growth in the cerebral cortex and lesions produced by monoenergetic deuterons. *International symposium of principles of sensory communication,* 1959.

Russell, R. W. *Brain, memory, learning.* Oxford: Clarendon Press, 1959.

Samuels, A. J., Boyarsky, L. L., Gerard, R. W., Libet, A., & Brust, M. Distribution, exchange and migration of phosphate compounds in the nervous system. *Amer. J. Physiol.,* 1951, **179**, 1–15.

Samuels, I. Reticular mechanisms and behavior. *Psychol. Bull.,* 1959, **56**, 1–25.

Sauders, F. K., & Young, J. Z. The influence of peripheral connexion on the diameter of regenerating nerve fibres. *J. exp. Biol.,* 1946, **22**, 203–212.

Schadé, J. P. A histological and histochemical analysis of the developing cerebral cortex. *Proc. roy. Acad. Sci. (Amsterdam)*, 1959a, **62**, 445–460.

Schadé, J. P. Differential growth of nerve cells in cerebral cortex. *Growth,* 1959b, **23**, 159–168.

Schadé, J. P. Structural organization of the cerebral cortex in normal and pathological brains. *International symposium on problems of the Brain.* Galesburg, Ill.: Galesburg State Research Hospital, 1963.

Schadé, J. P., & Baxter, C. F. Changes during growth in the volume and surface area of neurons in the rabbit. *J. exp. Neurol.,* 1960, **2**, 158–178.

Schleich, W. As cited by H. Klüver in *The brain and human behavior.* H. C. Solomon, S. Cobb, & W. Penfield, Eds. Baltimore: Williams and Wilkins, 1958.

Scoville, W. B., & Milner, Brenda. Loss of recent memory after bilateral hippocampal lesions. *J. Neurol. Neurosurg. Psychiat.,* 1957, **20**, 11–21.

Speidel, C. C. Studies of living nerves. II: Activities of amoeboid growth cones, sheath cells and myelin segments as revealed by prolonged observation of individual nerve fibers in tadpoles. *Amer. J. Anat.,* 1933, **52**, 1–79.

Speidel, C. C. Studies of living nerve. V: Alcoholic neuritis and recovery. *J. comp. Neurol.,* 1936, **64,** 77–113.

Speidel, C. C. Adjustments of nerve endings. *The Harvey Lectures,* Lancaster, Pa.: Science Press, 1940, **36,** 126–158.

Speidel, C. C. Studies of living nerves. VIII: Histories of nerve endings in frog tadpoles subjected to various injurious treatments. *Proc. Amer. phil. Soc.,* 1942, **85,** 168–183.

Sperry, R. W. The effects of crossing nerves to antagonistic muscles in the hind limb of the rat. *J. comp. Neurol.,* 1941, **75,** 1–19.

Sperry, R. W. Nature of functional recovery following regeneration of the oculomotor nerve in amphibians. *Anat. Rec.,* 1947, **97,** 293–316.

Sperry, R. W. Patterning of central synapses in regeneration of the optic nerve in teleosts. *Physiol. Zool.,* 1948, **21,** 351–361.

Sperry, R. W. Myoptic specificity in teleost motoneurons. *J. comp. Neurol.,* 1950, **93,** 277–288.

Sperry, R. W. Mechanism of neural maturation. In *Handbook of experimental psychology.* S. S. Stevens, Ed. New York: Wiley, 1951a.

Sperry, R. W. Regulative factors in the orderly growth of neural circuits. *Growth,* 1951b, **15,** 63–87 (supplement).

Sperry, R. W. Problems in the biochemical specification of neurons. In *Biochemistry of the developing nervous system.* H. Waelsch, Ed. New York: Academic Press, 1955.

Sperry, R. W. Corpus callosum and interhemispheric transfer in the monkey (*Macaca mulatta*). *Anat. Rec.,* 1958a, **131,** 297.

Sperry, R. W. Physiological plasticity and the brain circuit theory. In *Biological and biochemical basis of behavior,* H. F. Harlow & C. N. Woolsey, Eds. Madison: Univ. of Wisconsin Press, 1958b.

Sperry, R. W., & Deupree, N. Functional recovery following alternations in nerve-muscle connections of fishes. *J. comp. Neurol.,* 1956, **106,** 143–158.

Ström, G. Physiological significance of post-tetanic potentiation of the spinal monosynaptic reflex. *Acta physiol. scand.,* 1951, **24,** 61–83.

Tanzi, E. I fattie la Induzime ell odierne istologia del sistema nervoso. *Rev. sper. Freniat.,* 1893, **19,** 419–472.

Tello, F. La influencia del neurotropismo en la regeneracion de los centros nervioso. *Trab. Lab. Invest. biol.,* 1911, **9** (entire issue).

Thorpe, W. H. *Learning and instinct in animals.* London: Methuen, 1956.

Toennies, J. F. Die Erregungssteuerung im Zentralnervensystem. *Arch. Psychiat. Nervenkr.,* 1949, **182,** 478–535.

Verworn, M. Die Polare Erregung durch den galvanishen Strom. *Pflüg. Arch. ges. Physiol.,* 1889, **45** (monograph).

Waldeyer, W. von. Ueber einige neuere Forschungen im Gebiete der Anatomie des Centralnervensystems. *Berl. klin. Wschr.,* 1891, **28,** 691.

Weiss, P. Erregungsspezifität und Erregungsresonanz. *Ergebn. Biol.,* 1929, **3,** 1–151.

Weiss, P. Selectivity controlling the central-peripheral relations in the nervous system. *Biol. Rev.,* 1936, **11,** 494–531.

Weiss, P. Nerve patterns: the mechanics of nerve growth. *Growth,* Third Growth Symposium, 1941, **5,** 163–203.

Weiss, P., Ed. *Genetic neurology. Conference of the international union of biological science.* Chicago: Univ. of Chicago Press, 1950.

Weiss, P., & Hiscoe, H. B. Experiments on the mechanism of nerve growth. *J. exp. Zool.,* 1948, **107,** 315–396.

Weiss, P., & Taylor, A. C. Further experimental evidence against neurotropism in nerve regeneration. *J. exp. Zool.,* 1944, **95,** 233–257.

Willis, T. *Cerebri anatome qui accessit nervorum descriptio et usus.* London: Martyn and Allestry, 1664.

Windle, W. F. *Regeneration in the central nervous system.* Springfield, Ill.: Thomas, 1955.

Young, J. Z. The evolution of the nervous system and of the relationship of organism and environment. In *Evolution, essays presented to E. S. Goodrich.* G. R. de Beer, Ed. Oxford: Clarendon Press, 1938.

Young, J. Z. Structures degeneration and repair of nerve fibers. *Nature* (*London*), 1945, **156,** 132–136.

Young, J. Z. Growth and plasticity in the nervous system. *Proc. roy. Soc.* (*London*), B, 1951, **139,** 18–37.

Zanotti, F. M. *Della forza attrativa delle idee.* In *Opere de F. M. Zanotti.* Vol. V. Bologna: 1790 (originally published under false date 1747).

CHAPTER SIXTEEN

Biochemical Hypotheses

Traditionally, the process of learning and its end product—memory—have been thought to be the result of physiological and/or anatomical changes. It has been recognized for some time that these functional or structural alterations must, in turn, be based on more molecular events in the biochemical makeup of individual neurons. However, until recently no effort has been made to use biochemical processes as explanatory concepts for learning and memory because little or no relevant information about these processes was available. This trend has now been altered by a number of discoveries which have illuminated the biochemical basis of many inherited functional properties.

This development has raised many hopes that we may find the key to the problem of learning and memory in similar biochemical processes. Several speculative hypotheses have been advanced that promise more, at least to the nonexpert, than may be warranted at this time. It is premature to speak of biochemical *theories* of learning or memory or to propose that we abandon physiological or anatomical concepts in favor of a biochemical interpretation.

Before considering some of the biochemical speculations, a proper perspective, seemingly lost by some enthusiastic psychologists who have taken up the defense and dissemination of biochemical speculations, must be developed. All neural events must somehow be based on biochemical processes which, in turn, can be reduced to still more basic physical events. This does not call for the abandonment of anatomical or physiological concepts in favor of simpler levels of discourse. It is perfectly appropriate to attempt an explanation of specific phenomena by reducing the problem to a lower level of investigation, but there is no promise that such an approach will provide a complete answer to the problems. Explanatory concepts from all levels of discourse must be available if an understanding of the complex phenomena of learning and retention is to be achieved. Biochemical speculations can contribute valuable information in suggesting mechanisms capable of producing the general or selective facilitation which seems to be an essential aspect of all theories of learning. However, the need to investigate the structural and functional changes that occur as a result of these biochemical events will persist, and it remains to be seen how these individual, *local* changes are integrated and combined to produce the *specific pattern of functional changes* in the central nervous system that constitutes learning.

Aside from these general considerations, there are more serious objections to the unqualified enthusiasm of psychologists and physiologists. There is *no* direct evidence to link any of the proposed biochemical mechanisms *specifically* to learning and/or memory. The basic biochemical findings suggest merely that chemical events may take place inside a neuron as the result of use or repeated stimulation and that these reactions may somehow lower the cell's threshold to subsequent excitation. Even this general statement contains speculative elements. We have demonstrated only that repeated activation increases biochemical processes which are *assumed* to affect the threshold of the cell. These are, of course, important findings which may advance our understanding of neural functions. We should not conclude, however, that they explain the *selective* facilitation of *specific* neural pathways which develops not merely as the result of use but occurs under limited conditions of near-simultaneous excitation of particular neural pathways. Even the condition of near-simultaneity does not always produce learning or memory.

851

One of the stimuli must have special "motivational" properties, and we have no idea what this may mean in terms of either physiological or biochemical events. The presently available evidence indicates, in fact, that the proposed biochemical mechanisms are *not* specific to learning and/or memory. They may, nonetheless, explain important events that occur during learning and other neural processes and help us to understand the complex functional changes that take place during acquisition.

The appearance of biochemical concepts in psychology has created a unique and difficult situation. Few psychologists are qualified to evaluate the basic experimental literature or, for that matter, the often complex theoretical reasoning which leads to the statement that some sequence of biochemical events may be the basis of learning or retention. This situation is further complicated by the fact that the biochemists who have arrived at these conclusions have no training in psychology and consequently often define learning or memory in unsatisfactory terms. Facilitation of a neural pathway may be one of the events that must take place during acquisition, but learning and memory may require much more complex processes not explained by the same intracellular changes. If biochemical concepts are to play a significant role in future psychological theories, we shall have to acquire a sufficiently solid background in basic biochemistry to permit an intelligent, critical evaluation of biochemical findings. We cannot provide such a background in the framework of this discussion, but we would like to present a very condensed and rudimentary overview of basic biochemical concepts before discussing the theories of learning and memory proposed in recent years.

REVIEW OF BIOCHEMICAL CONCEPTS

Proteins

Proteins play an essential role in the structural and dynamic functions of all living matter. The term protein is applied to a great variety of complex nitrogenous substances which are made up of simpler components called amino acids. Proteins are commonly classified on the basis of solubility into *albumins* (soluble in water), *globulins* (soluble in salt solutions), *prolamines* (soluble in ethanol), *glutelins* (soluble only in acids), and *scleroproteins* (insoluble). A further distinction is made between "simple" proteins which de-

compose completely into amino acids and "conjugated" proteins which, on decomposition, liberate an organic component called "prosthetic group." The nucleoproteins that play such an important role in recent biochemical theories of learning are such conjugated proteins; nucleic acid is the prosthetic group. Generally, proteins are composed of hydrogen (6 to 7% of total dry weight), oxygen (20 to 23%), carbon (50 to 55%), and nitrogen (12 to 19%).

Amino Acids

Proteins are large molecules of high molecular weight. Literally thousands of carbon, hydrogen, oxygen, and nitrogen atoms combine to form a single protein molecule. It has been impossible to apply an elementary analysis to these complex structures. All proteins break down (hydrolyze) into smaller molecules called amino acids, which appear to be the basic building blocks of all proteins and hence of all living matter. About 30 different amino acids have been isolated to date, but not all appear in a given protein. The proportion of a specific amino acid varies greatly from protein to protein. Although it is not within the scope of this discussion to list and discuss all amino acids individually, an example may provide some idea of their composition and structure. The simplest amino acid is called *glycine* (NH_2 CH_2COOH) and is found abundantly in many proteins, particularly in skeletal proteins which form tendons and ligaments.

Amino acids combine by means of peptide bonds. The α-amino group of one amino acid attaches to the α-carboxyl group of an adjoining one; a water molecule is eliminated (hydrolysis) and an amide linkage is formed. *Peptides* are thus structural intermediaries between the simple amino acids and complete proteins. Several peptides combine in a chain-like structure (polypeptide chain) to form a complete protein. Recent experimental findings suggest that the nature of a protein molecule is determined not only by the type and proportion of the constituent amino acids, but also by the *sequence* of amino acids on the long peptide chains. The physical shape of the protein molecule is determined by the coiled structure of the polypeptide chain. A number of peptides occur in nature, and some of these have attracted much attention because they have marked antibacterial action. The actinomycins and penicillins are good examples of such "antibiotic" peptides.

Enzymes

Enzymes are proteins that are responsible for the catalysis of all chemical reactions in living tissues. A *catalyst* is defined as a substance that alters the rate of a chemical reaction. The chemical substance upon which a catalyst acts is called a *substrate*. Enzymes typically are highly selective catalysts which affect only specific chemical reactions or classes of reactions. The following analogy has been suggested (Fruton and Simmonds, 1958) to illustrate enzymatic functions. A living cell might be considered to be a factory in which individual enzymes act like different pieces of machinery to cooperate in the transformation of basic materials such as steel (the substrates) into complex products such as cars.

Nucleic Acids

Many of the more recent biochemical theories have postulated that changes in ribonucleic acid (RNA), deoxyribonucleic acid (DNA), or both are responsible for the functional facilitation which presumably accounts for at least some important aspects of learning and memory. These nucleic acids are relatively large and complex molecules which must be considered in some detail if we are to understand the nature of the proposed modifications.

A complete breakdown (hydrolysis) of the nucleic acids yields purine and pyrimidine bases, sugar, and phosphoric acid. Partial decomposition of the nucleic acids yields two intermediate products, nucleotides and nucleosides. We shall briefly consider each of these substances.

Pyrimidine bases. Four derivatives of pyrimidine are found in nucleic acids, each of which represents only a minor modification of the parent compound. *Cytosine* is made up of the basic pyrimidine structure, except that an amino group (NH₂) replaces the hydrogen at the second carbon. (The atoms of a ring structure of this nature are numbered, starting with the nitrogen atom

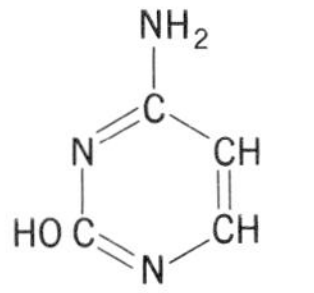

Cytosine
2–hydroxy–
6–aminopyrimidine

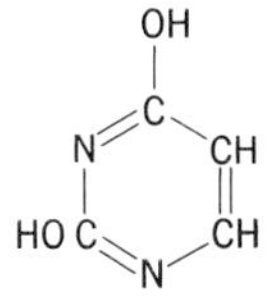

Uracil
2,6–dihydroxypyrimidine

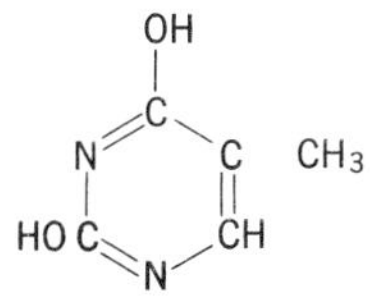

Thymine
5–methyluracil

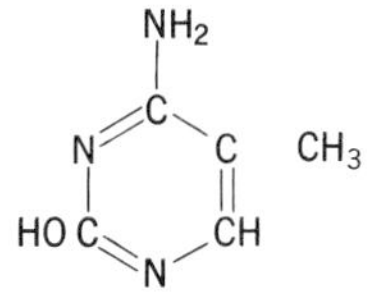

5- Methylcytosine

Fig. 16.2

in the upper left corner of the ring and proceeding in a counterclockwise fashion.) *Uracil* is formed by replacing the hydrogen atom at the second and sixth carbons with hydroxyl groups. *Thymine* represents a further modification of this structure. Like uracil it has hydroxyl groups at the second and sixth carbons, but it also has a methyl (CH₃) group in place of the hydrogen atom at the fifth carbon. The last of the pyrimidine derivatives that make up the nucleis acids is *5-methylcytosine* which resembles cytosine in having a hydroxyl group at the second carbon and an amino group at the sixth carbon. It differs from cytosine in having a methyl group in place of the hydrogen atom at the fifth carbon of the ring.

Purine bases. Ribonucleic acid and deoxyribonucleic acid both contain the purine bases adenine and guanine. These molecules are formed by replacing the hydrogen atoms normally attached to the second and sixth carbons of the basic purine ring structure with amino or hydroxyl groups. *Adenine* is formed by replacing the hydrogen at

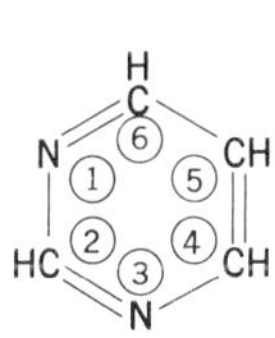

Pyrimidine

Fig. 16.1

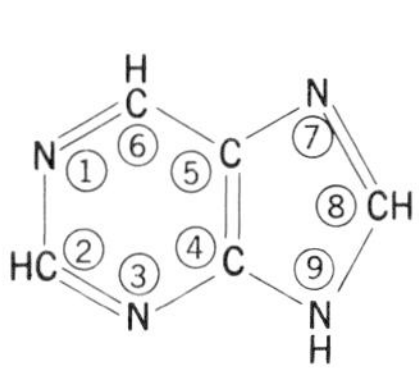

Purine

Fig. 16.3

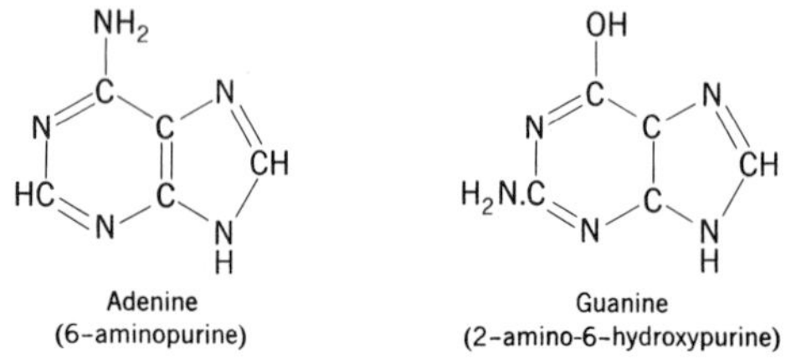

Adenine
(6-aminopurine)

Guanine
(2-amino-6-hydroxypurine)

Fig. 16.4

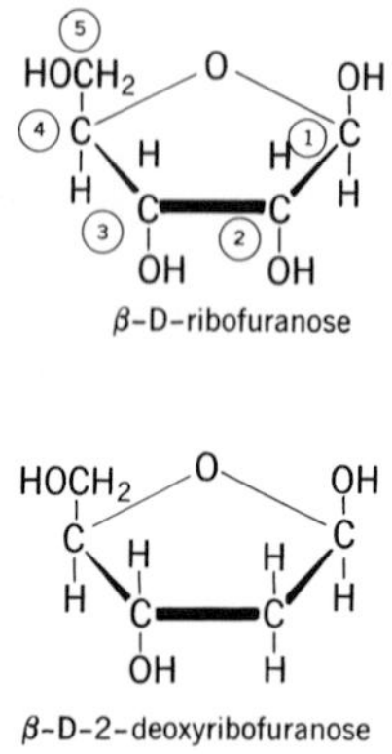

β–D–ribofuranose

β-D-2-deoxyribofuranose

Fig. 16.5

the sixth carbon with an amino group, and *guanine* shows a hydroxyl group at the sixth carbon and an amino group in place of the hydrogen atom at the second carbon of the purine ring.

Sugars. The nucleotides of the nucleic acids contain pentose sugars; these differ from the hexose sugars of common household use only in having five instead of six carbon atoms. One of the major differences between RNA and DNA is the structure of the sugar ring. Deoxyribonucleic acid (DNA) contains a sugar called *deoxyribose* and ribonucleic acid (RNA) contains *ribose*. The structure of these sugars is identical except that in the deoxyribose form a hydrogen atom replaces

the hydroxyl group found at the second carbon of the ribose sugar. (Note that the numbering system of these furanose ring structures differs from that previously described. It is customary to start at the first carbon on the top right portion of the ring and to continue *clockwise*.) As indicated by the term "deoxy," the difference between the two sugars lies in the absence of one oxygen atom from the ribose ring.

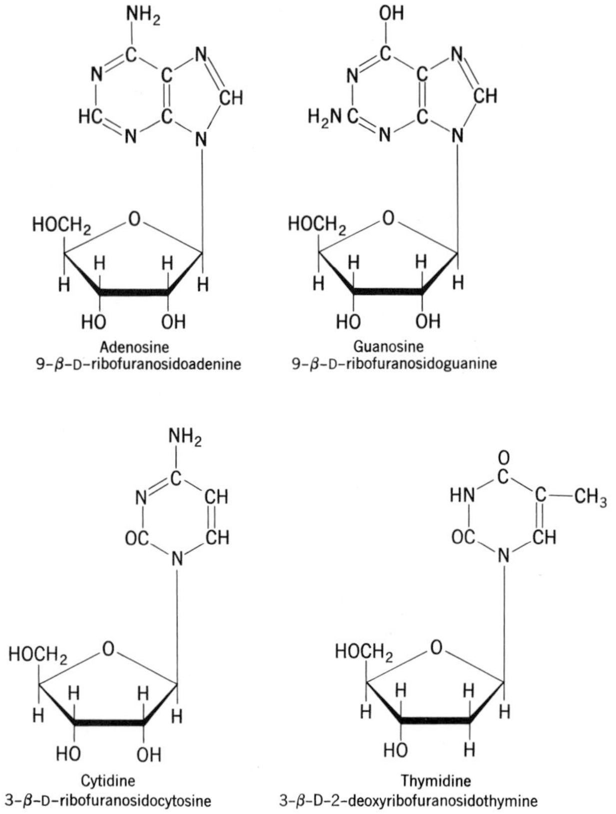

Adenosine
9–β–D–ribofuranosidoadenine

Guanosine
9–β–D–ribofuranosidoguanine

Cytidine
3–β–D–ribofuranosidocytosine

Thymidine
3–β–D–2–deoxyribofuranosidothymine

Fig. 16.6

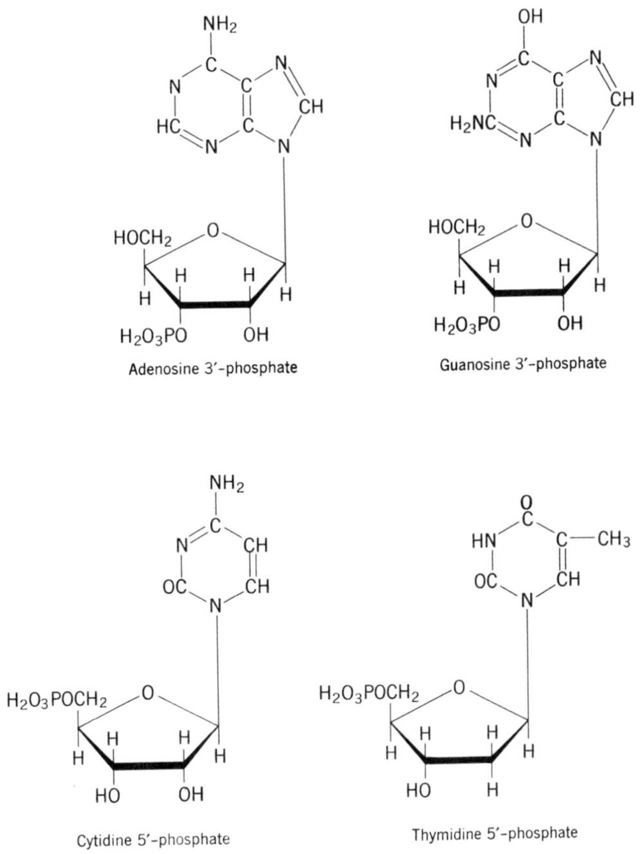

NH$_2$

OH

Adenosine 3'-phosphate

Guanosine 3'-phosphate

NH$_2$

Cytidine 5'-phosphate

Thymidine 5'-phosphate

Fig. 16.7

Nucleosides and nucleotides. Purine as well as pyrimidine bases combine with ribose and deoxyribose sugars to form nucleosides. Of particular importance to our present discussion are the ribonucleosides *adenosine* and *guanosine* (combinations of ribose sugar and the purine bases adenine and guanine) and *cytidine* and *uridine* (combinations of ribose and the pyrimidine bases cytosine and uracil).

Nucleotides are formed by the attachment of a phosphoric acid molecule to the third or fifth carbon of the pentose sugar of the nucleosides. Each of the nucleosides can form three types of such monophosphates; these are distinguished by retaining the name of the nucleoside and adding the phosphate and number of the atom to which it attaches. Adenosine, for instance, forms adenoside 5'-phosphate, adenosine 3'-phosphate, and adenosine 2'-phosphate. Collectively, the monophosphate combinations of adenoside are also called *adenylic acids*. Guanosine, cytidine, and uridine similarly form *guanylic acids*, *cytidylic acids*, and *uridylic acids*.

The nucleoside 5'-phosphate may be further phosphorylated to form di- and triphosphates. Well-known examples of this substance are the adenosine diphosphates (ADP) and adenosine triphosphates (ATP) which play an important role in energy transfer. These compounds are identical to the adenosine 5'-phosphates just described, except that additional phosphate groups are added to the one already present at the fifth carbon. We might also note that many important biological compounds (such as coenzymes) have a basic nucleotide structure.

The structure of nucleic acids. It was thought for a long time that the nucleic acid molecules contained equal (i.e., equimolecular) amounts of the four constituent bases adenine, guanine, cytosine, and uracil. Recent investigations have shown that this notion must be abandoned and that a different systematic scheme seems to be followed. In RNA the number of nucleotides made of adenine and cytosine bases is equal to the number made of guanine and uracil bases.

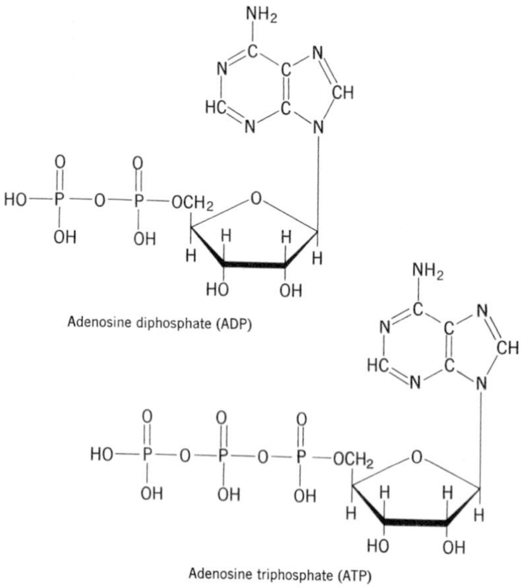

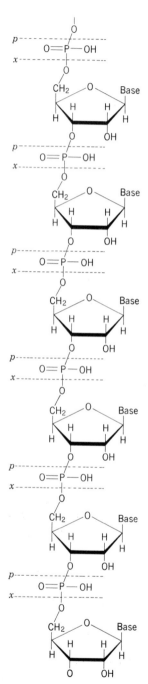

NH₂

Adenosine diphosphate (ADP)

NH₂

Adenosine triphosphate (ATP)

Fig. 16.8

A similar system characterizes DNA except that thymine replaces uracil. In addition, it now seems that the number of purine nucleotides is equal to that of pyrimidine nucleotides and that the *molar ratio* of adenine to thymine and guanine to cytosine is always one.

Ribonucleic acid (RNA). We shall ignore here the difference in nucleotide bases and examine how individual nucleotides form *internucleotide links* to develop long chains of interconnected nucleotides or *polynucleotides.* The main internucleotide links are phosphor-ester groups which connect the 3′ phosphate of the sugar in one nucleotide with the 5′ carbon of the sugar in the adjoining nucleotide. In this fashion, the long polynucleotide chains which make up all RNA molecules are constructed.

It follows from this structural limitation that RNA molecules can differ only in the sequence of bases in the nucleotide chain or in the actual length of the chain itself. RNA as it exists in the nucleoprotein of cells is heterogenous, and estimates of its molecular weight vary from 20,000 to 2,000,000. Although some of this variance may be due to differences in estimating techniques, we can get some idea of the general complexity and heterogeneity of RNA molecules from the following computation. Single nucleotides have an average molecular weight of about 350. Using the extreme values for RNA molecules just listed, we come to the conclusion that as many as 5700

Fig. 16.9 A section of the polynucleotide chain in the RNA molecule. The sites of hydrolysis by alkali and by 5′-phosphodiesterase are indicated by *p* and *x* respectively.

or as few as 57 nucleotides may interconnect to form a single polynucleotide chain or RNA molecule.

Deoxyribonucleic acid (DNA). The internucleotide links in DNA molecules are formed in the same general fashion as those of RNA chains. Phosphor-ester groups $(O=P—OH)$ link the third carbon of the sugar of one nucleotide with the fifth carbon of the sugar (furanose) ring of the adjoining carbon.

At present it is believed that the DNA molecule consists of a long, unbranched chain of nucleotides which form a stiff, rod-like structure. On the basis of the important work of Watson and Crick (1953) it is further assumed that this rod consists of a double helix containing two helical phosphate sugar chains which wind around the same axis and are held together by hydrogen bonds between their bases.

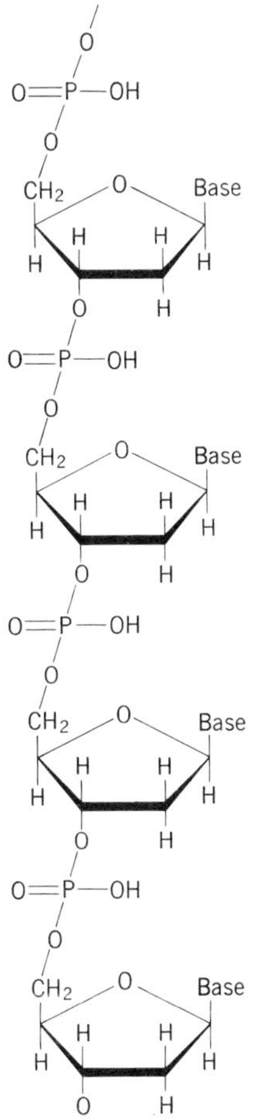

Watson and Crick's studies of DNA molecular models revealed that such a structure could be built only of pairs of one purine and one pyrimidine base and that the only pairings able to provide the necessary hydrogen bonds are adenine with thymine and guanine with cytosine. This, of course, would explain the reported 1:1 ratio of adenine to thymine and guanine to cytosine. In the double helix the following arrangement of bases could occur:

Phosphate____sugar____adenine..........thymine____sugar____Phosphate
Phosphate____sugar____cytosine..........guanine____sugar____Phosphate
Phosphate____sugar____guanine..........cytosine____sugar____Phosphate
Phosphate____sugar____thymine..........adenine____sugar____Phosphate

Perhaps the most interesting aspect of this arrangement is that the sequence of bases in one of the chains completely determines the sequence in the other; thus, a rupture of the hydrogen bonds (indicated by dotted lines) results in two individual strands which can form only exact duplicates of the original double helix by recombining with other nucleotide chains. This, as we shall see, may be an extremely important mechanism in the transfer of genetic information.

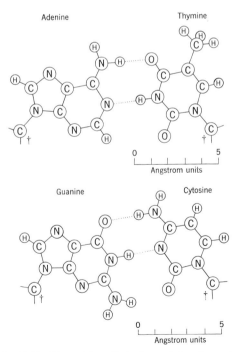

Fig. 16.11 The pairing of adenine and thymine and of guanine and cytosine. Dotted lines indicate the hydrogen bonds. The carbon atoms marked † belong to sugar rings.

Fig. 16.10 Part of the polynucleotide chain in DNA.

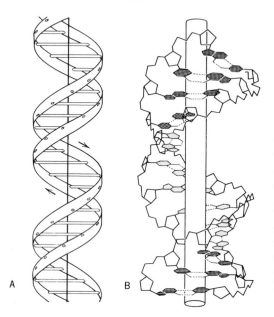

A   B

Fig. 16.12   A, the DNA molecule as proposed by Watson and Crick. The two phosphate sugar chains are represented by ribbons, and the pairs of bases holding the chains together are shown as horizontal rods. B, a model of the DNA helix. The dotted lines represent the hydrogen bonds binding the bases. (From Davidson, 1965.)

DNA molecules are extremely heterogeneous. Molecular weights varying from 4 to 15 million have been reported. The molar proportion of bases varies widely from species to species but appears to be constant for the different tissues of a given species.

The distribution of nucleic acids. The nucleic acid content of specific tissues varies widely. Highly cellular organs such as the spleen and pancreas are particularly rich in nucleic acids, whereas the brain and other fibrous organs have a much lower concentration. The DNA concentration tends to be high in tissues having a relatively large proportion of nuclear material and relatively little cytoplasmic substance. RNA, on the other hand, is particularly abundant in tissues with high cytoplasmic volume. Embryonic tissue tends to be richer in both nucleic acids than the corresponding adult tissue, but beyond that there appears to be little correlation with age.

The DNA content of a cell is the least variable of all cellular constituents, whereas RNA concentrations are subject to wide fluctuations. Fasting or protein-deficient diets, for instance, produce a marked reduction in the total RNA content of liver cells without affecting DNA at all. (Since nutritional changes are characterized by a loss of lipids, proteins, and other tissue constituents, it should be obvious that fasting produces a rise in DNA and even RNA in relation to total cellular constituents—even though the total content of the former is not changed and that of the latter is actually reduced.) It is noteworthy, in this connection, that even a sharp decrease in total liver RNA content does not result in a correspondingly reduced protein synthesis. Recent experiments have shown that the loss of RNA molecules is offset by an increased turnover rate in the remaining molecules so that the total amount of RNA synthesized per unit time remains constant. Activation of neural tissues by intense motor activity or sensory stimulation reduces the cytoplasmic RNA content.

The distribution of ribonucleic acids in the cytoplasm. Until the late 1930's and early 1940's it was generally assumed that the nucleic acids RNA and DNA are found only in the nuclei of cells (hence the name). This does, in fact, seem to be true for deoxyribonucleic acid, but recent investigations have shown rather conclusively that most ribonucleic acid is concentrated in specific portions of the cytoplasm of the cell.

Recent advances in phase contrast and electronmicroscopy have demonstrated cytoplasmic inclusions that are important in this context. The most interesting of these is a system of strands and vesicles called the *endoplasmic reticulum.* Tubules of this reticular structure are believed to form a complex network of canals which lead from the exterior of the cell to the nucleus. Electronmicroscopic analysis of these tubules has shown that two types of tube profiles occur. Smooth-surfaced profiles are commonly found in densely populated reticular nets. Rough-surfaced profiles, on the other hand, occur in nearly parallel strands which are covered with small (10 to 20 mμ) particles called *ribosomes.* These particles also occur individually in other portions of the cytoplasm. The endoplasmic reticulum makes up much of, if not all, the *microsomal fraction*; this is obtained by differential centrifugation, in addition to a nuclear fraction, a fraction of larger granules, and a supernatant devoid of sedimentable materials. If this microsomal fraction is treated further (with sodium deoxycholate), small particles which contain nearly all the microsomal RNA can be obtained;

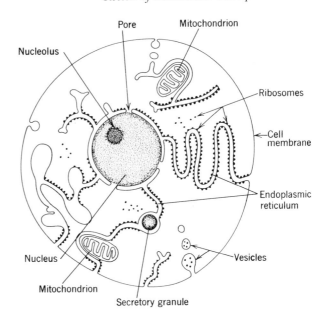

Fig. 16.13 A typical animal cell. (From Davidson, 1965.)

these particles appear to be identical to the ribosomes that have been identified by the electron microscope.

A comparison of the RNA content of the ribosomal fraction with that of the entire cytoplasm indicates the bulk of cytoplasmic RNA is concentrated in these particles. Microsomal RNA (mRNA) accounts for about 80% of the total RNA content of a cell. Mitochondria contain an additional 4%—believed to be derived from intramitochondrial ribosomes. There is also a relatively high concentration of soluble or transfer RNA (sRNA) in the cell sap which accounts for 10 to 15% of the total RNA. We must therefore distinguish at least two types of cytosomal (cRNA) ribonucleic acid, the microsomal RNA (mRNA) and the soluble or transfer (sRNA) type. They resemble each other closely with respect to the molar proportion of bases, but sRNA appears to have a much lower molecular weight than mRNA. It is believed that sRNA is involved in the transfer of amino acids to mRNA, and it appears likely that a different species of sRNA may be involved in the transfer of each amino acid.

The distribution of nucleic acids in the nucleus. The cell nucleus is chemically and cytoarchitecturally a complex structure which has not yet been studied sufficiently to permit an assignment of specific chemical components to particular cytological structures. As a whole, the nucleus contains large amounts of DNA, a small quantity of RNA (nRNA), a basic protein (either protamine or histone), lipids, other phosphorous compounds, and several inorganic elements. Deoxyribonucleic acid makes up nearly 50% of the dry weight of the nuclei of some cells (the average is nearer 30%).

In view of the suggested role of DNA in genetic mechanisms, it is interesting to note that the amount of DNA in the nuclei of spermatozoa is only about half of that in somatic cell nuclei of the same species. This finding is in marked contrast to the observation that the DNA content appears to be constant for different somatic tissues of a given species. Deoxyribonucleic acid is the least variable of all cellular constituents, and this stability has been used to calculate the number of cells in a piece of tissue. Some DNA has been found in the nucleolus, but the major portion of the total DNA content of a nucleus is found in the chromosomes. Approximately 90% of the mass of chromosomes is made up of nucleohistones which contain about 45% DNA and 55% histone. The remaining 10% of the chromosomal mass is composed of coiled threads called "residual chromosomes" which contain little DNA (1.5 to 2.6% in one study) but considerable amounts of nRNA.

Nuclear ribonucleic acid (nRNA) makes up only a small fraction of the total cellular RNA content but as much as 10 to 15% of the nucleic acid inside the nucleus. The total amount of nRNA varies widely between tissues, and all of it appears to be concentrated in the nucleolus and the chromosomes. The nRNA is composed of the usual four nucleotides, but the molar proportions of bases differ significantly from those found in cytoplasmic (mRNA and sRNA) RNA. More important, perhaps, is the observation that the metabolic activity of nuclear RNA is much greater than that of cytoplasmic RNA. It has been suggested, in this connection, that two types of nuclear RNA ($nRNA_1$ and $nRNA_2$) can be distinguished on the basis of pronounced differences in turnover and specific activity, but no corresponding functional differences have as yet been postulated. It has also been proposed that nRNA might be a "precursor" of at least part of the cytoplasmic RNA, but the obvious differences in molar composition between nRNA and cRNA make such an interpretation unlikely.

Enzymes that destroy RNA or DNA. A stable enzyme called *ribonuclease* has been purified;

this enzyme splits the linkage between ribonucleotides by selectively hydrolyzing the phosphate esters which attach pyrimidine nucleotides to purine nucleotides. This enzyme fragments RNA chains into (1) segments (oligonucleotides) of varying length and base sequence and (2) free pyrimidine (but not purine) nucleotides.

A similar enzyme called *deoxyribonuclease* I has been obtained from pancreatic tissue. Activated by magnesium or manganese ions, this enzyme fragments DNA molecules into mono- and dinucleotides. The mechanism of this action is not yet completely understood. Enzymes that also degrade DNA but do not require magnesium or manganese can be obtained from spleen tissue and are called *deoxyribonuclease* II.

The catabolism or breakdown of nucleic acids *in vivo* is poorly understood, but it is generally accepted that the initial step consists of the hydrolysis of RNA and DNA by a nuclease (such as the ribo- and deoxyribonucleases just discussed). The breakdown products are then con-

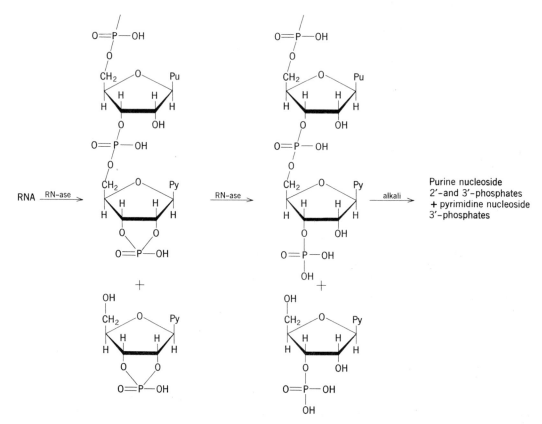

Fig. 16.14 The action of ribonuclease (RN-ase) on RNA showing the intermediate formation of cyclic phosphates.

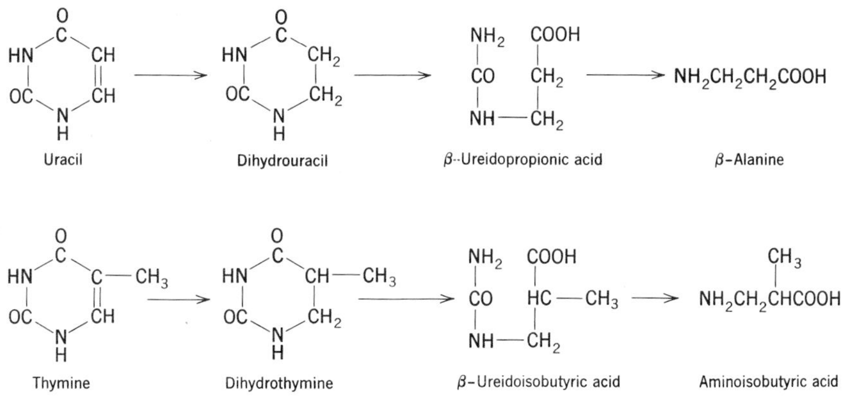

Fig. 16.15

verted to nucleotides and, eventually, nucleosides by a variety of phosphatases. Individual pyrimidine bases (uracil and thymine) are further degraded by a process involving (1) reduction to dihydro derivatives, (2) formation of ureido acids by ring opening, and (3) eventual loss of ammonia and carbon dioxide. The end product of this process is β-alanine or its methylated derivative.

Individual purine bases (adenine and guanine) are deaminated under the influence of specific enzymes (adenase and guanase) to hypoxanthine or xanthine. These intermediary products are then oxidized under the influence of xanthine oxidase to uric acid, the final product in man. In lower mammals, a further degradation of uric acid to allantoin takes place.

In vivo, DNA is remarkably stable and shows little or no tendency to break down, in spite of a relatively abundant supply of deoxyribonuclease in most tissues. Ribonucleic acid, on the other hand, shows relatively high turnover rates which indicate that as much as 10% of the available RNA is replaced every day. The reasons for this interesting difference between the two nucleic acids are not yet understood, but important theoretical deductions have been based on it.

The role of nucleic acids in genetic functions and protein synthesis. The functional properties of all cells and the nature of their interaction with other cells are basically determined by protein synthesis (i.e., the type of proteins manufactured and the rate of their synthesis). According to recent biochemical theories for which there is good experimental support, this crucial process is controlled by the ribonucleic acids. These acids, in turn, are regulated by genetically determined properties of the deoxyribonucleic acid. Messen-

ger or microsomal RNA (mRNA) molecules are manufactured inside the cell nucleus, using DNA molecules as models or "templates." These messenger RNA molecules then migrate into the cytoplasm of the cell; here they form ribosomal particles which attach themselves to the walls of

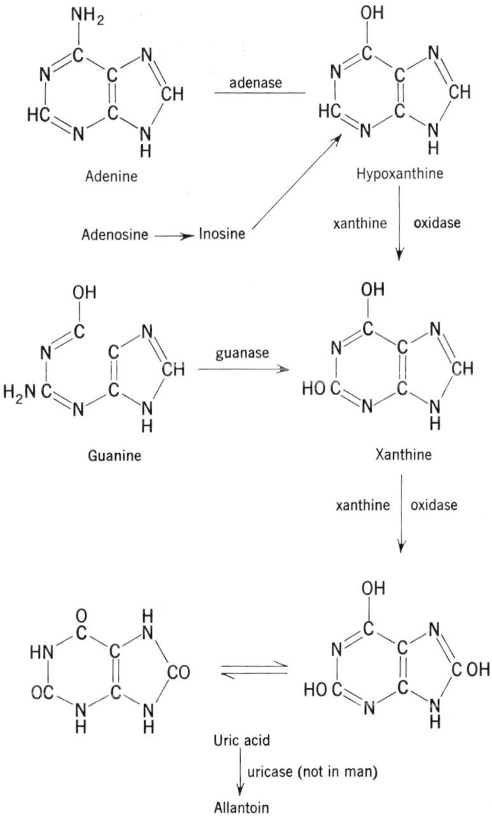

Fig. 16.16

the endoplasmic reticulum and serve as templates for protein synthesis. Soluble (or "transfer") RNA (sRNA) then picks up specific, enzymatically activated amino acids and transfers them to appropriate (as determined by the base sequence of the mRNA) site on the messenger RNA. In this fashion, specific chains of protein molecules, which are the basic ingredient of all cellular reactions, are developed. The manufacture of a specific protein depends directly on the availability of the appropriate mRNA model or template, and it is here that most biochemical theories of learning propose essential alterations. It should not be overlooked that the rate-limiting factor in this system is the presence of sRNA or, ultimately, the availability of essential amino acids.

Basically, the functional properties of each cell (i.e., the type and rate of protein synthesis) are determined by heredity. The genetic information is presumably coded in the base sequences of DNA molecules. During cell division each DNA molecule splits lengthwise all along its helical structure, so that one complete half of the original molecule is transferred to each of the daughter cells. Here the missing half is resynthesized, and an exact duplicate of the parent molecule is ready to serve as a model for the synthesis of mRNA; it can thus control the activities of the daughter cell, which will function precisely like the parent cell from which it was derived.

Before we see how learning (i.e., repeated and specific activation of such a cell) may produce permanent or at least long-persisting changes in this essential sequence, a closer look at the basic biological processes might be useful.

The starting point of all speculations about the functional properties of RNA was the series of discoveries which led to the hypothesis that genetic information might be transferred by means of reconstituting DNA molecules. It has actually been known for quite some time that the chromosomal structure of higher plants and animals contains high concentrations of this nucleic acid, but to demonstrate its role in genetic processes is quite difficult.

Much of the experimental evidence comes from *in vivo* or *in vitro* studies of bacterial transformations. These show quite unambiguously that the fundamental characteristics of at least certain types of bacteria can be modified by injections of DNA from related but functionally different strains. An example may clarify this idea. Pneumococci occur in active (virulent) as well as inactive forms. Inactive pneumococci are converted

to virulent organisms by injections of DNA extract from the active strain. The transformation is permanent, and the functional change appears to be due to DNA rather than some other compound, for the DNA "transferring principle" used in these studies did not contain proteins. Recent studies in this area have shown that a single specimen of DNA may simultaneously carry such different characteristics as resistance to penicillin, resistance to streptomycin, and ability to form capsules. Certain characteristics appear to be linked (i.e., always occur together on a DNA molecule), and it is easy to see how a more complex genetic program could be transferred by complex DNA molecules.

Just how this transfer might take place has been suggested by the work of Watson and Crick (1953) and Wilkins (1963). Working with theoretical and physical models of DNA molecules, Crick proposed that only a double helical structure with hydrogen bonds between opposing bases could account for the known properties of DNA. Wilkins added the important suggestion that the genetic information must be "coded" in terms of the sequence of bases along the polynucleotide chain. Since adenine can be paired only with thymine and guanine only with cytosine, this "code" can be maintained when the DNA molecule splits along its vertical axis during cell division. Each half of the original double helix can then serve as a template to form a complementary chain and thus reconstitute the parent molecule. (Synthesis of complete DNA molecules from single-stranded halves has been observed in the laboratory, although the structure of the reconstituted portion is, of course, open to conjecture.)

It was long thought that the ribosomal RNA provided a more or less permanent template for the manufacture of proteins. However, it has recently been observed that protein synthesis cannot continue for any length of time in the absence of DNA. This finding has led to the suggestion that the template function is perhaps performed by messenger RNA; this substance is continuously synthesized in the nucleus of the cell on the basis of DNA models and then migrates to the cytoplasmic inclusions. It is not clear whether messenger RNA then somehow transforms into ribosomal RNA or whether it merely attaches itself to the ribosomal particles.

Messenger RNA has only recently been discovered (Gros et al., 1961), and its role in protein synthesis has been established only on largely inferential evidence. It is known to have a "DNA-like" structure (Gros et al., 1961) and to be manufactured in the cell nucleus, using the DNA molecule as a template model. Its role in protein synthesis is inferred from studies showing that cell-free extracts continue to synthesize proteins as long as the DNA fraction is intact and appropriate nutrients are added. Protein synthesis was stopped in these studies by the addition of deoxyribonuclease, which presumably has no effect on the ribonucleic acids but destroys all DNA. Synthesis was reactivated by adding DNA to the denuded extract. Since DNA is believed not to have a direct role in protein synthesis, these findings suggest that the observed effects were due to an interference with the continuous synthesis of mRNA by DNA.

Several recent studies have provided additional support for the hypothesis that a continuous synthesis of messenger RNA is essential to protein synthesis. These findings are important because they indicate that the RNA molecule which serves as a template for protein synthesis has a very rapid turnover, requiring continuous resynthesis by DNA. Thus, the theoretical interpretations of the learning or memory process which rely on a change in template RNA can no longer be accepted. If memory is at all related to the nucleic acids or protein synthesis, it should involve changes in the DNA molecules which are responsible for the synthesis of specific messenger RNA molecules and show a sufficiently low rate of turnover to permit the storage of long-term memory. Such changes in DNA appear most unlikely, for DNA is a very stable molecule, as it indeed must be if it is to transmit genetic information faithfully.

We still do not know very much about the mechanisms involved in protein synthesis. There is a fairly good agreement among biochemists (Watson, 1963) that messenger RNA in some fashion serves as a model for the manufacture of specific proteins and that transfer or soluble RNA (sRNA) provides the mechanism by which the individual building blocks (amino acids) are conveyed to the appropriate place on the template molecule. However, the bulk of all cellular RNA occurs in the form of ribosomal (mRNA) ribonucleic acid, and there is no consensus about its possible role in protein synthesis.

Transfer or soluble RNA (sRNA) appears to have a double helical structure similar to that of DNA, except that the helix seems to be made up of a *single* strand which folds back upon itself to form the double helix (Wilkins, 1963). It has

been estimated that approximately 80 nucleotides make up the average sRNA chain, and diffraction pattern studies indicate that the individual bases on one-half of the folded chain join complementary bases on the other half. In view of the previously discussed limitations of base pairings (adenine attaches only to thymine and guanine only to cytosine), the pattern of bases appears to be far from random.

The double helical structure of sRNA differs in two important respects from that discussed for DNA. Recent studies suggest that the sRNA molecule is not a perfectly symmetrical structure but has a "tail" or terminal group; this has no counterpart in DNA and seems to contain free bases which, at least in the few samples studied so far, follow a cytosine-cytosine-adenine sequence. It is believed that the amino acids are attached to the sRNA molecules at this point. It is well known that sRNA is specific for particular amino acids of which there are at least 25 to 30 different types. This arrangement suggests that the sequence of the free bases at the tail of the sRNA molecule must be able to assume a variety of different codes to account for the observed specificity; however, the mechanisms of this coding are not yet understood.

Crick (1963) has discussed a possible mechanism for the selective combination of amino acids and sRNA molecules. On the basis of experimental studies (Crick et al., 1961), he argued that the code for amino acids must consist of a triplet of bases like that found at the tail of the RNA helix. Since there are four possible bases in the RNA chain, a total of 64 combinations and permutations of three bases (out of four) is possible, more than enough to account for the coding of the presently known amino acids. Several studies (Matthaei and Nirenberg, 1961; Matthaei et al., 1962; Weisblum et al., 1962) have obtained experimental evidence suggesting that specific base sequence triplets do, in fact, code for particular amino acids such as phenylalanine (uracil-uracil-uracil). Furthermore, some amino acids appear to be coded by more than one triplet, i.e., the code exhibits degeneracy. Leucine, for instance, appears to attach itself to uracil-uracil-cytosine as well as to uracil-uracil-guanine. We must remember, however, that these results have been inferred from complex findings and depend on the validity of a variety of assumptions which are tenable but far from well established at the present time.

Wilkins (1963) has suggested that three additional free bases may be located at the other end of the sRNA molecule at the point where the single strand begins to fold back upon itself to form the double helix. He believes that this "base triplet" may represent the code of the sRNA molecule which permits it to attach itself onto the appropriate spot on the messenger RNA template. If this attachment occurs by means of hydrogen bonding or base pairing as just discussed, the three free bases on the sRNA molecule would fit only into a complementary set of bases on the messenger RNA template, much as a key fits only a particular keyhole. Combined with the known amino acid specificity of the sRNA molecule, this would account nicely for the specific sequence of amino acids on the messenger RNA template which must occur if appropriate proteins are to be synthesized as demanded by the functional requirements of the cell. Recent investigations (Hoagland et al., 1957, 1958; Hoagland, 1959) have shed some light on the mechanism by which specific amino acids are transferred to the messenger RNA. The first step in this sequence is the activation of amino acids by adenosine triphosphate (ATP) to form high-energy complexes of amino acid and adenosine monophosphate. The activated amino acids then attach themselves to molecules of transfer RNA which are specific to the amino acid.

Rather than continue this discussion of basic biochemical mechanisms, we shall now consider some of the theoretical models that have attempted to apply biochemical processes to the problems of learning and/or retention. Further detail on the biochemical mechanisms is presented in such basic texts as that prepared by Fruton and Simmonds (1958) or more specialized treatments of nucleic acids such as Davidson's (1965) monograph.

INTRACELLULAR BIOCHEMICAL CHANGES AS POSSIBLE MECHANISMS FOR LEARNING AND THE STORAGE OF MEMORY

The rapid developments in biochemistry in the past decade have suggested that several mechanisms might be involved in the acquisition or storage of memory traces. Before we discuss particular hypotheses, it might be worthwhile to recall the functional requirements of a memory system. The principal problem is to discover how use or activation of a neuron *permanently* lowers its threshold to subsequent stimulation, and this is precisely the question most biochemical hypotheses have attempted to answer.

This nonspecific facilitation through use may not, however, provide a sufficiently selective

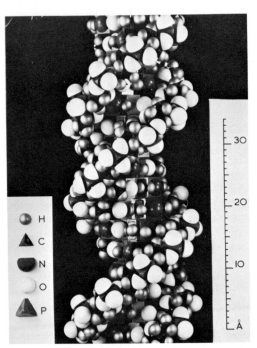 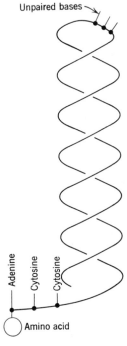

Fig. 16.17   Molecular model and diagram of a transfer-RNA molecule. (From Wilkins, 1963, © AAAS, and with permission of the Nobel Foundation.)

mechanism for the storage of particular memory traces. A question arises about how specific patterns of stimulation or excitation produce a more selective facilitation. It is, in fact, this latter requirement which has prompted the search for biochemical mechanisms, for it is difficult at present to conceive of physiological or anatomical changes that could possibly result in such specificity. Biochemical mechanisms, on the other hand, are sufficiently complex to permit the storage of many "bits" of memory in a single neuron.

Whether this is a strict requirement is open to discussion. It assumes that a particular neuron is necessarily part of more than one memory circuit, and it can be argued that the apparent specificity of CS-UCS connections argues against such an interpretation. As indicated briefly in our introduction to this chapter, there may be a more basic flaw in the reasoning that the establishment of memory traces requires only use or repeated use of a particular pathway. These questions will be disregarded here, and some of the biochemical hypotheses that have been proposed in recent years will be discussed.

The first biochemical theories of memory were proposed almost 20 years ago when the first major developments in biochemical cellular analysis suggested that genetic information might be coded in terms of specific protein templates. At this time each gene was believed to be a nucleoprotein molecule of specific spatial configuration and chemical composition. The functional properties of each cell were thought to be determined by these nucleoproteins, which act as the templates or models for the synthesis of *identical* protein molecules. The latter were then believed to move into the cytoplasm of the cell where they, in turn, would be used in the many enzymatic processes that determine the functions of each cell.

Monné's Hypothesis

Many of the earlier workers in this field pointed out that the storage mechanism for "genetic memory" could also serve "individual memory" if a modification of the nucleoproteins as a result of use could be postulated. Monné (1948), for example, proposed that the "synthesis of specific proteins is the essential physical phenomenon paralleling memory, fantasy, and intuition." He supported this hypothesis with evidence which suggested that protein synthesis is increased with demand (i.e., stimulation of a cell) and that neurons may be able to "learn" to synthesize particular proteins such as antibodies or specific enzymes. Monné further suggested that instinctive behavior might be directly related to specific patterns of protein synthesis in some neural structures and that modifications of these patterns (i.e., learning) could occur through repeated applications of particular stimulus configurations.

Katz and Halstead's Protein Hypothesis

Monné's rather sketchy hypothesis has been elaborated by Katz and Halstead (1950); their thorough treatment deserves to be called the first systematic attempt to account for learning and memory on the basis of biochemical processes. This theory did not attract as much attention as it deserved, partly because psychologists and physiologists were not yet ready to think in the novel biochemical terminology. Katz and Halstead's proposal has been ignored in recent years because its basic assumption (that nucleoprotein templates are the basic genetic mechanism) has turned out to be incorrect. This neglect is unfortunate because the essential aspects of the theoretical model are much more thoroughly developed than those of any of the more recent speculations; the theory can perhaps be modified in accordance with recent biochemical findings.

The basic premises of the Katz and Halstead hypothesis are as follows:

(*a*) In order for a neuron to become a functioning member of a neural network, involved in memory, a structural change in the neuron must occur consequent to the individual's experience. A neuron does not become a member of a network purely on the basis of its anatomical relationships. Neurons involved in vegetative (autonomic) behavior are functional *ab initio*, but neurons involved in memory become fully functional only after chemical and structural changes.

(*b*) An essential feature in a neuron's becoming operative is the formation of a new, specifically oriented protein molecule. The molecule is presumably a nucleoprotein and acts as the template for the synthesis of protein replicas. It now bears the same relationship to the neuron as a gene does. The protein replicas are utilized for the completion of the neural membrane so that it becomes capable of transmitting impulses, and this allows the neuron to become a functioning member of a neural network.

(*c*) A memory trace is distinguished by the chemical composition and geometrical orientation of the initial template molecule responsible for the initiation of a particular trace. Thus, each memory trace is differentiated by the composition and geometry of the repeating unit of a protein lattice, and the relationship between the traces is determined by the relationships of the various protein repeating units to each other.

Katz and Halstead propose that a memory trace develops when an impulse arrives at a neuron that is not yet "physiologically operative" in a cortical reception area. This causes randomly oriented protein molecules to assume a specific configuration, and a new template molecule arises; this molecule synthesizes replicas of itself which then become part of the membrane structure of the cell. When this process of "membrane organization" is complete, the neuron becomes capable of conducting impulses to adjacent cells. This organization is believed to involve other neurons by either the diffusion of oriented protein molecules across the synapse or the formation of new template proteins in the adjacent cells as a result of specific orienting forces. This organizing process is believed to spread through the cortex in a number of linear sequences until it encounters neurons that are either already organized or deficient in the particular protein needed to propagate the specific trace. In this way a complex protein lattice arises which differs from other memory traces by the chemical composition and geometrical configuration of its protein-repeating unit. Different memory traces may share all or part of a particular anatomical pathway and yet retain complete specificity. In agreement with recent findings, the hypothesis suggests that the neural pathways involved in a given memory trace may be very complex but not random and do not have a "circumscribed anatomical locus."

Before we discuss more recent biochemical models, it may be worthwhile to consider a unique aspect of the Katz and Halstead hypothesis. Most recent biochemical speculations agree that some modification of protein synthesis must be the mechanism of storage, but none of them discusses how this modification might affect specific functional properties of the cell. Katz and Halstead have postulated such a mechanism, and it may be instructive to discuss this model in spite of the fact that recent physiological as well as biochemical findings do not support the proposed mechanisms.

Katz and Halstead proposed that the protein lattice which represents the memory trace might be a structural component of the cell membrane essential to the conduction of impulses along the axon. Working with a "core conductor" model of nerve impulse propagation, they suggested that the protein lattice could itself account for most of, if not all, the electrical and chemical properties of the neural membrane. Visualizing the protein lattice as a "giant dipolar ion" which carries separate positive and negative charges, they proposed that such phenomena as the cell's resting potential, capacitance (dipolar ions are good dielectrics), and inductance might be explained without recourse to other mechanisms. On the basis of contemporary research (see Katz and Halstead, 1950, for a summary of this literature), they suggested that protein molecules may act as semiconductors which could form aggregates that conduct electrical changes along conduction bands common to the aggregate. The relationship between the energy levels of the conduction bands of adjacent protein aggregates determines whether or not an impulse is conducted across a synapse. The details of this interesting hypothesis are too complex to be discussed here; Katz and Halstead's excellent monograph presents a more detailed exposition (see also Halstead, 1951).

The Role of Nucleic Acids as Possible "Memory Molecules"

Hydén's RNA hypothesis. Katz and Halstead's nucleoprotein hypothesis failed to stimulate much interest and research, and the notion of intracellular memory traces was all but forgotten when Holger Hydén (1959) extended his findings on genetic mechanisms to the problem of memory. At the time of this proposal, evidence was rapidly accumulating that genetic information was carried by the DNA molecules in the cell nucleus; these molecules were found to influence cellular activities by serving as templates for the synthesis of ribonucleic acids which, in turn, serve as models for the manufacture of specific proteins.

Following a line of reasoning similar to that proposed by Katz and Halstead, Hydén suggested that the RNA molecules might be modifiable by cellular activity and thus be capable of storing memory traces. The flavor of this theory may be best represented in a brief quote from Hydén's writings (1959):

> First, we imagine that the electrochemical environment of the nerve cell can be sensitively altered by the pattern of nerve impulses entering the cell. A given impulse could, presumably, produce a change of a base in the chain

of an RNA molecule. This change would then remain. This new RNA molecule, although only slightly changed, would direct the synthesis of a protein molecule differing slightly but significantly from that previously produced.

Second, we assume that the new protein has the property of responding to the same electrical pattern that created the change in RNA. When the same electrical pattern does occur again, the new protein dissociates rapidly, causing an explosive release of the transmitter substance at the synapse. This allows the electrical pattern to bridge the synapse and be passed along by the second cell, then by a third cell, and so on.

Hydén further postulated that these sensitive protein molecules are perpetuated, presumably indefinitely, by uniquely shaped RNA molecules; these, in turn, are descended from RNA templates that were modified by cellular activity (i.e., the passage of a particular pattern of electrochemical activity). Each cell is believed to be capable of responding differentially to a great variety of stimulus patterns and thus to build up and store a large number of distinct memory traces.

This relatively simple hypothesis has generated a staggering amount of research, interest, and controversy during the past five years. It is much too early to unravel the resultant confusion. All we can do is mention some of the theoretical extensions of Hydén's original model which have been proposed in recent years and attempt a brief survey of the research literature which has grown up around it.

The most enthusiastic supporter of a molecular approach to memory has been Gaito, who has advocated the eclectic position that memory may be based on changes in either RNA, DNA, protein, or specific enzyme molecules. Suggesting that the recent developments in biochemistry herald the development of an area which he chooses to call "molecular psychology," Gaito (1961, 1963; Gaito and Zavala, 1964) has done much to popularize the idea that memory must have an intracellular biochemical basis which is open to experimental study with the techniques now available. Gaito has not himself proposed a coherent theory of memory, although several possible mechanisms are suggested in his writings.

Gaito has concurred with Hydén that changes in the linear sequence of bases in one of the RNA fractions may be the physical basis of memory, but he has suggested that the same or similar changes in the DNA molecule may provide a more permanent basis for memory storage. He

proposed more specifically that the genetic potential of a cell might be modifiable if stimulation could produce a "somatic mutation" so that adenine is changed to guanine and thymine to cytosine in the basic DNA structure. Alternately, memory might be related to "deletions, additions, and rearrangement" of bases in the DNA structure or, more simply, might reflect a primary change in the sequence of amino acids in specific protein molecules.

We shall discuss in some detail the evidence for each of these mechanisms; except the last which appears to be excluded on logical grounds. Proteins are not, as far as we know, self-duplicating. Their very high turnover rate does not permit the perpetuation of molecular changes which presumably result from stimulation. The best current estimates suggest that the *entire* protein content of nerve cells is renewed three times daily and that a particular protein has an average life of little more than 8 hr before being degraded. If no modifications are made in the basic mechanisms responsible for the protein synthesis (RNA or DNA), no long-term memory could possibly exist.

Hydén's basic hypothesis that memory reflects an alteration of RNA molecules which, in turn, determine protein synthesis was originally based on rather circumstantial evidence. He reported (1961a) that the RNA content of neurons is among the highest of all cells and that it shows an increase in man until about age 40. The RNA content remains stable to about age 60 and rapidly declines thereafter. This sequence represents at least a very rough analogue of the intellectual development of man, but we should not overlook the obvious fact that almost all the biochemical and physiological functions show a similar correlation with age.

Of perhaps greater relevance are findings which suggest that the composition, quantity, or concentration of RNA in nerve cells changes following normal or abnormal stimulation. Geiger et al. (1958), for example, reported that the cytidine and adenine content of the nucleic acids of cortical cells was significantly increased after 30 sec of electrical stimulation, whereas the uridine and guanine fractions remained constant. Edström and Eichner (1958) found that osmotic stimulation of cells in the supraoptic nucleus (presumably caused by intravenous injections of sodium chloride solutions) increased the total amount of cytoplasmic RNA by 80% and the nuclear RNA content by 35%.

Hydén (1962) has summarized a number of studies from his own laboratory and suggests that intense neural activity seems to produce a marked increase in RNA and protein synthesis. Analyzing cells from the vestibular nucleus, for instance, Hydén observed an increase of about 40% in the total RNA content and a marked increase in amino acid absorption following moderate passive rotatory stimulation of rats. He also pointed out that the biochemical development of neurons in unused sensory systems appears severely retarded. Anatomically, the gross structure of such cells appears quite normal, but the cell is impoverished in both RNA content and protein synthesis. All these observations are compatible with Hydén's hypothesis but do not represent compelling proof for it. In fact, the apparent lability of the RNA molecule following stimulation or use of a pathway has created more problems than it solved; it is next to impossible to distinguish the results of plain sensory stimulation from those that might take place during acquisition.

Since Hydén first published his hypothesis, a number of studies have lent somewhat more direct support to his model. Morrell (1961) produced an epileptogenic focus by spraying ethyl chloride on a small portion of the cortex and observed that spike discharges rapidly appeared in the contralateral hemisphere. This "mirror focus" was initially dependent on the original epileptogenic irritation (i.e., the contralateral focus disappeared when the connections between the hemispheres were cut). However, it became autonomous within several weeks to the point that even complete removal of the original focus did not reduce the activity of the contralateral mirror focus. The cells of this region appeared to retain this hyperexcitability even after months of inactivity (produced by isolation of the tissue); they showed a marked increase in total RNA content (as measured by special cell staining techniques) even months after the original focus had been excised. Morrell suggested that the acquisition and retention of this heightened activity might be similar to learning and memory and that these findings can be interpreted as supporting Hydén's hypothesis. This conclusion is, of course, open to the obvious criticism that the processes which account for seizure discharges, although reflected in RNA and protein synthesis, may have little or nothing in common with the molecular changes that perhaps take place during learning.

More directly related to the problem are a number of studies that report changes in RNA content or composition following exposure to a learning situation. Hydén and Egyhazi (1962) taught rats the relatively complex task of walking up a thin (1.5-mm), long (1-meter) wire, set at a 45° angle to the horizontal. Active and passive rotation were used on other animals to control for the activation of sensory cells in the vestibular system by this balancing act. After approximately $3\frac{1}{2}$ hr of practice spread over 4 to 5 days, the experimental animals mastered the task. The nucleic acids from the Deiters cells of the vestibular nucleus were analyzed. All animals showed an increase in total RNA content (presumably due to the repeated, intense activation of the vestibular system), but only the animals that had learned the balancing act showed a net synthesis of nuclear RNA with an increased adenine-uracil ratio. The cytoplasmic RNA failed to show base ratio changes, perhaps because (as Hydén suggested) these changes occur only in messenger RNA, which makes up such a small fraction of the cytoplasmic RNA that even major changes would be obscured.

In a subsequent experiment Hydén and Egyhazi (1963) discovered that the increased base ratio of the nuclear RNA disappeared within 24 hr after the last learning trial if adequate food was available in the home cages. This finding was interpreted as a change peculiar to the learning process, although it seems that a more permanent effect would be predicted by Hydén's notion that memory may be coded in this fashion. It was also observed that the glial cells surrounding Deiters' neurons showed marked RNA alterations after the learning of this complex sensory-motor task. The adenine content of glial RNA increased significantly in the animals subjected to the learning procedure, and the cytosine content showed a compensatory decline, producing a marked change in base ratios. The controls that received rotatory stimulation did not show significant changes in glial RNA base ratios, and "control" tissue taken from the reticular formation of rats subjected to the learning experiment showed a rise in total RNA but no change in base ratios. Combining biochemical hypotheses with recent speculations about possible functions of glial tissue in memory, Egyhazi and Hydén suggested that the glial cells may be particularly suited for the rapid and transient changes underlying short-term memory.

These findings lend support to Hydén's hypothesis, although we might question the adequacy of the experimental controls. There is no objective basis for the assumption that the active and passive rotation control did, in fact, result in vestibular stimulation identical or at least similar, either qualitatively or quantitatively, to that experienced by the animals who learned to balance on a thin wire. The observed differences in base ratios thus may reflect more intense or differential activation rather than learning or memory per se. This point may be supported by the observation that similar changes were observed in the RNA of surrounding glial cells. It is also not immediately obvious why Deiters' cells from the admittedly relevant sensory system should be expected to be selectively involved in memory, whereas cells from the reticular formation are used as control tissue. On the basis of behavioral and electrophysiological findings, the latter would, a priori, seem to be a more likely candidate for memory storage than the vestibular system. The extensive literature on the effects of central nervous system lesions and stimulation suggests that there may be no fixed, general locus for memory traces. This, however, does not justify the a priori assumption that learning must take place in the primary sensory pathways or associated relay nuclei. Studies of the type reported by Hydén and Egyhazi may have to be postponed until we can pinpoint the anatomical locus of conditioning more closely than is now possible.

Perhaps the strongest support for Hydén's hypothesis comes from a group of studies concerned with the effects of RNA or RNA inhibitors administered before or during exposure to a learning task. The most exuberant reports come from clinical investigations of the effects of RNA on senility. Cameron and Solyom (1961), for instance, administered RNA to senile patients (average age was 70 years) in an attempt to counteract the forgetfulness and general lethargy that characterize the aged. The patients were divided on the basis of pretreatment tests into two comparable groups, one to receive RNA, the other a placebo in a "double-blind" design (i.e., neither those administering nor those receiving knew whether RNA or the placebo was being given). The RNA treatment was reported to increase alertness and confidence and, most surprisingly, to produce an average improvement of 100% on tests of short-term memory. General intelligence did not appear to be affected. It is difficult to find fault with the

design of this study, except that it may have been important to control for the nutritional value of the yeast RNA which was administered in calorically significant quantities. Nonetheless, it is difficult to understand how the orally administered RNA could have increased the storage capacity of the individual brain cells, since only breakdown products could be expected to cross the blood-brain barrier.

Animal experiments have generally supported the conclusion that learning ability may be improved by RNA administrations, although the magnitude of this effect has typically been very small. (This is to be expected, for there is no logical reason to predict a major improvement following administrations of RNA to young animals presumably with an already adequate supply of the nucleic acids.) Cook et al. (1963) used a pole-climbing avoidance task to test the effects of long-term RNA treatment. Animals receiving daily intraperitoneal injections of RNA for 30 days before the beginning of training as well as during the testing period learned significantly faster and demonstrated greater resistance to extinction than placebo controls. Similar effects were observed when the pre-experimental treatment period was shortened to one or two weeks, but not when the experiment was begun only three days after RNA treatment.

Less convincing than these apparently positive results are a number of studies which have reported a decrement in learning ability (i.e., performance during acquisition or retention tests) after the administration of substances that modify or inhibit ribonucleic acids.

One of the most frequently cited of these is the experiment by Dingman and Sporn (1961) on the effects of 8-azaguanine on retention. This substance is thought to be a potent antimetabolite which is incorporated into RNA and inhibits adaptive enzyme formation. It is, perhaps, not the most suitable agent to use in studies attempting to relate RNA changes to memory because it may affect performance by modifying biochemical processes other than RNA synthesis. However, a number of interesting experiments have been done with it, and it may be worthwhile to discuss some of them briefly. Dingman and Sporn trained rats on a water maze task to a criterion of fifteen successive correct turns. The animals were then divided into two comparable groups and received injections of 8-azaguanine or a saline placebo, 15 min before a retention test. Although the experimental animals made more errors than the controls, this effect was so small that the differences were not statistically reliable. However, when animals were *trained* following 8-azaguanine treatments, a reliable impairment seemed to pervade all phases of the learning experiment. The experimental animals made more errors than the controls on each of the fifteen training trials. Since swimming speed was not affected by the experimental treatment, Dingman and Sporn suggested that the observed impairment could not be merely the result of a motor deficit. Paper chromatographic analyses showed that 8-azaguanine had been incorporated into brain RNA in both experiments.

The authors interpreted their findings as suggesting that the ribonucleic acids may play an essential role in acquisition but not in memory or retention. They recognize explicitly that the observed effects may not be related to RNA, learning ability, or memory mechanisms per se, but rather may reflect a change in some performance variable such as motivation. However, an additional comment should be made about the apparently differential effect of 8-azaguanine on acquisition and performance in the retention test. The negative results of the retention test are based only on half as many subjects (eight) as were used in the acquisition test, and it is conceivable that the observed differences might have reached statistical significance if a larger number of subjects had been used. Not too much importance can therefore be attached to the reported differential effect until the experiments can be replicated under more nearly equitable conditions.

That Dingman and Sporn's findings should be interpreted cautiously is further suggested by the results of a group of studies (Chamberlin et al., 1963) concerned with the effects of 8-azaguanine and tricyanoaminopropene on learning ability and memory. The latter substance has been reported to *increase* the RNA content of nerve cells by as much as 25% (Egyhazi and Hydén, 1963). Chamberlin and his co-workers (1963) trained three groups of rats in a lever-pressing avoidance situation following injections of 8-azaguanine, tricyanoaminopropene, and a saline placebo, respectively. No reliable differences were observed during acquisition, but the tricyanoaminopropene-treated animals performed reliably better on retention tests administered 1 and 2 days after the initial training. The performance of animals treated with 8-azaguanine did not differ reliably from that of the control group, either during learn-

ing or during the retention tests. Although none of the drugs produced measurable effects on general activity or food and water intake, it is not at all clear whether the superior performance of the tricyanoaminopropene-treated animals on the retention test can be attributed to a direct effect on memory mechanisms. There was no reliable difference between any of the groups on a subsequent task involving the acquisition of a Hebb-Williams-type maze habit for food reward. Perhaps the effects observed in the first part of the experiment were specific to the avoidance situation and reflect motivational rather than associative changes.

One of the most frequently cited reports in this area is Corning and John's (1961) study of the effects of ribonuclease (RN-ase) on retention in regenerated planaria. McConnell et al. (1959) previously reported that these flatworms can be conditioned in a classical defensive-conditioning paradigm and that the "CR" is retained in worms that regenerate from either the tail or the head portion of a conditioned animal. Corning and John reasoned that this apparent transfer of memory might involve the transmission of particular RNA molecules to the regenerating tissue and that this process might be interrupted by RN-ase. To test this hypothesis, worms were conditioned to perform a contraction CR in response to a photic CS. The animals were then transected into head and tail portions and allowed to regenerate either in pond water or in RN-ase solutions. After a complete worm had been formed, tests of retention showed that heads which regenerated a new tail in RN-ase (as well as heads or tails which regenerated in pond water) retained the CR. However, tails that grew a new head in RN-ase showed no evidence of retention. The authors suggested that RN-ase did not enter the tissue of the original worm but infiltrated the growing cells of the regenerating half. Since most of the rudimentary nervous system of these animals is located in the head portion, an incorporation of RN-ase into the regenerating tail would not be expected to interfere significantly with memory. However, a destruction of the RNA molecules of a growing head would make it totally impossible for the specifically modified RNA molecules, which presumably carry the memory trace, to enter into the developing head ganglia, thus causing complete forgetting.

These are extremely interesting findings, but several questions must be answered before we can agree with Corning and John's interpretation. First, it is not totally certain that the observed "conditioned" responses are the result of learning, even in the intact animal. It is difficult to rule out a possible interpretation of the apparent conditioning in terms of sensitization. Even if we accept that the initial appearance of the contraction response may be caused by conditioning, there always remains the possibility that the apparent memory for this response in the regenerated worm may be due to sensitization. The RN-ase might have produced a differential sensitization to light in the head and tail portions of the worm. This hypothesis is not altogether unreasonable, for the photic receptors are located exclusively in the head. Such an interpretation might account for the differential effects in Corning and John's experiment, even if one allows that the initial conditioning may have involved associative processes, since no test for sensitization was run in the postregeneration experiment. There are other problems with Corning and John's results. They reported that planaria which were regenerated in a 0.1 mg/cc ribonuclease solution showed structural abnormalities in the regenerated portion of the body. Since the conditioned animals were allowed to regenerate in solutions of 0.07 to 0.1 mg/cc, it is probable that structural deficiencies which may have involved the light receptors of the head are responsible for the observed effects. This objection is not totally answered by the demonstration that all animals could relearn the CR, for very similar results have been reported following central nervous system lesions which partially destroyed sensory pathways or projection areas.

The precise nature of the ribonuclease-induced deficit was unfortunately not clarified in a subsequent study of more complex learned behavior. John et al. (1961) found that injections of ribonuclease directly into the lateral ventricles of cats interfered with the performance of a food-rewarded pattern discrimination but not with a conditioned avoidance response to similar visual or auditory stimuli. Whether this difference can be explained on the basis of motivational or sensory factors is not clear at this time, but one should be careful in considering these data as evidence for an involvement of RNA in memory.

The possible role of RNA (or DNA) in learning and retention was questioned in an experiment on the effects of puromycin on protein metabolism and behavior (Flexner et al., 1962). The subcutaneous administration of puromycin produced an 80% inhibition of radioactively labeled amino acid incorporation into cellular proteins, suggesting a major interference with protein synthesis. The animals (mice) appeared drowsy but performed as well as normal controls in tests of acquisition and retention of shuttle box and Y-maze avoidance problems. Since only the amino acid valine was studied in these experiments, the negative results may be due to the coding of memory in protein molecules which do not contain this particular acid.

Flexner et al. (1963) subsequently reported an interesting series of studies which obtained positive effects of intracerebral puromycin injections on memory. It is difficult to understand why the route of administration should be so crucial if the puromycin effect reported in the second group of studies is, in fact, related to protein metabolism. However, the results appear to be highly selective, unambiguous, and—most importantly—reversible, suggesting that the negative findings of the initial study may be misleading.

Flexner et al. (1963) trained mice in a Y-maze avoidance situation to a criterion of nine out of ten successive correct responses using a massed-trial procedure to permit the completion of training in a single session. Intracerebral injections of puromycin (0.03 to 0.09 mg) were then given, one day after the training session for tests of short-term memory or 11 to 43 days after acquisition for tests of long-term memory. The first retention tests were administered 3 days after the puromycin injections.

The results suggested a very interesting anatomical differentiation between long-term and short-term memory as well as a remarkable estimate of the temporal parameters of memory fixation. Bilateral puromycin injections into the temporal lobe (fluorescein injections suggested that the area around the caudal rhinal fissure was primarily involved) completely destroyed short-term memory but had no effect on long-term retention. Similar injections into the ventricles or the frontal cortex did not affect either long-term or short-term memory. Long-term retention was consistently destroyed only by *combined* bilateral temporal, ventricular, and frontal injections. This marked effect did not seem to be produced by the increased dosage of puromycin, since injections of comparable or greater amounts into only one or two of the injection sites did not have reliable effects on long-term memory.

Bilateral temporal injections consistently destroyed memory 2 days after training, but not 6 days after acquisition. Variable results were obtained after 3, 4, or 5 days, suggesting that the transfer of short-term memory into permanent storage may require considerably more time than most behavioral studies have indicated.

Flexner and his associates provided an additional test of the differential effect on short-term and long-term memory. Three weeks after the initial learning, some animals received reversal training (i.e., learned to go to the previously incorrect arm of the maze) followed after 24 hr by bilateral temporal injections of puromycin. It was observed that all experimental animals reverted to the first learned habit, whereas all control animals continued to perform the reversal habit. The results of these experiments not only confirm the selective effect of temporal lobe injections but also suggest that the animals are physically capable of performing the required instrumental responses. It would be important to have a similar control for the apparent effects on long-term memory.

Agranoff and associates (Davis et al., 1965; Agranoff et al., 1965; Agranoff and Klinger, 1964) have reported similar effects of puromycin on memory in the gold fish. Animals trained to swim from a light to a dark compartment in a shuttle box to avoid electric shock showed a marked retention deficit when puromycin was injected intracranially within 30 min after the last of 20 training trials. This inhibitory effect appeared to be related to the antibiotic action of the drug since injections of puromycin aminonucleoside did not produce any retention deficit.

Davis et al. (1965) demonstrated a roughly parallel time course for the effects of ECS and puromycin. Maximal inhibition was obtained when the treatments were given immediately after training, and little or no effect remained 2 hr after the last training trial. Agranoff et al. (1965) reported that puromycin, injected 1 or 20 min *before* the first training trial, did not interfere with the acquisition of an avoidance response but significantly impaired recall as measured in a performance test 3 days later.

Landauer's extension of the RNA hypothesis. Landauer (1964) has attempted to account for the temporal aspects of conditioning by proposing a learning mechanism which depends on sequential rather than simultaneous activation of the CS-UCS pathways. He suggested that the conduction of impulses in the CS pathway might result in the production—by glia cells—of novel RNA molecules which somehow represent the CS. This novel RNA molecule might then be selectively transferred into neurons that are active shortly after the passage of the CS impulse. The incorporation of the RNA molecule into the neuron of the UCS pathway would render the latter selectively sensitive to the CS.

At first glance, this hypothesis appears rather implausible, for it is well known that macromolecules such as RNA do not, as a rule, cross cell membranes. Landauer attempted to answer this criticism by suggesting that the potential change across the neural membrane during the conduction of action potentials may promote the movement of RNA molecules into the neuron and that RNA may have a natural tendency to enter cells. Accordingly, this tendency would normally be blocked by the resting potential of the neuron. Although the physicochemical properties of neurons might permit such transfer, the notion is purely speculative.

Landauer's learning hypothesis is compatible with other current physiological and biochemical concepts and may deserve some experimental attention. Unfortunately, it is incorporated into a more general theory of neural function which is improbable. In this theory, Landauer suggests that neural impulses in the higher centers of the brain are not confined to specific neurons; rather, they are postulated to spread widely through the surrounding tissue "since the neurons in this region are unmyelinated." Conditioning is thought to consist not of a change in synaptic resistance but of an increase in the sensitivity of particular cell membranes to the spreading electrical activity generated by the CS. Specificity is achieved in this system by the postulation of finely "tuned" cell membranes which specifically respond to particular patterns of electrical activity. All of this is related to Landauer's learning hypothesis by the suggestion that the tuning of cell membranes is a function of an alteration of their biochemical composition by the movement of RNA molecules from the glia into the neuron.

Gaito's DNA hypothesis. It is too early now to judge the hypothesis that memory traces may be coded in terms of specific base sequence changes in ribonucleic or deoxyribonucleic acids. Hydén's speculations have stimulated much valuable and interesting research, and the hope that our understanding of associative mechanisms may be greatly advanced through a study of biochemical processes appears well founded. However, it is also too early to hope that all our problems will soon be solved, particularly since none of the theories now available is without major flaws.

There is, for instance, no direct experimental evidence for Gaito's speculation that memory may be related to base sequence changes in the DNA molecule, and much biochemical information against such an interpretation. The DNA molecule is known to transmit genetic information and must be an exceedingly stable structure in order to accomplish this task. It cannot be modified by environmental influences, as proposed by Gaito, without loosing basic properties essential to the coding of genetic information. The base sequence of a DNA molecule is determined by the base sequence of the template molecule on which it was originally formed (Kornberg, 1960), and there is absolutely no evidence for a modification of the basic process of polynucleotide synthesis by electrochemical changes in the cell. It has been shown, in fact, that this synthesis cannot take place in the absence of template molecules (Kornberg, 1960), and spontaneous coupling of polynucleotides does not, apparently, occur. Even if the DNA molecule were fragmented by an electrical impulse, there is no evidence that its constituents would recombine to form a new DNA molecule of differing base sequence composition. The only way in which the base sequence of a DNA molecule can be altered, as far as is known, is through the action of a mutagenic agent; this substance produces basic chemical changes in the pyrimidine and purine bases so that compounds not normally present in DNA are substituted for one of the four bases. Since no unusual bases have been detected in brain DNA, this cannot be the physical process responsible for memory.

Gaito has countered some of these criticisms by suggesting that the DNA of nerve cells may be essentially different from the commonly studied DNA of liver or pancreatic origin in being labile and modifiable by electrochemical events. This appears to be, at present, a most unlikely possibility, for all DNA molecules in the body derive from the same genetic template molecules and presumably have identical characteristics. Some research indicates that the molecule is as stable and invariant in the brain as in other portions of the body, and we have no experimental support for Gaito's suggestion.

Gaito's alternative hypothesis that memory may be directly related to changes in the amino acid sequence of particular protein molecules also appears unlikely at present. Proteins are not self-duplicating, and their very short life is measured in terms of hours rather than the necessary months or even years were they responsible for long-term memory. It is possible that such a mechanism might account for short-term memory, but even this appears doubtful if we consider that materials learned in situations designed to permit only short-term recall may positively affect subsequent acquisition in a long-term memory experiment.

The notion that has attracted most interest and support is Hydén's proposal that changes in the base sequence (or base ratio) of RNA may be the physical change underlying memory. In spite of the many methodological problems that have beset the experimental investigation of this hypothesis, it seems that the generally positive results provide a measure of support for it.

Briggs and Kitto (1962) have suggested in a critical review of this material that the apparent relation between ribonucleic acids and memory may be deceiving. The structure of the RNA molecule is known to be originally determined by the base sequence of DNA molecules which serve as templates or models for its synthesis. The messenger RNA then migrates into the cytoplasm of the cell and attaches itself to the ribosomes where it, in turn, serves as a template for the synthesis of specific proteins. The structure of proteins is determined by the base sequence of the RNA molecules and by the availability of the required amino acids. Briggs and Kitto contend that absolutely no biochemical mechanism would permit a modification of the basic RNA structure by bioelectrical events. They further suggest that even if stimulation of a neuron could in some fashion affect the base sequence of the RNA molecule, the desired effects would probably not be produced. Major alterations in the monomer sequence, they maintain, would have "disastrous" consequences for the cell because it would begin to manufacture foreign proteins totally useless in the normal processes of the cell. Small changes in the amino acid sequence of an established protein, on the other hand, would probably not affect its properties at all; however, if the active center on an enzyme protein were affected, its catalytic properties would be lost entirely.

These criticisms are themselves based on incomplete and perhaps faulty information. The possibility that one or more of the presently accepted biochemical assumptions may be incorrect cannot be ignored, and we should maintain an open mind with respect to all the suggested memory mechanisms.

The enzyme-induction hypothesis. After surveying the biochemical literature, Briggs and Kitto (1962) concluded that a primary change in the nucleic acids such as that suggested by Hydén and Gaito did not seem to be very likely. They conceded that Hydén's RNA hypothesis receives a measure of support from biochemical as well as behavioral investigations, but suggested an alternative explanation of these findings which is compatible with their own hypothesis about the physical basis of memory.

Briggs and Kitto (1962) proposed that the molecular basis of memory may be related to changes in the concentration of specific enzymes in neural tissue. These changes are only secondarily reflected in the RNA metabolism. This hypothesis is based on the following propositions. (1) All somatic cells contain the same genes, and each gene (consisting of DNA) is responsible for the synthesis of a specific enzyme protein. Hence, each cell is potentially capable of manufacturing all enzymes. (2) Cells do not, in fact, manufacture all enzymes, and different cells synthesize differing amounts of some enzymes. This indicates that some genes are totally inactive, whereas others operate below their maximum capacity. (3) The presence of a particular substrate within a cell initiates the synthesis of the related enzyme, and the concentration of the substrate determines the rate of enzyme production.

These apparently simple and straightforward mechanisms can be related to memory in the following manner. The transmission of neural impulses across a synaptic junction depends on the release of chemical transmitter substances. An impulse is transmitted to the next cell only if the concentration of the released transmitter is sufficient to produce threshold excitation in the postsynaptic membrane. It is assumed that the concentration of the transmitter substance released by a particular impulse is in part a function of the amount available in the cell as determined by the activity level of the biosynthetic enzyme system for the transmitter substance. If the enzymes of this system are inducible, as postulated in proposition 3, repeated stimulation of a cell will increase the neuron's ability to manufacture and release the transmitter; thus, each successive stimulation increases the probability of synaptic transmission.

This hypothesis does not postulate the storage of specific memory traces in a particular cell as suggested by the RNA hypothesis of Hydén. It merely proposes a mechanism for the nonspecific facilitation as a result of use which plays such an important role in all physiological theories of learning. Specific memories would be coded in terms of the particular pathways facilitated in this fashion. Although hypotheses of this type fail to explain why pathways interconnecting the CS and UCS systems should be preferentially facilitated (simultaneous excitation does not seem to be a sufficient condition), this approach to the problem of memory may be more fruitful than the more convenient postulation of intracellular mechanisms for the storage of many distinct memory traces.

Briggs and Kitto's hypothesis has received inferential experimental support. It has been shown that at least some enzymes are induced by the presence of their substrates (Dixon and Webb, 1958). The question whether the specific enzymes needed for the synthesis of transmitter substances are inducible in similar fashion is potentially testable. Some indirect support for this notion can be abstracted from the findings of Krech, Rosenzweig, and Bennett (to be discussed in detail) that the cholinesterase activity as well as the release of acetylcholine varies between bright and dull animals.

Perhaps most interesting is the fact that Briggs and Kitto's hypothesis predicts rather nicely some of the results of recent studies involving the measurement of neural RNA concentrations or the behavioral effects of RNA or RNA inhibitor injections. Thus, increases in enzyme concentration imply increases in RNA. A continual rise in total brain RNA would be predicted as long as an organism learns. Increases in RNA content have been correlated with age in several studies. Any interference with the RNA metabolism (such as might be produced by the administration of azaguanine) will disrupt enzyme induction and interfere with learning. A general increase in RNA metabolism (such as might be produced by tricyanoaminopropene), on the other hand, should facilitate these processes. Even the base ratio changes reported by Hydén and his associates can be explained by the enzyme induction hypothesis. It predicts an increase only in those RNA molecules required for the synthesis of the enzyme system which is involved in the manufacture of the transmitter substance. Since each of the RNA molecules probably has a unique constellation of base ratios, the analysis of total RNA reflects only an average of a very heterogeneous population. Changes in the base ratios of some of the RNA molecules would be expected to produce relatively small changes in the base ratio of this average. This prediction seems to be borne out by Hydén's recent work.

Briggs and Kitto's hypothesis appears to be the most promising approach to the problem of memory at the present time. It does not require basic assumptions that are incompatible with current biochemical knowledge or theory and appears to account adequately for a great deal of the experimental literature. Only time can tell whether its predictions can be further tested using presently available techniques, but the prospects seem to be brighter than those of other theories.

Before turning to a related area of research, it might be worthwhile to mention some of the biochemical mechanisms that have been proposed to account for the general phenomenon of enzyme induction. Platt (1962) has suggested that "regulator" genes (DNA) may produce a "repressor" substance which consists of RNA plus a specific protein. If this repressor substance complexes with an inducer substance, the function of structural genes (manufacturing particular messenger RNA molecules which, in turn, are responsible for the synthesis of an enzyme protein) is facilitated. Pardee (1962) has speculated that these repressor substances may be attached to the ribosomes, where they may normally block the deposition of amino acids on the RNA template. Smith (1962) has applied some of these notions to the transmitter substance acetylcholine as follows. Acetylcholine itself may be the inducer substance which facilitates the synthesis of the enzymes choline acetylase and cholinesterase. The initial release of acetylcholine would start an enzyme induction cycle which would cause greater and greater amounts of this substance to be released on each subsequent stimulation.

Briggs and Kitto's hypothesis receives a measure of support from a group of studies undertaken primarily at the Berkeley laboratories of Krech, Rosenzweig, and Bennett (Rosenzweig et al., 1956, 1960, 1962; Bennett et al., 1958a, 1958b; Krech et al., 1956, 1959a, b, 1962; Zolman and Morimoto, 1962). The basic assumption underlying these experiments is that the availability of acetylcholine in the brain determines the ease with which new connections are established and therefore the rate at which an organism will master a novel problem.

The earlier studies assumed that the level of cholinesterase (ChE) which hydrolyzes acetylcholine (ACh) is directly proportional to the level of the transmitter substance; they demonstrated that "maze-bright" rats (animals descended from parents that learned mazes rapidly) had a significantly higher cholinesterase level than "maze-dull" animals. When the two strains were crossed and the cholinesterase level of individual animals was correlated with their *own* learning ability, an inverse relationship appeared. Animals with higher ChE activity made *more* errors. It was subsequently learned that the synthesis of ACh is independent of the ChE level, and direct determinations of ACh activity were attempted to test the hypothesis that learning ability might correlate with the level of ACh at the synapse.

Although the observed differences are not large, it has generally been found in these studies that maze-bright rats tend to have either a higher ACh or lower ChE level than their maze-dull counterparts. Similarly, animals reared in complex environments, which presumably stimulate cortical activity and perhaps even learning, show a significant decrease in ChE activity, particularly in the sensory cortex. A marked increase in brain weight is also seen. Animals reared under conditions of environmental complexity tend to learn reversal problems more rapidly than controls reared in isolation.

A related observation has been reported by Russell et al. (1961), who found that chronically reduced ChE levels significantly retarded extinction but did not affect the course of simple conditioning. These findings are extremely interesting, although it is difficult to understand why one might expect an increase in total ACh activity following learning or exposure to a complex environment. If we are to understand the problem of memory, it will be necessary to show that the transmitter activity of specific synapses is increased during or following acquisition of a particular habit. This type of analysis is not feasible with presently available techniques.

Overton's calcium displacement hypothesis. Before we leave this fascinating subject we shall briefly discuss a very different theoretical approach; this theory conceives of memory as a biochemical change at the synapse which is largely independent of intracellular molecular events. Overton (1959) has proposed that learning may coincide with the displacement of calcium in the nervous system and has presented some experimental findings which can be interpreted to support this rather curious notion (Overton, 1958). According to this hypothesis, acetic acid is released as a consequence of the breakdown of acetylcholine during synaptic transmission. This acetic acid then combines with calcium to form a highly soluble salt, calcium acetate, which is rapidly absorbed into the bloodstream and is thus removed from the nervous system.

Overton suggests that this removal of calcium from the synaptic junction may increase the irritability of nervous tissue and produce a permanent or at least long-term facilitation which represents the memory trace. He points out that amnesia tends to be associated with diseases that involve a marked alteration in the calcium metabolism and describes an experiment (Overton, 1958) which indicated that rats maintained on a high-calcium diet tended to show more forgetting than normal controls or than animals fed a low-calcium diet. Chemical analysis of the brains of these animals showed an increased calcium concentration in the brain. We do not, however, have independent evidence for the suggested removal of calcium from the synapse following passage of a series of impulses. It is difficult to see how such a change, even if it could be demonstrated, would produce sufficiently permanent alterations to account for long-term memory. Any calcium that might be removed from a particular set of synaptic junctions would almost immediately be replaced by diffusion from neighboring tissues, perhaps producing a very small general fall in calcium concentration and an increase in irritability, but almost certainly no specific facilitation of a particular pathway. At present, it does not seem likely that this hypothesis could account for a significant aspect of the problem of memory. The theory has been mentioned here to illustrate the variety and diversity of biochemical speculations which have characterized the last decade.

Transfer of training studies. Before we leave the topic of biochemical mechanisms, some recent experiments on the possibility of memory transfer by brain extract must be described. The evidence for such transfer is controversial at best, but the potential importance of such a process for our understanding of learning requires discussion of this material.

Memory transfer was first reported in an investigation from McConnell's laboratories at the University of Michigan. McConnell (1962) conditioned flatworms, chopped them into pieces,

and hand-fed these pieces to untrained worms. When the cannibals were then trained on the same simple conditioning task, they made many more conditioned responses than normal control animals on the first day of training and continued to perform better than the controls throughout the first days of training. The difference tended to disappear as both groups neared asymptotic performance.

Zelman et al. (1963) reported that RNA extracts obtained from trained flatworms could be injected into the body cavity of untrained worms and produce comparable transfer of training effects. Jacobson et al. (1966a) have replicated these results in a series of experiments which attempted to rule out potential explanations in terms of pseudoconditioning or general sensitization.

These findings generated relatively little excitement because the flatworm is not a common laboratory animal. Serious questions have been raised about the basic learning phenomenon in this species; therefore demonstrations that the crude contraction response which can apparently be classically conditioned in these animals may be "transferred" to another animal via cannibalism or brain extract injections did not greatly impress most psychologists or physiologists concerned with the biochemistry of learning.

Serious interest in the transfer phenomenon was generated only recently when a group of Danish workers reported that similar transfer effects could be obtained in the albino rat. Fjerdingstad et al. (1965) reported that learning was facilitated when phenon-extracted RNA from the brains of trained rats was injected intracisternally into experimentally naive rats subsequently trained on the same problem.

Nissen et al. (1965) attempted to demonstrate the specificity of this effect in a two-alley apparatus which provided water reinforcements for selecting the lighted (or dark) alley. Somewhat surprisingly, animals that received RNA extract from rats trained to select the lighted alley performed better when reinforced for choosing the dark alley, whereas animals that received RNA extract from rats trained to select the dark alley performed better when reinforced for entering the lighted alley. Although it is clear in these experiments that the brain extracts contained something apparently related to the previous training of the donors, the relationship seems to be exactly the opposite of what might have been predicted.

Babich et al. (1965a) have reported similar

transfer effects. Rats were trained to approach the food magazine in an operant conditioning apparatus whenever a click was presented. After 900 training trials the animals were sacrificed and RNA was extracted from part of their brains (excluding the frontal lobes and olfactory bulbs and the brainstem posterior to the superior colliculi). Approximately 8 hr later this RNA extract was injected intraperitoneally (i.p.) into untrained rats. The response of the recipient animals to the auditory CS was tested at 4, 6, 8, 22, and 24 hr after the RNA injection. A correct response was recorded if the animal placed its nose inside a 63-cm² area surrounding the food cup. Using this somewhat unorthodox criterion, Babich et al. found that rats receiving RNA injections from trained donors performed significantly better than animals receiving injections of RNA from untrained donors.

The design of this experiment permits a number of interpretations other than a transfer of specific memories. A subsequent study by the same group of workers (Jacobson et al., 1965) was undertaken to remedy some of the more obvious problems, particularly the possibility of transfer of changes in general reactivity.

In this second experiment one group of rats was trained to approach the food cup in response to an auditory CS, and another was trained to respond to a blinking light. The animals were sacrificed following completion of training, and RNA was extracted from their brains as in the first experiment. Eight hr later the RNA extract was injected i.p. into untrained rats which were then exposed to a counterbalanced sequence of auditory and visual stimuli in the training apparatus. Jacobson's records show a small but statistically reliable tendency for animals receiving RNA from click-trained donors to respond preferentially to the auditory stimuli; animals receiving RNA from light-trained animals responded preferentially to the light.

Babich et al. (1965b) have replicated the first study of this series using hamsters as the trained donors and rats as the recipients. As before, the approach response to the food magazine appeared to transfer.

Jacobson et al. (1966b) have reported still another experiment designed to demonstrate that the transfer effect is not peculiar to their unorthodox training and testing procedure. The two-choice double-alley apparatus used in this study is unfortunately not the commonplace test situation we might hope for, since it is difficult to decide to what aspect of the stimulus situation the animal may have responded. One of the choices had a fine-mesh screen on the floor and a beaded chain hanging in the alley entrance; the other alternative had white contact paper with black-tape stripes on the floor and a vertical column of white jewel lights to one side of the alley entrance. Apparently no effort was made to guard against the acquisition of position habits. After 5 days of training in this apparatus (none of the animals made more than 2 errors on the last block of 25 trials), the animals were sacrificed and part of their brain (excluding frontal lobes, olfactory bulbs, pons, cerebellum, and medulla) was used to obtain an RNA extract. Approximately 8 hr later this extract was injected i.p. into untrained rats, which were then given five trials in the maze at 6, 9, 12, 22, and 25 hr after the injection. The recipient rats were subsequently trained to criterion and served as donors for subsequent tests. The results of this study show a small but statistically reliable transfer of training effect.

Rosenblatt and associates (Rosenblatt et al., 1966a, b, c) in a series of experiments demonstrated a weak but apparently consistent transfer effect in a variety of training and testing situations. The first of this series replicated the results reported by Babich et al. (1965a) in the same unstructured behavioral test. Subsequent experiments provided some evidence of transfer in more traditional behavioral situations. Among these are fixed-ratio performance in a standard operant conditioning apparatus; active and passive avoidance responses in a shuttle box apparatus; and discriminated operant behavior in a modified operant apparatus (rats were trained to press either the lever at the dark end of the box or the lever at the lighted end of the box; the position of the lights could be changed). Unfortunately, Rosenblatt gives many of the results only in terms of pooled data from a number of different experiments. Some of the differences reported for individual experiments are not statistically significant by commonly accepted standards. Several tentative conclusions nevertheless emerge from this interesting group of experiments.

1. Some evidence for a transfer of training effect was obtained in a variety of behavioral test situations, but the effects appeared most convincingly when the animal was required to respond to a definite cue (such as a click or light) rather than to an unchanging aspect of the environment (such as a lever). Situations that did

not require the expenditure of effort or very precise responses (such as merely approaching a food cup) showed the transfer effect more readily than more effortful and precise responses (such as lever pressing).

2. RNA extracted from cerebral or cerebellar portions of the brain as well as from the entire brain apparently contained relevant information, but the cerebellar extract was less potent than those from the whole brain or cerebrum. Incubation with RN-ase which destroys the RNA in the extract did not eliminate the transfer effect. A comparison of various extracts indicates that the information-bearing molecule, if such there be, appears to have the properties of a polypeptide rather than of RNA itself.

3. Of the various procedural factors which seemed to influence the magnitude of the transfer effect, dosage and stage of training at time of sacrifice appeared the most important. The best effects were obtained when the brain extract was taken just after the donor had reached asymptotic performance levels but had not been overtrained. Only marginal transfer could be obtained with one donor brain per recipient, and the magnitude of the transfer effect appeared to be a direct function of the dosage beyond this minimal level. Surprisingly, perhaps, there seemed to be no difference between the effects of extracts from single-donor brains as compared with those from pooled brains.

These observations may help resolve some of the controversy in this field. We should not, however, lose sight of the fact that many of these conclusions are based on marginal effects and that the basic phenomenon is itself still disputed. One notable question raised by Rosenblatt's experiments concerns the apparently idiosyncratic nature of the response to the brain extracts. The best transfer effects were demonstrated in a comparison of the top 50% of the experimental and control rats; few of the overall comparisons reached statistically reliable levels. In fact, some of the RNA-treated rats consistently performed more poorly than the poorest controls, indicating the possibility of adverse effects. Perhaps these adverse effects depended on the site or dosage of the injections as well as on the success of the extraction procedure. All these variables must be taken into account in future studies of this complex problem.

Ungar (Ungar and Oceguera-Navarro, 1965; Ungar, 1966) has reported interesting experiments on the transfer of drug tolerance and habituation effects via brain homogenates. In the first experiment rats and dogs were given repeated doses of morphine until they developed a marked tolerance to the drug. Brain homogenates from these animals were then injected i.p. into mice which had never before received morphine. The morphine tolerance of these animals was found to be significantly greater than that of control animals. The tolerance induced by a single injection lasted approximately 10 to 15 days. The degree of tolerance was a function of the amount of homogenate administered.

In the second experiment of this group, Ungar and Oceguera-Navarro habituated rats to a loud 400-cps tone (the criterion of habituation was an overt response to fewer than 10% of the stimuli). Brain homogenate from these animals was then injected i.p. into mice which had not been exposed to the sound. Sixteen hr later the first of fourteen daily habituation tests was conducted. Mice receiving brain extracts from habituated rats responded significantly less frequently to the tone than mice receiving extracts from naive rats.

The evidence for transfer of training is opposed by a very impressive array of negative results. The first published report of a failure to replicate the transfer effect appeared within a few months of Babich's publication.

In the first experiment Gross and Carey (1965) employed biochemical and behavioral procedures essentially identical to those used in the studies of Babich et al. and observed absolutely no evidence for transfer of training. In a second experiment the biochemical procedures were modified to increase the yield of RNA and eliminate phenol contamination. Again there was no indication of transfer of training or a relation between the amount of RNA injected and the number of approach responses.

A large number of studies conducted since then have similarly failed to obtain evidence for transfer of training. These experiments have not received the attention they deserve because it is difficult to publish negative results. A notable exception to this rule is a recent paper by Luttges et al. (1966) describing a series of experiments on the transfer of training problem.

In the first experiment mice were trained on a two-choice brightness discrimination task to swim to the nonpreferred arm of a maze. A control group was trained always to select the left arm regardless of the position of the light. After training was completed, the animals were killed and RNA was extracted in a procedure similar to that employed by Jacobson and associates. Eighteen hr after naive mice had received i.p. injections of this extract, their locomotor activity was tested. Two hr later they were given six trials in the water maze. Neither measure showed any significant effect of the RNA injection.

In the second experiment the extraction procedure was modified to follow that reported by Jacobson and associates even more closely. A spontaneous activity measure, taken 15 hr after the i.p. injection of this RNA extract, failed to show any effect. All animals were then given six trials in the water maze. Six additional test trials were administered 12 hr later. None of the measures showed any evidence for a transfer of training effect.

In the next experiment of this series, rats were trained on a light-dark discrimination in a shuttle box. After 10 consecutive days of criterion performance (nine correct choices in ten trials), the animals were sacrificed. Naive rats were tested in the shuttle box apparatus 18 and 42 hr after receiving i.p. injections of RNA extracts from the trained donors. The experimental rats did not perform significantly better than controls which received brain extracts from untrained animals.

In a further attempt to demonstrate transfer of training, this experiment was replicated but the donor animals received twice as much overtraining and the recipient rats were tested at 8, 16, and 40 hr after they had received i.p. injections of the RNA extract. Again, no reliable effects were observed.

Since many of the experiments which reported positive transfer effects were performed in appetitive situations, Luttges et al. next trained mice to run a modified Lashley type III maze for water rewards. After 18 days of training, eight mice that made no more than one error in the last 3 days of training were sacrificed. RNA extract from these animals was then injected into naive mice which were subsequently given one test trial in the maze every 8 hr. The performance of these animals did not differ from that of untrained mice given injections of saline or of RNA from naive animals.

In a subsequent experiment a less complex task was employed in order to keep the test situation comparable to those used by earlier investigators who had reported positive effects. Mice were trained to approach either the light or the dark compartment in a shuttle box in order to avoid painful shock. After completion of training, the animals were sacrificed and the RNA extracts pooled. A group of naive mice were then given i.p. injections of this extract in quantities equivalent to the amount extractable from three brains. Four hr later the animals were tested in the shuttle box. Absolutely no evidence of transfer of training was observed.

Perhaps the most telling argument against a transfer of memory via RNA which can be extracted from brains and injected into another animal comes from a further experiment in this group. Luttges et al. labeled RNA *in vivo* by injecting P^{32}-orthophosphate directly into the intraventricular cavity. This labeled RNA was then injected intraperitoneally into recipient rats. Radioactivity was measured in the animals blood, peritoneal fluid, and brain. It was found that most of the labeled RNA was rapidly excreted in the feces and urine and that no significant amounts were able to cross the blood-brain barrier.

No evidence of any transfer effect was obtained even when RNA extract from trained animals was injected directly into the brains of untrained animals. Thirty mice were thoroughly overtrained on a simple passive-avoidance task. RNA extract from these animals was then administered intraventricularly to naive mice 18 hr before their first training trial in the avoidance situation. The performances of these animals did not differ reliably from that of mice receiving RNA extract from untrained animals.

Particularly in conjunction with other reports of negative results (R. Leaf, A. Wagner, personal communication), these experiments suggest that the positive effects reported by Jacobson, Ungar, and others may reflect nonspecific sensitization rather than the transfer of memories. Many laboratories are currently engaged in efforts to clarify this important matter.

SUMMARY

A variety of hypotheses advanced in the past decade attempt to relate memory and, at least by implication, learning to intracellular biochemical events. The earlier proposals of Monné (1948) and Katz and Halstead (1950) centered around the possibility that memory might be related directly to the synthesis of specific proteins. Some of the basic assumptions of these hypotheses have been shown to be incorrect. The more recent speculations of Hydén (1961a) and Gaito (1963) have instead proposed primary modifications in RNA or DNA molecules as the basic biochemical correlates of memory. Hydén's influential writings rest on the assumption that the passage of a particular pattern of bioelectrical events changes the base sequence of RNA molecules. The novel RNA molecule directs the synthesis of new proteins which dissociate selectively, causing the release of transmitter substances at the synapse when the original bioelectrical pattern of excitation recurs. Gaito (1963) has suggested that memory might instead be related to the deletion, addition, or rearrangement of bases in the structure of deoxyribonucleic acids so that the genetic potential of the cell is permanently altered. There is as yet little or no experimental support for this notion.

Hydén's hypothesis is supported by a considerable body of experimental evidence, but Briggs and Kitto (1962) argue that the synaptic facilitation presumably related to learning and retention may be the result of an increase in the availability of neurohumoral transmitter substances. Repeated activation of a cell, according to this hypothesis, increases the neuron's ability to manufacture and release the transmitter substance and thus increases the probability of synaptic transmission. This hypothesis does not postulate the storage of specific memory traces in particular cells or cell assemblies as suggested by Hydén's RNA hypothesis. Instead, it relates memory to the synaptic facilitation of specific pathways. It does not explain the *selective* facilitation of connections between the CS and UCS pathways, but this problem is hardly unique to Briggs and Kitto's hypothesis. On the whole, this approach appears at present to be most fruitful.

BIBLIOGRAPHY

Agranoff, B. W., & Klinger, P. D. Puromycin effect on memory fixation in the goldfish. *Science,* 1964, **146,** 952–953.

Agranoff, B. W., Davis, R. E., & Brink, J. J. Memory fixation in the goldfish. *Proc. nat. Acad. Sci., (Washington),* 1965, **54,** 788–793.

Babich, F. R., Jacobson, A. L., Bubash, S., & Jacobson, A. Transfer of a response to naive rats by injections of ribonucleic acid extracted from trained rats. *Science,* 1965a, **149,** 656–657.

Babich, F. R., Jacobson, A. L., & Bubash, S. Cross-species transfer of learning: effect of ribonucleic acid from hamsters on rat behavior. *Proc. nat. Acad. Sci. (Washington),* 1965b, **54,** 1299–1302.

Bennett, E. L., Krech, D., Rosenzweig, M. R., Karlsson, H., Dye, N., & Ohlander, A. Cholinesterase and lactic dehydrogenase activity in the rat brain. *J. Neurochem.,* 1958a, **3,** 153–160.

Bennett, E. L., Rosenzweig, M. R., Krech, D., Karlsson, H., Dye, N., & Ohlander, A. Individual, strain and age differences in cholinesterase activity of the rat brain. *J. Neurochem.,* 1958b, **3,** 144–152.

Briggs, M. H., & Kitto, G. B. The molecular basis of memory and learning. *Psychol. Rev.,* 1962, **69,** 537–541.

Cameron, D. E., & Solyom, L. Effects of ribonucleic acid on memory. *Geriatrics,* 1961, **16,** 74–81.

Chamberlin, T. J., Rothschild, G. H., & Gerard, R. W. Drugs affecting RNA and learning. *Proc. nat. Acad. Sci. (Washington),* 1963, **49,** 918–925.

Cook, L., Davidson, A. B., David, D. J., Green, H., & Fellows, F. J. Ribonucleic acid: effect on conditioned behavior in rats. *Science,* 1963, **141,** 268–269.

Corning, W. C., & John, E. R. Effect of ribonuclease on retention of conditioned response in regenerated planarians. *Science,* 1961, **134,** 1363–1365.

Crick, F. H. C. On the genetic code. *Science,* 1963, **139,** 461–464.

Crick, F. H. C., Barnett, L., Brenner, S., & Watts-Tobin, R. J. General nature of the genetic code for proteins. *Nature (London),* 1961, **192,** 1227–1232.

Davidson, J. N. *The biochemistry of the nucleic acids* (5th ed.). London: Methuen, 1965.

Davis, R. E., Bright, Patricia J., & Agranoff, B. W. Effect of ECS and Puromycin on memory in fish. *J. comp. physiol. Psychol.,* 1965, **60,** 162–166.

Dingman, W., & Sporn, M. B. The incorporation of 8-azaguanine into rat brain RNA and its effect on maze-learning by the rat; an inquiry into the biochemical bases of memory. *J. psychiat. Res.,* 1961, **I,** 1–11.

Dixon, M., & Webb, E. C. *Enzymes.* London: Longmans, 1958.

Edström, J. E., & Eichner, D. Relation between nucleolar volume and cell body content of ribonucleic acid in supra-optic neurones. *Nature (London),* 1958, **181,** 619.

Egyhazi, E., & Hydén, H. Experimentally induced changes in the base composition of the ribonucleic acids of isolated nerve cells and their oligodendroglial cells, *J. biophysiol. biochem. Cytol.,* 1961, **10,** 403–410.

Fjerdingstad, E. J., Nissen, Th., & Røigaard-Petersen, H. H. Effect of ribonucleic acid (RNA) extracted from the brain of trained animals on learning in rats. *Scand. J. Psychol.,* 1965, **6,** 1–6.

Flexner, J. B., Flexner, L. B., Stellar, E., Haba, G. de la, & Roberts, R. B. Inhibition of protein synthesis in brain and learning and memory following puromycin. *J. Neurochem.,* 1962, **9,** 595–605.

Flexner, J. B., Flexner, L. B., & Stellar, E. Memory in mice as affected by intracerebral puromycin. *Science,* 1963, **141,** 57–59.

Fruton, J. S., & Simmonds, S. *General biochemistry* (2nd ed.). New York: Wiley, 1958.

Gaito, J. A biochemical approach to learning and memory. *Psychol. Rev.,* 1961, **68,** 288–292.

Gaito, J. DNA and RNA as memory molecules. *Psychol. Rev.,* 1963, **70,** 471–480.

Gaito, J., & Zavala, A. Neurochemistry and learning. *Psychol. Bull.,* 1964, **61,** 45–62.

Geiger, A., Yamasoki, S., & Lyons, R. Changes in nitrogenous components of brain produced by stimulation of short duration. *Amer. J. Physiol.,* 1958, **184,** 239–243.

Gerard, R. W., Chamberlin, T. J., & Rothschild, G. H. RNA in learning and memory. *Science,* 1963, **140,** 381.

Gros, F., Hiatt, H., Gilbert, W., Kurland, C. G., Risebrough, R. W., & Watson, J. D. Unstable ribonucleic acid revealed by pulse labelling of escherichia coli. *Nature (London),* 1961, **190,** 581–585.

Gross, C. G., & Carey, F. M. Transfer of learned response by RNA injection: failure of attempts to replicate. *Science,* 1965, **150,** 1749.

Halstead, W. Brain and intelligence. In *Cerebral mechanisms in behavior.* L. A. Jeffress, Ed. New York: Wiley, 1951.

Hoagland, M. B. Nucleic acids and proteins. *Scient. American,* 1959, **201,** 55–61.

Hoagland, M. B., Zamecnik, P. C., & Stephenson, M. L. Intermediate reactions in protein biosynthesis. *Biochem. biophysiol. Acta,* 1957, **24,** 215–216.

Hoagland, M. B., Stephenson, M. L., Scott, J. F., Hecht, L. I., & Zamecnik, P. C. A soluble ribonucleic acid intermediate in protein synthesis. *J. biol. Chem.,* 1958, **231,** 241–257.

Hurwitz, J., & Furth, J. J. Messenger RNA. *Scient. American,* 1962, **206,** 41–49.

Hydén, H. Biochemical changes in glial cells and nerve cells at varying activity. In *Biochemistry of the central nervous system. Vol. III.* Proceedings of the Fourth International Congress of Biochemistry. O. Hoffmann-Ostenhoff, Ed. London: Pergamon Press, 1959.

Hydén, H. Biochemical aspects of brain activity. In *Control of the mind, Part 1.* S. Farber & R. Wilson, Eds. New York: McGraw-Hill, 1961a,

Hydén, H. Satellite cells in the nervous system. *Scient. American,* 1961b, **205**(6), 62–70.

Hydén, H. The neuron and its glia—a biochemical and functional unit. *Endeavour,* 1962, **21,** 144–155.

Hydén, H., & Egyhazi, E. Nuclear RNA changes of nerve cells during a learning experiment in rats. *Proc. nat. Acad. Sci. (Washington),* 1962, **48,** 1366–1373.

Hydén, H., & Egyhazi, E. Glial RNA changes during a learning experiment with rats. *Proc. nat. Acad. Sci. (Washington),* 1963, **49,** 618–624.

Hydén, H., & Pigon, A. A cytophysiological study of the functional relationship between oligodendroglial cells and nerve cells of Deiter's nucleus. *J. Neurochem.,* 1960, **6,** 57–72.

Jacobson, A. L., Babich, F. R., Bubash, S., & Jacobson, A. Differential approach tendencies produced by injections of RNA from trained rats. *Science,* 1965, **150,** 636–637.

Jacobson, A. L., Fried, C., & Horowitz, S. D. Planarians and Memory. I: Transfer of learning by injection of ribonucleic acid. *Nature (London),* 1966a, **209,** 599–601.

Jacobson, A. L., Babich, F. R., Bubash, S., & Goren, C. Maze preferences in naive rats by injection of ribonucleic acid from trained rats. *Psychonom. Sci.,* 1966b, **4,** 3–4.

John, E. R., Wenzel, B., & Tschirgi, R. D. Unpublished observations, cited by Corning, W. D., & John, E. R. *Science,* 1961, **134,** 1363–1365.

Katz, J. J., & Halstead, W. C. Protein organization and mental function. *Comp. Psychol. Monogr.,* 1950, **20**(103), 1–38.

Kornberg, A. Biologic synthesis of deoxyribonucleic acids. *Science,* 1960, **131,** 1503–1508.

Krech, D., Rosenzweig, M. R., Bennett, E. L., & Krueckel, B. Enzyme concentration in the brain and adjustive behavior patterns. *Science,* 1954, **120,** 994–996.

Krech, D., Rosenzweig, M. R., & Bennett, E. L. Dimensions of discrimination and level of cholinesterase activity in the cerebral cortex of the rat. *J. comp. physiol. Psychol.,* 1956, **49,** 261–268.

Krech, D., Rosenzweig, M. R., Bennett, E. L., & Longueil, C. L. Changes in brain chemistry of the rat following experience. Paper read at American Psychology Association, Cincinnati, Ohio, 1959a.

Krech, D., Rosenzweig, M. R., & Bennett, E. L. Correlation between brain cholinesterase and brain weight within two strains of rats. *Amer. J. Physiol.,* 1959b, **196,** 31–32.

Krech, D., Rosenzweig, M. R., & Bennett, E. L. Relations between brain chemistry and problem-solving among rats raised in enriched and impoverished environments. *J. comp. physiol. Psychol.,* 1962, **55,** 801–807.

Landauer, T. K. Two hypotheses concerning the biochemical basis of memory. *Psychol. Rev.,* 1964, **71,** 167–179.

Luttges, M., Johnson, R., Buck, C., Holland, J., & McGaugh, J. An examination of "transfer of learning" by nucleic acid. *Science,* 1966, **151,** 834–837.

McConnell, J. V. Memory transfer via cannibalism in planaria. *J. Neuropsychiat.,* 1962, **3,** 1–42.

McConnell, J. V., Jacobson, A. L., & Kimble, D. P. The effects of regeneration upon retention of a conditioned response in the planarian. *J. comp. physiol. Psychol.,* 1959, **52,** 1–5.

Matthaei, J. H., & Nirenberg, M. W. The dependence of cell-free protein synthesis in *E. coli.* upon RNA prepared from ribosomes. *Biochem. biophys. Res. Commun.,* 1961, **4,** 404–408.

Matthaei, J. H., Jones, O. W., Martin, R. G., & Nirenberg, M. W. Characteristics and composition of RNA coding units. *Proc. nat. Acad. Sci. (Washington),* 1962, **48,** 666–667.

Monné, L. Functioning of the cytoplasm. In *Advances in*

enzymology. Vol. VIII. F. F. Nord, Ed. New York: Interscience, 1948.

Morrell, F. Lasting changes in synaptic organization produced by continuous neuronal bombardment. In *Brain mechanisms and learning.* J. F. Delafresnaye, A. Fessard, R. W. Gerard, & J. Konorski, Eds. Oxford: Blackwell Scientific, 1961.

Nissen, Th., Røigaard-Petersen, H. H., & Fjerdingstad, E. J. Effect of ribonucleic acid (RNA) extracted from the brain of trained animals on learning in rats. II: Dependence of RNA effect on training conditions prior to RNA extraction. *Scand. J. Psychol.,* 1965, **6**, 265–272.

Overton, R. K. An effect of high and low calcium diets on the maze performance of rats. *J. comp. physiol. Psychol.,* 1958, **51**, 697–699.

Overton, R. K. The calcium displacement hypothesis: a review. *Psychol. Rep.,* 1959, **5**, 721–724.

Pardee, A. B. Aspects of genetic and metabolic control of protein synthesis. In *The molecular control of cellular activity.* J. M. Allen, Ed. New York: McGraw-Hill, 1962.

Platt, J. R. A "book model" of genetic information transfer in cells and tissues. In *Horizons in biochemistry.* M. Kasha & B. Pullman, Eds. New York: Academic Press, 1962.

Røigaard-Petersen, H. H., Fjerdingstad, E. J., & Nissen, Th. Facilitation of learning in rats by intracisternal injection of "conditioned RNA." *Worm Runner's Digest,* 1965, **7**, 15–25.

Rosenblatt, F., Farrow, J. T., & Rhine, S. The transfer of learned behavior from trained to untrained rats by means of brain extracts, I. *Proc. nat. Acad. Sci. (Washington),* 1966a, **55**, 548–555.

Rosenblatt, F., Farrow, J. T., & Rhine, S. The transfer of learned behavior from trained to untrained rats by means of brain extracts, II. *Proc. nat. Acad. Sci. (Washington),* 1966b, **55**, 787–792.

Rosenblatt, F., Farrow, J. T., & Herblin, W. F. Transfer of conditioned responses from trained rats to untrained rats by means of a brain extract. *Nature (London),* 1966c, **209**, 46–48.

Rosenzweig, M. R., Krech, D., & Bennett, E. L. Effects of pentobarbital sodium on adaptive behavior patterns in the rat. *Science,* 1956, **123**, 371–372.

Rosenzweig, M. R., Krech, D., & Bennett, E. L. A search for relations between brain chemistry and behavior. *Psychol. Bull.,* 1960, **57**, 476–492.

Rosenzweig, M. R., Krech, D., Bennett, E. L., & Diamond, M. C. Effects of environmental complexity and training on brain chemistry and anatomy: a replication and extension. *J. comp. physiol. Psychol.,* 1962, **55**, 429–437.

Russell, R. W., Watson, R. H. J., & Frankenhaeuser, M. Effects of chronic reductions in brain cholinesterase activity on acquisition and extinction of a conditioned avoidance response. *Scand. J. Psychol.,* 1961, **2**, 21–29.

Smith, C. E. Is memory a matter of enzyme induction? *Science,* 1962, **138**, 889–890.

Ungar, G. Configurational and hydrolytic changes of proteins on excitation: their role in information processing. In *Protides of the biological fluids.* H. Peeters, Ed. Amsterdam: Elsevier, 1966.

Ungar, G., & Oceguera-Navarro, C. Transfer of habituation by material transferred from brain. *Nature (London),* 1965, **207**, 301.

Watson, J. D. Involvement of RNA in the synthesis of proteins. *Science,* 1963, **140**, 17–26.

Watson, J. D., & Crick, F. H. C. Molecular structure of nucleic acids. *Nature (London),* 1953, **171**, 737–738.

Weisblum, B., Benzer, S., & Holly, R. W. A physical basis for degeneracy in the amino acid code. *Proc. nat. Acad. Sci. (Washington),* 1962, **48**, 1449–1454.

Wilkins, M. H. F. Molecular configurations of nucleic acids. *Science,* 1963, **140**, 941–950.

Zelman, A., Kabat, L., Jacobson, R., & McConnell, J. V. Transfer of training through injection of "conditioned" RNA into untrained planarians. *Worm Runner's Digest,* 1963, **5**, 14–21.

Zolman, J. F., & Morimoto, H. Effects of age of training on cholinesterase activity in the brains of maze-bright rats. *J. comp. physiol. Psychol.,* 1962, **55**, 794–800.

ILLUSTRATION CREDITS

The illustrations of this book have been reproduced by permission, courtesy of the following publishing houses and journals.

PUBLISHING HOUSES

American Physiological Society, Washington, D.C.
Handbook of Physiology. Vol. I. J. Field, H. W. Magoun, and V. E. Hall, Eds., © 1959.
   2.121, 3.2, 3.28, 3.31
Handbook of Physiology. Vol. II. J. Field. H. W. Magoun, and V. E. Hall, Eds., © 1960.
   2.60, 2.84, 2.85, 2.95, 4.8, 4.10, 4.12, 5.9, 5.11, 5.12, 8.22, 8.23, 8.24
Handbook of Physiology. Vol. III. J. Field, H. W. Magoun, and V. E. Hall, Eds., © 1960.
   3.21, 3.22, 3.23, 4.18, 4.20, 4.21, 5.8
Physiological Triggers. T. H. Bullock, Ed., © 1957.
   8.21
Appleton-Century-Crofts, New York, N.Y.
Anatomy of the Nervous System. 2nd ed., O. Larsell, © 1951.
   2.34
Blackwell Scientific Publications, Ltd., Oxford, England
Symposium on Brain Mechanisms and Learning. J. F. Delafresnaye, A. Fessard, R. W. Gerard, and J. Konorski, Eds., © 1961.
   12.27, 12.28, 12.63, 12.64, 13.5, 13.19
William C. Brown Co., Dubuque, Iowa
Outlines of Neuroanatomy. A. T. Rasmussen, © 1943.
   2.119, 2.120
Clarendon Press, Oxford, England
The Neurophysiological Basis of Mind. J. C. Eccles, © 1953.
   15.12B, 15.13
Clark University Press, Worchester, Mass.
Handbook of General Experimental Psychology. C. A. Murchison, Ed., © 1934.
   3.15
Grune and Stratton, New York, N.Y.
Experimental Psychopathology. P. H. Hoch and J. Zubin, Eds., © 1957.
   10.12, 10.13
The Study of the Brain. H. S. Rubinstein, © 1953.
   2.9, 2.45, 2.87, 2.90, 2.91, 2.94
Hafner Publishing Co., New York, N.Y.
Atlas of Human Anatomy. Vol. III. 8th English ed., F. H. J. Figge, Ed., © 1963.
   2.62, 2.64, 2.65, 2.69, 2.70, 2.81
Holt, Rinehart and Winston, New York, N.Y.
Physiological Psychology. M. A. Wenger, F. N. Jones,

and M. H. Jones, © 1956.
   2.106
Houghton Mifflin Co., Boston, Mass.
The Perception of the Visual World. J. J. Gibson, © 1950.
   3.20
Hungarian Academy of Sciences, Publishing House, Budapest V, Hungary
Atlas of Human Anatomy. Vol. III. 17th ed., F. Kiss and J. Szentágothai, © 1964.
   2.22, 2.41, 2.42, 2.63, 2.67
Lea and Febiger, Philadelphia, Pa.
Gray's Anatomy of the Human Body. 27th ed., C. M. Goss, Ed., © 1959.
   Table 2.1, 2.113, 2.114, 2.117, 2.118
A Textbook of Neuro-Anatomy. 5th ed., A. Kuntz, © 1950.
   2.92
Little, Brown and Co., Boston, Mass.
Neurological Basis of Behavior. G. E. W. Wolestenholme and C. M. O'Connor, Eds., © 1958.
   12.18, 12.19
Henry Ford Hospital Symposium. *The Reticular Formation of the Brain.* H. H. Jasper, L. D. Proctor, R. S. Knighton, W. C. Noshay, and R. T. Costello, Eds., © 1958.
   1.32 right, 5.1, 5.2, 5.7, Table 5.1, 12.31, 12.32, 15.14
McGraw-Hill Book Co., New York, N.Y.
The Frontal Granular Cortex and Behavior. J. M. Warren and K. Akert, Eds., © 1964.
   13.13, 13.20, 13.21, 13.22, 13.23, 13.24, 13.25, 13.26, 13.29, 13.30, 13.31, 13.32
The Neuroanatomical Basis for Clinical Neurology. 2nd ed., T. L. Peele, © 1961.
   1.5, 1.6, 2.2, 2.3, 2.5, 2.6, 2.7, 2.8, 2.11, 2.16, 2.29, 2.47, 2.61, 2.66, 2.71, 2.72, 2.73, 2.74, 2.76, 2.77, 2.86, 2.103, 2.110, 2.111, 2.112, 2.116
Neuroanatomy. E. L. House and B. Pansky, © 1960.
   2.10, 2.13, 2.14, 2.15, 2.17, 2.20, 2.126, 2.127, 2.128, 4.22, 4.23, 4.24, 6.22, 6.23, 6.24, 6.25
Physiological Psychology. C. T. Morgan and E. Stellar, © 1950.
   1.12, 1.26
The Physiology of Man. L. L. Langley and E. Cheraskin, © 1958.
   4.25, 4.26, 4.27, 4.28, 4.31, 4.32, 4.33, 4.34, 8.1, 8.3
The Second International Symposium on Feelings and

883

Emotions. M. L. Reymert, Ed., © 1950.
9.10, 9.11, 9.12

Textbook of Histology. J. F. Nonidez and W. F. Windle, © 1949.
2.123, 2.124

The Macmillan Co., New York, N.Y.
The Cerebral Cortex of Man. W. Penfield and T. Rasmussen, © 1950.
2.75

Correlative Anatomy of the Nervous System. E. C. Crosby, T. Humphrey, and E. W. Lauer, © 1962.
2.28, 2.31, 2.33, 2.35, 2.37, 2.38, 2.39, 2.79, 2.104

The Electrical Activity of the Nervous System. 2nd ed., M. A. B. Brazier, © 1961.
1.8

The Pharmacological Basis of Therapeutics. 3rd ed., L. S. Goodman and A. Gilman, © 1965.
2.129

Josiah Macy, Jr. Foundation, New York, N.Y.
The Central Nervous System and Behavior. 2nd ed., M. A. B. Brazier, Ed., © 1959.
12.11, 12.20, 13.37, 13.38, 13.40, 13.41

Methuen and Co., Ltd., London, England
The Biochemistry of the Nucleic Acids. 5th ed., J. N. Davidson, © 1965.
16.12, 16.13

The M.I.T. Press, Cambridge, Mass.
Sensory Communication. W. A. Rosenblith, Ed., © 1961.
3.43, 3.53

The C. V. Mosby Co., St. Louis, Mo.
Neuroanatomy. 2nd ed., F. A. Mettler, © 1948.
2.21, 2.36, 2.43, 2.68, 2.88, 2.89, 2.93

Oxford University Press, Clarendon Press, Oxford, England
Degeneration and Regeneration of the Nervous System. S. Ramón y Cajal, © 1928.
15.1

Pergamon Press, London, England
Olfaction and Taste. Y. Zotterman, Ed., © 1963.
7.21

Thirst, First International Symposium on Thirst in the Regulation of Body Water. M. J. Wayner, Ed., © 1964.
7.20, 7.22

Pitman and Sons, Ltd., London, England.
The Electrical Activity of the Nervous System, 2nd Ed., Marie A. Brazier, © 1961.
1.8

The Ronald Press Co., New York, N.Y.
Physiological Regulations. E. F. Adolph, © 1943.
7.1, 7.33

W. B. Saunders Co., Philadelphia, Pa.
Comparative Animal Physiology. L. C. Prosser, © 1950.
8.4

Fundamentals of Neurology. 4th ed., E. Gardner, © 1963.
1.3, 1.4, 1.7, 1.11, 2.1

Neurophysiology. T. C. Ruch, H. D. Patton, J. W. Woodbury, and A. L. Towe, Eds., © 1961.
1.9, 1.10, 1.14, 1.17, Table 1.2, Table 1.3, 1.24, 1.25, 1.34, 1.35, 1.37, 4.1, 4.4, 4.5, 4.6, 4.7

Peripheral Nerve Injuries. 2nd ed., W. Haymaker and B. Woodhall, © 1953.
2.4

Textbook of Medical Physiology. 2nd illustrated ed., A. C. Guyton, © 1961.
6.3, 6.4, 6.5, 6.6, 6.7

A Textbook of Physiology. J. F. Fulton, Ed., © 1949.
8.2, 8.5, 8.6

Scheltema and Holkema N. V., Amsterdam, Holland
Atlas Anatonicum Cerebri Humani. G. Jelgersma, © 1931.
2.55, 2.56, 2.57, 2.58, 2.59

Charles C Thomas, Springfield, Ill.
Epilepsy and Cerebral Localization. W. Penfield and T. C. Erickson, Eds., © 1941.
1.23

Thirst: Physiology of the Urge to Drink and Problems of Water Lack. A. V. Wolf, © 1958.
7.2, 7.3, 7.4

University of Chicago Press, Chicago, Ill.
The Machinery of the Body. J. Carlson and V. Johnson, © 1949.
1.1, 1.2

The Structural Basis of Behavior. J. A. Deutsch, © 1960.
11.2

The Vertebrate Visual System. H. Klüver, Ed., © 1957.
2.107, 2.108, 2.109

University of Nebraska Press, Lincoln, Nebr.
Nebraska Symposium on Motivation, M. R. Jones, Ed., © 1961.
6.26

University of Pennsylvania Press, Philadelphia, Pa.
Electrical Signs of Nervous Activity. J. Erlanger and H. S. Gasser, © 1937.
1.18, 1.19

University of Texas Press, Austin, Texas
Electrical Stimulation of the Brain. D. E. Sheer, Ed., © 1961.
9.15, 9.16, 9.19, 9.25, 10.5, 10.11, 10.15, 13.33, 13.56

University of Wisconsin Press, Madison, Wis.
Biological and Biochemical Bases of Behavior. H. F. Harlow and C. N. Woolsey, Eds., © 1958.
13.11, 13.15, 15.2   Reprinted with permission of the copyright owners, the Regents of the University of Wisconsin

Cortical Connections and Functional Organization of the Thalamic Auditory System of the Cat. J. E. Rose and C. N. Woolsey, © 1958.
2.80   Reprinted with permission of the copyright owners, the Regents of the University of Wisconsin

Wetenschappelijke Uitgeverij, N. V. Excerpta Medica, Amsterdam C, Holland
Atlas of Human Anatomy. Vol. II. M. W. Woerdeman, © 1950.
2.130, 2.132

John Wiley and Sons, New York, N.Y.
  Handbook of Experimental Psychology. S. S. Stevens, Ed., © 1951.
    3.11, Table 3.1, 4.19, 9.13
  Light, Colour and Vision. Y. Le Grand, © 1957.
    3.1, 3.3, 3.4, 3.5, 3.6, 3.7, 3.8, 3.9, 3.10, 3.12, 3.13, 3.14, 3.16, 3.19, 3.33, 3.34, 3.35
  The Organization of Behavior. D. O. Hebb, © 1949.
    15.5, 15.6
Williams and Wilkins Co., Baltimore, Md.
  Bailey's Textbook of Histology. 15th ed., revised by W. M. Copenhaver, © 1964.
    2.102
  Human Sex Anatomy. R. L. Dickinson, © 1933.
    8.7
  Sex and Internal Secretions. 2nd ed., E. Allen, Ed., © 1939.
    8.16, 8.17, 8.34
  Strong and Elwyn's Human Neuroanatomy. 4th ed., R. C. Truex, © 1959.
    2.18, 2.23, 2.24, 2.27, 2.30, 2.82, 2.99, 2.100, 2.101, 2.125, 2.131
  Strong and Elwyn's Human Neuroanatomy. 5th ed., R. C. Truex and M. B. Carpenter, © 1964.
    2.19, 2.25, 2.26, 2.32, 2.40, 2.44, 2.46, 2.48, 2.49, 2.50, 2.51, 2.52, 2.53, 2.54, 2.83, 2.105, 2.115
Yale University Press, New Haven, Conn.
  Receptors and Sensory Perception. R. Granit, © 1955.
    3.36
Year Book Medical Publications, Chicago, Ill.
  Metabolic and Endocrine Physiology. Jay Tepperman, © 1962.
    4.29, 4.30, 4.35.

JOURNALS

Acta physiol. scand. (Acta Physiologica Scandinavica), Karolinska Institutet, Stockholm, Sweden
    5.4, 6.55, 6.56, 6.57, 7.14, 7.17, 7.18, 7.34, 7.35
Amer. J. Physiol. (American Journal of Physiology), American Physiological Society, Washington, D.C.
    1.30, 1.31, 3.44 right, 3.45, 6.1, 6.8, 6.9, 6.10, 6.11, 6.12, 6.18, 6.29, 6.30, 6.31, 6.32, 6.33, 6.34, 6.51, 6.52, 6.53, 6.58, 6.61, 7.5, 7.6, 7.7, 7.8, 7.9, 7.10, 7.11, 7.12, 7.13, 7.15, 7.19, 7.25, 7.26, 7.27, 7.28, 7.29, 7.30, 7.31, 7.32, 12.1, 12.2, 12.12, 12.13, 12.14, 12.45
Anat. Rec. (Anatomical Record), Wistar Institute, Philadelphia, Pa.
    2.12, 2.122, 7.23, 7.24
Ann. N.Y. Acad. Sci. (Annals of the New York Academy of Sciences), New York, N.Y.
    3.40, 3.41, 3.42
Arch. intern. Med. (Chicago) *(Archives of Internal Medicine),* American Medical Association, Chicago, Ill.
    6.54
Arch. ital. Biol. (Archives Italiennes de Biologie), Pisa, Italy
    12.4

Arch. Neurol. (Chicago) (Archives of Neurology), American Medical Association, Chicago, Ill.
    13.57
Arch. Neurol. Psychiat. (Chicago) (Archives of Neurology and Psychiatry), American Medical Association, Chicago, Ill.
    4.17, 9.17, 13.68
Ass. Res. nerv. ment. Dis. Proc. (Association for Research in Nervous and Mental Disease Proceedings), Williams and Wilkins Co., Baltimore, Md.
    4.9, 5.13
Bibl. biotheor. (Bibliotheca Biotheoretica), E. J. Brill, Leyden, Holland
    8.19
Brain (Brain, A Journal of Neurology), Macmillan and Co., Ltd., London, England
    2.78, 12.3, 13.14
Bull. Johns Hopk. Hosp. (Bulletin of the Johns Hopkins Hospital), The Johns Hopkins Press, Baltimore, Md.
    8.20
Comp. Psychol. Monogr. (Comparative Psychology Monograph), Williams and Wilkins Co., Baltimore, Md.
    8.11, 8.12, 8.13, 8.15, 13.16, 13.17
Doc. Ophthalmol. (Documenta Ophthalmologica), Advances in Ophthalmology, Den Haag, Holland
    3.27
Dtsch. med. Wschr. (Deutsche Medizinische Wochenschrift), Thieme Verlag, Stuttgart, Germany
    3.52
EEG clin. Neurophysiol. (Electroencephalography and Clinical Neurophysiology), Elsevier, Amsterdam, Holland
    4.13, 4.14, 5.14, 6.59, 6.60, 9.21, 12.9, 12.10, 12.16, 12.17, 12.21, 12.22, 12.23, 12.29, 12.30, 12.33, 12.34, 12.35, 12.36, 12.51, 12.52, 12.53, 12.54, 12.55, 12.56, 12.57, 12.58, 12.59, 12.60, 12.61, 12.62, Table 12.2, 13.39, 13.58, 13.69, 13.70, 13.71
Endocrinology, J. P. Lippincott Co., Philadelphia, Pa.
    8.30, 8.31
Exp. Neurol. (Experimental Neurology), Academic Press, New York, N.Y.
    12.15, 13.43
Harvey Lect. (Harvey Lectures), Charles C Thomas, Springfield, Ill.
    1.20
Helv. physiol. Acta (Helvetica Physiologica et Pharmacologica Acta), Schwabe and Co., Basel, Switzerland
    9.14
Ind. J. med. Res. (Indian Journal of Medical Research), Kasauli (Simla Hills), India
    6.49, 6.50
Int. J. Neuropharmacol. (International Journal of Neuropharmacologia), Pergamon Press, New York, N.Y.
    6.43, 6.44, 6.45, 6.46
Int. J. Physiol. Behav. (International Journal of Physiology and Behavior), Pergamon Press, New York, N.Y.
    6.40
J. cell. comp. Physiol. (Journal of Cellular and Comparative Physiology), Wistar Institute, Philadelphia, Pa.
    3.46, 3.47

J. comp. Neurol. (Journal of Comparative Neurology), Wistar Institute, Philadelphia, Pa.
4.16, 8.26, 15.3, 15.4

J. comp. physiol. Psychol. (Journal of Comparative and Physiological Psychology), © American Psychological Association, Washington, D.C.
6.13, 6.14, 6.15, 6.16, 6.17, 6.35, 6.37, 6.38, 6.39, 6.62, 7.36, 8.10, 8.14, 8.32, 8.33, 9.23, 9.24, 9.26, 9.27, 10.4, 10.10, 13.10, 13.18, 13.27, 13.28, 13.42, 13.44, 13.47, 13.49, 13.50, 13.51, 13.52, 13.53, 13.54, 13.59, 13.60, 13.62, 13.63, 13.64, 13.65, 13.74, 13.75, 14.1, 14.2, 14.4, 14.5, 14.6, 14.7, 14.8, 14.9, 14.10, 14.11

J. comp. Psychol. (Journal of Comparative Psychology), American Psychological Association, Washington, D.C.
8.25, 13.1, 13.4, 13.67, 13.73

J. exp. Psychol. (Journal of Experimental Psychology), American Psychological Association, Washington, D.C.
9.7, 9.8, 9.9, 12.46, Table 12.1, 12.47, 12.48, 12.49, 12.50

J. gen. Physiol. (Journal of General Physiology), Rockefeller University Press, New York, N.Y.
1.22, 3.17, 3.30, 15.7, 15.9A

J. gen. Psychol. (Journal of General Psychology), The Journal Press, Provincetown, Mass.
9.4

J. nerv. ment. Dis. (Journal of Nervous and Mental Disease), © Williams and Wilkins Co., Baltimore, Md.
8.29, 12.41, 12.42, 12.43, 12.44, 13.46, 13.48

J. Neuropath. exp. Neurol. (Journal of Neuropathology and Experimental Neurology), New York, N.Y.
13.2

J. Neurophysiol. (Journal of Neurophysiology), Charles C Thomas, Springfield, Ill.
1.13, 1.21, 1.32 left, 1.33, 3.38, 3.44, 4.11, 4.15, 5.3, 5.5, 5.6, 5.10, 8.27, 8.28, 11.3, 11.4, 12.5, 12.6, 12.7, 12.8, 12.24, 12.25, 12.26, 12.37, 12.38, 13.3, 13.6, 13.7(A), 13.7(B), 13.7(C), 13.8, 13.9, 13.12, 13.34, 13.35, 13.36, 13.61, 15.9B

J. Nutr. (Journal of Nutrition), Wistar Institute, Philadelphia, Pa.
6.19

J. opt. Soc. Amer. (Journal of the Optical Society of America), Optical Society of America, New York, N.Y.
3.37

J. Pharmacol. exp. Therap. (Journal of Pharmacology and Experimental Therapeutics), Williams and Wilkins Co., Baltimore, Md.
12.39, 12.40

J. Physiol. (Journal of Physiology), Cambridge University Press, London, England
1.15, 1.16, 1.27, 1.28, 1.36, 3.32, 3.48, 3.49, 3.50, 3.51, 6.27, 15.8, 15.11

J. Psychol. (Journal of Psychology), The Journal Press, Provincetown, Mass.
13.66, 13.72

J. Urol. (Baltimore) (Journal of Urology), © Williams and Wilkins Co., Baltimore, Md.
8.8

Kgl. Danske Vidensk. Selsk. Biol. Med. (Det Kongelige Danske Videnskabernes Selskab, Biologiske Meddelelser), Copenhagen, Denmark
8.18

Life Sci. (Life Sciences), Pergamon Press, New York, N.Y.
10.16

Nature (London), Macmillan and Co., Ltd., London, England
3.39, 15.10, 15.12A

Nobel Foundation, Stockholm, Sweden
16.17, © 1963, *Science,* by permission AAAS.

Proc. nat. Acad. Sci. (Washington) (Proceedings of the National Academy of Sciences of the United States of America), Washington, D.C.
3.26

Proc. phys. Soc. (London) (Proceedings of the Physical Society), Institute of Physics and Physical Society, London, England
3.18

Proc. roy. Soc. (London), B (Proceedings of the Royal Society), Burlington House, London, England
6.2, 6.28, 9.3, 9.5, 9.6

Proc. Soc. exp. Biol. Med. (Proceedings of the Society for Experimental Biology and Medicine), New York, N.Y.
6.20, 6.21, 6.41, 14.3

Psychiat. Res. Rep. Amer. psychiat. Ass. (Psychiatric Research Reports of the American Psychiatric Association), Washington, D.C.
10.2

Psychol. Rev. (Psychological Review), American Psychological Association, Washington, D.C.
6.42, 9.1, 9.18, 11.1

Psychosom. Med. (Psychosomatic Medicine), Hoeber Medical Journal, Harper and Row, New York, N.Y.
9.2

Quart. J. micr. Sci. (Quarterly Journal of Microscopical Science), Oxford University Press, London, England
4.2, 4.3

Res. Publ., Ass. nerv. Ment. Dis. (Research Publications, Association for Research in Nervous and Mental Disease), New York, N.Y.
1.29, 2.96, 2.97, 2.98, 9.29

Science, © post 1959, American Association for the Advancement of Science, Washington, D.C.
3.29, 6.36, 6.47, 6.48, 7.16, 9.22, 10.1, 10.3, 10.6, 10.7, 10.8, 10.9, 10.14, 13.45, 13.55, 16.17

Skand. Arch. Physiol. (Skandinavisches Archiv für Physiologie), Karolinska Institutet, Stockholm, Sweden
8.9, 8.35

Treatment Serv. Bull. (DVA Treatment Services Bulletin), Department of Veterans Affairs, Ottawa, Ontario, Canada
9.28

Z. Tierpsychol. (Zeitschrift für Tierpsychologie), Paul Parey Verlag, Berlin-Hamburg, Germany
6.63, 6.64, 6.65

AUTHOR INDEX

SUBJECT INDEX